The Handbook of Qualitative Research in Education

The Handbook of Qualitative Research in Education

Edited by

Margaret D. LeCompte
School of Education
University of Colorado, Boulder
Boulder, Colorado

Wendy L. Millroy
University of Cape Town
Cape Town, South Africa

Judith Preissle
Department of Social Science Education
University of Georgia
Athens, Georgia

ACADEMIC PRESS, INC.
Harcourt Brace & Company
San Diego   New York   Boston
London   Sydney   Tokyo   Toronto

Copyright © 1992 by ACADEMIC PRESS, INC.

All Rights Reserved.

ACADEMIC PRESS, INC.
A Division of Harcourt Brace & Company
525 B Street, Suite 1900, San Diego, California 92101-4495

United Kingdom Edition published by
Academic Press Limited
24–28 Oval Road, London NW1 7DX

Library of Congress Cataloging-in-Publication Data

The Handbook of qualitative research in education / edited by Margaret
    D. LeCompte, Wendy L. Millroy, Judith Preissle.
        p.   cm.
    Includes index.
    ISBN 0-12-440570-3
    1. Social sciences--Research.   2. Education--Research.
    I. LeCompte, Margaret Diane.   II. Millroy, Wendy L.   III. Preissle,
    Judith.
    H62.H2456   1991
    300'.72--dc20   91-19105
                                                                CIP

PRINTED IN THE UNITED STATES OF AMERICA
96 97   MM   9 8 7 6 5 4

Contents

CHAPTER 3
Systematic Ethnography: Toward an Evolutionary Science of Education and Culture   93
Marion Lundy Dobbert and Ruthanne Kurth-Schai

CHAPTER 4
Collaborative Research: Methods of Inquiry for Social Change   161
Jean J. Schensul and Stephen L. Schensul

CHAPTER 14
Validity in Educational Research   643
Margaret A. Eisenhart and Kenneth R. Howe

CHAPTER 15
Subjectivity in Qualitative Research   681
Golie Jansen and Alan Peshkin

Contributors

Numbers in parentheses indicate the pages on which the authors' contributions begin.

Michael Apple (507), Department of Curriculum Instruction, University of Wisconsin, Madison, Wisconsin 53706

Phil Francis Carspecken (507), Department of Educational Leadership and Cultural Studies, University of Houston, Houston, Texas 77204

Donna L. Deyhle (597), Graduate School of Education, University of Utah, Salt Lake City, Utah 84112

Marion Lundy Dobbert (93), Department of Educational Policy and Administration, University of Minnesota, Minneapolis, Minnesota 55455

Margaret A. Eisenhart (643), School of Education, University of Colorado, Boulder, Boulder, Colorado 80309

Frederick Erickson (201), Graduate School of Education, University of Pennsylvania, Philadelphia, Pennsylvania 19104

Gary Alan Fine (405), Department of Sociology, University of Georgia, Athens, Georgia 30602

James Paul Gee (227), Department of Linguistics, University of Southern California, Los Angeles, California 90089

Corrine Glesne (771), Department of Organizational Counseling and Foundational Studies, University of Vermont, Burlington, Vermont 05405

Linda Grant (405), Department of Sociology and Institute for Behavioral Research, University of Georgia, Athens, Georgia 30602

G. Alfred Hess, Jr. (597), Chicago Panel on School Policy and Finance, Chicago, Illinois 60604

Kenneth R. Howe (643), School of Education, University of Colorado, Boulder, Boulder, Colorado 80309

Evelyn Jacob (293), Graduate School of Education, George Mason University, Fairfax, Virginia 22030

Golie Jansen (681), College of Education, University of Illinois, Champaign–Urbana, Urbana, Illinois 61801

Ruthanne Kurth-Schai (93), Education Department, Macalester College, St. Paul, Minnesota 55105

Margaret D. LeCompte (597, 815), School of Education, University of Colorado, Boulder, Boulder, Colorado 80309

Joseph A. Maxwell (729), Graduate School of Education, Harvard University, Cambridge, Massachusetts 02138

Sarah Michaels (227), Education Department, Clark University, Worcester, Massachusetts 01601, and The Literacies Institute, Newton, Massachusetts 02160

Mary Catherine O'Connor (227), Program in Literacy, Language, and Cultural Studies, Boston University, Boston, Massachusetts 02215

Alan Peshkin (681), College of Education, University of Illinois, Champaign–Urbana, Urbana, Illinois 61801

Mary Anne Pitman (729), Department of Educational Foundations, University of Cincinnati, Cincinnati, Ohio 45221

Judith Preissle (815), Department of Social Science Education, University of Georgia, Athens, Georgia 30602

Richard A. Quantz (447), Department of Educational Leadership and Center for Education and Cultural Studies, Miami University of Ohio, Oxford, Ohio 45056

Leslie G. Roman (555), Department of Social and Educational Studies, and Women's Studies, University of British Columbia, Vancouver, British Columbia V6T 125, Canada

Jean J. Schensul (161), Institute for Community Research, Hartford, Connecticut 06105, and Department of Anthropology, University of Connecticut, Storrs, Connecticut 06268

Stephen L. Schensul (161), Department of Community Medicine, University of Connecticut School of Medicine, Hartford, Connecticut 06105

George and Louise Spindler[1] (53), Emeriti, Stanford University, Stanford, California 94305, and Ethnographics, Calistoga, California 94515.

Rodman B. Webb (771), Foundations of Education, University of Florida, Gainesville, Florida 32611

Harry F. Wolcott (3), College of Education, University of Oregon, Eugene, Oregon 97403

Peter Woods (337), School of Education, The Open University, Milton Keynes MK7 6AA, United Kingdom

---

[1] Visiting professors, University of California at Santa Barbara and University of Wisconsin at Madison.

Preface

Although qualitative researchers come from disciplines as disparate as anthropology, sociology, psychology, sociolinguistics, and political science, they share a common interest in analyzing data that are "sensory narratives," or accounts of verbal, visual, tactile, olfactory, and gustatory observations. These are rendered in field notes, recordings, interviews, transcriptions of audio- and videotapes, photographs, films, and other kinds of written human documents and artifacts. Qualitative narratives all have as their objective an authentic and holistic portrayal of an intact social or cultural scene. Because researchers also generate and approach their data from a variety of theoretical and interpretive perspectives, the issue of what constitutes an authentic and holistic portrayal has become hotly contested territory. In fact, as readers will discover in this volume, argument even rages over what constitutes, and which discipline or historical tradition has the authority to define, an ethnography.

In this handbook we have compiled a volume that spans the methodological and theoretical range of qualitative inquiry in the human sciences and present it as it has been used for research in education. One of our objectives in organizing this book was to establish, at this point in the history of educational research, what the "state of the art" is with regard to qualitative research in education. We have attempted to do so by letting distinguished practitioners of this method of inquiry define, at a high level of scholarship, the varying kinds of research that collectively are referred to as ethnographic and qualitative research designs. The work of the contributors represents, in our opinion, the very best in their respective traditions. These traditions range from those squarely located within a discipline, such as anthropology and sociology, to more eclectic and multidisciplinary approaches. Some address applications of qualitative research to teaching, evaluation, and community action. Still others elucidate theoretical issues such as subjectivity and validity. Each chapter presents a state-of-the-art analysis of important and current issues in, and applications of, qualitative and ethnographic research. They clarify the distinctions among variations in qualitative research design for potential users and provide the reader with access to examples of research from an array of qualitative styles, designs, perspectives, and substantive topics.

In the less than thirty years since qualitative research emerged as a serious approach to inquiry in education, its status has evolved from that of an upstart, marginal, and often pariah stepchild to a respected member of the research community. In some places, qualitative research methods are preferred over quantitative and experimental models. However, this evolution has been accompanied by considerable confusion of definitions, overlap of methods and agendas, and even attenuation of focus among its practitioners. Part of the confusion is inherent in a tradition that draws, as we have described elsewhere (Goetz and LeCompte, 1984), from many disciplines and perspectives. It is aggravated by the fact that both preservice and graduate training in education historically have failed to stress grounding in social science disciplines and their associated research methods. Until recently, in fact, the preoccupation with psychometric and quantitative approaches to inquiry in education obscured other modes of investigation and often led to the disparagement of alternative approaches. Ultimately, the narrowing of focus and procedures led to considerable dissatisfaction with the ability of conventional research practice to answer the questions that educators and social scientists were asking. Since the mid-1980s, qualitative methods have moved to center stage, achieving the status of "complementary" (Jaeger, 1988) methods rather than alternatives to quantitative and experimental designs. In fact, some of the pioneer qualitative methodologists and ethnographers in education—we, the editors, included—now find themselves in the peculiar position of having achieved orthodoxy. After having spent much of our professional lives defending the legitimacy of a position once held to be barely respectable, it is both comforting and disquieting to now find our work attacked for being part of the dominant methodological establishment! It is with relief, however, that we cast aside the defensive tone in which most of our earlier works were cast. We hope that this volume will enable readers both to disentangle the various strands that influence what we now call qualitative and ethnographic research and to view it as both accessible, which has seldom been a problem, and rigorous, a criticism for which alternative methods have long been held accountable.

Goetz, J. P., and LeCompte, M. D. (1984). *Ethnography and qualitative design in educational research.* Orlando, FL: Academic Press.

Jaeger, R. M. (1988). *Complementary methods for research in education.* Washington, D.C.: American Educational Research Association.

Acknowledgments

We would like to thank those people without whom this book would never have been possible. First, we want to acknowledge the support of our academic departments and graduate students in the production of this volume. We also would like to thank our contributors for timeliness beyond anything we could have expected from people whom we know to have so many demands on their professional and personal time. Many of them made substantial sacrifices to participate in this project. We also would like to express our deepest appreciation to our publisher, Academic Press, who encouraged us to pursue this project for at least three years before we were able to achieve a clear understanding of what we wanted to do. We also wish to thank our new editor, Nikki Fine, for seeing this project through to the end.

There is one person whose very special and integral role in our careers and lives must be made known, with the full realization that its real importance can never be fully acknowledged. Joe Ingram, former Senior Editor at Academic Press, sponsored our first ethnographic methods book (Ethnography and Qualitative Design in Educational Research), which we, Judith Preissle and Margaret LeCompte, feel was largely responsible for the direction and success of our careers. For almost ten years, he provided moral support through personal and professional crises that impeded the progress of our research and writing. He encouraged us to elaborate our work with the forthcoming second edition of our text. And it was he, more than anyone else, who continued to urge us to edit this volume. It is with the most heartfelt gratitude to a treasured friend and colleague that we dedicate this book to Joe Ingram.

Introduction

About the Choice of Authors

We solicited as contributors to this volume scholars whose empirical research we felt exemplified the range of approaches to qualitative methods. We then asked them to talk about their own work. Many of these individuals are well known and respected for their empirical work; the extent to which they have written methodological articles varies. We asked them to situate their work within an intellectual and historical tradition and distinguish between their own particular type of qualitative research and the way other researchers do it. Among the topics we asked them to address are how they view the world and subsequently define what is important to investigate, how they conceptualize their own research agendas, and how they carry out their work. Many have taken a rather personal approach to the task, detailing through their own experience the evolution of their unique contribution to inquiry. Others have situated their epistemological struggles within current debates over the conduct of inquiry. We made no effort to direct or "correct" the content of each chapter; the voice heard is that of the author alone. We wish to emphasize our belief in the legitimacy of each of the approaches presented in this volume.

The reader will notice that the contributors to this volume often generate conflicting interpretations about the field and its origins and evolution. In so doing, they have exemplified what Richard Quantz in this volume calls the "dialogue rather than the dialectic" of history. By this he does not mean that the purpose of debate in methodological circles ultimately should be to achieve a synthesis that annihilates or supersedes other positions. Rather, he advocates having debates that permit a multitude of new and old, interesting and interested voices to be heard. Each of these authors presents different ways of approaching the history of qualitative and/or ethnographic research. They also differ in the degree of involvement with participants assumed by the researcher, the level and units of analysis attended to, and the degree of linkage proposed between micro and macro levels of analysis in society. There even is within these pages considerable discussion over how to label what it is the authors do, including how they define the term "ethnography" itself.

Another interesting aspect of the volume is the intellectual lineages or relationships among the authors. Many of the contributors have chosen to coauthor their chapters with a former student, and some of those who have contributions of their own share equal billing with their former mentors. For example, Harry Wolcott was a student of the Spindlers, Mary Anne Pitman and Ruthanne Kurth-Schai were students of Marion Dobbert, Phil Carspecken and Leslie Roman were students of Michael Apple, and Corrine Glesne and Golie Jansen were students of Alan Peshkin. As the reader will notice, many of the authors have been colleagues: the Schensuls and Fred Erickson worked together during some of their first collaborative projects on Chicago's South Side; Donna Deyhle and Margaret LeCompte are currently working with similar schools in the Four Corners region of the American Southwest. Others have shared coauthorship—for example, Linda Grant and Margaret LeCompte with Judith Preissle-Goetz. There certainly are other formal and informal mentor–student and collegial relationships among the contributors of which we are unaware. Most of the authors, including the editors, came of age professionally and learned to respect one another's work in some of the same professional associations. Notwithstanding these ties, the frequency with which the reader will find that the authors reference each other's work was not planned by the editors but, rather, is a consequence of the importance of the contribution that each of these authors has made toward the development of more authentic, rigorous, and profound ways to investigate human behavior.

Selecting and generating labels for the authors has involved considerable negotiation, in good interactionist or interpretive fashion. We first surveyed the range of research approaches and the researchers best known for that type of work. We then made initial decisions as to who would best fit into each of the slots and contacted the people we had identified. We were delighted that, except for a few individuals who were committed to other projects, all of the people who were our first choice agreed to participate. However, once we told the researchers how and why we had categorized their work, what kind of researcher we thought they were, and what we believed they were doing, they started to slide out of or redefine our once-neat categories. Titles, text, and even the direction of the chapters underwent a long and continuous process of negotiation. The authors also redefined the divisions that we had made in the range of qualitative and ethnographic inquiry, largely as a consequence of their most current work. It is these most current perspectives that are, for the most part, represented in this book, although most of the authors have done so in a historical context. For example, many more authors call themselves "ethnographers" than we originally had envisioned, in large part, we think, because use of that term has begun to expand beyond the boundaries of its original disciplinary home in anthropology and to be applied to many kinds of interpretive and participative research. We also believe that there has been, over time, a shift from functional and descriptive research approaches to those that have a more critical, participative, and emancipatory flavor. As a consequence, the final version of this volume is different from what we originally intended. This is, we believe, a desirable consequence of encouraging people to define themselves and to construct their own terms. We say encouraging them to categorize themselves, because a few steadfastly refused to do so. We have, for this reason, made some assignments ourselves for the purposes of introducing the chapters to the reader; we ourselves are responsible for any errors of omission, commission, and interpretation in the categorization and description thereby introduced.

About the Organization of the Book

This volume is divided into three sections. In the first section, entitled "The Current Boundaries and the Future Directions of Ethnographic and Qualitative Research," we set the boundaries of current practice in ethnographic and qualitative research, as well as indicate the directions we think future practice might lead. The chapters by Wolcott; the Spindlers; Erickson; Gee, Michaels, and O'Connor; Jacob; and Dobbert and Kurth-Schai derive from what loosely can be called the traditions of anthropology and sociolinguistics. The chapter contributed by the Schensuls also is anthropological; their work is, however, uncompromisingly applied anthropology. It provides an important counterpoint to the complementary and sociologically informed work of applied and critical theorists whose chapters come later. The chapters by Woods; Grant and Fine; Carspecken and Apple; and Roman have their analytic and theoretical roots in sociology. Finally, Richard Quantz reviews the critical and sociological roots of critical ethnography from a historical and philosophical, as well as methodological, perspective. The chapters by Carspecken and Apple; Roman; and Quantz originally were intended to represent new directions in critical, feminist, and postmodern approaches to qualitative research; but as the readers will note, these issues also are reflected in the contributions of many of the other authors. These overlaps reflect what we feel has come to characterize the field: dialogue and cross-fertilization from multiple interested parties.

The second part of the book, entitled "Issues in the Execution of Ethnography and Qualitative Research," contains three chapters, each devoted to an issue that, while critical to all forms of empirical research, has particular importance to qualitative and ethnographic researchers. These chapters constitute the ingredients of both a familiar critique of such research and a continuing and evolving dialogue among its practitioners. These issues are ethics and the role of the researcher, by Donna L. Deyhle, G. Alfred Hess, Jr., and Margaret D. LeCompte; validity, by Margaret Eisenhart and Kenneth R. Howe; and subjectivity, by Golie Jansen and Alan Peshkin.

We have titled the last part of the book "Applications of Qualitative and Ethnographic Research." The varying applications presented in these three chapters include the use of ethnographic and qualitative research design in evaluation research, by Mary Anne Pitman and Joseph A. Maxwell; the teaching of qualitative and ethnographic research methods, by Rodman Webb and Corrine Glesne; and the meta-analysis of qualitative and ethnographic studies in education for synthesis and theory building, by Margaret D. LeCompte and Judith Preissle.

About the Authors and Chapters

Chapter 1 is by Harry Wolcott, who added anthropology to his career as an educator during his doctoral studies at Stanford University under the guidance of George Spindler. He conducted his fieldwork among the Kwakiutl Indians of British Columbia, producing the now-famous and reissued monograph *A Kwakiutl Village and School*. He joined the faculty at the University of Oregon after graduation and continues to hold an appointment as professor of education and anthropology. Professor Wolcott has been the editor of the *Anthropology and Education Quarterly*, a publication of the Council on Anthropology and Education, for which he also served as president. His *The Man in the Principal's Office* remains a classic of educational ethnography. In his chapter "Posturing in Qualitative Inquiry," Wolcott distinguishes between elements common to all qualitative approaches and elements unique to some of them, ethnography in particular. He provides a textual and visual introduction to the qualitative and ethnographic tradition, describing the strategic negotiations necessary to select the most appropriate approach for a particular project, given the many options available to qualitative researchers. In a comprehensive and laboriously achieved tree diagram, which we from time to time referred to (respectfully) as "Harry's 'burning bush,'" he introduces the reader to the roots, trunks, branches, and even some twigs of research approaches described in this volume. He cautions the reader about the disciplinary and conceptual antecedents of each of the approaches he reviews, indicating that researchers should attend not only to the problem they wish to investigate, but also to the roots and trunks of the traditions appropriate to the methods they choose before getting out on a methodological limb.

Chapter 2, "Cultural Process and Ethnography: An Anthropological Perspective," begins where the editors believe ethnography began: in anthropology. It is contributed by George Spindler, professor emeritus of anthropology and education at Stanford University, and Louise Spindler, lecturer in anthropology and education at Stanford University. George and Louise were among the founders of the Council on Anthropology and Education of the American Anthropological Association; they also served as its president. In 1988, the Council established the George and Louise Spindler Award in their honor for distinguished contributions to research and applied work in education. They have worked collaboratively in four cultures since 1948, studying the psychocultural adaptation of peoples to change, inside and outside of schools. In 1986, they were honored by the Committee on the Status of Women in Anthropology of the American Anthropological Association for their enduring relationship in the face of exigencies of fieldwork and collaboration. More than that of any other scholars, the work of the Spindlers has focused the attention of educators on the contribution of culture to issues in education. Through their many edited textbooks, their own published fieldwork, and the famous "Spindler series" of educational ethnographies published by Holt, Rinehart & Winston, their work has established the perspective of cultural anthropology and psychological anthropology as fundamental to qualitative research for generations of educational researchers. In their chapter, the Spindlers begin by analyzing the six collections of studies in anthropology and education and the ethnography of education, which they published between 1955 and 1987. Their analysis indicates that the research process, ethnography, has tended to overshadow the development of theory, and for that reason, the cross-cultural, comparative perspective unique to ethnography has, in their view, unfortunately been diminished. The first section of their chapter ends with a list of criteria for a "good" ethnography and lays out important issues to which researchers should attend while conducting fieldwork. The chapter reinforces the importance of the words of natives, their perspectives and understandings, and the meanings they assign to events, persons, and symbols. Because the social position *in situ* of research participants affects their perception of action and meanings, it is important to elicit responses from persons in all positions, including children, administrators, teachers, parents, and others in the study of schooling. The second part of the chapter describes the Spindlers' latest research approach, a cross-cultural comparative and reflective interview procedure, and gives examples of its application.

Although firmly within the discipline of anthropology, Chapter 3, "Systematic Ethnography: Toward an Evolutionary Science of Education and Culture," by Marion Lundy Dobbert and Ruthanne Kurth-Schai, represents a radical departure from the "classical" tradition of the Spindlers. Marion Lundy Dobbert is professor of anthropology and education in the Department of Educational Policy and Administration at the University of Minnesota. She believes that anthropology has isolated itself from the mainstream of science and, as a consequence, is losing a solid scientific perspective upon which to grow. She feels that this is particularly true in educational anthropology, because the sub-discipline has focused on schools and classrooms rather than on human learning from an evolutionary perspective. For these reasons, Dobbert considers herself to be a theorist whose concern is developing ethnography, and anthropology itself, into a science that dovetails seamlessly with historic theoretical traditions in the physical sciences, including the work of Darwin, Heisenberg, and Einstein. Her specialties include the study of the process of growing up among human and nonhuman primates, ethnographic methods, general systems theory, and the application of current developments in the physical sciences to research in the social sciences. Her books include *Ethnographic Research: Theory and Application for Modern Schools and Societies* (1982) and, with Pitman and Eisikovits, *Culture Acquisition: A Holistic Approach to Human Learning* (1989). Her coauthor, Ruthanne Kurth-Schai, began her career in alternative education, working in programs for "at-risk" junior high school students. She received her Ph.D. in social and philosophical foundations of education from the University of Minnesota and, since 1986, has served as assistant professor of education at Macalester College in St. Paul, Minnesota. Her scholarship is centered in social reconstructionist philosophy, which provides a framework for integration of studies in anthropological futures, general systems, and feminist and critical perspectives on education.

Dobbert and Kurth-Schai's chapter first describes the general systems framework, adopted from biological systems, with which they approach educational ethnography. They then review a variety of scientific developments, including chaos theory and various forms of mathematical modeling that inform their work. Finally, they describe the data collection techniques they have used in their own dimensional analysis of classrooms, using it to argue for the added insight that mathematical rigor can bring to ethnographic research.

Chapter 4, "Collaborative Research: Methods of Inquiry for Social Change," is by Jean J. Schensul and Stephen L. Schensul. We have placed it here, with the varying approaches to qualitative and ethnographic research, both at the request of the authors who see collaborative research as a distinct variant in anthropology and because the applied tradition never has been as marginal in anthropology as it has been in other social and behavioral sciences. Anthropologists traditionally have been as active outside of academia as they have been inside it, even maintaining long and respected careers with little institutional affiliation at all. Winners of the 1990 Solon T. Kimball Award for Public and Applied Anthropology of the American Anthropological Association, for their lifetime of commitment to research and practice in communities, the Schensuls are no exception to this tradition of applied research. Jean J. Schensul has served as president of the Council on Anthropology and Education and member of the board of directors and secretary of the Society for Applied Anthropology. She is the executive director of the Institute for Community Research, an independent nonprofit applied research and policy institute addressing issues of health, education, aging, and cultural policy, in Hartford, Connecticut. Stephen L. Schensul is associate professor of community medicine and executive director for the Center for International Community Health studies at the University of Connecticut School of Medicine. Both have published extensively in the areas of urban health planning, action research, and advocacy. While their educational work has concentrated primarily on community-based, nonformal settings, it consistently has informed the work of educators and scholars in the educational and academic establishment for more than two decades. Their chapter defines collaborative research as practiced in their own work and that of other social scientists who practice building multisectoral partnerships that link researchers, program developers, and members of the community into a study whose explicit purpose is to use research as a tool for joint problem-solving and policy change. The chapter first situates collaborative research within anthropological traditions. It then reviews a number of projects built on the principles of collaborative research and outlines the methods used in their execution.

Chapter 5 is contributed by Frederick Erickson, who is professor of education and director of the Center for Urban Ethnography at the Graduate School of Education at the University of Pennsylvania. Having served as both president of the Council on Anthropology and Education of the American Anthropological Association and vice president of Division G—The Social Context of Education for the American Educational Research Association, Fred Erickson's publications and research as well as his teaching activities have been instrumental in bringing legitimacy to the use of qualitative methods in the study of schools and classrooms. Of particular importance has been his 1985 review article "Qualitative Methods in Research on Teaching" in the *Handbook of Research on Teaching*, 3rd ed. Writing from the perspective of both sociolinguistics and cultural anthropology, his special gift has been to alert researchers to the specific kinds of questions about education that can be answered only by ethnographic and qualitative methods. In 1981 he received the American Educational Research Association's Award for Distinguished Service. His chapter in this volume focuses, at our request, on an area in which his work was seminal: microethnography. However, his own work spans the gamut of ethnographic studies from cross-cultural interaction and communication in classrooms to analyses of research methods to deeply introspective discussions of the social obligations of researchers to their research participants and to education.

Erickson's chapter first describes how microanalysis permitted researchers to open the "black box" of ordinary life in educational settings. He discusses how ethnographic microanalysis is a product of five streams of work: context analysis, ethnography of communication, studies of interaction and the self, conversational analysis, and the studies positing that communicative action is a manifestation of power relations among actors. He then discusses the logistics of executing microanalytic studies as well as how all five sets of theoretical influence are integrated into their practice.

Chapter 6, by James Paul Gee, Sarah Michaels, and Mary Catherine O'Connor, is titled "Discourse Analysis." James Paul Gee is a professor in the Department of Linguistics at the University of Southern California. After spending seven years in the Boston University School of Education, he became convinced that issues of language and sensemaking within educational institutions are a critical testing ground for theories of discourse and the development of a truly social linguistics. Believing that use of language is only meaningful within the larger context of social practice of sociocultural groups, he currently is working on development of a theory of discourse and language in use that reflects both psycholinguistics and sociolinguistics. Sarah Michaels is chair of the Education Department and director of the Literacy Institute at Clark University. Her primary area of research is discourse analysis oriented toward the relationship among students' out-of-school competencies, classroom processes, and the acquisition of multiple literacies. One of the first investigators to use ethnographic methods to study the way children use computers in the classroom, she has directed research on "sharing time" as oral preparation for literacy studies of talk and text in classroom writing, science, and mathematics activities. Mary Catherine O'Connor is assistant professor in the Program of Literacy, Language, and Cultural Studies and assistant director of the Literacies Institute at Boston University. Her most recent research involves how discourse shapes mathematical learning among middle school students. Her research interests include discourse and narrative analysis, development of school- and community-based language and literacies, and the influence of language and culture on standardized and alternative forms of assessment.

Like Erickson's chapter on microethnography, their focus is communications in small groups and dyads. Using many extended examples, their chapter illustrates not only how socio- and psycholinguists analyze data but also how the results of these analyses illuminate how meaning is constructed in the social context of the school. In particular, they describe how miscommunications occur and impede accurate information flow in educational settings.

Evelyn Jacob, an associate professor at George Mason University, is the author of Chapter 7, "Culture, Context, and Cognition." She served on the board of directors of the Council on Anthropology and Education and as chair of the Council's Committee on Cognitive and Linguistic Studies in Education. She was secretary of Division G—The Social Context of Education for the American Educational Research Association, and in 1991 she was elected to be its vice-president. With Cathie Jordan, she edited *Minority Education: Anthropological Perspectives* (Ablex Press; forthcoming in 1992). Her chapter in this volume describes a relatively new interdisciplinary area of inquiry that uses anthropology and psychology to study the social and cultural construction of cognition. It extends traditional psychology by explicitly examining the influence of context and meaning on cognitive performance; it extends anthropology by applying cultural analyses to acquisition of cognitive skills and knowledge. Jacob considers this approach particularly relevant for the field of education because it brings interpretive perspectives and methods to bear upon the traditional content of educational research: the teaching and learning of cognitive skills. Translation of works by the Russian scholar Lev Vygotsky recently provided a unifying theoretical and methodological focus for scholars interested in social and cultural influences on cognition. Jacob summarizes the work of these "neo-Vygotskians" and demonstrates how, in her own work, their insights and analyses are used.

In Chapter 8, "Symbolic Interactionism: Theory and Method," by British scholar Peter Woods, we change the disciplinary ancestry of the chapters from anthropology to sociology. Peter Woods is on the faculty of the School of Education at The Open University in Milton Keynes, England. His works have been among those most instrumental in bringing the "new sociology of education" from England to the United States. Peter Woods views himself as a symbolic interactionist whose main philosophical forbearers are G. H. Mead, James, Cooley, and Dewey. More contemporary influences include the interactionism of Blumer, Becker, Goffman, Hughes, and Strauss, phenomenology, ethnomethodology, and social anthropology with its emphasis on culture. All these place emphasis on the role of the self and the hidden assumptions behind appearance. They question the nature of knowledge and place more emphasis on process. Woods' chapter spells out the basic principles of symbolic interactionism and their methodological implications. It traces the involvement of the researcher's self through various stages of data collection and analysis and shows how, in this approach, the whole research process, including theory building, is grounded in the empirical world.

Chapter 9, by Linda Grant and Gary Alan Fine, is also from a sociological perspective but is more located in the fieldwork tradition of the "Chicago School." The authors have titled their chapter "Sociology Unleashed" to signify that while they are not departing from the traditional disciplinary categories of sociology, they are, however, calling for more flexible and adventurous questions, categories, and ways of doing inquiry. Linda Grant is associate professor of sociology and a member of the women's studies program at the University of Georgia. She also is a faculty associate of the Institute for Behavioral Research. Her study "Black Females' 'Place' in Desegregated Classrooms" (*Sociology of Education*, Vol. 57, 1984) won the American Educational Research Association Women Educators' Research Award. Her research includes studies of desegregated rural schools, the effects of entry of women and minorities into academia, and patterns of mentoring in the careers of male and female academics and physicians. Her work appears in *American Sociological Review, Anthropology and Education Quarterly, Journal of Marriage and the Family, Gender and Society,* and *The Elementary School Journal.* Gary Alan Fine received his Ph.D. from Harvard University. After spending much of his career at the University of Minnesota, where he also was editor of the journal *Symbolic Interaction,* he became, in 1990, professor and head of the Department of Sociology at the University of Georgia. His major research interests are small group interaction, peer relations among adolescents, and studies of folklore. His book *With the Boys* won an Opie Award; among his other books are *Shared Fantasies,* on videogames, and, with Kent Sandstrom, *Knowing Children: Participation with Minors.*

Fine and Grant's chapter begins with the statement that ethnographic fieldwork historically has been and currently is the heart of qualitative sociology. Reviewing the body of research studies in education and related fields, they highlight qualitative sociological work that challenges and expands the classical ethnographic tradition, either by using innovative investigative methods or creative combinations of methods, or by raising critical issues regarding relationships among researchers, subjects of research, and the audiences to which accounts are addressed.

Chapter 10, by Richard A. Quantz, is titled "On Critical Ethnography (with Some Postmodern Considerations)." Richard Quantz is a professor in the Department of Educational Leadership and associate director of the Center for Educational and Cultural Studies at Miami University in Oxford, Ohio. Quantz's contribution provides a historical and philosophical context for the subsequent chapters, which address critical and feminist perspectives. He describes critical ethnography as an empirical project located within critical discourse rather than as a particular set of methods for conducting research. He asserts that critical discourse can be best understood in its historical context. It is characterized by a set of themes that reflect particular approaches to knowledge, values, society, culture, and history. He indicates that critical discourse, which has stretched and changed to address issues current in any particular era, now is struggling to accommodate to apparently incommensurate themes embodied in contemporary postmodern theory and research.

Phil Francis Carspecken and Michael Apple wrote Chapter 11, "Critical Qualitative Research: Theory, Methodology, and Practice." Although he received his Ph.D. from the University of Wisconsin,

Carspecken did much of his graduate training at the Centre for Contemporary Cultural Studies in Birmingham, United Kingdom. Since the early 1970s, the Centre has been one of the focal points for the introduction of critical, interactionist, and interpretive approaches into educational research. Carspecken describes these influences as critical to his studies of play groups among Houston inner-city children, the illegal occupation of a Liverpool school by working-class residents, and experimental classrooms in inner-city schools. He now is assistant professor in sociology of education in the College of Education, University of Houston, University Park. Michael Apple's (1978) *Harvard Educational Review* article, "The New Sociology of Education: Analyzing Cultural and Economic Reproduction," first focused the attention of American scholars on British research, which revolutionized studies of the relationship between schooling and society in the United States. A former public school teacher and past president of a teachers' union, he now is professor of curriculum and instruction and educational policy studies at the University of Wisconsin, Madison, and has served as vice-president for Division G—The Social Context of Education of the American Educational Research Association. He, his former students, and his colleagues have generated some of the most thought-provoking and controversial analyses of schooling to emerge in the last two decades. Among his many books about the relationship between education and differential power are *Ideology and Curriculum* (1979, 1990), *Education and Power* (1982) *Teachers and Texts* (1988), and *The Politics of the Textbook* (1991).

Carspecken and Apple's chapter first defines the critical perspective, which informs their work. They then walk the reader through an extended example of how a critical theorist approaches critical analysis of actual field data. Beginning with initial issues of problem formulation, they use field note examples to illustrate how critical theory informs each of the five stages of the research process. They end with a discussion of how discrete field data is linked with structures of power in the larger social and cultural context.

Chapter 12, "The Political Significance of Other Ways of Narrating Ethnography: A Feminist Materialist Approach," by Leslie G. Roman, concludes our exploration of qualitative and ethnographic approaches to research in education. Having received her Ph.D. at the University of Wisconsin, Leslie Roman now is assistant professor in the Department of Social and Educational Studies at the University of British Columbia, where she teaches feminist theory, sociology of education, and critical ethnography. Her study of punk young women is one of the first in the United States to question the applicability to young women

of theories of accommodation and resistance to dominant cultural patterns that were generated primarily from studies of young working-
class men. She also has taken issue with traditional modes of investigation for what she perceives to be "voyeurism and intellectual tourism"
and a failure to confront the ethical responsibility of researchers to
those they study. Placing her discussion in what she defines as a
feminist materialist approach, she discusses these issues in the context
of developing a theory of method that she feels is more congruent with
the ethical realities of contemporary ethnographic fieldwork.

With Chapter 13, "Approaching Ethical Issues for Qualitative Researchers in Education," we depart from descriptions of ways to do
qualitative and ethnographic research and begin a discussion of perennial issues. The careers of the three authors vary, from Deyhle, who
has done both basic and evaluation research from a university base; to
Hess, whose studies of the Chicago public schools are based in an
independent research and advocacy organization whose stated purpose is to improve public education; and LeCompte, who has worked
as both a university-based researcher and an in-house evaluator for a
school district. These career differences form the basis for what has
proven to be a difficult task: developing a coherent statement on ethics
that balances the varying relationships that the authors had with people in the field as well as the differences in the stated purposes of their
research. Donna Deyhle is associate professor of anthropology and
education in the Department of Educational Foundations at the University of Utah. She also holds an appointment in Native American
studies and, for the past ten years, has been doing a study of Native
American adolescents in the Four Corners area of the United States.
Her work has been supported by two University of Utah Faculty Fellowships and two Spencer Fellowships and has been published in
journals such as *Curriculum Inquiry, The International Journal of
Multi-Lingual and Multicultural Research, The Journal of American
Indian Education,* and *Qualitative Studies in Education.* Trained as
an educational anthropologist at Northwestern University, G. Alfred
Hess, Jr., has been the executive director of the Chicago Panel on
Public School Policy and Finance since 1983. The panel is a multiracial, multiethnic coalition of twenty nonprofit agencies whose research
under Hess's direction has examined the financial and managerial
practices of the Chicago schools, school reform, desegregation,
adopt-a-school program assessment, and a nationally recognized series
of drop-out studies. Hess helped to draft the legislation that emerged
as the Chicago School Reform Act of 1988; he is the author of *School
Restructuring: Chicago Style* (Newbury Park, CA: Corwin Press,

1991). Margaret D. LeCompte is one of the editors of this volume. The experiences upon which her participation in this article is based include five years of service as the executive director for Research and Evaluation of the Houston Independent School District and a variety of research and evaluation projects in American and African public schools.

The chapter begins with a history of how and why professional social science associations in the United States developed a concern for codification of research ethics. It then presents one particular typology by which ethical choices may be categorized, given particular philosophical, ontological, and epistemological considerations. It then discusses how many educational researchers, including the authors, addressed ethical dilemmas arising at each of the many stages in the fieldwork process.

Margaret A. Eisenhart is associate professor of educational anthropology and research methodology and chair of the program area in Educational Foundations in the School of Education at the University of Colorado at Boulder. Kenneth R. Howe is associate professor of philosophy of education, also at the University of Colorado at Boulder. Their contribution is Chapter 14, "Validity in Educational Research." Margaret Eisenhart received her Ph.D. in anthropology from the University of North Carolina at Chapel Hill. Her research and publications focus on what students learn about gender and race in U.S. schools and the place of ethnographic methods in educational research. She is coauthor with Dorothy Holland of *Educated in Romance: Women, Achievement and College Culture* (Chicago: The University of Chicago Press, 1990). Ken Howe's interests include medical ethics, gender relations, the conceptual basis for ethics in teacher education, and epistemological debates in educational research. His publications include articles in the *Educational Researcher, Educational Theory,* and the *Journal of Teacher Education.* Their chapter in this handbook begins with a discussion of three conceptions of validity that have informed debates about standards that should apply to qualitative educational research. They then develop their own position, a crucial feature of which is a distinction between *general* and *design-specific* standards of validity. The thrust of their argument is that all educational research is subject to the same general criteria of validity, even though quite distinct and specialized criteria are required to conduct and evaluate specific research studies. The authors use the case of ethnography to illustrate their discussion.

Chapter 15 is "Subjectivity in Qualitative Research," by Golie Jansen and Alan Peshkin. Golie Jansen is a lecturer in social work at the University of Illinois and recently received her Ph.D. from the School of Social Work at that university. Within the qualitative research tradition, she aligns herself with feminist interpretive researchers. Alan Peshkin, who describes himself methodologically as a "pragmatic eclecticist," is a professor in the Educational Psychology Department at the University of Illinois at Champaign–Urbana. His orientation to qualitative research is in the tradition of studies of the relationship between communities and their schools in different subcultural settings. This tradition values long-term fieldwork and includes extensive opportunity for a range of multiple participant observation experiences and collection of documents. Since the publication of *Kanuri Schoolchildren* in 1972, his monographs on schools and communities in the United States, including *Growing Up American* (1978) and *God's Choice* (1986), have represented benchmarks in a particular genre of ethnographic research. Jansen and Peshkin's paper considers the "self" in the research process, addressing how different types of researchers who are more or less qualitative in their paradigmatic commitments conceive the nature and implications of subjectivity. The first part of their article is a review of historical and philosophical stances on the nature of subjectivity and objectivity. They then examine current issues in the debate over subjectivity and objectivity, in particular how practitioners of qualitative research engage their subjectivity, reflect upon it in the service of their research agendas, and address it in the presentation of research products.

In Part 3 of the book, we turn to practical applications, uses, and syntheses of the qualitative and ethnographic research tradition. Chapter 16, "Qualitative Approaches to Evaluation: Models and Methods," was written by Mary Anne Pitman and Joseph A. Maxwell. Mary Anne Pitman, a cultural anthropologist, is associate professor in the Department of Educational Foundations at the University of Cincinnati. Her research interests include the educative nature of rituals of social relations, cultural acquisition patterns among children from a rural intentional community who participate in home schooling, and the development of systematic and theory-grounded methods of ethnographic research; she was instrumental in institutionalizing Committee Four: Ethnographic Approaches to Evaluation in Education within the Council on Anthropology and Education. Her book with Marion Dobbert and Rivka Eisikovitz, *Culture Acquisition: A Holistic Approach to Human Learning*, details her approach to how cultures are transmitted and transformed in human groups; her edited volume with David Fetterman, *Ethnography in Theory, Practice and Politics* (Sage, 1986), was one of the first systematic presentations of the importance of holistic and anthropologically informed ethnography to evaluation research. Joseph A. Maxwell is assistant professor of qualitative research methods at the Harvard Graduate School of Education. Having conducted research on the cultural construction of social relations in a Canadian Inuit community, he also studies physicians' learning and the process of innovation in medical education in the United States. His publications include evaluations of medical education programs and articles on qualitative methods. Because the authors believe that qualitative evaluation is not constituted by one paradigm or model that can be contrasted to quantitative evaluation, their chapter first reviews the work of four of the most prominent practitioners of qualitative evaluation, highlighting their strengths, limitations, and implications for practice. They then discuss their own approach to qualitative evaluation, indicating that it is guided by a number of canons or checkpoints, including ethical constraints, data collection procedures, and reporting requirements.

Chapter 17, by Rodman B. Webb and Corrine Glesne, is called "Teaching Qualitative Research." Rodman Webb is professor of foundations of education at the University of Florida. Active in the American Educational Studies Association and the American Educational Research Association, he is editor of the journal *Qualitative Studies in Education* and, with Robert Sherman, of a textbook in qualitative research methods, *Qualitative Research in Education: Focus and Methods*. Corrine Glesne is assistant professor in the College of Education and Social Services at the University of Vermont. With Alan Peshkin, she has recently completed an introductory text on qualitative research methods; her substantive research interests include the study of education and rural development in the Carribean. Their chapter discusses the various approaches to teaching qualitative research in the context of the kinds of problems students have approaching and implementing a new way of thinking and engaging in inquiry.

Chapter 18, by Margaret D. LeCompte and Judith Preissle, is "Toward an Ethnology of Student Life in Schools and Classrooms: Synthesizing the Qualitative Research Tradition." The authors are two of the editors of this volume, and their biographies are summarized in the following section. Their chapter is a response to a challenge laid down to qualitative researchers and ethnographers by Dell Hymes in the late 1970s to begin developing an "ethnology" of education. Hymes' criticism was that ethnographic research remained a body of discrete, disconnected studies of specific phenomena and sites; he called for researchers to start specifying what it all meant in a more general way. This meant developing theories of educational phenomena that were grounded in the opus of existing studies. LeCompte and Preissle concern themselves with one type of research: qualitative and ethnographic studies of school and classroom experiences written from the students' perspective. Their analysis is twofold: First, they categorize the studies reviewed substantively, indicating what themes and concepts are shared among the studies; second, they group the studies according to the theoretical frames that inform them, indicating the way changes in theoretical perspectives have changed both the direction of research in education and the way educational participants are described and processes are interpreted.

About the Editors

We would like to close with some information about our own biographies. Margaret D. LeCompte and Judith Preissle, formerly Judith Preissle-Goetz, are, respectively, associate professor of sociology of education in the School of Education at the University of Colorado at Boulder and professor of educational anthropology in the Department of Social Science Education at the University of Georgia. Their coauthorship dates from 1977, with the presentation of their first joint paper, "Data Crunching, or, What Do I Do with the Five Drawers of Field Notes?," at the meetings of the Council on Anthropology and Education of the American Anthropological Association. Their subsequent articles have been published in the *Review of Educational Research, Educational Evaluation and Policy Analysis, Anthropology and Education Quarterly, The American Behavioral Scientist,* a number of handbooks on educational research in various disciplines, and a major text reference, *Ethnography and Qualitative Design in Educational Research* (New York: Academic Press, 1984). The latter work has been translated into Spanish and is slated for a second edition in 1992. Their professional activities include participation in professional associations serving sociologists, anthropologists, policymakers, and educators. Preissle served as secretary treasurer of the Council on Anthropology and Education, and LeCompte served as its president. LeCompte recently was elected secretary of Division G of the American Educational Research Association. Both are active in the Society for Applied Anthropology and the American Educational Studies Association. While much of their joint and separate authorship has been devoted to issues of research methodology, they also pursue empirical research interests. Preissle has done extensive studies on the role of schools and classrooms in the socialization of rural children to gender and other roles; like Preissle, LeCompte has had a long interest in studies of classroom interaction. In addition, she has done considerable research on school dropouts and on innovation and change in school pedagogy and organization.

Wendy L. Millroy was awarded a Fulbright Scholarship to pursue doctoral studies in mathematics education and received her Ph.D. in 1990 from the Department of Education at Cornell University. Her research interests include the teaching and learning of mathematics in formal and nonformal settings; for her fieldwork, she became a cabinet-maker's apprentice in her native South Africa, learning how a group of carpenters use mathematical reasoning and problem-solving in their trade. She currently is a research associate for the Elementary Science Implementation Project, funded by the National Science Foundation, at the University of Northern Colorado, Greeley.

PART 1

□ The Current Boundaries
and the Future Directions
of Ethnographic Research

CHAPTER 1

❑ Posturing in Qualitative Inquiry

Harry F. Wolcott

*The Handbook of Qualitative
Research in Education*

"Posturing" in qualitative inquiry? Yes, posturing. As one of base-ball's legendary figures liked to say (was it Casey Stengel?), "You can look it up." And that is what I did.

By conveying two different senses in which the term may be used, *posturing* draws attention to the issue I wish to discuss here. Accord-ing to my trusty Random House Dictionary (2nd edition, unabridged), as an intransitive verb *posturing* refers to "assuming" a posture, espe-cially an affected or unnatural one. *To posture* is to act "in an affected or artificial manner, as to create a certain impression." A negative connotation is implied; when we ourselves are chided for "academic posturing," no compliment is intended. As a transitive verb, however, *posturing* sheds its negative connotation: To posture is "to position, especially strategically"; "to develop a policy or stance," for oneself or one's group; or "to adopt an attitude or take an official position." In general, then, *posturing* describes behaviors ranging from assuming an affected pose to taking a strategic position. I suggest that the pos-turing we see among qualitative researchers in education exhibits that same range.

The purpose of this introductory chapter is to help researchers new to qualitative inquiry become effective strategists rather than affected poseurs. That is, of course, what other contributors to this volume are up to as well. In contrast to either their more theoretically inclined or more methodologically inclined chapters that describe specific ap-proaches, my intent here is to offer a broad overview to help readers find their way among the many alternatives presented.

Let me begin by offering an analogy for thinking about this hand-book and the "field" of qualitative inquiry that it ambitiously endeav-ors to portray. You probably realize that researchers interested in qual-itative approaches must come to terms with them in their own way. Even in educational research, where we seem on the verge of canoniz-ing it, qualitative research is not a field of study, and there is no clearly specified set of activities or identifiable group of specialists who prac-tice them. To claim competence in qualitative research is, at most, to claim general familiarity with what is currently being done, coupled perhaps with experience in one or two particular facets (e.g., to "be good at" collecting and interpreting life histories, or to "be" a symbolic interactionist). Claims to familiarity often amount to little more than a sympathetic attitude toward descriptive or interpretive work, ac-companied by a far more deeply expressed antagonism for that "other kind" of research to which we have begun attaching the negative label "positivist."

Partial though it must be, the range of approaches, issues, and applications presented in this handbook goes beyond what any one individual might ever know or need to know, except in a most general way. If you think of the chapters as houses, then among these authors some might not feel comfortable going as far as next door, and no one knows for certain what it would be like to visit the entire neighborhood.

I draw upon different analogies for my discussion, however, inviting you first to visualize the collection assembled here as a marketplace, a lively "marketplace of ideas" in which the various contributors might be regarded as independent vendors, or even as "hawkers" unashamedly touting their wares. Do not allow yourself to feel overwhelmed as you pass through the marketplace or feel obliged to examine in close detail everything proffered for your inspection. Realize that what you need for a successful visit to and through such a market is a clear idea of what is available that may prove *useful to you.* The advice I offer to anyone new to qualitative research is to "think like a shopper" as you approach the dazzling panoply and claims assembled before your very eyes.

"All very well if you *are* a shopper," you might reply, "but what about going to the marketplace just to have a look around, to see what's available?" Quite right; "having a look around" is reason enough for perusing a market—or perusing qualitative research. Feel free to "wander about," treating these pages like a shopper's catalog, pausing for a closer look when something catches your interest. And as you browse, size up not only the merchandise but the vendors as well. What does intuition tell you? What do you know of the reputations earned or the contributions made through the approaches represented? With which approaches do you feel anxious to get started, rather than anxious about whether or not you could ever conduct a competent piece of research on your own? Do you sense anyone trying to foist upon you a magic all-purpose elixir suitable for every research problem, without seeming regard for what that problem might be?

If you are in the qualitative marketplace but not really "in the market," with neither a research problem nor a problem with research as your pressing issue, enjoy the opportunity for a broad look around. Passing acquaintance with what is current should be sufficient for now. At a later date, with a research agenda of your own, you can return as a more discriminating shopper.

Alternatively, perhaps you anticipate being called upon to direct a tour of the qualitative marketplace, in spite of the fact that you feel a stranger here yourself—as have many academics who have had the teaching of a survey course thrust upon them in recent years. This handbook can also serve as a guidebook, to provide both you and your students with an overview and an introduction for topics to be explored later and in depth. Far less can be included in these pages than everything you may someday want to know about any *particular* approach, but what has been gathered here offers an excellent start, and bibliographic citations provide access to more extensive networks.

The readers I address are those whom, in my market analogy, I have dubbed "serious shoppers." You are not waiting demurely to be won over to qualitative approaches. Instead, you need to know how to make informed choices among them. How do you now decide in which sectors of the market to shop most closely? In brief, how does one gain entrée to qualitative inquiry itself? Let me review two ways to approach it.

The Initial Coin Toss

Like all research, qualitative inquiry has dual facets joined in complementary opposition, much like two sides of a coin. The two sides are the *ideas* that drive the work and the *inquiry procedures* with which researchers pursue them.

Sometimes these facets are pulled so far apart that they become hopelessly separated. We seem especially prone to discuss fieldwork procedures as though they are independent of the ideas we wish to explore. We are easily trapped into these positions, particularly when defending qualitative/descriptive approaches from the litany of our shortcomings concerning reliability, subjectivity, sample size, generalizability, and so forth.

On the other hand, once we recognize that ideas and procedures *are* forever joined—that they really are two sides of the same coin—then their complementary features offer alternative ways to approach qualitative study by variously emphasizing one dimension or the other. Two sides of a coin cannot "come up" together; on each toss, one side must prevail. Similarly, researchers assign priority either to ideas *or* to methodological approaches when addressing a new problem. One must begin somewhere. Research as preached says ideas come first, so I begin my discussion there. In research as practiced, particularly in educational circles, we seem to be forever preoccupied with method, a consequence of our psychometric heritage. My treatment of practice will address those concerns.

In bold relief, I first review how *ideas* help researchers to position themselves and make their moves strategically. In slightly greater detail, I then discuss how researchers orient themselves among the basic *strategies* of qualitative study. Qualitative researchers position themselves by identifying the underlying ideas and assumptions that drive their work and by identifying the procedures they intend to follow. These are the alternative ways to gain entrée into the seeming labyrinth of qualitative inquiry. Ultimately they must be joined as one, but that process occurs gradually, one step at a time.

Idea-Driven Research

To conduct an inquiry of any sort, *somebody* must have an idea. As inquiry proceeds, the idea that prompted it should become both better formed and better informed. The one critical attribute that qualitative and quantitative approaches share is that each begins with an idea that reflects human judgment. The severest critics of qualitative research sometimes appear oblivious to the fact that *all* research begins with a totally subjective, hopelessly human decision about what to study. Problem setting is the pivotal act of all science, social as well as not-so-social.

I have chosen the modest word *idea* as the umbrella term to refer to any and all of the thoughts that drive research. Ideas include everything from reported flashes of genius (how I long someday for one of my own!) to the more pedestrian notions and commonsense procedures that drive most of our work most of the time. I mean to draw attention to ideas themselves, without reflecting too harshly on the persona of the idea-getter.

For my purposes, three subcategories are sufficient to form a modest typology of the ideas that guide qualitative inquiry: theory-driven ideas, concept-driven ideas, and reform or "problem-focused" ideas directed toward redress. Let me say something about each category.

Theory-Driven Ideas

In the long run, we are all engaged in what Robert Merton has described as "the all-inclusive systematic efforts to develop a unified theory that will explain all the observed uniformities of social behavior, social organization, and social change" (1968:39). Those who "think theory" can link up in someone's—perhaps even their own— Big Theory everything that matters to everyone. Most people do not think in terms of grand design or regard themselves as theory builders, and qualitative researchers are not especially noted for their ability to either draw upon or contribute to theory. Personally, however, I am of the view that every human is a profound theory builder, so long as that activity is defined to include the myriad "little theories" necessary for each of us to negotiate our way through everyday lives.

In educational circles, both the term itself and the issues surrounding theory are often bandied about in threatening, counterproductive fashion. Theory is treated more like a moral imperative or a sacred rite than a potentially helpful guidepost. A dramatic instance occurs every time a student being initiated into the role of qualitative researcher is confronted with the terrifying (and often premature) query: "What's your theory?" That question does not necessarily invite intellectual dialogue, even when provoking such a dialogue can charitably be assumed as the intent of the questioner. As I have come to understand the ritual, a graduate student in such straits is expected to answer almost reflexively with a crisp response like "Symbolic Interactionism" or "Communication Theory." Unfortunately, big theoretical perspectives like these, which allow practiced scholars to communicate so much so quickly, are also bully phrases that can drive out little theories (e.g., hunches, notions) too modest to have fancy names or protective guilds. To be respectable, one dare not sink beneath what Merton (1968) called "theories of the middle range."

In an everyday sense, as William James observed, one cannot even "pick up rocks in a field without a theory" (noted in Agar, 1980:23). But researchers also use (or allude to) theory to convey social information about themselves in addition to its orienting function for their efforts. Whenever we identify our theoretical bent or expound on our theoretical underpinnings, we show—and show off—our competence in the research patois of particular professional subgroups. That is one of the major forms of posturing in qualitative inquiry. The names of others in our quoting circles, the labels we affix to our work, and our positioning of our work (and ourselves) within a context of other like-minded researchers all provide clues intended to be recognized within our cohort.

Authors are, of course, free to affix labels to their writing, just as they are free in writing itself, but the term *theory* in a title does not assure that an article will deal with theory, and one cannot entirely depend on authors to situate their work in the most appropriate theoretical milieu. Nor does absence of the term or failure to implicate theory suggest that theoretical bias—for better or for worse—is of no consequence to the researcher. But theory has become a power term among educational researchers, an enhancer sometimes employed to suggest a higher order than the business actually at hand. Just think how the term leads to the confusion that Grounded Theory is a theory (which it is not), that there is any such thing as a unified Literary Theory, or that any two individuals ever have or could have exactly the same thing in mind while nodding agreement about Communication Theory or Constructivism.

In my own struggle to remain theory-literate in the overlapping domains of cultural anthropology and the sociocultural foundations of education, I keep a watchful eye for scholars able to reveal the essence of, and note significant contrasts among, contemporary theories. Two circumstances where this talent is likely to appear are in efforts at "stock-taking" (the art of synthesis is certainly underdeveloped in our work) or when someone proposing a new theoretical framework, or revising an earlier one, provides the requisite overview of existing theories (predictably emphasizing their inadequacies) that prompted its formulation.

In one of their earlier papers, editors LeCompte and Goetz provided an excellent example of the kind of theoretical stock-taking to which I refer. Although their work in that instance was directed toward developing an ethnology of student life in classrooms, they placed their mission within a broader context of descriptive studies according to what they termed *theoretical frames* (Goetz, LeCompte, and Ausherman, 1988). They identified five such frames, assigning to each a brief title:

Structural Functionalism
Conflict Theory
Social Exchange Theory
Symbolic Interactionism
Critical Theory

I find succinct inventories like this informative and provocative. They serve as a resource for anyone seeking an authoritative citation or wanting to adapt an existing list for a new purpose. Although subject to the incontestable criticism that all such lists are necessarily oversimplified, this list, in identifying a manageable number of theoretical orientations, offers a useful means for locating major landmarks on the qualitative horizon. For me, the five theoretical positions are like topographical features on a map. True, pointing to major features draws attention from other noteworthy but less conspicuous ones that are the nuances of detail required by both the seasoned traveler and the casual explorer. And one can always ask "Why only five?" or "Why more than three?" But recognizing a few major features can be of great assistance to newcomers trying to get their bearings. Arguments about criteria for inclusion or level of detail can come later, after one gets a "feel" for the territory.

I also attend to how others writing about theory employ the term *theory* itself, noting particularly whether theory appears to be used strategically or simply to affect a pose or mask a persuasion. I have observed that those who use theory strategically are inclined to employ the word as an adjective rather than as a noun. That is what Goetz *et al.* (1988) did by inventorying Theoretical Frames rather than Grand Theories. Some authors avoid the potential entanglement of the "When is a theory?" issue altogether by employing alternative terms that do not beg the question such as *authoritative paradigms* or *reigning paradigms* (see, e.g., Guba, 1990).

I am neither especially eager to fix my exact bearings on theoretical maps nor especially anxious about my theoretical naiveté. Some researchers characterize themselves as "theory compulsive" or "theory shoppers," which seems to leave me in a residual category for the "theory reluctant." I take comfort in pithy statements such as A. N. Whitehead's depiction of theory as "conceptual entertainment of unrealized possibilities" (quoted in Gowin, 1990:82), or Gregory Bateson's reported insistence that one of his data sets was "sufficiently uncorrupted by theory" to allow for independent analysis.

I do not ordinarily use theory maps to find my way around or to locate my theoretical position vis-à-vis colleagues. I confess that I am awed by the "promise" of theory—what others keep reminding us it will and must accomplish. However, until educational theory gets better, or we get better at it—which will include a clearer idea not only of the various roles it can play but also of the distractions it can provide—I will continue to regard theory as a mixed blessing. It can serve as much as a bugaboo as a help, especially for beginning researchers liable to lose their way along pathways they are unable to discern.

Yet I often need to identify my theoretical position in some informative way, especially to communicate with others who carry only that kind of map in their heads. I am ever-mindful that theory is "out there somewhere." On the five-theory terrain described above I can, however reluctantly, locate myself (with Structural Functionalism). I can—but I would rather not. I prefer to think of myself as working on a gentle theoretical "plain" where distinguishing features are not so prominent, watersheds not so sharply defined. For me, Conflict Theory and Critical Theory may be on the other side of the mountain, but I definitely want to be able to see Symbolic Interactionism, and perhaps Social Exchange Theory, out of the corner of my eye.

Concept-Driven Ideas

Ranking well beneath the prestige level of Grand or Big Theories, or the acceptable but apparently minimum "middle-range" level, are ideas of all shapes and sizes that I will identify collectively as "concepts." Concepts are not flashy like theories; you have to press pretty hard to squeeze theory out of a concept, at least those of the "sensitizing" kind (a label Herbert Blumer [1954:7] proposed to distinguish them from the "definitive" variety). Concepts point in an orienting, consciousness-raising, but saucily independent manner. Linkages among them may be tenuous at best, and they often defy the rigorous definition and empirical basis demanded by "precise" thinkers. Those of us attracted to and satisfied with concepts for orienting our research must suffer accusations that we lack precision, like hunters who carry shotguns rather than rifles, or shoppers who are "just looking."

Nevertheless, for anyone who has not learned how at least to *appear* conversant with theory (which is not the same as actually *being* conversant—a good deal of academic posturing occurs in discussions of theory, as noted), let me commend "concepts" as an attractive level at which to begin. Working at that level—with a concept like "culture," for example—can provide structure without allowing the seeming absence of theoretical structure to become overbearing. This may be especially appealing for fieldworkers who find their mission in searching out interpretations for data rather than in seeking illustrations for theory. Most researchers who identify with a "school," or who conduct work within the canons of a recognized professional field or social science discipline, work with conceptual orientations. We sometimes describe that as working within an "academic tradition," another way of freeing ourselves from having to hook everything up with theory.

Most cultural anthropologists, for example, conduct research in an ethnographic tradition that commits them to cultural interpretation but is relatively noncommittal as to theory. Anthropologists do theorize— about Culture in general, about cultures in specific—and volumes have been written addressing issues of culture theory. Nevertheless, concepts like culture point with an elbow rather than a finger. That is not to render anthropologists theory-less, but to focus instead on the common *conceptual* focus that brings unity to their work.

At the risk of a whopping generalization, I hazard the opinion that anthropologists, like most educational researchers, seem more in-clined to "putter" with theory than to move it forward in systematic fashion. Trendy Big Theories are duly acknowledged, with an ever-watchful eye for what one anthropologist has described as the "demi-decadal trade-in of models" (Salzman, 1988:32), leaving everyone free to propose hypotheses and "little theories" at will. Once conceived, however, theories are pretty much left to fend for themselves. Because anthropologists prefer to propose new theories rather than subject theories already proposed to rigorous review, their "little theories," like those of educators, remain largely unattended. That also suggests that anthropological theorizing more often grows out of fieldwork than it is carried into it.

Theorizing among cultural anthropologists tends to be modest; to be called up during the latter, interpretive stages of research; and to become a preoccupation only in later, post-fieldwork years. Anthropo-logical theorizing is also more evident in orienting deskwork, when final accounts are prepared, than in orienting either fieldwork or fieldworker. But it should not go unnoted that some anthropologists, like some educational researchers, develop a strong theoretical bias. Margaret Mead was a proponent of the exploratory potential of fieldwork, yet she herself may have been the first American anthropol-ogist to take a research problem into the field rather than seek it there. (Note the subtitle to her 1928 study in Samoa: *A Psychological Study of Primitive Youth for Western Civilisation*.)

One might distinguish "up tight" (or, more charitably, "up front") theorists from "laid back" ones. Among the "up front" kind, I identify most sociologists, psychologists, and economists (i.e., researchers who tend to work deductively, with theory posing their problems and al-lowing them to maintain control of what they do). In the "laid back" category, I include the majority of anthropologists, historians, political scientists, and field-oriented or "Chicago School" sociologists. For researchers working in these traditions, theory tends to be enlisted to help understand what already has been observed rather than to dictate what one should be looking for. This same contrast—the "theory-first" and the "theory-after" proponents—might be an alternative way to divide educational researchers into opposing camps at least as distinc-tive as the oversubscribed qualitative–quantitative split.

One of the sometimes unrecognized functions of the labels we attach to our ideas, whether formal theories or casual notions, is that they allow us to communicate with others in-the-know without requir-ing extensive explanation. Another means of "telegraphing" that same information is to identify one's research interests in terms of broad academic disciplines, especially when communicating a conceptual orientation to audiences unaware of important nuances (and endless bickering) within academic traditions. The label of "biographer," "economist," "historian," or "literary critic," for example, may signal as much as the average outsider needs or wants to know about the scholarly endeavors of someone engaging in those specializations. Working in an anthropological vein and identifying myself that way among colleagues in education often prompted the response "Oh, sorta like Margaret Mead, eh?" in my early days as a field researcher in the 1960s, at least among those who recognized that not all anthropologists are archaeologists.

Like lists of currently popular theories, however, lists of dominant *themes*, or *paradigms*, or *traditions* can be finely honed to provide categories that lend conceptual order to the world of social research. Evelyn Jacob is an educational researcher who has described qualitative research by identifying what she has termed its major and currently fashionable "traditions." Jacob's initial taxonomy identified five traditions, with a bias reflecting her academic interest in anthropology (Jacob, 1987). Subsequently she added a sixth tradition that heads a slightly revised and reordered list of dominant traditions in educational research (Jacob, 1988):

Human Ethology
Ecological Psychology
Holistic Ethnography
Cognitive Anthropology
Ethnography of Communication
Symbolic Interactionism

Comparable lists are also compiled according to the labels assigned to cohorts who work in various traditions. Under the auspices of the Social Science Research Council, for example, Richard Shweder (1984:2) formulated a list described simply as "scholars of various denominations" to identify social scientists with a common interest in the concept of culture:

Symbolic or Interpretive Theorists
Cognitive Scientists
Ethnoscientists
Phenomenologists
Psychoanalytic Theorists

Critical Theorists
Contextualists

Those who propose such lists subject themselves to endless criticism, both for the particular categories they select (or omit) and for undertaking at all a task that can impose an unbecoming rigidity on the qualitative enterprise. Jacob's initial effort (1987), for example, was criticized by a team of British researchers who proposed two "important caveats" for readers of her work: "(a) 'Traditions' must be treated not as clearly defined, real entities but only as loose frameworks for dividing research and (b) good research does not stop at national boundaries" (Atkinson, Delamont, and Hammersley, 1988:243). Their concern focused on *defining* traditions too rigidly, rather than on list-making itself, for in providing a guide to British qualitative research, Jacob's critics countered with their own list offered under the heading "Approaches." Their seven approaches are

Symbolic Interactionism
Anthropology
Sociolinguistics
Ethnomethodology
Democratic Evaluation (or "Evaluation by
    Illumination")
Neo-Marxist Ethnography
Feminist Research

Such lists or maps also may be drawn with only the names of prominent researchers as reference points. Sometimes this is done by way of illustration, when a label is accompanied by the name of one or more widely recognized contributors to the field, as illustrated in a phrase like "Poststructural theory as reflected in the writing of Derrida and Foucault." Such lists can be pitched at a broad level or narrowed to scholars working within a particular tradition (e.g., "Poststructuralism as reflected in the writings of anthropologists like Clifford Geertz, Victor Turner, James Clifford, or George Marcus and Michael Fischer").

Just as often, labels may be avoided altogether, an author making reference only to individuals with whom the reader presumably is already familiar. Unfortunately, such blatant name dropping is both overused and abused in academic writing, with citations like "See, for example, Geertz," accompanied by no page references, no specific text, and probably no hint of what we are to look for so that we "see" what our guide wants us to see. (It is paradoxical that Geertz in general—and "Geertz 1973," his essay on thick description, in particular—has become the citation of preference among many qualitatively inclined researchers, for Geertz himself is a master of the erudite, forever referring or alluding to works and lives readers feel they *ought* to know, even if they do not.)

In spite of the excesses, situating one's work or dialogue with other like-minded scholars—and, even more helpfully, making references to specific pages in specific texts rather than to their persona—serves as a convenient shorthand for communicating frames of reference and keeping one's audiences oriented. Let me digress to recommend against ever assuming in your own writing that readers have read what you have read, know what you know, or could ever perceive *anything* exactly as you do. Write for an audience that you assume does *not* know what you are talking about and is *not* conversant with what others have written on the topic but that is keenly interested in knowing. Don't merely "drop" the names of authors, or texts, or theories; instead, weave them into your discussions with informative context.

Reform or "Problem-Focused" Ideas

"Whatever else he may be," anthropologist Ward Goodenough noted years ago, "Man is also a reformer" (Goodenough, 1963:15). Writing today, I doubt that Goodenough would modify anything except his gender language, and nowhere is his maxim better illustrated than in educational research. At about the same time, anthropologist Solon Kimball observed (but, I think, failed to jot down) that most educational reform is conducted under the guise of educational research. I have chosen the straightforward but admittedly loaded term *reform* for the third of my three categories encompassing idea-driven research. The word *reform*, if more widely used, might cast away doubts as to researcher intent; gentler labels mask the underlying commitment to change lurking in "problem-oriented," "decision-oriented," "action," and, most recently, "empowering" research.

What sets this category apart is that coupled with the act of inquiry is an underlying (and presumably conscious) assumption on the part of the researcher that things are not right as they are or, most certainly, are not as good as they might be. The avowed purpose of research is to bring about change directed at improvement. Theories or concepts have dual roles to play in reform: They not only orient the research, they rationalize it (i.e., they lend support to underlying assumptions that things are not right). Today's critical theorists and feminist researchers convene under the banner of theory but work on behalf of an explicit action agenda with a commitment to change. At the conceptual level, educator proponents of both "ethnographic evaluation" (e.g., Fetterman, 1987) and "critical ethnography" are researchers with an applied or action agenda. "Unlike other interpretivist research," as one reviewer has noted of the latter, "the overriding goal of critical ethnography is to free individuals from sources of domination and repression" (Anderson, 1989:249).

Discussion

My three categories—theory-, concept-, and reform-driven research—are neither mutually exclusive nor discrete. Ultimately, everything can be subsumed under theory, even the theory implicit in empiricism that holds sensory experience to be the only source of knowledge, or the theory of action implicit in reform. But I also think it useful to examine research in terms of the immediate concerns that drive it. Among educators, that means assigning priority to reform-driven work. For that reason, a first question to ask of any research effort is whether the end result is to solve a problem or bring about "needed" change, or both. Reform-driven efforts ought always to be clearly identified and recognized, for they employ research in a special way to serve predetermined goals. An incessant "change agenda" drives most educational research, including virtually all school-focused inquiry as well as a great deal of research focused more broadly on educational processes "writ large." The underlying assumption is that, whatever the problem, schools are the answer. (I'm not so sure that non-school-focused research ever finds schooling to be the answer, although schools are often implicated as part of the problem!)

That it is essentially reform-oriented or applied does not relegate school research to a lesser role than so-called pure or basic research. Schools are here to stay, the circumstances of formal education are infinitely improvable, and teachers themselves continue to demonstrate a willingness to engage in research that they perceive as relevant to their instructional programs. Perhaps the straightforwardness of qualitative/descriptive approaches has sparked new research interests among teachers. But these days—thanks also to the broadened perspective that qualitative inquiry has fostered—not all educational research is school-focused, and not every "outside" researcher is hell-bent on manipulating treatments or measuring classroom climates. We have been slow to recognize that a great place to learn about the processes of schooling is in schools. We don't yet seem ready to examine how schools may also be great places to learn about human social learning, including learning how to cope with the institution of school itself.

A critical feature of reform-driven research is the initial identification of the problem or program to which attention will be directed. Whether or not that is a happy circumstance for the individual researcher is often a function of personality and most always plays a role in the essential task of garnering institutional support. Problem setting is the epitome of the research act, but few researchers have or necessarily even want the freedom to decide which problems to pursue. The influences of both the politics of research and the proclivities of researchers are apt to escape us, enmeshed as we are in the social systems we purport to examine as objective investigators. I suspect that few if any researchers actually conceive and conduct their studies with anything like the freedom and detachment which they probably believe essential to their work. But that, as they say, is another story.

Procedure-Driven Research

Identifying a great question for a research study is no guarantee of a correspondingly great answer about how to pursue it. Neither theories, concepts, nor reform implicates specific methodological procedures, at least with any precision. An inclination toward Critical Theory or Cognitive Approaches is hardly a prescription for gathering relevant observational data. A seemingly straightforward, focused approach like Conversation Analysis takes on unexpected complexity with the realization that not even natural conversation is an ordinary by-product of researcher-present research. ("Just go ahead and talk. Pretend I'm not here.") Each social science offers the advantage of structured procedures for conducting research, but that advantage is gained at the cost of having to shape one's problem in terms of how it is customarily defined and investigated by others working in the same tradition. The "sedentary wisdom" of long-established traditions, as critics like Buchmann and Floden (1989:244) point out, offers legitimation rather than liberation; the biggest breakthroughs in scientific thinking have often required a break with investigative traditions rather than blind allegiance to them.

My anthropologist colleague Malcolm McFee used to lament, "Educational researchers are lucky. They always know what they are supposed to be looking at." If that is a blessing, however, it is a mixed one, to be weighed against the fact that educational researchers typically are not well versed in the theories, concepts, or methods of any particular academic tradition. Their career patterns reflect the practical experience of classroom teaching rather than theoretical grounding in a social science. As a consequence, they tend to be not only admirably eclectic but doggedly noncommittal, cheerfully proffering their receptivity to all approaches in lieu of thorough acquaintance with any of them. Furthermore, their experience as practitioners often has been gained in a climate overtly hostile to academia, with researchers perceived as doing things "to" or "on" teachers rather than for or in collaboration with them.

The question of calling forth appropriate procedures—of striking one's methodological posture—is every bit as critical as the issue of conceptualization. It is the central issue I address here, since several other contributors were assigned responsibility for presenting a range of conceptual and theoretical orientations. I have already suggested one might regard them as "hawking"—trying to get you to "buy into" qualitative study through particular conceptual orientations, established academic traditions, or calls for reform. Their sales pitches are convincing, their attentions flattering. But do not lose track of why you are in the marketplace—to assess options in terms of your own circumstances and talents.

These proponents are not only accomplished promoters, they are accomplished researchers as well. They know what can be done by pursuing each particular approach because they themselves have demonstrated success with it. In seeking ways to approach your own research, the important question is not whether these approaches work, but whether they are realistic alternatives because of the likelihood they will work for *you* and adequately address *your* problem.

Method is always adjunct to good science, we are told, and therefore nothing might seem more preposterous than a method (or methodologist) going in search of a problem. But that is part of the science myth, not its reality, as ethnographers of laboratory life have revealed (e.g., Latour and Woolgar, 1979; Traweek, 1988). In the real world of research, the most seasoned veterans probably are conversant with no more than one or two different approaches. Among experienced qualitative researchers, my impression is that the more senior one becomes, the less obliged one feels to demonstrate wide-ranging talents: One's own forte is already established. (Where I think senior qualitative researchers often err in later studies is in abandoning the painstaking efforts that distinguished their early work and established their reputations. The tendency is to escalate the *scale* of subsequent investigations in a way that works against achieving the level of thoroughness or intimacy of detail that gained them their reputations in the first place, i.e., a tendency to examine more phenomena, rather than to examine a particular phenomenon in more depth.)

Although method may be "secondary" or adjunct—i.e., necessary but not sufficient—it nonetheless offers an excellent way to position oneself strategically for initiating qualitative study. If you are not theoretically inclined, orient yourself by examining the techniques employed by other qualitative researchers. Make sense in terms of what you want to learn and ways that seem appropriate and realistic for going about learning it. In an effort to assist in that task, let me first strip these procedures to what I regard as the bare essentials. I will then examine how they are combined to form some (not all!) of the more readily distinguishable styles of qualitative inquiry employed by educational researchers.

The Basic Techniques in Qualitative Inquiry

I propose that the full range of data-gathering techniques employed in qualitative study can be subsumed under three categories of activity. In turn, the categories can be identified by common, everyday terms such as *watching, asking,* and what might be glossed as *reviewing.* Restated with more sophistication (but without further enlightenment), we often hear these activities referred to as *observing, interviewing,* and *archival research.* For alliterative as well as pedagogical purposes, the labels I have chosen to use here are *experiencing,* with emphasis on sensory data, particularly watching and listening; *enquiring,* in which the researcher's role becomes more intrusive than that of a "mere observer"; and *examining,* in which the researcher makes use of materials prepared by others.

These three techniques are so basic—and so unassuming—that when we employ any one of them as our sole research strategy we feel compelled to gussy it up in more esoteric language. We do not admit to "watching" studies or "asking" studies. Conducting an "observer" study also sounds a bit thin, although the phrase "observational data" has a nice ring. We elevate watching to the status of "participant observation," which clearly has become the label of choice for much descriptive or "naturalistic" research. (I caution, however, that most so-called participant observer studies in education warrant that label only in the sense that the researcher was physically present. "Outside" researchers seldom become involved as genuine participants in educational settings, and they are inclined to express ambivalence as to whether or not their own involvement is desirable or even acceptable. As a result, they become more preoccupied with potential observer effects than with finding ways to become more effective observers. Conversely, teacher researchers, the classroom's natural participant observers, encounter great difficulty disengaging sufficiently from personal experience to be convincing as "detached" observers.)

We do not speak of "listening" studies or "asking" studies or "enumeration studies." Instead, we dignify such work with grand titles like "oral history" or "ethnographic interviewing." Census-taking becomes "household survey" when we parade our techniques before others. We search out, and search in, libraries and other depositories of public and private documents, but "archival strategies" or "historical research" sounds more elegant than does "going to the library," "reading old newspapers and diaries," or "looking it up."

Some of the myriad combinations drawing upon these three basic ways of knowing have come to be regarded as distinctive approaches in qualitative inquiry. Any recognized approach may implicate not only a particular proportion of each of the three basic ingredients but also may imply some sense of priority among them and an idea of what we may rightly anticipate in the finished product.

In his classic article "Some Methodological Problems of Field Studies," Morris Zelditch laid the groundwork for analyzing field studies in terms of multiple methods in order to emphasize his major point—that "a field study is not a single method gathering a single kind of information" (1962:566). Consistent with his sociological orientation, the three "types" of method he identified were *participant observation, informant interviewing*, and *enumerations and samples*.

I have taken liberty with Zelditch's third category to make his list more broadly applicable to all qualitative inquiry. That third category, *enumerations and samples*, is adequately addressed through either of the first two; whether the systematic data collection essential for "enumerations and samples" is accomplished through *participant observation* or *informant interviewing* depends on researcher style and research purposes. Beginning fieldworkers need to recognize that observation and interviewing yield complementary rather than comparable data. What people tell us tends to reveal how they believe things *should be.* What we ourselves observe firsthand is more likely to reveal how things *are*, assuming that field observations extend throughout an adequate time period. In everyday life, of course, that is why the old days are so often portrayed as the good old days.

Zelditch specifically excluded the examination of documents from his three types of method on the grounds that they represent "resultants or combinations of primary methods." I do not concur that the role of document (and artifact) analysis in qualitative research should be so lightly dismissed. Instead, I have created a major category for that aspect of qualitative work under the broad label *archival research* or *examining*. I have done this not only in deference to the dominant research activity of biographers, historians, and philosophers but also to acknowledge that virtually *all* fieldworkers make use of materials prepared by others.

Zelditch's purposes were, first, to underscore that field study is not a single method and, second, to consider the kinds of questions that each component is best suited to address. As he noted, survey and sampling procedures provide frequency distributions. Participant observation provides information about incidents and histories. Through informant interviewing, we learn about institutionalized norms and statuses. In recent years we have witnessed a growing affinity for the idea (if not necessarily the actual practice) of "triangulation" as a way to respond to questions about the confirmability of data. A broad term like "field study" implies the use of multiple research techniques. Anthropologists make reference to a similar idea with their emphasis on fieldwork as a "multi-instrument approach" (e.g., Pelto and Pelto, 1978:121–122).

Anyone familiar with anthropological fieldwork but unfamiliar with Zelditch's article, or vice versa, might well wonder whether or not "field study" and "ethnography" are labels for the same thing. I take the position that they are related but are not the same. Making that distinction at this point presents the opportunity to examine qualitative approaches in terms of their common elements, rather than on the basis of the disparity suggested earlier by my "marketplace" analogy.

Field study and ethnography draw upon the three techniques basic to all field-oriented research: experiencing, enquiring, and examining. What distinguishes between them is that anyone doing ethnography makes a claim not only about procedures but also that the *result* will be ethnography. Ethnography is the end-product for the culturally focused description and interpretation that characterize anthropological fieldwork. Ethnography, therefore, is field study *plus* something special in the nature of interpretive emphasis, just as field study, in turn, draws upon disparate fieldwork techniques but combines them into something more than the product of pursuing any of them alone.

The sets of different labels that move us along from one or more of the three basic research approaches (e.g., interviewing) to a multi-method field study, and perhaps to something even more carefully specified, like ethnography, represent a series of discernible steps. Everyday experience is the starting point, which is then transcribed and transformed through the fieldworker's observing and recording to become the description and analysis presented in a scholarly mono-graph, article, report, or film. (It may also move toward an alternative objective to the traditional ones under review here.)

Along this progression, each researcher makes myriad choices that entail strategic decisions and differing expectations. Consistent with following any *particular* tradition, a bit more structure may be im-posed about how the reporting should be completed, including such mundane expectations as the "proper" number of pages, the "custom-ary" topics to be addressed, and perhaps even the "usual" sequence in which topics are announced and presented. Or a bit more may be necessary to help the researcher identify, and identify with, some subset of like-minded scholars who share an orientation to a particular set of procedures, a particular tradition, a particular subset of concepts, or a particular theoretical position.

This critical relationship between techniques and outcomes in qualitative inquiry is masked in a marketplace analogy that empha-sizes *differences in outcomes* rather than a *common set of procedures* for arriving at them. To emphasize interrelatedness, allow me to draw, and draw upon, a different analogy. Interrelatedness among qualita-tive approaches may be better illustrated by analogy to the branching structure of a giant shade tree, with strong limbs reaching out toward gradually thinning branches that extend from a sturdy trunk repre-senting a common "core" of research techniques (see Fig. 1). This qualitative "tree" beckons researchers to climb into its branches above the "soil of everyday experience" (to push the analogy a bit) to gain perspective on that experience. It is critical to keep in mind, however, that only the perspective from which events are viewed changes, not the events themselves.

Like all human observers, qualitative researchers rely on the same three general categories of techniques for gathering information: expe-riencing, enquiring, and examining. The difference between mere mortals and themselves is that qualitative researchers, like others whose roles demand selective attentiveness—artists and novelists, detectives and spies, guards and thieves, to name a few—pay special attention to a few things to which others ordinarily give only passing

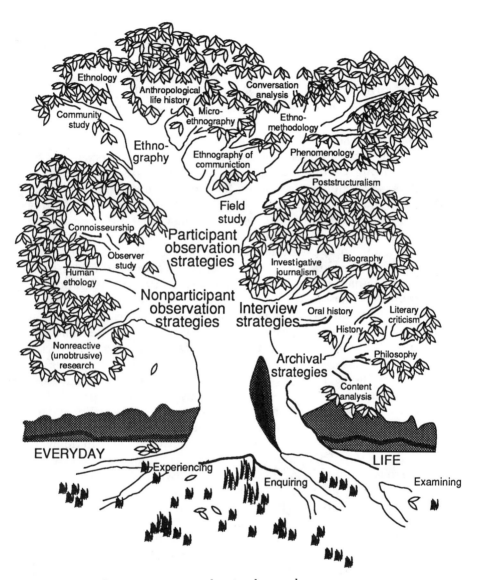

Figure 1 Qualitative strategies in educational research.

attention. Observers of any ilk do no more: We all attend to certain things, and nobody attends to them all.

When such everyday behaviors as watching and asking become the basis for a role definition as "qualitative researchers," small wonder that we look for impressive-sounding labels that help to validate us as the self-appointed observers of our fellow humans. We cannot escape either our humble roots in the events of everyday life or the preposterous goal we set for ourselves intellectually to make sense of them, as we endeavor, in Geertz's phrase "first to grasp and then to render" (Geertz, 1973:10). Alas, we must accept as accolade a judgment that may not always be intended as one—that we make the obvious obvious.

For the social researcher, however, the "tree" of qualitative inquiry entices with the prospect of a better view (i.e., perspective) for anyone willing to attempt the climb. The climb entails making choices along the way, choices that, for better and for worse—and literally as well as figuratively—can find one out on a limb. Inexperienced tree climbers are cautioned not to go higher than what feels secure and affords safe retreat. That is good advice for beginning qualitative researchers, too: not to pretend to be so far "above" the basic techniques that you lose your grasp of what you have observed and understood, nor to try too hard to impress others by extending your reach beyond the point necessary to see what you set out to see. I caution against posturing that entices you to make unwarranted claims about how far up or out you will go, at least until you are familiar with the choices to be made, where they lead, and the costs and risks likely to be involved. By costs and risks, I refer not to risks to human subjects but risks to researchers themselves in pursuing strategies that preclude reasonable alternatives, setting objectives that subsequently prove unattainable, or overreaching in the attempt to "transcend" observational data.

On the other hand, if you lay claim to being or becoming a qualitative researcher, you are making a claim about what you can do, what you have to offer. This should be "your kind of tree," and you should be able to get around in it. There are at least two questions facing you: How far do you need to get above the comforting security of data collected through the basic techniques, and what choices will you have to make to reach your intended perch? To be methodologically secure, the labels that derive from the data-gathering techniques on which they are based (in Fig. 1, the major strategy labels Archival, Interview, Nonparticipant Observation, and Participant Observation) offer the security of firmly rooted empirical data. Many a newcomer has been lured to qualitative study by the apparent ease of simply conducting some interviews, making some observations, or becoming a participant observer in order to "do research." A comforting myth is that objectivity and thoroughness are served if one faithfully observes, records, and reports "everything." It sounds so simple.

What is not apparent at first quickly becomes so once such wholesale data-gathering proceeds. Broad labels like Participant Observation or Interview offer no guidelines as to what to look at, what to look for, or what to record. They are no more helpful than being informed that to do archival research, a good place to start is the library. From the very first step up into the tree, then, there must be a guiding idea or purpose.

That purpose is not to be found among the qualitative strategies represented by the various branches. It is brought to the setting by the individual researcher. "Where is Theory?" my students queried when I presented them with an early sketch of the tree that would become Figure 1. They could not locate it as part of the tree itself, any more than a real tree has an idea of how it should be climbed—or why. What prompts the climb is a function of the climber, not the tree. Furthermore, there are other ways to get into a tree in addition to climbing its trunk—and there are other ways to pursue qualitative study. Theory, for example, can provide an external scaffolding from which a deductively oriented researcher can reach out and connect with even the most delicate branches without having to depend at all on the sturdiness of the tree for support or balance.

To follow the tree analogy, let me explore the branch of qualitative inquiry that leads toward ethnography and ethnology, terms heard with increasing frequency among educational researchers in recent decades. Starting at ground level, we encounter a sturdy trunk securely rooted in the techniques basic to all qualitative research. But the trunk of this figurative (and obviously oversimplified) tree soon presents options in the form of major forks and branches. The field-oriented researcher may be tempted to explore archival strategies only briefly—no more than necessary for the requisite literature review or a note on the historical context of a problem—while an educational historian may find no reason to proceed farther, his or her life's work spread out in an immediate network of limbs and branches all worthy of careful investigation.

Next, major forks beckon to one side or the other for the researcher whose problem (or personality) is best suited to emphasizing observer *or* interview strategies rather than trying to blend the two. Participant observation strategies immediately fork again. One becomes a major sociologically oriented branch leading out along established branches of phenomenology and ethnomethodology, and along a branch of the latter to conversation analysis, or out along slender, newly forming offshoots (only suggested in the diagram) toward poststructuralism and feminist perspectives. Another major branch opens out to anthropological alternatives, with an important offshoot among educational researchers leading to the ethnography of communication, and the suggestion of yet another, intertwined with sociology in the newly forming Interactional Sociolinguistics.

To pursue anthropologically oriented ethnography, one must follow a progression in which the procedures lead toward cultural interpretation. That view is unique; no other is quite like it. But to arrive at that perspective, one must forgo opportunities to explore other forks leading to other major branches (e.g., qualitative inquiry conducted in more sociological or psychological traditions, or stressing other strategies; the "tree" is far more complex than what is sketched here, and there is always the nagging doubt that a tree does not offer a suitable analogy at all). There are also critical choices to be made among lateral branches of any major one. Important anthropological alternatives, for example, lead out from macro- or "general" ethnography to community study, micro-ethnography, and anthropological life history. Like any tree, real or imagined, an individual can only climb "into" this one, not take command of it.

Now, consider. Is ethnography likely to provide the perspective you seek, the coign of vantage from which you want to observe some particular subset of the events of everyday life? Might your research purposes be served adequately by employing the basic *techniques* used by ethnographers (as well as most other field-oriented researchers) but making your way along a different "branch" instead? True, the label "ethnography" may enhance your work—if it really is ethnography. But keep in mind that if you announce at the outset where you expect to go, you will be expected to report back from that perspective. If you are uncertain how genuinely ethnographic your study may be, here is the moment for exercising restraint in making claims.

My choice of ethnography for illustration is not happenstance. Questions about employing that label first drew my attention to "posturing" in educational research, of both the strategy-devising and the impression-creating kinds. The problem surfaced with the growing recognition and acceptance of qualitative study that gained momentum through the 1960s and became well established in the 1970s. There were fewer distinguishable permutations in those early days. "Ethnography" had a special appeal; it was discipline-based, vaguely familiar, and neither associated with nor cowed by the reigning psychometric paradigm in educational research. Inadvertently, however, the term implied that *all* of education's new breed of qualitatively oriented researchers were conducting research "just like anthropologists" in general and "just like Margaret Mead" in particular.

But they weren't. Or, more accurately, not many of them were, and not many others were paying attention to the question of whether or not this "new" qualitative interest was meeting the requisite commitment to cultural interpretation that had always been a hallmark of ethnographic research. Most certainly it entailed some necessary but insufficient characteristics of ethnography, such as careful and detailed ("thick") description, attention to context, and data gathered *in situ* and in person. These characteristics also distinguished it from other forms of scholarship like history or philosophy, traditions well established but typically *contrasted with* research rather than regarded as *alternative forms* of it, if not dismissed summarily as humanistic rather than scientific endeavors.

A question still remains as to whether qualitative inquiry is—or should be—so broadly defined that it encompasses long-established traditions like biography, history, and literary criticism, or should be restricted to the field-based, descriptive approaches receiving attention here. Given the self-consciously methodological orientation that continues to (and will always?) dominate educational research, what probably joins all qualitative approaches in most minds is not a presumed uniformity of method as much as a prevailing notion among outsiders that what we "qualitative types" have in common is the absence of any method at all.

Qualitative researchers in education have never agreed among themselves about whether to make more of the differences among their approaches (as suggested by the marketplace analogy of competing and seemingly independent vendors) or to emphasize their commonality (as suggested by the tree analogy) in order to effect a common front. The latter position was epitomized several years ago in an important article written by Louis M. Smith, one of qualitative/descriptive research's earliest and most energetic proponents and practitioners. Although preparing a broad overview addressed to "the genre of research that is coming to be known by such varied labels as educational ethnography, participant observation, qualitative observation, case study, or field study," Smith elected to ignore distinguishing features among them. "For the most part," he stated, "I will use these terms as synonyms" (Smith, 1979:316).

A number of qualitatively oriented educational researchers, including some like myself of anthropological persuasion looking to protect fair Ethnography's name, have taken a different view. We feel that qualitative inquiry is better served not only by acknowledging the research techniques shared in common among qualitative approaches but also by recognizing how the techniques are variously employed, adapted, and combined to achieve different purposes. We take issue with the idea of treating the labels as synonyms. The tree we envision grows *out* like a massive oak rather than *up* like a tall pine.

I first approached this topic of "ethnographicness" in a 1975 article, "Criteria for an ethnographic approach to research in schools," followed in 1980 with "How to look like an anthropologist without being one." I felt awkward when confronted with the argument that the differences I sought to preserve were "only academic," but I held my ground, insisting that, after all, we *are* academics. We have an obligation to recognize genres. We may intentionally adapt or mix them, but we should not indiscriminately blur them or ignore the contribution each might make if pursued in its pristine form. However, I also recognized the frustration of researchers sympathetic to qualitative approaches who felt that, just when they finally had found a way to legitimate their naturalistic leanings by employing the label "ethnography," others were insisting that their work was not ethnographic after all and should not be so labeled.

Even today, Lou Smith insists that his case studies are ethnographies (e.g., Smith, Prunty, Dwyer, and Kleine, 1987:5; see also Smith, 1990) and can be regarded as ethnologies as well (Smith *et al.*, 1987:13–21). And I still argue that they are not. My argument follows the line of reasoning reviewed here, that Smith and his co-researchers effectively employ the fieldwork *techniques* used by (but are by no means exclusive to) ethnographers, but they do not make the requisite commitment to cultural interpretation. Nor do I argue that they should, for to do so would detract from Smith's own eclectic strategies and freewheeling interpretations clearly intended to help student and practitioner alike achieve an integrated and interdisciplinary (ethnography, history, and biography) approach to educational inquiry— rather than to make more astute anthropological fieldworkers of them.

We ethnographic purists don't really expect to convince Lou Smith, or other heavy "borrowers," of the need for preserving ethnographic purity. Nonetheless, in the prolonged but amiable dialogue that has ensued, we have been able to alert waves of qualitative researchers—who otherwise might have followed unquestioningly in those footsteps—to be cautious in choosing between "doing ethnography" and "borrowing ethnographic techniques." That distinction has proven salutary, I believe, as more—and more clearly distinguishable—styles for conducting qualitative inquiry have been introduced, styles developed out of field-based procedures but free of the exclusive dependency on ethnography for their validation as witnessed earlier. Among the better-established qualitative approaches today (including some talked about more than practiced) are human ethology, phenomenology, ethnomethodology, investigative journalism, and connoisseurship/criticism. Among "budding" newcomers are poststructuralism, interactional sociolinguistics, constructivism, and feminist perspectives. One would have to stretch to regard such varied approaches as "synonyms."

Some End-Products of Field-Oriented Studies in Education

In the previous section, I suggested that the common roots of qualitative inquiry can be found in three major data-gathering techniques basic to everyday life. By way of illustration, I followed these techniques along one important branch of research to show how they can lead to ethnography and ethnology. A researcher makes choices all along the way to arrive at any *particular* end product, and, of course, something must result from these efforts. In this section, I want to make note of a number of alternative end-products in field-oriented research. I have summarized this material in Table 1, which follows the same set of research strategies presented in the tree analogy. Here the focus is on outcomes in terms of the *customary product* of field-oriented research, the written report, rather than on alternative outcomes or processes. (For more on writing processes in qualitative research, see Richardson, 1990; Wolcott, 1990.)

This different emphasis calls for departures from the tree analogy and the tree diagram presented in Fig. 1. The first difference is that, in keeping with a focus on field-oriented research, I have not pursued the branch of inquiry that leads exclusively into archival research. Field-oriented researchers do make use of existing materials of all sorts. However, the scholarly approaches that rely most exclusively on such materials—historians, for example—have their own long traditions, and it is out of the question to try to encompass all that work here. Whether or not educational historians and philosophers (and biographers, to look at another established branch of inquiry) are to be, or wish to be, numbered among the constituents of the newly defined qualitative enterprise also remains at issue. This ambivalence is reflected in edited collections in the past few years in which historians, philosophers, and biographers sometimes make an appearance and sometimes do not. Eisner and Peshkin (1990), for example, invited educational philosophers to join their dialogue; Jaeger (1988) invited historical as well as philosophical contributions; and Sherman and

Table 1. Some End Products of Field-Oriented Studies in Education[a]

Genre	Illustrative types	Central concern	Variations	Foundations and procedures	Models of completed work
Case study	Broadly defined; virtually any type of study described below may be reported as a case study	The case itself is regarded as a bounded system	Sometimes categorized according to intent (e.g., descriptive, exploratory, explanatory)	Becker, 1990; Harvard Business School "cases" (e.g., Christensen, 1987); Merriam, 1988; Stake, 1978, 1988; Yin, 1984	Kyle, 1987; Reid and Walker, 1975; Schön, 1991; Stake and Easley, 1978
			Field study in formal organizations	*Administrative Science Quarterly* (Winter, 1980)	Lutz and Iannaccone, 1969; Popkewitz and Tabachnick, 1981
			Single subject or N = 1 research[b]	Hersen and Barlow, 1976; Kratochwill, 1977, 1978	
Nonparticipant observation study	Observer study	Observer acknowledged but not involved	Studies of behavior settings		Barker, 1968; Barker and Wright, 1955; Gump, 1967
			Studies of classroom interaction		Biddle, 1967; Bossert, 1979; Cazden, 1988; Erickson and Mohatt, 1982; Jackson, 1968
	Human ethology	Description of social behavior patterned on animal studies		Ambrose, 1978	Blurton-Jones, 1972; McGrew, 1972

				Conceptualized as a form of educational evaluation by Eisner (1976, 1977, 1981, 1985, 1991)	Alexander, 1977, 1980; Barone, 1983; McCutcheon, 1976, 1978
	Connoisseurship/criticism	Linking the art of appreciation and the art of disclosure			
	Portraiture; vignettes	The artist's shaping hand captures essential features in quick, broad strokes			*Daedalus* (Fall, 1981); Lightfoot, 1983; Perrone, 1985
Interview study	Investigative journalism	Event-focused and current	Journalistic reporting	Harrison and Stein, 1973; Lovell, 1983; Ullman and Honeymoon, 1983	Guba, 1981a,b[c]
			Depth reporting	Copple, 1964	
			Reform journalism		Mayer, 1961; Wiseman, 1969 (film)
			Precision journalism	Meyer, 1973	
	Oral History	Nonrecorded history	Oral history	Dollard, 1937; Hoopes, 1979; Thompson, 1978; Vansina, 1985	Altenbaugh, 1991; Precourt, 1982
			Anthropological life history	Goodson, 1980; Langness and Frank, 1981; Watson and Watson-Franke, 1985	

(*continued*)

Table 1. *Continued*

Genre	Illustrative types	Central concern	Variations	Foundations and procedures	Models of completed work
Participant observation study			Folklore; storytelling	Jackson, 1987; Richardson, 1975	Brauner, 1974; Connelly and Clandinin, 1990; Denny, 1978
	Participant observer study[d] (i.e., not claiming specific traditions such as those listed below)	Observer is present to participate, observe, and/or interview		Bruyn, 1966; Gold, 1958; Jorgensen, 1989; Kluckhohn, 1940; Smith, 1979; Whyte, 1955; Woods, 1986	Cusick, 1973; Peshkin, 1978, 1986; Smith and Pohland, 1974; Waller, 1932; Wylie, 1957[e]
			On-site research		Herriott and Gross, 1979
			Naturalistic research		Guba, 1978; Lincoln and Guba, 1985; Wolf and Tymitz, 1977
			Collaborative research	Adler and Adler, 1987	Filby et al., 1980; Jordan, 1985; Smith and Geoffrey, 1968
	Field study	Observe, interview, enumerate	Field study	Zelditch, 1962	Becker et al., 1961
			Grounded theory study	Glaser, 1978; Glaser and Strauss, 1967; Strauss and Corbin, 1990	Most of Louis M. Smith's work[f]

Phenomenology	"I am a camera"; all description of social action from view of the actor	Phenomenology[g]	Husserl, 1962; Mohanty, 1982; Natanson, 1979; Wann, 1964	Denton, 1974; Heshusius, 1986; Scudder and Mickunas, 1985; van Manen, 1990
		Phenomenological sociology	Schutz, 1967	
		Phenomenological psychology	Giorgi, 1970	
Ethnomethodology	How people make sense and make visible the rationality of their everyday lives		Douglas, 1970; Garfinkel, 1967; Handel, 1982; Heritage, 1984; Mehan and Wood, 1975; Psathas, 1979	Cicourel et al., 1974
		Focus on interpretations	Cicourel, 1973; Garfinkel, 1967	
		Focus on accounting practices		
		Conversation analysis	Moerman, 1988; Sacks, Schegloff, and Jefferson, 1974	
		Ethnography of communication	Gumperz and Hymes, 1964	McDermott, 1976; McDermott and Church, 1976; Philips, 1972, 1983

(continued)

Table 1. *Continued*

Genre	Illustrative types	Central concern	Variations	Foundations and procedures	Models of completed work
			Constitutive microethnography		Erickson, 1975; Mehan, 1978, 1980
			Specific or focused ethnography		Erickson and Shultz, 1981; McDermott, 1976; McDermott and Church, 1976
	Ethnography	Cultural description and interpretation	Macro-ethnography	Geertz, 1973; Malinowski, 1922; see also Kimball, 1955	Henry, 1963
			Community study	Arensberg and Kimball, 1940	Ogbu, 1974; Warren, 1967; Wolcott, 1967
			Microethnography		Chang 1991; Spindler, 1982; Wolcott, 1973
	Ethnology	Systematic comparisons across ethnographies		Brandt, 1982; Ettinger, 1983; Helm, 1985; Hymes, 1980	

[a] An earlier version of this table appeared in an article titled "Differing styles of on-site research" (Wolcott, 1982). The present version has been revised, updated, and, with technical help from Mark Horney, reformatted. Emphasis continues to be on identifying illustrative examples rather than providing a comprehensive survey.

[b] Single-subject research is design-rigorous; it is included here only as an exception to underscore the distinction between "one-subject" case studies and Single Subject or "N = 1" research.

[c] Guba proposes this procedure in educational research as a technique for checking the credibility of information, not as a full-blown method.

[d] The term participant observation appears as early as Lindeman (1924;191).

[e] Although Wylie's *Village in the Vaucluse* is not education-focused, it provides an excellent example of community study in the broad genre of participant observation rather than one of the more carefully prescribed types that follow.

[f] Given his proclivity for "grounded theory," and a customarily eclectic approach to research involving observation, interviewing, and enumeration, Louis M. Smith's work seems to fit here. See Smith's own discussion for an excellent review of the evolution of descriptive research in North America and Great Britain from the 1920s to the late 1970s (Smith, 1979).

[g] Phenomenology has evolved along two disparate lines, one following Husserl in the "Continental" sense, the other providing a more experiential tradition in its "American" sense.

Webb (1988) included biographical, historical, and philosophical views in theirs. I think qualitative inquiry is best served by leaving the door open to researchers who work in these traditions. Whether or not they themselves welcome this embrace is yet to be seen.

In passing, let me mention two techniques included in Fig. 1, Content Analysis and Nonreactive, or Unobtrusive, Research, that might seem to deserve places of their own in the table, although they usually augment some larger research effort rather than serve as end-products in themselves. Content Analysis procedures are employed by all kinds of researchers and have wide application. Paradoxically, Content Analysis beckons qualitative researchers into the opposing camp, requiring them to devise and follow systematic counting procedures. Yet it presents those of opposite persuasion, the quantitative researchers, with the ultimate qualitative question, "What counts?" Discussions about Content Analysis can be found in Krippendorff (1980) and Weber (1985).

The second set of procedures that may seem conspicuous by their absence in the table are those of Non-reactive Research (for the original source, see Webb, Campbell, Schwartz, and Sechrest, 1966). This type of observation is by definition so intentionally unobtrusive that researcher and research alike typically remain unknown to people in the setting. Although such observations may be made by any keen observer, I have not awarded Nonreactive Research the status of a full-blown approach that by itself leads to a major end-product of research.

Another major difference between the "tree" of Fig. 1 and Table 1 concerns Case Study and Case Study "Method." Case Study may have seemed conspicuously absent among the fieldwork strategies identified in Fig. 1. In Table 1, it makes a prominent appearance as an end-product of field-oriented research. Recognizing Case Study as an *end-product* rather than as a *strategy* represents a change in my own thinking. Heretofore, I have regarded Case Study as a way to conduct research and, thus, have included it in any discussion of strategies or methods (Wolcott, 1982, 1990:65). In trying to situate Case Study on the "tree," however, it seemed to fit everywhere in general, yet nowhere in particular. Although every strategy identified can be reported in Case Study format, Case Study does not implicate any particular approach. I suggest that case study can be most appropriately regarded as an outcome or format for *reporting* qualitative/descriptive work, but I propose that we examine critically the practice of regarding it as a qualitative "method" (cf. Merriam, 1988; Yin, 1984).

That "Case Study" and "Method" have been linked to create

"Case Study Method" seems both strange and telling. It is telling as a reminder of our pervasive defensiveness about method. To ward off accusations that we are lacking in method, we have acquired the habit of attaching that term to everything we do in qualitative inquiry. I make a conscious effort to use the word method reservedly, substituting "technique," "procedure," or "approach" whenever one of these alternative terms can be used instead. I avoid the word "methodology" altogether except when referring explicitly to *issues* (rather than *applications*) of method.

Perhaps we do interviewing and observing a disservice to label them as methods. With virtually all the end products identified in Table 1, a close inspection of origins usually reveals self-conscious efforts by early or vigorous proponents to emphasize that these are not methods at all. They are ways to conceptualize human social behavior and to describe and analyze it. Phenomenology is not a method. Ethnomethodology is not a method. Ethnography did not become a method until outsiders got hold of it; old-timers among cultural anthropologists still show a preference for the modest phrase "ethnographic research." We might speak and write with greater clarity and candor if we placed a moratorium on the term "method" for a few years, vowing to replace it in each instance with a carefully chosen alternative. In most cases, I believe we will discover that we are really talking about outcomes, although the language we use calls attention to method instead.

Before leaving the topic of Case Study, let me emphasize one further point from that section of the table—my inclusion of a category for Single-Subject, or "N = 1," research. As a footnote in Table 1 explains, these labels are included as exceptions, not as examples. Case Study can be defined in the broadest of terms and, as suggested above, seems improperly designated as a method; Single-Subject studies, as employed in the field of special education, are, by contrast, design-rigorous. Our own "cases of one" should not be described as "Single-Subject" research, and our Ns of one (i.e., one informant, one school, one village) should not be confused with "N = 1" research.

In similar vein, I admit to some tentativeness in including the category Human Ethology as a qualitative approach. As the study of animal behavior, ethology is an old science, but *human* ethology, particularly the study of very young children in school settings, is a relative newcomer. I doubt that ethologists of any ilk would feel comfortable finding themselves counted among qualitative rather than quantitative researchers. Although developed through "mere" description, their observations are of a most exacting nature, their work a reminder of how powerful *systematic* observation can be.

If you keep these caveats in mind, Table 1 should speak for itself as a guide to some of the more commonly found and frequently referred to outcomes in field-oriented research. Case Study is the first category, under the broad heading Genre, followed by Nonparticipant Observation Study, Interview Study, and Participant Observation Study. For each category, additional information is provided under the headings Illustrative Types, Central Concern, and Variations. Entries under the heading Foundations and Procedures call attention both to original sources and to methodological treatises; entries under Models of Completed Work call particular attention to studies in education.

I first drafted this table several years ago to track what I called "Differing Styles of On-Site Research" (Wolcott, 1982). Even then, my inventory of sources and models was necessarily incomplete. Today it is little more than a sampler, given the outpouring of new studies and the plethora of texts and articles devoted to procedures. Although recent works are included among the sources, particularly where they complement prior work or fill gaps, I have paid more attention to identifying earlier "classics" with which today's researchers may not be familiar. Among such classics cited in the table are Barker and Wright (1955), Becker, Geer, Hughes, and Strauss (1961), Henry (1963), Homans (1950), Jackson (1968), Smith and Geoffrey (1968), Whyte (1955), and Wylie (1957). The disciplinary roots of earlier studies are often more explicit, and researcher explanations of what they were up to in departing from traditional approaches may prove helpful to a current generation of researchers who find themselves subjected to the same questions.

Qualitative studies completed today often fail to show evidence of the disciplinary lineages that spawned them. As two colleagues observed years ago, the innovative process in educational practice tends toward adaptation rather than adoption (Charters and Pellegrin, 1972), and that also holds among those who investigate such processes. Some educational ethnography bears resemblance to anthropological ethnography, some educational ethnomethodology bears resemblance to sociological ethnomethodology, participant observation as practiced among some educational researchers reflects origins in anthropology or "Chicago School" sociology, and so on. But one does not ordinarily look to educational research for examples of these practices in their purest form. Most of the qualitative work in education shows more evidence of adaptation than of adoption. Nonetheless, adaptations can exhibit admirable hybrid vigor and serve as models for the work of others, outside the field as well as within it.

It is probably correct to say that there are as many versions of the work characterizing each major category as there are researchers working in it. *We are all self-styled researchers.* Individual differences we bring to our work only exacerbate the infinite variation that different problems and settings present. In Table 1, I have identified subcategories that highlight important variations within approaches yet allow me to hold to a manageable number of major categories. I urge interested readers to take up the task of revising and updating the table, using these headings and citations as a starting point for elaborating upon the contents and format in terms of a particular subfield or carefully specified set of interests and purposes.

A tablelike format is not intended to curb the tendency of today's researchers to be eclectic, but it is intended to help researchers recognize where they are coming from and what has happened before. It is too late to invent qualitative research, but it will never be too late to critique how it is conducted, to suggest new variations and combinations of basic data-gathering techniques, or to probe new theoretical possibilities. And the quest for exemplary models for research, qualitative studies that are quality studies as well, is never ending.

Teaching and Learning about Qualitative Research

My purposes for this introductory chapter are realized if the discussion and the material summarized in the figure and table accomplish three objectives. The first is to provide a broad overview emphasizing the range and variety of forms that qualitative research can take. As noted, qualitative researchers need not feel constrained by existing forms, but they should be able to recognize and distinguish among them.

My second objective has been to present these approaches as variations and recombinations of the fewest possible data-gathering techniques. I am satisfied to number those techniques at three. Wedded to the idea that three categories are sufficient, I am ready to perform any word magic needed to make the categories all-inclusive (e.g, "experiencing" is taken to embrace *all* the human senses, most certainly including listening; "enquiring" includes anything that puts an observer in an active, intrusive mode; "examining" can include examination of virtually any artifact produced by someone else, be it fax, footnote, furniture, or photograph).

Most assuredly, the number of possible approaches might be set higher. Buchmann and Floden (1989:243), for example, report "at least 30 different ways of conceiving and doing anthropology," which I interpret to mean that between them they know, or are familiar with the work of, 30 anthropologists. Their more astounding estimate of the "number of possible alternative schemes an individual investigator might choose from, on a conservative estimate," was 2^{20} or 1,048,576 (p. 247n, reporting an earlier discussion by Schwab [1978:245–246] on difficulties in settling boundary issues among disciplinary structures). On the other hand, anthropologists less self-conscious about method might take issue with my inflationary figure of three techniques, arguing that either of two inclusive terms "participant observation" or "fieldwork" is sufficient for identifying the taproot on which all cultural description is founded. If you are a serious candidate for qualitative research, you should feel at ease with a range between 1 and, give or take, 1,048,576. At the same time, your pattern-seeking proclivities should have alerted you to the seeming happenstance that, within that possible range, I identified *three* basic techniques, just as I divided idea-driven research into three subparts. I have a tendency to organize things in threes.

Third (see what I mean!), I hope the discussion, figure, and table serve not only to orient you to qualitative inquiry in general but also invite you to locate yourself in terms of the kinds of problems that attract you, the strategies by which you approach them, and the kind of end-product you seek.

An additional use the figure and table may serve is as an outline or syllabus for introducing others to qualitative research. For several years, I have offered a graduate seminar, "Qualitative Research in Education," a one-term survey course with a title that promises far more than can possibly be delivered. Used as an outline, Table 1 provides a useful synthesis for students and instructor alike as we set out to reconnoiter so huge a territory. Similarly, the "tree" of Fig. 1 emphasizes relationships among the strategies and, perceived as a working statement rather than *fait accompli*, poses questions about what goes where, what has been left out, and so forth. Students are better served to see themselves as part of that dialogue than to think the answers have all been worked out.

Among many issues on which I *do* agree with Lou Smith is the insightfulness of George Homan's observation years ago that "People who write about methodology often forget that it is a matter of strategy, not of morals" (Homans, 1949:330, cited *in* Smith, 1979:317). The notion of posturing presented here is intended to help qualitative researchers recognize that they make strategic choices. They also need to recognize an ever-widening array of well-specified alternatives from which to choose, and to understand that any alternative—whether a long tradition like ethnography or a newcomer like portraiture—is based on a variation of the same set of information-gathering techniques employed by all humans-as-observers. Humble origins, indeed! What Geertz has observed for anthropological insights holds true for *everyone* whose research stems from "intensive fieldwork in particular settings," that "like all scientific propositions, anthropological interpretations must be tested against the material they are designed to interpret; it is not their origins that commend them" (Geertz, 1968:vii).

After a professional lifetime of trying, I remain unconvinced that we can "train" people to be interviewers or participant observers, although we can help "natural" fieldworkers become better ones (see Wolcott, 1981). We can provide students with opportunities to experience fieldwork techniques for themselves under circumstances comparable to the research settings they anticipate. For anyone who must formulate strategies without prior fieldwork experience, I return to the "tree" analogy to make some obvious recommendations: Don't overextend your reach; don't get out on a limb trying to do (or claiming you are going to do) more than is appropriate for the problem you are addressing; and don't assume that any one approach is superior to any other without careful consideration of purposes.

As a case in point, I was once invited to join a research project for which my primary qualification was my experience as an ethnographer. My primary responsibility, however, was to produce a case study describing the introduction of a newly developed series of programs for instructional television. From the outset, the conditions were clearly explained to me: "We want an ethnographer, but we don't want you to give us a full ethnography" (Wolcott, 1984:182). Thus, even for ethnographers, ethnography is not always the answer.

Posturing: To Position, Especially Strategically

To conduct any inquiry one must have both an idea of what one is attempting to accomplish and an idea of how to proceed. But posturing is not only a matter of identifying a strategy and capitalizing on researcher talents, it is also a personal matter influenced by the kinds of information and kinds of memberships (e.g., discipline-based associations, formal divisions within the community of educational scholars) available to and valued by academicians individually. Prior professional commitments (e.g., to the improvement of classroom practice) and future professional aspirations (e.g., to educational research groups or social science disciplines) also exert an influence and extract a corresponding commitment over the problems we select and the data-gathering techniques with which we pursue them. Those commitments consciously and unconsciously influence our identification of problems or lead us to redefinitions of problems that make them amenable to study in some particular way rather than in others.

As as dyed-in-the-wool ethnographer, it is hardly surprising (but not always easy for me to remember or to admit) that the research problems that draw my attention are invariably recast so that ethnography becomes the answer. I feel at a decided advantage with ethnographic techniques in my kit bag and a general orientation toward discerning the cultural dimensions of social issues. My research posture is firm and unambiguous. I have always regarded "culture" as so neutral, so purely analytic a concept, that I almost went into shock when I encountered words by Martyn Hammersly and Paul Atkinson questioning that assumption:

> When setting out to describe a culture, we operate on the basis of the assumption that there are such things as cultures, and have some ideas about what they are like; and we select out for analysis the aspects of what is observed that we judge to be "cultural". While there may be nothing wrong with such cultural description, the kind of empiricist methodology enshrined in naturalism renders the theory implicit and thus systematically discourages its development and testing. (Hammersley and Atkinson, 1983:13)

I no longer insist on the neutrality I once claimed for ethnography. But I do insist that cultural interpretation is what ethnography is all about (see Wolcott, 1987). I also feel some obligation to commend ethnography as a highly suitable strategy in educational research. It has a long tradition, yet remains infinitely adaptable. I also have found the cultural orientation to be as insightful a perspective on my personal life as it has been provocative in my professional one. It has become the position, or strategy, from which I ordinarily pursue research. I cannot resist making a modest sales pitch of my own on its behalf. For anyone searching for structure to guide field research and willing to accept the commitment to cultural interpretation that it entails—with a corresponding emphasis on sociocultural influences rather than on individual volition—the work of earlier ethnographers may point the way. But if culture is unlikely to provide a helpful perspective on the issues you seek to understand, then feel free to avail yourself of the fieldwork techniques associated with it, and follow them out along some other branch that looks more promising.

Posturing in qualitative research is not something to avoid; it is something to approach with studied deliberation. No one can be "above" or "beyond" method, but with the new tolerance for qualitative inquiry, educational researchers need no longer feel mired in it either. Ideas are the heart of the matter. Malinowski's (1922:9) expressed enthusiasm for "foreshadowed problems" and his concomitant disdain for "preconceived ideas" notwithstanding, one cannot embark upon research without preconceived ideas. Feigning "immaculate perception" (as it has lightheartedly been called) is another affection to avoid. Allow time to grow into a posture that "fits" your interests and talents and permits you to be as natural as the settings and situations you are trying to describe and understand.

In the interim, while evolving and refining your own initial posture, do not fret that you might be contaminated by familiarity with the works and words of your predecessors. Read widely among several qualitative approaches and in depth among those you would emulate. Pay particular attention to completed studies, rather than to admonitions telling others how to proceed, for the ideals of research are sorely tested by the realities of the circumstances under which we work. Remain aware as well of an observation made earlier, that every qualitative researcher is a self-styled one. As Eisner notes, "In qualitative inquiry, personal stylistic features are neither liabilities nor elements that are easily replicable. Qualitative inquirers confer their own signature on their work" (1991:169).

No one "owns" ethnography, any more than anyone owns participant observation or case studies. Even those who have styled an identifiable approach—e.g., Blumer's symbolic interactionism or Garfinkel's ethnomethodology of the 1960s, Eisner's educational connoisseurship/criticism of the 1970s, or the postmodern anthropology of James Clifford and George Marcus in the 1980s—must watch it take shape in the hands of others.

The more you desire the security and safety afforded by a firm grasp on basic research techniques, the more you may feel you should try to compensate by trying to capture "everything" in your observations, your notes, and your reports. Keep in mind, however, that without setting your research problem, you have no basis for judging what you need in order to bring a study to fruition. No matter how tentatively you go about it, you must position yourself adequately to have a sense of purpose that includes some hunch about those data that may prove of greatest use. I have elaborated elsewhere on the paradox that the real secret in descriptive work is not to gather as much data as possible but, rather, to get rid of as much data as possible, as soon as possible (Wolcott, 1990:35ff.).

If it is your personal style to test and display prowess by venturing out into the unexplored, propose your study in terms of hopes and aspirations rather than promises, and do not cavalierly ignore the advice or accomplishments of those who have gone before. Others will be quick enough to remark on your attainments and to make comparisons. With both feet firmly on the ground, observers watching from below always have advice to offer those dangling high above.

"When in doubt," states an old maxim highly appropriate both for conducting qualitative inquiry and for reporting it, "tell the truth." Tell what you saw (and asked about, and found in the work of others), all the while maintaining an objective eye for your own objectivity. In simple, direct terms, describe your data-gathering procedures accurately and adequately, but discuss them in terms of intended outcomes and your strategies designed to realize them. Deal in a similar, straightforward manner with the ideas—hypotheses, hunches, whatever you choose to call them—that guided your pursuit and reveal how they, like your strategies, may have altered during the course of your work. Describe when and how theory played a role in your developing research—if it really did. Alternatively, describe what you seek in theory or how your work raises questions for colleagues more theoretically inclined. In what direction are you looking for the theoretical underpinnings that you feel might (or "ought to") be there?

In the absence of any apparent theoretical link to validate your work or make it seem more impressive, try candor. You can hope that others more theoretically inclined or discipline-oriented will recognize and accept an implicit challenge to make connections between your data and your interpretations, or to suggest how your work fits with—or raises questions about—the work of others. There is contribution enough to be made through astute and carefully reported observation, and modes and models aplenty to help you to achieve a posture rather than a pose while engaging in this work.

References

Adler, P. A., and Adler, P. (1987). *Membership roles in field research*. Newbury Park, CA: Sage.

Agar, M. H. (1980). *The professional stranger: An informal introduction to ethnography*. Orlando, FL: Academic Press.

Alexander, R. R. (1977). *Educational criticism of three art history classes.* Unpublished doctoral dissertation, Stanford University, Stanford, CA.

Alexander, R. R. (1980). "Mr. Jewell as a Model"—An educational criticism. *Studies in Art Education,* 21(3), 20–30.

Altenbaugh, R. J. (1991). *The teacher's voice: A qualitative analysis of teaching in twentieth-century America.* New York: Falmer Press.

Ambrose, A. (1978). Human social development: An evolutionary-biological perspective. *In* H. McGurk (Ed.), *Issues in childhood social development.* Longon: Methuen.

Anderson, G. L. (1989). Critical ethnography in education: Origins, current status, and new directions. *Review of Educational Research,* 59(3), 249–270.

Arensberg, C. M., and Kimball, S. T. (1940). *Family and community in Ireland.* Cambridge, MA: Harvard University Press.

Atkinson, P., Delamont, S., and Hammersley, M. (1988). Qualitative research traditions: A British response to Jacob. *Review of Educational Research,* 58(2), 231–250.

Barker, R. (1968). *Ecological psychology.* Stanford, CA: Stanford University Press.

Barker, R., and Wright, H. (1955). *The Midwest and its children.* New York: Harper and Row.

Barone, T. (1983). Things of use and things of beauty: The story of the Swain County High School Arts Program. *Daedalus,* 112(3), 1–28. (Reprinted in E. Eisner [Ed.], 1985, *The educational imagination: On the design and evolution of school programs* [2nd ed., pp. 275–295]. New York: Macmillan.)

Becker, H. S. (1990). Generalizing from case studies. *In* E. W. Eisner and A. Peshkin (Eds.), *Qualitative inquiry in education: The continuing debate* (pp. 233–242). New York: Teachers College Press.

Becker, H. S., Geer, B., Hughes, E., and Strauss, A. (1961). *Boys in white: Student culture in medical school.* Chicago: University of Chicago Press.

Biddle, B. (1967). Methods and concepts in classroom research. *Review of Educational Research,* 37, 337–357.

Blumer, H. (1954). What is wrong with social theory? *American Sociological Review,* 19, 3–10.

Blumer, H. (1969). *Symbolic interactionism: Perspective and method.* Englewood Cliffs, NJ: Prentice-Hall.

Blurton-Jones, N. G. (1972). *Ethological studies of child behavior.* New York: Cambridge University Press.

Bossert, S. (1979). *Tasks and social relationships in classrooms.* New York: Cambridge University Press.

Brandt, E. (1982). Popularity and peril: Ethnography and education. *Review Journal of Philosophy and Social Science,* 7, 139–153.

Brauner, C. J. (1974). The first probe. *In* R. Stake (Ed.), *Four evaluation examples: Anthropological, economic, narrative, and portrayal.* A.E.R.A. Monograph Series on Curriculum Evaluation. Chicago: Rand McNally.

Bruyn, S. T. (1966). *The human perspective in sociology; The methodology of participant observation.* Englewood Cliffs, NJ: Prentice-Hall.

Buchmann, M., and Floden, R. E. (1989). Research traditions, diversity, and progress, *Review of Educational Research,* 59(2), 241–248.

Cazden, C. (1988). *Classroom discourse: The language of teaching and learning.* Portsmouth, NH: Heinemann Educational Books.

Chang, H. (1991). *American high school adolescent life and ethos: An ethnography.* New York: Falmer Press.

Charters, W. W., Jr., and Pellegrin, R. J. (1972). Barriers to the innovative process: Four case studies of differentiated staffing. *Educational Administration Quarterly*, 9(1), 3–14.

Christensen, C. R. (1987). *Teaching and the case method*. Boston: Harvard Business School.

Cicourel, A. V. (1973). *Cognitive sociology: Language and meaning in social interaction*. London: Penguin.

Cicourel, A. V., Jennings, K. H., Leiter, K. C., McKay, R., Mehan, H., and Roth, D. R., (Eds.). (1974). *Language use and school performance*. New York: Academic Press.

Connelly, F. M., and Clandinin, D. J. (1990). Stories of experience and narrative inquiry. *Educational Researcher*, 19(5), 2–14.

Copple, N. (1964). *Depth reporting*. Englewood Cliffs, NJ: Prentice-Hall.

Cusick, P. (1973). *Inside high school: The student's world*. New York: Holt, Rinehart and Winston.

Daedalus (Journal of the American Academy of Arts and Sciences) 110(4). Special issue. America's schools: Portraits and perspectives. Fall 1981.

Denny, T. (1978). Story-telling and educational understanding (Occasional Paper 12). Kalamazoo, MI: The Evaluation Center, Western Michigan University.

Denton, D. (1974). *Existentialism and phenomenology in education*. New York: Teachers College Press.

Dollard, J. (1937). *Criteria for the life history*. New Haven, CT: Yale University Press.

Douglas, J. (Ed.). (1970). *Understanding everyday life*. Chicago: Aldine.

Eisner, E. (1976). Educational connoisseurship and criticism: Their form and functions in educational evaluation. *Journal of Aesthetic Education*, 10(3), 135–150.

Eisner, E. (1977). On the uses of educational connoisseurship and criticism for evaluating classroom life. *Teachers College Record*, 78(3), 345–358.

Eisner, E. (1981). On the differences between scientific and artistic approaches to qualitative research. *Educational Researcher*, 10(4), 5–9

Eisner, E. (1985). *The educational imagination; On the design and evaluation of school program* (2nd ed.). New York: Macmillan.

Eisner, E. (1991). *The enlightened eye: Qualitative inquiry and the enhancement of educational practice*. New York: Macmillan.

Eisner, E., and Peshkin, A. (Eds.). (1990). *Qualitative inquiry in education: The continuing debate*. New York: Teachers College Press.

Erickson, F. (1975). Gatekeeping and the melting pot: Interaction in counseling encounters. *Harvard Educational Review*, 45, 44–70.

Erickson, F., and Mohatt, G. (1982). Cultural organization of participation structures in two classrooms of Indian students. *In* G. D. Spindler (Ed.), *Doing the ethnography of schooling* (pp. 132–174). New York: Holt, Rinehart and Winston. (Reissued in 1988 by Waveland Press, Prospect Heights, IL.

Erickson, F., and Shultz, J. (1981). *Talking to the man: Social and cultural organization of communication in school counseling interviews*. New York: Academic Press.

Ettinger, L. F. (1983). *A comparative analysis of on-site descriptive research in art education: An initial contribution to educational ethnography*. Unpublished doctoral dissertation, University of Oregon, Eugene.

Fetterman, D. (1987). Ethnographic educational evaluation. *In* G. and L. Spindler (Eds.), *Interpretive ethnography of education: At home and abroad* (pp. 81–106). Hillsdale, NJ: Lawrence Erlbaum Associates.

Filby, N., Cahen, L., McCutcheon, G., and Kyle, D. (1980). *What happens in smaller classes?* San Francisco: Far West Educational Laboratory.

Garfinkel, H. (1967). *Studies in ethnomethodology*. Englewood Cliffs, NJ: Prentice-Hall.

Geertz, C. (1968). *Islam observed: Religious development in Morocco and Indonesia.* Chicago: University of Chicago Press.

Geertz, C. (1973). Thick description. *In* C. Geertz (Ed.), *The interpretation of cultures* (pp. 3–30). New York: Basic Books.

Geertz, C. (1983). *Local knowledge: Further essays in interpretive anthropology.* New York: Basic Books.

Giorgi, A. (1970). *Psychology as a human science: A phenomenologically based approach.* New York: Harper and Row.

Glaser, B. G. (1978). *Theoretical sensitivity: Advances in the methodology of grounded theory.* Mill Valley, CA: Sociology Press (PO Box 1431).

Glaser, B. G., and Strauss, A. L. (1967). *The discovery of grounded theory: Strategies for qualitative research.* Chicago: Aldine.

Goetz, J., LeCompte, M. A., and Ausherman, M. E. (1988). Toward an ethnology of student life in classrooms. Paper presented at the American Anthropological Association meetings, Phoenix, AZ.

Gold, R. (1958). Roles in sociological field observations. *Social Forces*, 36, 217–223.

Goodenough, W. H. (1963). *Cooperation in change: An anthropological approach to community development.* New York: Russell Sage Foundation.

Goodson, I. (1980). Life histories and the study of schooling. *Interchange*, 11(4), 62–76.

Gowin, D. B. (1990). Review of *Methodology of theory building*, by E. Steiner. *Educational Studies*, 21(1), 80–83.

Guba, E. G. (1978). *Toward a methodology of naturalistic inquiry in educational evaluation* (Monograph No. 8). University of California at Los Angeles: Center for the Study of Evaluation.

Guba, E. G. (1981a). *Effective evaluation.* San Francisco: Jossey-Bass

Guba, E. G. (1981b). Investigative journalism. *In* N. L. Smith (Ed.), *New methods for evaluation: Techniques* (pp. 167–262). Beverly Hills, CA: Sage.

Guba, E. G. (Ed.). (1990). *The paradigm dialog.* Newbury Park, CA: Sage.

Gump, P. V. (1967). *The classroom behavior setting: Its nature and relation to student behavior.* Washington, DC: US Office of Education.

Gumperz, J., and Hymes, D. (Eds.). (1964). The ethnography of communication. *American Anthropologist*, 66(6), Part 2.

Hammersley, M., and Atkinson, P. (1983). *Ethnography: Principles in practice.* London: Tavistok Publications.

Handel, W. (1982). *Ethnomethodology: How people make sense.* Englewood Cliffs, NJ: Prentice-Hall.

Harrison, J. M., and Stein, H. H. (1973). *Muckraking past, present, and future.* State College: Pennsylvania State University Press.

Helm, J. (Ed.). (1985). Social contexts of American ethnology, 1840–1984. *1984 Proceedings of the American Ethnological Society.* Washington, DC: American Anthropological Association.

Henry, J. (1963). *Culture against man.* New York: Random House.

Heritage, J. (1984). *Garfinkel and ethnomethodology.* Cambridge, England: Polity Press.

Herriott, R., and Gross, N. (Eds.). (1979). *Dynamics of planned change.* Berkeley, CA: McCutchan.

Hersen, M., and Barlow, D. H. (1976). *Single-case experimental designs: Strategies for studying behavior change.* New York: Pergamon.

Heshusius, L. (1986). Pedagogy, special education, and the lives of young children: A critical and futuristic perspective. *Journal of Education*, 168(3), 25–37.

Homans, G. C. (1949). The strategy of industrial sociology. *American Journal of Sociology* 54(4), 330–337.

Homans, G. C. (1950). *The human group.* New York: Harcourt, Brace and World.

Hoopes, J. (1979). *Oral history: An introduction for students.* Chapel Hill: University of North Carolina Press.

Husserl, E. (1962). *Ideas: General introduction to pure phenomenology.* New York: Collier Books. (Originally published in 1931.)

Hymes, D. (1980). Educational ethnology. *Anthropology and Education Quarterly,* 11, 3–8.

Jackson, B. (1987). *Fieldwork.* Chicago: University of Chicago Press.

Jackson, P. (1968). *Life in classrooms.* New York: Holt, Rinehart and Winston.

Jacob, E. (1987). Qualitative research traditions: A review. *Review of Educational Research,* 57(1), 1–50.

Jacob, E. (1988). Clarifying qualitative research: A focus on traditions. *Educational Researcher,* 17(1), 16–24.

Jaeger, R. M. (Ed.). (1988). *Complementary methods for research in education.* Washington, DC: American Educational Research Association.

Jordan, C. (1985). Translating culture: From ethnographic information to educational program. *Anthropology and Education Quarterly,* 16(2), 105–123.

Jorgensen, D. L. (1989). Participant observation: A methodology for human studies. Newbury Park, CA: Sage.

Kimball, S. T. (1955). The method of natural history and educational research. *In* G. Spindler (Ed.), *Education and anthropology* (pp. 82–85). Stanford, CA: Stanford University Press. (Reprinted in G. and L. Spindler [Eds.], 1987, *Interpretive ethnography of education* [pp. 11–14]. Hillsdale, NJ: Lawrence Erlbaum Associates.)

Kluckhohn, F. R. (1940). The participant observer technique in small communities. *American Journal of Sociology,* 46, 331–343.

Kratochwill, T. R. (1977). N = 1. *Psychological Bulletin,* 64, 74–79.

Kratochwill, T. R. (1978). *Single subject research.* New York: Academic Press.

Krippendorff, K. (1980). *Content analysis: An introduction.* Beverly Hills, CA: Sage.

Kyle, D. W. (1987). Life as teacher: Ms. Carr's second grade. *In* G. W. Noblit and W. T. Pink (Eds.), *Schooling in social context: Qualitative studies* (pp. 23–45). Norwood, NJ: Ablex.

Langness, L. L., and Frank, G. (1981). *Lives: An anthropological approach to biography.* Novato, CA: Chandler and Sharp.

Latour, B., and Woolgar, S. (1979). *Laboratory life: The social construction of scientific facts.* Beverly Hills, CA: Sage.

Lightfoot, S. L. (1983). *The good high school: Portraits of character and culture.* New York: Basic Books.

Lincoln, Y., and Guba, E. (1985). *Naturalistic inquiry.* Beverly Hills, CA: Sage.

Lindeman, E. C. (1924). *Social discovery: An approach to the study of functional groups.* New York: Republic.

Lovell, R. P. (1983). *Reporting public affairs: Problems and solutions.* Belmont, CA: Wadsworth.

Lutz, F. W., and Iannaccone, L. (1969). *Understanding educational organizations: A field study approach.* Columbus, OH: Charles E. Merrill.

Malinowski, B. (1922). *Argonauts of the western Pacific: An account of native enterprise and adventure in the Archipelagoes of Melanesian New Guinea.* New York: E. P. Dutton (Reissued in 1984 by Waveland Press, Prospect Heights, IL.)

Marcus, G. E., and Fischer, M. (1986). *Anthropology as cultural critique: An experimental moment in the human sciences.* Chicago: University of Chicago Press.

Mayer, M. (1961). *The schools.* New York: Harper.

McCutcheon, G. (1976). *The disclosure of classroom life.* Unpublished doctoral dissertation, Stanford University, Stanford, CA.

McCutcheon, G. (1978). Of solar systems, responsibilities, and basics. *In* G. Willis (Ed.), *Qualitative Evaluation.* Berkeley, CA: McCutchan.

McDermott, R. P. (1976). *Kids make sense: An ethnographic account of the interactional management of success and failure in one first-grade classroom.* Unpublished doctoral dissertation, Stanford University, Stanford, CA.

McDermott, R. P., and Church, J. (1976). Making sense and feeling good: The ethnography of communication and identity work. *Communication, 2,* 121–142.

McGrew, W. C. (1972). *An ethological study of children's behavior.* New York: Academic Press.

Mead, M. (1928). *Coming of age in Samoa: A psychological study of primitive youth for Western Civilisation.* New York: William Morrow.

Mehan, H. (1978). Structuring school structure. *Harvard Educational Review, 48,* 32–64.

Mehan, H. (1980). The competent student. *Anthropology and Education Quarterly, 11,* 131–152.

Mehan, H., and Wood, H. (1975). *The reality of ethnomethodology.* New York: Wiley-Interscience.

Merriam, S. B. (1988). *Case study research in education: A qualitative approach.* San Francisco: Jossey-Bass.

Merton, R. K. (1968). On sociological theories of the middle range. *In* R. K. Merton (Ed.), *Social theory and social structure* (pp. 39–72). New York: Free Press.

Meyer, P. (1973). *Precision journalism: A reporter's introduction to social science methods.* Bloomington: Indiana University Press.

Moerman, M. (1988). *Talking culture: Ethnography and conversation analysis.* Philadelphia: University of Pennsylvania Press.

Mohanty, J. N. (Ed.). (1982). *Phenomenology and the human sciences, 1981.* Denver, CO: Philosophical Topics, Inc.

Natanson, M. (Ed.). (1979). *Phenomenology in the social sciences.* Evanston, IL: Northwestern University Press.

Ogbu, J. (1974). *The next generation.* New York: Academic Press.

Pelto, P. J., and Pelto, G. H. (1978). *Anthropological research: The structure of inquiry* (2nd ed.). New York: Cambridge University Press.

Perrone, V. (Ed.). (1985). *Portraits of high schools.* Lawrenceville, NJ: Princeton University Press.

Peshkin, A. (1978). *Growing up American: Schooling and the survival of community.* Chicago: University of Chicago Press.

Peshkin, A. (1986). *God's choice: The total world of a fundamentalist Christian school.* Chicago: University of Chicago Press.

Philips, S. (1972). Participant structures and communicative competence. In C. Cazden, V. John, and D. Hymes (Eds.), *Functions of language in the classroom* (pp. 370–394). New York: Teachers College Press. (Reprinted in 1985 by Waveland Press, Prospect Heights, IL.)

Philips, S. (1983). *The invisible culture: Communication in classroom and community on the Warm Springs Indian Reservation.* New York: Longman.

Popkewitz, T. S., and Tabachnick, B. R. (Eds.). (1981). *The study of schooling: Field-based methodologies in educational research and evaluation.* New York: Praeger.

Precourt, W. (1982). Ethnohistorical analysis of an Appalachian settlement school. *In* G. Spindler (Ed.), *Doing the ethnography of schooling* (pp. 440–453). New York: Holt.

Rinehart and Winston. (Reprinted in 1988 by Waveland Press, Prospect Heights, IL.)

Psathas, G. (Ed.). (1979). *Everyday language: Studies in ethnomethodology*. Englewood Cliffs, NJ: Prentice-Hall.

Reid, W. A., and Walker, D. F. (Eds.). (1975). *Case studies in curriculum change*. London: Routledge and Kegan Paul.

Richardson, L. (1990). *Writing strategies: Reaching diverse audiences*. Newbury Park, CA: Sage.

Richardson, M. (1975). Anthropologist—The myth teller. *American Ethnologist, 2*, 517–533.

Sacks, H., Schegloff, E., and Jefferson, G. (1974). A symplist systematics for the organization of turn-taking for conversation. *Language, 50*(4), 696–735. (Reprinted in J. Schenkein [Ed.], 1978, *Studies in the organization of conversational interaction*. New York: Academic Press.)

Salzman, P. C. (1988). Fads and fashions in anthropology. *Anthropology Newsletter, May*, 32–33.

Schön, D. A. (Ed.). (1991). *The reflective turn: Case studies in and on educational practice*. New York: Teachers College Press.

Schutz, A. (1967). *The phenomenology of the social world*. Evanston, IL: Northwestern University Press.

Schwab, J. J. (1978). Education and the structure of the disciplines. *In* I. Westbury and N. J. Wilkof (Eds.), *Joseph J. Schwab: Science, curriculum, and liberal education* (pp. 229–274). Chicago: University of Chicago Press.

Scudder, J. R., and Mickunas, A. (1985). *Meaning, dialogue, and enculturation: Phenomenological philosophy of education*. Lanham, MD: University Press of America and Center for Advanced Research in Phenomenology.

Sherman, R. R., and Webb, R. B. (Eds.). (1988). *Qualitative research in education: Focus and methods*. Philadelphia, PA: Falmer Press.

Shweder, R. A. (1984). Preview: A colloquy of culture theorists. *In* R. A. Schweder and R. A. Levine (Eds.), *Culture theory: Essays on mind, self, and emotion* (pp. 1–24). New York: Cambridge University.

Smith, L. M. (1957). The micro-ethnography of the classroom. *Psychology in the Schools, 4*, 216–221.

Smith, L. M. (1979). An evolving logic of participant observation, educational ethnography, and other case studies. *Review of Research in Education* (Vol. 6). Washington, DC: American Educational Research Association.

Smith, L. M. (1990). Critical introduction: Whither classroom ethnography? *In* M. Hammersley, *Classroom ethnography: Empirical and methodological essays* (pp. 1–12). Milton Keynes, England: Open University Press.

Smith, L. M., and Geoffrey, W. (1968). *Complexities of an urban classroom*. New York: Holt, Rinehart and Winston.

Smith, L. M., and Pohland, P. (1974). Education, technology, and the rural highlands. *In* R. Stake (Ed.), *Four evaluation examples: Anthropological, economic, narrative, and portrayal*. A.E.R.A. Monograph Series on Curriculum Evaluation. Chicago: Rand McNally.

Smith, L. M., Prunty, J. P., Dwyer, D. C., and Kleine, P. F. (1987). *The fate of an innovative school*. New York: Falmer Press.

Spindler, G. D. (Ed.). (1982). *Doing the ethnography of schooling*. New York: Holt, Rinehart and Winston. (Reissued in 1988 by Waveland Press, Prospect Heights, IL.)

Stake, R. (1978). The case-method in social inquiry. *Educational Researcher, 7*, 5–8.

Stake, R. (1988). Case study methods in educational research: Seeking Sweet Water. *In*

R. M. Jaeger (Ed.), *Complementary methods for research in education* (pp. 253–300). Washington, DC: American Educational Research Association.

Stake, R., and Easley, J. (Eds.). (1978). *Case studies in science education.* Urbana: University of Illinois.

Strauss, A., and Corbin, J. (1990). *Basics of qualitative research: Grounded theory procedures and techniques.* Newbury Park, CA: Sage.

Thompson, P. (1978). *The voice of the past: Oral history.* London: Oxford University Press.

Traweek, S. (1988). *Beamtimes and lifetimes: The world of high energy physicists,* Cambridge, MA: Harvard University Press.

Ullman, J., and Honeymoon, S. (1983). *The reporter's handbook: An investigator's guide to documents and techniques.* New York: St. Martin's Press.

Van Maanen, J., Manning, P., and Miller, M. (1986). Series introduction. *In* J. Kirk and M. Miller, *Reliability and validity in qualitative research.* Beverly Hills, CA: Sage.

van Manen, M. (1990). *Researching lived experience: Human science for an action sensitive pedagogy.* Albany, NY: SUNY Press.

Vansina, J. (1985). *Oral tradition as history.* Madison: University of Wisconsin Press.

Waller, W. (1932). *The sociology of teaching.* New York: Wiley.

Wann, T. W. (Ed.). (1964). *Behaviorism and phenomenology.* Chicago: University of Chicago Press.

Warren, R. (1967). *Education in Rebhausen: A German village.* New York: Holt, Rinehart and Winston.

Watson, L., and Watson-Franke, M. (1985). *Interpreting life histories: An anthropological inquiry.* New Brunswick, NJ: Rutgers University Press.

Webb, E. J., Campbell, D. T., Schwartz, R. D., and Sechrest, L. (1966). *Unobtrusive measures: Nonreactive research in the social sciences.* Chicago: Rand McNally.

Weber, R. P. (1985). *Basic content analysis.* Beverly Hills, CA: Sage.

Whyte, W. F. (1955). *Street corner society* (2nd ed.). Chicago: University of Chicago Press.

Wiseman, F. (Producer). (1969). High school [Documentary film]. Cambridge, MA: Zipporah Films.

Wolcott, H. F. (1967). *A Kwakiutl village and school.* New York: Holt, Rinehart and Winston. (Reissued in 1989 by Waveland Press, Prospect Heights, IL, with a new Afterword.)

Wolcott, H. F. (1973). *The man in the principal's office: An ethnography.* New York: Holt, Rinehart and Winston. (Reissued in 1984 by Waveland Press, Prospect Heights, IL, with a new Introduction.)

Wolcott, H. F. (1975). Criteria for an ethnographic approach to research in schools. *Human Organization, 34*(2), 111–127.

Wolcott, H. F. (1980). How to look like an anthropologist without being one. *Practicing Anthropology 3*(1), 6–7, 56–59.

Wolcott, H. F. (1981). Confessions of a "trained" observer. *In* T. S. Popkewitz and B. R. Tabachnick (Eds.), *The study of schooling: Field based methodologies in educational research* (pp. 247–263). New York: Praeger.

Wolcott, H. F. (1982). Differing styles of on-site research, or, if it isn't ethnography, what is it? *Review Journal of Philosophy and Social Science, 7*(1,2), 154–169. (Special issue on Naturalistic Research Paradigms, edited by M. V. Belok and N. Haggerson.)

Wolcott, H. F. (1984). Ethnographers sans ethnograpy: The evaluation compromise. *In* D. M. Fetterman (Ed.), *Ethnography in educational evaluation* (pp. 177–213). Beverly Hills, CA: Sage.

Wolcott, H. F. (1987). On ethnographic intent. *In* G. and L. Spindler (Eds.), *Interpretive ethnography of education* (pp. 37–57). Hillsdale, NJ: Lawrence Erlbaum Associates.

Wolcott, H. F. (1990). *Writing up qualitative research.* Newbury Park, CA: Sage.

Wolf, R. L., and Tymitz, B. (1977). Toward more natural inquiry in education. *C.E.D.R. Quarterly*, 10.

Woods, P. (1986). *Inside schools: Ethnography in educational research.* London: Routledge and Kegan Paul.

Wylie, L. (1957). *Village in the Vaucluse.* Cambridge, MA: Harvard University Press.

Yin, R. K. 1984. *Case study research: Design and methods.* Beverly Hills, CA: Sage.

Zelditch, M., Jr. (1962). Some methodological problems of field studies. *American Journal of Sociology*, 67, 566–576.

CHAPTER 2

☐ Cultural Process
and Ethnography:
An Anthropological
Perspective

George and Louise Spindler

*The Handbook of Qualitative
Research in Education*

53

PART 1
Changes Exemplified in Six Collections, 1955–1987

This essay is divided into three parts: (1) a brief analysis of the changes over time in the ethnography of education as exemplified by six collections edited by George Spindler or by George and Louise Spindler from 1955 to 1987; (2) a discussion of the ingredients for a good ethnography of schooling; and (3) an exposition of relevant approaches developed by the authors in a long-term research project in Schoenhausen, Germany, and Roseville, Wisconsin, from 1968 to the present.

The mandate by the editors has allowed us the freedom to draw from our own work as an example of "classic" (editors' term) educational ethnography. We are not so sure about the "classic" properties of our studies, nor are we convinced that our approach is "traditional" (editors' term). What we are sure of is that what we are going to write about is what we have done over the past 40 years as anthropologists deeply interested in the educational process. We have changed and developed over time, and we are doing some of the same things now that we were doing in the 1950s, but a lot that we weren't. Though we will avoid an autobiographical stance, there is unavoidably a personal element in all of this that we hope will be useful and not merely evidence of egotism.

Six Collections

George Spindler began working in the schools as an anthropologist on a research project directed by Dr. Robert Bush, School of Education, Stanford University, in 1950. This project included case studies of teachers, children, and administrators and was responsible for bringing him (G.S.) into a life-long relationship with education. *Education and Anthropology* appeared in 1955. His next edited collection, *Education and Culture: Anthropological Approaches,* appeared in 1963 and combined a mix of reprints from the 1955 volume and new ones. The third volume appeared in 1974, *Education and Cultural Process: Toward an Anthropology of Education. Doing the Ethnography of Schooling: Educational Anthropology in Action* appeared in 1982, and *Interpretive Ethnography of Education at Home and Abroad,* edited by both Spindlers, appeared in 1987. *Education and Cultural Process* appeared in the second edition in 1987, and *Doing the Ethnography of*

Schooling was reprinted with a new Foreword in 1988. Together, these volumes constitute a record of the development of the field of educational anthropology and of educational ethnography as construed by cultural anthropologists. Because most of the articles are not written by the Spindlers, they afford a reasonably good cross-section of changes in the field.

Education and Anthropology

The conference that resulted in *Education and Anthropology* (G. Spindler, 1955a) was held from June 9 to 14, 1954, with Carnegie Foundation support, in a Carmel Valley hideaway and brought twelve cultural anthropologists and as many professional educators into a face-to-face situation for 4 days. They discussed papers prepared by George Spindler, Bernard Siegel, John Gillin, Solon Kimball, Cora DuBois, C. W. M. Hart, Dorothy Lee, Jules Henry, and Theodore Brameld. Margaret Mead prepared a summary entitled "The Anthropologist and the School as a Field" and Alfred Kroeber commented on the conference as a whole. This conference and the volume issuing from it have often been cited as the beginning of educational anthropology and the ethnography of education. This is not entirely accurate because various workers such as Solon Kimball, Jules Henry, and Margaret Mead were in the field before the conference and, in fact, the "anthropology of education" can be said to have started with Edgar Hewett in 1904 in an article in *American Anthropologist*. The appearance of this volume did, however, provide a substantial platform for the launching of serious anthropological research in the schools and credited the anthropology of education as a legitimate subdiscipline. Though the book was published 35 years ago, this legitimation both in education and in departments of anthropology has been slow to develop. It is probably correct to say that most professionals working as educational anthropologists feel themselves to be quite marginal in both disciplinary contexts even today.

Ethnography is listed only once in the index for *Education and Anthropology*, and that was in the context of the overview by George Spindler of the use of cross-cultural materials furnished by ethnography, not from the ethnography of education as such. In many cases throughout the volume, ethnography was clearly taken for granted as a source of information, both on other cultures and on our own. However, no one thought of "educational ethnography" or "the ethnography of schooling" as *special fields*. The emphasis throughout the book was on concepts and problems: models for the analysis of the educative process in American communities, the school in the context of the community, learning intercultural understanding, contrasting prepubertal and postpubertal education, discrepancies in the teaching of American culture, education and communications theory, the meeting of educational and anthropological theory, roles for anthropologists and educators, the school as a field of study for the anthropologist, and the educational consequences of the Supreme Court 1954 decision on segregation—*Brown v. the Board of Education.*

It all seemed so clear then. Anthropologists learned about culture by studying the cultures of others. They could put the insights thus gained in interpretations of education and schooling to use in their own (and other) societies. In this way, anthropology furnished the materials for a cultural critique. Education was seen as cultural transmission and as a major instrument in cultural survival, but the learning of culture, the school and the social structure, the exercise of power, the effect of culturally based values on teacher perceptions, the informal transmission of values, the roles of the school administrator and teacher, and American culture as a specific context for schooling were all considered relevant. There was a frank and unselfconscious eclecticism in both concept and method. There was also a clear, implicit understanding of what anthropology was and, thus, what it might do for, with, and in education. The volume is worth reading for the information it provides about the platform from which we have launched ourselves as well as for the feeling of both security *and* excitement that was in the air at the time.

Education and Culture

The term "ethnography" is not listed in the index of *Education and Culture: Anthropological Aproaches* (1963). In the overview article by George Spindler, the anthropologist is not described as an ethnographer but, rather, as a consultant, as a researcher in education whose "greatest contribution" is the holistic approach to research and analysis, and as a teacher—making explicit the cultural assumptions of educators. Ethnography, however, serves as the implicit data base for studies carried out and written about by the authors. Jules Henry writes on attitude organization in elementary school classrooms and spontaneity and creativity in suburban classrooms. Dorothy Eggan writes on instruction and affect in Hopi cultural continuity. George Spindler analyzes personality, the sociocultural system, and education among the Menomini. Melford Spiro describes education in a communal village in Israel. Jack Fischer considers Japanese schools for the natives of Truk (Caroline Islands). And Bernard Siegel writes about social structures, social change, and education in rural Japan. But no one talked about "ethnography" as such. It was taken for granted. The *problem* was the focus. All of the articles in this volume make for good reading. They are neither tedious, hung up on methodology, nor bound to single cases, except where appropriate. They are intellectually freewheeling and methodologically true to form. These studies employ structured and unstructured interview techniques, questionnaires, psychological tests, socioeconomic inventories, census reports, sociometric techniques, value-projective techniques—the whole range of procedures used in the social and behavioral sciences. Our field has always been methodologically eclectic. But underlying all of these usages is the constant attention to the flow of life around the participant–observer, the anthropologist, that gives meaning to the results of the specialized techniques. This basic approach to research in the field is very apparent in most of the chapters in *Education and Culture*. Jules Henry's two chapters are models for what needs to be done in the application of anthropology to the analysis of educational processes in our own society. The fact that the commitment to direct observation is more apparent in the papers that deal with educational process in non-Western societies than with those at home is an indication that anthropologists had only begun their work in our own society.

A quotation from the introductory chapter in *Education and Culture* by George Spindler indicated what, apparently, needed to be done in the future. "Probably the most substantial contribution that anthropology could make to education would be the building of a body of case materials based on direct observation in a variety of educational situations, but most of this work remains to be done." In the future volumes edited by the Spindlers, this development becomes clear.

Education and Cultural Process

Education and Cultural Process: Toward an Anthropology of Education (1974) is a departure from the first two books, both of which were essentially essay collections taking ethnography for granted but with some exceptions not presenting much direct ethnographic observation. In the 1974 collection, on ethnographic case studies are clearly the focus. John Singleton, in his paper on education as cultural transmission, distinguishes participant observation from other observational procedures and applies "these research perspectives to what I like to call 'educational ethnography'." He describes Harry Wolcott's (1973) study of an elementary school principal, Richard King's (1968) study of an Indian residential school in the Yukon, and Gary Rosenfeld's (1971) study of a slum school in Harlem as outstanding examples

of this application. He might well have added his own *Nichu*, a case
study of a Japanese elementary school (Singleton, 1967), as another
good example as well as Richard Warren's (1971) study of education in
Rebhausen, a German village. (Wolcott, King, Singleton, and Warren
were all Spindler Ph.D.s in the emerging education and anthropology
program at Stanford University.) Of 27 papers in this volume, 12 are
explicitly ethnographic and focus on single cases. Of these 12, only
McDermott, on achieving school failure, Spindler, on a case study of
culturally defined adjustment and teacher perceptions, Schwartz and
Merten, on the meaning of a sorority initiation ritual, and Wolcott, on
the elementary school principal, report on schools in our own society.

The 1974 volume is clearly cross-cultural in character and pays
more attention to other cultures than to our own. This may be one of the
reasons why educators have been slow to accept the work by anthropologists of education as relevant to their concerns. Why worry about
some other culture when you have so many problems in your own?
Therein lies a dilemma. Anthropology without its cross-cultural perspective becomes a kind of poor sociology. Whatever insights anthropologists have been able to bring to the analysis of educational process
have been derived in significant degree from a cross-cultural perspective. Much of the current work in educational anthropology lacks this
explicit reference to a cross-cultural perspective and, in our opinion, is
the poorer for it.

Education and Cultural Process contains the first explicitly "ethnographic" section ("Approaches to the Study of Schools and
Classrooms [Part IV]") on ethnographic method. The four papers in
this section diverge in various ways but have in common a concern for
the role of the researcher–ethnographer. Richard King characterizes
his role as that of "significant friend," and Harry Wolcott his role as
"enemy." Both characterizations must be seen in the context of their
articles to make full sense. But the concern with the role of the researcher indicates a growing awareness of the effect of researcher and
situation on the results of any study involving human beings. This
interaction is critical in the study of schooling for the anthropologist–
ethnographer and is particularly conspicuous in the small community
of the school and the classroom.

Doing the Ethnography of Schooling

Our next edited volume, *Doing the Ethnography of Schooling;
Educational Anthropology in Action* (1982), is explicitly ethnographic
throughout. Of the 15 papers in the book, 12 are based on ethnographic

research in school sites. Heath describes the problems of white teachers with black children in Trackton. Erickson and Mohatt describe participant structure in two classrooms of American Indian students. Varenne describes the symbolic expression of social interaction among American senior high school students. Gearing and Epstein do an ethnographic probe into the hidden curriculum in a working-class school. Hanna describes public social policy and the children's world in a desegregated magnet school. Finnan describes children's spontaneous play in an American school. Warren analyzes ethnic identity in two schools, one of them in the United States, the other in Mexico. Hart analyzes the social organization of reading in an elementary school.

This collection was developed in part as a response to a condition that had developed as educational ethnography became a fad. The book begins with a quote from a California State Department of Education official: "Anything anyone wants to do that has no clear problem, no methodology, and no theory, is likely to be called 'ethnography,' around here." One of the major purposes of the volume was to show that anthropological educational ethnography did have clear problems and that it had both methodology and theory. The papers speak for themselves and, on the whole, successfully counter this negative perception.

One of the significant themes that emerges in the papers in this volume is the attention to the "hidden" curriculum, to the covert, tacit, or implicit cultural patterns that affect behavior and communication, particularly in face-to-face social interaction, and that are largely outside the consciousness of the actor. This focus is clear in most of the papers, although not a primary preoccupation in all. Some analysts refer this orientation to the influence of a paralinguistic model. The editorial commentary draws attention to the fact that covert culture, hidden postulates, dynamic themes, and the like were a primary preoccupation on the part of many anthropologists of the 1940s and that they did not draw from a paralinguistic model.

Interpretive Ethnography of Education

The next collection, *Interpretive Ethnography of Education at Home and Abroad* (1987) includes 19 papers, 14 of which are based on direct ethnographic evidence from single cases. Another three are about ethnographic methods, one of which, by Solon Kimball, is reprinted from the 1955 conference volume. The other two are by George and Louise Spindler on teaching and learning how to do the ethnography of education and by Harry Wolcott on ethnographic intent, in which he tells us both what ethnography is and what it is not.

The editors take a strong position on education as cultural transmission. To quote from their first chapter:

> We see education as cultural transmission, and of course cultural
> transmission requires cultural learning, so learning and transmission
> are separated only by convention. Further, we see that aspect of
> cultural transmission in which we are most interested—education in
> the broad sense, schooling in the narrower sense (including initiations,
> rites of passage, apprenticeships, as well as schools) as *calculated
> interventions* in the learning process. We are not interested in all
> learning that takes place as children grow into adults, get older, and
> finally die. We are interested in the learning that takes place, whether
> intended or unanticipated, as a result of calculated intervention. It is
> our unique subject matter as educational anthropologists and without a
> unique subject matter as well as a methodology, there is no discipline.

In retrospect, this statement seems to eliminate learning that is not a result of calculated intervention from the purview of anthropologist–ethnographers. It could reduce the anthroethnographers' attention to learning in peer groups or to the concomitant learning that is tangential to calculated intervention. This would be an unfortunate effect.

The rationale for the emphasis on cultural transmission is that this focus exploits anthropological expertise on sociocultural structure and process and a focus on learning puts the focus on the individual. It is all too easy to slip into a "blame the victim" interpretation if one emphasizes the individual learner and not the context and circumstances of learning. We have not yet found the proper position between these two possible polar positions—cultural transmission as calculated intervention and learning as individualized process. Theory in educational anthropology is still in a fairly raw state, although there is quite a bit of it. We will undoubtedly eventually work out this problem.

Interpretive Ethnography of Education continues to recognize the importance of comparative and cross-cultural work in the ethnography of education with papers by the Spindlers on Schoenhausen (Germany), a first-grade class in a French school by Katherine Anderson-Levitt, interethnic images in multicultural England by Paul Yates, and a paper by Norman Chance on Chinese education in a village setting.

In 1955, and even in 1963, we could take for granted that the cross-cultural perspective was basic to the whole structure of the discipline. Today we have to make a self-conscious, purposeful attempt to get such material included in a collection or any other publications directed largely at educational ethnography. The contents of the quarterly *Anthropology and Education* indicate this to be the case as well. Few articles have been published in it over the past 5 years with an explicit cross-cultural frame of reference. The implications of this for the future of the anthropology of education and educational ethnography are significant. If anthropology does not contribute a cross-cultural perspective, then what does it contribute? Because ethnography has become a household word in most of the social science disciplines, it needs a distinguishing criterion for its anthropological subtype to avoid the possibility that we may simply disappear as a recognizable subdiscipline. Some feel this is happening to cultural anthropology as a whole. If so, it is not surprising that this may happen to educational anthropology. It will be one of the developments to watch over the next several years.

Other notable developments in the ethnography of education appearing in *Interpretive Ethnography of Education* include explicit attention, by David Fetterman, to evaluation done ethnographically; the appearance of the cultural knowledge framework, drawn initially from ethnoscience and cognitive anthropology, in a paper by Katherine Anderson-Levitt; the distinctions between voluntary and involuntary minorities and their responses to schooling in articles by John Ogbu and Margaret Gibson; the emphasis on transitions between home and school and the participation structures encountered in each in a paper by Concha Delgado-Gaitan; a focus on gender differences in the emergence of sexist behavior in four children's groups by Ruth Goodenough; the combination of attention to participation structures and hidden curriculum in an article by Reba Page on lower track classes at a college preparatory high school; and the problems attendant to computer literacy as related to curricula by Susan Jungck. One has a clear sense that educational ethnography is reaching out into new areas and beginning to formulate some fairly clear theoretical paradigms.

Education and Cultural Process: Anthropological Approaches

The last volume to be included in this review is the second edition of *Education and Cultural Process: Anthropological Approaches*. There is a 13-year separation between the first edition of this volume (1974) and the new one (1987). It adds 14 new papers on a wide range of topics, including the anthropology of learning and the relevance of learning theory to an anthropology of education; the historical roots of the subdiscipline; the relationships between anthropologists and educational institutions; primate behavior and the transition to human status; ethnography within a systematic methodological framework; the new immigrants and their patterns of academic success; controlled cross-cultural comparisons of schooling; comparative cognitive development in two countries; a comparative analysis of social bias in schooling; and the teaching of anthropology. The difference between *Education and Cultural Process* in both of its editions and the other collections is consistent in that both editions are about the relationships of anthropology to education and do not focus primarily on ethnography as a research tool. There seems to be a constant struggle between these two orientations. The "ethnography of education" framework has tended to supplant as well as supplement the broader concerns of an anthropology of education. The discipline has tended to become more case-centered and more exclusively ethnographic, in contrast to other methods such as surveys, questionnaires, archival research, and psychological tests, than anthropology itself has ever been.

The most important tension in theory represented in the 1987 edition of *Education and Cultural Process* is that between the cultural transmission focus and the learning of culture or cultural acquisition position referred to above. The dialogue is fairly well represented in a paper by Harry Wolcott on the anthropology of learning and a paper by George Spindler on cultural transmission in this volume; however, much remains to be said. A further contribution to the emerging debate is furnished by George and Louise Spindler in "Do Anthropologists Need Learning Theory?" (included in *Education and Cultural Process*). The article makes some move toward a combination of cultural transmission and cultural acquisition. In our course titled "Cultural Transmission," offered at Stanford since 1954, we have dealt with such concepts as concomitant learning, incidental learning, unintended learning, and latent learning. These concepts all take as a basic assumption that cultural transmission as intentional intervention is the starting point for analysis.

We acknowledge the credibility of the position taken by Wolcott and others who would start from the other end of the continuum between cultural transmission and the acquisition of culture, but we are concerned that starting thus will result in loss of the unique perspective that anthropology has furnished on the ways in which societies, using their cultural resources, organize the conditions and purposes of learning so that some things are learned and others are not. The situation is complicated by the fact that what is *not* to be learned through intentional interference may be precisely that content which is included in the list of processes just provided above, such as concomitant learning, and that these kinds of learning provide much of the impetus for sociocultural change, because they are "subversive" in their relationship to explicit, mandated learning. The relationships between the purposeful organization of educational resources, as in cultural transmission, and the forms and processes of learning, including forms of "resistance to learning" will constitute, we believe, an important arena for significant theoretical debate in our subdiscipline. A careful, sensitive ethnography of teaching and learning will be of the greatest significance in the development of systematic theory in the arena defined by cultural transmission and in the acquisition of culture by the individual.

Conclusion to Part 1

The conclusion we draw from this review of these collections is that educational ethnography is alive and well, moving energetically, but without a great deal of consistent theoretical guidance, in many directions. It has moved from a position of being taken for granted to a position where it tends to dominate the discipline for which it is a research tool. The emphasis on method will probably subside as stronger problem orientations and theoretical concerns reemerge in the field.

With this, we conclude the first part of this paper and proceed now to the second, which is intended as a somewhat informal and rather personal statement of what we think we do as ethnographers in schools and in other educational institutions or communities.

PART 2
Toward a Good Ethnography
of Schooling

In Part 2, we are concerned with ethnography as a distinctive approach to the study of education-related phenomena.

Direct Observation

The requirement for direct, prolonged, on-the-spot observation cannot be avoided or reduced. It is the guts of the ethnographic approach. This does not always mean *participant* observation. While participant observation is frequently possible in traditional anthropological fieldwork, it is particularly difficult, for most adults, in classrooms, playgroups, and other characteristic settings in the ethnography of schooling. One can participate in the teacher role, but it is difficult to participate as a child. Nevertheless, it is often desirable to go as far as one can to assume the role of the child. For example, in George Spindler's first study, in 1968, of the elementary school in Schoenhausen (reported in *Education and Cultural Process;* see Spindler, 1974b), he tried to do the work assignments the third- and fourth-graders were doing in class while also doing ethnography. This effort did help him to gain rapport with the children. They did their best to help him succeed as a pupil. He found it impossible at times to do ethnography and finish his lessons, so usually opted for doing the former. But he continued to go on hikes, climb towers, and eat lunch with the children. It was all useful—not so much because it made him empathic or gave him special insights into how it was to be a German child in the third grade but, rather, because it made him less threatening and more familiar. In our (G. & L. Spindler) recent restudies in 1977, 1981, and 1985 of the Schoenhausen school, we participated less and observed more. We don't know the children as well, but we know more about their behavior; we have more *data.* Of course the presence of two observers (of both sexes) helped. This in itself is important. We now have much more data on girls, which George Spindler did not obtain the first time around, and know much more about teachers, because they were all female (except for the Rektor) and the women related better to us as a couple than to G. S. as a lone man.

It is clear that the *role* of the ethnographer must vary from site to site. Kinds and intensity of participation that are appropriate, sex roles, obtrusiveness (participants may be more obtrusive than passive observers), and multiplicity of demands on the ethnographer all vary greatly. There are no hard and fast rules. A *sense* of what is appropriate and of what will probably work can be conveyed by training if the individual being trained already has well-developed sensitivities about social interaction, self–other relations, and obtrusiveness. Some people, who may be good people in numerous ways, do not possess these sensitivities and should not be ethnographers.

Above all else is the requirement that the ethnographer observe *directly.* No matter what instruments, coding devices, recording devices or techniques are used, the primary obligation is for the ethnographer to be there when the action takes place and to change that action as little as possible by his or her presence.

Sufficient Time on the Site

There is no hard and fast rule regarding what constitutes sufficient time on the site. Significant discoveries can be made in 2 weeks or less of ethnographic observation, but the *validity* of ethnographic observation is based on observation *in situ* that lasts long enough to permit the ethnographer to see things happen not once but repeatedly. Of course some things such as an earthquake, murder, fire, or mass hysteria are likely to occur only once during one's fieldwork, if at all, in which case we must do the best we can. But most of the things we are interested in happen again and again. We must observe these happenings often enough so that finally we learn nothing significant by their reoccurrence. A researcher knows when that point has been reached. Then one should observe still longer, to be sure that one's sense of that point in time is not premature nor the result of fatigue.

In the traditional anthropological fieldwork situation, we usually think of a year as being a reasonable, though a trifle truncated, period of time to execute the study of a complex community or phenomenon. Most well-received studies have taken longer than that. When George Spindler published his first ethnography on Menomini acculturation in 1955 (G. Spindler, 1955b), he had worked for a total of 19 months with the Menomini over a 6-year period. His German case study, *Burgbach: Urbanization and Identity in a German Village* (1973), is based on intermittent work over a 12-year period and the field studies of many students attending Stanford in Germany. Louise Spindler's (1962) *Menomini Woman and Culture Change*, is based on intermittent fieldwork from 1948 to 1954. George Spindler's first case study of a single teacher in a fifth-grade classroom in a California school took 6 months, with two afternoon-long visits, on the average, each week. The first Schoenhausen publication (Spindler, 1974b) was based directly on 6 weeks of very intensive fieldwork in 1968, but we had researched the area (Remstal, Germany) previously in 1960 and 1967.

In contrast to the time required for a community study, if we had to state a desirable time for an adequate study of a single classroom, or even a significant segment of a single classroom, such as a reading group, we would say 3 months, with observation continuing for a significant portion of every school day. It would be better if this 3-month period were spread over an entire school year, because some things just do not happen during a 3-month period. Every one of the papers submitted for *Doing the Ethnography of Schooling* and *Interpretive Ethnography of Education* is based on at least 9 months of direct observation. Some of them are based on observation over a 5- or 10-year period.

It must be emphasized that the relatively long periods of fieldwork mentioned here are for in-depth studies of significant and complex relationships where time is not limited by external conditions. Validity in ethnographic studies largely depends on an adequate period of study. At the same time, it is useless to deny that much of significance can be learned in short periods of time. Policy decisions usually have to be made on the basis of inadequate knowledge. A short-term ethnography may be better than no ethnography at all. But again, *validity* is not to be expected of short-term ethnography. This apparently is not generally understood. There are serious, or apparently to-be-taken as serious, ethnographic reports that are based on as little as 2 weeks of "ethnographic" study. Two weeks of reconnaissance can tell us a lot about the topography we would need to explore in-depth for a "real" ethnographic study, but 2 weeks is not sufficient time in which to do a serious cultural ethnography.

Volume of Recorded Data

Once upon a time, a prominent anthropologist stated at a national-level meeting of social scientists convened to discuss methodology and field equipment, "Just give us a pad of paper and a pencil and enough time . . . ." We have gone well beyond this and now use video cameras, tape recorders, film cameras, time-lapse photography, and various eliciting instruments and coding devices. However, we cannot let technical devices do our work for us. What such devices collect are data that can be analyzed (and reanalyzed) later.

There is no technological substitute for the alert individual observer, with all senses unstopped and sensitivities working at top efficiency. Of course this "turned on" observer is not simply collecting data impartially. A model of possible relationships exists in the mind of the ethnographer. And yet, there is no substitute for this observer, because only the human observer can be alert to divergences and subtleties that may prove to be more important than the data produced by any predetermined categories of observation or any instrument. True, the observer can keep on observing what is collected with tapes and visual devices long after the action is over, but these devices are so selective, so focused, that the *observer-in-situ* will often pick up what the camera or recorder leaves out. We have found it essential in our work with the Blood, Menomini, and Cree and in schools in Germany and America to collect as much visual and auditory material as possible but to always have a human observer turned on. A worthwhile field trip is usually marked by a high volume of collected data—both extensive field notes and extensive recorded material. Each of the ethnographically based papers for our edited volumes represents only a fraction of the data collected for each project.

The good ethnographer is also a good collector of artifacts, products, documents—anything that can conceivably be related to the object of study. We tried to scoop up anything and everything we could from teachers and students in the German classroom and in Roseville, and if we couldn't take it with us, we'd take a picture of it. One collects documents, such as lesson plans, books, directives from higher echelons, newspaper articles, letters to the principal, texts of speeches, and student products such as artwork and essays. More of this kind of material probably exists than any reasonable researcher will ever get around to analyzing, because things one sees no use for within a year after the field study is finished often suddenly appear important 10 or 20 years later. In ethnography, one is always dogged with the realization that what is happining will never happen again. The categories of happenings repeat themselves endlessly in human affairs, yet each event is unique.

The Evolving Character of Ethnographic Study

At least in the initial stages of a project, the ethnographer should not work out specific hypotheses, coded instruments, or even highly specific categories of observation. The reason for this is to avoid predetermining what is observed and what is elicited from informants. The problem that one thinks one is going to study is usually not the one actually studied. This does not mean that the ethnographer enters the field *in vacuo*. It is precisely our point, as anthorpological ethnographers, that ethnography is not merely a technique; it is a style of inquiry to which certain techniques (direct passive observation, participant observation, ethnographic interview, etc.) are germane, but, more importantly, it is a research process that starts with certain models of significant relationships. This model, for anthropological inquiry, is sociocultural and usually addresses cultural knowledge and social interaction in which cultural knowledge is used by actors (who may become informants but are often simply observed acting) to, as Ray McDermott has said, "make sense and feel good."

However, having stated that the ethnographer usually will not have the research problem and hypotheses all worked out beforehand, one is immediately assailed by doubts. Sometimes this is not true, and no hard and fast rule can be applied indiscriminately. The situation is usually something like this: The anthropologist gets interested in a problem *area*, such as reading competence and social context, school experience as mediating traditional versus modernization requirements, sex role differentiation in textbook content and its interpretation in classroom behavior, styles of verbal interaction between white teachers and black children, play behavior as related to social class, ethnicity, and gender, and so forth. As a rule, the specific problem, with related hypotheses, is developed as the fieldwork proceeds. The ethnographer knows something interesting is going on out there and tries to relate to it. Eventually, the observations begin to fall into categories and be governed by models. Of course, this creates a predisposition to certain foci and sensitivities, but not as concretely or as narrowly as when everything possible is worked out beforehand. The model or frame of reference in anthropological ethnography is usually broad enough to encompass a wide range of phenomena. The important criterion is that the ethnographer should preceed in the initial stages of investigation with as open a mind as possible, attending to a wide variety of possible relationships. Soon one begins to formulate hypotheses, more often resembling serious hunches than formal hypotheses, that are explored and tested by continued, repetitive observation and data elicitation.

Instrumentation

Recorded observations and recorded elicited data (such as interviews) are the base grist for the ethnographic mill. Although there is nothing wrong with using instruments such as questionnaires, they are rarely used in the first stages of work. When instruments are employed, they should usually only be used in the following circumstances. (1) When the investigator already knows what is important to find out. In such a case, a "survey" procedure can be used in which responses are collected efficiently from a relatively large sample of respondents. (2) When they are developed specifically for the field site and the focus of inquiry is judged significant in that site. This means that if instruments are used in an ethnographic study they will usually be generated during the specific research study by the ethnographer. This has been the case for our instrumental activities inventory (Spindler and Spindler, 1965, 1989), values projection technique (G. Spindler, 1977; Spindler, Spindler, Trueba, and Williams, 1990), the expressive autobiographical interview (1970), and the various interpersonal rating scales used in the Roger Harker case study (Spindler *et al.*, 1990). Their form will be determined by the information collected to date.

Nevertheless, their results will be viewed with a certain suspicion and must continually be checked against one's direct observations and directly elicited information.

Quantification

By nature, ethnographic data are qualitative, but this does not mean they are inexact, ambiguous, or intuitive (although intuition is important in fieldwork and in data analysis—one must just know when one is being intuitive). The observations collected by Shirley Heath on white teachers questioning black children are very precise, as are the data collected by Susan Phillips on teaching procedures in law school classes and by Fred Gearing and Joseph Epstein on "learning to wait" to learn to read (all in *Doing the Ethnography of Schooling*). Concepts such as "climate," "atmosphere," and "ethos" seem to be often judged proper subjects for ethnographic inquiry, whereas "hardware" questions must be turned over to quantifiers. This is a profound misconception. No research procedure is more rigorous than ethnography.

There is nothing wrong with quantification, when it is necessary, and many ethnographers find it essential once they attempt to make statements about the distribution of phenomena beyond the relatively small group or single institution or social segment in which they are working. We (G. S. and L. S.) almost always report our research in published form with fairly substantial quantification and some form of inferential nonparametric statistics. Most of our colleagues who publish on the ethnography of schooling do not report quantified data nor describe them statistically. Quantification is not the beginning point, nor is it the ultimate goal. There are many phenomena that are better tested out in relation to a hypothesis by doing another, or several, ethnographic probes in different sites than by using instruments that will permit surveys of larger samples and produce data appropriate for quantification and statistical analysis. Instrumentation and quantification are simply procedures employed to extend and to reinforce certain kinds of data, interpretations, and test hypotheses across samples. Both must be kept in their place. One must avoid their premature or overly extensive use as a security mechanism (see Devereux, 1967).

Object of Study

Our reading of ethnographic work in the schools suggests to us that some people doing ethnography do not know what they are doing it for except that it is "qualitative" and "descriptive" and that these are suddenly deemed desirable methodological attributes. Our aims in compiling the collection of work by anthropological ethnographers in *Doing the Ethnography of Schooling* and *Interpretive Ethnography of Education* were to define not only methods and techniques of research, but also the shape of intellectual goals.

A reasonable statement of intellectual purpose for ethnographic research will go something like this: The object of ethnographic research by anthropologists is to discover the cultural knowledge that people hold in their minds, how it is employed in social interaction, and the consequences of its employment. We assume that, although elements and patterns of cultural knowledge are shared in some degree by persons of the same age, sex, social status, etc., within the framework of a given cultural tradition, no two individuals have exactly the same cultural knowledge. When persons interacting in a given social setting are of different age, sex, etc. (i.e., white adult female middle-class teacher and black lower-class male and female children), their cultural knowledge will be disparate in many interactive scenes. This disparateness produces unanticipated consequences in social interaction that stabilize as tacit rules and expectations. These rules and expectations are held differently by different actors in any given setting but, to some extent, are shared (e.g., white teachers ask dumb questions; black children are slow to respond verbally) and ramify into other sectors of behavior (e.g., vandalism, impertinence, negativism).

For each social setting (i.e., classroom) in which various scenes (e.g., reading, "meddlin," going to the bathroom) are studied, there is the prior (native) cultural knowledge held by each of the various actors, the action itself, and the emerging, stabilizing rules, expectations, and some understandings that are tacit. Together these constitute a "classroom" or "school" culture.

The complexity of the relationships described earlier define as insufficient the position taken by some anthroethnographers—that the object of study is simply to elicit and report the emic knowledge of the native. It is imperative to discover what the native does not know explicitly (the tacit or implicit culture) and to examine the interaction of persons as actors in social settings. Knowing what natives know is not enough. We start with the emic position, the view of and the knowledge of the native, and work our way our to the etic, interpretive position. It is the interpretive product, however, that usually gets us into trouble with the natives when they read it. An interpretation is a cultural translation influenced, at least, and transformed, at worst, by our theories and models. These theories and models are always extraneous to the cultural knowledge of the native and, right or wrong, will be regarded with suspicion if not outright rejected.

Selective Holism and Contextualization

One often reads that ethnography is "holistic." This ascribed quality derives from the time when one ethnographer alone in a remote village or with a small band would try to record and report on everything from kinship to canoes. Of course, no one ever succeeded in reporting "everything," but there is no denying that traditional ethnographies often include an amazing range of notes and queries on a multitude of things (to borrow from the title of the first known manual for anthropological fieldworkers). Holism is still a desirable ideal if we can reduce its operational meaning to the pursuit of relationships beyond the immediate focus of our research to other relevant contexts. If we study social relationships in a reading group in a fourth-grade classroom, we may also need to study social relationships in the classroom, school, home, and community. We may also find ourselves studying the physical environment of reading, the value contexts of reading in American culture, and the use of information dissemination techniques that can serve as substitutes for reading. We allow ourselves to go wherever our expanding attention takes us as we try to describe and interpret a complex of relationships at the core of our attention.

One form of contextualization that is frequently neglected in ethnographic study is historical time. Most ethnography is synchronic, expressive of the here and now. Studies conducted intermittently over a period of years help correct this. We have worked in the Schoenhausen Grundschule intermittently since 1968, and we find that our understanding of the school expands each time we study it. Time produces new data that put the previously collected information in a different perspective.

Whose Ethnography Is It Anyway?

It should be clear that we are trying to define the criteria for a good *anthropological* ethnography of schooling. In doing so, we do not mean to deny doing ethnography to others. Psychologists, sociologists, historians, and various nondenominational inquirers are doing and will continue to do ethnography. Nevertheless, ethnography originated, and persists, as the field arm of cultural anthropology. Its emerging character definition will be greatly influenced by this origin and continuing status within anthropology. Ethnography is presently suffering from overuse, without specification, as a household word in the social sciences and, particularly, in education. This will eventually damage the reputation of this kind of research and erode its potential utility to social scientists, teachers, and policymakers. We are attempting to define the criteria of good anthropological ethnography and clarify its limitations as well as its assets. We must know what it can and cannot do if we want ethnography to assume a place as one of the credible methodologies in the study of the educative process.

Criteria for a Good Ethnography

Given the preceding observations, we posit the following as reasonable criteria for a good ethnography of education.

Criterion I

Observations are contextualized, both in the immediate setting in which behavior is observed and in further contexts beyond that setting, as relevant.

Criterion II

Hypotheses emerge *in situ* as the study continues in the setting selected for observation. Judgment on what may be significant to study in-depth is deferred until the orienting phase of the field study has been completed.

Criterion III

Observation is prolonged and repetitive. Chains of events are observed more than once to establish the reliability of observations.

Criterion IV

The native view of reality is attended through inferences from observation and through the various forms of ethnographic inquiry (including interviews and other eliciting procedures); however, in the ethnography itself, places are made from which native voices may be "heard." Cultural translations are reduced to the minimum, commensurate with effective communication.

Criterion V

Sociocultural knowledge held by social participants makes social behavior and communication sensible. Therefore, a major part of the ethnographic task is to elicit that knowledge from informant participants.

Criterion VI

Instruments, codes, schedules, questionnaires, agenda for interviews, and so forth should be generated *in situ*, as a result of observation and ethnographic inquiry.

Criterion VII

A transcultural, comparative perspective is present, although frequently as an unstated assumption. That is, cultural variation over time and space is considered a natural human condition. All cultures are seen as adaptations to the exigencies of human life and exhibit common as well as distinguishing features.

Criterion VIII

Some of the sociocultural knowledge affecting behavior and communication in any particular setting being studied is implicit or tacit, not known to some participants and known only ambiguously to others. Therefore, a significant task of ethnography is to make what is implicit and tacit to informants explicit to readers. In the modern world, this often means explicit to informants as well. Under controlled conditions, this may cause the ethnographer considerable trouble, for the *implicit* is often implicit to the native because it is unacceptable at the explicit level. We tread a thorny path here.

Criterion IX

Because the informant (any person being interviewed) is one who has the emic, native cultural knowledge, the ethnographic interviewer must not predetermine responses by the kinds of questions asked. The management of the interview must be carried out so as to promote the unfolding of emic cultural knowledge in its most heuristic, "natural" form. This will require the interviewer to "flow" with the informant's style of talk and organization of knowledge without imposing pre-conceived agendas in the interview interaction.

Criterion X

Any form of technical device that will enable the ethnographer to collect more live data—immediate, natural, detailed behavior—will be used, such as cameras, audio and video tapes, and field-based instruments (with the *caveats* mentioned earlier).

Criterion XI

The presence of the ethnographer should be acknowledged and his or her social, personal, interactional position in the situation de-scribed. This may result in a more narrative, personalized style of reporting than has been the case in the past in ethnographic reporting.

PART 3
A Case Study Example

Objectives

In this part of our chapter, our objective is to demonstrate at least some of the criteria for a good ethnography of schooling by reviewing, albeit in truncated form, some of the research methods developed and applied in a research project we began in Germany in 1968 and that has evolved into a comparative study of two schools (and their commu-nities) in Germany and Wisconsin, United States. We will be forced to condense interview material and observations to summaries rather than supply the full text. Interested readers may pursue a further exposition by examining our other publications (Spindler, 1974a; Spin-dler and Spindler, 1987a,c, 1991; Spindler *et al.*, 1990a).

Our overall objective for this long-range study (1968–present) has been to establish the role of the school in the preparation of children for an urbanizing Germany and a changing world. We have pursued the same general objectives in our study of the Roseville school, which began in 1983. We are particularly interested in the influence of cul-ture on the role of the school and, for this reason, have exploited the differences as well as the similarities exhibited by the two commu-nities. The project has taken many turns over time, and we have pur-sued a number of themes including gender differences, teacher styles, and changing perceptions of relationships between activities instrumental to goals variously linked to traditional and modern cultural contexts, curriculum adaptations to changing purposes, resistance to change, the use of film as evocative stimuli, and the effect of position in the situation (e.g., friend, informal leader, formal power position, age, gender, reputation, etc.) on the interpretations of perceived behaviors in classrooms. These goals, and the research methods attendant upon them, have produced a plethora of texts with which we are currently still struggling; so the project is far from finished and is undergoing continual change. We have experimented with a variety of research techniques, all generated by the field experience. The latest development is the comparative, reflective, cross-cultural interview, and we will devote more space to this technique than to other methods or techniques in the brief summary to follow (G. and L. Spindler, 1992). But first, permit us to describe the two research sites.

The Research Sites

Schoenhausen is a village of about 2000 in a semirural but urbanizing area in the *Land, Baden Württemberg,* in southern Germany. Schoenhausen was known, and still is to some extent, as an *ausgesprochner Weinort* (emphatically a wine-making place). The nativeborn are *Swaebisch* and Protestant. Most of the "newcomers" originally migrated from the former east zone, Sudetenland, or other areas from which Germans were expelled or from which they fled after World War II. These newcomers are somewhat more urbanized as a rule and more often than not Catholic (G. Spindler, 1973). The *Grundschule* (elementary school) is charged with the responsibility for educating all of the children and preparing them for a changing Germany and world. Its 127 children are distributed in four grades staffed by six teachers and a *Rektor* (principal) and various other special services personnel. The Schoenhausen Grundschule has enjoyed a good relationship with the community and with the parents whose children attend it. Partly, at least, this relationship is due to the benign influence of the *Rektor* who has been in that position since the beginning of our study in 1968.

The Roseville Elementary School, located in central Wisconsin, includes kindergarten through eighth grade and is somewhat larger than the Schoenhausen school, but it is comparable in every other respect. The school district is rural but has many commuters who work in nearby towns, some of them as many as 40 or 50 miles distant. The majority of children attending the school come from small dairy farms.

This school also enjoys good relationships with its community and with the parents who eagerly attend school functions whenever possible. The principal is himself a farmer as well as an educator and is well liked. The predominant ethnicity of the Roseville School District is German (G. and L. Spindler, 1987a and 1987b, G. and L. Spindler *et al.* 1990a).

Research Techniques Used

The Instrumental Activities Inventory

One of our first research projects in Schoenhausen was to elicit responses to a technique that we had developed in our studies of culture change—the instrumental activities inventory (I.A.I.). We had used the I.A.I. in two other field studies in Canada with native American populations (G. and L. Spindler, 1965, L. Spindler, 1978). The technique itself consists of line drawings of significant activities that are related to a traditional, as against a modernized, way of life in the specific research site. In the I.A.I. prepared for the research in Germany, "activities" may be living in a traditional versus a modern type of house, working in a factory or working in a vineyard, going out to a restaurant to eat supper or having a quiet meal at home, going to school, living in a *Bauernhaus* (a large dwelling sheltering both humans and animals), or an apartment house, and so forth. We administered the I.A.I. to all of the school children, all of the teachers, and a significant sample of parents in 1968 and 1977. Respondents produce choices of activities and the rationale for these choices. Comparisons of the 1968 and 1977 samples raised questions about the degree to which a wide-ranging modernization program implemented during this period had actually been accepted. The analysis of the texts thus produced was in part statistical—comparing the distribution of choices as related to various antecedent factors such as occupation, educational level, area of origin, degree of urbanization, sex, and age. We found that sex and age were by far the most determinant variables in the differentiation of choices (G. and L. Spindler, 1990). Another analytic procedure was to isolate clusters of supporting values for a traditional versus a modern, urbanized way of life from the rationales for choices provided by our respondents. This was easily done since there tend to be certain elements that are consistently present when one or the other choice of an instrumental activity is made (G. Spindler, 1974b; G. and L. Spindler, 1987b).

One of the surprises that analysis of the 1968 sample as against the

1977 sample revealed (which included all of the children, teachers, and most parents) was that there had been a decided swing back to traditional instrumentalities during this 10-year period. This was contrary to our expectations, since there had been a massive reform directed at education during that period. The curricula, the instructional materials, and even many of the teachers had been changed during this time (G. and L. Spindler, 1987a). Also surprising was the fact that females had turned more traditional than males (G. and L. Spindler, 1990b). In contrast, in the 1968 sample females more frequently than males had opted for instrumental choices that were oriented toward modernization and mechanization.

The I.A.I. responses were the least ambiguous and the most easily analyzed type of text that our research produced. The I.A.I. was very useful as a way of determining some parameters within which other research questions could be pursued, as well as being significant in its own right. It is important that although the I.A.I is a fairly complex "instrument," it evolved out of the research experience *in situ*. Although the initial development was with the Blood Indians of Alberta, Canada (G. and L. Spindler, 1965), the specific activities, their representation, and their relationship to the traditional versus the modern poles of the adaptive continuum must always be specifically site-oriented.

Field Notes

Of course we took extensive notes on activity in the classrooms and on interviews with teachers, administrators, children, parents, and others in the community. These notes are indispensable in that they provide in relatively short compass a holistic grasp of not only what is happening and what people have said but one's reactions to things said and done. Much of the rest of the data that we collected is cast against the notes that we have taken because the notes provide temporal ordering and sequence as well as content. However, notes by themselves would be grossly inadequate. No one can sit in a classroom and take notes on more than a very few of the things that come to one's attention simultaneously, and questions always arise as to why one's attention was focused in a given direction and not others. But the problem with much of what one collects using film, video, or audio recording is that these data are so complex and inclusive that one has, in effect, to do the fieldwork over again in order to analyze the materials thus collected. One's field notes alone will support or fail to support each one of the criteria for a good ethnography. They are the product of observation whether passive or participant. They are also the product of interviews both casual and formal, even if usually backed up by a tape recorder. Examining the taped interview in the light of field notes increases the efficiency of that examination. We have also found it very useful to include whatever interpretations occur to us as we are observing or interviewing, but we are careful to keep those interpretations separated by brackets or, in some cases, by different-colored inks. These interpretations or "hunches" are frequently the starting point for significant analysis later.

Films

We filmed activity in classrooms, playgrounds, and on excursions away from the school. Our initial purpose was to provide ourselves with a more complete record of those activities. Later, we used the films as evocative stimuli in interviews, following the lead of Collier and Collier (1986). Films are the most difficult kind of "text" to analyze, and we are still working on them. For us, the greatest utility of films as "records" is that we can "return" to the classroom years later. Unlike action in real life, the action recorded on film (or video) can be rerun again and again so that one can look at particulars with close attention.

In preparing this chapter, we reran nearly all of the films that we had taken from Schoenhausen in 1977, 1981, and 1985 and those that we had taken in Roseville in 1983, 1984, and intermittently since. This rerun made all of our other data come to life for us, but it also further informed us of things we already knew or of things we did not know at all.

One phenomenon, for example, that came to our attention through repeated viewings of the films was that despite great variations in the explicit aspects of teacher style in the management of classroom activity, all of the teachers in the Schoenhausen school were in constant charge of their classrooms. They never relinquished responsibility to the students. Although they might take a position in the back or along the side of the room and seemingly be quite relaxed about what was going on, we saw that teachers were giving signals, sometimes as subtle as pursed lips or raised eyebrows, to reinforce or intervene in student behavior—as in, for example, role playing or other group activities that did not require direct supervision by a teacher. At the same time, certain dramatic differences among teacher styles became even more apparent with film viewing. Some teachers spend all of their time in the front of the room in explicit control of the class. Others set up a task of some kind and then *appear* to relinquish control (but, as we have said, do not). Other teachers are always in the middle of their student groups engaging in a great deal of bodily activity as well as talk as the action proceeds. Some teachers are formal and keep distance, whereas others are seemingly quite relaxed and keep little distance, and so on (see Spindler and Spindler, 1987c).

Films are a part of the "collectors" orientation of the ethnographer, but they soon become essential as sources of data that can be re-examined with new hypotheses and new theoretical orientations. Films are also great correctors of conceptual and interpretive "drift." One tends to pay attention to the same phenomena revealed by one's other data banks time and time again. Over a period of years, a kind of mythology develops that, like all mythologies, is self-sustaining. Films are a great corrective for this tendency. Once one starts filming, a research project seems grossly inadequate without them.

Photographs

We also took hundreds of still photographs with a 35 mm camera and have found them very useful, not only for research but also for teaching (Collier and Collier, 1986). When one shows a film that has not been "cinematized," the flow of the action is usually either too fast and complex for the audience to understand it or so slow that it is boring. An image that stays on the screen in good detail for as long as one wants it to can be talked about and discussed. The pictures are also important as documentation and are easy to examine as one is either doing an analysis of other data or actually writing it up. It is important, of course, to have records of when and where photographs were taken. This applies to both film and still photographs. Again, taking photographs is a part of the collector's orientation of the ethnographer, and once taking pictures becomes habitual and accepted by the "natives," one does it without thinking much about it. In general, we have found that taking photographs and making films in our field situations did not seem overly intrusive. But by the time we started taking them, people knew us pretty well, with the exception of the Roseville school, where we entered the school with the explicit purpose of making films on the first day of the study. The purpose of doing this, however, had been discussed thoroughly with all the school personnel, including the children, before the first day.

Exchange

Another form of text was produced by the teachers and children themselves. After the 1985 revisit to Schoenhausen (we had already started fieldwork in Roseville), we implemented an exchange between students and teachers in the two locations. Each of the teachers wrote letters to their counterparts explaining their activities, where they lived, and their thoughts about the teaching profession. Children wrote to each other after they had seen films of the classrooms in their counterpart school and made comments about the action. These kinds of solicited documents are useful as an expression of the native point of view. An exchange of this sort must be regarded as a research device— that is, a situation is created by the ethnographers. A complex reflective process is instigated, while the teachers and children are explaining themselves in light of what they think the "others" might see or understand and, at the same time, asking questions that reflect their understanding of the others' situations.

Other Data

It goes without saying that ethnographers always explore available archival data and pay particular attention to demographic characteristics. The composition of the population was very important as a backdrop for the Schoenhausen school, in view of the fact that about half of the children were from *Einheimischen* (native) families and the other half were from migrant (German) families. This was particularly important in the earlier phases of our research, because we were working with a migrant adaptation and conflict model.

Other kinds of data collected include newspaper clippings, memos from the superintendent's office, changes in land ownership patterns in the community area, and changes in the residential composition of the community. In all of our research projects, we have paid a great deal of attention to the community context of whatever phenomena we were researching and have found this to be invaluable. Contexts expand in concentric circles from the target phenomenon. The only limits in pursuing context that we have discovered are those imposed by time, energy, and funding.

The Reflective Cross-Cultural Interview

The basic procedure in reflective cross-cultural interviewing is simple: We filmed in Schoenhausen and in Roseville, and we showed the teachers, children, and administrators the films from both places. We conducted interviews about what they saw in their own classrooms and in those of the "other" and how they interpreted what they saw.[1] We cannot replicate any substantial amount of this material in this paper and refer the reader to Spindler and Spindler (1991), where some text is provided. These interviews are of a different quality than anything that we had collected previously. They are *reflective* in depth and with a subtlety that had heretofore been lacking. The observed differences in the action in the two settings, Schoenhausen and Roseville, caused teachers and children to reflect back on their own behavior at the same time that they were pronouncing perceptions of the behavior of the other. In a sense, they were experiencing what we experienced as ethnographers. After working in the Schoenhausen school in 1968, 1977, and 1981, our visits to the Roseville school, beginning in 1983, allowed us to perceive differently and to reexamine what we were observing in Schoenhausen. This reorientation was fully implemented in our 1985 visit. We had come to accept the Schoenhausen school and community as "normal" and familiar, and it was increasingly difficult to see what it was we were observing. The Roseville experience sharpened our perceptions and caused us to think about them in a different way. To observe anything anywhere, it seems necessary to make it a little "strange" (Spindler and Spindler, 1982).

Diverse Reflections

Group Interviews with Children

We showed the films of the Roseville classrooms to the first and second grades combined and to the third and fourth grades during separate screenings in the Schoenhausen Grundschule. We showed the Schoenhausen films to the same grade groups in the Roseville Elementary School. We tape-recorded the responses by the children, which were in both cases very enthusiastic and "dynamic." But the Schoenhausen children far outdid the Roseville children in sheer animal enthusiasm. "What did you notice?" asked a Schoenhausen teacher of the children. "Some of them could work at a table with a teacher and some could sit alone." "They could work with another person if they wanted to." "They could go to the closet and get things to use if they wanted to and there were some of them listening to tape recorders." "Some of them are black-haired!" "The children are not fighting with each other!" "There's nobody tripping anybody else when they move around." "There's no fighting." And so on and so on.

The teacher in charge of the screening in Roseville asked the children the same question, and they responded with similar comments, but of different content. "I'd rather live away from the school."

"I like riding on the bus." "We have more recesses and they are a lot of fun and we have a gym—did they have a gym?" "I like having desks like ours where there's a special place to keep things." "I wouldn't like to get a table with other kids." "I like being in school a long time each day." "We like staying in school for lunch, it's fun." "It's too noisy in those classrooms." "How could you learn anything if it was so noisy?" "I couldn't work by myself if there was so much noise all the time." "I like being able to choose the things I want to do." "The teacher isn't always telling us what we have to do." "None of them wore hats." "The tops of their desks were messy." "The moving chalkboard is really neat." And so on and so on.

The Roseville children perceived the noise and activity of the Schoenhausen children as greater than that in their own classrooms, and most placed a negative value on it. They appreciated the long school day, the lunch period, and living out in the country, not "packed in" with other families and houses. They also recognized a facility such as the gymnasium and the modern school building as positive attributes. They were not particularly attracted by the apparent freedom to talk out loud or to engage in vigorous physical activity at times, as was frequently the case in the Schoenhausen school, and felt that this could actually be injurious to learning.

The "position" of the children is reflected in their comments, just as the position of the teachers and the administrator is reflected in their comments (in the following sections). These are the real conditions of the children's lives in the schools. These conditions are perceived through cultural screens provided by life in Roseville and life in Schoenhausen. We do not have to pursue this into "German" culture and "American" culture, writ large, for our purposes, although it is tempting to do so.

Schulamtdirektor

We showed the same films to the Schulamtdirektor, his staff, and the Schoenhausen teachers. We can excerpt only a few translated statements from the much longer reaction of the Schulamtdirektor.

> I must say that there is between the school in Roseville and that in Schoenhausen a clear difference. A decisive difference. Our teachers, our understanding about school, are situated in a specific system. This system is influenced directly from above, from the school system viewpoint. One always understands that there is a curriculum plan prepared beforehand that is binding and it gives a clear statement of what the instruction means. A very clear statement. Instruction is, as

we understand it, as a rule joined with a certain theme. Instruction is joined with a certain class. Instruction is linked to a certain preparation, a certain goal and a certain realization of these goals. The teacher is always at the front. The children sit before him. The teacher brings everything together under the same label, tries to reach the same goal, so that every hour a little piece of the mosaic (of learning) is laid down. And so goes the work in a given hour and in the next hour, week for week until finally the teacher, with the children, reaches a specific goal. This is characteristic for German instruction and for our understanding of instruction. If the pictures from Roseville are typical, it is very difficult for me to understand how instruction and progress can move together. There are many questions, many.

The Schulamtdirektor was very clear in his statement of what German instruction was and how the situation as he perceived it in Roseville would violate the assumptions behind this statement. His statement projects a clear cultural orientation. His interpretation is shared to some extent by the teachers, but much less vigorously. It is apparent that his position as a chief administrator at the apex of the local district system affects his interpretation of the "other" school situation. It is also apparent that he shares certain perceptions of the situation with the Schoenhausen teachers (following) and even with the children.

Two Teachers

All of the teachers in both the Schoenhausen and the Roseville schools were interviewed in the cross-cultural comparative reflective style that we are demonstrating. That is, each teacher was shown the same films from each school and interviewed both while they were being shown and after they had all been shown. The teachers, in effect, provided their own cultural interpretations, which are ordinarily supplied by the anthropologist ethnographers. This was part of our attempt to move the elicitation of data as far as possible into the cultural knowledge of the informant rather than impose our own on the observations or the elicited interview material. This does not absolve us from responsibility for interpretive analysis, but it provided us with a very different kind of data than any other technique that we have utilized.

We can select only a very few items from all of the interviews for the two teachers—both female, in their late 30s, and teaching in schools of comparable size. The complete interviews for these two teachers can be found in Spindler and Spindler (1992).

Mrs. Schiller   Mrs. Schiller, a third-generation American of German descent, has taught in the Roseville elementary school for 5 years and is considered to be one of the best teachers on the faculty. We had observed her classroom many times before this interview was held and before she had seen the films. We were impressed with how freely the children moved about in the classroom to pursue their own goals. She usually worked up front with a small group around the table while the children worked on lessons, listened to tapes, or pasted colored paper together to make turkeys (it was near Thanksgiving). We asked Mrs. Schiller how the children could work so well on their own and what she did to prepare them for that. She responded that the most important thing was that she and the children developed a trusting relationship, so she could rely on them to work without supervision. She was aghast at the idea that she could not carry on in this manner at the Schoenhausen Grundschule. She said "I have a lot of faith in kids. I think kids are neat! If you have high expectations, 98% of the time they will fulfill your expectations."

We asked her what she would feel like if she went out in the hall or someone called her to the phone and she came back in a few minutes and found things in disorder. She responded, "Well, I would tell them right off, I am very disappointed! I have this important phone call and you couldn't sit for five minutes while I answered it. I would let them know it hurt me personally. It's a kind of personal thing. Oh, yes! You start building that up the first day of school. Then they feel 'We can't hurt our teacher.' Oh, yes, that happened today! I had to take a workbook to a parent who was taking her little girl to the dentist so she could work on it if she had to wait and the class has the same assignment. When I came back to my room they had all finished that page that was assigned and they went right on to the next one. I praised them. 'It was really nice that I could count on you, and I could come back to a nice, quiet class.' And of course they all beamed. They just love praise!"

At other points in the interview, she was concerned with the development of individual responsibility and made it clear that with her praise for good behavior and her sorrow and personal hurt at bad behavior, she instilled a sense of guilt in the children. This and the emphasis on individual development were points of particular difference between Mrs. Schiller and Frau Wanzer, the Schoenhausen teacher. We now turn to Frau Wanzer.

Frau Wanzer   For the first few minutes, we talked with Frau Wanzer about what we wanted to do in her classroom in the next observation period. We indicated that we would like to present a systematic view of her classroom on film to the Roseville teachers in our exchange activity. We suggested that she spend some time before the class that we were to film explaining her procedure and her goals for the day and that we, in turn, could explain this to the Roseville teachers. She had seen the Roseville films at the same time as the Schulamtdirektor. She responded "Yeah! It would perhaps have been good if for the films you showed us (of the Roseville classrooms) they had this introduction. *Für mich in Jeden Fall* (for me in any case) it was really difficult to see what was intended. Perhaps that was also the ground for the feeling that many of us had, *"Was lernen sie eigentlich?"* (what are they learning, really?).

The film shows Mrs. Schiller working at the front of the room with a small group of children and the rest of them, as usual, pursuing their own ends, although many of them were catching up on lessons. Frau Wanzer was very taken by this and asked, "How did she know what the children were doing in the rest of the room? How did the children working alone know what they are supposed to do?" She went on to say that if she were to do this in the Schoenhausen Grundschule, disturbances would occur.

We explained that Mrs. Schiller was very proud that her classroom was productive and that she had explained to us that the children seek out the materials to use for their work or whatever on their own, although they usually ask permission to use them, and that she told us that of course the children "have specific lessons, but when they are finished—they can do what they will."

Frau Wanzer was impressed with this also, and she responded simply, *"Sie können tuen was sie wollen!"* (They can do what they want!). We responded, "they have various opportunities—such as tapes, computers, the library, flash cards, charts and posters, and so forth. Frau Wanzer replied, *"Da ist naturlich ein grossen Unterschied* (There is naturally a great difference) to our school. They (Roseville) have much more time to work, much more. With us one hour equals 45 minutes and one must in this time reach a goal. In America they have so much time and so when they are finished with their lessons they can do what they want, but with us there is no time. The more gifted children finish, but many do not and then they must be helped to reach the goal for the lesson." She goes on to talk about how much more time Roseville teachers have (the Schoenhausen academic school day is 8:30–11:30 A.M.) and about helping all of the children to reach at least the minimum goals defined in the curriculum plan. We then turned the discussion to the curriculum plan itself, and she pointed out that she has in her *Lehrerplan* (curriculum plan) the goals that "I must reach.

Every hour has a part goal. I must find out as the hour progresses if I am to have enough time to reach that goal. It depends on whether the hour goes well or badly—how much time I'll spend." The Lehrerplan for Frau Wanzer comes from the *Land, Baden Württemberg*—equivalent to province or state. She and the other teachers as well as the Schulamt-direktor were very surprised that the Roseville teachers actually had considerable control over their own curriculum plan.

The interview turned to what she would do if she did have the opportunity to have some free time that was not scheduled, and she explained that she would have tables arranged, each of them furnished with appropriate books and materials before the children arrived and that they could choose which one of these tables they would like to work at, and, at the end of the period, they would report, each group, to another group. But she was not enthusiastic about the notion of a "*volligfrei*" (totally free) classroom period. "*Dass macht nichts!*" (That makes nothing—that's of no use!) We then went on to talk about what would happen if she left the room and left the children in the room with no supervision: What would she do if she came back to find the children in boisterous or generally unruly activity? She said, "I would talk to the class. I would attempt to reach an understanding. Scolding does no good. Sometimes I have said that I am *traurig* (sad). We asked, "Would you say that you are *beleidigdt* (hurt)? Frau Wanzer replied that she would "No, never hurt. Only sad." And so we asked her if she tried to make the children feel guilty, and she said that children of that age did not understand guilt: "How can they understand who is guilty? The one who started the trouble or the one who responded to the trouble and carried it on further?"

Interpretation

The differences run deep. Mrs. Schiller assumes that her goal is to help each individual develop to his or her fullest degree—to the limit of their individual capabilities. Frau Wanzer assumes, as does the Schulamtdirektor, that her purpose is to help each child attain the standards set forth in the Lehrerplan—that some will meet them fully and others only minimally. Frau Wanzer takes for granted the existence of a Lehrerplan that is furnished to the school by the State school system and that will directly guide her management of her instruction. Mrs. Schiller takes for granted the fact that teachers from the school district develop their own curriculum and that it is only an approximate guide. Frau Wanzer assumes that the children eventually learn to continue working when she leaves the classroom, but that one cannot expect too much of the younger first- and second-graders. Mrs. Schiller expects her first- and second-graders to be responsible for keeping a quiet, on-task classroom when she is gone for a few minutes. Frau Wanzer would "talk" to her class if there were a disruption, but she would not act "hurt," only "sad," and she would not try to make her children feel "guilty." Mrs. Schiller would develop personal liking and trust with her children, would be "hurt" if they misbehaved, and would leave them all feeling guilty if they did. Furthermore, the two teachers have quite different conceptions of guilt. Mrs. Schiller was trying to encourage the children to internalize feelings of guilt about misbehavior, whereas Frau Wanzer was looking at guilt as a juridical process. For Frau Wanzer, guilt has to be established; there is a perpetrator, a reinforcer, and perhaps a victim; for Mrs. Schiller, there is a feeling state—guilt is internalized. The children feel guilty about their irresponsible behavior and hurting their teacher.

These are the assumptions, as we see them, that lie behind both the behaviors of the two teachers in their classrooms and their perceptions of each other's behaviors *in situ*. These are cultural differences, we believe, that are expressed in and derived from the German and American historical experience, respectively. The case for this extension is substantially beyond the scope of this chapter: therefore, we confine ourselves to the observation that in Schoenhausen and Roseville, respectively, these are assumptions that we regard as cultural, in the sense that they are pervasive within the dialogue of the school and school system and antecedent to the operations of the specific teachers and children we have observed.

The cross-cultural comparative reflective interview procedure furnishes clear evidence that the various audiences viewing the action all saw the same things in the films of classrooms. The children and teachers in Roseville saw the children in the Schoenhausen classrooms as noisy and enthusiastic. The children and teachers in Schoenhausen saw the Roseville classrooms as quiet and orderly. Each acknowledged that their own classrooms were more "noisy" or more "quiet" as well as seeing the other in those terms.

The cross-cultural comparative reflective interviews also gave us clear evidence of the ways in which position affects perceptions. The Schulamtdirektor, the children, and the teachers "saw" the same features of behavior in the "others'" setting but emphasized these features differently, and the children actually "saw" some things the adults did not. The Schulamtdirektor viewed the action from the top down, from the perspective of a system. The children interpreted the classroom action and setting from their perspective—desks, lunch, clothes, popcorn day, teacher's position in the classroom, blackboards, and so forth, but they still "saw" the quiet and order in the Roseville classroom and the noise level and boisterous activity in the Schoen-hausen classrooms. The teachers, represented by Mrs. Schiller and Frau Wanzer, interpreted behavior in their own and the other's classroom with clearly different assumptions about what each ex-pected of children and what their purposes as teachers were. These assumptions, we believe, are cultural.

All of the principals cited above are "natives," and they tell their "story" in their own way. The foreign observers—ourselves, the eth-nographers—also "saw" and "interpreted." We "saw" the same features of classroom activity and our interpretations are not wildly different from those of the natives at any point, but they are influenced by our anthropological goals, our persistent search for "culture," in its various expressions. The interested reader may find confirmation of this elsewhere (Spindler and Spindler, 1987a,c).

Conclusion to the Comparative Reflective Cross-Cultural Interview Technique: A "Postmodern" Comment

The reflective cross-cultural interview technique has been dis-cussed only briefly in our own publications (G. S. and L. S.) but was applied in a study by Fujita and Sano (1988) in which a Japanese and an American preschool furnished the cultural "brackets" for the inter-views.[2] For us, the first tentative application of the technique in our 1981 research visit to Schoenhausen came to full bloom only in the 1985 research visit. It was an experiment growing out of the field experi-ence and not out of the literature by fellow academicians. We find, however, that it is in line with modernist conceptions of ethnography characterized by the collaborative interaction between the ethnogra-pher and the natives, the emphasis on discourse and dialogue, and the critical dimension of the reflection in which all parties to the discourse are engaged. This mode of ethnography is less definitive, more processual, and less structural than traditional ethnography and asks the reader to do some work in striving to understand what is going on (Marcus and Fischer, 1986; Clifford and Marcus, 1986). Some features of the modernist approach to ethnography seem to grow naturally out of the kinds of criteria for a good ethnography that we developed in Part 3 of this chapter. None of our innovative research techniques will satisfy the radical postmodernist ethnographers such as Stephen Tyler (*in* Clifford and Marcus, 1986), who would most likely see the construction of a kind of experimental setting—such as the showing of films from two cultures, one of which is the native's own, and using films as brackets for interviews—as too manipulative.

Ethnography as a research tool (or procedure or orientation) is changing, and it is incumbent upon ethnographers of schooling and education to keep abreast of this change. However, it is worth pointing out that observing, filming, tape-recording, note-taking, and so forth in a classroom with 30 or so children and a teacher is quite different than trying to write a "realist" ethnography of a whole community, even though the classroom as a closed encounter has much in common with other events within communities such as rituals, councils, or even family situations. We need to explore further the difference between writing an ethnography of a community and writing an ethnography of a bounded encounter. The approach, in any event, must surely be interdisciplinary, and we must pay close attention to the hazards of cultural translation, letting the natives speak for themselves as much as possible.

We have found all of the techniques and methods that we use in the field to be indispensable. Our methods tend to have a dominant theme of creating situations, for some purposes, to which natives respond. This is true, for example, of the instrumental activities inventory and the cross-cultural reflective interview. This is also true of the "expressive autobiographical interview" technique that Louise Spindler (1962, 1978) developed in her studies of women and their adaptations to culture change and that we have applied in studies of teachers. However, we do spend a great deal of time interacting with people in our studied communities informally, becoming friends and participants in daily affairs and special occasions, and we do a great deal of observing where our presence is as passive and as unnoticeable as we can make it.

Whatever techniques of the more manipulative kind (such as those first mentioned) that we do develop and apply emerge, as indicated, from the more casual field experience.

Conclusion

In Part 3, we have tried to practice what we preached in Part 2. As we reflect on the criteria for a good ethnography, we think we have demonstrated, albeit sketchily, criteria I–XI—in short, all of them, but some more than others. We leave to the reader the specific relevances, as appropriate to modernist ethnography, which asks the reader to do some work. The anthropology of education and its field arm, ethnography, are in a dynamic and rather sensitive situation. Because our data are so complex, we need to become more interdisciplinary, while retaining the considerable virtues of our anthropological disciplinary base. We need to keep close to the natives' point of view, to the natives' meanings, while we provide cultural translations that make sense to our readers, most of whom are not anthropologists. We need to avoid entrapment by the call from applied researchers to provide advice, recommendations, and problem solutions. Our aim is to generate research and interpretations that can be used by professional educators to find their own solutions to serious problems and to contribute to the broad understanding of human life to which anthropology has always contributed. The life of the educational anthro–ethnographer is a hard one, full of frustration, vexation, and marginality, but it is exciting.

Notes

[1] Some parts of this discussion are paralleled in Spindler and Spindler (1992). The complete text of the teacher interviews is given in that paper as well.
[2] The first presentation of the reflective cross-cultural interview technique and some of its results was made by G. and L. Spindler at the American Anthropological Association meetings in 1986. Fujita and Sano (1988), both Stanford Ph.D.'s in anthropology, subsequently applied it in their field research in Riverfront City, Wisconsin, and in Japan.

References

Clifford, J., and Marcus, G. (Eds.). (1986). *Writing culture: The poetics and politics of ethnography*. Berkeley: University of California Press.
Collier, J., Jr., and Collier, M. (1986). *Visual anthropology*. Albuquerque: University of New Mexico Press.
Devereux, G. (1967). *From anxiety to method in the behavioral sciences*. Paris and The Hague: Mouton.
Fujita, M., and Sano, T. (1988). Children in American and Japanese day-care centers: Ethnography and reflective cross-cultural interviewing. *In* H. Trueba and C. Delgado-Gaitan (Eds.), *School and society: Learning content through culture* (pp. 125–163). New York: Praeger.
Hewett, E. (1904). Anthropology and education. *American Anthropologist, VI*, 574–75.
King, R. (1968). *School at Mopass: A problem of identity*. New York: Holt, Rinehart & Winston.
Marcus, G. E., and Fischer, M. (Eds.). (1986). *Anthropology as cultural critique: An experimental movement in the human sciences*. Chicago: University of Chicago Press.
Rosenfeld, G. (1971). *Shut those thick lips: The ethnography of a slum school*. New York: Holt, Rinehart & Winston. (Reprinted by Waveland Press, 1986.)

Singleton, J. (1967). *Nichu: A Japanese school.* New York: Holt, Rinehart & Winston.

Spindler, G. (Ed.). (1955a). *Education and anthropology.* Stanford, CA: Stanford University Press.

Spindler, G. (1955b). *Sociocultural and psychological processes in Menomini acculturation* (Vol. 5). University of California Publications in Culture and Society. Berkeley: University of California Press.

Spindler, G. (Ed.). (1963). *Education and culture: Anthropological approaches.* New York: Holt, Rinehart & Winston.

Spindler, G. (1973). *Burgbach: Urbanization and identity in a German village.* New York: Holt, Rinehart & Winston.

Spindler, G. (Ed.). (1974a). *Education and cultural process: Toward an anthropology of education.* New York: Holt, Rinehart & Winston.

Spindler, G. (1977). Anthropological perspectives on American culture, core values, continuity, and change. In G. D. Renzo (Ed.), *We the people: American cultural and social change.* Westport, CT: Greenwood Press.

Spindler, G. (1974b). Schooling in Schoenhausen: A study of cultural transmission and instrumental adaptation in an urbanizing German village. In G. Spindler (Ed.), *Education and cultural process: Toward an anthropology of education* (pp. 230–273) New York: Holt, Rinehart & Winston.

Spindler, G. (Ed.). (1982). *Doing the ethnography of schooling: Educational anthropology in action.* New York: Holt, Rinehart & Winston. (Reprinted by Waveland Press, 1988.)

Spindler, G. (Ed.). (1987). *Education and cultural process: Anthropological approaches* (2nd ed.). Prospect Heights, IL: Waveland Press.

Spindler, G., and Spindler, L. (1965). The instrumental activities inventory. *Southwestern Journal of Anthropology, 21,* 1–23.

Spindler, G., and Spindler, L. (1970). Fieldwork with the Menomini. In G. Spindler (Ed.), *Being an anthropologist: Fieldwork in eleven cultures* (pp. 267–301). New York: Holt, Rinehart & Winston. (Reprinted by Waveland Press, 1987.)

Spindler, G., and Spindler, L. (1982). Roger Harker and Schoenhausen: From the familiar to the strange and back again. In G. Spindler (Ed.), *Doing the ethnography of schooling* (pp. 21–43). New York: Holt, Rinehart, & Winston.

Spindler, G., and Spindler, L. (1987a). In prospect for a controlled cross-cultural comparison of schooling: Schoenhausen and Roseville. In G. Spindler (Ed.), *Education and cultural process: Anthropological approaches* (pp. 389–399). Prospect Heights, IL: Waveland Press.

Spindler, G., and Spindler, L. (Eds.). (1987b). *Interpretive ethnography of education at home and abroad* (pp. 143–170). Hillsdale, NJ: Lawrence Erlbaum.

Spindler, G., and Spindler, L. (1987c). Schoenhausen revisited and the discovery of culture. In G. Spindler and L. Spindler (Eds.), *Interpretive ethnography of education at home and abroad.* (pp. 143–163). Hillsdale, NJ: Lawrence Erlbaum.

Spindler, G., and Spindler, L. (1989). The self and the instrumental model in the study of culture change and modernization. *Kroeber Anthropological Society Papers, 19,* 67–70. Berkeley, CA.

Spindler, G., and Spindler, L. (1990). Male and female in four changing cultures. In D. Jordan and M. Swartz (Eds.), *Personality and the Cultural Construction of Society* (pp. 182–200). Tuscaloosa, AL, and London: University of Alabama Press.

Spindler, G., and Spindler, L. (1992). Crosscultural, comparative, reflective interviewing in Schoenhausen and Roseville. In M. Schratz (Ed.), *Qualitative voices in educational research* (pp. 150–175). London, and Bristol, PA: Falmer Press.

Spindler, G., Spindler, L., Trueba, H., and Williams, M. (1990). *The American cultural dialogue and its transmission*. London, and Bristol, PA: Falmer Press.

Spindler, L. (1962). *Menomini woman and culture change*. Memoir of the American Anthropological Association 91, Menasha, WI.

Spindler, L. (1978). Researching the psychology of culture change and modernization. *In* G. Spindler (Ed.). *The Making of Psychological Anthropology* (pp. 174–198). Berkeley: University of California Press.

Warren, R. (1971). *Rebhausen: A German village*. New York: Holt, Rinehart & Winston.

Wolcott, H. (1973). *Man in the principal's office*. New York: Holt, Rinehart & Winston. (Reprinted by Waveland Press, 1984.)

CHAPTER 3

☐ Systematic Ethnography: Toward an Evolutionary Science of Education and Culture

Marion Lundy Dobbert and
Ruthanne Kurth-Schai

Introduction

Systematic ethnography, the approach to ethnographic research described here, has evolved as we have reflected on our attempts to meet the challenges facing all qualitative researchers: how to record, to represent, and then to enhance understandings of the complexity of human thought and action in social settings. In doing so, we have struggled to balance our commitments to two tasks: (1) to capture the variability, spontaneity, and creativity of human social interaction by constructing richly detailed descriptions of classroom and community life, and (2) to search for patterns or regularities amid the chaos and complexity. We do not hope to discover prescriptions for the prediction and management of human behavior but, instead, to identify parameters or points of reference to assist educators, students, and community members in designing more desirable social and educational environments. Our designs have grown more holistic as we have attempted to address biophysical, emotional, and spiritual aspects of human activity as well as social and cognitive issues. These objectives have led us to adopt an approach to research that is increasingly systematic. Additionally, we have incorporated more formalized approaches including structured observational formats and mathematical techniques for pattern identification. These assist us in working more consistently and coherently with rising levels of complexity and detail.

More specifically, systematic ethnography is shaped by two themes. First, it views humans as biological beings who have evolved through processes common to all life forms on this planet. Evolutionary theory posits a developmental continuum ranging from processes shared by all life forms to emergent capabilities characteristic of only the most highly evolved organisms. Systematic ethnography attends to this entire continuum in its fieldwork. It thereby extends its focus beyond that typically addressed by current cognitive or social schools of anthropology to include the observation and analysis of biophysical, emotional, and spiritual dimensions of human activity. All are considered essential to the study of educational and sociocultural systems. Systematic ethnography implements its commitment to holism by adopting a broad-based and systematic approach to sampling, developing finely detailed and richly textured observational data, and employing multiple research methods.

Along with other anthropologists and ecologists, we believe that learned culture is essential to human evolution and adaptation. We perceive learning—the ability to process information and then respond accordingly—within an evolutionary framework. Thus, education must be understood in part through biologically based studies of human capacities for sociality, communication, and learning. The fact that humans are social mammals and group-dwelling primates leads systematic ethnography to focus on the texture of social interaction, as exemplified in the work of A. F. C. Wallace (1970). Additionally, the socially focused and biologically grounded theory of learning espoused by John Dewey (1916, 1929) provides an appropriate theoretical framework for a systematic ethnographic approach to the study of formal educational settings.

Second, systematic ethnography focuses on social structure and its regularities. Because information derived from the organization of physical and biological processes holds all living systems together, the theoretical base for systematic ethnography has been shaped by the concerns and procedures derived from the concepts of regularity in both British and American social anthropology, particularly the work of Nadel, Fortes, Radcliffe-Brown, Naroll and Cohen, and Arensberg and Kimball. Along with them, we share the position that one of the primary tasks of anthropology is to seek regularity in human action. The concept of regularity that characterizes systematic anthropology differs, however, from the understandings of systematized patterns held by social anthropologists of the mid-twentieth century (for further discussion, see the section on "Historical Approaches to a Comparative Social Science," pp. 128–129). Instead, it applies complex concepts of regularity similar to those represented in quantum and chaos physics and modern biology, which seek regularity, but not uniformity and predictability, in physical and ecological interactions. This aspect of systematic ethnography has been influenced particularly by the work of Prigogine and Stengers (1984) and the modern study of chaos (Gleick, 1987). Systematic ethnography implements its commitment to move beyond interpretive work in search for regularities by employing mathematical techniques designed to reveal patterned behavior within dynamic, complex systems.

Together, the focus on information-based evolutionary processes; the concern for careful detailed observation of biologically, socially, and spiritually intersecting factors in learning situations; the emphases on regularity derived from social anthropology and modern systems sciences; and the consequent adoption of formal approaches to analysis give systematic ethnography its name. In this chapter, these foundational tenets of systematic ethnography are elaborated to demonstrate how its field methods and data analytic strategies are derived from an evolutionary information theory base.

The habit of applying systems concepts to ethnographic data and theory and of trying to see sociocultural systems as wholes was fostered in students in the Anthropology Department at the University of Wisconsin in the late 1960s by Robert J. Miller (1965, 1966, 1978), who used it to solve some of the research problems he encountered in South Asia, for instance, to gain an understanding of the Buddhist revival in India and Ceylon (now Sri Lanka). Miller would join anyone interested in long conversations applying systems concepts to anthropological issues. Over the years, Beatrice Miller, who taught at Beloit College, also participated in these conversations. Her style of radically restructuring ethnographic concepts by rethinking them in a systems context (B. D. Miller, 1978a,b, 1979) has influenced both of us (M. L. D. and R. K.-S.). These conversations, which continued over a period of nearly 20 years, were both illuminating and provocative and have led to our continued belief that systems theory can be fruitfully and solidly applied to ethnographic work at the theoretical and fieldwork levels. We have attempted in various ways throughout our work to take this heritage seriously and to do as much as possible to develop it and pass it on to our students in an improved condition. The way we have developed the concept of order that underlies systematic anthropology is a case in point. Our position starts with a standard information-based approach to order taken from the systems theory of the late 1960s. This position has been further elaborated through the adoption of more recent concepts of order developed in physics and other physical and biological sciences.

We use these concepts to approach a selected set of issues taken from historical problems facing social and cultural anthropologists of the 1950s to 1970s, the solutions to which remain unrealized to this day. We attempt to address them by building an approach to their solution based on epistemological assumptions that were not part of the historic dialogues between social and cultural anthropology, therefore leaving the larger field of anthropology with a series of unfinished scientific agendas.

Evolutionary Process and the Study of Education and Culture

To establish a systematic framework for the study of complex human sociocultural systems and the processes of culture acquisition and transmission that perpetuate it, humans must be studied within the context of their evolutionary history. Humans as biological beings have evolved through processes common to all life forms. According to

James G. Miller (1978), an M.D. and leading systems theorist, the evolutionary process, which began with single-celled creatures, has resulted in a life system wherein each life form shares characteristics that have developed from the primitive forms over the past 3 billion years through the process of *shred-out*. Shred-out is a shorthand term for the evolutionary process of differentiation and increasing complexity:

> Each process is broken down into multiple subprocesses which are mapped upon multiple structures, each of which becomes specialized for carrying out a subprocess. If this allocation of process is not to be chaotic in the more complex systems which have more components involved in each process, the rationale for their division of labor must be derived from that which prevailed in their simpler progenitor systems. This shred-out or mapping of comparable processes from simpler structures at lower levels to more complex structures at higher levels is a chief reason . . . that cross-level generalizations will prove fruitful in the study of living systems. (J. G. Miller, 1978:26)

Through this same process, social systems evolved. Functions that were once properties of individuals were spread to groups of individuals, each of which specialized. We see the results of this process in social insects and in herd mammals. As functions shredded-out, increases in adaptability, control over the environment, independence, and self-regulation occurred. It is this process that leads to the real unity of all living systems because

> If at any single point in the entire evolutionary sequence any one of the . . . subsystems processes had ceased, the system would not have endured. That explains why the same . . . subsystems are found at each level from cell to supra-system. And it explains why it is possible to discover, observe, and measure cross-level formal identities. . . . (Miller, 1978:4)

The use of an evolutionary perspective, then, transforms the concept of the unity of life from a merely philosophical assertion to a set of facts grounded in all we know about biological systems.

Using this evolutionary logic, we can also propose, with J. G. Miller, that shred-out and subsequent integration have given rise to seven distinct levels of living systems: cell, organ, organism, group, organization, society, and supranational system, each having as components systems of the levels below. Thus, one way to define the holistic study of human sociocultural systems would be to examine the

Table 1   The Subsystems of All Living Systems[a]

Subsystems that process matter and physical energy	Name of subsystem
1. The subsystem that admits or brings in matter or energy	1. the ingestor
2. The subsystem that carries matter and/or energy around the systems to the places that need them	2. distributor
3. The subsystem that decomposes or otherwise changes matter and energy into more useful forms	3. converter
4. The subsystem that synthesizes or combines ingested matter, creating forms needed by the system	4. producer
5. The subsystem that serves as or creates deposits of matter, energy and holds them for later use or attention	5. storage
6. The subsystem that expels matter or energy from the system in the form of wastes or products	6. extruder
7. The subsystem that moves the entire system or moves parts of it in relation to its environment or other parts	7. motor
8. The subsystem that maintains the proper spatial relations between parts so that they do not interfere with each other	8. supporter

Subsystems that process information

9. The subsystem that receives information markers that signal significant change in the environment, such as chemical alterations, movements of other organisms, etc.	9. input transducer
10. The subsystem that receives information from internal systems and transforms it to internally transmissible patterns (e.g., the transformation of sound waves to the neuroelectrochemical patterns)	10. internal transducer
11. The subsystem that contains nodes and forms a transmission route for information distribution in a system	11. channel and net
12. The subsystem that creates meaning by using previously obtained programming to classify or map the information so that it can be used by decomposing it and recomposing it into internal codes	12. decoder

Table 1   (*Continued*)

Subsystems that process information	Name of subsystem
13. The subsystem that begins the learning process by synthesizing newly received and existing information	13. associator
14. The subsystem that stores information for later use	14. memory
15. The executive subsystem that selects information and sends it out to control other system parts or the whole system	15. decider
16. The subsystem that transforms internally coded information to codes that communicate with external systems	16. encoder
17. The subsystem that transforms the coded information into its physical analogy for output purposes	17. output transducer
Systems that process both matter and energy and information	
18. The subsystem that can give and/or create new systems like itself	18. reproducer
19. The subsystem that holds the system parts together and protects them from the environment	19. boundary mechanisms

[a] Adapted from James G. Miller (1978).

basic subsystems and processes common to all life. This information-based perspective allows us to find a starting point for our analyses of living systems.

All living systems from the cellular to the supranational, according to J. G. Miller's formulation, share 19 subsystems and their associated processes. These basic subsystems are essential for life functions. There is nothing magical about the number 19, and the subsystems of living systems could be analyzed in slightly different ways, as Miller notes in his work. But Miller's formulation is both complete and informative without being unwieldy; thus, we have chosen to adopt it as a framework for judging ethnographic completeness. Holistic research on sociocultural and educational systems would necessarily include study of all 19 subsystems, which are summarized in Table 1. The subsystems are divided into three groups: those that process matter and/or energy, those that process information, and those that process both.

The Study of Biophysical Dimensions

Because living systems cannot exist without physical energy processing and distribution, it is important to systematically focus on these aspects of educational systems. The work of anthropologists who adopt an ecological approach (e.g., Rappaport, 1984) suggests that there may be stronger relations between the physical and cognitive aspects of systems than we have generally acknowledged in the past. Our knowledge about schools reinforces this. Most educators will agree, for example, that dirty halls taint academic performance and social interaction, as do inadequate lunches, overly crowded classrooms, and insufficient recess time. However, rather than studying complete educational systems, including inquiry into biophysical aspects, much educational research focuses on arbitrarily limited subsystems of education, centering on issues that most closely reflect the cognitive and social priorities imposed on schools by contemporary societies. When the physical subsystems of social systems are ignored or played down, researchers are blinded to the fact that the provision of food for lunches, the use of cleaning compounds in the halls, the function of the storeroom, etc., are all essential. J. G. Miller's work points out that distinctions among biophysical, cognitive, and social aspects of learning cannot be maintained on any logical basis. His formulation eliminates the line between biophysical and cultural concerns by using the concept of information. This allows us to unify the study of these concerns by recognizing that biophysical, cognitive, and social processes collectively shape and limit educational systems.

The Study of Emergent Dimensions

The concept of shred-out also signals that we need to think about biology as applicable to all living systems, not only to animal and mammalian systems but also to the evolved complexity of human systems. Three emergent systems that have shredded-out of basic biological systems are of particular importance in the study of education. These are the human systems of individual emotions and their cultural organization into a larger communication system, the spiritual system, and the development of social learning in a cultural context.

The shred-out process explains that such complexes do have a biological base. In systems theory and in J. G. Miller's biology they are treated as "emergents." Miller (1978) explains emergents as any new type of system that arises by a change in template. The new template's complexity is likely to correlate positively with its ability to adjust to its environment, and, usually, a more complex template is more likely to survive stresses in the environment. Antithetically, a less complex system is less likely to survive. Thus, over time, the types of systems that tend to survive, on the average, become increasingly complex (J. G. Miller, 1978:76).

Emergents can be identified and described at each level of evolution. Life and self-reproduction emerge at the cell level, language arises at the organism level, and reproduction by the means of organizational charters at the group level. In general, emergents lead to longer duration of life, the ability to adjust to more and greater stresses, use and control of larger volumes of space, increasing amounts of matter, energy, and information inputs and outputs, increased efficiency, and increased genetic variety (J. G. Miller, 1978). Emergents above the level of the organism also tend to add the possibility of shifting subsystems processes among components, the ability to perform acts and make artifacts beyond the ability of a single organism, the sharing of a single component by multiple groups, and integration and coordination through symbolic languages. Miller (1978) goes on to note that if the emerged complexity did not lead to increased integration, the complexity would destroy the system. Thus, evolutionary progress tends to intensify both the range and degrees of integration by employing feedback controls toward a common purpose.

From this perspective, no gap exists between the sciences one may use to study the natural biological universe and to study human culture. Elaborate human cultural features are a normal manifestation of the evolutionary process that lead to increased complexity in life at all levels ranging from the cell to the organism and beyond to the group and society.

It should be noted, however, in proceeding from a position based on the functions of all living systems, we are *not* readopting the organismic analogy in which society is viewed as a quasibiological organism. Along with Miller (1978), we specifically reject this position. Rather, we have adopted a systems theory approach that assumes that complex systems are constituted from subsystems shredded-out from previous systems and that the *properties of each subsystem at each higher level are unique to that level*. All social systems—those of ants, herd-dwelling mammals, and primates including humans—are at least one level above that of the organism and are themselves made up of particular and specialized organisms. When their information-processing properties are combined, they yield unique social systems with equally unique information-processing properties. Cultural systems are still higher-order systems that combine social systems and result in still more complex types of systems with unique information-processing capabilities. By acknowledging this increasing emergent complexity, systematic anthropology seeks to avoid the reductionist stances inherent within cognitivist, materialist, or structuralist anthropology, which treat total human systems as derivative of their logically prior subsystem—be it language, economics, or social structure.

The Study of Emotion

It was Darwin who first pointed out that emotions and their expressions contribute to adaptation and survival potential (Lutz and White, 1986). This is in fact a primary reason for focusing on them in systematic ethnography; we believe that emotions are a part of the total human evolutionary adaptation. The best-known example of emotional adaptation is the mammalian fight-or-flight mapping of stressful situations, in which hormones play key roles in survival. Another emotional system that has a clear survival role is the affectional system, which binds social groups together (Harlow, 1986; Lancaster, 1975).

Emotions also serve to integrate various aspects of social life. Many social behaviors are at least partly controlled or motivated by the emotional attitudes that are socially expected to be associated with them. The American Configurationalists of the second quarter of this century, Mead and Benedict particularly (see Harris, 1968:402–423), recognized this and developed a form of anthropology in which the patterning of emotions was central. They were unable to sustain their research program because they did not really have an explanatory framework, because their interpretations of data proved to be selective, and because their philosophy was interpretive and evocative rather than scientifically comparative (Harris, 1968).

Recently, however, interest in emotional organization has become more central in several disciplines, including anthropology. Lutz and White (1986) point out that the increased interest is a response, among other things, to a dissatisfaction with positions that implicitly or explicitly treat humans as mechanical information processors. This concern has arisen through both interpretivist focuses on relational and communicative aspects of interchanges and more universalist concerns arising from ethological and evolutionary foci (Lutz and White, 1986:405–406). Our own interest in emotions derives from our systems perspective, which suggests that emotions are biologically fundamental and rest upon hormone production triggered by varied external stimuli. These stimuli may vary by culture, but that is not the point here; the focus is on the biological, information mapping, meaning based functions of hormonal systems. William Gray (1973) suggests that emotions also play an essential role in the ways humans communice, organize, and interpret cognitive information.

Lutz and White (1986) provide another reason for studying emotions in educational research on American culture—one that we had not considered in our original formulation. They cite D'Andrade's 1986 work on the American folk model of the mind. In his model, Americans are said to believe that feelings provide the link between perceptions and beliefs, on one hand, and desires and intentions, on the other, in a causal chain of reasoning. If this model is correct, we should expect to find that teachers, other school personnel, and students will often use feelings as an explanation for learning-related decisions and behaviors. Indeed, our own research shows this is frequently the case. Teachers, for example, will say that they cancelled their planned math activity for the afternoon and substituted a film because the kids were fidgety due to the upcoming holiday. Children will say that it is easy to do good work in Mrs. K's classroom because she is nice. Data such as these suggest that, to a significant extent, emotions "make the classroom-go-round." If we omit this aspect of classroom life to concentrate on curricula, materials, new teaching methods, etc., we will not be able to discover how and why classrooms really work, especially from the perspective of their resident populations. The fact that ethnographers are known for paying careful attention to the emotional side of life is one factor that has led to the popularity of ethnographic research in education. Even ethnographers, however, have a long way to go in developing a systematic approach to recording and analyzing emotions in educational research.

To quote from Lutz and White (1986:431), "Incorporating emotion into ethnography will entail presenting a fuller view of *what is at stake for people in everyday life* [their emphasis]." However, achieving this has been problematic because there has been a split between materialist and idealist positions, with the former school viewing emotions as biological muscle movements, blood pressure changes, and hormonal processes and the latter seeing them as cultural ideas about appropriate responses. From our perspective, this dichotomy is as meaningless as the dichotomy between individual and social approaches. We see both as continua that shade into one another at the center. Emotions are both biological and communicative, personal and social in various mixes. For fieldwork purposes, we employ a materialist focus in attempting to record emotions observed in the field by looking at behavioral markers of emotions. We also accept statements of emotions as conveying informants' associated cognitive meanings in interviews or other conversations. Detailed, systematic fieldwork attends to both biological and cognitive aspects of emotional systems.

The Study of Spiritual Dimensions

One of the most obvious forms of shred-out of the information handling processes in humans is the emergence of a spiritual capacity and the development of religion. This facet of information processing addresses the increasing complexity of data to which humans are sensitive through increased integration. It is an emergent element of the human decoding, association, memory, decider, and encoding subsystems. From the perspective taken here, it is an essential aspect of the biologically evolved characteristics of humans and must therefore be considered as part of any holistic study. Unfortunately, a concern for the spiritual dimensions of teaching and learning is usually absent from educational anthropology. This may in part reflect modern educational practice outside parochial schools. It may also reflect American cultural and legal biases. From a holistic, biologically derived perspective as well as from a standard cultural viewpoint, however, "Religion is one of the great driving forces in human activity, both individually and socially" (Firth, 1958:125).[1] It is scientifically indefensible to omit the powerful spiritual facet of human behavior and motivation just because omission is, and has been, the fashion in Western science and law for more than a century. Furthermore, setting the topic aside cannot be justified in light of what anthropologists have learned of human cultures.

As systematic ethnographers, then, we must include a focus on this critical aspect of human information processing. We are concerned with use of the spiritual realm in even the most ordinary circumstances. Thus, to use the concept of spirituality in the framework we are establishing here, we need to set it in a larger context than that usually adopted by anthropologists who study religion. Drawing from the work of general systems theorists, we will define spiritual and religious beliefs and observances as *spiritual information processing* and suggest that recognition of its existence and understanding of its impact is essential to a holistic and systematic study of humans: Spiritual information processing is that phenomenon whereby humans envision, encode, share, and respond to symbols of the transcendent—that which is dramatically different from and far superior to whatever currently exists. Descriptions of this creative, exploratory, and purposive activity run as a common theme throughout systems theorists' explanations of human behavior.

Kraft (1979), for example, attempts to interpret the writings of the French paleontologist–priest, Pierre Teilhard de Chardin, from a general systems perspective. Chardin (1959) hypothesized the existence of radial energy—a universal force of attraction that draws all things toward higher levels of consciousness and complexity. Radial energy is evidenced in the evolutionary progression from physical energy, to matter, to life, to thought, to spirit, and on toward Omega, a state of dynamic perfection, of eternal discovery and eternal growth. While tangential or physical energy is used to establish relationships among systems of the same level, radial or spiritual energy is exchanged among systems with different levels of complexity and consciousness. It extends beyond spatial and temporal dimensions, hence providing the possibility of intuiting aspects of the transcendent. Communication energy, centered in the intellect and emotions, bridges the gap between physical and spiritual energy. Applying Chardin's concepts of energy and/or information to his analysis of evolutionary history, Kraft proposes that the energy supply to the universe in the form of both communication and radial energy (knowledge and love) is everincreasing. This position is in agreement with contemporary biological perspectives that document the increase of information, in the form of organizational complexity, through the evolutionary process (Brooks and Wiley, 1988). Kraft also believes that although humanity has been preoccupied with physical energy as the key to prosperity on the material plane, now and in the future, the survival of humanity and the biophysical world will depend on continued development of spiritual information processing capabilities.

Moving from a universal to a human systems level of analysis, Ackoff and Emery (1972) provide further insight into the nature of spiritual information processing. They suggest that humans, in essence, are ideal-seeking systems. An ideal-seeking system is a purposive system that, upon attainment of one goal, will select another goal through which it can more closely approximate its ideal. An ideal is defined as an ultimate intended outcome that may be approached without limit but that is never fully realized. Ideal-seeking systems exhibit wisdom—the ability to generate and then choose specific goals from a series of alternatives, to anticipate long-term consequences of present actions, and to maintain progress toward an ideal through environmentally responsive and philosophically consistent behavior. Even though ideal-seeking is a transformational experience, it also functions as a stabilizing, organizational force, providing cohesion and continuity for human life as an extended and unpredictable process. Progression toward ideals depends on social cooperation.

Ackoff and Emery (1972) suggest that to pursue an ideal, any system must satisfy four conditions. It is these conditions that link the ideal-seeking, spiritual aspects of its subsystems intimately with the biological subsystems. First, the system must acquire resources to direct toward the achievement of the ideal, and these must be distributed, exchanged, protected, and maintained. Second, the system must acquire knowledge concerning itself and its environment so that it may develop and use tools and resources efficiently and create and disseminate new knowledge. Third, ideals are more effectively pursued in an atmosphere of internal and external peace. A system's goals will not be achieved if they seriously conflict with the goals of others. Psychological, religious, legal, philosophical, educational, and diplomatic institutions (i.e., emergent facets of subsystems) work toward achieving the necessary integration. Fourth, Ackoff and Emery suggest that ideals are best pursued in environments dominated by continual efforts to approximate the desirable, the unattainable. The inspirational function of aesthetic states created through artistic, philosophical, and religious institutions and subsystems designed for recreation and emotional release promote ideal-seeking. Ackoff and Emery caution that transformation through ideal-seeking cannot occur if any of the four functions are nonexistent or not fully integrated. Their caution is consistent with the holistic position we are discussing here and underscores the necessary connections between basic biological functions and the emergent, complex information-processing functions found in human systems. From an anthropological perspective, the intertwining of physical, resource-based subsystems and religious ritual subsystems was well illustrated by Rappaport (1984) in *Pigs for the Ancestors*, where he demonstrated the connections between cycles of pig populations, calories available for use in the entire system, and the cycle of ritual observances in a New Guinea setting.

Magoroh Maruyama (1972) reinforces Ackoff and Emery's conception of information processing as a complex social process thoroughly dependent on human interaction and collaboration. He suggests that setting goals is best accomplished in pluralistic social environments where human diversity is encouraged and accommodated. Cultural goals are built inductively with reference to people's opinions and values—they are diverse, dynamic, and highly interactive. Although spiritual information processing is a patterned, repetitive behavior, results of the process cannot be fully determined or predicted in advance. Cultural goals function as deviation-amplifying mutual causal networks, continually generating new structure, diversity, and complexity.

Taken together, the works of Kraft, Ackoff and Emery, and Maruyama suggest that spiritual information processing is perhaps the primary organizational and motivational construct regulating human existence. Although human experience is fully grounded in processes of biological and physical evolution, as ideal-seeking systems humans are not totally constrained by these processes. Instead, humans are drawn to imagine and to shape environmental transformations in a manner that reflects their continually evolving, socially defined value systems. Emotions, ritual, religion, and wisdom may be viewed as patterned behaviors that contribute to and are symptomatic of this higher order (i.e., broader, more complex, inclusive, and powerful) process.

To integrate this information theory perspective with a more standard anthropological view of the religious and the spiritual, we acknowledge Firth's (1958) definition of religion as an extended reality:

> Religious belief . . . involves to a large extent what may be called a shifting of the index-pointer of reality. It is not just a flight from reality. It is a series of assertions that reality extends to the ideas of God and the soul, to principles of good and evil; or that the ultimate reality is spiritual in nature. (pp. 127–128)

He goes on to note that religion attributes moral rightness to accepted beliefs and asserts that the truth embodied in such beliefs is final and absolute. This definition is very much in line with contemporary systems views of religion.

King (1987), in *The Encyclopedia of Religion,* supplies an additional conceptual link between information-based and traditional anthropological perspectives. He defines religion as the element of transcendental depth experience of culture and goes on to comment:

> It may be said that almost every known culture involves the religious in the above sense [transcendental] of a depth dimension in cultural experiences at all levels—a push, whether ill-defined or conscious, toward some sort of ultimacy and transcendence that will provide norms and power for the rest of life. . . . Religion is the organization of life around the depth dimensions of experience—varied in form,

> completeness, and clarity in accordance with the environing culture.
> [Later he adds] The truly significant element is precisely that
> ideational and emotional context. . . . the ideational system gives the
> experiences an identity. And by thus having a traditional religious
> identity, these experiences also have power to affect the whole
> life. . . . (p. 486)

Thus, King also links his position to Maslow's discussion of peak experiences that can be found both within and outside religious frames (cited *in* King, 1987). King accepts Maslow's position, although while qualifying it by stating that ecstatic, transic, and intense aesthetic experiences are found within both religious and nonreligious frameworks and have many features in common psychologically, the religious experience is religious precisely because it occurs in a religious context of thought, discipline, and value.

To summarize, religion and spirituality are fundamental modes of decoding, associating, using memory, deciding, and encoding in humans. Clearly, no analysis of human systems can be considered complete, scientific, or ethically sound without including consideration of the spiritual—as well as biological, physical, and social—aspects of species life. Thus, systematic anthropology will attempt to make visible the patterns of spiritual information processing at work within a community or intergenerational group under study. In addition to articulating a socially defined representation of what *is*—the existent, systematic ethnography requires delineation of a socially constructed image of what *should be*—the ideal. The principle of holism is thereby addressed in two ways: (1) knowledge of conceptual and value systems of the past, and how they developed into and are defined in the present, is extended to include consideration of how they may progress into the future (a temporal extension of traditional ethnographic frameworks); and (2) the impact of patterned behaviors typically considered peripheral to studies of conceptual process—emotion, wisdom, ethics and/or religion, the primary sources of inspiration and motivation by which humans work creatively to shape evolution—are accepted as appropriate and necessary foci for scientific investigation (an extension of traditional ethnographic frameworks to include analysis of higher levels of information processing).

To include the study of spiritual information processing in our work, we have made extended use of the Delphi—a standard method of futures research whereby issues are presented for group consideration through a process that is interactive yet confidential. Although originally developed as a quantitative method for acquiring expert consensus regarding technical forecasts, the Delphi has recently been more broadly defined as a method for enhancing group communication regarding complex issues (Linstone and Turoff, 1975). In light of this expanded definition, several variations of the original technique have appeared, including ethnographic variations (Poolpatarachewin, 1980; El-Shall, 1982; Palkert, 1986), those designed specifically to assist in the exploration and analysis of policy issues (Turoff, 1970; Rauch, 1979), and those adapted for use with children (Kurth-Schai, 1988a, 1991). We have found the Delphi very useful in studying schools and their potential for change. In an applied research project, we first used the method to determine both teachers' and students' views of ideal learning environments. We were then able to use these views as one approach to judging the effectiveness of a school innovation project (Kurth-Schai and Dobbert, 1990). In light of the holistic perspective taken here, it is interesting to note that children and teachers refer to necessary physical and resource conditions in addition to cognitive, emotional, and ideological issues in describing their ideal images of learning.

The Study of Learning in Evolutionary Perspective

From a biological perspective, evolution itself is perceived as a form of learning (Pringle, 1968) and a form of inductive logic (Campbell, 1970). Systems theorists contend that meaning-making and behavioral change are not limited to humans. The processing of matter, energy, and information is essential to all life forms. These processes rest upon the ability to perceive a recurrent pattern or a change in an environment, to relate perceived information to internalized information programs, and then to act accordingly. An amoeba, for example, demonstrates the capacity to make meaning from information when it perceives a thermocline, maps it on to its genetic programing, and then effects a motion toward or away from the new temperature environment. Classifying, mapping, and relating new information to old are common to all living systems. In fact, McPhail (1987) has argued that if an animal is to survive, it must have innate causal, associational, and pattern recognition processes preprogrammed into its brain, because prediction is required for life. His review of the literature indicates that complex learning has been demonstrated for all vertebrates, even fish. Gallistel (1989) goes even further and concludes that the experimental data suggest that animals use the equivalents of human formal mathematical processes including multiplication, equalities, subtraction, rates, division, ratios, and the concept of less than. These data support the view that there is a formal similarity between the structure of the biophysical world and brain processes—that is, all animal brains represent the world through well-defined complex processes formally mirroring its structure. Because all living beings map their environments to survive, all life maps life itself. This means that *all life is communal and social by definition* in any biosphere.

Moving to a cultural level, A. F. C. Wallace (1970) has taken a similar evolutionary communications-based approach. Wallace believes that culture is constructed through constant communication in a political negotiation process where each actor or group of actors maps, adjusts, and responds to the outputs of all other groups. Culture, like evolution, never reaches a fixed state and cannot really be considered as a body of information or material that can be passed down from generation to generation. Learning takes place within the confrontations of dynamic negotiations and cannot be studied apart from the ongoing processes of social life. In addition, the fact that we define humans biologically as social mammals and group-dwelling primates leads us to define learning as a process that occurs in the context of biophysical and social interaction.

Deweyan learning theory sheds additional light on the way one should pursue the study of learning processes in the social and biological context we are establishing here. Recent analyses of Deweyan philosophy (Colwell, 1985; Chaloupka, 1987) suggest that his conception of learning is fundamentally ecological and biocentric in scope. Among the false dualisms confronted by Dewey was the separation of humanity and nature. He contended that human and biophysical evolution are in essence interactive and interconnected, each occurring within the context of the other. Dewey further proposed that ultimately, all human knowledge and values are centered in experience, experience that is "of as well as in nature." (Dewey, 1929:4; see also Dewey, 1916). Human knowledge and values develop in response to interactions with the social and biophysical worlds and, in return, profoundly affect both human and nonhuman environments. Learning consists of those special interactions that enhance understanding of the "self-in-community" with other humans and the biosphere.

Committed to the centrality of experience, Dewey believed that learning does not solely depend on capacities for analytic abstraction, logical inference, and memorization of socially validated knowledge. Rather, learning is largely a function of our sensory and intuitive capabilities that develop in order to gain insight from the informational structures inherent within the environment. Dewey's emphasis on perceptual, as opposed to cognitive, ways of knowing is evident in his conception of science. As summarized by Chaloupka (1987), Dewey defined science as:

> . . . a structured pursuit of openness to experience . . . . Seeking to define what makes experience such an important aspect of learning, Dewey calls on the metaphor of the adventurer rather than the expert. The issue is not the discovery of laws through inquiry, but a more relative, tentative, and finally expressive goal—the continual reflective interaction with experience in which order is sought, but in which hubris is also a potential danger. (p. 256)

Deweyan learning theory is further extended beyond concerns addressed by cognitivists in anthropology or in educational theory because in the act of *experiencing,* not only thoughts, but also feelings and values, are activated and refined. Dewey was well aware of the complex and continuous interplay among social, political, ethical, and intellectual aspects of learning. Thus, the goal of science is not the disinterested pursuit of objective truth but, instead, the pursuit of wisdom—an information-based capacity to serve humanity and the environment through observation and analysis that seeks detachment from bias and, yet, is grounded in care for communal relationships as a prior criterion (Chaloupka, 1987). The goal of artistic activities is similar, only in this case; thoughts, values, feelings, perceptions, and intuitions all interact to produce wisdom articulated in the form of utopian images (spiritual information) necessary to inspire social progress and reform.

Dewey's emphasis on the role of humans in shaping, in addition to being shaped by, their social and biophysical environments distinguishes his work from that of enculturation theorists promoting social determinist interpretations. Again, the experience-based biological underpinnings of learning theory must be fully acknowledged, because social phenomena can be understood only within the context of prior understanding of physical conditions, regularities, and their interactions. For example, from a Deweyan perspective, attempts to promote social learning and change through exclusively social or political means—that is, by introducing technological innovations or by advocating a shift in ideological perspective—are conceptually flawed and, thus, result only in superficial improvements (Colwell, 1985). Dewey understood the futility of attempting to promote social learning through imposition of values—even highly noble ones—because such imposition cannot speak directly to people's experiences (Chaloupka, 1987). When separated from their experiential contexts, concepts become abstractions and lose their motivational power. Substantive and enduring reforms are grounded in, and developmentally responsive to, an intimate understanding of the patterns and processes of both human and nonhuman nature.

A fieldwork style consonant with this theoretical framework would recognize the evolutionary functions of all human interaction, including the information-gathering activities of anthropologists. Thus, the development of a systematic ethnography presents interesting challenges in the area of representing and interpreting conceptual and value systems. From this perspective, representation of community perception and opinion is most appropriately constructed through a process that encourages mutual exchange of ideas among participants and incorporates opportunities for thoughtful reconsideration of initial responses in light of opinions expressed by others. This criterion rests on the assumption that learning is a dynamic process grounded in social contexts. Traditional "one-shot" survey or interview techniques are not appropriate to the task because they restrict opportunities for reflection and refinement of ideas and commitments. In noniterative processes, human learning is artificially frozen in time, and impulsive, superficial, or highly tentative responses may be misconstrued as representative of culminating perceptions. The learning process is also obstructed by sole reliance on ongoing individual interviews of key informants because participants are placed in the position of abstracting their responses from the social context in which they originate and are subsequently fostered or challenged. Social interchange provides opportunities to shift patterns of thought and value to higher levels of complexity and integration, that is, to learn from others (Weingand, 1980; Palm, 1981; Kurth-Schai, 1988a). Noninteractive approaches to data collection deny such opportunities, thereby compromising the integrity of the data collected.

Adaptation—life-enhancing response to environmental change—is another key concept derived from evolutionary-based learning theory, which has significant methodological implications. Because humans process information in developmental and environmentally contextualized ways, flexibility and appropriate response to difference and to change are essential qualities of systematic ethnography. Adaptability plays a key role during the earliest phases of research when care is taken to ensure that methods of data collection are appropriate within constraints of the research context—that is, methods must be accepted by participants as cost-effective, time- and effort-conserving, and nonintrusive.

Adaptive methods are also essential to ensure that research processes are appropriate with respect to the varied needs and capabilities reflected in the community of research participants. Research processes must be flexible enough to function across differences, including age. We have worked, therefore, to adapt data collection techniques, originally designed for adults, to support increased participation by children. For example, at times drawing pictures may be substituted for written responses, a group discussion format may be substituted for individual interviews, or a child interviewer may be used rather than an adult, (Farrell, Peguero, Lindsey, and White, 1988; Boocock, 1976; Gamradt, 1990a, b, and c; Ottenheimer, Ottenheimer, and Ottenheimer, 1984 and 1986).

Finally, adaptability maintains its importance throughout the latter stages of the data collection process. To reflect conceptual patterns and values clearly, it is important to revise the wording or focus of questions, to introduce new issues for consideration, etc., as directed by initial responses of the research participants. This implies that researchers be well aware of the biases they bring to bear on the framing of key questions and issues and remain open to following the lead of the participants into divergent and unanticipated directions.

Linking Biology and Culture

Fortunately, a great deal of work has been done to develop linkages between biological and ideological aspects of human systems. From a holistic systems theory perspective, probably the most stunning work linking these two aspects of human systems was Rappaport's (1984) *Pigs for the Ancestors,* which addresses both the kind of detail needed in modern fieldwork and the use of holistic systematic frames for the study of anthropological problems. Through an ecological focus, Rappaport delves into the details of how complete systems map an environment for the necessary calories to survive. In selecting a focus on calories as a unifying framework, Rappaport opened potential links between cultural anthropological research and the natural sciences including physiological and ecological disciplines. The kind of careful measurement represented in his 10 appendixes include, among many other things, measurements of soil pH and nutrients, counts of forest species, measurements of garden yields, and human caloric expenditures obtained by counting numbers of arm strokes or hand movements as people did gardening tasks. The way he implemented an evaluation of diets, etc., makes other forms of anthropological and educational research look pale and weak with respect to depth, accuracy, and the potential for using holistic conceptual frameworks to examine biological–ideological links in detail. It is more common in contemporary anthropology to look at ritual in terms of internal meanings—that is, the subsystem processes of decoding and associating at several levels internal to a system, particularly among individuals, between social subgroups and individuals, and among varied social subgroups. Rappaport expands this aproach, which is too narrow and does fundamental violence to a cross-species mode for studying life, because it makes the basic processes of living in an environment peripheral and minor. He reintegrates ritual into a holistic systems perspective and rescues it from interpretivist perspectives where it loses any evolutionary functions.

Other links between the biological and ideological–cognitive aspects of human systems have been established by anthropologists concerned with the expression of emotions and with other nonverbal aspects of communication. Chapple (1970) took a physiological approach to the study of human behavior, evaluating expressive aspects such as human temperament and personality—which are often considered culturally based (Whiting *et al.*, 1966)—in terms of hormone flows and animal, particularly mammalian, behavior. In his study, he used careful, highly accurate timing to establish and demonstrate his behavioral hypotheses in these areas, which are so closely linked to communication and learning styles. His work points to the need to look at the physical features of behavior, particularly the external markers of internal physiological states such as flushing, muscle tension, level of activity, and bodily tension.

Hall (1959) linked the approaches of anthropologists to work done in biology on the meanings of time and space in animals and birds. He thus called attention to the influence of these factors on communication and the structuring of living systems. *The Silent Language* (1959) moves from a biological to a cultural frame as it discusses dimensions of time such as "lead time," Latino time versus Anglo–North American time, cultural meanings of night and day, or starting when things are ready versus starting by the clock. In later chapters, Hall directly compares the relations between human and animal uses of space and human cross-cultural examples of the significance of personal space, furniture arrangements, desk assignments, the ownership of space, and of space conceived on a grid versus space considered in terms of personal relationships. While we cannot accept Hall's (1959) cognitive definition of anthropology or his division of culture into the three levels of formal, informal, and technical, we have learned much from the way he sensitized the anthropology of his period to details of critical importance to the cultural shape of things. In addition, his point on the illusiveness of isolates in linguistics or elsewhere is well taken. As he notes, things come in systems. Norris Brock Johnson (1985) has followed up on Hall's work and has shown its great utility for educational anthropology in his studies of the manner in which classrooms are organized to convey meanings about educational status.

Birdwhistell (1970), following up on some of the concerns of Sapir, Chapple, and Hall, emphasized the need to look at nonverbal aspects of language coded in gesture, posture, and voice tone. It is Hall's and Birdwhistell's attention to the nonlinguistic sides of interaction that has taught us to see interaction in a way more compatible with a biological systems base that fits all living systems. Their foci have also indicated a need to include more detail on the biological aspects of communication in field notes, including the physical language of gestures; body movements, which vary by culture; positions and physiological states of bodies, which underlie our interpretations of situations; and uses of space for communicative and system structuring purposes.

Thus, the works of Chapple (1970), Hall (1956), and Birdwhistell (1970) contain both implicit and explicit clues about the types of fieldwork data that are needed to link the biological and cognitive–ideological facets of human systems. They attend to human physiological states, the human organism's mode of occupying space, to human cultural arrangements of space, to the importance of timing and sequencing in interaction, and to bodily aspects of communication. Birdwhistell's work is particularly useful at a practical level because it exemplifies and displays several formats for detailed recording of interactions, including verbal, spatial, voice tone, and gestural aspects of communication. From the perspective of a biologically based educational anthropology, all these are critical because they occur at the biocultural interface. They are also important because in the socially dense situations of classrooms it is easy to lose sight of the details in light of the simultaneous need to grasp the whole. It is the interweaving of the micro and macro aspects of such situations that will ultimately allow us to make strong theoretical interpretations of educational occurrences.

All of this work, then, points to how we must link macro and micro perspectives on sociocultural systems if we are to interpret them holistically as living systems. Another influence that prodded systematic ethnography toward the linking of the macro and micro levels in social analysis comes directly from the teaching of Arnold Strickon. In his Latin American work, Strickon (1972) was concerned with the interchanges in patron–client relations. His seminars at the University of

Wisconsin in the late 1960s made graduate students very conscious of the details of interpersonal interaction. He would insist that we indicate the type of ethnographically observable situation we were discussing, or he would, in typical anthropological fashion, challenge our vague and nebulous generalities by demanding a sample of actual interaction. This constant pin-pricking made it impossible for us to adopt the sort of systems theory that is vague, general, and purportedly universally embracing. It led, instead, toward the habit of grounding generalization in solid, ethnographically documentable detail, thus reinforcing the lessons of the works cited above—works that possess well-grounded perspectives and that link the biological and cultural spheres.

The ecological psychology of Barker (1968) and Barker and Wright (1954) also provides inspiration here. The very detailed types of data gathered by Barker and Wright on the young people they studied provide thicker description than do most anthropological forms of data gathering. In light of their commitment to capture the naturally occurring variability of human behavior and to do justice to the richness of environmental context in which such behavior occurs, they developed a system for collecting data on physical (physiological, spatial, and temporal), psychological, social, and educational dimensions of youth activity in addition to recording descriptions or personal goals and values provided by their subjects.

Designing Fieldwork to Implement an Evolutionary, Holistic Approach

An insistence upon gathering data that fills the requirements of such a broadly and technically defined holism creates a dilemma with respect to finite fieldwork done by less-than-omniscient researchers. Historically, in an attempt to resolve this dilemma, the varied schools of anthropology have selected one part—for example, culture and ideology, or social structure, or economic systems—and have avidly defended their selection as the logically prior foundation for the study of human systems. The evolutionary systems information-based approach we are using here suggests that this approach is inappropriate. In living systems, *no* subsystem is logically prior to a species' adaptation; *all* of its subsystems contribute to its survival. Consequently, we cannot select a subsystem such as language or economy and concentrate on it. In anthropology, we need to quit wrangling and defending our subdiscipline's preferential modes, while at the same time making a bow toward holism and gathering "background" data about all those other aspects of the sociocultural whole. When we focus our work on a particular subsystem of a living whole social system, we end up in a position from which we cannot properly analyze the very thing we are looking at. We are like people trying to build a 1000-piece jigsaw by studying one piece intently. Rather, we need to systematically and consistently *sample* from the entire living system so that we can build a science that actually speaks to the human condition, rather than to our individual preferences about its most critical parts.

Figure 1 summarizes what needs to be included in the study of whole systems. This figure can serve as a guide to a systematic approach to linking concern for both biological and ideological aspects of the human adaptation in fieldwork. It is organized according the 19 subsystems derived from Miller's work. The biologically based aspects of communication, emotions, religion, and spirituality and the social aspects of learning are integrated into the framework. The figure depicts the 19 subsystems specifically at the organic, sociocultural, school organization (district and building levels), and classroom levels. In the left-hand column, the basic biological systems are listed and defined. The second column sketches out the emergent subsystems that arose through the shred-out process. For the information-processing subsystems, the nature of the shred-out is keyed to the discussion in the text. The third and fourth columns examine the details of each subsystem as they apply specifically to schools.

To implement the systematic approach, then, we need to gather data on both the micro and macro aspects of any culture acquisition situation. To meet the requirements of a biologically and information theory-based anthropology, we must systematically gather simultaneous data on both individual biological behavior and social system behavior, so that both types of data appear linked in our field notes. From a practical perspective, we have developed the methods for collecting this type of data systematically along several lines. First, we have defined holism very broadly for operational purposes. We include biological and physical behaviors in observation and analysis. As discussed earlier, we assume that these are parts of human cultural patterns and that cultures shape and use the biologically based mammalian responses and physical potentials of human beings. Second, we define all ethnography as sampling. We take the principle that "you can't see everything" seriously and make conscious decisions about how to sample. We sample by time (e.g., every 10 minutes), by space (e.g., 33% of the classrooms), by status (e.g., student, teacher, administrator), or by sequence (e.g., every fifth child).

To make this possible, we design forms that incorporate all the items we want to sample. These forms are designed not to limit or

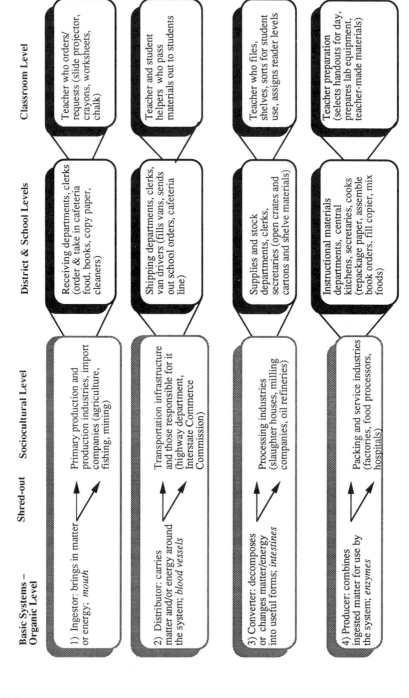

**Basic Systems –
Organic Level**   **Shred-out**   **Sociocultural Level**   **District & School Levels**   **Classroom Level**

1) Ingestor: brings in matter or energy; *mouth*

Primary production and production industries, import companies (agriculture, fishing, mining)

Receiving departments, clerks (order & take in cafeteria food, books, copy paper, cleaners)

Teacher who orders/ requests (slide projector, crayons, worksheets, chalk)

2) Distributor: carries matter and/or energy around the system; *blood vessels*

Transportation infrastructure and those responsible for it (highway department, Interstate Commerce Commission)

Shipping departments, clerks, van drivers (fills vans, sends out school orders, cafeteria line)

Teacher and student helpers who pass materials out to students

3) Converter: decomposes or changes matter/energy into useful forms; *intestines*

Processing industries (slaughter houses, milling companies, oil refineries)

Supplies and stock departments, clerks, secretaries (open crates and cartons and shelve materials)

Teacher who files, shelves, sorts for student use, assigns reader levels

4) Producer: combines ingested matter for use by the system; *enzymes*

Packing and service industries (factories, food processors, hospitals)

Instructional materials departments, central kitchens, secretaries, cooks (repackage paper, assemble book orders, fill copier, mix foods)

Teacher preparation (selects handouts for day, prepares lab equipment, teacher-made materials)

118

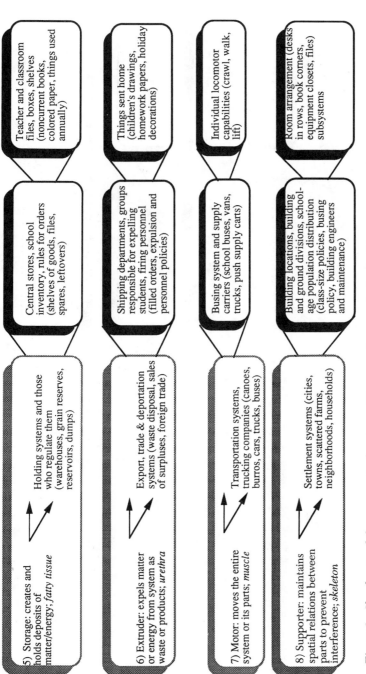

Figure 1 Shred-out and the emergent subsystems of human cultures and schools. (*Figure continues.*)

5) Storage: creates and holds deposits of matter/energy; *fatty tissue* — Holding systems and those who regulate them (warehouses, grain reserves, reservoirs, dumps) — Central stores, school inventory, rules for orders (shelves of goods, files, spares, leftovers) — Teacher and classroom files, boxes, shelves (noncurrent books, colored paper, things used annually)

6) Extruder: expels matter or energy from system as waste or products; *urethra* — Export, trade & deportation systems (waste disposal, sales of surpluses, foreign trade) — Shipping departments, groups responsible for expelling students, firing personnel (filled orders, expulsion and personnel policies) — Things sent home (children's drawings, homework papers, holiday decorations)

7) Motor: moves the entire system or its parts; *muscle* — Transportation systems, trucking companies (canoes, burros, cars, trucks, buses) — Busing system and supply carriers (school buses, vans, trucks, push supply carts) — Individual locomotor capabilities (crawl, walk, lift)

8) Supporter: maintains spatial relations between parts to prevent interference; *skeleton* — Settlement systems (cities, towns, scattered farms, neighborhoods, households) — Building locations, building and ground divisions, school-age population distribution (class-size policies, busing policy, building engineers and maintenance) — Room arrangement (desks in rows, book corners, equipment closets, files) subsystems

119

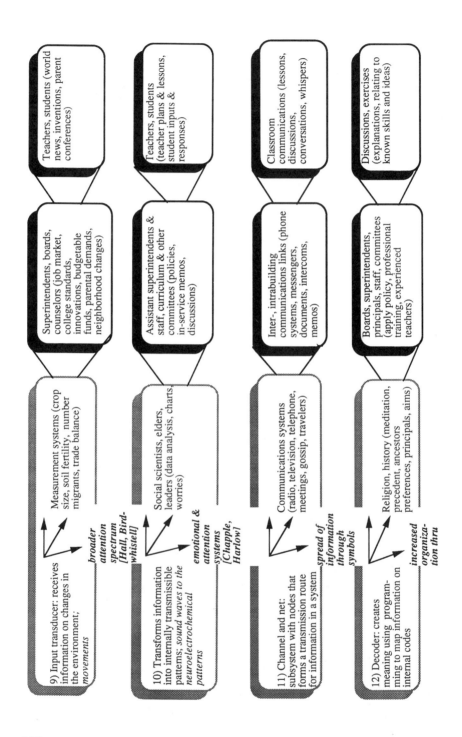

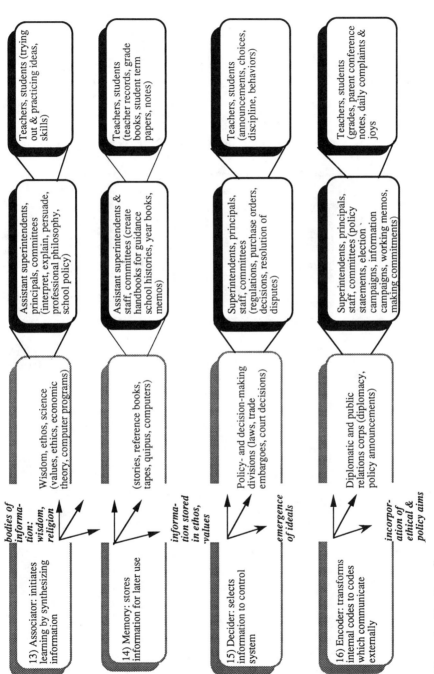

13) Associator: initiates learning by synthesizing information

bodies of information:
wisdom, religion

Wisdom, ethos, science (values, ethics, economic theory, computer programs)

Assistant superintendents, principals, committees (interpret, explain, persuade, professional philosophy, school policy)

Teachers, students (trying out & practicing ideas, skills)

14) Memory: stores information for later use

information stored in ethos, values

(stories, reference books, tapes, quipus, computers)

Assistant superintendents & staff, committees (create handbooks for guidance school histories, year books, memos)

Teachers, students (teacher records, grade books, student term papers, notes)

15) Decider: selects information to control system

emergence of ideals

Policy- and decision-making divisions (laws, trade embargoes, court decisions)

Superintendents, principals, staff, committees (regulations, purchase orders, decisions, resolution of disputes)

Teachers, students (announcements, choices, discipline, behaviors)

16) Encoder: transforms internal codes to codes which communicate externally

incorporation of ethical & policy aims

Diplomatic and public relations corps (diplomacy, policy announcements)

Superintendents, principals, staff, committees (policy statements, election campaigns, information campaigns, working memos, making commitments)

Teachers, students (grades, parent conference notes, daily complaints & joys

Figure 1 *(Continued)*

121

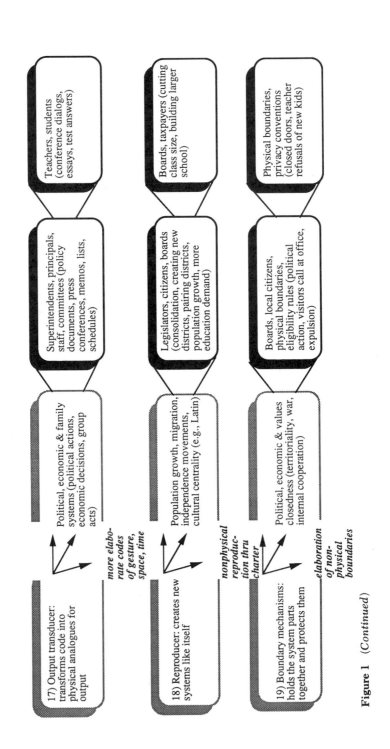

17) Output transducer: transforms code into physical analogues for output

Political, economic & family systems (political actions, economic decisions, group acts)

Superintendents, principals, staff, committees (policy documents, press conferences, memos, lists, schedules)

Teachers, students (conference dialogs, essays, test answers)

more elaborate codes of gesture, space, time

18) Reproducer: creates new systems like itself

Population growth, migration, independence movements, cultural centrality (e.g., Latin)

Legislators, citizens, boards (consolidation, creating new districts, pairing districts, population growth, more education demand)

Boards, taxpayers (cutting class size, building larger school)

nonphysical reproduction thru charter

19) Boundary mechanisms: holds the system parts together and protects them

Political, economic & values closedness (territoriality, war, internal cooperation)

Boards, local citizens, physical boundaries, eligibility rules (political action, visitors call at office, expulsion)

Physical boundaries, privacy conventions (closed doors, teacher refusals of new kids)

elaboration of non-physical boundaries

Figure 1 *(Continued)*

predefine the data gathered, but to guarantee that we collect dense and useful data in a consistent and comprehensive manner. Thus, interview forms, for example, are constructed on an "ethnographic" model, beginning with grand tour questions (Spradley, 1979). Observation forms are constructed systematically around our holistic theory, which insists on precise data concerning about a dozen factors in each observation (see e.g., Dobbert, Eisikovits, Pitman, Gamradt, and Chun, 1984a). These forms are carefully tested, reviewed, and revised throughout the early stages of each study to ensure that the format is theoretically sound and context appropriate. Table 2 provides an example of a form taken from a recent school study that is designed to embrace both the microcultural and macrocultural aspects of a classroom.

While forms such as that of Table 2 do not limit data gathered, they do promote uniform data collection. Our experience with the use of systematic forms leads us to agree with Mitchell (1967:21) that they ensure:

> . . . that the negative cases, which are important in any analysis, are not overlooked. As Richards comments on the use of census forms in anthropological inquiry: "Information collected on a regular form of this sort is, owing to the frailty of the observer, always more complete. I found in practice that I nearly doubled the information I had previously obtained by the more pious resolution to 'ask as many people as I could.' The blank column stares at the anthropologist accusingly". (Richards, 1938: 54)

The use of well-designed forms guarantees systematic, dense, and useful data.

We also think carefully about our commitment to holistic sampling when identifying the population of research participants. If we are to treat sociocultural systems as informationally interwoven, biologically and socially evolving wholes, research strategies must solicit and synthesize contributions from *all members of the community under study*. Each member of the community, regardless of their role or position within it, is actively involved in creating, evaluating, disseminating, and applying information. Due to their varying roles and positions, in addition to a wide variety of other personality factors, each individual interprets the world in reference to a unique perceptual framework and is, therefore, capable of providing distinctive intellectual, emotional, and moral insight. This essential information should not be lost or constrained by virtue of the research process. For systematic ethnographers, this suggests a necessity to include the perspectives of those most frequently overlooked in fieldwork, including chil-

Table 2   Fieldwork Form Permitting Attention to Biological and Social Dimensions of Classrooms[a]

Classroom Code: ____   No. Students in Room: ____   No. Staff: ___   Beginning Time: ____

Groupings: 1) number of groups, 2) average size of each, 3) locations, 4) type

Activity: 1) how organized, 2) who leads—roles, 3) who follows—roles, 4) name for activity

Av % on/off task:
Materials: name 1–3 central items

Foci/Excitement: 1) foci children's attention, 2) av. excitement abt activity/material-express/ posture, 3) degree curious/exploring/engrossed/involved, 4) differences by group

Av % on/off task:
Atmosphere: 1) markers general emotional atmosphere, noise, movement, 2) by group

Teacher Remarks: 1) verbal key words, 2) gestures, postures

Peer Orientation of Students: degree student orientation toward peers

Av % on/off task:
Play: 1) free fragmentation & sequence shifting, 2) energy, large muscle use, exaggeration

                                                                    End Time: _____

[a] ©1988 Marion Lundy Dobbert and Ruthanne Kurth-Schai.

dren and youth. Ignoring children, believing that their lives and thoughts are derivative, and feeling that they have less to say than adults is a long-standing Western European–derived prejudice (Lee, 1959; Goodman, 1970; Mead, 1978; Thorne, 1987; Kurth-Schai, 1988b). Although children can provide insights into their own constructions and interpretations of reality that are not accessible to adults, researchers fail to acknowledge the intelligence that children bring to social settings (Goodman, 1970; Mead and Wolfenstein, 1955; Roberts, 1970; Duke, 1987; Weinstein, 1983). Because children are not conceptually passive, and they actively participate as agents, actors, and creators of culture, their perceptions need to be understood directly (Thorne, 1987).

We recently incorporated the child's perspective in an applied study of schools involved in a statewide educational transformation project. To establish baseline data against which to measure later improvement, we asked first-grade to sixth-grade children to "Draw anything you want that shows something about 'My School and Me'." To guarantee that we would not misinterpret their work, the children were asked to give a title or short sentence explaining the drawing. Students at and above the middle-school level were asked to either write about their most memorable, good or bad, day in school or to describe the best school possible (CAREI, 1990). The results of this type of student expression clearly distinguished between schools and school atmospheres.

For example, the drawings of students in two of the elementary schools were largely positive. In one school, of the 65 pictures produced by sixth-grade children, 40 depicted people in school settings. On 29 pictures, they were clearly smiling, 5 pictures showed mixed positive and negative emotions, and 6 were hard to interpret. Twenty-five of the pictures carried titles with words such as "like" and "love" in them. Only three pictures from this school had ambiguous or negative titles (Gamradt, 1990c). In a second school in a different district, drawings were similarly positive. The writings of students from the junior high school in this same district, however, carried a different tone. Of the 17 students describing their most memorable day, 6 wrote about troubles and problems and 5 wrote of the difficulties of the first day at school. Of the 33 students who wrote about an ideal school, the majority suggested changes in their school, including changes in scheduling, class size, decreases in fighting, disappearance of racism, getting teachers who were not crabby, etc. (Gamradt, 1990b).

Such writing and drawing assignments can also indicate something about children's cognitive conceptions of school. The elementary drawing assignments from a third district showed pictures of schools where individualism was the organizing classroom principle. Pictures showed people sitting in desks working independently with smiling faces. The drawings showed nothing negative. But in the junior and senior high writings, the emotional expressions noted were negative. The writings emphasized rules and punishments, confrontations and adversarial relations with teachers, and showed little concern for academic learning (Lunak, 1990). The findings of increased negativity with increased age and higher school levels parallels the findings of an earlier study of youth we completed using the more conventional research techniques of interview and observation (Dobbert *et al.*, 1989).

If the sampling of research participant perceptions is to be truly holistic, care must also be taken to ensure that status and power differentials among research participants, or between participants and researchers, are not reinforced through processes of data collection and analysis. This issue can be addressed in both attitudinal and strategic ways. In terms of attitudes, Uma Narayan's (1988) work is particularly instructive. Narayan contends that whenever members of a powerful group ("outsiders"—in this case, researchers and powerful members of the community under study) attempt to learn about, or to work toward common goals with, members of less powerful group ("insiders"—in this case, less powerful community members including children), serious political and ethical issues are raised. For those of lower social status, the risks of collaboration are greater and the consequences of misguided efforts more severe. Additionally, the less powerful are especially vulnerable to insensitivities expressed by the powerful whom they have begun to trust. For these reasons, it is essential that the powerful exercise methodological caution and humility. Narayan explains:

> By the requirement of "methodological humility" I mean that the "outsider" must always sincerely conduct herself under the assumption that as an outsider, she may be missing something and that what appears to her to be a "mistake" on the part of the "insider" may make more sense if she had a fuller understanding of the context. By the requirement of "methodological caution" I mean that the outsider should sincerely attempt to carry out her attempted analysis of the insider's perceptions in such a way that it does not amount to, or even seem to amount to, an attempt to denigrate or dismiss entirely the validity of the insider's point of view." (1988:38)

In terms of strategic measures, encouraging full participation of the community, rather than selecting a representative sample, helps to avoid placing the less powerful in the position of acting as tokens. Steps may also need to be taken to prepare those whose knowledge and insight is seldom sought to assume roles as valued resources. Pedagogical strategies developed by critical and feminist theorists— whereby participants are encouraged to critically evaluate their position in society and then to actively address socially imposed inequities—provide useful references here and are also consonant with the adaptive focus of systematic anthropology (e.g., Carr and Kemiss, 1986; Freire, 1971; Weiler, 1988; Schniedewind and Davidson, 1983). Exercising careful judgment concerning when and how to protect anonymity, and when and how to provide opportunities for active exchange of ideas without concern for protecting their source, also helps to ensure full and meaningful participation on behalf of all participants.

To summarize, on the basis of all these considerations, the methodology of systematic ethnography tries to define the relevant whole for any piece of fieldwork and then to create a systematic, total system approach to sampling it as intelligently as possible. Here, again, we follow the lead of Arensberg and Kimball (1965:31), who commented with respect to community studies that ". . . a social scientist using community study must choose many, not just a few, techniques of observation and data collection." Following their lead, we use multiple methods and multiple foci in all our studies to cover the breadth of the 19 subsystems as well as yield samples from contrasting perspectives. We particularly try to include both cognitive and structural techniques as part of our designs. Thus, for the evaluation study in the Waterton Schools we used the observation form depicted earlier in Table 2, which focused on biology, behavior, and organization. We also conducted individual ethnographic interviews (Spradley, 1979) with teachers and group interviews with students to determine their views of actual and ideal educational environments. Additionally, we used a Delphi exercise to assist students and teachers in focusing on ideals in contrast to current school situations. Similarly, for a recent study of 36 schools in transformation, the team from the Center for Applied Research and Educational Improvement used a classroom observation form similar to the one depicted in Table 2, but with a stronger focus on the effects of the classroom on children; a more general observation of school climate, which included both behavioral and language foci; free association types of writing and drawing assignments to permit students to give us their uninhibited visions of their school; and interviews and focus groups with administrators, teachers, parents, the school board, teachers' union representatives, and community members.

Anthropology as a Comparative Science of Social Regularity

As indicated throughout the preceding sections, a major contribution of information-based evolutionary theory to the study of education and culture is its expanded operationalization of holism. Biophysical, emotional, cognitive, social, and spiritual dimensions of human existence are incorporated into an integrated, interactive, relational system rather than broken into subsystems and analyzed separately and, thus, out of context. As such, information-based evolutionary theory provides a framework for the development of richly textured descriptions reflecting the diversity, variability, spontaneity, and creativity of human interaction in social and educational settings. But ethnography grounded in an information-based evolutionary theory allows us to do more. The development of a broad-based, systematically structured, finely detailed data base makes it possible to pursue the study of regularity within and among human systems.

Historical Approaches to a Comparative Social Science

Historically, the idea that the central aim of anthropology is the search for social regularity has been most closely associated with British social anthropology. It can be summed up in this statement of Meyer Fortes (1953:35): "I hold . . . that there are regularities independent of period and place in social organization and culture, and that the main aim of social anthropology is to investigate the general tendencies, or laws, manifested in them." Radcliffe-Brown was probably the anthropologist who developed this conception of the field to its fullest extent. His view was that social anthropology ought to be a natural science and that fieldwork data should be collected to fit into the larger body of theory of that science. Science, he stated, does not proceed from observation to knowledge, but involves observation, classification, and generalization as parts of a unified complex process. Furthermore, the observation must be guided by some kind of hypothesis or framework. He laid out the elements of the comparative approach succinctly in the preface to Fortes and Evans-Pritchard's *African Political Systems:*

> The task of social anthropology, as a natural science of human society,
> is the systematic investigation of the nature of social institutions. The
> method of natural science rests always on the comparison of observed
> phenomena, and the aim of such comparison is by a careful
> examination of diversities to discover underlying uniformities.
> (Radcliffe-Brown, 1940: xi)

Similarly, Firth wanted to deal not with ethnographic data, but with comparative social structure: ". . . by the structural aspect of social relations we mean the *principle* [our emphasis] on which their form depends . . ." Firth, (1951: 28). Arensberg and Kimball, two American social anthropologists, agreed with this and took an even broader perspective in "The Community Study Method" when they identified "the comparison of the organizational forms of animal life and human culture" (1965: 47) as the fundamental anthropological issue.[2]

The goal of moving anthropology toward the status of a natural science of society through emphasis on human and cross-species comparison raises the question of what to compare. The earlier American comparativists, such as Wissler, Kroeber, and Dixon (note Harris, 1968), were often and rightly criticized for working with very small traits and comparing them out of cultural context. The British structural anthropologists were more conscious of context. Radcliffe-Brown (1957) pointed out that, because societies may resemble each other in one feature of social structure but differ greatly in others, it is necessary to compare them with reference to the entire economic, political, and kinship systems in which they are embedded. He repeatedly insisted that social science, like all science, must be done in a holistic context that goes well beyond that which we usually define as acceptable for the anthropological studies of education. Reviewing economics and cosmology (or comparative epistemologies), he shows how it is impossible to describe, explain, or understand them without reference to other connected aspects of society, beliefs, and ideals in the case of economics; language and the connection to the continuation of the social system in the case of cosmology. Thus, he concludes that *only* the study of whole societies as social systems is appropriate. His logic reinforces systematic ethnography's commitment to whole-system sampling discussed earlier.[3]

While allying ourselves with the concept of a social science of comparative regularity advocated by social anthropologists, we, nevertheless, do not accept the emphasis on unity, solidarity, or social determinism derived from Durkheim and Malinowski (Harris, 1968: 115), which characterized the British structural–functionalist approach. Attempts by both British social anthropology and Parsonian sociology to create a social science more closely reflecting the natural sciences, centered in theories assuming that the normal state of society was represented in a stable equilibrium, were, in the end, not successful. Without a theory specifying levels of systems with distinctive, emergent properties at each level; lacking a theory that could explain the mechanics of relations among systems through information, mapping, and feedback of various types; and forced to use an inadequate theory of stability, the creation of a social science of regularity has been impossible. To develop a social science of comparative regularity in the 1990s, a more complex theory of order than that available to the social anthropologists of the mid-century is required. To locate and develop a usable theory of order, we have turned to general systems theory and to modern work in quantum physics and chaos theory.

Contemporary Theories of Order

To develop a concept of order compatible with the biological, evolutionary perspective taken here, we adopt the information-based concept from systems theory that all life requires prediction and control and is not possible without it. A fundamental consequence of embracing an information-based perspective centered in the conception of an interlocked, *evolving* world is the necessary acceptance of an inherent order within the universe. Information is defined as constraint and order (Ashby, 1968). This means that all aspects of the universe are patterned in some way and that the relationships of all living things in this universe are predicated upon use of some subset of those patterns. The presence of regularity means that more than interpretation is possible in social science.

The existence of patterned information exchanges necessarily implies the development of structured systems. It is interesting that the most common definition of a system used by systems theorists, that of Hall and Fagen (1959:18), "a set of objects together with relationships between the objects and between their attributes," is almost perfectly parallel to Nadel's definition of social structure: "All the students of social structure are agreed that in studying 'structure' we study essentially the interrelation or arrangements of 'parts' in some total entity or 'whole' "(1959:6). This definition of a system is also directly compatible with Firth's idea of the central focus of anthropology: "It must be concerned with the ordered relations of parts to a whole, and with the arrangement in which the elements of the social life are linked together (Firth, 1951a:474). This whole, Nadel adds, is generally agreed to be society. In further specifying how we study social structure, he goes on to say,

> . . . people belong to a society in virtue of rules under which they
> stand and which impose on them regular, determinate ways of acting
> towards and in regard to one another. . . . Of the ways of acting so
> understood it is true to say that they are finite and always less
> numerous than the possible combinations of people: which means that
> the same ways of acting are repetitive in the population. (Nadel,
> 1957:7)

Nadel was so convinced of this regularity that in his major work, *The Theory of Social Structure* (1957), he proposed a formal, quasilogico-mathematical way of deriving structure by beginning with elementary propositions and building toward more complex structures.

While we do not accept Nadel's approach to creating a formalism, we do, building on information theory logic, accept this same faith in the order and patterning found in social life. But the concept of order that we are using is similar to that of quantum physics, chaos theory, and modern biology, which seek regularity, but not uniformity and predictability, in physical and ecological interactions. It is very different from the simple regularity of classical Newtonian systems and balanced, reversible chemical interactions.

Recent work on dissipative systems and in chaos theory has provided some clues to different and more complex types of order found in physical systems such as the weather, turbulent flows, and catalyst-based chemical reactions at a macroscopic level, which may provide models for the types of subtle order seen in social systems. It is a class of order where the general shape of a process may be determined. That is, the shape of the probability structure or phase space (to employ the correct term from physics) is known, but the specific individual happening cannot be predicted. Prigogine and Stengers (1984) contrast this type of order with the completely predictable, constrained order of the types of systems studied by classical physics, such as billiard balls and planetary systems, where all outcomes can be determined. Historically, by good fortune, physics stumbled onto this class of constrained systems of midlevel complexity and, in a short time, built an impressive record of prediction and control based on the principles developed.

Unfortunately for those who have taken classical physics as a model of and for science, completely predictable, constrained systems are rare. Cracks began to appear in classical science as early as 1811 with the work of Fourier, who essentially defined physical systems in terms of general probabilities over all molecules rather than in terms of constrained motions applying to each (Prigogine and Stengers, 1984:104–107). During the nineteenth and into the twentieth century, the major classical conceptions of order were undermined. Gleick (1987:6) quotes a physicist[4] as saying "Relativity eliminated the Newtonian illusion of absolute space and time; quantum theory eliminated the Newtonian dream of a controllable measurement process; and chaos eliminates the Laplacian fantasy of deterministic predictability." It would also be well to add that the concept of reversibility, the relatively simple, reversible order of classical physics and of balanced high school chemical equations, was destroyed with the development of rigorous, mathematical descriptions of dissipative or energy-consuming processes. The destruction of a requirement of reversibility, or classical balance, in rigorous scientific description opened the possibility of modeling processes in living systems that are bound to the one-way arrow of time—that is, which are all subject to the second law of thermodynamics, the law of entropy.

Of particular interest to social sciences are two types of order discovered by chaos theorists, neither of them deterministic. The first of these is stable, aperiodic order. It was this type of order which Lorenz found in his model of weather systems. A run of weather would almost repeat a previous one, but not quite; although one cycle might closely parallel another for a time, no point on his graph ever reoccurred. Then suddenly, the whole system would shift drastically and unpredictably to a totally different pattern. Nevertheless, the whole system stayed within the fixed bounds of a well-defined, complex track. It was "locally unpredictable but globally stable" (Gleick, 1987:48).[5] Contributing to this phenomenon was the very great sensitivity of the system to its precise local conditions; a change in a ten-thousandth of a part in a variable could precipitate a major shift in outcome. The amazing thing about Lorenz's system (see Gleick, 1987:48) is its hidden simplicity. The entire system's chaotic, but constrained, behavior can be generated from three rather simple non-linear equations with just three variables that feed circularly on the outcome of the last solution. In this respect, weather systems resemble the classes of far-from-equilibrium systems described by Prigogine and Stengers (1984), where very small variations can shift the entire system into a different state. They provide numerous examples ranging from the reproductive behaviors of slime molds, through the construction of termite mounds, to the development of turbulence in heated liquids. These sound very much like the kinds of order we find in cultural systems. The behaviors of individuals are unpredictable and may closely resemble, but do not duplicate, the behaviors of many others. In human systems, too, small behavioral variations may lead to a major shifts in system behavior. A good example is Watts' separation of the cylinder and condenser in already existing steam engines, which inaugurated the steam age.

The second type of order is the geometric type of fractal order found in complex shapes that infinitely repeat or nearly repeat themselves on smaller and smaller scales, creating boundaries of infinite lengths in finite spaces. A very interesting shape discovered by Hubbard (cited *in* Gleick, 1987), for example, has no real boundaries. On a map of four colors, every point in a boundary region of any given size borders on all four territories—if one looks within it, one finds smaller points of all four colors, and if one looks within them, other sets of points with all four colors, *ad infinitum*. Because this mapping describes the solution set for equations using Newton's method, its mathematics are well known (Gleick, 1987). Another example is the by-now-famous Mandelbrot set, which has appeared on calendars, in coffee table book form, and on numerous book jackets with its detailed and infinitely rich variations on a spiral and seashell-like theme at smaller and smaller levels where each level is made up of similar elements that are assembled in patterns unique to that level. This wealth of detailed order is generated by a very simple three-step process based on a single beginning number and incorporating a repeated feedback loop (Gleick, 1987). An example of a similar type of figure is shown in Figure 2a, where a simple nonlinear equation produces an evermore complex order folding inward on a decreasing scale. Figure 2b provides an illustration of a similar type of complex order, which appears to branch and spread out.

These types of order contain clues of major importance for the development of a natural science of society[6] because they suggest that formal models of nondeterministic human cultural systems, which allow for individual freedom of choice, may indeed be possible. They display both replication and variation inextricably intertwined, as we find it in sociocultural systems. The model of the boundaryless Newtonian mapping is reminiscent of the holistic notion that any part of culture can influence any other. They also suggest that the concept of intuitive formal models of cultural probabilities in the brains of ordinary people (and animals) is not necessarily the product of avid social (and biological) scientists' wishful thinking (see Naroll, 1970:27–28 and Gallistel, 1989:155–189). All the complexity in human brains may result from extremely simple formal rules, as does the complexity of the Mandelbrot set displayed in Fig. 2a. If we are trying to develop a social science that describes structure and regularity (in the modern sense), then we need to search for the type of underlying simplicity that generates the chaos and complexity of social life.

Developing Quasimathematical and Mathematical Methods of Searching for Order

Radcliffe-Brown has noted that we cannot find regularity in sociocultural data through direct examination of field notes:

> . . . we cannot hope to pass directly from empirical observations to a knowledge of general sociological laws or principles. The attempt to proceed by this apparently easy method was what Bacon so rightly denounced as leading on to a false appearance of knowledge. The immense diversity of forms of human society must first be reduced to order by some sort of classification; by comparing one with another we have to discriminate and define different types. (1957:72)

Figure 2a   Complex repetitive order based on simplicity. A Mandelbrot set based on the equation $Z > -\mu Z (1 - Z)$. [Developed by Paul Bourke, University of Auckland, New Zealand, while in residence at the University of Minnesota, and contributed to the University Microcomputers public-domain software.]

To understand the implications of this for educational anthropology, or to grasp its significance for ethnographic research in general, we need to understand the form of scientific generalization: First, it is critical to realize that the rule that explains a system does not resemble the system or replicate it in a verbal form. $E = MC^2$, for example, does not verbally or mathematically replicate the big bang that occurs when an atomic bomb liberates energy from matter. It further includes the speed of light squared (which never happens in nature). Additionally, no light forms an ingredient in the bomb. C^2 merely represents a way of accurately calculating the amount of energy to emerge from the matter in the bomb. In other words, the rules that explain system structure are different from the system. They exist on a different level of abstraction.[7] Figure 2a is an example. In its case, the simple rules that generate the elaborate pattern do not resemble the appearance of the pattern after any large number iterations.

The best example of a well-constructed explanation of the principles of structure in anthropology, one that illustrates the point

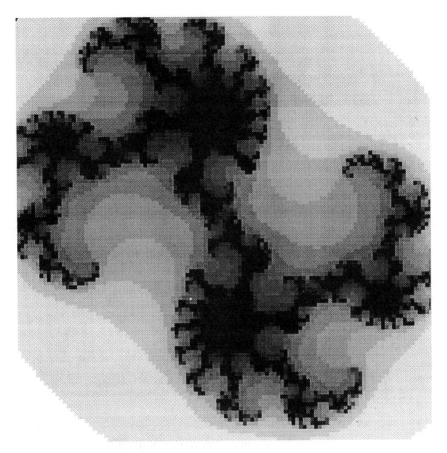

Figure 2b   Extremely complex repetitive order—a connected Julia set. [Reprinted with permission by Brian Lowry, Toronto, Ontario.]

about the different level of abstraction involved in explanation, is in Kroeber's (1909) work, "Classifactory Systems of Relationships." He explains that the level of the rules that generate a system are different in appearance and content from the system itself. He finds eight principles—generation, blood versus marriage, lineality/collaterality, sex of relative, sex of connecting relative, sex of speaker, age in generation, and condition of connecting relative—which generate hundreds or thousands of different classifactory kinship systems. While this work has been subject to minor modification since it was first published in 1909, it stands as a model of explanation in anthropology and, as a consequence, has been frequently reprinted in books of readings.

The aim of systematic anthropology is to find explanations for larger social systems and subsystems that expose the basic principles that generate the system in the same way that Kroeber generated his principles. To do this, systematic anthropology accepts the existence of information connections among living things. The patterning in these relations leads directly to the possibility of constructing formal analytic processes (i.e., analytic processes that replicate the form of the pattern and not the content). In the physical and biological sciences, the most common way to search for the patterning that generates order in systems is through locating an equation or system of equations that will model critical aspects of the system being studied.

Mathematical approaches in anthropology are not new. Unlike the cross-culturalists (later called holoculturalists in the American tradition) who used statistically based approaches, Radcliffe-Brown (1957:69–74) believed that in the natural science of society "relational mathematics will ultimately be required," and he sketched out a dimensional approach to scaling abstract characteristics represented by letters. But he did not make any suggestions about what these dimensions might prove to be.[8]

The most cogent article on the use of mathematical approaches in ethnographic work is J. Clyde Mitchell's "On Quantification in Social Anthropology" in A. L. Epstein's (1967) edited volume *The Craft of Social Anthropology*. Mitchell presents the history of quantification in social anthropology (Mitchell, 1967:18–19) and provides many examples of the uses of quantification in the contemporary anthropology of the period, including a few American examples. He also provides a strong rationale for the use of quantitative methods in conjunction with verbal description:

> . . . the more detailed knowledge which quantitative methods allow and the correlations between phenomena which statistical reasoning can educe should be the essential foundation on which anthropologists start to erect their generalizations about the social behavior of the people they study. Quantitative methods are essentially aids to description. They help to bring out in detail the regularities in the data the fieldworker has collected. Means, ratios, and percentages are ways of summarizing the features and relationships in data. Statistical measures based on the theory of probability go beyond the mere quantitative data and use devices to bring out the association between the various social facts the observer has collected. These are essentially analytical procedures and, as Fortes puts it, "are nothing more than a refinement of the crude methods of comparison and induction commonly used."

Although we would not rely on statistical methods as adequate for bringing out patterns in sociocultural data, for reasons we have explained elsewhere (Dobbert, McGuire, Pearson, and Taylor, 1984), we are otherwise in complete agreement with Mitchell's position.

By using mathematical techniques, we also increase our capacity to handle volumes of data within a coherent framework. Much information on social patterns is routinely overlooked by relying on purely verbal analyses. Mitchell (1967) demonstrates this when he shows that Gluckman's original formulation linking marriage stability prospects to patriliny and matriliny/bilaterality was both right and wrong—primarily because it did not consider enough variation in the potential linkages (pp. 23–24).

A Simple Mathematical Experiment

In our own experience, the ability of mathematical techniques to clarify patterns has proven valuable. In our studies of Waterton schools, we (Kurth-Schai and Dobbert, 1990) used simple correlations to reveal the interrelationships among classroom elements. Observations from each of 16 classrooms gathered using the form depicted in Table 2 was carefully analyzed to examine 14 specific elements of teacher role, classroom organization, and student role: (1) teacher remarks and gestures, (2) teacher activity level, (3) teacher instructional role, (4) teacher sociality, (5) materials in use, (6) groupings functioning during the observation, (7) size of groups, (8) degree to which the children could restructure and reorganize the assigned work to fit their personal preferences for learning, (9) general learning role taken by the children, (10) the emotional atmosphere, (11) children's physical activity level, (12) amount of peer interaction, (13) percent of children on task, and (14) degree of eagerness and involvement in the activity that the children displayed. Data on the 14 elements were then scaled and coded. Each of the 14 was then correlated with each of the 13 other elements. Thus, there were 91 pair-wise correlations since order of pairing is irrelevant.

All correlations were low. Only nine were correlated >0.5. Correlations among teacher variables and organizational variables, student behavior variables, and outcome variables were extremely weak; teacher remarks, gestures, and activity showed very little relation to any other factors in the classroom. Only one teacher variable, instructional role, was moderately correlated with the other 13 parts of the classroom system. In other words, our quantitative exploration indicated that teacher behaviors form an isolated system and do not appear to determine what happens in the classroom. Furthermore, when either percentage of students on-task or quality of focus were plotted against *all* the other teacher–student variables, analyses indicated that there were no correlations >0.17. Thus, the analysis indicated that *none* of the specific features of the classrooms that we observed produced high levels of learning as defined by quality of focus and percentage of students on-task. The strongest interrelationships found were between the student variables and general organizational variables. For example, the degree to which the students were permitted to reorder and reorganize assigned work activities had a 0.7 correlation with levels of peer interaction and a 0.6 correlation with their level of physical activity. The latter, in turn, was correlated with emotional atmosphere at the 0.6 level. Types of groups used, group size, and student learning roles were correlated with these variables (between 0.41 and 0.66) forming a cluster of behaviors thus revealed to be more closely related to each other than to teacher behaviors or to level of focus or to percentage of students on-task. Thus, it is not possible to interpret the behaviors we observed in these classrooms as caused by teacher direction or action and even less possible to attribute student learning behaviors to specific factors we observed. In this study, the clarity produced through mathematical manipulation of the data tore away some incorrect assumptions about how classrooms work and prevented us from focusing our analyses on teacher behavior.

Experiments with Coding and the Use of Dimensions

Another approach we have developed to locate patterning in data is through developing and applying coding systems, which can be consistently used to analyze data from many cultures and settings. Our approach to coding has been greatly influenced by mathematical, descriptive techniques that scale variation along a set of carefully specified dimensions. In systems information terms, codes need to replicate variation in well-defined sets. In our coding systems, as presumably in life, the dimensions represent the types of information to which an organism can attend. The system we have developed for coding emotions serves to demonstrate our approach to seeking rules that generate the system. Much of the scientific work on emotions has been devoted to searching for universal emotions (see, e.g., Plutchik, 1980); however, as we have indicated previously with respect to configurationalist views and to religion, a catalog approach cannot lead to a science because it omits the critical relations that hold evolving systems together. Consequently, to examine emotions from a relational perspective, we must adopt an approach that allows us to talk about *variation* in emotions so that we can observe how emotions are modified as we simultaneously examine how other factors vary. The two dimensions we use to describe emotions derive from measures that can be applied to any organism but can be uniquely applied to humans. The first dimension looks at physiological aspects of behavior. To use it, we note the degree to which the people we are observing display emotions related to the adrenal–cortical system (flushing, jerky movement, paralysis, etc.) or the parasympathetic system (smiling, relaxation, muscle looseness, etc.). The second dimension incorporates the attractive/aversive element and is open for informational input from the cognitive perspectives of informants gathered via interview.

The coding systems we seek to develop also embody another critical factor imported from the processes of description of physical systems in physics and chemistry. Complete descriptions *must* be based on more than one dimension. Thus, to use as an example a well-discussed issue from Lutz and White (1986), defining depression, we are not pressed to achieve the impossible task of finding a single concrete definition that fits both varied clinical and cultural situations and covers chronic and situationally induced cases. By using several dimensions (some of which can be cognitive and some physical), we can define an area and agree to call "depression" anything that falls within or close to this area. When we observe something in another culture that appears to be similar to "depression" and that falls partly in or near to this defined area, it will be irrelevant whether we call it "depression" or not because we will have fixed its location in the space determined by some carefully defined scales.

When investigating patterns of general culture acquisition, we have used dimensions on which to measure level of participation, dominance/subordinance, materiality/immateriality, good/evil, sacred/secular, degree of fixity in space and time, level of energy used, breadth of focus ranging from individual to the entire environment, degree of familiarity, relative sex (i.e., same/different), attractive/aversive, and degree of deliberate instruction (Pitman, Eisikovits, and Dobbert, 1989). To study schools, the dimensions we have developed include complexity of structure, dominance/subordinance, level of interaction, degree or intensity of focus, level of energy used, attractive/aversive, breadth of focus, and degree of fixity. We will not discuss here specific codes developed using these dimensions, nor the way we have used them to try to create system descriptions. Much of the work we have done was summarized thoroughly in Pitman *et al.* (1989). The point we wish to make here is that while coding systems must serve to replicate or map natural variety in a flexible, yet constrained way, the dimensions do not in themselves replicate the system. Like Kroeber's principals, they generate the system by their repeated intersections at particular points. Generally, we have used quasi-mathematical or mathematical approaches to find this order.

Computerization

To implement a mathematical approach for seeking regularity in data and to fully utilize the more detailed data that quantification allows, our strategy is to store data in a format that subdivides the entire body into small units. Such units can be reassembled as text, just as it was gathered, or can be examined by characteristics or topic through the use of codes. Previously, we subdivided data by hand onto separable slips or cards, as did earlier generations of ethnographers. Computerized data bases, however, are more flexible and permit easier coding and recoding, sorting and resorting. They also have an additional advantage. We are no longer forced to make a choice between collecting data in easily codable, sortable formats—which cause us to omit detail because we later have to do all the coding, sorting, and analyzing by hand and need to reduce the perceptual load—and collecting richly detailed data (for discussion of this issue in precomputer decades, see Mitchell, 1967:38–43).

Personal computers permit us to collect field notes that are as full of detail as we like and to code them in any number of ways without compromising context. By subdividing, coding, and entering our data into a computerized data base, we also increase the kind and number of analyses we can do in a short time. This has the function of increasing the depth with which we can deal with the information gathered. It is a truism that data cannot be used if it cannot be located; in fact, field notes are not data until the material in them has been made useable through some sort of an indexing or annotation system. Historically, *The Outline of Culture Materials* (OCM) (Murdock, Ford, Hudson, *et al.*, 1961) has provided a comprehensive coding system, and it is for its comprehension that it has been most used. Although the OCM codes are not dimensionalized, or scaled, our use of a detailed coding system to enhance retrievability and analyzability has been partly inspired by the permeability of data coded in Murdock's work and throughout the Human Relations Area Files system.[9]

By subdividing and disaggregating data through coding it—the opposite of text interpretation—we can see it in a new light. When we use a numerical or letter code system, we enable ourselves to see patterns that were hidden to us in texts because familiar surface patterns distracted our attention and obscured the patterns. The coding process formalizes data and allows us to see patterns in the abstract. This process also separates us from our preconceptions because we tend to have fewer (or different) preconceptions about abstract, formal patterns of numbers and letters. Computerization enhances our abilities to create novelty, because it permits endless flexibility in the way we call up patterns. We have been experimenting with various coding and data handling systems to enhance this process, including letter codes, translation to visual patterns (Pitman *et al.*, 1989), scaled numerical codes (Dobbert, 1988, 1989), and the mathematical formalisms of dimensional analysis. In the near future, we plan to experiment with three-dimensional graphics. These represent various ways of "making the familiar foreign," which Frederick Erickson (1973) considers a hallmark of ethnography.

Methods for Simplification of Patterns

In the search for the description of patterned regularity in social structure, chaos theory also provides inspiration for social scientists in the method used by its practitioners to solve complex problems. This is the method of simplification. When conventional methods did not result in solutions, they tried simplifications like graphs, generating pictures, or using letter strings to represent patterns. They looked at the "shapes" of their data qualitatively to achieve quantitative solutions.

One of our first major experiments in the creation of such abstract shapes was with the use of code "strings." First, we coded an entire observation of children for 13 elements and strung the codes together in a fixed order (Dobbert *et al.*, 1984a). The coded strings themselves cannot generate the principals of explanation because they are merely a replication of data and can only result in description. To generate principals, there is a need for simplification—that is, greater abstraction. Later, we generated a strategy based on the simplification algorithm of generative linguistics (Dobbert, 1989). We used the principal of markedness, which sorted data from three very different cultures into clearly explanatory clumps.

The combined use of strings and dimensions in the Waterton school studies gave very detailed views of classroom processes under different conditions. The simplification we used to sort data in this study was similar to that of determining a phase space in physics. We did this by examining five separate variables that our correlational analysis (described earlier) had determined were closely interrelated. We determined where each coded observation for every classroom fell with respect to traditional classroom formality (f), contemporary classroom informality (n), and primate learning styles (p). The variation in each of the five for each observation was reduced by assigning it to a type; f, n, or p. This was possible because the coded data were scaled on the dimensions discussed previously and each dimension could easily be divided into approximate f, p, or n thirds.

Thus, each code sheet was given a five-letter phase space designator. "Nnnnn," for example, indicated a classroom matching modern contemporary educational practice; ffnff designated a room where the observation noted a fairly traditional, formal, situation but the students were more active than usually associated with a formal desk-sitting pattern. This process reduced the variation from millions of possible patterns to just under 250 possible patterns and allowed us to sort our observations for similarity. By grouping the observations with the same letter patterns together, we found patterns in the entire set of observation of 16 classrooms over all 14 areas as fully coded. Our 210 observations of these classrooms fell into 29 primary patterns. We then arranged the patterns by decreasing order of teacher dominance and ascending order of fragmentation (student freedom to shift the order and sequence of task work) and student involvement with peers. As teacher dominance declined and fragmentation and peer involvement increased, the patterns also showed slight decreases in levels of teacher social interaction with students and in group size and slight increases in concreteness of materials, student directiveness and independence, student activity level, and pleasantness of the emotional atmosphere.

Analysis of these patterns indicated that eight sets of patterns where the teachers were less directive and socialized more with the children, where more fragmentation was possible, and where learners were somewhat more independent or dominant were slightly more successful in terms of the percentages of students on-task, focus quality, and the general happiness of the emotional atmospheres. Average percent of students on-task was 94.3%; in addition, the students were strongly focused on or very involved in the work. The nine most highly directive, structured traditional patterns where teacher–student social interaction was at a moderate level, little or no fragmentation was possible, and students were subordinate appeared slightly less successful overall. The percent of students on-focus was 89.4%, and the quality of focus fell, with students more loosely focused/involved or merely casually listening. There were also fewer happy and more clearly unhappy emotional atmospheres. The middle group of patterns with mid-level and mixed types of teacher and student patterns were least academically successful with 80.5% of the students on-task and the focus level was loosely lateral focus or represented partial listening. Emotional atmospheres, however, were slightly more positive than those associated with the formal traditional patterns. The processes of simplification and greater abstraction, then, permitted us to temporarily reduce data overload and enabled us to make sense of whole classroom patterns in our data.

The problem with this approach, although it works, is that it is necessary to redefine markedness for each type of situation observed. In studying classrooms at the Waterton school district, the classification and sorting rules used in the three cultures studies would not produce meaningful clumps of data. That is to say, we could not generate classroom structures with the same definitions of markedness and had to invent a different and weaker set of principals because there is more variety on the micro level than at the macro level.

Because it is necessary to redefine markedness for each new setting, it is clear that this approach to finding social structure is indirect at best. The formal abstraction is not adequate. Consequently, we have begun to develop another strategy. In the late 1970s, we began a series of experiments using dimensional concepts for analysis of data in comparative frameworks. We began with a formal mathematical approach to the analysis of whole cultures (Dobbert et al., 1984b), which appeared promising but a bit premature. To work more seriously with the development of appropriate dimensions for human cultures, we began to apply the concept to the more circumscribed concerns arising from a culture acquisition focus, using somewhat more focused dimensions. As mentioned earlier, in this series of experiments we first used the concept of dimensions to compare child-raising systems by employing a visual representation of the results, which displayed a culture acquisition space occupied by each culture studied (Dobbert and Eisikovits, 1989). This helped us locate some potentially usable dimensions. Later in our studies of Waterton schools, we further developed and formally tested through dimensional analysis still another set of modifications of the dimensions (Dobbert, 1988, 1989).

If we are to achieve the aims of the British structuralists and create a science of society, it is essential to locate a consistent, coherent set of dimensions that can be used to describe social systems. Furthermore, the sets of dimensions used to describe microcultural and macrocultural data must be completely consistent and at least partially overlapping. At this point in the development of a natural science of society, the search for such dimensions is the highest priority scientific task. Without the development of such dimensions, it will not be possible to achieve formal descriptions of qualitative, social data.

Unfinished Agendas

As we stated in the introduction, one of our goals in developing a systematic approach to ethnography is to address several unfinished agendas within the discipline of anthropology. Two agendas from the middle part of this century center around the need to incorporate into social science the study of those aspects of human life that were thought inappropriate for scientific study within the positivist tradition—the study of the emotions and spirituality.

A first item on this agenda was an increasing concern for the role of emotions in human sociocultural organization. A new emphasis on emotions was spurred in part by the work of Chagnon (1968) on the Yanomamo. The Yanomamo appeared to have an emotional organization clearly distinctive from our own in that competition was a major focus for all human energies and the role of anger was highly developed and elaborated. In their review of the anthropology of emotions, Lutz and White (1986) note that study of this area of human meaning and communications has been split by a dichotomy between the biological and cultural. The entire thrust of systematic ethnography is to eschew such dualism and unify biological and social approaches while still giving them due attention as physical and information-processing subsystems necessary for all life. Using dimensional theory, we frame emotional issues in a way that permits us to examine both regularity and variability. Since attention to emotions is part of our fundamental framework, this work, or similar work, should ultimately allow anthropologists to examine the relationships between emotions and social structure or emotions and belief systems, thus achieving the unrealized goals of the configurationalists.

Another factor that has allowed anthropologists to make increasing scientific sense of the meaning and functions of emotional relationships in human life has been the study of emotions in wild primates. As we have learned more and more about how emotions integrate primate social life and learning, we have discovered that emotional systems are primary and cannot be set aside as unsuited to scientific study. Nishida (1986), for example, has divided learning into three types: genetic, individual learning, and cultural transmission. Particularly the latter depends on the emotional organization of the primate troop or basic social group. Cultural behaviors in primates (i.e., those transmitted socially, shared by many members of the group, and persistent over generations) are not simply a result of local adaptation. Primate information such as knowledge of the home range, food selection within available items, food processing and tool use, and attitudes toward humans are spread within the group along the attention structure based in part on affection. The transmission of new behaviors or innovations in macaque troops has been particularly closely studied, and it has been well documented that the affection structure is the key to the pattern of information diffusion. New information is frequently introduced by one individual, often a juvenile. The customary flow of knowledge about innovations is from young to old (Nishida, 1986). From studies of Koshima and Takasakiyama troops, the author and a colleague concluded that the play group served as the main center for propagating new information, matrilines served as a second line of communication, and male paternal behaviors also led to acquisition of new behaviors. This pattern tends to reflect affectional interaction and attention structures.

The importance of an emotional component to learning has been confirmed in many primates. In chimpanzees, habituation to human contact by females new to a troop has been shown to occur within 1 month to 2 weeks when the females associated closely with habituated adult males. On the other hand, while the original habituation of the troop took many years, peripheral females remained shy for many more years (Nishida, 1986). Goodall (1986) has also contributed to information on the function of emotions in wild primates. For example, she reviewed the research and concluded that chimpanzees have the ability to impute motives or emotions to other individuals and cites many convincing incidents. She also cites an experiment during which they learned to lie. Here the best-known incident of the manipulation of emotions by a chimpanzee is seen in the story of Mike, a fairly small male of middle rank, who invented a new, noisy charging display with kerosene cans. On the basis of this novel emotional display, he brought himself to power when he was about 24–25 years old, still relatively young for a leader. Other primate researchers such as Harlow (1965), Hinde (1972, 1982), Chance and Jolly (1970), and Lancaster (1975) have contributed to our further understandings of the way to study emotions in all primates. Systematic ethnography builds on the results of such work, which relates human emotions to those in wild primates. We employ the insights of this research to examine the emotional structures of classrooms, as in our Waterton study, where we found the positive emotions are associated with higher levels of on-task behavior and stronger involvement in tasks. The insights on emotions gained from primate studies also apply to other learning situations, such as in adult learning, where most theorists agree that internal motivation is a key factor. Dobbert and Lunak (1989) have shown that systematic attention to emotions is, however, lacking but necessary to the creation of a stronger theory of adult learning.

A second item on our agenda from the mid-part of the century was a renewal of the study of the role of spirituality in anthropology. The necessity for a new approach is perhaps best represented in Evans-Pritchard's (1965) *Theories of Primitive Religion,* in which he notes that the anthropology of religion has been dominated by highly biased nonreligious or antireligious viewpoints:

> . . . with one or two exceptions, whatever the background may have
> been, the persons whose writings have been most influential have
> been at the time they wrote agnostics or atheists. . . . Religious belief
> was to these anthropologists absurd, and it is so to most anthropologists
> of yesterday and today. (pp. 15–16)

Among the influential writers he cites are Frazer, Marret, Malinowski, Durkheim, and Freud, in general the same group of theorists who are discussed in current reviews of the anthropology of religion—thus indicating that there has been no qualitative break in theorizing about religion among social scientists. Other indications of the need for further progress are the frequent and well-known strongly negative reactions of Native African and Native American respondents to ethnographic treatments of their spiritual systems.

Evans-Pritchard (1965) suggests that a primary problem in developing an anthropology of religion lies in the focus on origins. A proper science of religion, he states, would deal with relations between the religious aspects in a society and other empirical activities and beliefs. He cites works by Turner and Middleton, for example, as well as others as providing promising directions, but they are primarily studies of religions in single groups of people and do not move toward the making of general statements about religion. Outside of anthropology, he discussed the formulations of Pareto, Bergson, and Weber, who accept the "nonrational" as a fact of human existence and who attempt to set it in a general context of human necessity and evolution. But while he thinks that these works may be approaching the right questions, he does not find the answers impressive. Commenting on the theories of religion up to the time of his lectures, he states that ". . .

none of them is wholly satisfactory. We seem always to have come out by the same door as we went in" (Evans-Pritchard, 1965:121).

While this chapter does not represent a work on the anthropology of religion, we believe that the essential holism of the field of anthropology is severely compromised by the inability of ethnographers to fully define and study the religious and spiritual dimensions of human life. Consequently, we have put forward a theory of religion based on full acceptance of the ethnographically validated assumption that spirituality is indeed one of the great driving forces of human social and personal life. As such, we have established a framework for the inclusion of religious and spiritual issues consonant with the evolutionary, information-based approach used to underpin our general theoretical stance. In it, the spiritual aspects of life exist on a continuum of information handling and integration processes and do not stand out as exceptional and in need of separate explanation. Neither do they lose significance and ultimate dignity since the concepts of shred-out and emergent complexity permit the religious and spiritual realm a qualitative nature of its own.

A third major unfinished agenda of the 1950s and 1960s was the rapproachment of British social anthropology and American cultural anthropology:

> Looked at in the abstract, there are major differences between British social anthropology and American ethnology as to methods and points of view. . . . There is also an expressed difference in ultimate objective: the formulation of general propositions as to society versus descriptive integrations or processes of culture growth, though here the distinction is not so clear-cut. . . . But when the actual studies made by British and American anthropologists are examined, while there are differences in emphasis and selection, there is also a considerable area of common ground. If we can define and enlarge this area of agreement, anthropology as a whole will advance. (Eggan, 1955: 490–491)

An important attempt to unify the two anthropological schools was made by Eggan (1954) with the method of controlled comparison, which, even though little came of it, was much discussed. Harris, by way of comment on the failure of this agenda as of 1968, quotes Leach as saying of British anthropologists, "Most of my colleagues are giving up the attempt to make comparative generalizations; instead they have begun to write impeccably detailed historical ethnographies of particular peoples." This statement is equally applicable to the majority of American anthropologists, who have shown equally little interest in comparison and have equally devoted themselves to detailed ethnography.[10] But perhaps anthropologists on both sides of the Atlantic took the wisest course at the time since an adequate theoretical framework for comparison may not have been available. We have attempted to show, however, that such a framework—more accurately, several potential frameworks—became available with the advent of general systems theory and of modern physical science. Here we have used the general theory of systems, information theory, the theory of living systems, the theory of dissipative systems, and aspects of chaos theory to point out a potential route to this rapproachment in the 1990s. For us, this has been a very profitable endeavor. An eclectic approach, when taken deliberately within a defined comparative framework, leads not to a hodge-podge of meaningless multiple definitions, but to the honing of concepts and the strengthening of holism.

Closely related to this third agenda was the effort made in the 1950s and 1960s to create a *science of society,* attempted by both British social anthropology and Parsonian sociology. The best representative of this trend in anthropology is Radcliffe-Brown's *A Natural Science of Society,* cited earlier, which is based on notes taken at a seminar he presented at the University of Chicago in 1937 (posthumously published in 1957). This work presents us even now with several major unresolved issues in social science. As Radcliffe-Brown stated in the seminar, the possible existence of a natural science of society is "still questioned by some and by a few is even denied" (p. 3). This statement is probably more true now then was the case then. At any rate, Radcliffe-Brown notes that the development of the science will require continual improvement in methods, exact definition of fundamental concepts used for description, classification and analysis, and discovery of a way to systematically classify types of societies. But without a theory of systems that specifies levels of systems with distinctive, emergent properties at each level, and the mechanics of relations between systems, through information, mapping, and feedback of various types, the creation of a social science was impossible. Our efforts to develop systematic ethnography correspond exactly with Radcliffe-Brown's unfinished agenda but make use of scientific developments of the last two decades.

A fourth agenda was that of applying mathematical methods to anthropology in a fruitful manner. As indicated earlier, Radcliffe-Brown believed that a mathematical basis for a natural science of society would have to be developed. Gluckman (1967), in his introduction to A. L. Epstein's edited volume *The Craft of Social Anthropology,* saw progress in this respect:

As the subject has developed and analysis has become more
sophisticated, the standards by which data have to be collected
constantly rise, and the problems at which these data have to be aimed
become more complex and varied through the essays presented here
. . . is the consistent attempt to quantify variables. (p. xi–xii)

Despite the apparent movement that Gluckman saw in the late
1960s, the development of a mathematical social science of anthropology did not materialize. Part of the unfinished agenda in this area, then,
is to find types of mathematical formulations that do work. Because we,
like many anthropologists, are not convinced that the existing statistically based inferences used in psychology, sociology, and education
are fruitful in ethnographic work, we have attempted to start anew. We
believe it necessary to adopt a naive stance in the same way that
physicists working on an intractable problem realize that they often
must, if they are to have any chance of success where others have been
unable to move forward. Our willingness to work outside the normal
(in the Kuhnian sense) paradigm of anthropological work is fueled in
part by our training in holistic systems theory, with its technical concepts of negative and positive feedback that contribute to system stability and change. We are unwilling to surrender the dynamic pictures
of life available in this paradigm and substitute for them the static
pictures of ethnographic description.

Mathematical description used in physical sciences since the development of the calculus has been concerned with the representation
of patterning in dynamic systems. Those who lack the type of mathematical perspectives found in these fields often look at equations as
cold, static, and lifeless. To a theoretical physicist, who is as concerned
with real descriptions of real systems as are anthropologists, nothing
could appear to be farther from the truth. The excitement and beauty of
the process of working toward the development of a mathematical
statement that captures some of the real dynamics of complex situations drive the physicist. As we see our quantitative descriptions beginning to faintly reflect some of the reality of patterning in the sociocultural situations we observe, we experience some of this same
excitement. Although neither our work nor the directions we have
selected may prove to be the decisive breakthrough in the development of a dynamic, complex mathematical anthropology, we have explored some potential routes. We have alluded to them here in the
hope that they will spur further development either by proving themselves decisively dead-ends, which no one else need take, or that they
will spark follow-up or tangential work that will crystalize a system of

formal, dynamic descriptions on which to base a natural science of society.

Our Viewpoints Are Too Small

In developing the position taken in this chapter, we have worked to avoid a fundamental theoretical stumbling block identified by John Dewey—the construction of false dualisms. Rather than "taking sides" in the oppositional dialogue between anthropologists advocating structural interpretations and those whose work is influenced by interpretivist, cognitivist, poststructuralist, feminist, or critical perspectives, we have struggled to develop an alternative framework that informs, and is informed by, each of these competing traditions.

With structural-functionalists, we share the belief that anthropological inquiry should move beyond the cataloging of finely detailed accounts of human diversity and idiosyncrasy to search for order and regularity in social data. We share their commitment to the search for dimensions of cross-cultural and cross-species commonality, but not for the purpose of identifying static, universal invariants. Instead, we wish to identify boundary conditions or points of reference that—though providing information that is dynamic, partial, and indeterminant—can still be used to address the uncertainty, ambiguity, and risk that characterizes life in contemporary biological, social, and educational systems. We also share the structuralists' enthusiasm for the development of anthropology as a comparative science and their interest in the use of mathematical techniques for pattern identification. Mathematical techniques enhance data analysis by temporarily distancing the researcher from the subject, thus ameliorating the bias of immersed familiarity. By making the familiar look foreign (Erickson, 1973), mathematical and quasimathematical methods of data analysis promote the discovery of patterns. They also promote innovation by bringing to light patterns that researchers were unlikely to predict in advance.

With poststructuralists, feminists, and critical theorists, we share assumptions about the contextual, evolutionary, and political nature of knowledge. These issues have profoundly affected our decisions concerning what to study, how to do it, and what we hope will be the outcomes. We share their awareness of the epistemological and ethical damage done by promoting comparisons that are insufficiently sensitive to context. For this reason, we also agree with their objections to reductionist interpretations of regularity, which obscure human complexity and diversity. As a response to these concerns, we are committed to a radically holistic, carefully designed, and finely detailed approach to data gathering. Similar to ecological feminists in particular (e.g., Merchant, 1983; Warren and Cheney, 1991), we assume that a comprehensive understanding of biophysical—as well as ideological, spiritual, and ethical—conditions and processes is essential to the study of human learning and other forms of social interaction. Sharing with interpretivists the assumption that knowledge is not only socially but also historically situated, we have further attempted to expand our conception of holism by devoting special attention to the temporal dimensions of ethnographic inquiry.

In addition to enriching our awareness of both human diversity and dimensions of commonality, a primary purpose of research is to provide tools for enhancing the quality of life in social and educational settings. Similar to poststructuralists, feminists, and critical theorists, we view the act of research as intimately tied to emotional and spiritual information processing. It is, therefore, an inherently political activity —informed by ethical commitments, material interests, and power relations. We also view theory building as an embedded evolutionary activity, best developed in context, "from the ground up," in social situations that respect and value a broad diversity of goals and opinions. We are therefore concerned that structural forms of oppression— which prevent certain populations from contributing to processes of social and educational design—not be reinforced through ethnographic inquiry. Thus, our approach to ethnographic research must incorporate inclusionary perspectives on the definition of research populations, egalitarian approaches to data collection, attempts to promote the development of mutually beneficial relationships among researchers and participants, and careful consideration of potential political implications of the work for both those who will be affected as participants and those whose lives may be altered as results are translated into policy.

Donald T. Campbell (1970) labels as "evolutionary" the enlarged version of science we describe here. According to Campbell, a typical philosophical approach to knowledge initiates the investigation process by holding all achieved knowledge in abeyance until the very possibility of any knowledge can first be established. The evolutionary approach would assume, in general, all scientific and commonly accepted knowledge, would assume the achievements of modern physics and biology in particular, and would make use of this cumulative achievement in understanding the knowledge process itself. In evolutionary science, this knowledge is not assumed to be perfect or incorrigible. Rather, the tactic is one of assuming the correctness of the great bulk of knowledge while skeptically examining one fragment. This is the tactic that has enabled physics to continuously build while at the same time correcting its most basic assumptions. Clearly, the evolutionary approach is also the only tactic in line with an information-based perspective on life. If we believe in any version of Darwinian evolution, the science we develop must embrace the entirety of human life.

A major obstacle to the development of the type of evolutionary, holistic social science of society we have envisioned here has been the cultural gap between scientific and humanistic ways of viewing the world (Prigogine and Stengers, 1984). In this cultural climate, which divides the world between sciences, on one hand, and the arts and humanities, on the other, the use of mathematical expressions to describe dynamic social regularity arouses fear. Many are afraid that the attempt to develop an evolutionary social science will lead us back into the traps of classical science, where the phenomena observed were treated as objects totally outside of and disconnected from the observer and the moral order, or that such an attempt will return us to the crippling limitations of the positivist/empiricist approach. The perspective we propose here is neither classical, positivistic, nor empiricist. First, it does not posit an external, godlike view against which the truth can be measured. Rather, it is based on an interactionist theory of life, truth, and science. Second, it does not omit concern for and study of the emotional and spiritual aspects of human life and culture, labeling them irrational and not susceptible, therefore, to rational scientific investigation. It sees both of these central and arising from our biological heritage. Third, it uses very different concepts of order than those posited in earlier scientific traditions. In the end, perhaps, what we are arguing for is a social science that accepts the entirety of the knowledge of contemporary life and uses it creatively. We are trying to move toward an enlarged social science that is neither internally nor externally parochial.

The concept of order that we are using is similar to that of quantum physics, chaos theory, and modern biology, which seek regularity, but not uniformity and predictability, in physical and ecological interactions. It is a type of regularity that derives from the state of the entire system at a given point in time and is consistent with humanistic views of order in society. Among anthropologists, Naroll and Cohen (1970) explicitly argued that common sense reasoning is cross-culturally based on generalizations derived from the construction of subtle and complex probabilities, *an intuitive mathematics*, where the nature of the total universe sampled is unknown. In this sense, then, all humans (and animals) act as though they are evolutionary scientists operating on the notion that "the fundamental postulate of science is that reality is intelligible" (Radcliffe-Brown, 1957:6–7).

When Einstein developed the special and general theories of relativity, it became clear that the viewpoints of physicists working before him were too small. He introduced to physics a point of view that included the speed of light in a vacuum and gravity as a primary geometry or shaper of the known universe and said that these immensities were immediately relevant to everyday physics. In anthropology, we do not yet have a theory equivalent to relativity, but, based on the general discussion raised throughout this chapter, our viewpoints clearly are too small. We need to work systematically to enlarge our perspectives. We must attempt to develop ways to embrace simultaneously the diverse perspectives or subfields that have evolved within anthropology as well as the perspectives of the other social, physical, and natural sciences so that we can see where the whole of the discipline lies. Such goals have motivated and shaped our efforts to articulate the theory and methods of systematic ethnography.

Notes

[1] While quoting Firth here, we do not, however, accept his projection hypothesis on the nature of religion.

[2] Despite this quote from an American source, a prejudice against comparative analysis entered American anthropology early in this century with Boas' rejection of the then current and flawed comparative method and his insistence on a historical stance in which only social and cultural factors derived from common historical or psychological sources could be compared. This movement was a failure because it rested on an inadequate theory of classification and comparison; it could only catalog similarities, it could not generate explanations (Eggan, *1954: 743ff*). Unfortunately, its philosophy still contaminates American cultural anthropology and prejudices a large portion of it against comparative endeavors, despite the fact that the comparative method in anthropology and in other natural sciences has evolved and is no longer plagued by the problems that Boas protested against.

[3] An additional problem in comparative research, even beyond that of the obvious warping caused by culturally biased categories, has been that of finding cross-culturally valid categories. Naroll and Cohen (1970:15) provide an example of a clearly defined category, "cannibalism," which is nevertheless invalid because it "does not describe a behavior pattern which is functionally related to any other behavior pattern or trait. It lumps together a collection of unrelated behavior patterns. Therefore, one cannot learn much, if anything, about the general nature of human society or culture by a cross-cultural survey which has cannibalism for one of its categories." One way to attempt to circumvent this problem and define categories that are valid is to use categories compatible with and derived from the study of other living systems, particularly those derived from research on mammalian and primate biology and behavior. Considerable work has been done from this perspective over the last three decades, and we have attempted to

take advantage of it in formulating our own structures for data analysis (see Pitman, Eisikovits, and Dobbert, 1989).

[4] Gleick does not name the person he quotes.

[5] The entire discussion of Lorenz's work is based on Gleick (1987:16–31). We have generally quoted from secondary sources on chaos theory, because most anthropologists are not trained to read the original scientific papers.

[6] As noted previously (p. 128) this is Radcliffe-Brown's phrasing of the goal of anthropology and is quoted from the primary theme of his 1937 lectures given at the University of Chicago and published under the title *A Natural Science of Society* in 1957.

[7] The common failure to understand scientific generalization most likely has its roots in the way we educate children in science; when we teach the scientific method and the type of inductive reasoning associated with it, we use simple cases where it is not obvious that the logic of organization is different than the system observed. There is also a tendency to use the Aristotelian form of inductive generalization, which was what Bacon was inveighing against.

[8] In his discussion, the only abstract characteristic Radcliffe-Brown (1957) uses is religion. But it is characteristic that cannot work because it is based on an ethnocentric, nonscalable term.

[9] In working out earlier versions of our coding systems, in the late 1970s M.A. Pitman and M.L. Dobbert used *The Outline of Cultural Materials* (Murdock *et al.*, 1961) continuously to check the completeness of the code lists developed.

[10] Evans-Pritchard's (1940) work on the Nuer is almost as self-conscious about its fieldwork as is Mead in her Samoa (1961) and New Guinea (1975) works.

References

Ackoff, R. L., and Emery, F. E. (1972). On ideal seeking systems. *General Systems*, 17, 17–24.

Arensberg, C., and Kimball, S. (1965). *Culture and community.* New York: Harcourt, Brace & World.

Ashby, W. R. (1968). Principles of the self-organizing system. *In* W. Buckley (Ed.), *Modern systems research for the behavioral scientist* (pp. 108–118). Chicago: Aldine.

Barker, R. G. (1968). *Ecological psychology: Concepts and methods for studying the environment of human behavior.* Stanford, CA: Stanford University Press.

Barker, R. G., and Wright, H. F. (1954). *Midwest and its children: The psychological ecology of an American town.* Evanston, IL: Row, Peterson & Co.

Birdwhistell, R. L. (1970). *Kinesics and context.* Philadelphia: University of Pennsylvania Press.

Boocock, S. (1976). *Students, schools and educational policy: A sociological view.* Cambridge, MA: Aspen Institute.

Brooks D. O., and Wiley, E. O. (1988). *Evolution as entropy: Toward a unified theory of biology.* Chicago: University of Chicago Press.

Campbell D. T. (1970). Natural selection as an epistemological model. *In* R. Naroll and R. Cohen (Eds.), *A handbook of method in cultural anthropology.* New York: Columbia University Press.

CAREI (Center for Applied Research and Educational Improvement). (1990). Field work forms for an comparative school study project. University of Minnesota, Minneapolis.

Carr, W., and Kemiss. S. (1986). *Becoming critical: Knowledge, education and action research*. Philadelphia: Falmer Press.

Chagnon, N. (1968). *Yanomamo, the fierce people*. New York: Holt, Rinehart & Winston.

Chaloupka, W. (1987). John Dewey's social aesthetics as a precedent for environmental thought. *Environmental Ethics*, 9, 243–260.

Chance, M. R. A, and Jolly, C. J. (1970). *Social groups of monkeys, apes, and men*. London: Jonathon Cape.

Chapple, E. (1970). *Culture and biological man: Explorations in behavioral anthropology*. New York: Holt, Rinehart & Winston.

Chardin, T. de. (1959). *The phenomenon of man*. New York: Harper & Row.

Colwell, T. (1985). The ecological perspective in John Dewey's philosophy of education. *Educational Theory*, 35, 255–266.

Dewey, J. (1916). *Democracy and education*. New York: Macmillan.

Dewey, J. (1929). *Experience and nature* (reprinted ed., 1958). New York: Dover.

Dobbert, M. L. (1988). *Observing the children's component of positive learning cultures*. Paper presented to the American Anthropological Association, November 1988, Phoenix, AZ.

Dobbert, M. L. (1989). Methods for the discovery of patterns in cultural acquisition: Some comparative experiments. *In* M. A. Pitman, R. Eisikovits, and M. Dobbert (Eds.), *Culture acquisition: A holistic approach to human learning* (pp. 117–144). New York: Praeger.

Dobbert, M. L. (1989). *Testing dimensions for the study of classrooms*. Paper presented to the American Educational Research Association, March 1989, San Francisco, CA.

Dobbert, M. L., and Eisikowits, R. A. (1989). Facilitating comparison in research: Developing a coding system. *In* M. A. Pitman, R. Eisikovits, and M. Dobbert (Eds.), *Culture acquisition: A holistic approach to human learning* (pp. 145–168). New York: Praeger.

Dobbert, M. L., and Lunak, R. (1989). *Redesigning education for the 21st century: Contributions from primate learning research*. Paper presented to the World Futures Studies Federation Meeting, Nagoya, Japan.

Dobbert, M. L., Eisikovits, R. A., Pitman, M. A., Gamradt, J., and Chun, K. (1984a). Cultural transmission in three societies: Testing a systems-based field guide. *Anthropology and Education Quarterly*, 15, 275–311.

Dobbert, M. L., Lee, S. Y., Leonard, L., and Trombley, G. (Eds.) (1989). Cambridge today and tomorrow: Designing an optimistic future for 2010. A report for the planners, youth leaders, and citizens of the Cambridge area. Department of Educational Policy and Administration, University of Minnesota.

Dobbert, M. L., McGuire, D., Pearson, J., and Taylor, K. (1984b). An application of dimensional analysis in cultural anthropology. *American Anthropologist*, 86, 854–884.

Duke, D. (1987). What can students tell educators about classroom dynamics? *Theory into Practice*, 26, 262–271.

Eggan, F. (1954). Social anthropology and the method of controlled comparison. *American Anthropologist*, 56, 743–763.

Eggan, R. (1955). Social anthropology: Methods and results. In F. Eggan (Ed.), *Social anthropology of North American tribes* (pp. 485–551). Chicago: University of Chicago Press.

El-Shall, M. (1982). *A study of future cultural foundations of Egyptian education by the year 2000: An exploratory study using the ethnographic delphi technique*. Unpublished doctoral dissertation, University of Minnesota, Minneapolis.

Erickson, F. (1973). What makes school ethnography ethnographic? *Anthropology and Education Quarterly, 2,* 10–19.

Evans-Pritchard, E. E. (1940). *Thenuer.* London: Oxford University Press.

Evans-Pritchard, E. E. (1951). *Social anthropology.* London: Cohen & West.

Evans-Pritchard, E. E. (1952). *Social anthropology.* Glencoe, IL: The Free Press.

Evans-Pritchard, E. E. (1965). *Theories of primitive religion.* London: Oxford University Press.

Farrell, E., Peguero, G., Lindsey, R., and White, R. (1988). Giving voice to high school students: Pressure and boredom, "ya know what I'm sayin'?" *American Educational Research Journal, 25,* 489–502.

Firth, R. (1951a). Contemporary British social anthropology. *American Anthropologist, 53,* 474–490.

Firth, R. (1951b). *Elements of social organization.* London: C. A. Watts.

Firth, R. (1958). Religion in social reality. *In* Lessa, W. A., and Vogt, E. Z. (Eds.), *Reader in comparative religion* (pp. 124–133). Evanston, IL: Row, Peterson & Co.

Fortes, M. (1953). *Social anthropology at cambridge since 1900: An inaugural lecture.* Cambridge: Cambridge University Press.

Freire, P. (1971). *Pedagogy of the oppressed.* New York: Harper & Row.

Gallistel, C. R. (1989). Animal cognition: Representation of space, time, and number. *Annual Review of Psychology, 40,* 155–189.

Gamradt, J. K. (1990a). **Summary of findings: Student drawing assignments** (A supplement to elementary school report on educational change: Phase I by Linda Keller). Center for Applied Research and Educational Improvement, Technical Report, University of Minnesota, Minneapolis.

Gamradt, J. K. (1990b). **Summary of findings: Student writing assignments** (A supplement to junior high school report on educational change: Phase I by Linda Keller). Center for Applied Research and Educational Improvement, Technical Report, University of Minnesota, Minneapolis.

Gamradt, J. K. (1990c). **"Weston" Elementary School: O.E.L. phase I preliminary descriptive report.** Center for Applied Research and Educational Improvement, Technical Report, University of Minnesota, Minneapolis.

Gleick, J. (1987). *Chaos: Making a new science.* New York: Penguin.

Gluckman, M. (1967). Introduction. *In* A. L. Epstein (Ed.), *The craft of social anthropology* (pp. xi–xx). London: Tavistock.

Goodall, J. (1986). *The chimpanzees of Gombe: Patterns of behavior.* Cambridge, MA: Harvard University Press.

Goodman, M. (1970). *The culture of childhood.* New York: Teachers College Press.

Gray, W. (1973). Emotional–cognitive structures: A general systems theory of personality. *General Systems, 18,* 167–173

Hall, A. D., and Fagen, R. E. (1956). Definition of a system. *General Systems, 1,* 18–28.

Hall, E. T. (1959). *The silent language.* Garden City, NY: Doubleday & Co.

Harlow, H. (1965). The affectional systems. In A. Schreir, H. Harlow, and F. Stollnitz (Eds.), *Behavior of nonhuman primates: Modern research trends (Vol. 2;* pp. 287–334). New York: Academic Press.

Harlow, H. (1986). *From learning to love.* (The selected papers of H. F. Harlow, edited by C. M. Harlow.) New York: Praeger.

Harris, M. (1968). *The rise of anthropological theory.* New York: Thomas Y. Crowell.

Hinde, R. A. (1972). *Social behavior and its development in subhuman primates.* Eugene: Oregon State System of Higher Education.

Hinde, R. A. (1982). The uses and limitations of studies of nonhuman primates for the understanding of human social development. *In* L. W. Hoffman, R. Gandelman, and

H. R. Schiffman (Eds.), *Parenting: Its causes and consequences* (pp. 5–17). Hillsdale, NJ: Lawrence Erlbaum.

Johnson, N. B. (1985). *Westhaven: Classroom culture and society in a rural elementary school.* Chapel Hill, NC: University of North Carolina Press.

King, W. L. (1987). Religion. *In* M. Eliade (Ed.), *The encyclopedia of religion* (pp. 482–492). New York: Macmillan.

Kraft, W. R. (1979). What is energy? *General Systems,* 24, 209–240.

Kroeber, A. L. (1909). Classifactory systems of relationships. *Journal of the Royal Anthropological Society,* 39, 77–84.

Kurth-Schai, R. (1988a). Collecting the thoughts of children: A Delphic approach. *Journal of Research and Development in Education,* 21, 53–59.

Kurth-Schai, R. (1988b). The roles of youth in society: A reconceptualization. *Educational Forum,* 52, 113–132.

Kurth-Schai, R. (1991). Educational systems design by children for children. *Educational Foundations.* 5, 19–42.

Kurth-Schai, R., and Dobbert, M. L. (1990). Understanding positive learning environments: Organizational innovations and the quality of classroom life. Unpublished manuscript.

Lancaster, J. (1975). *Primate behavior and the emergence of human culture.* New York: Holt, Rinehart and Winston.

Lee, D. (1959). *Freedom and culture.* Englewood Cliffs, NJ: Prentice-Hall.

Linstone, H., and Turoff, M. (1975). *The Delphi method: Techniques and applications.* Reading, MA: Addison-Wesley.

Lunak, R. (1990). *Learning site culture: Site S-SC.* Center for Applied Research and Educational Improvement, Technical Report, University of Minnesota, Minneapolis.

Lutz, C., and White, G. M. (1986). The anthropology of emotions. *In* B. Siegel, A. Beals, and S. Tyler (Eds.), *Annual Review of Anthropology,* 15, 405–436.

Maruyama, M. (1972). Toward human futuristics. *General Systems,* 17, 3–15.

McPhail, E. (1987). The comparative psychology of intelligence. *Behavior and Brain,* 10, 645–695.

Mead, M. (1961). *Coming of age in Samoa.* New York: Morrow.

Mead, M. (1975). *Growing up in New Guinea.* New York: Morrow.

Mead, M. (1978). *Culture and commitment.* New York: Columbia University Press.

Mead, M., and Wolfenstein, M. (1955). *Childhood in contemporary cultures.* Chicago: University of Chicago Press.

Merchant, C. (1983). *The death of nature: Women, ecology, and the scientific revolution.* New York: Harper & Row.

Miller, B. D. (1978a). General systems theory: An approach to the study of complex societies. *Eastern Anthropologist,* 31(1), 15–30. (Republication of 1972 article.)

Miller, B. D. (1978b). People as biocultural systems: Concepts and analytic approaches for the anthropology of the future. *In* D. B. Shimkin, S. Tax, and J. W. Morrison (Eds.), *Anthropology for the future* (pp. 101–110). Urbana, IL: University of Illinois Press (with R. J. Miller).

Miller, B. D. (1979). Culture or culturing. *Cultural and Educational Futures,* 1, 7–12.

Miller, J. G. (1978). *Living systems.* New York: McGraw-Hill.

Miller, R. J. (1965). High altitude mountaineering, cash economy, and the Sherpa. *Human Organization* (Fall), 24(3), 244–249.

Miller, R. J. (1966). Background to Buddhist resurgence: Indian and Ceylon. *In Studies on Asia* (pp. 39–48). Lincoln: University of Nebraska Press.

Miller, R. J. (1978). Culture, civilization, system: Anthropological approaches to complexity. *Eastern Anthropologists* (January–March), 31, 1–14.

Mitchell, J. C. (1967). On quantification in social anthropology. In A. L. Epstein (Ed.), *The craft of social anthropology* (pp. 17–45). London: Tavistock.

Murdock, G. P., Ford, C., Hudson, A., *et al.* (1961). *Outline of cultural materials* (4th ed.). New Haven, CT: Human Relations Area Files.

Nadel, S. (1957). *Theory of social structure*. Glencoe, IL: Free Press.

Narayan, U. (1988). Working together across difference: Some considerations on emotions and political practice. *Hypatia*, 3, 31–47.

Naroll, R. (1970). The logic of generalization: Epistemology. *In* R. Naroll and R. Cohen (Eds.), *A handbook of method in cultural anthropology* (pp. 25–30). New York: Columbia University.

Naroll, R., and Cohen, R. (1970). Method in cultural anthropology. *In* R. Naroll and R. Cohen (Eds.), *A handbook of method in cultural anthropology* (pp. 3–24). New York: Columbia University.

Nishida, T. (1986). Local traditions and cultural transmission. *In* B. Smuts, D. Cheney, R. Seyfarth, *et al.* (Eds.), *Primate societies* (pp. 462–474). Chicago: University of Chicago Press.

Ottenheimer, H. with Ottenheimer, D., and Ottenheimer, A. (1986). *The secret language of the Comoro Islands*. Papers from the 1985 Mid-American Linguistic Conference, Kansas State University Press, Manhattan.

Ottenheimer, H., Ottenheimer, D., and Ottenheimer, A. (1984). *The family of an ethnographic team*. Paper presented to the Central States Anthropological Society, Lincoln, NE.

Palkert, L. (1986). *A Delphic perspective on the reactions of teachers to prospective future occurrences and their probable impact on K–12 education in Minnesota*. Unpublished doctoral dissertation, University of Minnesota, Minneapolis.

Palm, G. (1981). *Family perspectives on cable TV and home computers as information appliances in the future*. Unpublished doctoral dissertation, University of Minnesota, Minneapolis.

Pitman, M. A., Eisikovits, R. A., and Dobbert, M. L. (1989). *Culture acquisition: A holistic approach to human learning*. New York: Praeger.

Plutchik, R. (1980). *Emotion: A psychoevolutionary synthesis*. New York: Harper & Row.

Poolpatarachewin, C. (1980). Ethnographic Delphi future research: Thai University pilot project. *Journal of Cultural and Educational Futures*, 2, 11–19.

Prigogine, I., and Stengers, I. (1984). *Order out of chaos*. Boulder, CO: New Science Library.

Pringle, J. W. S. (1968). On the parallel between learning and evolution. *In* W. Buckley (Ed.), *Modern systems research for the behavioral scientist* (pp. 259–280). Chicago: Aldine.

Radcliffe-Brown, A. R. (1940). Preface. *In* M. Fortes and E. E. Evans-Prichard (Eds.), *African political systems* (pp. xi–xxiii). London: Oxford University Press.

Radcliffe-Brown, A. R. (1952). *Structure and function in primitive society*. London: Oxford University Press.

Radcliffe-Brown, A. R. (1957). *A natural science of society*. Glencoe, IL: The Free Press.

Rappaport, R. A. (1984). *Pigs for the ancestors* (2nd ed.). New Haven CT: Yale University Press.

Rauch, W. (1979). The decision Delphi. *Journal of Technological Forecasting and Social Change*, 15, 159–169.

Roberts, J. I. (1970). *Scene of the battle*. Garden City, NJ: Doubleday and Co.

Schniedewind, N., and Davidson, E. (1983). *Open minds to equality: Learning activities to promote race, sex, class and age equality*. Englewood Cliffs, NJ: Prentice-Hall.

Seymour-Smith, C. (1986). *Dictionary of anthropology*. Boston: G. K. Hall & Co.

Spradley, J. (1979). *The ethnographic interview*. New York: Holt, Rinehart & Winston.

Strickon, A. (1972). *Structure and process in Latin America: Patronage, clientage and power systems*. Albuquerque: University of New Mexico Press.

Thorne, B. (1987). Re-visioning women and social change: Where are the children? *Gender & Society*, 1, 85–109.

Turoff, M. (1970). The design of the policy Delphi. *Journal of Technological Forecasting and Social Change*, 2, 149–171.

Wallace, A. F. C. (1970). *Culture and personality* (2nd ed.). New York: Random House.

Warren, K., and Cheney, J. (1991). *Ecological feminism: What it is and why it matters*. Boulder, CO: Westview (in press).

Weiler, K. (1988). *Women teaching for change*. New York: Bergin & Garvey.

Weingand, D. (1980). *A Delphic perspective on lifelong learning in Minnesota: Focus on the public library as provider*. Unpublished doctoral dissertation, University of Minnesota, Minneapolis.

Weinstein, R. (1983). Student perceptions of schooling. *The Elementary School Journal*, 83, 287–312.

Whitten, P., and Hunter D. (1976). Religion. *Encyclopedia of anthropology* (p. 332). New York: Harper & Row.

Whitting, J. W. M., *et al*. (1966). *Field guide for the study of socialization*. New York: Wiley.

CHAPTER 4

❏ Collaborative Research: Methods of Inquiry for Social Change

Jean J. Schensul and
Stephen L. Schensul

The Handbook of Qualitative
Research in Education

This chapter discusses "collaborative research" as practiced in the work of the co-authors and other social scientists. Collaborative research may be defined as building multisectoral networks that link researchers, program developers, and members of the community or group under study with the explicit purpose of utilizing research as a tool for joint problem-solving and positive social change. Collaborative research is based on expressed organizational and/or community needs and is conducted in partnership with those most invested in the problem and its solution.

Participants in a collaborative research network may be members of a wide variety of organizations, communities, and groups. However, the network must include representation from at least one organization or community sector that does not usually engage in research and one organization or unit in which research is the primary or one of the primary activities. Examples of the first type would include schools and day-care centers, community organizations, businesses, neighborhoods, ethnic groups, unions, and other community-based groups. Examples of the second type include universities and non-profit research organizations.

The methods of collaborative research adapt standard research methodology to two major objectives of the collaborative research process: (1) ensuring the understanding and participation of all parties in all phases of the research process and (2) enhancing the potential of implementing the research and utilizing research results for the benefit of the population under study.

Collaborative research may begin in two interrelated ways: The researcher seeks the participation of nonresearchers in the research process for their expertise, for entry to the research population, to satisfy the requirements of funders, and/or to follow collaborative research guidelines; or program developers, organizations, or community residents seek the assistance of researchers for advocacy, for program direction, or for evaluation of the impact of programs. As relationships between these two sectors grow, a shared approach to research and programmatic goals may emerge from ongoing discussion and negotiation between both sectors. As rapport grows and programmatic and research products and experiences unfold, a collaborative research process develops between heretofore disparate sectors.

In this chapter, we will first discuss the various historical and ethical trends that have led to the development of collaborative research as an approach in the applied social sciences. Next, we will provide examples of a number of education-related collaborative research projects or activities, drawn primarily from our own work. These projects will act as a backdrop for a discussion of some of the methods used in collaborative research efforts. The chapter will conclude with a critical assessment of the approach.

Collaborative Research as an Approach in the Applied Social Sciences

The Problem of Making Social Science Knowledge Useful

What makes social science knowledge useful in the domain of education and community problem-solving? The problem of knowledge utilization has dominated these fields for the past several decades. Some anthropologists and other social scientists have claimed that knowledge is intrinsically useful. Others have claimed that knowledge becomes useful only in the social context within which it is to be used—that is, it is the impact of the knowledge in effecting positive change that makes it useful. Still others claim that the utility of knowledge depends on the process of dissemination to potential users.

Earlier models of knowledge utilization drawn from technological research and development were linear, involving production and dissemination. This model was found to be unsatisfactory because information went unused by those in the field (Hood, 1973). The problem of use then came to be viewed as a dissemination problem. Greater accessibility to the information through improved dissemination methods did not lead to use, however. Educators believed that knowledge was derived from experience, rather than from research. From their point of view, the models and conceptual frameworks derived from social science knowledge, even when "translated" and made culturally appropriate to lay audiences, were foreign to their perspective (Havelock, 1969; Sieber, Louis, and Metzger, 1972). The creation of information brokers, whose job was defined as integrating research-based knowledge with local user needs, solved some problems of dissemination but failed to create an independent link between the public and research-based knowledge (Rice and Rogers, 1980). If users were to interact directly with the producers of knowledge, they needed to understand the world of research through participation in it. The active participation of users in research would blur the distinction between researchers and practitioners in the field. This discussion led to the concept of educator-implemented research (cf. Lampert, 1984; Lytle and Cochran-Smith, 1989; Mohr, Grumbacher, Hauser, Mathews, and Willoughby, 1989, Cazden, Diamondstone, and Naso, 1989) and user-focused applied research centers.

Anthropologists, as one important group of educational researchers, have had mixed results in affecting educational policy and programs. In fact, despite the popularity of ethnographic research methods and the relevance of our research topics, anthropologists continue to face the same problem that our colleagues in other areas of educational research have been forced to address—that is, our general inability to relate our research methods and results to "practice" or application in classroom and/or community settings.

Anthropological knowledge in education is based on qualitative and quantitative data and focuses on cultural gaps in teacher–student interaction and relationships between school and community culture. The utilization of anthropological knowledge in education involves integrating a specific body of knowledge with efforts to resolve a particular problem in education (e.g., improving school–community relations, developing multicultural curricula). A measure of the usefulness of knowledge is the degree to which it has contributed to the ends for which it was planned.

Social science is concerned with answering social, economic, and cultural questions that can affect the general welfare. The co-authors of this chapter take the view that if social science can affect the general welfare of a social group, members of that group should participate in all aspects of the research in conjunction with the anthropologist. In addition to this ethical stance, there are two methodological reasons for this collaboration: The entry and understanding achieved when outside researchers collaborate with members of the group under study is far superior to the results that come from working alone, and the utilization of the information is greatly increased when the research is negotiated with others who share the same concerns (policymakers, actors, activists, administrators, and other primary change agents).

The collaborative dialogue defines not only the ends, but also the base and the context of research, key actors in the research process, a setting within which the research can be used, and parameters within which research questions can be framed. Although the following research process may vary in the degree to which all collaborators participate, the most critical element is a common belief in both the means and the ends.

Collaborative Research and "the Public Good"

Since Watergate, many authors have discussed the notion of ethics in public leadership and the notion of the "common good." The common good may be conceptualized within any social environment as maximizing the freedom or self-expression of the individual or ensuring distributive justice to individuals and groups. Liberal social theories support the first position; emancipatory dialectical theories support the second.

Liberal social theory suggests that "society is made up of irreducible individual actors whose rationality is based on information processing carried out in terms of self interests" (Cohen, 1985:257). "The common good" is that which maximizes benefit to the greatest number of individuals through negotiation. "The most satisfactory results occur when each actor is as free as possible to maximize within rules of order adapted for collective survival . . ." but maximal conditions of personal freedom help either to produce or to maintain unequal access to scarce resources. According to liberal social theory, the common good is achieved by reform through which unequal access can be modified. Emancipatory dialectical theories have to do with society in relation to the individual, society in relation to the environment, and intergroup relations, especially regarding the inequitable distribution of resources. These theories place definition of "the common good" in the hands of central administrations. As Minow (1988) indicates, neither of these solutions is satisfactory in complex multiethnic nation-states with a diversity of interests and perceptions of the common good. The principles of collaborative research offer a third position, which requires organized groups to advocate for the interests of the group *and* the individual, both to ensure access and to redefine the common good.

The History of Collaborative Research

The history of collaborative research can best be understood within the history of relationships between anthropologists and the people with whom they work. Anthropology depends on the ability to observe, reflect, and write about observations of ways of life of "the other." It is rooted in the expansion of entrepreneurial or colonial nation-states, which created the opportunity, in their self-interest, for literate explorers, priests, and administrators to describe ways of life that did not correspond with their own. These early culture historians wrote from a variety of perspectives; the best accounts are those that contain neutral descriptions rather than judgments and that are written by observers whose comments reflect relationships of close proximity and lengthy duration (Pelto and Pelto, 1979).

Over time, many anthropologists, recognizing the differences of education, class, and culture that have separated them from the peoples they have studied, have attempted to resolve these contradictions through the development of different strategies for conducting research and presenting ethnographies, Anthropologists have employed cultural relativism, have acknowledged the central role of hitherto unnoticed key informants, and have formally incorporated indigenous researchers into the conduct of research. Most recently, the postmodern practice of "writing ethnographies" has included the multiple perspectives of "indigenous" literate intellectuals. While these methods are increasingly collaborative and participatory in the collection of data and even in the manner in which information is presented, they do not reorder the relationship between the researcher and the researched, nor do they modify the uses of the research results.

A number of applied anthropologists in "state-of-the-art" articles on applied anthropology have reviewed this relationship and have emerged with several general approaches to research and practice. As expert witness, the anthropologist with many years of experience in the study of a particular community or ethnic minority group has been called upon to testify or to provide information in administrative or legal arenas (e.g., Native American land claims, bilingual education, cultural conservation, cultural survival; cf. Ablon, 1962; Lurie, 1955). This service is often an unintended consequence of basic ethnographic research (Hostetler, 1972).

Anthropologists in administration work within or administer local, state, national, or international projects or programs that are introduced or integrated into local communities. In such instances, anthropologists generally are expected either to identify and overcome barriers to acceptance or to interpret the local community's position to the administrative body. Anthropologists as administrators may have the opportunity to create consortia that include local communities. However, they are not usually able to assist local communities to make informed decisions about their participation or to advocate for their own involvement in the proposed programs. A handful of anthropologists have wielded political power over oppressed communities and have used their ethnographic knowledge of these communities and their links with national governments to develop structures that have supported community control over economic, educational, and social development, but this is uncommon.

Action or advocacy research stems from the recognition that anthropology as a discipline has focused on cultural entities (tribes, nation-states, communities, ethnic groups) that have been socially or politically marginal or marginated. These communities may be nonliterate and, as a result of their colonial or postcolonial histories, may not have enjoyed full control over their economic or cultural development, nor their integration into the global economy. In this approach, the anthropologist works in partnership with community organizations and leadership to integrate technical skills and insights based on ethnographic research, with community-initiated change programs and plans of action. In contrast to the administrative approach, the anthropologist engaged in action research prefers to understand and work to strengthen the position of a local community or ethnic group in a dialogue around policy or programming, rather than to determine the factors accounting for resistance to a program (Gearing, 1960; Peattie, 1968; Peterson, 1974; Piddington, 1960; Rubenstein, 1984; Tax, 1958).

Collaborative research extends this approach by facilitating the creation of networks of community organizations to use research as a means through which a community problem can be addressed. Eventually, the approach may, with consent of community networks, involve other larger institutions (including those that may constitute part of the "problem") in the problem-solving process (cf. Stull and Schensul, 1987). The following case examples illustrate ways in which approaches to collaborative research have been designed and carried out in urban areas of the United States by the authors and their colleagues.

Antecedents

Action Research in Chicano Communities

The work of Stephen L. Schensul and his colleagues in the 18th Street Mexican American Community of Chicago is well documented (S. L. Schensul, 1973, 1974, 1978; Bell, Schensul, and Just, 1974; S. S. Schensul and Bymel, 1975; S. L. Schensul and J. J. Schensul, 1978). Over the course of a 6-year period (1968–1974), and from a base as the director of the community research unit of a community mental health program, S. Schensul and his associates developed one of the earliest community action-research teams. This team consisted of university-trained anthropologists and other social scientists working hand in hand with community organizers and activists. Over time, the team documented significant needs and social problems in this large Chicano community and participated in the funding, development, implementation, and evaluation of over 20 significant community programs in bilingual education, maternal and child health, mental health, and alternative mental health programs, including traditional medicine, community-based mental health training, substance abuse, child abuse, sports and recreation, and gang prevention work.

By 1974, the team had determined that National Institutes of Health (NIH) basic research grants could be funded directly to community organizations rather than to universities or other large institutions. This led to the development of the Latina Mother–Infant Project, a community-based research project, funded by NIMH, to determine problems in access to perinatal health services among Mexican-American women. The Latina Mother–Infant Project was directed by an anthropologist, based in a community-run mental health program, and staffed by 13 trained lay community researchers who were also mothers and advocates. This project led to a number of published articles (cf. Gaviria, Stern, and Schensul, 1982) and, at the same time, to the development of Mujeres en Accion, the first community institution organized to advocate for the interests of Mexican-American women in Chicago (Stern, 1985).

Central to these developments was the decision to base research and action directly in the community of concern rather than in the state institution in which the community research unit was based. Placing the research team directly in the community—first through integration into block (facing sides of a city street) activities, later through assistance in the development of community institutions—ensured access to continuing research questions, community researchers, ideas for further program development, and continuing needs assessment. A further critical element was commitment to residence and long-term involvement in the life of the community. Anthropologists have maintained continued working relationships in the westside Chicano community from 1968 to the present. In 1991, the process has continued as Michael Schensul, son of Stephen and Jean Schensul, analyzed data on the homeless for El Centro de la Causa, under Felipe Ayala, its director and one of the key members of the original 1974 community research team.

From 1977 to 1990, Hartford, Connecticut, has been the location for a series of research approaches that build on the Chicago experience. These approaches emerged first as a result of collaborative efforts of the University of Connecticut Departments of Community Medicine and Anthropology with community activists in Hartford. During the time that Stephen Schensul (from the Department of Community Medicine in the School of Medicine) and Pertti Pelto (from the Department of Anthropology) were involved in community health research activities, these collaborative efforts facilitated the development of the hispanic Health Council, the Charter Oak Terrace Rice Heights Community Health Center, the Area Health Education Center, the Consortium of Primary Care Clinics, and the Hartford Community Mental Health Program (S. L. Schensul, 1981; and J. J. Schensul, 1978, 1982). Later, the University reduced its level of activity in the community, and other action-research networks continued in new directions. In 1984, Stephen Schensul, as Director of the Center for International Community Health Studies at the University of Connecticut, initiated a series of collaborative research projects with universities and communities in Peru, Sri Lanka, and, more recently, in Mauritius.

During 1978–1987, Jean Schensul was involved in community research as Associate Director and Research Coordinator of the community-based Hispanic Health Council. In 1987, she developed the Institute for Community Research, an independent, nonprofit action research institute whose consortia programs integrate research with training, interventions, health promotion, public education, or policy. Both the Institute for Community Research and the School of Medicine provided the co-authors with the opportunity to be involved in larger-scale projects in the 1980s and currently. In the sections that follow, we outline the general models that guided the development of these projects and offer some specific examples of implementation.

Large-Scale Planning Efforts

Large-scale planning efforts bring a wide variety of diverse constituencies together around one or more common problems. The first step is identifying a problem sufficiently broad and comprehensive to capture the interest of these constituencies. The problem may be captured as a "vision," a policy change, or a "domain" such as AIDS or teen pregnancy. The problem must by analyzed, its "causes" interpreted, and steps taken to address the problem through action or investigation. The challenge in these broad-based efforts is to promote and facilitate consensus across contituencies that may be very different in philosophy and approach from each other.

In the late 1970s and 1980s, the interface of health and elementary/secondary education proved to be an issue around which more than 50 agencies and individuals organized in Hartford, Connecticut, through the Area Health Education Center (AHEC) program. This program developed an independent community-based organization that, along with the University, acted as a base for organizing planning committees around the health of women, children, and the elderly and around school, clinic, and community prevention education programs. Multisectoral planning committees were organized and guided by systems-oriented facilitators with community health experience. Facilitation required the development of a long-range plan focused on program development and minority recruitment into the health fields, followed by goals, objectives, and immediate action steps. One critical function of the anthropologists was to integrate research and evaluation methods and the results of national investigations into the work of these committees.

An important effort of the Hartford Urban AHEC was the Hartford School Health Plan. This plan, created in 1979 by a multisectoral group facilitated by an anthropologist/health education administrator team, conceptualized a system-wide program of school health services and health education. In this system, elementary feeder schools and their communities were linked with middle schools, high schools, and a regionalized system of community clinics, secondary health resources, and hospitals. In 1990, more than 10 years later, the elements of this system-wide program were in place. As part of the program, members of the group agreed to produce a text on school-based health. While the text was never completed, school-based health service providers, educators, and teachers engaged in ethnographic documentation and analysis of their own programs. These analyses provided the basis for further program development, proposal writing, and curriculum creation and demonstrated to instructors the utility of qualitative research in a system that had heretofore been committed to experimental design.

The Rapid Sociodemographic Assessment Project is another example of a large-scale planning effort. Initiated in 1988 and funded with local foundation, United Way, and private sector resources, this project was designed to collect census-relatable sociodemographic information in the Hartford area in collaboration with neighborhood organizations, municipal planners, community organizations, and other potential users. The intentions of the project were to conduct an interim sample-based census update to track sociodemographic change at the neighborhood and town level in relation to 1980 and 1990 census data; to involve community residents and community leaders in the definition, collection, and use of the data; to establish a "public data base" consisting of primary and secondary data to be available and accessible to the public, especially to underserved users (including community organizations, planners, and advocates); and to define demographic trends of interest to planners, policymakers, educators, and others concerned with public and political welfare of residents of the Hartford area.

In the planning stages, over 75 municipal planning bodies, community-based agencies, and institutions participated in defining the scope of the project, the instrument, and potential uses of the data.

Twenty-one organizations participated in the collection of data. Some of these organizations are acting as distribution points for the data in various forms including reports, neighborhood profiles, and microdata sets. Much of our experience with community-based demographic survey work is derived from this project.

During the second phase of the project, distribution points will receive technical assistance in use and dissemination of the data, public and private users will be able to request additional analyses for a fee, and public and nonprofit agency staffs will be trained in uses of the data and interpretation of census and other secondary data sources that bear upon the region. Furthermore, the project is producing reports on specific topics such as urban men, children and youth, and women and employment. Each of these reports will be prepared by broad-based committees, which will use the results for policy and planning purposes.

Projects of this type fall within the domain of advocacy planning as outlined by Peattie (1968). Advocacy planning is defined by involvement of the "target population" to be affected by a "plan" or policy in the planning process. The collaborative research method ensures this involvement by requiring that members of the target population be involved in defining, collecting, and using qualitative and quantitative data in the planning process. Because most anthropologists are not formally trained as planners, nor in the dynamics of group process and conflict resolution, they should obtain training in group processes, or work with a facilitator team that includes planners, when attempting to build large collaborative research and planning networks.

Intervention and Evaluation Efforts

Ideally, collaborative research projects begin with research to identify the problem more clearly (cf. S. L. Schensul, 1985). In some instances, funding or other constraints make it impossible to conduct research prior to establishing an intervention. One strength of the collaborative research network is that its members are characterized by wide experience in the area to be addressed by the project. Thus, they can usually generate high-quality, substantive, community-responsive plans and programs based on their own experience. They can further use this experience to integrate research into such projects through pilot phase qualitative data collection, focus group discussions, participant–client tracking or management information systems, and outcome evaluation. Such efforts can be used to collect important data for the program and for others working in the field and can provide the basis for other related research projects.

In 1981, the Hispanic Health Council of Hartford received a grant through the Federal Bureau of Maternal and Child Health to initiate early entry and continuous use of pre- and postnatal services to pregnant Puerto Rican mothers. The project called for the development of a community education team and prevention-oriented education among networks of women of child-bearing age in the community. Anticipated outcomes were decreases in infant mortality and low birth weight and increases in frequency of breast feeding, first trimester entry to prenatal care, and postnatal follow-up care.

The project hired and trained a team of community perinatal health workers, who in turn trained networks of community perinatal health advocates. The health workers also acted as case managers for pregnant women entering the prenatal care system. The client case management program, which included detailed documentation of each case and the evaluation plan for the program, involved two research designs: time trend, which compared participants in the program to the national, state, and local trends, and a postintervention comparison design, which compared subsequent years of participant outcomes, using the first-year participants as a baseline (Pelto and J. J. Schensul, 1986; J. J. Schensul, Donelli-Hess, Martinez, and Borrero, 1987).

A second project, which exemplifies this approach, is a consortium project based at the Institute for Community Research entitled "Toward a Brighter Future for Hartford's Children." This consortium sets into place a system for early identification and assessment of children with potential developmental delays and language learning problems. The argument for the project was based on pediatric impairment and other otitis media studies and prevalance studies reports of day care providers about gaps in service for children with "special needs."

Members of the consortium met for 3 years to plan and obtain funding for this project, which began December 1990. Consortium members include the Institute as grantee, three ethnic-based organizations—The Urban league of Greater Hartford, the Hispanic Health Council, and La Casa de Puerto Rico—the city health department, and the regional birth to three service coordination center. Members of the Consortium contract for or deliver education, evaluation, or case-management services to the program, through the Institute for Community Research. The project's culturally appropriate outreach and education will improve parents' ability to recognize and address developmental problems before they become serious. Through evaluation, children needing treatment will be identified and referred with advocacy backup to appropriate services. The consortium is creating appropriate curriculum materials on early childhood development and developmental delays for use with parents, home day-care providers, and day-care personnel.

A management/evaluation information system will coordinate the information collection methods of consortium members and consolidate data in a single location. Data will include community needs assessments, intake forms, evaluation results, case records, and observational records and in-depth interviews with program outreach and case management staff. These data will be used by members of the Steering Committee to advocate for improvements in service delivery and the conditions which impede early identification and promote the illnesses known to result in impairments. Furthermore, the project will be used as the basis for conducting additional, more specialized research on otitis media, upper respiratory problems, behavioral problems, and other topics related to school performance.

Projects such as these should be developed with comprehensive tracking systems for monitoring both the progress of "clients" and issues and for documenting and addressing problems that may arise during the intervention or educational program. It is unfortunate that only national demonstrations projects receive sufficient research and evaluation funds to establish adequate informations systems for documentation and evaluation purposes. Anthropologists involved in developing educational demonstration projects should be especially persuasive in convincing national and local funders to support tracking systems and ethnographic documentation of project interventions and their outcomes.

Research and Demonstration Projects

Demonstration research projects are generally funded through the National Institutes of Health (NIH) and national foundations, to demonstrate the effectiveness of innovative approaches on a target population. Many of these approaches include a significant community educational component.

These studies often demand an experimental or quasi-experimental research design, with one or more comparison groups (cf. Cook and Campbell, 1979) and frequently conducted school or clinical settings where random or matched sample assignments are possible. It is exceedingly difficult, although not impossible, to conduct demonstration research projects with these characteristics in community settings because of problems in organizing and maintaining randomized assignment of participants, difficulties in standardizing the intervention(s) to ensure that all participants are exposed to the same experience, and difficulties in identifying and maintaining "natural" control or comparison groups.

One example of a community-based research and demonstration project was an NIMH-funded crisis research and demonstration project, referred to as the ARRIBA project. This project was designed by the Hispanic Health Council in conjunction with the Hartford Police Department to test two effects; (1) the ability of a culturally appropriate community-based crisis management system to prevent the acceleration of mental health-related crises in individuals or families, and (2) the potential for reorganization of the crisis management system in the area to provide more effective crisis services to Puerto Rican and other Latino clients.

The design called for the creation of a crisis intervention team that would work with the police to identify and resolve mental health problems before they became crises. The outcomes of clients in the ARRIBA system were to be compared with the outcomes of a "standard" crisis intervention program run by the police department. Staff of the program were hired from among experienced bilingual, bicultural candidates and were trained in case management, crisis intervention, qualitative case documentation, and record-keeping. Staff documenters working with the investigators described each case in-depth and maintained demographic, health, and mental health data on the individual and the household as appropriate. Project staff also documented through repeated observations, changes in the scope, staffing, and approach of the city-wide crisis intervention system. Case data were content-analyzed and -coded (J. J. Schensul, 1987).

The project design was altered when the police department, experiencing problems in the retention of Puerto Rican clients, declined to provide a control group. As a result, the primary independent variables in the design were redefined as degree of exposure of the client to the intervention, severity of the crisis situation as rated by the team of interveners, and the principle investigator and level of social support available to the primary client.

Project COPE (Community Outreach Prevention Effort) is one of over 60 street outreach demonstration projects funded over the past 4 years by the National Institute of Drug Abuse. This project, a consortium of five community-based organizations plus state and city health departments is testing the efficacy of culturally specific AIDS education for prevention programs with African-American, Puerto Rican, and Euroamerican intravenous drug users and their sex partners. The project has developed culturally distinct curricula and support and referral systems in African-American and Puerto Rican community organizations and has tested these components against a nonculturally targeted intervention located in a local drug treatment outpatient facility. One problem, typical of such projects, has been the early differentiation between research and outreach and education staff. The differentiation has been minimized by the participation of all research staff in interventions and intervention staff in some aspects of research.

Approximately 30% of the project's resources are directed to research and evaluation, using a panel design that includes a preintervention assessment and two postintervention assessments at 6 and 12 months. The project is directed by three anthropologists who have trained outreach and interview staff to collect qualitative data on intervention process and quantitative data on individual outcomes. Data collected by the project have been available to all project staff, and descriptive data have been presented in summary form by project administrators. Project nonresearch staff have recently expressed a strong desire to understand and participate in the analysis of quantitative data and are currently being trained to do so.

Demonstration research projects offer many challenges to collaborative researchers. Without careful organizing, projects can inadvertantly reinforce the traditional differences between research and intervention staff, making it difficult to maintain the rigor of the research design and standardized data collection. Although both the reseach team and many funders have conceptualized outreach or intervention staff as lay ethnographers, it is quite difficult to train nonethnographers to conduct ethnographic case-oriented research, which is so important in documenting the effects of an intervention process on individuals and groups. Furthermore, in consortium arrangements, key agencies critical to the research design may drop out of the project. Project investigators must be flexible in research design and methods in the field to continue the research under new circumstances.

Topic-Oriented Basic Research

Topic-oriented basic research may be conducted as KAB (knowledge, attitude, and behavior) studies or as lengthier studies of community phenomena. Quantitative/KAB studies fall within the traditions of the needs assessment of the planner or program developer and the epidemiologeal survey of the public health researcher. Generally, they are conducted when an organization or institutional network believes there may be a problem or issue to address but has little or not information about it. These studies are based on probability sampling techniques whenever possible and are not preceded by ethnographic analysis of the situation to be addressed. Needs assessments are localized; KAB studies often utilize questions obtained form instruments used elsewhere in the country or by a national or state department of health research. Both KAB studies and needs assessments are constructed so that they may be repeated to measure change through time. Both types of studies are based on self-report.

One example of a consortium-based needs assessment is a study of Puerto Rican elderly conducted by a network of organizations consisting of the Golden Age Senior Center of the San Juan Center, the Hispanic Health Council in Hartford, and the University of Connecticut Medical Anthropology Program. In this assessment, carried out in 1985–1986, an instrument was developed by knowledgeable community gerontologists working with the center as well as the executive and the research director of the Hispanic Health Council. Two students were paid to participate in the study and to assist in analyzing data. The instrument was written first in Spanish, and then translated into English and back-translated. Over a period of 6 months, 101 interviews with Puerto Rican elderly aged 60 years and over were conducted by the community gerontologists. A steering committee composed of representatives of the participating organizations was formed to review the data analysis process and assist in report writing. This project constituted the community's first experience in locating, interviewing, and beginning to promote the needs of Puerto Rican elderly, a heretofore unknown and unattended population in the area.

The AIDS Community Research Group was formed for community research to address AIDS on a city-wide basis. In 1988, the Centers for Disease Control funded the Institute as the grantee for an interagency consortium to do a two-phase AIDS KAB study in Hartford to provide a baseline for assessing changes in knowledge of AIDS, AIDS prevention, and risk behavior in the general community. The interagency consortium, referred to as the AIDS Community Research Group, conducted this study in six neighborhoods of Hartford. Community research staff coordinated the research and completed a total of 750 household interviews with eligible male and female respondents between the ages of 18 and 49. The instrument used by the project consisted of questions used for convenience sample interviewing by state epidemiologists and questions developed by the multiethnic steering committee for use in African-American, West Indian, Latino/ Puerto Rican, and other target communities in the city.

Over 35 community African-American, Hispanic, and white interviewers were trained to administer the survey instrument in three or four intensive training sessions and were able to complete a total of

over 750 interviews in seven neighborhoods and two public housing projects in the city. This study pointed to the disadvantage of em-
barking on new and sensitive research without an ethnographic phase.
It also demonstrated that, for the most part, gender was more important
than ethnicity in influencing respondents to participate. Furthermore,
it demonstrated the effectiveness of a research consortium consisting
of an ethnically representative group of community-based agencies
with different relationships with the community and different interests
in research data. Members of the consortium have all had access to the
raw data obtained through the project and are using reports and other
literature resulting from the project (ACRG, 1988, 1989). Other studies
that have utilized community researchers will be discussed in the
section referring to the training of community surveyors.

One example of more extensive basic research efforts conducted
by collaborative networks is an investigation of perceptions of
Alzheimer's disease among Puerto Rican and mainstream elderly to be
carried out by the Institute for Community Research in concert with a
private psychiatric institute and a public university's geriatric research
center (see Wetle, Schensul, Torres, and Mayen, 1989). A second is an
analysis of variations in adaptive strategies and choices of migrant
farmworkers in Florida, conducted by faculty of the University of
Miami Department of Psychiatry in collaboration with a farmworkers'
organization in south Florida. A third study explored variations in
breast- and bottle-feeding patterns among Puerto Rican mothers in
Hartford.

It should be apparent that virtually any topic can be examined
through consortium or collaborative arrangements provided that all
organizations understand and are committed to exploring the topic.
Each organization must be willing to support research without intervention. Finally, all organizations must be willing to participate in
planning and conducting the research and in utilizing its results. The
strength of the approach lies in improving the research design, instrument development, data collection capability, and quality of data analysis with the involvement of community-based collaborators familiar
with and in many cases, from the target population.

Research Training Programs

Community research training programs are different from projects
in which community researchers are trained to collect data because
they train lay researchers to understand and utilize research methods
to accomplish their own action or informational needs. Most research

training programs are intended for students or program planners and administrators rather than for community leaders, teachers, or activists. Thus there are few examples of programs such as these in the literature.

Collaborative community research training programs have been described for mixed groups of adults, women, youth, and teachers. As an example of the first, in 1980–1983 the National Institute of Education funded La Casa de Puerto Rico, and later the Hispanic Health Council, to train three cycles of community professionals to do education-related research as part of their effort to recruit black and Latino candidates into educational research (J. J. Schensul and E. Caro, 1982). This project was taught by an activist–anthropologist team and accredited first by the University of Connecticut and later by new Hampshire College School of Human Services.

A more recent example is the Urban Women's Development Project, a collaborative research consortium of five organizations representing African-American, Latino, and Anglo women and women's rights. The project is now in its third year of training urban women of all ethnic and class backgrounds to engage in problem identification, analyze policy, conduct survey research, and use the results to promote institutional or policy change. It is accredited by a local community college and has trained over 60 women since 1988. Many of these women have now entered higher education programs in sociology, anthropology, or planning. Another consortium project of the Institute for Community Research, the Teen Action Research Project, is using inquiry-based training and research methods to assist teens in understanding issues such as substance abuse that affect their daily lives and taking action to bring about positive change.

These programs all have in common the desire to help participants use research as a tool for improving critical thinking skills and understanding of the environment. Second, they try to erase the social, economic, and cultural distance between the instructor(s) and the participants by offering a collaborative learning experience. Third, they have as an important goal the intentional integration of participants of different ethnicities and backgrounds in an enjoyable learning environment. In each case, the curriculum is culturally targeted to include important historical and cultural dimensions of the experience of all participants. Each program has addressed one or more issues of state and/or national significance, thereby broadening the vision of the participants and orienting them as part of a national and global network. Finally, each of these efforts is committed to using the results of research to promote change.

While projects such as these are critical in demystifying research, these important limitations should be kept in mind. Instruction in research methods may not pay sufficient attention to theory. This can result in superficial or even undirected research, which can constrain the significance of the results. Second, these projects offer a review of research methods and can help participants to understand and to use research results, but they do not offer enough instruction to allow for the development of independent researchers. Finally, for their effectiveness these projects depend on the ability of the core staff to organize and analyze collected data and make it available rapidly and in an easily understood format, so that program participants can use it. Constraints of time and staffing may make rapid turnaround of data difficult, thus risking loss of the commitment of participants to use of the data.

Community Education Programs

Community education programs stem from the stated belief or recognition that community residents should be better informed about a particular topic. Ethnographic approaches to community education begin with qualitative data collection investigating the cultural beliefs and practices of the target population about the problem, and these approaches assume that residents' beliefs and practices are inherently logical and meaningful. Consequently, efforts to change them must make sense and must be cast in language, beliefs, and values that are culturally consistent with those of the target population. Community education programs incorporate research into the development of curriculum materials and dissemination strategies and may include comprehensive evaluation measures.

A typical example of the culturally appropriate community education program is the Puerto Rican Alzheimer's Education Project. The purpose of this collaborative, Administration on Aging–funded project, is to develop, test, and disseminate to service providers culturally appropriate educational materials and strategies designed to increase the capacity of these Puerto Rican elderly and their family caregivers to understand Alzheimer's disease and to utilize available services more effectively. The project is developing English and Spanish educational materials based on pilot work on symptom recognition, help-seeking behaviors, and service availability and accessibility carried out among Puerto Rican elderly and their caregivers in Hartford, Connecticut, between 1986 and 1989.

The best community education projects build on research, focus group discussions, and other forms of community participation to create a curriculum responsive in content and format. They should then utilize existing forms of community social organization (e.g., informal networks and community leaders, block clubs, churches, the media, cliques) to disseminate the information as rapidly and effectively as possible. Anthropologists are central to such programs because they are skilled in the qualitative research, focus group documentation, in-depth interviews, systematic data collection, and other methods useful in creating culturally appropriate curricula. Furthermore, their experience in community ethnography is important in determining which informal networks are likely to be most effective in distributing information in the target community.

Building the Community Base

The initiation of a research collaborative rests on three critical elements—the presence, influence, and insight of an applied social science researcher, the participation of skilled knowledge-oriented activists, and an issue or problem of passionate interest to a group of individuals, institutions, or agencies. For the researchers to be effective in influencing the creation of a collaborative, they must be embedded sufficiently in the life of the target community to have some idea of which topics are of interest and which individuals might be called together to discuss these topics. Thus, the first step for a committed collaborative researcher is involvement in the local community or communities in which research may take place.

The "community" may consist of school communities, a network of Headstart programs, a geographic area, or several target populations. Community researchers generally begin by entering one or more local communities. Educational researchers may identify a number of innovative or otherwise distinctive education programs and/or key people in a local board of education. Entry should follow the usual procedures outlined in a good ethnography text. Entry processes include identification of "key informants," attendance at (and participation in) important meetings, interviews with school personnel or agency heads, reviews of local newspapers, and talks with community residents, parents, and teachers.

For collaborative researchers, however, these entry methods take on an additional level of importance because researchers are seeking to identify important actors in relation to selected topics as well as to uncover important orienting information. The entry process may go on over a lengthy period, as one key informant leads to another and one sector is found to interface with another. Eventually, the collaborative researcher discovers key general community or instructional concerns, a network of interested, energetic, and committed key actors, and a set of institutions, programs, or individuals who may be called together to institute a collaborative research project. Once these networks are identified, they may be organized and reorganized into different configurations depending on the particular topic of interest.

Collaborative research projects are based on several principles of organization. The first important criterion for success is the selection of an experienced or knowledgeable facilitator. The chair or lead facilitator of the network should be someone familiar with all sectors of the community and committed to supporting the involvement of community-based organizations in policy and planning. This person should be sufficiently knowledgeable to ensure that all critical decision-makers to benefit in and/or be affected by the effort will be involved in the earliest planning stages.

A second criterion is inclusion. As many relevant organizations, agencies, and institutions should be included in the initial planning stages as possible. Decisions in favor of inclusion should rest on the potential scope of the project, the resources available, political implications of exclusion, and number of agencies and individuals with whom the facilitator feels comfortable working. A collaborative sometimes may include only two or three organizations; at other times, it may include up to 30.

In these projects, service/advocacy and research should be linked. The chair or lead facilitator should be familiar with the priorities of service providers and administrators and able to speak to and support these priorities while promoting the integration of research into program planning. Because research is frequently viewed as unnecessary, undesirable, or a costly appendage to "action" or program services, it is critical to demonstrate to doubting service personnel that information collection (and, later on, theory or model building) can be immediately useful to their work and, therefore, should be integrated into it.

Initiators should decide early on the cultural content of the project—that is whether or not the project will be multiethnic and multicultural in its approach and in what ways the development and implementing of multicultural interventions should be addressed. Inverventions may explore levels of cultural relevance. It is worth noting that ethnic minority organizations may not be well informed about the cultural characteristics of their constituencies and should be assisted in identifying these characteristics before they can build culturally appropriate interventions. It is critical to remember that "culture" is not monolithic, that each target population may have its own cultural profile, and that there may be "within-group diversity." Ongoing assessment of cultural characteristics and culture change should be built into the job descriptions of all project staff.

Incentives and equitable exchange of resources is critical to the success of the project. Exchange strengthens institutional commitment to the project. Organizations and community leaders will participate in action research efforts when incentives are strong and attractive. Incentives may be financial, social, or political. Furthermore, commitment to the effort is greatly strengthened when all participating organizations identify concretely both what they hope to gain and what contributions they can make to the program. Roles, expectations, and "in kind" and other contributions to a collaborative research project should be clearly and formally articulated before the project begins and should be reviewed regularly during the course of the project.

Identifying the Problem and Building the Program Model

Once a working group is identified, it must come to consensus on the direction of its work. A general topic or issue such as "art in education" or "the education of special needs children" may bring people together initially. But the general nature of these topics is insufficient to focus a project or program. How can a focus be identified? A simple procedure is as follows.

Identifying the "Dependent Variable" or the Central Problem

To arrive at the "dependent variable," members of the collaborative network are asked by a facilitator to identify a series of specific issues in the domain of general concern to the group. Such issues might include "substance abuse among high school youth," infant mortality, or ethnic differences in reading achievement level of first-graders. The group is then asked to define and implement each of the specific issues and to identify which issue is most significant. The most significant issue is then translated into the dependent variable and/or a problem statement. The dependent variable becomes the focus of research; the problem statement becomes the focus of the project or activity of the group or the problem to be affected or changed.

Identifying the "Causal" Factors that Appear to Influence the Issue or Problem

To complete the model, participants discuss and debate the multitude of factors that relate to, cause, or "precede" the dependent variable or problem. They then designate the relationships among those factors, as they themselves understand, and agree upon those relationships. If an hypothesized relationship cannot be clearly defined, the group must seek new information to clarify it. The result of this analysis is a "system" of interacting factors that impact on the issue or problem—a theoretical model. Once network members have decided on the central problem and the primary factors associated with it, they may choose from several different alternatives. If there is not information on the problem, they may wish to choose a basic research project intended to provide the basis for intervention. If there is prior information, or if funders will not fund research alone, network members may choose an intervention. A program might focus on basic research or needs assessment, research and development, intervention and evaluation, research and training, research for policy development, or some combination of all of these. The selection of program type will depend on the skills of the group, the availability and constraints of funding, and the degree to which sufficient information about the situation is determined to exist.

Building an Operational Model

To carry out this step, the group translates each factor from variable to problem to be addressed and works with both. For a research project, the group determines which of the independent variables are critical to the model and feasible to investigate given time, resources, and cultural sensitivity. For an intervention project, the group will determine which of the "factors" affecting the dependent variable can be modified or changed, given the preceding constraints. The result is an operational model for research or practice.

To summarize, the steps that permit transformation of a basic research model into an intervention model are as follows:

1. Determining which causal factors can be affected and which cannot, given the constraints of time, human resources, culture, and money.
2. Anticipating what changes might be brought about in the causal factors.
3. Anticipating what changes might result in the dependent variable.

Brokering Funding Possibilities

Apart from the urgency of the need, the most critical factor triggering the interest of members of a research network or collaborative is the promise of funding or additional resources. Researchers or action-research teams who call together potential consortia members must facilitate a set of ideas sufficiently compelling to bind the network into a joint vision and mission. At the same time, these ideas must be coordinated with funding sources, and funding sources must be identified and receptive to the ideas. Researcher–facilitators can expect no more than several "chances" to negotiate consortia that do not receive funding or other immediate benefits after a certain, relatively short period of time.

Often projects must be adapted to the interests of funders and changes must be negotiated with the research collaborative. In the case of the previously mentioned AIDS project, members of the consortium had earlier determined the need for a city-wide intervention project. The CDC, however, working through the State Department of Health Services, had determined that a probability-based KAB study was required to provide base line data for the state, and to interface with convenience samples in other parts of the state. The consortium agreed to accept the KAB study with the hope that it would provide the basis for generating a much-needed city-wide intervention. It is critical for those working with the funders to convey information to the research collaborative in an open and continuous way in order to avoid loss of trust and fear of manipulation.

Negotiating the Roles of Collaborating Members

When a collaborative research project includes a number of different organizations or institutions, the roles of each must be clarified. Even before a collaboration is agreed upon, the prospective roles of participating organizations should be considered. First, limited resources usually preclude duplication of services. Thus, conflicts may arise among organizations in the consortium that play similar roles in the community. Ways to address these potential conflicts in advance should be found and/or care should be taken to invite only the critical organizations to participate in the consortium. Second, participating organizations generally have agendas that should be discussed openly and, if appropriate, spelled out in advance contractually or in letters of agreement. If these agendas are not revealed until after the program is funded, unintended conflict may arise to threaten the collaborative network. Third, the situations of participating organizations may shift and change at any time during the implementation of a program. These changes may affect the mission, direction, resource level, supervisory capacity, reputation, and other dimensions of the institution. Such changes should be discussed, studied, and renegotiated as they occur and their implications communicated to the rest of the consortium to avoid gossip and misunderstanding.

One case in point is the AIDS Community Research Group. Each member organization in this research network took on a different set of responsibilities in relation to the project. The Institute for Community Research was responsible for overall management and coordination of field interviewing, coding of data and report writing, and data utilization. The Hispanic Health Council entered and managed data and participated in report writing. The Urban League completed an ethnographic study of the development of AIDS programming in the city, and the Hartford Health Department conducted training in AIDS and reviewed and disseminated results.

In the Brighter Futures Program, a consortium consisting of two independent but overlapping project networks, was brought together by the primary funder to integrate two early childhood intervention program concepts. In the process, the in-kind contributions and the anticipated benefits of membership of two of the participating service institutions were not fully defined. During the early months of the program, conflict occurred around the degree to which community educators–advocates in the program were to become directly involved in services to children with disabilities versus community education with parents at risk. After considerable debate, the Steering Committee eventually arrived at a compromise that included both.

Determining Informational Needs

After defining the problem, research collaboratives may determine whether or not to obtain more information. Rather than obtaining large amounts of general or demographic information, collaborative networks should concentrate on the collection of specific information pertinent to their selected direction. There are numerous ways in which guiding information can be collected. To explore the relationship between ethnicity and the arts, the Institute for Community Research held and documented a series of dialogues among artists, social scientists, planners, and arts consultants. These dialogues provided the basis for a report, a publication (Carroll and Schensul, 1990), and an National Endowment of the Arts grant to support the Connecticut Cultural Heritage Arts Program. Data obtained from the AIDS Community Research Group's study of AIDS knowledge, attitudes, and behaviors provided the basis for a city-wide AIDS prevention research and intervention project. A small pilot project involving in-depth interviews with Puerto Rican elders and their caregivers on normal versus abnormal aging provided the bases for the Puerto Rican Alzheimer's Education Project. Other ways of obtaining easily accessible initial information include panel discussions, community hearings, reports, and other secondary data and key informant interviews.

Research Methods in Collaborative Research Networks

Community research staff and interviewers constitute the core of the collaborative research effort. Community researchers are critical because, through membership, they are familiar with the target population(s) of the research. They are likely to have a vested interest in the quality of data collection and the significance of the results, and are known and trusted in the community. Community researchers generally have little or no prior involvement in any form of data collection and require thorough training. It is easier to train community researchers in quantitative survey research or other structured and systematic instrument-based data collection than in qualitative research techniques such as participant observation, in-depth or unstructured interviewing, or focus group interviews.

There are two approaches to involving community researchers. The first involves them in all aspects of the project from instrument development to data entry, analysis, and interpretation, to write-up. The second includes them only in the collection of quantitative (or occasionally qualitative) data. In this instance, the design for data collection and the analysis of the data are the responsibility of the investigators. The second approach is the most common because it is simpler and more cost-effective. Furthermore, community researchers, while they may be familiar with the environment of the project, may not have the theoretical experience or writing skills to observe, interview, and document a topic properly.

Involving survey researchers in data collection is cost-effective because they are paid by the completed interview or unit of time; involving them as full- or part-time staff is less cost-effective because their time is not always used effectively in the field. Project management must consider whether they need the ethnographic input of the community research staff in designing and testing the instrument or approach to data collection prior to a survey or they and their colleagues already know enough to avoid this step altogether or build it into field feedback and interview revisions. If project managers *are* members of the target community, is is more feasible to involve community researchers only as interviewers. If community members are not represented among project managers, community researchers should be hired as full-time, fully participatory staff.

Recruitment and Selection

Proper recruitment and selection of community researchers is critical to the success of the project. Researchers should be identified based on criteria established by each project. For example, a project involving the solicitation of responses to many open-ended questions can best utilize researchers who are comfortable with open-ended questioning and writing. A project involving the administration of a quantitative survey instrument will require interviewers who are rigorous in completing all questions and responses. A multiethnic sample benefits from a multiethnic research team whose members can support one another in ethnically diverse neighborhoods, classrooms, and other settings. We have found that in Connecticut matching by gender appears to be more critical than matching by ethnicity, especially in neighborhoods with large numbers of single women or elderly people, who may be especially cautious about whom they allow into their homes.

Recruitment for part-time researchers can be managed through personal networks, community-based agencies, local employment agencies, friends and relatives of staff, community newspapers, and presentations at church gatherings and other centers. We have found that recruitment through personal and agency networks is most effective in urban areas, through local newspapers, libraries, and municipal government networks in suburban areas.

Interviewers should be required to fill out application forms and to write a short essay if written responses or interviews are required. They should also be interviewed to find out how well they know the communities in which the research is to be carried out, what activities they have been involved in, how well they may be known, their prior experience in the field, including other research projects, and their feelings about interviewing in neighborhoods and communities with which they are not familiar. Vignettes requiring judgment in the field should be used to assess their ability to handle difficult situations in households or on the street.

The selection of an appropriate coordinator or project director is critical to the community research endeavor. The coordinator should be from the community from which data are to be collected and should be known to and knowledgeable about that community. Furthermore, coordinators should have a strong commitment to the usefulness of data in enhancing understanding of the community. The coordinator should know a broad network of community residents from among which interviewers or full-time community researchers may be chosen. Training or training coordination experience is useful. Well-developed organizational ability, ability to speak more than one language, and knowledge of the social and emotional stresses to which researchers may be exposed are also critical to the position.

Training

Community researchers who enter a project as core full-time staff should receive a full introduction to the history, theory, and methods of the project and participate as partners in the design of qualitative and quantitative data collection techniques. University-trained research-ers are familiar with standard research methods and procedures but are less likely to know whether or not they will succeed in the target community. Community researchers (or teachers) are familiar with the context of the research and play a major role in developing, critiquing, translating, and testing methods and techniques in the target commu-nity. The better each group understands the assumptions of the other, the more effective the partnership.

Researchers who enter a project during the data collection phase may also play an important role in pilot testing a developed instrument and/or in providing important feedback on the utilization of the instru-ment in the field. Furthermore, knowing the field context, they can assist the research team in gearing interviewing timing and interaction to the constraints of the field setting.

Survey researchers require a minimum of three or four training sessions (between 8 and 10 hours of training) to understand fully the project, the instrument, interviewing techniques, and questionnaire completion. If they are to be responsible for coding of their own instruments, they must receive additional training in proper coding techniques. Regardless of whether or not they are responsible for coding their own instruments, they should be instructed in the coding system because this will assist them to complete their answers thoroughly and in a form appropriate for coding by someone else.

Part-time community researchers should not be expected to engage in qualitative data collection unless they have received prior training in an academic environment. Qualitative data collection requires thorough grounding in inductive theory development, methods of content analysis, and interviewing and observing without bias. Qualitative researchers must also be able to translate observations and interviews into complete field notes. In some cases, these notes must be accurately translated from another language to English, either by the researcher or someone else on staff.

Training in service-oriented disciplines creates additional difficulties for community researchers. Social workers and other service providers are skilled in observing and interviewing individual clients to offer better assistance. The shift from the individual client to larger social units may be difficult unless they are oriented toward policy change or community advocacy.

Community researchers should undergo rigorous role play to be sure that they can accurately describe the project and the organization they represent. They should be able to answer most questions about the project or refer respondents to other staff of the project who can be more specific. They should carry an identification card with a picture of themselves and a letter from the organization signed by the director and the director of the project. In some cases, a letter of introduction from town or city officials assist researchers in obtaining the confidence of respondents. Project staff may decide to offer a modest gift, informational brochure, or referral guide as a way of expressing thanks to respondents for participation in the project. Occasionally, projects will offer a small fee to respondents. Project COPE is one unusual example of a project that pays respondents for participating in the pre- and postintervention interviews. The project staff makes it very clear that participants are being paid only for the pre- and postintervention interviews that they complete, which are designed to find new ways of preventing AIDS among people like themselves. They are not paid for participating in blood testing or the project interventions.

Monitoring and Supervision

All community researchers should be supervised closely and regularly, both in the field and in the office. Qualitative interviews should be reviewed and feedback provided in writing and face-to-face. Qualitative interviewers have greatest difficulties in documenting what they perceive to be insignificant details and in asking the full range of questions that will help the reader to understand the situation as completely as possible. Feedback and practice should focus on these areas, and field notes should be rewritten and resubmitted for review until they have improved.

Survey instruments and other quantitative tools for data collection should be reviewed for completeness, accuracy, and clarity of response. Interviewers should complete at least three interviews successfully before being given more responsibility. Field coordinators should inform interviewers that at least 10% of their interviews will be chosen randomly for verification by telephone or door-to-door repeat interviews. Furthermore, they should be informed that research staff have other ways of determining whether or not interviews have been constructed. Interviewers should receive payment for completed surveys as soon as possible after they have handed their surveys in. Often they undertake community survey research as an opportunity to supplement a modest income and are in much need of rapid payment.

Support Systems

Community researchers derive their strength from their knowledge and experience in their own communities. If the research takes place, as it often does, in economically marginated communities, they may be experiencing the same difficulties as the people they interview and need support and understanding to continue their work. Often times, community research staff do not expect to find the multiple problems and the extremely difficult and painful circumstances of the families they interview. They inadvertently come upon family crises, sickness, death, abuse, eviction, and any number of other problems for which they have no solutions and little to offer. Research staff have returned in tears or in anger and frustration. Investigators supporting community research and community researchers should be prepared to offer personal, social, referral, counseling, and other supports to research staff and should make sure that they spend some time in the field with the staff to understand and to experience directly the difficulties of community field research. Furthermore, the support resources and referral networks of the community-oriented organizations(s) sponsoring the research should be mobilized in advance in order to respond to crises or requests for information in the field. If possible, community interviewers may carry with them pamphlets, brochures, or lists of contact people in local agencies and health clinics known to respond to emergencies or to high-priority needs. These materials can be handed out after the interview and reviewed with the respondent in case of need.

Instrument Development, Data Analysis, and Dissemination

Whenever possible, community researchers or data collectors should be involved in instrument development, data analysis, and dissemination of research results. They bring expert knowledge of the "field," through their own experience and the ease with which they can collect additional qualitative or quantitative pilot data. Together, with the instrument development skills of the social science collaborator, they can create, pilot, and sometimes validate culturally and context-appropriate data collection methods. While joint instrument–questionnaire development may take more time, the end result is a more valid and reliable data set.

Involving community researchers in data analysis is both ethical and efficient. It is ethical because these researchers have collected the data from their own communities and should be able to reap the benefits of the data through analysis. It is efficient because these same researchers, once having learned from the data, are best positioned to disseminate the results in their own communities. Because they may never have been involved in analyzing either qualitative or quantitative data, however, they require some assistance from academically trained researchers as they approach the data. Once they learn to analyze and interpret the data, even on an initially superficial level, they contribute immeasurably to its interpretation because of their familiarity with the context of the project. It is important to leave enough time to allow for full participation of community researchers in analysis of data and to structure the data in a straightforward manner so that they can respond to it immediately.

Administrative and Organizational Issues and Problems in Building Collaborative Research Networks

Establishing Rules for Participation

Collaboration includes residents, members of the communities, and/or groups in which research is to be conducted. Collaborative research projects involve the development of action research partnerships among anthropologists, community activists and actors, and other sectors to address problems in a specific domain such as health or education. To ensure the active and equal involvement of those with less access to the domain in question, collaborative research efforts begin with the "affected" community. All projects are carried out in collaboration with organizations and communities involved in the research-related problem and its solution. Only when the problem or issue is identified, and its importance clarified from the community perspective, can other sectors be called in to participate.

Collaborative research must include a recognized need for information. A community's need for "more information" drives the collaborative research effort. Collaborative researchers are then better positioned to convince activists and program developers that information will be useful to their goals.

Before a project is negotiated, collaborative researchers must have a good sense of what types of projects can work in collaborative research settings. They must recognize the relative advantages of research, policy assessment, research training, research and demonstration, and evaluation and know how to select among these alternatives when negotiating a project. Furthermore, researchers must have a strong sense of research design and extensive knowledge of research methods to know which elements of a project can be negotiated and which cannot to maintain the integrity of the research design.

Collaborative research must involve joint negotiations and decision-making. Decisions should be made jointly by all members of a consortium on policy decisions such as hiring, methodology, target communities and agencies, new directions, and project structures. It benefits and strengthens a consortium if member organizations "cost share," especially when programs are allocated so that income flows roughly equally among consortium members. Because the conduct of research in local communities can be a sensitive matter, joint development and implementation of research (and intervention) methods is critical. Finally, research consortia must carefully plan ways in which they can collaborate in decisions on the use of information/results or dissemination.

Research networks must establish ground rules for operation early in the development of joint work. These ground rules relate to how roles and responsibilities, investigatorships, lines of authority, problem-solving, and fiscal management are decided, arranged, and monitored.

Regarding management, one (and no more than two) organization must take management or directorship responsibility. However, all project directors, principal investigators, and other managers must be prepared to share staff, resources, information, visibility, and credit with the members of the network.

For maintenance purposes, research consortia must be "bounded" (i.e., their boundaries must be defined and differentiated). Rules for recognizing participation in research network should be developed and clarified. Collaborative research projects involve individuals as well as organizations that do not necessarily have experience with research and that do not always value it equally with the other activities in which they engage. One of the responsibilities of the full-time, or university trained researchers is to ensure that all participants in a collaborative research project are involved and feel as if they are part of the research endeavor. A critical element in ensuring that this happens is to credit all participants in research-related activities including data analysis, data presentation, written articles, and other means of disseminating materials. The emphasis here is on recognizing participation (as distinguished from ensuring participation). Rules require that all participating entities be respected, remembered, included, referred to, and credited, even if they do not all participate at the same level all the time. Participating agencies or entities that pursue limited, irregular, or unpredictable involvement or who do not abide by the rules of the research network will be confronted by the designated management body.

Maintaining Stability in Collaborative Research Networks

Community consortia are not always successful. What leads to successful collaboration? Community research consortia are likely to run smoothly when the network is stable. Stable networks are defined by the stability of each participating organization and by the length of time and solidarity of relationship of the participants. The involvement of one or more new organizations without clearcut identities or sufficient staff or income is a constraint because the new organization is establishing its identity, does not have established funding, and may be forced to use consortium staff for other organization purposes.

Consortia accrue strength through planning. Although there is an ideal balance between planning and project funding and start-up, a longer planning period will consolidate working relationships among consortia members and provide the network with valuable experience needed to resolve the conflicts that must inevitably arise later.

It is critical to the stability of the consortium to obtain agreement of board and staff of participating organizations that research is important. If resistance to research and its uses exists at any level, consortium decisions involving data collection, publication, and use are likely to be questioned. Mistrust arising between one organization and the rest of the consortium around the conduct of research will negatively influence the rest of the network.

Finally, consortia are as strong as their individual members. When steering committee members are experienced directors or appointed substitutes with strong communication skills, conflicts and miscommunications among consortium members can be addressed easily. When participants understand and value data, the inevitable conflicts between research and service can be more easily minimized. When the administrative structures of participating organizations are clear and well established, consortium members can specify how they expect to operate under the consortium structure and can negotiate interagency differences when necessary.

Unstable networks are characterized by conflict among members at all levels. One common reason for conflict is inconsistency of internal supervision resulting in lack of compliance with work requirements. This problem can result in interagency resentments and/or competition and create ill will and lack of cooperation within the consortium.

Significant differences in personnel or institutional policies or operating procedures across consortium members can also create instability. Such differences may be reflected in differential pay scales and with consequent loss of personnel or internal competition for project personnel. Furthermore, differences in institutional policies may make it difficult or impossible to implement certain aspects of educational or other programs across all project sites in the same way.

Organizations may enter consortium relationships without being straightforward about their reasons for participating or with different reasons for participating among sectors or departments. Hidden or unknown agendas will appear and may conflict with expressed mutual interests.

Finally, an important destablizing influence is the failure to develop a shared language and set of meanings for the project. Failure may stem from different interpretations of the same conceptual vocabulary, from lack of understanding of the vocabulary of the project, or from discomfort with the project's conceptual framework.

Central Elements of Collaborative Research

First and foremost, collaborative research should be viewed as a tool for the empowerment of those groups within limited access to good data and the methods that produce such data. Populations that historically have had limited access to data and to quantitative research methods and results include women, ethnic minority groups, and the poor. Data enhance the ability of any group to understand its target population, promote its own interests, attract new resources, and see itself and its constituencies in relation to others (Hessler, New, and May, 1979).

Furthermore, collaborative research often may involve groups differing by ethnicity, gender, and class. The approach, while beginning in marginated communities, attempts to resolve contradictions among such groups by building bridges across structural, political, racial, and cultural barriers. It does so by building information collection or sharing around common issues and problems, by sharing human and financial resources across boundaries, and by creating structures that ensure the continued and equitable participation of all organizations in planning, conducting, and utilizing the results of research. Collaborative research may also involve "sympathetic sectors" of unresponsive institutions, By developing collaborative research links, such sectors can more effectively advocate for community-oriented positions or help to generate internal change.

Critical and Creative Thinking and Problem-Solving

Creative and critical thinking skills are central to collaborative research as problem-solving. Creative thinking generates the "aha" or innovative insights that motivate the problem-solver to move in new directions. Methods of critical thinking, about which more has been written, offer orderly approaches to framing, documenting, analyzing, and synthesizing information. This systematic approach to problem-solving leads to logical conclusions or directions for action. The conceptions of Ennis (1987) concerning critical thinking dispositions and abilities provide a set of definitions that assist in integrating research methods into critical thinking and problem-solving techniques. "Critical thinking is reasonable reflective thinking that is focused on deciding what to believe or do." As such it contains five key elements. It is practical, reflective, and reasonable and involves belief and action. These five elements can be further broken down into critical thinking dispositions or tendencies an critical thinking abilities. Ennis (1987) maintains that to truly incorporate these into educational settings we need to foster these dispositions and abilities several times, at various levels of difficulty and in various subject areas in a spiral curriculum fashion.

Action Research

Collaborative research projects are built on the principles of action research. Action research begins with the notion that most of the social, biological, and political problems affecting contemporary communities, nations, and the global community are complex and cannot be identified or solved without better sources of information and greater interpersonal and intersectoral collaboration. Research, as continuous inquiry, analysis, synthesis, and action, should be a tool for development in organizations and communities not traditionally involved in research. Furthermore, research and results of research should be readily accessible and useful to communities at a time when information is critical to improve access to other resources.

Action research holds that all parties or "stakeholders" must be involved in identifying, defining, and struggling to solve the "problem." Research as structured inquiry offers a means of bringing multiple sectors together to solve problems jointly. Strategies for solving problems may lie in investigating the dimensions of a problem, in testing and evaluating new approaches, in the continuous interaction of research and action, or in using research to influence policy or to promote political or economic change.

Fostering Cultural Pluralism and Cultural Transformation

Fostering cultural pluralism requires mutual respect for differences in ways of viewing reality, making decisions, organizing for action, and solving daily problems of survival and growth. Furthermore, it requires skills in negotiating differences so that common ground is apparent and both commonalities and differences can be understood, discussed, and appreciated. These differences must be negotiated so that all people are strengthened and confirmed rather than negated (J. J. Schensul, 1990).

Cultural transformation involves the selective discarding, creating, incorporating, and transforming of cultural elements on an ongoing basis (sometimes consciously, sometimes unconsciously) so that change occurs (J. J. Schensul, 1985). Change should occur such that individual and group identity are preserved but group boundaries are not fixed. Culture is continually transformed to accommodate new situations and contexts. We must perceive that it is and that we are actors in the transformative process in order to understand how to create an environment in which cultural pluralism can flourish.

An Ecological Perspective

To take an ecological perspective in collaborative research implies the understanding that we live an a complex environment in which our lives and ways of operating are inextricably bound up with those of others, both here and elsewhere. In this environment, we are linked by economic, political, biophysical, social, religious, emotional, and ideological principles and practices, which constitute the context in which we live and wish to change. The problems we may wish to solve are multidimensional and cannot be addressed by isolating them from their context or by trying to solve them alone. Finally, we have the power and capacity to plan together for the future. To do so requires an understanding of both the present and the past—that is, the future occurs in a historical context.

Summary

Collaborative research offers a method of agreeing on and working toward "the public good," which is built on a series of premises. We recognize that access to resources is not equitably distribued. Furthermore, structural and policy changes are necessary to ensure more equitable distribution of resources. In this context, individual development can be maximized while working collaboratively toward improved access. Taking cultural, class, gender, and other differences as well as commonalities into account is critical in understanding both the sources of inequity and their resolution. We believe that research can be an important tool in gaining power through access to information. In addition, critical thinking and participation in an investigatory process are crucial elements in enhancing the ability of individuals and groups to move toward satisfying community needs. Participatory research and analysis contribute to an understanding of the broader social context of any issue one might wish to address. Finally, collaborative research acknowledges that we are part of a global system of economic, political, and cultural exchanges and that we can and should participate in and borrow from approaches to social and cultural change found to be successful elsewhere in the world.

References

Ablon, J. (1962). The American Indian Chicago Conference. *Journal of American Indian Education*, 1, 17–23.

AIDS Community Research Group. (1988). AIDS knowledge attitudes and behaviors in a multi-ethnic neighborhood of Hartford. AIDS Community Research Group (Burke, Owens, Schensul, Singer, Torres, Uranga-McKane). Hartford, CT: Institute for Community Research.

AIDS Community Research Group. (1989). AIDS knowledge attitudes and behaviors in Hartford's neighborhoods. AIDS Community Research Group (Burke, Owens, Schensul, Singer, Torres, Uranga-McKane). Hartford, CT: Institute for Community Research.

Bell, M., Schensul, S., and Just, M. (1974). Coping in a troubled society: An environmental approach to mental health. Washington, DC: Lexington Books, and Lexington, MA: Fisher, W., and Heath and Co.

Carroll, T. G., and Schensul, J. J. (Eds.). (1990). Cultural diversity and American education: Visions of the future. *Education and Urban Society*, 22(4), August.

Cazden, C., Diamondstone, J., and Naso, P. (1989). Teachers and Researchers: Roles and relationships. *The Quarterly of the National Writing Project and the Center for the Study of Writing*, II(4), 1–27.

Cohen, R. (1985). Social theory and critical analysis in applied anthropology in collaborative research and social policy. *In* J. Schensul and S. Stern, (Eds.), *Applied behavioral scientist*, 29(2), 249–264.

Cook, T. D., and Campbell, D. (1979). *Quasi-experimentation: Design & analysis issues for field settings*. Boston, MA: Houghton-Mifflin.

Ennis, R. (1987). A taxonomy of critical thinking dispositions and abilities. *In* J. Baron and R. Sternberg (Eds.), *Teaching thinking Skills: Theory and practice,* (pp. 9–26). New York: W. H. Freeman.

Gaviria, M., Stern, G., and Schensul, S. (1982). Sociocultural factors and perinatal health in a Mexican American community. *Journal of the National Medical Association,* 74(10), 983–989.

Gearing, F. (1960). The strategy of the Fox Project. *In* F. Gearing, R. McNetting, and L. Peattie (Eds.), *Documentary history of the Fox Project.* Department of Anthropology, University of Chicago, Chicago.

Havelock, R. (1969). *Planning for innovation through dissemination and utilization of knowledge.* Ann Arbor, MI: University of Michigan.

Hessler, R., New, P., and May, J. (1979). Power, exchange, and the research-development link. *Human Organization,* 38, 334–342.

Hood, P. D. (1973). How research and development in educational roles can facilitate communication. *Journal of Research and Development in Education,* 17(4), 96–113.

Hostetler, A. (1972). Amish schooling: A study in alternatives. *Council on Anthropology and Education Newsletter,* 3(2), 1–4.

Lampert, M. (1984). Teaching about thinking and thinking about teaching. *Journal of Curriculum Studies* 16(1), 1–18.

Lurie, N. (1955). Anthropology and Indian claims litigation: Problems, opportunities and recommendations. *Ethnohistory,* 2, 357–375.

Lytle, S. L., and Cochran-Smith, M. (1989). Teacher research: Toward clarifying the concept. *The Quarterly of the National Writing Project and the Center for the Study of Writing,* II(2), 2–27.

Minow, M. (1988). A critique of pure harmonization: Problems of diversity and federalism. Paper prepared for the Georgetown University Law Center Conference on Federalism.

Mohr, M., Grumbacher, J., Hauser, C., Mathews, G., and Willoughby, K. (1989). Teacher–Researchers: Their voices, their continued stories. *The Quarterly of the National Writing Project and the Center for the Study of Writing,* II(2), 4–19.

Peattie, L. R. (1968). Reflections on advocacy planning. *Journal of the American Institute of Planners,* 34, 80–88.

Pelto, P. J., and Pelto, G. (1979). *Anthropological research: The structure of inquiry.* Cambridge, MA: Cambridge University Press.

Pelto, P. J., and Schensul, J. J. (1986). Theory and practice in policy research. *In* E. Eddy and W. Partridge (Eds.), edition of *Applied anthropology in America* (with Pertti J. Pelto in revised 2 ed). New York: Columbia University Press.

Peterson, J. (1974). The anthropologist as advocate. *Human Organization,* 33, 311–318.

Piddington, R. (1960). Action anthropology. *Journal of the Polynesian Society,* 69, 199–213.

Rice, R., and Rogers, E. (1980). Reinvention of the innovation process. *Knowledge: Creation, Diffusion, Utilization,* 1, 499–514.

Rubenstein, R. (1984). Reflections on action anthropology: Some developmental dynamics of an anthropological tradition. Paper presented at the Society for Applied Anthropology Annual Meeting, Toronto.

Schensul, J. J. (1985). Cultural transmission and cultural transformation: Educational anthropology in the eighties. *Anthropology and Education Quarterly,* 16(1), 1–7.

Schensul, J. J. (1987). Knowledge utilization: An anthropological perspective. *Practicing Anthropology,* 9(4), 2–4.

Schensul, J. J. (1990). Organizing cultural diversity through the arts. *in* T. Carroll and J. J. Schensul (Eds.), Cultural diversity and the future of education: Visions of America (special issue of the Education and Urban Society). Beverly Hills, CA: Sage Publications.

Schensul, J. J., and Caro, E. (1982). The Puerto Rican research and training project. Final Report to the National Institute of Education.

Schensul, J. J., Donelli-Hess, D., Martinez, R., and Borrero, M. Urban comadronas. *In* D. Stull and J. J. Schensul (Eds.), *Collaborative research and social change: Anthropology in action.* Boulder, CO: Westview Press.

Schensul, S. L. (1973). Action research: The applied anthropologist in a community mental health program. *In* A. Redfield (Ed.), *Anthropology beyond the university* (pp. 106–109). Athens: University of Geogia Press.

Schensul, S. L. (1974). Skills needed in action anthropology: Lessons from El Centro de la Causa. *Human Organization, 33,* 203–209.

Schensul, S. L. (1978). Commando research: Innovative approaches to anthropological research. *In Practicing anthropology,* 1(1), 1–3.

Schensul, S. L. (1981). The Area Health Education Center Program. *Practicing Anthropology,* 3(3), 15–16.

Schensul, S. L. (1985). Science, theory and application in collaborative research and social policy. *In* J. Schensul and S. Stern (Eds.), *Applied behavioral scientist,* 29(2), 164–185.

Schensul, S. S., and Bymel, M. (1975). The role of applied research in the development of health services in a Chicano community in Chicago. *In* S. Ingram and J. Altschuler (Eds.), *Topias and utopias in health* (pp. 77–96). The Hague: Mouton Press.

Schensul, S. L., and Schensul, J. J. (1978). Advocacy and applied anthropology. *In* G. H. Weber and G. McCall (Eds.) *Social scientists as advocates: Views from the applied disciplines,* (pp. 121–166). Beverly Hills, CA: Sage Publications.

Schensul, S. L., and Schensul, J. J. (1982). Self help groups and advocacy: A contrast in beliefs and strategies. *In* G. Weber and L. Cohen (Eds.), *Beliefs and self-help: Cross cultural perspectives and approaches* (pp. 298–336). New York: Human Sciences Inc.

Sieber, S., Louis, K. S., and Metzger, L. (1972). *The use of educational knowledge.* New York: Columbia University Bureau of Applied Social Research.

Stern, G. (1985). Research, action and social betterment in Collaborative Research and Social Policy. *In* J. Schensul and S. Stern (Eds.), *Applied Behavioral Scientist,* 29(2), 229–248.

Stull, D., and Schensul, J. (1987). *Collaborative research and social change.* Boulder, CO: Westview Press.

Tax, S. (1958). Values in action: The Fox project. *Human organization,* 17, 17–20.

Wetle, T., Schensul, S., Torres, M., and Mayen, M. (1989). Identifying symptoms of Alzheimer's disease among elderly Puerto Ricans and their family caregivers. *Newsletter of the University of Connecticut Travelers Center on Aging,* 3(2), 1–3.

CHAPTER 5

❑ Ethnographic Microanalysis of Interaction

Frederick Erickson

The Handbook of Qualitative Research in Education

The Interface between Ethnography and Microanalysis

Intellectual Antecedents and Aims of Microanalysis

One of the main purposes or ethnography in educational research is to reveal what is inside the "black boxes" of ordinary life in educational settings by identifying and documenting the processes by which educational outcomes are produced. Those processes consist of the routine actions and sensemaking of participants in educational settings, which, because they are habitual and local, may go unnoticed by practitioners and researchers alike. The close study of interaction through ethnographically oriented analysis of audiovisual records is a potentially useful component of an ethnographic study of education. It is not an alternative to more general ethnography but, rather, a complement to it.

To understand the relations between ethnographic microanalysis and more general ethnography, reviewing the intellectual roots of the approach to microanalysis of interaction that is being discussed in this chapter is useful. Ethnographic microanalysis of interaction derives from five streams of work, the first four of which are closely related substantively and historically.

The first approach, often termed *context analysis*, emerged in the early 1950s. It was influenced strongly by Bateson and Mead and involved anthropologists, linguists, and psychiatrists (see Kendon, 1990; Birdwhistell, 1970; McQuown, 1971; Pittenger, Hockett, and Danehy, 1960; Scheflen, 1973). A parallel effort was undertaken by Hall and Trager (1953) and by Hall (1968). Context analysis aimed to take account of the organization of verbal and nonverbal behavior as it occurs simultaneously during the conduct of interaction. This was done through detailed transcription of cinema film of naturally occurring interaction and by analysis of those transcripts. Because of cost and of technical limits in how long cinema film could be shot continuously, the events considered by context analysis tended to be single instances, usually lasting no longer than an hour and often much shorter than that.

The second influence on ethnographic microanalysis comes from the *ethnography of communication*. This approach was developed by linguistic anthropologists (see especially collections edited by Gumperz and Hymes, 1964, 1972; Bauman and Sherzer, 1974; and essays by Bauman and Sherzer, 1975; Hymes, 1974). The ethnography of communication focused on the social meaning of stylistic variation in communication within and across bounded cultural groups that were considered speech communities. Much of this work was done primarily by participant observation (e.g., Frake, 1975; Irvine, 1974). Gumperz especially was interested in the moment-by-moment organization of the conduct of interaction. For data collection and analysis, he used audio recording over several hours at a time and, more recently, used video recording as well (see Blom and Gumperz, 1972; Gumperz, 1982).

A third major influence was the perspective on interaction and on the presentation of self in encounters that developed in the work of the sociologist Goffman (1959, 1961, 1981; see also the review essays in Drew and Wooton, 1988). Goffman emphasized the encounter as an attentionally focused gathering in which aspects of the self were strategically revealed and concealed through ritual display and interactional routine. To collect evidence, Goffman primarily used participant observation. He also reviewed literature and still photography to glean insights on significant moments in interaction.

The first three of the influences noted here emerged before ethnographic microanalysis developed. The fourth and fifth influences developed contemporaneously with it. The fourth influence comes from *conversational analysis* in sociology (Schegloff, 1968; Sacks, Schegloff, and Jefferson, 1974; Schenkein, 1978). In contrast to the emphasis on cultural and linguistic patterning of ritualized aspects of interaction (exogenous sources of order in interaction) that characterized both the ethnography of communication and Goffman's work, conversational analysis has emphasized the emergent, endogenous organization of interaction and active sensemaking by its participants. Conversational analysis considers interaction as it is improvised by social actors who attend closely to what one another are doing and have just done in immediately present and past moments during the ongoing course of interaction.

A fifth influence on ethnographic microanalysis comes from various continental scholars who see communicative action as a discursive practice that manifests power relations among social actors (see Bourdieu, 1977; Habermas, 1979; Foucault, 1979; Bakhtin, 1981). From this perspective, certain key institutional relations manifested in interaction (e.g., those between jailers and prisoners, physicians and patients, supervisors and workers in industry, and educators and students) are seen as reproducing in microcosm symbolic relations of power asymmetry that obtain in society as a whole and are ramified throughout it. [Such analysis of large-scale modern societies recalls the interactionally focused analysis of a small-scale traditional society undertaken by Bateson in *Naven* (1958).] Interaction in institutional settings is seen as framing distinct definitions of self and voice, marking the boundaries of human agency that are possible in modern class-stratified societies. [It should be noted that this chapter presents a summary discussion of the orientation and conduct of ethnographic microanalysis. For richer notions of this work, the reader should consult especially Kendon (1990:15–49), Scheflen (1973), and McDermott and Roth (1978) and, on its intellectual antecedents and aims, Hymes (1974). More detailed discussions of method are found in Erickson (1982), Erickson and Shultz (1977, 1982), and Grimshaw (1982). Discussions of connections between ethnographic methods in education and in sociolinguistics are found in Erickson (1986/1990, 1988). Some examples of microanalytic research in education are found in Au (1980), Barnhardt (1982), Bremme and Erickson (1977), Erickson and Mohatt (1982), Fiksdal (1990), the chapters in Green and Wallat (1981), Heath (1986), McDermott and Gospodinoff (1979), Mehan (1979), Shultz, (1979), and Shultz and Florio (1979).]

We have considered the origins of and influences on ethnographic microanalysis of interaction. Now let us consider its substantive emphases within educational research. Ethnographically oriented microanalysis of interaction shares with more general educational ethnography the aim of specifying and describing those local processes that produce outcomes in educational settings, but its purpose is to document those processes in even greater detail and precision than is possible with ordinary participant observation and interviewing. Another purpose of taking a very close look at interaction is to test carefully the validity of characterizations of intent and meaning that more general ethnography may claim for the participants who are studied. Yet another purpose of microanalysis can be to identify *how* routine processes of interaction are organized, in contrast to describing *what* interaction occurs.

Given that ethnographic microanalysis is even more labor-intensive than ordinary ethnography, it should not be used unless it is really needed. Not all topics of inquiry are best addressed by this approach. What are some reasons for investing the time and effort that is necessary for the microanalysis of interaction within an ethnographic study of education?

Ethnographic microanalysis of audiovisual recordings is a means of specifying learning environments and processes of social influence as they occur in face-to-face interaction. It is especially appropriate when such events are rare or fleeting in duration or when the distinctive shape and character of such events unfolds moment by moment, during which it is important to have accurate information on the speech and nonverbal behavior of particular participants in the scene. It is also important when one wishes to identify subtle nuances of meaning that occur in speech and nonverbal action—subtleties that may be shifting over the course of activity that takes place. Verification of these nuances of meaning—especially of implicitly or cryptically expressed meaning—can help us see more clearly the *experience in practice* of educational practitioners—learners, teachers, administrators.

The microanalytic study of *how* interaction occurs is especially appropriate when one wishes to reproduce an exemplary practice (e.g., the kind of classroom conversation in which students and teachers are excitedly engaged in reasoning together, as contrasted to a conversation that never quite got off the ground intellectually or that failed to maintain group morale). Detailed analysis of the *how* of interaction, in contrast to emphasis on its *what,* is also appropriate when one wants to change an existing educational practice (e.g., to alter a conversation that never quite gets started or to the point so that it can become a rich and engaging interactional environment for learning).

In attempting to change interaction patterns, it is often important to see their social ecology as richly and precisely as possible—to see, for example, how listeners influence speakers while the speakers are talking, how the timing of speech and nonverbal action can make intellectual points more or less salient and coherent in group discussion, or how reinvoking something said earlier in a conversation can make clear to participants where their thinking together has been heading and how it has been developing. Advice to teachers such as "state goals first" or "clarify when students are confused" is not of much use unless the giver of advice can specify and illustrate the processes of oral discourse that are being recommended. As educators attempt to accomplish more richly intellectual instruction with a wide variety of learners—to teach more for reasoning than for knowledge of simple facts, to engage learners in interaction within their various "zones of proximal development," and to provide instruction in interaction that is inherently motivating—the organization of interaction itself as a medium for high-quality instruction becomes more and more significant as a focus of attention in educational research.

If, however, ordinary narrative description of events can report educational processes in sufficient detail so that their organization is clear to a reader (or if the most crucial kinds of social influence in the setting are mediated through writing or other indirect channels of communication that extend the exercise of social influence across time and space beyond immediate encounters), then the researcher is well advised not to attempt microanalysis of videotapes or films of naturally occurring interaction face to face. Such data collection and analysis would not be prudent in such cases because it is so labor-intensive.

Moreover, even microanalytic research, when it is done from an ethnographic perspective, always involves a combination of ranges in scope and specificity of attention and in more and less labor-intensive methods. In the work I will describe here, ethnographic interest in combining levels or aspects of social organization, describing broad patterns that characterize institutions and communities and focusing narrowly and precisely on the particular communicative actions of specific individuals, leads the researcher to attend not only to information that is available "on the screen" but to information that comes from beyond the screen, from wider participant observation and from social research more generally.

Ethnographic Microanalysis of Interaction

Ethnographic Microanalysis as Sampling: An Overview of the Research Process

Two issues are crucial for ethnographic microanalysis: (1) identifying the *full range of variation* in the organization of interaction in whatever setting, network, or community one is studying and (2) establishing the *typicality and atypicality* (relative frequency of occurrence) of various event types and modes of interactional organization (and of particular instances of these) across the full range of diversity in social relations to be found in the setting, network, or community. One determines the range of variation and the relative typicality or atypicality of instances in the data corpus through data collection that involves deliberate sampling. Sampling is fundamental in this research approach because of a primary substantive interest. This is to determine the range and conditions of variation in the organization of interaction within and across different social and cultural groups or networks and within and across particular interactional events that occur in the lives of members of those groups or networks.

To put it in slightly different terms, we are interested here in uniting what anthropologists have come to call the ethnography of communication with its microanalysis. Research begins by sampling comprehensively through general participant observation and then moving in successive stages to more restricted sampling through increasingly focused observation and audiovisual recording. Consider, for example, a particular social setting—the elementary school classroom in which all members are present during the school day. In beginning the study of such a setting, one would first do participant observation in that setting across the full day and then, ideally, videotape or film one or more full days, turning the camera or cameras on before school began and then continuing to record until after all the members had left the classroom. One would also observe and record the routine interactions of students outside school, in their homes and communities, as well as those of the teacher outside school, to compare the variation in the organization of interaction inside school with that experienced in the whole lives of school participants outside school.

Having collected instances along the full range of different types of events in the various settings of interest, the next issue is to determine the typicality of the events and modes of organization within events. This can be done in part by repeated participant observation and in part by somewhat more selective videotaping in which contrasting kinds of events during portions of the day would be repeatedly videotaped.

Making any film or videotape involves sampling decisions, of which the most obvious are when to turn the camera on and off and where to point it. Any audiovisual record is an incomplete document of what actually happened, even though a continuously shot film or tape is a more complete record than the participant observer's field notes. Decisions about what to record and how to record it, then, are not neutral. They are research decisions that should be informed by the overall conduct of participant observation in the study.

Videotapes are indexed according to the events and participants that appear on them. By reviewing contrasting events and sets of participants on the tapes and by reviewing the indexes, which show multiple instances of these contrasting events, the researcher can identify key contrasts—based on the scale, instrumental or expressive focus, mode of leadership, or any other dimension of theoretic interest in the study, according to which events can be characterized and contrasted. By this process, the researcher identifies a set of contrasting event types or a set of contrasting modes of interactional organization that appear in a variety of event types. Additional instances of these contrasting event types or modes of organization within an event are then collected.

Up to this point, attention has been focused mainly on recurring events. Once decisions have been made about key analytic contrasts according to which more focused sampling of instances of events can be done, rare events or unique events may become of interest. These may also be recorded, together with the multiple instances of frequently recurring events that are of special interest.

In this process, the researcher begins with exceedingly inclusive recording at the beginning of inquiry to ensure that a wide range of event types and modes of organization are present in the corpus of recorded material. The research moves, in later stages of the inquiry, to a more focused approach to recording to ensure that multiple instances of certain types are present in the corpus of research materials. Thus, the generalizability *within the corpus* of conclusions derived from close analysis of few instances can be tested. Having demonstrated generalizability *within the case* (here, one school classroom), the researcher can then conduct research to test the generalizability of findings *across cases* (other classrooms, other kinds of settings).

Comparison and Contrast with Participant Observation

Progressive problem-solving is inherent in the methods of ethnographic participant observation and in the methods of sociolinguistic microanalysis of audiovisual records of human interaction. In both approaches, the researcher is attempting to understand events whose structure is too complex to be comprehended all at once, given the limits on human information processing. These limits are compensated for in participant observation by spending time in the field setting. The limits are compensated for in microanalysis by spending time reviewing the audiovisual record and often by reviewing field notes as well.

In the fieldwork setting, the participant observer waits for particular types of recurrent events to keep coming around (e.g., disputes over land tenure, deaths, births, preparing the main meal of the day, seeing the next client at the unemployment office). The researcher may seek out particular sites within a field setting where a particular type of event is most likely to happen. This gives the participant observer a situation analogous to that of the subject in a learning experiment—the opportunity to have multiple trials at a similar task (in this case, the task of observing and analyzing a particular event type).

Across each trial at observing a recurrent event, the participant observer can alter slightly the focus of analytic attention, each time attending to some features of what is occurring and not attending to others. The observer can also vary the focus of attention in rereading field notes taken during the event. Despite the limits on the researcher's information-processing capacity, long-term observation and reflection enables the observer to develop an interpretive model for the organization of the event. These models are progressively constructed through learning across a series of partial observations. Hence, fieldwork can be thought of as a kind of naturally occurring learning experiment in which the learner acquires mastery across repeated trials.

In fieldwork, two sets of procedural decisions have special importance for correcting what is traditionally thought of as bias in sampling and observation: (1) the decisions the observer makes about where to be in physical and social space and time in the field setting and (2) the decisions the observer makes about the foci of attention in any one occasion of observation. The former affects the overall sampling of events that the participant observer makes; the latter affects the completeness of observations made cumulatively across a set of trials.

A major strength of participant observation is the opportunity to learn through active participation—one can test one's theory of the organization of an event by trying out various kinds of participation in it. Major limitations are the partialness of view of any single event and a tendency, therefore, toward bias in sampling in favor of the frequently occurring event types (because those are the ones one comes to understand most fully across time). There is also a bias toward the typical in another sense. Given the limits on what can be attended to observationally during any one trial, the observer's attention may become dominated early on by the focus of the emerging theory of organization. Observation may be devoted mainly to those aspects of action that confirm the theory, overlooking other aspects of action that might disconfirm it. Consequently, the potentially disconfirming evidence is less likely to be recorded in the field notes than is the potentially confirming evidence. I have called this elsewhere a tendency toward *hypertypification* in primary data collection (Erickson, 1988).

In contrast ot the participant observer, the analyst of audiovisual documents does not have to wait for instances of a particular event type to occur. The researcher *revisits* a particular set of instances by replaying the tape or film. The ability to revisit the same event for repeated observations is the chief innovation in audiovisual documentary research. In this way, the analyst is freed from the limits of the sequential occurrence of events in real time. He or she searches the recorded *corpus* of tapes for instances of events, moving as it were back and forth through time and space to identify analogous instances. This innovation of revisiting real-time records of interaction in events has distinctive strengths and limitations.

The first strength is the *capacity for completeness of analysis*. Because of the (theoretically) unlimited opportunities to revisit the recorded instance by replaying it, the instance can be observed from a variety of attentional foci. This enables a much more thorough description than those prepared by a participant observer from field notes.

A second strength is the *potential to reduce the dependence of the observer on premature interpretation*. Because a recorded instance can be replayed, the observer has opportunity for deliberation. He or she can hold in abeyance interpretive judgments about the function (meaning) of the actions observed. Especially in the early stages of fieldwork, these interpretive inferences can be faulty. In microanalysis, the opportunity to look and listen more than once relieves the observer's tendency to leap too soon to inferences of intent, interpretively shooting from the hip from moment to moment in real time.

A third strength in the analysis of audiovisual records is that it *reduces the dependence of the observer on frequently occurring events* as the best source of data. In participant observation it is the frequent event that one comes to understand best. The rare event can be understood only very partially. For the analyst of an audiovisual record, however, the rare event can be studied quite thoroughly through repeated reviewing.

Independence from the limits of real time in observation produces a profound qualitative difference in the conduct of inquiry from that which characterizes participant observation. However, the use of audiovisual records as a primary data source has two principal weaknesses, or limitations. The first and most fundamental is that replaying a film or videotape only permits the analyst to interact with it vicariously. No opportunity exists to test one's emerging interpretive theories by trying them out as an active participant in the scene. Such opportunity is the hallmark of participant observation, but that kind of learning is not available to the nonparticipant observer replaying an audiovisual record.

The second limitation is that in order to make interpretive sense of the recorded material the analyst usually needs to have access to contextual information that is not available on the recording itself. The everyday event of face-to-face interaction that is recorded is embedded in a variety of circumstances—in the life histories and social networks of the participants in the events and in the broader societal circumstances of the events, including the ethnic, social class, and cultural group membership of the participants. Marx said that persons make history, but not in circumstances of their own choosing. Analyzing the interaction that occurs in a particular event in relation to the broader circumstances of choice and constraint within which the event itself occurs is what makes ethnographic microanalysis "ethnographic."

Those broader circumstances are identified, documented, and collated by means other than audiovisual recording, transcription, and microanalysis.

Both limitations—the absence of participation as a means of learning and the absence of contextual information beyond the frame of the screen—can be overcome by combining participant observation and the collection and analysis of demographic and historical data with the analysis of audiovisual records (see Corsaro, 1982). The description of audiovisual data collection and analysis that follows presumes that participant observation was done in addition to filming or videotaping, so as to set the events on the tapes within the wider histories of which they are a part.

Methods of Data Collection: Entry, Ethics, and Obtrusiveness

Entering and working in a setting as a researcher involves a continuous process of negotiation, whether one is a participant observer who visits the setting intermittently or one is an "observant participant" who begins to study, as a researcher, the setting in which one is continuously present as a member.

My experience has been that entry to do participant observational research that also involves audiovisual recording is no more or less difficult than entry to do general participant observation. Current technology makes recording quite unobtrusive. The growing use of home video cameras demystifies the recording process. The ubiquity of "instant replay" in broadcasts of sports events makes intuitively sensible the notion that the researcher (and often those studied as well) will learn by reviewing tapes of everyday occurrences. Thus, audiovisual recording for research purposes is increasingly easy to explain and justify.

One chief stumbling block concerns people's fear of potential embarrassment. The most serious embarrassment might result from exposure of people's routine conduct to their supervisors in the setting, if those persons should somehow have access to the tapes. The possibility that anonymous audiences of researchers at conferences, or of students in classes at a university, might view the tapes seems far less threatening than does the possibility of scrutiny by one's peers and immediate superiors. Accordingly, if explicit assurances are made about strict limits on access to the tapes by others in the local setting, then the process of entry is greatly facilitated. Because of this, the discussion that follows emphasizes issues of access to the tapes and genuinely informed consent. When those issues are addressed directly, entry does not present special problems.

Before beginning to videotape in a setting, one needs to have explained one's purposes and to have gained written consent or oral assent from those concerned in the study. Appropriate procedures for gaining consent vary across situations. In most aspects, these procedures are the same for audiovisual recording and analysis as for the more usual kinds of participant observation. Consent procedures for ethnographic research are discussed generally in standard texts (e.g., Hammersley and Atkinson, 1983).

With audiovisual recordings, confidentiality is the ethical issue that seems most salient. It is indeed important, but not as an issue in itself. Rather, confidentiality can be seen as part of a larger issue—the fundamental ethical requirement of the researcher to prevent harm coming to those studied through the processes by which they are studied. "Harm" varies across different kinds of research. In medical research, harm can involve physical pain, illness, or even death. In social research, harm can involve embarrassment, administrative punishment, or legal punishment. Embarrassment is usually the most serious harm that occurs. Maintaining confidentiality by not revealing the individual identities of those studied is a means by which social researchers reduce the risk of harm to those studied.

However, in ethnographic research, it often is difficult to mask the identities of all the persons studied in a setting or community. People fear videotaping because it might blow their cover instantly. They might be recorded doing something wrong and then might be seen in that dereliction by those with the power to embarrass or punish. What is sensitive, then, is not necessarily what is recorded, but who might see it and when. Risk of harm through embarrassment or punishment can be minimized by recording only innocuous interaction, or by giving those recorded the right to ask to have material erased after it is recorded. Even more importantly, however, risk can be minimized through negotiated agreements about who will have access to the tapes once recorded. If those in a position to punish will never see the tapes, or will only see them long after the events that were recorded took place, then the risk of harm coming from being videotaped is dramatically reduced.

In a study of classroom interaction, for example, if the teacher knows that no fellow teachers or administrators will see tapes made in the classroom—or will only see footage previously reviewed by the teacher, and that footage only later in the school year—the conditions of risk are far different from those that would exist were access to the tapes left unrestricted when consent was negotiated. (It should be noted that students or classroom aides may need similar protection from instant review by the teacher if the students or aides are video-taped doing things the teacher could not attend to in the normal course of teaching.) Conversely, access to tape review might be wide, if care-fully negotiated. For example, in a collaborative action research project, a group of teachers and the principal might agree to review tapes across classrooms soon after the time of recording. In such a situation, access might be restricted to exclude those outside the colla-borative team, such as central office personnel and members of the school board. An agreement would stipulate that such persons would not seek access to the tapes, while access would be open within the action research team.

In each particular setting, researchers and those they study must determine together which kinds of people are liable to which kinds of harm if various individuals review particular kinds of recorded footage in specific time frames and in distinct social circumstances under which screening takes place. Written agreements can then be prepared that protect the interests of those most at risk, given the particular local circumstances. In all cases, storing the original tapes and files of notes using retrieval codes that do not identify individuals or sites by name can help reduce risk and anxiety.

Long-term uses of the footage should also be anticipated. During the initial negotiations, an ethics review committee can be established for the project. Such a committee could decide on future uses of the research footage. This is preferable to agreeing to destroy the original tapes after the fieldwork is completed or a final report is prepared. Because microanalysis takes so much time, it is in the researcher's interest to be able to keep the tapes for future study; however, this needs to be done in an ethically responsible way.

In my previous work, thorough negotiation of the uses of recorded footage, far from making people anxious, reduces their fears and makes the process of audiovisual recording something ordinary and under-standable. This is not only of value to those studied but also to the researcher. Especially when inexperienced in using audiovisual re-cording in an ethnographic study, the researcher may be overly anx-ious about the mystique of the machinery and its uses. If the researcher thinks of the camera as a penetrating eye and of the tapes as radioactive and pulsing while sitting on the shelf, that anxiety will be communicated to the persons who are being studied. In other words, prudence and explicitness in negotiating the ethical issues involved in videotaping not only prevents breaches of ethics but also reduces the sensitivity of videotaping and the projections that can arise around it for all parties involved, including the researcher.

The same is true for the process of audiovisual recording in the field. Byers (1966) noted that cameras don't take pictures—people do. Field recording is a human transaction, just as is all other interaction during participant observational research. If the researcher is trustworthy and unobtrusive at the scene of research, then the equipment will be too. If the person of the researcher is somehow suspect, then the equipment also will be suspect. The same activities by which rapport and trust are established by the human researcher in the setting—following ethically responsible negotiation of entry—are those by which the recording process becomes unobtrusive.

It follows that elaborate technical efforts to reduce the visibility of recording (e.g., one-way mirrors and concealed microphones) are not necessary. If the people being taped know about and agree with the purposes of the taping and trust the researcher, the video equipment will be no more obtrusive than a note pad or audio recorder. One cautionary note is necessary, however. It is important that the researcher be familiar with the equipment and its operation. Before coming to the setting, it is wise to rehearse recording thoroughly in all its stages—carrying equipment into a space, setting it up, recording, taking it down, and packing and carrying it out. This is especially important when working as a team of researchers. Every member of the team should be familiar with what needs to be done so that the equipment, and work relationships within the team, can be handled smoothly. When possible, it is also wise to bring equipment to the setting and test it out before regular recording is to begin, checking lighting conditions, microphone placements, sound and picture quality, and matters of teamwork.

Once recording begins, simplicity is the watchword. The most useful research footage is made in the most technically simple ways. The camera does not move much, as many people as possible appear within the visual frame, and shooting is continuous over long strips of interaction in the setting. That is the opposite of the way studio-edited documentary footage looks in a finished film or "camera-edited" home video footage looks, in an attempt to imitate the conventions of documentary film narrative. For use as a primary research document, a video record needs only three things: (1) visual framing that is consistent across time (not zooming in and out or panning from side to side for narrative emphasis), (2) a clear picture, and (3) a clear sound.

In the approach to microanalysis discussed here, continuous sequences of activity are emphasized, because *interaction* in its fullest sense is the phenomenon of research interest (i.e., what all the interactional partners' vebal and nonverbal activity is contributing to the total social ecology of communication in the event). Hence, in shooting primary research footage, it is not necessary to move equipment or adjust it as frequently as when one is shooting documentary footage. The camera can be put on a tripod, turned on, and walked away from frequently if the action being recorded remains stable in front of the camera. Even with a hand-held camera one can move slowly and smoothly. By judicious, slow use of a zoom lens, one can avoid coming close to the people whose interaction is being recorded.

It should be mentioned that there has been considerable debate about the relative merits of shooting for research purposes with a fixed camera or moving camera. Some of the issues in that debate are summarized by Grimshaw (1982:121–144), who argues for a moving camera. Given the approach to analysis taken in this chapter, however, relatively fixed camera shooting is the most appropriate, especially in the early stages of field recording.

Keeping a camera relatively stationary when on a tripod or when hand-held and including within the visual frame as much as possible of all the bodies of all the participants in the interactional event that is being recorded makes for the most comprehensive research documents. It is wise to begin recording a few minutes before the event in which you are especially interested begins and to continue recording for a few minutes after you think the event has ended. ("Beginnings" and "endings" are analytic judgments made by researchers and members. Early in a study, your notions of the boundaries of events may not match those of the members. Moreover, members' activity in preinitiation and postconclusion of events often appears to be significant when one is reviewing footage; thus, recording material that may seem on the scene to be extra footage often turns out to be useful later.)

There are tradeoffs, of course. One sacrifices visual and auditory detail for comprehensiveness in recording. As participant observation continues and you become more familiar with the organization of the routine events that are being recorded, you may wish to become more selective in recording to increase visual and auditory detail. For greater visual selectivity, you might tighten the shots somewhat using the zoom lens or you might hand-hold the camera. For greater audio selectivity, you might use microphones suspended from the ceiling, a

"shotgun mike" hand-held by an assistant, or a wireless radio microphone placed on one of the participants you are recording. Your shooting would be still wider (in visual and audio framing) than in ordinary
documentary or broadcast filming. This will make the pictures not
quite so pretty and the sound more penetrated by ambient noise than in
professionally shot footage, but your footage will be more useful for
microanalysis. Be sure to avoid the cinema and broadcast "talk show"
convention of moving the camera shot back and forth between
speakers as they alternate turns at talk. As much as possible, keep all
the relevant participants in the visual frame. The visual detail you
sacrifice (and the backs of some participants' necks you will shoot) will
be worth it because of the value of comprehensive footage that enables
you to see the reactions of listeners while the speaker is speaking.
Because *interaction* is the phenomenon of interest, and interaction is
mutually constructed in the simultaneous activities of speakers and
hearers, the visual frame needs to include as many hearers as possible
together with the speakers.

In classrooms especially, it can be useful to use two recording
systems simultaneously. One stationary camera shooting continuously
at wide angle and recording sound with the microphone on the camera
can be used in tandem with a hand-held camera that records sound
with an external microphone and records a more tightly focused visual
frame than the wide angle shot from the other camera. That way one
maximizes both scope and specificity in documenting events.

A final note on recording. When purchasing equipment, it is wise
to look for a camera with a digital stopwatch feature, by which time in
minutes, seconds, and microseconds can be printed on the tape as it is
initially recorded. During playback, the stopwatch is visible on the
screen. This is very useful for subsequent analysis. If you cannot
record a digital clock image on the original footage, then use a *time–
date generator* to record a clock image on a working copy of the
original. (Your research budget should include, in addition to the
footage you plan to shoot in the field, 25% additional footage for copying for later microanalysis. Do not use your original footage for analysis: Always copy it first.)

Footage should be stored with labels containing codes for individuals and sites—not the actual names—and the date of recording. If
field notes were written, they should be filed using the same identification code and same series order as the tapes. Even if it was not
possible to write continuous field notes while recording, one should
keep rough notes indicating the times at which events changed during
the time of recording. A card summarizing the recorded activities
and their durations can be attached to the tape or filed separately,

to be used as a rough index during subsequent analysis. Field notes should also indicate the actual times at which activity shifted during recording. Those notes then can also serve an indexing function. Having an index saves a great deal of time in later reviewing of tapes.

Issues in Data Analysis

As in ordinary participant observation, analysis actually begins while in the field. Choosing which events or persons to record involves making initial analytic decisions. Moving to greater visual and audio selectivity at later stages of recording represents another set of analytic judgments. Most of the analytic work, however, is done after fieldwork is completed.

The approach to analysis reviewed here is discussed in greater detail in Erickson (1982) and in Erickson and Shultz (1982). In essence, it proceeds similarly to the analysis of other kinds of participant observational data—one begins by considering whole events, continues by analytically decomposing them into smaller fragments, and then concludes by *recomposing* them into wholes. The latter of those three stages distinguishes ethnographic microanalysis from detailed analytic work such as morphophonemic and phonetic analysis in linguistics or microbehavioral analysis in psychology. In even more modern discourse analysis in linguistics, small units once identified analytically are not often recomposed in the research report. The ethnographic reconstruction of detailed phenomena of interactional behavior returns them to a level of sequentially connected social action, as regarded in a kind of narrative understanding that is akin to that held by the actors in the events themselves. The microanalytic case studies of interaction that result become part of the larger stories and sets of stories out of which an ethnographer's report is constructed.

Stage One: Reviewing the Whole Event

Using the original footage, one starts by reviewing a whole event at regular speed, without stopping at any point along the way. Beginning the review a few mintues before the event's putative beginning and continuing the review a few minutes after the event's putative ending, the researcher watches, listens, and writes the equivalent of field notes that describe the activity on the tape. The notes identify the approximate locations in time of major shifts in activity within the event and identify strips of talk or of nonverbal action that may be of special interest at various points.

Stage Two: Identifying Major Constituent Parts of the Event

The locations of major segment boundaries are checked in a second viewing, during which the researcher may play the tape back and forth across a putative boundary to identify it more precisely. Often there are at least three major sequential parts in an interactional event: a phase of getting started, a phase of main instrumental focus, and a phase of winding up on the way to the next event. The central portion of the event may sometimes be further differentiated, as may the opening and closing phases.

Shifts in the physical arrangement of participants in space often accompany shifts in the social arrangement of participation. Attention to changes in physical arrangement can provide clues to subtle shifts in the nature of activity in the event. Posture, shared gaze, and interpersonal distance define the patterns of physical relations among participants, termed *F-formations* by Kendon (1990:209–237). Relational roles, social identities, and rankings are aspects of the overall pattern of social organization, termed the *participation framework* by Goffman (1981:137) and the *social participation structure* by Erickson and Shultz (see Erickson and Shultz, 1977, 1982:17–18; Erickson, 1986/1990). Usually from one major constituent phase in an event to the next there is a rearrangement in both F-formation and social participation structure. As activity changes from moment to moment, so does the ecology of relations among the social actors.

Stage Three: Identifying Aspects of Organization within Major Parts of the Event

Having identified the boundaries of main segments in the event, the researcher examines particular main segments of interest. These will often be found to contain consitituent parts or subsegments. The boundaries of those parts are identified, using the same approach employed in stage two. Various sequential strips of activity will be identified. At this level of analysis, the strips of talk or nonverbal action may be defined by topically connected speech and various kinds of discourse routines, or they may be defined primarily by connected sequences of nonverbal action (e.g., a child piling a series of blocks up and then knocking them down, a teacher and student arranging laboratory apparatus for a chemistry experiment). Within the strips thus defined, the analyst identifies the social participation structure in even greater detail than in stage two, specifying the relative contributions of the various participants in the event. For example, in one strip a primary speaker may be accompanied by some listeners who speak a little while listening and by other listeners who show attention by gaze and nodding. In the next strip, three primary speakers may overlap in speech, while the remaining members of the audience show attention both nonverbally and in brief bursts of speech. We might characterize the two strips globally by saying that participation was more animated in the second than in the first. More precisely, however, we could identify a change in the ecology of social participation by noting that there was one primary speaker in the first strip, receiving two different kinds of attention from different parts of the audience, while in the second strip participation divided into two main types—that of the three primary speakers and that of the rest of the group as audience.

The emphasis here is on the dialectical, ecological relationships of mutual influence among participants in the event, not on the actions of individual persons considered in isolation from the actions of others.

Stage Four: Focus on Actions of Individuals

The fourth stage involves detailed transcription of the verbal and nonverbal behavior of individuals in the strips of sequentially connected action that were identified in stage three. Here the kinds of transcription done by linguists, discourse analysts, and researchers in nonverbal communication are prepared. Transcription is theoretically guided; that is, transcription conventions vary depending on the analytic purposes of the researcher (for discussion, see Ochs, 1979). Ideally a transcription should show relationships between the activity of the various participants. For example, if the speech of one person is shown, the simultaneous nonverbal listening actions of a listener should be shown in the transcript in such a way that not only the occurrence of the nonverbal action of the listener is noted, but its sequential position (and, possibly, its real-time duration) in relation to the speaker's speech is displayed.

At this level of detail, cultural differences in customary ways of organizing interaction become most fully apparent. Culturally differing ways of organizing the specific conduct of interaction may confuse students, making events that are organized in culturally unfamiliar ways quite distinctive kinds of learning environments for them subjectively, in contrast to events in which the patterns of interactional organization that occur are culturally familiar ones. Such differences in the detailed organization of interaction may make for the experience of events so organized as qualitatively differing kinds of learning environments for persons of differing cultural background or temperamental disposition. This is why a detailed understanding of the behavioral organization of interactional events has potential significance in educational research: It can help us understand why differing kinds of interaction in teaching and learning situations can be experienced as more or less educative (see the discussion in Cazden, 1988:99–135).

Stage Five: Comparative Analysis of Instances across the Research Corpus

Microanalysis at the level of detail described in stage four is done on strips of interaction that are either typical or atypical of interaction that occurs more generally within the recorded corpus of interaction and within the larger corpus of interaction that was observed and documented in the field notes but was not recorded. After preparing a microanalysis of a single instance, or of a few instances, demonstrating the representativeness of the instances is necessary. This is done by searching the corpus of recordings and field notes for further instances that are analogous to the first. Analogy may be at the level of the named event itself (e.g., all the reading lessons with a certain group of students may be searched for and then reviewed). Analogy could be at the level of a specific function or interactional activity (e.g., looking for all instances of interaction in which someone used humor to persuade, or all instances in which the teacher refocused the attention of the students after they had been distracted). Some sample from the full set of analogous instances may be microanalyzed at the same level of detail as the first instances to be analyzed and transcribed. Others within the set of analogous instances may be analyzed more globally, in less detail than the first. Typical and atypical cases are compared and their relative frequencies can be reported in synoptic charts or frequency tables. Even if every possible instance in the corpus is not analyzed, the researcher must demonstrate that he or she has searched the entire corpus exhaustively. In this way the researcher can claim that possible discrepant cases, which might invalidate the conclusions drawn, were not inadvertently ignored.

Systematic search for patterns of generalization within the corpus strengthens the argument for the representativeness of the instances chosen for microanalysis. Thus, ethnographic microanalysis proceeds by the method of analytic induction in identifying significant phenomena and dimensions of contrast. This is the same inductive approach in

progressive problem-solving that characterizes general ethnography
and related kinds of qualitative social research [see the classic discussion by Lindesmith (1947) and more recent discussion by Hammersley
and Atkinson (1983) and Erickson (1986/1990)].

How are analogous instances identified? Strips of interaction
within major constituent phases of whole interactional events may
exhibit functional relationships of interest (e.g., a particular way of
persuading or explaining, a particular configuration of audience attention and its influence on the speaker, a particular rhythmic organization of nonverbal activity and speech). These *activities* within events
may be identified and searched for across many different interactional
events that are named by participants. In classroom research, for example, patterns of audience attention that influence speakers can be
investigated by looking microanalytically at comparable strips of talk
to audiences in mathematics lessons, in language arts lessons, in opening morning discussion, and in interaction among students on the
playground. Does the organization of audience attention vary systematically across different kinds of speakers and different combinations of
audience membership? Does it vary across differing strategic moments
within events? Is audience attention typically different at the beginnings of certain kinds of classroom events from the way it is organized
near the ends of such events? Such questions of comparison can be
answered by identifying instances across different events and across
different phases within them. The general notes made in stages one
and two of videotape review serve as an index for comparison within
and across the events in the corpus of recorded interaction.

Information derived from participant observation and interviewing also has a place in the comparative microanalysis of instances.
Special local social identities, attitudes, and customs (as well as more
general identities and culture that vary along lines of class, gender,
race, or ethnicity) may bear significantly on the organization of the
interaction that is being studied. For example, in an early-grade
classroom, the best reader among the girls may typically receive a
different kind of attention from classmates from that received by a girl
who is not as good a reader, and Anglo girls who are mediocre readers
may typically receive different attention from their peers than Latinas
who are mediocre readers. The researcher's knowledge through acquaintance and interview of the intentions of a teacher or parent that is
gained through acquaintance and interview also can shape the analytic
interpretation of that adult's interaction with a child.

To avoid haphazard invocation of background information to "explain" what can be seen in the recorded research material, it is necessary to discipline the interpretive use of information from beyond the screen. A good rule is to locate background information only in relation to precise behavioral evidence available from the recording. For example, if certain tones of voice or facial expression were used in the listening behavior of students only when the best reader among the girls was speaking to them, then the inference that her social identity as an excellent reader was relevant to the kind of attention she received from her peers is more justified than if that particular kind of listening behavior were given to a wider variety of speakers.

Conclusion

Microanalysis of interaction in the ethnography of education has been discussed in a survey that began by comparing microanalysis with participant observation, continued by describing ethical and procedural issues in data collection, and concluded by reviewing issues of data analysis. The connections between general ethnography and microanalysis have been stressed throughout.

Notice that even when analytic focus is at its narrowest and most precise—in the transcription of the actions of individuals in fine-grained behavioral detail—this approach emphasizes the social and cultural ecology of meaning and action just as does more general ethnography. This is not "micro" study in isolation from macrosocial processes, nor is it behaviorist in orientation despite its close attention to details of interactional behavior. Transcription and analysis focus on relations of mutual influence that occur between participants, including the ecological relations between speakers and listeners that occur during the real-time enactment of interaction. The phenomenon of interest—interaction as it is socially and culturally organized—is thus seen analytically and characterized in reporting as fundamentally social, a matter of the actions of various participants constituting environments of meaning and influence for the actions of others. Thus, this approach does not simply report what an isolated social actor does at any particular moment. Rather, it shows teachers and learners, in whatever combinations and in whatever settings they may be found, as mutually constituting one another's activity in enacted learning environments that extend across successive moments in real time.

This, then is ethnographically oriented microanalysis, not only because it attempts a cultural description of communicative actions and their local meanings, but because such microanalysis provides an holistic perspective on the conduct of interaction and the processes by which human learning and change take place. Fundamentally, such analysis is not "micro" at all, but "macro" in its interests, just as microbiology and DNA/RNA have fundamental importance in the study of ecology. Ethnographic microanalysis portrays immediate human interaction as the collective activity of individuals in institutionalized relationships who, as they enact daily life locally in recurrent ways, are both reproducing and transforming their own histories and that of the larger society within which they live.

References

Au, K. (1980). Participation structures in a reading lesson with Hawaiian children: Analysis of a culturally appropriate instructional event. *Anthropology and Education Quarterly,* 11(2), 91–115.

Bakhtin, M. (1981). *The dialogic imagination.* Austin: University of Texas Press.

Barnhardt, C. (1982). "Tuning-in": Athabaskan teachers and Athabaskan students. *In Cross-cultural issues in Alaskan education* (Vol. 2). Fairbanks, AK: University of Alaska, Center for Cross-Cultural Studies.

Bateson, G. (1958). *Navén* (2nd ed.). Stanford, CA: Stanford University Press.

Bauman, R., and Sherzer, J. (Eds.). (1974). Explorations in the ethnography of speaking. London and New York: Cambridge University Press.

Bauman, R., and Sherzer, J. (1975). The ethnography of speaking. *Annual Review of Anthropology,* 4, 95–119.

Birdwhistell, R. (1970). *Kinesics and context: Essays on body motion communication.* Philadelphia: University of Pennsylvania Press.

Blom, J., and Gumperz, J. (1972). Social meaning in linguistic structure: Code switching in Norway. *In* J. Gumperz and D. Hymes (Eds.), *Directions in sociolinguistics.* New York: Holt, Rinehart & Winston.

Bourdieu, P. (1977). Outline of a theory of practice. Cambridge and New York. Cambridge University Press.

Bremme, D., and Erickson, F. (1977). Relationships among verbal and nonverbal classroom behaviors. *Theory into Practice,* 16(3), 153–161.

Byers, P. (1966). Cameras don't take pictures. *Columbia University Forum,* 2, 27–31.

Cazden, C. (1988). *Classroom discourse: The language of teaching and learning.* Portsmouth, NH: Heineman.

Corsaro, W. (1982). Something old and something new: The importance of prior ethnography in the collection and analysis of audiovisual data. *Sociological Methods and Research,* 11(2), 145–166.

Drew, P., and Wooton, A. (Eds.). (1988). *Erving Goffman: Exploring the interaction order.* Cambridge and Oxford: Polity Press.

Erickson, F. (1982). Audiovisual records as a primary data source. *In* A. Grimshaw (Ed.), *Sound-image records in social interaction research.* (Special issue of the *Journal of Sociological Methods and Research,* 11(2), 213–232.)

Erickson, F. (1986/1990). Qualitative methods in research on teaching. *In* M. Wittrock (Ed.), *Handbook of research on teaching* (3rd ed., pp. 119–161). New York: Macmillan. (Also, Quantitative methods; qualitative methods (with R. Linn). *AERA, Research in teaching and learning* (Vol. 2). New York: Macmillan.)

Erickson, F. (1988). Ethnographic description. *In* U. Ammon, N. Dittmar, and K. Matthier (Eds.), *An international handbook of the science of language and society* (Vol. 2, pp. 1081–1095). Berlin and New York: Walter deGruyter.

Erickson, F., and Mohatt, G. (1982). The cultural organization of participation structures in two classrooms of Indian students. *In* G. Spindler (Ed.), *Doing the ethnograph of schooling* (pp. 132–174). New York: Holt, Rinehart & Winston.

Erickson, F., and Shultz, J. (1977). When is a context? Some issues and methods in the analysis of social competence. *The Quarterly Newsletter of the Institute for Comparative Human Development,* 1(2), 5–10. *Also in* J. Green and C. Wallat (Eds.), *Ethnography and language in educational settings* (pp. 147–160). Norwood, NJ: Ablex.

Erickson, F., and Shultz, J. (1982). *The counselor as gatekeeper: Social interaction in interviews.* New York: Academic Press.

Fiksdal, S. (1990). *The right time and pace: A microanalysis of cross-cultural gatekeeping interviews.* Norwood, NJ: Ablex.

Foucault, M. (1979). Discipline and punish: The birth of the prison. New York: Random House (Vintage Books).

Frake, C. (1975). How to enter a Yakan house. *In* M. Sanches and B. Blount (Eds.), *Sociocultural dimensions of language use.* New York: Academic Press.

Goffman, E. (1959). *The presentation of self in everyday life.* Indianapolis: Bobbs-Merrill.

Goffman, E. (1961). *Encounters: Two studies in the sociology of interaction.* Indianapolis: Bobbs-Merrill.

Goffman, E. (1981). *Forms of talk.* Philadelphia: University of Pennsylvania Press.

Green, J., and Wallat, C. (Eds.). (1981). *Ethnography and language in educational settings.* Norwood, NJ: Ablex.

Grimshaw, A. (Ed.). (1982). Uses of sound and visual records in studies of social interaction. Special issue of *Journal of Sociological Methods and Research,* 11(2).

Gumperz, J. (1982). *Discourse strategies.* London and New York: Cambridge University Press.

Gumperz, J., and Hymes, D. (1964). The ethnography of communication. *American Anthropologist,* 66(6), Pt. II.

Gumperz, J., and Hymes, D. (1972). *Directions in sociolinguistics: The ethnography of speaking.* New York: Holt, Rinehart & Winston.

Habermas, J. (1979). *Communication and the evolution of society.* Boston: Beacon Press.

Hall, E. (1968). Proxemics. *Current Anthropology,* 9, 83–108.

Hall, E., and Trager, G. (1953). *The analysis of culture.* Washington, DC: American Council of Learned Societies.

Hammersley, M., and Atkinson, P. (1983). *Ethnography: Principles in practice.* London: Tavistock.

Heath, C. (1986). *Body movement and speech in medical interaction.* Cambridge and New York: Cambridge University Press.

Hymes, D. (1974). *Foundations in sociolinguistics: An ethnographic approach.* Philadelphia: University of Pennsylvania Press.

Irvine, J. (1974). Strategies of status manipulation in the Wolof greeting. *In* R. Bauman and J. Scherer (Eds.), *Explorations in the ethnography of speaking.* London and New York: Cambridge University Press.

Kendon, A. (1990). *Conducting interaction: Patterns of behavior in focused encounters.* Cambridge and New York: Cambridge University Press.

Lindesmith, A. (1947). *Addiction and opiates.* Chicago: Aldine.

Mehan, H. (1979). *Learning lessons: Social organization in the classroom.* Cambridge: Harvard University Press.

McDermott, R., and Gospodinoff, K. (1979). Social contexts for ethnic borders and school failure. *In* A. Wolfgang (Ed.), Nonverbal behavior. London and New York: Academic Press.

McDermott, R., and Roth, D. (1978). The social organization of behavior: Interactional approaches. *Annual Review of Anthropology, 7,* 321–345.

McQuown, N. (1971). *The natural history of an interview.* Microfilm collection of Manuscripts on Cultural Anthropology, 15th series, University of Chicago, Joseph Regenstein Library, Department of Photoduplication. Chicago, IL.

Ochs, E. (1979). Transcription as theory. *In* E. Ochs and B. Schieffelin (Eds.), *Developmental pragmatics.* New York: Academic Press.

Pittenger, R., Hocket, C., and Danehy, J. (1960). *The first five minutes: A sample of microscopic interview analysis.* Ithaca, NY: Martineau.

Sacks, H., Schegloff, E., and Jefferson, G. (1974). A simplest systematics for the organization of turn-taking in conversation. *Language, 50,* 696–735.

Scheflen, A. (1973). *Communicational structure: Analysis of a psychotherapy transaction* (formerly *Stream and structure in psychotherapy*). Bloomington: University of Indiana Press.

Schegloff, E. (1968). Sequencing in conversational openings. *American Anthropologist, 70,* 1075–1095.

Schenkein, J. (1978). *Studies in the organization of conversational interaction.* New York: Academic Press.

Shultz, J. (1979). It's not whether you win or lose, it's how you play the game. *In* O. Garnica and M. King (Eds.), *Language, children, and society.* Oxford: Pergamon.

Shultz, J., and Florio, S. (1979). Stop and freeze: The negotiation of social and physical space in a kindergarten first grade classroom. *Anthropology and Education Quarterly, 10*(3), 166–181.

CHAPTER 6

❑ Discourse Analysis

James Paul Gee, Sarah Michaels, and
Mary Catherine O'Connor[1]

The Handbook of Qualitative
Research in Education

The Multifaceted Nature of Discourse Analysis

By entitling a chapter "Discourse Analysis," we may seem to imply that a unified body of theory, method, and practice goes by that name. To the contrary, discourse studies are conducted in a variety of different disciplines with different research traditions, and there is no overarching theory common to all types of discourse analysis. Moreover, our intention in this chapter is not to provide a survey of the studies or the analytical tools that characterize this broad and diverse domain of work; a good and fairly current four-volume handbook on discourse analysis that attempts that task (van Dijk, 1985) already exists.[2] Instead, this chapter will focus specifically on discourse analysis as a method or set of tools for doing qualitative research in the field of education and in various related disciplines such as cognitive psychology, sociology of knowledge, and educational anthropology.

In this introduction section, we will review some general principles that inform all studies of discourse: (1) human discourse is rule-governed and internally structured; (2) it is produced by speakers who are ineluctably situated in a sociohistorical matrix, whose cultural, political, economic, social, and personal realities shape the discourse; and (3) discourse itself constitutes or embodies important aspects of that sociohistorical matrix. In other words, discourse reflects human experience and, at the same time, constitutes important parts of that experience. Thus, discourse analysis may be concerned with any part of human experience touched on or constituted by discourse.

In understanding the place and value of discourse analysis in the realm of educational research, it is important to distinguish between two research "stances" taken in discourse studies, both of which are represented in work we will discuss below. One emphasizes the study of discourse structure for its own sake, and the other focuses on the study of discourse as it relates to other social, cognitive, political, or cultural processes and outcomes.

Discourse Structure as an Object of Study

Grammatical theory has achieved a good deal of success in studying the internal structure ("grammar") of individual sentences (Chomsky, 1981; Radford, 1988). However, any society recognizes many different genres of language, which are typically longer than a single sentence (Bakhtin, 1986; Bauman, 1986; Bauman and Sherzer, 1974; Fowler, 1981; Sherzer, 1983; White, 1973). Following Hymes, we will call these "discourse genres." These genres are things such as stories, arguments, poems, descriptions, conversations of various sorts (e.g., classroom discussions, chats about the weather), and many more, with different cultural groups recognizing somewhat different genres. We will use the word "texts" for specific examples of these discourse genres collected at specific times and places. Texts can be oral, written, or signed (as in American Sign Language), and they can have more than one "author," as in a conversation.

Much discourse analysis focuses on the form, meaning, and regularities of these "suprasentence" texts as representative instances of particular discourse genres. Some analysts are concerned mainly with characterizing these regularities and features within and across languages and cultures, modalities, or historical periods. Such studies may be taxonomic and typological, or they may be a first step in answering a more complex question in which the discourse genre in question plays a role. Some examples of research questions that centrally involve the study of discourse structure for its own sake are the following:

- What forms do mythic narratives take across cultures? Are there universal characteristics that underlie each culture's central narratives?
- Can we characterize spoken versus written discourse by looking at the linguistic particulars of texts in these two modes?
- What are the recurring patterns that constitute cooperative conversation within a particular group?
- Is there a discernable, predictable discourse structure to classroom discourse?
- How does prosody signal text structure within a particular discourse genre?
- How are text-structuring devices that are found in orally coded languages expressed in visually coded languages such as American Sign Language?
- What are the characteristic features of expository versus narrative prose?
- In a particular language, how does the distribution of certain grammatical morphemes reveal the structure of a narrative?

These are generic versions of research topics that have been well represented in various scholarly literatures. Although the ultimate purposes of these studies range widely, all require a detailed analysis of some discourse genre, speech event, or specific instance of language use.

Discourse as Evidence in the Study of Social and Cognitive Processes

Other researchers take as their starting point the discourse or text and attempt to use it as evidence in their investigation of some larger social, cognitive, cultural, political, or psychological process. Because various forms of talk constitute our sociocultural, political, and mental lives, the study of discourse may provide a window into aspects of human life that are otherwise opaque to us. Some examples of questions that are representative of recent research of this kind are the following:

- By looking at the changes between a child's spoken narrative and a written version of that same narrative, what can we learn about the processes of literacy development?
- What can we learn about different cultural groups' folk theories of emotion by looking at the way language is used to socialize children into the affective realm?
- In students' talk about magnetism in a science class, are there discursive features that may reflect different mental models of that domain?
- What can we learn about social and interpersonal dynamics of power and control by looking at patterns of initiations and responses in conversations (e.g., who initiates topics; whose topic initiations are ignored)?
- What role do personal experience narratives play within the efforts of a particular group of adolescent boys to construct a gendered persona?
- Can the structures of conversation between doctors and patients tell us something about the negotiation of successful or unsuccessful working relationships?
- What can we learn about the traumatic disruption of language functioning through looking at cohesion processes in the discourse of aphasics?

Of course many researchers combine the stances of the first and second categories in their research. Some begin with a primary concern with understanding discourse structure, and they encounter larger social questions they might not have originally considered as they look closely at discourse data. Others discover more about the complexity of discourse structure as they are trying to answer social or political questions.

Interpretation and the Use of Discourse Analysis

The examples we discuss in this chapter all involve a back-and-forth progression between analysis of discourse structure and investigation of overarching issues in education. The work of Michaels (1981), which is discussed later in this chapter, is a good example of this kind of progression. In this study, Michaels called attention to the classroom speech event of "sharing time," in which certain discursive norms and practices prevail. This necessitated a description of the speech event within a particular socioculturally and socioeconomically diverse first-grade classroom. Next, Michaels investigated how children from different ethnocultural backgrounds in this classroom construed the event. This led to an examination of children's actual performances within Sharing Time sessions and a consideration of the relationship of these performances to the narrative conventions of the first-graders' home communities. These analyses enabled her to address a larger question: What are the educational consequences for children whose discursive norms differ from those of the school-based narrative event?

Michaels's study, however, is only one example of many possible combinations of purposes and methods. The term "discourse analysis" covers many dissimilar enterprises and analytic purposes. Ethnomethodological studies of conversation (Sacks, 1974; Sacks, Schegloff, and Jefferson, 1977; Schenkein, 1978), for example, or analyses of speech events within the tradition of ethnography of speaking (Hymes, 1962; Gumperz, 1982a; Ochs and Schieffelin, 1983) similarly entail the microanalysis of discourse. And yet these different traditions of work assume different views of the relationship between discourse and social structure and reflect different assumptions about the kind of evidence that is appropriate and acceptable in analyzing a given text. As such, it is not surprising that very different schools of discourse analysis exist, whose members share little with each other. Yet in all of these, as in any sort of qualitative research, the *interpretation* of one's analysis is perhaps the most forbidding part of the research process. Within the welter of different approaches and perspectives, and because of the complex relations between worlds and texts, the process of interpretation becomes central and problematic.

Students encountering discourse analysis for the first time often have a particularly difficult time with the limits of interpretation: What is one "allowed" to posit as the meaning of a text and what counts as adequate "evidence" for a particular conclusion? In this overview, we cannot give an answer to these central questions, because the limits of interpretation are largely determined by the purpose of the research and the conventions of the field within which the discourse analysis is being carried out. A study of mental models of text structure carried out by a cognitive psychologist will fall under quite different interpretive norms than will a study of a particular group's religious discourse carried out by a symbolic anthropologist. Similarly, descriptive linguists, social historians, educational practitioners, and literary critics may all engage in discourse analysis, for different purposes and with different bounds on the limits of interpretation.

Our purpose in this chapter is to argue for and illustrate some of the constructs, methods, and purposes for using discourse analysis in studies of educational settings and activities. We will not, however, offer a neutral survey of various extant approaches to discourse analysis. Rather, we will offer a view of the approach to discourse analysis that we use in our own ongoing work in studies of language, culture, and schooling. This will allow us to go into some depth but will, of necessity, be somewhat idiosyncratic. Our purpose here is to explicate and model certain approaches and methods in enough detail that the reader can see both some general principles and some specific techniques that might be applied in other cases.

The section entitled "Socially Situated Texts" provides an overview of some general characteristics of discourse analysis and lays out some general analytic tools and categories. The subsection "The Sociocultural Setting of Discourse Analysis" locates discourse analysis within a "sociocognitive" view of mind, a view that takes the mind to be constituted in social interaction. The subsection "Discourse Structure" presents, by example, ways of deriving structure and meaning from a text, with emphasis on some linguistic tools used in analysis.

The third section, entitled "Making Sense in Discourse," offers educationally relevant examples of discourse analysis within the wider sociocultural contexts discussed throughout the previous section. Each example highlights the discrepancies between the interpretive norms privileged in schools and middle-class homes and the ways of using language that nonmainstream students have developed and mastered outside of school. We do not mean to imply that these are the only questions or problems to be addressed or the only techniques to use in this kind of work. Rather, these examples illustrate a range of ways in which discourse analysis can be used to raise and answer questions of educational significance while addressing the complexities of social, cognitive, and linguistic processes in particular social institutions.

In each of the examples we include here, text interpretation is influenced and constrained by text structure and the social circumstances surrounding the production of the text. Even within these limits, we assume that our ability to say what a text means is always partial and incomplete. Nonetheless, throughout these examples we may seem to attribute inordinately rich meaning and structure to children's texts. This is purposeful. In our view, people's texts are not trivial outcomes of communicative needs. Rather, they function at many levels and are the product of a person's entire set of sociocultural, political, and psychological conditions and identities. Humans are constant creators of complex and multifaceted meanings. Therefore, particularly in educational research, we feel that to err on the side of overinterpretation is wiser. What we seek to avoid are analyses that misconstrue the discourse of any person as meaningless or impoverished.

Socially Situated Texts: An Overview of Structure and Function

The Sociocultural Setting of Discourse Analysis

In this section, we will give a general overview of the categories of analysis that we think are important in approaching the activity of discourse analysis. A text is always produced in social settings where a great deal more than language is present (Gee, 1990c; Cazden, 1988). While linguists are primarily interested in language, they cannot safely ignore the rest of what is going on around language, because this "other stuff"—actions, objects in the environment, gestures, glances, attitudes, thoughts, values—can determine what a text means. These things determine what sense people make of the text and what sense we can make of it as analysts. For this reason, we think it is important to present a view of discourse in which the social contexts are centrally integrated.

Genre and Performance

Any text is an example of some socially recognized and patterned use of language—You cannot start to tell a story or a joke unless you know what counts as a story or a joke among the group with whom you wish to communicate (Douglas, 1968; Sacks, 1974). As Hymes puts it, a discourse genre is a verbal form with a beginning, an end, "and a pattern to what comes in between" (Hymes, 1974:442). Genre terms, such as "story," "report," "discussion," "argument," "description," and "conversation," can be defined in two ways. They can be defined *etically;* that is, the researcher makes up a definition suitable to the study he or she wants to carry out, based on easily observable characteristics of the genre. Alternatively, they can be defined *emically,* that is, using terms that the community being studied understands and uses. For example, the term "story" can be defined etically as any narrative text that recapitulates some event or set of events in the past, in the order in which they occurred. Alternatively, it could be defined emically by its use in a particular discourse community to refer to "untrue," or highly embellished accounts of past events. Both *etic* and *emic* approaches are valuable, for different purposes.

A genre is *performed* within a particular context. The categories that follow include some of the most important dimensions in describing performances of discourse genres. Work in the "ethnography of communication" tradition has focused central attention on describing the range of discourse genres and performance characteristics across cultures and situations.[3]

Social Activity

We now turn to the nonlinguistic, social settings in which texts are produced. Any text in its particular genre is produced as part of some social activity (Leont'ev, 1978; Minick, 1989; Wertsch, 1981). A social activity involves conventional expectations about the roles participants will play and the characteristic ways in which people playing these roles are expected to act, interact, and appear to believe, value, and think. If we—as participants in discourse—lack an understanding of the social activity in which we are taking part, then we quite literally do not know what to do or how to talk, write, read, interact, or appear to think. We do not know what role to play, what "identity" to take on. Some examples of social activities are "show-and-tell" time at school, checking out at the supermarket, asking for a raise, asking someone for a date, giving a lecture, engaging in a teacher–student writing conference, and asking for directions. All these social activities involve language and more (Argyle and Cook, 1976; Atkinson, 1984; Birdwhistell, 1971; Goffman, 1971, 1974, 1981; Goodwin, 1981; Kendon, 1977; Lave, 1988; Rogoff and Lave, 1984).

Audience and the Dialogic Nature of Discourse

All thinking and all language use are social activities and, therefore, are inherently dialogic (Bakhtin, 1981; Vygotsky, 1987; Wertsch, 1985). Even when a person is engaged in a monologue of some type, whether an exposition, story, report, or description, his or her language, thoughts, and actions are still saturated with and fully influenced by the audience to which the monologue is directed. The monologue would take different forms in different contexts. Furthermore, it is influenced by how the audience behaves, how they sit, look, and respond. In this sense, the audience is still a participant, still in dialogue with him or her. For example, Scollon and Scollon (1979, 1981) have shown how even the head nods of hearers can shape and reshape a narrator's narrative.

Even when people engage in activities alone, with no overtly intended audience, they are still acting for and dialoguing with "imagined others." When a person sings alone in the shower, when a monk meditates alone in the desert, when one reads or writes privately, it is still a culturally grounded, social activity. One has to know how to behave, "how to go on" in Wittgenstein's (1958) famous phrase, in such a way that this is recognizably the sort of thing "people like us" do on occasions like this. The same is true of thought itself: Even private thought is social, directed toward these "imagined others," and assumes forms appropriate to the identities we choose at the time and place in which we think.

Activity Systems

Social activities are typically part of larger systems, which we will call "activity systems." Activity systems are conventions about the ordering of and relationships among various interconnected social activities, as well as the norms, rights, and obligations for speaking and acting that exist within each of these activities. For example, a given elementary school classroom might have a "writing system" that is composed of the activities of group brainstorming, writing first drafts on yellow paper, student–teacher conferences, revision on white paper based on conferences, final approval, and typing the final draft into the computer (Michaels and Bruce, 1989; Michaels, 1990). The activity system will have conventions about how these are ordered, how transitions between them are carried out, and how they are interconnected. Each individual activity and the roles participants play within them can only be fully understood in terms of their relations to the whole activity system.

Wider Sociocultural Settings

Social activities and activity systems are embedded within larger sociocultural systems that affect how participants carry out the roles prescribed for them within these systems. Social activities exist within ever wider cultural circles. For example, teacher–student writing conferences take place within the larger cultures of the classroom, the school, the local community, and the state and nation, and participants need not share all these levels of culture (e.g., they may come from different local communities). In addition, the participants in a given social activity each play other roles on other occasions, within different activity systems. Both cultural differences and differences in what other social activities people have mastered affect, more or less deeply depending on many other factors, their participation in any given social activity we wish to study. For example, a child who spends a great deal of time in one-on-one adult–child social activities outside school will engage in a teacher–student writing conference differently than one who doesn't; a member of certain Native American cultures (e.g., Navaho) may well engage in the social activity of class discussion differently than a member of middle-class, "Anglo-based" cultures (Tharp and Gallimore, 1988).

Of course, such sociocultural and activity differences interrelate in complex ways to ensure that not all people from a given group (African-American, Anglo, Navaho) are alike. It is important to remember, however, that a social role taken on as part of a social activity involves displaying characteristic ways of acting, behaving, talking, valuing, writing, and reading, and these can either reinforce or conflict with other ways of behaving, talking, and valuing that one has adopted and will adopt on other occasions (Edelsky, 1986; Heath, 1983; Ogbu, 1987; Rodriguez, 1981; Rosaldo, 1989; Ryan and Sackery, 1984).

Social activities, activity systems, and wider sociocultural settings are not the limit of the nonlinguistic social embeddings of discourse. There are yet three more layers that need to be considered, each of which can also affect the sense that a text makes: tradition, folk theories, and ideology. We discuss each of these in turn.

Tradition

Any social activity, whether it be storytelling within African-American culture or "sharing time" at school, has a *history*, is part of a *tradition* that transcends the individuals currently engaged in the activity. The social activity has changed through time by being acted out by actual individuals and by virtue of its complex relationships with other social activities, activity systems, and cultures (Callinicos, 1988; Giddens, 1984; Middleton and Edwards, 1990). For example, the values, attitudes, ways of acting, interacting, thinking, and talking, as well as the various roles for teller and audience that are part and parcel of the social activity of storytelling in African-American culture, stem from a very long history, with roots in Africa, in slavery, and in the modern struggles and social experiences of African-American people (Gates, 1984; Smitherman, 1977; Stucky, 1987). The social activity of writing an essay is also part of a long history, with important sociopolitical "origins" in the seventeenth century (Eagleton, 1984; Graff, 1987; Olson, 1977; Street, 1984).

Knowledge is historical and shared. People often engage in ways of acting, talking, valuing, and thinking within social activities that they as individuals do not fully understand. Social understandings are often partitioned among different members of a social group, with no one member necessarily understanding everything. In group interaction people "scaffold" and support each other so that together they can accomplish what one alone may be unable to do. This is, in fact, always the case with "apprentices" in social activities (Rogoff, 1991). Furthermore, people often do and say things that no one in the group necessarily understands, but that have become "routines" or "rituals" handed down through time and that may have "lost" their overt meaning (Douglas, 1986; Connerton, 1989). These routines serve functions for the group and accomplish social work of which participants are not consciously aware.

Finally, people often learn how to play roles within activities without learning completely why things are done this way. Basil Bernstein (see Atkinson, 1985) has argued that teachers in Schools of Education are often taught at "third hand"; that is, they are not directly given primary source material from fields such as developmental psychology or linguistics but, instead, "educators" (often not themselves in the relevant disciplines) "explicate" secondary sources for them, sources written for "nonprofessionals." Thus, the full social knowledge that undergirds a social activity is often not inside any one person's head.

Folk Theories

Another important level to consider in interpreting texts is an informant's perspective on the meaning of a text or of a particular discursive practice. People often have their own theories about what they are doing, however informal, implicit, or incomplete these theories may be. We will refer to these as *folk theories* (Boudon, 1986). [Holland and Quinn (1987) also refer to "cultural models."] Furthermore, people gain new knowledge from others and from the multiple ways in which social science filters into their everyday life, and this knowledge in turn modifies their folk theories and, thus, how they behave (Giddens, 1979, 1990).

Let us take as an example a teacher of a college English as a Second Language (ESL) composition class (Mitchell, 1990). This teacher has a folk theory that composition is or ought to be a "discipline," and that disciplines have their characteristic textbooks delineating the region of knowledge for which the discipline is responsible. This teacher took the Little Brown College Composition Handbook to be such a disciplinary text and saw it as her responsibility to teach its "content." However, she was teaching in an ostensibly "process-oriented" writing program (Graves, 1983), which purports to downplay teacher authority in an attempt to foster student voice and empowerment. The teacher undoubtedly had a folk theory about "process writing" as well. These theories, some of which may be tacit, will most certainly influence her participation in the activity systems in her classroom and college.

Ideology

A further layer to the text-making process is *ideology*, largely unconscious values and viewpoints within social activities that have implications for the distribution of power within society (Thompson, 1984). Social activities are inherently ideological in that they involve roles participants are expected to play. Each of these roles demands certain values and viewpoints. These values and viewpoints are often defined relative to other values and viewpoints that are to be taken up by others in subordinate or superior roles or are relative to values and viewpoints in other, often opposing, social activities (Gee, 1989d; Macdonell, 1986). Thus, hierarchy and power are almost always at stake in social activities (Bourdieu, 1977; Fairclough, 1989; Foucault, 1980, 1985). The role of being a feminist within many social activities is defined partly by opposition to certain types of male roles in other social activities. The role of being a manager within industry often involves taking on values and viewpoints that may subordinate workers and invite them, when engaged in mutual activity with managers, to adopt values and viewpoints complicit with their own subordination, in direct opposition to values and viewpoints they may hold in other social activities (e.g., union activities). And, of course, tradition, folk theories, and ideology interrelate in complex ways, with each other and with the diverse sociocultural settings of social activities (Jackson, 1989; Williams, 1981).

Discourse Structure

In this section, we turn to discourse structure and the specific analytic tools linguists use. Following this section, we will discuss specific examples of discourse analysis and ways in which discourse structure interacts with social activities, activity systems, sociocultural systems, history, folk theories, and ideology. In our discussion about discourse structure, we will confine ourselves to using one specific narrative as an example (Gee, 1990a; Toolan, 1988). We will deal with an oral text, although it will be clear where our remarks are germane to written texts as well.

The text is a "sharing time" turn recorded in a second-grade urban classroom in the United States. The student, whom we call Leona, was considered by her classmates to be one of the best "sharers" in the class. She shared willingly and frequently and often told long and highly developed narrative accounts. The teacher, Mrs. Williams, played the role of primary listener and responder, interjecting questions and comments in response to the children's sharing time contributions. She let the children talk at length but often found Leona's stories hard to follow and would frequently stop to ask her factual questions. Mrs. Williams also heard many of Leona's sharing time turns as "tall tales," as she called them, and at some point referred her to the school psychologist because of this.

Transcription as an Interpretive Lens

Before displaying the transcript of Leona's sharing time turn, it is necessary to say something about transcription conventions. In turning an oral text into a written one, or turning a handwritten piece of student writing into a text for analysis, one inevitably makes decisions about how to display the talk or writing on a page. In the case of an oral text, how much of the texture of the talk, the voice quality, pronunciation, rhythm, and intonation is necessary and appropriate to capture? In the case of student writing, how important is it to reproduce spelling errors or replicate the original layout of words on a line?

The organization of words on the page and the layout of dialogue (e.g., in script format, in parallel columns) have ramifications for what we notice and how we interpret the text.[4] In educational research, we are often dealing with students whose ways of speaking, writing, and reasoning diverge from those of the teacher (and researcher). In these cases, it is especially important to be mindful that the transcript will inevitably leave out some information or, by its display, make certain features more salient than others. Thus, the text as a written document may influence what we are capable of seeing and understanding.

This issue has been addressed most insightfully in sociolinguistic and anthropological work by Hymes (1974, 1981) and his colleagues. They pointed out the importance of combining linguistic, rhetorical, and ethnopoetic forms of analysis in research that aims to fully value the range of American Indian verbal art. Grappling with the form of a text brings the researcher to deeper questions of meaning and their expression in culturally specific genres. Recent extensions of this school of thought, such as the work by Gee (1990c), highlight the significance of this perspective for those primarily interested in the multiple discourses and literacies found in modern industrial societies and their educational consequences.

A striking example of how layout on the page can make a difference can be found in an article by Meier and Cazden (1982), in which they analyze a school composition written by a fourth-grade African-American boy from an urban school. They compare the text as it was originally produced, with invented spelling and punctuation idiosyncrasies, with a version presented in a poetic "lined" fashion, with spelling and punctuation standardized. The cultural and linguistic strengths of the child emerge from their "formatted" version. Meier and Cazden argue that teachers and researchers may get a clearer picture of the meanings and cultural sources of a student's text by imposing this additional structure on it. Our point is simply that formatting choices are a part of the analysis and may reveal or conceal aspects of meaning and intent.

Leona's Sharing Time Turn

Given the importance of transcription and formatting for interpretation, the analyst may wish to try more than one different approach to a text. In this example, we will provide two transcripts of the same turn, transcribed by different people (Michaels, 1981; Gee, 1990c), for their own purposes of analysis. In both transcripts, the discourse analyst began by dividing the flow of talk into audible chunks, using rising and falling intonation (akin to a comma and period) and pausing as cues. These chunks have been discussed in various ways by many different researchers as "tone groups" (Ladd, 1980), "breath groups" (Bolinger, 1986; Halliday, 1967), "intonational phrases" (Ladd, 1980), or "idea units" (Chafe, 1979, 1980).

Within each tone group, one syllable typically bears the primary pitch protrusion in the sentence (called a "pitch glide"), a movement in the pitch of the voice that falls, rises, rises-and-falls, or falls-and-rises in relation to the normal (base) pitch level of the sentence (Bolinger, 1986; Brazil, Coulthard, and Johns, 1980; Crystal, 1979; Ladd, 1980). In the first transcript, this information is captured with rising and falling lines over or under the syllable that receives primary stress. In the second trascript, this information is not included.

Transcript 1: *Leona's Puppy*[5]

L: L:a:st / la:st / yesterday / when / uh / / m' my fa:ther / in the morning / and he / there was a ho:ok / on the top o' the stairway / and my father was pickin' me up / and I got stuck on the hook / up there / an' I hadn't had breakfast / he wouldn't take me down until I finished a:ll my (breakfast) / cause I didn't like oatmeal either / / and then my puppy ca:me / he was aslee:p / and he was— he was / he tried to get up / and he ripped my pa:nts / and he dropped the oatmeal all over hi:m / and / my father came / and he said did you eat all the oatmeal / he said where's the bo:wl / / he said I think the do— / I said / I think the dog . . . took it / / well / I think I'll have t' make another can / / and so I didn't leave till seven / and I took the bus / and / my puppy / he always be following' me / he said / uh / my father said / um / h—you can't go / / and he followed me all the way to the bus stop / and I hadda go all the way back / by that time it was seven thirty / / and

then he kept followin' me back and forth / an' I hadda keep
acc
comin' back / / and he always be followin' me when I go
acc
everywhere / / he wants to go to the store / and only he could not

go to pla:ces / whe:re / we could go / like / to: / like / t' the stores

/ he could go / but he have to be chained up / / and we took him
acc
to the eme:rgency / and see what was wro:ng with him / and he

got a sho:t / an' then he was cry:in' / and . . . la / last yesterda:y /

and / now / they put him asleep / and / he's still in the ho:spital /

and th— doctor said that / he hasta / he got a shot because he: / he

was / he was ne:rvous / about my home that I had / and he / and

he could still stay but / he thought he wasn't gonna be a- / he

thought he wasn't gonna be able / to let him go: / / he's
∧
T: who's in the hospital Leona? / /

L: the do:g / he's ⌈vicious
         ∧

T: ⌊your puppy? / /

L: he's vicious / about my house / /
         p   ∧

T: what does that mean? / /

L: that's what the doctor said / /
         p

T: does anyone know what it means if / they say a dog is vicious? / /
         Keisha? / / ... take a guess / / ... do you think it's a good thing to
         say? / /

K: he doesn't like the house

T: he doesn't like it / and how does he show that he doesn't like it /
         maybe ... Joey? / /
         p

J: he's mad at it / / he wants to like / bite some stuff off of it or
     something /

T: perhaps / yeah / / how does your dog show that he's vicious /
     Leona? / /

L: he: / he bit my pa:nts / and he goes in my closet / and he ripped
     all my shoes

T: ahh ⌐

L: └ and then he rip- / he bi- / he tried to bite on the door and
     we took him to the hospital and he hadda get a shot and they put
                                            acc
     him to sleep / and / I didn't get my puppy back yet / if / the
     doctor said if / he doe- / if / he'll pay for another one if I can't
     have my other puppy / /

T: so where is your puppy now? / /

L: he's still in the hospital / /
     p

T: oh I see / and he may come home and he may not / /

L: he / I think the doctor called this morning / but I had left before
     the—then / / my dad said he'd talk to me when I come home /. . .
     I'll tell you Monday / what happened / /

T: Oh / O.K. / / so he w- / was he following you to the bus this
     morning? / /

L: yeah / / he likes me now /. . . but / once he got shot / he likes me / /

T: does he get to go outside a lot? / /

L: he plays in the grass a lot and I—

T: cause dogs need to run an awful lot / /

sometimes if they're in the house too much they / they get kinda

stra:nge / / because / ⌈ they don't have a chance to run
      ∧

L: ⌊ well / I don't get to take him out that much /

cause I have to clean the house / and sweep the walk / and he
                          ╵   ╵

always likes to / he he's tired / he thinks he's / w(ell) / he
              ╵ ╵   ∧∕

doesn't like goin' in his box / / I have a box around the house /
                        ∧   ╲   ╲

and he always pees on the floor / and I whacked him / /
              ╲   ╲   ╲╲

T: sounds like he needs some training / huh? / /
                              ╲   ╵

Notice that in this transcript, false starts and speech repairs (which occur in all speech) are included in the text. Tone grouping determines what occurs on a line. Michaels also included asides and the dialogue with the teacher following the narrative. In Gee's transcript, which follows, obvious false starts and speech repairs have been removed from the text, and the few subject nouns or noun phases that are idea units by themselves have been collapsed into the clauses to which they belong. Thus, in this second transcript, we get an "ideal" realization of the text. Such an ideal representation allows us to see patterns of structure and meaning more clearly.[6] In this transcript, the various elements of the story have been labeled, indicating their status as story parts, something that is derived from the analysis itself. This too makes structure and meaning more obvious. The point here is to allow the reader two experiences with the same oral text with different amounts and kinds of information included in the transcripts.

Transcript 2: *Leona's Puppy Story*

Part 1: Introduction

   1A: Setting

      Stanza 1

         1. Last yesterday in the morning
         2. there was a hook on the top of the stairway
         3. an' my father was pickin' me up
         4. an' I got stuck on the hook up there

Stanza 2

    5. an' I hadn't had breakfast
    6. he wouldn't take me down
    7. until I finished all my breakfast
    8. cause I didn't like oatmeal either

1B: Catalyst

Stanza 3

    9. an' then my puppy came
    10. he was asleep
    11. he tried to get up
    12. an' he ripped my pants
    13. an' he dropped the oatmeal all over him

Stanza 4

    14. an' my father came
    15. an' he said "Did you eat all the oatmeal?"
    16. he said "Where's the bowl?"
    17. I said "I think the dog took it"
    18. "Well I think I'll have t'make another bowl"

Part 2: Crisis

2A: Complicating Actions

Stanza 5

    19. an' so I didn't leave till seven
    20. an' I took the bus
    21. an' my puppy he always be following me
    22. my father said "he—you can't go"

Stanza 6

    23. an' he followed me all the way to the bus stop
    24. an' I hadda go all the way back
    25. by that time it was seven thirty
    26. an' then he kept followin' me back and forth
    27. an' I hadda keep comin' back

2B: Evaluation (Nonnarrative Section)

Stanza 7

    28. an' he always be followin' me when I go anywhere

29. he wants to go to the store
30. an' only he could not go to places where
    we could go
31. like to the stores he could go but he have
    to be chained up

Part 3: Resolution

3A: Concluding Episodes

Stanza 8

32. an' we took him to he emergency
33. an' see what was wrong with him
34. an' he got a shot
35. an' then he was crying

Stanza 9

36. an' last yesterday, an' now they put him
    asleep
37. an' he's still in the hospital
38. an' the doctor said he got a shot because
39. he was nervous about my home that I
    had

3B: Coda

Stanza 10

41. an' he could still stay but
42. he thought he wasn't gonna be able to let
    him go

[See Gee (1990c) for an extended anlysis of this particular story.]

The text above is demarcated into its "stanzas." A stanza (Gee, 1986, 1990a; Hymes, 1981; Scollon and Scollon, 1981) takes a particular perspective on a character, action, event, claim, or piece of information; each stanza has a particular point of view such that when character, place, time, event, or the function of a piece of information changes, whether in an argument, report, exposition, or description, the stanza must change. In our analysis below, we will see how stanzas function as the backbone of the meaningful development of a text.

All speech has stanzas, but different sociocultural groups "fill up" stanzas with language in different ways (Gee, 1989c). Leona (a member of the "African-American cultural tradition" shared by many African-Americans) uses a good deal of syntactic and semantic parallelism, as well as repetition of words and phrases, between the lines of her stanzas, just as do Biblical poetry [e.g., in the Psalms (Berlin, 1985)], the narratives of many oral cultures [e.g., Homer (see Foley, 1988)], and much "free verse" [e.g., the poetry of Walt Whitman (see Jannacone, 1985)]. Prosodically the lines in a stanza sound as if they go together, by tending to be said with the same rate and with little hesitation between the lines. Leona's stanzas show intricate structure and patterning, taking on some of the properties of stanzas in poetry (Gee, 1990b).

As just one indicator of how stanzas function to make sense in Leona's text, consider stanzas 3 and 4:

> an' then my puppy came
> he was asleep
> he tried to get up
> an' he ripped my pants
> an' he dropped the oatmeal all over him
>
> an' my father came
> an' he said "Did you eat all the oatmeal?"
> he said "Where's the bowl?"
> I said "I think the dog took it"
> "Well I think I'll have t'make another bowl"

Here Leona introduces one stanza by the line "an' then my puppy came" and the next by "an' my father came," setiing puppy and father into direct contrast. The first stanza has four physical events, whereas the second has four speakings or verbal events. Notice that in the second stanza, the second and third lines have "he said" and are questions, whereas the last two lines are statements and repeat "I think," giving the stanza something like the *aabb* rhyme structure in a stanza of poetry (Gee, 1989b).

Some levels of organization in Leona's stories are beyond lines and stanzas, and these are labeled in the text above. The story has a setting (at home), a catalyst (a problem that sets the plot in motion), a crisis (the puppy keeps following), a nonnarrative break called an evaluation (which signals the point of the story), and closes with a resolution (the puppy can't go home) and a coda.[7]

Before moving on, we comment on the nonnarrative portion of Leona's text (stanza 7):

> an' he always be followin' me when I go anywhere
> he wants to go to the store

> an' only he could not go to places where we could go
> like to the stores he could go but he have to be chained up

This portion of Leona's story involves habitual statements and stative verbs and depicts states or events that depart from the main narrative line. This section of Leona's story does not advance the plot but, instead, serves as what Labov (1972) has called "evaluation." Evaluation is material that gives an indication of the point of a story and what it is the narrator considers makes the story "tellable" (which, of course, can differ from culture to culture). Thus, this part of Leona's story is quite relevant to any interpretation we would offer for the story (see below).

An Interpretation of the Text

The meaning of a text flows from a combination of the words and structural organization of the text together with the inferences hearers draw based on their knowledge of the speaker and the context. The structure of a text serves as clues or guides to interpretive inferences. To show issues that arise in the consideration of meaning, we will offer one "reading" of this text, based on our inferences from the line and stanza structure, the linguistic patterns used in the story, and the overall organization of the story. A part of discourse analysis would involve taking such a reading as ours back to the community and seeing how members of that community, including Leona herself, make sense of the story, as well as situating our reading in the history and culture of the community.

The logic of this story seems clear, given its line and stanza structure. We first see the father (stanzas 1 and 2) as an adult authority figure, enforcing discipline in the home. Then, in stanzas 3 and 4, the father and the puppy are introduced in exactly parallel ways. The father comes on the scene and there are four instances of speech. The puppy comes on the scene and there are four nonspeech events, which together create chaos (lack of order and discipline) in the home. The puppy and father are thus juxtaposed as reflecting opposite values: adulthood, order, discipline versus youth, disorder, and exuberance.

In stanzas 5 and 6, the puppy's demand to go out and play leads to Leona's being "caught" (going back and forth) between two institutions of adult authority (the home and school), in danger of being in trouble with both. The puppy sees the outdoors as a realm of play, while the young girl is being enculturated to see it as a path from home to school, from one realm of order to another. The girl is caught between the values of the puppy and the father. (Note the "speech error" in line 22: "my father said 'he—you can't go.' " The young narrator conflates the puppy and herself; neither are allowed to go free and play).

A crisis is boiling, and in stanza 7 the little girl, in a nonnarrative interlude, explicates the nature of the crisis: The puppy always follows the young girl (see discussion in the next section about marking of habituality in Black English with the uninflected verb "be"). The puppy wants to go forth free (stanza 7 uses "go" five times), but in the end he has to be chained up and cannot go free. The puppy's nature is to follow her and entice her to play; thus, a conflict exists between the nature or essence of the puppy and the nature or essence of the father/home/adult world (see Bailey and Maynir, 1987).

Stanzas 8 and 9 prepare us for the final resolution to the crisis and the solution to the problem of the conflict between the puppy (child) and the father/home/adult world (note, by the way, that the child, apart from nonnarrative stanza 7, devotes two stanzas of four lines each to each of her major themes). The puppy, who woke up in stanza 3, goes back to sleep in stanza 8 (note that "sleep" means different things at home and outside the home). The puppy has gone to the hospital because he is "sick" (his conflict with the father is redefined as an illness), and he needs to be treated by a doctor, an adult authority figure in charge of diagnosing and treating "sick natures." The doctor's diagnosis is completely accurate: The puppy's problem is that he (and, by transfer, the little girl) conflicts with the home seen as a realm of adult order and authority (along with the school and hospital). The puppy's constitution (nerves) cannot put up with the home; the home makes him "nervous." In stanza 10, we find out the final verdict, the logical solution to the virtual logical argument that the story constitutes: The doctor (adult authority figure in charge of natures and their illnesses) cannot let the puppy go (which is precisely the puppy's "illness"—that he wants, like a child, to go free, to be free of the constraint and discipline of the adult human world).

The style of interpretation in which we have engaged here is not arbitrary. It takes the view that human sensemaking is based on trying to achieve satisfying resolutions of binary contrasts between important themes (e.g., constraint and freedom, life and death, adult and child, nature and culture), themes that are symbolized by concrete entities in the story. While such sensemaking is quite obvious in the myths of many cultures (Levi-Strauss, 1966) and in the oral storytelling that is an important part of many cultures (Finnegan, 1988; Foley, 1988; Ong, 1982; Stahl, 1989), including African-American culture (Abrahams,

1964), it is by no means unapparent even in "essayist" (Scollon and Scollon, 1981) speaking and writing, although here the contrasts are often left "abstract," rather than embodied in concrete entities and events (Eagleton, 1990; Myers, 1990).

We have argued above that all sensemaking involves ideology, values, and viewpoints about the distribution of power in social groups. Let us close this section by mentioning a few examples of the workings of ideology in Leona's story. First, she adopts a viewpoint that conflicts of styles are really conflicts of natures or essences, and these latter can be defined in medical or clinical terms and, thus, settled by authority figures specializing in natures and illnesses (i.e., doctors). This little piece of ideology is so pervasive in Western culture that it has been given a name: "the medical model" (Woodward, 1982), which has had many negative consequences for members of oppressed groups.

Second, note how obligation and authority are dealt with in the story. The father says, in stanza 4, "Well, I think I'll have to make another bowl." In stanza 7, the puppy "has to be chained up." In stanza 10, the doctor thinks that "he wasn't going to be able to let him [the puppy] go." Note that, in this story, obligation exists but its source is never apparent. This piece of ideology says that authority is actually imposed from somewhere outside the self or one's own social group. Such an ideology, not at all uncommon in social institutions like our schools, tends to license authority in a rather blanket way and to disempower individuals engaged in activities at the very site where authority is at issue (Apple, 1986; Giroux, 1988). The point here is not that Leona is a "dupe" to ideology, but that none of us can speak without being embedded in ideologies (Gee, 1990c). In our view, one function of discourse analysis is to uncover the workings of ideology.

Analytic Tools within Linguistic Discourse Analysis

Linguists have many microlevel tools with which to investigate the structural workings of language within discourse. Although we have tacitly used many of these in our preceding analysis, we do not have the space here to survey them in any detail. However, we will mention some of these tools and give relevant citations so that readers can pursue them in more detail if they wish. We will take a single sentence from our preceding text to exemplify the operation of these tools—"an' my puppy he always be following me," line 21, stanza 5—bringing in other material in only a limited way. The following sections describe several areas of linguistic discourse analysis that can be used separately or together.

Syntax and Morphology

Line 21 uses the so-called "naked be" of Black English to mark habitual aspect, that is, to signal that the puppy's following has happened repeatedly and is a long-term affair. We have seen in our analysis what role this plays in the meaning of the story. In general, perfective aspect or treating an event as a point in time, as in "My puppy followed me," is used in narratives for foregrounded, mainline plot events. Imperfective aspect or treating an event as ongoing in time, as in "My puppy was following me" or "My puppy always be following me," is used for background, expository, off-the-main-plotline information (Hopper and Thompson, 1980, 1982).

The syntactic form of line 21 is what linguists call "left dislocation" (Duranti and Ochs, 1979; Ochs and Schieffelin, 1983), where a noun phrase ("my puppy") has been placed in front of the sentence and repeated in the body of the sentence with a pronoun ("he"). This form is used to mark a shifted topic or a salient contrast. Line 21 is something of an aside, contextualizing the plot event of the puppy wanting to follow the girl to school on this particular day within the general habits of the puppy. Because the puppy has not been mentioned since stanza 3, the left dislocation form is used to reintroduce the puppy, who may have dropped to the background of the hearer's consciousness. The study of how the structural aspects of sentence grammar (syntax and morphology) are used in text building and textual sensemaking is a major part of discourse analysis in linguistics proper (Givon, 1979a,b, 1983, 1984, 1989; Haiman, 1984, 1985; Halliday, 1985; Longacre, 1983).

Cohesion

Cohesion is the way in which the lines and stanzas of a text are linked to or interrelated to each other (Halliday and Hasan, 1976, 1989; Halliday, 1989). Cohesion is achieved by a variety of linguistic devices, including conjunctions, pronouns, demonstratives, ellipses, and various sorts of adverbs as well as repeated words and phrases. In fact, any word, phrase, or syntactic device that causes two clauses to be related creates cohesion in the text. Such links are part of what stitches a text together into a meaningful whole; they are like threads that tie language together and, thus, also tie together the sense of a text. In stanzas 3 and 4, Leona repeats the form "my X came," thereby tying her talk about father and puppy together, as she does by also using the left dislocation in line 21 ("my puppy he ...") to reintroduce the puppy right before once again juxtaposing the father to the puppy (line 22: "my father said ..."). We have seen the role this juxtaposition of father and puppy plays in the meaning of the story. Such devices of connection and juxtaposition also help render this a unitary text.

Contextualization Cues

Contextualization cues are used by speakers to signal to the hearer what the speaker takes the context to be and how the speaker wants the hearer to construct that context in his or her mind (Gumperz, 1982a,b). These contextualization cues essentially tell the hearer what sort of person the speaker takes the hearer to be, what sort of person the speaker takes him- or herself to be, and what the speaker assumes the world to be like. As discussed above, line 21 uses a speech-based, informal form rarely found in essayist writing, namely left dislocation, as well as the "naked be" from colloquial black English. Both of these contextualize the occasion of the telling as informal, speech-based communication among friends/peers. As we will see later, this is decidedly not how schools often contextualize sharing time, which they often treat as early training in essayist literacy with its concomitant assumption that the hearer/reader is a "stranger."

Prosody

The prosody of the text, the way in which the speaker's voice rose and fell in pitch, the way in which she lengthened and shortened her syllables, the way in which she sped up and slowed down her rate of speech, and the places she hesitated and paused, constitutes the overall rhythmical organization of the text (Brazil *et al.*, 1980; Tannen, 1989). Such matters, which we introduced only in a limited fashion earlier, are crucial to how speakers express their viewpoints, attitudes, and the deeper sense they are trying to make above and beyond the literal meanings of words and sentences. Leona uses prosody to indicate that line 21 is, at this point in the text, "background information." At line 28, in stanza 7, she uses a different prosody on the same line to announce that she has exited the mainline of the narrative and is starting a section of "evaluation" material. This juxtaposition of same syntax and different prosody allows Leona to signal the structure of her text (e.g., the beginning of a new section), while stressing the importance of the puppy's ingrained behavior as a central theme of the story. In her stories in general, especially the ones we have from her as a

12-year-old, Leona can switch between the prosody of standard English and Black English to signal aspects of her identity as well as her attitude to her audience and to her material (Milroy, 1987; Milroy and Milroy, 1985).

Discourse Organization and Thematic Organization

Discourse organization and thematic organization are fairly well represented in our anlysis. Discourse organization is the macrostructure of the text, which we have represented in terms of stanzas and parts labeled with terms such as "setting," "crisis," and "resolution." Discourse organization has been looked at in a variety of different ways by psycholinguists, sociolinguists, ethnographers of speaking, and cognitively oriented text analysts (van Dijk, 1980; Labov, 1972; Hymes, 1981; Mandler, 1984; Peterson and McCabe, 1983; Wilensky, 1983). Thematic organization, which has been much less studied in the various subdisciplines of linguistics than it has been in literary theory, is the way in which images and themes are introduced, contrasted, and developed within a text (Birch, 1989; Cohan and Shires, 1988; Genette, 1980; Hasan, 1989; also Tannen, 1984, 1989). Such images and themes are an important part, not just of stories, but of all genres, including arguments, essays, and conversations, although they are "foregrounded" in stories, where they are often embodied in concrete entities (like the father and the puppy).

Making Sense in Discourse: Three Examples

We will now consider three specific examples of discourse analysis. Our emphasis will be on the issues that arise when discourse analysis is situated within the framework of social activities, activity systems, and sociocultural differences as well as traditions, folk theories, and ideologies.

Sensemaking in Discourse: Sharing Time

Our first example deals with sharing time in a first-grade urban classroom (Collins and Michaels, 1986; Michaels and Cook-Gumperz, 1979; Michaels, 1981, 1985; Michaels and Collins, 1984). Sharing time in this classroom was a social activity that occurred within a set of speech events (i.e., an activity system) that served to open the school day. It took place every morning within the context of "rugtime," a time when the children assembled on the rug for various teacher-structured activities such as taking roll and doing the calendar. Sharing time was thus an activity situated at the "border" between home and school. This border location is important in that sharing time served not only to prepare the students for the school day but was also a crucial bridge between home-based language practices and school-based language and literacy values. Sharing time proper opened with the teacher saying "OK, who has something important [exciting, special] to share?" The teacher, referred to as "Mrs. Jones," was a European-American middle-class woman with over 30 years of teaching experience and an outstanding reputation in her district. Mrs. Jones was actively involved in sharing time, holding her arm around each child as the child talked, helping the child hold the floor, and freely interjecting questions or reactions to the child or group at large.

Children saw sharing time as a specific social activity, as evidenced by their use of a highly marked intonation contour. This "sharing intonation," used primarily at the beginnings of sharing turns, was an integral feature of sharing discourse and did not occur in other classroom social activities. African-American and European-American children in this classroom differed a bit in this special sharing intonation: European-American children used vowel elongation and a gradual rising intonation on the focus, whereas African-American children used vowel elongation and a lilting high rise/mid-fall pitch contour on the focus.[8] This striking use of different prosodic systems to signal a common piece of knowledge raises from the start the question of how cultural diversity is or is not used as a resource in classrooms and how classrooms can become "commonwealths" made out of this diversity.

Sharing time is a speech activity in which the child who is sharing, the other children, and the teacher each have their roles (e.g., the sharer shares, the teacher can ask questions, and the audience is allowed to make short, topically relevant comments). However, the children are "apprentices." They do not have, in the privacy of their heads, full knowledge of the norms and values of the activity. The teacher plays a crucial role in structuring the children's discourse and providing an example of the kind and form of discourse that he or she considers appropriate. When a child neglected to provide explicit temporal or background information, for example, Mrs. Jones provided a slot for it by asking a specific question, such as "When did you go to the beach?" or "What beach did you go to?" Through an analysis of these teacher prompts, it became clear that the teacher had an underlying scheme (Fillmore, 1975; Quinn and Holland, 1987; Mandler, 1984) of what constituted "good" sharing, a schema that the children shared only to degrees, and in terms of which they were scaffolded and socially supported by the teacher.[9]

The teacher's schema had an implicit literate bias: While having something in common with everyday notions of narrative structure and logical temporal sequencing, the sharing time schema was far more restrictive. The child's account was expected to take the form of a simple statement and resolution centering on a single topic. Importance was attached, not to content per se, nor to the sequentially ordered structure of a narrative, but, rather, as in simple descriptive prose, to clarity of topic statement and explicitness. Although the teacher never overtly stated these requirements, her questions and comments indicated that what she was looking for was a decontextualized account centering on a single topic, whereby (1) objects were named and described, even when in plain sight; (2) talk was to be explicitly grounded temporally and spatially; (3) minimal shared background or contextual knowledge was to be assumed between speaker and audience; and (4) thematic ties needed to be lexicalized if topic shifts were to be seen as motivated and relevant.

Sharing time, then, is an interestingly complex (and somewhat misleading) genre. The child, fresh from the world of family and home, confronted with his or her first-grade peers, appears to be in a situation calling for a story to a group of peers. The child may well be tempted to tell this story in the style of informal face-to-face language used in communication with intimates [sometimes called the "pragmatic mode" (Givon, 1979a)]. However, the teacher does not want or expect the thematic intricacies of a fully emplotted story but, rather, the sequential "facts" of a narrative report, a report that resembles in some ways an expository essay. Both stories and reports are subgenres of narrative, but stories have plots with thematically developed "high points" of particular interest or drama to the narrator and audience, whereas reports are a sequential listing of "facts" or "events" (note, in fact, the ambiguity of the genre term "report": I can give you a "firsthand" report of the fire I saw or I can write you a report of the committee's findings). Sharing time is early training in the sort of literacy the school most values—"essayist literacy," language that is decontextualized from the shared knowledge of peers and from face-to-face settings. And this training takes place prior to the children being able to write expository prose. Situated at the border between home and school, sharing time seeks to transform the child's oral home-based language into the sort of explicit language school-based people use to "strangers" or readers of decontextualized, school-based prose.

We will look at two sharing time turns, the first a "successful" turn and the second an "unsuccessful" turn. In this classroom, and many others like it, African-American children from lower socioeconomic homes are disproportionately unsuccessful (in the teacher's eyes and ears) at sharing time compared with children from middle-class homes. We will see important differences in language and interaction within what is ostensibly the same social activity. The following is a reprint of a turn by a European-American child whom we will call "Mindy." The turn concerns making candles (for a different transcript of this turn and a fuller analysis,[10] see Michaels, 1981).

Mindy's Sharing Time Turn

M: When I was in day camp,
we made these, um candles,

T: You made them?

M: And uh, I-I tried it with different colors,
with both of them but,
one came out, this one just came out blue,
and I don't know, what this color is,

T: That's neat-o.
Tell the kids how you do it from the very start.
Pretend we don't know a thing about candles. [pause]
OK.
What did you do first? [pause]
What did you use?
Flour?

M: Um, there's some, hot wax,
some real hot wax,
that you, just take a string,
and tie a knot in it.
And dip the string in the um wax.

T: What makes it uh have a shape?

M: Um, you just shape it.

T: Oh you shaped it with your hand. mm.

M: But you have, first you have to stick it into the wax,
and then water,
and then keep doing that
until it gets to the size you want it.

T: OK.
Who knows what the string is for?

Mindy immediately announces her topic in her first two lines while holding up two small candles for the class to see. Mrs. Jones, then, uses an echo question to show how impressed and interested she is: "You made them?" (said with surprise). Without missing a beat, Mindy continues. However, her following talk about the color of the candles is lexically inexplicit and not elaborated; it relies heavily on the fact that the whole class can see the candles. Furthermore, the coloring of the candles is a rather peripheral part of the process of candlemaking, one that, however, lends itself to the visual presentation of the candles in this face-to-face setting. All of this is not the sort of talk that the teacher wants to encourage at sharing time, although it is typical of informal, face-to-face talk in the here and now to peers.

However, the teacher waits until Mindy pauses on a low falling tone (on "color") and reiterates her interest in the actual process but this time she does so more explicitly. She provides a clear and elaborate set of guides for how she wants Mindy to talk about making candles. "Tell the kids about how you do it from the very start. Pretend we don't know anything about candles." The last remark is, of course, an instruction to assume no shared knowledge and to be as explicit as possible, that is, to abandon the assumption that this is informal talk to peers who can obviously see the candles and who may well know as much as Mindy does about candlemaking. The teacher then pauses and gets no response. She rephrases her instruction as a question: "What did you do first?" She pauses again and then follows with an additional clue by offering an obviously wrong answer to the question, which nonetheless suggests to Mindy an example of the type of answer she has in mind. "What did you use? . . . Flour?" At this point Mindy responds, building on the base that the teacher's questions have provided. She describes what she used ("hot wax") and the steps involved. In addition to a description of the sequencing of activities involved in the business of making candles, this passage introduces several context-free lexical items ("some hot wax," "a string," "a knot").

The use of lexical items provides explicit information about the activity and the materials used in candlemaking. This contrasts with Mindy's use of anaphoric and deictic items that rely on the context for interpretation in her preceding talk about the candles. In addition, the use of definite and indefinite articles grammaticalizes the distinction between new and old information: "some wax" and "a string" become "the piece of string" and "the wax." When Mrs. Jones asks Mindy what gives the candles a shape (the candles had a patterned series of bulges and narrowings), Mindy says "Um, you just shape it," with a falling tone on "shape," indicating through the use of "just" and her intonation that "you do it the regular way." Mrs. Jones interprets her with no difficulty and then revoices Mindy's comment, adding in the explicit mechanisms that in Mindy's turn "went without saying:" "Oh you shaped it *with your hand.*" It is here, through the seamless mingling of voices (Mindy's and Mrs. Jones's), that one meaning is co-constructed.

The teacher and Mindy are able to coordinate their interaction in a smooth and flowing way so that Mindy, the apprentice, is scaffolded and supported by the teacher's greater expertise. Mindy's discourse in response to the teacher's questions and comments is far more complex than the spontaneous utterances she produced at the beginning of her sharing time turn without the teacher's guidance. Thus, we see in this example how a synchronization of exchanges and the teacher's revoicing of Mindy's contribution enables the student and teacher to co-construct a lexically explicit, coherent, and school-based account of a complex activity.

This interaction between Mindy and the teacher is very reminiscent of a type of verbal interaction between much younger children and their parents, which has been extensively studied in middle-class homes and which appears to occur much less frequently in nonmainstream homes (Heath, 1982, 1983; Wells, 1986). For example, consider the following breakfast-table conversation between a 29-month-old and his parents (from Snow, 1986:82):

Child: Pancakes away.
        Duh duh stomach.

Mother: Pancakes away in the stomach, yes, that's right.

Child: Eat apples.

Mother: Eating apples on our pancakes, aren't we?

Child: On our pancakes.

Mother: You like apples on your pancakes?

Child: Eating apples.
        Hard.

Mother: What?
        Hard to do the apples, isn't it?

Child: More pancakes.

Father: You want more pancakes?

Child: Those are daddy's.

Father: Daddy's gonna have his pancakes now.

Child: Ne ne one a daddy's.
            Ne ne one in the plate.
            Right there.

Father: You want some more on your plate?

Much research on child language development has shown that verbal interactions like the preceding one, coupled with certain types of interactive storybook reading, enhance a child's chance of later school success (Garton and Pratt, 1989). There is a sense in which both the teacher's interaction with Mindy and the preceding conversation above between parents and child are interactive slot-and-filler activities centered around adding more and more descriptive and lexically explicit detail around a single topic. In a verbal interation like the preceding one, an adult (or older peer) takes the telegraphic utterances of the young child and expands them into full and correct sentences. Investigators used to think that this worked because the adult was giving "grammar lessons" to the child by showing the child the whole adult sentences at which he or she was "aiming." However, we now know that if the adult merely provides extra conversation with the child built around the child's utterances, this will facilitate school-based sorts of language practices just as well (Snow, 1986). In fact, it turns out that the most facilitative practice an adult can engage in is what has been called "semantic expansions" of the child's language. Such expansions do not just fill out the structure of what the child has said, but they also incorporate the child's topic into the adult utterances and then add new information to it. Research has shown that the percentage of adult utterances that are semantically related to preceding child utterances is the best predictor of the child's "linguistic ability" (of the sort that enhances school success) and that a high correlation exists between the percentage of adult speech related to child activities and the size of the child's vocabulary.

Children like Mindy certainly do not fully know the sharing time scheme, nor do they know in any detailed way the nature of school-based literacy practices, but they are experts in engaging in the sorts of adult–child verbal scaffolding that we see in Mindy's sharing time turn and in the above conversation about pancakes. Both sorts of practices encourage lexically explicit and elaborated sequential reports on a single topic. For Mindy, school is like moving from the minor leagues to the majors. For her, sharing time, a transition from home to school at several levels, is a smooth transition; the interaction between teacher and child at sharing time is much like "games" Mindy has played at home.

Lower socioeconomic homes do not as regularly evidence the sorts of verbal practices seen in the preceding examples, nor the sorts of interactive one-on-one storybook reading that is typical of many middle-class homes (Adams, 1990; Chall, Jacobs, and Baldwin, 1990; Heath, 1983; Wells, 1986). This certainly does not mean they are not engaged in important linguistic practices. They are, in fact, engaged in rich language practices with deep historical roots, the sort that produce stories like Leona's, as well as many other dexterous and sophisticated language skills (Abrahams, 1976; Kochman, 1972; Labov, 1972; Smitherman, 1977). The school, however, is unaware of these, fails to use them as a resource and, in fact, actively, if unconsciously, devalues them.

In this regard, consider now a sharing time turn by a African-American child who we will call "Deena":

Deena's Sharing Time Turn

> T: Deena, I want you to share some one thing,
>   that's very important.
>   One, thing.
>   From where you are.
>   Is that where you are?
>   Is that where you were?
>
> D: No.
>
> T: OK.

Stanza 1

> D: Um. In the summer,
>   I mean, w-when um, I go back to school,
>   I come back to school, in September,
>   I'ma have a new coat,
>   and I already got it.
>   And, it's, um, got a lot of brown in it.

Stanza 2

> And, when, um, and I got it yesterday,
> and when I saw it,
> my um my mother was was going somewhere,
> and my when I saw it, on the couch,
> and I showed my sister,
> and I was readin' somethin out on on the bag,
> and my big sister said

C: [interrupts D] um close the door

D: my big sister said,
> Deena you have to keep that away, from Keisha,
> cause that's my baby sister,
> and I said no.
> And I said the plastic bag.

Stanza 3

> Because, um, when, um, sh-when the um she was um
> with me, wait a minute, my, cousin and her

T: [interrupts D] Wait a minute
> You stick with your coat now.
> I s-said you could tell one thing.
> That's fair.

D: This was about my co-

T: OK, all right, go on.

D: this was-

Stanza 3 continued

D: And yesterday when I got my coat,
> my cousin ran outside
> And he ran to tried to get him,
> and he, he he start, an' when he get in when he got in
> my house,
> he laid on the floor,
> and I told him to get up because he was crying.

T: Mm-what's that have to do with your coat?

D: H-he because he wanted to go outside,
> but we couldn't. [exasperated]

T: Why?

D: Cause my mother s-wanted us to stay in the house.

T: What does that have to do with your coat?

D: Bec- um uh

C: [whispers]

D: Because, I don't know.

T: Thank you very much Deena.

Cs: [talking]

T: OK, do you understand what I was trying to do?
Deena,
I was trying to get her to stick to one, thing.
And she was talking about her,

Cs: Coat.

T: Ne:w,

Cs: coat.

T: Coat.
It sounds nice Deena.

In this example, the teacher begins with a clear prescription of what she wants from Deena, with emphatic stress on "one thing." This is evidence of her well-grounded expectation that Deena will launch into a long and "rambling" (in Mrs. Jones's words) sharing time account, as she has done in the past. The teacher's expectations are met. In asking questions and prodding Deena to "stick to her topic," Mrs. Jones fails to collaborate with Deena to support a performance closer to the school-based sharing time schema. Neither Deena nor Mindy is yet a master of school-based, explicit, overtly connected essayist sorts of decontextualized talk. But while Mindy and the teacher can synchronize their contributions to build toward such an account, Deena and the teacher cannot. The teacher hears only a listing of what to her are disconnected, temporally contiguous events. The teacher continues to press for an explicit semantic link until Deena gives up and sits down.

There is no single, simple reason why Deena and the teacher cannot "pull off" sharing time together, and it is important not to fall into the trap of seeing the school failure of lower socioeconomic children in purely language-based terms, decontextualized from very real political issues concerning race and class (Hewitt, 1986; McDermott,

1987; Ogbu, 1978; Steinitz and Solomon, 1986; Trueba, 1989). However, part of what is going on between Mrs. Jones and Deena is this: Deena's home-based sociocultural notion of narrative favors stories over reports; her way of telling stories is culturally different from mainstream cultural practices; and her home does not regularly engage in early versions of school-like scaffolded verbal interactions such as the preceding pancake interaction.

It is clear that the teacher, in her school-based sociocognitive mode, does not know how to listen to Deena's story. Stanza 1 is a "preamble" to Deena's story, not its real beginning. Ironically, this descriptive preamble may have been an accommodation to the teacher's repeated earlier attempts to elicit what she saw as single-topic narratives or descriptions. This kind of narrative preamble did not occur in Deena's earlier sharing time turns or in her informal narrative accounts recorded with her sisters [although it is by no means uncommon in oral and folk narratives (Bauman, 1986; Stahl, 1989)].

In any case, because the teacher expects Deena, like Mindy, to announce her "topic" right at the beginning, the teacher assumes that stanza 1 is announcing the topic and that she is about to hear a report on Deena's new coat (a sequentially ordered set of events or facts about the coat). But "real" stories (elaborated and thematically developed plots) do not often announce topics in this way; rather, they have plot actions and accompanying expository background material that contextualizes the significance and dramatic interest of the basic plot (Chatman, 1978; Polanyi, 1989). Stanza 1 is such expository background material. The plot starts at stanza 2, with ". . . when I . . . got it yesterday . . . I showed it to my sister," which starts the first main-line event in the story (note that "showed" here is the first past-tense perfective event, thus the first true narrative mainline foregrounded event of the plot). This is typical of stories in many cultures, especially ones influenced by a rich oral tradition (Sternberg, 1985). We can now expect a series of "plot actions" in which the coat is a major protagonist but the agents of the action will be those who operate on or with the coat: Deena, her older sister, her baby sister, and her cousin.

The first plot action (stanza 2) is the older sister warning Deena that the coat's bag is dangerous just as Deena in fact reads the warning on the label. The second plot action (stanza 3) is the cousin running outside. The speech disfluencies at the beginning of stanza 3 are typical of real speech—people show such disfluencies as they plan a new section of their narrative (Levelt, 1989). Before Deena can get the planning done, she is interrupted and told that what she is about to say is irrelevant. When Deena continues stanza 3, we see that the plot action involves the cousin going outdoors. As good listeners to real stories, we should be trying to "guess" what this portends for the coat, but the teacher stops Deena again to ask the very question that in fact is supposed to be structuring her expectations about the story (and thereby giving her the satisfaction of suspense and participation in the storytelling act). Deena gives up, much as the writer of a detective fiction would give up if the reader refused to read furhter until he was told who had committed the murder.

From interviewing Deena (Michaels, 1981), it became apparent that stanza 4 may well have been something about the "naughty" cousin, who after having gotten dirty outside was about to put his hands on her new coat. There is no reason to believe that left to her own devices Deena would not have produced a story as imagistically and thematically compelling as Leona's. Her overall theme seems to have been that, left as a representative of "order" in the absence of her mother, Deena ends up trying to protect a baby from the dangers of her new coat, while having to simultaneously protect her coat from a disobedient, messy younger cousin. What, we may ask (and the story may have been asking), can we expect for this new coat from such inauspicious beginnings and, indeed, for the new school year it is meant to inaugurate?

We are not, however, claiming that Deena should have been left to her devices, although the teacher should have known (and the school should know) what those devices are. The teacher is not, in fact, intrested in hearing a fully plotted story with dramatic interest; she wants a more straightforward report that can be fairly easily shaped into the precursors of essayist talking and writing. However, for Deena, sharing time is a particularly deceiving enterprise, because it apppears to be a typical storytelling time among peers, a genre of special significance in African-American culture (certainly of as much significance and cognitive potential as semantically expanded conversations over pancakes in mainstream homes). Deena has little support from early home-based literacy practices (such as interactive storybook reading and semantically expanded conversations) and little support in the interaction with her teacher to enable her to cooperatively shape her performance into a version of early essayist literacy.

Our next example makes clear that while what children like Leona and Deena are doing at sharing time is not valued or assessed as successful, ironically, in a different social activity, somewhat similar behaviors are highly valued by mainstream cultures early in life and become the basis for later school success for some mainstream children.

Sensemaking in Discourse: Literature at Home

What Leona and Deena are attempting as young children, and what their culture has mastered in its oral storytelling, is of course highly valued in literary art (poetry, short stories, novels). And, in fact, such oral storytelling is the historical foundation of written literature (Bright, 1981; Tannen, 1982, 1989). Mainstream homes often engage in social activities around storybooks that introduce their children to literary discourse practices, practices that they will see throughout their schooling and in their continuing encounters with literature (Heath, 1982; Garton and Pratt, 1989). These home-based practices are also implicated in later school success.

We will look at one, rather typical, example of early interaction around storybooks and their implications for the nature of discourse in school and society (Gee, 1989a). Our example involves the speech activity of "pretend book reading," a variation of a regular home activity in which a young European-American middle-class mother reads storybooks to her two young daughters (ages 5 and 7 years). The 5-year-old, who we call Katie, has recently had a problematic birthday party at which a fight broke out among some of the children. In the next few days, Katie has told several relatives about the birthday party, reporting the events in "reportive" style ("the facts"). A few days later, when the mother is reading a storybook to her other daughter, the 5-year-old says she wants to "read" (she cannot yet decode print) and pretends to be reading a book, while telling what happened at her birthday party. Her original attempt at this is not very good, but eventually after a few tries, interspersed with the mother reading to the other girl, Katie produced the following story, which is not a report, or a typical "oral" story, but a "literary story" (the text is demarcated in terms of "lines" and "stanzas").

Katie's Story

Stanza 1 (Introduction)

    1. This is a story,
    2. About some kids who were once friends,
    3. But got into a big fight,
    4. And were not.

Stanza 2 (Frame: Signaling of Genre)

    5. You can read along in your storybook.
    6. I'm gonna read aloud.
    [storyreading prosody from now on]

Stanza 3 (Title)

    7. "How the Friends Got Unfriend."

Stanza 4 (Setting: Introduction of Characters)

    8. Once upon a time there was three boys 'n three girls.
    9. They were named Betty Lou, Pallis, and Parshin, were the girls,
  10. And Michael, Jason, and Aaron were the boys.
  11. They were friends.

Stanza 5 (Problem: Sex Differences)

  12. The boys would play Transformers,
  13. And the girls would play Cabbage Patches.

Stanza 6 (Crisis: Fight)

  14. But then one day they got into a fight on who would be which team.
  15. It was a very bad fight.
  16. They were punching,
  17. And they were pulling,
  18. And they were banging.

Stanza 7 (Resolution 1: Storm)

  19. Then all of a sudden the sky turned dark,
  20. The rain began to fall,
  21. There was lightning going on,
  22. And they were not friends.

Stanza 8 (Resolution 2: Mothers Punish)
  23. Then um the mothers came shooting out 'n saying,
  24. "What are you punching for?
  25. You are going be punished for a whole year."

Stanza 9 (Frame)

  26. The end.
  27. Wasn't it fun reading together?
  28. Let's do it again,
  29. Real soon!

The books that are part of the storybook reading activities that regularly occur in Katie's home encode language that is part of several specific genres. These include, of course, "children's literature," but also "literature" proper. Such books use linguistic devices that are simplified analogues of "literary" devices used in traditional, canonical "high literature." These devices are often thought to be natural and universal to literary art, although they are not. Many of them have quite specific origins in specific historical circumstances (although, indeed, some of them are rooted in universals of sensemaking and are devices that occur in nonliterary talk and writing).

One device with a quite specific historical reference is the socalled sympathetic fallacy. This is where a poem or story treats natural events (e.g., sunshine, storms) as if they reflected or were "in harmony" or "in step" with (sympathetic with) human events and emotions. This device was a hallmark of nineteenth century Romantic poetry, although it is common in more recent poetry as well (Abrams, 1953). Notice how in the 5-year-old's story the sympathetic fallacy is not only used but also is, in fact, the central organizing device in the construction of the story. The fight between the girls and boys in stanza 6 is immediately followed in stanza 7 by the sky turning dark, with lightening flashing, and thence in line 22: "and they were not friends." Finally, in stanza 8, the mothers come on the scene to punish the children for their transgression. The sky is "in tune" with human happenings.

The function of the sympathetic fallacy in high literature is to equate the world of nature (the macrocosm) with the world of human affairs (the microcosm) as it is depicted in a particular work of art (Abrams, 1953; Eagleton, 1983). It also suggests that these human affairs, as they are depicted in the work of literary art, are "natural," part of the logic of the universe, rather than conventional, historical, cultural, or class-based.

In Katie's story, the sympathetic fallacy functions in much the same way as it does in high literature. In particular, the story suggests that gender differences (stanza 4: boy versus girl) are associated with different interests (stanza 5: Transformers versus Cabbage Patches) and that these different interests inevitably lead to conflict when male and female try to be "equal" or sort themselves on grounds other than gender (stanza 6: "a fight on who would be which team"—the fight had been about mixing genders on the teams). The children are punished for transgressing gender lines (stanza 8), but only after the use of the sympathetic fallacy (stanza 7) has suggested that division by gender, and the conflicts that transgressing this division lead to, are sanctioned by nature, are "natural" and "inevitable," not merely conventional or constructed in the very act of play itself. Notice, then, how the very form and structure of the language, and the linguistic devices used, carry an ideological message (about the distribution of gender roles in this case). In mastering this social activity, the little girl has unconsciously appropriated a whole system of thought, embedded in the very linguistic devices she uses.

Let's consider how this text relates to the later participation of this child in various school literacy-based social activities. The child had started by telling a story about her birthday, to various relatives, over a couple of days, in a reportive fashion. Then, on a given day, in the course of repeated book-reading episodes, she reshapes this report into another genre. She incorporates aspects of the book-reading episode into her narrative. Note, for example, the introduction in stanza 1, the frame in stanza 2, the title in stanza 3, and then the start of the story proper in stanza 4. She closes the frame ("The end") in stanza 9. This overall structure shapes the text into storybook reading, although, in fact, there is no book and the child can't read. Note that traditional accounts of literacy as "the ability to read or write" are going to have deep conceptual problems here, because they trouble themselves too much over things like books and reading and too little over social practices.

Supported by her mother and sister, 5-year-old Katie is mastering the social activity of storybook reading. But this activity is itself an aspect of apprenticeship in another, more mature social activity, namely literature. This child, when she goes to school to begin her more public apprenticeship into the social activity of literature, will look like a "quick study" indeed. It will appear that her success was inevitable given her native intelligence and verbal abilities. Her success was inevitable, indeed, but because of her earlier apprenticeship. Note too how her mastery of this storybook reading social activity leads to the incorporation of a set of values and attitudes (about gender and the naturalness of middle-class ways of behaving) that are shared by many other dominant social activities in our society. This will facilitate the acquisition of and participation in other dominant social activities, ones that may, at first, appear quite disparate from literature or storybook reading.

It is as pointless to ask of Katie's story, as it would be of Leona's puppy story, "Did she really intend, or did she really know about, such meanings?" The social activities to which she is apprenticed "speak" through her or, rather, allow her to speak beyond herself (a different sort of "speaking in tongues," perhaps). Finally, we can note that Katie ingests an entire ideological perspective here, in the act of coming to be a participant in a social activity, but not in any way in which she could analyze it, verbalize it, or critique it. It is one of the jobs of schooling, at its best, to give children these latter metacritical abilities, not just to allow them to practice further the social activities they have already acquired at home.

It seems something of a paradox that the literary devices used by the mainstream child Katie, within the social activity of early storybook reading, translate into school success, whereas the somewhat different, but equally literary devices of children like Leona and Deena (e.g., parallelism, repetition, thematic development, contrasting images) are not used as a resource by the school, even in language arts activities. But this is a paradox only if we take a decontextualized and asocial view of language. The language of Katie and that of Leona are embedded at home in different social activities, and these social activities relate in quite different ways to the school's social activities. To take one example among many, the school in the early years tends to value narratives only to the extent that they can be used to facilitate the acquisition of written language and of essayist expository ways of thinking, talking, and writing (Michaels, 1990). Katie's early literary training takes place in the context of written language, whereas Leona's takes place in an oral context. Only in the later years of school is literary narrative valued in its own right, and by this time the many students such as Leona have already come to see themselves as out of place and out of step in the world of school.

Sensemaking in Discourse: Verbal Analogy Items

The examples covered so far involve a speaker interacting with an audience of one or more in the performance of a particular school-based discourse genre or speech event. We have tried to show how individuals' social, cultural, and linguistic backgrounds lead them to approach these speech events in ways that may or may not coincide with the expectations of the school culture.

In the following example, we again develop this theme, attempting to show how careful analysis of particular discourse practices can reveal what is actually demanded of students by the institutions that control elite education in the United States. We rely on some methods of discourse analysis to examine an activity that plays a central gate-keeping role in the world of mainstream schooling: standardized test taking. We will focus here on only one genre of test item, that of verbal analogy problems in the Scholastic Aptitude Test (SAT).[11] The SAT is widely used as an entrance requirement for matriculation at colleges and universities in the United States and as a criterion in decisions to allocate scholarship funds after matriculation.

Performance on verbal analogy problems is widely considered to be an excellent index of the ability to use analogical reasoning (Embretson *et al.* 1986; Anastasi, 1988). In traditional psychometric studies of this topic, the main requirements for successful solution of verbal analogy problems are thought to be vocabulary knowledge and analogical reasoning, as laid out in the work of Sternberg (1977, 1985) and others.

Our perspective on people's sensemaking in discourse would suggest that the picture is more complex. Analysis of this discourse genre and of various test-takers' interactions with it reveals that there is another crucial type of knowledge that supports successful sensemaking in this genre. This knowledge involves awareness of a particular kind of restriction on the role of language in these problems. Specifically, the words in a verbal analogy problem are to be understood as dictionary entries, not as expressions used in communication in everyday life. A great deal hinges on this seemingly straightforward understanding, as we will show in the following sections.

Test Performance as a Socially Situated Activity

Verbal analogy problems present an interesting case in the study of discourse genres viewed as social activities. Other than in standardized tests of "scholastic aptitude" (and in programs and curricular materials intended to help students prepare for such tests), verbal analogy problems are a rarely encountered discourse genre. Those who set the items, the test makers, tacitly hold certain expectations about the roles participants in the activity will play and the characteristic ways in which people playing these roles are expected to act, interact with the text, respond, and, we would claim, to believe, value, and think. A successful "reading" of one of these problems requires that the test taker understand, if not endorse, the precise nature of the test-maker's expectations.

In the discourse of standardized tests, whatever dialogic interaction exists is sharply limited by the differences in power and control between the two "interlocutors." This difference in power and control stems from the larger activity system of which a particular testing incident is a part. The individual activity of taking the SAT and the roles participants play within it can only be fully understood in terms of their relations to the whole activity system and the wider sociocultural setting. Tests like the SAT play a profoundly important role in shaping attitudes about schooling, aptitude, life chances, and matriculation at college.

To this scenario we bring two analyses proceeding in parallel: the analysis of verbal analogy discourse as presumably intended by the test maker, and the analysis of specific students' problem solutions, as evidenced in a think-aloud protocol.[12] We will only present a few examples—this does not constitute a full-blown analysis in any sense. We present these data in an attempt to illustrate how our vertical approach to the analysis of discourse can illuminate numerous facets of complex communicative practices. In doing this, we will suggest once again that within mainstream education, interpretive practices are often nontransparent. They may require experience with isomorphic practices based in the home or community discourse and are not the direct indicators of "pure" ability they are thought to be but, rather, are mediated through tacit understandings that are socioculturally provided.

What Does It Take to Solve a Verbal Analogy Problem?

What is an analogy? Simply, it is a way of understanding situations and entities in one domain in terms of situations and entities in a different domain. On this view, an analogy asserts that a relational structure that normally applies in one domain can be applied in another domain (Gentner, 1983:156). In an analogy like the following, we understand the domain of lawyers and clients in terms of the relations between doctors and patients.

DOCTOR : PATIENT :: LAWYER : CLIENT

(Typically, this is read as "Doctor is to patient, as lawyer is to client.") To solve an analogy problem, it is generally asumed that the problem-solver discovers the important relations and attributes in the first "base" domain (for instance, the relations between doctor and patient), maps these into another "target" domain (for instance, the world of lawyers and their clients), and then checks to see to what extent the relations and attributes in the base domain apply in the target domain.

In much of the literature on analogical thinking, the base domain and target domain are complex structures or situations in the world— for example, the realm of electromagnetism and the realm of flow dynamics (Gentner, 1983). In the problems we are considering, the test item stem (the base domain) consists of two words in relation to each other. The possible answer choices (target domain) are also pairs of words. But what are the objects and attributes in the base and target domains, and what is the nature of the important relations between the two? There are two possibilities.

Words as Expressions   First, words can function as instruments in human communication. They can be used to *refer*. As such, a word can call up, or index, a situation or entity in the world that it may refer to. The word "rain" may call up memories of the entity known as rain, or instances of situations in which that word was used in a referential way. Linguists sometimes refer to words in action as *expressions* (cf. Lyons, 1977:23).

If we see the words in an analogy problem as expressions, then the real objects to be mapped from the base domain to the target domain are events or situations in the world. As such, the systematic relationship between the base domain and the target domain will involve relations among objects or situations in the world.

Words as Lexemes   On the other hand, words can be seen as objects in themselves, outside of the actual situations of use, as *lexemes* (Lyons, 1977:7). Lexemes are words considered as objects in the mental lexicon or, more practically, as objects in the dictionary. They have properties that limit what they can be used to refer to, but they also have grammatical and lexical properties, such as belonging to the class of mass nouns or intransitive verbs, as well as numerous other properties. If the objects in the base and target domains of an analogy are lexemes, then we will see quite different relationships emerge as important in the solving of an analogy problem.

Our claim is that analogy test items can be construed two ways. The test-maker sees the set of objects that are being mapped and the basis for the higher-order relations as relative to the *lexeme*. The test-taker, on the other hand, may understand the analogy to be about a set of real world entities and situations.

If this is so, then the test-taker must perform in three different dimensions to succeed with the "interlocutor," the test and its maker. The test-taker must display analogical thinking, as discussed above. The test-taker must display word knowledge, and finally the test-taker must display an ability to reason about words as objects. This is different from thinking analogically about events and situations, with words functioning only as an index to the situation and its properties. If the reader fails in the third area, he or she will likely be labelled as unable to think analogically, as being deficient in vocabulary knowledge, or both. Our claim is that in fact the reader may be deficient in neither but, rather, may have a different understanding about the activity itself.

Words as Expressions: Indexing a Situation[13]

In the following example, an adult in her mid-thirties, Danielle, a former college student who was no longer enrolled, was asked to read through verbal analogies taken from the SAT[14] and "think aloud" as she solved them. The item is given first, followed by the transcript of her problem solution.[15]

PATTER : RAIN
   RAINBOW : STORM,
   CALL : TELEPHONE,
   CLANK : CHAIN,
   VOLUME : RADIO,
   ERUPTION : VOLCANO

Danielle: [reads aloud] Patter–rain, rainbow–storm, call–telephone, clank–chain,
volume–radio, eruption–volcano . . .
Patter–rain . . . eruption–volcano.

Researcher: Why?

Danielle: [she sighs] Patter . . . is the sound . . . of, . . . is a type of rain. In . . . in . . .
in this analogy, patter is to rain as eruption is to a volcano, because the patter of the rain, is something that you hear . . .

Researcher: mm-hmm

Danielle: Aaand the eruption of a volcano is something that most people hear, very
few of us are close enough to see it.
You could also get away with volume–radio. As patter
. . . patter is to rain, volume is to radio.
Aaand, maybe . . . volume to radio, call–telephone? No, I don't like call–telephone.
Clank–chain . . . these-this-this series is a little bit better because . . .

because clank is a sound of a chain.
Call is [D coughs] telephone . . . not relevant,
Rainbow–storm, not relevant 'cause they're not sounds.

Patter to rain. So we have the three sound choices.
Volume to radio is something, you can control.
Patter [rain] is not . . . is not controllable. Forces are
controlling that.
Clank–chain is also controllable, because you're the one
doing the clanking on the chain,
And the only—the only two natural functions here are
eruption and vocano,
as patter to rain.

Researcher: So which one do you pick?

Danielle: Eruption to volcano.

The "correct" answer is CLANK : CHAIN. Yet Danielle has followed a chain of analogical inference that evidences both adequate word knowledge and the appropriate process of mapping objects from the base domain into the target domain. What are the different assumptions and actual practices that distinguish her interaction with the test item from that intended by the test-makers?

First, consider the fact that Danielle correctly identified the semantic field delineated by the stem: that of sounds and their sources. She narrowed down the field of correct answers to the three that could be used to refer to situations in which a sound emanated from a source. She then proceeded to compare, not the words, but the situations themselves. She compared the situations with respect to the dimension of agency in the relation between source and sound. She was evidently looking for the most systematic higher-order set of relations between the two domains (cf. Gentner, 1983).

What would the test-maker, or a test-taker more attuned to the discourse of standardized tests, have made of this item? First, such a reader would have considered the words themselves, as lexemes, to be the objects of the analogy. As such, the relations would not have been between situations involving sounds and their sources, but between words that denote sounds and words that denote sources of sounds. Thus, VOLUME : RADIO could have been eliminated, because the word "volume" does not denote a sound but, rather, the degree or intensity of a sound. Similarly, ERUPTION : VOLCANO could have been eliminated, because the lexeme "eruption" does not denote a sound but, rather, a process or instance of violent explosion. CLANK : CHAIN would be the only item in which the first term has as its central semantic function the designation of a sound.

If the lexeme "eruption" does not denote a sound, how could it be that Danielle used it to call up the sound of a volcano? In ordinary language use, her assumption would have been warranted as an instance of *metonymy*, the process whereby a speaker refers to an entity by using instead a word that refers to another entity that subsumes or is associated with the first entity. There are many conventional expressions that rely on this figurative use of language, such as "the pen is mightier than the sword." However, less noticeable instances permeate everyday language use. Every time we say something like "Chomsky takes up two feet on my bookshelf," or "Without the emergency break on, the car rolled down the driveway," we are using this "figurative" means to refer. It is books authored by Chomsky and the wheels of the car to which we intend to refer. The most noticeable examples are those in which the association between the referred-to entity and the metonymic label are unusual, as in the hapless waiter's "The mushroom omelette left without paying the bill" (Fauconnier, 1985:6).

Often the pragmatic relation between the "label" and the referent is completely ordinary and arises from the nature of physical events: Objects have characteristic dimensions such as shape and size. Events have characteristic sounds. When these relations are the basis of reference, we barely notice the figurative use of language. Nevertheless, the ordinariness of such devices in conversational discourse does not sanction their use in the particular discourse genre of test taking.[16]

The next two examples involve a freshman at a large public university. Gloria, a bilingual speaker of Spanish and English from the Southwestern United States, was asked to participate in a study of analogy test items, in which she would read through verbal analogies taken from the SAT and think aloud as she solved them. She, like the other subjects, was told that the researcher was interested in studying "how people think" while they take standardized tests and was paid $10 for the hour-long session. Later, the researcher examined her written work on a midterm in an introductory course in cultural anthropology. The comparison of her "analogical reasoning" in these two discourse genres reveals how the social context within which a text is situated shapes the ways that people make sense of that text.

SPOUSE : WIFE::
  HUSBAND : UNCLE
  SON : MOTHER
  CHILD : DAUGHTER
  BROTHER : SISTER
  GRANDPARENT : PARENT

As conceived by the test-makers, this item involves an analogy between lexemes, not situations in the world, As such, it is trading on a
property of the lexeme "spouse", namely that it is unspecified as to
gender of the potential referent. The word it is paired with, on the
other hand, "wife," is semantically specified for gender. It is restricted
in reference to picking out the female half of a married couple. In other
words, the terms "spouse" and "wife" can both be used to refer to the
female partner in a married couple, but the word *spouse* can also be
used to refer to the male partner. The crucial relationship that determines the correct analogical mapping is this fact about the semantic specifications of the first word in relation to the second word. The
only other pair where the same lexical relationship holds is
CHILD : DAUGHTER.

Gloria does not construe this task as one about relationships between lexical items; rather, she seems to be searching for an analogical
mapping between the referents of those lexical items.

Gloria: Yeah . . . Spouse is to wife . . . say male and female,

Researcher: Sorry?

Gloria: Male and female?
I guess relationship.
I don't . . .
'cause they're all related, all those things are related to
each other.
Husband and uncle, and . . .
that's the only thing I would think of
and then I would say brother and sister.

Researcher: Ok. Ok, so you would pick brother and sister.

Gloria: Yeah.

Gloria starts out by considering the two stem lexemes as a pair of terms
referring to a male and female, as we can infer by her utterance

"Spouse is to wife . . . say male and female." She seems to be thinking about a use of these two terms together, in actual reference to a pair of individuals. If these two terms were used together to refer to the relationship between a pair of individuals, as the other terms in this item do, they would only be referring to that of a husband and wife. Her mention of the attributes "male" and "female" indicate that she is not thinking about the denotational potential of "spouse" but, rather, what it would refer to in tandem with "wife." Given that she is dealing with entities in the world, we can assume that she has isolated the dimension of opposite sexes as potentially holding across the two domains of analogy.

Thus, in this problem we can hypothesize that she sees the domain as being family relationships, between a male and female. Furthermore, the relationship may crucially be reciprocal—that is, if X is Y's wife, then Y is X's husband. With these facts in mind, only one or two of the five answer pairs fits the schema. In one of the pairs, CHILD : DAUGHTER, only the second term explicitly denotes a kinship relation. Two others, GRANDPARENT : PARENT and HUSBAND : UNCLE, do not denote reciprocal relationships. Moreover, they do not specifically involve male and female relatives. The others, BROTHER : SISTER and SON : MOTHER, do denote reciprocal relationships involving males and females. Although we have no evidence for this, we might guess that Gloria chose BROTHER : SISTER because those relations are on the same generational level, as are husbands and wives, by definition. Sons and mothers involve another dimension—that of lineal descent.

To summarize, if a reader construes this problem as being about relationships between people, rather than relationships between words, a very different picture of the correct answer emerges. What is clear is that Gloria is seeking, as did Danielle, the appropriate analogy. She is searching for higher-order relations, she appears to know the meaning of the words, and she seeks to find corresponding pairs that will preserve the crucial meaning links between the pairs. However, the objects she is manipulating are situations in the world, not properties of lexical items.

If this analysis is correct, then Gloria is misreading the intent of the test-makers. She has not understood the constraints on this particular discourse genre. However, it is also clear from her protocol that she is very uncomfortable with the whole procedure. She repeatedly mentions that she hates taking these tests, doesn't do well on them, and finds them very troubling. The reason she does not like them comes up again and again. Gloria claims that she does not understand what the test-makers want from her. This is the source of her discomfort. In the following brief excerpt, she has just chosen an answer for one question and spontaneously begins to display these feelings.

Researcher: So for that one you'd think it was- three, ok.

Gloria: It's that same feeling, I was like . . .
           I couldn't think and I was like . . .
           and that's why none . . . none!
           not even one I would feel positive about. None!
           So I'd come out of there like—I don't know what I did!
           I just- pbbbh! you know, crossed out whatever.

Researcher: Yeah.

Gloria: [sighs] Ok, paragraph is to prose. . . . mmm.
           Well, I guess prose has paragraphs?
           I don't know. [laughs]
           Uh, . . . [sighs] see that's- oh God, those feelings . . .

Researcher: I feel so bad, I feel like
               / I'm torturing you.

Gloria: / no! no! [laughs]
           Oh God, let's see . . . [G begins to scan the choices and
           stops thinking aloud]

Researcher: What are you thinking about?

Gloria: How these all relate to one another.
           'Cause they all make so much sense.
           You just read'em and you don't really know what ch-what
           they want from you.

This desire to know the rules of the discourse game is consonant with a larger pictue of Gloria's life as a freshman. She and other subjects in the study were observed during a semester-long study skills class given as an adjunct to their large, introductory cultural anthropology lecture course at the university. In this study skills class, she was one of the top two or three students. She clearly enjoyed learning, applying, and displaying her knowledge of new study techniques. Similarly, her work in the introductory anthropology class, for which she usually received A's, showed interest, diligence, and a desire to discover and meet the standards of this new field. Gloria's very vivid displays of frustration during the verbal analogy test quite plausibly result from her pronounced desire to command the discourse norms of her academic environment.

Another Discourse Setting for Analogical Reasoning

So far we have discussed Gloria's performance in an activity designed to elicit analogical thinking—the verbal analogy test. The following example is part of Gloria's midterm from her lecture course in cultural anthropology. It answers a question that required a paradigmatic example of analogical thinking and vocabulary knowledge. In presenting this example, we want to suggest that the cognitive activity that is the putative core of verbal analogy items (i.e., analogical thinking) emerges clearly within a discourse genre whose rules are clear to Gloria.

An introductory anthropology class requires that students learn to think analogically about cultural practices and institutions found in their own and other cultures. Two of the guiding questions in introductions to cultural anthropology concern the status of cultural differences and cultural universals. To consider cultural universals, students must begin to distinguish between cultural practices that are only superficially similar, and those that are deeply similar, that serve a similar function or have a similar positioning in the cultures being compared.

In this particular exam, Gloria was asked to identify and discuss several cultural universals. To do this successfully, she had to discuss superficially different cultural practices, creating a level of description at which the particulars of these practices serve as objects that can be mapped analogically from culture to culture. She chose the notion of reciprocity: the incurring of obligation in the exchange of gifts. She compared the systems of exchange whereby people incur obligations in Becedas, Spain, the Trobriand Islands, the Punjab, the Kalahari Desert, and the United States. In all examples, she laid out what is exchanged, the nature of the obligation, and the reciprocity of the obligation.

The text given below is transcribed directly from her handwritten midterm, although for ease of reading we have corrected superficial errors in spelling or punctuation.

Cultural universals are those occurrences of culture—aspects,
custom—that seem to appear in every culture. Many studies have been
done to question the existence of these universals.

The idea of reciprocity has been set to see if every culture has this
sense of obligation in the exchange of gift giving,—if in every culture
there exist total prestations. Those systems of exchange by which
people make contracts and are bound by obligations have been shown
in the Trobriand Islands with the system of Kula,—by which all the
islands engage in an intertribal and island exchange of shells,
necklaces, and arm shells. There is an obligation to take part in this
system, for it is part of the economy. Reciprocity exists in many forms
as has also been shown in Becedas, with the ofrecijo and hay stacking
customs. The donors at one time are the recipients the next time
around. There is definite obligation in both customs whereby some
member of the family must repay gifts or services the next time
around.

Reciprocity thus involves an obligation to give, receive and repay—as
is seen in both examples. Many other societies in the world have
customs of reciprocity. The !Kung share their meat—as a refrigeration
method—but there is the obligation to give meat to those who give to
you—failing to receive and repay in these cultures is not accepting the
culture—it is like declaring war. The !Kung also have their system of
gift giving which is called Hxaso. Reciprocity is also seen in the
Punjab—with their system of gift giving within the castes. Even in our
own culture we see reciprocity—during Christmas we feel the
obligation to give to family and friends or any others we know are
giving a gift to us. It is the exchange of gift for gift, and the obligation
to return if someone has given you a gift and you have not returned the
favor. These are all examples of reciprocity—and it does seem to be a
universal phenomenon. It is just a question of the degree it partakes in
the culture. . . .

In this example, Gloria maps objects from one cultural domain into
another. Her answer lays out an analogy between Becedas and its
customs of hay-stacking and ofrecijo, with the Trobriand Islands and
its custom of Kula, etc. She shows that the higher-order relations of
gift-giving and reciprocal obligation through cycles of gift-giving are
maintained in the mappings. This excerpt is only part of her answer;
Gloria continues to draw analogies between cultures to derive the
cultural universal of the incest taboo. She then shows the reader that
not all cultural practices are universal by laying out a failed analogy:
cultural practices that might seem to reflect a universal notion of "life
crisis," but in fact do not. She received 30 points, the highest possible
total, for her answer.

What are the differences between this midterm and the verbal
analogy test that gave Gloria so much trouble? Both are "tests," and
both require adherence to a fairly narrow and technical use of lan-

guage. Both require analogical thinking. The difference lies partly within the way the test-taker acquires knowledge of the acceptable objects and relations that constitute the analogy. In effect, the class lectures and text provide the workshop within which the student can forge that knowledge. The rules of the discourse are part of the learning enterprise, whether or not these are explicitly labeled. The verbal analogy test, on the other hand, requires that the student already know the appropriate objects and relations that constitute the targeted analogies.

In this example, discourse analysis plays two roles: It can assist us in looking at the relation between a cognitive process (analogical reasoning) and the settings within which this process takes place, thus giving us insight into the construct validity of some of our measures of that cognitive process. Discourse analysis also widens our understanding of the way the test itself embodies larger values, beliefs, and systems of social practices. Because the verbal analogy test imposes limitations that are quite different from the usage norms found in everyday conversation, we are left with a question: Where do students who succeed at this discourse genre derive their expertise? To answer that question, we would have to investigate discourse practices within various speech activities outside the test-taking situation.

Conclusion

We have used these three case studies as "exemplars" of discourse analysis to illustrate a range of techniques, tools, and ways of using textual analysis in understanding the complex relationships among social, linguistic, and cognitive processes (Mishler, 1990). While each example focuses on discourse deriving from a different kind of social activity and institutional context, they are all integrally related through themes having to do with sociocultural differences, relations between discourse at home and at school, and educational equity. Together, these three examples illustrate a particular approach to discourse analysis. In this approach, talk or writing must be understood as a particular genre of discourse, embedded within larger activities and activity systems, as well as traditions, folk theories, and ideologies.

The examples do not, however, represent a cookbook approach to using discourse analysis in educational research and theorizing. Each case under investigation requires somewhat different techniques and lends itself to different kinds and levels of analysis. Our point has been to make a range of analytic practices and tools visible to the reader, as exemplars to "think with," so that they might be critiqued, adapted, or extended in new directions. Our research suggests that discourse analysis can be a powerful tool in exploring practical and theoretical issues in education. Beyond this, however, it suggests that in discourse analysis there can be no neat distinction between theory and practice or between research and advocacy for change.

Notes

[1]The three listed authors were coequal in the production of this chapter. Order of authors is alphabetical. Support for this work comes partially from the Literacies Institute, which promotes interdisciplinary research on issues of language, culture, and literacy, across the curriculum in a multicultural society. The Institute is funded by the Andrew W. Mellon Foundation.

[2]For introductions to discourse analysis with an emphasis on linguistics, the reader should consult Brown and Yule (1983), Coulthard (1977), Levinson (1983), and Stubbs (1983). Those interested specifically in the analysis of talk from a sociological perspective should see Psathas (1979), Schenkein (1978), Garfinkel (1977), Atkinson and Heritage (1984), and Goffman (1981). Anthropological and sociolinguistic approaches are well represented in Gumperz (1982a), Hymes (1981), Tedlock (1983), Moerman (1988), and Gumperz and Hymes (1972). Readers interested in discourse analysis in service of the explication of social, cultural, and political institutions and relations should consult Fairclough (1989), van Dijk (1985), and Kramerae, Schulz, and O'Barr, (1984).

[3]Starting with Hymes' work (Hymes, 1962), numerous anthropologists and linguists have conducted ethnographic studies of communication practices in different cultural groups and social settings. Good introductions may be found in Gumperz and Hymes (1972) and Saville-Troike (1982).

[4]Ochs has explored this issue in great detail, especially as it relates to studies of child language acquisition, in an article entitled "Transcription as Theory" (1979).

[5]The notations used to indicate intonation and prosody in this transcript were developed by John Gumperz and his collaborators, based on the work of John Trim. Speech is first chunked into tone group units (i.e., segments with a continuous intonational contour). These units are then designated as minor tone groups (signaling "more to come," akin to a comma—indicated as /) or major tone groups (ending with some indication of utterance closure, akin to a period in writing—indicated as //). Within a tone group, several features are indicated: (1) location of the nuclei (i.e., the syllable or syllables marked by change in pitch or other manifestations of prominence): "\" low fall, "\\" high fall, "/" low rise, "//" high rise; (2) other accented syllables in the tone group: "ǀ" high, "ǀ" low, "–" level; ":" indicates vowel elongation; (3) paralinguistic features such as (a) shift to a high-pitch register "L" or shift to a low pitch register "L" (both applying to the entire tone group), (b) pausing: ". ." indicating a break in timing " . . . " indicating a measurable pause, and "=" indicating continous speech flow, (c) speech rate: "acc." indicating accelerating tempo and "ret." indicating slowing down, (d) loudness over an entire tone group is indicated by "p" (soft) or "f" (loud). Doubling of one of the above symbols indicates extra emphasis.

[6]However, it should be kept in mind that false starts and repairs are meaningful indicators of underlying planning, and so themselves are also guides to structure and meaning (Gee and Grosjean, 1984; Goldman-Eisler, 1968; Levelt, 1989). People tend to display such speech disruptions when they are planning a new part or major division of their text "on-line," as they are speaking.

[7]The sociolinguist William Labov (1972) has argued that this sort of structuring is typical of African-American culture storytelling as well as many other cultures.

[8]It is worth noting that the African-American children in this classroom were all from low-income families and all lived within a radius of eight blocks from one another in the working-class part of town. They were bused from this community to the school, which was located in an upper middle-class neighborhood. The European-American children in this class, without exception, walked to school from this neighborhood and were all from professional, middle- to upper middle-class homes. Thus, in this classroom, ethnicity, class, and community affiliation were thoroughly confounded.

[9]This sharing time schema existed not just (however partially) in the teacher's head or in the children's heads alone, but also in the social interaction between teacher and child, as well as in the physical and discursive "space" of rugtime within the classroom and the school.

[10]As discussed earlier, transcribing the intricacies of speech in terms of its pronunciation, prosody, hesitations, and overlaps is a complex and artful business (Atkinson and Heritage, 1984; Ochs, 1979). In any discourse analysis, researchers transcribe only as much detail as is needed for their analysis, and there is no such thing as a "fully detailed" transcription (speech has a massive number of details that might be meaningfully relevant in some context). For our purposes later, we simply place each tone group on a separate line, using a comma to mark a pitch glide that means "more to come" (a "continuation contour") and a period or question mark for a pitch glide that achieves somewhat more closure than the comma.

[11]This research was partially funded through support for M. C. O'Connor, from the Ford Foundation's Division of Human Rights and Governance, in a grant to establish the National Commission on Testing and Public Policy, a 3-year study of the role of standardized testing in the allocation of opportunities. This research is part of a larger work on analogy items, currently in progress.

[12]"Think aloud protocols" are records of a subject's verbalizations as he or she works through some sort of problem, noting as completely as possible the steps required to complete that problem. For an extensive discussion of the possible insights this method affords, as well as methodological constraints on its appropriate use, see Ericsson and Simon (1984).

[13]In the following examples, the sex and location of some of the subjects has been changed. All names used are psuedonyms. Other information provided reflects actual reports of subjects.

[14]The items were obtained from Roy Freedle, who is engaged in research for the Educational Testing Service on the topic of analogy items.

[15]In the transcriptions, pauses are indicated by dots: " . . . " indicates a noticeable pause. All transcripts are complete segments unless otherwise indicated. Comments and clirifications are given in square brackets.

[16]Put another way, we could say that metonymic extensions are a property of referring (or predicating) expressions, not of lexemes. Because lexemes are the objects of analogical reasoning here, patterns of metonymic extension are irrelevant and will probably lead the test-taker into "error."

References

Abrahams, R. D. (1964). *Deep down in the jungle: Negro narrative folklore from the streets of Philadelphia*. Hatboro, PA: Folklore Associates.

Abrahams, R. D. (1976). *Talking black*. Rowley, MA: Newbury House.

Abrams, M. H. (1953). *The mirror and the lamp: Romantic theory and the critical tradition*. Oxford: Oxford University Press.

Adams, M. J. (1990). *Beginning to read: Thinking and learning about print*. Cambridge, MA: MIT Press.

Anastasi, A. (1988). *Psychological testing*, (6th ed.) New York: Macmillan.

Apple, M. W. (1986). *Teachers and texts: A political economy of class and gender relations in education*. London: Routledge & Kegan Paul.

Argyle, M., and Cook, M. (1976). *Gaze and mutual gaze*. Cambridge: Cambridge University Press.

Atkinson, J. M. (1984). *Our masters' voices: The language and body language of politics*. London: Methuen.

Atkinson, J, M., and Heritage, J. (1984). *Structures of social action: Studies in conversational analysis*. Cambridge: Cambridge University Press.

Atkinson, P. (1985). *Language, structure and reproduction: An introduction to the sociology of Basil Bernstein*. London: Methuen.

Bailey, G., and Maynir, N. (1987). Decreolization. *Language and Society*, 16, 449–473.

Bakhtin, M. M. (1981). *The dialogic imagination*, M. Holquist (Ed.). Austin: University of Texas Press.

Bakhtin, M. M. (1986). *Speech genres and other essays*, V. W. McGee (Trans.) and C. Emerson and M. Holquist (Eds.)). Austin: University of Texas.

Bauman, R. (1986). *Story, performance, and event: Contextual studies of oral narrative*. Cambridge: Cambridge University Press.

Bauman, R., and Sherzer, J. (Eds.). (1974). *Explorations in the ethnography of speaking*. Cambridge: Cambridge University Press.

Berlin, A. (1985). *The dynamics of biblical parallelism*. Bloomington: Indiana University Press.

Birch, D. (1989). *Language, literature and critical practice: Ways of analyzing text*. London: Routledge.

Birdwhistell, R. (1971). *Kinesics and context: Essays on body communication*. Harmondsworth, England: Penguin.

Bolinger, D. (1986). *Intonation and its parts: Melody in spoken English*. Stanford, CA: Stanford University Press.

Boudon, R. (1986). *The analysis of ideology*, M. Slater (Trans.). Chicago: University of Chicago Press.

Bourdieu, P. (1977). *Outline of a theory of practice*, R. Nice (Trans.). Cambridge: Cambridge University Press.

Brazil, D., Coulthard, M., and Johns, C. (1980). *Discourse intonation and language teaching*. London: Longman.

Bright, W. (1981). Literature: Written and oral. *In* D. Tannen (Ed.), *Analyzing discourse: Text and talk* (pp. 271–283). Georgetown University Round Table on Languages and Linguistics. Washington, DC: Georgetown University Press.

Brown, G., and Yule, G. (1983). *Discourse analysis*. Cambridge: Cambridge University Press.

Callinicos, A. (1988). *Making history: Agency, structure and change in social theory.* Ithaca, NY: Cornell University Press.

Cazden, C. (1988). *Classroom discourse: The language of teaching and learning.* Portsmouth, NH: Heinemann.

Chafe, W. L. (1979). The flow of thought and the flow of language. *In* T. Givon (Ed.), *Syntax and semantics 12: Discourse and syntax* (pp. 159–181). New York: Academic Press.

Chafe, W. L. (1980). The deployment of consciousness in the production of a narrative. *In* W. L. Chafe (Ed.), *The pear stories: Cognitive, cultural, and linguistic aspects of narrative production* (pp. 9–50). Norwood, NJ: Ablex.

Chall, J., Jacobs, V. A., and Baldwin, L. E. (1990). *The reading crisis: Why poor children fall behind.* Cambridge, MA: Harvard University Press.

Chatman, S. (1978). *Story and discourse: Narrative structure in fiction and film.* Ithaca, NY: Cornell University Press.

Chomsky, N. (1981). *Lectures on government and binding.* Dordrecht, Netherlands: Foris.

Cohan, S., and Shires, L. M. (1988). *Telling stories: A theoretical analysis of narrative fiction.* New York: Routledge.

Collins, J., and Michaels, S. (1986). Discourse and the acquisition of literacy. *In* J. Cook-Gumperz (Ed.), *The social construction of literacy* (pp. 207–222). New York: Cambridge University Press.

Connerton, P. (1989). *How societies remember.* Cambridge: Cambridge University Press.

Coulthard, M. (1977). *An introduction to discourse analysis.* London and New York: Longman.

Crystal, D. (1979). *Prosodic systems and intonation in English.* Cambridge: Cambridge University Press.

Douglas, M. (1968). The social control of cognition: Some factors in joke perception. *Man, 3,* 361–376.

Douglas, M. (1986). *How institutions think.* Syracuse, NY: Syracuse University Press.

Duranti, A., and Ochs, E. (1979). Left-dislocation in Italian conversation. *In* T. Givon (Ed.), *Syntax and semantics 12: Discourse and syntax* (pp. 377–416). New York: Academic Press.

Eagleton, T. (1983). *Literacy theory: An introduction.* Minneapolis: The University of Minnesota Press.

Eagleton, T. (1984). *The functions of criticism: From the spectator to post-structuralism.* London: Verso.

Eagleton, T. (1990). *The ideology of the aesthetic.* Oxford: Basil Blackwell.

Edelsky, C. (1986). *Writing in a bilingual program: Habia una vez.* Norwood, NJ: Ablex.

Embretson, S., Schneider, L. M., and Roth, D. L. (1986). Multiple processing strategies and the construct validity of verbal reasoning tests. *Journal of Educational Measurement,* 23.1, 13–23.

Ericsson, K. A., and Simon, H. A. (1984). *Protocol analysis: Verbal reports as data.* Cambridge, MA: MIT Press.

Fairclough, N. (1989). *Language and power.* London: Longman.

Fillmore, C. (1975). An alternative to checklist theories of meaning. *In Proceedings of the First Annual Meeting of the Berkeley Linguistics Society* (pp. 123–131). Berkeley: University of California at Berkeley.

Finnegan, R. (1988). *Literacy and orality.* Oxford: Basil Blackwell.

Foley, J. M. (1988). *The theory of oral composition: History and methodology.* Bloomington: University of Indiana Press.

Foucault, M. (1980). *Power/knowledge: Selected interviews and other writings 1972–1977,* C. Gordon, L. Marshall, J. Meplam, and K. Soper (Eds.). Brighton, Sussex: The Harvester Press.

Foucault, M. (1985). *The Foucault reader,* P. Rainbow (Ed.). New York: Pantheon.

Fowler, R. (1981). *Literature as social discourse.* Bloomington: Indiana University Press.

Garfinkel, H. (1967). *Studies in ethnomethodology.* Englewood Cliffs, NJ: Prentice-Hall.

Garton, A., and Pratt, C. (1989). *Learning to be literate: The development of spoken and written language.* Oxford: Basil Blackwell.

Gates, H. L., Jr. (Ed.). (1984). *Black literature and literary theory.* New York: Methuen.

Gee, J. P. (1985). The narrativization of experience in the oral style. *Journal of Education,* 167, 9–35.

Gee, J. P. (1986). Units in the production of discourse. *Discourse Processes,* 9, 391–422.

Gee, J. P. (1989a). Literacy, discourse, and linguistics: An introduction. *Journal of Education,* 171, 5–17.

Gee, J. P. (1989b). "Literariness," formalism, and sense making: The line and stanza structure of human thought. *Journal of Education,* 171, 61–75.

Gee, J. P. (1989c). Two styles of narrative construction and their linguistic and educational implications. *Discourse Processes,* 12, 287–307.

Gee, J. P. (1989d). What is literacy? *In* C. Mitchell (Ed.), *Journal of Education,* 171, 18–25.

Gee, J. P. (1990a). A linguistic approach to narrative, *The Journal of Narrative and Life History,* 1, 15–39.

Gee, J. P. (1990b). Memory and myth: A perspective on narrative. *In* A. McCabe and C. Peterson (Eds.), *Developing narrative structure* (pp. 1–25). Hillsdale, NJ: Lawrence Erlbaum.

Gee, J. P. (1990c). *Social linguistics and literacies: Ideology in Discourses.* London: Falmer Press.

Gee, J. P., and Grosjean, F. (1984). Empirical evidence for narrative structure. *Cognitive Science,* 8, 59–85.

Genette, G. (1980). *Narrative discourse,* J. Lewin (Trans.). Ithaca, NY: Cornell University Press.

Gentner, D. (1983). Structure-mapping. A theoretical framework for analogy. *Cognitive Science,* 7, 155–170.

Giddens, A. (1979). *Central problem in social theory.* London: Macmillan.

Giddens, A. (1984). *The constitution of society.* Cambridge: Polity Press.

Giddens, A. (1990). *The consequences of modernity.* Stanford, CA: Stanford University Press.

Giroux, H. (1988). *Schooling and the struggle for public life.* Minneapolis: University of Minnesota Press.

Givon, T. (1979a). *On understanding grammar.* New York: Academic Press.

Givon, T. (Ed.). (1979b). *Syntax and semantics 12: Discourse and syntax.* New York: Academic Press.

Givon, T. (Ed.). (1983). *Topic continuity in discourse: A quantitative cross-language study.* Amsterdam: John Benjamins.

Givon, T. (1984). *Syntax: A functional–typological introduction,* (Vol. 1). Amsterdam: J. Benjamins.

Givon, T. (1989). *Mind, code and context*. Hillsdale, NJ: Lawrence Erlbaum.

Goffman, E. (1971). *Relations in public*. New York: Basic Books.

Goffman, E. (1974). *Frame analysis*. New York: Harper & Row.

Goffman, E. (1981). *Forms of talk*. Oxford: Basil Blackwell.

Goldman-Eisler, F. (1968). *Psycholinguistics: Experiments in spontaneous speech*. New York: Academic Press.

Goodwin, C. (1981). *Conversational organization: Interaction between speakers and hearers*. New York: Academic Press.

Graff, H. J. (1987). *The legacies of literacy: Continuities and contradictions in Western culture and society*. Bloomington: Indiana University Press.

Graves, D. (1983). *Writing: Teachers and children at work*. Portsmouth, NH: Heinemann.

Gumperz, J. J. (1982a). *Discourse strategies*. Cambridge: Cambridge University Press.

Gumperz, J. J. (Ed.). (1982b). *Language and social identity*. Cambridge: Cambridge University Press.

Gumperz, J. J., and Hymes, D. (Eds.)(1972). *Directions in sociolinguistics: The ethnography of communication*. New York: Holt, Rinehart and Winston.

Hiaman, J. (Ed.). (1984). *Iconicity in syntax*. Amsterdam: J. Benjamins.

Haiman, J. (1985). *Natural syntax*. Cambridge: Cambridge University Press.

Halliday, M. A. K. (1967). *Intonation and grammar in British English*. The Hague: Mouton.

Halliday, M. A. K. (1985). *An introduction to functional grammar*. London: Edward Arnold.

Halliday, M. A. K. (1989). *Spoken and written language*. Oxford: Oxford University Press.

Halliday, M. A. K., and Hasan, R. (1976). *Cohesion in English*. London: Longman.

Halliday, M. A. K., and Hasan, R. (1989). *Language, context, and text: Aspects of language in a social–semiotic perspective*. Oxford: Oxford University Press.

Hasan, R. (1989). *Linguistics, language, and verbal art*. Oxford: Oxford University Press.

Heath, S. B. (1982). What no bedtime story means: Narrative skills at home and at school. *Language in Society*, 11, 49–76.

Heath, S B. (1983). *Ways with words: Language, life, and work in communities and classrooms*. Cambridge: Cambridge University Press.

Hewitt, R. (1986). *White talk black talk: Inter-racial friendship and communication amongst adolescents*. Cambridge: Cambridge University Press.

Holland, D., and Quinn, N. (Eds.). (1987). *Cultural models in language and thought*. Cambridge: Cambridge University Press.

Hopper, P., and Thompson, S. (1980). Transitivity in grammar and discourse. *Language*, 56, 251–299.

Hopper, P., and Thompson, S. (Eds.). (1982). *Syntax and semantics 15: Studies in transitivity*. New York: Academic Press.

Hymes, D. (1962). The ethnography of speaking. *In* T. Gladwin & W. C. Sturtevant (Eds.), *Anthropology and human behavior* (pp. 13–53). Washington, DC: Anthropological Society of Washington.

Hymes, D. (1974). *Foundations in sociolinguistics: An ethnographic approach*. Philadelphia: University of Pennsylvania Press.

Hymes, D. (1981). *"In vain I tried to tell you": Essays in Native American ethnopoetics*. Philadelphia: University of Pennsylvania Press.

Inghilleri, M. (1989). Learning to mean as a symbolic and social process: The story of two ESL writers. *Discourse Processes*, 12, 391–411.

Jackendoff, R. S. (1972). *Semantic interpretation in generative grammar*. Cambridge, MA: MIT Press.

Jackson, P. (1989). *Maps of meaning: An intorduction to cultural geography*. London: Unwin.

Jannacone, P. (1985). *Walt Whitman's poetry*, P. Mitilineos (Trans.). Washington, DC: NCR Microcard Editions.

Kendon, A. (1977). *Studies in the behavior of social interaction*. Bloomington: Indiana University Press.

Kochman, T. (Ed.). (1972). *Rappin' and stylin' out: Communication in urban black America*. Urbana: University of Illinois Press.

Kramerae, C., Schulz, M., and O'Barr, W. (Eds.). (1984). *Language and power*. Beverly Hills, CA: Sage Publications.

Kuhn, T. (1962). *The structure of scientific revolutions*. Chicago: University of Chicago Press.

Labov, W. (1972). *Language in the inner city* (pp. 354–936). Philadelphia: University of Pennsylvania Press.

Ladd, R. D. (1980). *Intonational meaning*. Bloomington: Indiana University Press.

Lave, J. (1988). *Cognition in practice*. Cambridge: Cambridge University Press.

Leont'ev, A. N. (1978). *Activity, consciousness, and personality*. Englewood Cliffs, NJ: Prentice-Hall.

Levelt, W. J. M. (1989). *Production: From intention to articulation*. Cambridge, MA: MIT Press.

Levinson, S. C. (1983). *Pragmatics*. Cambridge: Cambridge University Press.

Levi-Strauss, C. (1966). *The savage mind*. Chicago: University of Chicago Press.

Longacre, R. E. (1983). *The grammar of discourse*. New York and London; Plenum Press.

Luke, A. (1988). *Literacy, textbooks, and ideology*. London, Falmer.

Lyons, J. (1977). *Semantics* (Vol. 1). New York: Cambridge University Press.

Macdonell, D. (1986). *Theories of discourse: An introduction*. Oxford: Basil Blackwell.

Mandler, J. M. (1984). *Stories, scripts, and scenes: Aspects of schema theory*. Hillsdale, NJ: Lawrence Erlbaum.

McDermott, R. (1987). Achieving school failure: An anthropological approach to illiteracy and social stratification. *In* G. Spindler (Ed.), *Education and cultural process: Anthropological approaches* (2nd ed.) (pp. 173–209). Prospects Heights, IL: Waveland Press.

Meier, T., and Cazden, C. (1982). A focus on oral language and writing from a multicultural perspective. *Language Arts*, 59, 504–512.

Michaels, S. (1981). "Sharing time:" Children's narrative styles and differential access to literacy. *Language in Society*, 10, 423–442.

Michaels, S. (1985). Hearing the connections in children's oral and written discourse. *Journal of Education*, 167, 36–56.

Michaels, S. (1987). Text and context: A new approach to the study of classroom writing. *Discourse Processes*, 10, 321–346.

Michaels, S. (1990). The dismantling of narrative. *In* A. McCabe and C. Peterson (Eds.), *Developing narrative structure* (pp. 303–351). Hillsdale, NJ: Lawrence Erlbaum.

Michaels, S., and Bruce, B. (1989). *Classroom contexts and literacy development: How writing systems shape the teaching and learning of composition*. Urbana–Champaign, IL: Center for the Study of Reading.

Michaels, S., and Collins, J. (1984). Oral discourse styles: Classroom interaction and the acquisition of literacy. *In* D. Tannen (Ed.), *Coherence in spoken and written discourse* (pp. 219–244). Norwood, NJ: Ablex.

Michaels, S., and Cook-Gumperz, J. (1979). A study of sharing time with first-grade students: Discourse narratives in the classroom. *Proceedings of the Fifth Annual Meeting of the Berkeley Linguistics Society.*

Middleton, D., and Edwards, D. (Eds.). (1990). *Collective remembering.* London: Sage Publications.

Milroy, L. (1987). *Observing and analysing natural language.* Oxford: Basil Blackwell.

Milroy, J., and Milroy, L. (1985). *Authority in language: Investigating language prescription and standardisation.* London: Routledge & Kegan Paul.

Minick, N. (1989). *L. S. Vygotsky and Soviet activity theory* (The Literacies Institute Technical Reports Special Monograph No. 1). Newton, MA: Education Development Center.

Mishler, E. G. (1990). Validation in inquiry-guided research: The role of exemplars in narrative studies. *Harvard Educational Review* 60: 415–442.

Mitchell, C. (1990). Process writing in theory and practice. Unpublished doctoral dissertation, School of Education, Boston University, Boston.

Moerman, M. (1988). *Talking culture: Ethnography and conversational analysis.* Philadelphia: University of Pennsylvania Press.

Myers, G. (1990). *Writing biology: Texts in the social construction of scientific knowledge.* Madison: University of Wisconsin Press.

Ochs, E. (1979). Transcription as theory. *In* E. Ochs and B. Schieffelin (Eds.), *Developmental pragmatics* (pp. 43–72). New York: Academic Press.

Ochs, E., and Schieffeling, B. B. (1983). Foregrounding referents: A reconsideration of left dislocation in discourse. *In* E. Ochs and B. B. Schieffelin (Eds.), *Acquiring conversational competence* (pp. 158–174). London: Routledge & Kegan Paul.

Ogbu, J. (1978). *Minority education and caste: The American system in cross-cultural perspective.* New York: Academic Press.

Ogbu, J. (1987). Variability in minority school performance: A problem in search of an explanation. *Anthropology and Education Quarterly, 18,* 312–334.

Olson, D. R. (1977). From utterance to text: The bias of language in speech and writing. *Harvard Education Review, 47,* 257–281.

Ong, W., S.J. (1982). *Orality and literacy: The technologizing of the word.* London: Methuen.

Peterson, C., and McCabe, A. (1983). *Developmental psycholinguistics: Three ways of looking at a child's narrative.* New York: Plenum Press.

Polanyi, L. (1989). *Telling the American story: A structural and cultural analysis of conversational storytelling.* Cambridge, MA: MIT Press.

Psathas, G. (Ed.). (1979). *Everyday language: Studies in ethnomethodology.* New York: Irvington Publishers.

Quinn, N., and Holland, D. (1987). Culture and cognition. *In* D. Holland and N. Quinn (Eds.), *Cultural models in language and thought* (pp. 3–40). Cambridge: Cambridge University Press.

Radford, A. (1988). *Transformational grammar: A first course.* Cambridge: Cambridge University Press.

Rodriguez, R. (1981). *Hunger of memory: The education of Richard Rodriguez, an autobiography.* Boston: Godine.

Rogoff, B. (1991). *Apprenticeship in thinking.* New York: Oxford University Press.

Rogoff, B., and Lave, J. (Eds.). (1984). *Everyday cognition: Its development in social context.* Cambridge, MA: Harvard University Press.

Rosaldo, R. (1989). *Culture and truth: The remaking of social analysis.* Boston: Beacon Press.

Ryan, J., and Sackery, C. (1984). *Strangers in paradise: Academics from the working class.* Boston: South End Press.

Sacks, H. (1974). An analysis of the course of a joke's telling in conversation. *In* R. Bauman and J. Sherzer (Eds.), *Explorations in the ethnography of speaking* (pp. 337–353). Cambridge: Cambridge University Press.

Sacks, H., Schegloff, E. A., and Jefferson, G. (1974). A simplest systematics for the organization of turn-taking for conversation. *Language*, 50, 696–735.

Saville-Troike, M. (1982). *The ethnography of communication: An introduction.* Oxford: Blackwell.

Schenkein, J. (1978). *Studies in the organization of conversational organization.* New York: Academic Press.

Scollon, R., and Scollon, S. B. K. (1979). *Linguistic convergence: An ethnography of speaking at Fort Chipewyan, Alberta.* New York: Academic Press.

Scollon, R., and Scollon, S. B. K. (1981). *Narrative, literacy, and face in interethnic communication.* Norwood, NJ: Ablex.

Selkirk, L. (1984). *Phonology and syntax: The relation between sound and structure.* Cambridge, MA: MIT Press.

Sherzer, J. (1983). *Kuna ways of speaking: An ethnographic perspective.* Austin: University of Texas Press.

Smitherman, G. (1977). *Talkin and testifyin: The language of black America.* Boston: Houghton Mifflin.

Snow, C. (1986). Conversations with children. *In* P. Fletcher and M. Garman (Eds.), *Language acquisition* (2nd ed.; pp. 69–89). Cambridge: Cambridge University Press.

Stahl, S D. (1989). *Literary folkloristics and the personal narrative.* Bloomington: Indiana University Press.

Steinitz, V. A., and Solomon, E R. (1986). *Starting out: Class and community in the lives of working-class youth.* Philadelphia: Temple University Press.

Sternberg, M. (1985). *The poetics of biblical narrative.* Bloomington: Indiana University Press.

Sternberg, R. J. (1977). *Intelligence, information processing, and analogical reasoning: The componential analysis of human abilities.* Hillsdale, NJ: Lawrence Erlbaum Associates.

Sternberg, R. J. (1985). *Beyond IQ: A triarchic theory of human intelligence.* New York: Cambridge University Press.

Street, B. (1984). *Literacy in theory and practice.* Cambridge: Cambridge University Press.

Stubbs, M. (1983). *Discourse analysis: The sociolinguistic analysis of natural language.* Oxford: Basil Blackwell.

Stucky, S. (1987). *Slave culture: Nationalist theory and the foundations of black America.* Oxford: Oxford University Press.

Tannen, D. (Ed.). (1982). *Spoken and written language: Exploring orality and literacy.* Norwood, NJ: Ablex.

Tannen, D. (Ed.). (1984). *Coherence in spoken and written discourse.* Norwood, NJ: Ablex.

Tannen, D. (1989). *Talking voices: Repetition, dialogue, and imagery in conversational discourse.* Cambridge: Cambridge University Press.

Tedlock, D. (1983). *The spoken word and the work of interpretation.* Philadelphia, PA: University of Pennsylvania Press.

Tharp, R., and Gallimore, R. (1988). *Rousing minds to life: Teaching, learning, and schooling in social context.* Cambridge: Cambridge University Press.

Thompson, J. B. (1984). *Studies in the theory of ideology.* Berkeley and Los Angeles: University of California Press.

Toolan, M. J. (1988). *Narrative: A critical linguistic introduction.* London: Routledge.

Trueba, H. (1989). *Raising silent voices: Educating linguistic minorities for the 21st century.* Cambridge, MA: Newbury House.

van Dijk, T. A. (1980). *Macrostructures: An interdisciplinary study of global structures in discourse, interaction and cognition.* Hillsdale, NJ: Lawrence Erlbaum.

van Dijk, T. (Ed.). (1985). *Handbook of discourse analysis.* Orlando, FL: Academic Press.

Vygotsky, L. S. (1987). *Collected works* (Vol. 1). New York: Plenum.

Wells, G. (1986). *The meaning makers: Children learning language and using language to learn.* Portsmouth, NH: Heinemann.

Wertsch, J. V. (Ed.). (1981). *The concept of activity in Soviet psychology.* New York: M. E. Sharpe.

Wertsch, J. V. (1985). *Vygotsky and the social formation of mind.* Cambridge, MA: Harvard University Press.

White, H. (1973). Metahistory. Baltimore: John Hopkins University Press.

Wilensky, R. (1983). Story grammars versus story points. *The Behavioral and Brain Sciences,* 4, 579–591.

Williams, R. (1981). *Culture.* London: Fontana.

Wittgenstein, L. (1958). *Philosophical investigations* G. E. M. Anscombe (Trans.). New York: Macmillan.

Woodward, J. (1982). *How you gonna get to heaven if you can't talk with Jesus: On depathologizing deafness.* Silver Spring, MD: T. J. Publishers.

CHAPTER 7

☐ Culture, Context, and Cognition

Evelyn Jacob

The Handbook of Qualitative
Research in Education

Within various arenas of educational practice, there is increasing interest in the influences of cultural factors and social context on student learning (e.g., Bossert, 1988; Fosnot, 1989; Poplin, 1984; Sharan, 1985). However, traditional approaches within educational research do not offer ready models for examining these concerns.

Educational anthropology, to be sure, offers a variety of theoretical and methodological resources for examining how culture and context are related to learning. However, traditional anthropological research has rarely focused on the cognitive activities in which educators and schools are interested (Eisenhart, 1988) and does not offer readily appropriate models to investigate issues of "taught cognitive learning" (Erickson, 1982).

Traditional educational and psychological researchers face the opposite problem. Although they have focused on cognitive activities, their reliance on experimental methods reflects an implicit assumption that cognitive activities are acontextual. Thus, these scholars rarely attempt to address the issues of how culture and context affect learning (Eisenhart, 1988).

In addressing the issue, it will not be enough for researchers to develop appropriate research designs and methods; in addition, productive research will require an integrative theoretical perspective to guide the work.

Neo-Vygotskian work (variously called "cultural cognition," "anthropology of cognition," "cultural psychology," and the "study of everyday cognition") offers a potential answer to this theoretical and methodological need. It views the relationships among culture, context, and cognition as complex, multilevel, and reciprocal, and it suggests a range of methodological designs and methods useful for answering significant questions.

In this chapter I review neo-Vygotskian research and the major influences on its development: prior Western research on culture and cognition, and the work of Vygotsky and the Soviet sociohistorical school. The focus throughout this review is conceptual and methodological, not substantive.[1] Although I discuss in some depth selected empirical studies that exemplify various approaches, I do not attempt to comment comprehensively on all relevant studies.

On a conceptual level I review how researchers in various traditions have viewed the relationships among culture, context, and cognition. I assume that those perspectives which provide the most complete, well-rounded picture of culture, context, and cognition will be the most useful in improving our understanding and in guiding research and practice.

On a methodological level I review how researchers have designed their studies and how they have collected and analyzed data. I assume that those designs and methods that are consistent with interpretivist principles will be the most useful in studying the complex human processes comprising culture, context, and cognition. By interpretivist principles, I mean a perspective toward research that includes attention to the meanings that humans create and use to guide their behavior, a recognition that in any situation meanings can vary and create multiple realities, an assumption that researchers should build meaningful generalizations from detailed understandings of specific contexts, and an understanding that the components of social life are mutually influencing (Erickson, 1986; Lincoln and Guba, 1985).

In this review I attempt to identify historical trends in approaches to the study of culture, context, and cognition. Earlier studies tended to view culture and cognition as essentially separate and in a unilinear causal relationship. More recently, neo-Vygotskian research views culture and cognition as interdependent influences that come together and create one another in specific contexts (Cole, 1985).

Although this volume focuses on qualitative research, I have avoided the term "qualitative" as a general characterization of the studies I review. Any research study comprises a variety of components: philosophical and theoretical assumptions, research designs, and methods of data collection and data analysis. The term *qualitative* has been applied to each of these various levels. Thus, qualitative research has referred to research that is interpretivist at the philosophical or theoretical level, that has an open-ended and iterative design, that involves the collection of qualitative data, or that involves qualitative analysis of data.

Not all researchers examining questions about culture, context, and cognition have conducted research that is qualitative at all these levels. For example, some have collected qualitative data but have not held interpretivist perspectives, with the result that their framework and analyses are in a more positivist vein. For the sake of clarity, I will use the term qualitative to refer to methods of data collection and analysis and the term interpretivist to refer to "qualitative" philosophical assumptions.

Culture and Cognition: Pre-Vygotskian Research in the West

In the West, pre-Vygotskian research has its roots in two main traditions: cultural anthropology and cross-cultural psychology.[2] Both traditions framed their questions in terms of culture's influence on cognition. Central questions of concern to each discipline were to what degree all cultures shared basic cognitive skills and to what degree they differed. Until the late 1960s each group of scholars operated within its own disciplinary assumptions, goals, and methods. In the late 1960s some scholars began to develop interdisciplinary approaches. I will discuss each discipline separately before addressing the more interdisciplinary approaches.

Disciplinary Approaches

Cultural Anthropology

Culture has been a central focus of anthropologists. Although definitions of culture have varied (see Kroeber and Kluckhohn, 1963), most approaches have referred to some facet of a group's learned experience and attitudes accumulated over time. Most broadly, culture refers to all that humans learn, in contrast to what is genetically endowed (Keesing and Keesing, 1971). Anthropologists generally have viewed what is learned as encompassing both patterns *for* behavior and patterns *of* behavior. Patterns for behavior are mentalistic phenomena, shared meanings, systems of "standards for perceiving, believing, evaluating, and acting" (Goodenough, 1971). In contrast, patterns of behavior are directly observable and are the material manifestations of these ideational patterns. These material manifestations include manufactured products, overt behavior, and social events (Goodenough, 1971). Anthropologists may use the term culture to refer to all shared, learned patterns or, more narrowly, to refer only to shared meanings.

Anthropologists have viewed shared cultural meanings as crucial for understanding behavior. Because observable behaviors can mean different things to different cultures, anthropologists have argued that one must understand the cultural meanings to truly understand and interpret behaviors.

Anthropologists have assumed that these shared meanings and behaviors lead to significant regularity across individuals within a cultural group (Goodenough, 1971; Pelto, 1970). However, diversity also exists within the cultural system because individuals are socialized into cultural norms in different ways and are influenced by different subgroups within their society. Although anthropologists have seen culture as exerting a powerful influence on behavior, they have not viewed it as determining behavior because individuals must decide whether or not and, if so, how to apply cultural guidelines for behavior in specific situations. Moreover, shared cultural meanings and behaviors are not static. Shared meanings are created, continued, changed, and transmitted through social interaction.

Anthropologists and psychologists have usually used the term cognition in different ways. For psychologists it generally refers to processes and for anthropologists it usually refers to content (Cole and Scribner, 1975; Edgerton, 1974). Cultural anthropologists have not considered cognitive processes as a major focus of their research. If cognitive processes were a focus at all, it usually was as a small part of a broader study of a non-Western, nonindustrialized cultural group.[3]

Although anthropologists recognized differences among cultural groups, they generally asserted that these were "surface" differences and that the basic underlying abilities of the human mind were constant across all cultures, a position forcefully argued by Boas as early as 1911.

In general, early anthropological studies followed traditional ethnographic research designs, used participant observation and informal interviewing as primary methods of data collection, and conducted qualitative analyses (for some recent discussions of this approach, see Fetterman, 1989; Hammersley and Atkinson, 1983; Jacob, 1987b). The findings were reported at the level of the cultural group, with little emphasis on individual variation. Moreover, these studies generally placed both cognition and education in their larger cultural contexts, describing the cultural activities, attitudes, and values related to the activities, and the relationships of behavior and attitudes to the larger social order. Examples of this approach span the history of the discipline and still continue in the present.

Many of these studies focus on children's cognitive activities, situating them within the broader topic of education (e.g., Middleton, 1970), defining education broadly as the learning of culture, which includes cultural symbols, ethical and moral attitudes, history and rituals, cosmological beliefs, and work-related tasks. Fortes' (1970) research on education among the Tallensi is a classic example. He described the "social sphere" of Tale children, indicating that few differences exist between the culture of children and that of adults, with the consequence that:

> . . . the child is from the beginning oriented towards the same reality as its parents and has the same physical and social material upon which to direct its cognitive and instinctual endowment. The interests, motives, and purposes of children are identical with those of adults, but at a simpler level of organization. Hence the children need not be coerced to take a share in economic and social activities. They are eager to do so. (p. 19)

Fortes then described adults' and children's attitudes toward learning processes, children's educational experiences, social relationships in which education is embedded, and how children's social relationships, environments, and experiences change as they develop over time, with consequent changes in children's educational experiences. Although Fortes reported that there was some direct instruction of Tale children, he asserted that much of their learning occurs through direct participation in everyday activities, with the children first learning an "interest" and gradually perfecting their skills over time through the learning processes of mimesis, identification, and cooperation.

Other studies examined cognitive activities outside the context of children's education, focusing more on adult activities. For example, Bateson (1958) reported on the memory skills of learned men among the Iatmul of New Guinea as part of a larger study of their society and culture. Bateson estimated that these men had memorized between 10,000 and 20,000 totemic names, which they used in debating and other activities. Drawing on his observations of men's debates and of the order in which these men recited lists of names, Bateson argued that their memory skills were not developed through rote memorization but probably through visual and kinaesthetic imagery. He further argued that because these specialists had such an influence in the culture and because the use of totemic names pervaded the culture, the emphasis on memory skills extended beyond the specialists.

Hallowell's (1967) work among the Saulteaux provides another example of attention to the cognitive activities of adults. In three chapters, he dealt with the cultural context of spatial and temporal orientation and measurement among the Saulteaux, describing relevant cultural behavior patterns and values and how these related to other cultural patterns.

These ethnographic studies provide models for describing naturally occurring cultural practices in which cognitive activities occur and for situating these practices within larger patterns of cultural attitudes and behavior, and social organization. However, because these studies have focused at the level of the cultural group and because cognitive activity has rarely been a central focus, the studies have not provided detailed descriptions of the cognitive activities themselves or of the behavior within which they are situated. As a result, such ethnographic descriptions have not provided data that would allow for detailed examination of cognitive processes. Psychologists Cole and Scribner (1975:266) sought to remedy this deficiency by challenging anthropologists to view cognition "as a *specific set of activities* engaged in on *specifiable occasions* for reasons deducible from . . . [their] *social* theory" [italics in original].

Cross-Cultural Psychology

Within the field of psychology, the subfield of cross-cultural psychology led the way in examining cultural influences on cognitive processes. Psychologists viewed cognitive processes as:

> . . . the manner in which information is extracted from incoming
> stimulation, the manner in which that information is conceptualized,
> the manner in which it is used, and finally the processes by which
> thought is organized to consider things real on the one hand and things
> theoretical on the other. (Glick, 1975:597)

Consequently, psychological studies dealt with topics such as perception, classification, logic, and analytic ability.

Building on the assumption that test scores measure some underlying cognitive competence or ability, their basic, decidedly noninterpretive strategy was to compare the test scores of groups of people with differing cultural backgrounds or experiences. These researchers treated culture as an independent variable and scores on cognitive tests as the dependent variables.

A major goal of this work was to test the generality of Western theories of cognition (Cole, Gay, Glick, and Sharp, 1971). Much of the earliest work in this vein compared a non-Western group to a Western group, often reporting little more than that " 'natives' fared worse than standardized groups at home" (Greenfield and Bruner, 1966:90).

In the 1960s there was increased effort directed toward identifying the relationships between more specific aspects of culture and specific aspects of cognition. Many studies compared intracultural groups in an attempt to specify important causal factors in a more detailed way.

The impacts of urbanization and Western schooling were central concerns, and a number of studies examined this topic. For example, Greenfield, Reich, and Olver (1966) compared three age groups of Wolof children in Senegal from three settings (unschooled rural, schooled rural, and schooled urban). The subjects were asked to identify pairs from arrays of three pictures objects that were most alike and to describe the reasons for their choices. Greenfield and her colleagues reported that although the degree of urbanization had some impact on subjects' responses, attendance at school had a more dramatic influence. Schooling influenced the way that the children made classifications and the kinds of reasons they gave for the classes they formed, with the result that schooled children gave more abstract, conceptual answers.

Wagner (1974) conducted a similar study in the Yucatan, Mexico, examining the effects of formal schooling on memory. Different age groups of schooled urban, schooled rural, and unschooled rural subjects recalled the position of one out of seven familiar items in a linear array. Each subject was shown pictures of the items on cards one-by-one. After each item was shown, the card was turned over. When all seven cards had been shown, the subject was then shown a duplicate of one card and asked to point to its location in the array of cards turned face-down. Based on this work, Wagner reported that formal schooling is an important factor in the development of mnemonic skills in short-term memory.

A strength of such psychological studies involving intracultural comparisons was that they began to link more specific factors (e.g., social class, education, urbanization, familiarity with specific objects and cognitive operations) to various aspects of cognitive development. However, these variables, while better than global comparison of cross-cultural groups, were still relatively nonspecific.

A major problem with the cross-cultural psychology approach is that the cultural components were poorly understood and only minimally examined. First, many of the "independent" variables (e.g., age, gender, schooling, social class) used to contrast groups were "packaged" [i.e., they included "clusters of correlated and often ill-defined traits" (Whiting, 1976:305)]. These variables needed to be "unpackaged" by identifying the components of the variables that accounted for their association with differences in cognitive performance. Second, these studies presented little information about either cultural attitudes and values or aspects of social organization related to the cognitive activities examined. Third, these studies provided little information about the daily experiences that contrast the lives of these groups of children (Bronfenbrenner, 1974; Cole and Scribner, 1975;

Goodnow, 1969). Schoggen and Schoggen (1971) stated the need as follows:

> Despite the widespread agreement on the importance of early experience, . . . there is surprisingly little empirical evidence in the research literature which documents the nature of the experience children actually have in early life. Most of the data on early experience comes from the laboratory, from the clinic, and from parental reports of their child-rearing practices and the behavior of their children. Particularly lacking are data based on direct observations of individual children in the natural situations of everyday life. (p. 1)

For example, although many researchers examined the influences of Western schooling on cognition by comparing schooled and non-schooled groups, they rarely discussed the place those schools have in the culture of the people being studied or what the experience of schooling actually entailed.

These studies also can be criticized because they were generally insensitive to contextual influences on cognitive activity (Cole and Bruner, 1971; Cole *et al.*, 1971). First, they generally assumed that subjects' test scores reflected some underlying ability or competence rather than performance related to the specific situation in which they were being examined. Second, they generally collected data in experimental situations far removed from the everyday life of subjects.

Disciplinary Approaches in Perspective

The disciplinary approaches of both cultural anthropologists and cross-cultural psychologists made important contributions to the study of culture and cognition. By providing descriptions of everyday cognitive activities, anthropological studies documented that non-Western peoples displayed complex and prodigious cognitive skills in everyday life. By moving from cross-cultural comparisons to a focus on specific intracultural variations, psychological studies began to suggest specific aspects of life that contributed to the development of specific cognitive skills.

The two approaches operated with very different assumptions about research. The anthropologists were generally committed to examining everyday life and, for the most part, used interpretive perspectives and qualitative methods of data collection and analysis. The psychologists viewed experimental situations as the only source of useful information about cognition and used primarily quantitative methods of data collection and analysis.

Although each disciplinary approach had strengths, each had serious weaknesses for a rich and detailed study of culture and cognition. Traditional anthropological descriptions lacked sufficient detail about cognitive activities. Traditional psychological approaches were severely limited in their treatment of cultural factors and relied almost exclusively on test scores collected in experimental situations. Concerns with the limitations of both the traditional anthropological and psychological approaches led scholars to try to overcome these problems by conducting interdisciplinary studies.

Interdisciplinary Approaches

In the late 1960s and during the 1970s, scholars in anthropology and psychology tried to deal with the criticisms of disciplinary approaches by conducting interdisciplinary work that drew on both traditions. This interdisciplinary focus was reflected in how the researchers themselves referred to their work. For example, Cole *et al.* (1971) termed their work "experimental anthropology," and Lave (1977) described her work as using a " 'hybrid' anthropological–psychological approach." In general, these studies attempted to get at least some background cultural information through naturalistic observation as well as some experimental cognitive test data, usually comparing groups within one culture.

Two approaches developed toward observational data. One approach was similar to conventional anthropology. For background information, researchers gathered participant and nonparticipant observations with an explicit focus on cognitive activities. In the other approach, focused, often quantifiable, nonparticipant observations were conducted to provide detailed information about the activities of specific individuals.

Although most researchers continued to include some form of cognitive testing in their research, two approaches developed toward such cognitive data. In one approach, researchers continued to use tests that were developed independent of the specific cultural setting examined. In the other approach, cognitive tests were developed from observations to present subjects with tasks somewhat similar to those they encountered in their everyday lives.

Michael Cole, John Gay, and their colleagues (Cole *et al.*, 1971; Gay and Cole, 1967) pioneered this interdisciplinary work in their major study among the Kpelle of Liberia.[4] In addition to drawing on previous ethnographies of the Kpelle for general background, the researchers added their own data from conversations, court cases, and school essays to provide more detailed information on relevant cultural activities. They used these data to develop experimental tasks in a variety of cognitive areas (e.g., classification, learning, memory) and to help interpret their experimental results by comparing intracultural groups of varying ages, education, language, and Westernization. The major conclusion of this work was that *"cultural differences in cognition reside more in the situations to which particular cognitive processes are applied than in the existence of a process in one cultural group and its absence in another* [italics in original]" (Cole *et al.*, 1971:233).

While traditional ethnographic data are crucial for placing cognitive activity in its larger cultural framework, one problem with group level data is that it does not provide the detailed data on individuals needed for detailed intracultural comparisons. To deal with this problem, some researchers collected a variety of data on individuals, including survey data and various kinds of nonparticipant observation data. In some cases, these focused data were collected in addition to general ethnographic data, whereas in other cases no general background data were collected.

Jacob (1977, 1982a,c, 1983, 1984) studied relationships between culture and cognition for young children in a Puerto Rican town. She combined basic ethnographic data of the town with more focused data for a sample of children. The more focused data included interviews with the children's parents and teachers, detailed nonparticipant observations of the children's activities at home and school, and their scores on cognitive tests. The nonparticipant observers followed methods developed by Barker and Wright (1971) to describe and tape-record each target child's activities and interactions during 15–30-minute segments at home and school. Jacob collated the transcriptions and expanded descriptions to produce narratives that described each focus child's activities and interactions and their contexts. From one analysis of the data, Jacob reported that geographical stability, fathers' education, and presence of extended family members were positively related to children's performance on a standardized measure of cognition. She interpreted these relationship in terms of the value Puerto Rican culture places on feelings of warmth and security. In a subsequent analysis of the children's informal education at home, Jacob found that children were responsible for initiating opportunities to learn knowledge and skills, and she related this pattern to the Puerto Rican notion of *capacidad,* which stresses that children will only learn when they are ready.

Another method used to examine individuals' experiences was spot observations, which involve instantaneous observations using precoded checklists. For example, Munroe and Munroe (1971) related easily measurable experiential variables to performance on cognitive tasks. Their interest in the specific topic studied grew out of their observations of sex differences among Logoli children of western Kenya in performance on tests of spatial ability. The researchers wanted to study sex differences in experiential factors that "might be similar to those involved in the tests" (Munroe and Munroe, 1971:16). They hypothesized that environmental experience (measured by distance from home) contributes significantly to spatial ability. An age-matched sample of boys and girls (3–7 years old) were observed (20 times each) in natural settings. Observers recorded how far each child was from home and whether his or her activities were directed by another or not. They found that on the average boys were farther from home than girls for undirected activities and that children who were farther from home on the average had higher scores on the tests of spatial ability.

In a similar mode, Nerlove and her colleagues (Nerlove, Roberts, Klein, Yarbrough, and Habicht, 1974) made spot observations of children in two rural Spanish-speaking Ladino villages in Guatemala. They recorded variables such as the following: persons with the child; whereabouts of parents; child's activity; objects child had; whether or not child was talking and, if so, to whom; and whether or not the child was directed to do this activity and, if so, by whom. They coded the observations for the children's self-managed activities and voluntary social activities. They found that scores on self-managed activities correlated positively with performance on an embedded figures test and a matching figures test, which are meant to measure analytic ability, and that voluntary social activities correlated with performance on a verbal analogies test.

The work of Lave and her colleagues (Brenner, 1985; Lave, 1977, 1982; Reed and Lave, 1979) is similar in its basic outline to other studies discussed here. They examined the impact of two different educational systems (apprenticeship and formal schooling) on arithmetic skills of tribal tailors in Liberia. The research involved participant observation, formal and informal interviewing, and experimental tasks developed from ethnographic data. However, their work made some important methodological contributions. First, in contrast to other studies that gathered comparatively brief focused observations, Lave and her colleagues conducted *extended* observations of tailors' arithmetic activities in their normal tailoring activities. Second, they collected their data in a cyclical fashion.

> We moved from observation to some experimental tasks that were relatively close to the everyday scene. From there, we went to more formal experimental tasks . . . and then back to observation, armed with hypotheses about what we ought to see if our experimental results were adequate descriptions of everyday arithmetic activities." (Reed and Lave, 1979:579)

Their data indicated that skills learned incidentally in everyday activities lead to generalizable skills such as those learned in formal school. Moreover, their data suggested that differences among groups of tailors on formal arithmetic tasks could be accounted for by "the practice opportunities available in the learning environment, and the social costs associated with various types of errors" (Reed and Lave, 1979:580).

Interdisciplinary Work in Perspective

The early interdisciplinary research on culture and cognition presented an increasingly complex picture of culture and cognition, demonstrating that cognitive performance is related to specific experiences in everyday life. In addition, research had begun to establish that factors in the immediate context (e.g., features of the experimental task) influence cognitive performance.

This early interdisciplinary work made some methodological advances. Although experimental tasks were still central to almost all studies, researchers were beginning to develop their tasks from previous ethnographic data. In addition, focused observational data had begun to unpackage cultural variables by providing more detailed information about cognitive activities in everyday life.

Despite these methodological advances, much remained to be done. Scholars continued to view culture and cognition as separate and in a unilinear relationship. The status of experimental data remained a problem. Lave's (1979) observations of arithmetic problem-solving in tailor shops raised questions about the validity of even those experimental tasks explicitly derived from everyday life because her observations "showed that experimental situations and everyday situations in the tailor shop tap quite different problem-solving approaches" (p. 2). Most nonparticipant observations still exhibited a dearth of information about everyday activities and their sociocultural context. Moreover, only a few studies explored the cultural values and attitudes associated with the cognitive activities they examined.

In addition to these methodological problems, a major challenge was the need for a theoretical framework that united the various levels of analysis. For example, at an early point in interdisciplinary efforts, Cole *et al.* (1971) stated that "no comprehensive theory of the relation between mundane activities and cognitive processes has proved acceptable" (pp. 218–219). Ten years later, Scribner and Cole (1981) echoed the earlier complaint:

> To give a satisfactory account of the nature and significance of the differences we found—and failed to find—we would need to draw on some well-specified theory of cognition, especially a theory spelling out the mechanisms by which social factors affect cognitive variation. No such theory was at hand when we commenced our work, and none is at hand today to help us interpret it. (p. 234)

As early as 1974, Cole and Scribner had suggested that Vygotksy's work might offer the needed synthesis. However, it was not until 1978 and the publication of *Mind in Society* that some of Vygotsky's work directly relevant to the topic of culture and cognition became available in English. Consequently, it was not until the late 1970s and early 1980s that Western researchers interested in issues of culture and cognition turned to the earlier work of Lev Vygotksy and the Soviet sociohistorical school as a possible integrating theoretical framework.

Vygotsky and the Sociohistorical Tradition[5]

Writing from 1924 until his death, 10 years later, Lev Vygotsky developed a theoretical framework that combined history, social institutions, cultural artifacts, cultural meanings, cultural signs such as language, activities, interpersonal interactions, and cognition. Vygotsky's work, that of Leont'ev and Luria (the other members of the Soviet sociohistorical "troika"), and subsequent Soviet work on activity theory has brought new life to Western investigations of culture, context, and cognition.[6]

It is beyond the scope of this chapter to present a detailed discussion of the ideas of Vygotksy and other members of the Soviet sociohistorical school. The aim here is to present an outline of their approach, highlighting features most relevant to the current discussion.[7]

Theoretical Framework

Vygotsky (1978) distinguished between elementary (natural) mental functions and higher (social or cultural) mental functions. Elementary mental functions operate according to a natural line of development, which represents physical and organic growth and can be explained primarily through biological principles. According to Wertsch (1985c), elementary mental functioning is characterized by "control by the natural environment, an absence of conscious realization, individual origins, and a lack of mediation by psychological tools" (p. 27).

Higher mental functions follow a sociocultural line of development. The cultural line of development, while building on and compatible with biological factors, is primarily culturally and socially influenced. According to Wertsch (1985c), higher mental functions are characterized by voluntary regulation, conscious awareness of mental processes, social origins, a social nature, and the use of signs for mediation. Higher mental functions include thinking, reasoning, problem-solving, voluntary attention, and logical memory. In both his theoretical and empirical work, Vygotsky focused primarily on the higher mental functions (Minick, 1987), which he saw as indicative of the mental life of human beings.

In Vygotsky's view, "technical tools" (e.g., pencils, computers, calculators) and "psychological tools" (e.g., language, counting systems, mnemonic techniques, writing, diagrams) mediate higher mental functions. However, these mediational means do not merely facilitate prior processes; instead, technical and psychological tools transform the processes and structure of the action being performed (Vygotsky, 1981). For example, writing and editing with word-processing software on a microcomputer is a different activity from writing and editing by hand with a pen or pencil.

Vygotsky asserted that society influences mediational means and the development of higher mental functions at two levels: sociocultural history and the immediate interpersonal environment. At the level of sociocultural history, society influences human cognitive activity through the technical and psychological tools it provides to facilitate cognitive activity (Vygotsky, 1978). These mediational means are influenced by and, in turn, create and maintain cultural, historical, and institutional contexts.

At the level of the immediate personal environment, society influences psychological development through face-to-face interactions because higher mental functions have their origins in such interactions.

> *An interpersonal process is transformed into an intrapersonal one.*
> Every function in the child's cultural development appears twice: first, on the social level, and later, on the individual level; first, *between* people (*interpsychological*), and then *inside* the child
> (*intrapsychological*) . . . . All higher functions originate as actual relations between human individuals [italics in original]. (Vygotsky, 1978:57)

In Vygotsky's view, the transition from interpsychological to intrapsychological activity can be accomplished because the same general mediational means (i.e., language) are used in both interpsychological and intrapsychological activities. How this occurs was one of Vygotsky's central concerns.

A basic process involved in this transfer is termed internalization. While internalization is not a process of copying external reality, Vygotsky saw external social reality as having an important influence on the nature of internal intrapsychological functioning. In summarizing Vygotsky's views, Rogoff and Wertsch (1984) discussed this relationship as follows:

> The composition, structure, and means of action are internalized from their social origins. This means that variation in the organization of social functioning can be expected to lead to variation in the organization of individual psychological functioning. For example, a child who has participated in joint problem solving will use the same task representation that proved effective in group problem solving when solving such a problem independently. Hence, Vygotsky's approach suggests that to understand individual cognitive growth it will be fruitful to examine specific patterns of social interaction in which children participate. (p. 2)

A concept closely related to the social nature of the development of higher mental functions is the "zone of proximal development."[8] Vygotsky (1978) defined the zone of proximal development as:

> *the distance between the actual developmental level as determined by independent problem solving and the level of potential development as determined through problem solving under adult guidance or in collaboration with more capable peers* [italics in original]. (p. 86)

Thus, the zone of proximal development is the dynamic region where an individual can move from interpsychological to intrapsychological functioning.[9]

The zone of proximal development is useful in thinking about instruction and its relation to development. Vygotsky was not interested in instruction in technical skills such as typing or bicycle riding but, rather, in forms of instruction that may impact on "all-round development"—for example, instruction in some formal, academic disciplines. According to Vygotsky, the zone of proximal development is determined jointly by a child's developmental level and the form of instruction involved. Different forms of instruction can create different zones of proximal development. Instruction is maximally effective when it proceeds ahead of development. In such cases, instruction *"awakens and rouses to life an entire set of functions which are in the stage of maturing, which lie in the zone of proximal development* [italics in original]" (Vygotsky, 1934a:222, cited *in* Wertsch, 1985c:71).

While Vygotsky's ideas were truly innovative, they needed to be elucidated and extended (Wertsch, 1984, 1985b).[10] For example, Wertsch argued that two concepts dealing with participants' understandings needed to be added to Vygotsky's formulations: situation definition and intersubjectivity. A situation definition is how a situation is defined by those operating in it. In Wertsch's view, when an adult and child are jointly carrying out a task in the child's zone of proximal development, they necessarily have different definitions of the situation. Thus, a primary task for the adult is to bring about a change in the child's definition of the situation so that it is closer to that of the adult.

Intersubjectivity refers to the degree that two collaborators on a task share the same definition of the task and its setting. The degree of intersubjectivity can vary from minimal sharing to nearly complete sharing when "two interlocutors represent objects and events in identical ways" (Wertsch, 1984:12).

Intersubjectivity is often created through the use of language—that is, semiotic mediation. A central task in this view becomes understanding the ways that adults (or more competent peers) use language to bring about higher degrees of intersubjectivity with the learner. Much of Wertsch's subsequent empirical work has been devoted to this task.

Leont'ev (1981), one of the original Soviet troika, developed the concept of appropriation, which helps explain how cognitive change occurs.[11] In Leont'ev's view, children actively construct their understandings through the process of *appropriation* in interaction with their environment. For example, the psychological and technical tools in a child's world have social meanings and functions that have developed over time. A child does not have to independently invent the tools; rather, a child appropriates (takes over) those aspects of a culture's meanings and functions that are needed for his or her purposes. This is done through involvement in culturally organized activities in which the tools are a part.

In a joint activity between a teacher and a learner, the two actors may participate in the activity with different understandings of the situation and its goals. In such a situation, the teacher can appropriate the child's behavior—that is, explicitly interpret the child's behavior to him or her as being within the teacher's system of understanding and contributing to the teacher's goals. This appropriation by the teacher helps the child see his or her behavior in a new way (i.e., within the teacher's frame of reference).

While this discussion has stressed the teacher's appropriation of the child's behavior, it is actually a two-way street, and the teacher can be influenced by the child's appropriation of the teacher's behavior (Newman, Griffin, and Cole, 1989b). A similar point needs to be made about Vygotsky's approach to the relationship between society and the individual in general. John-Steiner and Souberman (1978) summarize this aspect of Vygotsky's view: "He sees the relation between the individual and the society as a dialectical process which, like a river and its tributaries, combines and separates the different elements of human life. They are never frozen polarities to him" (p. 126).

Methodological Guidelines

The work of Vygotsky and Leont'ev encompassed several important methodological features. Vygotsky (1978) contended that it was crucial to focus not just on the product of development but also on the processes by which psychological development occurs. This contention formed the base of his developmental (or genetic) method, which was (and is) different from conventional psychological experiments. He argued that research should result in a "dynamic display of the main points making up the processes' history" (Vygotsky, 1978:61). When these processes occur over a short time, they are termed "microgenesis" (Wertsch, 1985c). In such cases, the researcher examines the short-term development of psychological processes. For example, by observing subjects' repeated trials of a particular task, the researcher in effect conducts a short-term longitudinal study.

Because Vygotsky was not focused on outcomes but on processes leading to outcomes, his work included narrative descriptions of how individuals accomplished tasks given to them. In discussing Vygotsky's methods, Cole and Scribner (1978) stated that this aspect of his approach helps break down barriers between the laboratory and the "field" and fits better than traditional experiments with the qualitative methods of anthropology and sociology.

Vygotsky's ideas called for a new unit of analysis beyond the traditional psychological focus on the individual. Vygotsky's original proposal for this new unit of analysis—word meaning—was soon seen as inadequate (Wertsch, 1985c). Leont'ev (1978, 1981) was central in developing "activity" as an alternative "holistic" unit of analysis.[12] The new unit has three levels. The first level, that of "activity," is tied to a motive that is socially constructed (e.g., getting food, making clothes). The second level, that of "actions," is tied to goals that are instrumental in achieving the motive of the activity (e.g., making a weapon or going shopping are related to the motive of getting food). The third level, that of "operations," involves how an action is carried out (e.g., writing a list or committing items to memory to remember items needed for cooking).[13] Leont'ev (1981) argued that to truly understand human activity it is important to analyze it at all three levels. The notion of activity has been critical in Western researchers' development of a more sophisticated approach to context as part of their discussions of culture and cognition.

Vygotsky provided a theoretical framework that integrates culture, context, and cognition and outlines mechanisms for their mutual influence. However, his broad outline was filled in unevenly, and, although subsequent Soviet work in activity theory has expanded on aspects of Vygotsky's framework, much work remains to be done both theoretically and empirically. Western neo-Vygotskians have contributed to filling these gaps.

Cognition in Context: Neo-Vygotskian Research

When Western researchers began to explicate and apply Vygotsky's ideas in the late 1970s and early 1980s, they did so in the context of previous Western research in culture and cognition. Thus, previous anthropological, psychological, and interdisciplinary studies influenced researchers' questions and methodology, resulting in a wide variety of foci and methodological approaches. Moreover, neo-Vygotskian researchers have drawn on other work from a wider range of disciplines to elaborate on the intellectual seeds planted by Vygotsky. The central theoretical contributions of this work have been situating the study of culture and cognition within specific contexts and explicating the mutual influences among culture, context, and cognition, primarily through the mediation of language in social interaction.

For our purposes here, I will discuss studies with an intrapsychological focus separately from those with an interpsychological focus. Studies with an intrapsychological focus are most continuous with previous interdisciplinary research. Studies with an interpsychological focus, while definitely influenced by previous interdisciplinary research, add new and significant dimensions to the study of culture, context, and cognition.

Although both bodies of research continue the earlier interdisciplinary emphasis on integrating the traditional designs and methods of anthropology and psychology, individual studies display a range of research designs and methods. Like the earlier interdisciplinary studies, some emphasize traditional experimental features and others stress observations of naturally occurring behavior.

Studies with an Intrapsychological Focus

Studies with an intrapsychological focus extend previous interdisciplinary work, adding an emphasis on examining cognition in relation to its immediate contexts in everyday life. Acting on concerns about the ecological validity of experiments (e.g., Bronfenbrenner, 1979; Lave, 1979, 1980) and drawing on Vygotsky's ideas, researchers increasingly became interested in studying "cognition in context." The intrapsychological studies reflect the dual approaches found in interdisciplinary studies. Some primarily used experimental data that has been "grounded" in observations of everyday life; others focused on documenting everyday life directly.

Experiments Developed from Observations

Scribner and Cole's (1981) study of Vai literacy sought to examine the assertion that literacy has broad effects on the content and processes of thinking. They collected ethnographic data on Vai literacy behavior to provide background for their experimental studies. To have individual level data, they also conducted a survey that gathered data on demographics and on the acquisition and use of literacy.

The experimental components of the Vai literacy study suggest that it can be viewed as a transition study because the researchers' approach to their experiments changed in the middle of the study. In their earliest experimental work, the researchers used the background ethnographic data to compose comparison groups (i.e., subjects who were schooled, literate in Vai script, or nonliterate) and to adapt tasks previously used with Western subjects. Their conclusion from their work was that nonschool literacy does not produce general cognitive effects. Literacy seemed to affect performance only on tasks whose requirements were similar to literacy activities among the Vai. These findings led Scribner and Cole to shift their experimental strategy. Drawing on ethnographic work that indicated that the Vai used Vai, Arabic, and English literacy in different activities and for different purposes, they developed experimental tasks explicitly based on literacy activities among the Vai and compared groups who differed in their involvement in these literacy activities (i.e., nonliterates, Vai script literates, Arabic literates, English literates). These studies confirmed their earlier conclusions that the effects of literacy are related to *specific* features of the activities in which the Vai used literacy, presaging the focus in more recent research on context.

Although Scribner and Cole (1981:235) did not explicitly plan their study based on Soviet theories, their discussion of their findings of terms of the "practice" of literacy was influenced by Soviet activity theory. Thus, they defined a practice as socially developed, patterned, recurrent, "goal-directed sequences of activities using a particular technology and particular systems of knowledge" (p. 236). In this framework they concluded that the specific cognitive consequences of literacy they found were related to the specific practices of literacy among the Vai.

This study by Cole and Scribner was significant in helping to change the approach to cognition and culture. Their conclusion that cognitive effects are related to specific everyday practices focused attention away from general effects, to concern with *specific* cultural *practices* and their consequences.

Another study in a similar vein was the Industrial Literacy Project. Between 1978 and 1981, Scribner and her colleagues (Jacob, 1982b, 1986; Scribner, 1984a,b,c,d,e, 1985; Scribner and Fahrmeier, 1982; Scribner and Schafft, 1982) examined the cognitive practices of workers in an American milk-producing plant. Scribner (1984b) explicitly discussed the role of activity theory in this project, indicating that it served as a "meta-theory offering basic categories for future development in the various subfields of psychology" (p. 3). In this view, occupations are sociocultural activities and specific work tasks within an occupation are goal-directed actions. Literacy artifacts, such as forms and signs, are culturally produced psychological tools.

Building on a descriptive case study by Jacob (1982b, 1986), Scribner selected specific job-related cognitive tasks for further examination. In several cases, detailed nonparticipant observations of these selected tasks were used to describe strategies that individuals employed in natural settings and to develop hypotheses.[14] These hypotheses were then tested in job simulations (some of which were videotaped) and experimental tasks, by comparing experts (persons who held a job involving the task being examined) and novices (persons who did not hold the relevant job).

In summarizing the results of the study, Scribner (1984e) identified several common features of skilled performance of various job tasks examined. Workers' performance of their job tasks involved diversity and flexibility in methods of problem-solving, economy of effort, dependency on situation-specific knowledge, and effective utilization of the material resources in the environment as aids for problem-solving.

In the Industrial Literacy Project, analyses of cultural and cognitive data remained separate. Culture was implicitly seen as producing practices and artifacts that lead to cognitive performance. However, the study did hint at the central importance of context: "on many dairy tasks the environment was more than an external 'context' in which problem-solving occurred; it was an integral component of the intellectual activity itself" (Scribner, 1984e:38). As we will see, more recent studies have given context center stage.

In the overall plan of this project experimental data and quantitative analyses were the core. Qualitative participant observations provided background information and a benchmark for evaluating experimental data, and they were used to develop experiments with features similar to everyday life. Nonparticipant observations went beyond previous short observations to provide continuous descriptions of behavior over time. Scribner (1984d) described her view of the relationship between the observational and experimental components:

> Observational methods are needed to determine what tasks are involved in certain practices, to describe their characteristics, and to discover the constraints the setting imposes. Experimental methods are needed to refine these descriptions and to analyze the component knowledge and cognitive processes involved in task accomplishment. (pp. 14–15)

In this view, observational data are limited to suggesting and situating experiments. Cultural meanings and links to larger social institutions are missing.

Studies of Processes in Everyday Life

Work by Jean Lave and her colleagues (de la Rocha, 1985; Lave, 1988; Lave, Murtaugh, and de la Rocha, 1984; Murtaugh, 1985) contrasts with studies with an experimental emphasis because their project shifted the focus to ethnographic observations and interviews. Their goal in the Adult Math Project was to understand everyday math activities. Beginning in 1978 they conducted studies of arithmetic activities occurring as part of grocery shopping, dieting, and cooking.[15] They used Soviet activity theory to frame their discussions so that arithmetic tasks in grocery shopping, for example, were viewed as being at the level of "action" in activity theory (Lave et al., 1984).

To study how Americans form and solve arithmetic problems while shopping for groceries, two researchers accompanied each participant to the grocery store on a shopping trip (Lave et al., 1984; Murtaugh, 1985; see also Lave, 1988). While one researcher took observation notes, mapping the route through the market and recording prices and quantities of items considered, the other conversed with the participant to produce "think-aloud" protocols of the thinking and decisions the participants made. The researchers documented when arithmetic was used and how "problems" were formed and solved. Murtaugh (1985) concluded that the way in which shoppers solve problems is related to the ways in which they formulate problems, and that problem formulation should be a focus of future research.

As part of the same project, de la Rocha (1985; see also Lave, 1988) examined the relationship between a culturally based "fund of knowledge" and how individuals use that knowledge in practice. To this end, she recruited 10 women interested in losing weight and asked them to participate in the Weight Watchers program for 5 weeks. The researchers selected this program because it has an explicit and elaborate body of general knowledge that includes an emphasis on precision measuring. To see how the women used this knowledge, de la Rocha collected the food diaries that Weight Watchers requires participants to keep and then interviewed the women every week about these diaries, focusing on the methods they used to measure and the characteristics (packaging and ease of handling) of the food items they prepared. She found that use of precise measurement depended on features of the environment and that conflicts arose around measuring when the participants' goals for cooking and dieting conflicted. To deal with these conflicts, participants developed measuring strategies other than the precise measuring encouraged by the program.

Lave *et al.* (1984) emphasized the role of context in cognitive activities. Drawing on previous work by Barker (1968) and by the Laboratory of Comparative Human Cognition (1982), they argued that context consists of two components. On one hand, a context has physical characteristics, out of the control of the individual, that reflect the larger social order. This they termed arena. On the other hand, a context is also created by individuals as they interact with the physical context and with each other.[16] This they termed setting. They argued that this view requires researchers to examine not only the stable, physical features of the context, but also how these are defined by the participants.

Furthermore, they argued that Soviet activity theory does not address the nature of the articulation between activity and context. They asserted that "activity is dialectically constituted in relation with the setting [personally defined context]" (Lave *et al.*, 1984:73). In their study of grocery shopping, this meant that "the setting both is generated out of grocery-shopping activity and at the same time generates that activity" (p. 73).

Intrapsychological Studies in Perspective

The studies examined in this section share the earlier focus on individual cognitive activity. They differ from pre-Vygotskian studies in that they all attempt to study how cognition is related to specific activities in which individuals engage. These studies have drawn on Soviet work to conceptualize their work in terms of "activities" and to examine how individuals use the "technical tools" in their environment to accomplish cognitive tasks. In addition, Lave and her colleagues discussed the meanings that activities have for participants and explicitly dealt with context and its dialectical role in cognitive activity.

As a group, these studies challenge earlier assumptions of universal, context-free cognitive processes. They indicate that in everyday life cognitive activities such as mathematics are part of other ongoing activities that significantly influence mathematics practice. The studies present a picture of everyday cognition involving persons who are active constructors of cognitive practices that are situated and mutually constituted in concrete activities that are influenced by co-occurring activities, material resources of the environment, individuals' subjective experiences, and individuals' social relations. In this view, processes are central, not just outcomes.

However, these commonalities should not mask the considerable variability in methodology across the studies. Some studies placed primary emphasis on experimental tasks, although the tasks were developed from observations. Other studies placed primary reliance on ethnographic observations and interviews, using experimental data in a more comparative strategy.

A gap in all these studies is that the researchers did not place primary emphasis on understanding what the cognitive tasks and their encompassing activities meant to the participants. Moreover, they dealt neither with interpersonal situations in which other persons are resources for the activity nor with the larger social, cultural, and historical contexts in which specific activities are generated. Recent studies of interpsychological functioning have begun to address these issues.

Studies with an Interpsychological Focus

A major area of interest arising from the sociohistorical approach is how interactions between an expert and a novice (e.g., mother–child, teacher–student, student–student) result in cognitive change in the novice (i.e., movement from interpsychological to intrapsychological functioning). This interest has led to a wide variety of studies focusing on interactional *processes*. With the centrality of interaction in this view, methods of discourse analysis have become increasingly important.

Researchers studying interpsychological functioning have used both experimental and observational designs. In addition, researchers have implemented a new design, termed formative experiments, which combines aspects of the other approaches.

Experimental Studies

These studies are essentially experiments in which data (usually video tapes) are collected to examine the processes occurring during the experiments. Analyses usually are quantitative. Such studies are "qualitative" only in the sense that they collect qualitative data.[17]

Palincsar and Brown (1984) followed a training study model in two studies to examine the effects of their reciprocal teaching method on students' ability to learn from texts. They developed the reciprocal teaching method in part from Vygotsky's ideas of social learning. Palincsar and Brown implemented their reciprocal teaching method with one group of students while another group served as the control. In one study, the instructor was Palincsar; in the other study, regular classroom teachers used the method with existing reading groups.

Palincsar and Brown collected a variety of quantitative assessments on students' performance before, during, and after the training period. In addition, they videotaped the instructional sessions and then coded the dialogue in the sessions. Qualitative data were provided as *examples* of the kinds of changes indicated from the quantitative analyses.[18]

Wertsch, Minick, and Arns (1984) also examined interpersonal interaction during instructional tasks in an experimental setting. Their goal was to examine the influence of "activity" (i.e., socioculturally defined systems of human endeavor such as work, play, and schooling) on psychological processes. In particular, they were interested in contrasting formal schooling with household economic activity. They studied 12 adult–child dyads in Brazil, half of the dyads consisting of a mother and her child and half consisting of a female teacher and a student. In contrast to the teachers, mothers had no more than 4 years of formal schooling and presumably were only minimally influenced by that activity. Each dyad was asked to construct a copy of a three-dimensional toy barnyard according to an identical model. The task took place in an empty classroom, and the sessions were audio- and videotaped.

Because the analytic scheme used by Wertsch *et al.* (1984) explicitly applied activity theory, I will review it in some detail. The researchers segmented transcripts into "actions," defined as the interaction between child and adult oriented toward selecting and placing a single piece on the model.[19] The analysis focused on three steps needed to successfully complete placement of a piece on the copy: looking at the model, picking of the needed piece, and placing this piece on the copy. The researchers coded each step using a three-stage scheme. The first stage involved coding for whether the adult or the child had carried out the step. For those instances when the child had carried out the step, the researchers determined if the child had done so independently or with some assistance from the adult. If the child received assistance from the adult, the researchers then determined whether or not the adult's assistance required the child to understand the strategic significance of their behavior, further distinguishing between direct and indirect forms of assistance. The researchers analyzed these data quantitatively.

In discussing the results of their analyses, Wertsch *et al.* (1984) used the three levels of activity theory: activity, action, and operation. At the level of goal-directed action, both sets of dyads sought the goal of making the copy in accordance with the model, and both groups completed nearly identical numbers of successful episodes. However, the dyads were different at the level of operation (i.e., the ways they reached the goal). Specifically, they differed in how they divided up responsibility for carrying out the subcomponents of the task. Wertsch, Minick, and Arns infer from these differences in operational strategies that the adults in the two sets of dyads differed at the level of activity; that is, they differed in how they defined or interpreted the setting of the task based on how the activities are related and organized at the societal level. They argued that the critical difference was the two groups' different levels of exposure to formal schooling and that, because of this differential exposure, teachers and mothers interpreted the task differently. For the teachers, the goal of teaching or learning functioned as their main motive and led to their operational patterns; for the mothers, the goal was "the correct and efficient completion of the task at hand" (Wertsch *et al.*, 1984:170), a goal consistent with learning in the context of household economics.

While Wertsch *et al.* (1984) linked their analyses of adult–child interactions to a discussion of the participants' definitions of the situation and to larger sociocultural contexts, their discussion was inferential and not as strong as it might be if they had had data to support their interpretations. Moreover, their treatment of context was static and the "context" of the experiment was still taken for granted.

Naturalistic Studies

Several studies have used the ideas of the sociohistorical approach to guide ethnographic studies. These studies focus on the face-to-face interactions that occur in instructional settings and on the sociocultural factors that influence them. They are particularly useful in showing how larger sociocultural factors influence the unfolding of face-to-face interactions.

Florio-Ruane (1991) examined the instructional writing conference between teachers and students, which in its ideal form is a model of dialogue in a child's zone of proximal development (*scaffolded dialogue*, in Florio-Ruane's terms), with the beginning writer (student) and the reader (teacher) free to change conversational places. She reported that much research on writing conferences indicates that they do not always achieve this potential, and much conference talk tends to resemble the typical unilateral conversation structure found in lessons. "The promise of writing conferences as scaffolded dialogue between teacher/experts and student/novices is tempered by the realities of classroom life" (p. 369) and by the "school's routine definitions of situation, status, and role, [which] continue to operate within writing conferences" (p. 370). In Florio-Ruane's view, particular instructional techniques or discourse strategies do not necessarily make a difference in learning; what is needed is the creation of "conditions under which social life serves to support intellectual development" (p. 383–384).

A study in progress by Jacob (1987a, 1989, 1990, 1991) is examining the interactional processes accomplished by elementary students in cooperative learning groups in three classrooms and the community, school, classroom, and peer contexts that influence these interactional processes. For this study, Jacob conducted pilot observations and interviews in early 1988 and then was a participant observer in the school during the 1988–1989 school year. Her data comprise the following: field notes from classroom observations and informal discussions with teachers and the principal, in-depth interviews with teachers and students, and video tapes of the cooperative groups.[20]

Preliminary analyses indicate a very complex web of multiple layers of mutually influencing processes. For example, various factors external to a particular classroom as well as classroom features (including the students themselves) contribute to the way each teacher organized the cooperative learning lessons. These different lesson organizations supported different kinds of social interactions in the cooperative learning groups. In addition, students' friendship patterns and norms appear to be relevant to the interaction processes that occur within the groups, and these friendship patterns are related to the demographic and cultural characteristics of the local neighborhood.

While comparatively few ethnographic studies have been conducted within a Vygotskian framework, such studies seem particularly suited to examine naturally occurring interactional processes and to link social interaction processes to larger sociocultural and historical factors. However, it is exactly this link to existing circumstances that some researchers have sought to overcome in their use of formative experiments.

Formative Experiments

To deal with the limitations they perceive in both experimental designs and naturalistic designs, some neo-Vygotskian scholars have used a new design, termed "formative experiments" (Davydov, 1988; Griffin, Belyaeva, and Soldatova, in press; Newman, 1990). These scholars criticize traditional experiments because they lack ecological validity. They also criticize studies that describe ordinary school situations, because, although such research can tell us about the current forms and content of schooling and larger societal influences on schooling, they tell us little about what *could* be.

> Pessimistic findings from data gathered under current pedagogical conditions can severely underestimate the power of instructional theory and practices to influence development and may fail to provide an impetus or ideas for designing better education. (Griffin *et al.*, in press)

Thus, such studies are explicitly concerned with improving instruction. To achieve their goals, researchers combine qualitative methods of investigation with interventions in learning situations.

Newman, Griffin, and Cole (1984, 1989b) conducted several studies to examine the social construction of psychological tasks and to see how different social environments help or hinder different students. For example, in one series of studies, they developed activities that incorporated the "same" combinations problem (i.e., identifying all possible sets of pairs from a set of items) in different social settings (i.e., small group work in a classroom, tutorials in a "laboratory" setting, and after-school clubs). In another series, they examined the "same" division lesson when taught to different math-ability groups of students.

Their analyses developed directly from Vygotskian concepts and focused on the processes by which the context and task interacted. Data were qualitative (field notes and video tapes) and analyses relied heavily on methods of discourse analysis. In studies that examined outcomes, the analyses were quantitative.

Analysis of the goals of the actors was central to their approach. They showed that teachers and students may have different goals and different understandings of a situation. If a student's understandings and goals are close enough to the teacher's, the teacher can appropriate the resulting behavior into his or her own understanding of the task, thus contributing to the child's cognitive change.

Their analyses also examined relationships between interactional processes and larger contextual issues. For example, they also found that different settings place differential constraints on the goals of the participants. The degree of constraint and who determines the goals has a significant impact on the nature of the resulting social interaction and cognitive processes.

Other researchers developed and examined instructional programs based on the principles of Vygotsky and his followers. In these "formative experiments" (Newman, 1990), researchers had a specific educational goal in mind. They then modified the materials or the social organization to bring about the desired goal. These approaches used traditional ethnographic methods, such as participant observation and videotaping, to identify problems, to propose possible solutions, and to document before, during, and after change.

Newman and his colleagues (Newman, 1990; Newman, Goldman, Brienne, Jackson, and Magzamen, 1989a) conducted such a study during 1986–1987 using local area network technology to simulate "real" scientific activity in the classroom and to let students use computers the way scientists do. To achieve these ends, the researchers "were prepared to modify the design of the technology, introduce new software, develop curriculum materials, and conduct staff development workshops as needed" (Newman, 1990:11). To document the project, they collected observations, interviews, and video tapes.

They found that the project involved an evolving relationship between their research and development goals, and the needs and goals of the teacher and students. The computer technology supported the increased use of small group work over the year, including areas outside the science classroom. Moreover, the local area network led to "coordinated investigations" in which various small groups contributed their individual results to a larger group data base. This allowed the teacher to appropriate these individual contributions into a larger framework.

Another team of researchers (Diaz, Moll, and Mehan, 1986; Moll and Diaz, 1987) used case studies to document their development of changes in the social organization of instruction to improve the education of minority students. Their general procedure was to use ethnographic and microethnographic methods to analyze problem settings (i.e., settings where minority students were not doing well), to conduct careful analyses of what was happening, and to use the theory of the sociohistorical school to reorganize instruction. In one case study, they described how students in a bilingual program were not reading well in English. They observed that, whereas the students were given a range of tasks in Spanish reading from decoding to more advanced comprehension activities, in the English reading class all the students, even those who had demonstrated advanced comprehension skills in Spanish, were given only low-level tasks in English reading. The authors modified the instructional situation to allow students to discuss English readings in Spanish, the results showing that the students could understand more about the English text than they could articulate in English. The researchers interpreted this change as providing students with the necessary support to allow them to display their skills.[21]

Interpsychological Studies in Perspective

Neo-Vygotskian studies with an interpsychological focus have incorporated more of the Vygotskian and neo-Vygotskian ideas than can successfully be used in studies with an intrapsychological focus. In the interpsychological studies, a new dimension has been added—a central focus on understanding the interactional processes that are related to cognitive change. In addition, some have explicitly used activity theory to develop their units of analysis and their analytic methods, and some have explicitly linked social processes (and their related cognitive operations) to aspects of the sociocultural order. Many have also explicitly focused on participants' definitions of the situation and on interactants' intersubjectivity.

These researchers have exhibited the same variability of designs as is displayed in the intrapsychological work, with some emphasizing experimental approaches and others more naturalistic approaches. In addition, several researchers have combined qualitative methods with an experimental framework in a new way to develop formative experiments. Their goal has been to maximize educational benefits rather than to understand the current status quo. To this end they recursively modify interactional structures, technical tools, etc., to bring about the desired learning outcomes. Overall, the focus on interpersonal interaction has led to an increased use of methods of discourse analysis.

The results of this work have contributed to a fuller and more dynamic view of cognitive change and of the relationships among culture, context, and cognition. Like the intrapsychological studies discussed earlier, these studies present a picture of situated cognitive activities. Cognitive change is an inherently social process in which language (semiotic mediation) is a central means through which change occurs. For example, a major component of cognitive change involves "experts" helping "novices" change their definition of the situation to one that is closer to their expert definitions. One way experts help novices learn a new definition of the situation, is explicitly to interpret something the novice is doing in the expert's frame of reference—that is, to appropriate it.

This work is also beginning to show that social interactions (and their related cognitive change) are in a dynamic and dialectical relationship to other sociocultural and historical aspects of the situation. For example, in schools, factors such as routine definitions of status and role, pressures on teachers' time, and student friendship groups are in a dynamic relationship with instructional social interaction patterns.

Discussion

The story told here is not the story of a well-defined tradition of normal science as Kuhn (1970) has defined it. It is the story of dynamic change over the past 30 years through the interplay and intertwining of a variety of assumptions, goals, designs, and methods for the study of culture, context, and cognition. The dialogue has moved from separate discipline-based approaches, to interdisciplinary efforts, to new perspectives and approaches (i.e., neo-Vygotskian work) that draw from the work of Vygotsky and other Soviet scholars working on activity theory and from previous work in the West.

Neo-Vygotskian work continued the earlier trend in Western studies toward interdisciplinary work and examination of specific relations between culture and cognition. However, it also broke with this tradition in several significant ways. Most notably, neo-Vygotskian work has shifted the focus to understanding the processes that occur in local contexts and away from comparative studies focused on outcomes. The unit of analysis has also shifted from the isolated individual to units that focus on an individual or individuals acting in a specific setting. The new units support a view of humans as active constructors who act as whole persons in activities and a view of social interaction as a central contributor to cognitive change. Individuals' behavior and interactions and the activities in which they operate are also influenced by and influence their definitions of the situation and goals, the technical and psychological tools available and used, their social relations, co-occurring activities, the physical context, the context they jointly create, and larger sociocultural and historical factors that influence the routine patterns in the context. This emerging view is consistent with interpretivist principles.

This perspective has led to an increasing use of methods of discourse analysis to help understand how social interaction contributes to cognitive change. It has also led to the implementation of formative experiments that seek to move from documenting what is, to exploring what could be.

Yet, although this area is filled with tremendous excitement, activity, and potential, there is much to be done both theoretically and empirically. Although Vygotsky presented a grand scheme linking social institutions, cultural knowledge, interpersonal interactions, and individual cognitive activities, his broad theoretical outline is filled in unevenly. Much remains to be done in explicating Vygotsky's vision, especially at the interpersonal and institutional levels. Some neo-Vygotskians are pursuing this need. Wertsch (Wertsch, 1985c, 1989, 1991; Wertsch et al., 1984), for example, has focused primarily on the interpersonal level, explicating the ways in which language is used to link the interpersonal and the intrapersonal. Recently, he has begun to explore the link between forms of language and the larger social order. Wertsch, Tulviste, and Hagstrom (1990) suggested that Bakhtin's notion of "social language" helps link society and language forms by suggesting that using any form of language as a mediational means involves appropriating some "social language" associated with a particular stratum of society. Thus, interpsychological functioning is linked with social life that is socially, culturally, and historically situated.

Lave (1988) drew on a range of social theory to develop a dialectical approach to explain situationally specific cognition. Her approach seeks to get away from the previous dichotomous approaches that emphasized social or cognitive behavior. Activities, rather than societies or individuals, become a central focus and are seen as the locus where the sociocultural external order meets individuals. The focus becomes the "relations between human action and the social or cultural system at the level of everyday activities in culturally organized settings" (Lave, 1988:14). Thus, in this view, activities "embody within themselves, the fundamental notions of temporal, spatial, and social ordering that underlie and organize the system as a whole" (Ortner, 1984:154, cited in Lave, 1988:14), and human actors are partially determined and partially determining (Lave, 1988:16).

Considerable empirical work also remains to be done. Vygotsky's own empirical work focused on the intrapsychological level, whereas much work by neo-Vygotskians has focused on the transition from the interpersonal level to the intrapsychological level. Although significant progress has been made in developing methods to examine interpsychological activity, more work needs to be done in linking this level of analysis to the larger constraints of the immediate context and larger institutional levels. Florio-Ruane's (1991) work raised important questions about the institutional and contextual constraints on actors that have important implications for interpsychological and, thus, intrapsychological activity. Other ethnographic work, not explicitly within the sociohistorical tradition (e.g., Mehan, Hertweck, and Meihls, 1986; Nespor, 1990) has raised similar questions.

Another issue that merits considerable further attention is the role of individuals' meanings. To date, this has been examined primarily in terms of individuals' definitions of the situation. Many other aspects of meaning can come into play and these need to be explored. Furthermore, the relationships between cultural meanings of a group and individual personal meanings in a particular situation need to be elaborated. Work in symbolic interactionism may be helpful in this regard.

Neo-Vygotskian researchers also need to clarify their stance toward experimental designs. While some neo-Vygotskian researchers have questioned the privileged status and acontextual assumptions of experiments, others continue to use only experimental designs and eschew naturalistic settings.

Although much work remains to be done, the literature discussed above presents educators and educational researchers with a broad theoretical framework and a range of methodological options for studying the relationships among culture, context, and cognition.[22] The emerging view of dynamic and dialectical relations among culture, context, and cognition has broadened and deepened our understanding of student learning. It has also shown that what currently *is* does not necessarily limit what *can* be, offering both hope and approaches for change.

Notes

[1] For examination of substantive aspects of this work, see reviews by Cole and Scribner (1974), Laboratory of Comparative Human Cognition (1979, 1982, 1983), Price-Williams (1975), and Rogoff (1990).

[2] Linguistics also entered into some of the discussions, but the main questions were formulated and discussed between anthropology and psychology. One central issue for which linguistics was involved was whether or not the structure of language determines the structure of thought (often discussed in terms of the Whorfian hypothesis). For a discussion of linguistic issues related to culture and cognition, see reviews by Cole *et al.* (1971:10–12) and by Cole and Scribner (1974:39–60).

[3] While the tradition of cognitive anthropology began to be developed in the 1960s and has continued to the present, its focus has been on describing cultural knowledge and identifying the organization of cultural knowledge (e.g., Dougherty, 1985; Holland and Quinn, 1987; Spradley, 1979; Tyler, 1969). Until recently, cognitive anthropologists have focused on studying the structure of semantic systems of cultural groups. Recent work (e.g., Dougherty, 1985; Holland and Quinn, 1987) has taken a broader perspective and begun to interact with relevant psychological theory and research. For a discussion of this literature in relation to the studies reviewed here, see Lave (1988).

[4] Cole (1988) later stated that this early work was influenced by Vygotksy's ideas. However, because Vygotsky is not explicitly discussed in the text, the project is included here.

[5] Although Vygotsky's ideas on sociocultural history were derived from others' writings (Wertsch, 1985c), they played such a central role in his theory that it is widely referred to as the "sociohistorical" or "cultural–historical" approach.

[6] Vygotsky and his Soviet colleagues have had their largest impact in the West through their theoretical and methodological ideas rather than through their empirical research. This is because Soviet and Western researchers have asked very different questions, because Soviet and Western psychologies have been based on very different philosophical premises (Wertsch, 1981). However, the distinction between Western and Soviet empirical research may soften as scholars begin to collaborate across former barriers (e.g., Griffin *et al.*, in press).

[7] To date, much of Vygotsky's work is available only in Russian. For a bibliography of his work in Russian and in English, see Vygotsky (1978:141–151). For further exploration, see work by Vygotsky (1962, 1978, 1981, 1987), Leont'ev (1978, 1981), and Luria (1976, 1979) or American sources reviewing the sociohistorical approach (e.g., Cole, 1988; Minick, 1987; Wertsch, 1979, 1981, 1984, 1985a,c; Wertsch *et al.*, 1984; Wertsch and Rogoff, 1984).

[8] A related concept is that of "scaffolding," discussed by Wood and Bruner (Wood, 1980; Wood, Bruner, and Ross, 1976).

[9] For a discussion of the zone of proximal development in relation to similar ideas by American scholars, see Griffin and Cole (1984). Drawing on work by Leont'ev (1981), Griffin and Cole discussed the idea of "leading activities"—that is, each stage in development is associated with a particular leading activity (e.g., play, formal schooling, peer activities, work). Using Polynesian data, Watson-Gegeo (1989) challenged two aspects of their notion of leading activities: the chronological order they propose and their suggestion that there is a one-to-one association between a leading activity and cognitive development.

[10] Although Vygotsky's general theoretical framework has remained robust, many of his specific ideas have been modified by subsequent research. Wertsch (1985c) provided a useful evaluation of Vygotsky's work in light of recent research.

[11] See also discussions of appropriation by Newman (1990) and Newman *et al.* (1989b).

[12] Although Leont'ev is widely credited for developing "activity" as a central unit of analysis in Soviet psychology, he (Leont'ev, 1981) credited Vygotsky's work as containing the basic ideas of activity theory.

[13] Wertsch and Sammarco (1985) presented a good example of applying the notions of action and operations to the analysis of an experiment.

[14] In other studies (e.g., Scribner, 1984c), only experiments were conducted. For example, recall of dairy items and categorization of dairy items were compared for various groups.

[15] Although Lave (1979) pointed out that problem-solving with math in everyday settings is always socially influenced and very often interactive, the studies in the Adult Math Project did not explicitly examine the interpsychological aspects of everyday math activity and, thus, are examined in this section.

[16] For a similar point of view, see Erickson and Shultz (1981).

[17] For other examples, see work by Forman (1989), Forman and Cazden (1985), Gauvain and DeMent (1990), Wertsch and Sammarco (1985), and Wertsch, McNamee, McLane, and Budwig (1980).

[18] The analytic approach followed by Palincsar and Brown (1984) contrasts with that in a later study by Palincsar (1986). In this latter study, Palincsar qualitatively examined the dialogues recorded during reciprocal teaching sessions with first-grade students. Her goal was to identify the ways that dialogue can be used to provide "scaffolded" instruction. For an example of their work that combines both the qualitative and quantitative analyses of dialogue, see Palincsar and Brown (1989).

[19] The development of methods for coding *dyads* instead of the behavior of individuals is a significant step and crucial for analysis within a Vygotskian perspective. See Rogoff and Gauvain (1986) for their discussion of the development of their work from coding individual behavior to ethnographic analyses of a small number of cases to a scheme for examining dyadic behavior across a large data base.

[20] In addition, Jacob collected quantitative pre- and postmeasures (attitudinal measures, language proficiency measures, and content measures) for the cooperative learning classes and comparable classes who did not use cooperative learning.

[21] The latest work in this tradition (e.g., Moll, 1990) added explicit teacher–researcher collaboration to the method. With the goal of improving Latino students' literacy learning, Moll used ethnographic methods to document the origin, use, and distribution of knowledge and skills in Hispanic households. Moll also used these methods (observation and videotaping) to examine existing methods of instruction. In an after-school "lab/study group," researchers and teachers used the household data among others to develop methods of literacy instruction that built on the resources of the community. "This study group represents a social context for informing, assisting, and supporting teachers' performances; it is an activity setting where teachers and researchers get together to study teaching, to learn about the households, and to develop innovations; it is also a self-assisting group where teachers help themselves" (Moll, 1990:8).

[22] Scholars have also used Vygotsky's approach to develop principles for educational practice (e.g., Brown, Collins, and Duguid, 1989; Collins, Brown, and Newman, 1989), to develop specific instructional methods (e.g., Brown and Palincsar, 1989; Palincsar and Brown, 1984), and to explicate programs, particularly those involving small group instruction (e.g., Tharp and Gallimore, 1988). Other scholars (Brown and Ferrara, 1985; Newman *et al.*, 1989b; Wertsch and Rogoff, 1984) have used the sociohistorical approach to suggest alternative assessment methods.

Acknowledgments

I would like to thank Bruce Davis, Beverly Mattson, and the editors of this volume for comments on earlier drafts of this chapter.

References

Barker, R. G. (1968). *Ecological psychology: Concepts and methods for studying the environment of human behavior*. Stanford, CA: Stanford University Press.

Barker, R. G., and Wright, H. F. (1971). *Midwest and its children*. Hamden, CT: Anchor Books. (Originally published in 1955.)

Bateson, G. (1958). *Naven: A survey of the problems suggested by a composite picture of the culture of a New Guinea tribe drawn from three points of view* (2nd ed.). Stanford, CA: Stanford University Press.

Boas, F. (1911). *The mind of primitive man*. New York: Macmillan.

Bossert, S. (1988). Cooperative activities in classrooms. *In* E. Rothkopf (Ed.), *Review of research in education*, 15, 225–250. Washington, DC: American Educational Research Association.

Brenner, M. (1985). The practice of arithmetic in Liberian schools. *Anthropology and Education Quarterly*, 16, 177–186.

Bronfenbrenner, U. (1974). Development research, public policy, and the ecology of childhood. *Child Development*, 45, 1–5.

Bronfenbrenner, U. (1979). *The ecology of human development: Experiments by nature and design.* Cambridge, MA: Harvard University Press.

Brown, A. L., and Ferrara, R. A. (1985). Diagnosing zones of proximal development. *In* J. V. Wertsch (Ed.), *Culture, communication and cognition: Vygotskian perspectives* (pp. 273–305). Cambridge, MA: Harvard University Press.

Brown, A. L., and Palincsar, A. S. (1989). Guided, cooperative learning and individual knowledge acquisition. *In* L. Resnick (Ed.), *Knowing, learning, and instruction: Essays in honor of Robert Glaser* (pp. 393–451). Hillsdale, NJ: Lawrence Erlbaum.

Brown, J. S., Collins, A., and Duguid, P. (1989). Situated cognition and the culture of learning. *Educational Researcher, 18*(1), 32–42.

Cole, M. (1985). The zone of proximal development: Where culture and cognition create each other. *In* J. V. Wertsch (Ed.), *Culture, communication, and cognition: Vygotskian perspectives* (pp. 146–161). Cambridge: Cambridge University Press.

Cole, M. (1988). Cross-cultural research in the sociohistorical tradition. *Human Development, 31,* 137–157.

Cole, M., and Bruner, J. S. (1971). Cultural differences and inferences about psychological processes. *American Psychologist, 26,* 867–876.

Cole, M., and Scribner, S. (1974). *Culture and thought: A psychological introduction.* New York: John Wiley.

Cole, M., and Scribner, S. (1975). Theorizing about socialization of cognition. *Ethos, 3,* 249–268.

Cole, M., and Scribner, S. (1978). Introduction. *In* L. S. Vygotsky, *Mind in society: The development of higher psychological processes* (pp. 1–14). Cambridge, MA: Harvard University Press.

Cole, M., Gay, J., Glick, J., and Sharp, D. (1971). *The cultural context of learning and thinking: An exploration in experimental anthropology.* New York: Basic Books.

Collins, A., Brown, J. S., and Newman, S. E. (1989). Cognitive apprenticeship: Teaching the crafts of reading, writing, and mathematics. *In* L. Resnick (Ed.), *Knowing, learning, and instruction: Essays in honor of Robert Glaser* (pp. 453–494). Hillsdale, NJ: Lawrence Erlbaum.

Davydov, V. V. (1988). Problems of developmental teaching: The experience of theoretical and experimental psychological research. Part 2. *Soviet Education, 30*(9).

de la Rocha, O. (1985). The reorganization of arithmetic practice in the kitchen. *Anthropology & Education Quarterly, 16,* 193–198.

Diaz, S., Moll, L., and Mehan, H. (1986). Sociocultural resources in instruction: A context-specific approach. *In* California State Department of Education, *Beyond language: Social and cultural factors in schooling language minority students* (pp. 187–230). Evaluation, Dissemination and Assessment Center, California State University, Los Angeles.

Dougherty, J. W. D. (Ed.). (1985). *Directions in cognitive anthropology.* Urbana: University of Illinois Press.

Edgerton, R. (1974). Cross-cultural psychology and psychological anthropology: One paradigm or two? *Reviews in Anthropology, 1*(1), 52–65.

Eisenhart, M. (1988). The ethnographic research tradition and mathematics education research. *Journal for Research in Mathematics Education, 19,* 99–114.

Erickson, F. (1982). Taught cognitive learning in its immediate environments: A neglected topic in the anthropology of education. *Anthropology & Education Quarterly, 13,* 149–180.

Erickson, F. (1986). Qualitative methods in research on teaching. *In* M. C. Wittrock (Ed.), *Handbook of research on teaching* (3rd ed., pp. 119–161). New York: Macmillan.

Erickson, F., and Shultz, J. (1981). When is a context? Some issues and methods in the analysis of social competence. *In* J. Green and C. Wallat (Eds.), *Ethnography and language in educational setting* (pp. 147–160). Norwood, NJ: Ablex.

Fetterman, D. (1989). *Ethnography: Step by step.* Newbury Park, CA: Sage Publications.

Florio-Ruane, S. (1991). Instructional conversations in learning to write and learning to teach. *In* B. Jones and L. Idol (Eds.), *Educational values and cognitive instruction: Implications for reform* (Vol. 2), (pp. 365–386). Hillsdale, NJ: Lawrence Erlbaum.

Forman, E. (1989). The role of peer interaction in the social construction of mathematical knowledge. *International Journal of Educational Research*, 13, 55–70.

Forman, E., and Cazden, C. (1985). Exploring Vygotskian perspective in education: The cognitive value of peer interaction. *In* J. V. Wertsch (Ed.), *Culture, communication, and cognition: Vygotskian perspectives* (pp. 323–347). Cambridge: Cambridge University Press.

Fortes, M. (1970). Social and psychological aspects of education in Taleland. *In* J. Middleton (Ed.), *From child to adult: Studies in the anthropology of education* (pp. 14–74). Garden City, NY: Natural History Press. [Reprinted from *Africa*, 1938, 11(4).]

Fosnot, C. T. (1989). *Enquiring teachers, enquiring learners: A constructivist approach for teaching.* New York: Teachers College Press.

Gauvain, M., and DeMent, T. (1990). *Shared social history as prerequisite knowledge in joint cognitive activity.* Paper presented at the annual meeting of the American Educational Research Association, Boston.

Gay, J., and Cole, M. (1967). *The new mathematics and an old culture: A study of learning among the Kpelle of Liberia.* New York: Holt, Rinehard & Winston.

Glick, J. (1975). Cognitive development in cross-cultural perspective. *In* F. Horowitz (Ed.), *Review of child development research* (Vol. 4, pp. 595–654). Chicago: University of Chicago Press.

Goodenough, W. (1971). *Culture, language, and society.* Addison-Wesley Module. Reading, MA: Addison-Wesley.

Goodnow, J. J. (1969). Problems in research on culture and thought. In D. Elkind and J. Flavell (Eds.), *Studies in cognitive development.* New York: Oxford University Press.

Greenfield, P., and Bruner, J. S. (1966). Culture and cognitive growth. *International Journal of Psychology*, 1, 89–107.

Greenfield, P., Reich, L., and Olver, R. (1966). On culture and equivalence: II. *In* J. Bruner, R. Olver, and P. Greenfield (Eds.), *Studies in cognitive growth* (pp. 270–318). New York: John Wiley.

Griffin, P., and Cole, M. (1984). Current activity for the future: The Zo-ped. *In* B. Rogoff and J. V. Wertsch (Eds.), *Children's learning in the "zone of proximal development"* (pp. 45–64). San Francisco: Jossey-Bass.

Griffin, P., Belyaeva, A., and Soldatova, G. (in press). Creating and reconstituting contexts for educational interactions including a computer program. *In* N. Minick, E. Forman, and A. Stone (Eds.), *Contexts for learning: Sociocultural dynamics in children's development.* Oxford: Oxford University Press.

Hallowell, A. I. (1967). *Culture and experience.* New York: Schocken Books. (Original work published in 1955.)

Hammersley, M., and Atkinson, P. (1983). *Ethnography: Principles in practice.* New York: Tavistock.

Holland, D., and Quinn, N. (Eds.). (1987). *Cultural models in language and thought.* Cambridge: Cambridge University Press.

Jacob, E. (1977). The influence of culture and environment on cognition: A case study in a Puerto Rican town. Doctoral dissertation, University of Pennsylvania: Philadelphia.

Jacob, E. (1982a). Combining ethnographic and quantitative approaches: Some suggestions with examples from a study in Puerto Rico. In P. Gilmore and A. Glatthorn (Eds.), *Ethnography and education: Children in and out of school* (pp. 124–147). Washington, DC: Center for Applied Linguistics.

Jacob, E. (1982b). *Literacy on the job.* Final report to the Ford Foundation. Washington, DC: Center for Applied Linguistics.

Jacob, E. (1982c). *Puerto Rican children's informal education at home.* Final report, NIE-G-80-0132, to the National Institute of Education. Washington, DC: Center for Applied Linguistics.

Jacob, E. (1983). Studying Puerto Rican children's informal education at home. In C. Rivera (Ed.), *A sociolinguistic/ethnographic approach to language proficiency assessment* (pp. 71–85). Clevedon, England: Multilingual Matters.

Jacob, E. (1984). Learning literacy through play: Puerto Rican kindergarten children. In H. Goelman, A. Oberg, and F. Smith (Eds.), *Awakening to literacy* (pp. 73–83). London: Heinemann.

Jacob, E. (1986). Literacy skills and production line work. In K. Borman and J. Reisman (Eds.), *Becoming a worker* (pp. 176–200). Norwood, NJ: Ablex.

Jacob, E. (1987a). *Culture and cognition: A case study of cooperative learning with limited-English-proficient students.* Research proposal, George Mason University, Fairfax, VA.

Jacob, E. (1987b). Qualitative research traditions: A review. *Review of Educational Research, 57,* 1–50.

Jacob, E. (1989). *Students creating culture: Cooperative learning in a multi-ethnic elementary school.* Paper presented at the annual meeting of the American Anthropological Association, Washington, DC.

Jacob, E. (1990). *Studying cooperative learning with minority students: An anthropological perspective.* Paper presented at the biennial meeting of the International Association for Cooperation in Education, Baltimore.

Jacob, E. (1991). *You can't jump into it all at once: One teacher's implementation of cooperative learning.* Final report to the Commonwealth Center for the Education of Teachers. Harrisonburg, VA: Commonwealth Center for the Education of Teachers, James Madison University.

John-Steiner, V., and Souberman, E. (1978). Afterword. In L. S. Vygotsky, *Mind in society: The development of higher psychological processes* (pp. 121–133). Cambridge: Harvard University Press.

Keesing, R., and Keesing, F. (1971). *New perspectives in cultural anthropology.* New York: Holt, Rinehart & Winston.

Kroeber, A. L., and Kluckhohn, C. (1963). *Culture: A critical review of concepts and definitions.* New York: Vintage.

Kuhn, T. (1970). *The structure of scientific revolutions* (2nd ed.). Chicago: University of Chicago Press.

Laboratory of Comparative Human Cognition. (1979). What's cultural about cross-cultural cognitive psychology? *Annual Review of Psychology, 30,* 145–172.

Laboratory of Comparative Human Cognition. (1982). Culture and intelligence. In R. Sternberg (Ed.), *Handbook of human intelligence* (pp. 642–719). Cambridge: Cambridge University Press.

Laboratory of Comparative Human Cognition. (1983). Culture and cognitive development. *In* W. Kessen (Ed.), *History, theory, and methods. Vol. 1. Handbook of child psychology* (pp. 295–356). New York: John Wiley.

Lave, J. (1977). Cognitive consequences of traditional apprenticeship training in West Africa. *Anthropology & Education Quarterly*, 8, 177–180.

Lave, J. (1979). *A model of mundane arithmetic problem-solving.* Paper presented at the Social Science Research Council Conference on Cultural Representations of Knowledge, La Jolla, CA.

Lave, J. (1980). What's special about experiments as contexts for thinking? *Quarterly Newsletter of the Laboratory of Comparative Human Cognition*, 2, 86–91.

Lave, J. (1982). A comparative approach to educational forms and learning processes. *Anthropology & Education Quarterly*, 13, 181–187.

Lave, J. (1988). *Cognition in practice: Mind, mathematics and culture in everyday life.* Cambridge: Cambridge University Press.

Lave, J., Murtaugh, M., and de la Rocha, O. (1984). The dialectic of arithmetic in grocery shopping. *In* B. Rogoff and J. Lave (Eds.), *Everyday cognition: Its development in social context* (pp. 67–94). Cambridge, MA: Harvard University Press.

Leont'ev, A. N. (1978). *Activity, consciousness, and personality.* Englewood Cliffs, NJ: Prentice-Hall.

Leont'ev, A. N. (1981). *Problems in the development of mind.* Moscow: Progress Publishers.

Lincoln, Y., and Guba, E. (1985). *Naturalistic inquiry.* Beverly Hills, CA: Sage Publications.

Luria, A. R. (1976). *Cognitive development: Its cultural and social foundations,* M. Lopez-Morillas and L. Solotaroff (Trans.) and M. Cole (Ed.). Cambridge, MA: Harvard University Press.

Luria, A. R. (1979). *The making of mind: A personal account of Soviet psychology.* Cambridge, MA: Harvard University Press.

Mehan, H., Hertweck, A., and Meihls, J. L. (1986). *Handicapping the handicapped: Decision making in students' educational careers.* Stanford, CA: Stanford University Press.

Middleton, J. (Ed.). (1970). *From child to adult: Studies in the anthropology of education.* Garden City, NY: Natural History Press.

Minick, N. (1987). The development of Vygotsky's thought: An introduction. *In* L. S. Vygotsky, *The collected works of L. S. Vygotsky: Vol. 1. Problems of general psychology* (R. Rieber and A. Carton, Eds.; N. Minick, Trans.) (pp. 17–36). New York: Plenum Press.

Moll, L. (1990). *Community-mediated instruction: A qualitative approach.* Paper presented at the annual meeting of the American Educational Research Association, Boston.

Moll, L., and Diaz, S. (1987). Change as the goal of educational research. *Anthropology & Education Quarterly*, 18, 300–311.

Munroe, R. L., and Munroe, R. H. (1971). Effects of environmental experience on spatial ability in an East African Society. *Journal of Social Psychology*, 83, 15–22.

Murtaugh, M. (1985). The practice of arithmetic by American grocery shoppers. *Anthropology & Education Quarterly*, 16, 186–192.

Nerlove, S. B., Roberts, J. M., Klein, R. E., Yarbrough, C., and Habicht, J.-P. (1974). Natural indicators of cognitive development: An observational study of rural Guatemalan children. *Ethos*, 2, 265–295.

Nespor, J. (1990). The jackhammer: A case study of undergraduate physics problem solving in its social setting. *International Journal of Qualitative Studies in Education*, 3, 139–155.

Newman, D. (1990). Opportunities for research on the organization impact of school computers. *Educational Researcher*, 19(3), 8–13.

Newman, D., Griffin, P., and Cole, M. (1984). Social constraints in laboratory and classroom tasks. *In* B. Rogoff and J. Lave (Eds.), *Everyday cognition: Its development in social context* (pp. 172–193). Cambridge, MA: Harvard University Press.

Newman, D., Goldman, S., Brienne, D., Jackson, I., and Magzamen, S. (1989a). Computer mediation of collaborative science investigations. *Journal of Educational Computing Research*, 5, 151–166.

Newman, D., Griffin, P., and Cole, M. (1989b). *The construction zone: Working for cognitive change in school*. Cambridge: Cambridge University Press.

Ortner, S. B. (1984). Theory in anthropology since the sixties. *Comparative Studies in Society and History*, 26(1), 126–166.

Palincsar, A. S. (1986). The role of dialogue in providing scaffolded instruction. *Educational Psychologist*, 21, 73–98.

Palincsar, A. S., and Brown, A. L. (1984). Reciprocal teaching of comprehension-fostering and monitoring activities. *Cognition and Instruction*, 1, 117–175.

Palincsar, A. S., and Brown, A. L. (1989). Classroom dialogues to promote self-regulated comprehension. *In* J. Brophy (Ed.), *Advances in research on teaching* Vol. 1 (pp. 35–71). Greenwich, CT: JAI Press.

Pelto, P. (1970). *Anthropological research*. New York: Harper & Row.

Poplin, M. (1984). Toward a holistic view of persons with learning disabilities. *Learning Disability Quarterly*, 7, 290–294.

Price-Williams, D. (1975). *Explorations in cross-cultural psychology*. San Francisco: Chandler & Sharp.

Quinn, N., and Holland, D. (1987). Culture and cognition. *In* D. Holland and N. Quinn (Eds.), *Cultural models in language and thought* (pp. 3–40). Cambridge: Cambridge University Press.

Reed, H. J., and Lave, J. (1979). Arithmetic as a tool for investigating relations between culture and cognition. *American Ethnologist*, 6, 568–582.

Rogoff, B. (1990). *Apprenticeship in thinking: Cognitive development in social context*. New York: Oxford University Press.

Rogoff, B., and Gauvain, M. (1986). A method for the analysis of patterns, illustrated with data on mother–child instructional interaction. *In* J. Valsiner (Ed.), *The role of the individual subject in scientific psychology* (pp. 261–290). New York: Plenum Press.

Rogoff, B., and Wertsch, J. (Eds.). (1984). *Children's learning in the "zone of proximal development."* New Directions for Child Development, No. 23. San Francisco: Jossey-Bass.

Romney, A. K., and D'Andrade, R. G. (Eds.). (1964). *Transcultural studies in cognition*. Special Publication of the *American Anthropologist*, 66(3, part 2).

Schoggen, M., and Schoggen, P. (1971). *Environmental forces in the home lives of three-year-old children in three population subgroups*. DARCEE Papers and Reports, Vol. 5, No. 2. Nashville, TN: George Peabody College for Teachers.

Scribner, S. (Ed.). (1984a). Cognitive studies of work. *The Quarterly Newsletter of the Laboratory of Comparative Human Cognition*, 6(1, 2).

Scribner, S. (1984b). Introduction to this issue. *The Quarterly Newsletter of the Laboratory of Comparative Human Cognition*, 6(1, 2), 1–5.

Scribner, S. (1984c). Organizing knowledge at work. *The Quarterly Newsletter of the Laboratory of Comparative Human Cognition*, 6(1, 2), 26–32.

Scribner, S. (1984d). Studying working intelligence. *In* B. Rogoff and J. Lave (Eds.), *Everyday cognition: Its development in social context* (pp. 9–40). Cambridge, MA: Harvard University Press.

Scribner, S. (1984e). Toward a model of practical thinking at work. *The Quarterly Newsletter of the Laboratory of Comparative Human Cognition*, 6(1, 2), 37–42.

Scribner, S. (1985). Knowledge at work. *Anthropology & Education Quarterly*, 16, 199–206.

Scribner, S., and Cole, M. (1981). *The psychology of literacy*. Cambridge: Harvard University Press.

Scribner, S., and Fahrmeier, E. (1982). *Practical and theoretical arithmetic: Some preliminary findings*. Industrial Literacy Project, Working Paper No. 3. New York: The Graduate School and University Center, City University of New York.

Scribner, S., and Schafft, G. (1982). *Literacy in unions: An interview account*. Industrial Literacy Project, Working Paper No. 2. New York: The Graduate School and University Center, City University of New York.

Sharan, S. (1985). Cooperative learning and the multiethnic classroom. *In* R. Slavin, S. Sharan, S. Kagan, R. Hertz-Lazarowitz, C. Webb, and R. Schmuck (Eds.), *Learning to cooperate, cooperating to learn* (pp. 255–262). New York: Plenum Press.

Spradley, J. (1979). *The ethnographic interview*. New York: Holt, Rinehart & Winston.

Tharp, R., and Gallimore, R. (1988). *Rousing minds to life: Teaching, learning, and schooling in social context*. Cambridge: Cambridge University Press.

Tyler, S. (Ed.). (1969). *Cognitive anthropology*. New York: Holt, Rinehart & Winston.

Vygotsky, L. S. (1962). *Thought and language*, E. Hanfmann and G. Vakar (Trans. and Eds.). Cambridge: MIT Press. (Original work published in 1934.)

Vygotsky, L. S. (1978). *Mind in society: The development of higher psychological processes*, M. Cole, V. John-Steiner, S. Scribner, and E. Souberman (Eds.). Cambridge, MA: Harvard University Press.

Vygotsky, L. S. (1981). The genesis of the higher mental function. *In* J. V. Wertsch (Ed.), *The concept of activity in Soviet Psychology* (pp. 144–188). Armonk, NY: Sharpe.

Vygotsky, L. S. (1987). *The collected works of L. S. Vygotsky: Vol. 1. Problems of general psychology*, R. Rieber and A. Carton (Eds.) and N. Minick (Trans.). New York: Plenum Press.

Wagner, D. (1974). The development of short-term and incidental memory: A cross-cultural study. *Child Development*, 45, 389–396.

Watson-Gegeo, K. (1989). *Heavy words and important silences: The social transfer of cognitive skills in Kwara'ae*. Paper presented at the annual meeting of the American Educational Research Association, San Francisco.

Wertsch, J. V. (1979). From social interaction to higher psychological processes: A clarification and application of Vygotsky's theory. *Human Development*, 22, 1–22.

Wertsch, J. V. (1981). The concept of activity in Soviet psychology: An introduction. *In* J. V. Wertsch (Ed.), *The concept of activity in Soviet psychology* (pp. 3–36). Armonk, NY: Sharpe.

Wertsch, J. (1984). The zone of proximal development: Some conceptual issues. *In* B. Rogoff and J. Wertsch (Eds.), *Children's learning in the "zone of proximal development"* (pp. 7–18). San Francisco: Jossey-Bass.

Wertsch, J. V. (Ed.). (1985a). *Culture, communication, and cognition: Vygotskian perspectives*. Cambridge: Cambridge University Press.

Wertsch, J. V. (1985b). Introduction. *In* J. V. Wertsch (Ed.), *Culture, communication, and cognition: Vygotskian perspectives* (pp. 1–18). Cambridge: Cambridge University Press.

Wertsch, J. V. (1985c). *Vygotsky and the social formation of mind.* Cambridge, MA: Harvard University Press.

Wertsch, J. V. (1989). Semiotic mechanisms in joint cognitive activity. *Infancia y Aprendizaje, 47,* 3–36.

Wertsch, J. V. (1991). *Voices of the mind: A sociocultural approach to mediated action.* Cambridge: Harvard University Press.

Wertsch, J. V., and Minick, N. (1990). Negotiating sense in the zone of proximal development. *In* M. Schwebel, C. A. Maher, and N. S. Fagley (Eds.), *Promoting cognitive growth over the life span* (pp. 71–88). Hillsdale, NJ: Lawrence Erlbaum.

Wertsch, J. V., and Rogoff, B. (1984). Editors' notes. *In* B. Rogoff and J. Wertsch (Eds.), *Children's learning in the "zone of proximal development"* (pp. 1–6). San Francisco: Jossey-Bass.

Wertsch, J. V., and Sammarco, J. G. (1985). Social precursors to individual cognitive functioning: The problem of units of analysis. *In* R. A. Hinde, A.-N. Perret-Clermont, and J. Stevenson-Hinde (Eds.), *Social relationships and cognitive development* (pp. 276–293). Oxford: Clarendon Press.

Wertsch, J. V., McNamee, G. D., McLane, J. B., and Budwig, N. A. (1980). The adult–child dyad as a problem solving system. *Child Development, 51,* 1215–1221.

Wertsch, J. V., Minick, N., and Arns, F. (1984). The creation of context in joint problem-solving. *In* B. Rogoff and J. Lave (Eds.), *Everyday cognition: Its development in social context* (pp. 151–171). Cambridge, MA: Harvard University Press.

Wertsch, J. V., Tulviste, P., and Hagstrom, F. (1990). A sociocultural approach to intelligence. Unpublished paper, Frances L. Hiatt School of Psychology, Clark University, Worcester, MA.

Whiting, B. (1976). The problem of the packaged variable. In K. F. Riegel and S. A. Meacham (Eds.), *The developing individual in a changing world* (Vol. 1, pp. 303–309). The Hague: Mouton.

Wood, D. J. (1980). Teaching the young child: Some relationships between social interaction, language, and thought. *In* D. R. Olson (Ed.), *The social foundations of language and thought* (pp. 280–296). New York: Norton.

Wood, D. J., Bruner, J., and Ross, G. (1976). The role of tutoring in problem solving. *Journal of Child Psychology and Psychiatry, 17,* 89–100.

CHAPTER 8

❏ Symbolic Interactionism: Theory and Method

Peter Woods

The Handbook of Qualitative Research in Education

Introduction

One of the main approaches in qualitative research among sociologists today is that of symbolic interactionism, deriving from the Chicago School of the 1920s and 1930s. One of the chief exponents of its ideas and their implications was G. H. Mead (1934). Mead's work was popularized by H. Blumer, who first coined the term "symbolic interactionism" in 1937. Blumer (1969) argued for three central principles: (1) human beings act toward things on the basis of the *meanings* that the things have for them, (2) this attribution of meaning to objects through symbols is a continuous *process*, and (3) meaning attribution is a product of social interaction in human society. The symbols are signs, language, gestures, or anything that conveys meaning, and the meaning is *constructed* in social interaction. This contrasts strongly with those approaches, prevalent at the time, that argued that human behavior was the product of internal psychological drives or that it was determined by structural forces in society. At its heart was a model of person as a constructor, creator, or coper, continually interacting with the world, adjusting means to ends, and sometimes ends to means, both influencing and being influenced by structures. As action builds up among groups of people, so cultures develop; however, like the person, these are processes continually under change and construction and with which the person has a loose, dialectical relationship.

This emphasis on the self, construction, interaction, and voluntarism owes much to the ideas of William James, C. H. Cooley, John Dewey, and W. I. Thomas as well as G. H. Mead. These ideas provided one of the main line of influences, although not the only one, on Robert Park and Ernest Burgess, who, during the 1920s at the University of Chicago, laid the basis of the field research tradition in sociology. The perspective required studying people in their natural environment, not through abstracted forms or in artificial experiments. The city itself was a "social laboratory," which "magnifies, spreads out, and advertises human nature in all its various manifestations. It is this that makes the city interesting, even fascinating. It is this, however, that makes it of all places the one in which to discover the secrets of human nature and society" (Burgess, 1929:47). These "secrets" are things we are usually "blind" to. Park, acknowledging this debt to James, argued that "the thing that gives zest to life or makes life dull is, as James, says, 'a personal secret', which has, in every single case, to be discovered. Otherwise we do not know the world in which we actually live" (Bulmer, 1984:93). This is not something that can be found in libraries or laboratories. Park thus urged his students to "go get the seat of your pants dirty in real research" (Bulmer, 1984:97).

The urban sociological studies, for which the Chicago School became so noted, were the result. They were not, as some have thought, purely empiricist. The hallmark of the Chicago School, according to Bulmer (1984:3) was a "blending of firsthand inquiry with general ideas, the integration of research and theory as part of an organized program." Thomas and Znaniekci's (1927) great work "The Polish Peasant in Europe and America" set the stage for this, to be followed by a series of studies, of which Shaw's (1930) "Jack-Roller", Cavan's (1928) "Suicide", Anderson's (1923) "The Hobo", Cressey's (1932) "The Taxi Dance Hall", and Thrasher's (1927) "The Gang" are some of the best known. They used a variety of methods—informal interviews and observation, documentary materials, personal documents, life histories—and established participant observation as a recognized research method in sociology.

The preeminence of the Chicago School began to wane with the rise of other institutions and the influence of Parsonian sociology during the 1940s and 1950s. Quantitative methods predominated during this period. It was in this context that Blumer mounted his assault and, with others, initiated a second generation of the Chicago School. Everett Hughes, Lloyd Warner, and Anselm Strauss were prominent in this activity. Some key works emerging were by Goffman (1959), Becker et al. (1961), Becker (1963), Davis (1963), Roth (1963), Glaser and Strauss (1965), and Becker, Geer, Riesman, and Weiss (1968). Although not as integrated as the earlier group, they shared a common approach in "getting their hands dirty" and developing theory out of their research. They were also concerned in developing a rigorous methodology, and a steady stream of articles, books and commentaries ensued (e.g., Becker and Geer, 1960; Becker, 1967, 1970; McCall and Simmons, 1969; Glaser and Strauss, 1967; Schatzman and Strauss, 1973). Their greatest achievement was the development and codifying of the technique of participant observation. They are still the main methodological influence on the field today.

Meanwhile, in the United Kingdom, a similar reaction against the prevailing structural functionalism in the sociology of education took place in the 1970s. Influential texts here were M. F. D. Young's (1971) edited collection *Knowledge and Control* and the Open University (1972) course *School and Society*. The influence of the Chicago School was evident from the list of authors in one of the readers of this course—Geer, Blumer, Becker, and Hughes, for example—although there were other influences. Shortly, this so-called "new" sociology of education (indicating the wish of its sponsors for it to be starkly separated from the "old") itself bifurcated into a more deterministic, Marxist-oriented line and a more interactionist one. Following Hughes and Burgess' example, and gathering strength from the new Chicagoans, British interactionists (more or less) used the school as a social laboratory, opening up the "black box" that hitherto had been impervious to the "input–output" studies that had prevailed hitherto. Here was a fascinating new world, where action did not simply take place as a product of external structural and cultural forces but, rather, was constructed within classrooms. How this occurred and with what consequences seemed a crucial question, not only for sociology but also for education. Sociology of education in Britain had only really begun in the 1950s, and while important work was done on background factors and their relationships to achievement, the standard survey approaches gave no assistance with understanding the processes of what actually went on in schools, how it was experienced by teachers and pupils, what different perspectives they brought to bear, how they related together, and how conflict was resolved if that was a consequence. It seemed that the broad sweep approaches took too much for granted; made assumptions too readily about what "teaching" and "learning" constituted; reified and overpsychologized things such as "intelligence," "achievement," "deviance," and "the curriculum"; and tended to regard teachers as a monolithic class of professionals with similar interests, kinds, and degrees of commitment and views on teaching, and pupils as incomplete adults.

They were not necessarily wrong, but they begged a host of questions about who teachers and pupils were and what they were doing to each other in schools and classrooms. The Chicago School was one of the main sources of inspiration for those attracted toward these questions and provided an epistemological and methodological platform for the pursuit of answers. During the 1970s and 1980s, a large number of educational ethnographies in the interactionist tradition were produced (Woods, 1983), accompanied by a number of methodological commentaries (Hammersley, 1983; Burgess, 1982, 1984a,b, 1985a,b; Hammersley and Atkinson, 1983; Woods, 1986; Finch, 1986). Specialist texts explored symbolic interactionism (Rock, 1979; Bulmer, 1984; Hammersley, 1989). While, like all methods, not above criticism and debate, the qualitative method in the interactionist tradition is now firmly established as one of the main modes of inquiry in educational research. In this article, I aim to explore its underlying rationale, its sociological relevance, its methodological apparatus, and its approach to theory.

Principles of Symbolic Interactionism

I will concentrate here on the "main" line of interactionism deriving from Mead and as popularized by Blumer, Becker, Glaser, Strauss, and others.

The Self

At the heart of Mead's thought is the "self." His conceptualization is "a complete reversal of the traditional understanding of the relation between society and the individual" (Luckmann, 1967:19). The self is "the lens through which the social world is refracted. It is the medium which realises the logic of social forms. Fundamentally, however, the self emerges *from* the forms" (Rock, 1979:146). Mead's view is behavioristic, but not in the sense that one starts from observable forms: It is centrally concerned with the inner experience of the individual and how the self arises within the social process (Mead, 1934:7–8). This "social behaviorism" is very different from the behaviorism associated with Watson (1913) or Skinner (1953). Certainly there is some nonsymbolic, unreflective behavior, where individuals react as if by instinct and without thought. Involuntary movements of defense, habitual activity, and training responses are examples of this, although habitual activity can be the product of symbolic activity by earlier generations. However, much activity is symbolic, involving construction and interpretation, both within the self and between the self and others. A teacher slapping a child on impulse for misbehavior, for example, is making a gesture that stimulates a particular response (the cessation of the misbehavior). But if the teacher assumes a stern countenance, moves nearer to the child, or produces a cane from a drawer and places it on the desk, these activities are symbolic. They convey meaning that is interpreted in the other's experience—in this case, "I know from my own past experience and by observing and listening to others that the cane is used to beat pupils who behave in a certain way. As the teacher looked at me as he placed it carefully on the desk, this is probably a warning to me as to the consequences of my present actions." One mind communicates to another. For joint activity to ensue, it is necessary that the same meaning is attached by the participants in the act to the symbol. An important component of this activity is that individuals have a developed ability to respond to their own gestures. Thus, the teacher knows from his or her past experience that the same consequences ensue as those inferred by the pupil; furthermore, each knows that the other assigns the same meaning to the act. This construction of meaning in interaction occurs by means of the ability to take the role of the other, to put oneself in the position of the other, and to interpret from that position. Thus, people imaginatively share each other's responses. This sharing and the mutual imbuing with meaning makes the behavior truly social, as it would not be if it were mere response.

Symbols can be nonverbal, as in the preceding example, but the most important are verbal, as expressed in language. The internalization of symbols and meaning patterns and stimulation of thought through language increases the human being's powers of reflectivity and the ability to see one's self as an object, to make indications toward one's self, and to act as one might toward others.

Defining the Situation

Social interaction, therefore, is a process of construction, not a mere response to factors playing on the person such as personality factors, psychological drives, social norms, or structural or cultural determinants. Human interaction is not a neutral mechanism that operates at the instigation of external forces but, rather, a formative one in its own right. The teacher in the earlier example must consider many things. He or she needs to interpret the behavior of the pupil; the consequences for the pupil, the teacher, and for others; the implications for the achievement of aims; and how this action might be received. Social life is composed of many such transactions: "a continuing matter of fitting developing lines of conduct to one another . . . through the dual process of definition and interpretation (which) operates both to sustain established patterns of joint conduct and to open them up to transformation" (Blumer, 1977:13). Schemes of interpretation become established through use but require continued confirmation by the defining acts of others. For example, a pupil might challenge a teacher's symbolic warning to test the resolve behind the meaning. The teacher must then act to confirm the initial definition and to sustain the continuing framework. But the interaction is open to redefinition. By "testing out" the teacher, the pupils may find new degrees of latitude. Similarly, the teacher may discover pupil interests and values, not to mention power, that have an influence on his or her teaching style. This is how cultures are established, but they are everchanging entities in a continuing process of internalization and externalization (Berger and Luckmann, 1967).

Symbolic interactionism is not simply consensual but can cover all modes of interaction, including confrontation, indifference, and conflict. It can cast an interesting light on the latter by revealing how different meanings may have been assigned. Consider this example, which follows a structure of the act suggested by Shibutani (1961), after Mead:

Symbol: A class comes into my room, and one of the boys calls out to me "Happy Christmas."

Perception: I wonder for a moment whether he is being impertinent, or just friendly. I could cuff him round the ear, or smile and say "Happy Christmas" back. The latter might help establish good rapport, and a relaxed, casual atmosphere. But my knowledge of the child (he doesn't like authority and is always trying to bring teachers down a peg or two); others like him (always "taking the mickey" to undermine the lesson so they need do no work), and the likely effect on others (respect for me diminished, virtue in impertinence, lesson ruined in consequence) lead me to decide that it is cheek.

Manipulation: I cuff him round the ear and say "Don't be impertinent, boy!"

Consummation: He scowls and goes to his desk in silence. I turn my attention to the class.

It may be that I have interpreted the boy's gesture rightly according to my cultural background and wrongly according to his. We might share different cultural expectations. However, the point here is that we each construct our realities in interaction, taking our cues from others. Perhaps the boy's went like this:

Prior perception: I feel happy today, it is near the end of term, nearly Christmas, the atmosphere is become casual, this teacher's not a bad sort, it is customary among my folk to show goodwill towards others and try to make them happy.

Gesture: I say "Happy Christmas" to him. He cuffs me round the ear.

Perception: I feel anger. It brings out in me all I detest in teachers. He's also made me look ridiculous in front of my friends. I resolve on revenge.

Manipulation: As soon as his back is turned, I get busy with the pea-shooter, jew's harp, and stink bombs.

Consummation: Teacher turns, clearly harassed, and shouts and threatens. I feel satisfied.

This illustrates how interaction can be built up through different constructions of reality and conflicting definitions of the situation with the result of conflict. Just as objects can be interpreted differently on different occasions or by different people (a ruler, for example, can be a measuring instrument, a weapon, an indicator, a musical instrument, an aid to reading and writing, and so on), so situations must be interpreted. This lays the basis for how we perceive and interact with others, and it guides the orientation of our conduct. For smooth interaction to occur, it is necessary that all interpret situations in the same way. For example, it is necessary for the pupils, as well as the teacher, to recognize that a "lesson" is taking place for teaching and learning to occur.

Socialization

The basis for the adult self is laid in childhood, notably during play and taking part in games. As the child acquires language, he or she can label and define objects in terms that have shared meaning. Others designate the child by name, facilitating the child's view of self as social object. At the play stage, however, the child relates to others as individuals, not as a group or groups. "Significant others"—parents, teachers, friends, perhaps—have particular influence in the emergence of the child's self, but, as yet, it is a segmented, uncoordinated self.

Coordination, and the ability to adopt the perspectives of a number of others simultaneously, develops during "the game stage." Games have sets of rules, and to take part successfully, the individual must be able to take the role of all the other participants simultaneously. This is different from the segmented and specific orientation to the particular attitudes of individuals.

What this means, in effect, is that individuals can see their own behavior not only from the point of view of significant others but also in terms of generalized norms, values, and beliefs in terms of a team in a game, or a subcultural group, or a society. Mead called this "the generalized other," and it is a crucial element in how he saw the relationship between self and society:

> It is in the form of the generalized other that the social process influences the behavior of the individuals involved in it and carrying it on, that is, that the community exercises control over the conduct of its individual members; for it is in this form that the social process or community enters as a determining factor into the individual's thinking. (Mead, 1934:155)

Some have taken this kind of statement by Mead to imply the determining force of society. But social organization provides a framework inside which people construct their actions. Structural features such as "social class" "set conditions for their action but do not determine their action" (Blumer, 1962:189–190). People do not act toward social class or social systems; they act toward situations. Social organization may shape situations to some extent and also provide "fixed sets of symbols which people use in interpreting their situations" (ibid.). This may be more rigid in primitive societies, but in modern societies, where social interaction is more complex, new situations arise more frequently, requiring more flexibility in schemes of interpretation.

We may take as an example the process of socialization. Some view this as largely a one-way process, by which the individual learns a set of meanings and values shared by members of society and which the individual is required to learn if he or she is to participate in society. Some theories emphasize identification with role models (see E. Becker, 1971); some "social learning," which rests on a system of rewards and punishments (Bandura, 1969); some "cognitive development," which argues that appropriate conduct is inferred from early knowledge that one is male or female. The symbolic interactionist would see the role not as a prescriptive list of behaviors to be selected from, nor as offering a how-to-do-it manual for all occasions, but, rather, as a more abstract model, offering general guidance. Appropriate conduct is worked out by an interpretive and interactive process. Thus, a young girl might like to play rough games, climb trees, and fight. As she grows older and becomes more conscious of her sex role, she will infer that girls do not behave in that way, and this might inhibit her conduct. She will have "taken the role of the other" and seen herself as others would. In the interplay, there is room for maneuver. The girl constructs her response from inferring the appropriate conduct for a female, from role taking, and from personal proclivity.

Thus, in "sex role socialization" theory, boys and girls learn and internalize the appropriate attitudes, beliefs, mental sets, and behaviors of males and females. The very way in which they assign meanings and make interpretations is dictated by their sex. The range of their symbolic universe is delimited by such activity. This became the most prominent explanation of gender differentiation. However, more recently, this view has been strongly attacked. Neither girls nor boys are passive recipients of existing culture but, rather, create their own responses in interaction with it. The point is well illustrated with respect to "passive" or "quiet" girls. On the face of it this may be taken as typical female behavior, in line with cultural prescriptions, but research has shown that, in some cases at least, this is a considered strategy in response to one kind of situation. It is not a release of propensities in line with any *natural* feminine behavior, nor is it a response directed by social conditioning, but an active adaptation to the circumstances they find themselves in. It may be a form of resistance (Anyon, 1981) or it can represent the most expedient means to an end, and it may be variably deployed (Stanley, 1986). Sex role socialization is more appropriately seen as a *factor*, therefore, in gender differentiation, not a determinant. Moreover, socialization is not an unmediated internalization of norms and values but a developed capacity to take the role of others effectively. Through this process, the individual learns an enormous number of meanings and values and, thus, actions through the communication of symbols with others.

As Rose (1962:13) points out, society—the related meanings and values through which individuals interact and which set up some expectations of appropriate behavior—exists before the individual. However, he lists a number of other reasons why this should not be regarded as cultural determinism. For example, some interaction is noncultural, or extracultural, and cultural expectations are for ranges of behavior, not specific behavior, and for role and general situations, not for individuals, who have choice as to how they move among these [although these "choices" may be structurally influenced (see later)]. Qualifications such as these considerably loosen the cultural framework and permit the individual to engage with it actively. This is done through the interplay of the two aspects of the self—the "I" and the "Me."

The "I" and the "Me"

The "I" part of the self is the more spontaneous, impulsive initiator of action. The "Me" is the product of viewing oneself as object, as one would be viewed by another. Thus, there will be a defined "Me" in relation to each of the roles that we perform. The "I" and the "Me" are in constant interaction with each other. Mead described the relationship in these terms: "The 'I' is the response of the organism to the attitudes of the others; the 'Me' is the organized set of attitudes of others which one himself assumes. The attitudes of the others constitute the organized 'Me'; one reacts towards that as an 'I' " (quoted in Rose, 1962, p. 12).

We can never know the "I" as we can the "Me." The "I" is embodied in present action. As soon as the action is complete and we reflect on it, it becomes part of the "Me." Thus, the "I" can only be inferred from observing the "Me." "It is only after we have done the things that we are going to do that we are aware of what we are doing" (Mead, 1934:203). For this reason, we can never know ourselves or others completely. The nature of and reasons for our behavior are only partially known and may be reconstructed in the light of new experiences over time (Mead, 1929).

Furthermore, although conceived of separately, the two parts of the self are involved in the same moment:

> "I" and "Me" are phases of consciousness, parts of a process, not concrete entities, and both present in the instant. At one moment in our conduct, we are alert to external stimuli and we respond to them. Almost immediately, we role-take, visualizing the direction of our conduct and the possible responses to it. In that moment our attention shifts to ourselves. (Hewitt and Hewitt, 1986:130)

The two parts of the self complement each other, both for the individual and for society. The creative "I" is the source of initiative, novelty, and change; the "Me" is the agent of self-regulation and social control. A mutual and beneficial dependence exists, unlike the antagonism Freud perceived between the "id" and the "super-ego." It is from the "I" that novel acts "emerge." There are many opportunities for these creative acts. They add interest to personal lives and are the main ingredient behind social change and adaptation. However, they might not all be beneficial or useful. The "Me" acts "to evaluate the innovations of the 'I' from the perspective of society, encouraging socially useful innovations while discouraging undesirable actions" (Baldwin, 1986:118). The "Me" is part of a social group, holding the values of that group, and those values are used to assess the initiatives of the "I." It is not an automatic check but, rather, a product of reflection whereby the individual chooses a course of action.

People differ in their abilities and willingness to "take the role of the other" and to employ self-control through the "Me." This self-reflection may operate variably depending on the situation. At times, it may result in degradation—"emphasizing the more violent sort of impulsive expression" (Mead, 1934:213), as in the unlicensed actions of a mob or during warfare. At other times, more beneficial consequences may ensue. Similarly, people develop different propensities for using the "I" or the "Me." The conventional form of the "Me" may be reduced in some cases. Mead gives the example of the artist, where "the emphasis upon that which is unconventional, that which is not in the structure of the 'Me' is carried as far, perhaps, as it can be carried" (1934:209–210). Reformers, radicals, and revolutionaries are others pursuing unconventional courses, although in all these cases, as with artists, they are sustained by reference groups with their own norms and values providing the parameters of their own "Me's."

On the other hand, some people may suppress the "I" and be guided almost entirely by the dictates of the "Me." In general, however, a mixture of the two is regarded as efficacious for both self and society. Neither could survive without a measure of routine but the health of both depends on the abilities and freedom of people to "think their own thoughts" and "express themselves" and "be original" (Mead, 1934:213). These thoughts, however, must feed back into the group if they are to be useful. People are never fully socialized in the sense that they know how to respond appropriately to all events and stimuli. However experienced we become, new problems and situations calling for new solutions and adaptation always arise.

Methodological Implications of Symbolic Interactionism

Respecting the Empirical World

The most important premise is that inquiry must be grounded in the empirical world under study. By the "empirical social world" is meant the minute-by-minute, day-to-day social life of individuals as they interact together, as they develop understandings and meanings, as they engage in "joint action" and respond to each other as they adapt to situations, and as they encounter and move to resolve problems that arise through their circumstances. This might be the study, among others, of (1) what teachers and pupils actually *do* in school (making no assumptions about "teaching" and "learning"); (2) how they themselves experience and perceive it; (3) how they undergo certain processes such as the social construction of matters of school experience (e.g., classroom order and classroom competence, "intelligence," "underachievement," "childhood," "deviance," "stress," "the curriculum"); (4) aspects of the pupil or teacher career, such as how they pass through certain stages, how they "become" pupils and teachers, or how they adapt to situations; (5) how decisions are made or policy formulated; (6) the construction of social situations, such as those teachers and pupils devise in classrooms and staffrooms; (7) their resolution of problems through social strategies; (8) school organization and its influence on attitudes and behavior; (9) social relations and the development of cultures and subcultures; and (10) pupil and teacher perspectives on matters such as their own interrelationships, the curriculum, and classroom activity. These are all lived experiences in real situations. This kind of activity is at the heart of the problems of social science at whatever level of abstraction.

Blumer (1976:13) argues that "every part of the act of scientific enquiry . . . is subject to the test of the empirical world and has to be validated through such a test." Research methods are the means to discover that reality; they do not themselves contain it. They should respect, therefore, the nature of that reality—hence the emphasis on "naturalism" (Matza, 1969), on "unobtrusive methods" (Webb, Campbell, Schwartz, and Sechrest, 1966), and on "grounded theory" (Glaser and Strauss, 1967). The latter is a reminder that the entire research process, not just data collection, should keep faith with the empirical world under study. The research design, the problems formulated for study, the specification of categories, the relationships among the data, explanatory concepts, and interpretative frameworks all must be tested for closeness of fit. They all received special emphasis from Blumer, writing at a time when, in some approaches, a considerable disjuncture often existed between some of these processes and the empirical world. Problems selected for study in these approaches might have been prominent in the mind of the researcher but not necessarily of major importance in the situations studied. Abstract concepts were devised with little attempt to trace through their linkage with the reality to which they were purported to relate. Theories were formulated to "explain" the data, being imposed on it *post hoc*, with the linkages not fully explored (see A. Hargreaves, 1980).

Respecting the empirical world means making as few assumptions in advance of the study as possible. Seeley (1966) made the distinction between the "making" and "taking" of research problems. By and large, sociologists have often "taken" educators' problems, without questioning their underlying assumptions. As Young (1971) notes, this may situate the research from the beginning in a system perspective—one that supports, tacitly or otherwise, the status quo. One example is

Dale and Griffith's (1966) study of pupil performance, which asked why some pupils' achievement deteriorated, and they took as their criterion of deterioration pupils' demotion to lower streams (tracks). School policy and processes and teacher practices were not considered, nor were pupil perspectives. Not surprisingly perhaps, the researchers found a strong association between deterioration and parental background. The possibility that teachers and pupils and subsequent interaction had been influenced as a *consequence* of streaming practices was not considered. Later studies researched the process holistically and from the inside without preordaining the issue and were able to chart these consequences (D. H. Hargreaves, 1967; Lacey, 1970; Ball, 1981; Abraham, 1989).

Mac an Ghaill (1989) gives an example from research on "race."[1] The predominant "race-relations" viewpoint in the 1970s and 1980s saw black pupils' educational achievement in terms of "cultural deficit." That is to say that black pupils' adaptation to school was hindered by features in their own culture. While he started with this viewpoint, however, Mac an Ghaill came to reformulate the research problem. As he accumulated material from his observations of and interviews with teachers and pupils, he went "beyond the white norm." The problem, he concluded, was racism, not cultural deficit (see also Mac an Ghaill, 1988). Sociologists, in short, must "make" their own problems, "among which may be to treat educators' problems as phenomena to be explained" (Young, 1971:2). The basis for "making" such problems will be experience in the empirical world. It was his growing, deep acquaintance with this experience that persuaded Mac an Ghaill that he had the wrong research design. Similarly, it was their close monitoring of streaming procedures, and everyone's experiences with them, that enabled D. H. Hargreaves (1967) and others to document the effects of streaming.

Layers of Reality

Social life is not only complex in its range and variability—It is also deep, in that it operates at different levels. Berger (1966:34) talks of social reality having "many layers of meaning. The discovery of each new layer changes the perception of the whole." Blumer (1976:15) talks of "lifting veils." I liken it to climbing mountains. Frequently, when you achieve one apparent peak, another appears beyond, and so on—but you do know when you do eventually reach the top. A school typically presents a "public face" to outsiders. A researcher who stays for 1 or 2 weeks might discover more than a casual visitor about how the school really works, because public facades cannot be maintained for long. But a longer stay is needed and much work is necessary to develop the knowledge, skills, and trust that will permit entry into those innermost arenas and confidences required for firsthand understanding of the situation.

Methodologically, this means, first, maintaining a certain openness of mind, not prejudging the matter under investigation, nor necessarily settling for first or even second appearances. As in all research, curiosity should be fostered, in this case to see beyond, to press on to the next "peak" until the summit is reached and the whole mountain can be viewed in perspective. What is presented is carefully noted, but the status to be attached to it is temporarily suspended. However, guesses might be made, tested along the way and abandoned, and changed or revised in the light of later discoveries. Second, this kind of exploration cannot be undertaken in a day or a week. Nor can it take place outside the actual situation of the object of study or by proxy. Depending on the area under investigation, it can take months or years of working "in the field." A typical formula for research students is "1 year fieldwork, 2 years writing-up," although many variations exist. Third, this mode of study has implications for the relationships the researcher fosters with subjects in the research. People are unlikely to allow total strangers into their private and confidential gatherings or to tell them their innermost thoughts and secrets without certain guarantees. They must be backed by a certain trust in the researcher and reflected in the "rapport" traditionally developed between researcher and subjects. The alternative is to engage in covert activities that are ethically suspect (Bulmer, 1982). The ethical matter is more fully discussed later.

Taking the Role of the Other

If we are to understand social life, what motivates people, what their interests are, what links them to and distinguishes them from others, what their cherished values and beliefs are, why they act as they do, and how they perceive themselves and others, we need to put ourselves in their position and look out at the world with them. Their reality may not be our reality, or what we think theirs is. We need to know how they define situations, because, in Thomas' (1928:572) famous phrase, "If men [sic] define situations as real, they are real in their consequences." This is a reprise of the interactionist viewpoint that people act on the basis of meanings that objects have for them. They do not respond to an objective reality or to how others perceive it but, rather, to how they interpret it.

Even so, researchers often do leave the other's constructions of reality out of account. In Bennett, Desforges, Cockburn, and Wilkinson's

(1984) noted work on pupil learning, for example, they investigated the "match" between teacher tasks and pupils' abilities. They found a high degree of mismatches, stemming, they argued, from faulty teacher diagnosis and teachers' overemphasis on procedures. They based these conclusions on their own observations and judgments. They did not consult the teachers about their theories of teaching and learning or how the tasks fitted within their general pedagogical context, nor did they observe the teachers over time, situating the tasks within a more general framework. These omissions had profound implications for the findings. The "faulty diagnosis," for example, may have been an accurate one if the teacher's intention had been to provide an "easy" task to boost confidence in a particular child. Similarly, there may have been good reason for the "emphasis on procedures"—part of a broader strategy, perhaps. Equally, this may not be the case, and Bennett *et al.* (1984) may have been right. However, we cannot judge on the evidence presented. The omission of teacher understandings severely delimited the research. Therefore, what was needed, in addition to researcher observation, was a means of discovering how the teachers observed viewed their own behavior. This might have been achieved by "taking the role of the other."

Taking the role of the other would allow researchers to obtain "inside" knowledge of the social life under study. If they are to understand peoples' outlooks and experiences, researchers must be close to groups, live with them, look out at the world from their viewpoints, see them in various situations and in various moods, appreciate the inconsistencies, ambiguities, and contradictions in their behavior, explore the nature and extent of their interests, and understand their relationships among themselves and with other groups—in short, if possible, to adopt their roles. To these ends, researchers have joined such groups as delinquent gangs (Patrick, 1973; Parker, 1974), the teaching staff of a school (D. H. Hargreaves, 1967), a group of hippies (Yablonsky, 1968), bikers (Willis, 1978), or pupils (Llewellyn, 1980).

We need to know, therefore, the subject's viewpoint, whether it be a disruptive child, a truant, a schizophrenic pupil, an anarchic pupil, or, indeed, a "conformist" pupil. The latter two cases are particularly instructive. Seemingly anarchic behavior, perpetuated by "vandals," is often described as "meaningless" behavior. Pupil behavior that does not conform to the adult norm is frequently described as "childish" and immature." But all this behavior is redolent with meaning. For example, vandalism can be "acquisitive" (to acquire money or property), "tactical" (a conscious tactic to advance some other end, such as drawing attention to a grievance), vindictive (to gain revenge), or malicious (an expression of rage or frustration) (see Cohen, 1968). As for "conformity," Hammersley and Turner (1980) have shown how the use of such a term raises a host of questions (Conformity to what? By whom? In what forms, and what situations?) In short, the bipolar use of deviant–conformist does no justice to the vast array of pupil reactions.

The question might be asked, how old do pupils have to be before one can start prioritizing their subjectivities? Is there not an age below which their interpretive competence is not sufficiently developed for us to be able to "take their roles"? To take this position is to be drawn into outmoded views of children's development that see such competence as limited until children have passed through certain essential stages. Developmental psychologists have identified considerable intellectual competence among young children (Tizard and Hughes, 1984; Richards and Light, 1986). Their views match those of interpretive sociologists such as Mackay (1973), who felt such approaches made "children available as beings who interpret the world as adults do . . . and that they . . . transform a theory of deficiency into a theory of competency" (p. 31). Nor is this an age of "innocence," as some would have us believe—a protected and separate world, wherein children engage only in "childish" things. Rather, children can handle difficult concepts and consider serious social issues. Researchers working in the field of "race," for example, have discovered that young children are perfectly capable of discussing the principles involved and of engaging in abstract thought in the area (Carrington and Short, 1989).

The methodological prescription for young children then is the same as for the search for all such understandings. The researcher must take the role of the other. But the younger the children, the further they are removed from adult interpretive practices. Silvers (1977) found

> . . . that only on those occasions in which we reflected back upon the taken-for-granted features of not simply sociological conceptualizations, but adult interpretations behind our initial sense-making, did we achieve an understanding. On those occasions we "lost" a particular adult way of seeing since its practice was called into focus against others; but that loss, in turn, permitted us to acquire an "innocence" to entertain alternatives. We also found that the acquiring of alternatives requires the experience of how things can be understood in the manner of children, which necessitates engaging in activities as the children do. (p. 137)

In summary, to understand social interaction, it is necessary to witness it as close as possible and in depth in all its manifestations and all the situations in which the form under examination occurs. Because social interaction is constructed by the people engaged in it, one should try to see it from their point of view and appreciate how they interpret the indications given to them by others and the meanings they assign to them and how they construct their own action. In addition, because this is a process, it must be sampled over time.

Appreciating the Culture

Groups in interaction develop a large number of symbols imbued with interrelated meaning that collectively constitute a culture or subculture. Oftentimes, symbols that seem of the merest significance to outsiders are the ones most redolent with meaning for participants. Such symbols may possess some alternative cultural significance for an observer, enabling reasonable, but false, interpretation. The observer, therefore, must "wash clean" of cultural frameworks and understandings that might be imposed on the data from outside. The task, then, is to capture the meanings that permeate the culture as understood by the participants. The consequences of not doing so have been occasionally illustrated in teacher–pupil studies. Dumont and Wax (1977), for example, showed how a teacher with many years of experience took her pupils' silence and docility as indicating respectful conformity, when, in fact, it had the opposite meaning within the culture of the tribal Cherokee community to which the pupils belonged. What she was doing was interpreting pupil behavior solely through her own perspective and not theirs.

A group culture often has a certain ambience or ethos, which the researcher needs to grasp. The best commendation one can receive perhaps about the accuracy of one's attempts to understand a group's ethos is from the group members. They, after all, are the ones who generate the meanings involved. Mac an Ghaill (1988), for example, showed what he had written to the black pupils he had been studying. One of them said, "It's really good. I've read through most of it. I think that you have really captured what it's like for black kids at school" (p. 142). This is not to say that "respondent validation" (i.e., insiders confirming the correctness of analyses) is always appropriate. We need to distinguish between everyday conceptions of reality and the sociological theory through which it may be interpreted (Denzin, 1978). I will discuss later how some interactionists strive to "generate" this theory from the data, rather than impose it on them. However, even if this is done successfully, it may bring a result not recognized and/or not liked by insiders. As Denzin (1978) puts it,

> Sociological explanations ultimately given for a set of behaviours are not likely to be completely understood by those studied; even if they

prove understandable, subjects may not agree with or accept them, perhaps because they have been placed in a category they do not like or because elements of their behaviour they prefer hidden have been made public. An irreducible conflict will always exist between the sociological perspective and the perspective of everyday life. (p. 9)

Taking the role of the other, therefore, does not mean "going native" (Paul, 1953). The researcher must try to maintain a delicate balance between achieving as complete an understanding of insiders' perspectives as possible and sociological distance, thus permitting rigorous analysis of them. However, while such work typically proceeds at two levels of construction—(1) fieldwork and gathering data and (2) analysis and attempting some conceptualization, explanation, or theory—the correspondence between them should be close. Thus, while the method is appreciative [this "empathetic fidelity" standing at "the root of symbolic interaction's finest achievements" (D. H. Hargreaves, 1978a:19)], the approach retains the sociologist's typical critical edge (Dingwall, 1980; Jordan and Lacey, 1989).

Learning the Symbols

One of the first requirements of symbolic interactionist research is to understand the symbolic meanings that emerge in interactions and are attributed in situations over time. Methodologically, this means learning the language of the participants, with all its nuances and perhaps special vocabulary. Other means of communication— gestures, looks, actions, appearance, and the whole area of "body language," which is intended to convey meaning to others—are also important. These symbolic expressions must be linked to observed behavior and the situations in which they occur, because they can vary among them and over time. Ideally one needs to show how meanings emerge in interaction. Thus, pupils might complain in interviews or on a questionnaire of being "picked on" or "shown up" by teachers. However, it is difficult (1) to understand fully what these actually mean and (2) to know how to interpret them without seeing them occur.

Scenes must be closely monitored if we are to identify their inner mysteries. Understandings between pupils and teacher can become extremely recondite, triggered by the briefest of signals among them, which are inaccessible to outsiders. For example, Delamont and Galton (1986) refer to a "Horace" joke. A child spelled "horse" "horace," and this was picked up by another child who called out "Look! There's a horace outside the window eating the grass." Thereafter misspellers were referred to as "Horace" or described as "doing a horace." This may seem unremarkable—simply an aside joke—but basically it is a reminder both of group identity and of underlying rules, very important ones concerning correct spelling, which are both dramatized and made more acceptable by being displaced in humor and by being deeply embedded within the classroom culture. Thus, the group collectively "owns" the mystery. It is something they have generated and that belongs to them and them alone as a group. The more impenetrable it is to outsiders, the more successful it is in these respects.

The interrelation between behavior and language and its embeddedness within the social structure of the classroom is well illustrated by Werthman (1963), who describes how "looking cool" emerges from interaction wherein teachers transgress certain unwritten but tacitly agreed upon rules. The heavy but ingenious symbolism of the behavior is expressed here:

> Of all the techniques used by gang members to communicate rejection of authority, by far the most subtle and most annoying to teachers is demeanour. Both White and Negro gang members have developed a uniform and highly stylized complex of body movements that communicate a casual and disdainful aloofness to anyone making normative claims on their behaviour. The complex is referred to by a gang member as "looking cool", and it is part of a repertoire of stances that include "looking bad" and "looking tore down". The essential ingredients of "looking cool" are a walking pace that is a little too slow for the occasion, a straight back, shoulders slightly stooped, hands in pockets, and eyes that carefully avert any party to the interaction. There are also clothing aides which enhance the effect such as boot and shoe taps and a hat if the scene takes place indoors. (p. 221)

The beauty of this behavior lies in its superb efficacy. Its message is clear, unmistakeable, and hurtful but gives little chance for counterattack. Werthman's point-of-entry was the boy's references to "looking cool," which the researcher then "unpacked" by observations. Subjects' own references cue one into important aspects of their culture, whether it is "dossing or swotting" (Turner, 1983), "blagging or wagging" (Willis, 1977), "bunking off" (Furlong, 1977), or "having mates" (Mealyea, 1989). Distinctive argot is not the only clue however. Subjects may use the same terms as the researcher but intend very different meanings. Cues indicating a term of special significance might be frequency of use, emphasis, and generality. Thus, pupils' references to "work" have been shown to have varying meaning among different groups (Woods, 1990b). Furthermore, what various pupils understand by "work" may be considerably different from the researcher's understanding. The words themselves are not enough, even though they may be the same as those of the researcher. They must be interpreted. The researcher aims for "shared meanings," when one feels part of the culture and can interpret words and gestures as the members of that culture do" (Wax, 1971:11). If this is not done, spurious explanations may be advanced. Furlong (1977) points out that research shows that

> . . . teachers usually "explain" pupil behaviour in purely educationist terms. Thus rather than refer to the pupils' reality, teachers have a tendency to draw on what they consider to be specialist knowledge to understand why children act as they do. For example, two common explanations of delinquency are, "She comes from a very deprived neighbourhood" and "She never had a father." Teachers using such explanations see themselves to be drawing on specialised "sociological" and "psychoanalytic" knowledge respectively. Whatever the apparent bases of these "specialist" explanations (and teachers have an infinite variety to choose from to fit every purpose) they have one factor in common—this is their uniform neglect of the pupils' perspective. (p. 163)

The same principle, of course, applies to pupils. Teachers may struggle at times to understand pupils. Pupils also may hear a teacher's words but apply a different meaning to them than the teacher intends.

Similarly, we need to know what meaning is attributed to actions by participants and beware of substituting our own. Wilson (1977) gives the example of "student hits other student" in a study on "interstudent aggression in the classroom." If we were using preconstructed categories, all observed instances of the action would have to be included (although there could be some difficulty over what constituted "hitting"). The interactionist, however, would want to know how the action was understood by those involved:

> How do the various participants (the hitter, person being hit, onlookers, teacher) perceive the event?
> Do they even see it as aggression?
> Do the hitter and person being hit concur on the meaning? (p. 252)

Wilson goes on to point out that hitting may not even be an act of aggression. It could, in fact, be the reverse—an act of affection or part of subcultural norms that indicate "playful demonstration of strength." It could also be a means of annoying the teacher or causing classroom disruption. Even if it is aggression, there are many subtleties involved. For example,

> The event could be an initiatory first act, or it could be a retribution for previous acts of aggression not necessarily linked immediately in space, time, or kind. The event could be part of a personal relationship between the two students involved, or it could be part of a larger interpersonal network of relations—for example, intergroup hostility. (*ibid*)

There are many other possible meanings for such an act, not all of them readily explainable by the participants. Although it may be impossible to comprehend them all, the researcher aims to uncover as many as possible through long-term observation and close discussion with the actors.

Situating the Interaction

To understand the interaction under study, one must also understand the context within which it occurs. This is because (1) the situation can affect perspectives and behavior, and (2) perspectives can affect situations. One of the best examples of the situation affecting perspectives is the transformation that comes over teachers when they enter the classroom. Lacey (1976:60) noted in his research that many of the teachers in the school of his research were "sincere in their desire to help and encourage their pupils to learn." However, on occasion, these "reasonable, kindly men" turned into "bellowing, spiteful adversaries. They left the staffroom in good order; it was in the classroom that things went wrong." Keddie (1971) also noted this phenomenon of teacher change and advanced an explanation based on the difference between two contexts. In the "educationist" context, which prevailed outside the classroom, teachers employed theoretically led definitions. For example, streaming (tracking) by ability was seen by teachers as an institutional reinforcement of class-determined inequalities. However, in the "teacher" context of the classroom,

> . . . what a teacher knows about pupils derives from . . . streaming, which in turn derives from the dominant organizing category of what counts as ability. The "normal" characteristics . . . of a pupil are those which are imputed to his band or stream as a whole . . . . This knowledge of what pupils are like is often at odds with the image of pupils the same teachers may hold as educationists since it derives from streaming, whose validity the educationist denies. (Keddie, 1971:139)

Thus, teachers are constrained by the circumstances of their work—large classes, examination pressures, mandated curriculum—which might bring about a profound transformation of their views, attitudes, and behavior (see also Gracey, 1972). Clearly the research methods need to be sampled across as many situations as possible if perspectives are to be fully understood.

Alternatively, perspectives can help determine situations. Thus, Denscombe (1980) shows how teachers, faced with an unpopular new policy of "open" classrooms, subtly "closed" them again. Pupils' understanding of the school situation can be vastly different from teachers (Corrigan, 1979; Willis, 1977). For example, they may see it as not a "place of learning" but an "arena for socializing," for which learning may be counterproductive. Several studies have shown how pupils transform situations to be more in line with their own interests. Turner (1983) describes how a pupil who conformed in some lessons was disruptive in others. This was because the school did not always meet his own ideal of wanting to do well by providing good teachers. Bad teachers did not give "proper lessons," therefore, but such lessons were functional in providing him with an opportunity to respond to peer group pressure and "mess about a bit." A similar example arose in our pupil transfer research (Measor and Woods, 1984). The school was attempting to dissolve some gender boundaries by having a common curriculum. But pupils noticeably "regendered" them. Boys used cakes as weapons and a sewing machine as a train. Girls protested about nasty smells and unisex goggles in physical science. In other words, these lessons were very useful to boys and girls in developing their gender identities. They also became very skilled in the practice of what we called "knife-edging," that is, making the most of their options by delicately balancing among a number of alternatives, some of which were contradictory (like the example from Turner, earlier—that is, "doing well" and "mucking around"). Students could define situations at will, switching between them with polished ease (see also Birksted, 1976; Stanley, 1989). Thus pupils "juggle their interests" (Pollard, 1980).

Much teacher–pupil conflict appears to be produced by opposing definitions of the situation. The "blazer-ripping incident" at a school of my research (Woods, 1979) is an illustration here. Here, the school blazer was a prime symbol of school authority and pupil oppression. The rules of school uniform were enforced with rigor in the interests of maintaining order—another illustration of the symbolic value of appearance. On the last day of term, it was traditional for a certain amount of "blazer-ripping" to occur—symbolic of pupils gaining their freedom. However, one year a boy's blazer was ripped to shreds early in the last week of term. This precipitated a major crisis. The teachers launched a major offensive to apprehend and punish the culprits. The boys simply could not understand what all the fuss was about. "They'd been writing all over blazers, writing their names on them, it's a traditional activity at the end of your school days" (Woods, 1979:119).

The symbols here are clear: the school uniform, the "ideal pupil" appearance and behavior. Unsurprisingly, at the end of compulsory schooling, the desecration of these symbols is a prominent part of the celebrations, part of the rites of passage that mark transition into the world of work. Such desecration is recognized, too, by teachers as legitimate activity—but only at the proper point of the passage, that is, the end of the week. The beginning of the week was still "school," requiring business as usual, governed by school rules. Hence, competing teacher and pupil definitions of the situation were the cause of misunderstanding, which precipitated conflict.

Clearly, the methods employed must be sensitive to both interpretations. Research methods must pick up the interaction between perspectives and situation to see how they bear on each other. Researchers must sample across time also, because the same props may mean different things on different occasions. If the research took the teachers' perspective, the pupils would be judged "deviant." If it took the pupils' perspective, the teachers would appear unreasonable. Neither deviance nor lack of reason was at the heart of the problem here.

Interaction as Process

In their interaction, people are continually interpreting the indications of others and constructing their behavior accordingly. It is not something that is done once according to some set pattern. There may be some general guidelines, but this does not alter the fact that social interaction is a moving process, with people defining, assigning meanings, aligning, and re-aligning their actions, seeing how they can best satisfy their interests, comparing and contrasting them with others, adjusting them if necessary, and devising strategies. Interaction and interpretation do not remain static, governed by determining features like group norms. An overemphasis on such norms was indeed a criticism of some of the early work on pupil subcultures. Furlong (1976), for example, criticized the "social psychological" approach employed by D. H. Hargreaves (1967) and Lacey (1970), which portrayed the emergence of pupil subcultures and the development of group norms in secondary schools in response to streaming practices. Using the concept of the "informal group" and assuming that "friends" will interact more with each other than with "nonfriends," they used sociometric questionnaires to find who was in which group. They could then identify the norms and values associated with each, which collectively formed distinctive and consistent "cultures." Social pressure and the desire for status induced conformity to these norms. Furlong (1976) makes three criticisms of this approach, as follows. (1) Interaction does not just "happen" in informal groups but is "constructed" by individuals—and is extremely variable over the course of a lesson, or day, depending on many circumstances. (2) There is no "consistent" culture for all circumstances. As far as "delinquent pupils" are concerned, "classroom situations change in the meaning they have for pupils, and, as they change, so will the pupils' assessments of how to behave" (p. 161). (3) Social behavior is portrayed as a controlled response to an external reality—a culture, rather than constructed interaction, which allows for some choice. While interactionists would accept these points, Furlong does take his criticism too far, almost to deny the existence of pupil cultures. They are still there, but pupils have an active engagement with them. L. Davies (1984:57) puts this well in her study of a group of "problem" girls in a secondary school when she says "sub-cultures are not a kind of superglue where pupils must instantly 'adhere' to the rules of the group, but at most a cavity foam filling with plenty of air space to manoeuvre."

Research methods can also strongly influence the outcome. This is well illustrated by studies of pupils' interethnic association. The great majority of work in this area, using predominantly sociometric techniques, had previously found pupils preferring their own ethnic group and not forming many interethnic friendships (e.g., Davey and Mullin, 1982). However, Denscombe, Szule, Patrick, and Wood (1986) state that this finding was contrary to many teachers' observations in the schools of their research. They studied two multiethnic classes, using a range of methods including extended fieldwork observation of free association in the classrooms and in the playground. They indeed found a high degree of racial integration, which supported the teachers' own observations. While this, of course, may be a product of those particular schools, it is also quite likely that the quantitative techniques of the earlier studies failed to capture the complexity of the situation, in which there could have been many forms of interaction, both conflictual and consensual, both between and within ethnic groups, varying among situations and over time and in nature and degree of "friendship." In the quest for "statistically significant" results over a larger sample, a great deal of this significant interaction is missed. The method compresses the process of social interaction into a particular, limited, "snap-shot" form (Blumer 1976:16). Furthermore, although the earlier work was about friendship, what this actually meant to the participants was not explored (for a study of how pupils construe and construct friendship, see B. Davies, 1982).

The research methods, therefore, need to grasp a sense of social flux. They may reveal that some forms of behavior are fairly stable, others variable, and others emergent and developmental. Some forms of interaction proceed in stages; the methods need to encompass each stage and its place in the whole. Consider, for example, the process of "labeling" deviants (Becker, 1963). Labeling may begin with some comparatively insignificant deviation from one's customary, law-abiding role, which in itself is easily normalized. This is primary deviance (Lemert, 1967). Secondary deviance arises out of the social reaction to the former. As D. H. Hargreaves, Hester, and Mellor (1975) put it:

> The labelling creates, under certain conditions, problems for the person who committed the deviant act which can be resolved by the commission of yet further deviant acts and by a self-designation as a deviant person. The paradox is that the social reaction which was intended to control, punish or eliminate the deviant act has come to shape, stabilize and exacerbate the deviance. (p. 6)

Consider the stages of the labeling process in this hypothetical example:

1. A girl in a class of schoolchildren likes socializing with her peers during lessons and often talks to her neighbors.
2. She is perceived by the teacher as a chatterbox, a bit of a nuisance, a low achiever, and, on occasion, a little "sly" in her perpetration of misdeeds.
3. She is disciplined, perhaps through sarcasm. The sarcasm stings and promotes feelings of revenge and antagonism, which encourage her to increase her deviant behavior.
4. Meanwhile, the teacher discusses the girl with colleagues, some of whom may have noted similar tendencies, and they collectively apply the label of

"nonconformist" to the girl, so that she is treated
similarly by all her teachers.
5. The girl responds with more persistent deviant
behavior, which becomes habitual. Eventually, the
role becomes internalized and the girl acts out her
teachers' expectations; this role may be reinforced by
her own peers' reactions to her. She has become a
"real" deviant.

The initial reaction by the teachers has been crucial in this development. The "primary" deviance, if treated in a different way, might
have remained at a low level, marginal to the girl's otherwise completely acceptable behavior (see D. H. Hargreaves, 1976). Clearly, it is
necessary for the research methods to encompass the whole of this
process and to delineate each part of it and their interconnections. If
only one part is sampled, the wrong conclusions may be drawn.

Researching the Self

So far we have considered the methodological imperatives of interaction among people. But the self itself is a social structure capable of
interaction, as the "I" and the "Me" make indications to each other. If
we are to understand the "I," we must explore people's innermost
feelings, their impulses and passions, their hunches and risk-taking,
the things they would like to do but cannot, what prompts them to act
in certain ways, and what gives them pleasure and what causes pain.
Some of this clearly addresses the affective and subconscious rather
than the cognitive and conscious domains. We have few studies in
these areas because of methodological difficulty rather than theoretical
imperative. Nias (1989) is one of the few to tackle the area. In a book on
primary teachers she argues that

> . . . no account of primary teachers' experience is complete if it does
> not make room for potentially dangerous emotions such as love, rage
> and jealousy, on the one hand, and intermittent narcissism and
> outbreaks of possessive dependence on the other. Although much of
> this book focuses upon teachers' socially-regulated "selves", their own
> descriptions of their feelings about pupils, and their relationships with
> them and with their colleagues, reminds us that the regressive,
> passionate and unruly aspects of human nature are always present in
> the classroom and may sometimes escape from rational control. (p. 203)

Feelings not only condition the self; they also help regulate its passage. We came across an example of this in our work on pupil transfer between primary and secondary schools (Measor and Woods, 1984). We encountered a number of pupil myths concerning the transition (e.g., "You get your head put down the loo on your birthday"). After studying these we concluded that they were a key factor in helping to prepare pupils, emotionally as well as socially, for quite a profound change to a bigger, tougher, more impersonal and altogether more demanding situation. Our method for studying them involved the following:

1. understanding the different levels at which myths operate,
2. knowledge of the formal properties of myths and of status passages,
3. appreciation of the myths' appeal to the subjective and emotional aspects of such a transition,
4. relating them to the general cultural context of pupils' experience and the general symbolic ambience of that context,
5. seeing them as a whole, as a collective commentary, and
6. relating them to pupil perspectives and frameworks of meaning.

Such an approach, we felt, grounds these myths within the social world of the pupils and is able to take account of the important unconscious element, linking interactionist analysis to both structuralist and functionalist approaches and to a Freudian analysis of the unconscious (Measor and Woods, 1983:74; see also Hunt, 1989). Such theoretical combination might be sought with respect to explaining other issues of pressing concern. For example, "teacher stress" is regarded as a psychological condition, but it is very much about the difficulty of sustaining the self in certain circumstances. "Burnout," I would argue, is a consequence of a breakdown of the self caused by the irreparable impaction of the "I" against the "Me" (Woods, 1990a).

The "I" also indulges in hunches, impulsions, ideas, guesses, and risk-taking, much of it consigned to the sub- or unconscious and instantly monitored and conditioned in the immediacy of the moment. It produces what Schön (1983) has described as "knowledge-in-action." It also involves innovation, inventiveness, and creativity, not just in planning major exercises, but also in minute-to-minute activity, demanding a number of varied decisions that characterize the teacher's work. Some of these may be based on routine and a well-formulated

"Me." Others bring the "I" into play. Because we cannot put ourselves in another's skin and "know" what he or she "knows" (Laing, 1967; Schutz, 1967), we would need to be actively involved ourselves to understand them fully. Otherwise, a very close monitoring of these processes is required, working beside a teacher as she deliberates, considers, weighs up the pros and cons, seizes upon a decision, makes a gesture, acts on impulse, or does something unexpected.

A focus on the self also demands a consideration of the person's interests and biography. Interests are an expression of the self, not a requirement of the role. Role requirement may vary with personal interests, although not necessarily. Thus, while we might assume a teacher's primary interests to be giving instruction and keeping order, Pollard (1985) has shown these to be secondary interests. The primary ones are, in fact, maximizing enjoyment (the affective element again), controlling the workload, maintaining one's health and avoiding stress, retaining autonomy, and maintaining one's self-image. In some circumstances, these primary interests may dictate behaviors other than instructing and controlling, such as that of "coping," which may involve a range of strategies designed to manage severe pressures and constraints (A. Hargreaves, 1978).

The fact that the self is a process with a past and a future as well as an ongoing present requires some attention to the formulation of the self. Frequently what one sees is only a small portion, with hidden layers of meaning and reality both laterally across the here and now and longitudinally back in time. A full understanding of the present "self" requires knowledge of its construction over time, of the formative years of primary socialization, of the influence of "significant others," of decision points and "critical incidents" (Strauss, 1959), of the search for means to ends and the reformulating of ends, of the identification of reference groups, and of the laying down of "side bets" (Becker, 1977a). Consequently, pupils' and teachers' lives and careers have become a popular subject for study in interactionist research (Ball and Goodson, 1985; Sikes, Measor, and Woods, 1985) and "biography" and "life history" popular methods.

Symbolic Interaction and Society

Symbolic interactionism typically deals with small-scale, everyday life, seeking to understand processes, relationships, group life, motivations, adaptations, and so on. In so doing, and because it places such emphasis on the importance of the empirical world, it has attracted criticisms of being "idealist," "situationist," and "empiricist" (Whitty,

1974; Sharp and Green, 1975). Critics claim that it is unable to theorize the larger system and to see how the "everyday" is affected by it; however, although this might be a legitimate criticism of some studies, it is not an essential feature of the approach.

Symbolic interaction does have a view on wider concerns—on social structures and system. In some approaches (for example, structural–functionalism or economic Marxism), the imperatives of the system are acted out directly in people's behavior. But people do not merely respond to imperatives in this manner; they construct a response, which in some respects might vary from what the wider system might lead us to expect. Thus, the broad claims of correspondence theory—that schools simply correspond to the structures and attitudes of the wider society (see e.g., Bowles and Gintis, 1976)—have been shown by a number of interactionist studies to be invalid. Schools do not reproduce docile workers for the labor force. There are too many rebels among them (see e.g., Willis, 1977). Thus, interactionism can be said to have a "corrective" function inasmuch as it can submit some of the claims of such theories to empirical test. In the process, the theory becomes modified (in this case, to one that recognizes the "partial and relative autonomy" of the school), lays emphasis on "cultural production," and begins to formulate theories of "resistance" (Willis, 1977; Aggleton, 1987). Interactionist studies can continue to monitor these for accuracy of representation—for example, with respect to the types of behavior defined as "resistance" (A. Hargreaves, 1984b). The point can be applied more generally. A detailed interactionist study can be used for comparative purposes in any area—for example, the study of black students may test some more traditional studies of the schooling of white youth (Mac an Ghaill, 1989:186).

This is one way, then, in which the approach bears on wider concerns, as a commentary on, or test of, broader theories about society and systems. However, interactionism can also approach society and social structure from below. By monitoring the attribution of meanings as well as how these sustain situations and processes, and how people define and redefine each other's and their own perspectives, patterns may be identified that exhibit both personal creativity and external constraint. This has been conceptualized in such devices as "coping strategies." These require the study

> . . . of the situational constraints in response to which they are
> fashioned, and of the relation (present or past) of such constraints to
> wider structural concerns. While the language of strategy analysis has
> so far been confined to interactionist research, this need no longer be
> the case. All too frequently, *the situation* [italics in original] has been

> regarded as the outer limit of constraint upon teacher and pupil
> behaviour. Concerns which have normally been thought to be the
> proper province of interactionist research should now be linked with
> and included in theories about the operations of social structure . . . .
> (A. Hargreaves, 1980:193).

Strategies are not only two-dimensional (micro–macro); they have historical referents. Pollard (1982) has pointed to the importance of personal biography and institutional history in their formulation. In recent years, this has further renewed the interest among some in "life histories." These have the advantage of monitoring a developing self within the context of local factors such as home life, parents, school and teachers, and significant others as well as wider concerns, which the passage of time has brought into focus, such as social class, religion, and social, political, and economic climate. Sensitively handled and portrayed, the influences of these can be seen in the acted-out life and on the formulating self (see Dollard, 1935; Goodson, 1980; Bertaux, 1981).

No one can pretend that the problem of linking micro and macro, situation and society, and process and structure has been solved. By and large, sociologists still tend to work in one sphere or the other. Where links are made, a common device is to "spot-weld" one onto another without fully tracing through the connections. A. Hargreaves (1980) has identified three such general models of schooling and society, which he terms "direct reproduction" (e.g., Althusser, 1971; Bowles and Gintis, 1976), "relative autonomy" (Willis, 1977), and "split-level" (Woods, 1979), all of which, he argues, have serious problems. Either the conceptualization appears to exist more in the mind of the researcher than in the empirical world of study or the analysis remains rooted in the latter—but does not grow.

However, some interactionist studies are more open to macro analysis than others. Among them, one may count the work on social strategies (Becker, 1964; Lacey, 1977; A. Hargreaves, 1978; Pollard, 1982), on "commitment," because this links the "self" to the system (Becker, 1960; Lacey, 1977; Nias, 1981; Thapan, 1986), on "control" and "choice," because these reveal the conditioned nature of "choice" (Ball, 1981), on the effects of school organization (such as streaming, or tracking) on group formation and individual adaptation, because the former is almost inevitably influenced by wider concerns (D. H. Hargreaves, 1967; Lacey, 1970; Ball, 1981), and on the many studies of social class (e.g., Becker, 1977b; Metz, 1990), gender (L. Davies, 1984; Mahoney, 1985), and "race" (Fuller, 1980; Mac an Ghaill, 1989). These have produced many rich studies of cultural formation and intergroup conflict and division that serve a potentially productive basis for macro studies. Currently in the United Kingdom, many researchers are studying the effects of the 1988 Education Reform Act in schools. The political connotations in the Act could hardly be more explicit. They provide a good opportunity to trace through the interconnections between political framework and school and classroom structure and process. This is a "natural experiment," which interactionists would want to make full use of—unlike artificial experiments, which, of course, are out of court for naturalistic investigators. Studying the interconnections helps to cultivate the "sociological imagination," which

> . . . enables its possessor to understand the larger historical scene in terms of its meaning for the inner life and the external career of a variety of individuals. It enables him [sic] to take into account how individuals, in the welter of their daily experience, often become falsely conscious of their social positions. Within that welter the framework of modern society is sought, and within that framework the psychologies of a variety of men and women are formulated. By such means the personal uneasiness of individuals is focused upon explicit troubles and the indifference of publics is transformed into involvement with public issues . . . . (Mills, 1959:11–12)

The sociological imagination enables us to grasp history and biography and the relations between the two within society. Life histories are clearly conducive to this, but so is qualitative research in general.

Mac an Ghaill (1989) argues that qualitative research is useful to the sociological imagination because it enables us "to bring into focus the three-dimensional social world of biography, culture and history" (p. 185). His own study of black youth revealed to him that much previous traditional research was "distorted, de-racialised and de-gendered" (p. 186). This "sociological refocusing" is necessary because it offers some micro—macro interconnections. In his case,

> In studying the schooling of black youth, student–teacher classroom survival strategies can be seen to be linked to the wider framework of racism and sexism, thus acknowledging that "race", class and gender are constitutive elements in the maintenance of hegemonic domination. Consequently, the transformation of these power relations requires a theory of social change that includes these interrelated elements. (p. 186)

The refocusing might be accompanied by an increase in the range of vision. This implies, firstly, observing in as many settings as possible within an institution—classroom, staffroom, head's office, subject department room, governor's meetings, meeting of the local council, and so on, because what happens in one of these has implications for what happens in others, and this can be perceived. By the same token, more than one site could be used in what A. Hargreaves (1985:43) has termed "linked micro studies," which could focus on processes in linked settings as well as situations. These might help us "gain a serious, well-grounded understanding of the complicated mechanisms by which economic, political, and social constraints on teaching and learning are filtered down to school level." Such a program would inevitably increase work loads if the typical depth of the research was to be maintained. Hammersley (1980:207), therefore, recommended the coordination of research studies, through, for example, the selection of "critical cases" ("identifying a location where evidence supporting or refuting a theory is most likely to be found"); "parallel studies" (e.g., of different forms of teaching or learning, which provides "comparative analytic leverage"); "team" research; and the micro analysis of historical settings and intercultural studies. Above all, in Hammersley's opinion, more testing of existing work is needed, without which coordination would be pointless (see also Hammersley, Scarth, and Webb, 1985; Scarth and Hammersley, 1988).

The micro–macro problem in sociology is far from being resolved. But symbolic interactionism has its part to play in the investigation and conceptualization of the interface. Some of the actual methods deployed are discussed in the next section, and "the generation of theory" in the section following that.

Research Methods and the Researcher's Self

The research methods most appropriate for symbolic interactionism fall under the general term "ethnography." Not all ethnographers are interactionists, but the term is used here within their field of reference. Several texts discuss the approach and its techniques (e.g., Glaser and Strauss, 1967; Lofland, 1971; Schatzman and Strauss, 1973; Bogdan and Taylor, 1975; Hammersley and Atkinson, 1983; Goetz and LeCompte 1984; Burgess 1984a; Woods, 1986; Strauss, 1987) as do many articles (including the collection in McCall and Simmons, 1969; Becker, 1970; Burgess, 1982, 1984b, 1985a,b; Sherman and Webb, 1988). A complete account of such methods is not given here; rather, the chief research instrument—the researcher—and how it interacts with theory and method is described. This applies symbolic interactionist principles to the research process itself. The researcher does not stand above and outside the research. The research is contextualized within situations and definitions of situation; research activities are constructed and interpreted in distinctive processes; and the researcher's self is inextricably bound up with the research. Reflexivity—the need to consider how one's own part in the research affects it—is therefore an essential requirement. This is illustrated by referring to some of the basic techniques.

Initial Commitment

In my student days, we were given courses in research methods designed to equip us with the knowledge and skills necessary to go out and do research. Any kind of research probably needs more personal engagement in the activity than this, but interactionist research above all cannot be taught in this way. To be meaningful, research methods need the involvement of the researcher's self. This means that knowledge of "how to do it" can only come from "going out and doing it." This was the basis of Park's (1920s) advice to his students to "go and get their hands dirty in real research" and of Becker's to his to "just go out there and do it" (Atkinson, 1977:32).

The initial guidance comes from the predisposition of the researcher to the approach and commitment to interactionist principles. The techniques follow generally from the methodological implications traced out in the previous section, but they flow directly from the self. This is not to say that things are done instinctively and to perfection but, rather, that one "learns on the job." Nor is it to say that research manuals are not important. Indeed, they are as essential as in any other approach, but their use is coterminous and interactional, rather than sequential. They only begin to make sense when one is involved, engaging with similar issues and situations. The "empathy" that is so important in one's feelings for the subjects of the research is also important for one's engagement with methods' texts. The excitement of discovery, the boredom of the "nothing happening" syndrome, the pleasure of meeting and interacting with people, the problems of effecting access and "coming up against brick walls," and errors and inadequacies as well as finding new ways of doing things or providing a new slant on a particular technique are all part of the endeavor, and the messages from others are seen from best advantage when placed on the comparative basis of one's own research processes and situations.

The texts themselves were produced from experience in the real world. In this way, the methodology *and* its study are grounded in the empirical world.

Researcher Skills

The ethnographer, thus, works to develop research skills *in situ* and to "fine-tune" the self. So much depends on what one sees and hears that much rests on one's powers of observation and listening. The kinds of skills that are involved are those of social management—interpersonal skills that facilitate the negotiation of access into both private places and private thoughts and that develop the kind of trust and rapport that encourage people to relax, be "natural," go about their everyday business in the researcher's presence in their usual way, and hold nothing back in interview. Good social management helps to ensure that some things to be seen and heard are worthwhile. To this end, some researchers have cultivated the "good guy" image, one sympathetic to the group under study (Lacey, 1976). Where two or more groups are in conflict under study, considerable personal skills are required to handle the consequent role conflict engendered in the researcher.

Although "naturalism" may be a keynote, things do not just happen and unfold before one's eyes. One's right to witness and take part in slices of other people's lives must be worked for and earned. Although just "hanging around" is not an uncommon activity among ethnographers, and quite appropriate in some circumstances, at other times one must make things happen in the sense of effecting entry to an important event or meeting, arranging interviews, or approaching people with a view to converse with them. For this, one needs interpersonal skills and fine judgment as to when to bring them into play and when to leave them alone. The inclination is to be as unobtrusive as possible (Webb *et al.*, 1966), but sometimes important situations are not immediately revealed or access offered. Without this kind of ingenuity, one fails to penetrate beyond the outer layer of reality.

If entry is achieved, one then needs observational skills. These involve, in the first place, vision—the ability to see and take in a wide range of activity over a period of time. Vision consists of a cultivated power of scanning, which ensures that as wide a portion of activity as possible is covered. Scanning will include the less as well as the more obvious places, people, and activities. At the same time, the ethnographer needs powers of *discernment*—selecting specific aspects for more concentrated scrutiny and greater definition (the criteria for which I discuss later)—which inevitably means letting other aspects go by. Once these are detected, one must consider how to record material. Filming and taping are useful aids where they do not intrude, but in many situations this is neither possible nor appropriate. The ethnographer therefore cultivates the art of photographing with, and logging in, the mind for commitment to written record as soon as possible. He or she notes key aspects or comments on scraps of paper, or even a sleeve, summarizing incidents with "key words" that will recall whole incidents, speaking into a dictaphone, punctuating the period of observation with "recording slots" to ensure against "drowning" in the data, performing all these activities smoothly in a seamless web both for efficiency and so as not to intrude on the action. Similarly, special skills are needed for interviewing, at their center a certain persona showing understanding of and empathy with the interviewee.

Such a disposition would appear to be necessary if we are to penetrate "fronts" (Goffman, 1971), achieve access to the other's self, and share in their innermost confidences. Once started, other skills are brought into play, notably *active listening*, which shows the other that you hear and react and construct interpretations occasionally, both with a view to maintaining the interpretative frame and keeping the other "warmed up"; the gentle art of *focusing*—that is, keeping the interviewer to the subject—and, in an unobtrusive way, *infilling* and *explicating* where material is incomplete, unclear, or ambiguous; and *checking* for accuracy by pressing points, seeking evidence, rephrasing, summarizing, playing devil's advocate, seeking contrary instances (Dean and Whyte, 1958), and identifying clues and indicators. There are few straight answers, there is always more to be said, and people are of almost infinite depth. In some instances, such as life histories, the discussion may be a voyage of discovery for the subject as well. They may find out new things about themselves or come to new realizations, which, in a curious way, empower them. One ex-teacher, whose life history we were compiling over a series of 10 2–3-hour conversations told me:

> Now the more we talk about it, the more the uncertain things become,
> you know, . . . the minute I put it into words, *my* [italics in original]
> words, I've got it. Now the only other way is for me to go away and
> write it all down, longhand. When I've written it again it's mine. So
> that's what I believe about this discussion thing. If you don't write
> copious notes, if you're not that sort of person, then you must sit down
> and talk about it. (Woods and Sikes, 1987:176)

The interview, therefore, is not just a device for gathering information. It is a process of reality construction to which both parties contribute and who are both affected by it. The interviewer puts some of him- or herself in—some contrasting, or complementary experiences perhaps, or some indications of own persona, or at the very least acts as a sounding board—and comes out reflecting on how the interview has affected his or her thoughts, ideas, viewpoints, and theories. However, the researcher is already looking to the next chain in the construction of the research, be it another interview in a different place, or at a different time, or with a different person, or be it observation, study of documents, questionnaire, or whatever.

The Researcher's Self

The researcher thus is a finely tuned instrument with considerable skills, but he or she is a person no less, with values, beliefs, and a self. Because these are all bound up with the research, ethnography is a very personal business. Each research project can take up to 5 or 6 years to complete, becoming major slices of one's life, calling for considerable personal investment. They frequently have as much to do with the understanding of oneself as of the world. The researcher's own background, interests, and values will be influential in selecting a topic for research. However, other criteria can be used in selecting subjects for study. These include balance, which will direct one to areas and subjects as yet uncovered; refinement and development, where previous studies have not "saturated" the topic (Glaser and Strauss, 1967); and relevance—that is, the research is deemed to be directed toward some social good.

Also, although the research subject is identified partly by personal interests and values, the conduct of the research is subject to rigorous scrutiny: exploration in depth to the extent of "saturation"; attention to sampling across people, places, and time; the use of multimethods (triangulation); naturalistic methods that are relatively free from researcher interference in the sense of misconstructing others' meanings and that penetrate through layers of reality to the innermost core; reflectivity and the keeping of a research diary and compilation of a research biography, so that the personal element is seen as part of the research, not separate and hidden from it; the search for contrary cases and alternative explanations; and tightness of fit among data collection, analysis, and theory (see next section). In these various ways, findings are tested and retested.

Yet even though the methods used are scientifically rigorous—and researchers continue to try to refine these techniques—the research is always a construction. This is because the researcher must put his or her own self into the research and interpret what he or she sees or hears. This is so whether one chooses to be a fully participant observer or "fully" nonparticipant. King (1978) took refuge in the "Wendy House" in his infant classroom so that he could better observe activity unaffected by his presence. But everyone knew he was there, and he had to make sense of what was happening. He would do this by observing, taking notes, talking to the people involved, writing up field notes after the event, reflecting on them, and doing some initial analysis, which might then guide further investigations, and so on. The research is thus gradually constructed over time. The people concerned, including the researcher, are continually making indications to each other, attributing meanings, and interpreting symbols. How the researcher does this depends on the kind of self he or she brings to the interpretation—experiences undergone, interests and values, personal reference groups, affective disposition toward those studied, and commitment to causes involved in the research.

This is most clearly illustrated in life histories or "historical ethnography." The subjects' memories, thoughts, and perceptions are of unknown scope and depth, even to themselves. Accounts are built up through successive discussions over a period of time as the life history or ethnography is "reconstructed." A first discussion reveals some parameters and sparks of ideas that are pursued in more detail in the next, and so on, until no new material emerges. Previous conversations are reviewed for accuracy and completeness. Subject and researcher work between meetings reflecting on the material, refining points, discovering new slants, spotting apparent inconsistencies and contradictions, and attempting some preliminary analysis. Again the researcher does not stand above or outside this activity but, rather, shares in it—not just as a trigger to release the other's thoughts, but as a contributor to "joint action," as a participant in a particular kind of situation, where both parties project part of their selves into the interaction and both construct meanings from it.

How the subjects interpret situations depends on similar factors to those influencing the researcher to some degree, but of key importance is how they perceive the researcher. Delamont (1984) shows how self-presentation might affect access by the different appearances she chose when first meeting different groups:

> When I saw heads I always wore a conservative outfit and real leather gloves. I had a special grey dress and coat, for days when I expected to see the head and some pupils. The coat was knee-length and very conservative-looking, while the dress was minilength to show the pupils I knew what the fashion was. I would keep the coat on in the head's office, and take it off before I first met the pupils. When

observing I tried to dress like the student teachers who were common
in all the schools: no trousers, unladdered tights, and no make-up.
(p. 25)

Similarly, it is necessary to know something about how subjects
construct the situation with the researchers in it. For example, in
interviewing pupils, it is possible that they may interpret the situation
as a counseling session, as a spying maneuver (in the interests, perhaps, of the teaching staff, inspectorate, or parents), or as an opportunity to promote various interests of their own (e.g., to wreak revenge, to
secure favors).

Clearly it is important to identify which scenario is in play and how
the subjects see the researcher before we can assess the outcome. No
information is straight and unidimensional—it must be seen within a
context of meaning.

Dilemmas of the Researcher Role

The fact that the researcher has a self, engages in interaction, and
interprets and imbues meaning gives rise to a number of dilemmas in
the researcher role. If handled sensitively, however, these can be a
source of strength.

Involvement versus Distance

A traditional problem for qualitative researchers is that between
involvement, immersion, and empathy on the one hand and distance
and scientific appraisal and objectivity on the other. The former is
necessary to understand others' perspectives as they see them, to see
how they see others, to identify their problems and concerns, and to
decode their symbolic behavior. It involves negotiating access, developing rapport, trust and friendship, sociability, inclusion, identification with the others involved, sensitivity to their concerns, and ability to appreciate their feelings as well as cognitive orientations.
However, the more one succeeds in doing this, the greater the danger
of the researcher's perspective being taken over by the subjects in the
well-known syndrome of "going native" (Paul, 1953). A frequent criticism of some ethnographers is that they romanticize their subjects,
seeing them through "rose-colored glasses," representing them with
great sympathy as well as empathy, while others who figure in the
subjects' world appear as pale shadows. There is also the risk of distortion—of letting the part represent the whole.

To guard against these dangers, one is advised to cultivate some social distance. The researcher is, after all, different from the subjects of the research. He or she is there to research, to plumb the depths and "get to the bottom of things" certainly, but of all groups involved in any specified interaction and in a way that recognizes put-ons, power positions, "line-shooting," and fairy tales. He or she is also there to analyze, to advance explanations, and to represent material in ways that might not otherwise occur to the inmates. Establishing comparative bases in and among groups, triangulation of methods to increase validity, reflectivity outside the situation, the consideration of material *post hoc*, the writing up of field notes and diaries all aid this process and enable the researcher, if involvement and distance are cultivated in a judicious mixture, to have the best of both.

Creativity versus Evaluation

This creativity versus evaluation dilemma reflects the tension in the researcher between the "I" and the "Me." To what extent should the "I" be given free rein; to what extent checked and disciplined by the "Me"? In "discovery" research, the "I" has to be given a certain license. As Mead says, "We don't know what wonders it's capable of." The "I" is important in several respects. First, in the realm of feelings, the "I" is responsible for the stirring of excitement, curiosity, and motivation so indispensable for any kind of research. This does much to counter the physical and mental fatigue one experiences during the intensive fieldwork period. It keeps the mind alert to a range of possibilities, in several situations and in interaction with a number of people throughout the day, often including "rest" periods [because these are (1) interesting in themselves and (2) useful for making up notes]. It keeps one going in writing up field notes at night. It supplies the drive and impulsion that keeps sloth and ennui at bay during difficult periods or that wins over it when promising openings beckon but one's stamina wilts. Second, the "I" creates opportunities for interaction. Some may feel they can witness things as they naturally happen with "fly-on-the-wall" techniques (although flies can be very distracting!). Others may feel the need to make things happen, at least with respect to creating openings and making appointments. There is always a tension here between "naturalism" and "arrangement," but access must be organized. Sometimes it is not clear where one goes next—the "I," unleashed, should come to the rescue. Openness of mind, willingness to follow hunches and take risks, and a certain stoicism if they do not work are all part of this. Third, it is the "I" that creates ideas, conceptualizes, identifies patterns, notices a relationship where no relationship was suspected before, detects a missing factor, recognizes a problem, and worries at its resolution.

All this is indispensable. But somewhere along the way the "I" must be subject to checks and discipline. The "Me" embodies the scientific community, the canons of social scientific research, and existing literature in the area. It will carry out tests, looking for negative cases and seeking contrary evidence. Some ideas will prove ephemeral and, thus, be discarded for lack of evidence or reshaped to fit that which exists. It will spot weaknesses in the use of only one method or only one informant and qualify findings accordingly. It will monitor for inadequate sampling and repair it. It will reveal ambiguities, inconsistencies, and lacunae and point to the need for more research. It will reveal leading questions and other errors on the tape transcript and, thus, condition one's approach. It will show how one's research is similar and dissimilar to others in the area. Thus, the "I" scanning freely detects critical items and themes for study; the "Me" locks them into place. The "I" and the "Me" are not phased in this neat way but are more or less in continuous interaction, although the "I" probably has more license in the earlier, discovery, and scene-setting part of the research. The conditioning of the "Me" helps to identify the worthwhile features of the research, sifting out elements that do not stand up by agreed criteria and highlighting those that do. It helps to make more "solid," as opposed to "indulgent," sense, "scientific" as opposed to "personal."

The dilemma is sometimes represented as intensification versus extension, or intensive examination of one particular area, kind of interaction or process, or subject versus extensive examination of many. Ethnography involves intensification, putting social life under the microscope, seeing the myriad detail of everyday life in fine relief, and leaving no stone unturned in the search for deeper focus and sharper definition. Critics have sometimes complained that this leads to myopia, tunnel vision, and getting bogged down in detail. However, the myopia is counteracted and the intensification made a virtue by attention to sampling; triangulation of sources, of researchers, or of methods; historical and social contextualization (for an example, see Lacey, 1970); and the search for formal theory (see next section).

Covert versus Overt Research

This is the main ethical problem in ethnography and reflects the tension between the public's right to know and the subject's right to privacy (Bulmer, 1980, 1982; Burgess, 1985c; Soltis, 1989). Such problems are most acute in ethnography, which rests on the deep personal engagement of the researcher and relationships established and developed during the study. Consider, for example, the ethical implications of researching in repressive institutions, such as a concentration camp, an authoritarian and punitive school, or in criminal activities, or in racist or otherwise biased institutions. It might be thought difficult for a researcher committed to principles of equality and social justice, for example, to work "overtly" in such institutions. There may be greater problems in access being granted in the first instance or being sustained once the purpose of such research was discovered. Yet it is important that such institutions be researched.

Such features might come to light in the course of the research. The researcher is then faced with the problem of whether or not to expose such injustices. This might run against the terms of his or her negotiated contract and the human decency implied by the relationships developed during the research. It might also be counterproductive in terms of promoting the cause (producing, for example, confrontation rather than conversion) and to the cause of research generally in prejudicing other researchers' opportunities. On the other hand, to say nothing might be to condone the wrong or injustice reinforcing the prevailing system. Worse, the researcher may act as a "provocateur," subjects rehearsing morally dubious activities possibly in exaggerated form in the belief that they are doing the researcher a service.

Participant observation has, on occasion, been likened to "spying" or "voyeurism," activities more in keeping with intelligence services and perversion than academic research. There is an unsavory feel to such a role so conceived. The researcher effects entry, carries out what observations are required, persuades subjects to "spill the beans," and then "cuts and runs," writing up the account in private in the service of humanity in general. The question is do the ends justify the means? If we accept that, are we any better than those studied? Is there a moral code that we should accept? How far would that prevent the truth from emerging?

Bulmer (1982) has argued strongly against covert research. It runs against the principle of "informed consent" (people agreeing to take part in research on the basis of knowledge of what it is really about); invades privacy, "contaminating private spheres of the self" (p. 220); involves deception, which is inimical to the qualities of trust, rapport, and friendship; breeds more and more problems, for example, of where to stop; harms sociology and sociologists; and carries a number of practical problems (e.g., the difficulty of sustaining such a front over a long period).

However, as Bulmer acknowledges, research is hardly that clear-cut. There are some who seek to justify covert research they have conducted (Humphreys, 1975; Homan, 1980; Holdaway, 1982) and others who see *some* as unavoidable (Denzin, 1968; Roth, 1962; Burgess, 1985c; Gans, 1968). "Consent" is not a straightforward business. As Dingwall (1980:878) points out, in stratified settings there is a "hierarchy of consent," senior personnel acting as "gatekeepers" and subordinates possibly being forced to participate. Also, one encounters so many people during a typical study, often casually, that it is impossible to secure the consent of all. The researcher is faced with a complexity of choices and is subject to a number of situational constraints. Public and private spheres are not always sharply defined, and "total openness" is probably unachievable. One cannot always predict the courses qualitative research will take or what surprises it will turn up. Covert methods in some instances, too, *have* advanced our understanding of society (e.g., Rosenhan, 1982; Festinger *et al.*, 1956). In large, complex organizations, covert observation is perhaps more acceptable, the self being cushioned here by bureaucracy. Douglas (1970) argues that the powerful hide behind secrecy, manipulation, and deceit and require similar methods to penetrate their armor. Bulmer (1982) is not impressed by these arguments, feeling that "sociologists need to think creatively about ways in which access may be gained other than by outright deception." He quotes from *The American Sociologist's* (1968) "Towards a Code of Ethics":

> Just as sociologists must not distort or manipulate truth to serve
> untruthful ends, so too they must not manipulate persons to serve their
> quest for truth. The study of society, being the study of human beings,
> imposes the responsibility of respecting the integrity, promoting the
> dignity and maintaining the autonomy of these persons. (p. 318)

It should be noted, too, that open fieldwork *has* been done with sociologically unsympathetic groups such as the National Front (Fielding, 1981). These ethical problems set up conflicts in the researcher's self. Whyte (1955) experienced considerable personal anguish over the deception he felt compelled to use in his study of "Cornerville"; Patrick (1973) felt obliged to conclude his research on a Glasgow gang because his covert involvement was pressing him into criminal activity; Humphreys (1975) later regretted the various deceptions he had deployed in his study of homosexual encounters.

The moral conflict arises from elements grating against each other in the self. The researcher engaging in joint action with subjects sets up an interpretive and moral frame that rests on a certain code of conduct involving certain mutual expectations. The interaction, in other words, is rule-bound, although most of the rules are implicit, just as the interaction being observed. It is constructed over time and reinforced by many interactions. The other's behavior toward you as researcher, as already noted, rests on the perception of who and what you are, why and for whom you are doing the research, what your interests are, your view of them, and your relationships with them and others. As Dean (1954) states,

> A person becomes accepted as a participant observer more because of the kind of person he turns out to be in the eyes of the field contacts than because of what the research represents to them. Field contacts want to be reassured that the research worker is a "good guy" and can be trusted not "to do them dirt" with what he finds out. (p. 233)

If most of this relationship is based on a sham, one is not only deceiving the subjects, but also one's self. If it offends one's own values and runs contrary to principles ingrained through years of socialization, not to mention allegiance to a professional code of ethics (all represented in the "Me"), one risks a damaged self and a "spoiled" project and possibly spoiled research career. In the course of a research study, many such issues will need to be confronted. The "I" will seek a creative resolution of them. Where partial deception is involved, the "Me" will monitor how, and with what justice, it is encased in a greater good, and, if it concludes "not much," the "I" in turn will seek early repair and recompense. If there are no such opportunities or the deception is too great, the researcher may experience agonies of conscience and a personal crisis. The appreciative element of symbolic interactionism, taking the role of the other, and seeing the world through other's perceptions all takes place in a moral context. So, too, do the indications one makes to oneself. Reflexivity involves a constant monitoring of the rightness of what one is doing. It may also involve a change in the researcher's self. Research is an educative process, not only for what one discovers about others, but for what one discovers about oneself. Taken-for-granted beliefs and assumptions, views on the world, and comprehension of one's own interests, abilities, and aspirations may all come under review.

Ethnographers will continue to debate these matters keenly. And, while general ethical parameters will be worked out in codes of professional ethics that apply to the community, there will be many particular instances requiring individual adaptations that depend on the construction of self. As Dingwall (1980:888) acknowledges, "competent fieldwork requires a clear conscience." In Soltis' (1989:129) opinion, this basically involves observing the "non-negotiable" values of "honesty, fairness, respect for persons and beneficence"—markers laid down by the professional community for personal struggles. But while they are "non-negotiable" in principle, in practice many decisions must constantly be made that contain the dilemma that observing these values in one form means not doing so in others (see e.g., Burgess, 1985c). At the same time, the underlying purpose of the research, which is to produce generalizable statements and theory, provides some ethical safeguards through close attention to how this theory is produced. It is to this subject that I now turn.

The Generation of Theory

Grounded Theory

During the 1970s and the unproductive debate about "positivism" versus "interpretivism," it was customary to draw the contrast between the hypothetico-deductive method and the "testing" of theory on the one hand and the qualitative inductive method and the "generating" of theory on the other. Today there is less emphasis on any epistemological contrast. Qualitative techniques can be used to both generate and test theory. The emphasis in fieldwork research to date, however, has been on the first, largely guided by the work of Glaser and Strauss (1967).

Their criticism of much verification work was not because verification of existing theories was not important but, rather, because many of the theories that were being tested were not "grounded" in the empirical world and were unsound in the first place. They were poorly generated in the social activity they sought to explain. They would, thus, have poor predictive value and be of little use in practical applications. The same criticism might be made of some qualitative studies that, after a detailed descriptive ethnography, present a theoretical section that may have only a loose relationship with the data. This practice is not unassociated with postgraduate folklore, which holds that there must be a "theoretical" chapter, just as there should be a "literature" chapter. This has been known as the "bolt-on" model. The aim, therefore, is to produce "grounded theory."

Generating Theory

Much qualitative work has been criticized for being merely descriptive, for being limited to "how" rather than including "why" questions. But these distinctions are not as clear-cut as they might seem. Ethnographic description is theory-laden in several senses. The researcher inevitably interprets what he or she finds through certain theoretical frameworks. The same applies to the subjects he or she studies in how they make sense of the world. The representation of findings, too, is no ordinary "description" that anybody could provide. In the rich detail of several "layers of reality," classifications, categories, and typologies, and conceptual refinement, representation amounts to what Geertz (1973) has called "thick" description, already heavily theoretically informed. That many ethnographies stop at this point may be an indication of the inferential difficulties in proceeding further or, of course, sheer exhaustion. Another possibility is that it could be the limit to which the researcher feels that "theoretically informed description" can go. But the research does not have to stop there, because theory is process, an "ever-developing entity, not a perfected product" (Glaser and Strauss, 1967:32). Analysis also is not a separate stage of the research but is done in interaction with ongoing fieldwork from the very beginning. One may be reluctant to "take" rather than "make" problems (R. H. Turner, 1962) or to specify the issue or problem to be examined in advance of the study. But then no ethnographer begins absolutely carte blanche. From readings, discussions, and experience, ethnographers will have developed a notion of the research. It may be a "foreshadowed problem" (Malinowski, 1922) derived from lacunae in the literature, either empirical or theoretical. It may involve some "mapping" of previously uncharted territory. The Chicago School excelled at this, with their fascination to understand the city in all its social aspects. The same applies to British ethnography of the 1970s and 1980s, which "mapped out" the field of the school and classroom and, in time, rectified certain imbalances, such as the early 1970s favoring of boys as a research interest over girls, the neglect of blacks, the emphasis on deviants and on older, secondary school pupils, and a period of "teacher-bashing."

Theoretically guided research may be used to test an existing theory or to modify or elaborate upon it. One of the best examples is the development of differentiation—polarization theory. D. H. Hargreaves' (1967) and Lacey's (1970) initial work in a secondary modern and grammar school, respectively, produced a theory that claimed that where pupils were differentiated by ability (as in stream-ing, or tracking), then a polarization of attitudes (into pro- and anti-school) would occur among them. Ball (1981) examined this theory in a comprehensive school, finding the process still held under "banding" (broad streaming arrangements) but very much modified when mixed-ability classes were introduced. Abraham (1989) set out to explore the extent to which the theory was applicable to a setted comprehensive school in the south of England. He discovered a similar syndrome but with variations, which led him to conclude that other factors helped to modify and promote polarization (such as examination and career pres-sure, and the onset of subject options). Others have used and devel-oped the theory in different settings: Burke (1986) in a college for 16–19-year-old students; Foster (1990) in a multiethnic comprehen-sive school working with a declared antiracist policy; and Rosie (1988) with a group of school-leavers with special needs who underwent Youth Training Scheme training. This, then, is an example of how qualitative researchers build on each other's work in a theoretically productive way.

In these various ways, the research is theoretically driven from the start. Once in the field, the search begins for new theory. Theory often is represented as being in the situation one studies or emerging from it. It is actually constructed in the researcher's head but is rigorously checked and rechecked against the ongoing data. It is not the product of some preconceived idea. Insofar as it "emerges," it does so from the strength of the indicators one identifies. The sheer weight and appar-ently disparate nature of data prompts motivation to structure and synthesize. Nias (1990:162) observes that "the extent and quality of the information I collected challenged me to search for and eventually find connections and relationships between apparently isolated ideas. In seeking not to drown in the data, I found unexpected reefs under my feet." What form do these indicators take?

They are signs that alert one to the fact that "something is up," that there is something odd about what is being witnessed, or that there is a connection between events previously unsuspected or a pattern that is gradually, over time, revealed. For example, Lynda Measor and I were keyed in to the importance of pupil myths surrounding school transfer when a number of pupils prefaced their comments with remarks like "I have heard that . . . ," "They tell me that . . . ," "There is this story that . . ." (Measor and Woods, 1984). In "The Divided School" (Woods, 1979), my examination of "teacher survival" led to the theory that in situations where constraints on action ex-ceeded the expectations of strong commitment a struggle for survival would result. It was initiated by the observation of what appeared to me to be some very strange behavior. One of these was a senior chemistry class, where the teacher taught a class for 70 minutes, complete with experiment and blackboard work, while the pupils manifestly ignored him. They were clearly doing other things. Only in the last 10 minutes of the lesson did they dutifully record the results in their exercise books at his dictation. In another instance, a teacher showed a class a film even though it was the wrong film and had nothing remotely to do with the subject that had been delivered. Such events had been delivered. Such events seemed to me to cry out for explanation. Why did people behave in these strange ways?

Inconsistencies and contrasts also arouse interest. Why, for example, should teachers change from kindly, friendly, considerate people in one situation (staffroom) to hostile, aggressive, intemperate people in another situation (classroom) (Waller, 1932; Lacey, 1976; D. H. Hargreaves, 1978b)? Why do they lay claim to certain values and beliefs in the one situation and act out others of strong contrast in the other (Keddie, 1971)? Why do they behave with such irrationality and such pettiness on occasion? Why do pupils "work" with one teacher and "raise hell" with another (G. Turner, 1983)? From this latter observation, Turner came to certain conclusions about pupil interests and school resources and refined notions of "conformity" and "deviance."

The investigation of key words is a common method for unpacking meanings. Becker *et al.* (1961) gave the example of "crock," a common term used by physicians about their patients, which the researchers used as a way of understanding medics' perspectives. Similarly, the identification and comprehending of pupil argot is a *sine qua non* of understanding pupil culture. Why did Willis' "lads" refer to another group of pupils as "ear' oles" (basically, because they were always "listening" and never "doing," but the term carries a wealth of meaning that stands in contrast and thus highlights the "lads'" own beliefs and activities). Other research has turned up "dossers" (idlers) and "swots" (hard-working pupils) (G. Turner, 1983). Beynon (1985) found the boys of his research indulging in an activity they described as "sussing-out." This was a sophisticated set of linked activities, which at first glance seemed anarchical and meaningless (cf. Cohen, 1968), but which were part of a "process of establishment" during the crucial phase of "initial encounters" (see also Ball, 1980). The pupils studied by Werthman (1963) and Rosser and Harré (1976) laid great emphasis on "looking cool." Sharp and Green's (1975) "progressive" teachers wanted their children to be "busy," which led them to formulate their concept of "busyness" as an organizing feature of such teachers' perspectives.

The Construction of Typologies and Theoretical Models

After the identification of key topics, one proceeds to investigate their types and properties. What kinds of sussing-out are indulged in? Beynon (1985) classified the major types—group formation and communication, joking, verbal and nonverbal challenges, intervention, and play—with subtypes within them. Some qualitative studies stop at this point, incurring the criticism that all they do is construct typologies. But typologies are not lacking worth in themselves, nor is cessation of analysis at this point an inevitable product of the method. What this activity does is ensure that the notion of sussing-out has substance and delineates its major forms. We would want to go on from there to consider how sussing-out works. How do teachers and pupils modify their behavior toward each other? Why does it take this particular form?

To answer these questions we would need to consider three things. First, we need to act upon the interactionist axiom of seeking to understand events from the point of view of the participants and try to discover the pupils' intention. The second factor is incidence. One would want to know when and where this kind of activity took place and with whom. Is it limited to initial encounters? If it is occurring at other times, another explanation is required. Under what sort of circumstances does it occur, and with what kinds of teachers and what kinds of pupils? Are all pupils involved, or only some? What proportion of total pupil behavior is taken up with this kind of activity? This is the contextual aspect. Comparisons need to be made with other sections of activity. Theory and methodology interact, the emerging theory guiding the next part of the investigation. If there is similar activity elsewhere, then the theory may have to be revised—although there may be another explanation for that activity. Third, what are the consequences of the activity? The theory would lead us to expect that where the required knowledge was ascertained, where teachers justified their claims to being able to teach and to control, different, more "settled" behavior would ensue; where it was not, the behavior would presumably continue and perhaps intensify because the boundaries of tolerance would be seen as lying further and further back. If this is not the case, again the theory may have to be revised.

It is also necessary to explore alternative theories. In the case of sussing-out, one would need to consider the possibility that the behavior was a cultural product (e.g., of male, working-class, or ethnic culture) or an institutional product (i.e., a function of a particular kind of school organization). Some of these, of course, may also be involved—that is, the behavior may be and probably is multifunctional.

Comparative Analysis

The development of the theory proceeds in a rigorous way, primarily by means of comparative analysis. Instances are compared across a range of situations, over a period of time, among a number of people, and through a variety of methods. Attention to sampling is important if the theory being formulated concerns a particular population. Thus, comparisons are made among a representative set. Negative cases are sought for these and perhaps may invalidate the argument or suggest contrary explanations. These comparisons may be made both inside and outside the study. These kinds of comparisons, however, can also be used for other purposes—establishing accurate evidence, establishing empirical generalizations, specifying a concept (bringing out the distinctive elements or nature of the case), and verifying theory (Glaser and Strauss, 1967).

Theorizing begins from the first day of fieldwork with the identification of possibly significant events or words. Field notes are not only recorded but coded, in a number of ways. There are alternative ways of doing this (Glaser and Strauss, 1967; Lincoln and Guba, 1985; Grove, 1988). I largely follow the Glaser and Strauss model. The first coding may arise directly from the data, taking subjects' classification. For example, in a study of "pupil perspectives," "being picked on," "being shown up," and "being made to do hard work" are some pupils' claims about their treatment by teachers that could form the initial classification. Re-examination of the material might reveal that some might be placed under several codes as well as force consideration of material that has not yet been but that must be coded, if the theory is to be all-inclusive—all aspects of pupil perspectives revealed by the research must be included.

Some provisional rules are now established for allocating to categories, and these become more refined, more clearly demarcated, and firmer as the research proceeds. These codes may have sufficient theoretical purchase to form the basis of the theory. This is true of "being shown up" and "sussing-out." Or they may be translated into higher-order constructs as with "teacher" and "pupil strategies." Such concepts should be analytic—"sufficiently generalized to designate characteristics of complete entities, not the entities themselves"—and *sensitizing,* which are more forward-looking and offer direction

(Blumer, 1954). Glaser and Strauss give the example of "social loss" generated in their study to explain nurses' differential treatment of the dying. I (Woods, 1979) advanced the notion of "teacher survival" to explain teachers' aberrant behavior; Sikes *et al.* (1985) developed a theory about different kinds of teacher commitment and how movement among them depended on socioeconomic circumstances in our study of teacher careers; A. Hargreaves (1984a) abstracted his notion of "contrastive rhetoric" as a political strategy in school policy discussions (for his account of the generation of this concept, see A. Hargreaves, 1987). All of these are based in the first instance on initial coding arising directly from the data. The whole process ensures the groundedness of the ensuing theory (for more detailed examples, see Strauss, 1987).

As categories and codes are suggested by the data, so they prefigure the direction of the research in a process known as "theoretical sampling." This is to ensure that all categories and codes are identified and filled or groups fully researched. Thus, Mac an Ghaill (1989) followed the observation of an antischool group, the "Warriors," with the collection of material from school reports and questionnaires on their attitudes toward school, enabling him to build case histories. This is a good illustration of how theory and methodology interrelate, leading to an "escalation of insights" (Lacey, 1976). Investigation goes on until "saturation" occurs—when no new theoretical forms are being generated and new data does not add to existing ones.

To aid this process, the researcher becomes steeped in the data but, at the same time, employs devices to ensure breadth and depth of vision. These include the compilation of a field diary, a running commentary on the research with reflections on one's personal involvement; marginal comments on field notes as thoughts occur on reading and rereading them; comparisons and contrasts with other material; further light cast by later discoveries; relevance to other literature; notes concerning validity and reliability; and aide-memoires, memos, and notes, committing thoughts to paper on interconnections among the data and some possible concepts and theories. Consulting the literature is an integral part of theory development. It helps to stimulate ideas and to give shape to the emerging theory, thus providing both commentary on and a stimulus to study. Consulting colleagues also is helpful, for their funds of knowledge and as academic "sounding-boards." The sounding-board is an important device for helping to articulate and shape ideas. What may seem to be brilliant insights to the researcher may be false promises to others. The critical scrutiny of one's peers at this formative stage is very helpful. It may be obtained by discussion (the mere fact of trying to articulate an idea helps to shape it), by circulating papers, or by giving seminars. Where appropriate, those featuring in the research may engage in "respondent validation," as discussed earlier. Although not always applicable for the reasons given, this can be useful in testing the salience of higher-order constructs. For example, explaining their relevance to respondents on matters of close concern to them can be particularly instructive (see also Ball, 1984). In one such life history study, I was persuaded to discard some concepts that I thought illuminated some aspects of the life, but that the subject saw as obfuscatory (Woods, 1985). More discussion ensued on the points in question, and as more empirical details emerged it became clear that he was right. The result was a tighter analysis more firmly grounded in the "life." For Mac an Ghaill (1988, 1989), the involvement of the pupils in his study in his analysis was crucial:

> There was continual critical discussion, among the students and myself, of the descriptions and interpretations of the data. More specifically, we were concerned primarily with the inter-relationship of the three dimensions of "race", gender and class. For the Black Sisters, racism was the main determinant of their lifestyles outside the domestic situation, though the interaction of class and gender with racism was acknowledged. (Mac an Ghaill, 1989:182)

Another important factor is time. The deeper the involvement, the longer the association, the wider the field of contacts and knowledge, the more intense the reflection, and the stronger the promise of groundedness. Nias (1990) remarks:

> The fact that I have worked for so long on the material has enabled my ideas to grow slowly, albeit painfully. They have emerged, separated, recombined, been tested against one another and against those of other people, been rejected, refined, re-shaped. I have had the opportunity to *think* a great deal over 15 years, about the lives and professional biographies of primary teachers and about their experience of teaching as work. My conclusions, though they are in the last resort those of an outsider, are both truly "grounded" and have had the benefit of slow ripening in a challenging professional climate. (p. 162)

Nias reminds us that a great deal of *thinking* must go into this process and that this is frequently *painful*. Wrestling with mounds and mounds of everaccumulating material; searching for themes and indicators that will make some sense of it all; taking some apparently promising routes, only to find they are blind alleys; writing more and more notes and memos; rereading notes and literature for signs and clues; doing more fieldwork to fill in holes or in the hope of discovering some beacon of light; presenting tentative papers that receive well-formulated and devastating criticisms—all these are part and parcel of the generation of theory. For most people, the pain barrier must be confronted and broken for quality theory to emerge (see Woods, 1986).

The criteria for a good grounded theory include a strong degree of fit with the data it purports to explain; explanatory power, accounting for the relationships among the elements under specific conditions, thus being able to predict outcomes under what circumstances; relevance, in being directed toward central concerns of the area under examination; flexibility, in being capable of taking into account new and different material; density, where the theoretical constructs are few but encompass a large number of properties and categories; and integration, indicating a strong relationship among the constructs (Glaser and Strauss, 1967, 1968; Hutchinson, 1988).

Substantive and Formal Theory

Glaser and Strauss (1967) make the distinction between substantive theory, which applies to theory developed for an empirical area such as patient care, classroom teaching, or delinquency, and formal theory, which is developed for a conceptual area of sociological inquiry such as stigma, socialization, or social mobility. They give the example of "social loss" from their own research. A hypothesis derived from the substantive theory would state "The higher the social loss of a dying patient (1) the better his care, (2) the more nurses develop loss rationales to explain away his death" (p. 42). The formal theory would state "The higher the social value of a person the less delay experienced in receiving services from experts" (p. 42). A teacher strategy example would be to associate it with a property of "teacher career-continuance commitment," which would produce the hypothesis "The greater the constraint on teaching activity, the more teachers who hold career-continuance commitment will be forced into survival rather than teaching." The formal theory would simply generalize this to all jobs. It has more explanatory power in this respect, and this is equally as desirable in educational research as in any other.

The more analytic, formal, or "generic" (Lofland, 1971) the theory or concept, the more generalizable the findings are likely to be. Atkinson and Delamont (1986) refer to Goffman's (1968) development of the notion of "total institution" from a comparison among a range of institutions, although his immediate point of reference was a mental hospital. Analytic concepts developed in other fields can enrich the area under study. For example, I (Woods, 1979) found interesting parallels with the medical profession in a study of teacher behavior in preparing school reports. Friedson (1972) observed how doctors protected themselves by the use of "avoidance techniques"; Goffman (1961) similarly developed the notion of "role-distance"; Sudnow (1971) alerted me (P. W.) to the fact that rapid identification with rather crude stereotypes is typical of institutional, functionary life, and not just of schools. Such comparisons can help initiate formal theory. Glaser and Strauss (1965) also give the example of "status-passage." They developed a formal theory on status passage involved in dying. It has proved its worth in informing areas as diverse as becoming a mother (Oakley, 1980), becoming divorced (Hart, 1976), becoming a trained bread salesman (Ditton, 1977), and pupils moving on to a higher school (Measor and Woods, 1984). These studies also fed back into the formal theory. For example, having discovered the prevalence of myths attending pupil transfer, Measor and Woods (1984) hypothesized that similar bodies of knowledge attend other status passages. The theory then informs educational policy. For instance, previous studies of "transfer" had indicated a fairly rapid "reincorporation" phase, echoing the rather functionalist theoretical line of Van Gennep (1960) in his work on "rites of passage." Our work suggested that this missed the provisional nature of early adaptations and that a longer time perspective was needed. It also argued that "reincorporation" was misleading, for the adaptations pupils made during the status passage were the product of negotiations in which pupils influenced the situation to some extent and were not simply "reincorporated" into it. This illustrates again the interactionist perspective that led to consideration of pupil interests, perspectives, and activities.

Although the end-product of qualitative research for some may be theory that helps to explain what is observed and to predict what will happen under similar circumstances (if A then B), others reject the search for causal connections and claim to study the nature of the social world and the "meanings" that are constructed and negotiated. They want to know what situations are "actually like" and how they are experienced by the participants. The interactionist emphasis on process, flux, voluntarism, inconsistencies, contradiction, dilemmas, and strategies makes it difficult to think in terms of "causes" and "truth." Rather, there are connections, influences, and tendencies that seem to resemble more closely the nature of the social world than hard-line theories dealing with unchanging facts and seeking to establish ultimate truths. The line taken in this paper is somewhere between these positions. Qualitative research can generate and test theories, but they need to be adequate at the level of meaning, not decontextualized, attenuated, and dehumanized.

Criticisms of Grounded Theory

Grounded theory has not been without its critics. Brown (1973), for example, has argued that Glaser and Strauss are not clear about the nature of grounded theory, nor about the link between such theory and data (see also Hammersley, 1989). They refer to categories and their properties and to hypotheses as "theory." Their examples are of a particular kind of data—classificatory, processual—amenable to that kind of analysis, but "some phenomena involve much greater discontinuity in either time or space or in the level of the systems studied" (Brown, 1973:6). Greater immersion in the field is unlikely to yield useful theories here. Equally plausible alternative explanations from elsewhere may be available, so questions of how one decides among them (i.e., methodological issues) must be considered at an early stage. We need a balance, therefore, among verification, exploration and formulation. Bulmer (1979) raises doubts about Glaser and Strauss' tabula rasa view of inquiry in urging concentration and a pure line of research on the matter in hand and discounting existing concepts (in case of contamination) until grounded categories have emerged. This must be very difficult to do in well-researched areas. More characteristic is the interplay of data and conceptualization. Also, he wonders, when should the process of category development come to an end? Possibly the method is more suited to the generation of concepts than of testable hypotheses (see also Williams, 1976).

In fairness, Glaser and Strauss (1967) do acknowledge the construction of theory on existing knowledge which already has claims to being well grounded. This is similar to my arguments for "stage 2 ethnography" (Woods, 1986). I argue here that where ethnographies have accumulated in a certain area to the point of "saturation" of concepts, we need to move to a higher level of analysis in which all these related studies are examined and their interconnections explored. Glaser and Strauss also recognize the importance of testing. Their complaint is about testing theory inadequately related to the material it seeks to explain. As for the confusion over theory and the identification of categories and their properties, the emergence of concepts and the formulation of hypotheses represent a clear and well-tried route. The fact is that many qualitative studies do not cover all these stages. This does not mean that they are without worth.

Detailed ethnographic description and theory-testing (of reasonably grounded theories) are equally legitimate pursuits for the qualitative researcher.

A call for a much greater emphasis on systematic theory-testing has been made by Hammersley (1987). He argues that there has been an overreaction against positivism, which made verification studies unfashionable. Symbolic interactionist studies produced a wealth of empirical research, mainly descriptive, with some "interesting theoretical ideas" but not much "cumulation of theoretical knowledge." The one exception to this, he feels, is "differentiation–polarization" theory (discussed earlier). There is much sense in this argument, which in some respects is similar to my call for "stage 2" work. However, if the argument for rigorous, systematic testing is taken to its extreme, we only end up with the kind of theory so strongly criticized by Blumer, Becker, Glaser, and Strauss.

Conclusion: The Promise of Symbolic Interactionism

D. H. Hargreaves (1978a) has drawn attention to the following strengths of symbolic interactionism: (1) its appreciative capacity, or its ability to explore social action from the point of view of the actor; (2) its designatory capacity, or its ability to articulate taken-for-granted, commonsense knowledge, thus providing a language for discourse about these areas; (3) its reflective capacity, or its ability to provide members or inmates with the means to reflect on their own activity; (4) its immunological capacity, or its ability to inform policy by providing knowledge and understanding of the everyday life of school, thus helping to protect the policy from failure; and (5) its corrective capacity, or its ability to offer a critique of macro theories that may be incorrect in their empirical assumptions—and, hence, serving as a means of strengthening them. Some of these were mentioned earlier.

We might add to these four others. (6) Its illuminative capacity, or the range, depth, and richness of detail it provides on individuals, groups, institutions, and issues. Interactionist ethnography has opened up and illuminated the "black box" of the school. It will be prominent in the investigation of issues—for example, in the United Kingdom in monitoring the consequences of the 1988 Education Reform Act, such as the impact of testing on pupils and teachers, the induction of new governors, how teachers adapt their subject, teaching, and their selves to the new imperatives, the repercussions for teacher careers, and the experiential consequences of institutional change. On all such issues, and others, there will be a continuing need for the kind of information the interactionist approach provides. (7) Its theoretical capacity. Symbolic interactionism has considerable theoretical possibilities. It can generate theory inductively, as discussed in the section "Research Methods and the Researcher's Self," leading to strongly grounded theory. It can exert strong influence on macro theory and lead to its re-formulation, as in resistance theory. It also offers good chances of conceptualizing the micro–macro interface. Also, it affords a means of testing theory, as in the line of work associated with differentiation–polarization. It is not, therefore, a purely descriptive endeavor, although its theoretical potential has not yet been fully explored. (8) Its policy-making capacity. Finch (1986) points out that the researchers of the Chicago School of the 1930s were not directly concerned with policy. Their work, however, did have direct policy implications, although "not of a kind which could be straightforwardly applied within the dominant political framework" (p. 132). Much interactionist work since has been similar. There are signs, however, that some interactionists are becoming more directly policy-minded. This was certainly true of the Manchester studies of D. H. Hargreaves (1967) and Lacey (1970), which conceivably had an impact on school organization policy. It is vividly illustrated by A. Hargreaves (1988), who shows how an analysis of classroom teaching drawing attention to the effects of such things as large classes, full timetables, examination pressures, and poor career prospects leads to vastly different policy implications from those promoted by the Department of Education and Science (1983) who were arguing that the most important factor in teaching was teacher's "personal qualities." It is much to the fore also in studies of pressing social issues such as gender and "race." Such studies would be expected to inform whole-school policies on these matters (see e.g., Stanley, 1986, 1989; Gillborn, 1990; Measor, 1983, 1989; Wright, 1986; Foster, 1990). An interactionist approach could be useful, also, in evaluating such policies (see e.g., Grugeon and Woods, 1990). (9) Its collaborative capacity. Interactionism provides opportunities for researchers and teachers to join together in doing research, thus promoting professionalism and helping to effect change from the inside, as it were. The researcher's theoretical and methodological knowledge and the teacher's practical knowledge of teaching make a strong combination, the one enriching the other (Pollard, 1984; Woods 1985, 1986, 1989; Hustler, Cassidy, and Cuff, 1986; Woods and Pollard, 1988). This entails a model of teacher as "reflective practitioner" (Schön, 1983), theoretically aware, and seeking ways of applying scientific knowledge to practical problem-solving. This is consonant with the "transformative," "emancipatory," "empowering" (i.e., of members) approach of critical ethnography (see Lather, 1986; Anderson, 1989; Troyna and Carrington, 1989). We might expect collaborative work to increase, therefore, in the future.

D. H. Hargreaves' article entitled "Whatever Happened to Symbolic Interactionism?" was intended as a rallying-cry for an approach that the author clearly feared was becoming less commonly practiced, due to change in fashion, before it had reached its potential. What he was witnessing, I suggest, was not necessarily a slackened interest in symbolic interactionism but, rather, the demise of "the paradigmatic mentality" (Hammersley, 1984), which had divided social scientific research into "positivists" and "interpretivists." The move away from paradigms was to herald a number of syntheses in which interactionism was to play its full part.

Prominent among these has been the increasing recognition that far from being mutually exclusive, qualitative and quantitative research methods gain strength from each other when used together. As King (1987) argues, "There is no best method in the sociology of education", only suitable and feasible methods, so we should try to use as many as possible" (p. 243). Webb *et al.* (1966) also argue for "multi-techniques" because each has its strengths and weaknesses, and the former can help bolster the latter. Trow (1957) points out that "The problem under investigation properly dictates the methods of investigation" (p. 33). Sieber (1972) has itemized the various ways in which fieldwork and surveys complement each other (see also Zelditch, 1963; Denzin, 1978; Jick, 1983; Atkinson, Delamont, and Hammersley, 1988).

We have noted how interactionism can help bring together cognition and affectivity, and micro and macro. It also amalgamates art and science. This manifests itself in various ways—the "brilliance of the prose," which "has to creep around inside our own belief systems and dig these elements and objects out and present them to our gaze" (Goffman *in* Taylor, 1987:155), "poetic eloquence" (McLaren *in* Newman, 1989), and the graphic, almost alive, evocations of interaction in Willis (1977), Riseborough (1981), or Beynon (1985). More important than these end-products is how art and science combine in the production of research. Nisbet (1962) argued that these had become separated in the nineteenth century, the one associated with genius, inspiration, and beauty, the other with carefully controlled method and objectivity [see also Bruyn's (1966) discussion of C. P. Snow's "The Two Cultures"]. But this is a false distinction, because both are concerned with reality and are necessary to each other. The one provides ideas, hunches, and "leaps of the imagination"; the other disciplines, regulates, checks, and tests. The one inspires to represent culture, biographies, and activities as they are lived and experienced in, sometimes, almost poetic terms; the other ensures that there is no poetic license, that this is really what happened. The one facilitates the identification of patterns, themes, and connections that will assist the emergence of concepts and theory; the other monitors these ideas, rejecting those that are unsatisfactory by scientific criteria, ordering and arranging others, and comparing them with others elsewhere.

This, some might argue, is no more than an expression of the "I" and the "Me" and their essential dialectic for the unity of the self. If art and science do need to be brought together, interactionism has good qualifications to promote the amalgamation and to help produce a most human science.

Note

[1] The term "race" is enclosed in quotation marks according to British practice, denoting that the concept has no scientific basis.

Acknowledgments

I am grateful to Margaret LeCompte, Wendy Millroy, Judith Preissle, and Martyn Hammersley for their comments on a previous draft of this article.

References

Abraham, J. (1989). Testing Hargreaves' and Lacey's differentiation–polarisation theory in a setted comprehensive. *The British Journal of Sociology*, 40(1), 46–81.

Aggleton, P. (1987). *Rebels without a cause*. London: Falmer Press.

Althusser, L. (1971). Ideology and ideological state apparatuses. *In* L. Althusser (Ed.), *Lenin and philosophy and other essays* (pp. 123–173). London: New Left Books.

American Sociologist, The. (1968). Toward a code of ethics. 3, 316–318.

Anderson, N. (1923). *The hobo*. Chicago: University of Chicago Press.

Anderson, G. L. (1989). Critical ethnography in education: Origins, current status and new directions. *Review of Educational Research*, 59(3), 249–270.

Anyon, J. (1981). Social class and school knowledge. *Curriculum Inquiry*, 11(1), 3–41.

Atkinson, J. M. (1977). Coroners and the categorization of deaths as suicides. *In* C. Bell and H. Newby (Eds.), *Doing sociological research* (pp. 31–46). London: Allen and Unwin.

Atkinson, P., and Delamont, S. (1986). Bread and dreams or bread and circuses? A critique of "case study" research in education." *In* M. Hammersley (Ed.), *Controversies in classroom research* (pp. 238–255). Milton Keynes, England: Open University Press.

Atkinson, P., Delamont, S., and Hammersley, M. (1988). Qualitative research traditions: A British response to Jacob. *Review of Educational Research,* 58(2), 231–250.

Baldwin, J. D. (1986). *George Herbert Mead: A unifying theory for sociology.* Beverly Hills, CA: Sage Publications.

Ball, S. J. (1980). Initial encounters in the classroom and the process of establishment. *In* P. Woods (Ed.) *Pupil strategies.* London: Croom Helm.

Ball, S. J. (1981). *Beachside comprehensive.* Cambridge: Cambridge University Press.

Ball, S. J. (1984). Beachside reconsidered: Reflections on a methodological apprenticeship. *In* R. G. Burgess (Ed.), *The research process in educational settings: Ten case studies* (pp. 69–96). London: Falmer Press.

Ball, S. J., and Goodson, I. F. (Eds.). (1985). *Teachers' lives and careers.* Lewes: Falmer Press.

Bandura, A. (1969). Social learning theory of identificatory processes. *In* D. A. Goslin (Ed.), *Handbook of socialization theory and research.* Chicago: Rand McNally.

Becker, E. (1971). *The birth and death of meaning* (2nd ed.). New York: Free Press.

Becker, H. S. (1960). Notes on the concept of commitment. *American Journal of Sociology,* 66(July), 32–40.

Becker, H. S. (1963). *Outsiders: Studies in the sociology of deviance.* New York: Free Press.

Becker, H. S. (1964). Personal change in adult life. *Sociometry,* 27(1), 40–53.

Becker, H. S. (1967). Whose side are we on. *Social Problems,* 14, 239–247.

Becker, H. S. (1970). *Sociological work.* Chicago: Aldine.

Becker, H. S. (1977a). Personal change in adult life. *In* B. R. Cosin *et al.* (Ed.), *School and society* (2nd ed., pp. 57–63). London: Routledge and Kegan Paul.

Becker, H. S. (1977b). Social class variations in the teacher–pupil relationship. *In* B. R. Cosin *et al.* (Eds.), *School and society* (2nd ed., pp. 107–113). London: Routledge and Kegan Paul.

Becker, H. S., and Geer, B. (1960). Participant observation: The analysis of qualitative field data. *In* R. N. Adams and J. J. Preiss (Eds.), *Human organization research: Field relations and technique* (pp. 267–289). Homewood, IL: Dorsey Press.

Becker, H. S., et al. (1961). *Boys in white: Student culture in medical school.* Chicago: University of Chicago Press.

Becker, H. S., Geer, B., Riesman, D., and Weiss, R. S. (Eds.). (1968). *Institutions and the person.* Chicago: Aldine.

Bennett, N., Desforges, C., Cockburn, A., and Wilkinson, B. (1984). *The quality of pupil learning experiences.* London: Lawrence Erlbaum.

Berger, P. (1966). *Invitation to sociology.* Harmondsworth, England: Penguin.

Berger, P. L., and Luckmann, T. (1967). *The social construction of reality.* Harmondsworth, England: Penguin.

Bertaux, D. (Ed.). (1981). *Biography and society.* Beverly Hills, CA: Sage Publications.

Beynon, J. (1985). *Initial encounters in the secondary school.* London: Falmer Press.

Birksted, I. (1976). School versus pop culture? A case study of adolescent adaptation. *Research in Education,* 16(November), 13–23.

Blumer, H. (1954). What is wrong with social theory. *American Sociological Review,* 13, 3–12.

Blumer, H. (1962). Society as symbolic interaction. *In* A. M. Rose (Ed.), *Human behaviour and social processes* (pp. 179–192). London: Routledge and Kegan Paul.

Blumer, H. (1969). *Symbolic interactionism.* Englewood Cliffs, NJ: Prentice-Hall.

Blumer, H. (1976). The methodological position of symbolic interactionism. *In* M. Hammersley and P. Woods (Eds.), *The process of schooling* (pp. 12–18). London: Routledge and Kegan Paul.

Blumer, H. (1977). Sociological implications of the thought of George Herbert Mead. *In* B. Cosin, I. R. Dale, G. M. Esland, D. Mackinnon, and D. F. Swift (Eds.), *School and society: A sociological reader* (pp. 11–17). London: Routledge and Kegan Paul.

Bogdan, R., and Taylor, S. J. (1975). *Introduction to qualitative research methods*. New York: John Wiley.

Bowles, S., and Gintis, H. (1976). *Schooling in capitalist America*. London: Routledge and Kegan Paul.

Brown, G. W. (1973). Some thoughts on grounded theory. *Sociology, 7*(1), 1–16.

Bruyn, S. T. (1966). *The human perspective in sociology: The methodology of participant observation*. Englewood Cliffs, NJ: Prentice-Hall.

Bulmer, M. (1979). Concepts in the analysis of qualitative data. *Sociological Review, 27*(4), 651–677.

Bulmer, M. (1980). Comment on the ethics of covert methods. *British Journal of Sociology, 31*(1), 59–65.

Bulmer, M. (1982). The merits and demerits of covert participant observation. *In* M. Bulmer (Ed.), *Social research ethics* (pp. 217–251). London: Macmillan.

Bulmer, M. (1984). *The Chicago School of sociology*. Chicago: University of Chicago Press.

Burgess, E. W. (1929). Basic social data. *In* T. V. Smith and L. D. White (Eds.), *Chicago: An experiment in social science research* (pp. 47–66). Chicago: University of Chicago Press.

Burgess, R. G. (Ed.). (1982). *Field research: A sourcebook and field manual*. London: Allen and Unwin.

Burgess, R. G. (1984a). *In the field: An introduction to field research*. London: Allen and Unwin.

Burgess, R. G. (Ed.). (1984b). *The research process in educational settings: Ten case studies*. London: Falmer Press.

Burgess, R. G. (Ed.). (1985a). *Field methods in the study of education*. London: Falmer Press.

Burgess, R. G. (1985b). *Issues in educational research*. London: Falmer Press.

Burgess, R. G. (1985c). The whole truth? Some ethical problems of research in the comprehensive school. *In* R. G. Burgess (Ed.), *Field methods in the study of education* (pp. 139–162). London: Falmer Press.

Burke, J. (1986). *Concordia sixth form college: A sociological case study based on history and ethnography*. D. Phil. thesis, University of Sussex.

Carrington, B., and Short, G. (1989). *"Race" and the primary school*. London: NFER–Nelson.

Cavan, R. S. (1928). *Suicide*. Chicago: University of Chicago Press.

Cohen, S. (1968). Vandalism: Its politics and nature. *New Society, 12 December,* 316–317.

Corrigan, P. (1979). *Schooling the Smash Street kids*. London: Macmillan.

Cressey, D. (1932). *The taxi dance hall*. Chicago: University of Chicago Press.

Dale, R. R., and Griffith, S. (1966). *Downstream*. London: Routledge and Kegan Paul.

Davey, A. G., and Mullin, P. N. (1982). Inter-ethnic friendship in British primary schools. *Educational Research, 24,* 83–92.

Davies, B. (1982). *Life in the classroom and playground: The accounts of primary school children*. London: Routledge and Kegan Paul.

Davies, L. (1984). *Pupil power: Deviance and gender in school*. London: Falmer Press.

Davis, F. (1963). *Passage through crisis: Polio victims and their families*. Indianapolis, IN: Bobs–Merrill.

Dean, J. P. (1954). Participant observation and interviewing. *In* J. Doby, E. A. Suchman, J. C. McKinnet, R. G. Francis, and J. P. Dean (Eds.), *An introduction to social research* (pp. 225–252). Harrisburg, PA: The Stackpole Co.

Dean, J. P., and Whyte, W. F. (1958). How do you know if the informant is telling the truth? *Human Organisation*, 17(2), 34–38.

Delamont, S. (1984). The old girl network: Reflections on the fieldwork at St Lukes. *In* R. G. Burgess (Ed.), *The research process in educational settings: Ten case studies* (pp. 15–38). London: Falmer Press.

Delamont, S., and Galton, M. (1986). *Inside the secondary classroom*. London: Routledge and Kegan Paul.

Denscombe, M. (1980). Pupil strategies and the open classroom. *In* P. Woods (Ed.), *Pupil strategies* (pp. 50–73). London: Croom Helm.

Denscombe, M., Szule, H., Patrick, C., and Wood, A. (1986). Ethnicity and friendship: The contrast between sociometric research and fieldwork observation in primary school classrooms. *British Educational Research Journal*, 12(3), 221–235.

Denzin, N. (1968). On the ethics of disguised observation: An exchange between Norman Denzin and Kai Erikson. *Social Problems*, 15, 502–506.

Denzin, N. (1978). *The research act in sociology: A theoretical introduction to sociological methods* (2nd ed.). London: Butterworth.

Department of Education and Science. (1983). *Teaching quality*. London: Her Majesty's Stationery Office.

Dingwall, R. (1980). Ethics and ethnography. *Sociological Review*, 28(4), 871–891.

Ditton, J. (1977). *Part-time crime: An ethnography of fiddling and pilferage*. London: Macmillan.

Dollard, J. (1935). *Criteria for the life history*. New York: Libraries Press.

Douglas, J. D. (1970). *Understanding everyday life*. Chicago: Aldine.

Dumont, R. V., and Wax, M. L. (1977). Cherokee school society and the intercultural classroom. *In* B. R. Cosin, I. R. Dale, G. M. Esland, D. Mackinnon, and D. F. Swift (Eds.), *School and society* (2nd ed.), pp. 70–78). London: Routledge and Kegan Paul.

Festinger, L., *et al.* (1956). *When prophecy fails*. Minneapolis: University of Minneapolis Press.

Fielding, N. (1981). *The national front*. London: Routledge and Kegan Paul.

Finch, J. (1986). *Research and policy*. London: Falmer Press.

Foster, P. M. (1990). *Policy and practice in multicultural and anti-racist education: A case study of a multi-ethnic comprehensive school*. London: Routledge.

Friedson, E. (1972). *Medical men and their work*. Chicago: Aldine.

Fuller, M. (1980). Black girls in a London comprehensive school. *In* R. Deem (Ed.), *Schooling for women's work* (pp. 52–65). London: Routledge and Kegan Paul.

Furlong, J. (1977). Anancy goes to school; a case study of pupil knowledge of their teachers. *In* P. Woods and M. Hammersley (Eds.), *School experience* (pp. 162–185). London: Croom Helm.

Furlong, V. J. (1976). Interaction sets in the classroom: Towards a study of pupil knowledge. *In* M. Hammersley and P. Woods (Eds.), *The process of schooling* (pp. 160–170). London: Routledge and Kegan Paul.

Gans, H. J. (1968). The participant observer as a human being: Observations on the personal aspects of fieldwork. *In* H. S. Becker, B. Geer, D. Riesman, and R. S. Weiss (Eds.), *Institutions and the person* (pp. 300–317). Chicago: Aldine.

Geertz, C. (1973). Thick description: Toward an interpretive theory of culture. *In* C. Geertz (Ed.), *The interpretation of cultures: Selected essays by Clifford Geertz*. New York: Basic Books.

Gillborn, D. (1990). Sexism and curricular "choice." *Cambridge Journal of Education,* 20(2), 161–174.

Glaser, B., and Strauss, A. (1965). *Awareness of dying*. Chicago: Aldine.

Glaser, B., and Strauss, A. (1968). *Time for dying*. Chicago: Aldine.

Glaser, B. G., and Strauss, A. L. (1967). *The discovery of grounded theory*. London: Weidenfeld and Nicolson.

Goetz, J. P., and LeCompte, M. D. (1984). *Ethnography and qualitative design in educational research*. New York: Academic Press.

Goffman, E. (1959). *The presentation of self in everyday life*. Garden City, NY: Doubleday.

Goffman, E. (1961). *Encounters*. New York: Bobbs-Merrill.

Goffman, E. (1968). *Asylums*. Harmondsworth, England: Penguin.

Goodson, I. (1980). Life histories and the study of schooling. *Interchange*, 11(4), 62–76.

Gracey, H. (1972). *Curriculum or craftsmanship: Elementary school teachers in a bureaucratic system*. Chicago: University of Chicago Press.

Grove, R. W. (1988). An analysis of the constant comparative method. *International Journal of Qualitative Studies in Education*, 1(3), 273–279.

Grugeon, E., and Woods, P. (1990). *Educating all: Multicultural perspectives in the primary school*. London: Routledge.

Hammersley, M. (1980). On interactionist empiricism. *In* P. Woods (Ed.), *Pupil strategies* (pp. 198–213). London: Croom Helm.

Hammersley, M. (Ed.). (1983). *The ethnography of schooling*. Driffield, England: Nafferton Books.

Hammersley, M. (1984). The paradigmatic mentality: A diagnosis. *In* L. Barton and S. Walker (Eds.), *Social crisis and educational research* (pp. 230–255). London: Croom Helm.

Hammersley, M. (1987). Ethnography and the cumulative development of theory. *British Educational Research Journal*, 13(3), 283–296.

Hammersley, M. (1989). *The dilemma of qualitative method: Herbert Bulmer and the Chicago tradition*. London: Routledge.

Hammersley, M., and Atkinson, P. (1983). *Ethnography: Principles in practice*. London: Tavistock.

Hammersley, M., and Turner, G. (1980). Conformist pupils? *In* P. Woods (Ed.), *Pupil strategies: Explorations in the sociology of the school* (pp. 48–66). London: Croom Helm.

Hammersley, M., Scarth, J., and Webb, S. (1985). Developing and testing theory: The case of research on pupil learning and examinations. *In* R. G. Burgess (Ed.), *Issues in educational research* (pp. 48–66). London: Falmer Press.

Hargreaves, A. (1978). Towards a theory of classroom strategies. *In* L. Barton and R. Meighan (Eds.), *Sociological interpretations of schooling and classrooms* (pp. 73–100). Driffield, England: Nafferton Books.

Hargreaves, A. (1980). Synthesis and the study of strategies: A project for the sociological imagination. *In* P. Woods (Ed.), *Pupil strategies* (pp. 162–197). London: Croom Helm.

Hargreaves, A. (1984a). Contrastive rhetoric and extremist talk. *In* A. Hargreaves and P. Woods (Eds.), *Classrooms and staffrooms* (pp. 215–231). Milton Keynes: Open University Press.

Hargreaves, A. (1984b). Marxism and relative autonomy. Unit 22, Course E205, *Conflict and Change in Education*. Milton Keynes, England: Open University Press.

Hargreaves, A. (1985). The micro–macro problem in the sociology of education. *In* R. G. Burgess (Ed.), *Issues in educational research* (pp. 21–47). London: Falmer Press.

Hargreaves, A. (1987). Past, imperfect, tense: Reflections on an ethnographic and historical study of middle schools. *In* G. Walford (Ed.), *Doing sociology of education* (pp. 17–44). London: Falmer Press.

Hargreaves, A. (1988). Teaching quality: A sociological analysis. *Journal of Curriculum Studies*, 20(3), 211–231.

Hargreaves, D. H. (1967). *Social relations in a secondary school*. London: Routledge and Kegan Paul.

Hargreaves, D. H. (1976). Reactions to labelling. *In* M. Hammersley and P. Woods (Eds.), *The process of schooling* (pp. 201–207). London: Routledge and Kegan Paul.

Hargreaves, D. H. (1978a). Whatever happened to symbolic interactionism? *In* L. Barton and R. Meighan (Eds.), *Sociological interpretations of schooling and classroom: A reappraisal* (pp. 7–22). Driffield, England: Nafferton Books.

Hargreaves, D. H. (1978b). What teaching does to teachers. *New Society, 9 March*, 540–542.

Hargreaves, D. H., Hester, S. K., and Mellor, F. J. (1975). *Deviance in classrooms*. London: Routledge and Kegan Paul.

Hart, M. (1976). *When marriage ends: A study in status passage*. London: Tavistock.

Hewitt, J. P., and Hewitt, M. L. (1986). *Introducing sociology: A symbolic interactionist perspective*. Englewood Cliffs, NJ: Prentice-Hall.

Holdaway, S. (1982). An "inside job": A case study of covert research on the police. *In* M. Bulmer (Ed.), *Social research ethics* (pp. 59–79). London: Macmillan.

Homan, R. (1980). The ethics of covert methods. *British Journal of Sociology*, 31(1), 46–59.

Humphreys, L. (1975). *Tearoom trade* (2nd ed.). Chicago: Aldine.

Hunt, J. C. (1989). *Psychological aspects of fieldwork*. New York: Sage Publications.

Hustler, D., Cassidy, A., and Cuff, E. C. (Eds.). (1986). *Action research in classrooms and schools*. London: Allen and Unwin.

Hutchinson, S. (1988). Education and grounded theory. *In* R. R. Sherman and R. B. Webb (Eds.), *Qualitative research in education: Focus and methods* (pp. 123–140). London: Falmer Press.

Jick, T. D. (1983). Mixing qualitative and quantitative methods: Triangulation in action. *In* J. Van Maanen (Ed.), *Qualitative methodology* (pp. 135–148). Beverly Hills, CA: Sage Publications.

Jordan, J., and Lacey, C. (1989). Teacher education, the sociological imagination and restricted case study. *In* P. Woods and A. Pollard (Eds.), *Sociology and teaching: A new challenge for the sociology of education* (pp. 117–138). London: Croom Helm.

Keddie, N. (1971). Classroom knowledge. *In* M. F. D. Young (Ed.), *Knowledge and control* (pp. 133–160). London: Collier–Macmillan.

King, R. A. (1978). *All things bright and beautiful*. Chichester: Wiley.

King, R. A. (1987). No best method—Qualitative *and* quantitative research in the sociology of Education. *In* G. Walford (Ed.), *Doing sociology of education* (pp. 231–246). London: Falmer Press.

Lacey, C. (1970). *Hightown grammar*. Manchester: Manchester University Press.

Lacey, C. (1976). Problems of sociological fieldwork: A review of the methodology of Hightown Grammar. *In* M. Hammersley and P. Woods (Eds.), *The process of schooling* (pp. 55–65). London: Routledge and Paul.

Lacey, C. (1977). *The socialization of teachers*. London: Methuen.

Laing, R. D. (1967). *The politics of experience*. Harmondsworth, England: Penguin.

Lather, P. (1986). Research as praxis. *Harvard Educational Review*, 56(3), 257–277.

Lemert, E. M. (1967). *Human deviance, social problems and social control*. New York: Prentice-Hall.

Lincoln, Y., and Guba, E. (1985). *Naturalistic inquiry*. New York: Sage Publications.

Llewellyn, M. (1980). Studying girls at school: The implications of confusion. *In* R. Deem (Ed.), *Schooling for women's work*. London: Routledge and Kegan Paul.

Lofland, J. (1971). *Analysing social settings: A guide to qualitative observation and analysis*. New York: Wadsworth Publishing.

Luckmann, T. (1967). *The invisible religion*. New York: Macmillan.

McCall, G. J., and Simmons, J. L. (Eds.). (1969). *Issues in participant observation*. Reading, MA: Addison-Wesley.

Mac an Ghaill, M. (1988). *Young, gifted and black*. Milton Keynes, England: Open University Press.

Mac an Ghaill, M. (1989). Beyond the white norm: The use of qualitative methods in the study of black youths' schooling in England. *Qualitative Studies in Education*, 2(3), 175–189.

Mackay, R. (1973). Conceptions of children and models of socialization. *In* H. P. Dreitzel (Ed.), *Recent sociology No. 5, Childhood and socialization* (pp. 27–43). New York: Macmillan.

Mahoney, P. (1985). *Schools for the boys*. London: Hutchinson.

Malinowski, B. (1922). *Argonauts of the Western Pacific*. London: Routledge and Kegan Paul.

Matza, D. (1969). *Becoming deviant*. Englewood Cliffs, NJ: Prentice-Hall.

Mead, G. H. (1929). The nature of the past. *In* J. Coss (Ed.), *Essays in honour of John Dewey* (pp. 235–242). New York: Henry Holt.

Mead, G. H. (1934). *Mind, self and society*. Chicago: University of Chicago Press.

Mealyea, R. (1989). Humour as a coping strategy. *British Journal of Sociology of Education*, 10(3), 311–333.

Measor, L. (1983). Gender and the sciences: Pupils' gender-based conceptions of school subjects. *In* M. Hammersley and A. Hargreaves (Eds.), *Curriculum practice: Some sociological case studies* (pp. 171–191). London: Falmer Press.

Measor, L. (1989). Sex education and adolescent sexuality. *In* L. Holly (Ed.), *Girls and sexuality: Learning and teaching*. Milton Keynes, England: Open University Press.

Measor, L., and Woods, P. (1983). The interpretation of pupil myths. *In* M. Hammersby (Ed.), *The ethnography of schooling* (pp. 55–76). Driffield, England: Nafferton.

Measor, L., and Woods, P. (1984). *Changing schools: Pupil perspectives on transfer to a comprehensive*. Milton Keynes, England: Open University Press.

Metz, M. H. (1990). Social class context, teacher's identity and daily practice in American high schools. Paper presented at International Sociological Association XIIth World Congress of Sociology, *Sociology for one world: Unity and diversity*, Madrid.

Mills, C. W. (1959). *The sociological imagination*. New York: Oxford University Press.

Newman, A. J. (1989). Review of P. McLaren (1989), Life in schools: An introduction to critical pedagogy in the foundations of education. *International Journal of Qualitative Studies in Education*, 2(3), 269–270.

Nias, J. (1981). Commitment and motivation in primary school teachers. *Educational Review*, 33(3), 181–190.

Nias, J. (1989). *Primary teachers talking: A study of teaching as work*. London: Routledge.

Nias, J. (1991). Primary teachers talking: A reflexive account of longitudinal research. *In* G. Walford (Ed.), *Doing educational research* (pp. 147–165). London: Routledge.

Nisbet, R. (1962). Sociology as an art form. *Pacific Sociological Review*, Autumn, 145–165.

Oakley, A. (1980). *Women confined: Towards a sociology of childbirth*. Oxford: Martin Robertson.

Open University. (1972). *School and society (course E282)*. Milton Keynes, England: Open University Press.

Parker, H. J. (1974). *View from the boys*. Newton Abbot, England: David and Charles.

Patrick, J. (1973). *A Glasgow gang observed*. London: Eyre Methuen.

Paul, D. (1953). Interview techniques and field relationships. *In* A. L. Kroeber *et al.* (Eds.), *Anthropology today* (pp. 430–451). Chicago: University of Chicago Press.

Pollard, A. (1980). Teacher interests and changing situations of survival threat in primary school classrooms. *In* P. Woods (Ed.), *Teacher strategies* (pp. 34–60). London: Croom Helm.

Pollard, A. (1982). A model of coping strategies. *British Journal of Sociology of Education*, 3(1), 19–37.

Pollard, A. (1984). Ethnography and social policy for classroom practice. *In* L. Barton and S. Walker (Eds.), *Social crisis and educational research*. London: Croom Helm.

Pollard, A. (1985). *The social world of the primary school*. London: Holt, Rinehart & Winston.

Richards, M., and Light, P. (Eds.). (1986). *Children of social worlds*. Cambridge: Policy Press.

Riseborough, G. F. (1981). Teacher careers and comprehensive schooling: An empirical study. *Sociology*, 15(3), 352–381.

Rock, P. (1979). *The making of symbolic interactionism*. London: Macmillan.

Rose, A. M. (1962). A systematic summary of symbolic interaction theory. *In* A. M. Rose (Ed.), *Human behaviour and social processes* (pp. 3–19). London: Routledge and Kegan Paul.

Rosenhan, D. L. (1982). On being sane in insane places. *In* M. Bulmer (Ed.), *Social research ethics: An examination of the merits of covert participant observation* (pp. 15–37). London: Macmillan.

Rosie, A. (1988). An ethnographic study of a YTS course. *In* A. Pollard, J. Purvis, and G. Walford (Eds.), *Education, training and the new vocationalism* (pp. 148–164). Milton Keynes, England: Open University Press.

Rosser, E., and Harré, R. (1976). The meaning of disorder. *In* M. Hammersley and P. Woods (Eds.), *The process of schooling* (pp. 171–177). London: Routledge and Kegan Paul.

Roth, J. A. (1962). Comments on "secret observation." *Social Problems*, 9(3), 283–284.

Roth, J. A. (1963). *Timetables*. New York: Bobbs–Merrill.

Scarth, J., and Hammersley, M. (1988). Examinations and testing: An exploratory study. *British Educational Research Journal*, 14(3), 231–249.

Schatzman, L., and Strauss, A. (1973). *Field research: Strategies for a natural sociology*. Englewood Cliffs, NJ: Prentice-Hall.

Schön, D. A. (1983). *The reflective practitioner: How professionals think in action*. London: Temple Smith.

Schutz, A. (1967). *Collected papers*. The Hague: Nijhoff.

Seeley, J. (1966). The "making" and "taking" of problems. *Social Problems*, 14, 382–389.

Sharp, R., and Green, A. (1975). *Education and social control*. London: Routledge and Kegan Paul.

Shaw, C. R. (1930). *The Jack-Roller: A delinquent boy's own story*. Chicago: University of Chicago Press.

Sherman, R. R., and Webb, R. B. (Eds.), (1988). *Qualitative research in education: Focus and methods.* London: Falmer Press.

Shibutani, T. (1961). *Society and personality.* Englewood Cliffs, NJ: Prentice-Hall.

Sieber, S. D. (1972). The integration of fieldwork and survey methods. *American Journal of Sociology,* 78(6), 1335–1359.

Sikes, P., Measor, L., and Woods, P. (1985). *Teacher careers: Crises and continuities.* London: Falmer Press.

Silvers, R. J. (1977). Appearances: A videographic study of children's culture. *In* P. Woods and M. Hammersley (Eds.), *School experience* (pp. 129–161). London: Croom Helm.

Skinner, B. F. (1953). *Science and human behaviour.* New York: Macmillan.

Soltis, J. F. (1989). The ethics of qualitative research. *International Journal of Qualitative Studies in Education,* 2(2), 123–130.

Stanley, J. (1986). Sex and the quiet schoolgirl. *British Journal of Sociology of Education,* 7(3), 275–286.

Stanley, J. R. (1989). *Marks on the memory: The pupils' experience of school.* Milton Keynes, England: Open University Press.

Strauss, A. L. (1959). *Mirrors and masks: The search for identity.* San Francisco: The Sociological Press.

Strauss, A. L. (1987). *Qualitative analysis for social scientists.* Cambridge: Cambridge University Press.

Sudnow, D. (1971). Dead on arrival. *In* I. Horowitz and M. S. Strong (Eds.), *Sociological realities: A guide to the study of society.* New York: Harper & Row.

Taylor, L. (1987). Interview with Bob Mullan. *In* B. Mullan, *Sociologists on sociology* (pp. 142–165). London: Croom Helm.

Thapan, M. (1986). Forms of discourse: A typology of teachers and commitment. *British Journal of Sociology of Education,* 7(4), 415–431.

Thomas, W. I. (1928). *The child in America.* New York: Alfred A. Knopf.

Thomas, W. I., and Znaniekci, F. (1927). *The Polish peasant in Europe and America.* New York: Alfred A. Knopf.

Thrasher, F. (1927). *The gang: A study of 1,313 gangs in Chicago.* Chicago: University of Chicago Press.

Tizard, B., and Hughes, M. (1984). *Young children learning: Talking and thinking at home and school.* London: Fontana.

Trow, M. (1957). Comment on participant observation and interviewing: A comparison. *Human Organization,* 16(3), 33.

Troyna, B., and Carrington, B. (1989). Whose side are we on? Ethical dilemmas in research on "race" and education. *In* R. Burgess (Ed.), *The ethics of educational research* (pp. 205–223). London: Falmer Press.

Turner, G. (1983). *The social world of the comprehensive school.* London: Croom Helm.

Turner, R. H. (1962). Role-taking: Process versus conformity. *In* A. M. Rose (Ed.), *Human behaviour and social processes* (pp. 20–40). London: Routledge and Kegan Paul.

Van Gennep, A. (1960). *The rites of passage.* London: Routledge and Kegan Paul.

Waller, W. (1932). *The sociology of teaching.* New York: Wiley.

Watson, J. B. (1913). Psychology as the behaviourist views it. *Psychological Review,* 20, 158–177.

Wax, R. H. (1971). *Doing fieldwork; Warnings and advice.* Chicago: University of Chicago Press.

Webb, E. J., Campbell, D. T., Schwartz, R. D., and Sechrest, L. (1966). *Unobtrusive measures: Nonreactive research in the social sciences.* Chicago: Rand McNally.

Werthman, C. (1963). Delinquents in school: A test for the legitimacy of authority. *Berkeley Journal of Sociology,* 8(1), 39–60. [*Also in* Hammersley, M., and Woods, P. (1984). *Life in school: The sociology of pupil culture* (pp. 211–224). Milton Keynes, England: Open University Press.]

Whitty, G. J. (1974). Sociology and the problem of radical educational change: Towards a reconceptualization of the new sociology of education. *In* M. Flude and J. Ahier (Eds.), *Educability, schools and ideology* (pp. 112–137). London: Croom Helm.

Whyte, W. F. (1955). *Street corner society.* Chicago: University of Chicago Press.

Williams, R. (1976). Symbolic interactionism: The fusion of theory and research? *In* D. C. Thorns (Ed.), *New directions in sociology* (pp. 115–137). Newton Abbott, England: David and Charles.

Willis, P. (1977). *Learning to labour.* Farnborough: Saxon House.

Willis, P. (1978). *Profane culture.* London: Routledge and Kegan Paul.

Wilson, S. (1977). The use of ethnographic techniques in educational research. *Review of Educational Research,* 47(1), 245–265.

Woods, P. (1979). *The divided school.* London: Routledge and Kegan Paul.

Woods, P. (1983). *Sociology and the school.* London: Routledge and Kegan Paul.

Woods, P. (1985). Conversations with teachers: Aspects of life history method. *British Educational Research Journal,* 11(1), 13–26.

Woods, P. (1986). *Inside schools: Ethnography in educational research.* London: Routledge and Kegan Paul.

Woods, P. (Ed.). (1989). *Working for teacher development.* Cambridge: Peter Francis.

Woods, P. (1990a). *Teacher skills and strategies.* London: Falmer Press.

Woods, P. (1990b). *The happiest days? How pupils cope with school.* Lewes: Falmer Press.

Woods, P., and Pollard, A. (Eds.). (1988). *Sociology and teaching.* London: Croom Helm.

Woods, P., and Sikes, P. J. (1987). The use of teacher biographies in professional self-development. *In* F. Todd (Ed.), *Planning continuing professional development* (pp. 161–180). London: Croom Helm.

Wright, C. (1986). School processes—An ethnographic study. *In* J. Eggleston, D. Dunn, and M. Anjali (Eds.), *Education for some: The educational and vocational experiences of 15–18 year old members of minority ethnic groups* (pp. 127–179). Stoke on Trent: Trentham Books.

Yablonsky, L. (1968). *The hippie trip.* New York: Western Publishing Company.

Young, M. F. D. (Ed.). (1971). *Knowledge and control: New directions for the sociology of education.* London: Collier–Macmillan.

Zelditch, M. (1963). Some methodological problems of field studies. *American Journal of Sociology,* 67, 566–576.

CHAPTER 9

☐ Sociology Unleashed: Creative Directions in Classical Ethnography

Linda Grant and Gary Alan Fine

The Handbook of Qualitative
Research in Education

Until recently an orphaned stepchild in the field of sociology, qualitative methodology has achieved some measure of prestige in the past decade, recapturing some of the centrality this methodology had in the first half of the century. For many academics, qualitative research is a rich and provocative methodology. Whether this is due to the maturation of a group of sociologists whose perspectives were formed in the 1960s, the decreased amount of funding available during the Reagan years, changes in the gender composition of sociology faculties, or the closer ties between the social sciences and the humanities, previously dominant survey research and other quantitative methodology is no longer so dominant, and qualitative research is on the upswing.

The rich, qualitative tradition in American sociology—traceable primarily to symbolic interactionists and urban ethnographers associated with the Chicago School—reached its nadir in terms of visibility in the 1970s, the period of hegemony of quantitative analysis in sociology and other social sciences (Mullins, 1983). Certainly during this period there was a body of significant qualitative research studies, such as *The Social Order of the Slum* (Suttles, 1968), *Tally's Corner* (Liebow, 1967), *Passing On* (Sudnow, 1967), and *Everything in Its Path* (Erikson, 1977), but it would be fair to say that the sociological mainstream was skeptical of this approach. Even the graduate students who had so advanced qualitative field research in the 1950s at the University of Chicago (e.g., Erving Goffman, Fred Davis, Howard Becker) were no longer actively conducting qualitative field research by the 1960s and 1970s.

By the late 1980s, the health of qualitative sociology was more robust. Three journals devoted to qualitative sociology—*Symbolic Interaction, Qualitative Sociology,* and *Journal of Contemporary Ethnography* (formerly *Urban Life,* formerly *Urban Life and Culture*)—organized in the 1970s, are stronger than ever, with expanding readership and increasing numbers of submissions. One, *Symbolic Interaction,* recently expanded from a semiannual to a quarterly to accommodate increased submissions and readership. Furthermore, although quantitative analysis still is more common than qualitative sociology in major national, regional, and specialty journals, the proportion of qualitative papers published in these journals has almost doubled in the last 15 years (Grant and Ward, 1991; Grant, Ward, and Rong, 1987; Ward and Grant, 1985). The increase is impressive, especially because many qualitative studies are published in book rather than journal form. Several respected research annuals, in particular *Sociological*

Studies in Child Development, Research in the Sociology of Health Care, and *Studies in Symbolic Interactionism,* also have helped disseminate qualitative sociological work to wider audiences, as have edited volumes composed of qualitative studies in many substantive subareas of sociology.

The teaching of qualitative methods also expanded in the 1980s. Graduate departments in sociology offered required or elective course work in qualitative and/or sociohistorical methods (*Footnotes,* 1988). Teaching of qualitative sociology has been facilitated, not only by an outpouring of qualitative studies in sociology, but also by a dramatically greater availability of discussions of qualitative sociological inquiry. The Sage series of qualitative methods monographs, launched in the 1980s to parallel the publisher's successful and longer-standing series in quantitative analysis, is a notable instance of the expansion in pedagogical tools. A decade ago, most sociological teaching of field methods relied heavily on a few classic works: Glaser and Strauss' (1967) theoretical statement of the logic of inductive inquiry; Schatzman and Strauss' (1973) "how-to" manual for conducting qualitative inquiry; Spradley's richly detailed volumes on participant observation (Spradley, 1980) and ethnographic interviewing (Spradley, 1977); McCall and Simmons' (1969) text-reader on participant observation; and Denzin's (1970) volume on links between theory and research.

In the last decade, qualitative sociologists (along with their cousins in the other social science disciplines) in the United States and abroad have published articles and books that substantially expand the theoretical grounding of qualitative methods and provide resources for teaching and self-learning (see e.g., Becker, 1985; Clifford and Marcus, 1986; Denzin, 1989; Emerson, 1983; Fetterman, 1987; Goetz and LeCompte, 1984; Lofland, 1984; Mishler, 1986; Patton, 1990; Shaffir, Stebbins, and Turowetz, 1980; Warren, 1988; Fine and Sandstrom, 1990; Van Maanen, 1988). These volumes provide guidance on research techniques and also contain candid accounts of researchers' doubts, errors, missteps, and recoveries, hopefully a source of encouragement to novice researchers (Adler and Adler, 1987; Richards, 1985).

In addition, renewed emphasis on the reflexivity and the standpoint of the researcher, sparked recently by writings of feminist and minority researchers (Aptheker, 1989; Collins, 1990; Cook and Fonow, 1986; Eichler, 1987; Farganis, 1986; Smith, 1987) has encouraged scholars to locate themselves in the body of their work. The illusion of the researcher as a "fly on the wall" is increasingly difficult to justify. This requires detailed reporting of fieldwork roles and also revelation of personal history and biography affecting orientations toward topics and research subjects (Collins, 1990; Denzin, 1987a,b; Hochschild, 1989; Krieger, 1983; Millman, 1980; Oakley, 1981, 1984a,b; Reinharz, 1983a,b; Rubin, 1976; Smith, 1987).

The regeneration of qualitative sociology can be traced to several sources. First, as Fine (1990) has noted, despite perennial predictions of demise and decline, symbolic interactionists never really disappeared but continued to produce important fieldwork and theory from various departmental sites, even through the period of greatest dominance of quantitative sociology (see also Saxton, 1988). Many major departments in the United States contained at least one productive symbolic interactionist engaged in fieldwork or writing about theory.

Second, the large core group of sociologists trained at the University of Chicago in the late 1940s and 1950s were reaching the pinnacle of stature and influence in the discipline. Even though many of them were no longer actively conducting field research, they had been trained in this tradition, were sympathetic to it, were able to teach qualitative methods and direct qualitative dissertations, and were critical of quantitative methods.

Third, the economic structure of qualitative research helped the growth of this approach during a period of lean times for granting agencies and suspicion from policymakers. Whereas quantitative research is often capital-intensive, qualitative research is labor-intensive—a boon for graduate students, who could conduct research as competent and innovative as that of their mentors. The movement of concern from political and economic issues to cultural domains also helps to make qualitative research seem a more appropriate tool. Qualitative sociologists were more accepted by cultural elites than were quantitative researchers by political elites, and this sociopolitical reality helped make cultural and interpretive sociology seem to be "where the action is." The flowering of literary theory and cultural sociology in this age of political conservatism seems not accidental. Although we doubt that many qualitative sociologists voted for Reagan, given academic politics, without cutbacks in social science funding traceable to Reaganism qualitative research would have been diminished.

Fourth, some observers have linked the increased usage of qualitative methods to changes in the gender composition of sociology (Mackie, 1985; McNamee, Willis, and Rotchford, 1990; Nielson, 1990; Grant et al., 1987; Grant and Ward, 1991). Although there is considerable debate about whether or not women played central roles in the development of qualitative sociology (cf. Deegan and Hill, 1987; Lorber, 1988), contemporary women sociologists use qualitative methods more so than men sociologists in journal publication (Grant *et al.*, 1987). Sociology is a rapidly feminizing discipline (Kulis, 1988), a factor that might encourage further development of qualitative research in the discipline or might contribute to its marginalization.

Dimensions of the Method

The heart of qualitative sociology, historically and currently, has been ethnography or fieldwork. In fieldwork, a researcher or team of researchers assumes a quasipublic role in a social setting and attempts to interpret that setting from the perspective of actors within it. As Hammersley and Atkinson (1983) and Agar (1980) note, ethnography is both a process and a product. The process can be flexible and typically evolves contextually in response to the lived realities encountered in specific field settings, which researchers enter as at least peripheral members (Adler, 1985; Adler and Adler, 1987; Gold, 1969; Schatzman and Strauss, 1973; Lofland and Lofland, 1984). The product is a written or performed account, providing a sociological interpretation of the setting, joined by a history of the process by which the interpretation was generated. Ethnography draws upon techniques of participant observation and ethnographic interviewing, often in tandem. The ethnographic account also can be informed by review of the scholarly literature, document analysis, collection and interpretation of artifacts, responses of informants to the researcher's tentative accounts, and personal history and reflection by the researcher (Agar, 1980, 1986; Becker, 1985; Denzin, 1989).

The goal of any method is to collect and present descriptive material that can be analyzed by others. Because of the richness and fullness of the description of qualitative research, this approach is particularly valuable in understanding important social situations. Indeed, the ethnographic approach has the longest history of any methodology, being at the heart of all personal narration.

New Directions in Qualitative Sociology

Today qualitative researchers are pressing at the boundaries of classical ethnography. Many are combining ethnography with other forms of data collection and analysis. Recent works have combined ethnography with field experimentation, survey research, or socio-linguistic discourse analysis (Lever, 1983; Eder, 1988; Goodwin, 1990). Others are combining ethnography with cultural analysis (Becker and McCall, 1990; Goodwin, 1990a, 1990b; Gubrium, 1988a,b; Millman, 1980; Reinharz, 1986).

Qualitative sociologists also are challenging and expanding the traditional modes of ethnographic presentation. Such challenges include the orienting of sociological work to popular as well as scholarly audiences (Hochschild, 1989; Richardson, 1985, 1987, 1990b; Riessmann, 1987; Rubin, 1976).[1] Other scholars are experimenting with presentation of ethnographic work in forms other than written (Becker and McCall, 1990; McCall and Becker, 1990; Myerhoff, 1978; Paget, 1990; Schwartz, 1990).

Cross-cutting, but not entirely synonymous with, these challenges is a re-examination of issues of power and control in qualitative sociology. Reconsideration of these themes in the 1980s has been sparked by qualitative feminist researchers (Cannon *et al.*, 1989; Eichler, 1987; Krieger, 1983; Smith, 1987; Stacey, 1988; Warren 1988), but they always have been present in qualitative sociological research (Broadhead and Rist, 1976; Rainwater and Pitman, 1967). Two related ethical concerns have been prominent in recent literature: appropriate relationships between researchers and those researched in the course of fieldwork and the relative power of the researcher and the subjects of research to control the production and use of the account that results from fieldwork.

In this review, we focus on qualitative sociological work that challenges and expands classical ethnography, either by using innovative methods or creative combinations of methods or by raising critical issues regarding relationships among researchers, subjects of research, and audiences to which the accounts are addressed. We argue that the renewed attention to the later issues affects methods. Researchers adapt methods to minimize ethical risks or to provide more faithful representations of subjective (emic) perspectives. These adaptations, in turn, provoke further controversies—we choose to believe healthy ones—about the purpose and future of qualitative sociology.

To examine the new directions and challenges in qualitative sociological research, we first examine how researchers have attempted to combine classical ethnography with other modes of research. We focus on selected works, illustrative of creative approaches adopted by contemporary researchers.

Melding Methods

The Ethnographic Site
as a Research Laboratory

Traditionally, ethnographies have conducted their studies of a particular research site and then moved on to another site—perhaps another area of research entirely. Few qualitative researchers in sociology, in contrast to some in anthropology (who returned to the same village year after year), were content with a single site. Often the excitement was gone; the juice was sucked from the orange and the peel thrown away—a model quite unlike that in the physical sciences, where the researcher spends a lifetime working on a fairly narrow range of issues.

One of the most remarkable attempts to emulate the careful examination of a single research setting is the research program of Donna Eder and her students, who are examining a middle school and a high school in a small Midwestern community, using a number of methodologies and with several substantive interests, but each focusing on the culture and social structure of these youngsters. Together these studies of adolescent peer cultures in schools and school-related extracurricular activities carried out by Eder (1985, 1988, 1990, in press a,b) in collaboration with her students (Eder and Enke, 1991; Eder and Parker, 1987; Enke, 1990; Evans and Eder, 1989; Kinney, 1989; Simon, Eder, and Evans, 1989) and by her students (Enke, 1990; Kinney, 1989) provide scholars with a longitudinal data base virtually unique in qualitative research—information that is wide and deep, although from a single locality.

Male and female researchers observed and informally interviewed middle school and high school students in classrooms, lunchrooms, extracurricular activities, such as sports and cheerleading, and off-campus clubs and parties over several years. Observations identified naturally occurring groups of peers who interacted in and out of school. Members of these groups later were video- and audiotaped as they engaged in informal discussions on topics of their choice in a school cafeteria learning center and on bus rides. Groups were same-gender, paralleling patterns of social relations apparent in the middle school. This provided a useful strategy as talk emerged as a critical component of social relations and cultural creation among adolescents, especially among the girls. Ethnographic observations of behavior revealed regularities of girls' peer cultures—for example, that popularity and romance are cyclical and ephemeral (Eder, 1985; Simon *et al.*, 1989) and that a few students are social isolates in school settings (Evans and Eder, 1989)—and their discourse provided the clue to uncover how these roles and relationships emerge and are maintained and transformed. The analysis of all of these data was important to gain a sense of this social world.

For instance, Eder (1985) found that for girls the relationship between being popular and being liked varies over the cycle of popularity. In the middle school setting, girls become popular by being cheerleaders or being friends of cheerleaders. Popular girls typically receive more friendship bids and social invitations than they can accept. As popular girls decline bids for friendship, they are apt to be redefined in discourse of peers as "stuck up," whereupon others' liking for them declines, although they might still be popular because of their visibility. The analysis suggests that being liked or disliked is not wholly a function of personal qualities of individual students but, rather, complex social dynamics in combination with students' skills in managing problematic interactions.

In a later, related paper, Evans and Eder (1989) traced interactional dynamics confronting students who are socially isolated in middle schools. Social isolation, like popularity, generally has been attributed primarily to individual characteristics of children. Eder and Evans suggest that social isolation is a dynamic process in which both linguistic and self-presentational skills play a critical component. Peers present isolated students with unique challenges that never are directed toward popular students [e.g., "reverse insults" (teasing implying that popular students of the other gender are attracted to the isolated students)]. Isolated students find it difficult to respond to reverse insults in an effective manner, so students who are their targets either fail to respond or react in a manner that peers judge to be inept. The isolate's response becomes the basis for further teasing and exclusion. Thus, the status of isolate becomes successively more difficult to discard. The treatment of social isolates by peers involves insulting language and intentional cruelty, debunking theories that social isolation derives primarily from ineffective socialization or communication skills on the part of the isolate.[2]

In other papers by Eder and her team, ethnography is used to delineate the different structures of male and female peer groups in school settings. Girls, in particular, build cohesion and solidarity through gossip (Eder and Enke, 1991), teasing (Eder, in press a,b), humor (Sanford and Eder, 1984), collaborative problem-solving (Enke, 1990) and storytelling (Eder, 1988).

Whereas other studies have shown that boys' discourse typically is characterized by dominance, boasting, and competitive bids to control the floor (Best, 1983; Goodwin, 1985, 1990, 1991; Schofield, 1982), girls' discourse is used instead to build cohesion. Girls pick up, repeat, and expand on conversational elements of prior speakers. Enke's (1990) study of female high school athletes extends Eder's research by illustrating that this process occurs even among girls who do not like one another. When required to work together on group tasks (in Enke's case, on a high school basketball team), the girls nevertheless use conversation to strengthen connections and resolve problems critical to task-related group cohesion. Enke provides a detailed example of how two teammates who expressed dislike for one another and spent no time together outside team activities nevertheless collaborated effectively to devise a strategy for resolving one girl's dispute with the team's coach.

Kinney (1989) extended Eder's research to examine the transition of students from middle school to high school, analyzing how social context affects not only social relationships but self-identity. Middle schools usually are smaller than high schools and considerably less diverse in range of activities and peer cultures. Within the context of the middle school, some students become defined by peers as "dweebs," or deviants. The definition, typically accepted by the boys themselves, is partially related to development, and males who mature late, suffer from acne, or are easily embarrassed in interactions with girls are likely prospects for labeling as dweebs.

By the time they reach high school, many former dweebs become redefined by themselves and others as normals. Maturation explains only part of this transition. The wider, more diverse social atmosphere of the high school also is an important supportive factor in identity transition. The high school is considerably larger, offers a wider range of curricular and extracurricular options, and embodies distinctive, sometimes competing peer groups rather than a single elite. Students of both genders are less concerned than their counterparts of middle school age about conformity to a single standard of behavior. The likelihood is greater that larger numbers of students find comfortable niches and like-minded peers in the high school environment.

The works of Eder and her collaborators show that many phenomena attributed to personalities and developmental phases of adolescents actually have a sociological base. They also suggest that certain problems (e.g., social isolation) probably cannot be resolved by counseling of individual students but, rather, require an intervention into ongoing social relationships—relationships that adults in school may not be aware of because they are explicitly structured to elude adult scrutiny. These conclusions would not have been as powerful if they had been based on a one-shot study by a single investigator. The aggregation of data collected by multiple researchers over time adds to the confidence with which we accept the results.

Ethnography as Sociolinguistic Analysis

The analysis of talk has always been critical to ethnographic research, and the presentation of talk has always been central to ethnographic description. Indeed, too often it seems that all that people described in ethnographies do is to talk. The presentation of talk has always been central to ethnographic description. However, until recently, talk has not been examined *as talk*. There has been a need for an ethnography of speaking: discourse analysis in the field. Sociolinguistics was virtually unknown 20 years ago; today it is an important and creative area of the discipline, well connected to qualitative research. A large body of research produced in the last decade has focused on the role of language in social situations and social organization. These studies reveal how social actors, even very young children (Corsaro, 1988, in press; Corsaro and Rizzo, 1988) use language in a purposive manner to construct identities and manipulate social relationships. Slightly older children are even more attuned to the niceties of language in constructing meaning (Fine, 1987; Heath, 1983; Goodwin, 1991).

Marjorie Harness Goodwin (1990a, 1990b) has substantially advanced sociolinguistic and conversational analysis in a long-term study of language use in play of black children in West Philadelphia. Goodwin (1990b) argues that talk is used by children to "build their ongoing social organization and the phenomenal world they inhabit." Goodwin transcends what might be termed formal linguistics by emphasizing not only the autonomous, formal system of language but the ways in which production of talk is contextual, a form of social action critical to human discourse and the building and maintenance of social organization. Talk creates what she terms *participation frameworks,* in which an entire field of action is made relevant by forms of speech. The speaker may transform the social order of the moment by invoking different speech activities.

Goodwin argues that studying talk provides added rigor and comparability to qualitative accounts of social action. Researchers present examples of materials they analyze, so that other researchers might peruse them for alternative interpretations. The documentation typically provided in sociolinguistic analysis advances methodology and facilitates comparative research. She contends that such an approach avoids the pitfalls of interpretive anthropology, which focuses attention on the ethnographer/informant dialogue. Sociolinguistic analysis instead directs attention to how people themselves perform meaningful activities in nautralistic settings.

In several papers and a recent book, Goodwin (1985, 1990a, 1990b) uses ethnography combined with sociolinguistic analysis to challenge popular theories of "separate spheres" or "different voices" of discourse used by females and males. Goodwin shows that there are both similarities and dissimilarities in forms of talk used by boys and girls but that greater variability exists among the girls.

Context is far more critical for girls than for boys in forms of discourse. In informal play activities, the discourse of boys and girls is structured distinctively. Boys use asymmetrical forms of speech and nonverbal actions to construct leader-directed, hierarchical forms of organizations, while girls use other nonhierarchical, collaborative forms of discourse to form more egalitarian groups. When girls play house, however, and assume roles that in society have normative status differences (e.g., mother–child), they use forms of discourse more similar to those of boys to construct and maintain status-differentiated forms of organization. Goodwin also challenges the popular notion that girls' games are less complex than boys' (see Gilligan, 1982; Lever, 1976, 1978), thereby preparing girls less well for interaction within the context of large formal organizations. She demonstrates the complex negotiation and coordination required to play "house," a favorite activity of girls she observed. Furthermore, she shows that girls who play subordinate roles (e.g., young children) engage in active negotiation to define the boundaries and options associated with their positions, rather than experience socialization for passivity.

Corsaro (in press) and Corsaro and Rizzo (1988) in cross-cultural studies of American and Italian nursery schools demonstrate how forms of interaction and of discourse among even very young children reflect distinctive patterns reflective of norms of the adult cultures in which they are immersed. For example, Italian children engage in much more overt, verbal discourse in routine interactions than do American children, and they do so at an earlier age. These patterns parallel adult discourse in the two societies.

West (1984) and Fisher (1986) use ethnography in combination with discourse analysis to reveal how male doctors exert control over encounters with female patients, although in works of these writers, discourse analysis is more central than ethnography. Mehan (1979) has analyzed how clashes about norms of language use in classrooms disadvantages students whose cultural backgrounds differ from those of teachers. Within American schools, such students are labeled as academically deficient. Maynard (1985) explores language use in stratification processes in peer relations. Condit (1990) has analyzed rhetoric aspects of private and public discourse about abortion in context with ethnographic data exploring women's intent in producing discourse. Riessman (1987) shows how organization of speech—in her case, into temporal or episodic presentations—varies across class and race–ethnic statuses and impedes clear communication between subjects and researchers and clients and therapists.

The combination of ethnography and sociolinguistic analysis seems especially powerful in studying experiences of little-researched and dominated groups. Language often is the medium of translation of ideology into social control, and the detailed study of language within relations of dominance reveals the legitimating rationale for dominance and the means by which control is maintained.

Ethnography and Field Experimentation

Janet Schofield's (1982) detailed study of social relationships in a desegregated magnet middle school provides an illustration of the effective use of field experimentation and structured observation in conjunction with ethnography. Schofield and a team of researchers studied responses to desegregation among students and teachers in grades six through eight. Structured observations can be distinguished from ethnography in that the former involves a predetermined focus and form of data collection by researchers (McCall, 1984). In structured observations, researchers determine *a priori* the phenomena on which they will concentrate as well as the form in which data will be recorded (such as checklists or other coding sheets).

Ethnographic observations by Schofield and her collaborators determined how race and gender, in combination, affected student perceptions and social relationships in schools. Effects were magnified as children moved from sixth to eighth grade. By the latter grade, gender effects on racial interaction were more salient as students began to date and became preoccupied with larger societal standards of what constituted beauty and attractiveness and appropriate dating partners. Black male students, in particular, were perceived by white girls and their parents as more threatening as these students became more mature.

Schofield supplemented naturalistic observations with structured observations of freely chosen lunchroom seating patterns to test tentative hypotheses about separation by race and gender derived from ethnographic observations. Structured observations recorded seating patterns by race, gender, and grade level. Schofield found support for her contention that racial separation increased with student grade level (Schofield, 1981; Schofield and Sagar, 1977).

To illuminate perceptions of threat and the influence of perceived threat on student social relationships, Schofield designed a field experiment, using samples of students of varying race, gender, and grade level configurations. She provided thematic apperception cues to students evoking potentially ambiguous cross-racial themes (e.g., "Black students in this school usually . . . " with students completing the paragraph). Student responses revealed different interpretations based on combined race–gender configurations. White females felt a heightened sense of threat that increased with grade level in comparison with other students. They were more likely to provide responses to cues indicative of threat, whereas students of other race–gender configurations interpreted them as routine and nonthreatening. The field experiment proved an effective means to get students to talk about issues of race and of threat. The ethnographic component of the research had discovered that within the context of the school, race was a taboo topic. Teachers and administrators avoided explicit mention of race, a common tactic in desegregated schools in this era. Schofield suggests that the practice created interactional dilemmas (e.g., confusion on the part of teachers about how to respond to overt racist remarks made by students) and in the long run may have been counterproductive to successful desegregation. Within the school, for example, there was no mechanism for discussing or responding to the white girls' fears or their parents' concerns about their safety.

In Schofield's work, ethnography preceded other forms of data collection. Structured observations on lunchroom seating took place only after ethnographic research had verified that this would be a valid indicator of natural peer groups and friendship choices. The experimental materials were generated inductively, symbolizing recurrent and meaningful events that took place in the setting. Schofield has analyzed her data using both qualitative and quantitative strategies.

While Schofield's data triangulation is more explicit and carefully conducted than most, these forms had been used earlier in qualitative research. For example, Whyte (1948) used similar methods in his attempt to examine the effect on status on achievement (bowling scores) among the Cornertown boys while Schofield cites the brilliant mixture of experimental analysis and ethnography by Muzafer and Caroline

Sherif in their studies of summer camps and youth groups (Sherif, 1962; Sherif and Sherif, 1964).

Ethnography and Survey Research

Ethnography and survey research often are viewed as antithetical, proceeding from different assumptions about the nature of reality. Nevertheless, they have been successfully combined by some researchers. One example is Janet Lever's (1983) study of soccer in Brazil. Lever uses eclectic methods, including participant observation, intensive interviewing, reflective introspection, and extensive archival and documents analysis, to probe the meaning of soccer in Brazilian society. She develops a complex argument proposing that soccer rivalries reflect potentially divisive ethnic and class divisions in Brazilian society and that avidly followed soccer competitions provide a means to articulate but also to resolve some of these factional disputes.

Although the core of her work is ethnographic, she develops a questionnaire to explore behaviors and perspectives of soccer fans and the phenomenon she labels "fandom." Developed toward the end of her study, the questionnaire was administered to industrial workers representative of distinctive class and ethnic groups. According to Lever's prior ethnography, the groups selected were representative of factions of Brazilian society apt to be fans of particular teams. Via the questionnaire, Lever verified that soccer was indeed a preoccupation of Brazilian males of all classes, who attended soccer matches frequently, watched soccer on television, regularly followed newspaper accounts of soccer matches, and could identify prominent soccer players more reliably than they could name prominent political and civic leaders. The questionnaires verified other tentative conclusions from her ethnographic data, including the relationship of class background to preferences for certain teams and the greater participation of higher-class women, as compared to lower-class women, in soccer "fandom."

Another example of the successful combination of survey research and ethnographic techniques is Wright's (1988) study of marriages where one spouse is afflicted with Alzheimer's disease. Wright interviewed 30 married couples in which one spouse had been diagnosed at an early stage of Alzheimer's and a smaller sample of control couples with no evidence of the disorder in either spouse.

One component of Wright's research was a questionnaire, generated only after months of qualitative inquiry, about the division of labor in household tasks before and after the onset of Alzheimer's. The questionnaire was used creatively in analysis in several ways. First, it provided detailed and specific information on the variability of the effects of Alzheimer's on division of house labor based on the genders of the afflicted and nonafflicted spouse, chore distribution prior to the onset of illness, the couple's economic resources, and the availability of family-based and other social support. Administration of the questionnaire often provoked unanticipated but valuable insights, such as Wright's discovery that some husbands attached positive value to performing domestic chores for afflicted wives, viewing this as repayment to wives for years in which they had provided domestic labor for the men.

Second, administration of the questionnaire provided further evidence for Wright's judgment about the progression of the disease in the afflicted spouse. On some occasions, persons who appeared composed and alert in interviews became frustrated or confused when responding to the brief and straightforward questionnaire, a process that Wright (an experienced nurse with training in gerontology) observed. Administering the questionnaire allowed her to assess the progression of the disease, verifying or contradicting the physicians' diagnoses of the progression of the disorder and enriching her empathetic understanding of the caretaker's perspective on interactions with afflicted spouses, most specifically the minute-to-minute variation in mental alertness and capability. Some afflicted subjects, for example, became so upset by the questionnaire and a related problem-solving diagnostic instrument used in the research that Wright had to spend hours in the household restoring emotional calm before terminating the interview.

Using questionnaires or structured interviews provides a means by which an ethnographer can gain systematic data about an audience of interest. Fine (1990), in his ethnographic research on mushroom collectors, sent questionnaires to members of a local mycological society, a 20% sample of the national society of mushroomers, and included a set of questions on a random household survey in Minneapolis–St. Paul. Coupled with lengthy in-depth interviews with two dozen amateur mushroomers in Minnesota, this permitted a clearer understanding of the various perspectives of these groups on environmental and nature activities. In this case, the interviews proved to be a valuable tool to supplement 3 years of detailed ethnographic research.

Ethnography as Theory

Traditionally, the primary purpose of fieldwork was to collect descriptive material: to find out what was really happening in a setting, so that we better understand a group, social category, activity, organization, or institution. This emphasis on careful, painstaking depiction played a critical role in uncovering hidden arenas but led to an understandable claim that some ethnography was atheoretical, in that it refrained from making claims that could be generalized beyond a narrow range of settings to more general sociological principles.

With the reinvigoration of sociological theory in the 1980s came a concern on the part of ethnographers with making their research speak to general claims. Even a journal that had been as robustly descriptive as *Urban Life* by the late 1970s expressed a desire for "more systematically theoretically grounded papers" (Manning, 1978:283).

Arlie Hochschild's (1983) admirable ethnography, *The Managed Heart*, is ostensibly about how airline flight attendants are trained to use emotion. Yet, her work fails as standard ethnography in that the reader is told precious little about the work life of flight attendants. It is not an occupational study, in the sense that it would have been if presented by one of Everett Hughes students, who would have provided much greater detail on the organization of the occupation and its routine activities. Rather, Hochschild presents a focused, theoretical ethnography. Material extraneous to seeing emotion as a form of impression management, structured through industrial demands, has been eliminated. Furthermore, unlike many traditional, descriptive ethnographies, Hochschild incorporates those materials from other sources that help her make her point.

Other studies make similar attempts to address the construction of deprofessionalization; for example Kleinman (1984) uses liberal Protestant ministry students. The interest is not in religion, still less in a particular religious community, but, rather, in the manipulation of core values, such as equality and community. Fine, (1987, 1990), in focusing on the work lives of cooks, is actually attempting to develop a sociology of aesthetics rather than a description of a fascinating occupation.

Contemporary ethnographers believe that they can build general theory from any set of data (see Glaser and Strauss, 1967); under this model, theory is emergent from data. One can enter a field setting because it is convenient, without desiring to document that setting, and emerge with a new concept, an important substantive approach, or a contribution to "grand theory."

Policy-Relevant Ethnography

Increasingly common in the last several decades are ethnographies relevant to policy issues. These ethnographies have been particularly prominent in the sociology of education. Some works have been explicitly designed to address policy issues, whereas others have been more theory-driven. Some authors have been based in traditional sociology departments, while others have worked from interdisciplinary departments or institutional bases outside academia. Some have been supported by external grants specifically addressing policy issues. In most instances, these studies have made simultaneous contributions to policy development around critical social issues and to the generation of important lines of sociological theory, challenging the common assumption that policy-relevant work is incompatible with theory production.

Several works already discussed, including studies of peer relations in schools by Eder and Schofield, fall into these categories. These studies have been valued by sociologists for theoretical advances in the newly emerging subarea of sociology of adolescence but have also been used by scholars and practitioners in educational policy-making.

Ray Rist's (1973, 1978) studies of all-minority and desegregated schools illuminates bases of stratification within the daily life of schools. Rist's (1973) research analyzes rarely studied within-race stratification and compares and contrasts processes of stratification in single-race and cross-racial schools. His works challenge the once-common assumption that classrooms are largely autonomous settings, shielded from outside influences via the closed door and norms of professional autonomy that give teachers substantial authority for determining the internal life of the classroom. Rist traces the multiple means by which elements of external culture sift into classrooms and bring in forms of race and class stratification that teachers and administrators profess to want to keep out. Rist also provides a powerful critique for assumptions that teacher behaviors are primary influences in classrooms, demonstrating the powerful influence of peer cultures on the construction of classroom life. Rist also illustrated how non-academic, class, and race-based criteria (dress style, language, grooming, performance of older siblings) entered into evaluations and placements of students despite adherence to a rhetoric of merit within schools. These perspectives have been expanded on by scholars in many disciplines carrying out qualitative research in diverse, multi-ethnic, and class variable settings (e.g., Clement, Eisenhart, and Harding, 1979; Furlong, 1984; Fuller, 1980; Gaskell, 1985; Grant and Sleeter, 1986; Irvine, 1990; Lesko, 1988; Luttrell, 1989; Moore, 1983; Mullard, 1985; Roman, 1989; Scott-Jones and Clark, 1986; Thorne, 1985; Valli, 1986).

Work by Grant (1984, 1985, in press a,b,c) shows how desegregation, changes in the tracking system, and other forms of organizational change have differential impacts on students based on combined race–gender status. Black females, in particular, stand to lose much when schools contain more white students. Typically the highest-ranking pupils and recipients of the most teacher attention in all-black classrooms, they lose centrality to white students in desegregated rooms. Furthermore, complex classroom interactions nudge black females toward social, rather than academic, achievement in desegregated settings. Macrocultural norms about appropriate placements of various groups and school organizational factors affect everyday interactions in classrooms, pressing different students in the same classrooms and schools toward variable outcomes. Studies in Midwestern and Southern elementary classrooms illuminate the ways in which inequality operates within a system professing adherence to ideologies of equality and highlights the importance of theory-building to explain contextual effects or, what McCarthy (1990) calls, "asynchronies" in experiences of different groups within organizations. Other researchers working at higher levels of the education system have underscored the importance of using ethnography to develop theory encompassing race, class, and gender variations in schooling experience (see e.g., Connell, 1982; Gaskell, 1985; Kessler, Ashenden, Connell, and Dowsett, 1985; Luttrell, 1989). These works demonstrate the need for theoretical frames that incorporate intersections of race, gender, and class in understanding social experience in educational settings and the labor force.

Metz' studies of authority relations in desegregated schools (Metz, 1978) and of the contexts of three magnet schools in the same city (Metz, 1986) have raised important policy issues as well as made contributions to organizational theory. At the policy level, Metz' first study pointed out that teacher authority behaviors were differentially perceived across tracks enrolling different social classes. While democratic forms of instruction were well received in high tracks, low-track students and their parents perceived such teaching styles as indicative of poor teacher preparation and little concern about student learning. These perceptions created crises of authority. Metz' second ethnography showed how three magnet schools, ostensibly constrained by the same overarching school systems, developed dramatically different internal climates. Metz also probed the contradictions related to equality issues produced by magnet schools: they were designed to minimize inequalities by race and class, yet in some ways exaggerated these inequalities by producing some schools that were better and had more resources than others. Furthermore, more elite parents had the cultural knowledge to enroll their children successfully in the superior magnet schools, whereas less-affluent parents did not. But Metz' work also makes important contributions to organizational theory related to authority and control. Metz argues that the "loosely coupled" nature of school systems in large urban areas permitted the wide variation in climates of magnet schools as long as a certain level of symbolic conformity was maintained on paper and in public. Her work speaks more generally to conditions under which large bureaucracies can and cannot exercise control over subunits.

Sociological Analysis of Text

Qualitative sociologists increasingly analyze written texts, ranging from literary works to personal documents, such as letters, diaries, to graffiti. These analyses involve both historical and contemporary materials. These techniques do not constitute ethnography by our definition, because researchers do not assume a public role and negotiate a relationship with subjects, but techniques used to analyze ethnographic data are applied to the analysis of documents. Furthermore, some researchers engaged in ethnographic work (Lever, 1976, 1978; Gubrium, 1988a,b) elicit the production of personal documents for sociological analysis. Lever, for example, supplemented ethnographic analysis of fifth-grade children's play on school grounds with diaries that children kept about their out-of-school play activities. Gubrium urged Alzheimer's-afflicted individuals and their caretakers to keep diaries of their experiences, which he used to supplement observations about the ways in which care of afflicted individuals is carried out in the home. In work in progress, Fine is using the text of speeches in high school debates to understand the structure of argumentation, in addition to his ethnographic analysis. Denzin (1987a,b) used self-reflection, personal diaries, and other documents in the analysis of the process of recovery from alcoholism.

Extended Case Studies

Extended, comparative case studies are another vital line of research in contemporary qualitative sociology and represent a revival of a classical qualitative technique that fell out of favor with researchers during the periods of greatest dominance of quantitative analysis. These studies have been most prominent in the study of organizations, where detailed, contextual fieldwork studies have modified organizational theory and highlighted the dangers of overgeneralization in quantitative analysis. Among the better-known works of this genre is Michael Burawoy's (1979) *Manufacturing Consent*. Midway through fieldwork, Burawoy discovered that, coincidentally but fortuitously, he was studying the same firm as had been studied decades earlier by Donald Roy (1952, 1958). Burawoy's replication permits the examination of the ways in which the microlevel relationships between workers and managers in the firm had been altered in the course of three decades of social and cultural change.

More explicitly than other forms of qualitative sociology, the "extended case method," as Burawoy terms the approach, explores macrostructural influences on everyday life. Rather than building a portrait of macrosocial relationships from the examination of micro-order phenomena, the perspective starts explicitly from the vantage point of macrostructural forces to analyze how microsituations are affected by larger social structures. Contemporary sociologists have applied variations of the extended case method to studies of workers and managers (Burawoy, 1985; Garson, 1988; Kanter, 1977; Silfen Glasberg, 1989; Smith 1990) and comparative studies of women workers in U.S. industries (Statham, Miller, and Mausch, 1988) and in developing countries (Ward, 1990). These studies reveal that large-scale social forces affect work places in context-specific ways and warn against overgeneralization in theories derived and tested with quantitative data. The case studies also illustrate creative strategies used by workers to negotiate options within rigidly bound work settings. The analytical technique has applicability to a broad range of sociological subfields and likely will become more prominent in the 1990s.

Ethnographic Analysis of Published Materials

A recent example of sociological analysis (or reanalysis) of materials published for other purposes is Reinharz' (1986) interpretive account of the meaning of miscarriage in women's lives. Reinharz notes that the life history method she used revives a technique employed by symbolic interactionists in the 1920s and relies on sympathetic introspection, or "interpreting her experience as if it were my own" (Reinharz, 1986:230). Reinharz writes that the sympathetic introspection was facilitated by her somewhat-similar personal experience (Reinharz, 1988).

Reinharz' analysis is based on a published personal account of one woman's experience (Pitzer and Palinski, 1980). The author of the account and subject of Reinharz' analysis, Chris, had one successful pregnancy, but then experienced three miscarriages over a 2.5-year period before bearing a second child. As Reinharz notes, personal documents represent a form of unobtrusive data in that such documents are not created for study and, thus, are not as seriously affected by reactivity as are other forms of data collection. Reinharz focuses her analysis on Chris' use of words and an explication of "the range of meanings behind particular words" by reference to contemporary literature on reproduction. Chris' experience is personal, yet her actions and her responses to experience are framed by historical and macrosociological factors such as the state of medical knowledge related to miscarriage and the organization and discourse of the medical profession.

Reinharz explores how her subject's understanding and feelings toward pregnancy are transformed by her successive miscarriages and by her interactions with significant others, physicians, hospitals, and social support providers. Prior to the first miscarriage, Chris anticipates a normal and uneventful pregnancy, as her first had been. She shares news of pregnancy with important others, including her 4-year-old daughter, visualizes the child-to-be, begins contemplating names and room arrangements, unpacks and launders baby clothing, and forms mental images of the expected baby. Early signs of the miscarriage are misinterpreted as nonthreatening, until her encounters with physicians define them otherwise. Chris is stunned by what she terms the insensitivity of the physicians. The them, miscarriage is a routine, nonserious event. To her it is emotionally devastating. She describes how lack of acknowledgment in medical discourse of her sense of loss intensified her pain.

By drawing on written materials on reproduction and contraception, Reinharz demonstrates that most women, as a by-product of realizing that they can control contraception, also come to believe that they can control conception and birth. Babies are timed to fit other sociological events (e.g., Chris' summer hiatus from her school counseling job, her husband's completion of a training course). This orientation represents a shift from other historical eras, where pregnancies and birth were not regarded as controllable. Miscarriage violates not only one's sense of control over conception and birth but also produces doubts about the usually taken-for-granted assumption that one's body functions normally. This can produce a fundamental shift of identity, a viewing of oneself as abnormal rather than normal.

Reinharz analyzes contradictions in Chris' reflections about the causes of and her responses to her miscarriages. Although Chris overtly professes no sense of guilt about "causing" her miscarriages, her words and actions sometimes belie these expressions. Furthermore, she develops a contradictory orientation toward physicians. Although Chris determines that she needs the help of physicians to complete a successful pregnancy, she simultaneously mistrusts physicians for their lack of understanding of her emotional responses and becomes angered by the lack of medical knowledge about miscarriage.

She also experiences clashes in perspective in dealing with social institutions. After one miscarriage, Chris goes to a Catholic hospital for treatment (a dilation and curettage, a common, although controversial, operation usually performed after a miscarriage). This hospital refuses surgery until she has had a negative pregnancy test, forcing upon her an emotionally painful delay in treatment. The distress results from different interpretations of the event held by her and by hospital policymakers. Chris resolves not to use Catholic hospitals for such treatment and to recommend that friends avoid such hospitals. Thus, her personal experience is transformed by interaction in the context of a large institution and her response to this encounter.

When, after a third miscarriage, Chris' physician reluctantly orders a barrage of tests and identifies a possible physical cause of miscarriages (a treatable infection), Chris is overjoyed. This is an inversion of the usual response of individuals who learn that they suffer from an illness. Chris and her husband overzealously follow the treatment regimen (he takes medication, even though there is no evidence of illness in him), in part to exert control over a situation in which the couple feels they have lost control. After treatment, a successive pregnancy results in the birth of a normal, healthy son. Throughout this pregnancy, however, Chris' outlook remains tentative. Instead of visualizing the child-to-be, Chris uses and thinks in medical terminology: fetuses, trimesters, and the like. She avoids public disclosure of her pregnancy until it is forced on her by biology and by responses of others (she was literally bursting out of her clothing and others remark on her pregnancy). When her son is born, she celebrates him as "perfect." Her obstetrician, who actually missed the birth because Chris' labor was fast, is restored to a position of high esteem, although her reactions to him over the course of treatment have been variable and ambivalent.

Reinharz' reanalysis of these materials portrays the phenomenology and emotion of this experience from the perspective of women. The reanalysis also illustrates the power of textual analysis to bridge the links between personal experience and social structure in historical context. Furthermore, it has implications for practice. Medical treatment practices surrounding miscarriage, and even counseling and theraputic materials written to assist women who have undergone this experience, are relatively insensitive to the emotional impact and indentity transformation women experience in recovering from a miscarriage.

Conrad (1988) uses another type of textual analysis that is linked to his ethnographic studies of medical students' socialization. A recent paper (Conrad, 1986), for example, challenges the widely held stereotype that premedical students engage in cut-throat competition with classmates to obtain entry into medical school. Moving from his observational work on premedical and medical education, Conrad (1988) analyzes several examples of the recently published accounts of the medical school and residency experience written by physicians in training. One account he chooses as an example was written by a Ph.D. anthropologist who subsequently completed medical school (Konner, 1987). Essentially, the writers become ethnographers for Conrad's purposes. The contrasts between the etic perspective of the researcher and the emic perspectives of the articulate subjects he has chosen enrich the reader's understanding of the medical school experience, but the study blurs the boundaries between literature or journalism and sociological analysis.

Walker and Moulton (1989) use family photographic albums as bases of qualitative analysis. They examine the content and layout of albums as they convey images and presentations of family life, but the researchers also analyze ways in which subjects present and account for the contents of these personal materials to the researchers.

Presenting Worlds

In addition to analyzing literary works, sociologists have struggled to find appropriate formats in which to convey sociological works to diverse audiences. As sociology has been pushed out of the policy arena, it has attempted to find niches elsewhere. One of the most promising of these is in the popular market, particularly in that part of the market that buys books and magazines—intelligent lay readers. Topics that appeal to female readers have seemed particularly effective in capturing publishers' attention. Writers who attempt to write for this market often strive to reach the academic market as well, sometimes with greater impact, sometimes with less.

Perhaps most notably in this regard, Laurel Richardson (1987) ventured on the interview and talk-show circuit to disseminate her work on single women who have affairs with married men (Richardson, 1985). As Richardson (1990a,b) notes in a recent account, she welcomed opportunities to discuss her work-in-progress with general audiences in the course of its preparation because these forums provided a means to recruit diverse subjects for interviews. Adler (1985), observing a nationally ranked collegiate basketball team, demonstrated that while publicity could harm research-in-progress, it can also add to the range of information that it is possible to obtain.

Richardson's work has been favorably reviewed in disciplinary journals for its theoretical contributions and for the methodological quality of its execution, but it has also been devalued because of the form of dissemination chosen by its author. Although sometimes such a rejection can be attributed to jealousy, writing for a popular audience involves, as Richardson recognizes, a series of compromises, some of which involve the kinds of qualifications that one can make regarding one's "truth claims," the complexity of the analysis, and the extent and form of field notes included. Some of these popular ethnographies violate norms of academic discourse and read like novelizations of the life of their central "characters."

Arlie Hochschild (1989) also attempts to reach a popular audience in her most recent work, *The Second Shift*. The work is written as case histories, with the avowed goal of being accessible to those researched and persons whose lives are similar to them. The heart of the book is a series of vignettes, focused on the experiences of families she interviewed and observed, that are easily accessible to lay audiences. Hochschild (1973, 1983) directed prior works primarily toward scholarly audiences.

Although these works directed toward lay readers surely do help persons who are struggling with similar issues, such as the role of dual-career families as described by Hochschild in *The Second Shift*, they run the danger of dismissal as nonserious scholarship by the professional reader, who must infer theoretical relevance and methodological precision rather than find these laid out in the traditional scholarly mode. Thus, Richardson's decision to publish some material in popular format and other material in academic format seems particularly effective. Each form of discourse has its own rules.

Popularization is not the only, or even the most significant of the "experiments" in which qualitative researchers are engaging. Significantly, Howard Becker, in collaboration with Michal McCall and Marianne Paget, has experimented with the presentation of qualitative sociology as performance, terming it "performance science" (Becker and McCall, 1990; McCall and Becker, 1990; Paget, 1990). Becker teaches seminars on this topic to undergraduate and graduate students. Field notes as performance is the latest in a series of innovations in presentation of qualitative work by Becker, who also has written a widely consulted handbook on writing for social scientists. Becker and McCall believe that re-living and re-presenting interactions studied by ethnographers allows examination of these encounters from multiple perspectives. The researcher(s) gain useful insights into the meaning of events by observing responses of diverse audiences to their re-creation. Even more radically, some qualitative researchers, mostly anthropologists such as Dan Rose (1990), are experimenting by incorporating poetry into ethnographies. Filmed presentations of anthropological work have long been accepted in that discipline (Rollwagen, 1988). Annual meetings of the American Anthropological Association feature ongoing screenings of anthropological films. Sociologists have used this form of presentation less readily. Sociological films usually are pedagogical outgrowths of published written texts, not the primary forms in which findings are presented.

The written register is not the only area in which experimentation has occurred. Becker and several other sociologists have used photographs and other visual materials to convey to audiences more than can be transmitted in written accounts (Becker, 1974, 1978, 1981). The ethnographic investigations of Douglas Harper (1982) on hoboes and a rural repairman dramatically demonstrate that understanding can be facilitated by interpreted photographs, particularly when the informants contribute to the interpretation. Likewise Naomi Bushman's photographs, used in conjunction with Marcia Millman's (1980) written text, explore the social meaning of being overweight in America. In her methodological appendix, Millman discusses ways in which viewing the photographs and reflecting on the messages they conveyed were part of the process of thinking through her analysis.

Anthropologists have made greater strides than have sociologists in using film and video to present ethnographic accounts. One notable example is Barbara Myerhoff's (1978) film *Number Our Days*, an outgrowth of her ethnography of the same title. Her work is a sensitive, detailed ethnography of a senior citizen center in Venice, California, that serves a population of nonaffluent, elderly Jewish citizens living far from kin. In the print version of the work, Myerhoff explicitly discusses the variations in perspectives presented in the book and the film and the justifications for the divergence. She observes that the preparation of the film was, in part, a response to her subjects' insistence that they receive public recognition. Many objected to the use of pseudonyms and the disguising of identifying personal life details—standard practices in research (Fine, 1990). Her subjects wanted to be noticed and recognized, to leave a permanent mark of their existence before they died. The film provided such an opportunity.

The Role of the Researcher

Another area of debate among contemporary qualitative sociologists is the appropriate relationships among researchers, informants, and audiences of research. We wonder: What is the appropriate role of the researcher in relation to subjects in the process of fieldwork? Should researchers maintain an objective (if such is ever possible) or a subjective stance? Finally, whose voices and perspectives should guide the account?

Roles in Data Collection

Several writers argue that qualitative approaches minimize risks to informants because researchers are acutely aware of their perspectives. The long-lasting, close relationships developed in qualitative work are thought to make researchers especially sensitive to issues of exploitation and misrepresentation. This viewpoint has been challenged forcefully by Judith Stacey (1988), who argues that these very relationships allow the researcher greater opportunities for emotional manipulation of research subjects and that the exchanges of intimate knowledge that occur in such settings maximize rather than minimize ethical risks. In a presentation to the American Sociological Association meeting of the later-published paper, Stacey (1987) discussed her difficulty in grappling with knowledge that a key subject in her account was struggling with issues of sexual orientation and finally "came out" as a lesbian to close associates and to the researcher. Initially, the subject asked Stacey to withhold this information in her account. This produced an ethical dilemma for Stacey, who believed the information was essential for understanding the account. The dilemma was resolved when the subject, without pressure from the researcher, informed Stacey that it would be acceptable for the researcher to discuss the informant's sexual orientation in her account.

Stacey, like many researchers who have carried out both qualitative and quantitative research, found qualitative research to be more emotionally demanding on the researcher than quantitative analysis. She hints that issues of potential emotional manipulation might be more critical for women, who are socialized to be proficient in this form of influence (see also Rollins, 1985).

Sociologist Lillian Rubin (1976) formed controversial relationships with research subjects in producing *Worlds of Pain*, a book about working-class families. Rubin shared with her respondents a childhood in a working-class family, although as a married adult she held middle-class status. Rubin acknowledges that coming to grips with issues in her personal life and challenging what she believed were stultifying, stereotypical, elitist portraits of working-class family life by sociologists was an important impetus guiding her work. Rubin provided portions of her text to selected respondents prior to its publication, in some (but not all) instances modifying her account in light of their responses. Checking out tentative interpretations with key actors in a social setting is a common practice in qualitative sociology, but sharing prepublication drafts of sociological accounts with lay subjects is far less frequent. Rubin was aware that interviews stirred up painful memories and sometimes difficult after effects for some subjects. Trained as a therapist, she offered limited, cost-free therapy to subjects who desired it, a controversial procedure that has drawn lavish praise and also bitter criticism (see e.g., Jackall, Laslett, and Skolnick, 1978; McCourt, 1977).

Judith Rollins (1985) struggled with emotion, exhaustion, and ethical dilemmas to research and write *Between Women*, an ethnographic account of relations between domestic workers and their employers. Rollins combined archival analysis and interviewing of domestic workers and their employers with participant observation. She worked as a domestic for several employers, an experience she found to be sometimes exhausting, occasionally satisfying, and always emotionally draining. Her experience and her emotional response to it are used reflexively to enrich the accounts of her interview subjects who worked as domestics as well as to provide insights into roles of employers. She struggled with issues of deception, as when she intentionally altered dress or language to be accepted as a "real" domestic worker in the eyes of potential employers. She ultimately made a personal decision that it was acceptable in this context to deceive employers but unacceptable to deceive relatively less-privileged domestic workers in the course of data gathering.

Despite controversial reviews, these works are achieving some measure of reward within the American Sociological Association. Rollins' book won the Jessie Bernard Award given by the association to the best book-length work about women's lives, and Hochschild's (1989) *The Second Shift* was a nominee for the prestigious Cooley award.

British sociologist Ann Oakley (1981) characterizes traditional forms of qualitative interviewing as potentially exploitative of research subjects. Oakley's sensitivity to this theme was heightened in the course of her long-term qualitative research on women's experiences during pregnancy, childbirth, and transition into motherhood (Oakley, 1981, 1984a, 1984b). Initially attempting to maintain the stance of the "objective" researcher and revealing only the bare outlines of her personal history in interviews with pregnant women, Oakley constantly was pressed for medical information and details of her own confinements by respondents who knew she had children. She discovered that many women lacked knowledge of fundamentals of pregnancy and childbirth (asking her, for example, which hole in their bodies the baby emerged from) as well as information on nutrition, exercise, the dangers of smoking and drug-taking, and the like. Oakley decided that to withhold such information was immoral. She answered questions where she could and urged women to confront their physicians more assertively where she could not provide answers.[3] Oakley (1981) suggests that a more appropriate orientation for researchers and subjects is what she terms *inter-viewing*, in which both researcher and subjects are conscious of one another's agendas and attempt to mold the research to address both. Relatedly, Carolyn Ellis (1991) recently has advocated greater use of what she terms "sociological introspection" on emotional experience as a means to explore in greater depth how emotions are felt and how they affect social action. Ellis argues that self-introspection (detailed analysis of one's own feelings) and interactive introspection (sharing of emotional experience with subject-collaborators) can yield valuable data not attainable by other methods.

Involvement as collaborators with research subjects provokes criticism from some classical ethnographers who argue that researchers must attempt to maintain the "fly-on-the-wall" role and intervene as little as possible in research (Bogdan and Taylor, 1975). Such critics are suspicious of research that combines ethnography with techniques such as experimentation or survey research, because by structuring the form in which information is elicited, the researcher is intruding on and thereby transforming the setting. They also question those research projects in which the researcher maintains an active role in a setting and those in which the researcher develops close relationships with informants. In fact, these "fly-on-the-wall" studies have often been more espoused in principle than in fact, as most researchers involve themselves in the situation (e.g., Erikson, 1977). But today the principle is being questioned in a more public way than before, especially by researchers writing from a feminist perspective.

Objectivity versus Subjectivity

The debate about whether sociologists should carry out research on topics in which they have strong or little emotional investment and personal involvement is a long-standing one in sociology and one not limited to qualitative work (Merton, 1972; Gouldner, 1962; Lee, 1978). Often the debate is a fraud, in that it is hard to find a sociologist who has no concern about what he or she studies. The illusion is that the researcher wants "Just the facts, ma'am." Yet, all research has some element of subjectivity. In fieldwork, such concerns are more overtly central, because ethnographers must give some sort of account of their interest in the phenomena they observe to subjects and to readers within the discipline. Thus, a recentering of fieldwork—and especially that by women and minority scholars who work from feminist and/or critical perspectives—raises the role of self anew.

The rift between prevailing theory and ideology and one's subjectivity is the inspiration for revisionist analysis (Cook and Fonow, 1986; Farganis, 1986; Keller, 1985; Smith, 1987). These theorists view self-reflection and emotion as valuable sources of data, a controversial position that leads to criticism that works are "polemical" if they address controversial issues of concern to the researcher. This raises anew the old charge that qualitative research is nothing but advocacy or journalism and that the conclusions are nothing more than personal opinions. For 20 years, some qualitative researchers have tried to emulate a scientific model with its concern with validity and reliability; however today the trend in sceptical circles is to see qualitative research as more akin to literary criticism (see Krieger, 1983).

What often is labeled "action research" falls into this category of controversial work, and it often has a qualitative focus. The researcher forms and acknowledges a specific commitment to individuals or groups involved in a social relationship, frequently to a "have not," less powerful, or stigmatized group. The research is organized and interpreted at least partially according to the needs of the group to which the researcher has partisan ties. Some theorists, most prominently Becker (1967) and Gouldner (1962), approach the matter differently, arguing that researchers inevitably have partisan ties, acknowledged or not, in the research alliance. When partisanship is unacknowledged, some suggest that it serves the interests of the elites, whereas others believe that qualitative researchers, like many social scientists, tend to identify with the oppressed in their "hidden" beliefs.

Studies of families of children with cancer carried out by Mark Chesler and colleagues are qualitative forms of action research (Barbarin and Chesler, 1983; Chesler and Barbarin, 1987). Chesler, whose own child successfully battled leukemia, had a personal stake and substantial emotional investment in the project, as did other members of the collaborative team. The research was designed to address issues defined as relevant by families whose children were undergoing treatment for cancer more so than to address theoretical issues in sociology. In some sense, Chesler was speaking for a group of which he was a member.

Representatives of critical actors—afflicted children, family members, medical professionals, social workers—influenced and criticized the work at each step. The emotional responses of participants and datagatherers were addressed throughout the research process and incorporated into the final product. Although the focus was on the production of "useful" information, the research also makes contributions to sociological theory by, for example, clarifying sources of social support and differentiating between useful and destructive forms of intended support. Sections of the work addressing the experiences of cancer survivors returning to school, sometimes with noticeable signs of their ordeals such as amputated limbs, not only provides practical information for educators and parents of children with special needs but also advances theory about stigma and its operation in social settings.

Collaborative ethnography may or may not be a form of action research. Collaborative ethnography is employed with the intent of representing multiple perspectives in the final account. Collaborative ethnography sometimes is, and sometimes is not, linked to action research. Indeed, the traditional collaborative approach was merely an attempt to gain more sources of data, rather than being oriented to social change (Becker et al., 1961; Sherif, 1962; Strauss, Schatzman, Erlich, and Sabshin, 1963). One prominent example of collaborative ethnography is an Australian ethnographic study of schools which involved researchers of varying race, gender, ethnicity, and sexual orientation and included public school teachers as well as university-based researchers (Connell, 1987; Connell et al., 1982; Kessler et al., 1985). Members of the research team varied in the degree to which they were merely interested in application of research results and indentified with the interests of specific groups in the schools and larger society. Their intent was not simply to ensure that the interests of all these parties were addressed by the research but that the account insofar as possible incorporated perspectives of diverse groups. In the United States, collaborative ethnography is used particularly often in evaluation research. Despite a few large-scale projects, ethnography still is largely a solo-authored enterprise, although increasing numbers of scholars are collaborating with subjects in the production of their accounts (Hochschild, 1989; Oakley 1984a,b; Rollins, 1985; Rubin, 1976).

Writing Qualitative Accounts

The relative control exercised by researchers and informants in the production and use of the final account has been problematic within qualitative sociology. Feminist sociologists, in particular, have objected to the obliteration of informants' voices in the accounts of "expert" sociologists who intend to speak primarily to specialists in their disciplines. Emphasis on the expert's voice has been attacked not simply as morally inappropriate but also as producing limited-vision scholarship that generalizes too facilely and makes false claims to universal truths (Smith, 1987).

Smith (1987) argues that all sociology is written from a standpoint: the subjective reality of the researcher, denying claims to objectivity. Those who claim otherwise typically are writing from the perspective of what she terms "the relations of the ruling." Highlighted in their accounts are phenomena, language, ideologies, and ways of knowing which are important from the perspective of elites. Such analyses typically are presented as theory and/or generalizable accounts, presumably incorporating significant experiences of all social actors.

Smith (1987) argues that white women and nonprivileged white men and minority women and men (i.e., those outside the ruling elites and who have not been participants in the construction of the prevailing discourse and ideology) frequently experience a rift between lived experience and the "generalized" theories that supposedly explain important components of their lives. Smith recognized the rift when she realized an unbridgeable gulf between the core of sociology she studied as a graduate student and her after-school life as the single mother of two small children. Smith argues that the rift can be the starting point for a creative, revisionist sociology that captures standpoints of less privileged social actors. She also recognizes the fundamental challenge that such a perspective raises for mainstream sociology, whether qualitative or not.

Smith (1987) details a strategy, based on research in progress with her colleague Alison Kelly, by which social organizations, from local neighborhood groups to the global economy, can be studied from the perspective of nonprivileged groups. They are concerned with the time-consuming but often unrecognized work that mothers have done for generations to articulate their children to school. The analysis begins at the immediate, face-to-face level. As it moves to successively larger and more abstract levels of social organization, the phenomenological perspective of the participant, not the expert, is used to define the relevant questions for inquiry and the meaningful sources of data. For example, mothers identify problematic intersections between home and school life. The mothers' perspectives, rather than the perspectives of school officials, become the basis for framing questions posed at the next level of organization: the schooling environment.

Susan Krieger (1983) grappled with the dilemma of how much abstraction and generalization were appropriate in *The Mirror Dance*, her participant observation study of a lesbian community. Krieger found conflicting, nonreconcilable visions of the community. Some participants saw it as a loose amalgamation of persons sharing intellectual concerns, while others viewed it as a tight-knit, intimate group providing emotional sustenance as well as intellectual stimulation. She reports a myriad of other visions about the community's functions and boundaries. Krieger consciously resists endorsing any one perspective, however, by not revealing her judgment about what the "real" community might be from her perspective as the "expert." To do so, she notes, would be to render invisible the fact that the community meant different things to various members. Knowing the divergent views of various members of the community made some of the conflicts that emerged within it comprehensible.

Krieger noted in a session on qualitative methods at the 1981 American Sociological Association meetings that her refusal to insert the voice of the expert into her accounts caused some scholars to label her work as journalistic rather than sociological.

Similar themes are raised by Blauner's (1987) discussion of the difficulties of presenting oral history materials as sociology. Oral history is a relatively new technique in sociology, and, Blauner argues, there are no disciplinary norms about the appropriate treatment of such materials and substantial disagreement about how much "processing" by sociologists of such first-hand materials is appropriate. Sociologists commonly select, arrange, edit, and otherwise manipulate qualitative materials forming accounts. Yet, to do so distorts the lived reality of the subjects and obliterates the subjects' ordering of events and meanings. Refusing to cast the materials into familiar scholarly forms risks having it delegitimated as nonscholarly or non-sociological. At the least the sociologist is expected to offer histories as representative types within a conceptual scheme justified as having sociological significance.

Such editing, however, distorts the coherence and order of the account from the perspective of the subject. The subject's voice and mode of presentation is lost in the process of translating the account into one more easily comprehensible by sociologists. Blauner, like Krieger, argues for less processing of these materials. The question that critics will ask is whether or not these accounts tell us anything beyond themselves and whether or not to "simply" learn about a particular scene is sufficient. Is the writer abdicating her or his responsibility to generalize, while leaving it to the reader, who will have no such qualms?

Reissman (1987) raises a related concern in connection with her research on women's accounts of the dissolution of marriages. Reissman found that researchers and therapists, who overwhelmingly are white and middle class, were able to "hear" and comprehend accounts given by those women undergoing divorce whose backgrounds were similar to their own. White middle-class subjects tended to organize accounts temporally, reporting significant events in the time sequence in which they occurred. Such a reporting style coincided with the ways in which researchers analyze data and construct accounts. Women of different ethnicity and social strata organized accounts thematically and episodically, a style that researchers and therapists find harder to comprehend. The closer links between discourses of researchers and middle-class white women created temptations to give these subjects' voices more centrality in the written account.

Aptheker (1989) writes that women's lives often are constructed in nonrelated fragments, which she compares with bits of fabrics composing tapestries. Women talk of goals and motives in a manner different from that of men, who usually have the power to exert more control over the course of their lives. Women's conversations ramble more than those of men and are interrupted more frequently. Furthermore, women's accounts leap back and forth between the private and the public domains that some have suggested are in reality more easily separable for men than for women (DeVault, 1990; Lengermann and Niebrugge-Brantley, 1990). Yet sociological accounts of women's lives often attempt to "organize" these rambling conversations under topical headings so that the very form of presentation distorts the ways in which women experience and perceive their lives.

Discussing one's life, like making a tapestry or a quilt, can be a long and convoluted practice that often seems to lack momentum and direction. The end result often is a creative integration of fragments into an object with both instrumental and artistic worth. The norms of presentation of sociological work, these writers argue, obliterate the form of women's experience, casting it as more goal-directed, less emotional, and more linear than it actually is.

Conclusion

Twenty years is a long time in the life of the mind. We have argued that over the past two decades ethnography in sociology has changed dramatically—in its popularity, its justification, its procedures, its openness to other methodologies, its relationship to theory, and its presentation. While some may consider ethnography in sociology to be simply "going about to see what's up," we suggest that this methodology is complex, tightly argued, and beset with important and stimulating controversies. It is appropriate that many of these controversies are found in qualitative research in sociology, because it was in sociology that ethnography was transformed from the examination of the "other" (common in anthropology ethnographies, travel writings, and missionary accounts) to the examination of our own communities. Anthropologists, scholars in journalism, educational researchers, and others have followed sociologists back to home territory to uncover the depth and richness of our own lives.

Notes

[1] Hochschild's (1989) recent study of dual-career families, *The Second Shift*, was explicitly written to be accessible to popular audiences and was, during 1989, a selection of the Quality Paperback Book Club. Hochschild's (1973, 1983) earlier books had been directed primarily to scholarly audiences.
[2] The authors find that when they present the paper, they typically are interrupted by the audience, who seem to want to end quotations of field notes that they find to be painful.
[3] Women researchers' identification with interests of women as subjects is by no means a recent phenomenon. Margaret Hagood (1977), a demographer conducting research with poor rural women in the 1930s in the United States, discusses ways in which she collaborated with subjects to provide them with information about contraception, even though she was accompanied on interviews by a male chaperon whose expressed duty it was to see that such information was not transmitted!

Acknowledgments

We are grateful for comments on earlier drafts by William Finlay and Margaret D. LeCompte.

References

Adler, Patricia A., and Adler, Peter. (1987). *Membership roles in field research.* Beverly Hills, CA: Sage Publications.
Adler, Patricia A., and Adler, Peter. (1990). *Backboards and blackboards.* New York: Columbia University Press.
Adler, Peter. (1984). The sociologist as celebrity: The role of the media in field research. *Qualitative Sociology,* 7, 2–32.
Agar, M. (1980). *The professional stranger: An informal introduction to ethnography.* New York: Academic Press.
Agar, M. (1986). *Speaking of ethnography.* Beverly Hills, CA: Sage Publications.

Aptheker, B. H. (1989). *Tapestries of life: Women's work, women's consciousness, and the meaning of daily experience.* Amherst: University of Massachusetts Press.

Barbarin, O., and Chesler, M. (1983). *Children with cancer: Views of parents, educators, adolescents, and physicians.* Maywood, IL: Eterna Press.

Becker, H. S. (1967). Who's side are we on? *Social Problems,* 14, 239–247.

Becker, H. S. (1974). Photography and sociology. *Studies in Visual Communication,* 1, 3–26.

Becker, H. S. (1978). Arts and crafts. *American Journal of Sociology,* 83, 862–889.

Becker, H. S. (1981). *Exploring society photographically.* Chicago: University of Chicago Press.

Becker, H. S. (1982). *Art worlds.* Berkeley: University of California Press.

Becker, H. S. (1985). *Writing for social scientists.* Chicago: University of Chicago Press.

Becker, H. S., and McCall, M. (Eds.). (1990). *Symbolic interaction and cultural studies.* Chicago: University of Chicago Press.

Becker, H. S., et al. (1961). *Boys in white: Student culture in medical school.* Chicago: University of Chicago Press.

Best, R. (1983). *We've all got scars: What boys and girls learn in elementary school.* Bloomington: Indiana University Press.

Blauner, B. (1987). Problems of editing 'first-person' sociology. *Qualitative Sociology,* 10, 46–64.

Bogdan, R., and Taylor, S. J. (1975). *Introduction to qualitative research methods.* New York: Wiley.

Broadhead, R. S., and Rist, R. C. (1976). Gatekeepers and the social control of social research. *Social Problems,* 23, 325–336.

Burawoy, M. (1979). *Manufacturing consent: Changes in the labor process under monopoly capitalism.* Chicago: University of Chicago Press.

Burawoy, M. (1985). *The politics of production: Factory regimes under capitalism and socialism.* London: Verso.

Cannon, L. Weber, Higginbotham, E. and Leung, M. A. (1988). Race and class bias in qualitative research on women. *Gender & Society,* 2, 449–462.

Chesler, M. A., and Barbarin, O. (1987). *Childhood cancer and the family.* New York: Bruner/Mazil.

Clement, D., Eisenhart, M., and Harding, J. (1979). The veneer of harmony: Social race relations in a desegregated elementary school. In R. C. Rist (Ed.), *Desegregated schools: Appraisals of an American experiment* (pp. 15–64). New York: Academic Press.

Clifford, J., and Marcus, G. (1986). *Writing culture.* Berkeley: University of California Press.

Collins, P. Hill. (1990). *Black feminist thought: Knowledge, consciousness, and the politics of empowerment.* New York: Allen and Unwin.

Condit, C. M. (1990). *Decoding abortion rhetoric: Communicating social change.* Urbana: University of Illinois Press.

Connell, R. W. (1987). *Gender and power.* Stanford, CA: Stanford University Press.

Connell, R. W., et al. (1982). *Making the difference: Schools, families, and social division.* Sydney: Allen and Unwin.

Conrad, P. (1986). The myth of cut-throats among premedical students: On the role of stereotypes in justifying failure and success. *Journal of Health and Social Behavior,* 27, 150–160.

Conrad, P. (1988). Learning to doctor: Reflections on recent accounts of the medical school years. *Journal of Health and Social Behavior,* 29, 323–332.

Cook, J. and Fonow, M. M. (1986). Knowledge and women's interest: Issues of epistemology and methodology in feminist sociological research. *Sociological Inquiry*, 56, 2–29.

Cosaro, W. (1988). Routines in the peer culture of Italian and American nursery school children. *Sociology of Education*, 61, 1–14.

Cosaro, W. (in press). Cultural context and peer cultures of Italian and American nursery school children. In Philip Wexler (Ed.), *The classroom experience*. London: Falmer.

Cosaro, W., and Rizzo, T. (1988). Discussione and friendship: Socialization procedures in the peer culture of American and Italian nursery school children. *American Sociological Review*, 53, 879–894.

Deegan, M. J., and Hill, M. (Eds.). (1987). *Women and symbolic interaction*. Boston: Allen and Unwin.

Denzin, N. (1970). *The research act*. Chicago: Aldine.

Denzin, N. (1987a). *The alcoholic self*. Beverly Hills, CA: Sage Publications.

Denzin, N. (1987b). *The recovering alcoholic*. Beverly Hills, CA: Sage Publications.

Denzin, N. (1989). *Interpretive interactionism*. Beverly Hills, CA: Sage Publications.

DeVault, M. L. (1990). Talking and listening from women's standpoint: Feminist strategies for interviewing and analysis. *Social Problems*, 37, 96–116.

Eder, D. J. (1985). The cycle of popularity: Interpersonal relations among female adolescents. *Sociology of Education*, 58, 154–165.

Eder, D. J. (1988). Building cohesion through collaborative narration. *Social Psychology Quarterly*, 51, 225–235.

Eder, D. J. (1990). Serious and playful disputes: Variations in conflict talk among female adolescents. *In* Alan Grimshaw (Ed.), *Conflict talk: Sociolinguistic arguments in conversations*. Cambridge, MA: Cambridge University Press.

Eder, D. J. (in press a). The role of teasing in adolescent peer group culture. *In* Spencer Cahill (Ed.) *Sociological studies of child development*.

Eder, D. J. (in press b). Teasing activities among adolescent females. *In* Deborah Tannen (Ed.), *Gender and talk*. New York: Morrow.

Eder, D.J., and Enke, J. (in press). The Structure of gossip: Opportunities and constraints. *American Sociological Review*, 56, 494–508.

Eder, D. J., and Parker, S. (1987). The cultural production and reproduction of gender: The effect of extracurricular activities on peer group culture. *Sociology of Education*, 60, 200–213.

Eichler, M. (1987). *Nonsexist research methods*. Boston: Allen and Unwin.

Ellis, C. (1991). Sociological introspection and emotional experience. *Symbolic Interaction*, 14, 23–50.

Emerson, R. (1983). *Contemporary field work*. Boston: Little, Brown.

Enke, J. (1990) Informal talk among female athletes in a high school setting. Paper presented at the American Sociological Association meetings, Washington, DC.

Erikson, K. (1977). *Everything in its path: Destruction of community in the Buffalo Creek flood*. New York: Simon & Schuster.

Evans, C. and Eder, D. (1989). No exit: Process of social isolation in the middle school. Presented at the American Sociological Association meeting, San Francisco.

Farganis, S. (1986). Social theory and feminist theory: The need for dialogue. *Sociological Inquiry*, 56, 50–68.

Fetterman, D. (1987). *Ethnography: Step by step*. Beverly Hills, CA: Sage Publications.

Fine, G. A. (1986). Mushrooms, birds or old bottles? Mushroomers and their concerns. *McIlvainea*, 7, 23–30.

Fine, G. A. (1987). *With the boys: Little league baseball and preadolescent culture.* Chicago: University of Chicago Press.

Fine, G. A. (1989). Aesthetic contraints: The culture of production in restaurant kitchens. Paper presentecd at the American Sociological Association meeting, San Francisco.

Fine, G. A. (1990). Symbolic interactionism in the post-Blumerian Age. *In* G. Ritzer (Ed.), *Frontiers of social theory: The new synthesis* (pp. 117–157). New York: Columbia University Press.

Fine, G. A., and Sandstrom, K. L. (1990). *Knowing children: Participant observation with minors.* Beverly Hills, CA: Sage Publications.

Fisher, S. C. (1986). *In the patient's best interest: Women and the politics of medical decisions.* New Brunswick, NJ: Rutgers University Press.

Footnotes. (1988). Methods courses in U.S. sociology departments. Washington, DC: American Sociological Association.

Fuller, M. (1980). Black girls; in the liberal comprehensive. *In* R. Deem (Ed.), *Schooling for women's work.* London: Routledge and Kegal Paul.

Furlong, J. (1984). Black resistance in the liberal comprehensive. *In* S. Delamont (Ed.), *Readings on interaction in the classroom* (2nd ed.). London and New York: Menthuen.

Garson, B. (1988). *The electronic sweatshop.* New York: Penguin.

Gaskell, J. (1985). Course enrollment in high school: The perspective of working-class females. *Sociology of Education,* 58, 48–59.

Gilligan, C. (1982). *In a different voice: Psychological theory and women's development.* Cambridge: Harvard University Press.

Glasberg. D. Silfen (1989). *The power of collective pursestrings: The effects of bank hegemony on corporations and the state.* Berkeley: University of California Press.

Glaser. B., and Strauss, A. (1967). *The discovery of grounded theory.* Chicago: Aldine.

Goetz, J. P., and LeCompte, M. D. (1984). *Ethnography and qualitative design in educational research.* Orlando, FL: Academic Press.

Gold, R. L. (1969). Roles in sociological field observations. *In* G. J. McCall and J. L. Simmons (Eds.), *Issues in participant observation* (pp. 30–38). Reading, MA: Addison-Wesley.

Goodwin, M. H. (1985). The serious side of jump rope: Conversational practices and social organization in the frame of play. *Journal of American Folklore,* 88, 315–330.

Goodwin, M. H. (1990a). Cooperation and competition across girls' play. *In* A. D. Todd and S. Fisher (Eds.), *Gender and discourse: The power of talk* (pp. 55–96). Norwood, NJ: Ablex.

Goodwin, M. H. (1990b). *He said–she said: Talk as social organization among black children.* Bloomington: Indiana University Press.

Gouldner, A. (1962). Anti-minotaur: The myth of a value-free sociology. *Social Problems,* 9, 199–213.

Grant, C., and Sleeter, C. (1986). *After the school bell rings.* Philadelphia: Falmer Press.

Grant, L. (1984). Black females 'place' in desegregated schools. *Sociology of Education,* 57, 58–76.

Grant, L. (1985). Race–gender status, system attachment, and children's experience in desegregated classrooms. *In* L. C. Wilkinson and C. B. Marrett (Eds.), *Gender influences in classroom interaction* (pp. 57–77). New York: Academic Press.

Grant, L. (in press a). Go-betweens, enforcers, and helpers: Black girls in elementary school classrooms. *In* B. T. Dill and M. B. Zinn (Eds.), *Women of color in American society.* Philadelphia: Temple University Press.

Grant, L. (in press b). Race and the schooling of young girls. *In* J. Wrigley (Ed.), *Education and gender inequality*. Philadelphia: Falmer Press.

Grant, L. (in press c). Reduction of tracking and students' experiences in classrooms: Variations by race and gender. *In* P. Wexler (Ed.), *The classroom as experience*. Philadelphia: Temple University Press.

Grant, L., and Ward, K. B. (1991). Gender and publishing in sociology. *Gender & Society*, 5, 207–223.

Grant, L., Ward, K. B., and Rong, X. L. (1987). Is there an association between gender and methods in sociological research? *American Sociological Review*, 52, 856–862.

Gubrium, J. F. (1987). Structuring and destructuring the course of illness: The Alzheimer's disease experience. *Sociology of Health and Illness*, 9(1), 1–24.

Gubrium, J. F. (1988a). Incommunicables and poetic documentation in the Alzheimer's disease experience. Paper presented at the Southern Sociological Society meeting, Nashville, TN.

Gubrium, J. J. (1988b). The social preservation of the mind: The Alzheimer's disease experience. *Symbolic Interaction*, 9, 37–51.

Gubrium, J. F. (1990). *The home care expeience*. Beverly Hills, CA: Sage Publications.

Gubrium, J. F., and Lynott, R. J. (1985). Alzheimer's disease as biographical work. *In* W. A. Peterson and J. Quadagno (Eds.), *Social bonds in later life* (pp. 349–367). Beverly Hills, CA: Sage Publications.

Hagood, M. J. (1977). *Mothers of the South: Portraiture of the white tenant farm woman*. New York: Norton. (Originally published in 1930).

Hammersley, M., and Atkinson, P. (1983). *Ethnography: Principles in practice*. London: Tavistock.

Harper, D. A. (1982). *Good company*. Chicago: University of Chicago Press.

Heath, S. B. (1983). *Ways with words: Language, life, and work in communities and classrooms*. Cambridge: Cambridge University Press.

Hochschild, A. R. (1973). *The unexpected community*. Englewood Cliffs, NJ: Prentice-Hall.

Hochschild, A. R. (1983). *The managed heart: The commercialization of human feeling*. Berkeley: University of California Press.

Hochschild, A. R., with Machung, A. (1989). *The second shift: Working parents and the revolution in the home*. New York: Viking.

Irvine, J. J. (1990). Black students and school failure: Policies, practices, and prescriptions. New York: Greenwood.

Jackall, R. (1988). *Moral mazes: The world of corporate managers*. New York: Cambridge University Press.

Jackall, R., Laslett, B., and Skolnick, A. (1978). Symposium review of Lillian Rubin's *Worlds of pain*. *Contemporary Sociology*, 7(2), 131–139.

Kanter, R. M. (1977). *Men and women of the corporation*. New York: Basic Books.

Keller, E. F. (1985). *Reflections on gender and science*. New Haven: Yale University Press.

Kessler, S., Ashenden, D. J., Connell, R. W., and Dowsett. (1985). Gender relations in secondary schooling. *Sociology of Education*, 58, 34–48.

Kinney, D. (1989). From dweeb to normal: Identity change during adolescence. Paper presented at the American Sociological Association meeting, September, San Francisco.

Kleinman, S. (1984). *Equals before God: Seminarians as humanistic professionals*. Chicago: University of Chicago Press.

Konner, M. (1987). *Becoming a doctor: A journey of initiation in medical school*. New York: Viking.

Krieger, S. (1983). *The mirror dance*. Philadelphia: Temple University Press.

Kulis, S. (1988). The representation of women in top-ranked sociology departments. *American Sociologist, 19*, 203–217.

Lee, A. M. (1978). *Sociology for whom?* New York: Oxford University Press.

Lengermann, P. M., and Niebrugge-Brantley, J. (1990). Feminist sociological theory: The near-future prospects. In G. Ritzer (Ed.), *Frontiers of social theory: The new synthesis* (pp. 316–346). New York: Columbia University Press.

Lesko, N. (1988). *Symbolizing society: Stories, rites and structure in a Catholic high school*. New York: Falmer.

Lever, J. (1978). Sex differences in the complexity of children's play and games. *American Sociological Review, 43*, 471–483.

Lever, J. (1983). *Soccer madness*. Chicago: University of Chicago Press.

Liebow, E. (1967). *Tally's corner: A study of Negro streetcorner man*. Boston: Little, Brown.

Lofland, J., and Lofland, L. (1984). *Analyzing social settings: A guide to qualitative observation and analysis* (2nd ed.). Belmont, CA: Wadsworth Publishing.

Lorber, J. (1988). From the editor. *Gender & Society, 2*, 5–8.

Luttrell, W. (1989). Working class women's ways of knowing: Effects of gender, race, and class. *Sociology of Education, 58*, 34–47.

Mackie, M. (1985). Female sociologists; productivity, collegial relations, and research style examined through journal publications. *Sociology and Social Research, 69*, 189–207.

Manning, P. K. (1978). Editor's remarks. *Urban Life, 7*, 283–284.

Maynard, D. W. (1985). On the functions of social conflict among children. *American Sociological Review, 50*, 207–223.

McCall, G. S. (1984). Systematic field observation. *Annual Review of Sociology, 10*, 263–282.

McCall, G., and Simmons, J. L. (1969). *Issues in participant observation*. Reading MA: Addison-Wesley.

McCall, M., and Becker, H. S. (1990). Performance science. *Social Problems, 37*, 117–132.

McCarthy, C. (1990). *Race and curriculum: Social inequality and the theories and politics of difference in contemporary research on schooling*. Philadelphia: Falmer.

McCourt, K. (1977). Review of Lillian Rubin's *Worlds of pain*. *American Journal of Sociology, 83*, 813–816.

McNamee, S. J., Willis, C. L., and Rotchford, A. M. (1990). Gender differences in patterns of publication in leading sociology journals, 1960–1985. *American Sociologist, 21*, 99–115.

Mehan, H. (1979). *Learning lessons: Social organization in the classroom*. Cambridge, MA: Harvard University Press.

Merton, R. K. (1972). Insiders and outsiders. *American Journal of Sociology, 77*, 9–47.

Metz, M. H. (1978). *Classrooms and corridors: The crisis of authority in desegregated secondary schools*. Berkeley: University of California Press.

Metz, M. H. (1986). *Different by design: The context and character of three magnet schools*. Boston: Routledge and Kegan Paul.

Millman, M. (1980). *Such a pretty face: Being fat in America*. New York: Norton.

Mishler, E. G. (1986). *Research interviewing: Context and narrative*. Cambridge, MA: Harvard University Press.

Moore, H. (1983). Hispanic women: Schooling for conformity in public education. *Hispanic Journal of Behavioral Science, 5*, 45–63.

Mullard, C. (1985). Multiracial education in Britain: From assimilation to cultural pluralism. *In Race and gender: Equal opportunities in education* (pp. 39–52). Oxford: Pergamon.

Mullins, N. J. (1983). Theories and theory groups revisited. *In* R. Collins (Ed.), *Sociological theory*. San Francisco: Jossey-Bass.

Myerhoff, B. (1978). *Number our days*. New York: Dutton.

Nielsen, J. M. (1990). *Feminist research methods: Exemplary readings in the social sciences*. Boulder, CO: Westview.

Oakley, A. (1981). Interviewing women: A contradiction in terms. *In* H. Roberts (Ed.), *Doing feminist research*. London: Routledge.

Oakley, A. (1984a). *The captured womb: A history of the medical care of pregnant women*. New York: Oxford.

Oakley, A. (1984b). *From here to maternity: Becoming a mother*. Harmondsworth, England: Penguin.

Paget, M. (1990). Performing the text. *Journal of Contemporary Ethnography*, 19, 136–155.

Patton, M. Q. (1990). *Qualitative evaluation and research methods* (2nd ed.). Beverly Hills, CA: Sage Publications.

Pitzer, H., and Palinski, C. O. (1980). *Coping with a miscarriage*. New York: Doubleday.

Rainwater, L., and Pitman, D. J. (1967). Ethical problems in studying a politically sensitive and deviant community. *Social Problems*, 14, 357–366.

Reinharz, S. (1983a). Experiential analysis: A contribution to feminist research. *In* G. Bowles and R. Duelli-Klein (Eds.), *Theories of women's studies*. London: Routledge and Kegan Paul.

Reinharz, S. (1983b). *On becoming a social scientist*. San Franscisco: Jossey-Bass.

Reinharz, S. (1986). The social psychology of a miscarriage: An application of symbolic interaction theory and method. *In* M. J. Deegan and M. Hill (Eds.), *Women and symbolic interaction (pp. 229–249). New York: Allen and Unwin*.

Reinharz, S. (1988). What's missing in miscarriage?   *Journal of Community Psychology*, 16(1), 84–102.

Richards, P. (1985). Risk. *In* H. Becker, *Writing for social scientists* (pp. 108–120). Chicago: University of Chicago Press.

Richardson, L. (1985). *The new other woman: Contemporary single women in affairs with married men*. New York: The Free Press.

Richardson, L. (1987). Disseminating research to popular audiences: The book tour *Qualitative Sociology*, 10, 164–176.

Richardson, L. (1990a). Narrative and sociology. *Journal of Contemporary Ethnography*, 19, 116–129.

Richardson, L. (1990b). *Writing strategies: Reaching diverse audiences*. Beverly Hills, CA: Sage Publications.

Richlin-Klonsky, J., and Strenski, E. (1991). The ethnographic field research paper. *In A guide to writing sociology papers* (pp. 93–126). New York: St. Martin's Press.

Riessman, C. K. (1990). Worlds of difference: Contrasting experience in marriage and narrative style *In* A. D. Todd and S. Fisher (Eds.), *Gender and discourse: The power of talk* (pp. 151–176). Norwood, NJ: Ablex.

Rist, R. C. (1973). *The urban school: Factory for failure*. Cambridge, MA: MIT Press.

Rist, R. C. (1978). *The invisible children: School integration in American society*. Cambridge, MA: Harvard University Press.

Rollins, J. (1985). *Between women: Domestics and their employers*. Philadelphia: Temple University Press.

Rollwagen, J. R. (1988). *Anthropological film-making*. Chur, Switzerland: Harwood Academic Publishing.

Roman, L. (1989). *Becoming feminine: The politics of popular culture*. Philadelphia: Falmer.

Roy, D. (1958). Banana time: Job satisfaction and informal interaction. *Human Organization*, 18, 158–168.

Roy, D. (1952). Quota restriction and goldbricking in a machine shop. *American Journal of Sociology*, 57, 427–442.

Rose, D. (1990). *Living the ethnographic life*. Newbury Park, CA: Sage Publications.

Rubin, L. B. (1976). *Worlds of pain: Life in the working-class family*. New York: Basic Books.

Sanford, S., and Eder, D. J. (1984). Adolescent humor during peer interaction. *Social Psychology Quarterly*, 47, 235–243.

Saxton, S. (1988). Comments in Society for the Study of Symbolic Interaction Notes, November, pp. 1, 3.

Schatzman, L., and Strauss, A. (1973). *Field research: Strategies for a natural sociology*. Englewood Cliffs, NJ: Prentice-Hall.

Schofield, J. W. (1982). *Black and white in school: Trust, tolerance, or tokenism?* New York: Praeger.

Schofield, J. W. (1981). Complementary and conflicting identities: Images and interaction in an interracial school. *In* S. R. Asher and J. M. Gottman (Eds.), *The development of children's friendships* (pp. 53–90). Cambridge: Cambridge University Press.

Schofield, J. W., and Sagar, H. A. (1977). Peer interaction in a desegregated middle school. *Sociometry*, 40, 130–138.

Schwartz, D. (1990). Visual ethnography: Using photography in qualitative research. *Qualitative Sociology*, 12, 119–154.

Scott-Jones, D., and Clark, M. (1986). The schooling experience of black girls: The interaction of gender, race, and socioeconomic status. *Phi Delta Kappan*, 67, 520–526.

Shaffir, W. B., Stebbins, R. A., and Turowetz, A. (Eds.). (1980). *Fieldwork experience: Qualitative approaches to social research*. New York: St. Martin's Press.

Sherif, M. (1962). *Reference groups: Explorations into conformity and deviation of adolescents*. New York: Harper & Row.

Sherif, M., and Sherif, C. (1964). *Intergroup relations and leadership: Approaches and research in industrial, ethnic, cultural, and political areas*. Norman: University of Oklahoma Institute for Group Relations.

Simon, R., Eder, D., and Evans, C. (1989). The development of feeling norms underlying romantic love among adolescent females. Paper presented at the Midwest Sociological Society meetings, St. Louis.

Smith, D. E. (1987). *The everyday world as problematic: A feminist sociology*. Boston: Northeastern University Press.

Smith, V. (1990). *Managing in the corporate interest: Control and resistance in an American bank*. Berkeley: University of California Press.

Spradley, J. P. (1977). *Ethnographic interviewing*. New York: Holt, Rinehart & Winston.

Spradley, J. P. (1980). *Participant observation*. New York: Holt, Rinehart & Winston.

Stacey, J. (1987). Does ethnography solve ethical dilemmas? Paper presented at the American Sociological Association meeting, Chicago.

Stacey, J. (1988). Can there be a feminist ethnography? *Women's Studies International Forum*, 11, 21–27.

Statham, A., Miller, E. M., and Mausch, H. O. (Eds.). (1988). *The worth of women's work: A qualitative synthesis*. Albany, NY: SUNY Press.

Strauss, A. L. (1987). *Qualitative analysis for social scientists*. Cambridge, MA: Cambridge University Press.

Strauss, A., Schatzman, L., Erlich, D., and Sabshin, M. (1963). The hospital and its negotiated order. *In* E. Friedson (Ed.), *The hospital in modern society* (pp. 147–169). New York: The Free Press.

Sudnow, D. (1967). *Passing on*. Englewood Cliffs, NJ: Prentice-Hall.

Suttles, G. (1968). *The social order of the slum*. Chicago: University of Chicago Press.

Thorne, B. (1985). Boys and girls together . . . but mostly apart: Gender arrangements in elementary schools. *In* W. Hartrup and Z. Rubin (Eds.), *Relationships and development*. Hillside, NJ: Lawrence Erlbaum.

Valli, L. (1986). *Becoming clerical workers*. London: Routledge and Kegan Paul.

Van Maanen, John (1983). *Qualitative methodology*. Beverly Hills, CA: Sage Publications.

Van Maanen, J. (1988). *Tales of the field: On writing ethnography*. Chicago: University of Chicago Press.

Walker, A., and Moulton R. K. (1990). Photo albums: Images of time and reflections of self. *Qualitative Sociology*, 12, 155–182.

Ward, K. B. (Ed.). (1990). *Women workers and global restructuring*. Ithaca, NY: ILR Press.

Ward, K. B., and Grant, L. (1985). The feminist critique and a decade of publishing in sociology journals. *The Sociological Quarterly*, 19, 139–158.

Warren, C. A. B. (1988). *Gender issues in field research*. Beverly Hills, CA: Sage Publications.

West, C. (1984). *Routine complications: Troubles with talk between doctors and patients*. Bloomington: Indiana University Press.

Whyte, W. F. (1948). *Street-corner society: The social structure of an American slum*. Chicago: University of Chicago Press.

Wright, L. K. (1988). Alzheimer's disease as developmental asychrony: A dialectical paradigm of the marital relationship of older couples. Unpublished Ph.D. dissertation, Department of Sociology, University of Georgia, Athens.

CHAPTER 10

❑ On Critical Ethnography (with Some Postmodern Considerations)

Richard A. Quantz

The Handbook of Qualitative Research in Education

Introduction

What is critical ethnography? The question begs for a definitive answer, one that clearly demarcates the boundaries of a "critical" ethnography from all other forms. Unfortunately, no answer is likely to satisfy critical ethnographers themselves, because to define the term is to assume an epistemological stance in which the social world can be precisely defined—a position that is not very critical. Still several attempts have been made in the last decade to provide a working idea of critical ethnography. For example, in the introduction of a 1980 special issue of *Urban Life*, dedicated to "critical perspectives on ethnography," T. R. Young, the issue's editor, wrote "As a collection these articles examine how human consciousness is organized in late capitalism and how social action is constrained in the interests of profit, growth, and control by the various knowledge-producing industries, especially social science and related disciplines" (Young, 1980:133). Masemann (1982:1) wrote " 'Critical ethnography' refers to studies which use a basically anthropological, qualitative, participant-observer methodology but which rely for their theoretical formulation on a body of theory deriving from critical sociology and philosophy." Simon and Dippo (1986) wrote

> For ethnographic work to warrant the label "critical" requires that it meet three fundamental conditions: (1) the work must employ an organizing problematic that defines one's data and analytical procedures in a way consistent with its project; (2) the work must be situated, in part, within a public sphere that allows it to become the starting point for the critique and transformation of the conditions of oppressive and inequitable moral and social regulation; and (3) the work must address the limits of its own claims by a consideration of how, as a form of social practice, it too is constituted and regulated through historical relations of power and existing material conditions. (p. 197)

None of these definitions really provides specific boundaries for critical ethnography, and, in this essay, I too will not so much define critical ethnography as I will place it within a discourse. Critical ethnography is one form of an empirical project associated with critical discourse, a form in which a researcher utilizing field methods that place the researcher on-site attempts to re-present the "culture," the "consciousness," or the "lived experiences" of people living in asymmetrical power relations. As a "project," critical ethnography is recognized as having conscious political intentions that are oriented toward emancipatory and democratic goals. What is key to this approach is that for ethnography to be considered "critical" it should participate in a larger "critical" dialogue rather than follow any particular set of methods or research techniques.

If, in fact, research methods do not seem to be crucial in the conceptualization of critical ethnography, then one might feel compelled to address the topic of critical ethnography by concentrating on what makes critical ethnography "ethnography"; however, I have chosen to focus on what makes critical ethnography "critical." I did not make this decision lightly, because I am all too aware of two apparently opposite reactions of ethnographers to critical ethnography. One reaction is to ask "What does this have to do with ethnography?" and the other is to ask "But isn't critical ethnography just good ethnography?" My simple answer to the first question is to reply that if "ethnography" is only some derivative of Franz Boaz' or Bronislaw Malinowski's work then "critical ethnography" has little to do with "ethnography," but if by "ethnography" we mean the re-production or rewriting of a social group's culture then it has everything to do with it. My simple answer to the second reaction is that, while I would like to believe that critical ethnography is just "good" ethnography, too many examples of ethnography have some claim to excellence that just aren't very critical.

I have decided to focus on the critical side of critical ethnography because one of the commonly expressed ideas in critical ethnography is the refusal to bifurcate theory from method; that is, those engaged in critical ethnography find any discussion of method outside of theory to be not only sterile but distorted. Method is fully embedded in theory and theory is expressed in method. This is not to say that lively debate does not exist among those engaged in various forms of critical ethnography concerning method (see e.g., Hollands, 1985; Carr and Kemmis, 1986; Gitlin, Siegel, and Boru, 1988; Lather, 1986; Anderson, 1989) but that method must never be reduced to technique. This position is in agreement with Thomas (1983:478–479), who lamented that social ethnography had been reduced from its "critical potential" in the Chicago School days to no more than "the application of methodological rules and the practice of normative techniques rather than the development of social insights." For these reasons, I have opted to explore the discourse and some examples of what might be called critical ethnography rather than attempt to lay out some basic (but mythical) rules that govern its methods.

Describing the parameters and rules of any research method is risky, but attempting to codify the research approach often referred to as critical ethnography is foolish. For one thing, those engaged in research that might be labeled "critical ethnography" often have

Method vs. theory

C/E ⇒ Utterance in an ongoing critical dialogue

widely varied projects arrived at through unique personal histories. For another thing, those of us who have some interest in things "critical" are often more comfortable critiquing the institutionalized forms of others' works (even "critical" work) than asserting the codification of our own. In fact, many of us are just plain skeptical of any codification. For this reason, this essay has been extremely difficult for me to construct. I became uncomfortable attempting to formalize critical ethnography, because its form has consistently required me to gloss over real differences among a wide variety of research projects, often to "celebrate" examples of which I may be somewhat critical and to leave out altogether certain issues, ideas, or arguments that may be relatively important to certain aspects of critical research. I finally settled on a strategy that lays out one particular understanding of the chronological development of critical ethnography based on the different histories in Great Britain and in North America and draws out five themes often found in the discursive practices of critical ethnography. My argument is that any ethnography that claims to be "critical" must be understood as an utterance in an ongoing "critical" dialogue, and, as such, one can understand critical ethnography better by rereading some of the past dialogue and by elaborating some of the repeated themes of that dialogue. This is not to claim that other approaches are not also very appropriate for those trying to understand critical ethnography (see Anderson, 1989; Fay, 1987; Masemann, 1982; Simon and Dippo, 1986; Thomas, 1983), but only that this is one approach that, I believe, is both consistent with critical thought today and constitutive of the background necessary for newcomers to understand and to participate in the critical dialogue in education. What follows then are two sections: The first briefly reviews some of the crucial, important, or interesting ethnographies in the critical dialogue, and the second elaborates the central themes of society, culture, history, knowledge, and values. In the second section, I also attempt to very briefly introduce some of the challenges to critical discourse from postmodernism and feminism, which are forcing those in the area of critical studies to reexamine the discursive practices that orient their research.

A Chronological Development of Critical Ethnography

In the late 1960s, sociologists of education, like other educational scholars, began to challenge the accepted role of scholar as apologist for the status quo. One of the most important influences on this new

education research → challenge the status quo

mood in educational sociology was the work of the deviance studies, which had developed in the 1950s and 1960s. As a form of symbolic interactionism, deviance research centered around case studies of groups such as prostitutes, drug cultures, youth gangs, and night people. Perhaps the most important spokesperson for these studies was Howard Becker, whose books *Outsiders* (1963) and *The Other Side* (1964) became dominant perspectives in the sociological definition of social problems. By treating the viewpoints of subordinated people seriously, these deviance studies challenged the accepted worldview of the status quo. By legitimizing the views of subordinates in their dealings with social institutions such as the justice, health, welfare, and educational systems, marginal groups became defined as victims of narrow-minded managers rather than miscreants who deserved the scorn of ordinary people. The deviants that sociologists came to know through these studies, in the words of Howard Becker (1967:240), were "more sinned against than sinning." And while the deviants became defined as victims, the caretaking institutions ostensibly designed to alleviate social problems were defined as the constructors of deviance. By turning to symbolic interactionism with its relativist legacy (best formulated in W. I. Thomas's "definition of the situation"), deviance sociologists could assuage their sentiments toward the underdog and develop a set of concepts and a methodology that advanced the cause of those marginalized people they studied. In 1966, Howard Becker (1967), in his presidential address to the Society for the Study of Social Problems, boldly asked sociologists, "Whose side are we on?" While Becker himself adroitly avoided answering the question directly, he left little doubt that he sided with the underdog and so, he implied, should all well-meaning researchers.

Becker's call to sociologists to take the side of the underdog when combined with his pathbreaking book *Boys in White* (Becker, Geer, Hughes, and Strauss, 1961), became an important call to educational sociologists. Clearly the job of educational sociology should be to document the way in which students are victims rather than to act as a mechanism for the improved efficiency of schools in their continued victimization of students. In Britain, such a study was already coming to fruition. The Department of Social Anthropology and Sociology of the University of Manchester, long a center of symbolic interactionism and very influential in the development of social anthropology, was completing an extensive series of case studies on British schooling. In 1967, David Hargreaves published the first of a series of books from this study. His *Social Relations in a Secondary School* (1967) utilized participant observation and documented the manner in which schools themselves work to differentiate and polarize students. An important study, Hargreaves' book shifted attention away from the home life of "disadvantaged" students and centered it on the very processes of the school as a mechanism in the construction of student deviants. More importantly, his book showed the power of field study in "naturalistic" settings and launched extensive numbers of "ethnographic" studies of schooling in Britain over the next two decades. With its emphasis on participant observation and its legitimation of the perspective of deviant student groups, Hargreaves' study became an important forerunner of critical ethnography.

But Hargreaves' study suffered from some important omissions in his understandings of social life as well as from his methodology. To explain this problem, it might prove fruitful to return to Howard Becker's "Whose Side Are We On?" In his speech, published later in the journal *Social Problems*, Becker (1967) argues that sociologists cannot conduct objective research because they cannot help but be biased. As he summarizes his argument (in the gender-biased language of the 1960s),

> . . . no matter what perspective he [a sociologist] takes, his work either will take into account the attitude of subordinates, or it will not. If he fails to consider the questions they raise, he will be working on the side of the officials. If he does raise those questions seriously and does find, as he may, that there is some merit in them, he will then expose himself to the outrage of the officials and of all those sociologists who award them the top spot in the hierarchy of credibility. Almost all the topics that sociologists study, at least those that have some relation to the real world around us, are seen by society as mortality plays and we shall find ourselves, willy-nilly, taking part in those plays on one side or the other. (p. 245)

While Becker shows us that social interaction requires interpretation, he fails to provide us with a convincing basis for choosing one side or the other, apparently satisfied that sociologists, who primarily are social liberals, will choose the side of the underdog. In a response to Becker's article, Alvin Gouldner (1968) took issue with this unprincipled relativism, which he labeled "the devotional promiscuity of sacred prostitution" (p. 104). Gouldner points out that Becker's "sentimental disposition to see the world of deviance from the standpoint of the deviant conflicts with his theoretical disposition to take the standpoint of whichever group he happens to be studying" (p. 104). In other words, Becker's sentiment and his methodology may be in opposition whenever he makes superordinates the object of his study. And given that any particular group is a subordinate to someone as well as a superordinate to others, the task of identifying with the underdog becomes contextual and contradictory. Therefore, Gouldner argues, committing oneself to working for the underdog cannot rely on intuition and goodwill. If researchers are to commit to the underdog, they need grounding. "A commitment made on the basis of an unexamined ideology may allow us to feel a manly righteousness," writes Gouldner, "but it leaves us blind" (p. 105).

Gouldner (1968) further attacks Becker's approach as "romanticism" more interested in displaying exotic lives than in tearing down the barriers that restrict freedom and empowerment:

> It expresses the satisfaction of the Great White Hunter who has bravely risked the perils of the urban jungle to bring back an exotic specimen. It expresses the Romanticism of the zoo curator who preeningly displays his rare specimens. And like the zookeeper, he wishes to protect his collection; he does not want spectators to throw rocks at the animals behind the bars. But neither is he eager to tear down the bars and let the animals go. The attitude of these zookeepers of deviance is to create a comfortable and humane Indian Reservation, a protected social space, within which these colorful specimens may be exhibited, unmolested and unchanged. The very empirical sensitivity to fine detail, characterizing this school, is both born of and limited by the connoisseur's fascination with the rare object: its empirical richness is inspired by a collector's aesthetic. (p. 106)

This romanticism is particularly problematic when one recognizes that Becker's approach makes the deviant a victim of a society instead of a rebel against it. By failing to place the caretaker institutions (e.g., courts, hospitals, welfare agencies, schools) within a larger societal context, deviance studies, according to Gouldner, cannot recognize the broader social forces at work in the construction of deviance and, therefore, provide no basis for justifying their position.

This Becker–Gouldner debate marks some of the fundamental disagreements between more traditional ethnographies and critical ethnographies. While in sympathy with the underdog sentiments of traditional ethnography in education, critical ethnographers are suspicious of the romanticism and the lack of grounding that such studies imply. While appreciative of the methods used, critical ethnographers are suspicious of the conceptualization of the situations that are presented in traditional school ethnographies. These problems are concretely represented in the Manchester studies. Hargreaves seems to embody, at least in spirit, Becker's relativistic underdog sociology, while Colin Lacy's (1970) study of a British grammar school seems to lean toward the Gouldner interest in grounding case study research in broader social and political forces.

Lacy's book, *Hightown Grammar* (1970), was researched as part of the same Manchester study that Hargreaves participated in, but whereas Hargreaves seemed to center on the world as constructed by students in interaction with each other and with agents of the school, Lacy wished to broaden his study by placing such interactions within broader social and political factors. While not ignoring the area explored by Hargreaves, Lacy also showed how extra-school factors influence school behavior and help to shape school practices. For example, parental interpretations of their children's abilities plus knowledge of school and ability to cope with problems all work to increase close supervision of children's school behavior. While both books center on the process of school differentiation and pupil polarization, Lacy was interested in placing such understandings in a larger social and political framework. His study became more than just siding with the underdog in their interaction with a caretaker institution, it opened the door to understanding how schools work as part of a larger social ordering.

The Manchester studies clarified the way in which symbolic interactionism could be used in research on the school deviant. As a result, case study methods based on participant observation, interview, and field observation became an important tool for educational research. Its interest in underdog research and labeling/deviance theory and (with Lacy) political context provided educational sociology an incentive to move toward new methods of research and new theories of society. An explosion of participant observer–case study research in education occurred throughout the United Kingdom and came to be labeled "ethnography." Examples of some studies can be found in such "new sociology" anthologies as M. F. D. Young's *Knowledge and Control* (1971), Chanan and Delamont's *Frontiers of Classroom Research* (1975), and Hammersley and Woods's *The Process of Schooling* (1976).

While most of the studies in these "new sociology" anthologies were firmly within the Becker symbolic interactionist school of research, others began to search for the grounding that Gouldner calls for and that Lacy points to. Influenced by continental forces in social thought, particularly the work of Althusser, these researchers sought a foundation on which to stand while conducting ethnographic studies of schools and deviant youth. One of the earliest of these was Sharp and Green's (1975) ethnographic study of progressive primary education. In *Education and Social Control* (1975), Sharp and Green rejected the idealism that is implicit within the symbolic interactionist and phe-nomenological approaches found in the "new sociology of education" and substituted an Althusserian perspective, which attempted to get beneath the social consciousness to the material basis for that con-sciousness. As a result, their study utilizes power as a central concept around which their observations and their findings revolved. But while Sharp and Green were strongly influenced by contemporary develop-ments in continental Marxism (i.e., Althusserian structural Marxism), their methodology was equally influenced by the case study research methods of symbolic interactionism and deviance studies. Their book became, perhaps, the first clear example of "critical" ethnography in its utilization of ethnographic methods to describe a social conscious-ness constructed within particular power relations and located within a broad social and political framework.

Perhaps the strongest, most sustained development of the research methods that would later be called "critical ethnography" occurred at the Centre for Contemporary Cultural Studies (CCCS) at the Univer-sity of Birmingham. CCCS, an interdisciplinary center strongly influ-enced by Raymond William's work in literary studies, performed its work through study groups of faculty and students. The adoption of ethnography as a major approach to research at the Centre resulted from an interest in tying theory to reflected experience. While the theoretical perspectives of continental Marxism, especially those es-poused by Althusser, show skepticism of empirically derived data, many members at the Centre apparently felt a need for personal expe-rience within the phenomena being studied to force reflected thought. If experience without theoretical grounding is in danger of ideological distortion, theoretical developments outside experience encourages myopic and irrelevant formalism. In the words of Grimshaw, Hobson, and Willis (1980), "One of the foci of our work has been to analyse and gauge the complex relations between representations/ideological forms and the density or 'creativity' or 'lived' cultural forms. If the 'structuralist revolution' has warned against an inflation of the latter on any naive humanist trust, its 'theoreticist' descendents warn against the all-engulfing power of the former" (p. 74). To those at the Centre, culture, while materially based, could not be simply or mechanically reduced to material relations. Culture, while necessarily located within material contexts, must also always be understood to form in complex relations.

We can find the movement from a symbolic interactionist eth-nography to a critical ethnography in the work of Paul Willis. For his 1972 doctoral dissertation at CCCS, Willis conducted an ethnography of drug use in a "hippie" subculture. Later published as *Profane Culture* (1978), Willis's ethnography of a drug subculture with its emphasis on the social construction of drug use and its relation to life style was clearly within the Becker tradition of deviant studies. However, in 1977 Willis published *Learning to Labour: How Working Class Kids Get Working Class Jobs*, an ethnographic study which neatly placed a deviant student culture within the material relations of broader society. While the recipient of much criticism as well as praise, *Learning to Labour*, more than any other single piece of research, radically altered the way many scholars would begin to think about ethnographic research. The work very clearly showed how ethnography could be tied to Marxist theory to elaborate and develop an understanding of schooling.

Shortly after *Learning to Labour* was published, David Robins and Philip Cohen published *Knuckle Sandwich: Growing Up in the Working-Class City* (1978), another ethnography with well-developed theoretical grounding. In *Knuckle Sandwich*, Robins and Cohen spent much time developing a concept of territoriality, which they then used to explain much of the violence found in working-class youth life. Besides grounding social consciousness in material relations, Robins and Cohen conducted their research while they worked to alter the conditions of their informants. They therefore acted as more than eavesdroppers and chroniclers; they acted as transformative agents as well. Their "ethnography" was a scholarly reflection on their attempts as youth directors to create and sustain a youth center in a London housing estate.

Through the rest of the 1970s, several ethnographic studies were produced by individuals who had studied or worked at the CCCS at Birmingham. Paul Corrigan's *Schooling the Smash Street Kids* (1979), Dick Hebdige's *Subculture: The Meaning of Style* (1979), and, of course, the anthologies of working papers, including *Culture, Media, Language* (Hall, Hobson, Lowe, and Willis, 1980) and *Resistance through Rituals* (Hall and Jefferson, 1976). Besides introducing Marxist theory into ethnographic work, many scholars at CCCS began to utilize feminist theory to ground their ethnographic studies.

While some feminist work is evident in the anthologies mentioned above, feminism in critical ethnography found its strongest presence in the anthology titled *Women Take Issue* (CCCS, 1978) (especially Angela McRobbie's well-known "Working Class Girls and the Culture of Feminity"), but it was not until the 1980s, in Christine Griffin's *Typical Girls?* (1985), that a Centre scholar published a fully developed feminist ethnography. A conscious response to Willis's *Learning to Labour*, Griffin's *Typical Girls?* built an ethnographic study of

female consciousness in patriarchal society

adolescent female consciousness while located within a patriarchal social world. Griffin (1985) nicely linked culture to the material world by arguing that "cultures are produced as groups make sense of their social existence in the course of everyday experience" (p. 202). By recognizing patriarchy as a fundamental organizing principle of the material world, Griffin, McRobbie, and the members of the CCCS gender study group (1978) both challenged and altered critical ethnography.

Through the work of the Birmingham Centre, the case study methods of symbolic interactionism were located in a theoretically organized material world (patriarchal and capitalist). Such research came to elaborate the world of youth both in and out of schools. And through the work of the Centre's ethnographies, particularly that of Willis's *Learning to Labour*, resistance theory became the primary orientation for critical ethnography.

As the 1980s drew to a close, it had become clear that the impact of the CCCS at Birmingham had had the single greatest influence on the theory and practice of critical ethnography both in Britain and North America. Certainly British ethnography must be credited with the first explorations in conducting educational ethnography from a critical perspective. Besides the pathbreaking work of the Willis, Sharp and Green, and Robins and Cohen studies, many other British ethnographers showed evidence of critical influence on their methodology. Some of the more interesting of those ethnographies include Roger Hewitt's *White Talk Black Talk* (1986), Lynn Davies' *Pupil Power: Deviance and Gender in School* (1984), and Peter Aggleton's *Rebels without a Cause: Middle Class Youth and the Transition from School to Work* (1987).

While critical ethnography received a strong beginning in Britain during the 1970s, in North America critical ethnography developed most strongly in the 1980s. By the 1980s, ethnographic and other field study methods had had a relatively long if minor tradition in educational research. Perhaps the classic educational sociology study was Waller's 1932 study *The Sociology of Teaching* (1965). In the 1950s, Becker *et al.*'s (1961) *Boys in White* established the labeling/deviance tradition of symbolic interactionism as an important approach to the sociology of education. In the 1960s, several other qualitative approaches began to influence educational research in the United States. Cicourel and Kitsuse's *The Educational Decision-Makers* (1963) established phenomenological sociology as an important research approach and the anthology of Cazden, John, and Hymes, *Functions of Language in the Classroom* (1972), showed the power of sociolinguistics in the study of schooling. However the strongest tradition of qualitative

examples

*C/E ⇒ Britain 70s.
U.S.   80s*

study in the sixties was that of cultural anthropology in the Boas/ Malinowski tradition. Case studies of education, done in the grand anthropology tradition, began to be published. Wax, Wax, and Dumont's *Formal Education in an American Indian Community* [1980 (1964)], Wolcott's *A Kwakiutl Village and School* (1967) and *The Man in the Principal's Office* (1973), and Rosenfeld's *Shut Those Thick Lips!* (1971) are some of the more important of these "case studies." However, all these studies failed to link culture to a material base. Only Jules Henry's *Culture against Man* (1963), the work of Henry's student, Ray Rist, *The Urban School: A Factory for Failure* (1973), and Phillip Jackson's *Life in Classrooms* (1968) attempted to place ethnographic research within a broader socioeconomic context.

In the 1970s, these foundations had led to a large number of studies using ethnographic methods in various ways. The microethnography of Erickson (1975, 1977), McDermott (1977) McDermott and Gospodinoff (1979), and Mehan (1974, 1978); the classic Malinowskian ethnography of Peshkin's *Growing Up American* (1978); the Mertonian systemic anthropology of Ogbu's *The Next Generation* (1974); and the Chicago style case study of Cusick's *Inside High School* (1973) and Metz's *Classrooms and Corridors* (1978) are some of the important ethnographic works of the 1970s. For American educational researchers, ethnography, while not the dominant tradition, was readily available for those interested in alternative approaches to the study of schooling. With the publication of Bowles and Gintis's *Schooling in Capitalist America* (1976), the English translation of Bourdieu and Passeron's *Reproduction in Education, Society, and Culture* (1977), the importation of the British ethnographies of education, and the introduction of continental thought through the work of Michael Apple and Henry Giroux, North American educational scholars were positioned for the development of a critical ethnography: a research method built on the various traditions of qualitative research, grounded in the critical social theory of continental philosophy and the growing influence of feminist theory, and committed to a liberatory political project.

One of the first influential attempts was Everhart's *Reading, Writing and Resistance* (1983). Everhart apparently approached his study of a junior high school with a traditional anthropological distrust of theoretical positioning. However, while attempting to write his ethnography, he began to realize the importance of bringing a theoretical perspective to bear on his research. His belated turning to Marxism as a grounding theory may appear to be the classic example of "letting the data generate theory," but Everhart's reconstruction of his ethnography (his written construction of the culture) actually indicates his understanding that the data become meaningful to the researcher only when the researcher brings a theoretical focus to it. This is one of the important understandings of critical ethnography: One does not simply catalog a culture like a librarian and then seek a theory that explains it. While practitioners of other forms of ethnographic research may acknowledge the formative aspects of theory, their practice of "selecting" the theory that best "explains" the data assumes that the data are themselves obtained outside of theory. So despite their protestations to the contrary, whenever they claim to "let the data generate theory," they are acting as if the data were "collected" rather than "produced" by the researcher. While certainly not the only ethnographic approach to realize the importance of this point, critical ethnographers have made it a central aspect of their method.

At the University of Wisconsin at Madison, a group of educational scholars began to publish their ethnographic studies first in an anthology (Apple and Weis, 1983) and then as separate studies (Valli, 1986; Weis, 1985). Drawing from the theoretical work of Apple and influenced by Willis's ethnographic methods, the Wisconsin scholars developed an approach to school ethnography that explored the complexity and contradictory nature of reproduction and resistance. Weis's study of black students attending an inner-city community college portrayed the culture of the students as a logical response to their positioning within the practices of the college and the experience of their lives in a racist capitalist society. Valli's ethnographic study of high school business students revealed how complex and contradictory the career choices of adolescent females are when located in a patriarchal, capitalist society. Both studies are important in their attempt to make lived cultures more complex and resistance more contradictory.

Linda McNeil's (1986) study of the contradictions of control embedded in school administrative practices and organization patterning, while more influenced by Chicago-style case study sociology than the other Wisconsin ethnographers, shows the influence that reproduction and resistance theory was having at Wisconsin–Madison. Through her emphasis on power as a central category and her use of history as an explanatory concept, McNeil showed the extent to which critical ethnography was influencing researchers who were not primarily located in critical theory.

One of the other important North American centers for the promotion of critical ethnography was the Ontario Institute for the Study of Education (OISE). Roger Simon, while primarily known for his work in curriculum theory, along with Don Dippo, began an ethnographic study of "work education" (i.e., vocational education). While the completed manuscript of this study is not yet in print, a few preliminary articles from the study have been published (see Simon, 1983). Perhaps more important for its impact on critical ethnography than the publication of any particular ethnography was the Simon and Dippo (1986) article on methodology. By publishing their piece in *Anthropology and Education Quarterly*, Simon and Dippo not only made critical ethnography an active topic of discussion among ethnographers of education but also gave the research method a legitimacy in anthropology it may not have had before.

The study for Peter McLaren's *Schooling as a Ritual Performance* (1986) was conducted for a doctoral dissertation at OISE. McLaren's ethnography is one of the most original ethnographic studies within the critical dialogue. While McLaren's study is squarely within the resistance theory tradition, his reliance on continental structuralism as found in Turner's anthropology and Grime's ritualogy [the systematic study of ritual (see Grimes, 1982)] brings to his study a deeper and more sophisticated understanding of social science thought than generally found in educational ethnographies. His development of ritual performance as an explanatory concept for schooling has pointed the way toward newer social theories associated with semiotics and postmodern thought.

Several other important critical ethnographies must be mentioned. One is the early work of Jean Anyon (1980, 1981). Anyon's work, while only minimally ethnographic, was one of the earliest American attempts to use qualitative research methods to conduct critical research in education. While trapped in the logic of reproduction without the corrective of the resistance theory most frequently utilized by critical ethnographers since Willis's *Learning to Labour* (1977), these studies were very influential in the development of critical ethnography in North America. One of the very best critical ethnographies is *Making the Difference* (Connell, Dowsett, Kessler, and Ashendew, 1982). This Australian ethnography was crucial in its recognition of the independent influences of class and gender. By recognizing the interplay of these two factors, Connell *et al.* (1982) clarified the way in which aspirations and success in school are mediated by class and gender. Kathleen Weiler's *Women Teaching for Change: Gender, Class and Power* (1988) is an excellent example of how feminist theory must be an integral part of critical ethnography. Weiler also shows how critical ethnography can be used not only to critique reactionary schools but also to understand the possibilities of critical pedagogy for feminist teachers. Jay MacLeod's (1987) study of two adolescent male groups in a low-income housing project was the first extensive critical ethnography to focus at least part of its study on a working-class group trying to succeed in school. MacLeod's study of a group of African-American youths, called the "Brothers" and "Hallway Hangers," was similar to Willis's study of the "ear'oles" and the "lads"; however, MacLeod takes their aspirations and conformity seriously and allows us to see the contradictory nature of their compliance. While MacLeod focuses on class as an organizing concept, at least two studies on Blacks in Britain (Fuller, 1980; Furlong, 1984) suggest that his findings may have been more confounded by race than he perceives. Both Fuller and Furlong found that Afro-Caribbean Blacks in Britain engaged in, apparently, school-conforming behavior while either unwittingly failing due to a lack of understanding (Furlong, 1984) or by knowingly resisting the school's attempt to reproduce their subordinate position by combining academic success with antischool sentiments and behavior (Fuller, 1980). Other good examples of North American, Australian, and New Zealand critical ethnographies in education include Fine (1986, 1987, 1988), Gaskell (1984, 1985), Sola and Bennett (1985), Lankshear (1987), Roman (1988), and Britzman (1986, 1991).

As can be seen in this review, critical ethnography has its methodological roots in the same methodological discourse as other ethnographic approaches to educational research, yet somewhere in the late 1960s and early 1970s some researchers began to join the conversations of educators who were suspicious of the idealist tendency in standard educational theory to treat their abstractions as more real than the lived reality. At the same time, some of the neo-Marxist and feminist theorists began to see the advantages and necessity for qualitative research methods. This coming together of two traditions, one in social theory and the other in research methods, has been well elaborated by Anderson (1989), who considers it an historical dialectic. While I am personally hesitant to label the relationship a "dialectic," clearly the two traditions have influenced each other: The discursive traditions of critical theory have been strengthened by a method to incorporate experience, and the experiential methods of educational ethnography have been deepened by critical discourse. Ethnography without theory grounded in the material relationships of history can too easily become a romantic display of the exotic life-styles of the marginal, a voyaristic travel log through the subcultures of society. Such studies, while claiming underdog sympathies, do little to address the marginal and subordinate status of those whom they might study. Critical ethnography has evolved to address these shortcomings in traditional research. At the same time, theory without empirical knowledge of lived cultures is too easily reduced to mere formalism; it remains an elitist exercise in academic conversations, which does more to advance the careers of university professors than it contributes to the empowerment of ordinary people. Critical ethnography has also evolved to address these shortcomings in radical social theory.

Although this short historical review has focused on the ethnographic studies in critical research, empirical study and social theorizing are not separate activities. One must be familiar with both the discourse of social theory informing critical ethnography and its method. With this thought in mind, the next section will explore some of the important themes found in the discourse of critical ethnography.

Themes in the Discourse of Critical Ethnography

Critical ethnography exhibits a multiplicity of voices around particular topics; therefore, I do not expect to find any particular methodological discipline or specific conceptual categories when I read a "critical ethnography." On the other hand, I do expect to find the critical ethnographer engaged in an ongoing dialogue related to issues of emancipation in an historically structured society. Critical ethnography's contribution to this dialogue lies principally in its ability to make concrete the particular manifestations of marginalized cultures located in a broader sociopolitical framework. To understand this dialogue, I will concentrate on a few themes found in critical discourse that seem to distinguish critical ethnography from other approaches to ethnography. The following section will explore five themes (knowledge, values, society, culture, history) that may help clarify critical discourse in educational ethnography.

Knowledge

In the critical tradition, knowledge is seen as utopian and transformative, built on self-revelation and verified in praxis. Truth is embedded in the social relations of material practices, revealed in the demystification of ideology and culture, conceived in a vision of freedom, and proved in the emancipation of people. As Marcuse (1968) wrote,

> When truth cannot be realized within the established social order, it always appears to the latter as mere utopia. This transcendence speaks not against, but for, its truth. The utopian element was long the only

Praxis

progressive element in philosophy, as in the constructions of the best state and the highest pleasure, of perfect happiness and perpetual peace. The obstinacy that comes from adhering to truth against all appearances has given way in contemporary philosophy to whimsy and uninhibited opportunism. Critical theory preserves obstinacy as a genuine quality of philosophical thought. (p. 143)

In critical discourse, truth is often found in the free society that does not yet exist but must be arrived at through the negation of that which is. "The purpose of scientific theory is to engender self-knowledge and so to liberate people from the oppressiveness of their social arrangements" (Held, 1980:89). This is often referred to as "praxis."

Praxis and Ethnography

Praxis may be understood to be one resolution to the theory and practice dualism that has plagued Western intellectual thought. The concept of praxis has long been associated with the critical tradition, but its influence has also been felt in more mainstream research.

Praxis and Symbolic Interactionism.   Paul Rock (1979) explains the place of praxis in the logic of symbolic interactionism:

Praxis

Participant observation emerged directly out of the central concerns of symbolic interactionism. It transforms the sociology into a particular kind of praxis, refracting and condensing the special vision of knowledge which was prepared by the formalist and the pragmatist. There are no "data" in that vision. Materials do not simply await discovery by the social scientist. Instead, facts are principally produced in the symbolic work of social encounters. They are not "given" but created. (p. 193)

In Rock's analysis, praxis is created as the researcher interacts with the researched. While "culture" is located in the intersubjective experiences of the participants, ethnographic "knowledge" is located in the interactive experiences of an academically informed researcher with those participants. Because this interaction creates dualistic claims to legitimacy (on the one hand, the theoretical formulations of the academy and, on the other, the pragmatic patterns of the people being studied), the researcher is encouraged to conform to the perceived meaning system of the participants—privileging their constructions (i.e., emic) to those of the researcher (i.e., etic). The problem created by the dualism of thought and practice, then, is thought to be solved

emic/etic

through the construction of thought while participating in practice. To protect such thought construction from the perceived inappropriate influence of academic discourse, traditional ethnography places heavy emphasis on reflexivity or the "bracketing" of knowledge and values. Such strategies call for the separation of one's own theoretical positions from those being studied through an emphasis on reflexivity. In this way, praxis is achieved in the construction of knowledge through concrete experience and is unencumbered by the researcher's own biases.

Praxis and Critical Theory. The understanding of praxis as knowledge generated through theory constructed in practice, while similar to a critical meaning, is, nonetheless, different. The difference lies in that symbolic interactionists define praxis as arising in experience while critical theorists define it as arising in transformation. In *The German Ideology*, Marx and Engels (1947) make clear that critical theory must be integrated with revolution to accomplish effective social change. For Marx, the dualism of thought and practice was resolved through the unity of philosophy and revolution rather than theory and experience. "Theory and experience" implies a knowledge located in the present and, therefore, constrained by the sociopolitical constructions of the moment; on the other hand, "philosophy and revolution" implies a knowledge that is an active construction of the future and, therefore, obligated only to that future. In other words, for Marx, theory is the basis for transformative action and truth can only be determined by the future, while, for the symbolic interactionist, theory is the basis for understanding experience and truth is located in the present.

The idea of a "critical" praxis becomes fully developed in the "negative dialectic" of the Frankfort school. For Horkheimer, "Truth is a moment of correct practice" (see Held, 1980:191–192) aided by the intellectual's "negative critique." "Negative critique" forms a necessary, although insufficient, basis for addressing the particular historical situation (see Held, 1980:185). The intellectual's "own thinking," Horkheimer wrote, "should in fact be a critical, promotive factor in the development of the masses" (Horkheimer, 1972:214). He continued,

> If the theoretician and his specific object are seen as forming a dynamic unity with the oppressed class, so that his presentation of societal contradictions is not merely an expression of the concrete historical situation but also a force within it to stimulate change, then his real function emerges. (p. 215)

Horkheimer made it clear that through critique future action can alter present circumstances and result in praxis.

> The thinking subject is not the place where knowledge and object
> coincide, nor consequently the starting-point for attaining absolute
> knowledge. . . . In reflection on man, subject and object are sundered;
> their identity lies in the future, not in the present. (Horkheimer,
> 1972:211)

The recognition that praxis requires an active theory made concrete is re-iterated in Adorno's "immanent method" and "non-identity thinking," which confront an object with its own justification seeking the contradictions that formulate its shape. Through the construction of "constellations" of concepts, Adorno argued we can come to know the utopian vision of the possible and, therefore, to reveal the discrepancy between the actual and the potential. Adorno's immanent method uses the constructions of the object to critique the object and to demystify the present society. Such an approach to praxis requires the researcher to approach the concrete practice with the ideological constructions overtly identified and utilized for analysis. This approach is diametrically opposite to that of the participant observation promoted by symbolic interactionism.

In traditional ethnography, praxis is found in the field: The researcher, conscious of the reflexive nature of researcher–participant interaction, carefully separates self-vision from that of the cultural group and, through the interaction of the researcher's thinking and the informant's action, knowledge is formed. For many critical ethnographers, however, praxis does not occur until the critical theory is fused in the practice of transformation. Critical theorists hold that what occurs in the field between the researcher and the observed should never be confused with praxis but is, instead, merely an aspect of theory. Knowledge is not found in the research itself but in the actions of people creating history. This implies that ethnography cannot, by itself, be an example of praxis, although it can help produce praxis. It also implies that while praxis can only be achieved in the forces of history, not in the researcher's field activities, the researcher can, and must, play a part in that history. For some in the critical tradition, the advancement of theory is itself transformative. In his discussion of Adorno, Held (1980) wrote,

> Thinking is a form of praxis, always historically conditioned; as
> physical labour transforms and negates the material world under

> changing historical circumstances, so mental labour, under changing
> historical conditions, alters its object world through criticism. (p. 204)

Recently, many critical ethnographers seem to share the view that praxis requires material transformation, not simply symbolic emancipation (see e.g., Lather, 1986). By demanding that critical ethnographers work for material, not just theoretical, transformation, they are claiming that ethnographers have an ethical responsibility not only to the transformation of history in a general and broad way but also to the transformation of the particular and concrete history of the people being studied. But even in this case, praxis is not to be found in the work of the ethnographer but in the work of the people to transform and make their own history. In either case, praxis is found in the transformations of society rather than in the experiences of researchers.

The renewed emphasis on material transformation in recent years has been particularly influenced by the work of Michel Foucault. As Foucault stated, "The problem is not changing people's consciousnesses—or what's in their heads—but the political, economic, institutional regime of the production of truth" (Foucault, 1980:133). Truth, according to Foucault, is found in the struggles of everyday politics and the "wars" of institutional practices. Praxis always requires both symbolic and material transformation because knowledge is always formed through power and power is always located in knowledge. Foucault (1980) wrote,

> Knowledge and power are integrated with one another and there is no
> point in dreaming of a time when knowledge will cease to depend on
> power; this is just a way of reviving humanism in a utopian guise. It is
> not possible for power to be exercised without knowledge, it is
> impossible for knowledge not to engender power. (p. 52)

Power/knowledge can be found in popular knowledge and requires researchers to return to the "daily struggles at grass roots level, among those whose fight was located in the fine meshes of the web of power . . . where the concrete nature of power became visible" (Foucault, 1980:116). This search for "power/knowledge" among "the daily struggles at grass roots level" and the "fine meshes of the web of power" (p. 116) as well as the "localized systems" and the "strategic apparatuses" (p. 102), clarifies the critical project in educational ethnography as an attempt to recognize the complex and contradictory manifestations of asymmetrical power relations in cultural formations in the lives of ordinary people.

The Object of Critical Ethnography

The critical aspects of praxis (the relationships between symbolic and material transformation, between present constructions and future potentials, and between power and knowledge) makes clear that critical and traditional ethnographers differ fundamentally on the role of the empirical project. Whereas the traditional ethnographer understands the ethnographic project as either complete in itself or as a part of the idealist project of ethnology, the critical ethnographer sees the ethnographic project as an aspect of critical theory, which must eventually be completed in political and social action.

For the traditional ethnographer, the empirical re-presentation of a native life world is the project. Because each society constructs a range of different visions given their particular cultural dynamics, the ethnographer enters the research project with the distinct intent to discover what that particular vision is. When located, the job of the ethnographer is to describe that vision as carefully as possible to give outsiders an insiders' view. Most of the methodological arguments in traditional ethnography revolve around which methods most appropriately recognize and reconstruct the insiders' view, not over the nature of the goal.

Many critical ethnographers agree that different social groups often construct different cultural visions, but these different cultural views result not from some autonomous response to environmental conditions or social context, but from the actions of people located in historically structured situations. The critical ethnographer assumes the integral formation of structure and culture. That is to say that in the study of subgroups, the researcher knows before entering the field that subcultures are marginally positioned. The important question is not whether they are or are not marginal, and certainly not whether or not those identified with the group perceive their marginality, but how has their political, social, and material disempowerment been manifested in cultural formations. Novice readers of critical ethnography often think the purpose of critical ethnography is to show that a group is oppressed and, therefore, critical ethnography is often criticized as having the answer before the research is conducted and of "not respecting the indigenous culture." But such opinions assume a much larger degree of autonomy and coherence in cultural construction than critical ethnographers are willing to assume. Those who accuse critical ethnographers of having the answer before they begin misunderstand the question that is being asked. The researcher may assume that those to be studied are disempowered, but there is no assumption about how that disempowerment is represented in cultural forms, how participants respond to their positioning, that they recognize their response as anything other than individual choice, or even that they agree that they are disempowered. The role of empirical study is, therefore, to clarify how material relations become manifested in differing life experiences, not to generate descriptions of autonomous units.

For example, Weis (1985) shows how black, inner-city, community college students positioned as marginal persons in a castelike society inhabit a culture committed to the ideas of social mobility, the personal value of school knowledge, and the legitimacy of the faculty while, at the same time, maintaining commitments to the "collectivity" of their poor, black, urban communities; adherence to "street time"; and specific antagonisms to teachers who fail to give them a "fair exchange." The contradiction of these conflicting positions guarantees their ultimate failure. Willis (1977) provides us with another example by revealing that the "lads'" inevitable future on the shop floors and their genderization of school success as masculine failure leads to the ultimate reproduction of class relations. McLaren (1986) shows how Portuguese students in Toronto, limited to interstitial spaces for the playing out of their street culture, experience a school life marked by contradictory rituals. Robins and Cohen (1978) explain the organized physical violence in English soccer stadiums as an attempt to "magically" control territory that in reality is owned and controlled by an absentee bourgeoisie. McRobbie (1978) found that young working-class women, while committed to traditional feminine values, perceived their inevitable future without optimism. These young women retreated to an ideology of romance and often engaged in antischool behavior by interjecting sexuality into their school lives. Roman (1988) shows how femininity is produced differently among different young women as they participate in the ritual construction of punk slam dancing. In all these cases, the ethnographers show different concrete actions of people marginally positioned in asymmetrical power relations. That all of these groups are oppressed and marginalized is not the question. The question is, rather, how are marginalized people positioned in material and symbolic relations, how do they participate in these relations, and how can our understanding work toward the restructuring of these relations.

How are they positioned materially + symbolically?

Some Contemporary Influences

While critical ethnography works toward the elimination of the theory/practice epistemological dualism through the idea of praxis, recent work in postmodernism has attacked the division that is held between aesthetics and epistemology. While most critical ethnographers attempt to dissolve the categorical distinctions between theory and practice and between epistemology and ethics (see next section), most still accept a firm distinction between knowledge and rhetoric. This distinction has come under increasing attack since Derrida (1973, 1976) questioned the relationship between the signifier (the actual sound or visual stimulus of a sign) and the signified (the concept that we have in mind). Since Saussure, the assumption has been that the signifier and signified are inseparable; that a signifier without a signified is meaningless and a signified without a signifier is unnamed and, hence, meaningless. Derrida challenged this idea by suggesting that meaning is actually found in the relationships of (or actually the differences between) signifiers with other signifiers, not with a signified. The effect of this argument is to shift attention away from that philosophical area referred to as epistemology and center it on rhetoric. The question for these postmodern thinkers is not how do we ground what we know, but how do we rhetorically claim authority to advance what we say as that which is known?

This shift in attention from the content to the form of knowledge has led to an interesting exploration of the rhetoric of ethnography as a textual genre. The work of Clifford (1983, 1986a,b), Crapanzano (1985), Marcus (1980), Marcus and Cushman (1982), Marcus and Fischer (1986), Rosaldo (1989), Said (1978), and many others builds on the more traditional work of Geertz (1973, 1983) to question the traditions of ethnography as well as to advance new forms for its practice as text. While certain aspects of this new work in anthropology point favorably toward critical ethnography in education [see e.g., Marcus's analysis of Willis's *Learning to Labour* (Marcus, 1986)], critical ethnographers, with few exceptions (see Brodkey, 1987), have not yet seriously analyzed the form of their work. Despite its theoretical complexity, the rhetorical form of this work is remarkably ordinary and constrained by the language games of the academy (see Quantz, 1989). As a result, critical ethnography may be trapped in rhetorical strategies that serve the professional advancement of the ethnographers more than the transformation of society or the liberation of the people they are describing, despite their best intentions. As critical ethnographers come to realize that their own liberatory epistemology may be blinding them to an equally oppressing rhetoric, they will have to begin seeking strategies for overcoming this bias within their work. Critical ethnographers might turn to the work of Lather (1986), who strongly advances a more active, participatory, and "reciprocal" form of ethnography, or to that of Brodkey (1987), who analyzes ethnography as a narrative process, or to that of McLaren (in press), who places the whole ethnographic project within "a field of competing discourses," or to Fine who argues for an "activist" approach to research (Fine, 1990). These theoretical discussions may provide some help in addressing, what to me seems to be, a very difficult issue for critical ethnography, but while these writers, like myself, can point out some of the difficulties and possible directions, I have yet to see a published ethnography in education that steps outside the normal form of the academy [except, perhaps, the work of P. D. R. Corrigan (1988, 1989)]. And to the extent that someone can get a form-breaking ethnography published, it will be interesting to see if this person is successful in the academic language games that control promotion, tenure, and other institutional rewards.

Summary

Critical ethnographers are likely to understand knowledge as something located in theoretical practice achieved through radical transformation. The particular published ethnography should not be approached as the truth revealed in the concrete as much as another statement in the critical dialogue that is working toward emancipation. Its truth claims lie not in some generalizable statistical procedure nor in an appeal to eyewitness accounts as to the future possibilities of democracy. Its goal is not to present some objective or emic representation of a particular culture but is to clarify the myriad ways in which historical relations become manifested in cultural constructions. These clarifications inform those who are working for democratic transformation of the hidden forces that underpin social relations. While the elimination of the theory/practice dualism through transformative praxis provides both critique and possibility, it fails to recognize the implications of rhetoric on what we accept as knowledge. As a result, critical ethnographers are vulnerable to the criticism that their work benefits their own careers more than it does the forces of emancipation. While a few writers have begun to address this issue, the failure to produce any new ethnographic forms in education may continue to work against the transformative potential that critical ethnographers define as their *raison d'etre*.

Values

Critical ethnographers are occasionally criticized for imposing their values on the group they are studying. This criticism is unfair because it is never a matter of whether or not researchers impose their values but the implications of the values that they are imposing. Ever since the development of quantum mechanics in physics, researchers have come to understand the manner in which they partially construct the event being studied. Research is never without interest; all forms of research impose values. Critical thought rejects the division of knowledge and interest as artificial and disingenuous. Critical ethnographers impose a value system that requires the researcher to place any culture into a wider discourse of history and power, which serves an emancipatory interest, whereas other ethnographers impose a value system that requires the researcher to treat every culture as if it were independent of or, at most, interactive with history and power. From a critical perspective, these studies ultimately serve the interest of the status quo. While having an ethical orientation does not separate critical ethnography from other educational ethnography, the pointed effort of critical researchers to reveal their own value perspective to the reader may differentiate critical ethnography from other forms and it may be this openness about their values that prompts criticism more than anything else.

For Simon and Dippo (1986:200), the need to reflect on the intrusion of values into research is one of the three central features of critical ethnography. According to them, critical ethnography "must reflexively address its own situated character. This means that we must acknowledge that the knowledge we produce is inevitably limited by our own histories and the institutional forms within which we work." This realization leads to "a commitment to study the character and bases of one's own work practices and their relation to the knowledge such practices produce." The commitment to reflexivity is a fundamental theme in critical discourse, but it is also a central theme in noncritical ethnographic discourse (see particularly Hammersley and Atkinson, 1983). Today, nearly all ethnographers would accept the view that there is no such thing as value-free research.

In traditional ethnography, the recognition that both the researcher and the researched have the capacity for self-reflection and that the researcher can use that capacity to gain insights of social and cultural practices has been long discussed. In fact, Hammersley and Atkinson (1983) believe that reflexivity is the hallmark of all ethnography.

> Neither positivism nor naturalism provides an adequate framework for social research. Both neglect its fundamental reflexivity, the fact that we are part of the social world we study, and that there is no escape from reliance on common-sense knowledge and on common-sense methods of investigation. All social research is founded on the human capacity for participant observation. We act in the social world and yet are able to reflect upon ourselves and our actions as objects in that world. By including our own role within the research focus and systematically exploiting our participation in the world under study as researchers, we can develop and test theory without placing reliance on futile appeals to empiricism, of either positivist or naturalist varieties. (p. 25)

For Hammersley and Atkinson, the concept of reflexivity suggests that ethnographers should conduct research in a manner that treats the researcher as part of the researched. That is, ethnographers should treat themselves as part of the social event being studied. Because recent thinking in ethnography does not pretend to be value-free, the important question cannot be *should* we impose our values but *how should* we, as researchers, deal with our values. When Becker raises the question "Whose side are we on?" he provides us with the crucial question. As researchers, we are unable to be neutral, we must choose a position. Becker chooses to pick the side of the underdog, assuming that those whom he studies are the underdogs. Gouldner suggests that such a position may be contradictory because those one studies may not always be the underdog. He argues that researchers must have a grounding to their research, and critical ethnography finds that grounding in historical structures.

Critical researchers, while sympathizing with Becker's underdog commitments, are unconvinced that one should present informant culture from the value positions of the group being studied instead of some other value position. Three points come to mind. First, such a task is impossible given the assumptions of reflexivity. That is to say, the researcher will always understand the cultural patterns in terms of the values of a researcher. The very act of researching and reporting the results of the research to a group of outsiders is likely to contradict the value position of the informant culture. The whole *raison d'etre* of the research project contradicts the value orientation of those being researched. Edward Said's (1978) analysis of "orientalism" in Western ethnography as an intellectual construction that promotes the subjugation as Asian societies explains the point.

Second, critical ethnographers talk about culture in terms of alienation, self-estrangement, hegemony, or ideology (terms that indicate the failure of participants in a culture to discuss their culture in terms of historical/structural constraints), all of which suggest that the mere acceptance of their "meaning" is to remain trapped in a hermeneutic circle that fails to transform. Emancipation requires people to overcome their historically structured culture, which, in turn, requires that they step outside of their cultural views and reflect on their positioning in the world.

Third, the choice to present the values of the participants' culture without the critical analysis of the researcher is itself a value position. One must always ask, what interest is being served by such a value position. Habermas (1971) suggests that research that takes this "hermeneutic" position serves the "practical" interest. The practical interest is one oriented around social relations and symbolic order. The practical interest seeks harmony and integration at the expense of freedom. The practical interest is a special interest that serves the status quo and those who benefit from the present order, while it works against social change and those who are oppressed by the present order. The Habermasian argument leads us to conclude that ethnography that attempts to limit historical–structural analysis, far from being free of values, actually serves the interests of the ruling elite. Because values must always enter into research and because some interest is always being served by research, critical ethnographers opt for those values that promote transformation of oppressive societies toward emancipation and democracy. This is what Habermas labels the "emancipatory interest" (Habermas, 1971).

While all critical research should serve the interest of emancipation, the researcher should not seek out or report only empirical evidence that supports the researcher's view. All cultural evidence needs to be observed, described, and analyzed, and that which appears to counter researcher assumptions must be revealed. But keep in mind that all evidence, supporting or refuting, must be considered within historical/structural conditions and pointed toward emancipatory possibility.

The critical argument is as follows: Because all research is value-laden and serves some interest, research should be conducted in such a manner as to reflect the value of freedom and serve the interest of emancipation. To reflect freedom and serve emancipation requires complete description and honest analysis of empirical findings, not consciously edited or distorted empirical evidence. Criticism of critical ethnography often confuses the first for the second. "Open" description and analysis that reflects a critical perspective should not be attacked on the basis of improper intrusion of values because description and analysis always reflects values—it cannot be otherwise. Evidence that has been edited or distorted by ignoring counterevidence should be criticized, but, I believe, is as rare in good critical ethnography as in any form of good ethnography. There is much reason to believe that value choices must be addressed in ethnographic research, and critical ethnographers are likely to argue that the failure to consciously choose values that have an emancipatory interest is to choose values that serve the status quo.

Some Contemporary Influences

Trapped in its modern discourse, critical ethnography opens itself up to postmodern critique in its concepts of society, culture, history, and knowledge. However, in the area of ethics, its modern discourse provides critical ethnography with a transformative possibility missing from much postmodern writing. Certainly in response to the postmodern privileging of the aesthetic, critical theory's continued commitment to democracy and emancipation as a real alternative is reason enough for our continued interest in this form of research. While Habermas's insistence on the possibility of an "ideal speech act" in which individuals with full understanding engage in rational dialogue around social and political issues seems rather naive given a postmodern understanding of discourse, his unwillingness to abandon transformative possibility demands respect. Just because his enlightenment faith in rationality hides a Eurocentric and patriarchal bias does not mean there may not be other ways to construct democratic possibility, ways that keep the modern emancipatory project alive while overcoming its androcentric and racist discourse. Critical ethnographers must move away from their traditional understanding of democratic ethics and begin to entertain the ethics of others. I have in mind the liberation theology of writers such as Gutierrez (1984) and West (1982); the gender politics of postmodern feminists such as Benhabib and Cornell (1987), Flax (1990), Fraser and Nicholson (1990), Hutcheon (1989), Kipnis (1988), and Morris (1988); the race–gender politics of womanists such as bell hooks (1989), Lugones and Spelman (1983), Fox-Genovese (1988), Jordan (1985), and Walker

(1983); and the critical postmodernism and critical pragmatism of educators such as Cherryholmes (1988), Giroux (1988a, 1988b, in press a,b), McCarthy (1988), and McLaren (1988). Some of these influences have begun to find their way into critical ethnography (see Britzman, 1991; Roman, 1988), and, I expect, the latest work in critical ethnography will continue the trend.

Summary

For critical ethnography, the key to reflexivity is to recognize the activity of research as itself located in historical/structural constraints positioned by asymmetrical power conflict and embedded in an overall project. When we do so, the difference between reflexivity as Simon and Dippo refer to it compared to the way in which Hammersley and Atkinson use it should be clear. No matter what the approach, the researcher's insinuation into the social reality of a disempowered group is itself an act of power/knowledge and the academic authoring of ethnographic description is wrought with contradictions that claim projections of emancipation while alienating people from their own cultural descriptions. Reflexivity suggests that the critical researcher must understand these contradictions and act to reveal them either in the written description or in the lived reality of the people. While much critical ethnography is still locked within a modernist discourse, unconsciously constructing a Eurocentric and androcentric perspective, the critical project of ethnography can potentially be retained through the appropriation of liberation theology, feminism, womanism, and certain critical educators. When one realizes that values order and influence all research, then the critical ethnographer's emphasis on openness and his or her conscious effort to serve an emancipatory interest should be praised rather than criticized.

Society

In critical discourse, social processes are discussed in terms of asymmetrical power relations embedded in particular historical/structural conditions. While different critical ethnographies may lead to varying understandings of the relationship between material and cultural relations and the meaning of power, they tend to share an interest in detailing the exercise of and resistance to particular, concrete powers within structural/historical constraints and attempt to point to the reformulation of power in more democratic social relations.

Material Relations and Cultural Forms

For Marx, of course, material constraints are primary. Because the dialectic of historical materialism is defined in terms of the mode of production, human agency, in a Weberian or idealist sense, has little impact on social conditions. In the "Preface to a Critique of Political Economy," Marx (1977) wrote,

> In the social production of their life, men enter into definite relations that are indispensable and independent of their will, relations of production which correspond to a definite stage of development of their material productive forces. The sum total of these relations of production constitutes the economic structure of society, the real foundation on which rises a legal and political superstructure and to which correspond definite forms of social consciousness. The mode of production of material life conditions the social, political, and intellectual life process in general. It is not the consciousness of men that determines their being, but, on the contrary, their social being that determines their consciousness. (p. 388)

The singularity of Marx's emphasis on the mode of production has been continually argued among critical thinkers. Most neo-Marxist ethnographers seem to be influenced by cultural Marxists such as E. P. Thompson and Raymond Williams. They place strong emphasis on a dialectic between material conditions and human consciousness, which together produce particular historical constraints. Those critical ethnographers influenced by Althusser and French structuralism are more likely to seek deep structures that organize and determine social life and place little emphasis on the role of human consciousness in the social construction of reality. But whether more influenced by cultural Marxists or French structuralism, Marx's initial statement on the material foundation of social life has contributed one continuing theme in critical discourse: Cultural relations must always be tied to material relations.

In response to Marx's singular emphasis on "materiality," Thompson and Williams stress a dialectic in which human agency plays a significant role in social reproduction. For example, E. P. Thompson (1966) wrote, "The working class did not rise like the sun at an appointed time. It was present at its own making . . . owes as much to agency as to conditioning, . . . the working class made itself as much as it was made" (p. 213). The idea that human agency does effect concrete practice has been very influential in the ethnographic work of the CCCS in Birmingham. Paul Willis (1977) was obviously influenced by Thompson in his ethnography of the "lads." Willis warns us against "a too reductive or crude materialist notion of the cultural level. . . . In its desire for workers of a certain type the reach of the production process must pass through the semi-autonomous cultural level which is determined by production only partially and in its own specific terms" (p. 171). Willis's statement emphasizes the need to recognize the influence of both human agency and material relations in the construction of culture.

The idea of constraints embedded in cultural forms such as language and discourse discourages critical ethnographers from overemphasizing human agency at the expense of historical structures. Althusser's emphasis on the material embeddedness of ideology suggested to some ethnographers the need to move beyond human consciousness and to uncover social reproduction in concrete practices. As Sharp and Green (1975) wrote,

> The task of the social scientist therefore, far from attempting some hermeneutic understanding of the individual acting subject in all his idiosyncrasy and uniqueness, should be to look behind the level of immediacy in order to try to develop some sociology of situations, their underlying structure and interconnections and the constraints and contingencies they impose. (p. 25)

They therefore suggest that "some insights might be gained by bringing the debate down from the formal level to substantive empirical reality" (p. 23). However, even ethnographers clearly influenced by Althusser are unwilling to ignore human agency. "Suffice it to say that an adequate theoretical perspective must be able to take into account human coherency and the creative power for individuals in acting in and transforming the world—and the relationship between conscious activity and objective reality" (see Sharp and Green, 1975:23).

Critical ethnographers are likely to believe they face a social reality that is strongly structured by "material" relations embedded in cultural forms. Although the relative emphasis given to the role of material production or to human consciousness may exhibit a wide range among critical ethnographers, their work is usually situated within this wider dialogue and a discussion of material conditions will usually constitute a crucial element of their analysis. In this way, critical ethnographers may appear quite different from ethnographers who have been strongly influenced by the phenomenological and hermeneutic traditions. The work of Peter Woods (1978a,b, 1979, 1981) in Britain and Alan Peshkin (1978, 1986) in the United States are clear examples of ethnographies that make human agency and consciousness primary and reduce material relations to mere whispers if included at all. By contrast, the work of Willis (1977) and Sharp and Green (1975), as discussed above, while perhaps placing different emphases on material–culture relationships, nonetheless place material relations at the center of their ethnographies.

Power and Society

While the central location of structured material relations is one important theme of critical discourse, including social structure as a fundamental analytic concept does not necessarily make an ethnography critical. Critical discourse places that discussion of structure or material relations within asymmetrical power relations rather than within a systemic whole. Therefore, ethnography that is built on a systemic metaphor for society [such as the work of John Ogbu (1974) and that of James Macpherson (1983)] is less likely to be considered in the critical tradition. Ogbu, who utilizes the sociology of Merton, and Macpherson, who bases his work on Parsons, construct a concept of structure that subsumes power to system. By doing so, Ogbu and Macpherson never actually challenge the systemic organization of power, but only the mobility of that system. Critical discourse, on the other hand, is more likely to challenge the very basis of the organization of power no matter how mobile it is, because critical discourse recognizes social structures or social "systems" to be the result of particular asymmetrical power relations. Certainly critical ethnographers are not the only ones to discuss power, but they are almost alone in treating power as a central concept either to be explained or to help explain the research.

Power often enters more sociological forms of ethnography such as those based on symbolic interactionism, phenomenology, or functionalism, but in these participant observation studies power tends to be seen as only one possible factor among many with which to analyze data. One need only look at the discussion of differentiation and polarization by Lacy (1970), Hargreaves (1967), Ball (1981), in which it is clear that schools have some power in social stratification, or the Beynon and Atkinson (1984) essay on "mucking and sussing," in which students and teachers engage in a struggle to control the direction of the classroom, to realize that power has a part in many educational ethnographies. However, these studies, like most, choose to interpret such findings in terms of negotiation among groups who have different cultural constructions. They suggest that the conflict arises from the different perspectives rather than that the different perspectives arise from the conflict embedded in wider historical–structural conditions.

If we look at the language of differentiation and polarization as presented by Lacy (1970), the point may become more clear. Differentiation is defined as

> . . . the separation and ranking of students according to a multiple set of criteria which makes up the normative, academically oriented, value system of the grammar school. Differentiation is defined here as being largely carried out by teachers in the course of their normal duties. . . . [Polarization] takes place within the student body, partly as a result of differentiation, but influenced by external factors and with an autonomy of its own. It is a process of subculture formation in which the school-dominated, normative culture is opposed by an alternative culture which I refer to as "anti-group" culture. (p. 57)

Lacy claims that polarization arises from the conflict of different cultures and different value systems (partially constructed through differentiation) rather than polarization (and, therefore, different cultures and values systems) arising from asymetrical power relations embedded in material structures. As explained earlier in this essay, Lacy did, to a minimal extent, place his findings within a broader sociopolitical context. Critical ethnographers, however, probably would like this context more fully described as contradictions within particular social relations. They also hope to make such a context an integral part of the analysis. The failure of the Manchester studies to discuss differentiation as an example of asymmetrical power relations or as an example of conflict between historically constructed social groups is a serious shortcoming. Teacher duties that result in differentiation are an example of power embedded in structure, not just the result of a "socially constructed reality" based on teachers' "definitions of the situation." Lacy, Hargreaves, and Ball, for all of their concern for the abuse of power and the plight of the school failures, owe more to the discourse of symbolic interactionism and Chicago School sociology then they do to critical traditions.

Ray McDermott's studies of Rosa are a more typical example of the failure to raise questions of asymmetrical power relations. In one discussion, McDermott (1977) concludes that the young pupil, Rosa, fails to engage in appropriate learning activities during reading lessons due to an unconscious collusion between Rosa and her teacher to help Rosa out of an uncomfortable and unproductive social situation rather than as a result of Rosa's submission (and perhaps her teacher's submission) to the overwhelming power of the learning situation as defined by the school.

Compare McDermott's studies of Rosa with Gitlin's (1983) ethnography on teacher work, in which he elaborates on the power embedded in curricular forms that control teacher behavior without any administrative directives. In other words, Gitlin defines the teachers' practices as fundamentally constituted within power relations. Or examine Paul Corrigan's (1979) "Smash Street Kids," who find themselves in trouble with the police as a result of "doing nothing" while on the streets. According to Corrigan, the "kids" are continuously surprised that the police interfere with their "weird ideas" and find no legitimate authority for the actions of the police. As Corrigan writes,

> This reflects very strongly the model of control in the school, where there was no real recognition of the moral or legal rights of the teacher to interfere. Similarly with the police, the only way in which their rights of interference are recognized is through their *power* and that is recognized, like the teacher, *only* in physical presence. (Corrigan, 1979:137)

Some Contemporary Influences

While critical approaches generally utilize historical structure and materiality as a basic approach to social reality, one should not assume that history and concrete life can only be approached as a "structuralist" phenomenon. The "poststructural" thought of Foucault, for instance, has begun to have strong influence on critical thinking. For Foucault, power is not something that is merely wielded by the powerful when they wish to control specific actions of the less powerful but, rather, is something that defines in a profound way the very relations themselves, the actual relationships that create the powerful and the disempowered. As Foucault (1980) has said, "individuals are the vehicles of power, not its points of application" (p. 98). Power is embedded in historical discourse and, therefore, is a fundamental concept for describing the concrete practices found in the study of everyday life. Foucault (1990) wrote,

> Power's condition of possibility . . . must not be sought in the primary existence of a central point, in a unique source of sovereignty from which secondary and descendant forms would emanate; it is the moving substrate of force relations which, by virtue of their inequality, constantly engender states of power, but the latter are always local and

> unstable. The omnipresence of power: not because it has the privilege
> of consolidating everything under its invincible unity, but because it is
> produced from one moment to the next, at every point, or rather in
> every relation from one point to another. Power is everywhere; not
> because it embraces everything, but because it comes from
> everywhere. . . . One needs to be nominalistic, no doubt: power is not
> an institution, and not a structure; neither is it a certain strength we
> are endowed with; it is the name that one attributes to a complex
> strategical situation in a particular society. (p. 93)

While the description and analysis of these "complex strategical situations" may be the greatest contribution that critical ethnography could
make to critical theory, few critical ethnographers have yet to fully
exploit the possibilities of a poststructural understanding of power.

Philip Corrigan is one researcher who recognizes power as integral
to the construction of our consciousness. In the following quotation,
Corrigan (1989) points to his desire to reconstruct the history that
(in)forms his personal history. Notice the manner in which Corrigan
integrates power into consciousness in such a way as to recognize both
the empowering and constraining effects of the social and cultural
forces unleashed in 1968.

> I am also trying to recover, and thus trace the lineaments of the
> specific empowering involved, the revolutionary kernel of "1968" for
> me: we do not only have to make different Xs (name your own favorite
> cultural production/form) but we have to make different Xs, *differently*
> [italics in original]. This may well entail a lot of hesitation, uncertainty,
> a welcoming of a "loss of the old verities" and of the multivarious
> "crises of Marxism" because it involves being careful: taking care that
> we do not replicate (with our bodies, in our voices, behind our backs)
> the old forms that constrain and maim in our embracing of the political
> romance and the leadership drives and performance instincts
> associated with both avant-gardes and vanguards. The suffering male
> Artist; the agonizing, dismal male Intellectual: being smart, being
> clever. (p. 70)

For Corrigan, power is not some force to wield or resist but something
that permeates the very fabric of our ways of life. While critical ethnography has taken an important step by making power the central
focus of social analysis through the development of reproduction/
resistance theory, it must take the next step and place power/
knowledge (and power/desire) at the center of our understanding of
culture.

Feminism has also contributed to an understanding of power that
fractures and particularizes the domination of subordinated persons,

but also one that imbues it with possibility. Nancy Hartsock (1990), for example, draws on well-developed feminist themes in her critique of Foucault's concept of power, claiming it as an example of the work of a "colonizer who refuses" and who is, therefore, left unable to act. Drawing on the work of Jewish Tunisian Albert Memmi, Hartsock asks, "Has one . . . ever seen a serious political demand which did not rest on concrete supports of people or money or force? The colonizer who refuses to become a part of his group fellow citizens faces the difficult political question of who might he be" (p. 164). In place of the historically convenient (given the new challenges from the margins) desolution of the Subject (the postmodern claim of the end of an ideal integrated and centered self), Hartsock calls for a feminist theory of power that reconstitutes the subject in history, reclaims the possibility of transformation, and locates understanding of the world in practical daily activity. A postmodern feminism such as Hartsock's repositions the discourse of power within ethnography by requiring that it maintain its transformative possibility even while acknowledging its cultural dispersion.

Summary

In critical discourse, society is understood to involve some kind of constitutive relationship between material and cultural relations; therefore, any ethnographic study that does not examine the relationships between the material and the cultural fails to bring the insights of critical discourse to bear on its project. While there is disagreement as to the strength of the effects of the material on the cultural or the cultural on the material or whether the relationship is dialectical or complex and contradictory, critical ethnographers are likely to locate the material as a central aspect of their ethnographies. While incorporating the material in any cultural study, critical ethnographers are likely to understand those material relations in terms of power. By this I mean that power is not just one aspect of particular societies but that power is the basis on which particular societies arise. Modern societies are not merely marked by the rise of capitalism, patriarchy, and Eurocentrism; capitalism, patriarchy, and Eurocentrism have formed modern societies. People must always construct their cultural lives within and against these constraints with varying degrees and focuses of understanding and recognition. Ethnography that fails to examine culture as embedded in such complex and conflictual social life has failed to describe its object. Finally, critical ethnographies have for too long operated within a concept of material—cultural relations and power that fails to recognize the complexity and contradictions of the present historical moment. If critical ethnographers hope to push their conversation forward, they must find ways of incorporating postmodern/poststructural concepts of power into their discourse of society while holding on to the transformative possibility, which has always marked critical thought and which has been reconstructed by certain feminist writers (see Giroux, in press b; Nicholson, 1990).

Culture

④ While the critical tradition does place an emphasis on material relations in social analysis, human consciousness has also become of central concern. Critical theorists recognize that, while material relations are represented in human consciousness, human consciousness has some part to play in material and cultural relations. This knowledge has led them to explore issues of ideology, hegemony, and culture in human studies. It has also led to the belief that the transformation of society through the critique and demystification of culture should be a fundamental goal of critical discourse. This particular project is ideally suited to the processes of ethnographic research with its emphasis on describing cultural assumptions and patterns. But because such assumptions and patterns only gain critical meaning in the larger social context, a critical concept of culture requires an understanding of the complex relationships among the material, the historical, and the cultural. Rather than accepting culture as an entity constructed by the subjective acts of bounded groups to provide meaning and order to life, critical discourse suggests that *culture is an ongoing political struggle around the meaning given to actions of people located within unbounded asymmetrical power relations.* This recognition that culture is intimately connected to historical/material relations encourages some critical ethnographers to approach the study of culture in a manner that stresses a plurality of cultures competing with each other over the representation of their identity and their positioning within larger social formations. They suggest that culture is better understood as contested terrain than as a set of shared patterns.

The Demystification of Culture

The idea that culture does not develop solely, or even largely, through subjective acts of bounded groups but, rather, as a consequence of the political struggles of various groups to name their experiences and represent their identity distinguishes the critical tradition

- name their experiences ⇒ culture
- represent their identity

from most other approaches to ethnography. To understand one's positioning within society requires some attention to the social relations that organize cultural constructions. In traditional critical discourse, this understanding is usually approached through some form of demystification of cultural representations. While our consciousness may be formed within certain material relations, we do have agency and this agency can, potentially, be used for the transformation of historical structures. As Marcuse (1968) wrote,

> Critical theory's interest in the liberation of mankind binds it to certain ancient truths. It is at one with [Western] philosophy in maintaining that man can be more than a manipulable subject in the production process of class society. . . . [Critical theory] opposes not only the production relations that gave rise to bad materialism, but every form of production that dominates man instead of being dominated by him: this idealism underlies its materialism. Its constructive concepts, too, have a residue of abstractness as long as the reality toward which they are directed is not yet given. Here, however, abstractness results not from avoiding the status quo, but from orientation toward the future status of man. (p. 153)

This transformative possibility assumes that humans are potentially able to demystify cultural constructions and to understand their historical structuring as we are able to do when we read the above quotation and recognize the political ideology embedded in its patriarchal language. This attempt at "self-transparency" (Fay, 1987:80) becomes a signature of critical discourse.

Critical discussions of culture assert the potentiality of self-transparency because they also assume that historical or material structures play an integral part in culture production. Without the constitutive role of historical or material relations in the formation of culture, any concept of self-transparency is meaningless. But given the constitutive role of history and the material in culture construction, the possibility of demystification remains. Traditionally, ethnography has presented culture as something constructed by participants in family, neighborhood, or peer groupings. If the complex society at large is considered at all in relation to the cultural constructions (and it frequently is not), it is presented as something that interacts with or conflicts with an already self-defined cultural group. But Marcuse argues that "The particular exists only in and through the totality of relations of which it is a part" (Held, 1980:230). In critical ethnography, then, the group's construction of culture is a complex activity that must always include oppositional relations with potential group formations as defining forces, not just interactive forces, in the construction of cultural patterns. Culture is not just heritage passed on from one generation to the next but is constructed out of the lives of people located in particular historical relations. As Marcus and Fischer (1986) state,

> What makes representation challenging and a focus of experimentation is the perception that the "outside forces" in fact are an integral part of the construction and constitution of the "inside," the cultural unit itself, and must be so registered, even at the most intimate levels of cultural process. . . . (p. 77)

For example, Dick Hebdige argues, in his analysis of the mod youth subculture of the 1960s (Hebdige, 1976; see also Hebdige, 1979), that the "fetishising of style" was an "imaginary" expression of their real social relations. In their appropriation and redefinition of Edwardian style, the mods were able to express resistance to the powerlessness of their working-class position. Of course such construction of style, according to Hebdige, is only "imaginary" and can never replace their materially defined relationships in a capitalist system. The mod subculture is constructed, he suggests, by a certain group of working-class youths given particular relations with the larger capitalist society. In other words, the mod subculture is not the result of a preexisting working-class culture in *interaction with* a self-defined middle-class culture but is, rather, formed in the same asymmetrical power relations that we represent as class cultures. The cultural constructions of the mod youth are the manifestations of power relations rather than the results of the interaction of different cultures: It is tied to social relations rather than to cultural consciousness. The existence of particular historical forms that underpin and constrain cultural constructions makes "self-transparency" a possibility, because it permits any particular cultural construction to be placed within the wider historical moment.

The demystification of cultural hegemony is a key characteristic of critical discourse, but demystification alone is not enough to place an ethnographic study in the critical tradition. To claim a voice in the critical dialogue, demystification must always be tied to power relations. After all, demystification has always been a common element of phenomenology. Nell Keddie (1971) gives us an example of demystification alone in her classic study of school discourse. The contradictions illuminated by Keddie's identification of "educationist" and "teacher" contexts certainly demystify school discourse, but she does not place these contradictions into the broader context of historical/material relations and, therefore, fails to raise cultural power to the rank of an analytic tool. Her analysis remains too simplistic to serve as a catalyst for effective transformative action. Compare Keddie's study with that of McLaren (1986:104–108), who defines teacher talk as sacred ritual and its effects as complex and varied, but whose practice is fundamentally an exercise in power. McLaren shows us where and how power is exercised through complex ritual performances and, therefore, provides a potentially important site to begin to restructure school practice. For the critical ethnographer, then, demystification of cultural hegemony is of primary concern, but demystification must be within a dialogue of social processes as asymmetrical power relations embedded within particular historical/material constraints.

Cultural Politics

Because culture is always constructed in relation with others and within structural constraints, one cannot talk about culture without some conception of cultural politics. For those at the CCCS, cultural power represents the power a particular cultural view has in controlling the symbolic realm in a particular site.

> But just as different groups and classes are unequally ranked in relation to one another, in terms of their productive relations, wealth and power, so *cultures* [italics in original] are differently ranked, and stand in opposition to one another, in relations of domination and subordination, along the scale of "cultural power." (Clarke, Hall, Jefferson, and Roberts, 1976:11)

Social processes must be understood as mechanisms of conflict, in which cultural power plays an active role. The critical ethnographer's interest in observing cultural action lies in the extent to which that culture acts to support or subvert ideology, to mystify or to demystify social conditions. In this way, critical ethnography attempts to clarify political struggle.

Culture should always be understood to refer to both the structured patterns of a group and the meanings members give to those patterns. As the youth subcultures group at the Birmingham CCCS expressed it, "We understand the word 'culture' to refer to that level at which social groups develop distinct patterns of life, and give *expressive form* to their social and material life-experience" (Clarke *et al.*, 1976:10). These scholars present youth cultures as subordinate to both parents with their working-class culture and agents of the state (teachers, social workers, police, etc.) with their middle-class culture.

Youth feel compelled "to magically express and resolve the contradictions of parent culture" (such as their commitment to physical labor and their belief in fair reward for fair work) as well as their opposition to middle-class culture through styles that celebrate low status traits such as physical and sexual aggressiveness. By raising to high status that which is low status, they attempt to create "ideological resolution to unsolvable material contradictions" in their lived experiences (Clarke *et al.*, 1976:13–33). This emphasis on "imaginary responses," "magical expressions," and "ideological resolutions" suggests that the youth do not adequately understand the material basis for their choice of style and, in turn, reveals why critical ethnographers are less likely to accept participants' meanings as fully accurate representations of their cultural constructions unless these constructions are located in the historical conditions that help form them. "Cultures are webs of mystification as well as signification," Roger Keesing (1987:161) points out, suggesting that any attempt to represent culture outside of societal forces will misrepresent it.

Although some recent anthropological theory influenced by literary criticism (see Geertz, 1988; Clifford and Marcus, 1986; Marcus and Fischer, 1986) has elaborated a complex discussion of culture, traditional educational ethnography still emphasizes conventions that understand culture to be the common and intersubjective agreements of a group. For example, Spradley's well-known definition that culture is "the knowledge people use to generate and interpret social behavior" (Spradley and McCurdy, 1972:8) leads him to develop methods of semantic ethnography, which tend to overreport consensus and tend to overlook the contradictions, variety, and struggle within the actions people take to construct a meaningful world. As Henry Giroux has suggested in the critical tradition "culture is analyzed . . . not simply as a way of life, but also as a form of production that always involves asymmetrical relations of power, and through which different groups in their dominant and subordinate positions struggle to both define and realize their aspirations (Giroux, 1989:126). Culture is not so much the area of social life where people share understandings as that area of social life where people struggle over understandings. For this reason, many critical ethnographers prefer to use the plural "cultures" rather than the singular "culture." Such a convention reminds us that culture is a contested terrain with multiple voices expressed through constitutive power relations.

Though the nature of this struggle over culture can never be reduced to a simple opposition, it is crucial to replace the notion of "culture"

plurality of cultures
no single culture

with the more concrete, historical concept of "cultures"; a redefinition
which brings out more clearly the fact that cultures always stand in
relations of domination—and subordination—to one another, are
always, in some sense, in struggle with one another. (Clarke *et al.*,
1976:12)

In using the plural form, we are unlikely to fall into the Becker roman-
ticization of deviant groups as Spradley does when he defines "the
culture of tramps" as "urban nomads" whose choice of life-styles is
incompatible with modern life, instead of recognizing the displaced or
oppositional nature of homeless, unemployed men who have turned to
alcohol (Spradley, 1970).

Some Contemporary Influences

In the preceding discussion, I have claimed that the concept of
self-transparency or demystification requires some understanding of
historical or material structuring. Such appeals to history or the material are too often appeals to a grand narrative—that is, to some referent
story such as the march of modernism or enlightenment or liberalism
or capitalism or communism. Lyotard (1984) brings our attention to the
contradiction of grand narratives that take patriarchy, Eurocentrism,
and modernity outside of history. Because the grand narratives are
themselves constructs of history, the appeal to them as a basis for
demystification falsely lays claim to a true state of affairs. When critical
ethnographers such as Willis (1977), Robbins and Cohen (1978), and
Paul Corrigan (1979) appeal to class as an unproblematic construction
of history and fail to explore the patriarchal, Eurocentric assumptions
of their ethnographies, they have relied on grand narratives to organize
their analyses. To assume "self-transparency" is often to assume that in
some way one's position in the world is unitary, that is, defined by
singular narratives such as Marxism or certain forms of feminism. On
the other hand, with the rejection of grand narratives as found in
postmodernism (Laclau and Mouffe, 1985) and some forms of feminism
(Fraser and Nicholson, 1988), one's identity becomes defined through
the multiple "subject positions" one holds (referring to the position
one occupies in a discourse; see Laclau and Mouffe, 1985; Rosaldo,
1989). The rejection of grand narratives does not permit the kind of
self-transparency assumed in critical discourse; however, by introducing subject positions, we might claim the possibility of "self-
articulation." Self-articulation implies the ability to reconstruct discourse and, therefore, the possibility of altering one's own subject

multivocality

position. Critical ethnography might focus on how marginalized groups work for self-articulation instead of self-transparency.

Another relevant contemporary theme is that of multivocality or multivoicedness. Developed from the work of the Bakhtin Circle (primarily Mikhail Bakhtin, Valintin Volosinov, and P. N. Medvedev), multivoicedness points us toward the recognition that neither cultures nor individuals can be understood in terms of unity; both individuals and cultures are best understood in terms of multiple voices engaged in dialogue (for an elaboration of some important "Bakhtinian" themes that can be used in ethnographic writing, see Quantz and O'Connor, 1988). The dialogic conception of individuals and culture extends the critical sense of a plurality of cultures discussed previously by recognizing not only that society is complex and contradictory but that the "elements" of society (individuals and culture groups) are themselves internally complex and contradictory. The idea of multivoiced and dialogic individuals and cultures further complicates our understanding of "self-transparency" because no unitary or centered Subject or culture exists. On the other hand, the Bakhtin Circle presents us with a sense of history that, when combined with the idea of subject positions, points to the continued possibility of some form of active agency in the discursive positioning of historical actors.

While these contemporary themes create problems for the traditional critical concept of demystification, they reinforce the critical emphasis on cultural politics. Whether we are talking about the contentions around narratives, the positioning of the subject, or the multivocality of individuals and cultures, the political aspects of culture become even more obvious and central. Clearly, critical ethnography must find some way to move from "self-transparency"—implying an ability to see things as they really are—to "self-articulation"— implying an ability to construct discourses that reposition the subject. It also must find techniques for representing the multivoicedness of people and their cultures. Only in this way can a critical discourse around culture continue to be relevant to educational ethnography.

Summary

As it does with discussions of society, critical discourse must always recognize culture to be in some way located in an historical/material world. Because of this emphasis on the location of culture within larger social forces, critical ethnographies tend to view cultures of particular groups as at least partially constituted through their relations with other cultures. Culture is not constructed within a bounded

Self-articulation   vs   *Self-transparency*

group. The idea of "holistic" ethnography, in which the "whole" of the culture is observed, is an absurd idea. Any culture, even the most remote [see Rosaldo's (1980) study of the Ilongots], is constituted, at least in part, by others. To assume that the meaning of cultural activity can be defined only within a cultural hermeneutic of emic study fails to recognize the fundamental and constitutive role played by larger social forces. Consequently, critical ethnographers have been skeptical of discourses in which cultural meaning arises only from within an autonomous group, choosing instead to place cultural meaning within the larger context of history and material relations. The idea that cultural meaning cannot be restricted to the hermeneutic of the group makes possible the concept of self-transparency. If we reconstruct our understanding of history without appealing to grand narratives and our understanding of culture and individuals in terms of multivocality and subject positions, we should be able to reconstitute self-transparency as self-articulation. In this manner, culture comes to be understood as a terrain of struggle in which the attempt at self-articulation becomes, in itself, an act of power.

History

History is a recurring theme in critical ethnography, and yet it is rarely elaborated in a direct manner. I have argued in this essay that both society and culture must be understood in terms of history, and, in my discussions, I have frequently intertwined history with structure and with material relations. However, while history is almost always an integral force in critical ethnographies, it is usually an implied rather than overtly referenced or acknowledged aspect of critical ethnography. The importance and understanding of history in critical discourse can be traced to Marx's conception of material history. This teleological understanding of history is a central organizing theme, even for those critical ethnographers who consciously reject a Marxian historical materialism. For one thing, because society and culture can be understood only in historical terms, critical ethnographers are likely to approach their studies as asynchronous events and are unlikely to lapse into the "ethnographic present" in their writings.

On the other hand, history seems to play only a supporting role in traditional ethnography, if it plays any role at all. As Marcus (1986) has written,

> Ethnographies have always been written in the context of historic change: the formation of state systems and the evolution of a world

critical ⇒ asynchro

interpretive focus

political economy. But aside from the use of a few well-established techniques for taking into account change, history, and political economy, ethnographers of an interpretive bent—more interested in problems of cultural meaning than in social action—have not generally represented the ways in which closely observed cultural worlds are embedded in larger, more impersonal systems. Nor have they portrayed the role of these worlds in the sort of events and processes that make history, so to speak, perhaps because ethnography as description has never been particularly ambitious in this way. (p. 165–166)

traditional

synchro

As Marcus points out, traditional ethnographers have been more interested in the elaboration of meaning within a synchronous system. They have paid little attention to culture embedded in broader historical movements. To the extent that traditional ethnographers have been interested in history at all, it has been understood to be localized and only indirectly connected to broader historical trends.

While, in theory, many ethnographers call for an active inclusion of history, in practice, few ethnographers seem comfortable with its use. Of course, traditional ethnography has been heavily criticized for the use of the "ethnographic present" and, as a result, one finds fewer and fewer examples of the use of the forever-present tense in ethnography. But even with the decline of the ethnographic present, ethnography still appears locked into a synchronous understanding of culture. Such synchrony becomes apparent in the concepts that Rosaldo (1980:10) has called "cultural homogeneity" and "cultural continuity."

The doctrine of homogeneity allowed practitioners . . . to posit a basic personality shared by all members of a culture. The assumption of continuity across generations allowed them to sidestep longitudinal studies and instead to study parents and their infants at a single point in time, in order to infer (without asking whether the character of children might differ from that of their parents) how child training practices (which themselves might have changed) had produced adult character. Their assumption that primitive cultures were timeless, as static as they were uniform, grew in large part out of a mistaken perception of the limitations imposed by the short term of field research. They restricted themselves unduly to what they could observe during their brief time in the field; for them, seeing was believing. (Rosaldo, 1980:10–13)

This emphasis on "seeing is believing" necessarily restricts most ethnographers to what they actually observe in the field (after all, this is the hallmark of ethnography) and leads most traditional ethnographers to assume cultural homogeneity and continuity in their ethnographic descriptions, even when they attempt to write in a style that acknowledges the temporal particularity of their field experience.

To argue that history plays a supporting or background role in traditional ethnography is not to argue that it has no part at all. However, I want to argue that history has a more methodological influence than an analytic influence in traditional ethnography. For example, one way in which history has been incorporated into ethnographic studies in education is through the requisite brief institutional and community history found in an introductory chapter (see Guthrie, 1985; Metz, 1978; Peshkin, 1978, 1986). Unfortunately, such brief historical sketches are soon forgotten and are rarely used for analytic purposes. It is as if history is one aspect of "setting the stage" (see Delamont, 1983), but, because interpretive ethnography places such strong emphasis on the human capacity to construct meaning in an immediate context, the stage (and, therefore, history) has, at best, a minor role to play in explaining cultural patterns.

Perhaps a more integral place for history in traditional ethnography is in the form of the "career." Career, a concept developed in labeling/deviance theory, is used to explain the life of individuals as they move through time and is often approached through the use of "biography" or "life history" (see Woods, 1985). Such concepts do make history an active *methodological* concept, but still do not make history an active *analytic* concept in educational ethnography. That is to say that biography and life history may be used to describe, categorize, and report changes in various student or teacher responses (see Ball and Goodson, 1984), but history is not used to explain the production of present cultural constructions in the context of broader historical trends.

Critical ethnographers, on the other hand, seem to make history an important analytic tool but fail to take advantage of the methodological use of history in ethnography (for an exception, see Quantz, 1985). Perhaps, the clearest use of history in a critical ethnography can be found in Robins and Cohen's book *Knuckle Sandwich: Growing Up in the Working-Class City* (1978). In *Knuckle Sandwich*, Robins and Cohen spend many pages developing the concept of "territoriality" as a present-day construction embedded in the particular history of the British working class. They then use the concept of territoriality as an analytic concept in their explanation of violence at English soccer matches. By tying a present cultural pattern to the changing historical conditions of housing patterns for working-class neighborhoods, Robins and Cohen have clearly embedded history in culture. Roger Hewitt (1986) also places cultural practices within the changing historical conditions of housing patterns. In *White Talk Black Talk*, Hewitt shows how black language patterns may be adopted and abandoned by white youths depending on the racial patterning of their neighborhoods. In both cases, present-day youth culture is not merely an evolution of some previous cultural patterns but is also produced by particular social conditions constructed by specific historical practices.

In another example, Robert Everhart (1983) uses the concept of "regenerative knowledge" in *Reading, Writing, and Resistance* to explain the system of meaning used by junior high school students to organize their social life. To Everhart, "regenerative knowledge" can be explained as

> . . . legitimated and reinforced through, and based upon the collective ties between, individuals whose relationship to productive forces is roughly equivalent and who share common world-views that grow out of and eventually may re-create those very productive forces—a social class. Such a knowledge system, based on mutuality of communication within a "community" (such as that of students), may be termed "regenerative" because it is created, maintained, and re-created through the continuous interaction of people in a community setting and because what is known is, in part, dependent upon the historical forces emerging from within the community setting. (Everhart, 1983:124–125)

History must be understood to be both the "march of time" and an active force in structuring the moment, so that we cannot limit our concept of history to "setting the chronological stage" and "the shoulders upon which we stand," but we must also recognize that history is continually expressed through constraining cultural formations and that it is an active force in constructing the future.

History includes both the constraints and the possibilities of cultural and social life. It is more than an analytic tool for unpacking present-day cultures; it provides the potentiality for transformation by negating reification. For critical research, social structures are always historical: created by humans and potentially alterable by humans. As Adorno (1973) wrote, "What man ought to be as such is never more than what he has been: he is chained to the rock of his past. He is not only what he was and is, however, but equally what he can come to be . . ." (p. 51). This emphasis on historical interpretation of cultural patterns and, therefore, on transformation leads critical ethnography away from statements calling for the preservation of subordinated cultures in some pristine form. Because cultures are always produced in a complex of historical forces rather than by some isolated, collective self-will, present subordinated cultures must always be understood in terms of their subordination. The naive call for cultural preservation is a concealed act for continued social and cultural domination. When history is presented as a productive force rather than as a mere contextual factor, then history must play a productive part in the ethnographic presentation of the concrete practices of subordinated people.

Some Contemporary Influences

While critical ethnography is inseparable from an active contemplation of history, its sense of history has come under increasing attack in recent years. While most critical ethnographers have rejected historical materialism as an iron law of historical progress, they have not so easily abandoned a dialectical and teleological sense of history. Certainly the classic "critical ethnographies" have been tied to a dialectic located in class relations under capitalism. In recent years, this neo-Marxist analysis has been replaced by an only slightly more complex analysis that either brings gender into the analysis with class (Connell *et al.*, 1982; Gaskell, 1985; McRobbie, 1978; Valli, 1985, 1986) or subsumes discussions of class to gender (Griffin, 1985). While postmodern and certain feminist discourses have brought the concept of a historical dialectic into question, relatively few ethnographers have introduced a complex understanding of the relationships among class, race, and gender (see Grant and Sleeter, 1986; Roman, 1988). The attacks on foundational thinking and the unified Self suggest that history involves many more fluid conflicts than can be represented in a dialectic. History is multifaceted, multivoiced, and contradictory. Historical actors occupy many subject positions at the same moment. Such everchanging positioning challenges a dialectical and teleological sense of history.

Postmodern feminists such as Young (1990) and Lugones (1987; Lugones and Spelman, 1987) bring our attention to the intolerance of difference that any teleological concept of history implies. If history is moving to some all-defining, unitary community, then the indeterminate, multifarious, and contradictory aspects of concrete lives must, by definition, become determinant, singular, and coherent. Yet such qualities are fundamental organizing principles of patriarchy. As Young (1990) puts it,

> The ideal of community . . . privileges unity over difference, immediacy over mediation, sympathy over recognition of the limits of one's understanding of others from their point of view. Community is an understandable dream, expressing a desire for selves that are transparent to one another, relationships of mutual identification, social closeness and comfort. The dream is understandable, but politically problematic, I argue, because those motivated by it will tend to

suppress differences among themselves or implicitly to exclude from
their political groups persons with whom they do not identify. (p. 300)

Instead of a politics oriented around community, Young argues for a
politics of difference, one in which she locates a "concrete political
vision of inexhaustible heterogeneity" (p. 301). In a similar vein, Lugones (1987) argues for a "pluralistic feminism, a feminism that affirms
the plurality in each of us and among us as richness and as central to
feminist ontology and epistemology" (p. 3). She advocates what she
calls the exercise of " 'world'-travelling."

> Without knowing the other's 'world,' one does not know the other, and
> without knowing the other one is really alone in the other's presence
> because the other is only dimly present to one. Through travelling to
> other people's "worlds" we discover that there are 'worlds' in which
> those who are the victims of arrogant perception are really subjects,
> lively beings, resistors, constructors of visions even though in the
> mainstream construction they are animated only by the arrogant
> perceiver and are pliable, foldable, file-awayable, classifiable.
> (Lugones, 1987:18)

Through Lugones "world"-travelling and Young's politics of difference, it becomes impossible to imagine the dialectical advancement of
a teleological history.

As I have written elsewhere (Quantz, in press),

> That history might be understood as the evolution of culture toward
> more advanced and better forms of civilization has formed the
> foundation of both liberal and Marxist thought. While different
> historians may argue about the directness of the progression and point
> out regressive moments in our history, they more or less agree that
> civilization generally advances—the present being a more progressive
> moment than the past.

But if individuals and their cultures are multivoiced and contradictory,
how does one recognize a more progressive moment from a less progressive moment? In the past, when critical ethnographers were challenged for imposing a personal vision on a subordinated culture, they
were always able to claim some grounding in history, but without such
a teleological and dialectical understanding of history, how do critical
ethnographers justify the intrusion of history into their analyses?

Perhaps one solution to this problem is to approach history dialogically instead of dialectically. Anthropologists and other Western
scholars, drawing from the work of the Bakhtin Circle, have begun to
recognize the possibilities of a dialogical approach to history.

> For Bakhtin dialogic consciousness is not only social, it is historically and ideologically located within specific material and symbolic realms. Because individuals must construct their private thoughts and their public communication within the limit of language opportunities available at a given time and place, the individual human utterance is formed within historical constraints. Accordingly, Bakhtin chooses to call speech "behavioral ideology." As part of a historically situated social dialogue, behavioral ideology represents the concrete manifestation of these limitations on the speech used by an individual. (Quantz and O'Connor, 1988:98)

Certainly ethnography lends itself to a dialogic conception of history. By locating history in the utterances of the moment, history can be located and described through ethnography as much as ethnography can be contextualized and elaborated through its connections to history.

The theoretical work of Laclau and Mouffe (1985) also provides a possible approach to our understanding of history in culture. In their analysis of hegemony, Laclau and Mouffe provide a strategy for radical democratic activity, which, while not abandoning utopian directions, assumes neither a dialectic nor a teleological history. Through their emphasis on subject positions and the particularity of social struggles, they provide discursive potentials for describing history and orienting political transformation. By focusing on the way in which discourses position subjects, Laclau and Mouffe reject a conception of history as the momentary conclusion of prior events and refocus our attention on history as an active construction of present events where temporary allegiances occur as different people come to share, momentarily, similar discursive positions. Constructions such as those of Young, Lugones, and Bakhtin Circle, and Laclau and Mouffe are only now beginning to enter the critical education discourse (see Giroux, 1988a,b, in press a,b); Quantz and O'Connor, 1988). Whether or not their work will help critical ethnographers address the patriarchal and Eurocentric biases that organize their sense of history without abandoning either the analytic potentialities or the political project that has been the hallmark of critical ethnography will be known in the next decade.

Summary

While history plays an integral part in critical ethnography, it seldom appears in as overt a fashion as it does in Robins and Cohen's *Knuckle Sandwich* (1978). Whether or not it is overtly addressed, history becomes one of the central themes of critical ethnography. By emphasizing interrelationships among society, culture, and history, few critical ethnographers fall into the trap of the ethnographic present and are unlikely to become overly reliant on the concepts of cultural homogeneity and cultural continuity. On the other hand, because of the reliance on a dialectical and teleological understanding of history, critical ethnographers may present an overly deterministic and simplistic description of cultures as well as one filled with androcentric and Eurocentric constructs. Perhaps the work of the Bakhtin Circle, postmodern feminists such as Young and Lugones, and postmodern theorists such as Laclau and Mouffe may provide a way for critical ethnographers to address these problems.

Conclusion

Critical ethnography is a recent development in educational research that is still evolving. As one empirical aspect of a larger political project, critical ethnography has begun to play a role in the way we construct and think about schooling in this country. While any one ethnographic study may not have much force, the large number of ethnographic studies mentioned in this essay have gone a long way to provide empirical shape to the theoretical ideas that schools are sites of cultural politics. But many are still dissatisfied with the effective results of critical ethnography on school politics. After all, for a research approach that sets its conception of truth against the transformation of society, practical results are absolutely necessary. For those such as Gitlin, Siegel, and Boru (1988), Lather (1986), and Fine (1990), who essentially argue that praxis should be located in the present and should involve the particular individuals being studied, critical ethnography has seemed too academic, too removed, too oriented toward the life of the academy and not enough toward the politics of the everyday. While I happen to share their concern for a more active form of research, one whose object might not be oriented toward the representation of rewriting of cultures (i.e., ethnography) but, rather, toward the transformation of people's lives, I am convinced that there is still a place for critical ethnography in the critical dialogue surrounding schooling. By exploring the concrete particulars of cultures located in historical material relations with theoretical commitments to democratic transformation, critical ethnography has contributed much to our present discourse. While I believe that critical ethnographers must begin to reconsider their work in light of postmodern and feminist writing, I also continue to believe that ethnographic fieldwork of some sort will contribute to the overall critical project. While I advocate a decentering of culture and of critical discourse, decentering does not require me to think of the study of particular realities and voices as isolated research activities—unified and complete in themselves. While I share the desire to see more activist research, I do not wish to see the complete abandonment of a critical ethnography whose purpose will be realized in a larger sense of history and community than action research implies. I hope to continue to see academics willing to participate in the critical dialogues that have been outlined in this paper, and I continue to believe that they can, in a limited way, contribute to the democratic transformation of schooling.

Acknowledgments

I would like to thank the Institute of Education, University of London, for making possible the time and resources I needed to begin considering this topic and especially Tony Green for his many suggestions on early drafts of this essay.

References

Adorno, T. (1973). *Negative dialectics*, E. B. Ashton (Trans.). New York: Seabury.

Aggleton, P. (1987). *Rebels without a cause: Middle class youth and the transition from school to work*. London: Falmer Press.

Anderson, G. (1989). Critical ethnography in education: Origins, current status, and new directions. *Review of Educational Research*, 59(3), 249–270.

Anyon, J. (1980). Social class and the hidden curriculum of work. *Journal of Education*, 162, 67–92.

Anyon, J. (1981). Social class and school knowledge. *Curriculum Inquiry*, 11(1), 3–42.

Apple, M. W., and Weis, L. (Eds.). (1983). *Ideology and practice in schooling*. Philadelphia: Temple University.

Ball, S. (1981). *Beachside comprehensive: A case-study of secondary schooling*. Cambridge: Cambridge University Press.

Ball, S., and Goodson, I. (Eds.). (1984). *Defining the curriculum: Histories and ethnographies of school subjects*. London: Falmer Press.

Becker, H. S. (1963). *Outsiders: Studies in the sociology of deviance*. London: Free Press.

Becker, H. S. (Ed.). (1964). *The other side: Perspectives on deviance*. New York: Free Press of Glencoe.

Becker, H. S. (1967). Whose side are we on? *Social Problems*, 14(3), 239–247.

Becker, H. S., Geer, B., Hughes, E. C., and Strauss, A. L. (1961). *Boys in white: Student culture in medical school*. Chicago: University of Chicago Press.

Benhabib, S., and Cornell, D. (1987). *Feminism as critique*. Minneapolis: University of Minnesota Press.

Beynon, J., and Atkinson, P. (1984). Pupils as data-gatherer: Mucking and sussing. In S. Delamont (Ed.), *Readings on interaction in the classroom* (pp. 255–272). London: Methuen.

Bourdieu, P., and Passeron, J. C. (1977). *Reproduction in education, society, and culture.* Beverly Hills: Sage Publications.

Bowles, S., Gintis, H. (1976). *Schooling in capitalist America.* New York: Basic Books.

Britzman, D. P. (1986). Cultural myths in the making of a teacher: Biography and social structure in teacher education. *Harvard Educational Review,* 56(4), 442–455.

Britzman, D. P. (1991). *Practice makes practice.* Albany, NY: SUNY Press.

Brodkey, L. (1987). *Academic writing as social practice.* Philadelphia: Temple University.

Carr, W., and Kemmis, S. (1986). *Becoming critical: Education, knowledge and action research.* London: Falmer Press.

Cazden, C., John, V., and Hymes, D. (1972). *Functions of language in the classroom.* New York: Teachers College Press.

Centre for Contemporary Cultural Studies. (1978). *Women take issue: Aspects of women's subordination.* Women's Studies Group, University of Birmingham.

Chanan, G., and Delamont, S. (Eds.). (1975). *Frontiers of classroom research.* Slough, England: National Foundation for Educational Research.

Cherryholmes, C. (1988). Power and criticism: Poststructural investigations in education. *In Advances in contemporary educational thought* (Vol. 2). New York: Teachers College.

Cicourel, A., and Kitsuse, J. (1963). *The Educational decision-makers.* Indianapolis: Bobbs-Merrill.

Clarke, J., Hall, S., Jefferson, T., and Roberts, B. (1976). Subcultures, cultures and class. *In* S. Hall and T. Jefferson (Eds.), *Resistance through ritual: Youth subcultures in post-war Britain* (pp. 9–79). London: Hutchinson.

Clifford, J. (1983). On ethnographic authority. *Representations,* 1(2), 118–146.

Clifford, J. (1986a). Introduction: Partial truths. *In* J. Clifford and G. Marcus (Eds.), *Writing culture: The poetics and politics of ethnography* (pp. 1–26). Berkeley: University of California.

Clifford, J. (1986b). On ethnographic allegory. *In* J. Clifford and G. Marcus (Eds.), *Writing culture: The poetics and politics of ethnography* (pp. 98–121). Berkeley: University of California.

Clifford, J., and Marcus, G. (1986). *Writing culture: The poetics and politics of ethnography.* Berkeley: University of California.

Connell, R. W., Dowsett, B. W., Kessler, S., and Ashendew, D. J. (1982). *Making the difference.* Sydney: George Allen & Unwin.

Corrigan, Paul. (1979). *Schooling the smash street kids.* London: Macmillan Press.

Corrigan, P. D. R. (1988). The making of the boy: Meditations on what grammar school did with, to, and for my body. *Journal of Education,* 170(3), 142–161.

Corrigan, P. D. R. (1989). Playing . . . Contra/dictions, empowerment, and embodiment: Punk, pedagogy, and popular cultural forms (on ethnography and education). *In* H. Giroux and R. Simon (Eds.), *Popular culture: Schooling and everyday life* (pp. 67–90). Critical Studies in Education Series. Granby, MA: Bergin & Garvey.

Crapanzano, V. (1985). *Waiting: The whites of South Africa.* New York: Random House.

Cusick, P. (1973). *Inside high school: The student's world.* New York: Holt, Rinehart & Winston.

Davies, L. (1984). *Pupil power: Deviance and gender in school*. London: Falmer Press.

Delamont, S. (1983). *Interaction in the classroom* (2nd ed.). Contemporary Sociology of the School Series. London: Methuen.

Derrida, J. (1973). *Speech and phenomena and other essays on Husserl's theory of signs*, D. B. Allison (Trans.). Evanston, IL: Northwestern University. (Original French publication in 1967.)

Derrida, J. (1976). *Of grammatology*, G. Chakravorty Spivak (Trans.). Baltimore: Johns Hopkins University. (Original French publication in 1967.)

Erickson, F. (1975). Gate-keeping and the melting pot: Interaction in counseling interviews. *Harvard Educational Review*, 45, 44–70.

Erickson, F. (1977). Some approaches to inquiry in school/community ethnography. *Anthropology and Education Quarterly*, 8, 58–69.

Everhart, R. (1983). *Reading, writing, and resistance: Adolescence and labor in a junior high school*. Critical Social Thought Series. Boston: Routledge and Kegan Paul.

Fay, B. (1987). *Critical social science: Liberation and its limits*. Ithaca, NY: Cornell University.

Fine, M. (1986). Why urban adolescents drop into and out of high school. *Teachers College Record*, 87, 393–409.

Fine, M. (1987). Silencing in public school. *Language Arts*, 64, 157–174.

Fine, M. (1988). Sexuality, schooling, and adolescent females: The missing discourse of desire. *Harvard Educational Review*, 58(1), 29–53.

Fine, M. (1990). Ventriloguy and 'voices' . . . Coming clean about smoke, mirrors and politics in activist research. First Annual Laurie McDade Memorial Lecture, Miami University, OH.

Flax, J. (1990). Postmodernism and gender relations in feminist Theory. *In* L. Nicholson (Ed.), *Feminism/postmodernism* (pp. 39–62). New York: Routledge.

Foucault, M. (1990). *The history of sexuality, volume I: An introduction*, R. Hurley (Trans.). New York: Vintage.

Foucault, M. (1980). *Power/knowledge: Selected interviews & other writings, 1972–1977*, C. Gordon (Ed.). New York: Pantheon Books.

Fox-Genovese, E. (1988). *Within the plantation household: Black and white women of the old south*. Chapel Hill: University of North Carolina.

Fraser, N., and Nicholson, L. (1990). Social criticism without philosophy: An encounter between feminism and postmodernism. *In* A. Ross (Ed.), *Universal abandon?: The politics of postmodernism* (pp. 83–104). Minneapolis: University of Minnesota. [Also published in Nicholson, L. J. (Ed.), *Feminism/postmodernism* (pp. 19–38). New York: Routledge.]

Fuller, M. (1980). Black girls in a London comprehensive school. *In* R. Deem (Ed.), *Schooling for women's work* (pp. 52–65). London: Routledge and Kegan Paul.

Furlong, J. (1984). Black resistance in the liberal comprehensive. *In* S. Delamont (Ed.), *Readings on interaction in the classroom* (pp. 212–236). London: Methuen.

Gaskell, J. (1984). Gender and course choice: The orientation of male and female students. *Journal of Education*, 166(1), 89–102.

Gaskell, J. (1985). Gender enrollment in the high school: The perspective of working-class females. *Sociology of Education*, 58, 48–59.

 Geertz, C. (1973). *The interpretation of cultures*. New York: Basic Books.

Geertz, C. (1983). *Local knowledge*. New York: Basic Books.

Geertz, C. (1988). *Works and lives: The anthropoloigst as author*. Stanford, CA: Stanford University.

Giroux, H. (1988a). Postmodernism and the discourse of educational criticism. *Journal of Education*, 170(3), 5–30.

Giroux, H. (1988b). Border pedagogy in the age of postmodernism. *Journal of Education*, 170(3), 162–181.

Giroux, H. (1989). Schooling as a form of cultural politics: Towards a pedagogy of culture, power, and knowledge. *In* H. Giroux and P. McLaren (Eds.), *Critical pedagogy, the state and cultural struggle* (pp. 125–151). Albany, NY: SUNY Press.

Giroux, H. (in press a). Postmodernism as border pedagogy: Redefining the boundaries of race and ethnicity. *In* H. Giroux (Ed.), *Postmodernism, feminism and cultural practice*. Albany, NY: SUNY Press.

Giroux, H. (in press b). Rethinking the boundaries of educational discourse: Modernism, postmodernism, and feminism. *In* H. Giroux (Ed.), *Postmodernism, feminism and cultural practice*. Albany, NY: SUNY Press.

Gitlin, A. (1983). School structure and teachers' work. *In* M. Apple and L. Weis (Eds.). *Ideology and practice in schooling* (pp. 193–212). Philadelphia: Temple University Press.

Gitlin, A., Siegel, M., and Boru, K. (1988). *Purpose and method: Rethinking the use of ethnography by the educational left*. Paper presented at the annual meeting of the American Educational Research Association, New Orleans.

Gouldner, A. (1968). The sociologist as partisan: Sociology and the welfare state. *American Sociologist*, 3(2), 103–116.

Grant, C., and Sleeter, C. (1986). *After the school bell rings*. Barcombe, England: Falmer Press.

Griffen, C. (1985). *Typical girls? Young women from school to the job market*. London: Routledge and Kegan Paul.

Grimes, R. (1982). *Beginnings in ritual studies*. Washington, DC: University Press of America.

Grimshaw, R., Hobson, D., and Willis, P. (1980). Introduction to ethnography at the center. *In* S. Hall, D. Hobson, A. Lowe, and P. Willis (Eds.), *Culture, media, language* (pp. 73–77). Centre for Contemporary Cultural Studies, University of Birmingham. London: Hutchinson.

Guthrie, G. P. (1985). *A school divided: An ethnography of bilingual education in a Chinese community*. Hillsdale, NJ: Lawrence Erlbaum.

Gutierrez, G. (1984). *A theology of liberation: History, politics, and salvation*, Sr. Caridad Inda and J. Eagleson (Trans.). Maryknoll, NY: Orbis Books.

Habermas, J. (1971). *Knowledge and human interests*, J. Shapiro (Trans.). Boston: Beacon Press.

Hall, S., and Jefferson, T. (1976). *Resistance through rituals: Youth subcultures in post-war Britain*. Centre for Contemporary Cultural Studies, University of Birmingham. London: Hutchinson.

Hall, S., Hobson, D., Lowe, A., and Willis, P. (1980). *Culture, media, language*. Centre for Contemporary Cultural Studies, University of Birmingham. London: Hutchinson.

Hammersley, M., and Atkinson, P. (1983). *Ethnography: Principles in practice*. London: Tavistock.

Hammersley, M., and Woods, P. (1976). *The process of schooling*. London: Routledge and Kegan Paul.

Hargreaves, D. (1967). *Social relations in a secondary school*. London: Routledge and Kegan Paul.

Hartsock, N. (1990). Foucault on power: A theory for women? *In* L. Nicholson (Ed.), *Feminism/postmodernism* (pp. 157–175). New York: Routledge.

Hebdige, D. (1976). The meaning of mod. *In* S. Hall and T. Jefferson (Eds.), *Resistance through ritual: Youth subcultures in post-war Britain* (pp. 87–98). London: Hutchinson.

Hebdige, D. (1979). *Subculture: The meaning of style*. London: Methuen.

Held, D. (1980). *Introduction to critical theory: Horkheimer to Habermas*. London: Hutchinson.

Henry, J. (1963). *Culture against man*. New York: Random House.

Hewitt, R. (1986). *White talk black talk: Inter-racial friendship and communication amongst adolescents*. Comparative Ethnic and Race Relations Series. Cambridge: Cambridge University Press.

Hollands, R. G. (1985). *Working for the best ethnography* (Occasional Paper). Birmingham, England: Centre for Contemporary Cultural Studies.

hooks, bell. (1989). *Talking back*. Boston: South End.

Horkheimer, M. (1972). Traditional and critical theory. *In* M. J. O'Connell *et al*. (Eds.), *Critical theory.* (pp. 188–243). New York: Herder & Herder.

Hutcheon, L. (1989). *The politics of postmodernism*. New York: Routledge.

Jackson, P. (1968). *Life in classrooms*. New York: Holt, Rinehart & Winston.

Jordan, J. (1985). *On call: Political essays*. Boston: South End.

Keddie, N. (1971). Classroom knowledge. *In* M. F. D. Young (Ed.), *Knowledge and control: New directions for the sociology of education*. London: Collier–Macmillan.

Keesing, R. (1987). Anthropology as interpretive quest. *Current Anthropology* 28(2), 161–176.

Kipnis, L. (1988). Feminism: The political conscience of postmodernism. *In* A. Ross (Ed.), *Universal abandon? The politics of postmodernism* (pp. 149–166). Minneapolis: University of Minnesota.

Laclau, E., and Mouffe, C. (1985). *Hegemony and socialist strategy: Towards a radical democratic politics*. London: Verso.

Lacy, C. (1970). *Hightown grammar: The school as a social system*. Manchester: Manchester University.

Lankshear, C. (1987). *Literacy, schooling and revolution*. New York: Falmer Press.

Lather, P. (1986). Research as praxis. *Harvard Educational Review*, 56(3), 257–277.

Lugones, M. (1987). Playfulness, 'world'-travelling, and loving perception. *Hypatia*, 2(2), Summer, 3–19.

Lugones, M., and Spelman, E. (1983). Have we got a theory for you! Feminist theory, cultural imperialism and the demand for 'the woman's voice.' *Women's Studies International Forum*, 6(6), 573–381.

Lyotard, J. (1984). The postmodern condition: A report on knowledge. *In* G. Bennington and B. Massumi (Trans.), Theory and history of literature Series (Vol. 10). Minneapolis: University of Minnesota.

MacLeod, J. (1987). *Ain't no makein' it: Leveled aspirations in a low-income neighborhood*. Boulder, CO: Westview Press.

Macpherson, J. (1983). *The feral classroom: High school students' constructions of reality*. Melbourne: Routledge and Kegan Paul.

Marcus, G. (1980). Rhetoric and the ethnographic genre in anthropological research. *Current Anthropology*, 21, 507–510.

Marcus, G. E. (1986). Contemporary problems of ethnography in the modern world system. *In* G. Marcus and M. Fischer (Eds.), *Anthropology as cultural critique* (pp. 165–193). Chicago: University of Chicago.

Marcus, G., and Cushman, D. (1982). Ethnographies as text. *Annual Review of Anthropology*, 11, 25–69.

Marcus, G., and Fischer, M. (Eds.). (1986). *Anthropology as cultural critique*. Chicago: University of Chicago Press.

Marcuse, H. (1968). *Negations: Essays in critical theory*. Boston: Beacon.

Marx, K. (1977). Preface to a critique of political economy. *In* D. McLellan (Ed.), *Karl Marx: Selected writings* (pp. 388–392). Oxford, England: Oxford University.

Marx, K., and Engels, F. (1947). *The German ideology*. New York: International Publications.

Masemann, V. L. (1982). Critical ethnography in the study of comparative education. *Comparative Education Review*, 26(1), 1–15.

McCarthy, C. (1988). Marxist theories of education and the challenge of a cultural politics of non-synchrony. *In* L. Roman and L. Christian-Smith (Eds.), *Becoming feminine: The politics of popular culture* (pp. 185–203). London: Falmer Press.

McDermott, R. (1977). Social relations as contexts for learning in school. *Harvard Educational Review*, 47(2), 198–213.

McDermott, R., and Gospodinoff, K. (1979). Social contexts for ethnic borders and school failure. *In* A. Wolfgang (Ed.), *Nonverbal behavior: Application and cultural implications*. New York: Academic Press.

McLaren, P. (1986). *Schooling as a ritual performance: Towards a political economy of educational symbols and gestures*. London: Routledge and Kegan Paul.

McLaren, P. (1988). Schooling the postmodern body: Critical pedagogy and the politics of enfleshment. *Journal of Education*, 170(3), 53–83.

McLaren, P. (in press). Critical ethnography and field relations: Collaboration in our own ruin. *In* R. Stebbins and W. Shaffir (Eds.), *Experiencing fieldwork*. Beverly Hills, CA: Sage Publications.

McNeil, L. M. (1986). *Contradictions of control: School structure and school knowledge*. New York: Routledge and Kegan Paul.

McRobbie, A. (1978). Working class girls and the culture of femininity. *In* Centre for Contemporary Cultural Studies (Ed.), *Women take issue: Aspects of women's subordination*. Women's Studies Group, University of Birmingham. London: Hutchinson.

Mehan, H. (1974). Accomplishing classroom lessons. *In* A. V. Cicourel, K. H. Jennings, S. H. M. Jennings, K. C. W. Leiter, R. MacKay, H. Mehan, and D. R. Roth, *Language use and school performance*. New York: Academic Press.

Mehan, H. (1978). Structuring school structure. *Harvard Educational Review*, 48, 32–64.

Metz, M. H. (1978). *Classrooms and corridors: The crisis of authority in desegregated secondary schools*. Berkeley: University of California.

Morris, M. (1988). Tooth and claw: Tales of survival and *Crocodile Dundee*. *In* Andrew Ross (Ed.), *Universal abandon? The politics of postmodernism* (pp. 105–127). Minneapolis: University of Minnesota.

Nicholson, L. J. (1990). *Feminism/postmodernism*. New York: Routledge.

Ogbu, J. (1974). *The next generation: An ethnography of education in an urban neighborhood*. New York: Academic Press.

Peshkin, A. (1978). *Growing up American: Schooling and the survival of community*. Chicago: University of Chicago Press.

Peshkin, A. (1986). *God's choice: The total world of a fundamentalist Christian school*. Chicago: University of Chicago Press.

Quantz, R. (1985). The complex visions of female teachers and the failure of unionization in the 1930s: An oral history. *History of Education Quarterly*, Winter, 439–458.

another initial of example

Quantz, R. (1989). *Ethnography in education: A postmodern view*. Paper presented at the American Educational Studies Association, Chicago.

Quantz, R. (in press). Interpretive method in historical research: Ethnohistory reconsidered. *In* R. Altenbaugh (Ed.), *The teacher's voice: A qualitative analysis of teaching in twentieth-century America*. London: Falmer Press.

Quantz, R., and O'Connor, T. (1988). Writing critical ethnography: Dialogue, multivoicedness, and carnival in texts. *Educational Theory*, 38(1), 95–109.

Rist, R. C. (1973). *The urban school: A factory for failure*. Cambridge: MIT Press.

Robins, D., and Cohen, P. (1978). *Knuckle sandwich: Growing up in the working-class city*. Hammondsmith: Penguin Books.

Rock, P. (1979). *The making of symbolic interactionism*. London: Macmillan.

Roman, L. G. (1988). Intimacy, labor, and class: Ideologies of feminine sexuality in the punk slam dance. *In* L. G. Roman and L. K. Christian-Smith (Eds.), *Becoming feminine: The politics of popular culture* (pp. 143–184). London: Falmer Press.

Rosaldo, R. (1980). *Ilongot headhunting, 1883–1974: A study in society and history*. Stanford, CA: Stanford University.

Rosaldo, R. (1989). *Culture and truth: The remaking of social analysis*. Boston: Beacon Press.

Rosenfeld, G. (1971). *Shut those thick lips!: A study of slum school failure*. New York: Holt, Rinehart & Winston.

Said, E. (1978). *Orientalism*. New York: Pantheon.

Sharp, R., and Green, A. (1975). *Education and social control: A study in progressive primary education*. London: Routledge and Kegan Paul.

Simon, R. (1983). But who will let you do it? Counter-hegemonic possibilities for work education. *Journal of Education*, 165(3), 235–256.

Simon, R., and Dippo, D. (1986). On critical ethnographic work. *Anthropology and Education Quarterly*, 17, 195–202.

Sola, M., and Bennett, A. T. (1985). The struggle for voice: Narrative, literacy and consciousness in an East Harlem school. *Journal of Education*, 167(1), 88–110.

Spradley, J. (1970). *You owe yourself a drunk: An ethnography of urban nomads*. Boston: Little, Brown.

Spradley, J., and McCurdy, D. (1972). *The cultural experience: Ethnography in complex society*. Chicago: Scholastic Research Association.

Thomas, J. (1983). Toward a critical ethnography: A reexamination of the Chicago legacy. *Urban Life*, 11, 477–490.

Thompson, E. P. (1966). *The making of the English working class*. New York: Vintage Books.

Valli, L. (1985). Office students and the meaning of work. *Issues in Education*, 3(1), Summer, 31–44.

Valli, L. (1986). *Becoming clerical workers*. Boston: Routledge and Kegan Paul.

Walker, A. (1983). *In search of our mothers' gardens: Womanist prose*. San Diego: Harcourt Brace Jovanovich.

Waller, W. (1965). *The sociology of teaching*. New York: John Wiley. (Originally published in 1932.)

Wax, M., Wax, R., and Dumont, R. (1989). *Formal education in an American Indian community*. Prospect Heights, IL: Waveland Press. (Originally published in 1964.)

Weiler, K. (1988). *Women teaching for change: Gender, class and power*. South Hadley, MA: Bergin & Garvey.

Weis, L. (1985). *Between two worlds: Black students in an urban community college*. Critical Social Thought Series. Boston: Routledge and Kegan Paul.

1977 - initial C/E work? key to Δ in approach

West, C. (1982). *Prophesy deliverance! An Afro-American revolutionary Christianity.* Philadelphia: The Westminster Press.

Willis, P. (1977). *Learning to labour: How working class kids get working class jobs.* Farnborough, England: Saxon House.

Willis, P. (1978). *Profane culture.* London: Routledge and Kegan Paul.

Wolcott, H. (1967). *A Kwakiutl village and school.* New York: Holt, Rinehart & Winston.

Wolcott, H. (1973). *The man in the principal's office.* New York: Holt, Rinehart & Winston.

Woods, P. (1978a). Negotiating the demands of schoolwork. *Journal of Curriculum Studies,* 10(4), 309–327.

Woods, P. (1978b). Relating to schoolwork: Some pupil perceptions. *Educational Review,* 30(2), 167–175.

Woods, P. (1979). *The divided school.* London: Routledge and Kegan Paul.

Woods, P. (1981). Strategies, commitment and identity: Making and breaking the teacher role. *In* L. Barton and S. Walker (Eds.), *Schools, teachers and teaching.* London: Falmer Press.

Woods, P. (1985). Conversations with teachers: Some aspects of life-history method. *British Educational Research Journal,* 11(1), 13–26.

Young, I. M. (1990). The ideal of community and the politics of difference. *In* L. Nicholson (Ed.), *Feminism/postmodernism* (pp. 300–323). New York: Routledge.

Young, M. F. D. (Ed.). (1971). *Knowledge and control.* London: Collier–Macmillan.

Young, T. R. (1980). Introduction. *Urban Life,* 9(2), 133–134.

CHAPTER 11

☐ Critical Qualitative Research: Theory, Methodology, and Practice

Phil Francis Carspecken and
Michael Apple[1]

The Handbook of Qualitative
Research in Education

Introduction

The Orientation of Critical Social Research

In one of his more compelling statements, the French sociologist Pierre Bourdieu states that "Taste classifies and it classifies the classifier" (Bourdieu, 1984:6). That is, to call something "good culture" is not simply a neutral description. It sets up a polarity between the classifier and the classified. It signifies a relation of power. *Someone* thinks this is good, and it can only be good if someone else's culture is bad.

Notice what is being argued here. Rather than seeing cultural phenomena as isolated entities, we must situate them back into the social relations that give them meaning. They are profoundly social constructions. However, it is not just the fact that culture is a social construction that counts, for this is a widely recognized and by now almost trivial point. What Bourdieu adds is the relationship between such social constructions and the ability of some groups to enhance their own authority, to regulate others, and to control the social space for their own benefit. Culture and power, then, are not part of different language games but, rather, form an indissoluble couplet in daily life.

This recognition has provided the starting point for a generation of critically oriented work in education. From the early and somewhat economistic and reductive analyses of the early 1970s (e.g., Bowles and Gintis, 1976) to the more dynamic models that characterize such research today (see Apple, 1985; McCarthy and Apple, 1988), schooling is seen in a particular way. It is intimately connected to the patterns of unequal benefits and losses that organize societies like our own. These patterns are not simply "there," however. They are built into the very warp and woof of our society. As Adam Smith—surely no Marxist for temporal as well as ideological reasons—reminds us, for every one rich person there must be five hundred poor ones. Education is not immune from these patterns of differential benefits.

During the past two decades, we have become increasingly conscious of the way education functions in terms of class, gender, and race. Not only have the outcomes of schooling been closely examined, by tracing out the utterly complex relationship between schools and the reproduction of cultural hierarchies and of the social division of labor, but the internal practices that go on within educational institutions have been rigorously scrutinized as well. Questions concerning the content and form of the curriculum, the pedagogy, and the evaluative mechanisms (plus the social assumptions that lay behind all of this) have become even more powerful. Whose knowledge is considered legitimate? Why is it organized in this way? Why is it taught to this group? In this way? What is the relationship between "cultural capital" and "economic capital" (Bourdieu and Passeron, 1977; Apple, 1990).

These are complicated issues, as you would imagine. They also are among the most important questions one might ask. Education does not stand alone, a neutral instrumentality somehow above the ideological conflicts of the society. Rather, it is deeply implicated in the formation of the unequal cultural, economic, and political relations that dominate our society. Education has been a major arena in which dominance is reproduced *and* contested, in which hegemony is partly formed and partly fractured in the creation of the common sense of a people. Thus, to think seriously about education, like culture in general, is also to think just as seriously about power, about the mechanisms through which certain groups assert their visions, beliefs, and practices. While education is not totally reducible to the political, not to deal with the structural sources of differential power is not to deal with education as a cultural and social process as well.

These points may be clearer if we reflect on the recent efforts in countries such as the United States and Britain to bring education more closely into line with industrial needs. With the disintegration of the postwar social democratic accord, capital, right-wing, and new middle-class groups have been able to shift the terms of the debate over education to the language of efficiency, standards, the "Western tradition," and productivity. The altered discourse of the debate has become part of the cultural production of a new hegemonic accord in which educational policies are rearticulated around rightist principles (Apple, 1988; Shapiro, 1990).

It is difficult to distinguish among educational, cultural, and political processes in this arena. Of course, one of our problems is that we tend to assume that such a distinction is easy to make. That there is a close connection between culture and power in the real world is well argued by Richard Johnson (1983). As he states, there are three reasons for not making a hard and fast separation between the cultural and political:

> The first is that cultural processes are intimately connected with social
> relations, especially with class and class formations, with sexual
> divisions, with the racial structuring of social relations, and with age
> oppressions as a form of dependency. The second is that culture
> involves power and helps to produce asymmetries in the abilities of

individuals and social groups to define and realize their needs. And the third, which follows the other two, is that culture is neither an autonomous nor an externally determined field, but a site of social differences and struggles. (Johnson, 1983, p. 3)

Those approaching education from this perspective have a different task. They need to see schols as existing in a social context that sets limits on what education can and cannot accomplish. These limits are structured around the class, gender, and race dynamics and conflicts that organize society. In the process, critical investigators will interpret schools as *institutions* that are under considerable pressure to perform vital "functions" for the larger political economy.

Yet this is but one part of the task. Such an approach does see educational institutions as related to a larger structuring of institutions and understands what education does from the outside. However, people are not simply the carriers of external sets of determinations. They have agency. Schools can be and are arenas in which alternative and oppositional cultural practices evolve. We already intuit this in our everyday language. Think of the word "subject." People can be both the subjects of a ruler (they can be led, legislated, and controlled) *and* they can be the subjects of history. That is, they are not simply objects at the mercy of structural determinations, but also agents of change, of social forces they continually create beyond themselves (Therborn, 1980; P. Anderson, 1980; Giddens, 1979). It is this dual recognition— what is often called the issue of structure and agency—that is so important to critical work.

Agency does not exist "in general," however. It too occurs in patterned ways, because people are not abstractions. They are embodied as classed, raced, and gendered subjects themselves, acting within differential relations of power. Therefore, an understanding of the meanings they construct in the institutions in which they live—like schools—also requires a recognition of these embodiments and these relations.

It is important to stress here that these prior understandings about the nature of power serve as an orienting framework. They are *not* preordained and unquestionable; rather, they provide a conceptual and normative orientation that organizes the *questions* critical researchers ask. Questions are asked about the role of schools in the context of an unequal society; however, this does not mean that the answers are known beforehand. It is those questions and the vision of society that stands behind them, not only the method, that sets critical work apart from other ethnographic research.

The best ethnographies within this tradition ask a series of questions about both the *experience* of and the *outcomes* of cultural forms in schools. What is the meaning of particular relations? For whom? Do these forms tend to reproduce or contest existing forms of subordination or oppression? Do they permit a questioning of existing relations by pointing to alternative social arrangements? Often some contradictory combination of all these issues exists in people's daily lives (Johnson, 1983:48).

What Distinguishes the Critical Approach from Other Qualitative Approaches?

Here, we stress the idea of orienting *questions* because of a number of issues that have been raised about critical ethnography. Issues of "ideological bias" and "theory drivenness" have surfaced in discussions of critical analysis (G. Anderson, 1989). Our own position on this is clear. All social research is informed from its very beginnings as a set of concerns or questions in the mind of the researcher by a particular orientation that implicitly or explicitly bears a theoretical view. The "orienting theory" (Whyte, 1984)[2] of the critical researcher has just been described as consisting of concerns about inequality and the relationship of human activity, culture, and social and political structures. It is this orienting theory that initially motivates the critical researcher to conduct research and makes it possible for questions to be formulated and field sites chosen for study.

Orienting theory, however, does not provide the answers that the critical ethnographer seeks, nor does it make critical inquiry subject to bias any more than orienting theory may bias any piece of research. Critical qualitative research begins the process of inquiry in much the same way as does other qualitative research—with the collection of data and with attention to the same criteria for "trustworthiness" (Lincoln and Guba, 1985) as other approaches. As shown in this chapter, it is possible to divide the actual research process followed during a critical field study into five stages, and it is only the stages in which various forms of analysis are worked on data collected in fieldwork that the distinctive features of the critical approach emerge. Moreover, at all stages of a critical field study, key features of the orienting theory of this approach are subject to refinements and alterations. A critical field study is aimed not only at making an empirical–descriptive contribution but also a theoretical contribution—deepening our understanding of core social–theoretical concepts such as "action," "structure," "culture," and "power."

Thus, to summarize, the critical approach to field research is distinguished first of all in terms of the motivation of the researcher and the questions that are posed. Critical researchers are usually politically minded people who wish, through their research, to aid struggles against inequality and domination. The orienting framework of the critical investigator is itself placed in dialogue with the research process, and this means that a literal dialogue between researcher and the researched is actually created. It is an effort to build up our most fundamental concepts of the social world through interacting with it or, as Roman and Apple (1990) argue, by acting on the world with others in democratic ways so that this world may be changed. Secondly, specific theoretical models that demarcate this particular approach from others are employed in critical social research. These models are used to investigate the location of the social routines and cultural forms reconstructed in the first stages of inquiry within broad patterns of social inequality and relations of domination.

We will focus here largely on the potential of critical research to enhance our understanding and explanation of social phenomena, not on its important place in social transformation, because this has been argued for in greater detail in a previous treatment of the political role of qualitative research (Roman and Apple, 1990). We also will not engage in a thorough literature review. Recent reviews of critical research can be found elsewhere (G. Anderson, 1989). Rather, we will outline the general theoretical features through which critical ethnographies are conducted. We want to do this as clearly as possible, because critical research has too often limited its primary audience to those neo-Marxists and others already committed to its principles and we believe that the methods of inference employed in good critical ethnography would be useful in all qualitative studies of social life.

The Five Stages of Critical Qualitative Research

It is useful to divide a typical critical field sudy into five stages. Roughly, the first three stages of a typical study begin with the collection of observation data, construction of a preliminary analysis on this data, and generation of another set of data based on interactions with the subjects of study. The last two stages perform additional analyses on the information generated in stages one through three. In stage four, relationships between the routines and cultural forms exhibited by one group of people on a single social site are compared to routines and cultural forms exhibited in other social sites to reveal "system relationships," a term defined and exemplified later in this chapter. In stage five, reasons for these system relationships are sought by building the findings "outward" toward a general model of society. Once stages one through three have been followed sequentially, the investigator may reemploy them—that is, conduct further observations and further interviews between periods of analysis. Therefore, the five stages are not meant to be strictly sequential, although we recommend *beginning* with a temporal sequence of stages one through three for reasons explained later on.

Note that only two of these five stages concern the actual collection of data and compilation of field notes: stages one and three. The first of these emphasizes observation techniques and the second interactive methods of producing data. The real distinguishing feature of these two stages, however, does not consist of the *methods* employed but, rather, the epistemological status of the data produced. To emphasize this point, the first stage may be called "monological data collection" and the third stage "dialogical data generation."

The first stage may be called monological because it emphasizes the passive observer role. It produces a set of data taken from a third-person perspective. The observer produces an account monologically[3]—without entering into a dialogue with the people being studied. In principle, certain types of interviewing is also monological in this sense. Interviews that seek only to acquire demographic information or reports provided by the subjects of study about their life routines, without any real interaction between the ideas of the researcher and those of the subjects of study are monological.

In stage three, by contrast, the researcher generates new data *with* the subjects of study through both one-on-one and group discussions. Stage one consists of an effort to observe a naturalistic setting with minimum interference on the part of the researcher, but stage three deliberately becomes a nonnaturalistic affair in which subjects of study are asked to reflect on their lives in ways that may be new to them and to share in the production of a theory relevant to their lives. It is important to conduct the monological, naturalistic stage before conducting the dialogical stage because the routines and forms of life in question may well be altered through the methods we recommend in stage three. The five stages, then, are as follows:

1. Monological data collection
2. Preliminary reconstructive analysis
3. Dialogical data generation
4. Describing system relationships
5. Explaining system relationships

To be conducted, each stage requires the grasp of a number of core concepts on the part of the researcher. Each stage also corresponds to diverse field techniques and methods of inference. We are now ready to examine each stage in-depth to carefully explain the methods and concepts pertaining to them. A segment of field notes produced during a recent critical study conducted by one of us (P.F.C.) will be used to illustrate many of the points we will make below. At times, the work of other critical researchers will be referred to to exemplify certain concepts and procedures.

We will first introduce five individuals who were the subjects of this recent study and present a segment of field notes. Then we will discuss the various stages of a critical study by reference to these notes. As we advance through the stages, we will slowly lengthen the field note segment and unfold a sort of real life "story" in this way.

Project TRUST

These field notes were taken during the spring of 1990 as part of a study of an education program we will call Project TRUST. Project TRUST was designed to enhance the self-esteem and social skills of especially disruptive pupils attending an inner-city elementary school. The rationale of the project was both to remove such students from normal classrooms, because teachers found it difficult to conduct lessons with them present, and to alter their behavior patterns so that they could be returned later as less-disruptive pupils. Only four pupils were in the TRUST classroom at a time. The names of the participants, as well as of the project, have been changed. It will be important to know something of the cast of characters:

Alfred: A young white male teacher hired especially to run Project TRUST.

Mary: A 9-year-old Afro-American female, referred to
TRUST for consistently getting into fights with other pupils.
Jorge: An 8-year-old Hispanic male, referred to TRUST for
not obeying teachers and talking loudly in class at
inappropriate times.
Simione: A 9-year-old Afro-American male, referred to
TRUST for frequently defying teachers, refusing to work,
and picking fights with other pupils.
Jason: An 8-year-old Afro-American male, referred to
TRUST for fighting with other students and defying
teachers. Jason comes into latter sequences of field notes
and is not present in the notes first displayed and analyzed
below.

Like most children in this school, Mary, Jorge, and Simione all come
from low-socioeconomic, single-parent homes. Jason comes from a
dual-parent home, which is also of low socioeconomic status.

These field notes were taken by two observers writing in notebooks and a tape-recorder capturing all speech acts. The observers
used a method in which each took a different person in the room for
concentrated attention. This person was called the "focal person." As a
first priority, everything this person did and said was written down. As
a second priority, the actions and speech acts of others affecting this
person were written down. Everything else going on in the room was
written down as a third priority. Thus, although various events were
unavoidably missed when jotting down the observation notes, the
observers controlled the missed events through this system of prioritizing. Approximately every 5 minutes, each observer changed to a
new focal person. The actual notes presented below, then, were reconstructed from the notebooks of the two observers and by listening to
the tape, which made it possible to capture much of the detail.

Alfred has just called all the students from their study carrels to a
table near a blackboard. Mary and Jorge come immediately but Simione delays. Alfred begins the lesson anyway, handing out "feeling
thermometers," which they are already familiar with. These paper
devices allow the pupils to move a red indicator from "cool" through
various feeling degrees like "upset" to "hot" and "blow your top!".

Alfred: Mary, how do you feel when someone keeps on bugging
you and keeps on and keeps on? Show me how that makes
you feel on the feeling thermometer. [Alfred standing by

blackboard, which is very near the table. He is busy with something else as he speaks, a sheet of orange construction paper on which he writes by leaning over one part of the table. He asks Mary the question in between writing on the paper, looking up from the paper at Mary, then back to writing as he waits for an answer.]

Jorge: Wow man! She blows her top! [Jorge is leaning over Mary's desk looking at her thermometer. Mary doesn't look at him. She looks at Alfred but doesn't say anything.]

[Simione joins the group. He comes from his study carrel later than the other two. Alfred makes no acknowledgment.]

Alfred: [Looking up again, moving eyes from Mary to Jorge and back to Mary.] It makes her blow her top. Can any of you think of something people do that make you upset? Not blow your top but just be upset? [Returns to writing on the orange paper.]

Jorge: Nothing. [Shifting about in chair a good deal, twisting his body right and left, elbow on table with hand in chin.]

Mary: Anything. [Looking in direction of Alfred. Body is rigid-looking with no movement, hands clasped in lap, no eye movements toward other pupils.]

Alfred: Anything? Let's be specific. Tell me one thing that makes you upset. [Looking at Mary, ignoring Jorge, has stopped writing on orange paper, and is standing fully up.]

Mary: Getting called a name.

Simione: Getting called a name makes *me* almost upset!

Jorge: If someone calls me a name I feel happy.

Simione: Happy? You feel *happy* when someone calls you a name?

Jorge: Yup.

Alfred: [Looking first at Simione and then at Jorge.] OK, it makes him happy [bland voice].

Jorge: [Quick, immediate response to Alfred.] No, *upset*. [Smiling at Alfred.]

Stage One: Monological Data Collection

Primary Data

The preceding field notes represent what we can call the "primary record," or the "primary data" of the qualitative study. The critical social researcher constructs a primary record in much the same way as any qualitative researcher does; therefore, we will keep our comments about stage one brief. The principle point we wish to emphasize about primary data is the ontological category to which it belongs. Primary data is "objective." Its objectivity pertains to two important characteristics: It is accessed through the senses, and it entails validity claims concerning "what is" and "what took place." Thus, primary data is totally open to multiple recording devices (e.g., two observers and a tape-recorder as used here—a video tape could also have been used). And when the researcher constructs this record, he or she does so with the claim that other people would agree with it, as it is written, if they were present at the time. This claim will be strengthened if more than one observer takes notes, if a low-inference vocabulary is used in compiling the notes, and if an audio and/or video record is made on tape. Member checks, in which the participants themselves are asked to read field notes and comment on them, will also strengthen this particular claim.[4]

Stage Two: Preliminary Analysis of the Data

The primary record will be constructed over a period of time, during which many observations will be conducted with the same group of people and/or on the same social site. As the record is built, the researcher will usually also begin to make a preliminary analysis of it. Stage two is concerned with this preliminary analysis and involves a number of new concepts and procedures.

Below we have reproduced portions of the same field notes presented above but have added two distinctive types of comments to them. We have made provisional "counts" of certain patterns of behavior illustrated in these notes that occur repeatedly throughout the entire set of field data compiled in this study. This form of analysis remains close to the objective realm, although some additional interpretation may often be involved. We have also interpreted the interactions described in these notes for their possible meanings. As the discussion following the field notes below will explain, inferring meaning from field notes requires familiarity with two other ontological categories: the subjective realm and the intersubjective, normative realm.[5] We have italicized the comments to distinguish them from the actual field notes, and we have placed a "1" just before comments that remain close to the objective realm, a "2" just before comments that concern the other two realms.

Alfred: [While working on his construction paper.] Mary, how do you feel when someone keeps on bugging you and keeps on and keeps on? Show me how that makes you feel on the feeling thermometer. *[(1) Alfred often "keeps busy" with something while talking to the students.] [(2) Comment: "Keeping busy" seems to dilute the attention Alfred is extending to pupils, here to Mary. It seems to increase the distance between teacher and pupil—like "I'm very busy with this important work, which is at least as important as talking to you. It is work I've told you nothing about because its importance concerns only me." Because this activity comes up frequently, this could be the pupil's interpretation of it.]*

Jorge: Wow man! She blows her top! *[(1) Jorge often uses terms like "man," "guy," "wow," "awesome," "radical," typical of pupil, out-of-school discourse rather than "in-school" discourse between pupil and teacher.] [(2) Comment: Jorge's use of such discourse might slightly challenge the norms advocated by Alfred and increase Jorge's autonomy from the teacher.]*

[. . .]

Jorge: Nothing. *[(2) Comment: Jorge many times replies to Alfred in a way that Alfred seems not to wish for—as if, in this case, he thinks Alfred is fishing for an affirmative reply plus some examples to further illustrate his point and Jorge answers in the negative to block what he takes to be Alfred's project—this needs exploration.]*

Mary: Anything. *[(1) Mary often contradicts Jorge and / or Simione—takes a position opposite to theirs.] [(2) Comment: Mary often takes an extreme position affirmative of Alfred's point, as if she anticipates what he wishes pupils to say and provides an exaggerated response.]*

[. . .]

Alfred: OK, it makes him happy [bland voice]. *[(2) Comment: As* *if he is saying, "right, some people might feel happy when called a name and that's OK."]*

Jorge: No, *upset. [(1) Jorge often will offer a certain response to Alfred and then, when Alfred accepts it as a valid response, will change it.] [(2) Comment: It seems that Jorge offers a challenge in this way but gets a response he did not wish for, plus a switch in attention away from him. So he changes the response to make a new "offer." Alfred does not accept the new offer—a sort of covert "punishment"—explore further.]*

Inferring Meaning: The Subjective and Normative Realms

The actual analysis of meaning involves three principle steps. First, that of noting possible meanings, as we have already done, and writing them within the field notes in which they occur. Writing such comments in a speculative form and embedding them within the actual field notes makes it relatively easy to revise one's interpretations later on. It also facilitates thorough member checks, where the subjects of study are invited to read the investigator's interpretations and comment on them.

Second, after a number of such comments have been written alongside the field notes, the researcher can conduct another level of analysis on them to reconstruct *normative* factors, which make these meanings possible. Social acts carry meaning only because they reference unstated, background sets of rules [in Giddens' sense of the term (Giddens, 1979:65–68)] and assumptions. These implicitly referenced rules and assumptions make it possible for the actor, the people acted toward, and all people observing the interaction to interpret or "read" various meanings from the act. Understanding meaning, then, involves taking first-, second-, and third-person positions with respect to an act, and this can be done only with reference to certain norms assumed to be in play.

In our preceding comments, for example, we speculate that Jorge's act of saying "nothing" to Alfred could be read as a type of challenge to Alfred. We also speculate that Mary's act of saying "everything" could be read as a statement of support for Alfred and a counterchallenge to Jorge. To make such speculations, we must refer to a normative rule that states that students should anticipate the projects of their teachers and cooperate to help bring these projects off. This normative rule may be reconstructed, or discursively articulated, by us. It is a normative rule, moreover, which itself implies further, more general rules: rules of action concerned with cultural statuses, roles, and identities ("teacher," "student," "male," "female"), with culturally constructed authority relations ("teacher–student," "adult–child"), and with modes of conveying politeness, rudeness, and so on. The senses of "challenge" and "support," which can be read from Jorge and Mary's remarks, depend on this implicit reference to a set of social norms. In a following section, we will return to this idea of a normative "set" and discuss ways in which such sets possess *structure*.

Third, the researcher can conduct yet another analysis in which speculations about the *subjective states* of the individuals under study are reconstructed. Thus, to continue with the example just presented, we are not only interested in implicit sets of social norms referenced by Jorge's assertion that nothing will make him upset and Mary's claim that "everything" will make her upset, we are also interested in whether or not Jorge consciously *intends* to challenge Alfred and in whether or not Mary consciously intends to counter this challenge to align herself on Alfred's side. We are interested as well in how Alfred actually interprets these acts. This is quite a separate issue and refers to a distinctively different ontological realm—the subjective, as opposed to the normative, realm. Mary might, for example, be aware of the norm that students should cooperate with teachers and construct her act of saying "everything" in light of this norm, but she may actually *sympathize* with Jorge, only taking a position contrary to his in order to stay in good with Alfred, who has the power of keeping her in this classroom or allowing her to return to her normal classrooms. She may wish to keep her real sympathies "hidden" within her subjectivity. Thus, normative reconstruction makes it possible to investigate *potential* meanings carried by social acts and as such yields a *meaning field* within which the action takes place. But a further analysis of subjective states is necessary to approach the actual interpretations made by the actors of this meaning field.

Normative Reconstructions

Let us now return to our field notes and note further normative and subjective interpretations, which could be worked upon some portions of them. First, we will consider normative interpretations and then elaborate our discussion of the normative realm. In the next section, we will consider subjective reconstructions.

- "Being busy" on the part of Alfred while talking to students conveys a *potential meaning* that Alfred has only partially invested himself or risked himself in the interaction. The *norms* involved refer to modes of displaying attention, intimacy, and respect. It can be interpreted to be a *legitimate* activity because he, as teacher, has the authority to convey this meaning without it being taken as "rude" behavior. It is, thus, referenced to an assumed *authority relation* between Alfred and pupil, distances their relationship accordingly, and is implicitly claimed to have more implications with respect to Mary's *identity* than Alfred's (Mary is "worthy" of only so much attention).

- Jorge's use of terms like "wow," "man," and so on convey a meaning referenced to a distinction and even an opposition between a school *setting* and a street *setting*[6]—a realm of maximized **teacher** autonomy and power and a realm of maximized **pupil** autonomy and power. Its legitimacy is understood to be contentious by Jorge, who probably assumes that Alfred also considers it contentious. Thus, Jorge claims the legitimacy of the opposition and takes a side with respect to it. Alfred does not respond at all to this language and, thereby, does not acknowledge the legitimacy of the claim or the opposition it rests upon.

We have set in italics terms that refer to "objects" or "elements" in the normative realm where they first appear, carefully avoiding terms that reference subjective realms. A fuller list of such elements would include concepts developed within symbolic interactionism. Roles, role sets, statuses, and "projects" are all examples of such terms. Qualitative researchers are always free to coin new terms of their own to represent normative objects. "Identity" has a special meaning as a normative element and is discussed in contrast to subjectivity in sections that follow.

The validity of a reconstruction depends once again on consensus requirements. Usually member checks and multiple observers or peer debriefers can build a sufficient case for the validity of a reconstruction. "Strip analysis", as explained by Agar (1986), is another way to strengthen the claim that a particular reconstruction is valid. If sequences of primary data ("strips") can be predicted and explained consistently with a given normative reconstruction, the reconstruction is all the more likely to be a coherent one. Dialogical data generated in stage three by asking participants to articulate the normative structures they think they made use of in an interaction is an excellent way to perform further reconstructive analysis and validate the findings. More is said about this later.

Subjective Objects of Study

As already mentioned, the process of inferring meaning automatically leads to a series of assumptions about the *subjective* states of actors as well as about intersubjective, normative references. Let us go back to Alfred, Simione, Mary, and Jorge and list some of the subjective states we might infer from their interactions. Recall the sequence in which Jorge says "nothing" when Alfred asks which situations in life can make him feel "upset." The norm we think might be referenced by this statement is one stating that pupils will anticipate the projects of teachers and should cooperate in bringing the projects off. Jorge acts in opposition to this norm. The possible subjective states implied are:

- Jorge violates the rule in a *deliberate* manner. On some level of awareness he is *conscious* of violating it and he *assumes* that Alfred assumes he is aware of the rule and, thus, that he is deliberately violating it.
- Alfred is aware of Jorge's *intention* to violate the rule but *deliberately* redefines what constitutes a violation of the rule by introducing a new norm: Student's statements about their subjective states are to be accepted no matter what form they take.
- Mary is *aware* of the rule and of Jorge's violation of it and *wishes* to show Alfred and Jorge that she will not violate it. Her remark of "anything" after Jorge says "nothing" is intended to show support for Alfred's definition of the situation and his authority as teacher and to show her refusal to join Jorge in offering challenge.
- Jorge is in some way *disappointed* in the response of Alfred to his challenge and accordingly offers a new response.

Subjective objects of study include terms like those italicized: intentions, deliberations, wishes, feelings, and states of awareness are all examples. The normative and subjective worlds of reference are, thus, closely linked but distinct. Participants use intersubjective normative rules to give other participants impressions of their own subjective states and to make inferences about the subjective states of others. People can, and often do, use intersubjective rules to deceive others about their subjective states.

Qualitative researchers may only be interested in the normative worlds of their subjects of study, but they usually wish to gain some understanding of the subjective worlds as well. Most ethnographers of education will want to know, for example, not only what intersubjective rules are at play within a classroom but also whether or not students like their teachers, are bored with lessons, actually intend to disrupt classes, feel embarrassed when called to the board, and so on. It is also frequently important to try to discover whether or not participants are *aware* of the normative rules that others think they are aware of.

Normative and subjective objects of study differ in important ways and must be approached with different techniques. Speculations about subjective states will be made when making preliminary interpretations of monological data, but a case for the validity of these speculations must be made through the use of dialogical techniques (stage three). Unlike normative objects of study, subjective states are not constructed by taking a first-, second-, and third-person perspective; rather, they prioritize the first-person perspective. To be sure, *representations* of subjectivity must make use of intersubjective material, even when a person tries to formulate a feeling or thought to him- or herself alone. But in all such activities, the distinction between the normative and subjective is ontologically drawn. We can be mistaken about representations of our own states and about our interpretations of others' states. The ethnographer must therefore dialogically facilitate self-exploration and self-representation with an individual to gain some understanding of subjectivity (stage three).

Identity versus Subjective Objects of Study

Under the influence of Foucault, Derrida, and their various disciples, much has recently been written about subjectivity and its social construction (see e.g., Derrida, 1979; Foucault, 1979; Dreyfus and Rabinow, 1983). However, what is usually meant by subjectivity in these works is what we would call features of intersubjectivity—the normative realm. As already mentioned, structures of the normative realm are used by participants in any interaction to represent the self publicly, to make inferences about the selves and subjective states of others, and to make inferences about how others perceive one's own self. Different cultural groups provide diverse structures through which to claim and maintain an identity—different ways of being a male, a teacher, a pupil, a parent, and so on. These are normative structures—identities are just one more category of elements within the normative realm that can be reconstructed in ethnography and should not be confused with subjectivity.

Returning briefly to our sample field notes, we can surmise that the full meaning of the interactions recorded there can only be understood if the claims to identity made by each participant are understood. When Jorge consistently uses terms like "man," "wow," and so on and when he consistently challenges Alfred's efforts to win his cooperation in the construction of lessons, he is presenting an identity to the rest of the group that he wishes to claim as valid and wishes to maintain throughout series of interactions. Of course Jorge, like everyone else, has a personal repertoire of identities, and he will change his identity claims even among the same group of people, depending on various conditions. But his personal repertoire is constructed from a larger, normative set of possible identities from which he selectively draws. Identity is a feature of the normative world and not the subjective world *per se*, although one will use intersubjective forms to interpret one's own subjectivity so that these two realms interpenetrate each other.

Let us extend the field note sequence a bit to look more closely at the identities being claimed and constructed in the interactions. We have left it with Jorge stating that he would actually feel upset if someone called him a name rather than happy as he had first claimed. Alfred next began asking Simione how he would deal with a situation if he were mad:

Simione: [Sitting slumped in chair, chin in hand, looking only at Alfred.] If I *were* mad? I'm not *were*, I *am* mad.

Alfred: Why?

Simione: He's [Jorge] sticking his tongue out at me. [Continues to look only at Alfred, as if ignoring Jorge.]

Alfred: Umm, Mary, if you saw someone sticking their tongue out . . .

Jorge: [interrupting] If that happened to *me* I would want to beat them up—kill them. [Moving about in his chair, speaking rapidly and with volume, looks towards Simione as he says "kill them."]

Alfred: Umm, would you really Jorge? Can you tell us about a time in the past when you acted that way?

Jorge: [excitedly] Yeah, there was someone kicking me and calling me names. I got mad. I hit him in the face and he fell on the ground. [Gives dramatization of it by standing up and giving mock kicks and punches to the air.]

[Simione has head on table and not very responsive; not making eye contact with anyone.]

Jorge: [starts taunting Simione] I bet *you* couldn't fight like that.

Jorge is clearly asserting a particular identity in this sequence, which involves bravado and prowess. He makes use of a number of intersubjective norms to once again assert a challenge to Alfred by affirming a street norm (fighting when angry) against Alfred's view that anger should be handled without violence, a view Alfred has presented in various ways during previous classes and was once again approaching in his questioning of Simione. Jorge is challenging Simione even more than Alfred by first provoking him with a protruded tongue and then claiming that he would beat up anyone who dared do the same thing to him. The meaning of his utterance rests on several normative elements:

- A street norm that one ought to fight when angered by someone else and that failure to do so is (probably) unmanly.
- An *identity claim* that he is capable of acting on that norm.
- A challenge to Simione's *identity* through the suggestion that Simione is not capable of acting on this norm because he has not followed or even attempted to negotiate the norm in this present situation.

We might suspect that Jorge's identity claim is bound to certain conceptions of masculinity claimed valid by Jorge although we cannot be sure of the gender attributes of his self-presentation from the preceding short passage. We do have more evidence from the notes that this particular claim for selfhood is based on an opposition to school norms, as it is embedded within a sequence of activities performed by Jorge in which Alfred's claims for valid norms are consistently challenged. We note that Alfred's strategy was once again to try to outmaneuver Jorge by interpreting his statements to be reports on feelings and responses worthy of an objective analysis rather than as challenges. He tries to draw Mary into the discussion in order to disassociate Jorge's statement from what could be construed as a "challenge" and an assertion of identity. But this time, Jorge persists with his challenge, getting out of his seat and openly taunting Simione.

Identities are constantly claimed, alongside norms and values, in human interactions. In fact, they are internally bound to them. Participants use norms and values to claim identities. Claims that certain norms or values are valid are often simultaneous claims to be a certain kind of person. One's own interpretation of self, one's self concept, is in fact a normative interpretation based on interactions with others. One's self-interpretation is built through interactions and is dependent on the responses one receives.

Hence, identities are intersubjective and ontologically distinct from subjective states. Because of this distinction, human actors must constantly reassess their suppositions about the inner states of another throughout an interaction. It is because one's own identity is not the same as one's subjective states that one must constantly claim to be a certain kind of person in social interactions and look toward the reactions of others to gain a degree of certainty about it. It is this distinction between subjectivity and identity that makes the latter a product in need of continuous maintenance through public performances—dramaturgical acts.

Cultural Power

By noting the distinction between subjective states and cultural identity structures, one is in a position to theorize about power relations shaping interactions. For example, we may speculate about power relations between Jorge and Simione in the preceding interactions. Although dialogical data generation would be necessary to really explore Simione's subjective state when challenged by Jorge, the reader will notice, when the interaction sequence is continued below, that Simione becomes much more talkative and exhibits more of his physical presence when Jorge leaves the table to go back to his carrel. Jorge has rather forcibly suggested that Simione can have a valid identity, at the moment of Jorge's challenge, only if he responds aggressively. Jorge claims a limited repertoire of acceptable identities for Simione, which Simione fails to contest. Simione does not attempt to claim alternative ways of being a valid male student but, rather, withdraws. The power in this particular situation falls on Jorge's side, and it consists of the power to define valid identities and modes of self-expression *for others*. Simione may be experiencing a mismatch of his subjective side and the identity structures of the normative realm constructed by Jorge. Subjectively, he may believe or hope that he is in fact a valid human being worthy of a sense of dignity. But publicly, at this particular moment, he cannot claim the necessary norms with which he could make an alternative identity claim. Jorge appears to have control over the norms governing the definitions of valid identity claims. In all such situations, people are oppressed. This is one form of cultural power, and it is based on the subjective–intersubjective distinction.

Cultural power is of major interest to critical researchers and its exploration is one of the distinctive features of our approach. However, critical ethnographers will want to discover, through their ethnographies, the ways in which entire classes of people experience a mismatch between subjective and intersubjective realms. The particular interaction between Jorge and Simione in our example may not directly indicate a wider pattern. Although inferences from particular instances of cultural power to societal-wide patterns of power relations mediated by culture involve theoretical concepts not yet introduced in this chapter, we will extend the field notes a bit here to show where a specific instance of cultural power may well indicate a broader pattern.

The reader will recall that we left the scene with Jorge standing up (in violation of a formal class rule) and openly taunting Simione. Simione has his head on the table and is not making eye contact with anyone.

Alfred: [Hasn't looked at Jorge at all during his performance— looks at Simione now.] Simione, how do you feel now?

[Simione shrugs.]

Alfred: Do you want to show me on your thermometer?

[Simione shakes his head no.]

[Jorge sits down.]

Alfred: OK. I'll show you how I feel. Uhh, Jorge, can I borrow your thermometer?

Jorge: NO! [Head is low on hand and turned to side; no eye contact with anyone.]

Alfred: [Standing through all this.] No? OK. Mary can I borrow yours?

[Mary starts to push her thermometer across the table toward Alfred.]

Jorge: [Quickly sitting straight and looking at Alfred—voice at normal volume.] NO, I'll let you borrow mine.

Alfred: No, you said you didn't want to, that's OK., maybe later. [He takes Mary's thermometer.] Thank you Mary!

[Jorge crumples up his thermometer, casts it to the floor, and stamps on it. Jorge leaves his chair, kicking it toward the wall to make a great deal of noise, and goes to his carrel. He sings a song in Spanish, something about Mexico, loudly as he goes.]

Simione: How do *you* feel right now Mr. Taylor? [Simione is now sitting up straight and moving his arms as he talks.]
[(2) Comment: use of teacher-initiated normative frame, effort to reduce teacher–pupil distance.]

Alfred: Calm. [Moves the thermometer to "calm" and shows Simione and Mary.]

[Mary and Simione have heads down on table.]

[Jorge tears up papers at his carrel very loudly; starts a new song in Spanish.]

Alfred: [Moving eyes between Mary and Simione.] I'd like to talk to you about the incident yesterday between you two [an incident in which Simione and Mary had nearly come to physical blows].

[Jorge keeps making loud noises at desk—rumples papers.
Alfred shows no sign of hearing Jorge nor do Mary or Simione.]
[(2) Comment: performance team, tacit agreement to ignore Jorge.]

On one level, we can approach the power implications of these interactions by trying to determine what concerns Jorge has with the *subjectivities* of the other people he is interacting with. In particular, we wish to know which people Jorge is primarily performing for, and what impressions he wishes to make on them. Or, to say it differently, *whose regard* does Jorge seek and what sort of regard does he wish. "Regard" or "recognition" is a subjective phenomena, so no matter how others respond to Jorge, Jorge will have to "guess" what their real views of him are. Jorge's actions carry identity claims that would require a subjective affirmation from specifically targeted others to be validated. This validation is always elusive, but only certain responses from others could make Jorge feel a degree of certainty about their perceptions of him.

When Jorge first denied Alfred's request and then tried to reverse his position with respect to the request, it seems quite clear that Alfred's subjectivity was a primary concern of his. Alfred's refusal to accept his change of mind sparked Jorge into another series of defiant actions, which Alfred chose not to respond to. It is not clear what impression Jorge wished to make or what perception he wished Alfred to have of him, but it is clear that Alfred's subjectivity was in some way an important reference for Jorge. This accorded Alfred the power of granting or withholding some form of recognition to Jorge. Further observations and interviews could help to clarify what form of recognition Jorge sought, but we can hypothesize that it has something to do with Jorge's own power—his autonomy from the rules of Alfred tries to maintain *and* Alfred's recognition of this autonomy. The pattern Jorge displays is that of (1) rejecting the terms through which Alfred offers to affirm Jorge's identity (i.e., rejecting the identity Alfred offers for Jorge) and (2) then changing his response (and identity claim) when Alfred disappoints his anticipations. This clearly shows that Alfred is important to Jorge's efforts to construct a valid identity—that Alfred is not just an authority figure to be fully resisted but a significant other whose recognition is desired by Jorge.

We have used the terms recognition and regard in the preceding analysis. Identity claims are basically claims for recognition—the recognition an other can give to one's subjectivity, one's autonomy, worth, potential capabilities. People desire affirmation, self-certainty, dignity, and respect. These desires are fundamental and tied to what Anthony Giddens (1979) calls "ontological needs"—needs to *be* that require having an identity. People can only *exist* by constructing themselves through social interactions in which identities are continuously claimed and these claims responded to. This implies a motivation for self-affirmation or recognition, a set of "social–psychological needs." Because there is no direct access to subjectivity (even to one's own subjectivity), recognition needs are a continuous affair and take specific forms mediated by intersubjective, normative orders.

On another level, critical theorists claim that entire populations of people are systematically misrecognized through lack of control over the normative contexts in which identity repertoires constructed. *Misrecognition* refers to systematic mismatches between subjective states and intersubjective identity structures. One can exist as a self in a truncated, impoverished manner when one is forced to use limited normative realms for identity claims. Subordinate populations in crucial social settings like schools are forced to use identity repertoires dominated by others to win recognition. Alternative identity claims may not be conceivable within such sites or, if conceivable to the actors, are not possible to use because they are not seen, or heard, by the powerful others in the setting.

Again, we have not yet developed the concepts and methods necessary to move from a single ethnography to claims about entire groups of people throughout society, but we will soon do so. Let us now consider those features of the interactions between Alfred and his pupils, which would seem to indicate group relations expressed in a single interaction.

Obviously it is the use of Spanish and of a song about Mexico by Jorge as he moves to his carrel that would cause the ethnographer to wonder about broader relations of cultural power than those immediately before her or his eyes. Jorge sings in Spanish as an act of defiance. Because the use of Spanish and other symbols of ethnic identity on the part of Jorge comes up frequently in the entire study, it clearly is an important way for Jorge to assert a subjective state of independence and power through the affirmation of an ethnic identity. The claim made rests once again on a contrast of two settings: a non-Hispanic classroom setting and an Hispanic neighborhood and home setting. Jorge's self-assertion works in such a way as to place these two settings in opposition to each other. Jorge's singing is probably a way for him to assert an identity *for* those present, which has the strength of a claimed distant group of supporters. Jorge's behavior is like saying "I'm Hispanic, there are lots of Hispanics who know who I am, and I (we) think your class is crap." *Possibly* Jorge finds more opportunities within his neighborhood and home cultures for successfully claiming valid identities that fit his subjective states than he does in Alfred's classroom; however, more research would be necessary to find this out. Meanwhile, it remains significant that Jorge appears to desire Alfred's recognition of his claimed oppositional identity.

Stage Three: Dialogical Data Gathering

The first two stages we recommend for a critical field study consist of collecting data monologically and performing a preliminary analysis on it. But it will be necessary to engage in discussions with the subjects of study at some point to gain more clarity on the subjective and normative reconstructions begun in stage two. We suggest delaying the introduction of interviewing and group discussion techniques because use of them will often alter the routine forms of interaction and modes of speech that are of interest to the ethnographer. Hence, we have suggested use of interview and group discussion techniques as a third stage of the critical study.

Because the actual field techniques involved in generating dialogical data are well described elsewhere (see Spradley, 1979; Morgan, 1988), we will save space by avoiding any discussion of technique here and focus instead on the analysis of dialogical data.

There are several reasons why dialogical data generation is essential in critical fieldwork. The first is that it allows the people under study some control over the research process, yielding a more democratic form of knowledge production. The second is that it is really the only way to complete normative reconstructions begun in the second stage. The researcher alone is limited in inferring the normative contents of cultures and must begin a dialogue with those people being studied to check and alter her or his speculations about them. The third is that dialogical methods are empowering to the groups being studied. Sensitive questioning can often help people articulate features of their culture, and their feelings, for the very first time. Since articulating formerly tacit conditions helps one to distance one's identity from the structures within which it is frequently embedded, this method can be empowering to the subjects of study, and it can change the ways in which they routinely act. The fourth reason is that dialogical techniques yield contrast data and the fifth is that they aid in the discovery of normative structure. "Contrast data" and "normative structure" are concepts worthy of some elaboration and are discussed accordingly just below.

Contrast Data

Theoretically, dialogical data collection consists of the generation of "public realms," normative realms specifying what can and cannot be said or done, which are usually not commonly found within the life routines of the subjects of study. An interview or a facilitated group discussion creates a new normative context for the subject through which slightly new identities may be claimed and new norms referenced. This is the reason why people can and will express themselves in new or at least less common ways in an interview or group discussion than they do in the situations observed by the ethnographer.

Thus, the use of dialogical methods provides highly useful sets of *contrast data:* contrasts between the way people act and speak in naturalistic settings and the way these same people talk about their behaviors in an interview or group discussion. If a subject can talk about feelings and thoughts in an interview that they feel are not "allowed" expression within the normative realms observed by the researcher, then the researcher has learned something important about the norms operating in the routine contexts.

A study conducted by Carspecken (1991a,b) on a school illegally occupied and run by working-class residents well illustrates the use of contrast data. Members of the action committee, which had taken over the school, indicated in interviews that they felt stifled during action committee meetings and that certain "rules" were in play, which made questioning of the committee leaders impermissible. This was particularly true of the female committee members, who constituted the majority. When this was probed further, the interviewees indicated two principle reasons for these rules: that the opinions of women were not supposed to mean very much, especially when they opposed the views of the male leadership, and also that the leadership had "done all they could" for the rank and file activists and were, thus, owed "loyalty." Loyalty, they explained, meant not questioning. Thus, it was possible to elicit articulations of sexist and solidarity norms operating in the culture that the interviewees themselves had not previously verbalized—at least in a distancing and critical manner. Many of the women interviewed, for example, explained the situation as due to the fact that "women need to be led" and only after some facilitated discussion began to relate their feelings of frustration to their beliefs about their own sex. At this point, these same women could counter their former views and express themselves with the belief that women do not need to be led after all. In this way, features of the informal power structure of the committee were revealed without undue speculations on the part of the ethnographer. These interviews actually helped to spark challenges to the leadership simply because the interviewees had articulated formerly tacit norms and, thus, could take a critical perspective on them. The routine activities studied consequently changed after interviewing took place.

Normative Structure and "Social Texts"

In our earlier discussion of the normative realm, we indicated that a single normative element is almost always related to other normative elements. To return to an example we used there, the norm that students should anticipate the projects introduced by their teachers and cooperate with them is related to more general cultural expectations pertaining to the statuses of teacher, student, adult, youth, and polite behavior. Social action does not make implicit reference to discrete norms but, rather, to sets of normative terms. In this section, we discuss the ways in which such normative sets display *structure* and explain that dialogical data collection is particularly suited to elucidating such structures.

Let us begin by clearing up a possible misunderstanding. The term "structure" has often been used in sociological studies to denote "social structure" rather than "normative structure." Social structure usually refers to relations between distinctive groups in society, such as the relations existing among social classes, between males and females, and among various racial and ethnic groups. Thus, the term structural analysis in sociology often refers to an analysis that takes broadly spread class, gender, and racial relations into account. This use of the term structure is similar to what we mean by system relations in following sections.

Normative structure is distinctively different from social structure. Normative structure is analogous to the generative grammar implicated in speech acts. Each speech act implicitly refers to an entire grammar, and an understanding of this grammar is necessary both to produce the act and to understand it. Normative structures are similarly implicated in single social acts and must be grasped to both produce and understand the act.[7]

The field note sample we have been referring to will come up again to exemplify points we make below, but it is too short to be used as an illustration of normative structure. Instead, let us refer to one of the classical texts in critical ethnography, *Learning to Labour*, by Paul Willis (1977).

Willis reconstructed a number of core themes existing within the culture of "the lads"—the group of working-class male students he studied. These themes included "masculinity," antagonism to authority, nonconformity with the establishment, and a dislike of mental work. Each of these themes translated into diverse rules for self-presentation, expected behavior toward different types of people (teachers, other "lads," conformists, girls), the production of jokes and antics (what is and is not considered humorous), and so on. These are the sorts of things we have been calling "normative elements" above.

Willis showed further that each core theme was paired with an opposite: masculinity was in opposition to femininity, nonconformity to conformity, physical work to mental work, street knowledge to school knowledge, and so on. In structural anthropology, these would be called "binary oppositions." To understand any single element, one must understand what specifically it is *not*—its opposite. One must understand both to understand each singly.

Moreover, the four binary oppositions just listed were linked to each other homologously: masculine is to feminine as nonconformity is to conformity as physical work is to mental work as street knowledge is to school knowledge, and so on. This meant that to fully understand "masculinity" from the perspective of these boys, one would have to simultaneously understand other items in the homologous chain. Thus, for example, conformity, mental work, and school knowledge were all "femininelike."

Willis thus reconstructed the normative structure used by the lads to interact with others. This structure involved the binary opposition and the homology. Just as in the case of a generative grammar, this structure did not strictly *determine* the lads' behavior but, rather, allowed for a large variety of creative, original activities. It is a structure implicated as a whole in single acts but one that allows any number of individual acts to be generated.

Dialogical techniques are important in the pursuit of normative structure. Willis used group discussions to arrive at his structure of binary oppositions and homologous relations, which were operative in the culture of the lads. When a key category, like that of "physical work," emerged in the discussions, he probed its meaning through paraphrasing and direct questioning so that the boys in his study themselves articulated the homologous structure. When asking the lads to discuss the meaning of work, for example, Willis elicited the contrast between physical and mental work because the lads themselves used this contrast to explain their views. Willis could then compare the normative structure emerging from his conversations with the lads to the behaviors he observed them to regularly engage in. He found that the behaviors could be consistently understood as implicitly drawing on the same structure of oppositions that the lads more explicitly formulated in his discussions with them.

Normative structures need not always involve binary oppositions and homologies, or at least not these forms of implication exclusively. In a recent book, Carspecken (1991a) examines other types of intersubjective structure and their relationship to the binary opposition and homology. Thus, diverse forms of normative structure are possible.

In light of the previous comments on normative structure, then, it is possible to indicate where an analysis of this type might go in the case of Alfred, Simione, Mary, and Jorge. Jorge seems to be making oppositions between his home culture and the school culture, and street culture and school culture. His assertions of bravado should be explored for their relation to his concept of masculinity. His style of masculinity clearly differs from that of Alfred. His reference to an opposition between his out-of-school Hispanic culture and the classroom culture when exhibiting defiance and bravado may possibly indicate a linkage between gender and ethnic terms. The issue would have to be pursued through the collection of much more data.

Stage Four: Describing System Relationships

Beginning with stage four, the distinction between social and system integration becomes an important feature of the theoretical model employed by critical qualitative researchers. We will adopt the distinction between these two terms formulated by Giddens, which is sufficient for the analytical requirements of stage four (Giddens, 1979). Social integration refers to the coordination of action in face-to-face settings, whereas system integration refers to the investigation of relationships between the normative orders on diverse social sites. In stage four, then, the critical researcher begins to examine relationships between social sites and social groups. The most common site relationships investigated by early critical ethnographies of education have been much the same as sites studied by all sociologists of education: home and neighborhood, school and classroom, job and job market. More recent studies, however, have added media production and distribution institutions, publishing companies, teacher training institutions, and local, state, and federal government institutions (see G. Anderson, 1989).

Isomorphisms and Locking

We will explain two types of system relationships, which have been studied by critical researchers. Once again, Willis's study serves as a paradigm case for the first type of system relationship. This type of relationship is what Giddens calls the homeostatic system—a system relationship that works through the volition of those acting it out but that, as a system relationship, is unintended, unnoticed as a system relationship, and basically unmonitored (Giddens, 1979).

Willis discovered a "reproductive loop" characterized by the movement of (some) working-class children from the home of origin into an informal oppositional group within school, to a working-class job of roughly the same nature as the jobs worked by the children's parents. Thus, we see the reproduction of one segment of the working class across a generation. This occurred despite the existence of compulsory schooling, which offered some opportunities for social mobility—for a rise out of the working class into the middle class. It occurred despite the intentions of teachers and, as a reproductive loop, was also not intended by the working-class lads themselves. The loop occurred in an unplanned, unmonitored way.

Willis was able to reveal this reproductive loop by comparing the culture he reconstructed for the lads with the cultures of their homes and the culture of the work environments into which the lads moved after finishing school. His comparison of these cultures displayed *isomorphic* relations between them (for his use of this term, see Willis, 1983).

Isomorphism used in this context refers to similarities between the cultures of each site. The lads' opposition to school authority, their skills at producing "a laff" in situations that they found stifling and boring, their efforts to express and maintain masculine identities, and their affirmation of physical over mental labor all made use of themes they would find again in the shopfloor cultures of their future jobs. Willis also found that many of the same cultural themes could be found in the homes of the lads as well—presumably a major source of cultural material used by the lads in constructing their antischool culture. The similarity of the themes resulted in the production of isomorphic cultures on each site. These themes "worked" for the lads in each site— "worked" in the sense that they allowed the lads to produce affirmed identities and a sense of dignity within each realm. The fact that these themes *could* work in each case is significant—a circumstance discussed just below as "locking." The cultures on each site were not, of course, identical because actors would claim masculine identities and confront authority figures with different styles and different cultural contents on each site. But the point is that the normative structure drawn on in each case was highly similar—isomorphic.

"Locking" is Willis's term for describing the system processes that correlate with isomorphisms. Willis argues that the similarities of the normative realms existing among these three sites have "locked" these sites together in an unintended reproductive loop. As the term implies, locking refers to *contingent* relationships between sites. Various conditions had to be present in each site for locking to occur. The fact that the school was predominantly attended by working-class kids, the fact that the jobs the lads took on later used technological and organizational processes that facilitated the formation of a workers' culture (rather than a group of physically isolated workers unable to interact on the job), and a host of other conditions were necessary but contingent factors. Isomorphisms must therefore be explained by reference to conditions on various sites, and these conditions must be regarded as contingent, rather than determined.

However, the conditions that supported the formation of isomorphic cultural realms across the three sites studied by Willis may be distinguished by degrees of contingency. Many of the conditions that played a crucial role in the formation of this particular system loop owe their existence to general economic relations in capitalist society, such as the physically demanding conditions of shopfloor work and the lack of control workers have over the most general features of their labor. Thus, the discovery of system relationships in stage four begs larger questions about their place within an entire social system. These questions are dealt with in stage five and will be discussed in the relevant section. But first we will explain a second type of system relationship, which should be first studied as a contingent, empirical phenomena in the fourth stage of a critical field project.

The Circuit of Cultural Production

Willis's (1977) study demonstrates how a system loop can be formed through isomorphic relations between normative orders on diverse social sites. In his study, isomorphisms supported system locking through the *progressive movement of the lads from one site to the next* during the course of their life cycle. Other types of system relationships, however, do not depend on the same people moving across the sites in question but, rather, involve links between sites based on "system media" (Habermas, 1987). System media include the complex flows of money, information, consumer products, and other cultural items in society. There are various ways of bringing these diverse media flows into the analysis of an ethnographic study. A theoretical model that is particularly effective for the study of cultural products and their impact on diverse normative realms is the "circuit of cultural production," developed by Richard Johnson (1983) at the Centre for Contemporary Cultural Studies in England.

Before introducing the specifics of this model, we will ground the discussion by returning to Alfred and his Project TRUST students. An interaction sequence recorded on a different day from the sequence referred to earlier follows. Jason, an 8-year-old Afro-American boy, has now joined the class and Simione is out of the room—sent earlier to a counselor for some offense. All three students are having a group discussion with Alfred about fear, when Jason suddenly asks about a television program he watched the night before.

Alfred: Now, how do we handle being scared? There are lots of ways, let's think of some.

Jason: Kill someone! [Laughs.]

Alfred: No, well . . .

Jason: [interrupting] Mr. Taylor did you see *Jackson High* last night [TV program]?

Alfred: Yeah. How many of you saw *Jackson High* last night?

[All three pupils raise their hands.]

Alfred: That was an interesting program. What did the new principal do in the school?

Jason: Oh yeah! He went fum, pum pum, beat you bloody! [Stands up and swings arms in the air—loud and excited voice.]

Alfred: Why did he do that?

Jason: Because there was drugs and gangs.

Alfred: There were drugs and gangs in the school and the principal . . .

Jorge: [interrupting] If those guys came here I'd go [mock hits to air with "pum," "bum," "bamb bamb bamb"] beat those people up!

Alfred: Yeah but were those people really bad people, do you think?

Mary: Yeah.

Alfred: Yeah?

Mary: They took drugs.

Alfred: Yeah but was that because they were bad people or because they made bad choices?

Mary: They made bad choices.

Alfred: So they weren't really that bad, just the choices they made.

[Jason and Jorge are both fidgeting in their chairs, eyes attending mostly to the walls or each other.]

Alfred: At first it was hard to change wasn't it?

Mary: Uh huh. They didn't like him.

Alfred: They didn't like the new principal because he was trying to change the school, stop the drugs and fighting.

Mary: He did change it.

Alfred: Yeah, eventually he changed it. So, Jason, did you like the program?

Jason: Yeah! They beat this guy bloody!

Jorge: They didn't really 'cause it was just a TV show.

Alfred: To make you think about real life.

Jorge: My Dad has a gun!

Alfred: Yeah, but . . .

Jorge: [interrupting] He has a license. If someone pointed a gun at me I'd [gets out of seat and gives a mock kick to the air, as if kicking a gun out of a hand, then punches the air many times making noises].

Alfred: [to Jason who has turned in his seat to look at Jorge] That's not a very good choice Jorge's making right now is it?

Jason: No. [Not looking at Alfred, staring at Jorge.] Ohhh! Beat them bloody!!

In this sequence of interactions, the importance of television to the students and the incorporation of media messages into their own culture is apparent. Alfred tries to use the television program watched by all the children the night before to reinforce points he has previously made in class about *choices*. Certainly this program contained many messages suiting Alfred's interests, and he tries to lead the pupils into a reading of it consistent with his own. Mary anticipates Alfred's direction and cooperates with it. But Jason and Jorge seem to be tuned into the exciting and violent features of the program alone, reading the program in an alternative manner.

The culture of any group will have been partly constructed by its members through the selective appropriation of cultural items generated elsewhere in society. The qualitative researcher can ask (1) *where* do cultural themes come from, (2) *what* possible meanings do they bear, (3) *how* do the subjects of study interpret the meanings, and (4) *in what ways* do these interpretations affect the daily lives and routines of the people being studied. These four features of cultural products are the four components of Richard Johnson's "circuit of cultural production."

Johnson (1983) notes that cultural products may be regarded through the metaphor of a circuit that begins with the conditions in which the products are produced and ends with the take-up of certain selected readings of the product by a cultural group. A "circuit" is generated because the influence of a cultural product on a form of life will affect the production of new culture. The closing of a circuit takes place in two ways. Cultural products become resources for people to draw on in their daily production of local culture, and producers of marketable cultural items monitor reactions to their products to make decisions about the nature of future products. Television producers, for example, monitor the amount of viewer time they can capture from consumers and at times conduct surveys to monitor product "demand."

Johnson recommends analyzing this circuit with respect to a particular product by examining the cultural and economic interests of those who produce the cultural item. This will help the investigator understand why such products exist and why they carry some of their messages. Next, the investigator should consider the product itself, as autonomous from the conditions of its production. All cultural products carry ranges of explicit and, especially, implicit, meanings, which may not have been intended by the producers, just as works of literature need to be read and interpreted on their own, aside from the intentions of the authors who wrote them. Next, the researcher should examine precisely how the group of people she or he is studying interprets the cultural items they come in contact with. Some of the potential meanings of the product will be ignored or missed, others given emphasis. Finally, the way in which people talk about cultural products is not always identical to the ways in which such interpretations enter into their real life routines. Jorge and Jason both expressed much enthusiasm over the violent features of the television program on *Jackson High School*, but more research would have to be conducted to see whether or not (and precisely how) this enthusiasm translates into the ways they actually handle conflict in their own lives.

Culture is, of course, continuously produced in new forms by all people throughout society. But it is the *system relationships* of a particular society that determine the societal-wide patterns of distribution and impact of various cultural forms. Willis's lads produced a cultural form that had little direct impact on other groups of people in society. This is because their cultural form was not intended to enter nor capable of entering the major system media in present-day societies: marketable commodities.[8] On the other hand, cultural forms congealed into marketable commodities, like television programs, books, movies, computers, toys, and innumerable other objects, will become distributed broadly. Thus, the circuit of cultural production model is a way of revealing system relationships among various cultural sites.

The type of system relationship revealed by the circuit of cultural production model differs from the homeostatic loop discussed earlier. The distribution and reception of cultural products are usually monitored by producers because they are produced with intended effects. Products produced for economic gain such as music and films are *partially* monitored, because the producers are primarily concerned with sales, not with the full range of cultural effects caused by their products. Advertisers who display pictures of sparsely clad females standing near an item for sale monitor their profits, not the effects of their advertising on cultural views of women and sexuality. Products produced for political reasons or ideological reasons, on the other hand, will be monitored more closely for their effects on people's beliefs, attitudes, and behaviors.

Critical researchers working in education will be concerned with cultural products of all types. Important items included among them are textbooks, curricular and pedagogic theories, music, clothing, films, videos, music, and educational reports (for a study of textbooks and educational reports at all four points of the circuit of cultural production, see Apple, 1986).

Stage Five: System Relationships as Explanation

In the introduction, we stated that critical research on education begins with questions about the role played by schools within an unequal society. The fifth stage of a critical field study most fully addresses this concern. Efforts are made to relate the findings of stages one through four to a broad view of society as a whole. This will involve a search for the complex ways in which specific cultural realms both contribute to and contest more general social relations of inequality found throughout a society.

In critical social research, a theoretical model of society (e.g., a neo-Marxist model, a theory of patriarchy) is usually used to interpret field findings (in which specific processes discovered in the field are cited as *instances* of general processes) and to alter the model itself (in which certain features of the model are refined or reconceptualized). The models themselves should have been developed and presented with supportive evidence before the critical field researcher makes use of them. We will not review the various models in use nor the debates that continue with respect to them for want of space. Instead, we will provide a very partial discussion of a few concepts that are central to most critical analyses on this level.

Social System

The models of society used by critical social theorists all concern conditions of life that large categories of people face in common. When conducting a field study through the fourth stage previously outlined, the investigator will become cognizant of economic, political, and cultural conditions that are not unique to the particular sites being studied but, on the contrary, are general. For example, the home and work environments that Willis's lads were born into bore many features shared by an entire class of people—working-class males. Thus, Willis's findings tell us something about cultural processes developed to cope with conditions of life produced by an economic system (the capitalist system of England in the early post–World War II era) and widely prevalent views of gender (patriarchy). The reproductive loop he discovered was based on a number of contingencies, as indicated in the discussion of stage four, but some of the central features of this loop were contingent only on capitalist and patriarchal relations. McRobbie's (1978) study of working-class school girls, on the other hand, discovered a reproductive loop for female members of the same class, but once again, some of the central conditions contributing to this loop were contingent only on the most general economic and gender relations of society as a whole.

In principle, a single theoretical model of society can help us to make sense of both of these studies—a model that captures the complex intersections of class and gender relations in society generally. Such models express patterns in the system relationships of society—the processes that integrate the many diverse sites of society into consistent social relations. As such, these models represent society as a *system*. Society is seen as a highly complex system that differentiates groups of people and establishes relations between them.

The trick in moving from stage four to stage five, then, involves separating out the highly particular features of the sites under study from those features that characterize entire social groups. A theoretical model of society that represents class, gender, race, and other groupings is needed to recognize what is general in the situation. In the following, we will discuss a few concepts that help the researcher find general conditions within specific settings.

Interests

The first concept is that of "interests." There has been much theoretical discussion about the status of interests, the distinction between interests and needs or desires, and the question of whether or not interests are "objective" phenomena (see e.g., Saunders, 1983). Without begging too many questions, we think it possible to clarify the concept of interests and its distinction from needs and desires by referring to the three ontological categories we have consistently used in this chapter: subjectivity, intersubjectivity, and objectivity. All human acts suggest some sort of subjective impetus, or motivation, on the part of the actor of which no one (including the actor him- or herself) has direct knowledge. Rather, subjective states, including the subjective experience one has of needs and desires, become objects of reflection and discourse only through a culturally mediated (intersubjective) interpretation. Needs and desires may thus be imperfectly represented—there can be a mismatch between a subjective state and its cultural expression. Needs and desires fall within the subjective pole of the complex references carried by an act and, as such, possess an *internal* relationship to human volition.

Interests, on the other hand, can be conceived to fall toward the objective pole of the references carried by an act. They have an *external* relationship to human volition. *Interests may be defined as the socially constructed means through which needs and desires are pursued or secured.* Actors can talk and think about their interests only through cultural representations of them; therefore, people may also be misinformed about their interests. There may be a mismatch between one's interests and the culturally shaped ways in which one thinks and talks about them.

Because many needs and desires require forms of economic and/or political power to be satisfied, the study of interests leads rather quickly to the study of economic and political systems. The amount of access to material resources people have (their economic power) and the access they have to legal–political decision-making procedures (their political power) are key determinants of their interests. Because people need food and shelter, economic conditions characterizing society as a whole (e.g., wage rates, job opportunities) and political conditions characterizing society as a whole (e.g., welfare provisions, housing policies) will directly shape some of the specific interests of all people. When inquiring about the ways that people satisfy their needs, the researcher is learning about the socially constructed interests of these people—learning about their location within a social and political system.

The examples of interests we have just presented favor a special *type* of interests, which could be called "material" because they relate to the material conditions of human existence: food, shelter, and so on. Later, we will introduce another category of interests, which we call "cultural" and which relate to the social–psychological conditions of human existence. First, however, we will continue to discuss other features of interests in general, and the reader is invited to conceptualize them primarily in material terms for the time being.

The Hierarchical Nature of Interests

Interests have a hierarchical quality to them. There is usually an *immediate interest* related to a need or desire and a series of *broader, longer-term* interests associated with that same need or desire. Needs for food and clothing, for example, necessitate securing an income for most people in society. If you are unskilled, female, and/or a member of a minority ethnic group, a "job ceiling" (Ogbu, 1990) will work to limit the ways in which you can secure this income. You will probably have to work for low wages or depend on state benefits. It is in your short-term interests to take such a job or register for such benefits. But longer-term interests would involve such things as increasing the minimum wage, passing legislation that improves social benefits, ensuring that public schooling gives your children a full chance to enter into occupations suiting their abilities and interests, and, finally, changing social arrangements altogether so that the privileges enjoyed by higher classes in society do not depend on the existence of a lower class like the one you belong to. Short-term interests, then, refer to what must be done to survive within given social relations, and long-term interests correspond to making alterations in these arrangements themselves— in the economic, political, and cultural systems of society. Cultural misperceptions of interests usually involve the obfuscation of their less-immediate dimensions—their location within a broad system of inequality.

To conduct an analysis of the interests and, thus, the social location of a group of people, the critical researcher should begin by examining how they meet basic needs and what constraints they face in doing so. This will reveal the amount of control they have over material resources in society and over the legal–political processes that affect their lives. Then, the researcher should refer to a theory of society to help clarify the relationship of this group with other groups in society. The most general groupings about which inequalities are drawn are delimited by gender, race, and class.

Culture and Living Conditions

An understanding of the political and economic resources available to a particular group will help in understanding key environmental conditions affecting the culture of the group. Low-income groups, for example, often must work boring and physically demanding jobs and/or live in crowded residential areas characterized by higher-than-average rates of crime. These are specific environments that are coped with through the production of culture. For a poor group possessing little political power, various cultural themes that help the members cope may exist. There could be a "grin and bear it" cultural theme or an "enjoy it while you can" theme or, as in the case of Willis's lads, a series of themes that make potentially boring environments settings for jokes and acts of defiance. Some of these themes will be produced through systematic readings of various cultural products, the nature of the reading being shaped by its usefulness for coping with specific living environments.

Thus, the researcher will be concerned with the interests of a social group given by its location within society at large and with the ways in which members actually respond to these interests culturally. So far, critical research has done much to increase our understanding of such responses. Members of subordinate groups often do mis-perceive their full interests but develop cultural forms which nevertheless partially contest their subordinate position. Willis's lads developed a culture which won them some control over events in school and lessened the boredom to which they would otherwise be subject. The same cultural form which obscures a full perception of a group's position in society often also partially contests the powers which lock the group into that position.

Cultural Power and Interests

Because so many relations of inequality in society are maintained only because cultural forms serve to justify and perpetrate them, we encounter forms of "cultural power" when we investigate the relationship of interests to the cultural response they engender. One form of cultural power consists of cultural interpretative schemes, which keep subordinate groups from fully challenging the social relations that disadvantage them. A counter form of cultural power consists of the cultural themes used by subordinate groups to partially challenge these relations and win small realms of greater autonomy and freedom within stifling living conditions.

Another form of cultural power, however, has been partially addressed already in our previous section on "contrast data." People do not have needs and desires given only by the biological prerequisites of life—needs for food, shelter, and so on. People also have social–psychological needs. Symbolic interactionist theory has long recognized the fact that human interaction is necessary for the existence of "selves" (see especially Mead, 1967). The human self is a constantly constructed phenomenon that depends on interactions to exist. Social acts carry identity claims that are based on the distinction, ontologically drawn, between subjective states and public representations of these states. Humans are, moreover, *motivated* to make these claims. They are motivated to exist—not only biologically but also socially.

As argued earlier, humans do not merely need to have an identity but also desire to experience a match between their subjective states and their public identities. Normative realms provide repertoires from which identities may be claimed but provide restricted, inadequate repertoires for certain groups of people. Thus, it makes sense to speak of "nonmaterial interests," or "cultural interests." For some groups, culture limits the opportunities for gaining recognition by limiting the available repertoires of identities that others *will* recognize. Consequently, one may experience a mismatch between subjective states and normative realms. One can meet recognition requirements *immediately* in such situations only through coping in some way with this experience of mismatch. Coping can involve the repression of impulses, the loss of self-esteem through *believing* in the impoverished identities that one is forced to use to gain any sort of recognition at all, or the careful construction of several identities used in diverse social environments—only some of which allow for full self expression.

Once again, we find the hierarchical nature of interests in operation, this time with respect to social–psychological needs. Once again, people will have various degrees of awareness of their full interests. For subordinate populations, full nonmaterial interests involve fundamental alterations in typical normative realms—alterations in cultural definitions of "female," "Black," "unskilled worker," and so on.[9]

Interests and System Relationships

Material interests reflect one's position within economic and political systems of a society. Nonmaterial interests are also features of system relationships. One such system relationship involves a "fit" between one's material position in society and the normative realms one lives through. This fit is usually a complex one whereby a cultural form both enables people to cope with their conditions of life and limits their ability to change it for the better. This is the type of system relationship Willis discovered. Examining another example may clarify this type of system relationship.

Societies that perceive women as "naturally" self-sacrificing, "intrinsically" nurturing, and generally less capable than men in positions of managerial work have, in the past, fostered such views for women themselves, internally. Women who perceive themselves in this way will be more likely to accept lower-paying jobs and culturally restricted occupational categories. This is a complex system relationship that may be relatively unmonitored and the product of an unintended locking mechanism. The subordinate position of women, in this simplified example, is reproductively looped through the normative realms that limit the possibilities for challenging or even questioning an asymmetrical distribution of resources and constraints. Both material and nonmaterial interests are involved in such a reproductive pattern. Women have experienced oppression in terms of their access to positions of political and economic power in society at the same time that they have experienced limitations on their possibilities for self-expression.

The reason system loops such as those that have affected women get locked and reproduced is their fit with the material positions of the people involved. Once a reproductive loop, even an unmonitored one, becomes locked into complex system relationships in this way it becomes all the harder to attempt to change those relationships. Trying to change such patterns will affect the interests, material and nonmaterial, of other groups of people who have benefitted from the system relationship. Efforts to make such changes result in conflicts, and asymmetries in the distribution of economic and political resources may be decisive in the outcome of such conflicts.

A second type of system relationship, through which both cultural and material interests can initially be revealed, is the circuit of cultural production. Let us stay with the example of women's position in society for purposes of illustration. Many media products in society propagate limited notions of feminine (and masculine) identities. Movies, television programs, advertising, and so on all contribute to commonly held, limiting images of femininity. These cultural products will affect various cultures in a variety of ways, depending on the reading given to them. Readings, in turn, will vary according to living conditions and already intact normative orders. The ethnographer can study the origins of some identity repertoires by studying the readings given to cultural products important to a particular group. McRobbie's (1978) working-class school girls, for example, appropriated sexy, exaggerated, feminine images prevalent in teenage girl magazines as a way of resisting school authority and leaving school early to get married. These readings *worked* for the girls because of their negative experiences with school—ultimately rooted in their class background and the gender identities of their homes and neighborhoods. But the readings also limited the girls' ability to control many life possibilities by getting them married early and having them shun opportunities present in the school. To understand the full phenomena, the ethnographer needs to understand sources of cultural items and the *material interests that drive their production* as well as the conditions of life that favor certain readings.

This type of analysis goes beyond that described in stage four because interests and power relations are referred to as explanatory factors. The investigator makes use of theoretical models of society to provide a broad interpretation of his or her field findings.

Finishing a Research Project

We relegated dialogical data generation, data generation that proceeds through establishing an intensive dialogue between the researcher and those researched, to stage three of a typical field project. The dialogical approach, however, should be reintroduced repeatedly after stage three so that the inferences made in stages four and five are also freely discussed with the subjects of study. This serves both the validation and political requirements of critical qualitative research. In terms of validation, subjects of study are always capable of coming up with their own theories of system relationships and interests. By discussing one's own views on these matters with the subjects of study, the researcher remains open to being mistaken in his or her interpretation of a way of life. Politically, dialogical methods allow for a democratic form of theory production. This is because researchers enter the field with an unfair advantage over those who are subjected to their studies; they possess the means for representing a way of life to society at large, while most groups of interest to critical researchers do not.

This advantage must not be abused. People should not be analyzed without having some input into the analysis and the development of theories explaining what they do. A critical study should never be completed, therefore, without a full discussion of the findings with those who were the objects of the research. If it proves to be impossible to gain a consensus between the researcher and the people under study, alternative accounts should be placed side by side in the final write-up. Dialogical methods also serve political purposes by raising the awareness of subordinate populations so that they may be empowered to gain more control over their lives. True critical research is a collaborative endeavor.

Conclusion

In this chapter, we have focused on concepts, methods, and politics. We have demonstrated through selective examples how critical qualitative research proceeds. We have done this in recognition of one of the primary tenets of critical work: Think *relationally*. Think about the connections between what goes on in institutions such as schools and the assemblage of differential power relations—and how they are continuously produced, mediated, and/or transformed in our daily lives.

Thinking relationally requires the development of a set of concepts that are specific to the task. Thus, we have spent considerable time in this chapter elaborating this conceptual apparatus and giving examples of how it can be used. In the process, we have sought to avoid the dichotomy, one that we believe is partly false, between critical and more mainstream qualitative approaches. As we have argued here, critical and more mainstream qualitative research brings concepts and tools to bear on educational phenomena that are of great importance to the entire qualitative research tradition, both at the level of theoretical sophistication and at the level of understanding the relationship between commitments and the researcher. Critical research is no more theory-driven than other forms of research and, if done well as we have argued here, can and must produce testable (in the broadest meaning of that term) and falsifiable formulations.

Yet, it is crucial to remember that critical models of research are intended to be exactly that—*critical*. While we have focused on the descriptive and explanatory parts of the critical project, this does not exhaust what it is about. It is also, and profoundly, linked to what Raymond Williams (1961) so eloquently called "the long revolution," the set of social movements that seek to democratize our economic, political, and cultural relations. For differential power still exists and we—as researchers and as raced, classed, and gendered actors ourselves—are not divorced from these unequal relations. In a social context in which millions of people live in conditions that can only be described as tragic, the question remains: What can we do, with others, to keep "the long revolution" on course?

Notes

[1] Phil Carspecken has written the sections of this paper that deal with the ontology and epistemology of critical qualitative studies, the sections on making inferences from field data and the interpretation of field data through the concepts central to critical theory. The organization of a critical ethnography through five stages and the actual field notes used in this chapter to illustrate analysis are also his contributions. Michael Apple has written the introduction and conclusion to the chapter. Everything in this chapter was discussed by the two authors and although both authors might have some reservations about certain statements contributed by the other, these reservations are in every case very minor.

[2] Whyte distinguishes among different categories of theory involved in qualitative studies, and his use of "orienting theory" roughly meets our purposes here. What the reader must bear in mind, however, is that orienting "theory" is usually only *implicitly* theoretical. As "conventionalist" philosophies of science point out, all uses of language are "theoretical," whether or not those who use them are explicitly aware of the implicated theories (see Keat and Urry, 1975:ch. 3). However, we do not think that a beginning theoretical orientation renders the data collected and the initial inferences conducted by any social researcher, critical or not, "incommensurate" with data generated through other orienting frameworks. There are methods and validation procedures that should be followed by all qualitative researchers and that make field notes and primary cultural reconstructions "commensurate" to a large variety of orientations [see Whyte (1984), and for the commensurability of research findings, see Bernstein (1983)].

[3] Strictly speaking, the collection of data in this way is not monological but dialogical, because the very idea of doing research, of recording behaviors and speech acts, and the use of language itself in this process are all dialogical phenomena. That is, they implicitly refer to a community of researchers that gives these social routines sense. But this type of data collection proceeds as if it were monological through its failure to include the subjects of study in the actual process of research. At this stage, the subjects of study have been objectified. That is why this is called monological data collection. For discussions of monological and dialogical epistemological theories, see Habermas (1981, 1988).

[4] Strictly speaking, objective data is "preinterpreted data" insofar as a number of primary inferences must be made in all observations and recordings. That is why the validity claim associated with objective data is worded in terms of *consensus* in our discussion. The researcher must attempt to use a low-inference vocabulary and take other measures designed to maximize conditions for gaining a consensus among people present or potentially present at the research site. The consensus *aimed for* concerns only what was done or said, as could be captured in a video record, and not the meaning of what was done or said.

[5] We follow Habermas (1981, 1988) here with the term "normative" but are not entirely happy with it. Habermas also uses the term "social" to describe this realm but, once again, the term, or at least its English translation, is less than perfect. The realm of norms, values, and identities is usually *directly intersubjective* in that it consists of shared but tacit items. As intersubjective, it is not available to the senses but also not directly related to the internal states that we, following Habermas, will call "subjective." It is a set of suppositions each participant must make through taking the roles of others. Each participant must *suppose* a common understanding of norms, values, and identities held by others in the group but is constantly *testing* these suppositions through interaction. Habermas does not call this simply the "intersubjective realm" because objectivity and all *representations* of subjectivity (including one's self-perceptions and private thoughts) presuppose intersubjective interpretations. The normative realm, however, remains intersubjective, whereas the objective realm uses intersubjective schemes in conjunction with the senses and the subjective realm remains an ontological domain in privileged distinction from intersubjectivity *per se*. The subjective realm is necessarily impenetrable to others and is, thus, the reason why the normative realm must be a continuously shifting field of suppositions. One can and often does feel a degree of certainty about norms and identities prevailing within a group at the same time as one may be doubtful of the subjective states of others. These two realms are both fundamentally distinct and mutually dependent on each other.

[6] Peter McLaren (1986) used a similar analysis of "settings" in his critical ethnographic study *Schooling as a Ritual Performance*. He called them "states," however, and conceived of the processes involved as one of "switching states" rather than as one in which various settings may be *referenced* within a single interaction. McLaren's book is recommended reading for its unique incorporation of ritology (ritual theory) into critical ethnographic methods.

[7] We are using the term normative structure in much the same way that Anthony Giddens (1979:ch. 2) uses the term virtual structure.

[8] Of course, cultures like that of the lads have taken commodity forms in rock music, "new wave" music, and so on; however, in these cases, market forces will often alter the shape of such cultural forms to ensure steady demand.

[9] For a path-breaking analysis of what we are calling cultural needs and their place in critical theory, see Giroux (1988). Giroux approaches these issues through the concepts of "ethics" and "morality."

References

Agar, M. (1986). *Speaking of ethnography*. Newbury Park, CA: Sage.

Anderson, G. (1989). Critical ethnography in education: Origins, current status, and new directions. *Review of Educational Research*, 59, (3), Fall, pp. 249–270.

Anderson, P. (1980). *Arguments within English Marxism*. London: Verso.

Apple, M. (1985). *Education and power* (ARK ed.). New York: Routledge.

Apple, M. (1986). *Teachers and texts: A political economy of class and gender relations in education*. New York and London: Routledge.

Apple, M. (1988). Redefining equality. *Teachers College Record*, 90 (Winter), 167–184.

Apple, M. (1990). *Ideology and curriculum* (2nd ed.) New York: Routledge.

Bernstein, R. (1983). *Beyond objectivism and relativism: Science, hermeneutics, and praxis*. Philadelphia: University of Pennsylvania Press.

Bourdieu, P. (1984). *Distinction*. Cambridge: Harvard University Press.

Bourdieu, P., and Passeron, C. (1977). *Reproduction in education, society and culture.* Beverly Hills, CA: Sage Publications.

Bowles, S., and Gintis, H. (1976). *Schooling in capitalist America.* New York: Basic Books.

Carspecken, P. (1991a). *Community schooling and the nature of power; the battle for Croxteth comprehensive.* New York and London: Routledge.

Carspecken, P. (1991b). Parental choice, participation, and working class culture. *In* Education Group II, CCCS (Ed.), *Education limited: Schooling and training and the New Right since 1979* (pp. 237–264). London: Unwin Hyman.

Derrida, J. (1979). Structure, sign, and play in the discourse of the human sciences. *In* R. Maksey and E. Donato (Eds.), *The language of criticism and the sciences of man: The structuralist controversy.* Baltimore: Johns Hopkins Press.

Dreyfus, H., and Rabinow, P. (1983). *Michel Foucault, beyond structuralism and hermeneutics.* Chicago: University of Chicago Press.

Foucault, M. (1979). The subject and power. *Critical Inquiry,* 8(4), 777–795.

Giddens, A. (1979). *Central problems in social theory: Action, structure, and contradiction in social analysis.* London: Macmillan.

Giroux, H. (1988). *Schooling and the struggle for public life: Critical pedagogy in the modern age.* Minneapolis: University of Minnesota Press.

Habermas, J. (1981). *The theory of communicative action, volume one: Reason and the rationalization of society.* Boston: Beacon Press.

Habermas, J. (1987). *The theory of communicative action, volume two: Lifeworld and system, a critique of functionalist reason.* Boston: Beacon Press.

Habermas, J. (1988). *The logic of the social sciences, methodology philosophy, and social theory.* Cambridge, MA: MIT Press.

Johnson, R. (1983). *What is cultural studies anyway?* (Occasional Paper SP No. 74). Centre for Contemporary Cultural Studies, University of Birmingham.

Keat, R., and Urry, J. (1975). *Social theory as science.* London and Boston: Routledge and Kegan Paul.

Lincoln, E., and Guba, E. (1985). *Naturalistic inquiry.* Beverly Hills, CA: Sage Publications.

McCarthy, C., and Apple, M. (1988). Race, class and gender in American educational research. *In* L. Weis (Ed.), *Class race and gender in American education.* Albany, NY: SUNY Press.

McLaren, P. (1986). *Schooling as a ritual performance: Towards a political economy of educational symbols and gestures.* London and Boston: Routledge and Kegan Paul.

McRobbie, A. (1978). Working class girls and the culture of femininity." *In* Centre for Contemporary Cultural Studies (Ed.), *Women take issue: Aspects of women's subordination. Women's Study Group, University of Birmingham.* London: Hutchinson.

Mead, G. H. (1967). *Mind, self, and society from the standpoint of a social behaviorist.* Chicago: Phoenix Books.

Morgan, D. (1988). *Focus groups as qualitative research.* Newbury Park, CA: Sage Publications.

Ogbu, J. (1990). Social stratification and the socialization of competence. *In* K. Dougherty and F. Hammack (Eds.), *Education and society, a reader.* New York: Harcourt Brace Jovanovich.

Roman, L., and Apple, M. (1990). Is naturalism a move beyond positivism? *In* E. Eisner and A. Peshkin (Eds.), *Qualitative inquiry in education.* New York: Teachers' College Press.

Saunders, P. (1983). *Urban politics, a sociological interpretation.* London: Hutchinson.

Shapiro, S. (1990). *Between capitalism and democracy: Educational policy and the crisis of the welfare state.* New York: Bergin and Garvey.

Spradley, J. (1979). *The ethnographic interview.* New York: Holt, Rinehart & Winston.

Therborn, G. (1980). *The ideology of power and the power of ideology.* New York: New Left Books.

Whyte, W. F. (1984). *Learning from the field; a guide from experience.* Beverly Hills, CA: Sage Publications.

William, R. (1961). *The long revolution.* London: Chatto & Windus.

Willis, P. (1977). *Learning to labour: How working class kids get working class jobs.* London: Gower.

Willis, P. (1983). Cultural production and theories of reproduction. *In Race, class and education.* London: Croom Helm.

CHAPTER 12

❑ The Political Significance of Other Ways of Narrating Ethnography: A Feminist Materialist Approach

Leslie G. Roman

The Handbook of Qualitative Research in Education

Introduction

Feminist researchers working across a variety of theoretical and political traditions (radical, liberal, materialist, and poststructuralist) have repeatedly challenged masculinist ways of knowing and describing the world. Feminists have attempted to revise and reconceive traditional research epistemologies and modes of representation to understand and transform women's gender-specific experiences of subordination (Barrett, 1982; Coward, 1980; Jaggar, 1983; Haraway, 1988; Lather, 1986; Mascia-Lees, Sharpe, and Cohen, 1989; McRobbie, 1982; Oakley, 1981; Scott, 1985; Smith, 1974, 1988). And although we disagree on exactly what constitutes a feminist understanding of women's subordination or whether or not a single feminist understanding is possible, we strenuously reject the subject–object dualism or, what feminist philosopher of science Sandra Harding (1986, 1987a) calls, "objectivism." By objectivism, Harding means the stance often taken by researchers in attempts to remove, minimize, or make invisible their own subjectivities, beliefs, and practices, while simultaneously directing attention to the subjectivities, beliefs, and practices of their research subjects as the sole objects of scrutiny. Objectivism, she argues, is predicated upon the idea that objectivity can only be satisfied by an empiricist quest for value-neutrality in research praxis. With the exception of those working within the liberal feminist tradition, most feminist researchers have rejected the idea that research can be conducted in a value-neutral or interest-free way.

Feminists, however, must be equally concerned with overcoming the implied obverse stance of "subjectivism," the relativistic assumption that no value-directed inquiries can be objective and, therefore, all are equally justifiable.[1] By subjectivism, I mean the stance often taken by researchers in attempts to valorize the subjectivities, experiences, and knowledge of their research subjects (and conceivably themselves), while simultaneously relying on notions of subjective experience that are unmediated by the historically specific analyses of the underlying structures, material conditions, and conflicting sets of unequal power relations. Because both stances are premised on the subject–object dualism, neither subjectivism nor objectivism can provide adequate causal analyses of the connections between the structures and processes that give rise both to these unequal power relations and to people's experience and knowledge of them.

In this chapter, I intend to argue for a feminist materialist alternative to the subject–object dualism in the context of educational ethnographic research. Like other research methods, ethnography can be used either to transform or to reproduce existing social inequalities and divisions. Feminist materialist ethnography is grounded in an ethical, politicized, and scientific articulation of research practice not only because it makes an explicit commitment to democratize knowledge and theory, but also because it connects research to an emancipatory and transformative vision of society.

The theoretical and political project of feminist materialist ethnography would be to engage women (or other groups differentially subordinated by race, class, national culture, age, and sexual orientation) in collectively and democratically theorizing what is common and different in their experiences of oppression and privilege. The act of theorizing together to represent the world from the standpoints of women and/or other subordinate groups renders theory, method, and practice inseparable. The aim would be action on the everyday world in order to transform such subordination in various cultural institutions by developing systematic theoretical alternatives to prevailing masculinist, class, and racially exploitative modes of interpreting the world. In the practice and conception of research methods, women or other subordinate groups would then be considered both the subjects and objects of their own experiences. Hence, subjectivity and objectivity could less easily be claimed to live in a separate polarized relation to one another.

I will argue that developing such an alternative requires a radical break from the positivistic tendencies within naturalism, the prevailing discourse for the practice of ethnography. By naturalism, I mean the claim that the methodology of the natural sciences can be applied unproblematically to the social sciences (Keat, 1971:3). Naturalism, as philosopher of science Roy Bhaskar explains, refers to the thesis that "there is (or can be) an essential unity of method between the natural or social sciences" (Bhaskar, 1979:3). According to Bhaskar, to posit an essential unity of method between the natural and social sciences is to provide an account that conceives of the sciences in the form taken by scientific knowledge, the reasoning through which it is produced and the concepts that enable its adequate theorization (1979:24). While striving to develop a new critical naturalism that rejects its long entanglement with positivist science and epistemology, Bhaskar identifies and refutes two dominant conventions of naturalism that accomplish no such rejection: "*reductionism*, which asserts there is an actual identity of subject matter as well; and *scientism*, which denies that there are actually any significant differences in the methods to studying social and natural objects, whether or not they are actually (as in reductionism) identified" (Bhaskar, 1979:3). For my purposes, it is to the dominant conventions of naturalism and its affinities with positivism, and not some conceivable antipositivist and critical variant along the lines suggested by Bhaskar (1979, 1986) and Keat and Urry (1982), that my critique of naturalistic ethnography is directed. Later, we will have occasion to define naturalism's affinities with positivism more closely. Suffice it to say for now, however, that naturalism generally presumes and often embodies the mistaken contrast between the implied objectivity of the natural sciences, whose aim is explanatory understanding as defined by positivism, and the implied subjectivity of those studies of social reality that involve interpretive understanding (Keat and Urry, 1982).

Although I will use the discourse of naturalistic ethnography as my example of the polarized stances of objectivism and subjectivism, the conclusions I draw have political and ethical implications for forms of critical theory and research praxis across a wide range of fields. I will critique the ways in which the practices within the institutionally constituted discourse of naturalistic ethnography fail to permit systematic analyses of the inseparability of subjectivity and objectivity within historically specific contexts of unequal power relations. As will become clear, though, I do not mean to suggest that individual researchers who work within this discourse consciously intend to deceive their research subjects or their readers when they take objectivist or subjectivist stances in their involvement with research subjects or in their written accounts of fieldwork. Nor do I mean to suggest that naturalistic ethnographers deny moments of subjectivity when they confront the ethical and political dilemmas of conducting and representing field research. I do intend to argue, however, that the failure of ethnographers to challenge the discourse of naturalism, which is predicated on the subject–object dualism, may reify and mystify the knowledge required to understand and transform unequal power relations, not only between researchers and research subjects, but also those that structure the wider society. Moreover, I will contend that the failure to challenge naturalism may block the theoretical and practical capacities of ethnographers to imagine and develop emancipatory research praxis.

While I will make the case that feminist materialism is politically preferable to other stances that might inform the prior commitments of ethnographic research, my argument is not naively or solely grounded in a political rationale for feminist materialist ethnography. An equally compelling argument is that it provides the most systematic explanatory account of the persistence or transformation of existing fundamental social divisions, inequalities, and forms of oppression. Therefore, I will compare the explanatory accounts of different forms of feminist and materialist epistemology in terms of their conceptions of social justice and transformation as well as the ways in which these conceptions may contribute to or stand in the way of emancipatory research praxis.

I will propose a feminist materialist alternative to the subject–object dualism that makes it possible to think of the relationship between subjectivity and objectivity as something not static, fixed, historically unknowable, or unnameable. Rather, I conceive of this relation as a dialectical and shifting one, which operates through multiple and conflicting sets of discourses, material interests, and power relations by race, class, gender, age, and sexual orientation. I conceive of this relationship as *politicized (politicizing) subjectivity* and *historically specific (historically contextualizing) objectivity*. By conceiving of the relationship between subjectivity and objectivity in this historically conjunctural manner, I mean to part ways with those versions of Marxism and feminism that are class- or gender-essentialist and, therefore, cannot account for the asymmetric or contradictory interests at work in the formation of people's consciousness and practice.[2]

On the other hand, I also desire to distance myself from those strands of postmodernism or poststructuralist feminism that imply that any attempt to explain the material and ideological bases underlying the experiences of women or any other subordinate group necessarily results in a falsely totalizing or universalizing master narrative of domination.[3] At this present and purportedly postmodern moment in history, many attempts to grasp systematically the relationship between different forms of subjectivity and diverse, but nonetheless objective, conditions of oppression can be treated as mere textual maneuvers devoid of radical political effects. It is therefore important once again to ground notions of multiple or polyvocal subjectivities not only in different discourses but also in specific material and ideological conditions.

The value of a politicized conception of feminism, which I believe feminist materialism represents, is its explanatory power to provide feminist struggles and analyses with the theoretical and practical resources of historical specificity (Moi, 1988). Thus, while I do not believe there is one *a priori* speaking position for feminism, I will argue that an ethnography informed by a feminist materialist critique of existing social inequalities is capable of providing concrete, historical, and structural analyses of specific lived cultural and social relations and material conditions in ways that may contribute to social transformation and political transformation as well as to critical scholarship.

Examining the Subject–Object Dualism

Working for feminist materialist alternatives to the subject–object dualism entails self-consciously confronting several questions. For whom is research or inquiry conducted? This issue concerns the function of social research in empowering certain social actors and silencing or disempowering others. Who decides what the "problems" of a research agenda are? Both questions require all those involved in research to examine the links between people's cultural practices and the structural conditions underlying them in and around the educational contexts we research. These contexts include the differential power relations between the researcher and the researched. Is the objectivist stance of the prevailing subject–object dualism one consequence of adhering to a masculinist and positivistic position, in which the more one distances oneself from the "object of study," the better one is as a researcher? Conversely, is naturalistic ethnography—a method involving a great degree of intimacy and apparent mutuality in the potential for self-exposing subjectivity between the researcher and the researched—in more danger of exploiting subordinate groups than allegedly more positivistic, quantitative, and masculinist research methods (Stacey, 1988)? How might the relationship between objectivity and subjectivity be reconceived as alternative to the polarized stances of objectivism and subjectivism?

In short, how are the beliefs, practices, and interests of the researcher by gender, class, race, national culture, age, and sexual orientation constitutive of the evidence for or against the ethnographic descriptions and analyses the researcher advances about his or her research subjects? What ethical principles and epistemological traditions can be evoked to guide ethnographers facing the contradictions invariably entailed in the often unacknowledged and asymmetrical power relations of conducting fieldwork and writing ethnographies? These questions serve as a backdrop against which I judge not only the adequacy of the procedures used by many qualitative researchers in education but also their claims regarding the justification for research and the context of discovery.

The Research Context and Methods

I base my arguments on the politics of conducting and writing an ethnography (Roman, 1987, 1988, 1989, in press). This work examines how middle- and working-class Punk young women formed their gender and class identities and relations within the extramural curriculum and rituals of their subculture while they also traversed their families and schools. The study (Roman, 1987, in press) was conducted in a midwestern city I call Jamison. Jamison employs much of its population as professionals and technical administrative staff in three of its largest employers, the state and local government and the state university. It is, however, also the home of a meat-processing plant, several word-processing firms, hospitals, and insurance companies, which employ a substantial female working-class population. Recently, Jamison has begun to attract working-class youth from large urban areas, where employment in the industrial sectors of the economy is rapidly disappearing.

Of the 32 Punks participating in the study, 19 (12 females and 7 males, ages 14–27 years) were determined to have secure middle-class backgrounds. In contrast, the backgrounds of 13 Punks (8 females and 5 males, ages 15–31 years) are best located within the working class, according to criteria drawn from Wright's (1980a,b) analysis of class and contradictory class locations. At the conclusion of the study, all 19 of the middle-class Punks were completing or had completed high school in one of two schools in which the majority of the students were college-bound. Six of the seven post–high school Punks, five of whom were females, continued to live at home with their parents as economic dependents or had moved in and out while receiving economic assistance and casually pursuing postsecondary coursework at Jamison's vocational–technical college or at the state university. Five of the post–high school women have worked for wages only in part-time jobs, such as waiting tables in coffee bars, baking for continental restaurants, or doing graphic arts or photography for small businesses.

In contrast to the middle-class Punks, while 12 of the 13 working-class Punks were completing or had completed high school, 7 of these (5 females and 2 males) were old enough to have completed four years of college, yet only 2 had done so. Moreover, of crucial significance is a pattern that emerged among the working-class Punks concerning the relatively short number of years they economically depended on and lived at home with their parents. Unlike the pattern of prolonged economic dependency among the post–high school middle-class Punks, by the conclusion of the study, 8 of the 13 working-class Punks (5 females and 3 males) had, between the ages of 15 and 17 years, emancipated themselves economically from their families of origin. In addition to having worked in jobs that constituted working-class locations previous to their emancipation, they have subsequently begun to establish their own independent class trajectories by working in jobs that, for the most part, follow a complex pattern of employment in working-class locations. The pattern is complex because it is interrupted by periods of underclass subsistence when these Punks were either employed part-time in jobs constituting working-class locations or unemployed altogether.

Ethnographic field research consisting of observation, participant observation, and informal and formal interviewing with self-identified Punks, began in the fall of 1981 and was completed in the summer of 1984. For the duration of the spring of 1984, I conducted field research in the Punks' schools, observing their classroom interactions among themselves and with other students. I interviewed their teachers, counselors, and principals. During this same period, I also made a number of visits to the 26 homes of those Punks whose families of origin lived within geographic reach, where I interviewed their parents. Some of the interviews with the Punks' teachers, school personnel, and parents confirmed reports given to me by the Punk young women of their direct experience or witness of family violence and/or sexual abuse in or outside their families.[4]

For the first several months of fieldwork, I familiarized myself with the Punks and their member-generated categories and distinctions regarding groups within the subculture. Initially, I spent most of my time observing Punks interacting with each other and interviewing them within subcultural contexts exclusive of their families and schools. These contexts, which included record shops, cafes, skateboard ramps, band practices, "fanzine" (fan magazine) production sessions, and gigs, were seen by Punks as "subcultural" because of their perceived freedom from the intrusions of other youth groups, parents, and school personnel. Observations and interviews in such contexts allowed me to identify five clearly demarcated Punk subcultural rituals concerning modes of participation in the consumption and production of style or bodily presentation, fanzines (fan magazines), slam dancing and pogoing, and skateboarding. I found discernible differences in the meanings for and modes of participation in these rituals, which were demarcated not only by class and gender but often by family form and histories of prior family violence and/or sexual abuse in the women's experiences.

Elsewhere (Roman, 1987, 1989, in press), I narrate the practical and ethical dilemmas produced by my first forays into the subculture in which I failed miserably at attempts to "go native," that is, to "dress Punk" and participate as a pretend Punk who could be conversant with Punks about the music and other subcultural practices. While I came to overtly reject the "going native" approach to conducting the fieldwork,

I found myself unintentionally easing over to the other extreme, the "fly-on-the-wall" approach to fieldwork. This approach involved my thorough immersion as an observer into the subculture in order to determine the various rituals and spatial and temporal maps underlying the Punks' cultural practices and social relations. I quickly discovered, however, that this stance also produced its own set of ethical dilemmas regarding the level and nature of my involvement in the daily gender and class issues facing the young women (Roman, 1987, 1989, in press).

The Dialectics of Theory and Practice

In the aforementioned work (Roman, 1987, 1989, in press), I describe in detail the dialectical interaction, which I call *double exposure*, between my fieldwork practice and emergent theory. I show how and under what conditions I developed a feminist materialist alternative to the subject–object dualism. Because I present my arguments largely in the absence of the practical social relations that helped give rise to them, I would like to clarify two points at the outset. In fact, the arguments advanced in this paper emerged from a specific set of social relations—a middle-class, white, academic researcher studying a predominately white group of middle- and working-class Punk young women in the context of their interactions with Punk young men.

First, the issues of practice and ethics surrounding my ethnographic research did not emerge out of nor were they derived from my rigid adherence to feminist materialist theory. Rather, it is more accurate to say that my ethnographic practice and ethics in the field emerged and were transformed as I attempted to square the conflicts and contradictions they presented with my training as a naturalistic ethnographer and my prior conscious political beliefs as a feminist materialist. The interaction of practice with my deeply held political beliefs and theoretical commitments was dialectical; that is, as practical ethical dilemmas shaped and transformed my feminist materialism, the resultant emergent theory in turn caused me to rethink my ethical stances toward the young women I researched.

Second, ethnographic decisions are not a matter of choosing between the priorities of politically and ethically motivated methods and those that are scientific and epistemologically founded. My fieldwork relationships with the Punk young women and men reveal the epistemological reasons why it is wrong, if not impossible, to evade political and ethical decisions in making methodological choices. To crystallize these arguments, I am not proposing a "feminist materialist method or procedure" for the conduct of ethnographic research; rather, I am advancing those theoretical and methodological features of my research that may indicate possible applications of a general structure of social scientific theory to the conduct of research on women and gender.[5] These features are epistemological because they entail the production of theories of knowledge that offer an alternative to masculinist science and social science and because they challenge different forms of essentialism often assumed in neo-Marxist and feminist subcultural ethnographic work.[6]

Naturalism as Discourse and Ideology

The Appeal of Naturalistic Ethnography

Initially, I selected the naturalistic approach to ethnography as the primary method for my study (Roman, 1987) for two compelling reasons. First, ethnography insists on rendering "thick" contextual descriptions of social subjects as they actively and creatively make sense of their social worlds (Geertz, 1973). As Woods (1985) states:

> Ethnography by definition is descriptive. In anthropology it means, literally "a picture of the way of life of some interacting group . . ." Faithfulness to a culture as it is found is one of the guiding principles of ethnography, and immersion in the culture under study is the general strategy towards this end. (p. 52)

The idea of thoroughly immersing myself as a participant–observer in a setting in order to render a picture of people's common-sense knowledge, cultural practices, and agency within their subcultures, families, and schools had a particular appeal for me. Such a method seemed consistent with the culturalists' political critique of the determinism embedded in structuralist theories of social reproduction. Like some other critically oriented researchers, such as Willis (1981), I shared those elements of such a critique that were opposed to reducing human agency and social subjectivity to the mere passive effects of social structure. Ethnography, I reasoned, with its focus on microlevel patterns of social interaction among people, would provide a useful antidote to the tendency of structuralist reproduction theories to abstract grossly and overtheorize about what goes on in the daily life of cultural institutions or informal settings, whether they are schools, families, or youth subcultures.

Second, I was drawn to naturalistic ethnography because, for the most part, structuralist theories of social reproduction relied on methods that were either opaque or overly formalistic and totalizing in their account of social subjects' collective self-making processes. I wondered whether Willis's (1977) lads or the young women in McRobbie's (1978) influential study of the role of the school in reproducing class and gender relations would have recognized themselves in the resultant theoretical accounts had their subcultural practices and subjectivities been interpreted strictly through Bernstein's (1977) structural and linguistic schema of classification and framing or through Bourdieu and Passeron's (1977) typology of linguistic and cultural competence. Could such structural approaches account for the richness and complexity that occurs in daily life?

In contrast, ethnographic accounts, as they had been used by culturalists such as Willis (1977), McRobbie (1978), and others, seemed at first glance to be explicit in their methods and rationales for participant observation. Willis (1977) even went so far as to include a methodological appendix that attempted to provide a reflexive account of his field research as well as the lads' responses to his theoretical interpretations of their subcultural practices and subjectivities. Unlike the overbearing formalism and inaccessibility of structuralist theories of social reproduction (Bowles and Gintis, 1976) and their attendant methodologies, ethnographies seemed immediately available to a wide range of readers. They appeared to invite the readership into dialogue with the research subjects themselves. Moreover, the texts of these culturalist ethnographers appeared to function as written proxies for the agency of working-class people and the "oppositional" or "resistant" aspects of working-class culture. As such, interview data, descriptive accounts, and extracts from fieldwork with working-class groups, much like narrative realist texts, seemed to clarify powerfully—as if told in their own voices—the underlying structural mechanisms and material conditions that enabled society's cultural and social reproduction.

Given such a politically and intellectually compelling rationale for "doing" ethnography, I worked toward my adoption of the conventional role and subject position of the naturalistic ethnographer. According to the discourse of naturalistic ethnography, I would enter the Punks' subculture as an anthropological stranger, explore them in the context of their own natural settings, and, yet, remain careful not to disturb the ecology of their social world by introducing my own subjectivity, beliefs, or interests as a white, middle-class, academic researcher.[7]

As an ethnographer of a Punk subculture, I would participate

. . . covertly or overtly in people's lives for an extended period of time, watching what happens, listening to what is said, asking

questions; in fact, collecting whatever data are available to throw light
on the issues with which he or she is concerned. (Hammersley and
Atkinson, 1983:2)

And I would enter the field research heeding the words of Schatzman
and Strauss (1973):

The naturalistic researcher will not in advance presuppose more than
the barest rudiments of social order and value. What he [*sic*] will do is
maximize the possibilities of discovering these as they are developed
within the situation. (p. 14)

Thus, a key element of naturalistic ethnography is the attempt by the
researcher to hold in abeyance any of his or her prior political assumptions and theoretical commitments about what is happening in the
world under study. According to the naturalistic view of ethnographic
research, I would arrive in the Punk subculture only to discover that
much of what I took for granted as knowledge about how the social
world works would be disconfirmed or proven false in the context of a
new environment. As an ethnographer, my tasks would then be to gain
an insider's knowledge of what was going on and to gradually and
inductively generate theory to explain what I saw. As Schutz (1964)
argues, entering the field in such a manner would allow me to acquire a
certain objectivity not available to the Punks themselves, whose underlying assumptions regarding their own practices would remain fundamentally and unconsciously obscure to them.

According to Schutz (1964), I as researcher might expect to find
some overlap in assumptions, beliefs, and world views between myself
and the researched, given that we live in the same society; however,
this would not minimize the value of the ethnographic account as a
social science method. Ethnography could still render a description of
the cultural patterns and practices that vary across and within society,
especially those that shed light on the social meanings and contexts
that constitute such variations. By seeking to ascertain the Punks'
everyday ways of perceiving the world, the naturalistic ethnographer
could glimpse the ongoing constitution of social reality. I would conceive of social reality mainly as the situations and meanings widely
available among the people being studied in order to construct and
reconstruct the social world of their own culture (Reynolds, 1980;
Sharp and Green, 1975).

Writing the ethnography would entail my documenting and preserving an accurate description of how the Punk young women saw

things in the context of interactions with other Punks, their fellow students, teachers, parents, and so forth. My analysis would emerge out of the Punks' accounts as members of a particular "taken-for-granted" reality. I would therefore be describing the commonsense rules—whether tacit or explicit—that organized the various practices and subjective meanings constituting social reality in the subculture, families, and schools. The analysis then would emerge inductively out of the field research alone (Edwards and Furlong, 1985; Schatzman and Strauss, 1973).

According to such a view of naturalistic accounts, anything more would constitute an *imposition* of my own "arbitrary and simplistic categories on a complex reality" (Hammersley and Atkinson, 1983).[8] If I followed the main tenets of naturalistic ethnography as Hammersley and Atkinson have summarized and ambivalently critiqued them, I would be reassured by the claims of numerous ethnographers representing a variety of disciplines and political traditions (including neo-Marxist sociologists of education) that naturalistic ethnography diametrically opposes and provides a methodological alternative to the allegedly intrinsic positivism of the natural sciences, quantitative sociology, and experimental research. In the process, I would feel comforted by the idea that the methodological criteria of naturalism would "solve" the "problem" of subjectivity as it is represented and reified in the subject–object dualism.

According to this view of the naturalistic ethnographer, I would not place the Punks in a laboratory setting, introduce them to standardized questionnaires written in neutral-sounding observational language, or subject them to artificial simulations (the plans for which some educational psychologist may have already conceived). I therefore could take heart that both the field research and the written account of the ethnography would be free of such unnatural and intrusive measures. Having alternated in the researcher's role between acting as a fully immersed participant–observer, who surrenders herself to the "native" experience and account of their subculture, and participating as an unobtrusive fly on the wall, who gleans privileged knowledge and insight into the participants' culture, I could proceed unproblematically to write the ethnography. Because the ethnography itself would not rely on the deductive mode of explanation or universal covering laws that would attempt to posit, predict, or generalize from the observations of the subjects' interactions, I could rest assured that I had not succumbed to positivism[9] (Giddens, 1979; Hammersley and Atkinson, 1983; Keat and Urry, 1982).

Naturalistic Ethnography's Affinities with Positivism

A research method that closely attends to the ways social subjects form their commonsense knowledge in their everyday contexts and situations undeniably makes some important modifications to the assumptions traditionally associated with a positivistic conception of scientific method. For example, while positivistic science usually asserts the experimental mentality, with its emphasis on the discovery of universal laws and deductive explanations that rely on value neutrality and quantifiable precision, naturalistic ethnography forsakes generalizations in favor of the image of contextually and inductively built qualitative description and theory. Now, certainly one of the values of naturalistic ethnography is its potential to generate theory that may challenge unwarranted preconceptions or conclusions on the parts of researchers. It is also important to recognize, however, that beneath such distinctions, *naturalistic ethnography often constitutes an extension of rather than a break from positivism.*

First, whereas positivism usually employs the discourse of hypothesis-testing and controlled experiments to speak of the research process, naturalistic ethnography uses the discourse of the discovery and exploration of the culture of "others." Both discourses take for granted the assumption that the researcher is a detached observer who "minimizes" the research subjects' "reactivity" to the researcher (Aggleton, 1984; Hammersley and Atkinson, 1983; Hargreaves, Hestor, and Mellor, 1975; Lofland, 1971). Just as positivistic science and, more particularly, quantitative sociology have been accused by naturalistic and qualitative researchers of standardizing the research process to minimize the effects of the researchers on the data or the research subjects, naturalistic ethnographers have been equally obsessed with the effects of their presence in creating "distorted" or "unnatural" interactions among those they research.

Aggleton (1984) provides one typical example of an ethnographer who works to erase his presence in the fieldwork and in the written account of it. Aggleton set out to study a group of what he termed "new middle class," subcultural youth, whom he identified as "underachievers," attending an English college of further education. Because he had been a teacher at the same college in which he hoped to conduct the research, Aggleton went to elaborate lengths to disguise the nature of his research with former faculty colleagues and the students who were the prospective research subjects for the study.[10] Inside the school and with his former teaching colleagues, Aggleton represented himself in admittedly "vague" terms as taking a leave of absence from his teaching, allowing them to draw their own conclusions that he was either conducting research on "something to do with youth culture" or "taking time off dossing at the University" (Aggleton, 1984:110). Outside school, however, he represented himself to the students as just another person who, like themselves, had become "disillusioned" with school, was "pissed off with teaching," and who was having "difficulty" with his "work."

Of course, the very idea that the ethnographer works to "increase naturalism" or gain rapport by reconstructing accounts of her or his self-presentation and purposes with different groups of research subjects exposes the discourse's own contradictory ideology. It is analogous to women being sold cosmetics to use in creating a natural appearance. The researcher uses nonreciprocal and nondialogical means of entry and communication to gain access into sets of social relations (e.g., subcultures and school faculties) that are themselves structured by their interactive and dialogical features among and between groups. Aggleton's attempts to build rapport in this manner, which I (Roman, 1987, 1989, in press) have called "going native," shares with positivism the assumption that one can simply refrain from making and/or revealing the ethical considerations that motivate and are embedded in the practice of field research. Maintaining these different and less-than-open accounts with the students and faculty appears to pose no major ethical problems for Aggleton in examining how he obtained his data or the conditions under which people opened up to him. Instead, like most ethnographers who work within the discourse of naturalism, Aggleton—though very sensitive in other ways—tends to construct himself as a "neutral" and "unobtrusive observer" whose main interest in establishing rapport or "building commonality" (Aggleton, 1984:111) with the research subjects is the quest for better data.

It is this similarity in the underlying logic and methods of positivism and those of naturalistic methods such as participant observation and ethnography that prompts Willis (1981)—in one of the rare discussions of the limitations of naturalistic ethnography by a neo-Marxist—to warn against creating a false distinction between quantitative research as intrinsically positivistic and qualitative research as free of positivism.

> The duality and mutual exclusivity of the overly neatly opposed categories, "qualitative methods" and "quantitative methods," suggests already that the "object" is viewed in the same unitary and distanced way even if the *mode* is changed—now you measure it, now you feel it. (Willis, 1981:88)

In either "mode" of research, Willis argues, the researcher assumes that knowledge of the social world can be constructed by drawing inferences from immediate sensory experiences of the "object" under study. These inferences are then made distant from the researcher's own subjectivity, interests, and values.

Like the positivistic concern to create the aura of neutrality on the part of the researcher, naturalistic ethnographers generally offer a similar rationale for minimizing the reactivity of their research subjects to themselves. They do so by adopting various field roles, such as "going native" to become a fully immersed participant or becoming the unobtrusive "acceptable incompetent" (Lofland, 1971). They stress their concern not to contaminate the natural relations and interactions among research subjects with the "biases" of the researcher (Popkewitz, 1981; Schatzman and Strauss, 1973). Such preconceptions on the part of the researcher are seen as ultimately distorting or falsifying the results of the study. According to this view, data retrieved under conditions that acknowledge the researcher's presence and her or his possible effects on what the research subjects said in interviews or how they interacted among themselves pose a threat to the ecological validity of the analysis.

Instead of treating the inevitable reactions to and interactions with the researcher by the research subjects as valid data occurring within a specific set of social relations, a good deal of naturalistic ethnography legitimates a number of misconceived distinctions premised on the positivistic logic that neutrality in research and on the part of the researcher's established field role is both attainable *and* desirable. The apparent prevalence of such a premise operating in naturalistic ethnographies inspired Johnson (personal communication, March 1982) to coin the phrase "the phenomenon of the missing researcher." Johnson uses this phrase to describe how researchers adopt authorial voices in their written accounts in which they do not acknowledge that they held any prior theoretical assumptions or nascent hypotheses when they entered and conducted the field research.

One fundamental problem with such a logic is its affirmation of the false distinction between "natural," or ecologically valid, and distorted, or "artificial" or "imposed," modes of doing ethnographic field research. Such a distinction holds in common with positivism the assumption that the social reality and social relations associated with field research can be treated as entirely distinct from the social relations of the wider society, which are structured, in part, by the inequitable power relations and divisions of gender, class, race, age, and sexual orientation. One could imagine different practices, behaviors, and social meanings arising in the field when a researcher is physically present among the research subjects and when she or he is physically absent. How a group responds to and understands the presence of the researcher is as informative as how it makes sense of the researcher's absence; in either case, the group's responses and understandings constitute meaningful sets of social relations.

It is difficult, however, to argue that the context in which the researcher is present can somehow be seen as less meaningful or less socially constructed than one in which the researcher is absent, because in both cases there are underlying power relations structuring social life that affect whatever understandings and accounts of reality the given groups generate to articulate "what is or is not going on" for them. To ignore an account of such power relations as they underlie the field research is to assert an argument that reinforces naive realism and empiricism. It presumes that social reality is atomistic (Jaggar, 1983) and can, therefore, be reduced to descriptions of "the way things are," that is, the appearances of social life as they are observed by the research subjects (Jones, 1986:34). Just as critically, in sanctifying the absolute primacy of how subject members see their social reality, naturalistic ethnography fails to account for any of the structural mechanisms and material conditions that might contribute to the determination of how members see things or articulate what they understand.

Taking such a view also asserts the erroneous notion that inductive reasoning, or what Glaser and Strauss (1967) call "grounded theory" (p. 55) and the cultural description it renders in ethnographic accounts, can be separated from the researcher's *prior* assumptions, theory development, testing, and explanation. In response to such a view, Hammersley and Atkinson (1983) find themselves most critical of naturalistic ethnography's affinities with positivism. They first make the rather obvious but still crucial argument that all research methods, whether they are more quantitatively or more qualitatively structured, involve processes of selection and interpretation in which the researcher describes and explains a limited or partial construction of the social totality under study. In their view, no researcher is privy to the structural totality of the culture under study, because "even in a small-scale setting we [ethnographers] could not begin to describe everything, and any description we [ethnographers] produce is inevitably based on inferences" (Hammersley and Atkinson, 1983:13).

However, they later advance a more sophisticated argument, implying that all description is theory-laden. Hence, they critique the assumption within naturalistic ethnography that limits the project of ethnographers to cultural description:

> While there may be nothing wrong with such cultural description, the kind of empiricist methodology enshrined in naturalism renders the [researcher's] theory implicit and thus systematically discourages its development and testing. (Hammersley and Atkinson, 1983:13)

In pursuit of this argument, Hammersley and Atkinson come close to a critical break with naturalistic ethnography. This near-break occurs when they challenge the restriction placed on ethnographers merely to describe the social world under study rather than to theorize systematically and explicitly one's transforming relationship to it. By refusing to accept naturalistic ethnography's distinction between description (seen as value-neutral) and theory (seen as value-laden or as the consequences of the researcher's imposition of her or his prior assumptions), they implicitly reserve a role for the ethnographer's reflexive[11] development and testing of theory as a form of "critical praxis," that is, as a way of transforming the differential power relations that exist between the researched and researcher and within the social setting itself. However, the boundaries and principles of that role remain unclear as their discussion ultimately seems to vacillate, casting the ethnographer in either a relativistic or an objectivistic position. They do little more than recognize that ethnographers are part of the social worlds they study. Beyond equating such a recognition with reflexivity, Hammersley and Atkinson's critique of naturalism gives us little purchase on the relation of ethnographers and ethnographic research practice to understanding and transforming (however modestly) the structural power relations underlying the field research.

Toward a Feminist Materialist Practice of Ethnography

Although specific critiques of naturalistic ethnography by materialists and feminist materialists, particularly within cultural studies, remain nascent and rare, far-reaching criticisms of naturalism's affinities with positivism and the ways it is predicated on the subject–object dualism can be found in the elaboration of materialist and feminist theories outside debates on naturalistic ethnography *per se*. I draw on both sets of debates to extend my own critique of naturalistic ethnography from a feminist materialist perspective. The purpose of the critique is not merely to say what feminist materialist ethnography is by way of negation, that is, by way of saying what it is *not* in its opposition to positivism; I also aim to elaborate the principles and practices that might inform the practice of feminist materialist ethnography. By comparing various feminist and materialist approaches, I will engage in neither political sectarianism nor cultural relativism. I do, however, believe that it is incumbent on critical ethnographers of all varieties to show how our prior epistemological and political assumptions about what constitutes a socially just society are linked dialectically to emancipatory research praxis.

As I have just shown, the discourse of naturalistic ethnography gives primacy to the subjective or intersubjective states of social members' accounts. Because this discourse still prizes a positivistic notion of objectivity and an atomistic view of knowledge, it renders the researcher a purportedly distant and neutral observer who merely describes the "appearances of social life." Yet as political philosopher Jaggar (1983) so persuasively argues, every method entails at least an implicit commitment to a certain theoretical understanding of the social world and to particular criteria for imperial and theoretical adequacy. And it is at this level of analysis that it becomes clear that naturalistic ethnography affirms a social world that is meant to be *gazed upon but not challenged or transformed.*

The Implications of Materialism for Ethnography

In her superb analysis of social reproduction in a New Zealand secondary school, Jones (1986) cogently summarizes a representative materialist critique of naturalistic ethnography. She quotes Rachel Sharp (1982), who maintains that

> . . . ethnography reinforces ontological and epistemological social atomism: the atoms of social life are individuals; their beliefs, intentions, assumptions and actions form both the starting point of, and dictate the explanatory procedures for grasping social reality. (Sharp, 1982:49, *in* Jones, 1986:35)

Jones draws on Sharp's theoretical critique of naturalistic ethnography to explain the theoretical and epistemological basis of her own materialist ethnography. She draws the implication from Sharp's language that ethnographers cannot afford to ignore the fact that social subjects are born into and socially constituted by "a world already made," and that "structured patterns of social relations pre-exist the individual and generate specific forms of social consciousness, . . . linguistic and, hence, cognitive possibilities that socially structure available life chances . . ." (Sharp, 1982:50). Furthermore, to get beyond the phenomenal level of analysis, ethnographers need to explain the underlying social relations that set objective limits on the "appearances" of people's practices and their accounts of the social world.

According to Jones, such an analysis would make explicit use of the crucial materialist distinction between the appearances of social life and the material conditions and social relations structuring them. This call for a method that works dialectically on the relation between the phenomenal appearances of social life and the objective nature of the social relations that structure them is a dramatic departure from naturalistic ethnography, but it is also one that enables researchers to generate and test theories in the process of doing the research. Jones concurs with the statement of sociologist E. O. Wright (1978) about the value of examining such a distinction:

> The point of the distinction between appearances and underlying reality is not to dismiss appearances, but rather to provide a basis for their explanation. The central claim [in Marxist theory] is that the vast array of empirical phenomena immediately observable in social life can only be explained if we analyze the social reality hidden behind those appearances. If we remain entirely at the level of appearances we might be able to describe social phenomena, but we cannot explain them. (p. 12)

Thus, a materialist conception of ethnography provides an explanatory theory that situates the understandings of the research subjects and the researcher within the underlying social reality (i.e., the modes and forces of material production and their relations of domination and subordination) (Sharp, 1982).

In contrast to naturalistic ethnography's assertion of value-neutrality as a criterion for theoretical and empirical adequacy, materialism makes an explicit commitment to understand and transform the various forms of subordination that exist in society (Jaggar, 1983). Rather than seeing knowledge as the construct of either the social members under study or the researcher-as-detached observer, materialism views knowledge as arising through practical social struggle to change the social world, struggle that in turn changes the human subjects themselves. Speaking very generally, because all human productive activity grows out of specific material conditions and social relations of society (namely, capitalism, patriarchy, and racial domination), social knowledge constitutes definite historical forms.

Given such a premise, it follows that doing ethnographic research entails asking several related questions that are grounded in the issues raised at the outset of this article: What are the social locations and backgrounds of the researcher and the research subjects? Whose knowledge gets articulated in the field as well as in the written account? Who benefits from the research? Is it possible within the confines of naturalistic ethnography to capture the active agency of people without ignoring or minimizing the structural determinants that set limits on people's practices and subjectivities?

These questions clearly raise a particular set of epistemological issues concerned with attempts to ground accounts of the social world in a basis that is less distorting than dominant atomistic and traditional modes of social and scientific inquiry. In this aim, materialist and feminist perspectives agree; however, materialist and feminist strategies for responding to these questions and extending the issues they raise into areas of ethnographic research practice differ in at least one way that is germane to our discussion. Broadly speaking, materialist epistemology (as reflected in the work of neo-Marxist ethnographers and sociologists of education) tends to maintain the subject–object dualism without question,[12] while feminists of various orientations have attempted to challenge the masculinist rigidity of the categorical bounds of this dualism. As Harding (1987b) argues in her edited volume *Feminism and Methodology*, if women's perspectives and knowledge claims were already legitimate within both traditional and Marxist approaches to social and scientific inquiry, then the development of specifically feminist approaches would no longer be necessary.

Hereafter, the focus in this essay will be on the implications of different feminist epistemologies for ethnographic research. The issues raised by feminist epistemologies pertain to all forms of qualitative research and inquiry in which the primary goal is the development of a self-critical stance toward the ethics and politics of the power relations between the researcher(s) and the researched in the constitution of emancipatory research praxis.

The Implications of Forms of Feminism for Ethnography

Feminists of various orientations (particularly radical and materialist) have worked to revise Marxism's gender-blind epistemology and appropriate its conceptual arguments to understand and transform women's gender-specific experiences of subordination (Barrett, 1982; Coward, 1980; Jaggar, 1983; Lather, 1986; McRobbie, 1982; Oakley,

1981; Scott, 1985; Smith, 1974; Spender, 1980). We disagree, however, as to what constitutes a feminist understanding of women's subordination. Feminists widely debate such questions as: Is a research method and theory feminist simply because it is developed by a woman or consists of women as research subjects? Are research methods and theories feminist because they raise the question of women's subordination in the context of focusing exclusively on women's experiences of it? Can it be assumed that there are enough commonalities in women's experiences across and within groupings by class, race, age, and sexual orientation to speak of a shared experience of subordination?

One position taken by some feminists implies uncritically that feminist research, methods, theories, and practice consist of any research done by women about women or with women as research subjects (Bernard, 1973; Scott, 1984; Spender, 1980). Such a position assumes that an understanding, whether it is tacit or explicit, exists among women about what feminism is or what gender interests may unite them. Insofar as it applies to interactive or qualitative research methods, it holds in common with radical feminism the assumption that women researchers and research subjects form a natural bond based on their identification with each other as women.

Although the specifics of their argument vary, researchers working within this paradigm frequently view traditional academic social science research—with its surveylike interviewing techniques; its positivistic canons for establishing rigor, validity, and truth; and its gatekeeping for publishing—as inherently masculinist and therefore objectifying of female research subjects (McRobbie, 1982; Oakley, 1981; Spender, 1980). In contrast, for example, they characterize the practice of qualitative research methods as necessarily feminist and politically egalitarian. They argue that qualitative methods encourage more democratic social relations between researchers and research subjects by employing dialogical interview strategies in which female respondents "talk back" and pose questions to a female researcher as an instance of woman-to-woman identification based on their common experiencs of motherhood, childbirth, using a "female language," and so forth (McRobbie, 1982; Oakley, 1981; Spender, 1980). They then argue that the rapport established among female researchers and their research subjects is a special and *natural one,* representing their common understanding of women's experiences. Because this position affirms the validity of women's active agency as unmediated by asymmetries in power and material conditions, it holds a naive view of the universality of women's experiences of feminine subordination and, hence, of the basis for rapport between female researchers and research subjects. This view of what makes research feminist, whether one speaks of method, theory, or practice, tends to romanticize the biological nature of the origins of rapport between women researchers and research subjects, establishing a gender essentialist argument as its basis for challenging the masculinist research methods, while still upholding naturalism.[13] It is questionable, though, whether a feminist epistemology that upholds naturalism can be linked to emancipatory research goals and praxis.

As an overreaction to the gender essentialism of the first position, as well as to the class essentialism of Marxism, some feminists articulate an admittedly minority view by asserting quite the opposite.[14] They hold that feminist research can be separated from the issue of whether it is conducted by women, about women, and/or with women. Such a position rejects the assumption that a shared interest, unity, or reality around women's experiences can be said to unite women researchers and research subjects and, hence, be presumed to constitute feminism. As feminist poststructuralist Rosalind Coward (1980) argues:

> Feminism can never be the product of the identity of women's experiences and interests—there is no such unity. Feminism must always be the alignment of women in a political movement with particular political aims and objectives. It is a grouping unified by its political interests, not by its common experiences. (p. 63)

Yet, as Barrett (1982) contends from a feminist materialist position, whatever problems may be generated by premising feminism (and, for our purposes, feminist research methods, theories, and practices) on the effort to understand and transform what is shared in women's experiences of subordination, far greater problems emerge in the attempt to separate feminism (as a political effort) from women's experiences of specific material and ideological conditions. Divorcing feminism from women's experiences of gender-specific material conditions could lead to the position that women researchers and their women research subjects experience nothing in common with regard to shared experiences of gender oppression in the process of the field research or in the attempt to construct a feminist alternative to such experiences, for example.

As an alternative to the first two positions, feminist materialists argue along the lines of Jaggar (1983) that, while there is no unified experience of feminine subordination, "a primary condition for the adequacy of a feminist theory . . . is that it should represent the world from the standpoint of women" (p. 370). By "the standpoint of women" Jaggar means uncovering the ways in which

> . . . women's perceptions of reality are distorted both by male-dominant ideology and by the male-dominated structure of everyday life. The standpoint of women, therefore, is not something that can be discovered through a survey of women's existing beliefs and attitudes. . . . Instead, the standpoint of women is discovered through a collective process of political and scientific struggle. The distinctive social experiences of women generates [sic] insights that are incompatible with men's interpretations of reality and these insights provide clues to how reality might be interpreted from the standpoint of women. The validity of these insights, however, must be tested in political struggle and developed in ways that promote the interests of women above men. (p. 371)

These remarks by Jaggar imply a tendency to universalize or disregard the plural standpoints within women's experiences of subordination. The major import of her argument, however, with which I agree, refines the concept of "the standpoint of women" in such a way as to consider the epistemological and political consequences for feminist theory and practice when the *differences* as well as commonalities in women's lives are taken into account. For Jaggar as well as for Smith (1974), Hintikka and Harding (1983), Harding (1986, 1987a,b), and Barrett (1982), the criterion that distinguishes whether or not a research method and theory is feminist is not its claim that women's experiences are homogenous or unified in a common viewpoint of subordination. Rather, research is feminist when its methods, theory, and practice draw on the differences among groups of women to theorize about what is common or different in their experiences of various forms of oppression and privilege.

Jaggar (1983) identifies both the research goals and the political praxis underlying genuinely feminist materialist methods. In fact, quite unlike the assumption of naturalistic ethnography, feminist materialist epistemology renders theory, method, and praxis inseparable from one another, especially in their aim to transform women's subordinate positions within and across dominant power relations of our cultural institutions. She argues that to develop a systematic theoretical alternative to the prevailing modes of interpreting the world:

> . . . a way must be found in which all groups of women can participate in building theory. Historically, working-class women and women of color have been excluded from intellectual work. This exclusion must be challenged. *Working class women, women of color, and other*

> *historically silenced women must be able to participate as subjects as well as objects in feminist theorizing.* . . . Within a class divided and racist society, different groups of women inevitably have unequal opportunities to speak and be heard. *For this reason, the goal that women should begin to theorize together is itself a political goal and to succeed in collective theorizing a political achievement.* Women who theorize together can work together politically; indeed, in theorizing they are already doing one kind of political work [italics added]. (pp. 386–387)

For Jaggar as well as for most feminist materialists, the test of adequacy for any research method, theory, and practice is its usefulness in developing a "scientific reconstruction of the world" from their own standpoint(s). The integration of feminism as both theory and practice comes when the "representation of reality" is tested "constantly by its usefulness in helping women transform that reality" (p. 387).

In contradistinction to naturalistic ethnography's naive and structurally unfounded realism, which does not question the constitution of existing power relations (particularly those that manifest themselves in procedural norms for observation and interviewing), the *contested realism*[15] to which feminist materialism aspires seeks to democratize the production of theory and the research process itself. The aim is action on the everyday world by women as subjects and objects of their own experiences. The test for adequacy is measured not in absolutist, atomistic, or relativistic terms, in which all competing knowledge claims can be reduced to an essential women's standpoint. Instead, the test constitutes the success of actual struggles in transforming for women "what constitutes fully human activity" (Jaggar, 1983:387), a test that has social ramifications that go well beyond the confines of any one ethnography.

Furthermore, according to Jaggar, most feminist materialists are open to the possibility that the development of theories, methods, and practice from the standpoints of women is accessible to men. In fact, the vision of social change entailed in feminist materialism encourages women to build alliances with men who actively critique patriarchal values and practices in the context of discovering how not to become dominated by them. This said, however, feminist materialists do predict that men would have less incentive for comprehending such gendered perspectives than women. They also predict that the threat to male privilege posed by women acting collectively on their own behalf would militate against such perspectives being widely accepted by or worked for among men (Jaggar, 1983).

Ethnography as Socially Transformative Praxis

If we take feminist materialist epistemology seriously, then the implications for ethnographic research practice are significant. First, within such a position, positivism in principle finds no place in establishing either the relationship of theory to data or the relationship between the researcher and the research subjects. Second, there is no role for positivism in the relationship between tests for theoretical adequacy and the political usefulness of research praxis in making social change. One implication that can be drawn from a feminist materialist epistemology is a clear statement against ethnographers depicting themselves or their research as denying their subjective experiences, or as being distinterested and neutral.[16]

Third, a genuinely feminist materialist ethnographer would attempt to show how the specific social relations and material conditions underlying the field research set limits on the access and rapport she or he could establish with particular groupings of research subjects. The ethnographer would take into account her or his own class background, race, gender, age, and sexual orientation, as well as those of the research subjects, in any account of the field research. Clearly then, a crucial task for the ethnographer is the *elaboration of the structural power relations* that formed the basis for conducting the field research and the study and not just a simple recounting of method as a set of techniques to gain rapport with people so as to have access to better data.

It is important here to give readers a sense of the practical dilemmas and contradictions I faced in the attempt to integrate practice with my feminist materialist theory in a dialectical manner during the course of the fieldwork and writing of the ethnography on which I base these theoretical insights. After spending significant amounts of time with the Punk young women (alone or in groups) in the context of observing their subcultural rituals and everyday lives in their schools and families, I was often confronted with their telling me, much as a younger sister confides to an older sister, of problems that demanded I define and voice an interested feminist materialist ethical stance. On many occasions, the young women themselves demanded that I respond to particular conditions facing them in their gender relations with the male Punks or in class relations among themselves. On these occasions, I found that it was simply impossible and politically untenable to remain a silent or passive observer. Otherwise, through my silence and obtrusiveness,I would lapse into what I call elsewhere (Roman, 1989, in press) as *voyeurism and intellectual tourism.*[17]

For example, in gender terms, middle- and working-class young women alike individually approached me with their dilemmas in dealing with such issues as unwanted pregnancies, boyfriends harassing them verbally or physically, and the intrusion of parents and school personnel into arenas of their sexual lives, which they felt were private. I was frequently consulted as a sympathetic adult friend who would listen and/or perhaps give advice on such matters as where to seek an abortion, obtain birth control, or get tested for venereal diseases. In a number of painful interviews, several of the young women spoke of histories of sexual abuse and family violence. In terms of class relations, especially during the individual interviews when middle-class Punks were not present, the working-class young women spoke angrily of their exploitation by middle-class Punks through forms of cultural appropriation of Punk styles of bodily presentation or dance, or their domestic spaces, a practice they called "crashing." Conversely, middle-class young women Punks frequently expressed jealousy of the time I spent interviewing the working-class young women, especially if one of these young women happened to be their "best girlfriend."

I mention these examples (even if only briefly) as a way of suggesting how they compose the specificity of the social relations out of which the resultant theorizing of my ethnographic research practice grew. These social relations were produced conjuncturally and therefore cannot be addressed adequately with absolutist, global, or universalizing language, which would fail to locate in the written accounts of fieldwork the researcher's interests (at the intersections of the so-called personal and public experiences) within them.

For example, in the academic written account of my fieldwork (Roman, 1987, 1989, in press), I explained why it was easier for me as a middle-class university researcher initially to gain access to and establish rapport with the middle-class Punks and their families than with the working-class Punks and their families, who more often (and rightly) viewed me as an intruder. I also described how the young women came to see me as a "big sister," "friend," or "adult intruder," while the young men treated me as a potential "groupie" to their bands, "Dear Abby" confidante, or threat to their relationships with their girlfriends. By taking such interests and social relations into account, I began to analyze critically the social functions of my attempts to establish rapport with the Punks. I had to question whether the alliances I had made (intentionally or unintentionally) reproduced or transformed forms of class exploitation and gender oppression that existed between myself and the Punks and among the Punks themselves.

This kind of reflexivity engages the researcher in confrontations over the tendencies within naturalistic ethnography to affirm the idea that ethnographers ought to present themselves to research subjects and later to their readers as having become either the fully immersed, gone-native or the fly-on-the-wall fieldworker. Similarly, many ethical dilemmas posed by the fieldwork's social relations caused me to question as well as to provide an alternative to the ethnographers' convention of presenting themselves in the written account as the absent presence, or what historian and cultural analyst Richard Johnson calls "the missing researcher" (Personal Communication, March 1982). I argued through the use of painful examples from the fieldwork that by not challenging these dominant positivistic tendencies within naturalistic ethnography—tendencies that limit the subject positions and authorial voices of ethnographers—researchers are likely to find themselves maintaining residual or creating emergent forms of domination and exploitation of the research subjects, which I (Roman, 1987, 1989, in press) earlier call *voyeurism* and *intellectual tourism*.

Given the centrality of feminist materialism's fundamental theoretical commitment to understand and transform women's (and, in other contexts, other people's) subordination, "emancipatory praxis" would play an integral role in conducting the ethnographic fieldwork and in generating and testing theory. In this regard, Lather (1986) argues, "emancipatory theory-building" (p. 262) sharply contrasts with inductive or grounded theory-building. The aim is to use feminist materialist theory in an explicitly open-ended, dialogical, and reciprocal manner with research subjects while struggling against any tendency to impose her or his theory where it is unwarranted.

Of course, there are enormous tensions here concerning what counts as "theoretical imposition" on the part of the researcher. Does any explanation offered by the researcher that disagrees with those of the research subjects constitute imposition? Clearly, as I have argued earlier, the importance of a feminist materialist analysis is its attempt to understand the structural conditions that underlie social subjects' everyday actions without resorting to a phenomenological explanation. As Lather (1986) puts it:

> How does one avoid reducing explanation to the intentions of social actors, by taking into account the deep structures—both psychological and social, conscious and unconscious—without committing the sin of theoretical imposition? (p. 262)

This tension is further connected with the underlying realization, as argued earlier, that social subjects (including the researcher) have different stakes and contradictory interests in maintaining or challenging their own or others' oppression. Any analysis that attempts to get beyond the appearances of social life to examine the historically specific and objective forms taken by oppression and power relations "therefore must be premised on a deep respect for the intellectual and political capacities of the dispossessed" (Lather, 1986:262), which does not equate contradictory subjectivity or "commonsense" with "false" or inferior consciousness.[18] This places a rigorous demand or precondition on the researcher to honor the subjectivities of and possible criticisms to be made by those women research subjects from a different class, race, culture, sexual orientation, gender, and age than that of the researcher.

Consistent with such a precondition is the commitment on the part of the researcher to allow her or his prior theoretical and political commitments to be *informed* and *transformed* by the lived experiences of the group she or he researches as well as by her or his own experiences as an ethnographer involved in the specific social relations with the research subjects. An ethnography in which theory is produced democratically—that is, as a collective effort among the researcher and the research subjects—is less likely to generate propositions that are imposed by the researcher and more likely to be responsive to the logic of evidence that does not fit the researcher's preconceptions. Unlike the process of naturalistic ethnography, an ethnography that is dialogical and aims to build theory democratically encourages the research subjects' empowerment through systematic reflection on their own situations and roles in reproducing or transforming existing power relations. Introducing this subjective element and its jointly constructed interaction into the research, in fact, increases the potential for historically specific forms of objectivity rather than objectivism, which does not disclose this evidence or the dialogue that produced it. It also decreases the possibility that theoretical imposition on the part of the researcher will occur as the result of unexamined subjectivism.

For example, in keeping with the logic of emancipatory praxis in my study (Roman, 1987, in press) I attempted to work collectively with the young women Punks, holding small group interviews and discussions, which eventually operated in a fashion similar to women's consciousness-raising groups in the building and testing of theory. I described how I encouraged the young women to give me feedback that would check my emerging hypotheses and descriptions of particular subcultural practices and rituals for unwarranted interpretations and conclusions. I provided examples in the written account where the young women's interpretations of the subculture's gender and class relations differed from or concurred with mine. Full collaboration at every stage of the research was not attempted or achieved—far from it. Yet even though successful moments of genuine democratic and collective dialogue as well as theoretical reciprocity were modest and few, I found them worthy of mention because they represented times when the young women and I knew that some of the inequalities imposed by class and by virtue of being a researcher or research subject were not as great as our efforts to struggle against them.

Theoretical and Political Adequacy

The tests for theoretical and political adequacy that ought to be applied to the ethnography can be framed in the following questions. I have sought to preserve the reference to the Punk young women as a reminder of their centrality in the process of formulating these questions, although one could imagine other or additional questions emerging in the context of racially mixed groups or groups of researchers and research subjects from different backgrounds than those participating in this study. The parenthetical remarks within the questions serve to broaden the issues raised regarding the implications of feminist materialist ethnography for ethnographic research in education. The parenthetical remarks are useful for asking how these questions may apply or could be transformed in order to be relevant to research contexts with different groups: Does the ethnography (as a research process and as an interpretive account) resonate with the Punk young women's actual lived experiences? Is the ethnography useful to the young women in terms of enabling them to comprehend systematically their experiences of feminine subordination, some of which varied by class (and with other groups could vary by race, age, or sexual orientation)? Did the process of meeting in groups (or whatever strategy developed mutually between the research subjects and the researcher to foster dialogue and democratic theory-building) lessen the structural divide between my own intellectual work (or that of other mostly middle-class researchers) and the research subjects' "commonsense"[19] ways of articulating their identities and relations of gender, class, race, age, and sexual orientation? Are my theoretical understandings and concepts accessible—that is, written in language that is neither pretentious nor condescending? Did the young women find that the written account demystifies or clarifies the underlying structural power relations that shaped their everyday experiences? Equally important, how have the young women's theoretical understandings and interpretations modified or challenged my theoretical understandings of what it meant to become Punk (or in other contexts to belong as a member of a specific social or subcultural group)? Have I taken seriously these issues, which are simultaneously methodological, ethical, and political, or have I sought refuge in the subject positions of the "voyeur" or "intellectual tourist," who watches and takes from the community of research subjects, giving little back that is of value to them?

Conclusion: The Political Significance of Other Ways of Narrating the Relationships between Cultural Selves and Others

In this essay, I have made a variety of arguments that challenge the practice of naturalistic ethnography—a discourse whose affinities with positivism reify the existing dominant social relations. I have offered a provisional feminist materialist alternative to the subject–object dualism in naturalistic ethnographic research—one that requires a radical break from conducting "ethnography as usual" by challenging the practices by which ethnographers become "intellectual tourists" and "voyeurs."

I describe this alternative as "provisional" both because it is a work in progress and because I do not view feminist materialism as a set of abstract utopian principles to be applied in an absolutist or formalistic framework removed from historically specific material and ideological conditions as well as power relations. Clearly, the ethical, political, and epistemological implications on which I base this alternative emerge out of a specific configuration of power relations—a white middle-class feminist studying white middle- and working-class Punk young women. Such a configuration is not unique to my ethnography, particularly in terms of the asymmetries of class and symmetries of gender and race generated between myself as researcher and the young women as research subjects.

But while my proposed feminist materialist alternative raises issues that may be relevant and applicable to those ethnographies involving similar configurations of class, race, and gender, its implications should not be generalized in any absolutist way to those studies that emerge from radically different ones between researchers and research subjects. Among other particulars, the feminist materialist implications one could draw from this study presume the model Sandra Harding (1987a) calls "studying down," that is, the insistence by feminist researchers on the importance of either studying ourselves reflexively as members of one or more oppressed groups by gender, class, or race or studying the standpoints of "others" whose interests are clearly subordinate to our own as class, gender, and racial subjects.

Recently, feminists have joined others in recognizing the need to examine the cultural practice, social relations, and material conditions that structure the daily experiences of more powerful groups—that is, the idea of "studying up," where the sources of social, economic, and ideological power are wielded, albeit in contradictory ways. Even in such contexts, a feminist materialist alternative to the subject–object dualism would still demand that the race, class, gender, and beliefs of the researcher be scrutinized critically on what Harding (1987a) calls the "same critical plane as the overt subject matter" of such studies. Thus, the researcher appears not as an absent presence, a removed authorial voice, but rather as an historically located social subject with specific interests and normative desires. Clearly, in the context of such studies it may be neither possible nor desirable for researchers to embrace emancipatory means and ends by engaging in the degree of reciprocal self-disclosure and democratic theory-building directly with research subjects that were the specific strategies in my own study. What constitutes emancipatory means and ends—as well as the justificatory grounds for research—would, as in all other contexts, have to be deliberated at the outset and negotiated in light of what is known about the specific configurations of power relations between research-ers and research subjects.

It is clear, however, that to produce relational studies of power across as well as within dominant and subordinate social formations, feminist materialist explanatory accounts would require carefully chosen contexts for "studying up" as well as "studying down," al-though the ethical, political, and epistemological implications of such studies would vary accordingly and could not be prescribed in advance from radically different sets of social relations and material conditions. Feminist materialist ethnographers who desire to move in the direc-tion of doing relational studies of power might draw on the recent work of sociologist Dorothy Smith (1988). Smith suggests ways in which researchers may avoid the pitfalls of particularism and methodological individualism that are usually associated with ethnographic meth-ods by moving toward a conception of "institutional ethnography" (pp. 151–179). Institutional ethnographies would attempt collaborative, parallel, and simultaneous studies of dominant and subordinate social formations within the same or related institutions in order to explain the structural rather than the merely particularistic dimensions of unequal power relations in one context of an institution or social formation.

In this essay, I have shown that while feminists have not avoided discussions of the political implications of research methods, such debates have at times oscillated between the claim that qualitative research methods such as ethnography represent an inherently feminist alternative to the masculinism of traditional social science quantitative methods (Oakley, 1981; Scott, 1984) and the more recent insistence that qualitative methods inevitably exploit research subjects (Stacey, 1988). I have offered an alternative to such polemics as well as to the defense of naturalistic specific power relations, interests, and ethical concerns. If we no longer think of ethnography as either inherently egalitarian and feminist or as an essentially reifying and masculinist method, and if we think of ethnography as historically and politically constituted in specific power relations, more promising emancipatory and socially transformative possibilities can be accomplished. Ways of narrating "otherness" and "difference" as well as the relations between cultural selves and others in ethnographic work become practices for political deconstruction, struggle, and transformation.

Notes

[1] As Harding (1986) argues, relativism is problematic for feminists because if all theories are equally justifiable, then we have little recourse to determine among them which one(s) adequately explains or represents women's activities as fully social and their gender relations with men as real and important dimensions of human history.

[2] For example, see the works of Hebdige (1979), Willis (1977), and Everhart (1983), which have been widely criticized for their unselfconscious overidentification with their white male research subjects and their failure to consider the young men's gender relationships with women and the sexual division of labor within and across the contexts of their leisure practices, waged work, schools, and family lives. For a critical analysis of the class and gender essentialism of early culturalist work, see the "Introduction" in Roman and Christian-Smith with Ellsworth (1988:1–34). In the same collection, also see McCarthy's (1988:185–203) critique of the class and racial essentialism of recent debates in neo-Marxist work on schooling and my (Roman, 1988:143–184) analysis of the Punk "slam dance" for an example of a feminist alternative to productivist, masculinist, and class essentialist accounts of subcultural rituals.

[3] Most notably, see Gallop (1985), Jardine (1985), and Spivak (1987). For feminist materialist critiques of this position, see Moi (1988) and Alcoff (1990).

[4] Six of the 12 middle-class young women reported experiencing some forms of family violence and/or sexual abuse. Four of these were sexually abused by an adult familial

intimate: two were abused by their fathers exclusively, one by both her father and mother, and another by her mother's female friend. Two others were sexually assaulted by unknown adult males outside their families. Two of the young women who experienced sexual abuse in their families were battered or witnessed battery in their families. During the fieldwork, 6 of the 12 middle-class young women attempted suicide through drug overdoses and wrist slashings. Four of these attempts involved young women who reported experiencing some form of family violence and/or sexual abuse. Four were battered or witnessed battery by their fathers, and, of these, one had also been sexually abused by a father. Two others experienced one or more incidents of sexual assault outside their families by a boyfriend and/or an adult male stranger. Other cases of abuse may not have been reported.

[5] The concept of gender here is not meant as a synonym for women as research subjects or as researchers; rather, it is meant to describe the relational categories of and meanings for masculinity and femininity. These meanings may differ within and among classes, races, and cultures, as well as among conceptual systems as ways of naming the social world—that is, the way social actors know "what" they know. Thus, to study gender in a feminist relational manner is to include the possibility that men as well as women can be the subjects of a feminist study and that male researchers can meet the requirements for producing less distorted masculinist or androcentric descriptions, explanations, and understandings of the social world. The issue of whether or not women and men have experiences that can serve as equally reliable guides in the production of undistorted social research is taken up later in the discussion on the feminist materialist standpoint position.

[6] See footnote 2.

[7] For an accessible and typical account of the ethnographer as "professional stranger," see Agar's (1980) ambivalently proscriptive discussion of the ways ethnographers attempt to handle the "strain" of negotiating across the roles of "detached involvement" from and through immersion into groups or cultures under study, or what he calls "going native" (pp. 50–51). Elsewhere, I (Roman, 1987, 1989, in press) argue that to the extent that naturalism coheres as discourse and as ideology, it does so chiefly through researchers having to negotiate ambivalently across the conflicting stances of objectivism and subjectivism—what I call, respectively, "being a fly on the wall" and "going native"—instead of having to develop alternatives to them that have democratizing ethical and political consequences for research praxis.

[8] While Hammersley and Atkinson (1983) are liberal critics of some of naturalism's affinities with positivism, they nonetheless fail to challenge the subject–object dualism within naturalism, a dualism that can also be found in the epistemology and discourse of positivism.

[9] Although *positivism* has become a term of abuse, its use for my purposes refers to what some philosophers of science have called the "received model" of natural science. This model has been influenced strongly by logical empiricist conceptions of knowledge and a hypothetico-deductive method. Such conceptions of knowledge aspire to formulate deductively related covering laws in which observations and events can be separated from their context and subsumed under such laws. Giddens' (1979) and Hollands' (1984) discussions provide illuminating histories and critiques of positivistic logic.

[10] I do not mean to suggest that all naturalistic ethnographers work to disguise their identities to research subjects or their purposes for conducting their research. Nor am I suggesting that naturalistic ethnographers never have confessional moments of subjectivity when they acknowledge in a more reflexive manner the frequency of the emotional crises and anxieties generated by their attempts to manage the ethical and political

consequences of adhering to the stances of subjectivism and objectivism that are part of the discourse of naturalism. For examples of the tensions for researchers generated by their attempts to achieve objectivist or subjectivist stances simultaneously, see Dentan (1970:104–107) and Keiser (1970:234–235); for a more critical example of a reflexive account of fieldwork by a naturalistic ethnographer, see Rabinow (1977). My point is, however, that such examples fail to challenge the subject–object dualism, which permits ethnographers to treat their "subjectivities" as incidental moments rather than as historically contextualized and interested within specific social and power relations.

[11] Ruby's (1980) provocative conceptualization of reflexivity is defined as the action of anthropologists (or researchers more generally) revealing their methodology and themselves as the "instruments of data generation." However, Ruby neglects how the plurality of voices and perspectives, particularly on the parts of research subjects, shape the generation of ethnographic data and narrative (whether or not self-consciously disclosed by ethnographers). The issue then becomes whether or not the concept should be used when researchers do not take a genuinely dialogical approach to the disclosure of such pluralities, even though they themselves may have been thoughtfully personal and autobiographic in their ethnographies.

[12] The differences between feminist and materialist theories and epistemologies on the utility and adequacy of the subject–object dualism is worthy of a paper in and of itself. In this limited space, however, it is important to note that this dualism in neo-Marxist ethnographic research takes several forms under the guise of other binary oppositions, most notably the opposition between description and analysis, which is exemplified in the bifurcation of Willis's (1977) narrative voice. The first part of the book, called "Ethnography," is arranged thematically and contains verbatim interview data and dialogue from the lads. Willis is self-consciously present only as an interlocutor who sometimes brings into their dialogue the structural and material world in which the lads' practices are situated. By marginalizing his own gender and class relation to and affinity and identification with the lads, Willis speaks through the first part as methodologist, clearly distinguishing the first part as narrative, realistic "description." Willis represents the authenticity of the lads' voices on the basis of both using verbatim extracts from interviews and by constructing these interviews as unmediated and uninterrupted by the lads' social relations with him.

The second part, labeled "Analysis," rhetorically and theoretically analyzes and expounds on the first. In this part, Willis's narrative voice sounds much more authoritative, summative, and "objective" than in the first part. While the second part refers back to the first part, it relies heavily on theorized abstractions and academic language to elaborate Willis's analysis of the lads' resistances to their schooling and capitalist social relations. The second part gains is authorial validity by referring back to and relying on the verbatim data—the data that methodologically symbolize naturalness, authorial nonselection, neutrality, and authenticity. The bifurcation in Willis's narrative voice between description and theory/analysis serves a partcular bifurcation. It masks the degree to which he participates in the lads' subculture and, hence, can claim to know and understand the very sensemaking process he describes exclusively as "theirs." It is then another form of the subject–object dualism as represented through the ethnographer's bifurcated narrative voice.

[13] By rejecting gender essentialism, I obviously do not mean to suggest that only research that theorizes about women's direct experiences of subordination is feminist. There is a danger in ignoring the social relations and constitution of male power when feminists claim that only researching the powerlessness of women can help transform women's oppression. We also need to know how men experience their positions of

power across varying class and racial formations. The incentive for men to conduct such research as it specifically relates to the constitution of their gender interests, however, is less self-vested than the interests of women in understanding their own subordination. Scott (1985) makes this point well.

[14] For critiques of this position, see Haraway (1988), who calls for embodied "situated knowledges" (p. 581), and Alcoff (1990), who argues against reductionism and political retreat by feminists taking subjectivist or relativistic positions.

[15] By the term "contested realism," I mean to acknowledge the conjunctural aspects of conflicting power relations by race, class, and gender that mediate contradictory and different experiences of subordination and privilege. I, however, also maintain that analyses of specific social relations and material conditions must eschew both voluntarism and reductionism when it comes to assessing the limits imposed on what subject positions get taken up by whom. A notion of contested realism acknowledges different experiential realities without resorting to a position of classical realism. At the same time though, it calls for an analysis of persistent forms of oppression and unequal material conditions that require us to once again reassert "the real," acknowledging its contested and diverse states as a struggle for hegemony between dominant and subordinate groups.

[16] As will become clear, this does not mean that the obverse of positivism is naive subjectivism. In my study (1987, in press), I attempt a synthesis between culturalist and structuralist interpretive approaches, using semiotics to discover the discursive codes at work in the young women's verbal and nonverbal practices. The strategy used avoids the subject–object dualism, because it takes biography and historical moments into account, attempting to locate those moments within the structurally determined limits of the discourses available to produce them.

[17] Although these are exaggerated "ideal types," I use the terms to refer to the dominant conventions proscribing roles and narrative authorial voices for ethnographers. By the concept of "voyeur," I refer to the discursive codes and cultural practices to which an ethnographer consents when she or he accepts a privileged vantage point from which she or he discloses minimally the *prior* theory she or he uses to describe, view, interpret, and frame questions in the process of representing the knowledge and meanings of the research subjects. A subject position of ethnographic voyeurism is secured both when the use-value of the research subjects' knowledge is transformed within exchange relations into the commodified pleasure (sexual or economic) of the researcher and when the group under study feels intruded upon by the researcher. The voyeur's rapport is short-lived, having been premised on the idea that the ethnographer's role is to extract the research subjects' commonsense knowledge and withdraw from the intimacy established when the research is completed.

The concept of "intellectual tourist" refers to the discursive codes and cultural practices to which an ethnographer consents when she or he conducts research as a brief excursion, foray, or sightseeing tour into "other" people's lives. Unlike the voyeur, the ethnographer as intellectual tourist may, for brief periods of time, become deeply involved in the daily lives of the research subjects so as to achieve "cultural immersion" or the status of a participant observer. Even though the intellectual tourist has worked quite arduously to establish rapport with the research subjects, she or he strains to write an account in which she or he appears as distant and disengaged. She or he recalls copious fieldnotes as "snapshot" descriptions taken on the scene of the research subjects' cultural practices. Yet in the final account, the researcher draws on dense theoretical language recognizable to those in her or his field but possibly obscure to those studied. Such language often has the effect of mystifying to the research subjects the very conditions of their lives about which the researcher theoretically aims to develop critical understanding. In either case (voyeurism or intellectual tourism), the research subjects may find the ethnographer's account of little use in grasping or transforming various inequalities they experience in their daily lives.

[18] A Gramscian understanding of commonsense knowledge and consciousness as "contradictory" avoids the empiricist trap of seeing social subjects' practices as mere reflections of material conditions in the "real world" in which they take practical action. It makes a distinction between those intellectuals who have the material resources and time to develop a more systematically theoretic view of their activities and those whose material positions of subordination do not permit such reflections. Yet the distinction is not premised upon the idea that subordinate classes or social groups necessarily are limited to less systematic understandings of the social world. As Gramsci (1971) writes referring erroneously only to men:

> The active man-in-the-mass has a practical activity, but no clear
> theoretical consciousness of his practical activity. One might say he has
> two theoretical consciousness (or one contradictory consciousness): one
> which is implicit in his activity and which in reality unites him and all
> his fellow workers in the practical transformation of the real world; and
> one which, superficially explicit or verbal, he has inherited from the
> past and uncritically absorbed. (p. 333)

[19] See footnote 18.

Acknowledgments

As always, I wish to express my appreciation to the Punk young women who participated in this study for their generous, challenging, and good-humored criticisms of my descriptions and analyses of their subculture's rituals. I also wish to acknowledge the thoughtful comments of Margaret LeCompte and Wendy Millroy on revisions of this chapter.

References

Agar, M. H. (1980). *The professional stranger: An informal introduction to ethnography*. Orlando, FL: Academic Press.

Aggleton, P. J. (1984). *Reproductive "resistance": A study of the origins and effects of youth subcultural style amongst a group of new middle class students in a college of further education*. Unpublished doctoral dissertation, University of London-King's College, London.

Alcoff, L. (1990). The problem of speaking for others. Paper presented at the Second Biennial New Feminist Scholarship Conference, State University of New York at Buffalo, March 31, 1990.

Barrett, M. (1982). Feminism and the definition of cultural politics. *In* R. Brunt and C. Rowan (Eds.), *Feminism, culture and politics* (pp. 37–58). London: Lawrence & Wishart.

Bernard, J. (1973). My four revolutions: An autobiographical history of the ASA. *American Journal of Sociology, 78*, 773–791.

Bernstein, B. (1977). *Class, codes and control: Vol. 1. Theoretical studies towards a sociology of language*. London: Macmillan.

Bhaskar, R. (1979). *The possibility of naturalism: A philosophical critique of the contemporary human sciences*. Sussex: Harvester Press.

Bhaskar, R. (1986). *Scientific realism and human emancipation*. London: Verso.

Bourdieu, P., and Passeron, J. (1977). *Reproduction in education, society, and culture*, R. Nice (Trans.). London: Sage Publications.

Bowles, S., and Gintis, H. (1976). *Schooling in capitalist America*. New York: Basic Books.

Clifford, J., and Marcus, G. E. (Eds.). (1986). *Writing culture: The poetics and politics of ethnography*. Berkeley: University of California Press.

Coward, R. (1980). This novel changes lives: Are women's novels feminist novels? A response to REbecca O'Rourke's "Summer Reading." *Feminist Review*, 5, 53–64.

Dentan, R. K. (1970). Living and working with the Semai. In G. D. Spindler (Ed.), *Being an anthropologist: Fieldwork in eleven cultures* (pp. 85–112). New York: Holt, Rinehart & Winston.

Edwards, A. D., and Furlong, V. J. (1985). Reflections on the language of teaching. In R. C. Burgess (Ed.), *Field methods in the study of education* (pp. 21–36). Lewes, UK: Falmer Press.

Everhart, R. (1983). *Reading, writing and resistance: Adolescence and the labor process in a junior high school*. London: Routledge and Kegan Paul.

Gallop, J. (1985). *The daughter's seduction: Feminism and psychoanalysis*. Ithaca, NY: Cornell University Press.

Geertz, C. (1973). Thick description: Toward an interpretive theory of culture. In C. Geertz (Ed.), *The interpretation of cultures: Selected essays by Clifford Geertz* (pp. 3–32). New York: Basic Books.

Giddens, A. (1979). *Central problems in social theory: Action, structure and contradiction in social analysis*. London: Macmillan.

Glaser, B., and Strauss, A. (1967). *The discovery of grounded theory*. New York: Aldine.

Gramsci, A. (1971). *Selections from the prison notebooks*, Q. Hoare and G. N. Smith (Trans.). New York: International Publishers.

Hammersley, M., and Atkinson, P. (1983). *Ethnography: Principles in practice*. London: Tavistock.

Haraway, D. (1988). Situated knowledges: The science question in feminism and the privilege of partial perspective. *Feminist Studies*, 14 (3), 575–599.

Harding, S. (1986). *The science question in feminism*. Ithaca, NY: Cornell University Press.

Harding, S. (1987a). Introduction: Is there a feminist method? In S. Harding (Ed.), *Feminism and methodology* (pp. 1–14). Bloomington and Indianapolis: Indiana University Press.

Harding, S. (1987b). Conclusion: Epistemological questions. In S. Harding (Ed.), *Feminism and methodology* (pp. 181–190). Bloomington and Indianapolis: Indiana University Press.

Hargreaves, D. H., Hester, S., and Mellor, R. (1975). *Deviance in classrooms*. London: Routledge and Kegan Paul.

Hebdige, D. (1979). *Subculture: The meaning of style*. London: Methuen.

Hintikka, M., and Harding, S. (Eds.). (1983). *Discovering reality: Feminist perspectives on epistemology, methodology and the philosophy of science*. Dordrecht, The Netherlands: Reidel.

Hollands, R. G. (1984). *Working for the best ethnography.* Unpublished paper. Birmingham, UK: University of Birmingham, Centre for Contemporary Cultural Studies.

Jaggar, A. (1983). *Feminist politics and human nature.* Totowa, NJ: Rowman and Allenheld.

Jardine, A. (1985). *Gynesis: Configurations of woman and modernity.* Ithaca, NY: Cornell University Press.

Jones, A. (1986). *At school I've got a chance . . . Social reproduction in a New Zealand secondary school.* Unpublished doctoral dissertation, University of Auckland, New Zealand.

Keat, R. (1971). Positivism, naturalism, and anti-naturalism in the social sciences. *Journal of Social Behavior,* 1(1), 1–17.

Keat, R., and Urry, J. (1982). *Social theory as science.* London: Routledge and Kegan Paul.

Keiser, R. L. (1970). Fieldwork among the Vice Lords of Chicago. *In* G. D. Spindler (Ed.), *Being an anthropologist: Fieldwork in eleven cultures* (pp. 220–237). New York: Holt, Rinehart & Winston.

Lather, P. (1986). Research as praxis. *Harvard Educational Review,* 56, 257–277.

Lofland, J. (1971). *Analyzing social settings.* London: Wadsworth.

Mascia-Lees, F. E., Sharpe, P., and Cohen, C. B. (1989). The postmodernist turn in anthropology: Cautions from a feminist perspective. *Signs: Journal of Women in Culture and Society,* 15(11), 7–33.

McCarthy, C. (1988). Marxist theories of education and the challenge of a cultural politics of non-synchrony. *In* L. G. Roman and L. Christian-Smith with E. Ellsworth (Eds.), *Becoming feminine: The politics of popular culture* (pp. 185–203). London: Falmer Press.

McRobbie, A. (1978). Working class girls and the culture of femininity. *In* Women's Studies Group (Ed.), *Women take issue: Aspects of women's subordination* (pp. 96–108). London: Hutchinson of London.

McRobbie, A. (1982). The politics of feminist research: Between text, talk and action. *Feminist Review,* 12 (October), 46–57.

Moi, T. (1988). Feminism, postmodernism, and style: Recent feminist criticism in the United States. *Cultural Critique,* Spring (9), 1–22.

Oakley, A. (1981). Interviewing women: A contradiction in terms. *In* H. Roberts (Ed.), *Doing feminist research* (pp. 30–61). London: Routledge and Kegan Paul.

Popkewitz, T. S. (1981). The study of schooling: Paradigms and field-based educational research and evaluation. *In* T. Popkewitz and B. Tabachnick (Eds.), *The study of schooling: Field-based methodologies in educational research and evaluation* (pp. 1–26). New York: Praeger.

Rabinow, P. (1977). *Reflections on fieldwork in Morocco.* Berkeley: University of California Press.

Reynolds, D. (1980). The naturalistic method of educational social research—A Marxist critique. *Interchange,* 4, 77–89.

Roman, L. G. (1987). *Punk femininity: The formation of young women's gender identities and class relations within the extramural curriculum of a contemporary subculture.* Unpublished doctoral dissertation, University of Wisconsin–Madison.

Roman, L. G. (1988). Intimacy, labor and class: Ideologies of feminine sexuality in the punk slam dance. *In* L. G. Roman and L. Christian-Smith with E. Ellsworth (Eds.), *Becoming feminine: The politics of popular culture* (pp. 143–184). London: Falmer Press.

Roman, L. G. (1989). Double exposure: The politics of feminist materialist ethnography. Manuscript solicited and submitted for publication. Paper also presented at the Second Biennial New Feminist Scholarship Conference, State University of New York at Buffalo, March 31, 1990.

Roman, L. G. (in press). *A tenuous sisterhood: Women in an American punk subculture.* New York: Routledge, Chapman & Hall.

Roman, L. G., and Christian-Smith, L. (1988). Introduction. *In* L. G. Roman and L. Christian-Smith with E. Ellsworth (Eds.), *Becoming feminine: The politics of popular culture.* London: Falmer Press.

Rosaldo, M. Z. (1983). Moral/analytic dilemmas posed by the intersection of feminism and social science. *In* N. Haan, P. Rabinow, and W. M. Sullivan (Eds.), *Social science as moral inquiry* (pp. 76–95). New York: Columbia University Press.

Ruby, J. (1980). Exposing yourself. Reflexivity, anthropology, and film. *Semiotica,* 30(1/2), 153–179.

Schatzman, L., and Strauss, A. L. (1973). *Field research: Strategies for a natural sociology.* New Jersey: Prentice-Hall.

Schutz, A. (1964). The stranger: An essay in social psychology. *In* A. Schutz (Ed.), *Collected papers* (Vol. 2, p. 91–105). The Hague: Martinus Nijhoff.

Scott, S. (1984). The personable and the powerful: Gender and status in sociological research. *In* C. Bell and H. Roberts (Eds.), *Social researching: Politics, problems and practice* (pp. 165–178). London: Routledge and Kegan Paul.

Scott, S. (1985). Feminist research and qualitative methods: A discussion of some of the issues. In R. Burgess (Ed.), *Issues in educational research* (pp. 27–46). Lewes, UK: Falmer Press.

Sharp, R. (1982). Self-contained ethnography or a science of phenomenal forms and inner relations. *Journal of Education,* 164, 48–63.

Sharp, R., and Green, A. (1975). *Education and social control: A study in progressive primary education.* London: Routledge and Kegan Paul.

Smith, D. (1974). Women's perspective as a radical critique of sociology. *Sociological Inquiry,* 44, 7–13.

Smith, D. (1988). *The everyday world as problematic: A feminist sociology.* Milton Keynes, UK: Open University Press.

Spender, D. (1980). *Man-made language.* London: Routledge and Kegan Paul.

Spivak, G. C. (1987). *In other worlds: Essays in cultural politics.* New York: Methuen.

Stacey, J. (1988). Can there be a feminist ethnography? *Women's Studies International Forum,* 11(1), 21–27.

Willis, P. (1977). *Learning to labor: How working class kids get working class jobs.* Westmead: Saxon House.

Willis, P. (1981). Notes on method. *In* S. Hall, D. Hobson, A. Lowe, and P. Willis (Eds.), *Culture, media, language* (pp. 88–95). London: Hutchinson.

Woods, P. (1985). Ethnography and theory construction in educational research. *In* R. C. Burgess (Ed.), *Field methods in the study of education* (pp. 51–78). Lewes, UK: Falmer Press.

Wright, E. O. (1978). *Class, crisis and the state.* London: New Left Books.

Wright, E. O. (1980a). Study of job characteristics and social attitudes: Questionnaires for employed. Institute for Social Research, University of Michigan–Ann Arbor (Summer). Survey employed in the Comparative Project on Class Structure and Consciousness.

Wright, E. O. (1980b). Varieties of Marxist conceptions of the class structure. *Politics and Society,* 9, 323–358.

PART 2

❏ Issues in the Execution
of Ethnography and
Qualitative Research

CHAPTER 13

❑ Approaching Ethical Issues for Qualitative Researchers in Education

Donna L. Deyhle, G. Alfred Hess, Jr.,
and Margaret D. LeCompte

The Handbook of Qualitative
Research in Education

Ethical Being

It is now a half century since the outbreak of World War II, which was perhaps the greatest cataclysm in recorded human history. In and around that event, the issues of morality dominated the intellectual scene. Whether in religion or science, politics or teacher preparation, people were asking great questions about the meaning of life (e.g., Frankl, 1963) and the meaning of their work (Oppenheimer, 1989). In the social sciences, which Cassell and Wax (1980) point out were originally called the "moral sciences" but are now more normally thought of as the "behavioral sciences," whole new schools of thought and discipline emerged from the experiences of the Holocaust. One of these, logotherapy, sometimes called the third school of Viennese psychoanalysis, was built explicitly on a definition of humanness in which morality was central. "Responsibility for its promulgation is the very essence of human existence" (Frankl, 1963:172f). Morality, then, could be no mere abstraction.

Writing in the midst of the European conflagration in the 1940s, Dietrich Bonhoeffer (1961) wrote:

> An ethic cannot be a book in which there is set out how everything in the world actually ought to be but unfortunately is not, and an ethicist cannot be a man who always knows better than others what is to be done and how it is to be done. An ethic cannot be a work of reference for moral action which is guaranteed to be unexceptionable, and the ethicist cannot be the competent critic and judge of every human activity . . . . Ethics and ethicists do not intervene continuously in life. They draw attention to the disturbance and interruption of life by the *shall* and the *should* which impinge on all life from its periphery. Ethics and ethicists do not wish to represent goodness as such, that is to say, as an end in itself . . . . (p. 236f)

Bonhoeffer warns us that ethical behavior is not the scrupulous observance of some code of moral acts and immoral acts. Instead, he suggests, the observance of such codes deludes us into thinking we have acted properly when we actually have avoided our responsibility. The Nuremburg war trials at the end of World War II built on this principal by rejecting the defense by Nazi subordinates that they were simply doing as they were told. Writing in the midst of those actions, Bonhoeffer suggests we cannot so easily shrug off our responsibility for life. He further suggests that living in blind adherence to such codes abstracts individuals from real living. In his opinion, the ethicist's job is ". . . to help people to learn to share in life . . . and not hold themselves aloof from the processes of life as spectators, critics, and

judges . . . in humorless hostility towards every vital force . . ."
(1961:237). His assessment of ethicists who reduce the life of professionals and other individuals to following canons of acceptable action
is ". . . in that case . . . the limits of the *ethical* are in the end so
grotesquely stretched that the last paragraph of a[n] . . . ethic must
have as its subject *morally permitted behavior* . . . [italics in origi-
nal]" (1961:237).

Bonhoeffer's words, written and edited in the shadow of a Nazi
prison cell, ask us to examine our living in larger terms than whether or
not we have followed a generally accepted code of professional behavior. In fact, they stand as a reprimand to the many who blinded themselves to the larger moral questions of their time, while they followed
the canons of scientific behavior in their daily professional lives.

The radical Christian theologian, Paul Tillich, points to the ethical
collapse encountered when confronting the rise of national socialism.

> The intellectual defense of Anglo-Saxon civilization against fascist
> ideologies is extremely weak. Common-sense philosophy and
> pragmatism are not able to provide criteria against the dynamic
> irrationalism of the new movements; and they are not able to awaken
> the moral power of resistance necessary for the maintenance of the
> humanistic values embodied in Western and Anglo-Saxon civilization.
> It is not positivism and pragmatism, but the remnants of the
> rationalistic-progressive solution of the ethical problem on which the
> future of that civilization is based. (Tillich, 1963:86)

Tillich describes the development of ethics in Western civilization
as the replacement of Catholic supranaturalist ethical absolutism by a
rational absolutism, rooted in the Enlightenment, which undergirded
the development of the bourgeois society from the seventeenth century onward. But, he asserts, the ethics of bourgeois rationalism were
not up to the challenge posed by Nazism.

> Therefore, as the Catholic system was not able to adapt itself seriously
> to the modern period of bourgeois growth, so the bourgeois-
> progressive rationalism was not able to face the breakdown of the
> bourgeois world. Supranatural and rational absolutism in ethics both
> proved to be unable to adapt themselves to a fundamental change in
> the historical situation. (Tillich, 1963:87f)

And what of qualitative researchers during the middle of the
twentieth century? Qualitative researchers who hope to find in this
chapter a list of rules for ethical research in education should be
warned now that we do not intend to provide here a list of "morally
permitted behaviors." Rather, we discuss a set of approaches that we

find useful in our own work, and we highlight the research of authors who faced some of, perhaps, the most exquisitely delicate ethical issues of current researchers in education and the social sciences.

Anthropologists, the most active of qualitative researchers in the 1940s, were concerned with the relationship between personality and culture. Their work described the cultures of natives on Pacific islands to be invaded by American forces or detailing how our Asian enemy might best be ruled, once defeated (Benedict, 1946). It is instructive to note, as Margaret Mead did, that one of the first efforts at formulating a code of ethics for qualitative researchers sprang from that experience.

> Immediately after World War II, when practically every anthropologist in the country had been active as an applied anthropologist, the Society for Applied Anthropology began to struggle with a code of ethics which was eventually passed in 1962 as the Statement of Ethics. As a member of the original committee, I took medical ethics as a provisional model, and asked about analogous requirements: What was to be the overriding value within which applied anthropologists would act, as the physician was faithful to life and the judge to the law? What were our obligations to our clients? What were our responsibilities as a profession to train and certify the fitness of our members to act as applied anthropologists? What were our obligations to one another as fellow practitioners? (Mead 1978:431)

However, Mead goes on to bemoan the fact that this effort was not ". . . embodied in any recognized set of institutional practices . . ." (Mead, 1978:431). Specifically, she decried the relaxed standards of membership for the Society for Applied Anthropology (SfAA) which carried no standard for minimal education or of responsibility within the profession. She longed for a more recognized way of anthropology becoming a profession.

> How are the overriding values of anthropology to be defined, so that an anthropologist might indeed take an oath of loyalty to them, and so that they might become the basis on which his or her loyalty could be attested by colleagues? Under the influence of the group who worked with the Harvard School of Business, the early discussions at the Society for Applied Anthropology centered on the matter of wholes. Anthropologists, we said, dealt with wholes—whole systems, whole institutions, whole societies, ultimately the whole world. Our task, in any particular case, was to define the whole within which we were working—a factory, a school system, a hospital, a political unit, an ecological unit—and then act in terms of the good of the whole. (Mead, 1978:432)

Following the lead of the SfAA, other professional associations adopted their own codes. In 1971, the Council of the American Anthropological Association (AAA) adopted a set of Principles of Professional Responsibility (last revised at the 1989 AAA Annual Meeting). Not long after the AAA's 1971 action, the American Political Science Association adopted its Rules of Conduct and the American Psychological Association approved, in 1981, its Ethical Principles of Psychologists. In the same year, the Council of the American Sociological Association approved a Code of Ethics (all of these codes are reproduced in Reynolds, 1982).

As bourgeois capitalism experiences a period of resurgence after the decades in which its values were questioned by socialists, communists, and other critical thinkers, professional researchers have once again become respected members of the social elite, supported handsomely by salaries and government grants. We believe it unfortunate that morality among professional researchers often has degenerated into a preoccupation with adopting and revising, by majority votes, codes of professional ethics that spell out for uncritical researchers what is "morally permitted behavior."

The authors of this chapter are not ethicists. We are not philosophers of science or practicing theologians. We are qualitative researchers in education, seeking an understanding for ourselves and our colleagues of how we may act ethically in the midst of doing educational research. We approach the question of ethics by grappling daily with difficult questions about what to do in concrete situations. And we find most of the codifications that reduce professional ethics into sets of "morally permitted behavior," to cite Bonhoeffer again, inadequate.

This chapter will focus on wrestling with ethical issues faced by qualitative researchers. It will try to provide some perspectives for each researcher to utilize as they face their own concrete situations. The chapter will not provide a simple list of "dos and don'ts." Neither will it seek to review the history and scope of ethical dilemmas faced in qualitative research; that task has been more thoroughly explored elsewhere (e.g., Reynolds, 1982; Rynkiewich and Spradley, 1976). However, we would be remiss if we did not provide some perspective from the field of ethics to help focus our thinking.

Ethical Theories and Their Bearing on Fieldwork

In the interest of interactive communication, we ask the reader to participate in the following multiple-choice question. Please circle the letter next to the alternative that best completes the following sentence.

Qualitative research is:

1. A means to discovering general knowledge not accessible through quantitative approaches.
2. An effective way to improve practice in a particular field (e.g., education) so that the field may benefit as many people as possible.
3. A research approach that has its own well-defined principles determining appropriate practice.
4. A method for enhancing the lives and concerns of otherwise neglected and oppressed peoples.
5. A research method that maximizes the "people-oriented" skills and capacities of a particular type of person.

We suspect that most readers would find some truth in each of the above statements; however, if the readers have been obedient to the instructions and have chosen the option that best reflects their understanding of qualitative research, they may also have indicated which of several potential ethical perspectives they will find most likely to be persuasive. We now turn to a discussion of these different ethical perspectives.

Five Ethical Theories

William F. May (1980) summarizes the relationship between ethical positions and fieldwork in his article, "The Bearing of Ethical Theories on Fieldwork." Having spent more than a year doing fieldwork on ethics and researchers' behavior at professional meetings of anthropologists and sociologists, he synthesizes ethical positions into five theories of moral behavior.

May's analysis helps qualitative researchers to understand the roots of differences within the qualitative research community about the question "What is ethical research?" Too often debates about research ethics are carried out by adherents of differing fundamental moral philosophies without acknowledging the differences in fundamental assumptions that divide the debaters. In those cases, neither side to the debate can undestand why the other holds positions that appear to them to be untenable. We present May's analysis in an effort to provide perspective as we address the more limited field of ethical issues in qualitative research in education. We make no judgments about the adequacy of May's interpretations of the various philosophers to whom he refers, nor do we claim that May would be completely happy with how we condensed his effort for this article. But even with those reservations, we think the model of five ethical perspectives he provides is very useful as a reference point for qualitative researchers grappling with ethical issues.

The Teleological Ethic

May first examines the teleological ethic, a term that he notes derives from the Greek term *teleos*, a target in archery.

> A teleological ethic orients each action or activity toward that goal or
> target which constitutes its good . . . . A teleological ethic orients
> actions to ends . . . the end of academic inquiry (ethnographic
> research included) is the truth: the discovery and transmission of
> knowledge . . . . Knowledge is a fundamental good in that it is so
> basic to the human enterprise that it does not have to be justified by
> virtue of its contribution to some other good. As the philosophers say,
> it is an *intrinsic* rather than an *instrumental* good . . . . (May,
> 1980:358)

According to May, one implication of adopting a teleological ethic is that truth is defined as an end in itself. Activists may use research findings, but research results should not be manipulated so as to better serve the ends of advocacy. May also notes the implications of seeing knowledge as a fundamental good. First, it is a good that must compete for support with other goods; this is particularly true in terms of support for research. May worried that "Researchers will become more and more vulnerable to the sweet talk of outside money" (1980:359).

Second, May argues that under a teleological ethic, ". . . the good of knowledge is not such that one can use any and all means in its pursuit." Instead, May asserts that the doctrine of the proportionality of means to ends applies to the search for knowledge. The means must be appropriate to the end sought. Therefore, because truth is the goal, deceptive means for acquiring knowledge are automatically ruled out.

The Utilitarian Ethic

Next, May turns to the utilitarian ethic, which he associates with a cost–benefit approach to determining what is ethical. He notes that utilitarians had until recently dominated ethics in the social sciences by applying as their chief test of human action an assessment of the goods or harms produced by research. "Utilitarians are result-oriented, consequentialist thinkers. They usually measure actions by their utility in producing the greatest good for the greatest number" (1980:360). May notes that the cost–benefit techniques of such an ethic closely resemble the methods of quantitative science and, thus, have an appeal to such researchers and to policymakers who equally rely on cost–benefit analyses.

May notes that utilitarians can end up on either side of substantive ethical debates. For some, covert research can be justified as producing an end that cannot be otherwise accomplished (e.g., in studying up the social scale or in examining oppression). Other utilitarians, and May cites Wax (1980) as an example, favor candor in research because it will promote the profession and will arouse fewer suspicions in those being studied. May concludes, "For all these reasons, lying gets rejected not because it is disproportional to the truth, but because it lacks utility" (1980:361).

May criticizes the utilitarian ethic for its imprecision in calculating harms and benefits. He further asserts that simple cost–benefit analyses do not adequately take into account the principle of distributive justice.

> In more complex social situations, benefits shower on some and harms on others. A mere adding up of their totals does not solve the problem of their just distribution . . . . Fieldworkers might avoid this morally dubious feature of utilitarianism by insisting that the analysis only consider the goods and harms accruing to the people studied—to keep from sacrificing them to fieldworkers' more remote philanthropic purposes or narrower careerist aims.
>
> Even so restricted, cost/benefit analysis does not solve the problem of distributive justice within a research population that includes diverse constituencies and interests. (1980:361f)

May then asks the question that qualitative researchers involved in policy-related issues regularly confront: "Whose benefit should be served?" When studying administrators, teachers, students, and parents in a local school setting or a school district, which constituency should derive the greatest benefit? Which can best tolerate suffering harm, as a result of the research? And among each constituency, which students should benefit and which can do with less? Codes of ethics that tell researchers to do nothing to harm their subjects are impotent before such questions, but a utilitarian evaluation of the benefits and harms is not enough either. One answer, May suggests, is the ". . .

principle of the greatest good for the greatest number" but even that falls short.

> Its democratic majoritarianism is a distinct improvement over an artistocratic ethic that lets kings and dukes count for more than serfs and scullery maids . . . . The principle is less successful, however, in protecting a minority when a great good can be produced for a great number but at severe cost to some who in no way participate in that good. (1980:362)

May further criticizes the utilitarian ethic for reducing categorical rules to mere items in a mechanical calculation. "Elemental principles of moral conduct—integrity, honesty, confidentiality and respect for persons—should never be reduced to mere factors in a cost/benefit equation . . . . This conviction leads to the quest for categorical imperatives" (1980:363).

The Categorical Imperative

May's third moral theory is a deontological ethic of categorical duties, which he suggests is associated in a common sense way with the issue of ethics: ". . . principles that have a categorical force irrespective of results" (1980:363). May traces the history in Western thought of duty as derived from the will of God. Kant found this conceptualization to be too parochial; in its place, he sought a universally grounded categorical imperative. ". . . Kant stated that all persons should act in such a way that the maxim (or principle) by virtue of which they act can be universalized" (1980:363). May notes that such an approach rules out self-contradictory behavior such as lying, breaches of confidence, and covert research. In this second form of the categorical imperative, May notes, focus ". . . shifts from the *form* of action to its *content:* one must always treat other persons as ends rather than means [italics in original]" (1980:363). It reinforces the sanction against lying, breaches of confidence, and covert action in that they are not only inconsistent but also disrespectful. In language reminiscent of Martin Buber's *I and Thou* (1958), May continues, "It reduces others from subjects to objects, from ends to means."

May criticizes the deontological ethic as a basis for field research on three grounds. First, because it allows for no exceptions, he suggests that it deals too lightly with consequences. He notes that Sir David Ross' (1930) distinction between absolute and *prima facie* obligations helps to deal with this problem in that exceptions are recognized but must be argued for as suspensions of the obligation. This,

May suggests, argues for peer review panels of disinterested colleagues to judge whether or not sufficient grounds are given to suspend specific obligations, such as, for example, a request to conduct covert research in a specific situation.

May's second criticism goes to the underlying individualism within which Kantian thought developed. He points out what anthropologists know well, that researchers must respect not only individuals but also communities. Because communities represent many interests, universal categorical imperatives for any given community may be difficult to uncover. Finally, May suggests, ". . . the Kantian imperative . . . concentrates on general rather than special obligations. It deals with categorical duties of one human being to another irrespective of special ties . . . the respect that one human being owes another, *qua* human being, irrespective of the historical accidents of birth, proximity, role, and shared experience" (1980:364). May sees this as leading to a minimalist ethic that ignores the special relationships between a researcher and host population that creates special obligations.

Critical Theory and Advocacy

May's fourth moral theory is built on critical theory and its application for advocacy research. By unnecessarily narrowing his focus to the positive ties between the researcher and the researched, May mistakenly suggests that advocacy research ". . . requires that the researcher make a positive contribution to the well-being of those researched and implies that this commitment take precedence over obligations to the wider community or other special communities" (1980:365). May suggests that an advocate both writes *about* and *on behalf of* his subject population. We would suggest that, while this may be true, other advocates may study and write about one subject population *on behalf of* either another population or the wider society as a whole.

May continues:

> Adversary research operates, as the term implies, chiefly within the legal model. The researcher functions as adversary to the established and the powerful who already control the media and the levers of power. Because these elites usually operate within the relatively closed world of bureaucratic authority, the researcher is under no obligation meekly to seek permission to study them. (1980:365)

May suggests that the interventionist understanding of research attacks the distinction between abstract and applied research. In such an understanding, the academician, discovering and transmitting truth, but not applying it, is simply serving the interests of those now established in power. But critical theorists hold that ". . . there is no reason why knowledge should be placed exclusively at the service of official policy-makers (in the fashion of current utilitarian practice) and not at the service of the unauthorized and the powerless" (1980:366). May worries, however, that without some independent commitment to the truth, the participant observer may vanish in the crowd of participants.

It is only after this analysis of current advocacy research practice that May turns to its theoretical basis in the Frankfurt School of Critical Philosophy. He suggests that Jurgen Habermas and his American counterparts are seeking ". . . to rehabilitate the notion of interested knowledge" (1980:366). He notes Habermas's argument against the positivists (see also Chapter 14, later in this volume) that ". . . the 'objective' knowledge of the empirical sciences is hardly interest-free" (1980:366). Instead of seeking to surmount the taint of interest, Habermas suggests there is a "critical" interest, an interest in emancipation, which should govern the social sciences.

> Thus Habermas does not seek to eliminate interest from research but rather [seeks to] engender an interest in liberation. He encourages a social research which is unapologetically and unashamedly oriented to advocacy and criticism . . . . The critical sciences are oriented to the future, rather than to the past. They are defined by anticipation rather than reminiscence. As knowledge, they interestedly press for human emancipation." (1980:366)

However, May worries that critical theory, by reacting against an impoverished notion of objective knowledge, ". . . too easily rejects a commitment to it" (1980:366). On the contrary, he feels the proper response to positivistic reductionism is to insist on deepening objective knowledge, not disdaining it. "Fully objective knowledge is obdurate; it refuses to be wholly pliable either to the controllers or the emancipators" (1980:367).

May adds one further criticism. Because society does not easily divide into the powerful and powerless, social change often contains tragic ingredients: Benefits to some are often disadvantages to others who may also be powerless. Furthermore, the host community for advocacy research probably itself is fractured into competing power groups, which often intensify with the arrival of a fieldworker. In this context, May implies, a morality built on critical theories of emancipation may not match the sophistication of the fieldworker's research methods.

Covenantal Ethics

May's own preference, which he calls covenantal ethics, has a particular attractiveness to qualitative researchers. It involves "Obligations to host societies, to the public, to students, sponsors, colleagues, and one's discipline . . ." (1980:367). Covenants characterize significant relationships between husbands and wives, professionals and clients, and researchers and their subjects.

> At the heart of a covenant is an exchange of promises, an agreement that shapes the future between two parties . . . . Since a covenantal ethic acknowledges the indebtedness of one to another, it tends to encourage a somewhat more specific set of virtues than the generalized benevolence of the utilitarians or the rectitude of the Kantians. It emphasizes gratitude, fidelity, even devotion, and care. (1980:367)

In a personal judgment, May suggests that the 1971 Principles of Professional Responsibility of the AAA moved in the direction of a covenantal ethic by acknowledging the specific obligations anthropologists incur

> . . . with colleagues, students, spouses, subjects, governments, the particular individuals and groups with whom they do their field work, and other populations and interest groups in the nations with which they work. But the statement makes clear that the researchers' paramount responsibility is to those he [sic] studies' . . . . This paramount obligation to the people studied derives from mutual personal exchanges. (1980:368)

May acknowledges that, for all its attractiveness for field researchers, a covenantal ethic does not solve all ethical problems. In particular, he notes that a covenantal ethic does not resolve the conflict of commitments many researchers face. May acknowledges that researchers simultaneously participate in numerous commitments. Thereby, he acknowledges the primary difficulty with a covenantal ethic—that, like the Kantian categorical imperative, it may too easily degenerate into individualism. The predecessor of both the categorical imperatives and covenantal ethics is rooted in the Hebraic tradition of a covenant with God. However, in lacking an initial and primary covenant with God to determine universal imperatives, it appears to us that covenantal ethics share the same drawbacks as the Kantian imperative. The constraints of covenants with those who are or were close at hand (informants, professional colleagues) may obscure obligations from covenants with those less immediate (the nation, other similar communities, other oppressed peoples, etc.).

As indicated earlier, we do not necessarily agree with all of May's characterizations of the preceding philosophical positions, and our condensation may not do justice to his argument. We clearly do not agree with many of May's judgments and criticism of the positions he has presented. But we feel that May's analysis can help qualitative researchers to understand the roots of differences within the qualitative research community about the question "What is ethical research?"

We ask readers to refer back to the question we asked at the beginning of this section. Each answer can be loosely connected to May's five ethical theories.

If you selected (1), you would adopt a teleological
    position.
If you selected (2), you would adopt a utilitarian
    position.
If you selected (3), you would adopt a deontological
    position.
If you selected (4), your ethics would be informed by
    critical theory.
If you selected (5), you would adopt a covenantal
    position.

However, readers should be cautioned that these are loose, debatable connections. Just as readers might have chosen several answers, researchers, too, might adhere to several ethical positions, depending on the issue, the context, and the participants. We turn now to ethical positions in the arena faced by qualitative researchers in education.

Special Concerns for Qualitative Research in Education

Education, as a special arena for qualitative research, presents some special concerns. Education is an integral aspect in the life of any society. It is one of the dimensions of culture that field researchers traditionally have examined when studying a community. Almost by definition, research in schools does not involve a whole culture, which Margaret Mead defined to be the interest of anthropologists. It is conceivable to consider a school system as a whole culture, but most anthropologists, we suspect, would feel somewhat uneasy disconnecting the school system from the rest of the larger society. And those of us who have worked within school systems know that our work regularly involves other societal systems: homes from which students come to school, political systems that establish the governance structures for schools, economic systems that both shape the schools and in which schools prepare students to participate, and symbol systems that control the behaviors and loyalties of students and teachers alike.

In addition, we are highly conscious that schools are only one of the institutions that work to educate young people, particularly if we restrict our attention to public elementary and secondary schools. Many other formal institutions educate the young and many informal ways teach the young how to become adults and to recreate their society for the next generation. Thus, qualitative researchers have some inherent reluctances when they focus their research activities on the field of education, reluctances that regularly push their concerns beyond their own self-delimitation of focus.

Education, as a delivery system, is unlike other fields of knowledge such as physics, or mathematics, or literature. In itself, education is not a body of knowledge. Thus, most research in the field of education, by definition, is not seeking fundamental truths, though it may involve so-called basic research when it is focused on cognition or other similar arenas. We would argue that research in education, whether quantitative or qualitative, is primarily applied research. The results of such research almost always have immediate or potential practical applications or implications.

But education may be seen in different ways by different observers. For the followers of Horace Mann and Thomas Jefferson, education was a social good that benefitted all of society. They believed that an educated citizenry was a prerequisite for a functioning democracy. Similarly, functionalists believe that in a complex urban society an institutionalized public education system is critical to the reproduction of the society for the next generation.

Others, however, look more cynically on that reproductive function. Bowles and Gintis (1976) and their followers suggest that the education system works to reproduce the current class system of our society despite the democratic rhetoric about its potential role for upward mobility. From this vantage point, it can be argued that the inequities in public schools (not to mention access to higher-quality education through private schools) are intentionally maintained by those in power to pass along to their children their current advantage.

In a somewhat similar analysis, education can be seen as a commodity whose distribution must be determined. Some will argue for the "home rule" right of individuals to purchase differing levels of education for their children, either on the open market (e.g., private schools) or through choice of a community in which to live. Others argue, with some recent success in Kentucky, Texas, and New Jersey, that education is a fundamental right of all citizens and is not to be withheld or diminished due to the happenstance of where one's parents live. Still others, particularly business leaders, argue that our nation cannot be competitive unless we more adequately educate our emerging work force.

We would suggest that the perspectives held by educational researchers about the public education system will interact with the ethical posture in which they feel most comfortable. Similarly, the understanding of qualitative research with which one most closely identifies is likely to influence the ethical perspective with which a particular researcher is most comfortable. Thus, one's view of society, perception of preferred research method, and ethical perspective are intertwined.

Ethical Preferences of Educational Researchers

Because most educational research is applied research, it is difficult for most researchers to address the questions of ethics in educational research from a teleological moral stance. It is, perhaps, for this reason that Chester Finn's (1988) (former Assistant Secretary for Educational Research and Improvement) criticism of the worthlessness of much educational research has dominated recent discussions in this field. If educational research adds little to the repository of fundamental knowledge and, furthermore, has little direct effect on practice, what is its justification? Three subsequent presidential addresses at the American Educational Research Association have sought to deflect Finn's criticism, but the underlying question remains.

As long as academic recruitment and tenure are predicated primarily on publication of new knowledge resulting from so-called basic research, professors in schools of education will be caught in a fundamental economic bind. Their positions depend on publication of basic research, but their research focus is essentially an applied field. Over the years, there have been numerous accommodations to this dilemma, including the proliferation of journals and edited volumes on educational research, which has had little direct application to the delivery of education within formal schooling systems. This was the basis of Finn's criticism, which had to be taken extremely seriously because it was made by the government official responsible for providing much of the funding for such research. Given this situation, it is not surprising to us that many academics, seeking to enhance their contribution to the academy of scholars, are attracted to a teleological ethic, which sees the advancement of knowledge as a good in and of itself.

However, we suspect that many more academics, and other educational researchers in nonacademic jobs, are attracted to the utilitarian ethic. Much educational research is focused on the question "How can we improve the delivery of educational services to children?" A variant upon that question is "How can we make schools better places in which to work and to learn?" We will return to examine the differences between these questions a bit later, but both questions are very compatible with a cost–benefit ethical approach, both for the researcher and for the administrator deciding whether or not to authorize or cooperate with proposed research.

Administrators regularly must ask themselves whether or not the proposed research will have such a great potential benefit that it is worth the disruption to the school that will result from conducting it. At the American Educational Research Association's 1990 Annual Meeting in Boston, a whole session was devoted to this question. On the panel was an assistant superintendent in charge of research in a suburban Boston school district whose paper focused on giving graduate students advice about how to address exactly this question (Baker, 1990). In this context, it is obvious that research designs that minimize disruption and promise direct benefit to the individuals (i.e., students, teachers, staff), schools, and administrators involved most easily pass the cost–benefit administrative decison-making process. Those that are most disruptive and have the most potential for causing real problems, particularly political problems, for the administration have the least chance of passing this screen regardless of their perceived value in enhancing knowledge. Teleological concerns about the ultimate increase of knowledge may be acknowledged but are unlikely to have much effect if the potential for disruption of the school or the system is high. If the cost–benefit analysis is essentially neutral, some administrators might be willing to tip the decision toward allowing the research on the principle that the pursuit of new knowledge is a good that should be encouraged if all else is equal. In other words, if the utilitarian ethical analysis does not result in a negative determination, then the teleological ethic may have some sway.

Of course, such situations immediately raise the question of cost to whom and benefit to whom. Most ethical codes seem focused to protect subjects of research from bearing the costs of research in which the academic researchers derive all of the benefits, a virtually unarguable defense of the relatively powerless from the self-serving academically powerful. However, in most educational research, the costs and benefits are usually distributed among the various subject populations.

In some research designs, all of the cost may be to students and teachers in the classroom and all of the benefit to the administrators (e.g., in evaluating a program installed by administrators but not well liked by teachers and students). Of more concern are those projects with potentially large benefit to students but with resulting high costs for teachers and administrators, such as research to determine and make public accurate drop-out rates for a school district (Hess and Lauber, 1985; Deyhle, 1989; LeCompte and Goebel, 1987). The potential problems for administrators making such information public, thereby attracting public criticism of the administration, make it unlikely such research will be authorized unless the administrators are facing other costs that might be even higher if they do not try to assess and address the problem. In either case, a utilitarian ethic is much more likely to be employed by the administrator faced with such a question and more likely to be appealed to by the hopeful researcher than by a teleological ethic, which says this piece of information should be pursued for its own end.

Unfortunately, in the resurgent bourgeois society of the late twentieth century, some educational researchers are simply glad to have a relatively high-status job (e.g., professor in a university, researcher for the government or a school system), doing work that is not too onerous and making a comfortable living. For such comfortable researchers, the primary concern is to avoid stepping over some irrevocable moral line. For those persons, and for new entrants into the field of educational research, a set of categorical guidelines of what is and what is not ethical research is very attractive. Such persons seek the assurance of knowing that what they did was not prohibited under existing laws or guidelines. Some such persons have little commitment to the ultimate results of their research ("I don't care what my dissertation subject is, just give me a problem I can attack with an ANOVA so I can get my degree."). They do not anticipate any significant benefit from their research, except to themselves for having completed the dissertation at a cost that is not too high and with procedures sufficiently correct to avoid undermining their own efforts. Their focus is not on *being* ethical but, rather, on *not doing* something immoral. For such persons, a categorical ethic is particularly attractive. Others with more altruistic motives but a low tolerance for ethical uncertainty also prefer a clear cut set of *dos and don'ts*.

For reformers, who are deeply offended by persistent social evil that they feel "called" to address, critical theory provides a philosophical rationale that frees them from attacks by positivists, gives them a reason to surmount unfavorable cost–benefit analyses, and justifies their transgressions of majoritarian codes of acceptable behavior. They focus on the ways school systems abuse and oppress students, from the high numbers of push outs in the inner city to the rote learning approaches that do not encourage critical thinking in some of the better suburban schools. Many reformers are quite willing for administrators and teachers to pay any price to correct these evils. How to emancipate those whom they perceive to be the beneficiaries of their research dominates their thinking, colors their opinions of administrators, teachers, and support staff, and undergirds their resolve to push forward despite personal cost. An emancipatory ethic pervades their life, probably well beyond their research activities.

For researchers, particularly qualitative researchers, who highly value the interactions they have with participants in their research, a covenantal ethic is especially appealing. While this ethic would justify the extremes of "going native" (though the validity of such research might then be called into question), it is also an attractive position for those who emphasize a collaborationist advocacy strategy or for those enamored of the practitioner–researcher (teacher as researcher) model. The temptation that those adopting a covenantal ethic have is to shut out the larger world. However, some would suggest they thereby ignore covenants with others beyond their immediate participants. The cost of covenantal ethics may be higher than many researchers anticipate on initial entry to the field, because covenants cannot be presumed to end upon departure from the field. Covenants, by their very nature, usually are not time-bound.

We do not pretend that these brief vignettes are either comprehensive or exhaustive. However, it is obvious that researchers with differing life agendas will vary in the degree to which they find each of these moral theories attractive. More significantly, individual researchers may find these various ethics attractive in different situations and may appeal to more than one ethical base in consideration of any one situation. There are arenas of overlap with each of these moral theories. Still, we believe that as educational researchers examine their own lives, they will find that one of these ethical frameworks characteristically dominates their work.

For these reasons, we do not expect that there will be general agreement on ethical stances appropriate for many specific dilemmas. We are not sure that there is a way to resolve differences of perspective that derive from fundamental choices of ethical paradigms. As Kuhn (1970) observes, persons in different paradigms frequently talk past each other. However, we suggest that if researchers are aware of the differing ethical options available, they may better understand each other's positions, even if they disagree with them.

Special Issues for Qualitative Researchers

A distinction is often made between the differences in ethical issues faced by "basic" and "applied" researchers. We agree with William Bevan that this distinction is spurious. In the first place,

> To be preoccupied with the primacy of pure, as contrasted to applied, science is to reify a specious distinction, for science is, in its most fundamental sense, only an approach to solving problems—an approach based on logic tempered by experience—and its goals may be both specific and general, concrete and abstract, practical and theoretical, and immediate and long-range. Indeed, history has taught that fundamental knowledge often emerges in the course of attempting to solve practical problems. (Bevan, 1972:990)

Traditional ethnographic research has been seen by some as "basic" in nature; the researcher attempts (with varying degrees of success) to intrude as little as possible into the culture of the subject group in the process of gathering information about human life. The research purpose is to add to scientific knowledge. The goal is to develop an understanding of the "world" as it is experienced by its various "natives," whether they be located on an isolated Pacific island, on a North American Indian reservation, in a city jail, or in a school classroom. The "laboratory" is to remain as untouched as possible. Reports are published in societies far distant in both geography and time from the research site and have little impact on the studied peoples. To the extent that the ethnographer can maintain a neutral role in basic research, ethical considerations may be minimal. If this position were accurate, major ethical dilemmas would be faced only by applied researchers who necessarily cannot maintain neutrality.

As should be obvious by now, we argue that such distinctions between basic and applied research are false and delude the positivist researcher who seeks to maintain them into an illusory ethical security. Ethical issues are serious considerations for all qualitative researchers. They range from assessing the real impact of the researchers' presence on their subject population (both for methodological veracity and for sociological and psychological impact) to examining the nature of the relationships that result from their research effort.

In contrast to the practice common a century ago, few ethnographers today go into communities merely with a descriptive intent. Today, few indigenous peoples will tolerate being studied without extracting promises of some tangible benefit. Instead, people being researched seek help from researchers in addressing specific social, political, and economic problems. These concerns include overpopulation, juvenile delinquency, crime, drug use, poverty, war, political and educational oppression, the uneven distribution of wealth, racism, and prejudice. Increasingly, at the end of the twentieth century, these are the research topics of qualitative researchers. To undertake this effort, researchers have moved into the corporate board room, courts, schools, jails, and inner-city communities in complex societies. As the focus of research moves from small isolated traditional societies, both the purposes and clients of research have changed. Practicing anthropologists and sociologists, and applied educational researchers, enter the research site with a different conception of their role and task from that of the positivist, basic researcher; they come as self-conscious intervenors and problem-solvers. As we have suggested, such an approach presents particular ethical concerns for the qualitative researcher.

Ethical Issues in Early Fieldwork

Formal fieldwork by anthropologists began in the late nineteenth century. Prior to this time, historical, or "long-distance," research was the norm. With the beginning of formal fieldwork came the issue of dealing with roles and relationships as anthropologists met the "natives" on their own grounds. As Evans-Pritchard put it:

> It is indeed surprising that, with the exception of Morgan's study of the Iroquois, not a single anthropologist conducted field studies till the end of the nineteenth century. It is even more remarkable that it does not seem to have occurred to them that a writer on anthropological topics might at least have a look, if only a glimpse, at one or two specimens of what he spent his life writing about. William James tells us that when he asked Sir James Frazer about natives he had known, Frazer exclaimed, "But Heaven forbid!" [Evans-Pritchard (1951) 1964:71f; Evans-Pritchard credits Benedict, 1948:587, with this anecdote]

Developing an insider's perspective is the basic presupposition of most qualitative research. Seeking that insider's perspective, as May has suggested, gives particular significance to interpersonal ethical issues. As ethnographers came into contact with the groups they were studying, their role as an "outsider" trying to become an "insider" created unique ethical problems. Issues such as reciprocity, exploitation, paternalism, colonialism, and deception came to the consciousness of researchers. As early as 1919, Franz Boaz, in a letter to *The Nation*, challenged the deception of anthropologists who really were acting as spies for the United States government. He wrote, "The point against which I wish to enter a vigorous protest is that a number of men [anthropologists] . . . have prostituted science by using it as a cover for their activities as spies." For his stand against covert research activities, he was censured by the AAA, removed from the governing Council, threatened with expulsion from the Association itself, and pressured into resigning from the National Research Council. Their action exemplifies a majoritarian determination of ethics. Today, the condemnation of clandestine political research, as well as taking positions on other social and ethical issues, has become a major focus of attention in the Association.

Ethical and policy issues are often intertwined in the social sciences. Since 1946, anthropologists have struggled with many of these issues, starting with a resolution to study the effect of the use of atomic energy, the dangers of its use, and the promises it offered. A sampling of other AAA resolutions over the last 40 years shows the variety of the Association's concerns:

- A 1952 resolution to investigate the nature of what was then the stated policy of the Bureau of Indian Affairs to "disrupt" Indian cultures.
- A 1962 resolution that reaffirmed that no scientific evidence existed to support contentions that blacks were biologically and mentally inferior to whites.
- Two 1967 resolutions, one the need to end the armament race in the interest of future survival of the human race and another calling for anthropologists to support peaceful settlement of the Vietnam war.
- 1970 resolutions that covered land rights of Native Alaskans, U.S. weapons use in Latin America, sexual discrimination, secret or classified research, and the confidentiality of informants and communities studied.

The Nature of Relationships in Qualitative Research

> Yet I soon recognized I was being *too* careful, to the degree that some students found me somewhat disinteresting. I reflected on the problem and realized I was being too distant and aloof and not enough of a friend; consequently, some of the students perceived me as just a trifle "square." After all, how long could I go along replying "darn it" when the groups whose way of life I was attempting to become a part of used "barracks" language? . . . Therein, I decided, lay my problem: I was not human enough! (Everhart, 1977:8)

A paradoxical tension exists between the different roles field-workers assume conducting research in other cultures or societies. At the same time that one is trying to "get inside" and be a part of the group studied, there is a concurrent pull to remain "objective" and maintain a perspective as an outsider. The two extremes of the roles are those of the "friend" and the "stranger." The anthropologist starts fieldwork as a stranger and seeks to balance friendships earned during the course of the research with activities designed to gain from those friends an understanding of those studied. Tension emerges from the effort required to balance these roles. Hortense Powdermaker (1966) said of fieldwork:

> Its practice is both an art and a science. Involvement is necessary to understand the psychological realities of a culture, that is, its meanings for the indigenous members. Detachment is necessary to construct the abstract reality; a network of social relations including the rules and how they function—not necessarily real to the people studied. (p. 9)

Unique ethical considerations are inherent in designing a qualitative study because the success of such research is based on the development of special kinds of relationships between researchers and informants. Almost all site-level ethical questons in qualitative research center on variations of this theme. Two of the foremost are how researchers structure their relationships with those they study and the ways in which they gain information and disclose it. While these problems hold for all social science researchers, they are particularly relevant to qualitative researchers. Anthropologists, sociologists, fieldworkers, and even some ecological and clinical psychologists must take fieldwork relationships very seriously, for both methodological and ethical reasons. Successful qualitative research almost always mandates the establishment of a network of competent informants, who also may become special friends.

Like most friendships, relationships with fieldwork participants are far more complex than those with survey or questionnaire respondents or experimental subjects with whom interaction is limited and constrained by both time and the positivistic restrictions of scientific controls on subjectivity. Like most friendships, which they frequently become, traditional fieldwork relationships are of long duration; they mandate patterns of nurturing, caring, and reciprocity; and they permit and necessitate deeper personal disclosure on the part of both researcher and researched than is the case in other forms of research. The risks and rewards are great. The level of shared knowledge and the sense of responsibility felt by researcher and participants is high. Traditional ethnographers simply cannot do their work adequately without such relationships.

Some trainers of ethnographers even feel that without a people-oriented "ethnographic personality" one is not a good fieldworker. Others, however, would point to the personal journals of archetypal ethnographers such as Bronislaw Malinowski to indicate that good fieldwork may not necessarily require mutual friendship.

The early stages of traditional fieldwork may be quite agonizing. The fieldworker frequently experiences loneliness and alienation, because "no one will talk to me." But the personal agony is compounded by the professional frustration of not being able to accomplish his or her job. In a study of Navajo and Ute youth, Deyhle (1986) wrote about the process of developing friendships with one group of break dancers. She had been a month in her field site with very few "serious" conversations with Indian youth outside of school. A group of Indian students were practicing break dancing on an open cardboard box in the dirt across the street from her house. After sharing side glances for over an hour, they cautiously came to the edge of the porch. "We saw you at school. In Mr. Brown's class. They say you want to talk to us Indians" (1986:114). After several hours of talk about break dancing, favorite movies, personal "horror" stories, other students, school, and clothing, the topic moved to "cool" breaker pants—black zippered parachute pants. Admitting she owned a pair, which were passed around for verification of authenticity, Deyhle was pressed to wear them to school. Deyhle (1986) continued:

> I begged off (concerned about the school administration's response to their resident anthropologist dressed as a breaker), used the hot weather as an excuse, and for the next two weeks faced the daily question, "When are you going to wear your breaker pants?" By Halloween I had become close to this group of students and was invited to join them for a planned event. "We are going to all dress as

breakers and show those whites. Wear your breaker pants. And take your camera; we will be out there—to show the whites." I did. The teachers and administrators didn't notice. The Indian students were visibly pleased and told me, "You look cool, just like us." For the next four months the awareness of my pants surfaced in conversations with other Indian students. I moved from "stranger" to "friend" as Indian students sought me out in school and at home to talk about friends, enemies, school, or to just pass time between social engagements. (p. 115).

In stepping over the boundary separating observer from participant, the researcher is rewarded with a deeper understanding of those they have come to learn about. However, by "marking" oneself as a member of a particular group, the researcher perhaps forfeits access to "opposing" groups. This is not an unfamiliar problem in qualitative research (Agar, 1980; Cusick, 1973; Wax, 1971).

But the step across the boundary poses an ethical issue as well. What did joining the students mean for Deyhle's covenants with teachers and administrators? The fact that they did not notice, nor considered her action important, did not mean it had no effect on her relationships with school and district staff members. Ultimately, Deyhle was forced to take sides between the students and the administrators. Was the outcome of that decision predestined in crossing this boundary?

Boundary Spanning: Friendships between Opposing Groups

In moving toward an understanding of the people they study, ethnographers seek some form of friendship from individuals in the group they are studying. Often these friendships are with different, even opposing, groups. Goetz and LeCompte (1984) (using the term "boundary spanning" as first used by Schensul, Schensul, Gonzales, and Caro, 1981) explain this issue. "Boundary spanning in some sense is similar to cultural brokering, insofar as ethnographers often act as intermediaries or go-betweens for several groups each of whose actions or motivations need to be explained to the other" (p. 99). Tension exists when friendship leads to a stance of advocacy between opposing groups.

The anthropological literature is replete with descriptions of relationships with one group or individual affecting friendships with other groups during fieldwork and affecting the quality of the data itself (Wax, 1971; Briggs, 1970; Turnbull, 1972; Everhart, 1977; Deyhle,

1986; Agar, 1980). In traditional ethnographies, the anthropologist frequently "chose" one family or individual through which to develop an understanding of much of the culture. Powerful or powerless families, political or religious leaders, Westernized or traditional families—each painted different pictures of "reality" for the anthropologist. Conflict often resulted as the anthropologist tried to move between these different groups. The ability to transcend intragroup segmentation is important for the completeness of the portrayal of the studied community. However, it creates ethical considerations for researchers as they anticipate differing impacts of their research on each separate group.

Applied researchers in complex modern settings experience the same conflicts. Different goals and agendas often exist between students, parents, teachers, school administrators, police, politicians, street people, the poor and the rich. Because the researcher is often the only relatively nonaligned person in a setting, he or she may be the recipient of all sorts of confidences from warring factions. In one day of fieldwork, for example, LeCompte interviewed one teacher whom the principal subsequently revealed was about to be fired. She then was told by the superintendent that the issue of how she handled the firing would be critical in the principal's evaluations. She also was told by another distraught teacher about child-care problems and an ailing spouse that were impeding her participation in after school required meetings. With feminist sympathies aroused, LeCompte was about to mention the teacher's problem to the principal when the principal informed her not only that she had real ethical problems about being told to fire the first teacher, but also that the other teacher with child-care problems was a chronic whiner in need of professional disciplinary action. LeCompte felt that each of the parties—teachers, principals, and central office staff—saw her as a sounding board and possible intervenor in their plight. Yet, each had asked her to view the information as confidential. Being the repository of so many secrets often makes comfortable interaction difficult. Often, it is up to the fieldworker to mediate among these groups somehow during the course of the research.

Everhart wrote that in the process of attaching himself to the "jocks" in the junior high school he was studying, he accepted "his" group's ridiculing of another student group, the "brains." Given his interest in all groups, he could not seek identification with only one student group. His attempt at boundary spanning was aided by a student who explained the researcher's interest in spending time with "those weirdos," "Because, you dummy, we're not the only ones in this school. He has to understand how everybody thinks and what they do—even the weirdos like Robin" (Everhart, 1977:6).

As the role of the fieldworker shifts from that of a stranger to friend, qualitatively different data is obtained. When in the field for an extended period of time, the most effective role for an ethnographer often is as an informant's friend. In discussing how the historic role of ethnographers within the cultures or groups they studied has been critical to the scientific merit of a study, Goetz and LeCompte (1984) reported,

> Ethnographers shared houses, raised their children, became ill, and
> had emotional crises around the people they studied. To the extent
> that they became a part of the community and had the same
> experiences as natives did, the quality of their data was improved.
> (p. 94)

The intimate interactions of researchers and researched have repercussions and ethical problems for both the fieldworker and his or her informants and community. A heavy burden is placed on the researcher to expose his or her true "person," to function as a solver of local problems, to express personal opinions, to act less like a "passive researcher," and to function as a direct connection between opposing groups. On the other side, an equally heavy burden is placed on those in the community who choose to befriend and assist the researcher in the gathering of information and insight into local political, economic, and social situations.

The laboratory that qualitative researchers view and seek to understand is alive with human beings who are themselves trying to define and redefine their roles as mothers, fathers, sons, daughters, and members of various social and cultural groups. For the researcher, gaining a clear and deep understanding of these behaviors means moving on stage with the actors. To remain a "stranger" or an observer of the actors only results in gaining a picture of their "costumes and makeup" rather than an understanding of the meaning behind their actions. Maintaining an "objective" role stance enhances the pretense that one's own actions have not affected the participants or actors.

Our own experiences belie this argument. We would argue that the researcher who does not acknowledge the effects of his or her presence on the community being studied is not aware of the realities of the drama unfolding around him or her. Embedded in this drama are ethical issues the researcher must face.

In the remainder of this chapter we will examine these ethical issues, noting that as fieldwork progresses, like a widening net, these problems encompass increasingly larger and more politically volatile concerns.

Assuming a Fake Persona: False Personal Knowledge

Because the anthropologist or qualitative fieldworker is the key data collection instrument, impression management (how one presents oneself) or "posturing" is critical to types of relationships formed in the field. How and as whom does one present oneself in the field? Is it ethical to pretend to be something you are not to

1. gain knowledge you otherwise would not be able to get,
2. gain access to a site from which you otherwise would be banned, or
3. preserve access to a site whose accessibility has become endangered?

The answer to this question, faced by every qualitative researcher, may vary, depending on the ethical perspective adopted and the aim of the intended research. In most cases, the answer is "No." Teleologists, most utilitarians, categoricalists, and covenantors would find that deception on the part of the researcher is inappropriate, although for different reasons. Teleologists cite the inappropriateness of the means to the end sought; utilitarians refer to the long-range damage to the discipline; categoricalists believe deception violates the doctrines of informed consent; and covenantors hold that it is disrespectful of one's research subjects. Researchers with these ethical perspectives refer to Humphreys' (1970) study of homosexuals in public toilets, *The Tea Room Trade,* as a classic example of a study executed in an ethically questionable manner. Humphreys posed as a "Watch Queen," someone who keeps a lookout at the toilet door for police or others considered undesirable by the male homosexuals under study. He clearly would not have been able to obtain the data he got without this cover. He engaged in clear deception and obtained data that could greatly harm his subjects without their consent. However, some utilitarians could argue that the risk was worth the result. Some reformers might argue that, without the knowledge he was able to build up, the rights of this persecuted minority would have been continually abused, and their emancipation indefinitely delayed.

A different example is Peshkin's study of a school in a fundamentalist religious community (Peshkin, 1986). Peshkin, who is a practicing Jew, negotiated with the community's leaders for over a year before they would grant him permission to enter their community for a study without joining the group. Rather than hide his religious affiliation, which would have made access easier in the short run, Peshkin was able to use it as a basis for fruitful negotiation and discussion with community gatekeepers, maintaining his integrity and theirs, as well as gaining useful knowledge about the constraints under which both researcher and those studied operated (Peshkin, personal communication).

More subtle than whether or not to present a false persona is the question of which "you" do you present at the field site? Each researcher is a different person, depending on the relationships in which he or she is participating. A father is quite different from a husband; a graduate student in class is quite different from the teacher he or she may actually be in a fourth-grade classroom. In the research site, researchers may reveal information about these other roles but are unlikely to play them out in the field. In many situations, which roles are revealed may significantly affect the research undertaken. The most commonly faced ethical decisions about role presentation by the researcher are probably not about presenting a false persona, but whether or not and, if so, which of a researcher's multiple roles he or she shares at the field site.

A further issue is raised by the prospect of qualitative research, which involves no participation. Experimental schools frequently are built with one-way glass observation rooms. Often those rooms are used for prospective teachers to observe the actions of a master teacher or to monitor the progress of particular pedagogical innovations, without intruding on that teacher's interactions with his or her class. In these cases, where judgments are made without the knowledge or participation of those being observed, are all such "deceptive" efforts unethical? Are any of them ethical?

Exchange of Information about the Study: Can the Truth Hurt?

Because traditional ethnographers must interact with the participants of their study for long periods of time and are present in the field so that participants can get in touch with them frequently, they are subjected to a constant barrage of questions about the purpose, design, and consequences of their activities. Ethical dilemmas arise with regard to the amount of information that researchers feel they can or should give out without unduly biasing the information provided by informants. Agar (1980:56) found, for example, that the degree to which people would talk with him about narcotics use depended on the extent to which they believed he was just another employee of the Narcotics Addiction Control Commission. When he altered his approach to emphasize the research task and its confidentiality, people were more receptive. Thus, from a utilitarian perspective, a truthful approach that focused on his researcher's role, rather than his federal employee's role produced greater benefits.

The question always arises, "If people really know I am studying them, will they tell me what I need to know?" It is tempting not to disclose the purposes of one's research, especially when doing so might work to shut off communication because the topic under investigation involves secret, shameful, or privileged information. From the utilitarian perspective, the danger in avoiding full disclosure is that the researcher frequently gets caught, if not during the study, then afterward when the results are published. In the first instance, researchers are no more adept at keeping up a front than are their informants; the longevity in the field during traditional ethnography that overcomes contrived behavior on the part of the informants also mitigates against deceptive behavior by the researcher.

However, in shorter studies or in more controlled field sites, a utilitarian approach might justify lack of full disclosure about the study. Similarly, where research participants are oppressed, critical theorists might argue that partial disclosure, while uncomfortable for the researcher, might be necessary to uncover the information necessary to emancipate those suffering from current oppressive conditions.

The issue of how much to "release" and to whom is complicated by the multiple "voices" or subjects encountered by educational researchers working in complex communities. When the school district where Deyhle (1987) was working decided to apply for a federal "At Risk" grant, they pressed her into releasing the drop-out data she had compiled on Navajo youth from the past 10 years. With her data showing a 50% drop-out rate, a strong case could be made about the need for the grant. Several teachers urged her not to cooperate with the district. The district already had been under court order since 1974 to build additional high schools on the reservation so Navajo students would not have up to 4-hour bus rides to the existing schools located off the reservation and to provide a bilingual–bicultural program for all of its students. While the high schools were built, the bilingual–bicultural curriculum plan remained on a library shelf gathering dust. These teachers argued the existing power structure would use the grant for Anglo employment and exclude any Navajo involvement. However, working from an ethic of advocacy, Deyhle helped the district write the drop-out prevention grant.

The grant was funded for almost $300,000 over a 2-year period, and the teachers' prediction came true. Deyhle watched the"dividing of the spoils" from the grant exactly in accordance with the existing sociocultural biases of the community. Anglo Mormon males assumed all administrative positions. Counselor positions, required by the grant to be bilingual, were filled with Anglo locals; it was argued that "qualified Navajo" could not be found. The few Navajo who filled the home school liaison positions were all members of the Mormon church. This happened despite the fact that the local population to be served by the grant were non-Mormon Navajo. The conflict between these groups of Navajo was strong. Control of the grant represents, or is a reproduction of, the larger religious, political, and racial problems among groups in this county. While the grant was awarded to alleviate conditions among the powerless, it remained controlled by the powerful as a means of enforcing Navajo assimilation.

Although the school district was "granted" federal funds because of its poor record of achievement with Navajo youth, they publicly refused to believe that the 50% drop-out rate reported by Deyhle in the grant proposal was accurate. Claiming she did not"know the kids," school officials instead reported to the State Education Agency a drop-out rate less than 10%. At this point, the local Navajo decided to use the higher drop-out rates to their own advantage: to prove discrimination in the schools and demand educational equity for their youth. The Justice Department is now using Deyhle's study in its investigations of the school district.

LeCompte (1985; Borman and LeCompte, 1986) has noted that as fieldwork progresses, like a widening net, these ethical problems encompass increasingly larger and more politically volatile concerns. Or as McDermott and Gospodinoff (1981) remind us, the politics of everyday life in the classroom will be identical to the politics of everyday life outside of the classroom. In the case of Deyhle's study, different groups benefitted differently by using her research results. The powerful colonized and coopted the grant. Now the powerless are using the data to support their struggles. From the advocacy position of critical theory, critique and transformation are goals of research. But what "voice" does the qualitative researcher listen to in complex communities? What does "transformation" mean when one group's core religious beliefs require the transformation of the other group against their

will? Ethically, what does "taking sides" mean in educational research? And whose side should the researcher take?

Reciprocity

The successful fieldworker will work hard to cultivate the special
friendships of informants and trusted participants. Reciprocity is critical at this stage; initially it involves an exchange of visits; later it may
become an exchange of services, material goods, access to prestige,
mutual confidences, and interdependencies. One of the most important commodities exchanged involves the sharing of mutually beneficial bits of information.

Fieldworkers, from whatever discipline, are frequently people
who are better educated than their participants, especially if the participants are from societies with less advanced technologies. Fieldworkers have access to facts and techniques not possessed by their
informants. Nonetheless, informants possess information that is critical to researchers on many levels. It is not uncommon in underdeveloped areas for the researcher, with his or her medical kit, to
become an informal and often unwilling barefoot doctor. McCurdy
(1976) was unable to refuse aid to his villagers, given that the problems
and services required were relatively minor—ointments, transportation to the hospital, and first-aid advice. The difficulty for the researcher was that visits by the sick to his home came to occupy all of
every morning, greatly interfering with time for fieldwork. He was able
to arrange for his chief informant to perform some "medical" duties,
enhancing the native's credibility among the villagers and allowing
McCurdy to continue his work. Similarly, LeCompte (1969, 1974,
1978) routinely helped her teacher subjects find materials, evaluation
studies, and bibliographies from university libraries that were inaccessible to them. Borman (1979), whose research was conducted among
urban Appalachian children and their families, resulted in her use of
the perspective she acquired to become an officer of an advocacy group
in Cincinnati, Ohio—the Urban Appalachian Council. An opposite
reciprocity is exemplified by the case of a European naturalist in Brazil
who was poisoned by touching a toad whose venomous properties he
did not recognize. He was treated successfully by a Txcumarrae tribal shaman after all attempts to use European medicine had proven
ineffective (Riding, 1986). Closer to home, LeCompte's current research on school restructuring has been facilitated by data collection
surveys and questionnaires developed by the principal whose school
she is studying. Deeming them as good as any she could devise, she

obtained his permission to incorporate them into her own survey instruments.

Each side in the research enterprise benefits from the exchange of information and services but the level of reciprocity must be negotiated with each person and group. This gives rise to an inescapable ethical issue: How much *should* be given? Frequently the question becomes, how much *can* be given before the researcher's own North American notions of equity and fairness are violated and the researcher feels the demands have become too large for what has been given in return. At that point, the researcher may feel he or she is being used. However, the exchange may be equally unsettling for the host community, operating from a completely different set of cultural mores about appropriate levels of exchange. Especially in cross-cultural settings where definitions vary, the issue of reciprocity inevitably becomes a stumbling block for Western researchers.

In educational research sites with multiple participants or clients, the issue of reciprocity is more complex. Deyhle (1987) reported her attempts as she worked with conflicting groups of Navajo, Ute and Mormon Anglos, adolescents and their parents and teachers, and the school district and the Navajo Nation. She taught university courses for the district's teachers and designed a drop-out study to assist the school district in determining who was leaving school and why. When tax time came, she became the tax preparer for the local Navajo. She also helped with college application forms, translated notes from the schools, helped repair broken cars, transported students home to the reservation when buses were missed, and worked as a spokesperson between the Navajo parent organization and the school district. Conflicting groups, however, interpreted and were affected by her efforts differently. The school district felt she was on "their" side because of the teacher training attempts. The Navajo community, on the other hand, saw the teaching training efforts as evidence she supported the Navajo parents' concerns over poorly trained and racially prejudiced teachers. Similarly, LeCompte, who worked as an "in-house" evaluator for a large urban school district, wore "many hats," including that of administrator, methodological expert, negotiator, and often hatchetman! She saw to it that teachers and other participants received summaries of the evaluation reports for which they had been subjects. She assisted teachers in developing and funding innovative curricular projects; participated in a study of voter behavior, which resulted in sufficient redrawing of electoral districts to elect the first Hispanic member to the school board; served as an advocate for teachers, administrators, and staff whose programs had been unsuccessful because needed supplies or funding failed to arrive; and helped staff members to achieve public recognition of their research through publication and presentation at professional meetings. She and her evaluation staff also often were deployed by the superintendent to meetings when he wished to emphasize the gravity of topics; if "research" was there, the matters under consideration *must* be important (LeCompte, 1985)!

In other educational contexts, the issue of reciprocity can be somewhat different. For example, frequently, those controlling the field site have more power regarding access and permitted behavior than does the researcher. In these situations, as compared with traditional ethnographic field sites, the power balance is reversed. Yet even then, because the researcher is usually involved in some initiatory activity and in some intrusive behavior, the issues of reciprocity are important.

In 1988, the Illinois General Assembly adopted legislation mandating the creation of Local School Councils at every Chicago public school. These councils were to have real governance authority over the school's instructional program, budget, and selection/removal of the principal. The Chicago Panel, under Hess' direction, set out to monitor the implementation of these councils through a participant observational study of 12 schools (Hess and Easton, 1991; cf. also Hess, Wells, Prindle, Kaplan, and Liffman, 1986). Several schools were interested but wanted to know what was in it for them. The Panel was able to focus another study surveying past high school graduates on four of the sample schools, with the promise of making the survey results available to the council for their own planning purposes. The Panel also promised to hire current students to make the anticipated follow-up calls on those who had not returned their surveys. In this way, the Panel created a formal exchange, symbolic of other less formal exchanges that were sure to transpire, in negotiating entrance to the field site.

In other situations, more tangible exchanges may be required. When the Panel set out to interview 85 young mothers in a study of the effects of teen pregnancy on dropping out, a more direct approach was required. Youth workers who provided clients to be interviewed required as a virtual condition of access, that the Panel pay each interviewee a $5 stipend for their time (Hess, Green, Stapleton, and Reyes, 1988).

What are the ethical questions involved in such exchanges? Is "bought" information different from "given" or "volunteered" information? Is the information from either of these contexts different from that derived from involuntarily observed behavior? Do the differing exchanges involved in securing information create different obligations in the use of that information? Adhering to different ethical perspectives might lead to different answers to each of these questions.

Exploitation: The Effect of the Researcher on the Host Community

Because they possess more power in the form of access to desired exchangeable goods, researchers usually can define what constitutes a fair exchange on the basis of their own cultural values. Almost always, in traditional ethnography, the researcher gets more from the study than do the subjects. At some point in all fieldwork, these one-sided decisions begin to seem unfair, onerous, and even unethical to sensitive researchers.

As we have indicated, McCurdy resolved the medical issue in a way that, by his account, was felt to be fair by everyone. By contrast, Richard Lee, trying to pay back his Bushman informants and tribes people by giving them a huge Christmas feast, exceeded, and therefore violated, Bushman norms regarding sharing, generosity, and humility (Lee, 1969). By one ethical analysis, the issue involves the point at which people, otherwise defined as friends and associates, begin to feel exploited or embarrassed. At what point do the participants feel they are not being respected (Kantian) or begin to stop being cooperative (utilitarian)?

And what if the researcher's very presence results in conflict within the community? Even when the researcher has been sensitive in the host community, unforeseen repercussions can be harmful to individual community members. Such was the case with Deyhle's study of a Navajo community and schools. First, the young children from the family she was living with were pressured overtly. At the swimming hole and at ceremonies they were teased by other Navajo. "What are you doing with the *bilagáana* [Navajo term for 'white person']? Is she your wife? Do you love her? Why are you not with Navajos? Are you a white person?" (Deyhle, 1987:11). For the adults in the family, a more serious incident illustrated the "danger" families from a community face when accepting an outside researcher. Deyhle was invited to attend a 3-day healing ceremony with a family responsible for transporting the ceremonial drum and prayer sticks to the dance. Because their 1957 Chevy was not running, the family, along with the sacred objects, food, and blankets, filled her Honda station wagon. After the first night, on a part of the reservation in which both the family and Deyhle were strangers, unfriendly eyes followed their unloading of the car. After several hours, conscious of the discomfort her presence was causing the sick person's family and wanting to avoid any embarrassment for her friends, she left the ceremony. Several days later she again saw the family and asked how the last night of the ceremony had gone. She was told several youths had tried to set fire to the hooghan in which the ceremony had taken place and that the police had to be called to remove two Navajo who were drunk. The mother related, "It was bad. The fights and then the water drum broke, the one that was in your car. And then that man [relative of the patient] said the drum should not have been in your car. It was not traditional. I told him that was not true. You did not touch the drum so it was all right." She seemed unconcerned and the conversation moved to sheep shearing. A month later Deyhle found out, from the youngest daughter, that the situation was not "all right." Because of pressure from relatives, the family had to have a medicine man perform a 1-night ceremony to avoid "bad luck" because of the broken drum and to allay the suspicion that its cause was connected to her presence. It was clear that the presence of an outside researcher affected this Navajo family's "normal life"—positively in some situations, painfully in others. Within formal educational settings, the very presence of researchers causes conflict and suspicion, whether they are outsiders such as Hess and his associates or district employees such as LeCompte and her staff. Researchers can tell people "what they do not want to hear" (McDade, 1985); that information in the hands of administrative authorities or the courts can put reputations, jobs, and even whole programs in jeopardy.

Saying Goodbye

An anthropologist has failed unless, when he says goodbye to the natives there is on both sides the sorrow of parting. [Evans-Pritchard (1951) 1964:77–79]

Almost as many researchers have written about the problems of leaving the field as have written about the problems in gaining access (see e.g., Bowen, 1954; Powdermaker, 1966; Wax, 1971). This is because, having spent a great deal of time getting to know people intensively and having established mutual dependencies, the anthropologist feels ethically responsible for the fate of the people who depend on him or her. This responsibility may extend only so far as mourning the loss of companionship or status associated with knowing the researcher, but it may also encompass an economic void such as the loss of jobs, services, and goods provided by the researcher. For one

African village, LeCompte's departure meant cessation of the twice-monthly mail plane, which was arranged by the government primarily to keep the American in touch with the world, but probably also to keep an eye on her activities. It also meant the loss of a job for her housekeeper who subsequently had to migrate away from her extended family network to the capital city to find work. It meant the closing of the night school, because LeCompte's kerosene lamp, which illuminated it, broke and could not be replaced. Similarly after determining how to limit his medical activities to protect his fieldwork time, McCurdy's second concern about his role as the village barefoot doctor was how to continue these badly needed services after he had gone. Is it moral, or even practical, for the researcher to leave people stranded who have become dependent on his or her assistance?

Qualitative educational researchers working in the United States face a slightly different twist when saying "Goodbye" to the people they have "researched." In many cases, they live in the same town or within driving distance. Leaving might mean finishing the study, but the demands and needs of people do not stop with the completion of the research study. Although Deyhle lives 350 miles from her research site, she feels she never has really "left." Requests for curriculum and teacher training, visits from Navajo families, and discussion with Legal Aid lawyers occur monthly. Poems and letters are exchanged with young women seeking advice on topics as wide-ranging as birth control and college admission. Several runaways have shown up on her doorstep. One teenage mother came to the city with a hospitalized baby. She stayed 6 weeks. When reflecting on her continued involvement, Deyhle sometimes admits to feeling annoyed, tired, used, and angry, "I remember thinking, this is my own separate life here. The fieldwork belongs down there!" Qualitative researchers deal with people and their total lives—a research design that comes with responsibilities.

Ethical Issues during the Postfieldwork Phase of Analysis and Publication

Assuring Confidentiality

The successful fieldworker, having established a network of good friendships with informants in the field, will gain access to all sorts of confidences, trusted and privileged information, secrets, and observations of unguarded behavior. As a consequence of these activities, all necessary to the execution of a legitimate qualitative study, researchers sooner or later will be faced with the uncomfortable realization that their friendships have not been untainted. In addition to establishing intimacy, they have become voyeurs (Hansen, 1976; see also Chapter 12, earlier in this volume). A critical ethical issue is raised at this point: What is to be done with very sensitive data, especially when informants may not want it reported, when it may identify them in ways that could harm or embarrass them, or when the data, although interesting, may not be of critical importance to the study?

Qualitative research brings one into close and prolonged proximity with the people they study. Anonymity in the research site is impossible and unwanted. For even the most casual contacts, the researcher must keep a running case record of who people are, their occupations, places of residence, kin and friendship ties and affiliations. This material can be damaging if used by persons wishing harm to the group. Protecting the anonymity of informants whose disclosures have been quite detailed or of individuals identifiable by their specialized roles or idiosyncratic behavior becomes extremely difficult. Names can be changed, but that does not always disguise the individuals. In fact, a determined investigator could almost always discover who had worked with the resident fieldworker. Even the informed consent forms required by committees for the protection of human subjects can be used to identify individuals in a study, because participation is indicated by their signatures on the forms.

On the other hand, researchers may have discovered information about the unjust treatment of members of the studied population, which, if published, could lead to significant alternatives in the life of the studied community. How do researchers assess their ethical responsibilities in such cases? Teleologists may feel the information itself is its own justification: that others should have access to what the researcher now knows. Utilitarians may weigh the benefits of revelation against the costs to various members of the society. Categoricalists might examine codes of ethics related to the discovery context. Critical theorists might assess the effects of publication on the most oppressed. Covenantalists may focus on the rupture of relationships with the informants. Each might come to a somewhat different conclusion.

Changing Topics in Midstream Despite Prior Agreements

Qualitative research frequently uncovers previously unforeseen research questions that must be explored to accomplish the intended research. Recursive analytic strategies frequently cause changes in direction of and questions addressed in the typical ethnographic research report. During the ongoing process of investigation, new questions are formulated and initial ones may be found inadequate, erroneous, or nonsensical, given feedback from the field (see Goetz and LeCompte, 1984). While this cyclical process of analysis and interpretation of data may disturb positivist experimental researchers, it is a defining characteristic of much qualitative research and is construed as a means for improving the validity of a study. However, it is not a rationale for engaging in unethical practices such as avoiding disclosure or engaging in a research equivalent of "bait and switch" scams. But the practical setting often leaves the researcher in a situation that appears to have practiced exactly that sort of deception.

In 1986, the Chicago Panel set out to study differences in high schools that might explain why some schools had higher drop-out rates than did others who enrolled similar students (Hess *et al.*, 1986; Hess, Wells, Prindle, Kaplan, and Liffman, 1987). The study was a matched pairs, ethnographic study in eight Chicago high schools, designed to replicate previous efforts in the effective schools literature. Hess and his colleagues were looking for school-level variables that would explain differences between more effective schools and those that were less effective. However, in the course of the 16 weeks of observations in the schools by four ethnographers, interviewing students, teachers, and administrators, doing detailed observations in a sample of classrooms, and general observation in the public areas of the schools, it became evident that a number of factors, common to all eight schools, contributed to generally higher city drop-out rates. The final report included both the between-school distinguishing variables (effectiveness of principal, orderly discipline, more active teaching in the classroom, and more interactive teaching) and the contributing factors common to all eight schools (reduced instructional day through excessive use of study halls, lower weekly minutes of instruction in all subjects due to shorter class period, existence of a culture of cutting, and, in a number of schools, student sanctions against success). When the report was issued, even though it had been thoroughly discussed with the Deputy Superintendent and the Superintendent for High Schools and the General Superintendent had had a draft of it for a month without response, the administration was embarrassed and publicly accused the research team of improperly shifting the focus of the study and of "trashing the Chicago schools" (*Chicago Tribune*, December 8, 1986). Did the research team act ethically in reporting the negative data applied to all schools rather than just a few?

From a teleological perspective, the study did produce knowledge about the drop-out problem in Chicago high schools, its explicit aim. The knowledge was the direct result of the means adopted to secure the knowledge, a recursive research strategy built on participant observation in eight schools. This knowledge was not limited to differences between schools, the primary focus of the original research design.

From a utilitarian perspective, the release of the data common to all schools was likely to benefit many more individuals (Chicago high schools enroll, in four grades, about 100,000 students each year) than it would impinge on (a few administrators and about 5000 high school teachers). Furthermore, the benefits might derive to generations of high school students, not just those currently enrolled. On the cost side, however, was the likelihood that future cooperative research with this school administration was endangered.

From the perspective of the categorical imperative, making available information that pointed to some root causes of the drop-out problem seemed to be an obviously universalizable action. Secondly, the staffs of the individual high schools and the key administrators were given drafts of the study for review far in advance of its publication, and none commented negatively on the inclusion of the material common to all schools, although several were concerned about figuring out what to do about these problems. Thus, it can be argued, the individuals involved were all treated with respect.

From an emancipatory perspective, the study revealed the systematic short changing of Chicago high school students; they were being denied the same exposure to instructional opportunities, which their suburban counterparts were routinely receiving. This was not just appropriate research; it was mandatory. And, in fact, this study played an important role in the eventual decision of the state legislature to enact a systemwide school reform plan 2 years later.

From the covenantal perspective, however, the researchers encountered a more troubling situation. They had interviewed 20 students in each school, but they had also interviewed 20 teachers and observed in half of those teachers' classes and in the classes of another 10 teachers. They had built up informal relationships with both students and teachers. Most teachers were convinced their students could not sit still for a 50-minute period. While the researchers were convinced the teachers were wrong and were simply "blaming the victim" in a typical example of how low expectations by professionals become a self-fulfilling prophecy, many students, on the other hand, participated in a culture of cutting impeded by racial intimidation the progress of students seeking to be successful in school ("You trying to be like Whitey?"). Deciding how to act in light of their obligations and covenants with different teachers and students was troubling to the research team.

We present this situation to point out that, from different perspectives, different ethical conclusions can be reached, depending on the ethical perspective adopted and the vantage point of those making the assessment. There was some uneasiness within the research team itself. The General Superintendent clearly thought the team had acted unethically. Because most of the research team, and clearly the sponsoring agency of the research, operated from a critical theoretical approach and were dedicated to the effort to improve the educational prospects for Chicago high school students who were then suffering from a 43% drop-out rate, there really was little choice but to release the study, which the team entitled, *"Where's Room 185?" How Schools Can Reduce Their Dropout Problem.* By so naming it, the team recognized it would focus public attention on the phantom study halls used in most of the schools to shortchange their students, thereby focussing on the very heart of the ethical issue, the expansion of the study to common findings.

Searching for Rival Hypotheses

Qualitative data are always held up to the charge that they only constitute the single opinion of a subjective observer. As a counter argument, ethical treatment of the data requires that the researcher be scrupulously honest in seeking out negative cases, discrepant cases, and alternative explanations of phenomena. Survey rsearchers and experimentalist who use probabilistic sampling techniques assume that their design procedures assure inclusion of potentially negative cases in the populations they study. Qualitative researchers are honorbound to seek out anomalous cases, explain how this was done, and report results.

Thus, ethical questions include the thoroughness of the methodology employed by qualitative researchers. Because their sampling techniques usually do not lend themselves to generalizability, there is an obligation, some would argue, to secure and present as objective a data base as possible. In fact, in many situations, qualitative researchers can utilize appropriate sampling techniques to assure the presence in their data of negative cases. So, in the study reported above, *Where's Room 185?*, the research team drew its sample of students and teachers to be interviewed and/or observed from a stratified random sample of all students and teachers in each school. Still, some advocacy groups might argue that the emancipatory case is so critical that it is appropriate simply to portray the evil being studied so graphically that people will be forced to act. However, enhancement of knowledge is slighted at the point where such an approach may lead to the suppression of relevant disconfirming information, compilation of an inaccurate portrayal of the real-life situation of those whose plight is being described, or where all the alternatives available to address that plight are ignored. In such cases, we would agree with May, that the critical theoretical perspective suffers when it is disconnected from objective knowledge to highlight interested knowledge.

Ethics during the Years After

The problem of ethical relationships with participants in the field often does not end after the publication of the monograph or the series of articles related to the research. As traditional ethnographic informants have become more sophisticated, or become graduate students themselves and, ultimately, colleagues, they have begun to talk back and ask pointed questions about the nature of the fieldwork done in their cultures. They have questioned the validity of data gathered and have contested the interpretations generated by nonnative researchers (Said, 1978). They also have questioned the sensitivity of relationships maintained with "their" anthropologist. In 1984, the AAA hosted a symposium in which rueful anthropologists discussed with their informants their respective roles over time. Mentor, parent, friend, subject, child, sibling, scholarly colleague were analogues used to describe the delicacy of such relations and how fraught they were with a need for sensitivity to the exercise of ethical behavior.

In addition to redefining the ongoing and changed relationships with people who once were informants, anthropologists also may have to attend to later demands made by former informants and their families. Many researchers talk of simple requests such as hospitality during visits, requests for materials, medicines and supplies, and books. LeCompte, for example, received a preemptory request 3 years after leaving the site for a 4-year supply of antipsychotic drugs for an informant's schizophrenic uncle. Harrell-Bond (1976) speaks of entertaining her Liberian friends when they came to visit in England. Sometimes, however, the demands are more onerous and resemble those made on members of an extended family. A son of LeCompte's tribal family showed up in New York City, expecting LeCompte to put him through college. Or, as was recently documented in the *Anthropology*

Newsletter (November 1985), one can be asked to perform the same custodial duties for aging and disoriented "adoptive" parents as are other native members of the family. The ethical issue is, given what one has gained from the long-gone relations in the field, how can one refuse to help? In the case of the care of aging parents, the fieldworker in question did set aside her fieldwork goals, endangering her status with the agency that funded her, and spent a summer pinch-hitting for the absent "adopted" sisters and cousins. As a happy consequence, her relationship to the community deepened and subsequent fieldwork was much more fruitful. In LeCompte's situation, the son was assisted in finding admission to and financial aid from a university appropriate to his interests.

In educational research, it is not uncommon for researchers to maintain ongoing efforts in the same research site over a series of years, with school staffs as active participants in the research effort. It is also not uncommon for those same individuals to interact in the university context as professor and student. Similarly, the same individuals may relate as consultant and contractor. The multiplicity of relationships among the same individuals could be described as incestuous. The ethical issues raised by the multiplicity of overlapping roles can be quite confusing. From a utilitarian perspective, it all might be seen as quite cost-effective. From an emancipatory perspective, on the other hand, it might all be seen as quite self-serving on the researcher's part.

Conclusion

Ethical issues, as Bonhoeffer suggests, are not the initial focus of qualitative research in education. Few empirical researchers state that their purpose for being in schools to do "ethical research." Rather, people begin doing research in schools or other educational contexts and discover they are forced to make decisions that require ethical choices. Frequently, such choices are not seen as ethical choices at the time. They look like practical decisions about what to do next, either methodologically or strategically. Only later, upon reflection, do they appear to have been ethical choices.

In this chapter, we have tried to bring the *shall* and the *should* from the periphery of research life and apply them to the practical issues encountered in doing qualitative research in general and qualitative research in education in particular. We do not claim to have examined every situation that the qualitative researcher might encounter. We have tried to highlight some fairly frequently encountered situations, to focus on the ethical issues involved in them, and to try to provide some perspective for both the neophyte and the experienced researcher to reflect on these situations.

Only the advocate of a categorical imperative perspective of ethics, consumed with formulating ethical codes that he or she can then seek to impose on other practitioners, would presume to tell others which decision in each situation is ethical or unethical. We believe that to codify ethical decisions for others in this way turns the search for an ethical way of being into a mundane list of moral or immoral acts. It reduces the fullness of human living. Instead, we believe that ethics in qualitative research in education is not an issue one faces when he or she goes into a field site but, rather, is a reflection of the entire way in which one lives his or her life. One is not suddenly faced with ethical decisions when one goes into the field. He or she is faced with behaving in an ethical manner at every moment; doing qualitative research in the field simply creates specialized situations with more extensive ramifications that must be examined. We have sought, in this chapter, to bring the *shall* and the *should* to bear upon some of these situations.

References

Agar, M. (1980) *The professional stranger: An informal introduction to ethnography.* New York: Academic Press.

American Anthropology Association. (1985). *Code of ethics.*

Baker, G. (1990). Evaluation and the middle sized school system: Conditions of cooperation with out-of-school organizations. Unpublished paper presented at the Annual Meeting of the American Educational Research Association by the Assistant Superintendent of the Acton (Mass.) Public Schools, April.

Benedict, R. (1946). *The chrysanthemum and the sword.* Boston: Houghton Mifflin.

Benedict, R. (1948). Anthropology and the humanities. *American Anthropologist, 50(4),* pt. 1, 583–593.

Bevan, W. (1972). Welfare of science in and era of change. *Science,* 176(June 2), 990.

Boaz, F. (1919). Scientists as spies. *The Nation,* 109, 797.

Bonhoeffer, D. (1961) *Ethics.* New York: The Macmillan Company.

Borman, K. M. (1979). Children's situational competence: Two studies. *In* O. Garnica and M. L. King (Eds.), *Language, children and society,* (pp. 81–113). Oxford: Pergamon.

Borman, K. M., and LeCompte, M. D. (1986). Qualification and why it doesn't work. Paper presented at the American Educational Research Association, San Francisco.

Borman, K. M., and Meuninghoff, E. (1983). Lower price hill's children: Family, school and neighborhood. *In* A. Batteau (Ed.), *Appalachia and America,* (pp. 210–226). Lexington: University Press of Kentucky.

Borman, K. M., Lippincott, N., and Matey, C. M. (1979). Family and classroom central in an urban Appalachian neighborhood. *Educational and Urban Society,* 11(1), 61–86.

Bowen, E. S. (Pseudonym). (1954). *Return to laughter.* New York: Harper and Brothers.

Bowles, S., and Gintis, H. (1976). *Schooling in capitalist America.* New York: Basic Books.

Briggs, J. (1970). *Never in anger.* Cambridge: Harvard University Press.

Buber, M. (1958). *I and thou*. New York: Charles Scribner's Sons.

Cassell, J., and Wax, M. L. (1980). Editorial introduction: Toward a moral science of human beings. *Social Problems*, 27(3), February, pp. 259–264.

Cusick, P. (1973). *The egalitarian ideal and the American high school*. New York: Longman.

Deyhle, D. (1987). *The role of the applied educational anthropologist: Between schools and the Navajo nation*. Paper presented at the Society for Applied Anthropology annual meetings, Oaxaca, Mexico.

Deyhle, D. (1986). Break dancing and breaking out: Anglos, Utes, and Navajos in a border reservation high school. *Anthropology and Education Quarterly*, 17, 111–127.

Deyhle, D. (1989). Pushouts and pullouts: Navajo and Ute school leavers. *Journal of Navajo Education*, VI(2), 36–51.

Evans-Pritchard, E. E. (1951). *Social anthropology*. London: Cohen & West. (Reprinted with additional essays as *Social anthropology and other essays*. New York: Free Press of Glencoe. Paperback edition, 1964, FP90987.)

Everhart, R. B. (1977). Between stranger and friend: Some consequences of "long term" fieldwork in schools. *American Educational Research Journal*, 14(1), 1–15.

Finn, C. (1988). What ails education research? *Educational Researcher*, 71(1), 5–8.

Frankl, V. (1963). *Man's search for meaning*. New York: Washington Square Press.

Goetz, J. P., and LeCompte, M. D. (1984). *Ethnography and qualitative design in educational research*. New York: Academic Press.

Hansen, J. F. (1976). The anthropologist in the field: Scientist, friend and voyeur. *In* M. A. Rynkiewich and J. P. Spradley (Eds.), *Ethics and anthropology: Dilemmas in fieldwork* (pp. 123–154). New York: John Wiley and Sons.

Harrell-Bond, B. (1976). Studying elites: Some special problems. *In* M. A. Rynkiewich and J. P. Spradley (Eds.), *Ethics and anthropology: Dilemmas in fieldwork* (pp. 110–122). New York: John Wiley and Sons.

Hess, G. A., Jr., and Easton, J. Q. (1991). Monitoring the implementation of radical rhetoric: Restructuring the Chicago public schools. *In* N. P. Greenman and K. M. Borman (Eds.), *Changing schools: Recapturing the past or inventing the future?* Norwood, NJ: Ablex (in press).

Hess, G. A., Jr., and Lauber, D. (1985). *Dropouts from the Chicago public schools*. Chicago: Chicago Panel on Public School Policy and Finance.

Hess, G. A., Jr., Wells, E., Prindle, C., Kaplan, B., and Liffman, P. (1986). *"Where's room 185?" How schools can reduce their dropout problem*. Chicago: Chicago Panel on Public School Policy and Finance.

Hess, G. A., Jr., Wells, E., Prindle, C., Kaplan, B., and Liffman, P. (1987). Where's room 185? How schools can reduce their dropout problem. *Education and Urban Society*, 19(3), May, 330–355.

Hess, G. A., Jr., Green, D. O, Stapleton, A. E., and Reyes, O. (1988). *Invisibly pregnant: Teenage mothers and the Chicago public schools*. Chicago: Chicago Panel on Public School Policy and Finance.

Humphreys, L. (1970). *The tearoom trade*. Chicago: Aldine.

Jackson, P. W. (1990). The functions of educational research. Presidential Address delivered to the Annual Meeting of the American Educational Research Association, Boston, April.

Kuhn, T. S. (1970). *The structure of scientific revolutions*. Chicago: The University of Chicago Press.

LeCompte, M. D. (1969). *The dilemmas of inner city school reform: The Woodlawn experimental school project*. Unpublished M.A. thesis, University of Chicago.

LeCompte, M. D. (1974). Styles and the development of student work norms. Unpublished Ph.D. dissertation, University of Chicago.

LeCompte, M. D. (1978). Learning to work: The hidden curriculum of the classroom. *Anthropology and Education Quarterly*, 9, 22–37.

LeCompte, M. D. (1985). Wearing many hats: A culture conflict model for survival in applied research settings. Paper presented at the annual meeting of the American Anthropological Association, Washington, D.C., December.

LeCompte, M. D., and Goebel, S. D. (1987). Can bad data produce good program planning? An analysis of record keeping on school dropouts. *Education and Urban Society*, 19(3), May, pp. 250–268.

Lee, R. B. (1969). Eating Christmas in the Kalahari. *Natural History, A Naturalist at Large*, 78(10), 14–22, 60–63.

May, W. F. (1980). Doing ethics: The bearing of ethical theories on fieldwork. *Social Problems*, 27(3), February, 358–370.

McCurdy, D. W. (1976). The medicine man. *In* M. A. Rynkiewich and J. P. Spradley (Eds.), *Ethics and anthropology: Dilemmas in fieldwork* (pp. 4–16). New York: John Wiley and Sons.

McDade, L. M. (1985). Telling them what they do not want to know. Paper presented at the American Anthropological Association meetings.

McDermott, R. P., and Gospodinoff, K. (1981). Social contexts for ethnic borders and school failure. *In* H. Trueba, G. Guthrie, and K. Au (Eds.), *Culture and the bilingual classroom*. London: Newbury House.

Mead, M. (1978). The evolving ethics of applied anthropology. *In* E. M. Eddy and W. L. Partridge, *Applied anthropology in America* (pp. 425–437). New York: Columbia University.

Oppenheimer, J. R. (1989). *Atom and void: Essays on science and community*. Princeton, NJ: Princeton University Press.

Peshkin, A. (1986). *God's choice*. Chicago: University of Chicago Press.

Powdermaker, H. (1966). *Stranger and friend: The way of an anthropologist*. New York: W. W. Norton and Company, Inc.

Reynolds, P. D. (1982). *Ethics and social science research*. Englewood Cliffs, NJ: Prentice-Hall.

Riding, A. (1986). Shaman and the dying scientist: A Brazilian morality tale. *New York Times*, February 4, p. A2.

Ross, Sir D. (1930). *The right and the good*. Oxford: Oxford University Press.

Rynkiewich, M. A., and Spradley, J. P. (1976). *Ethics and anthropology: Dilemmas in fieldwork*. New York: John Wiley & Sons.

Said, E. (1978). *Orientalism*. New York: Pantheon.

Schensul, J. J., Schensul, S. L., Gonzales, M., and Caro, E. (1981). Community-based research and approaches to social change; the case of the Hispanic health council. *The Generation*, 12(2), 13–26.

Tillich, P. (1963). *Morality and beyond*. New York: Harper & Row.

Turnbull, C. M. (1972). *The mountain people*. New York: Simon and Schuster.

Wax, M. L. (1980). Paradoxes of "consent" to the practice of fieldwork. *Social Problems*, 27(3), 272–283.

Wax, R. H. (1971). *Doing fieldwork: Warnings and advice*. Chicago: The University of Chicago Press.

CHAPTER 14

❑ Validity in Educational Research

Margaret A. Eisenhart and
Kenneth R. Howe

The Handbook of Qualitative
Research in Education

Introduction

Validity—generally defined as the trustworthiness of inferences drawn from data—has always been a concern in educational research. Questions about validity historically arose in the context of experimentalist research and, accordingly, so did their answers. The emergence of nonexperimental, so-called "qualitative," methods in educational research over the past two decades, however, poses new questions. In particular, should experimentalist conceptions be applied to alternative research designs? If so, how? If not, what conceptions should be applied instead?

These are the kinds of questions we entertain in this paper. We begin with the conventional conception of validity as defined by Campbell and Stanley in the early 1960s and used by a generation of educational researchers working in the 1960s and 1970s. Next, we discuss several kinds of alternative conceptions that grew out of and responded to the special features of qualitative research as used in education. With these alternative conceptions of validity as our point of departure, we then develop our own position. A crucial feature of the position we develop is our distinction between *general* and *design-specific* standards of validity. The import of this distinction will become clear as the paper unfolds. Its basic thrust is that all educational research is subject to the same general criteria of validity even though quite distinct and specialized criteria are required to conduct and evaluate specific kinds of research studies. We end the paper with a discussion of how general validity and design-specific instances fit together.

The Conventional Approach

Conventional conceptions of validity in educational research derive most directly from Campbell and Stanley (1963).[1] Focusing on experimental and quasi-experimental designs, they divided validity into two kinds, internal and external. Internal validity, referred to as the *sine qua non* of good experimental design, pertains to the credibility of inferences that experimental treatments (factors) cause effects under certain well-defined circumstances. To meet the requirements of internal validity, other factors that reside in the way the study was conducted (i.e., "internal" to the design of the study) and that may have caused the effect must be ruled out. External validity pertains to generalizing the effects observed under experimental conditions to other populations and contexts. To meet the requirements of external validity (or to define its limits), factors that limit the study's application to other situations—factors such as the characteristics of the people, settings, or variables investigated (i.e., that are "external" to the conduct of the study)—must be ruled out.

Campbell and Stanley's basic approach was thus to require evidence that each type of validity has been met or approached. In the case of internal validity, the researcher must show that various "threats" (to be described later) that might affect the interpretation of results are controlled for in the research design. For external validity, the researcher must show that the characteristics of the people, settings, and variables that define the experimental conditions are unlikely to matter when the treatment is applied to other targeted populations and situations. It should be noted that despite Campbell and Stanley's claim that internal validity is the *sine qua non* of good research design, they emphasized the importance of external validity, particularly for educational research. According to them, because of the practical nature of educational research, "generalizations to applied settings of known character is the desideratum" (Campbell and Stanley, 1963:5).

As we indicated earlier, the emergence and subsequently acknowledged legitimacy of alternative, so-called qualitative, methods in educational research over the past two decades posed a challenge to the conventional conception of validity. Questions were raised about the appropriateness of using the conventional conception as a guide or standard for qualitative research. Some suggested that the conventional approach is epistemologically unsuited to be a general standard for most educational research. Others wondered, "If not this standard, then what?" There have been three major responses to this challenge: adaptations of the conventional approach, alternatives to the conventional approach, and eclecticism.

Adaptations of the Conventional Approach

Norman Denzin, a sociologist and author of *The Research Act: A Theoretical Introduction to Sociological Methods,* a textbook now in its third edition (1970, 1978, 1989), is frequently cited in papers about qualitative educational research. Denzin's book is devoted to descriptions and comparisons of research designs—Denzin calls them "methodologies"—commonly used by sociologists (specifically symbolic interactionists). In the 1989 edition, Denzin compared seven methodologies: experiments, surveys, participant observations, unobtrusive methods (techniques used by a researcher who is physically removed from the events being studied), life histories, interviewing, and filming.

Validity is a basis for Denzin's comparison of these research methodologies. He relied on Campbell's (1963a,b) list of eight factors that threaten internal validity and four factors that threaten external validity as criteria for assessing the methodologies. The eight threats to internal validity are historical events occurring between measurements, maturation of subjects between measurements, subject selection effects on results, interaction of maturation and selection effects on results, loss of subjects, testing effects, changes in instrumentation, and statistical regression toward the mean of groups originally chosen for their extreme scores. The four threats to external validity are differences in likely response to testing (reactive effects of testing), differences in likely response to treatment (reactive effects of experiment), multiple treatment interference, and subject selection efffects on applications. With only minor alterations to his definitions of the threats, Denzin compares each of the seven methodologies in terms of their ability to minimize the 12 threats.

Denzin explained, however, that minimizing the threats is not addressed in the same way in each research design. Threats may be approached experimentally, in which case the researcher can manipulate subjects, variables, and conditions, and threats can be controlled through this manipulation. When such direct manipulation is not possible, threats may be treated with multivariate analysis, whereby the researcher uses statistical manipulations to approximate the controls possible in a true experiment. In both experiments and multivariate analysis, causal inferences are accepted as valid when the probability that observed correlations are spurious or accidental is very low. A third and quite different approach to handling threats to validity is analytic induction. Using this approach, the researcher aims to identify directly time order, covariance, and other threats. This approach is used in the most qualitative of the designs Denzin discusses— participant observation and life history. Analytic induction requires that a researcher consider every piece of data before inferring causality. Support for (read: the validity of) the inferences advanced is strengthened by demonstrations that researchers have searched for data expected to severely test or negate inferences and that the researchers' emerging inferences accommodate, explain, or account for the variations discovered.

Denzin showed that each design has strengths and weaknesses with respect to minimizing threats, and he found experiments *and* participant observation especially strong overall (see the table on p. 30, 1989 edition). Because designs differ as to which threats they address most strongly, Denzin argued that when experimental and nonexperimental designs are compared, threat-by-threat, they tend to compensate for one another's weaknesses. Because different designs are more or less vulnerable to different threats, Denzin claimed (as did Campbell) that the most valid studies are those that rely on several research designs, thus reducing threats in as many strong ways as possible.

Judith Goetz and Margaret LeCompte, an educational anthropologist and an educational sociologist, respectively, adopted a strategy similar to Denzin's in their discussion of ethnographic analogues for Campbell and Stanley's internal and external validity. In their book, *Ethnography and Qualitative Design in Educational Research* (1984), they outlined threats to internal and external validity following Campbell and Stanley and illustrated ways of dealing with these threats within the context of ethnographic design (see especially pp. 220–232).

Like Campbell and Stanley [and also following Hansen (1979) and Pelto and Pelto (1978)], Goetz and LeCompte (1984) wrote:

> Establishing validity requires (1) determining the extent to which conclusions effectively represent empirical reality and (2) assessing whether constructs devised by researchers represent or measure the categories of human experience that occur. . . . *Internal validity* refers to the extent to which scientific observations and measurements are authentic representations of some reality; *external validity* refers to the degree to which such representations can be compared legitimately across groups [italics in original]. (p. 210)

Goetz and LeCompte imply that the spirit of Campbell and Stanley's threats can be translated into terms applicable to nonexperimental designs like ethnographies. For example, they suggest that the internal validity of ethnographic studies can be addressed in part by adopting procedures that increase the likelihood that an authentic picture of the participants' reality is elicited. Thus, the internal validity of ethnographic research is judged to be strong when researchers spend long periods of time in the field so as to get to know participants, their views, and situations; when the researchers' actions and interviews are conducted in the idiom of participants; and when the researcher is directly involved in the lives of those being studied. Goetz and LeCompte's approach to external validity is the same. They suggest, for example, that careful and extensive descriptions of the settings and people being studied, of the social conditions of study, and of the constructs being used give other researchers the information necessary to assess the typicality of a situation, to identify appropriate comparison groups and translation issues, and thereby to meet the requirements of external validity in the context of ethnographic research (see also Eisenhart, 1988).

Relying on Cook and Campbell (1979), Goetz and LeCompte also translate a third kind of conventional validity: construct validity, or the extent to which abstract ideas ("constructs") used in research studies (e.g., self-esteem, culture) match the empirical evidence used to indicate or measure the abstraction. Although construct validity has conventionally been used to assess the correspondence of test constructs to test items, Goetz and LeCompte (1984:225) argue that construct validity can be straightforwardly translated into ethnographic research practice when ethnographers demonstrate that the categories they are using are meaningful to participants or reflect the way participants actually experience reality.

Goetz and LeCompte also include in their discussion more global considerations that figure into the determination that an ethnographic study is valid. (Their global considerations foreshadow our general standards of validity.) They stress, for example, that the theoretical orientation guiding the research project—in their case, the structural–functional perspective of cultural anthropology—influences the way the general meaning of validity is translated into a research design, the factors that threaten validity, and the means of minimizing such threats. They emphasize that because the *primary* criterion for selection of a research design must be whether the design allows the researcher to address the research questions posed, the answer to *this* question may lead to an amalgamation of two or more of what they call the "ideal-typical abstractions" (Goetz and LeCompte, 1984:47–48) of research designs such as those set forth by Denzin.[2] Furthermore, they add to their list of attributes of a good study: completeness (does the report of the study contain all the elements considered necessary for a research report of this kind?), appropriateness (are the approach and design used effective and suitable for the research questions posed?), clarity (is it easy and straightforward to figure out what the study is about and why it is approached and designed in the way it is?), comprehensiveness (is the scope of the study large enough to address convincingly the questions posed?), credibility (are the conduct and results of the study believable?), and significance (does the study make an important contribution?) (pp. 233–245).

In summary, Goetz and LeCompte's adaptation of the conventional conception of validity entails a translation of the tenets of the conventional approach into criteria that make sense for ethnographic design. They also add more global considerations to their criteria for determining a study's validity. Their basic approach—to translate the conventional meanings of validity into ethnographic terms—differs from Denzin's approach, which is to consider how various designs, when used together, meet the requirements of the conventional approach. Yet both adapt Campbell and Stanley's definitions of internal and external validity so as to encompass nonexperimental as well as experimental research designs.

Alternatives to the Conventional Conception

A second response to the challenge posed by the emergence of alternative research methods is deep skepticism toward (e.g., Erickson, 1986) or outright rejection of (e.g., Lincoln and Guba, 1985; and, for different reasons, Roman, 1989) the notion that the conventional conception of validity may be fruitfully applied to alternative methods.[3] The ultimate basis for these more radical forms of divergence from the conventional conception is to be found in the various facets of the positivist–interpretivist–criticalist controversy, a discussion of which is beyond the scope of this paper (but see e.g., Bredo and Feinberg, 1982; Howe, 1985, 1988; Howe and Eisenhart, 1990; Roman, 1989; Roman and Apple, 1990). For present purposes, it is sufficient to note the emphasis that our first two exemplars of this more radical form of divergence—Erickson (1986) and Lincoln and Guba (1985)—place on the so-called "insider's perspective" and the emphasis that Roman (1989) places on exposing and transforming the power relations constituting research practice.

According to Erickson, the "basic validity criterion" of alternative methods is *"the immediate and local meanings of actions,* as defined from the actors' point of view [italics in original]" (Erickson, 1986:119). This criterion applies to the audience as well as the subjects of research.

Erickson discusses many of the same issues as Goetz and Le-Compte, but in a way more commonly used for discussing literature. In Erickson's view, the crucial piece of "ethnographic validity" is the way the "story" is told and evidence for its authenticity provided [see also Van Maanen (1988) who argues for more "narrative ingenuity" in the way ethnographic accounts are written]. Erickson (1986) points out that the presentation of text-based data, most often in some kind of story form, has rhetorical, analytic, and evidentiary functions:

> The [story] persuades the reader that things were in the setting as the
> author claims they were, because the sense of immediate presence
> captures the reader's attention, and because the concrete particulars of
> the events reported in the [story] instantiate the general analytic
> concepts (patterns of culture and social organization) the author is
> using to organize the research report . . . . In sum, richness of detail
> in and of itself does not make a [story] ethnographically valid. Rather,
> it is the combination of richness and interpretive perspective that
> makes the account valid. Such a valid account is not simply a
> description; it is an analysis. Within the details of the story, selected
> carefully, is contained a statement of a theory of organization and
> meaning of the events described. (p. 150)

Erickson also emphasizes the need to meet criteria of quality with
reference to how the results will be understood and used by various
audiences. In his version of validity, concerns about clarity, appropriateness, and so forth take on the added burden of being clear,
appropriate, and *useful* to potential audiences [e.g., teachers (see especially Erickson, 1986:153–156)]. This is a point we will return to later.

Lincoln and Guba (1985) have taken a more extreme position with
regard to standards for nonexperimental educational research designs.
Because of the special character of what they call "naturalistic studies," they advocate developing an entirely different set of standards by
which to judge the soundness of naturalistic research. In their view,
the two prime directives of naturalistic research, or "inquiry," are that
the researcher does not influence or manipulate (or does so to a very
limited degree) the conditions of study and that the researcher imposes
no *a priori* categories on the results of the study (p. 8). They view
naturalistic research as an "alternative research paradigm," an approach with a distinctly different ontological and epistemological basis
from that underlying experimental research. As such, they propose that
distinctly different research designs and different standards for validity must be used when conducting naturalistic research.

To refer to the overall quality of a piece of research, Lincoln and
Guba (1985) use the term "trustworthiness" of research. They write,
"The basic issue in relation to trustworthiness is simple: How can an
inquirer persuade his or her audiences . . . that the findings of an
inquiry are worth paying attention to, worth taking account of? What
arguments can be mounted, what criteria invoked, what questions
asked, that would be persuasive on this issue?" (p. 290).

Interestingly, despite the different labels and their contention that
the different paradigm of naturalistic inquiry demands that standards
be developed specifically for it, Lincoln and Guba begin their discussion with standards that are close analogues to those of Campbell and

Stanley. In particular, they list four kinds of trustworthiness, two of which, "truth value" and "applicability," are analogous to internal validity and external validity, respectively. Truth value refers to the accuracy (or "truth") of the findings for those beings studied. Applicability refers to the likelihood that the findings will pertain to other groups in other situations. The other two kinds of trustworthiness are consistency (or reliability in experimentalist terminology) and neutrality (or objectivity). Lincoln and Guba argue that all inquirers are concerned about these general standards of trustworthiness, but the meaning of each standard, the nature of threats, and the means of minimizing them will be distinctly different within experimental (what they call "positivist") and naturalist paradigms. Thus, each paradigm will need its own ways to handle the threats.

Lincoln and Guba argue that naturalistic inquiry is fundamentally *not* about determining causes and, thus, that it is inappropriate to pursue truth value (internal validity) by demonstrating that causes and their effects have been isolated. They propose that the analogous standard for naturalistic inquiry—where the major aim is to reconstruct the perspectives of those being studied—is the demonstration that the researcher's interpretations of data (the findings) are credible to those who provided the data. Meeting this standard has two parts: first, carrying out research in such a way as to increase the chances that respondent categories rather than researcher categories will dominate the findings and, second, having respondents approve the researchers' interpretations (Lincoln and Guba, 1985:296). Specific "techniques" for meeting the standard of credibility are described by Lincoln and Guba (1985:301–316). These techniques are examples, meant to illustrate ways in which the naturalist's special form of validity may be operationalized. They include techniques for prolonged involvement with those being studied, techniques for systematically considering many sources of data, techniques for obtaining and analyzing data so as to be able to consider them from different angles and perspectives, techniques for refining working assertions or themes pertaining to the data, and techniques for respondents' review of researchers' findings.

Lincoln and Guba argue that the experimentalist's procedures for external validity—assuring the representativeness of treatment conditions to application conditions, particularly through randomization— *prime facie* do not apply to naturalistic inquiry. They believe that naturalistic inquirers are responsible only for clearly and comprehensively describing the contextual conditions of their studies. They argue that the establishment of external validity in naturalistic inquiry is an empirical matter and must be determined by those who wish to apply

Provide "thick description"

the findings somewhere else. Potential audiences for research findings must themselves determine whether the context in which they are interested is sufficiently similar to the context from which research findings derive to make their transfer possible and reasonable (Lincoln and Guba, 1985:298). Because the determination of external validity is made by potential users, no techniques are provided by Lincoln and Guba to meet this standard (see p. 316). Rather, they contend that the researcher is obligated to provide the "data base" or "thick descriptions" necessary to make judgments about application possible.

Leslie Roman has taken a very different extreme position on the validity of nonexperimental research (Roman, 1989; Roman and Apple, 1990). From her perspective as a feminist materialist, she contends that *both* experimental and naturalistic researchers have incorrectly assumed that they could achieve validity primarily by limiting the researcher's involvement ("subjectivity" or "bias") in the collection, analysis, and reporting of data. Experimentalists use various procedures, such as random assignment, double-blind controls, and statistical manipulations in an attempt to limit the researcher's influence and to constrain the generalizations drawn from specific results; naturalistic researchers attempt to hold their own views in abeyance to permit the emergence of the insiders' perspective and the inductive development of theory to explain and extend the results from a specific case or group. Drawing on a criticalist approach to educational research (see also Anderson, 1989), Roman argues that experimental and naturalistic researchers do not question the ways in which power relations of the wider society are perpetuated in research practice. Neither group takes seriously the possibility that research constructs, procedures, and results (be they in the form of variables or people's conscious models) sustain historically specific power relations and material interests. From the alternative perspective of the criticalist, control over who to study, what to study, how to conduct the study, and the relationship of the researcher to participants or subjects is always worked out in terms of the power relations governing the wider society, unless steps are taken to ensure that research studies are democratically designed and results are democratically produced. Democratization of educational research is the goal of critical education research (see also Lather, 1986). From Roman's standpoint as a feminist materialist (within the criticalist tradition), she argues that valid research must use a methodology that (1) resonates with the lived experiences of the group being researched, (2) enables members of the group to comprehend and transform their experiences of subordination, (3) reduces the divide between the researcher's intellectual work and group members' ordinary ways of describing and understanding their experiences, and

(4) allows the researcher's prior theoretical and political commitments to be informed and transformed by understandings derived from the group's experiences (Roman and Apple, 1990:63–64). Needless to say, these features of a valid study are quite different from those suggested by either the conventional approach or the alternative approaches exemplified by Erickson or Lincoln and Guba.

Eclecticism

Many educational researchers who perceive important differences between experimental and alternative research designs nonetheless continue to have respect for and to be significantly influenced by Campbell and Stanley's two kinds of validity. Thus, a third response to the challenge to conventional validity posed by the emergence of alternative methodologies is a form of eclecticism in which criteria for validity accommodate ideas emanating from both experimental and alternative methodologies.

For example, Mary Lee Smith and Gene Glass, educational researchers, begin their book, *Research and Evaluation in Education and the Social Sciences* (1987), with a set of criteria for interpreting and judging the merits, that is, the validity, of educational research studies (pp. 2–6). They indicate that the criteria are generally applicable to any research design. However, as they proceed, they find that they must exempt one kind of research—naturalistic studies—from these general criteria.

Extending the tradition of identifying different kinds of validity, Smith and Glass (1987) list four: logical, construct, internal, and external. They write, "If the study has *logical validity*, the reader should be able to follow the argument and assess whether the hypothesis follows logically from the problem, whether the methods follow logically and consistently from the hypothesis, the findings from the methods, and the conclusions from the findings [italics in original]" (p. 2). A study has *construct validity* when the measures used by the researchers can be shown to correspond to the abstract "construct" under investigation (p. 4). Consistent with Campbell and Stanley, Smith and Glass add *internal validity*, which depends on ruling out alternative causes for the results of the study (p. 5), and *external validity*, which depends on demonstrating the generalizability of the results to other groups or situations (p. 6). Smith and Glass also say with reference to external validity, "In research, the people involved directly, the *sample*, are only of interest to the extent to which they inform us about similar groups of people not directly involved in the study [italics in original]" (p. 6). All but the first of these criteria have a decidedly experimental bent, by which control, randomization, and statistical manipulation are the primary means for establishing validity. However, the first standard, logical validity is a more extensive albeit inexact standard—one that focuses on the logic of decisions made in the design and course of the research project, rather than on the use of orthodox technical procedures. (This is yet another idea we will return to when we develop our general standards of validity.)

Smith and Glass's book also includes a discussion of "naturalistic studies," in which they find themselves unable to use three of the four criteria for validity outlined earlier. In striking contrast to their preceding statement about the role of the sample, Smith and Glass (1987) define the purposes of naturalistic studies to be "to understand the persons involved, their behavior and perceptions, and the influence of the physical, social, and psychological environment or *context* on them." They define the researcher's job to be "to describe [the persons involved] and interpret their actions for persons who have not been there and seen them directly—that is, for the readers [italics in original]" (p. 253). In fact, they go on to exempt naturalistic studies from all but the first criterion—logical validity—by arguing that the idiosyncracies of naturalistic studies defy the application of the kind of uniform standards that can be applied to the other research designs they treat, namely, experimental, quasi-experimental, causal-comparative, correlational, and survey studies. In lieu of standards, they propose some "issues" to be considered in assessing the quality of naturalistic studies. These issues include length of time in the field; the researcher's access to data from various sources; the researcher's subjectivity and biases; the clarity, completeness, and logic of the researcher's reasoning about the study; and the demonstration that final results have been obtained through triangulation (p. 278).

Their approach of listing "issues" for consideration as a guide for the conduct and assessment of naturalistic research is similar to the position described by J. K. Smith (1990, from Feyerabend). Smith suggests that the standards for some kinds of research are best thought of in terms of open-ended "lists" of general concerns that a researcher should address in some way in the research, rather than in terms of rules for admitting evidence or extending conclusions (the conventional approach).

Appraisal

Each of these three general responses to the challenge posed by the advent of alternative methods to the conventional conception of validity makes a significant contribution: adaptations of the conventional conception illustrate substantial commonalities that exist between experimental and alternative methods; alternatives to the conventional conception illustrate substantial differences; and eclecticism suggests that educational research can (perhaps) accommodate both.

In our judgment, however, more needs to be said, particularly with regard to explicating a general approach to validity that accommodates both "quantitative" and "qualitative" research designs. Because we deny that quantitative methods can be separated off and justified by appeal to a peculiar scientific (read: positivist) epistemology (Howe, 1985, 1988; Howe and Eisenhart, 1990), we think the pursuit of some general standards is appropriate and useful and, given a proper understanding of validity, unavoidable. On the other hand, we recognize that specific research designs have their own logic and coherence. Thus, a general approach to validity must accommodate differences among specific research designs.

Our aim is not to refute or dismiss the conceptions we have considered so far but, rather, to distill a more comprehensive account of validity. Our approach is to identify research studies with arguments (Dunn, 1982; House, 1977) and to define a valid argument as one that is credible in a general as well as a design-specific way.

The metaphor of research study as argument is useful in educational research for three reasons (following Dunn, 1982). First, the metaphor of argument discourages "facile distinctions between 'science' and 'ordinary knowledge,'" and the "patently false conclusion that knowledge derived from one source is inherently superior." Second, the metaphor "provides a conceptual framework that not only accommodates the experimental metaphor—including 'threats to validity' and their philosophic justification—but also permits a radical enlargement of standards for assessing and challenging knowledge claims." And third, the metaphor encourages the idea of public debate and scrutiny of research processes and results (Dunn, 1982:295).

Characterizing all educational research studies in terms of the general concept of an argument leads rather straightforwardly to a general concept of validity that can be applied across all such arguments regardless of their particular contents (for the application of this conception of validity to testing practice, see Messick, 1989). On the other hand, judgments regarding the validity of a particular argument also turn on whether the argument is credible to relevant audiences, allowing that the kinds of evidence and associated principles employed in particular arguments vary substantially. (This is a general point, not confined to validity in educational research: Consider valid argumentation in law versus physics.) Viewed in this light, the three approaches to validity in nonexperimental research described earlier (adaptation of the experimental or conventional approach, alternatives, eclecticism) fall somewhat short insofar as they encourage the view either that all arguments must be evaluated in terms of precisely the same criteria (adaptation) or that there must be different *kinds* of validity (alternatives to the conventional conception and eclecticism). In our view, it is more fruitful to think in terms of one *kind* of validity with different *design-specific instances.* Such a general conception of validity helps vitiate methodological imperialism and, at the same time, is consistent with the different kinds of knowledge and technical skills that go into marshalling and evaluating research-based arguments.

The position we will advance in the remainder of this paper has three parts. First, we argue that the field of educational research as a whole has certain concerns that transcend or are separate from those of specific disciplines or designs for research and that, for this reason, some *general standards* for the conduct of educational research that cut across all forms of educational research can and should be articulated. In our view, general standards should require that research studies be cogently developed, competently produced, coherent with respect to previous work, important, ethical, and comprehensive. We describe each of these features in more detail later.

Second, we think that although general standards of validity establish broad boundaries, they do not thereby dictate the specific strategies and techniques that researchers use when employing specific research designs. Instead, *design-specific standards*—which are subsumed by the general standards and which articulate the particular evidence, knowledge, principles, and technical skills that differentiate alternative designs—are required. Moreover, and as we have argued elsewhere (Howe and Eisenhart, 1990), such design-specific standards necessarily undergo revision and reconceptualization as scholars within various traditions conduct their work over time.

Finally, we consider how issues of substance and methodology peculiar to specific research designs may be construed as instances of variously interpreting and applying our general standards of validity. We will illustrate this relationship in the case of one specific design: educational ethnography.

Before turning to the articulation of our conception of validity, one further introductory point is in order. It has been suggested by some [e.g., J. K. Smith (1990)], that the emergence of alternative research designs (notably what he labels "constructivism," including the recent work of Lincoln and Guba; cf. Lincoln, 1990) may lead to the conclusion that standards of validity are ephemeral at best and can be no more precise than the everyday norms governing social interactions and negotiations. In our estimation, this view is far too extreme. Although neither static nor mechanically applicable, articulated standards of validity serve at least three important functions: They allow economy of thought in designing and evaluating educational studies; they provide the starting point for reflection on and improvement of the educational research enterprise; and they serve as the vehicle both for communicating within and across research traditions and for orienting newcomers (indeed, facilitating such forms of communication presumably is one of the major aims of this handbook).

Five General Standards for Validity in Educational Research

The five general standards we are about to advance can be usefully employed as guides for making valid arguments in educational research and can encompass, without undue constraint, distinct disciplinary and methodological arguments associated with specific research designs. Our first three standards are rules of thumb for systematic consideration of research studies *qua* arguments; they may be appropriately invoked across substantially different arguments, even though their precise application in a given study requires sophisticated and specialized knowledge. The fourth and fifth standards address more global requirements, whose application is not necessarily dictated in ways peculiar to specific designs.

Standard 1: The Fit between Research Questions, Data Collection Procedures, and Analysis Techniques[4]

Hilary Putnam remarks, "If you want to know why a square peg doesn't fit into a round hole, you had better *not* describe the peg in terms of its constituent elementary particles" (Rorty, 1982:201; attributed by Rorty.) Although Putnam's target is reductionism in scientific explanation, his remark also has a more prosaic meaning: The data collection techniques employed should fit, or be suitable for answering, the research question entertained. A corollary of this standard is that research questions should drive data collection techniques and analysis rather than vice versa.

We were certainly not, as graduate students or newly minted professors, the first to realize that the research designs presented to us in our courses and textbooks did not always fit the questions we most wanted to answer. As a graduate student, the expedient thing to do may be to whittle down the question so that a conventional research design could be used to address it. As researchers in a field in which major problems confront us, where significant debates about educational practice rage, and where person power and money to conduct research are limited, such an expedient solution is not justified. Instead, we think that methods sometimes must be modified, combined, and even created to address the research questions that need study.[5]

Correctly ordering research questions and methods, and developing their fit, is of course a complex issue. We do not mean to suggest that researchers can proceed as if they are blank slates—free of prior interests, commitments, and methodological expertise. Neither can they behave as if they have super intellects—capable of competently choosing from all of the relevant questions and methodologies. Nor, finally, can they operate as if they had available infinite time and resources. In some sense, then, research methodology will indeed drive research. On the other hand, the degree to which this occurs should be minimized. Research studies *qua* arguments have questionable validity when methodological preferences or matters of convenience, rather than research questions, drive the study design. Valid studies require cogently developed designs.

Standard 2: The Effective Application of Specific Data Collection and Analysis Techniques

In addition to deriving coherently from research questions, data collection and analysis techniques also must be competently applied, in a more-or-less technical sense. Research studies *qua* arguments cannot be valid without credible reasons for a specific choice of subjects, data-gathering procedures, and analysis techniques. Various principles guide how interviews should be conducted, how instruments should be designed, how sampling should proceed, how data should be reduced, and so forth, such that rather immediate "low-inference" conclusions are rendered credible. If credibility is not achieved at this level, then the more general (and more important) conclusions that ultimately rest on these low-inference conclusions will be suspect.

It is not the case that educational researchers must create brand new principles and procedures for competently conducting their work. Principles and systematic procedures for the conduct and assessment of numerous qualitative (as well as quantitative) research designs have been formulated and debated for years within the social science disciplines. Although some modification of technical standards from the social sciences may be necessary for educational research purposes, it is incumbent on educational researchers, who wish to demonstrate that their techniques have been competently applied, to locate their work in the historical, disciplinary, or traditional contexts in which the methods used have been developed.

Standard 3: Alertness to and Coherence of Prior Knowledge

Linking research questions with data collection and analysis techniques and competently applying the latter do not assure that a study will render credible conclusions, because studies also must be judged against a background of existing theoretical, substantive, or explicit practical knowledge. For arguments to satisfy this standard, they must be built on some theoretical tradition or contribute to some substantive area or practical arena. In other words, the assumptions and goals embedded in the development and conduct of the study must be exposed and considered. Only if this is done can the arguments derived from a new study be placed in their appropriate context and the arguments of one study appropriately compared to those of other studies.

Perhaps less obvious is the researcher's own prior knowledge, or "subjectivity" (Peshkin, 1988). Peshkin has argued that subjectivity is the basis for the researcher's distinctive contribution, which comes from joining personal interpretations with the data that have been collected and analyzed. As with assumptions derived from the literature, subjectivities must be made explicit if they are to advance, rather than obscure, the validity of research *qua* argument.

Standard 4: Value Constraints

Gone are the days when it was philosophically respectable to believe it possible (and desirable) to bracket values in the design and conduct of social research, particularly in "applied" areas such as education. The conduct of educational research is subject to both "external" and "internal" value constraints (Howe, 1985). Valid research studies *qua* arguments must include discussion of values, that is, of the worth in importance or usefulness of the study and of its risks.

External Value Constraints

External value constraints concern whether the research is valuable for informing and improving educational practice—the "so what?" question. Research might be well designed and conducted in a *technical* sense, but that alone is an insufficient criterion of worth. Valid studies must be worthwhile. The concern with important issues, when considered in the context of educational practice, has several implications. One is that research investigations be comprehensive enough to convey and expose the important and profound problems and issues that arise for practitioners. This is not primarily a matter of increasing the scope of research projects so that more data can be collected and analyzed, or of developing sophisticated technical means for more rapidly and precisely handling data. Rather, it means committing the educational research community to multifaceted investigations of major educational issues—whether they be at the level of pedagogy, policy, or social theory—and then demanding that researchers ground their methodology in the nature of these issues.

Admittedly, judgments of the worth of research projects can be very difficult to make. They have the potential to be exceedingly biased, as anyone who has served on a human subjects committee can attest. However, these are not judgments from which researchers can (or do) forever run and hide [witness the recent exchange in *Educational Researcher* between Finn (1988) and Shavelson and Berliner (1988) in which they debate whether educational research has or has not made an important contribution to the improvement of educational practice; also see the more recent discussion by Philip Jackson (1990), also in *Educational Researcher*]. Researchers are best advised to put questions about the worth of research immediately on the table, lest implicit judgments about worth or lack of it operate behind the scenes, as a kind of hidden agenda. Clearly, even if others might be puzzled about the study's worth, educational researchers themselves should be able to communicate what value their research has (if only potentially) for educational practice.

The conclusions of educational research also should be accessible to the general education community. That is, the language of the results and implications must be cast in a form that is understandable to and debatable by various audiences (those who might read accounts of the research) or stakeholders (those who have a material interest in the results or uses of the research) in a particular setting—teachers, administrators, and parents, as well as educational researchers with varying perspectives and expertise. Accordingly, researchers must give attention to the social, political, and cultural features of the contexts and individuals they investigate and to which the results might be applied (Erickson, 1986; House, 1980:Chap. 12; Weiss, 1983). Researchers must also be sensitive to the inevitably value-laden language that they employ—terms such as "at risk," "developed," or "culturally different"—to avoid mystifying their findings and cloaking them in a false "scientific objectivity."

Valid research studies *qua* arguments, then, should explicitly address, in language that is generally accessible to the community of interested parties, the importance of the research and its (potential) usefulness. This requirement facilitates and encourages public debate of educational issues and of the implications of research results.

Internal Value Constraints

Internal value constraints refer to research ethics. We call research ethics "internal" because they concern the *way* research is conducted vis-à-vis research subjects, not with the (external) value of results. For example, Stanley Milgram's (1974) research on obedience to authority rendered valuable insights regarding the power of researchers to elicit compliance from subjects to perform ethically objectionable actions. The way Milgram treated his subjects was highly objectionable, however—so much so that he would not be permitted to do his research today. (Ironically, Milgram's findings, at least indirectly, underpin current requirements for informed consent, especially those that require researchers to communicate clearly to subjects that they are free to withdraw from research at any time and without penalty.)

Internal value constraints are distinguishable from other concerns about validity insofar as observing them sometimes requires reducing the precision and certainty of findings. For instance, randomized double-blind experiments are notorious for the kind of trade-off they engender between the risk : benefit ratio that applies to the subjects of such research and the value of the knowledge that can be obtained for guiding future action. These concerns are especially relevant to "qualitative" researchers because they must weigh the quality of the data they can gather (and whether they can gather any data at all) against principles such as confidentiality, privacy, and truth-telling. Although internal value constraints, or research ethics, can be distinguished from more conventional issues of research credibility, they are nonetheless crucial to evaluating the legitimacy of research designs and procedures, and thus we believe to the validity of a research study.

Standard 5: Comprehensiveness[6]

Our fifth standard—comprehensiveness—encompasses responding in a holistic way to and balancing the first four standards as well as going beyond them. We mean "comprehensiveness" in three senses. First, with regard to standards 1–3, standard 5 demands a judgment about the overall clarity, coherence, and competence—what might also be called "overall theoretical and technical quality"—of the study. Second, with respect to standards 1–4, standard 5 requires a balancing of the overall technical quality, the value and importance of the study, and the risks involved in the study. As indicated earlier, meeting one standard, such as protection of human subjects, may require tradeoffs against other standards. This second aspect of standard 5 calls for thoughtful consideration and explanation of such tradeoffs.

Third, standard 5 requires comprehensiveness in the sense of being alert to and able to employ knowledge from outside the particular perspective and tradition within which one is working and being able to apply general principles for evaluating arguments. For example, Denzin (1989), Goetz and LeCompte (1984), and Shulman (1988) argue that "triangulation by theory"—or application of various explanations to the data at hand and selection of the most plausible one to "explain" the research results—is a powerful strategy for establishing the validity of a theoretical explanation. It may also be considered a strategy for comprehensiveness by demonstrating that a study, competently and ethically conceived and conducted, can stand up to the challenge posed by other approaches or different results. When researchers demonstrate that, or explain the reasons why, other relevant approaches should be rejected or disconfirming data should be questioned, their studies are more comprehensive than when they do not.

Our discussion of general standards in the context of educational research can be summarized and concluded as follows: All instances of valid research-based arguments in educational research, regardless of design-specific peculiarities, take the same general form—that is, important educational issues must serve as the basis for formulating important research questions and an appropriate and ethical research design; research questions and methods must be competently linked, methods must be competently applied, prior commitments must be exposed; the potential worth of the results must be weighed against the risks associated with the study; and, overall, a comprehensiveness must be achieved that balances design quality and importance against risks and permits the robustness of conclusions to be assessed. As these requirements were discussed, it should have become clear that the understanding of validity we are proposing is a unitary construct. The five standards are not independent of each other; they cannot be applied separately. They are interrelated and must be considered together. The import of a unitary and holistic construct of validity is clarified in the next section.

Design-Specific Standards

Our five general standards are designed to encompass, without undue constraint, the specific standards and norms of particular research designs (e.g., ethnographic research, quasi-experimental research, survey research). In this way, valid arguments in educational ethnography or test construction, for example, become instances (not kinds) of our general conception of validity. At the specific level, building a case for validity requires meeting the requirements of the general standards with reference to the underlying assumptions, topics, and methodological techniques associated with a given design. However, design-specific tenets may have little to do with investigations in education, because often the designs have been developed in the social or natural sciences for inquiry into other phenomena. Thus, the requirements of our five standards must be sufficiently general to accommmodate considerable variation among specific designs that might be used in educational research, yet be discriminating enough to differentiate the validity of various studies *qua* arguments for educational research. What would it mean in practice, then, to apply the five general standards to a particular research design or an individual study?

In the next three sections we will focus first on one specific research design—educational ethnography—and then on one ethnographic study—reported by Holland and Eisenhart in *Educated in Romance: Women, Achievement, and College Culture* (1990)—to illustrate how the five standards might be applied and how the fit between general and design-specific standards might be achieved.

Assessing Educational Ethnography

One major assumption guides our discussion of the validity of specific research designs: What counts as a valid argument in the context of a specific research design and what steps are sensible to take to establish that an argument is valid will depend on the tenets of the specific design tradition. In other words, the design must be informed by the work and workers within that tradition (even if only to indicate how a study will depart or diverge from that tradition). Furthermore, within traditions, what constitutes a valid study will change over time (Howe and Eisenhart, 1990). Thus, we expect that the manner of addressing our five general standards will be affected by the history, norms, and ongoing debates of the tradition in which a particular study is conducted.

Using the case of educational ethnography, we illustrate that standards 1–3 are not meaningful as criteria for validity unless considered together; they are not independent criteria that can be separately applied and met in some studies but not others. Furthermore, in the case of educational ethnography, meeting the requirements of standard 3 (identification of the relevant body of previous work and the researcher's commitments) is prior and crucial to determinations of whether standard 1 (cogent development) or 2 (competent application) can be met. Although statements about the ethnographic logic of standard 1 or the ethnographic criteria for standard 2 are sometimes made in the abstract, we argue that the application of either one of the first two standards cannot stand without standard 3. Similarly, standard 3 is a hollow component of research validity unless tied to the requirements of standards 1 and 2.

Second, meeting the requirements of standards 1–3 can be pointless, costly, or even harmful without also satisfying the requirements of standards 4 (value constraints) and 5 (comprehensiveness). In other words, the validity of ethnographic research, or any other specific research design, for educational research depends on all five standards taken together.

We begin our discussion of ethnographic research with reference to the first three standards. We find that the first three general standards (cogent design, competent application, and connection to previous work) can be addressed largely from within the ethnographic tradition. That is, ethnographers and others can rely on traditions of scholarship and established norms in cultural anthropology and fieldwork sociology to locate and appropriately design their ethnographic research studies. When we then turn to standards 4 and 5, however, we find that they require consideration of matters not customarily treated within the ethnographic tradition.[7] This is really no surprise, because standards 4 and 5 help define research as relevant to the practice of education.

Our Standards 1–3 and the Ethnographic Research Tradition

To determine whether our first three standards of general validity for educational research are met in the case of an educational ethnography, we must ask "Is there credible evidence, pursuant to the disciplinary tenets underlying ethnography, that data collection and analysis procedures were cogently developed from research questions, and that these procedures were competently applied?" To answer these questions for an ethnography, we would begin by trying to identify the disciplinary context in which the study and its methodology were conceived. For purposes of illustration, we will focus on the context of cultural anthropology or, more specifically, on one of its subareas— educational anthropology.

Identification of the appropriate disciplinary context is not necessarily a simple matter. Because disciplinary traditions of scholarship are multifaceted and often divided into distinct subareas, it is of paramount importance to identify the specific subarea of work in which a study is located. For example, although the general purposes and assumptions of educational anthropology can be identified (Eisenhart, 1988), many subareas, in which small groups of researchers pursue particular topics in specialized ways, also exist [see, for example, the authors writing about systematic ethnography, microethnography, feminist materialist ethnography, and discourse analysis in this volume, and, for a general discussion of these subareas, see Jacob (1987, 1988) and the rejoinder by Atkinson, Delamont, and Hammersley (1988)]. The subareas share some general orientations, such as a commitment to identify the sociocultural processes that constitute education in a particular setting, and general assumptions, such as that human behavior and human learning are responsive to a context that is pervaded by patterns of culture and social relations that are, as well, interpreted and reconstructed by participants. However, within subareas, educational anthropologists make different decisions about the topics of major importance, the primary assumptions, and methodological preferences. It is these subareas to which particular studies are addressed and in which research designs including procedures are actually worked out.

The importance of clearly defining or identifying with certainty the scholarship tradition before attempting to assess the research design or methods used can be elucidated with a simple illustration of the implications of using one or another definition of culture when conceiving an ethnographic study. Many cultural anthropologists take the theoretical position that culture consists of the meanings that society, by partitioning the world through its institutions, language, and the collective activities of groups, encourages members to hold. But cultural meanings might take several empirical forms. Meanings can be represented in the organization of social life; that is, in the way institutions (schools, families, occupations, religions, etc.) allocate and represent roles, responsibilities, and rewards (Geertz, 1987). Meanings also can be represented in the words that people use to describe the world and their place in it (Quinn and Holland, 1987). (There are many other ways meanings might be represented; we use these two for illustrative purposes only.) When studying any kind of meaning, anthropologists may consider insider perspectives (those meanings recognized by members of the group), outsider perspectives (usually those meanings identified by a researcher), or interactive perspectives (those meanings that arise when insiders and outsiders communicate with each other).

To anticipate the research designs and procedures necessary for a particular study of meaning then, it is first necessary to identify the kind(s) of meaning of interest [i.e., to identify the tradition of scholarship and/or the commitments of the researcher (standard 3)]. In the first case (institutional meanings), the research design and procedures must address at least two research questions to meet the standard 1 requirement for cogent development: What is the evidence that the meanings attributed to the institution are understood (through compliance, resistance, or opposition) by those who participate in or observe it? And what is the evidence that meanings attributed to an institution are pervasive in the society where it exists? Given these research questions, methodological procedures must be devoted to competently collecting relevant evidence and triangulating evidence from numerous participants in and observers of institutions, as well as across institutions, of the society. Where evidence of similar interpretations by insiders and outsiders is provided, the findings are stronger than if evidence were provided from only one source. Where patterns across institutions can be provided, confidence is increased that the findings (meanings) are pervasive.

In the case of the second type of meaning (cultural models), first-person accounts of events and actions, such as those given by participants or those given by "observers" about their own experiences (cf.

Kirkup, 1986; Van Maanen, 1988), are especially necessary to provide a basis for researcher inferences about collective meanings. Accounts made by ethnographers who try to become insiders could be considered useful in this sense too, although less so than true insider accounts. Similarly, insider corroboration of outsider accounts is weaker evidence for a finding—in this case—than insiders' own accounts. When meanings are provided by researchers who infer them from first-hand accounts, evidence is needed to demonstrate that inferred meanings can encompass or predict actions of the people to whom the models are attributed (cf. Eisenhart and Holland, in press). Finally, when interactive perspectives are of interest, evidence is needed that people from different positions or backgrounds come to take the same or similar meaning from observed actions or during their activities together (cf. Tobin, Wu, and Davidson, 1989).

Thus, for the validity of an educational ethnography to be judged in terms of our first three general standards, the study's place in a subarea tradition must be identified first. From there, the criteria used within the subarea to identify a good ethnography can be provided, thus establishing the design-specific norms by which standard 1 (cogent development of the research design from the research questions), standard 2 (competent application of procedures), and the remainder of the standard 3 requirement (to make clear the researcher's prior commitments or subjectivities) can be meaningfully assessed.

Our position on the interdependence of the first three standards differs from the position of those who would use salient characteristics of ethnographic methodology alone to develop a good (valid) ethnographic study. Spindler (1982), perhaps taking for granted a set of theoretical commitments, proposed such a list, which he called "criteria for a good ethnography." His criteria included observations must be contextualized, prolonged, and repetitive; hypotheses, questions, and instruments for the study should emerge as the study proceeds; judgments about what is most significant to study should be deferred until the orienting phase of the field study has been completed; participants' views of reality are revealed by inferences drawn primarily from direct observation and various forms of ethnographic interviewing; sociocultural knowledge—both implicit and explicit—that participants bring to and generate in social settings should be revealed and understood (Spindler, 1982:6–7). Although these criteria can be taken as features of many ethnographic studies, they cannot serve well as guides to cogent research designs or the competent application of techniques unless researchers can show that the features make sense, given specific research purposes.

In the context of this discussion of validity in ethnographic research, orthodox ethnographic techniques (e.g., participant observation, spending a long period of time in the field, learning the customs and language of the group, triangulating data sources and methods)—about which a great deal has been written both by educational anthropologists and educational researchers—may be ways to achieve validity, but their presence in a study is not sufficient to demonstrate that validity has been achieved. Evidence that these procedural steps were taken cannot stand in place of answers to questions about why the research topic was conceived as it was, the nature of the assumptions or commitments made, and a rationale for the research questions asked. The mere presence of familiar procedural steps cannot, by themselves, provide convincing evidence for the validity of anthropological or ethnographic arguments, nor should the steps be constraints on efforts to meet demands for evidence in other relevant or innovative ways. The test of a valid argument in light of our first three standards, in educational anthropology as elsewhere, lies fundamentally in the appropriateness of methods used given purposes selected. And scholars well-versed in the purposes of a subarea are in the best position to make good selections and to pass judgments on the appropriateness of methods.

The application of our fourth and fifth general standards (regarding value constraints and comprehensiveness) to educational ethnography takes a different form. To meet these requirements, ethnographers must take additional steps beyond those normally considered sufficient by the community of educational anthropologists.

Meeting the Requirements of Standard 4, or Establishing the External and Internal Value of Ethnographic Research

Regarding external value constraints, cultural anthropologists usually assume that their research questions and findings will be of interest primarily to other anthropologists or other students of human behavior. These uses are thought to be informational or advisory—as food for thought—by others interested in explaining or understanding sociocultural phenomena. For educational anthropologists who participate in the educational research community, another use (whether intended or not) is to interpret, affect, or change educational practice. Although some educational anthropologists have argued that they do not intend their research to be used in "applied" contexts, we argue that the general standards of validity proposed earlier do and should call upon educational anthropologists to put their purposes, interests, and insights pertaining to educational practice into plain language for public debate, even if ethnographic convention does not. Educational anthropologists should be asked to clarify their claims for the worth or power of sociocultural theories in contrast to, for example, claims by psychologists or economists. Anthropologists' claims about the worth of their studies for the improvement of educational practice must, we think, be made explicit and face the challenges brought by other educational specialists and practitioners. By and large in educational anthropology/ethnography, this has not been a major concern, although we know of no good reasons why ethnographers should not engage in such debates.

Turning to our standards pertaining to internal value constraints, the issues here include: Whose privacy is threatened, or peace-of-mind disrupted, by the research? For what or for whom will knowledge gained from the research be used? What are the personal and social implications of eliciting such knowledge, knowing it, and using it? In other words, who is privileged or disadvantaged, who receives the benefit, and who pays the price? In summary, is there evidence indicating that the study's purposes and results outweigh any risks?

Considered in this light, it is startling to realize how infrequently educational ethnographers have discussed the internal value of their work, at least publicly. In fact, the lore of educational anthropology includes the recommendation that researchers not divulge their ideas, plans, or worries to those being studied until after the work has been completed. Although this approach is consistent with ethnographic convention, it is not consistent with our general commitment to internal value constraints as outlined in standard 4. To meet our general requirements for validity in educational research is, we think, to make these internal value considerations explicit and thorough-going in the entire design and conduct of educational ethnography. This requirement places a new limit on what ethnographers can study—covert studies or studies in which informed consent cannot reasonably be obtained would be prohibited. The requirement also extends the ethnographer's obligation to apprise research participants of what the study is about and what its likely outcomes will be throughout the entire period of the study.

Meeting Standard 5, or Establishing the Comprehensiveness of Ethnographic Research

To meet the additional requirements (beyond what is required to meet standards 1–4) of comprehensiveness in the conduct of educational anthropology/ethnography is to balance the requirements of the first four standards and to place one study's arguments and evidence alongside alternatives, both from within educational anthropology and without it, that is, from the educational research community. Educational anthropologists must make their design standards and conventions, as well as their decisions about ethical and other tradeoffs, clear to others outside their own community of scholars. Then, they must enter into debates about the most compelling explanations, the most convincing evidence, and the most useful and least harmful ways of thinking about educational reform and taking action pursuant to it. To some extent, educational anthropologists already do this, as do research specialists in other fields. However, many of these so-called debates occur among close associates or specialists within a subarea and never reach a level where divergent perspectives clash and must be reconciled if reform of practice or policy is to follow. As we said about external value constraints, we do not think educational ethnographers have good reasons to remain outside the fray.

In the next section, we discuss the validity for educational research of a specific educational ethnography. In using this example, we suggest what must be debated and decided by educational researchers with the assistance of educational ethnographers. We emphasize that a determination of the validity of an individual study for educational research purposes depends on two things: (1) an application of our five general standards that is sensitive to the research conventions of the tradition in which the study was conceived and (2) the researcher's ability to clearly, cogently, and comprehensively describe the study with respect to the general standards.

Assessing One Educational Ethnography

The book *Educated in Romance: Women, Achievement, and College Culture* (1990), by Dorothy Holland and Margaret Eisenhart, analyzes the college experiences and career commitments of a small number of academically talented black and white women who began college in 1979. The research reported in the book included an ethnographic study of the women during their first 2 years of college, followup interviews with the women in 1983 and 1987, a survey, and a series of ethnosemantic studies of a larger number of college women and some men. Here we discuss the ethnographic study only.

If we were to assess the validity of this ethnographic study according to the position we have taken earlier, we would have to ask: "Does this study make a valid argument in a general way (for educational research) as well as a design-specific way (for educational anthropology)?" In other words, does this study measure up to our standards for general validity as well as to design-specific standards for ethnography?

It should be noted at the outset that at the general level we are applying standards to this work that Holland and Eisenhart did not anticipate. They did not write their book primarily for an educational research audience. Anthropologists themselves, they wrote for their colleagues in anthropology. One question before us is whether the argument developed in this book meets design-specific standards for a good ethnography. A second question, and more important for this paper, is whether the argument in the book also meets the requirements of general validity for educational research as described in our five general standards. Because the two of us are not in a good position to make a conclusive judgment about the validity of this study—we do not, after all, constitute either the community of educational anthropologists or educational researchers—we use the example primarily to illustrate the kinds of questions that come up and must be decided when the validity of a specific study for educational research is being considered.

If we begin with the standard 3 requirement to locate the ethnography within a subarea tradition of educational anthropology, we find that the ethnographic study reported in *Educated in Romance* was originally designed within the context of one subarea (devoted to explorations based on theories of symbolic interactionism), but the ethnographic data were eventually used to address research questions derived from another subarea (devoted to explorations based on theories of social reproduction). In the book, the authors devote considerable space—two chapters—to locating their final work in a tradition of scholarship. Part of a third chapter is devoted to an explanation of the two authors' own interests, attitudes, and biases pertinent to the study and its evolution. In general, we found extensive coverage of information relevant to assessing how well the study measures up to standard 3.

But given the standard 1 requirement for cogent development of the research design, what are we to make of the switch from one scholarship tradition to another? On the one hand, the authors provide considerable information about the fit between both their original and final research questions and design. They discuss in some detail how they came to realize that their original ideas about how college life would influence the career-related decisions of college women—the ideas that led to their research questions and design—were not borne out by their data. Based on previous research including some of their own, the authors originally anticipated that student peer groups would exert a direct influence on women's thinking and actions related to majors, careers, and other plans for adulthood. The ethnographic study was designed to investigate this influence by addressing the following four research questions (Holland and Eisenhart, 1979:16–17): (1) What is the content of male versus female roles and identities as promoted by the peer groups of college-age females? (2) What is the process through which college-age women are affected by their peer group in choice of college major? (3) What variation is there among peer groups of college-age women with respect to content of male versus female roles and identities and what seem to be factors promoting these inter-peer-group differences? (4) To what extent can peer-group characteristics "explain" differences in choice of majors by college-age women?

However, the authors found that the women's peers had very little information about each other's career-related plans and cared very little about them. The authors were forced to ask themselves a different question: What were the women and their peers interested in and what did they spend their time doing on campus? The need for the second question became obvious only after most of the ethnographic data had been collected and a preliminary analysis of some of the data had been completed. At about the same time, new theoretical perspectives and debates were emerging in educational anthropology and affected the authors' thinking about their study and data. Thus, the data were ultimately used to address a different set of research questions than originally intended (Holland and Eisenhart, 1990:59–60). These questions were the following: (1) What were the women's responses to the university? (2) How did their responses oppose, if they did, the patriarchal conditions that they faced? (3) How did their everyday experiences, their "lived culture," enter into the "choices" and "decisions" that they were making about their future careers and domestic arrangements? (4) What role did the peer group play in affecting university women's "choices" and "decisions" about their future lives? (5) What were the important divisions within the peer group and the important issues of "gender politics" within the student body? The final research questions were derived from the researchers' experiences with their data and new ways of thinking; these questions would not have occurred to them in 1979.

Did method drive research in an invalid way here? Yes and no. In one sense, the data obtained from the ethnographic study determined the future course of the study. On the other hand, ethnographic research is well known for just the sort of flexibility illustrated in this study. According to ethnographic research tradition, flexibility is valuable to the extent that it permits the researcher to adjust her or his original research questions or procedures to fit the special characteristics of those being studied (see Goetz and LeCompte, 1984; Spradley,

1980; also Spindler, 1982, cited earlier). Often, changes in research design, questions, and procedures are considered *necessary* to produce valid ethnographic results, that is, to demonstrate that the participants' culture, not that of the researchers, is being described and analyzed. In this light, unexpected evidence, not the method *per se*, made the change necessary and served to validate it, at least in the eyes of ethnographers. However, with respect to our standard 1 for educational research, a question remains about the fit between the original methods and the later research questions. Were the methods appropriate for the new questions?

Additional light can be shed on this question by referring again to ethnographic convention. At the time Holland and Eisenhart (1979) formulated their study, subareas of educational anthropology devoted to studies of symbolic interaction and social reproduction shared some commitments to ethnographic research design [compare for example the symbolic interactionist purposes and ethnographic designs described in Spindler's *Doing the Ethnography of Schooling* (1982) or Erickson and Shultz' *The Counselor as Gatekeeper* (1982) with the social reproduction purposes and ethnographic designs in Everhart's *Reading, Writing, and Resistance* (1983) or Willis' *Learning to Labor* (1977)]. In both subareas, the criteria for a good ethnography as outlined by Spindler (1982) would have applied in 1979. Holland and Eisenhart's study met all these criteria. However, by the mid-1980s, when Holland and Eisenhart were analyzing and writing up their findings, ethnographic research design criteria for studies based on theories of social reproduction (and their various revisions) were being reconceptualized along lines similar to Roman's position discussed earlier in this paper (Roman and Apple, 1990). Thus, it seems that the research design used in *Educated in Romance* was cogent, for its time and place in ethnographic tradition, but it might not be were the study conceived today.

Regarding our general standard 2 (requiring competent use of procedures), the authors of *Educated in Romance* took the approach of describing their procedures in the appendix of their book. Like most ethnographers, they did not comment directly on their reasons for selecting the procedures they used or on the limitations of their procedures. They relied primarily on the conventions and shorthand descriptions in which they had been trained as cultural anthropologists and on the power of the data revealed in the book to establish the appropriateness and quality of their techniques. This is standard operating procedure for cultural anthropologists (Geertz, 1988) and, thus, may be considered adequate, among ethnographers, to establish their competence in using ethnographic procedures. However, although enough information is provided to know *what* procedures the authors used, we cannot learn enough about the authors' reasons for using certain procedures to meet the spirit of standard 2. If educational researchers are to translate among diverse studies of similar topics, they must be told about the reasons for as well as the conduct of their methodological procedures.

Not surprisingly, Holland and Eisenhart also followed ethnographic convention regarding value constraints in their study. Before the study began, they apprised potential study participants of the nature of their involvement (e.g., that researchers would be spending large amounts of time with participants, that researchers would try to get to know participants as friends and to understand their worlds as they did). They explained the topic of the study at the time. They promised confidentiality and obtained written consent. However, they felt no special compunction to alert participants to later decisions to change the topic of the research or to have participants review or approve the researchers' interpretations. In fact, their silence was so complete that during the final follow-up interviews in 1987, some of the participants told the interviewers that they did not want to give any more information until they could read what had been written about them.

Again, this approach is consistent with ethnographic convention, but it is not consistent with our general commitment to internal value constraints in educational research as outlined in standard 4. To meet our general requirements for validity in educational research is, we think, to make these internal value considerations explicit throughout the design, conduct, revision, and interpretation of a research study.

With respect to standard 5 (comprehensiveness), the overall quality, balance of tradeoffs, and durability of *Educated in Romance* remain to be debated within the ethnographic and educational research communities. Our brief review of the book indicates some of the questions that must be addressed in the debate. Because the book is so new, the relevant communities are just now beginning to read it and assess it.

Summary

Returning to our general standards with the illustrations from educational anthropology and *Educated in Romance* in mind, we find that adhering to the first three general standards means identifying the subarea of scholarship to which a particular anthropological study of education is intended to contribute, formulating timely research questions (for the subarea), and choosing research methods that will permit the questions to be addressed, in that order. Although a commitment to meet our general standards 1–3 may require more explanation of background assumptions and methodological strategies than would be necessary within anthropology, meeting the general standards does not necessarily require steps different or additional to those ordinarily required in educational anthropology. In other words, the first three standards do not constrain or change the focus of work within the subarea. This is not the case for the other two standards. Standards 4 and 5 require researchers to address more general but serious questions about the significance of the research, the use and manipulation of human subjects as a part or consequence of the work, the researchers' commitment to and success at explaining and using the study's results and its implications for constructive change, and the ability of the research to stand up to public debate of its merits and worth.

In general, the treatment we have given above to educational anthropology and ethnography serves as an illustration of how we could assess the validity of arguments based on other specific research designs (both qualitative and quantitative) for educational research. We think it likely, however, that other specific designs will measure up to our standards for general validity in different ways. For example, those who conduct experimental studies seem to have very well-developed conventions for handling and describing their methodological competence (standard 2), yet their articles may include very little about the scholarship traditions and commitments that underlie or motivate their work (standard 3). Naturalistic inquirers, on the other hand, seem to have well-developed ideas about handling value constraints but lack clear or agreed-upon standards for research design or procedures. Naturalistic inquirers may be able to rely on the standards developed within their own tradition to meet the requirements of standard 4 but may have to look elsewhere for help to meet the requirements of standard 2. In another contrast, educational ethnographers, who have well-developed standards for research design but only limited conventions for handling value constraints, may rely on their subarea tradition to meet the requirements of standard 2 and look elsewhere for advice about how to meet standard 4.

Conclusion

We observed at the outset of this chapter that the appearance and subsequent growth of the use of qualitative methods in educational research spurred interest in developing formal standards for assessing the validity of qualitative research. Explicating such standards is important because it serves in general to legitimate qualitative educational research and in particular to make possible economy of thought in designing and evaluating research, to provide a starting point for reflecting on and improving the research enterprise, and as a vehicle for communication among researchers about what constitutes effective and defensible practice.

In our view, however, the three basic approaches to standards of validity for qualitative research that we labeled adaptation of the conventional approach, alternatives to the conventional approach, and eclecticism each fall short of providing an adequate conception. To reiterate, adaptation of the conventional approach encourages the view that all educational research must conform to the same standards—standards such as internal validity, external validity, and construct validity—whereas alternatives to the conventional conception and eclecticism each encourages the view that different types of educational research, particularly quantitative versus qualitative, must conform to quite different, even exclusive, standards.

In virtue of our appeal to the distinction between general and design-specific standards, our alternative conception construes validity as unitary but nonetheless two-tiered. In particular cases, fully informed validity judgments will require a grasp of design-specific standards (and the other papers in this volume no doubt have much more to contribute regarding these standards). With regard to educational research, we would emphasize, however, that design-specific standards are only necessary requirements insofar as they are subsumed by the requirements of the general standards. Related to this, we would also emphasize that design-specific standards should not serve to cut off discussion across research traditions, to foster "paradigm cliques" (Howe, 1988). Here, as elsewhere, we advocate a unity of purpose within educational research that nonetheless permits a diversity of approaches. As Abraham Kaplan (1964) remarks regarding science more generally,

> It will not do to say, "You people simply don't understand our problems!" or, "We have our own logic, our own standards of truth." There are indeed differences among the various disciplines, and these differences are important to the conduct of inquiry in each case. But they do not serve to cut the sciences off from one another . . . . In the one world of ideas there are no barriers to trade or travel. (pp. 3–4)

Notes

[1] In this section and the next two (on adaptations and alternatives to the conventional approach), we summarize positions on validity that are frequently cited and have influ-

enced the work of educational researchers from the 1960s through the 1980s. Readers should be aware, however, that these positions are now historical artifacts and that in many cases authors have extended, changed, or recanted their earlier views. Furthermore, many others, not cited here, have written about validity. Our intent is not to provide a comprehensive and detailed discussion of the history of positions on validity and changes in these positions over time but, rather, to highlight major themes in positions that we think have been most influential on educational research of the past several decades. However, to alert readers to more current or revised positions, we direct them to the following: For a compendium of the development of Campbell's thinking, including his work with Stanley, see Campbell (1988; edited by E. Samuel Overman); for a review and update of the work of Lincoln and Guba, see Lincoln (1990); for a revision of the work of Goetz and LeCompte, see LeCompte and Preissle (in press), Preissle-Goetz (1989), and Borman, LeCompte, and Goetz (1986); and for a revision of Erickson's position, see Erickson (1989).

[2] We agree with this point and have elsewhere extended it by pointing out that idealtypical research designs may also be altered or significantly reconceived when research questions are posed in accord with new or different theoretical positions (Howe and Eisenhart, 1990). Research designs are neither immutable nor are they independent of their contexts of use: They are changed over time, as the nature of theories, researchable questions, and methodological approaches change.

[3] For an argument that the idea of validity does not at all serve as a good criterion for qualitative research, readers are advised to consult Wolcott (1990). In referring to his own ethnographic work, Wolcott writes, "I try to understand, rather than to convince" (p. 148).

[4] Portions of our discussion of general standards are taken from Howe and Eisenhart (1990).

[5] We will address the issue of *important* research questions under "Value Constraints," our fourth standard.

[6] This is a revised version of the standard labeled "overall warrant" in Howe and Eisenhart (1990).

[7] Because we expect the logic of each research design to dictate both the manner and the order in which the five general standards are appropriately addressed, we do not expect the pattern described for ethnographic research to be true in every case. We take up this issue in more detail later in the paper.

References

Anderson, G. L. (1989). Critical ethnography in education: Origins, current status, and new directions. *Review of Educational Research, 59*(3), 249–270.

Atkinson, P., Delamont, S., and Hammersley, M. (1988). Qualitative research traditions: A British response to Jacob. *Review of Educational Research, 58*(2), 231–250.

Borman, K. M., LeCompte, M. D., and Goetz, J. P. (1986). Ethnographic research design and why it doesn't work. *American Behavioral Scientist, 3*(1), 43–57.

Bredo, E., and Feinberg, W. (Eds.). (1982). *Knowledge and values in social and educational research.* Philadelphia: Temple University Press.

Campbell, D. T. (1963a). From description to experimentation: Interpreting trends as quasi-experiments. *In* C. W. Harris (Ed.), *Problems in measuring change* (pp. 212–242). Madison, WI: University of Chicago Press.

Campbell, D. T. (1963b). Social attitudes and other acquired behavioral dispositions. *In* S. Koch (Ed.), *Psychology: A study of Science. Volume 6. Investigations of man as socius.* New York: Rand McNally.

678   Margaret A. Eisenhart and Kenneth R. Howe

Campbell, D. T. (Overman, E. S., Ed.). (1988). *Methodology and epistemology for social science: Selected papers*. Chicago: University of Chicago Press.

Campbell, D. T., and Stanley, J. C. (1963). *Experimental and quasi-experimental designs for research*. Chicago: Rand McNally.

Cook, T. D., and Campbell, D. T. (1979). *Quasi-experimentation: Design and analysis issues for field settings*. Chicago: Rand McNally.

Denzin, N. (1970, 1978). *The research act: A theoretical introduction to sociological methods* (1st and 2nd eds.). New York: McGraw-Hill.

Denzin, N. (1989). *The research act: A theoretical introduction to sociological methods* (3rd ed.). Englewood Cliffs, NJ: Prentice-Hall.

Dunn, W. N. (1982). Reforms as arguments. *Knowledge: Creation, Diffusion, Utilization*, 3(3), 293–326.

Eisenhart, M. (1988). The ethnographic research tradition and mathematics education research. *Journal for Research in Mathematics Education*, 19(2), 99–114.

Eisenhart, M., and Holland, D. C. (in press). Gender constructs and career commitment: The influence of peer culture on women in college. In T. L. Whitehead and B. Reid (Eds.), *Gender constructs and social issues*. Champaign, IL: University of Illinois Press.

Erickson, F. (1986). Qualitative methods of research on teaching. In M. Wittrock (Ed.), *Handbook of research on teaching* (pp. 119–161). New York: Macmillan.

Erickson, F. (1989). Validity in qualitative research. Paper presented at meeting of the American Educational Research Association, San Francisco, March.

Erickson, F., and Shultz, J. (1982). *The counselor as gatekeeper: Social interaction in interviews*. New York: Academic Press.

Everhart, R. B. (1983). *Reading, writing, and resistance: Adolescence and labor in a junior high school*. Boston: Routledge and Kegan Paul.

Finn, C. E. (1988). What ails education research? *Educational Researcher*, 17(1), 5–8.

Geertz, C. (1987). Interpretive anthropology. In H. Applebaum (Ed.), *Perspectives in cultural anthropology* (pp. 520–524). Albany: State University of New York Press.

Geertz, C. (1988). *Works and lives: The anthropologist as author*. Stanford, CA: Stanford University Press.

Goetz, J. P., and LeCompte, M. D. (1984). *Ethnography and qualitative design in educational research*. New York: Academic Press.

Hansen, J. F. (1979). *Sociocultural perspectives on human learning: An introduction to educational anthropology*. Englewood Cliffs, NJ: Prentice-Hall.

Holland, D. C., and Eisenhart, M. A. (1979). Women's peer groups and choice of career. Proposal for research project. Washington, DC: National Institute of Education.

Holland, D. C., and Eisenhart, M. A. (1990). *Educated in romance: Women, achievement, and college culture*. Chicago: University of Chicago Press.

House, E. R. (1977). *The logic of evaluative argument*. CSE Monograph Series in Evaluation. Los Angeles: Center for the Study of Evaluation, University of California.

House, E. R. (1980). *Evaluating with validity*. Beverly Hills, CA: Sage Publications.

Howe, K. (1985). Two dogmas of educational research. *Educational Researcher*, 14(8), 10–18.

Howe, K. (1988). Against the quantitative–qualitative incompatibility thesis (or, dogmas die hard). *Educational Researcher*, 17(8), 10–16.

Howe, K., and Eisenhart, M. (1990). Standards for qualitative (and quantitative) research: A prolegomenon. *Educational Researcher*, 19(4), 2–9.

Jackson, P. W. (1990). The functions of educational research. *Educational Researcher*, 19(7), 3–9.

Jacob, E. (1987). Qualitative research traditions: A review. *Review of Educational Research*, 57(1), 1–50.

Jacob, E. (1988). Clarifying qualitative research: A focus on traditions. *Educational Researcher*, 17(1), 16–24.

Kaplan, A. (1964). *The conduct of inquiry*. San Francisco: Chandler.

Kirkup, G. (1986). The feminist evaluator. *In* E. R. House (Ed.), *New directions in educational evaluation* (pp. 68–84). London: Falmer Press.

Lather, P. (1986). Research as praxis. *Harvard Educational Review*, 56(3), 257–277.

LeCompte, M. D., and Preissle, J. (in press). *Ethnography and qualitative design in educational research* (2nd ed.). San Diego: Academic Press.

Lincoln, Y. (1990). The making of a constructivist: A remembrance of transformations past. In E. Guba (Ed.), *The paradigm dialog* (pp. 67–87). Newbury Park, CA: Sage Publications.

Lincoln, Y., and Guba, E. (1985). *Naturalistic inquiry*. Beverly Hills, CA: Sage Publications.

Messick, S. (1989). Validity. *In* R. L. Linn (Ed.), *Educational measurement* (3rd ed., pp. 13–103). New York: American Council on Education and Macmillan Publishing.

Milgram, S. (1974). *Obedience to authority: An experimental view*. New York: Harper & Row.

Pelto, P. J., and Pelto, G. H. (1978). *Anthropological research: The structure of inquiry* (2nd ed.). Cambridge: Cambridge University Press.

Peshkin, A. (1988). In search of subjectivity—One's own. *Educational Researcher*, 17(7), 17–22.

Phillips, D. (1987). Validity in qualitative research: Why the worry with warrant will not wane. *Education and Urban Society*, 20(1), 9–24.

Preissle-Goetz, J. P. (1989). Validity in qualitative research. Paper presented at meeting of the American Educational Research Association, San Francisco, March.

Quinn, N., and Holland, D. (1987). *Cultural models in language and thought*. Cambridge: Cambridge University Press.

Roman, L. (1989). Double exposure: Politics of feminist research. Paper presented at the Qualitative Research in Education Conference, University of Georgia, Athens, GA, January.

Roman, L., and Apple, M. (1990). Is naturalism a move away from positivism? Materialist and feminist approaches to subjectivity in ethnographic research. *In* E. Eisner and A. Peshkin (Eds.), *Qualitative inquiry in education: The continuing debate* (pp. 38–73). New York: Teachers College Press.

Rorty, R. (1982). Method, social science, social hope. *In* R. Rorty (Ed.), *Consequences of pragmatism* (pp. 191–210). Minneapolis: University of Minnesota Press.

Shavelson, R. J., and Berliner, D. C. (1988). Erosion of the educational research infrastructure. *Educational Researcher*, 17(1), 9–12.

Shulman, L. (1988). Disciplines of inquiry in education: An overview. *In* R. M. Jaeger (Ed.), *Complementary methods for research in education* (pp. 3–17). Washington, DC: American Educational Research Association.

Smith, J. K. (1990). Alternative research paradigms and the problem of criteria. *In* E. Guba (Ed.), *The paradigm dialog* (pp. 167–187). Newbury Park, CA: Sage Publications.

Smith, M. L., and Glass, G. V. (1987). *Research and evaluation in education and the social sciences*. Englewood Cliffs, NJ: Prentice-Hall.

Spindler, G. D. (1982). General introduction. *In* G. D. Spindler (Ed.), *Doing the ethnography of schooling: Educational anthropology in action* (pp. 1–13). New York: Holt, Rinehart & Winston.

Spradley, J. P. (1980). *Participant observation.* New York: Holt, Rinehart & Winston.

Tobin, J., Wu, W., and Davidson, D. (1989). *Preschool in three cultures: Japan, China, and the United States.* New Haven: Yale University Press.

Van Maanen, J. (1988). *Tales of the field.* Chicago: University of Chicago Press.

Weiss, C. H. (1983). The stakeholder approach to evaluation: Origins and promise. *In* A. S. Bryk (Ed.), *Stakeholder-based evaluation.* New Directions for Program Evaluation (no. 17, pp. 3–14). San Francisco: Jossey-Bass.

Willis, P. (1977). *Learning to labor: How working class kids get working class jobs.* New York: Columbia University Press.

Wolcott, H. (1990). On seeking—and rejecting—validity in qualitative research. *In* E. Eisner and A. Peshkin (Eds.), *Qualitative inquiry in education: The continuing debate* (pp. 121–152). New York: Teachers College Press.

CHAPTER 15

❏ Subjectivity in Qualitative Research

Golie Jansen and Alan Peshkin

*The Handbook of Qualitative
Research in Education*

Introduction

As a concept, subjectivity usually does not stand alone. It is the historically less-celebrated partner of the objectivity–subjectivity dyad. Although strongly linked, the partners have not enjoyed equal respect and treatment. Objectivity undoubtedly has been the favorite, subjectivity the stepchild. In scholarly circles where "rigor" reigns, the terms objective and objectivity still carry the stamp of acclaim and acceptance, whereas subjectivity does not. However, as post-positivist voices become increasingly vocal in current paradigm and methodology debates, the status of subjectivity has risen to the point of being called "virtuous" (Peshkin, 1985).

Thinking about subjectivity and objectivity in qualitative research takes place in the larger context of science and culture, where the "assumptions, commitments and metaphors that have shaped these oppositions . . . are being called into question (Bernstein, 1983:2). Bernstein observes an "uneasiness" about these oppositions in academic circles, likened to "Cartesian Anxiety," which he and other scholars are ready to exorcize. At the root of the current so-called paradigm debates, century-old questions still exist, such as the following. Is there a "real world" out there? What is the nature and scope of truth, reason, and rationality? In the education community, these debates are described variously as the "paradigm dialog" (Guba, 1990a), paradigm conflict (Schwandt, 1989), and paradigm wars (Gage, 1989). The debate is often unsettling, in light of the same century-old desire for certainty. The unease may relate to the fact that the debate is not just an expression of an intellectual issue. According to Bernstein (1983:4), "perplexing questions concerning human beings: what we are, what we can know, what norms are to bind us, what are the grounds for hope" are at the core of the debate.

In the course of the epistemology and methodology debates, we see a noticeable shift in thinking about the understandings and definitions of subjectivity. Terms associated with subjectivity, such as distortion and bias, face competition from perspectives that see subjectivity as a unique, useful, personal quality of a researcher (Krieger, 1985; Peshkin, 1985, 1988; Rubin, 1981; Smith, 1980) or as a tribute that marks the interaction between researchers and their research participants (Eisner, 1990; Guba, 1990a; Reinharz, 1983; Roman and Apple, 1990). When subjectivity is seen as distortion and bias, the literature offers more or less prescriptive advice; when seen as an interactional quality, we learn about personal, reflexive, or political and theoretical stances.

In this chapter, we will place subjectivity and its illustrious partner, objectivity, in a historical context, discussing the roots of various definitions and understandings of subjectivity. We will then discuss how subjectivity is treated by scholars belonging to different "schools of thought," such as ethnographers, critical theorists, feminists, and other theoretically unspecified qualitative researchers in education. Finally, we will address methodological issues, such as the relationship between researcher and researched, strategies to "manage" subjectivity, and the role of subjectivity in constructing a text.

Subjectivity in Historical Perspective

The idea of objective knowledge discloses from the beginning a curious irony, a division within itself. For it shares with any conception of knowledge the necessity that it appear within the consciousness of an active subject; yet almost the very definition of the objective requires that it be other than the active subject who is aware of it. An object is something that appears within a man's consciousness which is not himself because it has existence and form of its own which he cannot control; in this sense, it opposes him. (Diefenbeck, 1984:3)

This "curious irony" has dominated the history of Western thought. Reason, truth, and objectivity as prevailing concepts in ideas about knowledge are always considered in relation to ideas about the subject. Ontology (the nature of reality), epistemology (the knower–known relationship), and methodology all originate in concerns about objectivity and subjectivity.

These concerns were no stranger to the Greeks. We find in Plato, who sought a normative solution to the establishment of objective truth, and in Aristotle, who sought truth in description of observable forms, an interest in subject–object relationships (Diefenbeck, 1984). Central in their thinking was their search for truth and certainty, for what is the "real" world. Parminedes developed the concept of a real world independent of sense perceptions that can be known with certainty (Diefenbeck, 1984), whereas as Caton (1973) states, "Socrates reminds us of the necessity to acknowledge the distinction between what appears to us and what is in reality, i.e., between opinion and knowledge" (p. 28). The result of such knowing is objective knowledge, which means in these views that "there is a world of objective reality that exists independently of us and that has a determinate nature or essence that we can know" (Bernstein, 1983:9).

Descartes and Kant, as founders of modern scientific thought, attributed a dual nature to reality, creating the either/or reasoning that still underlies modern thinking. Descartes brought the "dualities of subjective knower and objective known, of mind and matter, of consciousness and body . . . [to] conceptual adulthood" (Barone, 1990:4). Descartes, like Kant and the Greeks, was anxious to establish a universal objective foundation of knowledge. While Plato and Aristotle understood ideas as ultimately derived from Divine Reason, Descartes placed the authority of reason within the thinking subject, thereby becoming the founder of modern philosophy (Judovitz, 1988; Madison, 1988). His project is a search for truth as certainty. In his *Discourse*, searching to prove his existence, Descartes rejects everything that could be doubtful: "because our senses sometimes play us false, I decided to suppose that there was nothing at all which was such as they cause us to imagine (Descartes, 1968:53). Reflecting on himself as a thinker, and giving primacy to his mind in establishing truth, he self-consciously declared "I am thinking, therefore I exist" (p. 53). This principle, The Cogito, is the first "subjective" principle from which Descartes deduced his philosophy.

In his *Meditations* (Descartes, 1968), he further clarifies his essence as being a "thinking thing," while establishing a body–mind duality: "that is to say my mind, by which I am what I am, is entirely and truly distinct from my body, and may exist without it" (p. 156). Descartes' introduction of subjectivity, according to Judovitz (1988), "implies a new worldview, defined by theoretical priority of the subject and the reduction of the world to an object" (p. 2). This duality paved the way for modern science in which man is seen as "the master and possessor of Nature" (Descartes, 1968). As a method to establish truth, Descartes found certainty in the rationality of mathematical principles that would be the basis for a science that emphasized method rather than insight. In such a science, the question of what is true is settled by the ultimate premise of objective knowledge. In summary, "at the heart of Cartesian . . . philosophy has been the conviction of the universality of reason and the belief that there are universal standards and criteria of rationality" (Bernstein, 1983:29). As a paradigm, positivism fits these standards and, according to Barone (1990), represents the "mature" half of the dyad. He cites the *Encyclopedia of Philosophy* (1972) characterization of positivism as claiming "that science is the only valid source of knowledge, and facts the only possible objects of knowledge . . . [Positivism] opposes . . . in general, any procedure or investigation that is not reducible to scientific method" (p. 14 *in* Barone, 1990:5).

The philosophical debates after Descartes are all about different notions of subjectivity (knowing subject) and an objective world; ontological debates that continue to struggle with this dualism, yet often privilege one side of this subjectivity–objectivity dyad over the other.

Historically, different terms have been used for dichotomized ontologies underlying scientific methodologies. These sides are variously known as the objectivists and relativists (Bernstein, 1983), objectivists and subjectivists (Couch, 1987; Giddens, 1986), or the empiricists and idealists (Riley, 1974). Notwithstanding the appearance of changing issues, scholars still debate the questions of what is true, real, or rational. The following discussion offers examples of various ways scholars understand the subjectivity–objectivity dyad, but it is by no means a complete treatment of this debate.

The Dyad Defined

Objectivism is variously contrasted with relativism (Bernstein, 1983) by philosophers or with subjectivism (Couch, 1987; Giddens, 1986) by social scientists. Bernstein (1983), for example, defines objectivism as ". . . the basic conviction that there is or must be some permanent, ahistorical matrix or framework to which we can ultimately appeal in determining the nature of rationality, knowledge, truth, reality, goodness or rightness" (p. 8). He considers this position strongly related to foundationalism and states that this ontological view led to the acceptance of an epistemological distinction between the subject and the object. "What is 'out there' (objective) is presumed to be independent of us (subjects), and knowledge is achieved when a subject correctly mirrors or represents objective reality" (Bernstein, 1983:9). Relativism, in contrast, is defined as a context-dependent philosophical definition. It is, says Bernstein (1983),

> . . . the basic conviction that when we turn to the examination of those concepts that philosophers have taken to be the most fundamental— whether it is the concept of rationality, truth, reality, right, the good or norms—we are forced to recognize that in the final analysis all such concepts must be understood as relative to a specific conceptual scheme, theoretical framework, paradigm, form of life, society or culture. (p. 8)

Couch (1987), a sociologist, discusses the "objective–subjective controversy" (p. 105) as stemming from different ontologies and competing epistemologies. He contrasts objectivism with subjectivism.

Subjectivists claim that "all observations of human life are subjective," whereas objectivists claim that "the existence of an 'objective' world . . . can be comprehended" (p. 116). In tracing the different ontologies, he brings in perspectives from the natural sciences, rather than from philosophy, and presents the objectivist perspective as derived from the Newtonian ontology of the early inorganic physical sciences. According to this ontology, there are objects, not processes, to be studied. There is no intentionality, no variation. He quotes Galileo as one such proponent who studied natural phenomena with standardized instrumentation following quantitative procedures of data analysis. His point of view influenced the development of positivism in academia, with methods that, according to Couch, are more compatible with the bureaucratic ethos of modern academia.

Darwin challenged this positivist notion of constancy, or the existence of permanent regularities. Instead, he saw transformations and variations and emphasized processes, rather than objects, as the focus of study. If Darwin were right about an empirical world of variation, Couch notes, then the possibility of "true and everlasting laws" (Couch, 1987:108) was threatened.

Following a Darwinian ontology of change as inherent in organic existence underlies the development of naturalistic procedures in science and social science. In social science, subjectivists support a "naked-eye" enterprise and call for naturalistic procedures to study people and groups in everyday life.

Subjectivists assume a qualitative difference between natural and social phenomena, a distinction that most objectivists deny. In other words, subjectivists see human artifacts as distinct from other objects because they reflect intentionality or future-oriented action. Whereas objectivists assume that human beings are actors without purpose in an objective world, subjectivists see human actions as purposeful. Objectivists and subjectivists also do not agree about what is to be observed. Objectivists study objects (following Durkheim and Comte), while subjectivists study processes, people, or events (see Blumer, 1969; Denzin, 1978, *in* Couch, 1987; Glaser and Strauss, 1967).

Giddens (1986), another sociologist, treats the objectivist–subjectivist dyad as a difference in the perspectives of social theory. In his view, objectivists consider the primacy of social objects (society and social institutions) over individual agents as the core of social analysis, while subjectivists consider the human agent (as an intentional, reasoning actor) as the focus of analysis. Giddens considers that what is generally understood as opposing perspectives are, on closer examination, complementary. He rejects the functionalist notion of structure as external to action; rather, he sees structure as "both the medium and the outcome of human activities" (Giddens, 1986:533). In this understanding, institutions and human agents are mutually interdependent. Giddens criticizes (as do the structuralists and post-structuralists) subjectivist approaches for taking subjectivity for granted. Subjectivity is often "not regarded as a phenomenon to be explicated but is taken to be the basis of what it is to be a human agent" (p. 534). He does not agree, however, with the post-structuralist notion of "decentering of the subject," a concept that could entail a "disappearance of the self as agent" (p. 535).

Giddens (1986) reacts to the post-structuralist's understanding of the unconscious, which is understood as "structured as a human language" (p. 536). Although he sees some benefit in this conceptualization, he also sees limitations in terms of the relationship between consciousness and unconsciousness. To explain his view of this relationship, he introduces the concept of "practical consciousness," a concept that is not used in post-structuralist approaches. Practical consciousness, "the underlined center of human practical activity" (p. 537), refers to the ability of actors to explain their intentions and the reasons expressed in what they say about the circumstances of their actions. Only part of how actors know why they act as they do, however, is communicated discursively; part of this knowledge, while enacted, is not available to discursive awareness. Agency is more than discursive awareness. He concludes:

> Any account of social activity which eliminates the significance of practical consciousness is therefore massively deficient in respect of identifying the forms of knowledgeability that human agents display in the context of social life. I would include all variants of objectivism. (p. 537)

In Giddens' view, practical consciousness is the connection between individual human agency and the institutions that are shaped and reshaped in the daily life of individuals. Rather than viewing the text and writing as the most important explanation of meaning, as post-structuralists do, Giddens suggests that the conversation in the context of time and space is essential to explain meaning. This view affects social theory considerably in that it involves "rescuing the knowledgeable agent as the conceptual center for social analysis, and situating what 'knowledgeability' is in the context of the ongoing practices of social life" (Giddens, 1986:541). Giddens rejects a concept of social life as external to agency and, instead, sees it as "produced and reproduced in the moments of social activity stretching across the time/space context of action" (p. 541). Thus, in his view, the difference between objectivists' and subjectivists' perspectives in social theory is not a dichotomized, but a dialectical relationship. That is, institutions and human actions are mutually constitutive, and human agency in context remains a vital unit of analysis, irreducible to just text for the explanation of meaning.

Subjectivity as a concept enters indirectly into debates about the place of values in social science. After the turn of the century, the prevalent scientific standards included the Weberian notion of science as value-free. Weber saw science as the "arbiter of values" (Barone, 1990:7), holding that one's personal orientations should be separated from the scientific project. Weber's view of science "insured the preservation of the objectivity–subjectivity hierarchy" (Barone, 1990:6). The empiricist's tradition [with proponents such as David Hume, Charles Pierce, and John Dewey (Riley, 1974)] resulted in the logical positivism that became basic to major epistemological assumptions of science and social science. These assumptions are (1) the world exists, independent of human wishes and beliefs; (2) it is possible to know this independently existing world through perception and supportive judgments; and (3) observations and canons of logic provide a check on hypotheses and theories (rather than that the latter determine perceptions and dictate principles of truth and validity) (Riley, 1974:6). This is the "standard view" of science (Scheffler, 1982).

This empiricist tradition is opposed by the idealist tradition [with proponents such as Kant, Hegel, Marx, Mannheim, Wittgenstein, Polyani, and Kuhn (Riley, 1974)], which adheres to the following beliefs: (1) perception is not neutral but, rather, is shaped by linguistic categories and the mental attitudes and interests of observers; (2) truth and validity claims reflect historically determined values and interests of different groups; and (3) reality is mediated by conceptual schemes (Kant), ideologies (Marx), language games (Wittgenstein), and paradigms (Kuhn) (Riley, 1974:6–7). This view sees the world as constructed rather than as discovered. It understands perceptions as "colored" rather than neutral, and assumes that beliefs determine what counts as data, rather than that data and facts constrain belief. Truth and validity are seen as historically relative rather than as derived from common canons (Riley, 1974). The value debates, following these different epistemologies, often reflect anxiety, similar to the Cartesian Anxiety discussed above. They take on a similar either/or quality: Either there is a value-free or objective social science, or social science is "self-consciously political" (Riley, 1974:5).

Subjectivists and Subjectivity

We now turn from the various expressions of the dichotomy to look at those schools of thought that have developed the subjective side of the dyad or transcended the dual perspective of society. As previously shown, subjectivism and subjectivity have different meanings and are understood differently by authors from different schools of thought. They use terms such as interpretive, phenomenological, and hermeneutics to indicate their more subjective approaches to social inquiry.

Two German philosophers, Edmund Husserl and Wilhelm Dilthey, are historical heirs to the subjective side of the objectivity–subjectivity dyad. Their focus is against positivism and the use of methods from the natural sciences to study human life. In *Formal and Transcendental Logic,* Husserl (1969) reacts strongly against the regulative orientation of science. He states, "It is high time that people got over being dazzled, particularly in philosophy and logic, by the ideal and regulative ideas and methods of the 'exact' sciences—as though the In-itself of such sciences were actually an absolute norm for objective being and for truth" (p. 278).

Husserl, called a transcendental subjectivist (Bernstein, 1983), intended to discover the essence of consciousness through which reality can be known. For Husserl, "object" or "reality" are not separate from consciousness but constituted by it: "Neither a world nor any other existence of any conceivable sort comes 'from indoors' into my ego, my life consciousness. Everything outside is what it is in this inside and gets its true being from the givings of it itself. . ." (Husserl, 1969:250). Husserl's thoughts are complicated; however, he makes it clear that in terms of the objectivity–subjectivity debate, he considers the mind and spirit subordinate to material reality and, thus, more trustworthy (Barone, 1990). Although Barone says that few contemporary subjectivists would agree with this position, Husserl does enjoy renewed attention in postmodernist scholarship because he "effectively deconstructed both the 'epistemological subject' and the 'objective world' " (Madison, 1988:xi). Husserl is nevertheless a foundationalist who seeks to establish universal truth and a permanent base for knowledge.

The same can be said about Dilthey, who introduced hermeneutics, a theory of interpretation (Madison, 1988), into the human sciences. Dilthey was interested in sociocultural phenomena and their meanings. He "considered cultural products as expressions of meaning comparable to literary texts—texts written in a variety of scripts such as behavior artifacts and social structure. As expressions of meaning these 'texts' have to be interpreted" (Bulhof, 1980:3). Since

Dilthey was interested in a philosophy of life, he considered the individual as "the point of intersection of cultural systems and organizations into which his existence is woven" (Dilthey, 1964–1966:Vol. VII, p. 251). He was critical of an epistemology in which experience and knowledge are expressed in abstractions:

> There is no real blood flowing in the veins of the knowing subject fabricated by Locke, Hume, and Kant, but only the diluted juice of reason as mere mental activity. But dealing with the whole man in history and psychology led me to take the whole man—in the multiplicity of his power: this willing-feeling-perceiving being—as the basis for explaining knowledge and its concepts. (Dilthey, 1964–1966:Vol. I, p. xviii, *in* Dilthey, 1988:13)

Dilthey rejects transcendence. He looks at experience, "lived experience," as a focus for truth and reality. He, like Husserl, transcends the subjectivity–objectivity dyad, the inner and outer world: "Of course we know nothing about any real world which lies outside of our consciousness. We know of reality (i.e., an external world) only insofar as our will and our positing of goals are determined" (Dilthey, 1964–1966:Vol. VI, *in* Dilthey, 1988:21). In hermeneutics, subject and object are not detached but, rather, engage in a "communicative relationship" (Bleicher, 1982:63). The construction of meaning is based on intersubjective support for individual interpretations and the contexts in which they occur. However, an important question for Dilthey has been "how hermeneutic interpretation of meaning can be made objective" (Bleicher, 1982:63). Concerned with subjectivity as a possibly biasing factor, he stated that "What is shared by all must further be objective in the sense of transcending and encompassing the merely subjective as the private or idiosyncratic" (Dilthey *in* Bleicher, 1982:63). Subjectivists, following Dilthey, then focus on how individuals give meaning to their situation, while often still reflecting the Cartesian anxiety over the existence of objective truth.

Symbolic interactionists, such as Mead and Blumer, believe that positivists have distorted the meaning of naturalism by their focus on objectivity. Instead, they claim that the naturalistic study of behavior is on subjects rather than on objects. Subjects as "selves" act upon situations in terms of their perceptions. Symbolic interactionism accepts the existence of " 'objective' structural features in social reality; but it denies that they exert any determining influence over actions since the latter issue from interpretations which generally vary between actors and contexts" (Bleicher, 1982:107). To understand human behavior as subjective and willful, researchers must participate in these contexts. We can understand "the fundamental human processes . . . because we too are humans with the same subjective capabilities" (Irwin, 1987:41). Symbolic interactionism, then, affirms the principle of subjectivity and is expressed in methods that allow for inductive analysis. However, as Bleicher (1982) finds, Blumer "gives little consideration to the relationship between subject and object—or conceives it in objectivist terms" (p. 111).

Members of the Frankfurter Schule challenged the positivists by charging them with neglecting rational discussions of meanings, values, and experience (Grady and Wells, 1985–1986). They connected value-free science with a kind of irrationality that was characterized by the Nazi movement. They also objected to the idea of a disinterested science that gave no place to the unconscious or to ideological points of view. Habermas, a member of the Frankfurter Schule, proposes intersubjectivity as a central term, both as a critique of positivism and as a refocus on the hermeneutic tradition. For Habermas, the theory of intersubjectivity contrasts with theories that take individual consciousness as the basis for truth. Truth, he considers, is arrived at through the interactions of many individual subjectivities. It is a rational, negotiated agreement among responsible individuals. Thus, as Grady and Wells (1985–1986) state, "The Frankfurter Schule attacked the widely held notion that valid knowledge is restricted to empirically testable propositions arrived at through disinterested, value free inquiry" (p. 34).

Rabinow and Sullivan (1979) discuss the interpretive approach and its focus on particularity and contexts. They take a stand against either objectivity or subjectivity as a useful concept for the understanding of meaning in the interpretive approach. The authors indicate that in all human sciences both the object of investigation and the methods used for investigation "share inescapably the same pervasive context that is the human world" (p. 5). However, this acknowledgment does not give subjective awareness a prime place over detached objectivity. Rather, they state, "the interpretive approach denies and overcomes the almost de rigueur opposition of subjectivity and objectivity" (p. 5). In nineteenth-century interpretive approaches, the major explanation of meaning was based on individual self-consciousness, whereas current interpretive approaches emphasize the "shared world of meaning within which the subjects of human discourse constitute themselves" (p. 5). The recognition of intersubjectivity as the grounding of discourse and opinion in "modes of social relations" surpasses the understanding of meaning as a result of individual subjectivities (p. 6). In this sense, the marking of meaning as either objective or subjective is overcome. Both terms are transcended beyond their individual significance.

Rabinow and Sullivan (1979) joined others who addressed the crisis of the social sciences, which emerged in the 1960s and which is still the focus of much debate. Weberian canons about the separation of fact (empirically observable matters) and value (knowledge of what should be, of ultimate purpose), until then the mainstay of social science research, were questioned (Bredo and Feinberg, 1982; Johnson, 1975). Serious doubts were raised about whether or not any standards, methods, or canons could be claimed for scientific or rational thinking (Fiske and Shweder, 1986).

Since the 1960s, the objectivity–subjectivity debate centered around various issues. A major one was whether the purpose of social science is to produce universal generalizations. Rosenberg, for example, viewed such generalizations as "renunciations of the idea that human subjectivity identified with human will and the human spirit, can be studied scientifically" (1983, in Fiske and Shweder, 1986:5). Thus the use of methods developed for studies in the natural and physical sciences came under attack. Studying people, not objects, requires a method that captures their points of view (Johnson, 1975). This outlook was accompanied by a renewed interest in participant observation.

Another serious issue was at stake: The claim of the value neutrality of science became hotly contested. The questions that Riley (1974) raised—"Is a value-free social science possible? If so, is it desirable? . . . If a value-free social science is a myth, is an objective social science also a myth?" (p. 1)—were common. Riley also made the point that, although never explicitly stated, values imply subjectivity, whereas objectivity does not. The very term scientific is often equated with objectivity. This questioning of science as value-free, objective, and detached caused strong reactions on both sides of the dyad. Scheffler (1982) staunchly defended the ideal of objectivity, arguing that scientists should be impartial and detached, adhering to "an ideal that subjects all scientific statements to the test of independent and impartial criteria, recognizing no authority of persons in the realm of cognition" (1982:1). And sociologist Nisbet (1974), fearing nihilism in academia, reacted similarly: "One is obliged by the evidence . . . to conclude that the most unbelievable thing is the astonishing reversal of belief in the scientific, that is the objective, the detached, the dispassionate character of the social sciences" (in Riley, 1974:15).

Surkin (1974), also a sociologist, reacts just as strongly to the contrary: "In the face of . . . technological explosion and increasing institutionalization and professionalization of knowledge, to claim a neutral or 'objective' role for social science is clearly to fall under the onus of what Merleau-Ponti called 'non-sense'" (*in* Riley, 1974:32). He criticized proponents of the standard view of science for ignoring its political meanings and ideological functions. Value neutrality and the claim to objectivity, he states, "function as a guise for what is in fact becoming an increasingly ideological, nonobjective role for social science knowledge in the service of the dominant institutions in American society" (*in* Riley, 1974:22).

In a similar vein, Bredo and Feinberg (1982) problematize the easily accepted positivist position of the object–subject distinction. As regards the myth of a detached scientist, they say that "The way of looking at things—the scientist's subjectivity—is itself created as the scientist becomes socialized into the scientific community" (1982:116), which, according to them, shapes the scientists' explanations in terms of how to define and use conceptual distinctions.

In these ongoing debates, the positivists' premise of objective knowledge is undermined by claims that "knowledge is at least to some extent dependent on the knowing subject" (Johnson, 1975:17). This shift in epistemology evokes many uncertainties, such as Fiske and Shweder's (1986) questions about "whether a science of subjectivity is possible, [and] what that science of subjectivity might look like" (p. 7). One can conclude that, since the 1960s, positivistic research has not provided the uncontested norm for knowledge building.

Feminists joined post-positivist voices in questioning the standard view of science. The feminist critique converges with the interpretive critique of social sciences in that it also focuses on experiences rather than on abstract categories, although it views knowledge, constructed through dialogue, as discovery (Westcott, 1979). However, feminist scholarship diverges from the interpretive paradigm in its critique of androcentrism in all traditional epistemologies and methodologies: "Feminism overtly challenges the credibility of patriarchal narratives, and at the same time recognizes their persistence as submerged narratives—not least, within theory itself" (Balsamo, 1987:65). Feminists emphasize the absence of women as agents of knowledge (Harding, 1987) and the lack of attention to women's experiences in social science theories (Harding, 1987; Lather, 1986; Smith, 1987a,b; Westcott, 1979). Feminists "claim that the voice of science is a masculine one; that history is written from only the point of view of men (of the dominant class and race); that the subject of a traditional sociological sentence is always assumed to be a man" (Harding, 1987:3).

To Westcott (1979) and Smith (1987b), this feminist critique derives from the personally felt alienation that many women scholars experience. Women as social scientists, argues Westcott (1979), live in a contradictory world: They are engaged through their discipline, yet being a woman alienates them from the content and methods of the social sciences. Smith (1987b) calls this "externalization of sociology" a double estrangement for women (p. 91). Feminists reject the notion of women as "other," inferior, or objects of knowledge (Harding, 1987; Lather, 1986; Reinharz, 1983; Smith, 1987a,b; Westcott, 1979). They criticize the empiricists' notion that subject matter and method are independent; instead, feminists see this relationship as inseparable.

"The canon of objectivity" say Cook and Fonow (1986:9), comes under critical feminist scrutiny. We see this mainly in points of view about the researcher–researched relationship. They oppose the positivists' impersonal and dichotomized relationship and the corresponding belief that this creates more valid knowledge (Cook and Fonow, 1986; Harding, 1987; Lather, 1986; Oakley, 1981; Reinharz, 1983; Smith, 1987a,b; Westcott, 1979). Feminists consider women as participants or agents of knowledge; they connect researchers and subjects of knowledge in dialogue, thereby demystifying objectivity and the objectification of women (Cook and Fonow, 1986; Lather, 1986; Reinharz, 1983). In this view, in the words of the feminist singer Chris Williamsen (quoted *in* Lather, 1986), both the researcher and the researched become "the changer and the changed" (p. 5). In other words, knowledge of self and knowledge of the other are mutually informing (Westcott, 1979).

Harding (1987) posits that "epistemologies assumed in the new analysis of women and gender directly conflict with traditional ones, and they do so in ways that are not always recognized" (p. 181). She points out that the centrality of women's experience in research, and the researcher's position "in the same critical plane" (p. 181) as the research subjects, makes traditional epistemological assumptions impossible. Moreover, the purpose of change in feminist scholarship contradicts a value-free concept of science. Nonetheless, feminist research is thought to yield outcomes that are "more plausible (better supported, more reliable, less false, more likely to be confirmed by evidence, etc.) than the beliefs they replace" (p. 182). Committed to politicized inquiry, but also to objectivity, some feminists are at odds on how best to respond. They do not agree on a uniform epistemology, nor do they agree with the traditional epistemologies from which they borrow their views.

Harding (1986, 1987) views feminists as embracing three possible epistemologies. Feminist empiricists consider androcentrism to be a bias (like any other bias), which can be eliminated by stricter application of scientific methodology. They see the objectivity of an inquiry increased by challenging traditional theoretical concepts and by focusing on the inclusion of women's perspectives in problem definition, data collection techniques, and data analysis. However, while challenging the traditional empiricist notion that gender is not an issue in the production of results, they claim, instead, that women researchers are more likely to produce unbiased results. Driven by feminist concerns, feminist empiricists still adhere very closely to standard empiricist rules (Harding, 1987).

Other feminists, such as interpretive social scientists, criticize objectivity in the belief that the results of research are conditioned by the assumptions and values of feminist researchers. To that end Harding (1987:9) writes, "The best feminist analysis . . . insists that the inquirer her/himself be placed in the same critical plane as the overt subject matter, thereby recovering the entire research process for scrutiny in the results of research." Harding advocates placing the researcher's "class, race, culture and gender assumptions, beliefs, and behaviors . . . within the frame of the picture that she/he attempts to paint" (p. 9). She believes that "Introducing this 'subjective' element into the analysis in fact increases the objectivity of the research and decreases the 'objectivism' which hides this kind of evidence from the public" (p. 9). Smith (1987b) agrees. Critical of sociology's claim to "objective knowledge independent of the sociologist's situation" (p. 91), she claims that the researcher can know a phenomena only from within a socially constructed world.

Knowledge of the world comes from the researcher's relationship with those who know their own world, but whose voices, in an objective sociology, are silent. This perspective is called the feminist-standpoint epistemology. According to Harding (1986), its advocates include Flax (1983), Hartsock (1983), Rose (1983), and Smith (1974, 1979). They believe that taking the gendered social identity of the researcher into consideration can contribute to the potential objectivity of an inquiry. That is, the researcher and the researched are connected through the experience of everyday life. Both the feminist empiricist and the feminist-standpoint epistemologies still want to make scientific accounts more objective (Harding, 1987). Representing the world from the viewpoint of women better serves this purpose than through "incomplete and distorting accounts provided by traditional science" (p. 187).

A third position, that of feminist postmodernism, challenges both the feminist empiricist and the feminist-standpoint epistemologies. Postmodern feminists criticize universal, objective, theoretical claims about women. Although the "master narratives" have changed into feminist narratives, these narratives still represent a universality about women, which women of color, lesbians, and third-world women challenge (Balsamo, 1987). Therefore, postmodern feminists—opposed to universalism—seek to base their inquiry on "the fractured identities modern life creates: Black-feminist, socialist-feminist, women-of-color, and so on" (Harding, 1986:28). Their goal is to focus on and uncover partialities, rather than to discover universalities (Balsamo, 1987). This approach requires ". . . seeking a solidarity in our oppositions to the dangerous fiction of the naturalized, essentialized, uniquely 'human' (read 'manly') and to the distortion and exploitation perpetrated on behalf of this fiction" (Harding, 1986:28).

Postmodern feminists alert us to the point of view that being a woman does not suffice to make all women's experiences similar. Oppression takes on different forms depending on one's race, class, and culture (hooks, 1983). Therefore, "There could not be a feminist standpoint, as the generator of true stories about social life, [but] only . . . feminist oppositions, and criticisms of false stories" (Harding, 1987:188).

Closer to home in the field of education, the paradigm debate, including the debate about subjectivity, has not gone unnoticed. Bredo and Feinberg (1982) discuss a "relatively confusing period, since methodological standards are largely up for grabs" (p. 3). However, most educational research texts still favor the positivistic stance and objectivity as a regulative ideal (Barone, 1990). For instance, for Kirk and Miller (1986), the purpose of research is verification and discovery; objectivity is what makes research reliable and factual. In contrast to objectivity, subjectivity is bias that derives from the predispositions of the researcher. These predispositions—variously seen as to be avoided or as a positive force—influence the process and outcome of research, as we discuss later.

Eisner (1990) addresses the confusion in the use of the term objectivity: ". . . its meaning is not particularly clear, nor . . . are the consequences of the tacit, almost unexamined assumptions upon which it rests" (p. 1). According to him, objectivity refers to (1) the elimination of bias, (2) being fair and open to all sides of an argument, (3) a method or procedure to get information, such as in an objective test, and (4) seeing things the way they are. Eisner distinguishes between ontological objectivity (perceiving the world as it is) and procedural objectivity (referring to the methods used to eliminate personal judgment). He argues that both understandings lead to problems in the conduct of empirical research because they lead researchers to study only measurable phenomena and they reinforce a problematic view of knowledge.

For Eisner, the problematic part of ontological objectivity is its reference to the correspondence theory of truth, which assumes that our views of reality and reality itself are congruent. To satisfy this assumption, states Eisner, one needs to know reality and one's views of it; yet, he says, if we know reality, we do not need a view of it! Eisner also argues the impossibility of knowing the world as it is and affirms the ideas of a context-dependent view of knowledge. "What we come to see depends upon what we seek, and what we seek depends . . . on what we know to say" (p. 7).

Ontological objectivity is further complicated by limitations of representation and perceptual structures. In terms of procedural objectivity, Eisner (1990) addresses the possibility that people could agree on procedures that eliminate judgment. This consensus, however, "provides no purchase on reality" (p. 9). Accordingly, Eisner defines objectivity as "a concept built upon a faulty epistemology that leads to an unrealizable ideal in its ontological state and a matter of consensus . . . in its procedural state (p. 12). Letting go of the ideal of ontological objectivity does not mean that the alternative is "solipsistic subjectivism" (p. 10). Instead, following Dewey, Piaget, and others, Eisner (1990) believes that "whatever it is we think we know is a function of a *transaction* between the qualities of the world we cannot know in their pure, non-mediated form, and the frames of reference, personal skills and individual histories we bring to them [italics in original]" (p. 10). He considers himself a pluralist, believing that there is no single way to make sense out of the world. Multiple voices are needed for the different people who will express understandings and who will receive them.

Eisner sees truth, rather than objectivity, as a regulative ideal. "In so far as our understanding of the world is of our own making, what we consider true is also our own making" (1990, p. 12). While dismantling the concept of objectivity and replacing it with a transactional concept, he, curiously, never addresses the concept of subjectivity.

Barone (1990), however, dismantles both objectivity and subjectivity. He quotes Bernstein (1983), who, following Heidegger, calls into question the objective–subjective dyad as signifying the basic epistemological distinction. Like Eisner, Barone also refers to the "post dyadic mentality" (p. 14) of Dewey and James. Dewey uses experience as a concept basic to the construction of meaning; he sees reality as a transaction between the external objective world and the subjective mind of the observer. This view denies fixed boundaries between object and subject in inquiry. Barone notes the "dual service of the dyad" (p. 13): On the one hand, it provides researchers with criteria for trustworthy knowledge; on the other, it serves therapeutic purposes, because "belief in the dyad offered a sense of safety and security, for it presumed that phenomena were indeed predictable and controllable" (1990:13). However, like Eisner, Barone sees no use for a conception that embraces either ontological or procedural objectivity. Moreover, in a dyadic relationship, he reasons, if one member of the pair no longer is useful, neither is the other: If objectivity loses its value as a regulative ideal, subjectivity follows in the demise of its partner. Subjectivity is a "goner" (p. 9).

Barone proposes to use terms such as useful and persuasive. He explains his stance by turning to books with stories that challenge common understandings of social phenomena. Books such as *Uncle Tom's Cabin* and *Les Miserables* give readers an opportunity to reflect on and reconstruct their own views of reality. Such usefulness is what Barone seeks in educational research. Barone is not alone in believing that when one side of the dyad loses significance, so does the other. Bernstein (1983), for example, says that "If we question, expose and exorcise Cartesianism, then the very opposition of objectivism and relativism loses its plausibility" (p. 19).

Schwandt (1989) is less radical, yet he too claims that the traditional subjectivity–objectivity dichotomy cannot be maintained. In his consideration of the paradigm conflict, he asserts that knowledge is always uncertain. Referring to recent works in physics and philosophy of science (which now also reject a rigid distinction between objectivity and subjectivity), he states that what once was a dichotomy is understood more as a continuum. To this point Schwandt quotes Toulmin (1983):

> As we now realize, the interaction between scientists and their objects of study is always a *two-way* affair. There is no way in which scientists can reduce the effects of their observations on those objects without limits . . . . In the physical sciences, objectivity can now be achieved only in the way it is in the human sciences: the scientist must acknowledge and discount his own reactions to and influence on that which he seeks to understand. (p. 103 *in* Schwandt, 1989:395)

Schwandt emphasizes that differences between paradigms persist even when the objectivity–subjectivity dichotomy is diminished. Paradigms differ in their goals in that the quantitative paradigm seeks prediction and control, whereas the qualitative paradigm seeks understanding. Schwandt asserts that because neither one has a claim to certainty, it is "unproductive to debate which paradigm is scientific, normative, or superior in some other sense" (p. 396).

In education circles, the subjectivity–objectivity debate receives attention as one of the "most fundamental issues in research" (Eisner and Peshkin, 1990:15). At a recent conference on qualitative inquiry, Philips (a post-positivist philosopher) joins Roman (a feminist-materialist ethnographer) and Guba (a proponent of the constructivist perspective) in discussing subjectivity and objectivity. The following is an account of the three positions. We present them to illustrate the divergence of current views and how, when adhering to very different assumptions, one seems to become limited to the internal logic of one's own argument.

Philips calls his paper "Subjectivity and Objectivity: An Objective Inquiry." To begin with, Philips refers to the objectivity-is-dead literature. This includes Eisner, who sees no warrant for the claim of objective or value-free research, believing that "all methods and all representations are partial" (Eisner, 1986:15, *in* Philips, 1990:20).

Philips wonders why anyone doubts that qualitative research, or any research, can be objective. He attributes the decline of objectivity's importance to a shift in epistemologies, from a foundationalist to a nonfoundationalist approach. He credits Popper, Kuhn, Hanson, Feyerabend, and Lakatos with facilitating a move to relativism, thereby enabling the attack on objectivity. However, Philips asserts that an undermined notion of objectivity does not necessarily follow from this shift in epistemology, because objectivity cannot be equated with certainty or truth, and those, he says, are the concepts under attack in the new epistemologies. He sees good reason not to equate certainty with objectivity, because this would mean that if all knowledge is subjective, distinctions are impossible. Nor does the Hansonian view that all observations are theory-laden undermine the notion of objectivity. Scientists can reach a high level of agreement in instances of low-level observations, meaning that they can be high in objectivity.

Unlike Eisner, Philips (1990) sees that inquirers within a particular framework can escape from biases through the practice of peer reviews. These reviews can safeguard the objectivity of judgments. This is the key to Philips' position. "Objective" is a judgment made on the basis of procedural standards, yet he is aware that certainty is not guaranteed. He says, ". . . neither subjectivity nor objectivity has an exclusive stranglehold on truth," and adds, "At any one time, the viewpoint that is the most objective one is the one that is currently the most warranted or rational" (p. 24). From this point of view, objectivity becomes a yardstick to measure inquiry; it gives us criteria to distinguish between "shoddy" and "careful" inquiry.

Following Myrdal (1969) and Popper (1976), Philips sees in the scrutiny of a community of inquirers the basis for the establishment of objectivity in a qualitative sense. Philips agrees with Popper that scientific objectivity is social agreement, not the consequence of an individual scientist's work. Philips (1990) thus defines objectivity as a "stamp of approval" (p. 35) that is given to inquiry that holds up to the critical scrutiny of reviewers. Inquiry that fails to meet such scrutiny is "subjective." It is the inquiry that becomes trustworthy, not the objectivity of the inquirer. Given this outlook, objectivity is very much alive. Philips' ultimate aim is for inquiry to "earn a full stamp of approval" (p. 35).

Roman, who was joined by Apple in preparing her paper (Roman and Apple, 1990), takes a different approach in the paper "Is Naturalism a Move Away from Positivism? Materialist and Feminist Approaches to Subjectivity in Ethnographic Research." Roman and Apple bring explicit *a priori* values to their considerations. They amount to a political agenda that calls for the democratization of knowledge, especially in ethnographic studies of education. They consider the issues relating to the choice of methods and design, and to the validity of conclusions, to be political as well as technical in nature. Their purpose for reexamining epistemological questions in ethnography is to link this mode of research to democratization.

Roman and Apple (1990) understand the subjectivity–objectivity relationship as more than a binary opposition. They view subjectivity as

> . . . a signpost that distinguishes human consciousness of the social and material world. Its interaction with objectivity is a point of contention in which different but related power struggles take place between and among subordinate and dominant groups over what counts as "true" knowledge. (p. 39)

In this conception, subjectivity is not merely one's individual mindset; it encompasses human consciousness, too. It is shaped by power relations based on class, race, gender, age, and sexual orientation. Our subjectivities are affected by these power relations. Subjectivity and objectivity determine each other as "the conflicting sets of historically specific power relations and material interests" (p. 39).

In terms of theory and methodology, Roman and Apple place themselves in the tradition of critical ethnography and feminist materialism (see Harding, 1986; Lather, 1986; Oakley, 1981). While critical of ethnographers who advocate "purging of the researcher's subjectivity" (p. 43), they nevertheless find the most promise in ethnographic research.

Although there are major differences between positivistic methods (experiments, deduction, quantification) and ethnographic methods (contextuality, induction, qualitative description), Roman and Apple (1990) equate them in their concern for objectivity. In both discourses there are assumptions of a detached researcher and similar concerns about reactivity and distortion. Roman and Apple criticize ethnographic research for upholding the positivistic practice of separation between researcher and researched, while assuming that the reality of their setting can be seen as distinct from the inequitable power distribution in the social relationships of the wider society. To ignore these power relationships underlying field research is to think that "social reality is atomistic" (Jagger (1983), cited in Roman and Apple, 1990:51). Roman and Apple contend that when ethnographers emphasize how subjects see reality, they fail to indicate the underlying material conditions that play a role in how subjects come to their views and how they present them. In other words, the researcher, as neutral observer, claims to describe the "appearance of social life" (p. 53), while overlooking, as Jagger (1983) argues, that an implicit theoretical stance is inherent in every method.

According to Roman and Apple (1990), the implications of a materialist–feminist approach to ethnography are that (1) it is antipositivist in both the relationships between theory and data and between the researcher and the researched, (2) it pays attention to the subjective experiences of researchers, (3) researchers account for how underlying power relations affect access to and rapport with research subjects, and (4) researchers take into account their own class background, race, gender, age, and sexual orientation in the conduct of their research and in their writing.

Guba (1990b) responds to both Philips and Roman and Apple. He observes that objectivity is crucial for Philips and it is irrelevant for Roman and Apple. According to Guba, Philips admits to certain arguments against objectivity, yet "devises new definitions that make the concepts more tolerable" (p. 80). He reads Philips as believing in a mandatory accommodation to objectivity as it is conventionally understood, whereas he understands Roman and Apple as having no comparable concern because of their redefinition of subjectivity. They celebrate subjectivity. Guba sees in these two reactions "a complete[ly] different philosophic base from which to project the nature and meaning of inquiry" (p. 81), because they operate from different ontological, epistemological, and methodological premises.

Guba places Philips among the critical realists, who espouse a point of view as described by Cook and Campbell (1979). This point of view is realist because it assumes ". . . that causal relationships exist outside the human mind, and it is critical realist because these valid causal relationships cannot be perceived with total accuracy by our imperfect sensory and intellectual capacities" (p. 29 *in* Guba, 1990b:87). In this perspective, truth is a regulative ideal, and knowledge must be certain. Guba (1990) quotes Philips as saying, "If no knowledge is certain, then there is no possibility for any viewpoint to be objective" (p. 87). Guba agrees with this statement yet draws different implications from it. He agrees that the criterion for objectivity only makes sense when knowledge is certain in principle. However, only within the framework of a realist ontology can objectivity be a useful criterion. Thus he disagrees about the meaning of the term objectivity. His position is that "The term *objectivity* is not a descriptor for the reality that an inquiry (partially) discovers, but for the *process* whereby the putative discovery takes place. Remove the realist ontology and the possibility of an objective epistemology disappears. *The need for objectivity is gone* [italics in original]" (Guba, 1990b:87).

Guba considers Philips' position as consistent with his ontological convictions but sees a problem in Roman and Apple's subjectivist position. Despite their challenge of the positivistic tendencies of ethnography, Guba believes that they themselves adhere to a realist ontology. By their use of expressions such as "underlying social reality" and "structural conditions underlying social subjects' everyday actions" they assume a "real state of affairs" (Guba, 1990b:88). Guba, therefore, invites materialist feminists to adopt a relativist ontology. He denies the need to claim a fixed reality out there for phenomena that are socially constructed. Realities can be negotiated and transformed. Roman and Apple's appeal for democratic change makes sense to Guba, who argues that under the ontological assumption of a socially constructed reality, the epistemological assumption of subjectivity is the only logical alternative.

Guba (1990b) likens his reconstructed version of a materialist feminism to the constructivist paradigm that Lincoln and he propose. This paradigm is based on a relativist, consensual ontology, and it shares an interactive, subjective epistemology with materialist feminism. The constructivist paradigm parts with materialist feminism in terms of methodology. Roman and Apple propose a dialogic, transformative methodology, whereas Lincoln and Guba (1990b:89) term their methodology hermeneutic–dialectic and reconstructive.

Subjectivity and Method

Notwithstanding those who declared the demise of objectivity, and therefore concluded that subjectivity is irrelevant (Barone, 1990), many authors currently focus on how subjectivity plays out in the actual conduct of research. Just as scholars advance different critiques of objectivity on an abstract level, they do not agree on how to respond to subjectivity in the practical conduct of research. They offer varying definitions of subjectivity. Some see subjectivity as taking sides and reject the idea of value neutrality (Boros, 1988; Roman and Apple, 1990); most accept that the emotions and predispositions of researchers influence the research process (Agar, 1980; Krieger, 1985; LeCompte, 1987; Peshkin, 1985, 1988; Rubin, 1981; M. L. Smith, 1980; Stake, 1981) and either term subjectivity as bias (Agar, 1980; Ginsberg and Matthews, n.d.; LeCompte, 1987), a quality of the researcher to capitalize on to enhance understanding (Krieger, 1985; Peshkin, 1985, 1988; Rubin, 1981; Smith, 1980), or interactivity (Eisner, 1990; Guba, 1990a).

Following these differences in definition, there are differences in how to view the researcher–researched relationship, differences that some scholars explore on a epistemological level and that others work out in terms of strategies to become consciously aware of one's subjectivity while engaged in the research process. And, finally, differences are expressed in the making of text, in the ways researchers conceptualize description and interpretation, and how the researcher is present in the account (Geertz, 1988; Rosaldo, 1989).

Subjectivity in the Conduct of Research

The quest should not be for the fools' gold of objectivity, but for the real gold of self-awareness. For it is not our subjectivity that entraps us, but our belief that somehow we can be free of it. (Rubin, 1981:103)

That subjectivity is an "invariable aspect of social research" (Peshkin, 1988) captures the belief of many who have examined subjectivity in the conduct of research. Examining subjectivity from strong ideological positions or from more pragmatic considerations, all the authors we discuss in this section struggle with how and to what extent personal qualities or attributes (such as emotions or one's position as researcher) influence, or should influence, the research process. The following is an account of how various authors have devised ways to "discipline," "manage," or engage their subjectivity.

Stake (1981) called for "a needed subjectivity in educational research." Contrary to the standard emphasis on objectivity, he felt that research, and especially evaluation, "should rely more on personal experience and personal meaning as its data, and more on participant observation and introspection in its method" (p. 1). Stake's concern is for relevance, more than the rigor of measurements. Relevance is enhanced when researchers participate in the lives of the observed and learn about their perspectives as well as their behaviors. Stake (1981), following Rist (1977), advocates the tradition of *Verstehen* (Weber, 1964) as a method that "honors subjectivity" (Stake, 1981:2). He sees value in this outlook because of his special interest in pedagogical practice: ". . . [through] subjectivity we can bring our observations and interpretations more in line with what practitioners perceive to be the processes of education" (Stake, 1981:1).

M. L. Smith (1980) is concerned that the personal emotions of researchers can distort their perceptions. In naturalistic inquiry, "we cannot with assurance separate in the written account the characteristics of what is studied and the characteristics of the researcher" (p. 1). She states that we never know for sure if different researchers conducting the same study will reach similar conclusions. Differences between such accounts are called errors by positivists. While valuing objectivity, naturalistic researchers also acknowledge the unavoidability of the personal equation, which "involves affect, either conscious or unconscious, aroused in either the observer or the person observed, which changes the nature of the account" (M. L. Smith, 1980:2).

Smith's greatest concern is for the emotions of the observer—not the familiar, predictable anxiety of a new situation—but those emotions that are idiosyncratic to the researcher, and therefore unpredictable, evoked by a particular setting or subjects. These unarticulated emotions can distort the research process. Smith came to this position from a fieldwork experience in a high school. As she began to collect data in this high school, she felt isolated, self-conscious, and resentful. She tried to ignore these feelings, believing that they had no place in her study. With the help of a therapist, she realized that she held still unresolved feelings from her own high school days: "In a time, place, and role that were ambiguous and anxiety-provoking, I had filled in the ambiguities . . . not with what was truly there, but with nostalgic and fantasized memories of my own unsuccessful past experiences" (Smith, 1980:5).

Emotional reactions, however, can also enhance the accuracy of an account. Smith (1980) illustrates this by reference to a study in which she explored the special education staffing process. She observed a child whose behavior was problematic but, that, in Smith's eyes, was not severe enough to be labeled behaviorally or emotionally disturbed. She was outraged by the decision to place this child in a learning-disabled class for emotionally disturbed children, because the decision was based on a superficial evaluation process. Although Smith rejected this placement as a researcher, she felt she could not intervene. What she could do was become more committed to find out about the staffing process for special education placements. She notes that "rage is not a dependable emotion with which to interpret experience" (Smith, 1990:9), yet, in retrospect, she believed that this feeling helped to reveal the meaning of the event—a powerful institution exercising rules to unfairly evict a child from a classroom, because the child was seen as obnoxious—better than any facts from folders, transcripts, and conferences.

On the basis of these experiences, Smith (1980) urges researchers to engage in self-examination when they find themselves in a "heightened state of emotion" (p. 10), the better to distinguish between emotions that are generated from the situation and those that may be self-generated and irrational. She identifies several ways to test "the validity" of these feelings. Researchers can check their research journals to recall whether they are angry with someone, dislike someone, or have a personal axe to grind. They also can "gather evidence to test the pet hypothesis against an alternative one" (p. 10). For instance, her hypothesis in the case mentioned earlier was that the student was not learning-disabled; she was placed in a special education classroom because she was disruptive. Smith concludes that "Personalistic bias, though affective in nature, is neither random nor wholly explicable, and may either distort the truth or help one find it" (p. 14).

LeCompte (1987), a sociologist in the Chicago tradition of fieldwork, writes about bias and subjectivity in ethnographic research. She locates bias in the researchers' personal history and professional training. Personal biases derive from the historical time period in which one grows up and from one's sex, social class, and ethnicity. Sources of professional biases may derive from one's identification with a specific research focus in a given time period, from the tradition of ethnography one pursues, from one's adherence to a particular intellectual paradigm, and from the impact of people and opportunities in one's professional life. Perceptions are partial because they always are influenced by the statuses of the researcher. By being conscious of these influences and thereby identifying the sources of their bias, researchers can enhance the quality of their studies.

LeCompte (1987) uses the term "disciplined subjectivity" (p. 43) to describe a practice for determining conscious and unconscious sources of bias. It is a form of intellectual psychoanalysis that she terms "ethnography of the mind" (p. 43). This mode of analysis is similar to the one Hansen (1982) developed for anthropology of learning. Hansen advocates analyzing process, structure, context, and history as well as the relationships between biological and cultural variables. LeCompte (1987) concludes, "These are the ways in which good ethnographers analyze other people; should we not use the same care in analyzing ourselves?" (p. 45).

Agar (1980), an anthropologist, also addresses the biases of ethnographers. He considers being biased as unavoidable. Rather than questioning if ethnographers are biased, he asks what kinds of biases they have, how they play a role in the ethnographic account, and how one can document the way biases operate. Researchers should bring these biases to consciousness, understand them as part of one's methodology, and acknowledge them when drawing conclusions. Though never addressing subjectivity as such, Agar brings up the notion of how ethnographers shape the responses of subjects. By getting to know the ethnographers in their research roles, subjects develop expectations of what the ethnographer wants to learn and thereby decide what they will reveal. Agar states that ethnography is "much more complicated than collecting data," and that "objectivity is perhaps best seen as a label to hide problems in the social sciences" (p. 41). We can infer the inevitability of subjectivity in research from Agar's observation that,

> as you choose what to attend to and how to interpret it, mental doors slam shut on the alternatives. While some of your choices may be consciously made, others are forced by the weight of the personal and professional background that you bring to the field. (Agar, 1980:48)

Agar (1980) does not strive to eliminate biases, but he wants to justify them and make them public. He notes the importance of documenting one's learning and then showing one's readers how certain experiences can potentially falsify conclusions when they become the basis for one's conclusions. In this way, one shows that somebody said or did something that supports the bias. Another strategy Agar proposes is disciplining oneself to look at one's material in different ways, to reduce one's findings to basic premises, and, as a result, to make one's biases conscious. Researchers can then describe these biases as well as indicate how the biases guided their research.

Agar (1980) also describes exercises for fieldwork students that will enhance awareness of their biases. One exercise asks a group of students to describe the same physical setting. Since individual descriptions usually will differ, students can explore the reasons for the different descriptions. The point he makes is that different personal biases lead to different descriptions.

To Ginsberg and Matthews (n.d.), bias and subjectivity result from intensive interactions between the researcher and the researched. Qualitative researchers are greatly concerned with bias and subjectivity because of the potential for "inaccurate outcomes" (p. 13) when the unconscious reactions of the researcher to the researched go unnoticed. Although the authors use bias and subjectivity interchangeably, they characterize bias as an umbrella term covering many forms of contamination, whereas subjectivity is only one form of bias. Ginsberg and Matthews see bias and subjectivity as rooted in the psychoanalytic processes of transference and countertransference. Drawing on the concept of transference from psychiatry, whereby a patient's feelings are projected onto the analyst who represents somebody from the patient's past, Ginsberg and Matthews illustrate how similar processes may happen in a field situation: ". . . the informant who immediately takes to the researcher and bares his or her soul, or the informant who ignores the researcher or refuses to discuss various situations, may reflect transference between the informant and researcher similar to that between the patient and therapist" (p. 8). To them, ethnographic countertransference is a reality for all ethnographers; it is "the unconscious needs and conflicts that are aroused within the researcher while interacting with others in conducting field research" (p. 4). This process affects all choices a researcher makes, including who to study and who not to study, what is perceived as right or wrong, and what to record and what not to record. Accordingly, they call for ethnographers to explore their countertransferences "both for the purpose of making better decisions and discovering if the reactions themselves are important sources of data for understanding what is happening in a particular setting" (p. 13). The result of these reflections is a higher degree of accuracy.

To limit bias and subjectivity, Ginsberg and Matthews (n.d.) list a number of techniques to focus on countertransference. Researchers should explore their own feelings toward people to distinguish between "what is real for the setting versus what is some underlying operation within the researcher" (p. 15). They should engage in "personal inspection," a form of clinical supervision by a colleague to explore biases and assumptions and to generate more questions about the research. In addition, they should keep a checklist of possible contaminating influences on the data, as proposed by McCall (1969), or the "inquiry audit," as proposed by Halpern (1983) and Lincoln and Guba (1985), which could be modified to include the exploration of countertransference.

Lillian Rubin (1981) is a sociologist in the symbolic interactionist tradition. In discussing the "subjective dimension" (p. 97) of sociological research, she speaks about the importance of knowing one's own subjectivity as a researcher. First, referring to Freud, she states that "the only way we can be trapped by our subjectivity is for it to be out of awareness" (p. 103). Second, she states "that the beginning of all knowledge lies inside the individual—in the subjective experiences of a lifetime and the meaning imputed to them" (p. 103).

Rubin does not deny that objective material conditions shape human behavior and social life. She asserts, however, that knowledge is subjectively gained because we all give meaning to our personal experiences. These meanings are not necessarily unique; common experiences and their meanings are often shared by people living in the same sociocultural setting. For sociologists to deny their subjectivity is to deny the basic assumption of the discipline that people are shaped by their social environment.

Rubin sees training in clinical psychology as a valuable way to become aware of self and others. The skills gained not only help to understand unconscious meanings but also help to interpret them. Rubin came to this idea as a result of her first research project in which she carefully listened to and questioned people, but she still felt frustrated. "I knew intuitively there was more to know and I didn't yet know how to go about getting it" (Rubin, 1981:104). This frustration led her to seek clinical training, which helped her to listen for what was not said. She also learned to use and interpret her own reactions. In her study of working-class families (Rubin, 1976), she discovered, contrary to accepted research findings, that parents were ambivalent about and even rejected the idea of their children attending college. Parents feared their children would be lost to the family if they got too "high," and fathers looked down on men who were "pencil pushers." They only expressed these fears when Rubin discussed the cost of college with them. Most had no idea of the cost. When told, they were quick to express their ambivalence, after which it was easier to talk about their real fears and feelings. Rubin felt that three things helped her to do this research. First, she understood the pain of upward mobility, having come from a working-class family herself. Second, her clinical training helped her to establish rapport, to detect ambivalence, and to give importance to what is said and not said. Third, using a particular method of data collection—formal, in-depth, focused interviews, but also an informal style of hanging out—allowed for better understanding. She considered the informal hanging out very important. Without taking notes or using a tape recorder, she sat around while having a drink. She talked about the interview or about herself or helped solve problems in childrearing or marriage. She says, "It was then—when the structure of the interaction bespoke some kind of rough equality—that often they were open about many things, including whatever criticism they may have had about my conduct of the research" (Rubin, 1981:105). At those times identities changed; a researcher–researched relationship no longer existed. She was a guest in their homes. Rubin felt that situations like these elicited usefully different responses from those that were available in the formal interview situation.

Rubin gives another example from her research on friendship to emphasize the importance of clinical training. In an interview, one respondent told her about the importance of trust and helpfulness in defining friendship. He told her he could always count on his best friend, always trust that he was welcome. Rubin felt "bored" and "restless" during this interview. By "pushing" him, she learned that her respondent did not know where this best friend lived; he had moved away a couple of years ago. Afterward, when Rubin wondered about her reaction during this interview, she realized that she had never felt that way before. Through a similar experience with one of her clients, in which she again felt bored, she understood that this boredom was an expression of being disconnected from her client or interview respondent. Likewise, she realized that the man's words were disconnected from his feelings, causing "a state of empty, bored restlessness, a state that serves to sustain the denial and repression of emotionally loaded material" (Rubin, 1981:107). Rubin had picked up on that through understanding countertransference. She wanted to check the validity of her insight and called him to ask how he felt after the interview. He reported having felt "kind of low for the rest of the afternoon" (p. 108). When he asked her whether she knew why that was, she suggested that perhaps he was not that sure about what he had told her about friendship; she probably was right, he said. Through this example Rubin draws a parallel between the skills of a therapist and the skills of a researcher; in both practices, self-understanding is central to understanding and responding to others.

Peshkin (1985, 1988) studies the relationship between communities and their schools. He understands subjectivity as the personal qualities of an investigator that interact with the research phenomenon. Subjectivity is "an amalgam of dispositions stemming from one's class, statuses and values" (1985:276). He contends that subjectivity operates during the entire research process, from the choice of topic, to data gathering and analysis, to the writing up of the findings. Peshkin submits that if researchers are aware of their subjectivity, then they can inform readers about where self and subject have been joined. When subjectivity remains unexamined, it is beyond control in the research process.

Peshkin writes about catching himself "redhanded, with my values at the very end of my pen—where I believe they belong" (1985, p. 277). This awareness came when writing up the findings from his study of a fundamentalist Christian community. On closer examination, he realized that he did not feel the same strong positive feelings for the Christian school and its community that he was about to describe that he had felt for the rural school and community he had previously studied. Having discovered his subjectivity at work, he actively sought out his subjectivity in subsequent research.

Peshkin addresses the objectivity–subjectivity dichotomy by noting that if one's findings are to be acceptable, they must square "with the real or imaginable perceptions of others, [otherwise] I may have had an interesting personal experience, but I have missed the boat" (Peshkin, 1985:279). When objectivity draws the researcher's attention to "the use of facts without distortion by personal feelings or prejudices" (p. 279), it makes them conscious of a useful distinction between distortion and personal dispositions.

Peshkin now "monitors" himself as he conducts his research, looking for the "warm and the cold spots," to identify how he feels when engaged in research, because "untamed subjecitivity mutes the emic voice" (Peshkin, 1988:21). The purpose of this systematic monitoring of self is to keep one's lines of subjectivity open and to avoid the trap of perceiving just that which one's sentiments seek out and serve up as data. Peshkin identified his "subjective I's," as he calls them, as aspects of himself that emerged under the particular circumstances of his research in a multiethnic school. Because different research circumstances may elicit different subjective I's, he argues, subjectivity should be seen as "situational" (1988:18). For example, he calls one of his I's the "Ethnic Maintenance I," derived from being Jewish.

Peshkin comments on the hazard of the Ethnic Maintenance I, that is, by "valuing the behavior of those who chose to perpetuate their ethnic identity, I may ignore the lives of those who chose not to" (1988:8). Therefore, Peshkin values uncovering his subjective I's throughout the research process, so that he can acknowledge them in the interest of cautioning readers. Focusing on values and commitments that his research evokes, he identifies the particular orientation that will guide the story he writes. This particular orientation is the one he has come to see as one's "virtuous subjectivity." (Peshkin, 1985).

All the previously reviewed writers are concerned with subjectivity as a personal quality that emerges through interaction with subjects and events in the field. Krieger's (1985) narrower focus is on how to discern subjectivity in working with data. She retrospectively analyzes the observer–observed relationship and notes the restimulation of interest in this relationship through the development of feminist scholarship.

Krieger did fieldwork on privacy inside and outside a lesbian community. After finishing her 78 interviews, she could do nothing with them. Because she found no themes her data could support, she gave up, feeling that she did not have appropriate analytic distance from her data. After 2 years, she wrote a personal account about what it was like for her to live in that community, discovering that it was not that she did not have enough distance, but that she had too much. She felt estranged. However, to write in a sociologically useful fashion, she needed to overcome this estrangement and touch the experience. She came to see that her data were not just her interview notes but also included her year-long participation in the community and the feelings that she had at the time.

To once again feel or touch her experience of living in the community, Krieger engaged in a process of self-analysis she termed "reengagement." She asked herself: "Why did certain things move me? What had unfolded over the year's time? Why had I felt estranged? What did I want? What did I receive? What was I afraid of? How could I bridge the gap between myself and the data?" (1985:312).

Krieger subjected herself to a systematic analysis of her total research experience in a way that is comparable to LeCompte's (1987) "ethnography of the mind." She reexamined her entry into the field, her personal involvements, her emotional responses, and her feelings about leaving. By "separating out" (Krieger, 1985:312), a process that facilitates self-understanding and interpretation of qualitative data, she identified and examined her responses to all 78 interview cases in terms of her feelings both before and during the interviews. For example, she wrote about one preinterview experience: "I knew of V that she was a straight woman in one of the core support groups in the community. Was V afraid she would be distant and would withhold. Also K had told me V played 'poor me' so I worried I might get impatient with her" (p. 313).

After reviewing her preinterview experiences, Krieger went through her interview experiences to "identify my prejudices and any hidden personal agenda I might have had" (1985:313). From these notes she learned that she had often been uncomfortable, even afraid. She realized that some respondents made her angry when she felt that they expected her to be like them, whereas with others she felt she could just be herself. These feelings were strong because of her close identification with the women in the community. Upon closer reflection, however, she came to identify her anger as fear because "each interview situation was an intimacy situation for me and an occasion which I felt required proof of myself" (p. 315).

After this analysis, Krieger reviewed the content of her interview notes, while comparing the insights gained of herself with the analysis of her notes. Finally, she wrote a paper about the collective reality of participation in the lesbian community. She realized that her description was only a part of how community members felt, that is, the portion that she could relate to through her own experience. After coming to terms with her involvement through fear, she felt she could use her own experience "as a guide, a source not only of personal but of sociological insight" (1985:320). Krieger, like all of the above-mentioned researchers, discovered the importance of self-reflection for gaining insight into how personal qualities affect the research process.

Subjectivity in the Construction of Text

The objectivity–subjectivity debate in the social sciences not only raised questions about the conduct of research, and the researcher–researched relationship, but also has gained increasing significance in discussions about writing. Description and representation are not taken for granted anymore: The concern is with how the text is constructed, how the position of the author figures into the written account, and how "the subject–object distinction" (Van Maanen, 1988:34) plays out in different textual styles. In other words, the investigators' subjectivity is at stake in the creation of a text. Rosaldo (1989) cites Turner (1982), who criticized the objectivity of the older ethnographies. "Cartesian dualism," says Turner, "has insisted on separating subject from object, us from them. It has, indeed, made voyeurs of Western man . . ." (p. 41).

This reflection on the method of ethnography, particularly around questions of cultural representation and description, led Marcus and Fischer (1986) to observe that ethnographic fieldwork and writing is "the most lively current arena of theoretical discussion and innovation" (p. vii). Feminist authors (Balsamo, 1990; McRobbie, 1982; Strathern, 1984) and ethnographers (Clifford, 1986; Geertz, 1988; Marcus and Fischer, 1986; Rosaldo, 1989) have drawn attention to this debate about the "authorial voice," as have Erickson (1973), Barone (1990), and Eisner (1990).

Ethnographers, although considered to be users of the "softer" methods of the social sciences, traditionally sought respectability in the tenets of objectivity, just as other social scientists did. They presented the results of their fieldwork, obtained as detached observers of the "natives," as neutral descriptions of timeless traditional societies that manifest universal norms and structures (Rosaldo, 1989). In ethnography, the objects of research were "others"; ethnographers held authority over "truth." Said (1978) criticizes this approach, stating that "seemingly neutral, or innocent forms of social description both reinforced and produced ideologies that justified the imperialist project" (in Rosaldo, 1989:42).

Clifford (1986) comments on participant observation as a method that "presuppose[s] a standpoint outside—looking at, objectifying . . . a given reality" (p. 11). Participant observation, he notes, balances subjectivity and objectivity by recognizing the centrality of the investigator's experiences in the research process, while maintaining objectivity and distance. "In classical ethnographies the voice of the author was always manifest, but the conventions of textual presentation and reading, forbade too close a connection between authorial style and the reality it represented" (Clifford, 1986:13). This very process is now challenged because of the authority it gives to the observer. There is a growing realization that the "objects of analysis are also analyzing subjects" (Rosaldo, 1989:21) and that they themselves can have a voice. Moreover, Rosaldo sees both ethnographers and subjects as "positioned subjects" (p. 19). For ethnographers, their age, gender, and relationship to institutional structures influence what is learned.

This rejection of a detached, objective ethnography influenced a shift of the ethnographic metaphor from one of seeing and observing to one of speech and voice [or of style, according to Geertz (1988)]:

> In a discursive rather than a visual paradigm, the dominant metaphors
> for ethnography shift away from the observing eye and toward
> expressive speech . . . . The writer's "voice" pervades and situates
> the analysis, and objective, distancing rhetoric is renounced. (Clifford,
> 1986:12)

Clifford (1986) adds that ethnographers in the 1960s and 1970s started to write "about their field experience in ways that disturbed the prevailing subjective/objective balance" (p. 13). Using self-reflection in the ethnographic account (Rabinow, 1977) became more acceptable and was expressed in different textual strategies, such as writing in the first-person singular, staging dialogues (Crapanzano, 1980; Shostak, 1981), or integrating personal experience in the text as a means to understand the topic under study (Rosaldo, 1989).

A focus on self-reflection in ethnography is similar to the feminist's intent, but neither feminists nor ethnographers mean to "replace 'self' for the 'other'" (Balsamo, 1990:50). They mean, rather, to recognize the construction of knowledge as dialogical and interactive (Balsamo, 1990; Clifford, 1986). The examples of Rosaldo (1989) and Walkerdine (1986 *in* Balsamo, 1990) may exemplify this self-reflexive practice.

Rosaldo (1989) describes how he studied headhunting among the Ilongots in the Philippines. They engaged in the practice of headhunting after a death. For years Rosaldo distrusted Ilongot explanations of this practice as shallow and unsatisfying. They simply told him "how the rage in bereavement could impel a man to headhunt" (p. 3). Over the years, Rosaldo tried to come to a "deeper" understanding of this practice by exploring different theoretical frameworks—to no avail. Rosaldo could not understand the "force of anger possible in bereavement" (p. 7) until 14 years later when he lost his wife and colleague, Michelle Rosaldo. Rosaldo felt enraged. Following her death, he recalls the force of his anger in bereavement, an experience that allowed him to grasp the rage of the Ilongots. Their headhunting is a way to cope with grief. Rosaldo wrote in his journal that he

> . . . wish[ed] for the Ilongot solution; they are much more in touch
> with reality than Christians. So I need a place to carry my anger—and
> can we say a solution of the imagination is better than theirs? And can
> we condemn them when we napalm villages? Is our rationale so much
> sounder than theirs? (p. 11)

Rosaldo did not take this self-reflection lightly. He hesitated to put himself into the text of his account because of the traditional taboo, but also because of his awareness that self-reflection can become too self-absorbed. He notes the risk of "easy dismissal" (1989:11). To explain his "deeper" understanding, however, he could not leave himself out of his text: "My use of personal experience serves as a vehicle for making the quality and intensity of the rage in Ilongot grief more readily accessible to readers than certain more detached modes of composition" (p. 1).

Balsamo (1990) describes how Walkerdine (1986), a feminist researcher, engages in self-reflection, and shows how biography interacts with ethnographic practice in the production of knowledge. While studying family-interactional patterns as a participant observer, Walkerdine realized that ethnographic work is inherently unequal because of the interpretive choices open only to the investigator. She comments on participant observation as a nonintrusive method; however, she considers it as "voyeurism in its will to truth, which invests the observer [rather than the observed] with the knowledge . . . . In addition, the observer becomes the silent Other who is present in, while apparently absent from, the text" (Walkerdine, 1986:167, *in* Balsamo, 1990:50).

Walkerdine (1986) also reflects on her multiple subjectivities as a researcher. The family she studies is a working-class family. Walkerdine is a middle-class academic who came from a working-class family herself. Self-reflexivity is brought out in the way Walkerdine positions herself in her account of the family watching the movie *Rocky II*. She describes herself later, watching this movie alone, and how she was painfully reminded of class struggles as a working-class child. She uses her recognition of these feelings to put forward her understanding of the meaning of the family's interaction.

Rosaldo as griever and Walkerdine as working-class girl consciously insert themselves in the text and thereby abandon the language of distance and objectivity. By placing themselves on the same plane as their subjects, they and their readers gain a deeper understanding of the topics under study. Both examples also show that the construction of text is more than description or representation of culture. The textual strategies authors use in engaging their subjectivities is an integral part of the meaning they convey.

Reflections on Subjectivity: A Continuing Challenge

In 1968, sociologists Sjoberg and Nett published *A Methodology for Social Research*. It is informative in many ways, two of which have relevance here. In their preface, the authors state their intent: first, to clarify the place of theory in social research and, second, to examine "the impact of the researcher upon each step of the research process" (p. ix). To accomplish the latter, the authors draw on the "nonpositivist tradition" of Dilthey, Weber, and Mannheim, believing that doing so brings researchers to "the first step toward objectivity" (p. 10). Objectivity reigns supreme. Sjoberg and Nett endorse knowledge of self to best achieve positivist standards. Their book's index, accordingly, has entries for objectivity, sociology of knowledge, and *Verstehen*, but none for subjectivity.

The scholarly outlook of Sjoberg and Nett could not include what at the time barely existed—a nonpejorative construal of subjectivity and qualitative inquiry. Begrudgingly, they concede some merit to the nonpositivist work of fellow sociologists Reisman (1950) in *The Lonely Crowd* and Goffman (1959) in *The Presentation of Self in Everyday Life*, while making clear their professional allegiance:

> Although most logical empiricists admit that prediction has met with limited success . . . they view current theory and research as . . . worthy of societal support, for this enterprise articulates with . . . the industrial-urban order. It is no accident that positivists have envisioned a utopia resting upon scientific endeavor. Today this utopia includes bureaucratic systems that can readily control many aspects of the physical and social environments . . . . (Sjoberg and Nett, 1968:293)

That there is a quaint, archaic, even alien sound to these words suggests how far social researchers in general have traveled since the 1960s, as have qualitative researchers in particular.

Twenty years later, Berg and Smith (1988) followed Sjoberg and Nett (1968) in declaring an interest in the impact of the researcher, but otherwise their edited volume is a great conceptual distance from the positivism of Sjoberg and Nett:

> We are sure some of our critics will dismiss what we have to say here with the off-handed retort "Are you talking about art or science?" That is exactly our point. When we no longer can distinguish between art and science as separate processes but experience their holism we will have tapped the real meaning of the term clinical—knowledge through encounter, valid because it fits with experience, real because it touches the core, the universal and particular simultaneously. (Berg and Smith, 1988:34)

Today, qualitative researchers do not advocate subjectively shaped products that need only meet the personal standards of their maker. No one can get away with thinking that what he or she writes will fail to be tried on by others with varying degrees of experience, knowledgeability, and concern for what they read. The old concern for subjectivity is that it renders findings untrustworthy. The new interest in subjectivity, as we see it, is considerably less with whether or not our work is trustworthy (which virtue we do not scorn) and considerably more with how self and subject have intersected and with what effects. Trustworthiness (see Lincoln and Guba, 1985) will be judged by readers who personally ascertain the fit between what they read and what they know and have experienced.

Those in qualitative research who have become comfortable with subjectivity as an invariable but not necessarily negative fact in their research lives are reconciled to the absence of an ultimate authority to appeal to for certainty and of a reality out there that they can aspire to know with some sort of finality. They are reconciled to phenomena that they perceive, interpret, and construct and that they take as ambiguous, protean, and complex.

We do not believe that it is just a matter of time before scholars will abandon traditional views of objectivity or before qualitative researchers will reach a common view of the nature of subjectivity. We do believe that, at least among the growing ranks of qualitative researchers, subjectivity as a personal quality—as the involvement of self—will be accepted as unavoidably present in social research and as a fact without invariably negative consequences for the outcomes of inquiry. If the foundations of the old dyadic thinking about objectivity and subjectivity are not yet undermined, we do see the signs and shaking and cracking when 20 social researchers, most of them associated with university schools of management, prepare papers for a volume devoted to "encouraging all social investigators to reflect on what we do with ourselves while we conduct our inquiry" (Berg and Smith, 1988:10).

The redefining and reinventing of terms and procedures by qualitative researchers and methodologists (see Lincoln and Guba, 1985) encompasses subjectivity but has not yet included an alternate term for subjectivity. Perhaps it is time for a renaming that will not conjure up the old polarization with its history of praise and blame, of good and bad. We have no new appellation to offer, but many questions occur to us as we reflect on the current state of thinking about subjectivity. For there is much that remains unsettled and, thus, much that methodologists and practitioners of qualitative research can usefully explore.

Distinctions of ontology and epistemology are marked clearly at the level of words, but do practitioners with different views of subjectivity actually conduct their research differently? What differences make a difference? If, as we surmise, the differences do not make a difference, is it because qualitative researchers cannot translate conceptual distinction into practice, are perhaps unaware of how to do this, or, possibly, are so strongly socialized into established procedures of conduct that they do not even explore alternative ways of proceeding?

In the residual sounds of support for objectivity voiced by qualitative researchers, do we hear no more than vestiges of early socialization, or are they unexamined yearnings to have it both ways, objectivity still on the pedestal and subjectivity now enshrined as well? Or is objectivity no more than a sacred cow, so long revered that the habit of belief is deeply engrained and endures even if at some level we no longer believe?

Can objectivity be reconstrued as a viable concept for qualitative researchers? Is there some place for some form of objectivity so that we will not relinquish what surely is a compliment in ordinary language usage: Who among us would refuse the compliment of being called "objective?"

For example, Peshkin's (1986) study of a Christian school was reviewed in Christian and non-Christian journals; it was labeled fair, nonjudgmental, balanced, representative, unbiased, and objective. There was interreviewer agreement about the book's characterization of a religiously conservative institution. Do these labels about the product of inquiry also say something about the process of inquiry? About the analysis of data? Does objectivity in some form retain value as an attribute of the products of qualitative research and, thus, as a reflection of the conduct of the researcher? Which is to say that though we cannot see researchers in the act of being objective as they engage in participaton observation or interviewing, we can perhaps assume they were, somehow, "objective" by inspection of the outcomes of their data collection procedures. And what would the designation of objective mean if so applied?

Peshkin accepts these observations as compliments, as a "stamp of approval" (Philips, 1990). We think it merits exploring what there is about a narrative, and what is happening among readers and between readers and writer, that leads to the sort of labeling we associate with the supposed goodness of objectivity, no doubt in its nontechnical conception. In the bathwater of objectivity are there babies we can't help keeping? Are a "stamp of approval" and "objectivity" identical, similar, comparable, or what?

What, if anything, do qualitative researchers gain or lose if they relinquish objectivity as an attribute of their research process? Should the same question be raised about subjectivity? Should objectivity always appear in quotation marks when used by qualitative research-ers to call attention to its variable, equivocal usage? And should subjec-tivity, in fairness, be similarly marked for the same reasons? What does it mean for the conduct of inquiry if a qualitative researcher remains committed to objectivity? Does remaining committed really "hide problems," as suggested by Agar (1980:41)? Does it lead to other scholarly misdeeds as well? Can the concept of objectivity transfer to qualitative research from its home in the quantitative paradigm? Do we need to sunder the dyad once and for all, as did some subjectivists (Husserl, 1969; and Dilthey, 1964–1966) and some contemporary fem-inists (e.g., Harding, 1986; Westcott, 1979) so that they no longer are inevitably linked and opposed? As the simplistic good and bad, are both dishonored? If reconstructed as nondyadic terms, divested of their historically dichotomous pigeonholing, are we free to discover merit in each concept?

As previously discussed, Smith (1980), Peshkin (1988), and Le-Compte (1987) consider procedures for leashing subjectivity. Krieger (1985) and Rubin (1981) examine the necessity of an awareness of self to understand their research respondents and their research experi-ence. Do writers need to acknowledge their exorcisms and introspec-tions in their texts? These several writers speak of the benefits of their self-delvings, but do readers benefit by the disclosure of these del-vings? If so, how? If so, should we think of such disclosures as obliga-tory (see Lincoln and Guba, 1985:262–263)? And if so, do we elevate the capacity for effective self-analysis to a condition for the successful conduct of qualitative inquiry, with moreover, implications for the education and training [see e.g., Rubin's (1981) suggestion of clinical training] of qualitative researchers?

Are there, however, elements of our subjectivity that bear on the conclusions we draw but nonetheless should not be disclosed? For example, we think of Wolcott's (1973) ethnographic account of an elementary school principal. Although readers can infer Wolcott's per-sonal feelings about the pseudonymous Ed Bell, they might have benefitted from hearing from Wolcott how he felt about this man and whether or not he would have wanted his own child to be a student in Bell's school. What would be useful for readers to know about writers is limited by their proprieties of what writers are allowed to disclose. Learning the limits of propriety is another consideration.

With regard to disclosure in the construction of text, contemporary writers inform us of the variety of forms our narrative can take and the possibilities for, if not the necessity of, including the writer in the text.

In the interest of enhancing "truth" in writing, do we need to identify the types of "tales" we tell in education, much as did Van Maanen (1988) for ethnography? By seeing the types of tales we can and do tell, we might learn about different ways of positioning ourselves in our texts. We can learn when the form of our positioning goes too far and our tales feature us more than they should and more than they do others.

We conclude, as we reflect on the many questions we have raised and the many papers that generated them, that our awareness of the nature and meaning of subjectivity, and our understanding of the means and possibilities for writers and readers to react to it, is incipient. Thus, we can imagine methodological studies devoted to exploring some aspect of subjectivity as well as nonmethodological studies that include a focus on subjectivity either during or after the conduct of a study, or both. If, for example, we had the results of many researchers keeping track of their subjectivity during data collection, and the results of many researchers who grappled with their subjectivity as they analyze and write up their data, then we would have the basis for better-grounded analyses and interpretations of subjectivity as a factor in qualitative inquiry. Surely with subjectivity now unbound, we are ready to acquire a more sophisticated grasp of both objectivity and subjectivity. Having long coexisted as Prince Charming and the Ugly Duckling, can they both be reborn as swans?

We see nothing if not ferment of the broad field of qualitative research, in general, and in the discourse on subjectivity, in particular. The unsettled nature of this discourse testifies to the ferment. Clearly, this is not a time of certainty; canons of belief and conduct are not in the picture anymore. Under the circumstances, we might do well to find satisfaction in the occasion for growth, resisting the dispositions of schools of thought to harden into orthodoxies, while seeing in their disparate advocacies the spur to deliberation, reflection, and reformulation. In the process, concept and practice possibly may better inform and reform each other, with benefits compounded.

We can rely on the attention of qualitative researchers to subjectivity as long as the paradigm is perceived as a viable means for the conduct of inquiry. Qualitative researchers, whether in interviewing or in participant observation, are so palpably, inescapably present that they cannot delude themselves that who they are will not make a difference in the outcomes of their study. To be sure, most social research entails interaction—covert researchers are a notable exception—between researcher and researched. All social research is directed to topics that bear directly or indirectly on the life of the researcher. Accordingly, continued attention to subjectivity is rooted in the very nature of any social research that uses qualitative methods. (We believe it is rooted in social research pursued by any means, but that is another story.)

Subjectivity is not a "goner," Barone (1990) notwithstanding, although it may be going in its conventional depiction as objectivity's netherworld offspring, as, for that matter, is objectivity as the favorite child. To the extent that an inverse relationship exists between the terms, so that as one rises in favor the other correspondingly falls, this rising and falling happens within a paradigm. If, however, we sever the terms and their presumed logical tie, then the inverse relationship no longer is operative. Such severing, we suggest, is important to facilitate thinking about the potential meanings of the terms and the implications of these meanings for research. It will take more than the seeming logic of believing that when objectivity no longer is useful, then neither is subjectivity. The inescapable fact of our presence in research means that we are present to make choices. Choices equal subjectivity at work. How these choices may result in good or bad should be the continuing work of conceptualizers and practitioners of qualitative research.

Susan Handelman (1982), writing in *The Slayers of Moses*, poses a question that we cite to close our chapter. We chose to so end our discussion of subjectivity primarily to convey our sense that the asking of questions is what must be done to advance the needed dialogue on this most provocative concept. Handelman writes,

> The question is whether the validity of science depends on the
> achievement of a completely objective, noninvolved, nonprejudicial
> point of view, or whether the acknowledgement of the necessary
> relativity, subjectivity, and prejudice involved in any act of perception
> is, in fact, a truer and more scientific approach to knowledge. (quoted
> *in* Berg and Smith, 1988:10)

References

Agar, M. H. (1980). *The professional stranger. An informal introduction to ethnography.* New York: Academic Press.

Balsamo, A. (1987). Un-wrapping the postmodern: A feminist glance. *Journal of Communication Inquiry.* 11(1), 64–72.

Balsamo, A. (1990). Rethinking ethnography: A work of the feminist imagination. *Studies in Symbolic Interaction*, 11, 45–57.

Barone, T. (1990). *On the demise of subjectivity in educational inquiry.* Paper presented at the Annual Meeting of the American Educational Research Association, Boston, April.

Berg, D., and Smith, K. (1988). *The self in clinical research*. Newbury Park, CA: Sage Publications.

Bernstein, R. J. (1983). *Beyond objectivism and relativism: Science, hermeneutics and praxis*. Philadelphia: University of Pennsylvania Press.

Bleicher, J. (1982). *The hermeneutic imagination*. London: Routledge and Kegan Paul.

Blumer, H. (1969). *Symbolic interactionism*. Englewood Cliifs, NJ: Prentice-Hall.

Boros, A. (1988). Being subjective as a sociologist. *Journal of Applied Sociology, 5*, 15–31.

Bredo, E., and Feinberg, W. (1982). *Knowledge and values in social and educational research*. Philadelphia: Temple University Press.

Bulhof, J. M. (1980). *Wilhelm Dilthey: A hermeneutic approach to the study of history and culture*. The Hague: Martinus Nyhoff

Caton, H. (1973). *The origin of subjectivity. An essay on Descartes*. New Haven: Yale University Press.

Clifford, J. (Ed.). (1986). *Writing culture: The poetics and politics of ethnography*. Berkeley: University of California Press.

Cook, J. A., and Fonow, M. M. (1986). Knowledge and women's interests: Issues of epistemology and methodology in feminist sociological research. *Sociological Inquiry, 56*(1), 2–29.

Cook, T. D., and Campbell, D. T. (1979). *Quasi-experimentation: Design and analysis issues for field studies*. Chicago: Rand McNally.

Couch, C. J. (1987). Objectivity: A crutch and club for bureaucrats/Subjectivity: A haven for lost souls. *The Sociological Quarterly, 28*, 105–118.

Crapanzano, V. (1980). *Tuhami: Portrait of a Moroccan*. Chicago: University of Chicago Press.

Denzin, N. K. (1978). *The research act* (2nd ed.). New York: McGraw-Hill.

Descartes, R. (1968). *Discourse on method and other writings*, F. E. Stucliffe (Trans.). Middlesex: Penguin Books.

Diefenbeck, J. A. (1984). *A celebration of subjective thought*. Carbondale: Southern Illinois University Press.

Dilthey, W. (1964–1966). *Gesammelte schriften* (Vols. I–VII). Leipzig and Berlin: B. G. Teubner.

Dilthey, W. (1988). *Introduction to the human sciences*, Ramon J. Betanzos (Trans.). Detroit: Wayne State University Press.

Edwards, P. (Ed. in Chief). (1972). *Encyclopedia of philosophy*. New York: Macmillan.

Eisner, E. (1986). *The primacy of experience and the politics of method*. Lecture delivered at the University of Oslo, Norway.

Eisner, E. W. (1990). *Objectivity in educational research*. Paper presented at the Annual Meeting of the American Educational Research Association, Boston, April.

Eisner, E. W., and Peshkin, A. (Eds.). (1990). *Qualitative inquiry in education*. New York: Teachers College Press.

Erickson, F. (1973). What makes school ethnography "ethnographic?" *Council on Anthropology and Education Newsletter, 4*(2), 10–19.

Fiske, D. W., and Shweder, R. A. (Eds.). (1986). *Metatheory in social science. Pluralisms and subjectivities*. Chicago: University of Chicago Press.

Flax, J. (1983). Political philosophy and the patriarchal unconscious: A psychoanalytic perspective on epistemology and metaphysics. *In* S. Harding and M. Hintikka (Eds.), *Discovering reality: Feminist perspectives on epistemology, metaphysics, methodology and philosophy of science* (pp. 245–282). Dordrecht: Reidel.

Gage, N. L. (1989). The paradigm wars and their aftermath: A "historical" sketch of research on teaching since 1989. *Educational Researcher, 18*(7), 4–10.

Geertz, C. (1988). *Work and lives: The anthropologist as author.* Stanford, CA: Stanford University Press.

Giddens, A. (1986). Action, subjectivity, and the constitution of meaning. *Social Research,* 53, 529–545.

Ginsberg, R., and Matthews, B. (n.d.). Ethnographic countertransference: Beneath bias and subjectivity on qualitative research. Unpublished paper available from Ginsberg, University of South Carolina, Charleston.

Glaser, B. G., and Strauss, A. L. (1967). *The discovery of grounded theory.* Chicago: Aldine.

Goffman, E. (1959). *The presentation of self in everyday life.* Garden City, NY: Doubleday.

Grady, H. H., and Wells, S. (1985–1986). Toward a rhetoric of intersubjectivity: Introducing Jurgen Habermas. *Journal of Advanced Composition,* 6, 33–47.

Guba, E. G. (Ed.). (1990a). *The paradigm dialog.* Newbury Park, CA: Sage Publications.

Guba, E. G. (1990b). Subjectivity and objectivity. *In* E. W. Eisner and A. Peshkin (Eds.), *Qualitative inquiry in education* (pp. 74–91). New York: Teachers College Press.

Halpern, E. S. (1983). *Auditing naturalistic inquiries: The development and application of a model.* Unpublished doctoral dissertation, Indiana University, Bloomington.

Handelman, S. A. (1982). *The slayers of Moses.* Albany: State University of New York Press.

Hansen, J. F. (1982). From background to foreground: Toward an anthropology of learning. *Anthropology and Education Quarterly,* 13, 189–202.

Harding, S. (1986). *The science question in feminism.* Ithaca, NY: Cornell University Press.

Harding, S. (Ed.). (1987). *Feminism and methodology.* Bloomington: Indiana University Press.

Hartsock, N. (1983). The feminist standpoint: Developing the ground for a specifically feminist historical materialism. *In* S. Harding and M. Hintikka (Eds.), *Discovering reality: Feminist perspectives on epistemology, metaphysics, methdology and philosophy of science* (pp. 283–310). Dordrecht: Reidel.

hooks, b. (1983). *Feminist theory from margin to center.* Boston: South End Press.

Husserl, E. (1969). *Formal and transcendental logic,* D. Cairns (Trans.). The Hague: Martinus Nyhoff.

Irwin, J. (1987). Reflections on ethnography. *Journal of Contemporary Ethnography,* 16, 41–48.

Jagger, A. (1983). *Feminist politics and human nature.* Totowa, NJ: Rowman and Allenheld.

Johnson, J. M. (1975). *Doing field research.* New York: The Free Press.

Judovitz, D. (1988). *Subjectivity and representation in Descartes.* Cambridge: Cambridge University Press.

Kirk, J., and Miller, M. L. (1986). *Reliability and validity in qualitative research.* Sage University Paper Series on Qualitative Research Methods (2). Beverly Hills, CA: Sage Publications.

Krieger, S. (1985). Beyond "subjectivity": The use of the self in social science. *Qualitative Sociology,* 8, 309–324.

Lather, P. (1986). *Feminist perspectives on empowering research methodologies.* Paper prepared for the Eighth Annual Curriculum Theorizing Conference, Dayton, OH, October 22–25.

LeCompte, M. D. (1987). Bias in the biography: Bias and subjectivity in ethnographic research. *Anthropology and Education Quarterly,* 18(1), 43–52.

Lincoln, Y. S., and Guba, E. G. (1985). *Naturalistic inquiry.* Beverly Hills, CA: Sage Publications.

Madison, G. B. (1988). *The hermeneutics of postmodernity.* Bloomington: Indiana University Press.

Marcus, G. E., and Fischer, M. M. J. (1986). *Anthropology as cultural critique.* Chicago: University of Chicago Press.

McCall, G. J. (1969). Data quality control in participant observation. *In* G. J. McCall and J. L. Simmons (Eds.), *Issues in participant observation: A text and reader* (pp. 128–141). Reading, MA: Addison-Wesley.

McRobbie, A. (1982). The politics of feminist research: Between talk, text and action. *Feminist Review,* 12, 46–57.

Myrdal, G. (1969). *Objectivity in social research.* New York: Pantheon.

Nisbet, R. (1974). Subjective si! Objective no! *In* G. Riley (Ed.), *Values, objectivity, and the social sciences* (pp. 14–20). Reading, MA: Addison-Wesley.

Oakley, A. (1981). Interviewing women: A contradiction in terms. *In* H. Roberts (Ed.), *Doing feminist reearch* (pp. 30–61). London: Routledge and Kegan Paul.

Peshkin, A. (1985). Virtuous subjectivity: In the participant-observer's I's. *In* D. Berg and K. Smith (Eds.), *Exploring clinical methods for social research* (pp. 267–282). Newsbury Park, CA: Sage Publications.

Peshkin, A. (1986). *God's choice: The total world of a fundamentalist Christian school.* Chicago: University of Chicago Press.

Peshkin, A. (1988). In search of subjectivity—One's own. *Educational Researcher,* 17(7), 17–22.

Philips, D. C. (1990). Subjectivity and objectivity: An objective inquiry. *In* E. W. Eisner and A. Peshkin (Eds.), *Qualitative inquiry in education* (pp. 19–37). New York: Teachers College Press.

Popper, K. (1976). The logic of the social sciences. *In* T. Ardono *et al.* (Eds.), *The positivist dispute in German sociology* (pp. 87–104). New York: Harper.

Rabinow, P. (1977). *Reflections on fieldwork in Morocco.* Berkeley: University of California Press.

Rabinow, P., and Sullivan, W. M. (1979). The interpretive turn. *In* P. Rabinow and W. M. Sullivan (Eds.), *Interpretive social science. A reader* (pp. 1–24). Berkeley: University of California Press.

Reinharz, S. (1983). Experiential analysis: A contribution of feminist research. *In* G. Bowles and R. Duelli Klein (Eds.), *Theories of women's studies* (pp. 162–191). London: Routledge and Kegan Paul.

Riesman, D. (1950). *The lonely crowd.* New Haven: Yale University Press.

Riley, G. (Ed.). (1974). *Values, objectivity, and the social sciences.* Reading, MA: Addison-Wesley.

Rist, R. C. (1977). Overview on the relations among educational research paradigms: From disdain to detente. *Anthropology and Education Quarterly,* 8, 42–49.

Roman, L. G., and Apple, M. W. (1990). Is naturalism a move away from positivism? Materialist and feminist approaches to subjectivity in ethnographic research. *In* E. W. Eisner and A. Peshkin (Eds.), *Qualitative inquiry in education.* (pp. 38–73). New York: Teachers College Press.

Rosaldo, R. (1989). *Culture and truth. The remaking of social analysis.* Boston: Beacon Press.

Rose, H. (1983). Hand, brain, and heart: A feminist epistemology for the natural sciences. *Signs,* 9(1), 73–90.

Rubin, L. B. (1976). *Worlds of pain.* New York: Basic Books, Inc.

Rubin, L. B. (1981). Sociological research: The subjective dimension. *Symbolic Interaction*, 4, 97–112.

Said, E. (1978). *Orientalism*. New York: Pantheon Books.

Scheffler, J. (1982). *Science and subjectivity* (2nd ed.). Indianapolis: Hackett Publishing Company.

Schwandt, T. A. (1989). Solutions to the paradigm conflict: Coping with uncertainty. *Journal of Contemporary Ethnography*, 17, 379–407.

Shostak, M. (1981). *Nisa: The life and words of a !Kung woman*. Cambridge: Harvard University Press.

Sjoberg, G., and Nett, R. (1968). *A methodology for social research*. New York: Harper & Row.

Smith, D. E. (1974). Women's perspective as a radical critique of sociology. *Sociological Inquiry*, 44, 7–13.

Smith, D. E. (1979). A sociology for women. *In* J. A. Sherman and E. T. Beck (Eds.), *The prism of sex: Essays in the sociology of knowledge* (pp. 135–187). Madison: University of Wisconsin Press.

Smith, D. E. (1987a). *The everyday world as problematic: A feminist sociology*. Boston: Northeastern University Press.

Smith, D. E. (1987b). Women's perspective as a radical critique of sociology. *In* S. Harding (Ed.), *Feminism and methodology* (pp. 84–96). Bloomington: Indiana University Press.

Smith, M. L. (1980). *Solving for some unknowns in the personal equation*. CIRCE occasional paper. Urbana: University of Illinois.

Stake, R. E. (1981). A needed subjectivity in educational research. *Discourse*, 1(2), 1–8.

Strathern, M. (1984). Dislodging a world view: Challenge and counterchallenge in the relationship between feminism and anthropology. Lecture at the Research Center for Women's Studies, University of Adelaide, Australia, July 4.

Surkin, M. (1974). Sense and non-sense in politics. *In* G. Riley (Ed.), *Values, objectivity, and the social sciences* (pp. 21–38). Reading, MA: Addison-Wesley.

Toulmin, S. (1983). The construal of reality: Criticism in modern and postmodern science. *In* W. J. T. Mitchell (Ed.), *The politics of interpretation* (pp. 99–117). Chicago: University of Chicago Press.

Turner, V. (1982). Dramatic ritual/ritual drama: Performative and reflective anthropology. *In From ritual to theater: The human seriousness of play* (p. 89). New York: Performing Arts Journal Publications.

Van Maanen, J. (1988). *Tales of the field: On writing ethnography*. Chicago: University of Chicago Press.

Walkerdine, V. (1986). Video replay: Families, films and fantasy. *In* V. Burgin, J. Donald, and C. Kaplan (Eds.), *Formations of fantasy* (pp. 167–199). New York: Methuen.

Weber, M. (1964). *The theory of social and economic organization*, A. M. Henderson and T. Parsons (Trans.). New York: Free Press.

Westcott, M. (1979). Feminist criticism of the social sciences. *Harvard Educational Review*, 49, 422–430.

Wolcott, H. (1973). *The man in the principal's office: An ethnography*. Prospect Heights, IL: Waveland Press.

PART 3

◻ Applications of
Qualitative and
Ethnographic Research

CHAPTER 16

☐ Qualitative Approaches to Evaluation: Models and Methods

Mary Anne Pitman and
Joseph A. Maxwell

The Handbook of Qualitative
Research in Education

729

One of us (M. A. P.) can recall standing in the back of a meeting room at the Annual Convention of the Evaluation Research Society in 1977 with two applied anthropologist colleagues. We were in a standing-room only crowd listening to an evaluator, an organizational psychologist by training, presenting his case for the state licensing of evaluators. Job security, a serious concern in that time of disappearing academic employment, had drawn many in the room into evaluation research. The notion of a license and its often concomitant resource guarantees were intriguing. The speaker's proposed licensing criteria would have mandated a gate-keeping structure that would "keep the charlatans out of the field." It soon became clear to the three of us, however, that *we* were the charlatans. Qualitative researchers, according to the speaker, were threatening the integrity of evaluation, particularly the rigor of its procedures and the validity of its findings.

Ten years later at the Annual Convention of the American Educational Research Association, a panel of educational researchers presented basic procedures for conducting evaluations using qualitative methods. These panelists also spoke to a standing-room-only crowd. The charlatans had become the experts.

In some ways in *both* of these venues, as in the educational evaluation literature of that decade, the presentations were framed by the same assumption: namely, that qualitative evaluation research is one thing and one thing only, and that it is different from and (mostly) oppositional to quantitative evaluation research. This dichotomous thinking continued throughout the 1980s, despite attempts by some authors and editors to recommend and demonstrate a reconciliation (see Reichardt and Cook, 1979). While the literature on qualitative research, *per se*, grew tremendously, indicating, among other things, the multitude of options that it encompassed, the public discussions of qualitative approaches to educational evaluation remained focused on the "paradigm wars" of qualitative versus quantitative or naturalistic versus positivistic.

We wish to enter the conversation on qualitative evaluation by encouraging a consideration and discussion of the multiple perspectives that do indeed guide the conduct of qualitative evaluation research.

Our review of current empirical and philosophical literature has convinced us that there is considerable diversity in philosophical and methodological paradigms among qualitative evaluators. Still that review also emphasizes the fact that most of the writing on philosophical issues in the educational evaluation literature has focused on the so-called paradigm wars between qualitative and quantitative approaches. Our claim is that this focus has obscured the differences that exist among qualitative approaches to educational evaluation. Because the debate has been framed in terms of an assumed dichotomy between positivist and interpretivist positions, it has largely ignored other important perspectives that have informed qualitative evaluation, such as pragmatism and critical realism. In addition, the philosophic debate has become increasingly detached from the actual conduct of qualitative evaluation.

The fact remains, then, that the paradigm debate still dominates much of the discussion of qualitative evaluation. Not only are numerous books and papers being written about paradigms in qualitative research and evaluation (e.g., Guba, 1990), but even authors of methodological works who do *not* see paradigms as fundamental (e.g., Patton, 1990) seem to feel compelled to lay out their philosophical positions, if only to distance themselves from those who argue for the overriding importance of paradigm affiliation. We, therefore, will begin this chapter by discussing different philosophic positions that qualitative evaluators have taken and examine specific and substantive issues in qualitative evaluation from these perspectives.

We will claim that various qualitative "paradigms" or models exist for educational evaluation along with definable qualitative methods that are applicable to evaluation research. There are canons that guide its conduct to ensure validity. These have been written about and, to a lesser extent, demonstrated.

To clarify what we consider to be the current state in the discussion of models or paradigms for qualitative evaluation, and therefore the appropriate starting point in the design and conduct of such research, we will examine what we consider to be four distinctive and influential approaches to qualitative evaluation. These four approaches have been articulated by well-known and respected evaluators who have published explicit descriptions of their philosophy and methods of doing evaluation.[1] In the process of examining these approaches, we will compare and contrast them, indicating the diversity in epistemology. Our main intent is not to make philosophical evaluations of the positions taken by different qualitative evaluators; instead, we want to present the positions that these authors have taken, the implications they draw from these positions, and the relationship between these positions and the practice of qualitative evaluation. Insofar as we compare and criticize these positions, it is in terms of their consistency and consequences, not their philosophical correctness.

We will then delineate what we consider to be the appropriate procedural checkpoints in the conduct of any qualitative approach to evaluation research. As convinced as we are that qualitative evaluation is not one thing, that it is, and in fact should be, informed and guided by a number of philosophical and empirical positions and processes, we nevertheless believe that it is possible and desirable to identify several guidelines, checkpoints, or canons that are characteristic of all qualitative approaches to evaluation, in education and elsewhere.

The Relationship of Paradigms to Methods

Our major premise is that the relationship between paradigms and methods is an empirical question and must be answered by looking at the actual writing and work of qualitative evaluators. We do not believe that paradigms either determine practice or are irrelevant to it, but that they can facilitate or hinder its usefulness in attaining specific goals, clarify or obscure different ways of collecting or interpreting data, and emphasize or downplay specific issues of validity or ethics in the research.

In contrast to Ryan (1988), who presents the main features of three major paradigms and discusses the implications of each for program evaluation, we take an inductive approach. We will look at the guidelines for qualitative evaluation given by four authors from different paradigms and then attempt to determine both the differences among these approaches and the apparent connections between paradigms and methods.

In choosing the statements to review, we have used the qualitative technique of purposeful sampling (Patton, 1990:169). We have selected works that present clear and explicit statements of the philosophic stances of the writers and, among them, adequately represent the diversity of philosophic approaches among qualitative evaluators. The four statements we have selected are the following:

Michael Quinn Patton, Qualitative Evaluation and Research Methods (2nd ed., 1990). Patton has been an influential and prolific evaluator and writer, with numerous books on evaluation. He describes his philosophic position as "pragmatist."
Egon Guba and Yvonna Lincoln, Fourth Generation Evaluation (1989). Guba and Lincoln are also

influential and prolific authors; they have written
several books on evaluation and qualitative research,
including *Effective Evaluation* (Guba and Lincoln,
1981) and *Naturalistic Inquiry* (Lincoln and Guba,
1985). They characterize their position as
"naturalistic" (Lincoln and Guba, 1985) and
"constructivist" (Guba and Lincoln, 1989).

*Matthew Miles and A. Michael Huberman, Qualitative
Data Analysis: A Sourcebook of New Methods (1984b).*
Miles and Huberman have published mainly on
qualitative research and on school improvement. They
are not self-identified as "evaluators," but much of
their work has been on the evaluation of schools and
educational innovations. They are the most "scientific"
in orientation of all the authors; they call themselves
"soft-nosed positivists," but their actual philosophy
seems to be more realist than positivist.

*Elliot W. Eisner, The Enlightened Eye: Qualitative
Inquiry and the Enhancement of Educational Practice
(1991).* Eisner is another influential writer on
evaluation, with numerous works on education and
evaluation. His approach is the farthest from
"scientific"; he sees his approach to evaluation as
artistic rather than scientific, and he has explicitly
modeled this approach on art criticism.

These authors represent the range of currently important paradigms and approaches in qualitative evaluation fairly well. Miles and
Huberman are explicitly "scientific"; Eisner is explicitly "artistic."
Miles and Huberman are fairly close to a "realist" position; Guba and
Lincoln are strongly antirealist and relativist. Guba and Lincoln insist
on the compatibility of paradigm and methods; Patton denies that
evaluators need to be concerned with paradigms and warns of the
dangers of paradigm adherence.

We will present each author's philosophic stance, their definitions
of and approaches to qualitative research and qualitative evaluation,
their views of the goals and products of qualitative evaluation, and the
issues (including ethical and political issues) that they see as most
important. We conclude this review section by comparing their philosophies and methods and discussing the relationships among these as
we see them.

Michael Quinn Patton

Patton is the most "mainstream" of the qualitative evaluators to be considered here. His approach is similar to that of the majority of qualitative evaluators, and his numerous books on evaluation have probably played some part in this. The first edition of *Qualitative Evaluation Methods* (1980) was extremely popular and influential; the revised and expanded second edition, entitled *Qualitative Evaluation and Research Methods* (1990), could easily be used as a textbook on qualitative research in general.

Patton labels his philosophical position "pragmatist." He draws two main conclusions from pragmatism. First, stating that "qualitative inquiry is not a single thing with a singular subject matter" (1990:65), he describes the variety of theoretical orientations that have informed qualitative research. He sees each of these approaches as sharing the methods of qualitative inquiry, but as addressing different questions, interpreting the results from different frameworks, and using the methods of qualitative research for different purposes (p. 87).

Patton describes his own approach as simply one of several possible choices, presenting the approaches Guba and Lincoln and that of Eisner as legitimate alternatives. He characterizes his own approach as "utilization-focused evaluation," stating that it "represents an attempt to move beyond formal models to the practice of evaluation. It is an explicit recognition of the expanded options available . . . . [It] is not a recipe or even a 'model'—it is a strategy for making evaluation decisions . . . . The focus is on intended use by intended users" (Patton, 1990:121–122).

The second conclusion that Patton draws from pragmatism is that methods deriving from different paradigms can validly and usefully be combined within the same study. Arguing that the primary concern in qualitative inquiry is with research strategies rather than paradigms, he goes on to discuss the value of different mixes of designs, data, and analyses, including using experimental and quantitative methods in combination with qualitative ones for studying a single program. He concludes that "all kinds of variations, combinations, and adaptations are available for creative and practical situational responsiveness" (Patton, 1990:39).

Patton argues that it is meaningless to ask which of these "mini-paradigms" is right, best, or most useful, because the answer depends on what the researcher wants to do. Each has its own strengths and limitations. He goes further and argues that, for evaluators whose primary goals are practical, a concern with paradigms is not only unnecessary, but dangerous, because it leads to decisions based on disciplinary prescriptions rather than situational appropriateness. He claims that one can use open-ended interviews or participant observation without studying phenomenology, and that qualitative methods can now stand on their own as reasonable ways to find out what's going on in programs and other human settings. "In short, in real-world practice, methods can be separated from the epistemology out of which they have emerged" (Patton, 1990:90).

Consistent with Patton's pragmatist views, he eschews any concern with Truth as a singular, absolute goal of qualitative research. He argues that what is true depends on one's perspective, and that evaluators should seek "pragmatic validation" of results, based on their relevance to and use by the intended audience, rather than some illusory certainty. For Patton, providing this audience with a report that has practical utility and credibility—which includes accuracy, validity, and even truthfulness in the common-sense meaning of this term—is the goal of qualitative evaluation.

Patton (1990) defines evaluation as "any effort to increase human effectiveness through systematic data-based inquiry" (p. 11). His approach emphasizes rigor and validity; for Patton, qualitative evaluation is evaluation *research,* and must meet the standards for research to be valid. However, two points are important in understanding this assertion. First, Patton's definition of "research" is quite broad, including action research and formative evaluation as well as "basic" research (pp. 150–162). Second, Patton sees "rigor" and "validity" as political rather than purely technical terms, and, although the definition of these will differ for different types of research, he refuses to concede their use entirely to "basic" research. He also emphasizes the differences between quantitative and qualitative approaches, citing the latter's emphasis on flexibility rather than standardization, understanding rather than generalizability, and a commitment to many valid perspectives rather than a single truth.

In discussing the methods and products of qualitative evaluation, Patton emphasizes both rigor and multiple perspectives. He devotes considerable space to methods for assuring the quality and credibility of qualitative analysis, including testing rival explanations, examining negative cases, triangulating methods and sources, and determining the researcher's effect on the findings. He emphasizes that the credibility of results requires the empathic neutrality of the researcher toward the phenomenon studied—that the researcher does not set out to reach some particular conclusion.

Patton distinguishes two tasks of qualitative analysis: description and interpretation. The first task, description, includes description of the beliefs and values of the participants as well as of their behavior and the physical setting. Interpretation, which Patton defines as explaining the descriptive findings, drawing inferences from them, and attaching significance to them, is secondary to detailed description (1990:374–375, 422–423). For Patton, the discipline and rigor of qualitative analysis depend on solid description.

Patton sees serious dangers in using qualitative methods for causal interpretation. He argues that qualitative inquiry is a holistic process that seeks illumination and understanding, rather than a linear process that seeks causal determination and prediction. He warns that qualitative researchers who begin to make causal interpretations often fall back on the linear assumptions of quantitative methods, and that "simple statements of linear relationship may be more distorting than illuminating" (1990:423–424).

Patton does see qualitative evaluation as being concerned with verification as well as with discovery. He claims that creativity (the artistic side of qualitative research) is an important part of qualitative analysis. However, he emphasizes that qualitative research involves science (being rigorous and critical) as well as art.

Patton's pragmatist approach extends to his treatment of political and ethical issues in qualitative evaluation. In discussing covert research, for example, he presents a range of opinions, from Edward Shils's (1959) complete opposition to covert research to Jack Douglas's (1976) conflict model of society that legitimizes covert methods in the search for truth. Patton (1990) recommends full and complete disclosure but recognizes that this recommendation may not be appropriate for all circumstances—for example, evaluating a corrupt or abusive program (pp. 210–213). Elsewhere, he lists the ethical issues that a qualitative evaluator should deal with; he does not attempt to provide prescriptive solutions to these but, rather, to raise concerns and suggest ways of dealing with them (pp. 356–357).

Patton's principle of user-focused evaluation is also a key ethical component of his approach. For example, in discussing covert research, he asserts that the evaluator alone cannot make the decision about what is to be kept secret. This principle also informs his view that evaluators have an obligation to monitor and report the procedures used to reach their conclusions.

The pragmatism that is at the core of Patton's approach is the source of many of its strengths. *Qualitative Evaluation and Research Methods* is a predominantly practical work that provides concrete and specific guidance on aspects of qualitative evaluation ranging from entry negotiation and research design to data analysis and presentation of results. There are numerous examples from Patton's own research and an ecumenical openness to different strategies for resolving problems. Of all of the works considered here, Patton's is clearly the most useful for someone without much background in qualitative research who is attempting to use qualitative methods, or for a qualitative researcher who is new to evaluation.

However, we see some disadvantages in this pragmatic approach. Patton's ecumenism regarding paradigms leads him to occasionally treat all alternatives as equal. For example, in discussing the theoretical traditions of qualitative inquiry (1990:66–91), Patton begins by describing ethnography, phenomenology, and some other influential approaches, but the list continues with discussions of systems theory, chaos theory, and other perspectives whose influence on qualitative evaluation is not as yet significant; he concludes with an admonition that "readers must make their own decisions" (p. 89). Other parts of the book also lean toward this "laundry list" presentation, failing to distinguish established and significant concerns from emergent and peripheral ones.

Similarly, in presenting possible combinations of quantitative and qualitative design, data, and analysis, Patton describes these combinations as having equal intrinsic merit. He acknowledges that there are strong arguments for maintaining the purity and integrity of either a qualitative-naturalistic or quantitative-experimental approach but concludes that the practical mandate of the evaluator outweighs concerns about methodological purity (1990:186–198). What we miss here is a discussion of *why*, in a given circumstance, one might choose one combination rather than another, and what the tradeoffs would be.

Elsewhere in his work, Patton (1990:162–168) does consider tradeoffs involved in breadth versus depth and in selecting units of analysis, but again there is little guidance as to when to choose breadth over depth or vice versa; he asserts that "there is no rule of thumb that tells a researcher precisely how to focus a study. The extent to which a research question is broad or narrow depends on purpose, the resources available, the time available, and the interests of those involved" (p. 166). Patton's position is that all of these issues should be pragmatically negotiated with users and that explicit criteria would be incompatible with this.

Egon Guba and Yvonna Lincoln

The approach to qualitative evaluation taken by Guba and Lincoln is quite different from that advocated by Patton. Whereas Patton sees qualitative inquiry as having an essential scientific component, Guba and Lincoln see qualitative inquiry as fundamentally opposed to scientific inquiry, which they largely equate with "positivism." They argue that evaluation is an inherently social, political, and value-oriented activity and is, thus, incompatible with a scientific approach. They take as the goal of evaluation the enfranchisement of the stakeholders in an evaluation rather than the production of some "findings" in an evaluation report. Thus, they view qualitative evaluation in an applied or action context and as a political act (1989:35), rather than as "research" in the conventional sense.

Guba and Lincoln call the philosophical stance that they take "constructivist," a term they now prefer to their previous choice of "naturalistic" (Lincoln and Guba, 1985). They equate this stance with an interpretive or hermeneutic one. They see the meaningful constructions of individuals and groups, created through interaction, as the only reality that can be studied; "there *is no reality* except that created by people as they attempt to make sense of their surroundings [italics in original]" (1989:12–13). These realities are constructed rather than "out there" and depend on an observer for their existence. Guba and Lincoln's epistemology is thus radically relativist rather than realist, subjective rather than objective, and monist rather than dualist; they argue that an evaluation *creates* the reality that it presents, rather than discovering some objectively existing reality (1989:8).

They place this view in opposition to what they refer to as the "dominant," "conventional," or "scientific" paradigm and present an extensive critique of the assumptions of the latter; these include the existence of a real, objective world governed by natural laws, the validity of the concept of causality, a duality between observer and observed, and the view that inquiry can be value-free. In sharp contrast to Patton, they see no possibility of accommodation between the scientific and constructivist paradigms, because the basic assumptions of the two are fundamentally in conflict. They acknowledge, however, that a new paradigm may emerge that is more informed than either of these and argue that this is the only way to reconcile the differences between the two paradigms.

Guba and Lincoln distinguish between methods and methodologies, arguing that the use of naturalistic (qualitative) methods within a positivist framework, which they claim is easily done, is very different from "thinking naturalistically." The latter requires a revolutionary shift from positivism, a shift that changes both the meaning and practice of evaluation. They see the sort of qualitative evaluation that they advocate as having a "resonance" between the constructivist paradigm and the evaluation model. Thus, they criticize writers such as Patton and Miles and Huberman, who see evaluation methods and paradigms as independent and therefore advocate the mixing or ignoring of paradigms.

The approach to evaluation that Guba and Lincoln present is based not only on a constructivist epistemology, but also on the concept of responsive focusing. By this, they mean including the constructions of *all* stakeholders and not just those of the evaluator or the defined "client." For them, this entails negotiating the terms of the evaluation with all of the stakeholders, eliciting their constructions, facilitating a mutual critique of these constructions, and working toward a consensus among stakeholders, all conducted via a hermeneutic and dialectic process. The final product is a "case report" that is a joint construction of all participants, rather than the depiction of some "objective" situation. Its purpose is to help the reader vicariously grasp the constructions and motives of the stakeholders; they see the "New Journalism" as the best model for such a report. No judgments are made by the evaluator except insofar as these are concurred with by the relevant respondents.

In addition to this hermeneutic/dialectic process, Guba and Lincoln see the following as requirements for their approach, which they call Fourth Generation Evaluation (4GE):

1. A natural setting, because the realities with which it is concerned depend on the specific time and context of the constructors.
2. An inductive approach, which assumes that the evaluator needs to discover what questions to ask.
3. The use of qualitative methods.
4. The incorporation and use of the tacit knowledge (subjectivity) of the evaluator.

They deal at length with the criteria for judging the adequacy of such an evaluation, presenting two sets of standards. The first, which they term "trustworthiness," was originally presented by Lincoln and Guba (1985); it consists of four categories—credibility, transferability, dependability, and confirmability—which parallel the conventional criteria of internal validity, external validity, reliability, and objectivity. They also argue that the hermeneutic process itself is a form of quality control, claiming that this process virtually eliminates the possibility that the evaluator's biases can shape the result.

Guba and Lincoln (1989:245; Lincoln and Guba, 1986) now see

this first set of criteria as flawed, because it is based on positivist assumptions. In contrast, the second set of criteria, which they call "authenticity," is fully grounded in the constructivist paradigm. The latter consist of fairness, ontological authenticity (improvement in stakeholders' constructions), educative authenticity (stakeholders' appreciation of others' constructions), catalytic authenticity (stimulation to action), and tactical authenticity (empowerment to act).

Guba and Lincoln argue that both the scientific and constructivist methodologies are forms of disciplined inquiry, with the data and processes subject to public inspection and verification. However, much of their argument for 4GE is based, not on rigor or "trustworthiness" but, rather, on ethical and political concerns, which are incorporated in their standards for "authenticity." They repeatedly emphasize that 4GE serves to empower stakeholders who are frequently disenfranchised by conventional evaluations. They see the risk to stakeholders from an evaluation, and the potential educative benefit to these stakeholders, as primary reasons for the adoption of 4GE.

We see Guba and Lincoln's emphasis on the social, political, and ethical context of evaluation as the main strength of their approach. Their highlighting of these issues is an example of the point we made earlier—that paradigms can emphasize and clarify issues that other approaches may dismiss or downplay—e.g., the ways in which traditional evaluations have focused on the identified "client" to the exclusion of other stakeholders. We feel that after reading Guba and Lincoln's arguments for stakeholder empowerment, we can no longer see this issue in the same way that we did before.

However, while we agree that scientific views of evaluation have at times provided a warrant for ethical abuses, many of Guba and Lincoln's social and ethical concerns neither require nor are required by the constructivist paradigm. Some of the points they make about the need to consider stakeholders' perspectives are found in other approaches as well, including such "scientific" evaluators as Miles and Huberman. Furthermore, a constructivist epistemology could in principle be combined with strategies that Guba and Lincoln would consider unethical, such as Jack Douglas's use of covert research, described earlier.

Also, despite their strong stances on ethics, Guba and Lincoln do not address the almost unavoidable "symbolic violence" (Rabinow, 1977; cf. Miles and Huberman, 1984a) that occurs when privately held constructions are made visible to other groups, which is an inherent part of their method. They cite stakeholders' willingness to participate in the hermeneutic/dialectic process as one of the conditions for 4GE, but they do not address the possibly legitimate motives stakeholders may have to refuse to participate. Their view that the incorporation of stakeholders' values in a shared construction necessarily empowers those stakeholders seems questionable to us.

Second, we believe that much of Guba and Lincoln's attack on both "science" and "conventional" evaluation consists of setting up and then demolishing what is to some extent a straw man. They equate "science" with an array of assumptions that many scientifically oriented qualitative researchers would reject—for example, that science can address only verification, not discovery, and is therefore incompatible with soliciting concerns and issues from stakeholders (Guba and Lincoln, 1989:59). Some of these assumptions are old positivist views that have long been abandoned by philosophers of science. Their critique of these assumptions may be valuable in combating these vestigial remnants of positivism that still influence educational evaluation, but it would be more credible if they acknowledged that these views are rejected even by many "conventional" evaluators.

Their disavowal of validity as a positivist notion also leads them to disregard the credibility of the *information* the evaluator obtains, as opposed to the credibility of the *accounts* that the evaluator produces. They argue that one prerequisite for a successful hermeneutic/dialectic negotiation is the integrity of all parties in not deliberately offering misconstructions (Guba and Lincoln, 1989:149), but they ignore the possibility of ideological distortion and the ideological functions that stakeholders' constructions can serve. Indeed, their constructivist paradigm makes the concept of "distortion" meaningless, because it presumes an "actual" state of affairs that these constructions could be a distortion of.

In addition, Guba and Lincoln's assertions of the unity of paradigms remain largely assertions, without any real demonstration of these claims. This assertion is critical to their argument, because they insist on a dichotomous choice between the "scientific" and "constructivist" paradigms. This unity is not something that can be assumed, as has been demonstrated by McCawley (1982). In *Thirty Million Theories of Grammar* (1982), McCawley argued that two opposed positions in linguistics—generative semantics and interpretive semantics—that had generally been taken as unitary paradigms were in fact two packages of positions on a fairly large number of issues, each package corresponding to the views held by some prominent members of two communities of linguists. However,

> . . . neither of these communities was completely homogeneous, no member of the community retained exactly the same set of views for very long, . . . and the relationships among the views that were packaged together as "generative semantics" or as "interpretive semantics" were generally far more tenuous than representative members of either community led people (including themselves) to believe (McCawley, 1982:1)

One of our goals in this chapter is, like that of McCawley, to "take apart the various packages and to demonstrate where possible the independence of the views that comprise the package" (McCawley, 1982:1).

However, we also see a more fundamental problem with Guba and Lincoln's paradigm—that is, despite their avowal of multiple perspectives, their understanding of culture is to a significant extent "uniformist" in its assumption that what is most important to the functioning of a group is what the members share or come to share. This is an assumption that has been increasingly challenged in anthropology (Pelto and Pelto, 1975; Maxwell, 1986). Guba and Lincoln see the goal of 4GE as the creation of a single construction that will be accepted by all stakeholders; for them, "resolution" of an issue is equated with arriving at a shared construction of it, at which point the required action is self-evident (Guba and Lincoln, 1989:222). They do not assume that such sharing will be easy, or even possible, to achieve in all cases but see it as fundamental to successful action. This view largely ignores the fact that constructions are *socially situated* and, thus, unlikely to come to be shared by individuals in very different social positions (cf. Wallace, 1970). Also, we question the view that shared understanding will eliminate conflict and that it is a prerequisite to successful resolution of an issue.

Our critique of Guba and Lincoln here is similar to Rorty's (1989) critique of Habermas. Rorty argues that "Habermas . . . still insists on seeing the process of undistorted communication as convergent, and seeing that convergence as a guarantee of the 'rationality' of such communication" (1989:67). Guba and Lincoln, like Habermas, seem to see convergence on a shared construction as evidence, not of the "truth," but at least of the "authenticity" of that construction. Rorty, although he accepts the political ideal of "freely arrived at agreement . . . on how to accomplish common purposes," wants "to see these common purposes against the background of an increasing sense of the radical diversity of private purposes" (1989:67).

For all of these reasons, we feel that the greatest strength of Guba and Lincoln's work is as a critique of other approaches; its greatest weakness is as a model for actually conducting an evaluation along naturalistic or constructivist lines. They give no actual examples of such an evaluation, and the guidelines that they provide strike us as abstract and programmatic. Ironically, they may be ignoring the most fundamental sense of Kuhn's (1977) use of "paradigm": as an exemplar of research, a concrete problem solution against which abstract assumptions and principles are interpreted. Kuhn argues that "exemplary problem solutions are one of the essential vehicles for the cognitive content of theory . . . . The same generalizations combined with different exemplars would develop in different directions and would thus constitute a somewhat different cognitive system" (1977:501). Without such exemplars, we cannot judge the feasibility of Guba and Lincoln's approach.

Matthew Miles and A. Michael Huberman

As noted earlier, Miles and Huberman present the most explicitly "scientific" of the four approaches to qualitative evaluation. Both Miles and Huberman came to qualitative evaluation from a quantitative background and were drawn to qualitative methods because of their perceived value for understanding the process of innovation in schools. Like Patton, Miles and Huberman (1984a) see their approach as "pragmatic"; they say they will use any method that will help them to produce good analyses and endorse an epistemological ecumenism.

Miles and Huberman (1984b) also refer to themselves as "logical positivists who recognize and try to atone for the limitations of that approach" (p. 19) and are criticized as positivists by Guba and Lincoln. However, they elsewhere equate "neopositivism" with realism (Huberman and Miles, 1985:353) and identify their position with that of Manicas and Secord (1982) and others who explicitly adopt a critical realist approach. Because current post-positivist philosophy of science is predominantly realist rather than positivist, this term seems to fit Miles and Huberman's position better than "positivist."[2]

Miles and Huberman believe that social phenomena exist not only in the mind, but also in the objective world, and that these phenomena exhibit some stable regularities. They acknowledge that making sense of data is a construction, for both researchers and informants, rather than something that is "discovered." However, they also emphasize that both researchers and informants' constructions can be *wrong*. They devote a great deal of their book (a much greater proportion than for any of the other authors discussed) to ways in which researchers can identify and correct errors in their accounts.

Despite these views, which are quite different from those usually associated with qualitative inquiry, their approach clearly falls within the definition of "qualitative evaluation." They emphasize their concern with the meaning of events for participants, the importance of context, and the need for an inductive approach; one of their main strategies for determining the validity of their conclusions is to employ feedback from informants. They also point out the shortcomings of quantitative methods for understanding educational innovation.

A key concept in Miles and Huberman's approach to qualitative evaluation is "local causality." Arguing that *why* things happen is a central issue in qualitative research, they claim that qualitative methods are far better than purely quantitative ones at identifying the specific causal relations and processes that are occurring in a particular site. Their methods are aimed at the understanding of contextualized causal processes, rather than on relating abstract variables out of context, and they cite in support of their position Geertz's (1983) view that "local knowledge" is the first goal of qualitative research.

This emphasis on context is central to Miles and Huberman's methodology. Although they are less committed to purely inductive strategies than many other qualitative researchers, arguing that bitter experience (an inductive process) has taught them the value of some prestructuring of questions and methods, they repeatedly emphasize the dangers of "context-stripping" and the importance of keeping one's data and conclusions linked to the particular contextual features that gave rise to them.

Miles and Huberman's (1984b) *Qualitative Data Analysis* differs from the statements of the other three authors discussed here in three important ways. First, it is not explicitly about *evaluation* but about qualitative research. Second, it deliberately devotes very little space to issues such as entry negotiation, rapport, and data collection; it focuses on design, data analysis, and presentation of results. Third, it is not intended to present a systematic model or approach but, rather, to serve as a sourcebook, a set of tools that qualitative researchers can draw from. These three characteristics make it somewhat harder to assess Miles and Huberman's overall approach to evaluation than the other three approaches. However, some significant features stand out.

Miles and Huberman's focus on design and analysis provides the most detailed and explicit discussion of these issues of any of the four statements. They devote considerable space to discussing the development of a conceptual framework for a study (an issue barely touched on by the others), and they provide specific methods for doing this. They also present a vastly greater number of techniques for data analysis and interpretation than the other authors. They cover the standard methods, such as coding and memos, but emphasize what they call "displays"—graphic strategies (such as matrices and network diagrams) for reducing the sheer amount of data with which the researcher must deal and presenting it in a compressed, ordered way, which permits the analysis and conclusions to be seen as a whole. They see these displays as complementary to and interactive with narrative accounts and as a qualitative alternative to quantitative techniques for condensing and presenting findings.

One of Miles and Huberman's major concerns is with the possibility that the researcher will "get it wrong;" they argue that the most serious need in qualitative research is explicitness about the ways in which researchers draw and test conclusions. They discuss the dangers of erroneous assumptions, premature closure, self-delusion, judgmental error (citing the work of Tversky and Kahneman), elite bias in selecting informants, and accepting participants' perceptions as accurate accounts of what really happened.

Their strategies for dealing with these validity threats include the following: systematic attention to the quality of one's data; continuous revision of one's data collection methods; keeping data contextualized; various types of triangulation, including member checks; using several analysts to check each other's interpretations; the use of outliers and negative evidence; the development and testing of rival hypotheses and alternative accounts; and making predictions. They also emphasize the need to preserve the evidential chain that led to the conclusions, crediting Guba and Lincoln with the concept of an "audit trail" for evaluations.

Miles and Huberman do not deal systematically with ethical issues, but they raise these issues at several points. They acknowledge the "betrayal" that is involved in making participants' private constructions public, but they see this as intrinsic to field research, no matter how careful and well intentioned the researcher. They do not seem particularly concerned about the "adversarial" research style of people like Douglas, citing it as a strategy for learning about what is going on when participants are reluctant to reveal this. On the other hand, they do discuss the possible risks to some participants that arise in giving data and interpretations back to people in the site. They also argue that asking participants to review and comment on preliminary findings is professional work and that, on ethical grounds, people who do this should always be offered some recompense.

One of the main strengths of Miles and Huberman's work is the way in which it presents new methods and systematizes old ones, providing a far more detailed account of qualitative data analysis than exists anywhere else. Indeed, one could fault them for oversystematization; in the hands of someone who lacks familiarity with other approaches to qualitative research, their methods could become a rigid "cookbook" that would destroy the very openness and inductiveness that drew them to qualitative methods, despite the authors' warnings against such rigidity. Their residual neopositivism also occasionally causes them, in our opinion, to slide into overly linear and variable-oriented approaches. However, we believe that their emphasis on the possibility of error and their detailed discussion of ways to deal with this serve as a major contribution and corrective to the literature on qualitative evaluation methods.

Elliot W. Eisner

Of the authors discussed, Eisner is, in many ways, the farthest from Miles and Huberman. His approach to qualitative evaluation, which he calls "educational criticism," is explicitly artistic in nature rather than scientific, being based on connoisseurship and criticism in the arts. Although Eisner's previous work (e.g., Eisner, 1985a) emphasized the differences between art and science and contained extensive criticisms of "scientific" approaches to evaluation, *The Enlightened Eye* (Eisner, 1991) seems much less disputatious, possibly as a result of the imminent waning of the "paradigm wars." Nonetheless, his philosophic stance is quite different from that of the other authors discussed.

Eisner identifies two central concerns in art—seeing and representation, which are the basis for his approach to qualitative inquiry. Seeing, as opposed to mere looking, requires connoisseurship, an "enlightened eye" that is sensitive to what is subtle and significant in the subject. Representation, which he views as the main task of criticism, is the making public of what one has seen, enabling others to see this as well. He believes that the importance and difficulty of both of these is underappreciated, and that greater attention to them can result in important contributions to evaluation (Eisner, 1991:1–7).

However, Eisner also grants a legitimate role to scientific and quantitative approaches to evaluation. He argues that different modalities convey different types of understanding, and he sees his approach to qualitative inquiry as a complement rather than an alternative to scientific evaluation; neither is inherently superior to the other, but only more appropriate for different purposes (Eisner, 1991:186–187; cf. Eisner, 1985b:210–213). Elsewhere, he describes a study by a student at Stanford that combined quantitative methods and educational criticism and argues that "it is to the artistic that we must turn, *not* as a rejection of the scientific, but because with both we can achieve binocular vision [italics in original]" (1985a:199).

Eisner is troubled by the frequent equating of qualitative inquiry with ethnography. He feels that qualitative inquiry is far broader than this and legitimately includes artistic and humanistic as well as social science approaches (Eisner, 1991:15, 228–230). It is not even limited to "research" but is a pervasive part of our everyday experience: the perception of qualities. Such perception depends both on the existence of the qualities perceived and on our learned ability to experience them; it involves a transaction between our subjective life and a postulated objective world and, thus, transcends both "objectivity" and "subjectivity" (Eisner, 1991:16–22, 52–53).

Eisner identified six characteristics of a qualitative study: a focus on natural settings and their products, rather than laboratory manipulation; the use of the self as an instrument; an interpretive purpose (in two senses—meaning and explanation); the use of expressive (as well as literal) language and the presence of "voice"; attention to particulars in their own right rather than simply as a means to generalization; and believability that is based on coherence, insight, and instrumental utility (Eisner, 1991:32–41). This list differs only in minor ways from that of Patton (1990:40–41) or from the view of Guba and Lincoln or Miles and Huberman.

The most striking difference between Eisner's position and those of the other authors is his disavowal of any explicit method for doing qualitative research. He explains at some length how he trains educational critics, but his description of what such critics *do* in conducting a study is considerably less detailed than that of the other authors, although much more explicit with each subsequent publication. This is consistent with his repeated emphasis on the importance and value of diversity and on the drawbacks of structure and standardization. Although he is often asked for a framework that educational critics could use to observe and describe classrooms, he replies, "For readers who seek a procedure, a formula, or a set of rules for doing qualitative inquiry, this chapter will be a disappointment . . . . in qualitative matters cookbooks ensure nothing" (Eisner, 1991:169). He does provide some of the considerations and dimensions on which an educational researcher could focus and a brief discussion of different sources of data and forms of representation (Eisner, 1991:176–195). Still, *The*

Enlightened Eye contains considerably less information on data collection and analysis methods than most other works on qualitative research. Eisner sees the risk of encumbering the critics vision with rigid procedures as more serious than the risk of inadequate support for the process of collecting data and drawing conclusions.

This deliberate refusal to specify methods for qualitative research does not mean that Eisner is unconcerned with validity; he devotes an entire chapter to this issue. He argues that, "because we can secure no unmediated grasp of things as they 'really are,' we cannot ever be certain of having found Truth. We are always 'stuck' with judgments and interpretations" (Eisner, 1991:109). Nevertheless, there are evidentiary bases for our judgments, similar to those found in clinical settings and in law. He gives three sources of evidence for establishing the credibility of an educational criticism: structural corroboration, consensual validation, and referential adequacy.

Structural corroboration is similar to what is often known as triangulation: the use of multiple sources and types of data to support or contradict an interpretation. Acknowledging that qualitative research allows more scope for researchers to see what they choose and, thus, greater chance for the intentional neglect of evidence contrary to one's values or interests, Eisner argues that, "*it is especially important not only to use multiple types of data, but also to consider disconfirming evidence and contradictory interpretations or appraisals* when one presents one's own conclusions [italics in original]" (Eisner, 1991:111)—a statement that might easily have come from Miles and Huberman.

Consensual validation rests on the agreement of competent others that the researcher's account is valid. This does not entail that different critics would produce identical criticisms; different researchers will see different things in complex phenomena such as schools, and the goal is not a single uniform view but a diversity of valid and useful views (Eisner, 1991:112–113; cf. Eisner, 1985b:242–244). Finally, referential adequacy is based on the major function of an educational criticism: to enlarge the reader's perception and understanding of its subject. The referential adequacy of criticism is tested in the reader's ability to perceive the qualities it describes.

The generalizations that can be drawn from educational criticisms are those of ordinary life rather than statistical inference. Eisner sees generalization as a from of transfer of learning and views statistical generalization as a special case of this broader process. In qualitative research, it is primarily the readers who determine whether the study or evaluation generalizes to their situations. Eisner urges that this not be taken

. . . as an invitation to irresponsible description, interpretation, or
evaluation, but rather as reflection of the realization that
generalizations are tools with which we work and are to be shaped in
context. They are part of the substantive exchange between
professionals with their own expertise, not prescriptions from the
doctor. (Eisner, 1991:205)

In contrast to Eisner's previous work, *The Enlightened Eye* explicitly addresses ethical issues such as entry negotiation and possible risks to participants in an evaluation. His discussion of negotiating access has a strong ethical component, and he devotes a separate chapter to the problems of informed consent, confidentiality, and the right to withdraw from a study. However, he is skeptical of the view (e.g., Lincoln, 1990) that some general principle can be found to guide ethical conduct arguing that rigid adherence to either a "rights" or a "consequences" principle is inadequate to deal with the ethical issues in qualitative research. He provides a detailed description and analysis of an ethical error from his own research, stating that this incident has increased his concern with ethical considerations. His goal is to identify and illuminate the ethical dilemmas, not to resolve them; "with such consciousness we are in a better position to exercise sensibility, taste, and that most precious human capacity, rational judgment" (Eisner, 1991:226).

The advantages that we see in Eisner's artistic model of evaluation derive from the two features of art that he emphasizes: informed, critical perception and the value of nonliteral forms of representation. As Eisner argues, educational criticisms can present an illuminating portrait of what goes on in some setting, to show us what we had looked at but never "seen." In this task, his use of artistic methods of presentation, and in particular his emphasis on the importance of nonverbal methods of perceiving and communicating, seem to us to redress a common shortcoming of qualitative evaluations, which is that they are often written in a manner that emulates the supposed "objectivity" of quantitative research.

In an earlier work, Eisner (1985a:158–159) lists as one of the disadvantages of educational criticism its costliness and lack of efficiency. We tend to disagree; when its conclusions are valid, educational criticism seems more cost-effective than many other methods of qualitative evaluation, which require extensive field research to establish their conclusions. A trained educational critic, visiting a classroom, may develop an illuminating portrait after one visit, whereas a classroom ethnographer might take months to fashion an understanding of the same environment. Thus, educational criticism could contribute importantly to the improvement of current methods of supervision and administrative evaluation in education, in which cost-effectiveness is at a premium.

The other disadvantages of educational criticism listed by Eisner are those that we tend to agree with. Eisner (1985a:158–159) cites the method's lack of precision (reliability), which results from reliance on the critic's judgment; the inference by many readers that artistic language implies a biased or nonfactual account; and the difficulty that criticism has in drawing conclusions without doing violence to the criticism as a whole.

We are also concerned about the deliberate lack of attention to the methods used in educational criticism, especially the methods for analyzing data. The warnings by Miles and Huberman about the dangers of self-delusion, particularly the dangers involved in going directly from data to narrative, seem to us to be real and serious issues for educational criticism. Eisner recognizes these dangers, but his refusal to provide explicit guidance for dealing with these, as a result of his legitimate concerns about the negative consequences of structure, seems to us to leave qualitative researchers without systematic methods that could increase the credibility of their data and conclusions at a relatively small cost to their perception.

Our overall assessment of educational criticism, then, is similar to Eisner's in that we see it as a complement rather than an alternative to other approaches, one that can provide important perspectives and lead to insights that other approaches miss. However, we see it not just as a complement to quantitative or "scientific" methods but also to other forms of *qualitative* evaluation, which provide tools and perspectives that educational criticism does not emphasize.

A Comparison

In comparing the four approaches we have discussed, we note that their differences are evident in the following six categories.

The Existence of Reality

One of the key differences among the four positions is over the existence of some reality external to the mental constructions of individuals and groups. Guba and Lincoln strongly deny the existence of such a reality. Eisner, perhaps surprisingly, seems the most clearly realist in his statements, particularly in his emphasis on structural corroboration and referential adequacy. Patton and Miles and Huberman at times take what seems to be a realist view, but in other places they say things that seem inconsistent with a realist perspective.

Definition and Goals of Qualitative Inquiry and Qualitative Evaluation

As noted, Patton's views of qualitative inquiry are the most typical of qualitative evaluators, emphasizing an inductive and holistic approach in natural settings, the use of personal contact and insight, a focus on the specific context and the participants' perspective, and an orientation to the particular case studied. Miles and Huberman's views are similar but allow more prestructuring, more focus on specific variables, and more latitude for generalization from specific cases. Eisner, despite his portrayal of educational criticism as essentially artistic in nature, emphasizes many of the same characteristics as Patton: the importance of holism and context, the personal involvement of the investigator, and the concern with process, meaning, and diversity. Eisner's main differences with Patton pertain to the product of qualitative inquiry.

Guba and Lincoln's definition of what they call "constructivist inquiry" incorporates their rejection of "truth" as correspondence with reality, of causality, and of generalizability and emphasizes the inextricable link between facts and values. They argue that qualitative methods by themselves are not necessarily consistent with the constructivist paradigm and describe an approach that they feel *is* consistent with this paradigm. They also take a much more action-oriented view of evaluation than the other authors, emphasizing the empowerment of stakeholders rather than the "findings" of the evaluation.

Design and Methods

Patton's account is the most explicit and "how-to" of the four accounts and incorporates most of the characteristic features of qualitative research in general. Miles and Huberman's account is similar but pays much more attention to research design and analytic methods. Guba and Lincoln give extensive guidelines for 4GE, but these are not very explicit about how to actually do it. In keeping with their orientation, they say much more about political and ethical issues than about "research" issues such as analysis and conclusions. Eisner refuses on principle to specify particular designs or methods.

Validity

All of the authors emphasize validity or some analogous concept; their differences are over its definition. Miles and Huberman make the strongest case for the importance of validity in a conventional sense and provide a detailed discussion of how to deal with threats to validity. Patton's views seem similar, but are less extensively developed. Eisner's discussion, surprisingly, is quite similar to that of Patton and most other qualitative researchers; however, his treatment of referential adequacy emphasizes the *reader's* ways of determining this, rather than how the *critic* can do so. In addition, it is hard for us to see the application of his views in the examples of criticisms he gives. Guba and Lincoln's discussion of "authenticity" emphasizes ethical and political issues rather than "validity," which they consider a positivist concept.

The Product of Evaluation

For Guba and Lincoln, the desired product of an evaluation is its impact on stakeholders' constructions, rather than any sort of "findings." Patton discusses reports of findings in some detail but argues that there are no rules for producing a report; its nature will depend on the study's purpose and audience. Miles and Huberman's position seems similar to that of Patton, but they also emphasize displays as reporting techniques.

Attitude toward Other Approaches

Both Eisner and Patton explicitly state that they consider other approaches to be legitimate alternatives to the one they propose, while this attitude seems implicit in Miles and Huberman's account. Guba and Lincoln, despite their philosophical relativism, seem the most critical of alternative evaluation strategies, defining most of the other approaches discussed here as "positivist."

From Models to Methods

Clearly, we do not think that rigid views of "consistency" between paradigms and methods can adequately account for the specific features of the different approaches described earlier. The connections between philosophic assumptions and methods do not fit a simple linear model in which one mirrors the other. Instead, these relationships are context-dependent and, as such, allow for numerous possibilities from one study to the next within the overall domain of qualitative evaluation.

In our own approach, which we delineate in the next section of this chapter, we value and, in fact, insist on variation and adaptation in defining and selecting methods for particular qualitative evaluation studies; however, this context-dependent variability is not haphazard or chaotic. It is founded in what Miles and Huberman (1984a) refer to as a "shared craft." Indeed, we are struck by the amount of recent convergence among the authors discussed earlier (especially Patton, Eisner, and Miles and Huberman). We recognize in their work a common approach to the *practice* of evaluative qualitative inquiry, despite continuing disagreements about philosophical assumptions and paradigms. While the prospect of agreement or reconciliation among philosophical perspectives remains illusive for evaluation research, agreement on the conduct of that research appears feasible and also far more productive.

Our identification and endorsement of this convergence does not mean that we feel that paradigms are irrelevant to the practice of qualitative evaluation. It means only that we see no possibility of a philosophical reapproachment, nor do we believe that one is necessary. We think that qualitative researchers may be able to work together without agreeing on fundamental principles. Rather than a "top-down" approach that insists that evaluation practice be rigorously derived from paradigmatic assumptions, we prefer a "bottom-up" approach that sees paradigms as grounded in, and in dialectical relation with, the practice of qualitative evaluation. To explicate what we mean by this and how it looks in practice, we now turn to a presentation of our position on the actual conduct of qualitative evaluation.

Qualitative Research as a Paradigm of Choices and Decisions

All qualitative research, including qualitative evaluation, is and must be guided by a continual process of researcher decisions and choices. This fact necessitates procedural diversity even within paradigms and is itself necessitated by three factors. First, qualitative evaluation research has an inherently emic component. That is, the researcher seeks to describe not simply what he or she sees people doing and hears people saying, but primarily what the members of that human community see themselves doing and hear themselves saying (see Spradley and McCurdy, 1972). This is often referred to as the natives', participants' or insiders' perspective. To capture, understand, and, eventually, classify and compare that perspective, the qualitative evaluator must choose, assess, and redesign research methods and schedules to fit the community being studied. The evaluator needs to be guided by this emic perspective from the very beginning of the project, regardless of her or his epistemological model. Thus, for example, in the pragmatic model of Patton, what is sought is the solution to dilemmas that are defined by the school or agency initiating the study *and* by the actual informants in the study. In the constructivist model of Guba and Lincoln, what is sought is an approach to defining both dilemma and solution via a process of interaction between evaluator and evaluated. The voices and the point of view of the people studied are never absent from an evaluation that is qualitative.

The second factor that necessitates continual decisions as the basis of the qualitative approach to evaluation is that the researcher him- or herself is the instrument of data collection. No other process or product mediates between phenomena *in situ* and qualitative data, such as field notes. For this reason, qualitative evaluation research always has an idiosyncratic component. Procedures for recording data, for example, should be those that work for that person in that setting.

This second factor is the one that has been most likely to generate the criticism that qualitative approaches to evaluation are hopelessly subjective. We concede at the outset that indeed they are—in the sense that all research is subjective. We call this the Heisenberg principle of indeterminacy. Heisenberg claimed that quantum mechanical reality could not be studied as it existed because to measure one principle, namely position, inherently altered or made inaccessible another, namely velocity. As a result, what is known is not the properties of the phenomenon itself but, rather, the relationship between the design of the study and the phenomenon being studied. The natural sciences and especially their quantitative derivatives in the social sciences have developed elaborate statistical mechanisms for minimizing and accounting for this relationship. Similarly, qualitatively conducted evaluation research must attend to, acknowledge, and control for the nature of the research instrument.

This monitoring and control is accomplished via a parallel process of recording, which minimizes bias in the researcher's point of view, the main research instrument. The qualitative evaluator records physical, social, and cognitive/ideological data while recording his or her responses to that data and to the experience of recording it. The subjective response of the evaluator is tracked, noted, made conscious, reflected on, monitored, and assessed. These reflective field notes may take the form of a field diary in the tradition of cultural anthropology, or of parallel columns on each page of field notes, or some other method of recording that best fits that researcher's idiosyncratic predilections. In this way, one's response is used to monitor bias to the advantage of more accurate data. Personal reactions are clues to emic perspectives, especially when the two differ (Agar, 1980). They allow the evaluator to note bias in the form of implicit assumptions so as to return to the research site to attempt to generate alternatives. In this sense, subjective responses are critical to the conduct of qualitative evaluation, and, more importantly, to the interpretation of its results.

The locus for researcher decisions is the research setting. Qualitative evaluators base their research decisions on the exigencies of the research setting, what Miles and Huberman refer to as context. Decisions about who to observe and/or talk to, what to participate in and how, what questions to ask, and so on all depend on what is possible and appropriate in this situation for these stakeholders at this time. Similarly, qualitative evaluators interpret their data with reference to the context in which it originated. This attention to the total ecology of place derives from the traditional "holism" in cultural anthropology. All four of the approaches discussed earlier warn against taking data out of context, of reducing complex networks of influence to simple, linear relationships between isolated variables.

Researcher decisions, then, form the basis of the recursive process of qualitative evaluation research. Qualitative evaluators go to "the field." They conduct their research within the context of the real lives of real people. Their stance within this context, whether "context" is viewed as social, ideological/cognitive, or physical, is, ideally, empathically neutral and nonjudgmental. They observe, listen, and read, and then note their responses to this input. They query established theory and similar studies for additional responses, and then they make the next layer of decisions. We talk and write about this method one sentence at a time, a linear process. Qualitative evaluation is not conducted in a linear fashion, however. All aspects are ongoing. It is the evaluators' decisions that will shape the process for each particular study. Their decisions should be informed rather than merely subjective. They are informed by the data gathered to date, by an egalitarian and utilitarian querying of related theoretical explanations, and by scholarly and creative reflection on all information available.

Ethics

For an evaluator using qualitative methods, one of the earliest decisions will be to determine whether or not the evaluation can ethically be conducted at all. One ethical constraint is the necessity for confidentiality when disclosure would put participants at risk. A second constraint is the necessity for sufficient honesty on the part of the evaluator and understanding on the part of the participants so as to constitute, minimally, informed consent and preferably, for evaluation research, active interest. Third, there should be provision for reciprocity, for fair return in terms of service or remuneration for participants' time and other less tangible contributions.

Ethical decisions, like all other decisions in qualitative evaluation, are ongoing. One cannot expect that once an ethical determination has been made that the evaluation can be conducted without harm, that the ethical issues will then dissolve. Rather, one must expect and be prepared for the regular occurrence of ethical dilemmas in qualitative evaluation.

Confidentiality in applied evaluative research may differ considerably from that expected in research conducted solely in the interests of scholarship. On the one hand, the community or persons under study may request that their real names and locations be identified. They may wish to be known. The researcher must consider very carefully whether or not to comply with such a request by determining the possibility of harm. On the other hand, some informants and/or locations will need to be layered in confidentiality to prevent threat, manipulation, or some other form of harm to those who have engaged in a relationship of trust with the evaluator.

Informed consent is not an ethical consideration that can be set aside because the research is intended to be an evaluation. Clandestine investigation may be inherently unethical in the qualitative tradition. Evaluations that cannot be conducted by communicating an honest statement of intent to the research community may need to be rejected (for elaboration on this point, see Dobbert, 1982).

Finally, the principle of reciprocity applies to evaluation research as it does to any field-based study that admits an outsider into the private spaces of the real lives of real people. In traditional ethnography, one was always obligated to contribute in such a way that the research setting would not be significantly altered due to the presence of the researcher *while the research is in process.* In qualitative evaluation, however, the weaving of research findings with researcher involvement for change may be an appropriate approach to reciprocity.

As noted earlier, for Guba and Lincoln, such an action-oriented partnership is essential to constructing an evaluation at all. A form of reciprocity that has a respected tradition in the form of action research and applied anthropology is to assist in making the changes that are suggested by the evaluation after the research is completed. Indeed, there are those who have claimed that the only honest and effective way to conduct ethnographic or qualitative evaluation research is for the evaluator to guide the implementation of the recommendations, as far as possible (Pelto and Schensul, 1987). Reciprocity may be simple in cases where the persons being investigated are the ones who have requested the evaluation, and they both expect to be, and in fact will be, advantaged by its findings. However, when the evaluation is being conducted for one or a number of agencies, then the researcher must, minimally, determine some respectful, locally valuable form of fair return.

Evaluators, therefore, should hold themselves to the same ethical standards as do all qualitative researchers who derive their findings from relationships of trust. The scholar, basic or applied, who does field-based research has two obligations. The first is to the community studied. No harm should come to any of its members as a direct result of the study. This may include an obligation to seriously consider and, if possible, judiciously modulate potentially damaging data in one's final report. Observing the requirements of confidentiality, honesty, and reciprocity as previously described are typically sufficient to ensure this safety. The second obligation is to the profession. Having represented oneself as an evaluator, the researcher is obligated to produce an evaluation. The findings of the research must be presented and/or published in some appropriate format. Although the product resulting from evaluation research *may* be made available in the scientific community, it must first be made available in the community that requested the evaluation in the first place.

Ethical considerations, therefore, are a constant in qualitative evaluation. For Guba and Lincoln, they are the *raison d'etre* that motivates and guides all qualitative evaluation. But even for pragmatists like Patton, realists like Miles and Huberman, and critics like Eisner ethical considerations are imperative. In fact, because we cannot always predict the impact of our research, and because as evaluators we may have dual and competing group memberships, the ethical constraints typical of all qualitative research are that much more complicated and therefore carry that much greater an imperative in an evaluation research project.

Entree

Entree is understood as that phase of the qualitative evaluation process in which one selects or specifies a research site and obtains the necessary agreements from participants to conduct the research in their space. In evaluation research, this phase can differ considerably from entree procedures employed for basic research, and the latter will vary depending on the epistemology of the researcher. The informant–researcher collaboration characteristic of current participatory research, for example, collapses the entree process into the agreement to collaborate and places the negotiation of the research relationship squarely at the center of the ongoing project. In contrast, in the holistic community studies in the tradition of cultural anthropology, entree is a layered and extended process. Qualitative evaluators are likely to find themselves at many different places on the entree continuum, depending on at whose behest the research is being conducted.

The entree choices a qualitative evaluator will make regarding the number of sites and one's location within each specific site will be constrained by the same three factors that affect location and design of any qualitative investigation. These are the constraints imposed by the size of the research staff, the schedule for data collection, and the availability of financing to support research activities (see Dobbert, 1982). Qualitative evaluation can be conducted using a number of personnel configurations: a single researcher in a single site, a team of researchers in a single site, and multiple sites with either a single researcher or a team in each. Entree must be negotiated in each setting, in each human community within each setting, and eventually by each researcher who will be engaging in on-site participant observation or informant interviewing.

Schedule and budget constraints will vary widely also. Some evaluations may need to be conducted according to the model of what some have referred to as clinical anthropology and what others have called "rapid assessment procedures" (Scrimshaw and Hurlado, 1987). This refers to qualitative evaluation conducted more in the manner of organizational psychology. In such a study, a group such as a company, neighborhood, unit, department, school, or classroom requests input on a particular diagnostic issue around which some kind of tension appears to exist. A single researcher proceeds to gather basic qualitative data during a specified and limited time frame from several days to several weeks and produces a verbal and written report at the end of that time. As budgets increase, the schedule for data collection can be more generous and less intense, can make use of multiple data collection technologies, can employ nonparticipant research assistants and consultants, and can provide financial remuneration to participants affected by but not initiating the request for the evaluation. One's location along these several continua of defined constraints in regard to budget, staff, and schedule must be ascertained before designing the evaluation to assure that access will be possible.

Entree procedures are affected by two additional factors: the stance of empathic neutrality and the competing stance of adherence to particular theories. Regarding neutrality, the evaluator should hold to the tradition of nonjudgmental learning that is generically characteristic of ethnography and qualitative research. In negotiating entree, the qualitative evaluator communicates a genuine respect for, and humility in the face of, the particulars of peoples' lives. She or he requests permission to learn from rather than to study; to request instruction or, in some cases, interaction rather than information. This stance is mediated by the second factor, the particular theoretical orientation that frames the evaluation researcher's investigation. So, for example, if one takes the perspective of critical social theory, it may be incumbent on the researcher to represent either to funders or to informants his or her ability and intent to elicit and name inequities, especially those related to power and status. Similarly, if one's epistemological orientation is constructivist, as defined by Guba and Lincoln, entree would entail explaining that interaction between researcher and informants necessarily will be regular and ongoing and require a considerable time commitment from all involved.

Both of these factors, then—one's personal stance of learner (in the tradition of the researcher as instrument) and one's theoretical orientation—exert considerable influence in the early stages of qualitative evaluation and continue into the phase of role negotiation.

Role Negotiation

Having decided that the research can be conducted ethically and having gained access to the necessary locales, the qualitative evaluator begins to negotiate a role while designing the research schedule and rationale and preparing the formal proposal for acceptance or approval. As noted earlier, it is at this participatory juncture that evaluation research seems most contested. We claim that an improvisational approach to participant observation and informant interviewing and a comfort with ambiguity are necessary qualifications for the qualitative evaluator negotiating a role in an evaluation research setting.

In the initial stages, the evaluator begins to look for a possible fit, a role, and to assess how long it will take to negotiate an appropriate stance. The interactive, socially constructed nature of this process can be frightening for people who tend to rely on known social rules and boundaries for personal comfort. Such persons may occasionally be inclined to retreat into paradigmatic rigidity or formulaic approaches to data collection. As Spradley and McCurdy (1972) have said in their introductory methods text, "Fear of people can be one of the most significant barriers" to the conduct of ethnographic or qualitative research (p. 42). Keeping a field diary or journal can relieve the feelings of incompetence, confusion, or rejection that often characterize the initial stages of research and can help the evaluator understand the effects that these feelings may have on the research.

Second, initiation anxieties can be relieved by using established networks or skills. Qualitative evaluators can identify who they know within the setting or who is willing to acknowledge or assist them. They can establish what they can do or know about that may be of use to people. Making these early connections can ease initiation anxieties.

Finally, then, evaluators, like other qualitative researchers, whether interviewing or observing, need to ease into the evaluation research situation gradually, learning and using the amenities of appropriate social intercourse in specific settings or with specific persons (including dress and manners). By going slowly and concentrating on developing a routine for writing and later rewriting and labeling field notes and other field data, the qualitative evaluator initiates an inductive approach to data acquisition. Patterns of belief and behavior can emerge from descriptive, detailed data that has been gathered unobtrusively and nonjudgmentally from a position of acceptance within the community under study.

Design and Data Collection

Once the qualitative evaluator has determined that the requested evaluation study can be conducted ethically, has secured the necessary permissions, and has concluded that the resources exist to conduct the research in this setting, the next step is to design the particulars of the study. It is at this point that the qualitative evaluator more systematically begins to query self and site regarding the specific data collection methods that will fit both the researcher and the research setting. In all approaches to qualitative evaluation, there are two essential questions for this design process. First, what is the empirical unknown in this situation? That is, what do the folks here want to find out that is different from what they already know? Second, what is the best procedure for generating that information? That is, what constellation of methods will produce the kind of information that will address these questions and concerns? While it is very likely that a qualitative evaluator might not have pursued an evaluation project to this point without some sense that the project would fit an essentially qualitative data collection procedure, it is at the stage of design that that assessment is made more formally.

In addition to selecting procedures, the evaluation design should also address the theoretical constructs that appear to the evaluator to be the most likely to guide data collection and analysis. In the sense that data are already theory-laden, design is already analysis. The evaluator's theoretical perspective will structure the research design, whether or not that perspective is made explicit. This level of theory, what Pelto (1970) has called "meta-theory," is not typically made explicit in standard scientific research. Such "theoretical predispositions," as Patton (1980:276) terms them, have an essential implicitness. Because the researcher will structure the evaluation's data collection plan around these underlying theoretical systems, being more explicit in articulating them is essential in delineating the rationale for the components of the evaluation design. According to Simon (1986), explicating theory in this way helps to clarify for clients the intent and possible outcomes of an evaluation project.

Because evaluation research is conducted not solely for the benefit of the researcher's own scientific questions, but also for the benefit of the client's pragmatic questions, the qualitative evaluator needs to be more egalitarian and utilitarian in the application of particular theoretical constructs. Potentially useful theories should be reviewed and noted prior to initiating the data collection process. During the process of collecting and organizing data, the querying of the theoretical literature should be ongoing, with the evaluator expecting some theoretical approaches that initially appeared useful to drop out and others to emerge from data-based patterns. In the recursive process of designing, collecting data, analyzing, redesigning, collecting new data, analyzing and reanalyzing, diverse social scientific theories should be given a hearing for the potential contribution they may make to understanding the phenomenon under investigation. For this reason, an ideological purist may not make an excellent qualitative evaluator. However, if that person's meta-theory or implicit theoretical orientation is articulated, it may be that everyone involved in the project will agree that this is exactly the perspective—and none other—that they wish to have on the issue at hand. A qualitative evaluator is still not free to pursue theoretical questions that require abandoning the issue, program, staffing, impact, allocation of resources, or other such practical applied pragmatic questions that gave rise to the need for the evaluation in the first place. Therefore, we would agree with the intent of Patton's (1980) claim—that "In qualitative evaluation research, theory construction is inductive, pragmatic, and highly concrete" (p. 276).

Data collection itself will involve appropriate (to the question) use of the standard qualitative data collection techniques of participant observation, informant interviewing, and document review supplemented by other appropriate methods such as surveys and focus groups. Participant observation in evaluation research sometimes may be more observational, sometimes more participative. The stance may vary and be located at different points along this continuum at different stages in the data collection cycle. Similarly, interview procedures may be highly informal, of the "chatting with folks" variety, and at another stage in data collection they may approach a kind of questionnaire structure. Document review, when appropriate, should be ongoing and thorough so as to inform the continuing decisions regarding focus and process in interviewing and observation.

It is not our purpose here to delineate the specifics of these data collection techniques; that has been done for qualitative research *per se* by Pelto (1970), Bogdan and Biklen (1978), Goetz and LeCompte (1984), Dobbert (1982), Hammersley and Atkinson (1983), Lincoln and Guba (1985), and numerous others and for qualitative evaluation in particular in works such as that by Patton (1990). What we would highlight regarding method is that a system for data collection and data management must be devised and monitored.

A qualitative evaluator's data collection system should include at least the following five components. First, field notes, both those resulting from observation and those constructed from summaries and transcriptions of audio and video tapes, must be assessed for their detail, relevance, and evaluative bias. Detail consists of descriptive markers such as the exact description of behaviors, groupings, objects, and movements, rather than summary statements derived from observing the markers. Such a consistent system of assessment assures that one is observing the phenomenon at hand and not one's own expectations regarding it. Second, a regular procedure for rewriting, labeling (as in "date, time, place, focus"), and indexing all field data should be established early on and revised if necessary, but never abandoned. Indexing makes data accessible and retrievable and, thus, available for the necessarily recursive assessment of emerging themes, issues, and patterns prior to redesign and collection of new data. A third component of an adequate data collection and data management system would include a process for tracking and noting researcher bias. This may be accomplished via the field diary, reflective memos, or other recording procedures peculiar to each researcher's predilections, but it should minimally include noting and then extracting hidden inferences, veiled judgments, and other taken-for-grantedness in field notes themselves. Fourth, the qualitative evaluator must conduct preliminary analyses early and often. Through the use of indexing, rereading, and reflecting, one looks for patterns and themes in the data but also queries what is missing to determine if gaps are due to researcher focus or reflect actual patterns. This process also should suggest new areas of theory, previous research, and additional data that could be investigated. Fifth, evaluators must have multiple sources of evidence regarding any claim of regularity, discrepancy, or other pattern constellation. Sometimes referred to as triangulation, this layering of data across time, informants, events, documents, and so on is an essential validation technique for conclusions and recommendations. These five components of an adequate data collection and data management system ensure validity and provide the basis for some form of replicability.

Analyzing Evaluation Data

The implementation of analytical procedures as well as the results of those procedures in evaluation research should not be presented in an indulgently opaque, inaccessible, indecipherable, or literary fashion, as they often are in qualitative and particularly ethnographic research. This is not to say all qualitative evaluators must become as "scientific" in their orientation as, for example, Miles and Huberman. But some accounting for analytic procedures must be provided so that clients can assess the usefulness or appropriate application of the information and follow-up evaluations can be either deliberately comparable or deliberately different. We recommend, therefore, that a methods discussion in the final report include a description of the evaluator's analytic framework.

Such an analytic accounting can be structured around some kind of "describe and display" format. The first level of description is physical. At this level, the evaluator completes the statement: "I have available for analysis the following kinds of data." At the initiation stage of final analysis, this level of physical description serves to reacquaint the evaluator with all data collected to date, while simultaneously serving as an outline for the data collection section of the methods discussion. To complete the statement, the researcher would list information such as "I hold x pages of field notes representing x hours of participant observation that occurred x hours at a time x times a week over x weeks/months; I hold x pages of interview summaries and/or transcripts representing x interviews lasting x hours/minutes in duration; I hold the following documents collected in the following ways from the following persons." Data collection methods that are more participatory would produce different kinds of records including such things as protocols, informant responses to field notes, and so on. Nevertheless, the cataloging of physical records can be accomplished regardless of one's methodological preferences. It initiates analysis in such a way that the analytical process can be thorough and accounted for adequately. An example of how this catalog can become the basis for a description of data collection methods is evident in the following excerpt from a report on a team evaluation conducted by one of us (M. A. P.) in a child-care center:

> The fieldwork was conducted primarily during the five weeks between April 24 and May 22. During that time, approximately 120 hours per person were spent on data gathering and related field analysis. Each team member was assigned, by a process of consensus, to accomplish one of five different data collection tasks. Several fieldworkers were assigned to document the physical and human settings through observations, informal discussions, and attendance at staff meetings. Another fieldworker was assigned to shadow each of the lead teachers and to note the observable daily patterns, including the kinds of work done, other activities engaged in, interactions with children, staff, and others, and communication processes used. Three members of the team were assigned to contact and interview present and former practicum students. Finally, a single investigator was assigned to contact and interview the center's coordinator and the several academic personnel who were responsible for placing and supervising the practicum students. (Pitman and Dobbert, 1986:83)

The second level of description is conceptual. At this level, the evaluator completes the statement: "I hold data about the following." If an adequate procedure for managing, labeling, indexing, or otherwise structuring data records has been used during the process of data collection, then this level of conceptual description can be achieved in fairly short order. If not, this step will be longer and more laborious. The evaluator combs each section of the entire body of the data for the purpose of identifying and listing themes, patterns, topics, roles, and other or whatever conceptual content can be named or elicited. Again, a description from the child-care center study illustrates:

> Patterns were identified separately for each role in the program—lead teachers, practicum students, coordinator and placement personnel—and for each of two major analytical categories. The first involved a social analysis of patterns relating to statuses, activities, and values for the whole center. The second was a cognitive analysis of expressed values and belief patterns of all lead teachers, other staff, practicum students, and college staff. (Pitman and Dobbert, 1986:84)

This conceptual description is an analytic device for initiating the process of identifying explicit categories. Category construction is what qualitative researchers do in the process of analysis. Qualitative evaluators may have to tend to some predetermined categories. In the previous study cited, for example, "practicum students" was such a category. That was the group about whom information had been requested and was being sought. By beginning analysis at the level of conceptual description, such predetermined categories are necessarily viewed within the context of all other data-based categories and the entire body of data begins to take some kind of categorical shape.

The analytical structure can then move from data description, physical and conceptual, to data display. At this stage, the evaluator assesses which of the data topics are background, descriptive findings, which are extraneous, and which are critical to the question at hand. Descriptive findings become the basis of that discussion in the final report that one thinks of as "description of the research setting and population." It provides the context for the evaluative findings upon which the evaluator will base recommendations.

Remaining categories that emerge as critical, central, or focal are best presented in some kind of data display derived from and facilitative of further analysis. That is, one labels, codes, indexes, classifies, or otherwise names units of data. The logic of the coding system derives from the creative and theoretical background of the researcher in all qualitative research. In qualitative evaluation, the coding system must also reflect the questions that initiated and structured the evaluation in the first place. Returning to one's reflective notes on entree and role negotiation often reintroduces the evaluation researcher to the research questions and the rationale for the study and, thus, facilitates emicly sensitive coding. The evaluator's own theoretical predispositions also will be particularly influential at this stage of the evaluation. This is not necessarily either beneficial or harmful; however, it is critical that these be made explicit.

The categorical display may be a matrix, decision tree, tree diagram, or dimensional diagram or, instead, it may be a list, an outline, a typology, or other textual display. The purpose is to identify the categories, patterns, or themes that either emerged from or were applied to the concepts that described the data held. If warranted, the display should also show the relationship between categories. At some point, the categorical display should include a listing of each instance of raw field data that was clearly in that category, either by page and line or by short summary (the advantages of word-processing and data base management programs are evident here). The latter process indicates things such as where the load of the data is thickest and thinnest, how it is distributed, and so on.

In the final step of data analysis, the display and its accompanying data bits are used to produce a narrative description of evaluative findings.

Reports and Recommendations

A report of evaluation findings must be made. Indeed, as we noted earlier, the evaluator has an ethical obligation to structure and present findings. This is based on the principle of fair return. Having had access to the private workings of a group's beliefs and behaviors, the qualitative evaluator must represent the results of that access. Otherwise, no matter how participatory the research, one can be said to have engaged in little more than social voyeurism.

The form of the report depends on three factors: who requested the evaluation in the first place; what agreements, if any, were made regarding the nature of the outcome; and what was the nature of the relationship between the evaluator(s) and the community or persons under study. Once again, the qualitative evaluator's improvisational skills will be essential in negotiating a response to each of these factors and determining the appropriate format for each evaluation report. Meeting the terms of the original agreement, for example, may involve telling participants what the evaluator knows they do not want to hear. In such a case, maintaining accuracy while at the same time not jeopardizing the potential for application will require both political and rhetorical skills on the part of the evaluator. In reporting on just such an evaluation, McDade (1987) has said,

> I tell you in all forthrightness that if I had been more exacting in my
> role in relationship to this program, and had attained the enlightened
> position of being able to say "no" (to one or several of her multiple

roles within the agency of "researcher, volunteer, consultant, and evaluator") with diplomacy and tact, I may not have had the opportunity to discover the complex intricacies of the politics of evaluation as it evolved in this one situation and the pressure that can be brought to bear on evaluators reporting negative results. (pp. 5–6)

She later concluded, "I would like to think that this course of events in delivering messages of failure to an audience with a vested interest in not hearing the message can be addressed by successful tactical strategies in ethnographic evaluation." More importantly, however, this situation highlighted—for her and for us—the dilemmas in qualitative evaluation "about how to report on failure, how to maintain the integrity of ethnographic research as not just 'hearsay,' and how to ethically represent the responsibilities of evaluation to funders and to agency professionals" (McDade, 1987:13).

The actual form of an evaluation report will vary greatly. Sometimes it will be oral, sometimes written, usually both. Some presentations will involve advocacy, whereas others will be submitted, almost impersonally, as written text to be collated into a larger document.

Regardless of the format, qualitative evaluators will make their presentation as researchers. Their recommendations are a result of having conducted research. They engage in the tasks of data collection according to the tenets of their meta-theory and disciplinary or theoretical specialty. Eventually, when they formulate an explanation of the data, they offer that explanation in the form of recommendations. The evaluator is a consultant invited or given the opportunity to interact with some human group or phenomenon for the purpose of arriving at some perspective not achievable otherwise. These recommendations should be based on the evaluator's most creative, rigorous, insightful, carefully conceptualized, and demanding application and extension of known theory. This is why we advocate an egalitarian approach to theory in qualitative evaluation. By that, we mean that qualitative researcher evaluators should take as expansive an approach to the application of known theory within their fields as is conceivable, exploring every possible point of view with which they are familiar to shed light on the question at hand.

Models and Methods

The main point that we want to make regarding the four exemplars of qualitative evaluation and our own guidelines for the conduct of such research is that simple dichotomies such as positivist–

interpretivist and realist–relativist are not adequate for understanding the complexity and diversity of the different approaches available to the qualitative evaluator. We have claimed that the connections between philosophic paradigms and research methods are not adequately represented either by a "reflectionist" determination of one by the other (Maxwell, 1978) or by an attitude that sees paradigms as largely irrelevant to the actual conduct of research. Indeed, we have claimed that the decisions that the evaluator must make, decisions that are ongoing and recursive, must always be informed by a variety of explicit theoretical perspectives. What we advocate is the application of multiple theoretical approaches to educational evaluation. We are attracted to the richness of possibilities for understanding that can attend a chorus of theoretical voices, even when the sound is cacophonous. Listening to the data stories, to the stories of theory, and to one's own stories about the other two continually inform the evaluator at each stage of the research project through the point of making recommendations and, often, beyond.

All of this is intellectually challenging, physically demanding, time-consuming work. In Bogdan and Biklen's (1982:57) words, qualitative research "is labor-intensive research." In conducting that labor, the ethical labor and the interactive labor, the labor of writing and often the labor of advocacy, the qualitative evaluator mines the theoretical landscape to contribute a richly contextualized, emically sensitive, and humble wisdom to the understanding of human processes, structures, struggles, and possibilities.

Notes

[1] We have chosen not to look at actual evaluation reports for two reasons. First, it is difficult to determine philosophy and methods from evaluation reports. Second, most of the methodological statements we discuss contain specific examples of evaluation practice. We believe that this detailed examination of the statements of current major contributors to the definition of the field will be more useful to all qualitative evaluators.

[2] As Meehl (1986) and Phillips (1990) point out, the last real logical positivists abandoned that position in the late 1940s, as a result of devastating critiques of both the assumptions of the approach and its validity as an account of how science is actually done. A major goal of positivism was to eliminate from scientific discourse such "metaphysical" concepts as "cause" and to ground scientific theories entirely in "objective" sense data. Realists, in contrast, take theoretical concepts such as "cause" to refer to something about a real world external to our perceptions of it. For discussion of the fundamental difference between positivist and realist assumptions, see Norris (1983) and Phillips (1990).

References

Agar, M. H. (1980). *The professional stranger*. New York: Academic Press.

Bogdan, R. C., and Biklen, S. (1982). *Qualitative research for education: An introduction to theory and methods*. Boston: Allyn and Bacon.

Dobbert, M. L. (1982). *Ethnographic research: Theory and application for modern schools and societies*. New York: Praeger.

Douglas, J. (1976). *Investigative social research*. Beverly Hills, CA: Sage Publications.

Eisner, E. W. (1985a). *The art of educational evaluation: A personal view*. London: Falmer Press.

Eisner, E. W. (1985b). *The educational imagination: On the design and evaluation of school programs* (2nd ed.). New York: Macmillan.

Eisner, E. W. (1991). *The enlightened eye: Qualitative inquiry and the enhancement of educational practice*. New York: Macmillan.

Geertz, C. (1983). *Local knowledge: Further essays in interpretive anthropology*. New York: Basic Books.

Goetz, J. P. and LeCompte, M. D. (1984). *Ethnography and qualitative design in educational research*. New York: Academic Press.

Guba, E. G. (Ed.). (1990). *The paradigm dialog*. Newbury Park, CA: Sage Publications.

Guba, E. G., and Lincoln, Y. S. (1981). *Effective evaluation*. San Francisco: Jossey-Bass.

Guba, E. G., and Lincoln, Y. S. (1989). *Fourth generation evaluation*. Newbury Park, CA: Sage Publications.

Hammersley, M., and Atkinson, P. (1983). *Ethnography: Principles in practice*. London: Tavistock.

Huberman, A. M., and Miles, M. B. (1985). Assessing local causality in qualitative research. *In* D. N. Berg and K. K. Smith (Eds.), *Exploring clinical methods for social research*. Beverly Hills, CA: Sage Publications. (Reissued in 1988 as *The self in social inquiry: Researching methods*.)

Kuhn, T. S. (1977). Second thoughts on paradigms. *In* F. Suppe (Ed.), *The structure of scientific theories* (2nd ed., pp. 459–517). Urbana: University of Illinois Press.

Lincoln, Y. S. (1990). Toward a categorical imperative for qualitative research. *In* E. Eisner and A. Peshkin (Eds.), *Qualitative inquiry in education: The continuing debate*. New York: Teachers College Press.

Lincoln, Y. S., and Guba, E. G. (1985). *Naturalistic inquiry*. Newbury Park, CA: Sage Publications.

Lincoln, Y. S., and Guba, E. G. (1986). But is it rigorous? Trustworthiness and authenticity in naturalistic evaluation. *In* D. D. Williams (Ed.), *Naturalistic evaluation* (pp. 73–84). San Francisco: Jossey-Bass.

Manicas, P. T., and Secord, P. F. (1982). Implications for psychology of the new philosophy of science. *American Psychologist*, 38, 390–413.

Maxwell, J. A. (1978). The evolution of Plains Indian kin terminologies: A non reflectionist account. *Plains Anthropologist*, 23, 13–29.

Maxwell, J. A. (1986). The conceptualization of kinship in an Inuit community: A cultural account. Unpublished doctoral dissertation, University of Chicago.

McCawley, J. (1982). *Thirty million theories of grammar*. Chicago: University of Chicago Press.

McDade, L. (1987). *Telling them what they do not want to hear: A dilemma in ethnographic evaluation*. Paper presented at the Annual Meeting of the American Anthropological Association, Chicago.

Meehl, P. (1986). What social scientists don't understand. *In* D. W. Fiske and R. A. Shweder (Eds.), *Metatheory in social science* (pp. 315–338). Chicago: University of Chicago Press.

Miles, M. B., and Huberman, A. M. (1984a). Drawing valid meaning from qualitative data: Toward a shared craft. *Educational Researcher*, 13(5), 20–30.

Miles, M. B., and Huberman, A. M. (1984b). *Qualitative data analysis: A sourcebook of new methods.* Newbury Park, CA: Sage Publications.

Norris, S. P. (1983). The inconsistencies at the foundation of construct validation theory. *In* E. R. House (Ed.), *Philosophy of evaluation* (pp. 53–74). San Francisco: Jossey-Bass.

Patton, M. Q. (1980). *Qualitative evaluation methods.* Newbury Park, CA: Sage Publications.

Patton, M. Q. (1990). *Qualitative evaluation and research methods* (2nd ed.). Newbury Park, CA: Sage Publications.

Pelto, P. J. (1970). Anthropological research: The structure of inquiry. New York: Harper and Row.

Pelto, P., and Pelto, G. (1975). Intra-cultural diversity: Some theoretical issues. *American Ethnologist*, 2, 1–18.

Pelto, P., and Schensul, J. J. (1987). Toward a framework for policy research in anthropology. *In* E. M. Eddy and W. L. Partridge (Eds.), *Applied anthropology in America* (2nd ed., pp. 505–528). New York: Columbia University Press.

Phillips, D. C. (1990). Postpositivistic science: Myths and realities. *In* E. G. Guba (Ed.), *The paradigm dialog* (pp. 31–45). Newbury Park, CA: Sage Publications.

Pitman, M. A., and Dobbert, M. L. (1986). The use of explicit anthropological theory in educational evaluation: A case study. *In* D. M. Fetterman and M. A. Pitman (Eds.), *Educational evaluation: Ethnography in theory, practice and politics* (pp. 78–100). Newbury Park, CA: Sage Publications.

Rabinow, P. (1977). *Reflections on fieldwork in Morocco.* Berkeley: University of California Press.

Reichardt, C. S., and Cook, T. D. (1979). Beyond qualitative versus quantitative methods. *In* T. D. Cook and C. S. Reichardt (Eds.), *Qualitative and quantitative methods in evaluation research* (pp. 7–32). Newbury Park, CA: Sage Publications.

Rorty, R. (1989). *Contingency, irony, and solidarity.* Cambridge: Cambridge University Press.

Ryan, A. G. (1988). Program evaluation within the paradigms: Mapping the territory. *Knowledge: Creation, Diffusion, Utilization* 10, 25–47.

Schrimshaw, S. C. M., and Hurlado, E. (1987). Rapid assessment procedures for nutrition and health care: Anthropological approaches to improving programme effectiveness. Tokyo: United Nations University/Los Angeles; UCLA Latin American Center Publications.

Shils, E. (1959). Social inquiry and the autonomy of the individual. *In* D. Lerner (Ed.), *The human meaning of the social sciences.* Cleveland, OH: Meridian Press.

Simon, E. L. (1986). Theory in educational evaluation: Or, what's wrong with generic-brand anthropology. *In* D. M. Fetterman and M. A. Pitman (Eds.), *Educational evaluation: Ethnography in theory, practice, and politics* (pp. 51–77). Newbury Park, CA: Sage Publications.

Spradley, J. P., and McCurdy, D. W. (1972). The cultural experience: Ethnography in complex society. Prospect Heights, IL: Waveland Press.

Wallace, A. F. C. (1970). *Culture and personality.* New York: Random House.

CHAPTER 17

❑ Teaching Qualitative Research

Rodman B. Webb and Corrine Glesne

The Handbook of Qualitative Research in Education

Introduction

For reasons William James clarified a century ago in *The Principles of Psychology* (1890/1950), the whole world cannot become problematic at once. In that masterpiece of naturalistic inquiry, James details the process by which things (objects, acts, situations, ideas, observations) come to our attention as problematic. We see something and define it as a problem only because it stands out against a background of habits and taken-for-granted knowledge that are themselves, for the moment at least, unproblematic.

Teaching qualitative research methods in colleges of education is challenging and exhilarating precisely because such courses call into question students' taken-for-granted assumptions about so many things: the purpose of research, the uses of method, the nature of knowledge, and what it means to be human, to name but a salient few. In this chapter, we will examine some common difficulties and consummate pleasures that students and professors experience in qualitative research courses.

Unity and Variety in Qualitative Methods

Qualitative research has come of age in education. New courses are being offered every year, formal qualitative research programs are being established, special interest groups are being formed that cross department and college boundaries (e.g., the Qualitative Special Interest Group at the University of Georgia), qualitative research centers have been established (e.g., at the University of Tennessee, at the University of Aarhus in Denmark, at the University of Gothenburg in Sweden), and numerous professional meetings are devoted exclusively to the presentation of qualitative research findings (e.g., the Ethnography Forum at the University of Pennsylvania, the Qualitative Research in Education meeting at the University of Georgia, the St. Hilda's Conference at Oxford, the Human Sciences Group that meets annually at different locations in North America and Europe).

New outlets for the publication of qualitative research are becoming available. Journals that once were the exclusive domain of quantitative research now welcome qualitative work, and two journals (*Anthropology and Education* and *The International Journal of Qualitative Studies in Education*) publish only qualitative studies in education. A growing list of publishers (Cambridge University Press, Falmer Press, Sage Publications, Waveland Press, Westview Press, and the State University of New York Press) regularly publish books and monographs reporting qualitative research studies.

Not long ago, only a few textbooks dealt specifically with qualitative research in education. Professors teaching such courses often used books written for anthropology or sociology or built reading assignments around collected articles that students were asked to reproduce. Today, many texts on qualitative research in education are available, more are being written, and editors stalk the halls of academe seeking professors willing to add another title to the growing list of available texts (see Appendix for a list of such texts). It is a good indication that a field has established itself when profit-driven publishers look for people to produce texts and are willing to pay advances upon the signing of a contract.

The obvious vitality of qualitative research in colleges of education masks several problems in the field. Qualitative research is not a single entity and not, as many believe, a mere synonym for ethnography. Instead, qualitative research is an umbrella term that covers an enormous variety of methods and approaches to the study of human behavior. These approaches share some common characteristics (*viz*, an interest in the world as it is perceived by those we study, a focus on everyday life, a determination to study behavior as it occurs in "natural" settings, and a shameless reliance on interpretation) (Sherman and Webb, 1988:2–19). Qualitative methods can be distinguished from one another, however, by examining their deep and significant differences (see Eisner and Peshkin, 1990; Guba, 1990).

Given the variety of methods nestled under the qualitative umbrella, it should not be surprising that qualitative methods courses vary greatly, that they are taught under a variety of titles,[1] and that they are housed in several different departments in colleges of education. Many who teach qualitative research methods, especially recent hires, took qualitative methods courses in their own graduate studies. Some senior faculty members have done the same, but others report they are self-taught and "fell into" the area after they had finished their graduate studies (see Glesne and Webb, in press). Thus, what from the outside appears to be a unified and harmonious area of inquiry, from the inside looks less tidy and tranquil.

There are at least as many ways to teach qualitative research methods as there are qualitative research methods to teach. No useful review of the field can cover all teaching methods or research methodologies, and we will not try. Instead, we will focus on those teaching approaches that have applicability across a variety of qualitative methodologies. We acknowledge differences among research methodologies as necessary, but our focus will be on the unity we find in the variety of qualitative methods. Most of what we have to say, however, will have particular relevance to those methods that employ interviewing and participant observation techniques.

The formal literature on teaching qualitative research methods is sparse, and few professors in the field consult that literature when designing their courses. Instead, they consult their own experience as students and researchers and the growing list of textbooks in the area. They also draw on whatever folk knowledge they can gather from discussions with others who teach such courses. In this chapter, we look at relevant literature but also tap and organize the professional folk knowledge alive in the field. We have drawn on interviews with leading researchers and questionnaires that were filled out by 75 teachers of qualitative research courses in U.S. colleges of education (Glesne and Webb, in press).[2] We reviewed 55 course syllabi and drew information gathered from conversations with 14 qualitative researchers. We focus on common practices and successful teaching strategies and try to account for the apparent success of those methods. We also look at perennial problems faced by those who teach and learn qualitative methods and propose possible solutions to those problems. We turn first to some general problems associated with students' assumptions about qualitative research and the difficulties they have in learning to think as social scientists.

On Assumptions and the Problem of Relativity

Students who come to their first qualitative research course seldom realize what they are in for. Despite the warnings of fellow students and the cautionary tales of professors, few are prepared for the volume of work, the intense concentration, the psychological dislocations, the profound uncertainties, or the occasional exhilarations that are part and parcel of qualitative inquiry. Qualitative methods are difficult to master and most students are not use to devoting so much time and discipline for a course. Most come with a host of assumptions and biases that are likely to be challenged before the course is over. Many students find it difficult to examine everyday life with the sensitivities of social science. We will discuss these problems under several headings: Challenging Assumptions about Research Methodology, The Psychologist's Fallacy, The Sociologist's Fallacy, and the Problem of Relativism. In each section, we explore from somewhat different perspectives issues related to social science and multiple reality.

Challenging Assumptions about Research Methodology

Some students assume that a qualitative research class will provide procedures that, if followed faithfully, will produce warranted research results. This mechanistic (and, incidentally, thoroughly modern) view reduces methods to a set of *techniques*, a recipe to be followed. Students who confuse method with technique hope to learn a set of procedures but have little interest in understanding how or why those procedures "work." These expectations exist on the fringe of students' consciousness, and few bring them forward for conscious attention. However, if a student was to translate such assumptions into assertions, he or she might say,

> Look, I do not need to understand how a telephone works in order to place a call. The internal combustion engine is pure mystery to me, but I drive my car to school every day. I was a top student in my statistical methods courses, but I never understood the logical underpinnings of multivariant analysis. Yet, I can run data with the best of them and I have discovered "significant findings." Now that I think about it, my quantitative research classes only dealt with application. No one expected us to understand how or why a particular method of analysis worked, only how and when to apply it.

Quantitative methods professors might cringe at what our fictitious student has to say about statistical methods and methods courses. But we are not making a point about how such methods are being taught. Our point is about modern consciousness and the dangerous tendency to equate method with technique in many areas of contemporary life. Others have made the point before us (see Berger, Berger, and Kellner, 1973; Ellul, 1964; Gehlen, 1980), but these scholars have not fully examined the implications of their analysis for social science. The issue is important for our purposes because equating method with technique in qualitative research is twice alienating: It distances the researcher from the situation under study and from the research act itself. For students who see methods as a type of recipe, *doing research* simply means following proper procedures, attending to form, and allowing outcomes to "take care of themselves" (Gehlen, 1980:36).

Such students become anxious when they learn that fidelity to method, although necessary, will not assure the discovery of anything important or interesting.

Another assumption flows from confusing methods with techniques. Techniques are assumed by many students to be orderly, well tested, predictable, and efficient. Like other forms of technology, they are designed to reduce human input and human error. Techniques allow us to distance ourselves from the messy unpredictability of human experience. Some students are surprised to learn that qualitative research methods do not lift them safely above the murky stuff of human experience and that these methods are designed to bring them into close contact with the experiences of others and with the research experience itself. Such students are disappointed to learn that qualitative methods do not free them from the untidy necessity of interpretation. It falls to the researcher, not the method, to make sense of what has been observed.

Qualitative research professors may want to discuss these issues early in the course. Some assign provocative readings, such as Berger and Kellner's (1981) *Sociology Reinterpreted,* to help students dislodge and talk about their various research assumptions. That work is difficult, however, and must be thoroughly discussed in class before students fully grasp the authors' major contentions. Those interested in the complexity of interpretation might follow Maxine Greene's (1988) lead and assign literature that deals with social structure, multiple realities, and differences in perspective. Greene assigns *Moby Dick* and *The Scarlet Letter* for these purposes. Wolfe's (1987) *Bonfire of the Vanities* may have more contemporary appeal. An example of a useful short story is Herman Melville's "Bartleby the Scrivener." The aim of such assignments, Greene explains, is to gain

> . . . a double consideration of perspective and the achievement of
> meaning: on the part of the student (inquirer, questioner, scholar,
> reader) and on the part of the . . . participants in whatever social or
> cultural scene is being studied. This entails an effort to comprehend,
> not only the many modes of social grouping and arrangements in the
> culture, but also the ways in which all this is experienced by
> individuals. (Greene, 1988:182)

Some professors, especially those who require that students do an ambitious research project, find that they do not need to question students' basic assumptions about research at the start of the course. The act of doing qualitative research forces most students to question their own assumptions. Observing and interviewing puts students in close contact with the experiences of others. They soon learn that the research methods serve as guides for intelligence, not as a technical substitute for thought. The act of data analysis rids most students of the naive assumption that the data will somehow speak for themselves and that researchers can avoid interpreting what they have seen and heard. We do not mean to say that the issues we have discussed in this section will miraculously take care of themselves. They won't. We only suggest that assigning research projects is a powerful way to bring these questions to students' attention and to make class discussions on these topics more profitable. Those teaching the course, however, must be alert to when students are confronting their own misconceptions about methods and must focus the class's attention on these matters when the time is right.

The Psychologist's Fallacy

Most education students come to qualitative research classes underprepared in the social sciences. Unlike students in departments of sociology and anthropology, those in education generally have not taken a wide range of social science courses before coming to their first research methods class. If they (and we) are lucky, students will have taken enough humanities courses to have challenged what James (1890/1950:Vol. I, p. 196) called "the psychologist's fallacy." That fallacy refers (at least by extension) to the human tendency to bestow our own versions of reality on others and, when different versions of reality are inadvertently found, to criticize them as naive, foolish, or wicked (Barzun, 1983:39).[3]

Professors find the psychologist's fallacy difficult to discover and hard to dislodge. Sometimes it shows itself in students' field notes, but more often it comes into clear view in their final research reports. Only then do we see that a student has used research, not to understand the life-world of others but to caricature and criticize that world.

Criticism is an inviting activity for education students, who often do their research in schools and come to those settings with well-established notions of what classrooms should be like and what teachers and students should be doing. Thus, it is tempting for students to use qualitative research to promote their own vision of what is proper and to criticize everything else. Such reports have a self-righteous, muckraking tone, and though they may describe events in compelling detail, their discussion often lacks "explanatory power"

(Homans, 1967:79–109). One way to lead students away from criticism is to help them begin a line-by-line analysis of their data, a topic we will discuss later in this chapter.

Much that we say and do in qualitative research courses feeds the reformist inclinations of well-intended students. Social science is, after all, a debunking enterprise. Doing social science demands a certain detachment from the situation under study and a well-honed skepticism about dogmas and the taken-for-granted assumptions that support them. Lynd and Lynd (1937:402) called such dogmas "of course statements" to indicate that much in everyday life is accepted without question. Any query about taken-for-granted beliefs is likely to be answered with raised eyebrows and an incredulous, "Of course!" "Should schools prepare students for citizenship?" "Of course!" "Is the purpose of schooling to impart knowledge?" "Of course!" When students read qualitative accounts of schooling, they find much that contradicts the official dogma. Social science often exposes the difference between official claims and actual practices.

It does not miss the attention of most students that questioning people's basic assumptions [prying open what Schutz (1962b:287–356) called "the world of the taken-for-granted,"] has a downright subversive quality. What Berger (1977) says about the debunking motif of sociological consciousness applies, in varying degrees, to all worthy social science:

> Simply by doing its cognitive job, sociology puts the institutional order
> *and* its legitimating thought patterns under critical scrutiny. Sociology
> has a built-in debunking effect. It shows up the fallaciousness of
> socially established interpretations of reality by demonstrating that the
> facts do not jibe with the "official" view, or, even more simply, by
> relativizing the latter (by showing that it is only one of several possible
> views of society). *That* is already dangerous enough. . . . But
> sociology, at least in certain situations, is more directly subversive. It
> unmasks vested interests and makes visible the manner in which
> [those interests] are served by social fictions. Sociology can be political
> dynamite [italics in original]. (p. xiii)

The debunking motif of social science is misinterpreted by some students (especially those burdened by the "psychologist's fallacy") as giving them free license to criticize. Of course, that is not the message Berger intended. If students do their work well, they may (indeed, they probably will) uncover invisible forces [Merton's (1957) "latent" functions] that contradict the manifest dogmas of officialdom. Such findings may challenge the social order because they reveal that in the social world things are not necessarily what they seem. But it is one thing to expose the contradictions within a group's activities and quite another to criticize that group because its activities and ideologies do not please the researcher's normative sensibilities.

If students are ever to understand and accurately describe the facts before them, they must possess what Karl Mannheim (1971:374)—writing, interestingly enough, to educators—called a "readiness to see." The issue concerns value-free social science, a subject we address again later. For present purposes, it will do to point out that for Berger and Kellner (1981), Mannheim's *readiness*

> . . . is above all *a passion to see*, to see clearly, regardless of one's
> own likes or dislikes, hopes or fears. [It] implies a systematic
> openness to the values of others as they are relevant to the situation
> being studied—even if those values are quite repugnant to oneself:
> seeing is not approving, but I cannot see at all if I constantly voice my
> own disapproval [italics in original]. (p. 52)

Dislodging the psychological fallacy is difficult, but students are generally willing to participate in its exorcism. Most want to do good research and will try to heed their professor's suggestions. As we have already shown, it is not enough to simply put students in the field to do research. Students who mistake social criticism for scientific discovery will go about their work with enthusiasm, believing they are making important discoveries. It is hardly fair to let students do all that work only to find at the end that the reports amount to little more than a celebration of their own world view. Initiation into the social science vocation demands that we help students develop an ability to see beyond the walls of their own ideological assumptions. One way to develop students' readiness to see is to assign and carefully examine examples of good qualitative research. It is particularly useful to assign what we will call "empathic studied," by which we mean sensitive investigations of groups or individuals that students might find normatively suspect. Examples of research that serve this purpose include Joseph T. Howell's (1973) *Hard Living on Clay Street* (the story of southern migrants holding blue-collar jobs in Washington, D.C.), Terry Williams's (1989) *The Cocaine Kids* (an ethnography of teen-agers who work in Harlem's cocaine trade), Alan Peshkin's (1986) *God's Choice* (a sensitive protrayal of a fundamentalist school), and George Riseborough's (1988) "The Great Heddekashun War" (a life history of a teacher who suffered a nervous breakdown at the hands of his students). To be avoided are worthy but inherently condemnatory studies such as Jules Henry's (1965) *Culture against Man*. Studies of the latter variety are better addressed later in the course because they tend to reinforce rather than redress the psychologist's fallacy. On the other hand, a "deep reading" and attentive discussion of "empathic tales" can help students better appreciate the nature of the social scientific task.

Another method for helping students confront the taken-for-granted knowledge of everyday life has been developed by ethnomethodologists, most notably by Harold Garfinkel (1964). Garfinkel has shown that the mundane rules of everyday life come into clearest view when they are violated. To help students see the social rules that existed in their own homes, he asked them to systematically break the commonsense rules of family life and record the results. To make the job easier, he gave students a new perspective from which to examine their home world. He did not ask them to behave like social scientists at home but, rather, to behave as they would if they were paying boarders. Students were "instructed to conduct themselves in a circumspect and polite fashion. They were to avoid getting personal, to use formal address, to speak only when spoken to" (Garfinkel, 1964:232). The goal was to make a meaning-filled situation artificially senseless. Students were asked to record their observations without calling on their vast stock of family knowledge to make sense of what happened.

Garfinkel's assignment brought students into conscious contact with their own everyday habits. Almost any change of role or perspective probably would have accomplished the same ends. For example, Garfinkel could just as well have asked his pupils to cognitively switch genders, to act 10 years younger, or to answer all requests negatively. When common-sense expectations are violated, the taken-for-granted comes into view. That which is hidden in what James (1890/1950:Vol. I, pp. 104–128) called "the fringes of consciousness" is dislodged by events and brought to the foreground of students' attention. The results were more complex than Garfinkel had predicted. For one thing, parents were terrified by the new and unintelligible behavior of their children. They got angry when their offspring acted inappropriately, and some worried that their children were going crazy. Their anger and worry continued even after the children explained what they had been doing and why. Rules are rules and, for reasons detailed by philosophers and social scientists (Kestenbaum, 1977; Ostrow, 1990; Webb, 1976), their violations are sometimes emotion packed. Despite these significant difficulties, the exercise gave students insights into the complexity of everyday life. They came to appreciate the truth of

Geertz's (1973:5) remark that human beings are "suspended in a web of significance that they themselves have spun." Simultaneously, they began to understand that the "web of significance" is not ordinarily an object of our attention and comes into view only when we take extraordinary measures, such as breaching the rules or adopting a social science perspective.[4]

The Sociologist's Fallacy

It is not unusual for social scientists to become so absorbed by the people they are studying that the researcher becomes indistinguishable from the researched. When we overidentify with a particular group, we are no longer a participant observer but simply a participant. Our own relevance structures fall away (including those supplied by social science) and we "go native." The possibility of being resocialized into a new culture is increased if we are separated from our home culture and the "reality checks" that culture provides. Because education students usually do their work in familiar territory, they are less likely to lose their cultural bearings.

Education students are not likely to go native, but they do sometimes identify with one group to the exclusion of others in the social settings they study. For example, they may describe a reading group entirely from the point of view of the slow readers, or a classroom discipline system only from the teachers' perspective. In the spirit of fair play, we will call this tendency the *sociologist's fallacy*.

Seeing social events from the perspective of one group has its benefits, especially when the researcher gives voice to people who are seldom heard. Erving Goffman's (1961) *Asylums* would have done a service had it done no more than describe the "social world of the inmate[s]" at St. Elizabeths Hospital as they experienced it (p. ix). Such monolensed reports can expand the reader's vision of social reality. However, Goffman understood that we do not live in a monolensed world. In the second essay in *Asylums*, Goffman spells out the complex interaction between patients and care-givers. In every social setting, superiors interact with subordinates, the oppressed interact with their oppressors, the powerful interact with the powerless. To appreciate the complexities of such interaction, researchers must examine events from multiple perspectives. Willis (1981) and MacLeod (1987) would have told a diminished story had they looked only at what the working-class Lads and the underclass Hallway Hangers said about their world. The work of these researchers has had lasting impact because they took a wide perspective and showed how the interactions of many groups (antischool students, proschool students, teachers, parents, and the workplace culture) interact to limit the life chances of certain students. That accomplishment can be appreciated whether or not students share the commitments these authors bring to their work. Those seeking less ideological fare, however, might assign Howell's (1973) *Hard Living on Clay Street* or Rubin's (1976) *Worlds of Pain*.

It is difficult to solve problems for students before they have experienced them for themselves. Thus, beginning-of-the-semester discussions about the interactive nature of social systems do not often free students from overidentifying with one or another group in the social setting they chose to study. When students are in the midst of their own research, however, questions of perspective have powerful relevance. For that reason, it becomes important that students have multiple occasions to discuss their data collection and analysis with the professor and, just as importantly, with their classmates. This point is reflected in the discussion-oriented, seminar structure of most qualitative research methods courses being taught in colleges of education. Of the 55 syllabi we collected from teachers of such courses, all included class discussions and many scheduled times for students to discuss their research (Glesne and Webb, in press).

The Problem of Relativism

Social science demands that we make the familiar strange so that what is taken for granted in everyday life can be seen more clearly. Seeing the life-world from a social science perspective can cause students some unexpected problems, and instructors should be on the lookout for them. Such problems usually come in stages, the first of which we call *discovering relativity.*

Students who discover relativity have adopted Mannheim's (1971:374) readiness to see, but with peculiar vengeance. Everyday events that hitherto escaped notice become objects of intense scrutiny. This comment from a graduate student we will call Jane is typical of someone who has discovered the relativizing power of social science:

> This class is changing the way I see the world. It literally is changing my mind. I find myself examining everything: the way a driver looks at passing traffic when a policeman is writing him a speeding ticket, the way my boss extricates herself from unwanted conversations, the way my husband makes amorous advances, the way strangers avoid eye contact on the subway. It is all so interesting and . . . , well, so funny.

Jane has learned that we live in a world of multiple realities, and that every aspect of human behavior can be analyzed from more than one perspective. In Jane's case, two perspectives are operating: the point of view she adopts in the natural attitude of everyday life and the point of view she adopts as a budding social scientist. From the first perspective, Jane sees things such as roles, events, and motives in the same commonsense way as her fellow citizens. The natural attitude of everyday life is Jane's paramount reality (Schutz, 1962a). The things Jane observed—the roles (policeman, boss, husband, stranger), events (exceeding the speed limit, having a conversation, riding subways), motives (sidestepping conversation, suggesting amorous dalliance, avoiding eye contact)—come to her preselected and preinterpreted in the commonsense constructs of everyday reality. They are the standard categories (or typifications) that all sane citizens use to make sense of what they see. Schutz (1962a) calls such typifications "first-order constructs."

The everyday world (the paramount reality within which first-order constructs operate) has its exhilarating moments, but common events are usually so taken for granted that much within it escapes our notice. As Berger and Berger (1972:78) have put it, "Familiarity breeds not so much contempt as blindness." However, when the same world is examined from a social science perspective, interesting things begin to happen—portions of the familiar become strange, things that were invisible become visible, and, at least for Jane, the humdrum becomes humorous.

Jane's excitement is explained by her new-found ability to move back and forth between the perspective of everyday life and the perspective of social science. To be sure, the latter is rooted in the former, and the two share some common characteristics. But, as Schutz (1962b) has detailed, each perspective has its own rules, systems of relevance, and structures of plausibility and legitimacy. That is to say, Jane thinks and acts one way as a citizen of the everyday world and another way as a citizen of the social science community (Berger and Kellner, 1981:46). Thinking as a social scientist demands a higher degree of awareness and a calculated effort to structure events so that taken-for-granted habits, motives, and beliefs of others show themselves. It demands that Jane bracket her own everyday values and view the scene before her objectively or, more accurately, that she do all she can to approach the ideal of objectivity. As she begins to build social science explanations for what she observes (Schutz's *second-order constructs*), she must look for data that contradict those explanations and give up or change her interpretations if the evidence so demands. Doing social science requires from Jane an allegiance to the community of scholarship to whom she will report her findings and a sensitivity to the people about whom she eventually will write.

Jane has not yet adopted all the skills, rules, and habits necessary for full citizenship in the realm of science. She is new to the scientific enterprise. She is able to view everyday events from a social science perspective and to relativize any tidbit of social reality instantly. She tells us that even mundane events are now of keen interest to her and that these events have a new and unexpected comic quality.

It is easy to see why the movement from one world to another can make the ordinary intriguing, but why does Jane find humor in the enterprise? There are two answers to this question, and neither one suggests that Jane suffers from some giddy psychological affliction for which she needs psychological counseling. (Indeed, if we referred Jane to the local counseling center, she would relativize that activity too and, no doubt, would find its rituals both fascinating and farcical.) One answer to our question is that humor itself is a relativizing act that puts the ordinary into unexpected contexts.

The second answer is more problematic than the first. Relativizing someone else's social reality is funny for the same reason that pratfalls get laughs. We find it amusing when people momentarily lose social bearings or when their social pretensions are unmasked and we see them stripped of their social props. Allen Funt has made a fortune exploiting this single insight. What makes good humor, however, does not necessarily make good social science.

It is tempting for students to use their newly acquired tricks of the social science trade as a kind of intellectual recreation. Their aim is not to criticize (as was the case with the psychologist's fallacy) but simply to practice their new-found skills. This seemingly benign activity has benefits and dangers. For example, some students get stuck in the social science perspective and, to the great annoyance of family and friends, see almost every ritual and routine as a topic for study and discussion. The work of everyday life is disrupted when someone continuously interrogates the mundane. Thus, we cannot but sympathize with Jane's husband when he found that his amorous suggestions peaked interests that were more scientific and jocular than romantic. He understood immediately what it took Jane a bit longer to learn; that one cannot spend every waking hour as a social scientist without putting the fragile order of one's personal and intimate life at painful risk.

Some years ago, one of us worked next door to a newly minted anthropologist who had just returned from 2 years of fieldwork in New Guinea. Like any good anthropologist, he was intrigued by what made people tick, but, unlike most of his colleagues, he found it hard to step out of a social science perspective that guided his fieldwork. Back home he put his considerable social scientific skills to recreational use. For example, he liked to give dinner parties. Instead of following the custom of choosing guests who would enjoy one another's company however, he invited people he knew would not get along. His unwary guests would sit down to the meal, lubricated by a few predinner drinks and ready to make appropriately polite (mundane) conversation. The host, however, would bring up topics that were calculated to disrupt the taken-for-granted rituals of polite conversation. "So Sophie," he might ask a prochoice nurse, "how are things going down at the abortion clinic?" Only after Sophie was well into her answer would the host mention that the person sitting next to her was the vice president of an antiabortion league in a nearby city.

The story of this anthropologist has an interesting ending. After just a year of systematically challenging the mundane in his everyday life, he realized that he was living too close to the edge and began to long for the comforts that society affords members who play by its rules. He wanted to return to order, continuity, and triviality (Berger, 1977:xv; O'Leary, 1986:196). He made a conscious choice to reenter the paramount reality of everyday life and to limit the doing of anthropology to his world of work. He changed universities ("I want to live in a more conventional environment," he told us); bought a track house in the suburbs ("I want it to look as much like my neighbors' houses as possible"); joined the PTA ("I want to join the tribe"); and became conventional ("I want to blend in"). He followed the advice that Max Weber (1946) gave to those who are bothered by the relativity of social science (those he said "who cannot bear the fate of the times") and returned "to the arms of the old churches" (p. 155). As far as we know, he lived happily ever after.

Our anthropologist friend had relearned what Jane finally learned in her qualitative research course (or maybe at home!)—that the backbone of social order is found in the trivial and mundane. Berger (1977) makes the point:

> *Triviality is one of the fundamental requirements of social life.* It is sociologically, and probably anthropologically, and perhaps even biologically, *necessary* that good portions of social life take place in a state of only dim awareness—if you will, in a state of semi-sleep. It is precisely to permit this to happen that the institutional order imposes "programs" for the individual's activity.

> Society protects our sanity by preempting a large number of choices, not only of action but of thought. If we understand this . . . then we will see there are limits not only to disorder and discontinuity, but also to the frequency of "significant events." We will then become very

careful how we view "meaningless rituals," "empty forms," or "mere routines" in social life—simply because we will recognize that if social life in its entirety were charged with profound meaning, we would go out of our minds [italics in original]. (pp. xvi–xvii)

The task of teaching qualitative research methods is full of tensions and contradictions. Some students find it difficult to surrender their ethnocentric biases and must be pushed to examine everyday life from a social science perspective. Other students must be helped to hold their newly acquired relativizing skills in reasonable check. Sometimes the very student who resists the social science perspective early in the course must be urged later to set limits to its use. There are no recipes to guide teachers as they steer students through these qualitative tensions, but the problems associated with relativizing the social world suggest that qualitative research courses must be taught in a seminar setting. If we are to know what students are experiencing as they shift perspectives, they must discuss their research and psychological experiences with us. The point is that Jane was right, doing qualitative research does change the way that students think and experience the world, and instructors must keep aware of those changes.

On Teaching Qualitative Methods

To this point we have been discussing some problems associated with students' assumptions about research and the difficulties they encounter in learning to take a social science perspective. We now turn our attention to the organization and content of qualitative research courses. We will begin by examining the kinds of qualitative research courses typically taught in college of education graduate programs in the United States.

Kinds of Qualitative Research Courses

Those teaching qualitative research methods courses must make a choice whether they will teach *about* research methods or engage their students in a semester-long, field-based research project. (There are increasing requests for two-semester courses or for sequences of two or three research methods courses.) Faculty responding to our survey about the teaching of qualitative research methods were asked to send us copies of their course syllabi. Fifty-five course descriptions were sent. Of those, 39 required that students do a major piece of qualitative research, 6 assigned mini-projects, 4 gave students options, and 6 required no field project.

Introductory Courses

Those who teach *about* qualitative research usually teach introductory courses that cover "the fundamentals" and review a variety of research methods. Some teach skills-based courses that require mini-projects. For example, students may be asked to gain access to a setting and spend a few hours to a few weeks observing, writing field notes, and analyzing data. When they are finished, they write a short paper discussing what was learned. They then reenter the field to do interviewing and after a few weeks write another paper. They may go to different settings or back to the same setting several times, each time to apply a new technique. At the end of the course they may be asked to write a longer paper compiling their research findings or reviewing the several methods they applied and what they learned about each one. Skills-based courses usually serve as the prerequisite introduction to a qualitative methods sequence.

Another type of introductory course focuses on broad categories of qualitative research (ethnography, life history, grounded theory, educational criticism, feminist research methods, phenomenology, and so on), not on components of a specific method. These courses are designed to give students an overview of several methods, to help students appreciate what those methods have in common, and to prepare them to choose methods appropriate to various kinds of research problems. Methods-based courses may require short papers about each method studied. They may also require that students use their knowledge about a variety of methods to critique dissertations or published qualitative studies.

Design and Theory Courses

Courses that do not include any field-based research are of two kinds. The first, which we call *design courses,* usually come early in the qualitative sequence. Such courses focus on some underlying principles of qualitative research and help students plan qualitative studies. Students may read and critique qualitative studies and often are required to write a research proposal. The second category of courses, which we call *theory-based courses,* usually come later in the research sequence. These courses typically examine the theoretical underpinnings of qualitative inquiry. Students in these courses typically read books and articles by philosophers such as Richard Bernstein (1976), Jürgen Habermas (1971, 1981), William James (1890/1950), Maurice Natanson (1962, 1973), D. C. Phillips (1987), Paul Ricoeur (1976, 1981), and Peter Winch (1971). These courses may also examine sociological theories often used by qualitative researchers. Students in these courses are likely to read the work of Peter Berger (1977), Herbert Blumer (1969), George Herbert Mead (1934), and Alfred Schutz (1970).

Field-Based Research Courses

Field-based research courses guide students through a complete research cycle. The most common pattern requires that students gain access to an appropriate research setting, gain Human Subjects Committee approval for the project, collect the consent of gatekeepers and participants (and, in the case of children, written consent of appropriate guardians), spend a specified number of hours in the field, type and submit protocols, complete observations and interviews, submit interview transcriptions, begin data coding, read related literature, bring coding categories to class for discussion, develop organizational schemes that make sense of the data, develop taxonomic or other data displays, and write a final report. There are variations on this pattern. In some courses, for example, students work together on a single project suggested by the instructor, and in others students team up on topics of their own choosing. But whatever the arrangement, the goal is to give students guided experience doing field-based research. Some instructors limit the research project to interviewing or to observing. Others focus on evaluation. But the goal of the course (or, occasionally, a sequence of courses) is to take students through an entire research project.

Field-based research courses generally are taught in seminar fashion and, when possible, instructors limit enrollment to 15 students. When the number of students grows larger than 15, instructors report that discussion is hindered and they cannot adequately monitor students' work. Most instructors do some didactic teaching at the beginning and again periodically throughout the course as the class turns its attention to a new topic or is faced with a new problem. In seminars, instructors typically guide discussions and raise pertinent questions. They work to help students overcome the problems they encounter in the field, adopt the social science perspective, and find the undergirding logic of qualitative research. Discussions must draw out those who are reluctant and rein in those who would dominate the discussion. Anselm Strauss (1988) describes his research seminar:

> I make it clear from the beginning that the class is a workshop; it is a working group. . . . Therefore, I have to teach it in such a way that students very quickly begin to work together. What I want to prevent is people presenting themselves rather than working closely with others. (pp. 92–93)

The first task of the instructor is to create an atmosphere in which students can reflect on and openly discuss the research they are doing. The long-range aim is to help students develop the habits of continual reflection and of questioning their data, their methods, their theories, and themselves. It is to help develop not only a "social science imagination," but also what Mills (1958) called "intellectual craftsmanship." Mills suggests that instructors avoid abstract discussions of research techniques and address instead how methods develop and are applied in real research situations. The working seminar avoids the "methodological asceticism" that Mannheim (1932) believed characterized American social science and allows the kind of methodological discussion typical of intellectual craftsmanship. As Mills (1959) put it,

> Of the method-and-theory-in-general, I do not here need to say any more. I am nowadays quickly made weary by it; so much discussion of it interrupts our proper studies. I . . . should much rather have one account by a working student of how he is going about his work than a dozen "codifications of procedure" by specialists. (p. 28, quoted *in* Strauss, 1987:305)

Those looking for guidance on how to conduct an effective qualitative research seminar will find no better advice than that offered by Strauss (1987) in *Qualitative Analysis for Social Scientists.*

Perennial Problems

Predictable problems crop up throughout the research cycle that instructors must be alert to and help students overcome. In this section, we pay special attention to problems students are likely to face when doing field-based research. We will discuss these problems under four general headings: Early Issues, Data Gathering Problems, Data Analysis Problems, and Writing. Each area is further divided into subheadings. The last three categories and their several subheadings are all part of a single research process; what we have separated for ease of discussion cannot be separated in practice.

Early Issues

We have already dealt with the issues of students' assumptions and problems associated with learning the social science perspective. Although these problems crop up early in the course, instructors report that they must be addressed many times as the course evolves. We turn now to other problems and issues that often show themselves in the first weeks of qualitative methods courses.

Choosing Appropriate Settings and Identifying Appropriate Problems

Finding an accessible site and a researchable problem is more difficult than most students imagine. Everett Hughes used to tell his students at the University of Chicago that a good sociologist finds a researchable question in just about any social behavior. His point, as Strauss (1987:272) explains, was that "comprehensive scholarly reading plus confrontation with any kind of data would set [a good] researcher's brain into whirling and effective action." Strauss also quotes Barney Glaser's advice that researchers should "study the unstudied" (p. 272; see also Glaser, 1978).

Students in education seldom have much background in social scientific theory. What theory they have read is often drawn from psychology or education and misfocuses their attention on personal troubles instead of structural issues (Mills, 1959:8). Instructors cannot make up students' theoretical deficits in one course, and, for that reason, many colleges are adding theory courses to their qualitative research sequence. (It is our opinion that the intellectual future of qualitative research in education depends on what gets taught in these theory courses, but that is a topic for a separate essay.)

Students who have had little exposure to theory are well advised to study in settings that interest them, where behavior is public and repetitive and where those being observed are likely to cooperate with the researcher. Of these criteria, none is more important than the issue of personal interest. Students who do rewarding research are usually working on a problem about which they feel deeply even though they are unable to define its exact dimensions at the start. It is difficult for some students to understand that qualitative researchers begin their work without the guidance of a predefined research problem. Instead, they should have "foreshadowed questions" (Malinowski, 1922:8–9) that may grow from theoretical literature, from the researcher's own experience, or from the researcher's own values and ideological commitments. The first task for the student is to ask, "What really interests me, puzzles me, arouses my curiosity?"

Instructors report that they are most helpful when they ask students difficult questions about their topics. Some students propose topics that are not appropriate to qualitative study (Is phonic instruction or whole-language instruction more effective in increasing the test scores of first-grade students?); others ask questions that are too ambitious for a semester-long project (What is the relationship between school structure and student–teacher relations in two kinds of high schools?); and still others ask questions that are too vague (What are the qualities of a good teacher?). Problem questions must be dealt with early, or students will waste time (their own as well as that of the instructor and the class).

Once an interest is identified, an accessible setting must be found. Some students believe that gaining access is the same as gaining entry, and they need to be warned of potential difficulties. For example, an instructor told us about a student who gained access to a used car lot. The owner and sales people agreed to a study of how cars are sold on a lot. The instructor was worried that the student would not be allowed to see what was really going on, but the student insisted that he had gained permission and that all would be well. After a few weeks on the site, the student realized he was getting no useful data. Interviews were postponed and, when finally completed, yielded little information. Sales personnel worked to divert the researcher during sales pitches, and when the researcher discovered the ruse, he was explicitly asked to keep his distance. Just when the student began to gather some useful data, he was asked to leave the research site and he dropped the course in frustration. The instructor believes he could have saved the student much difficulty had he voiced his objections more forcefully at the outset of the study.

Clarifying the Question and Early Data Analysis

Once a setting has been found and foreshadowed questions have been identified, students must be aided in further narrowing the topic they will study. As Hammersley and Atkinson (1983) explain,

> . . . the aim . . . in the early stages of data collection is to turn the foreshadowed problems into a set of questions to which a theoretical answer can be given, whether this be a narrative description of a

sequence of events, a generalized account of the perspectives and
practices of a particular group of actors, or a more abstract theoretical
formulation. (pp. 32–33)

To narrow the research question, students must begin the data
analysis process (a topic we will address later). Students often feel
overwhelmed at this stage because so much of what they are doing is
new and challenging. They are trying to negotiate the problems of
entry and access and learn to take field notes. Their assumptions about
research may be coming into sight and into question. Understandably,
students do not leap with glee to the question-narrowing task. Instructors report, however, that students who have the greatest difficulty
later in the research process are those who have not worked early to
clarify their research questions. Students will not achieve complete
clarity on their research questions until much later, but attention to the
task early in the course will increase the likelihood that the question
will become clear by the end of the course.

When research courses are taught as seminars, students are asked
to report on their research and to discuss the problems they experience. Instructors do students a favor if they insist that students narrow
topics that are too ambitious and clarify topics that are too vague. There
is a danger, however, in giving students too many suggestions.
Students are best advised to return to their data for answers to the
issues raised by the instructor.

Keeping a Journal

Our questionnaire to instructors revealed that less than one out of
every seven required students to keep journals, a fact we found surprising. We are not referring here to the kind of personal journals that Mills
(1959) describes in *The Sociological Imagination,* although there is
much to be said for them. We mean, instead, that students should keep
a log of their research project. In this log, the student should keep the
history of the research, describe issues of entry and access, record the
dates and times of observations and people interviewed, collect the
minutes of meetings, organize notes on collateral reading, and store
research memos (Glaser, 1978:81–91; Strauss, 1987:109–150). Research memos can cover a variety of topics such as student hunches,
reactions to events, worries, discoveries, definitions (and redefinitions) of codes, comparisons among codes or categories, and more. It is
also useful for students to record their evolving conceptions of social
science in their journals.

Students will want to organize their memos in their own ways. They
should be warned, however, that loose-leaf notebooks or files will be

needed because journals grow quickly and must be organized to facilitate easy access to what has been recorded. Some may want to use a computer to make journal entries, and this makes good sense. Students often need reminding to keep journals up to date and to review them frequently.

Studying Familiar Terrain

The interests of education students often lead them into schools, and the difficulties in gaining access to these institutions (especially in university communities) lead students into settings where they know people who trust them and are willing to do them a favor. Studying familiar people and places is fraught with difficulties. First, there is the problem that familiarity breeds blindness. The student will have to work hard to render the familiar strange. Second, there is the problem of role conflict. Students who are also teachers may be expected by others in a school setting to act as aids and not as researchers. Such expectations can be beneficial, but more often they confound the research task and aggravate (or at least confuse) the actors. Third, there is the problem of bias. Students who study familiar terrain can seldom rid themselves of their own vested interests. Those interests may limit what the researcher can see and may distort that which does come into view. Fourth, there is the potential problem of uncovering "dangerous knowledge" or information that could change the nature of the student's previous relationships with people and places.

Most instructors report that they do what they can to discourage students from studying in familiar terrain. In cases where exceptions must be made, instructors and students must remain sensitive to the issues of familiarity, role bias, role conflict, and dangerous knowledge and must deal with them as such issues arise. Reading in these areas early in the course sometimes proves helpful. Schutz's essays "The Stranger" (1964b), "The Homecomer" (1964a), and "The Well-Informed Citizen" (1964c) can give students the theoretical ground for understanding the difficulty of familiarity and perspective. Students also can benefit from reading novelists who explore their own worlds in minute detail. Few social scientists have the eye for familiar detail displayed by Jane Austin, Charles Dickens, E. M. Forster, Sinclair Lewis, John Updike, or Tom Wolfe.

How Many Is Enough?

Students sometimes get frustrated when they ask clear and direct questions of instructors and invariably get the answer, "It depends," followed by a long discussion of the variables that might affect a student's choice. This is certainly the case with the straightforward questions such as "How many hours do I need to observe in this setting?," "How many people do I need to interview?," or "Does it matter what time I do my observing?" It will lessen frustration if, early in the course, the instructor makes explicit that his or her aim is not to answer such questions for students but to show them how they can answer the questions for themselves.

It will help students if information about sampling is assigned and discussed in class. Students find LeCompte and Goetz (1982) and Patton (1990) particularly useful in clarifying sampling issues and answering what we call the "Who?," "When?," and "How often?" questions. Those working at theory construction simply must read Strauss (1987), Glaser and Strauss (1967), or Glaser (1978).

Data Gathering

Some qualitative research programs split data gathering methods (interviewing, observation, photography, and so on) and data analysis into separate courses. For example, graduate students come to Strauss's Grounded Theory course already having mastered data gathering skills. However, in most education research programs, students are introduced to both data gathering and data analysis in one course. The task is formidable.

Instructors report devoting many classes to discussions of how to take field notes and conduct interviews. Some begin the class with a common assignment. Many follow Spradley's (1980) advice and ask students to observe events in a single setting such as a trial in a local traffic court, take notes on what they see, type out protocols, and bring protocols back to class where they can be discussed and compared. It helps if the common assignment brings students to an accessible but somewhat unfamiliar setting where a lot is going on, where behavior is repetitive, and where front- and backstage events are likely to catch students' attention. If you want to give students an initiation experience they will long remember, we suggest you send students to professional wrestling matches (Twitchell, 1989) or tent revival meetings.

Those prone to less exotic fare may wish to follow J. P. McDermott's practice of showing video tapes of public school events to familiarize students with the ethnographic enterprise and help develop their "readiness to see."[5] Those without access to such tapes are advised to consult their university's film library. Almost anything by Frederick Wiseman, whose explorations of total institutions have won international acclaim, will prove useful. His movie *High School* (Wiseman, 1968), however, is of particular relevance.

Most instructors provide advice on what students should bring with them to the site and what they should begin looking at. Spradley's (1980:77–79) "grand tour" is a useful device to get students started. It is also helpful to tell students how and when field notes should be typed into final protocol form. It is helpful, too, to begin data analysis early. Analysis will not only help students narrow their focus and clarify their research questions but will also help students begin to see that their efforts have a purpose and may yield results. Without the feedback that analysis supplies, the experience of transcribing field notes becomes like the task of Mr. Jabez Wilson in Arthur Conan Doyle's "The Red-Headed League," as endless and meaningless as copying the encyclopedia in longhand.

Some professors have students begin interviewing by practicing on one another in class or by interviewing a group (teachers, parents, administrators) on a common topic. For example, Ivor Goodson (1989) asks his students to do life histories of teachers before doing classroom studies. He argues that classrooms are the point of teachers' highest vulnerability and that beginning students are likely to gain greater trust and richer information if they begin their research by taking an interest in the teachers' past. It also helps to begin interviewing in a topic area where there is a built-in story and sequence of significant events.

It is worth reiterating that fledgling researchers are well advised to avoid institutional studies. One-semester courses simply are too short to allow a student to understand the complexities of a complex social environment. It is wiser to examine a small and manageable part of the institution in fine detail rather than to look at an entire institution superficially.

Data Analysis Problems

A famous William Blake etching depicts a figure ready to ascend a ladder that reaches from the earth to the moon. At the bottom of the etching, Blake wrote, "I want! I want!" Because human rapacity is insatiable, it is dangerous to speculate about the desires of Blake's lonely figure. Jacob Bronowski (1978) suggests that the figure wants something akin to a new perspective from which to view his life and his world. New perspectives bring a new order to the things before us. The wish to bring order to experience is at the center of the scientific enterprise and, more fundamentally, at the heart of the human condition. Bronowski was no phenomenologist, but he understood that the origins of science are found in the world of everyday experience and the findings of science must return to that world for verification (Schrag, 1980; Webb, 1976). Science is a sophisticated expression of the human desire to understand.

As we discussed earlier, much of the world comes to us endowed with cultural meaning, so individual "knowing is fundamentally collective knowing" (Mannheim, 1936:28). Actions and events come predefined by meanings supplied by what Schutz (1967) called our predecessors, contemporaries, and consociates. If we are to break through the taken-for-granted structures that we inherit from everyday life, we must learn to see from a different perspective and think in a more disciplined way. We must ascend Blake's ladder.

Finding a Unity in the Wild Variety of Nature

Science, including social science, is one way to gain a new perspective on everyday events. As Bronowski (1978:ix) explains, scientific methods and human imagination allow us to find "the hidden likeness in diversity," the unity hidden in the "wild variety of nature" (Bronowski, 1956:16). But, finding unity in what appears disparate taxes human abilities. Connection, said Bronowski (1956:14), "is not there for the mere looking. There is no way of pointing a finger or a camera at it; order must be discovered and, in a deeper sense, it must be created."

The descriptions and theories we produce are never mirror images of nature (Rorty, 1979). Although we speak of them as *true* when they are verified by experience, that does not mean that they are "the accurate representation of reality." As James (1890/1950) explains, they are merely "what it is better for us to believe" (quoted *in* Rorty, 1979:10). In James's view, "truth is made, just as health, wealth, and strength are made, in the course of experience" (quoted *in* Barzun, 1983:86). To check the truth of an idea (scientific or otherwise), we must test it in experience to see if it "works" or, to expand the point, to see if it helps us understand and accurately anticipate events.

Constructing Unity through Coding

Qualitative data analysis is an effort to construct order out of the booming, buzzing confusion that stands before the researcher. The task is difficult and students often resist it. About the time the instructor turns the class's attention to analysis, students are ensconced in their research sites, getting comfortable with their new data gathering skills, and intrigued by their fieldwork. To even think about data analysis introduces new, unappealing uncertainties. Research texts are not of much help because, with a few happy exceptions (Goetz and LeCompte, 1984; Miles and Huberman, 1984; Spradley, 1980; Strauss, 1987; Strauss and Corbin, 1990), texts say surprisingly little about how data analysis actually is done. What the books do say leaves students with the impression that unity will *emerge* almost magically from the data and present itself to researchers as a reward for their perseverance. Analytical methods are not described as tools to aid researchers in the creative work of analysis. Instead, they are presented as though analysis procedures are a sorcerer's ritual that, if performed correctly, will conjure truth from the depths of the data. Helping students see that data analysis is a creative act in which researchers strike a balance between introspection and objectification is the instructor's most difficult task (Agar, 1986).

Reading qualitative studies is not of much help because, at this point in the research cycle, students are befuddled by the reports' seamless findings and self-assured tone. In most published reports, nothing suggests that authors were ever swamped in or bewildered by their data. There is no hint that the authors ever doubted their ability to find patterns, to see the connections among patterns, or to report those patterns in a way that did justice to what was observed. There are some helpful confessional tales (Van Maanen, 1988) available, but many are more self-congratulatory than insightful. Without models to guide them, it is little wonder that students worry about data analysis.

As students gaze helplessly at voluminous field notes and interview transcripts, most doubt that they will ever find patterns and connections. Because they have already put weeks of work into their research, they are not inclined to drop the class. Instead, most dedicate themselves to working even harder. Unfortunately, most assume that they cannot find unity in the chaos because they do not have sufficient data. Therefore, they are inclined to stay in the field and gather more. The accumulation of data, of course, makes analysis even more frightening. We have found that conscientious students often collect too much data and, as a result, spend too little time analyzing what they have collected. Wolcott (1990) says that analysis and writing are a way to get rid of irrelevant data.

Students like to hear from peers who have recently completed qualitative projects or dissertations, and it is a good idea to invite them to address the class. The only way to help students get over their fear of analyzing data, however, is to get them to begin the analysis. The work is hard, but problems are lessened if data analysis starts early and continues throughout the research cycle. Some instructors follow Strauss's (1988) advice and begin data analysis in the first weeks of the course. They invite students to bring some part of their data to class so that everyone can help work out a problem some student is facing. Typically, students are asked to do unrestricted, line-by-line coding during initial analysis sessions. The coding methods differ depending on what qualitative approach is being stressed in the course, but Strauss (1988) describes what he does in his seminar on grounded theory:

> Each week someone will present and there will always be a backup person in case the first person gets sick or is unable to attend . . . . The presentation portion of the seminar begins and the first student presents his or her materials. The materials may consist of a portion of an interview or a portion of a fieldnote. I don't want the student to present too much material, just enough for the class to work on [between two and five pages]. Sometimes students will get the material to their classmates ahead of time, but when that is impossible we read that material at the beginning of the class. Then we start.
>
> I try to show students the difference between just looking at an interview or fieldnote in search of general themes and what I call intensive coding. One of the ways to do it, and I do it several times at the beginning of the course, is to let the class read an interview. Then I ask them what they see in it. After they have discussed the interview, we go back and I get them to look again at the first sentence. In fact, I may even ask them to take a look at the first word or two.
>
> When we look at the first two words, we discuss what those words mean or what they could mean. Sometimes we spend 30 or 40 minutes on a single phrase before moving on to the next phrase.
>
> The effort here is to show students that they should not skim over things when doing analysis. They have to read every sentence very closely, for words and phrasing will suggest all kinds of possible hypotheses that are worth exploring. The name of the game at the outset is not to know exactly what's going on in that interview; you can only know that after you have analyzed the whole interview and gone back to reinterview. The name of the game at the start is to open the whole field of inquiry.
>
> At the end of an hour and a half students sometimes think I'm a genius because we have opened up an array of questions, hypotheses, possibilities. (p. 93; see also Strauss, 1987:Chap. 3)

One advantage that Strauss's approach has over other methods— such as Spradley's (1980) system of language domaining—is that open coding gives students a sense of achievement early in the coding process. Strauss (1987) explains,

> The excitement of this analytic game, combined with "results," gives them confidence in this procedure, so much so that students characteristically look forward to trying it again in the next class sessions. Many make a personal challenge of mastering the procedure, understanding very well that it is one of the most important steps in becoming generally competent at analysis. (p. 268)

Strauss's procedure has another benefit: Because early coding is done in public and under the guidance of the instructor, students overcome the worry that there is only one meaning alive in the data and that they must get it fast and get it right or it will be forever lost. Because many voices are heard when students work together, a host of speculative—but ultimately checkable—possibilities are introduced.

Finding Unifying Patterns and Second-Order Constructs

Once data have been disassembled through coding, they must be reassembled (unified) as descriptive findings or theories. The first-order constructs that actors use to make sense of daily life must be transformed through coding and further analysis into the second-order constructs of social science. The models of the social world that we build must meet certain tests, although the nature of the tests vary depending on the methods used and the theoretical stance of the researcher.

Finding unity and pattern and building second-order constructs is an act of disciplined imagination, or what Dewey (1939:255) called "speculative audacity." Hutchinson and Webb (1990) quoted Bronowski (1956) to show how imagination serves scientists who are building second-order constructs:

> Newton made a daring imaginative leap when he hypothesized that the dropping of an apple and the flight of the moon around the earth were "two expressions of a single concept, gravitation. Faraday did [the same] when he closed the link between electricity and magnetism. Clark Maxwell did [the same] when he linked both with light" [Bronowski, 1956:15]. Science is made possible by the workings of the human imagination.[6] (Hutchinson and Webb, 1990:315)

Speculative hunches may be brilliant or worthless, but we cannot tell much about their value until they are tested against the data. The nature of such testing is a matter of considerable debate (Kuhn, 1970; O'Leary, 1986; Schrag, 1980; Webb, 1976). Berger and Kellner (1981), following Popper (1972), suggest that researchers must take their speculations back to the data in search of contradictory evidence. If the researcher's hypotheses stand up against Popper's falsification criteria, researchers may let them stand—until future evidence proves them inadequate. Luckmann (1978:234) suggests that hypotheses must also be taken back to what Pierce called the "republic of scholars" for debate and intellectual adjudication. Geertz (1973) suggests another way to test the veracity of our social science speculations. He would have us judge the products of "scientific imagination" by asking how close the findings "bring us into touch with the lives of strangers" (p. 16).

None of the instructors we interviewed was willing to claim that speculative audacity could be taught, but most agreed that students' imaginations can be nurtured and that most students eventually become competent researchers. Attending to the procedures of data analysis is as important as providing a working atmosphere in seminars. Modeling speculative moves and encouraging a focused playfulness during coding sessions makes classes more fun and more productive.

As codes are being developed, students must begin to search for unifying themes or core categories. Students worry that they will not recognize possible unifying themes in their data and that what they have taken apart through coding will remain forever disassembled. Here again, in-class work sessions are helpful. Students get to see how others develop ideas for themes and identify possible core variables. Writing research memos is particularly important at this juncture. Getting ideas down on paper helps students recognize what is still unclear. The process is helpful in itself, but it also improves the quality of class discussions because students come to the class with a clearer idea of what has been accomplished and what remains to be done. Strauss and others encourage students to discuss their memos in the seminar.

Occasionally instructors will work individually with students to help them search for theories. There is a danger, however, when instructors provide too much help. An example was reported by a professor who had helped a student spot a unifying theme in an ethnographic study:

> [The student] came to me the next semester to report that he was continuing his research and planned to make it the topic of his dissertation. He asked sheepishly if I would mind if he used *my theory*. I thought he was referring to something I had written, but I soon came to realize he was talking about the cultural theme we had developed when analyzing his domains. I told him it wasn't my theory;

that we had drawn the theory from his data and that it was his. If it held up after more work, that was great. He was pleased and acted grateful. Before he left he asked how he should footnote *my theory*. Then I understood that I had done too much for him and, even though my intentions were good, I had robbed him of the pleasure of finding something on his own.

Collateral reading helps students hone their speculative skills. Many become so absorbed in their data they find it difficult to relax and turn their minds to other things. Such students can find guiltless rest by reading novels, magazine, newspaper stories, or histories on topics related to their research. They may also watch movies and television programs on the topic. Students needing to justify such activity should read the wide-ranging and often entertaining footnotes in any of Erving Goffman's works.

Computer Programs

Computer programs are available to aid researchers in organizing data. Such programs do not code or analyze data, but they do speed the coding process and help in the management of information. Use of such programs, however, assumes computer literacy, and even seasoned computer users may find such programs difficult to master. Not all programs are of equal worth or are equally suited for every qualitative method. Therefore, it is important that students do careful research before spending money on what might be the wrong program.

The difficulty associated with finding and learning how to use the right program discourages many instructors from making computer use a part of their qualitative research courses. Some will demonstrate a program or two in class, but most suggest that students do their first research project without using data analysis programs. Students wanting guidance, however, will find Renata Tesch's (1990) *Qualitative Research: Analysis Types and Software Tools* a valuable resource. Tesch reviews available programs, explains what they can (and cannot) do for researchers, discusses how they work, and even suggests which programs are appropriate for what kind of research. Furthermore, an upcoming issue of *Qualitative Sociology* will be devoted entirely to the use of computers in qualitative research.

Writing

Until recently, little attention had been paid to the relationship that writing has to qualitative research. Writing up findings has been viewed as something researchers do when the analysis is complete.

But as Atkinson (in press) has made clear, every aspect of the qualitative process entails "the textural reconstruction of reality." Just about everything researchers do (recording field notes, keeping a research journal and memos, defining codes, drafting the final report) demands that they translate events, actions, facts, motives, or ideas into written form. Writing is "intrinsic to" the researcher's craft and "the success or failure" of a project depends on the researcher's ability not only to write clearly but to write in different ways for different tasks.

Few researchers discuss the stylistic issues entailed in writing field notes (Atkinson, in press). Textbooks usually supply useful advice about what to include in field notes. They suggest that students pay close attention to folk terms, that they try to get verbatim quotes, and that they describe details in concrete terms avoiding high-inference language (Spradley, 1980:68). Beyond that, not much is said.

Because field records are not generally available to anyone but the researchers who wrote them (we have given up the practice of saving our field notes so that others could check our work), "the construction of these 'primary' texts remains unexplored," and we have "no systematic analysis of fieldnotes as texts" (Atkinson, 1991). Even if we have no literature exploring what Atkinson calls the "poetics of fieldnotes," we can use classes to draw students' attention to what is written and the way in which style informs (and transforms) content. Later in the course, similar work can be done with other forms of writing.

The Final Report

Strauss (1987:259) suggests that students who "lack confidence in their analysis" find it difficult to start writing their final reports. Students write clearly only when they are thinking clearly. A thorough analysis of data will make writing easier. It is dangerous to overstate this point, however. We do not want to leave the impression that writing is begun only when the analysis is finished. Many a dissertation has languished while students struggled to clarify every finding before sitting down to write. Wolcott (1990:25, 45, 48) emphasizes that writing is an integral part of analysis, not something done when the analysis is complete. Writing, when we are attentive, exposes the flaws in our thinking and moves us back to our analysis when it needs further work. Often, we do further analysis during the writing phase.

The single primary obstacle to report writing is that students lack the time it takes to do it well. Understanding this, instructors are less critical of writing issues than they otherwise might be. Students write better reports when they begin writing early and pay attention to writing issues throughout the course.

We pointed out earlier that many colleges with a sequence of qualitative research courses have developed an introductory course where students read and critique qualitative studies. The qualities of good research are reviewed (Smith, 1987), and students apply those criteria to a variety of studies. Such courses are strengthened if attention is paid to how the studies are written. Fortunately, some wonderful books are available that draw students' attention to the minute particulars of qualitative writing (Atkinson, 1990; Becker, 1986; Clifford and Marcus, 1986; Geertz, 1983; Van Maanan, 1988). Aided by these books, students can explore macro-questions about power, voice, and the politics in qualitative research; middle-range issues about authorial authority, the marshalling of evidence, and the relationship between researcher and the researched; and micro-issues such as whether or not a piece should be written in the first person, whether or not its tone changes when the author moves from data to theory, and how the story is told. Early attention to such matters may sensitize students to these issues and help them be more careful readers and writers of qualitative research. Nonetheless, just as there is no way to learn how to do research other than doing it, there is no way to learn to write qualitative accounts other than writing them.

Students appreciate practical advice when they are getting ready to write. Some instructors advise students to find a place where they can write without distraction and to set out a work schedule that provides large chunks of uninterrupted time. All data, codes, memos, and journal entries should be readily available, and data displays (taxonomies, flow charts, integrative diagrams) should be put on the wall where they can be seen. The question of audience should be established at the outset, and students should be warned against writing from the assumption that the instructor is well acquainted with the data. Whether the paper is being written for class or for publication, the author should assume a naive audience. Having students present their findings to the seminar helps them clarify their thoughts and strengthen their evidence. Such assignments also help students avoid procrastination.

Completing the Report

When students are writing their reports, good books about writing in general and writing qualitative reports in particular have immense value. Students (and their professors!) are lucky to have excellent books from which to choose. Becker's (1986) *Writing for Social Scientists* and Wolcott's (1990) *Writing Up Qualitative Research* are particularly noteworthy. Becker's book grew out of a course he teaches on social science writing and Wolcott's book grew out of his own reflections on the writer's craft. Linda Brodkey's (1987) *Academic Writing as Social Practice* takes a more general look at academic writing, but a large portion of it will be of interest and use to qualitative researchers. Brodkey makes the point that writing may appear to be a solitary activity, but it is profoundly social and carries moral obligations, two of which are fidelity and clarity.

By fidelity, we mean accurately representing the data and our analysis of it, showing what we did and how we did it, and in all other ways respecting our obligations of citizenship to the "republic of scholars." This may entail showing ourselves in our writing, not as reporters of objective facts, but as instruments in the research process. Ball (1990) claims that methodological rigor requires qualitative researchers to include in their reports "a reflective account of the conduct of the research" and to reveal the problems they encountered and the choices, and errors, they made along the way (p. 170). Not all instructors require students to include this kind of *research biography* in their final reports. The seminar activities described by most instructors, however, encourage students to undertake radical self-reflection that Ball is calling for.

Berger and Kellner (1981) also address the issue of fidelity, but from another perspective. They claim that a social scientist has a moral obligation to be "*a listener of the many stories of human meanings—and . . . to retell the stories as faithfully as one is able* [italics in original]" (p. 75). The second-order constructs that social scientists use to make sense of peoples' lives must grow from and refer back to the first-order constructs those same people use to define themselves and fill their lives with meaning. Moving gracefully between first- and second-order constructs in social science writing is difficult.

We have suggested that students have a moral obligation to be clear; otherwise, the reader is separated from the lives of the people under study and from the researcher's analysis. We are not suggesting that students should "dumb-down" their text or simplify what is complex just to make reading easier. We are suggesting that the professional dialect of academics, like the lingo of bureaucrats, too often is a contrivance. It is designed, as Richard Mitchell (1979:51–52) says, to keep the reader subservient, confused, and inattentive to what is (or is not) being said. Mitchell (1981) is perhaps the world's harshest critic of unclear writing and is particularly ruthless when he examines the written words of "educationists." Assigning one or two of Mitchell's essays, however, helps students appreciate the importance of writing clearly and warns them against using jargon to make their writing sound intelligent.

Conclusion

We began by saying that the whole world cannot become problematic at once. We have proceeded to show that learning qualitative research methods generally throws large segments of a student's taken-for-granted world into question. Fortunately for all concerned, students generally focus on one problem at a time, thereby avoiding terror. But the closer students come to understanding what it means to take a social science perspective on the world, the more satisfying they find the experience. Instructors report that students enjoy qualitative research more than most other courses.

It is appropriate to end this chapter with a discussion of why qualitative research courses can be so appealing. Part of the reason, no doubt, is related to the self-selection process that goes on before students ever come to the qualitative research classroom. Students who have an affinity to quantitative research seldom choose a qualitative course, and those who do often do so with the conscious intent of broadening their research horizons.[7] Students report that they find in qualitative courses a way of looking at the world that is new but also vaguely familiar. As one student put it, "I didn't realize it before, but I've always seen the world from the edges. Now I've found a research method that matches the way I think."

The work that qualitative research requires is time-consuming and difficult. Nevertheless, most students do that work willingly and often joyfully. They distinguish between that which is difficult and that which is merely fatiguing; as Barzun (1959:254) has said, "The difference between work and wearisome futility lies in that distinction." Qualitative research methods courses provide students with a tangible (and marketable) skill. It gives them a way to bridge the gap between the abstraction of theory and reality of everyday life. It is both liberating (in that it provides new perspectives from which to view human activity) and conserving (in that it gives students insight into ultimate necessity of order and triviality) (Berger, 1977:x–xix).

Seminar discussions engage students because they deal (often simultaneously) with the practical and the profound. Practical discoveries have intrinsic value, but they are made more powerful because of what they suggest about larger matters such as the nature of inquiry. Learning to see events from a social science perspective relativizes the world of everyday life, debunks its pretensions, and to some degree frees students from culture's "iron cage." Many of the instructors we surveyed and with whom we spoke referred to the sense of liberation their students experienced in the course. Here are some examples:

- I see students "come alive," eyes sparkling, feeling liberated.
- It is exciting watching the empowerment of students who realize that they can create credible knowledge through human interaction with their informants.
- Students find this approach (to research) so involving and so valid that it changes their way of thinking.

It is precisely the liberating nature of qualitative research that we believe makes it a humanistic (in contrast to vocational) activity and unites it with the aims of a liberal education. We also believe that it is the deeply intellectual nature of the work that makes it so appealing to students. Qualitative research offers one perspective from which to view the world; it is one mode of experience among many open to us. It is not a privileged mode, and it certainly does not provide ultimate truth or a picture of the whole of experience. Every perspective leaves things out in an effort to make experience coherent. Students find the perspective of qualitative research satisfying because it makes them constructors of knowledge as well as consumers. It confirms their own powers of rationality and imagination. This is potent stuff.

Taking on the social science perspective, however, can do still more for students. As Berger and Kellner (1981) have put it, "The same methods of analysis that disclose the relativity of the beliefs of others will, invariably, disclose the relativity of one's own beliefs—if, that is, these methods are consistently applied" (p. 65). Once the relativizing genie is out of its bottle, no perspective, discipline, or mode of experience is safe. Social science can relativize itself (Latour and Woolgar, 1986; Woolgar, 1988).

As Fuller (1989:8) has pointed out, "Most people most of the time are content to understand the world within the ordinary framework of a particular mode's construction of the world." Even scholars are content to be practitioners of their disciplines. They "get on with the business of giving their respective lines of thought greater organizational clarity in terms of more or less unquestioned postulates or assumptions" (p. 9). Nevertheless, humanistic social science is more profoundly relativizing than most disciplines and pushes its most serious students beyond the comforting confines of its own postulates or assumptions.

We do not mean to suggest that social science is ultimately useless; quite the contrary. We mean only that humanistic social science can engender in students a healthy skepticism about all claims to truth. Attempts to understand experience from within the confines of any discipline are inherently limiting, abstract, and reductionist. As Fuller (1989:10) explains, "Every mode of interpretation of experience is reductionist in seeking to complete itself by explaining all experience in terms of its own postulates of interpretation." Paradoxically, social science also can engender a deep respect for the truth-seeking enterprise and the power of human beings to create meaning through experience. A relativized social science need not leave us without intellectual ground to stand on. Instead, it moves us back to a contemplation about the nature of human experience, the origins of human knowing, and what it means to be human.

Notes

[1] A recent survey found that qualitative methods were being taught under titles such as Action Research, Ethnographic Methods in Education, Introduction to Field Methods, Advanced Field Methods, Field Studies in Education, Naturalistic Inquiry, Participant Observation, Educational Anthropology, Educational Connoisseurship and Criticism, Disciplined Inquiry in Administration and Policy Studies, Curriculum Theory and Development, Scholarly Thought and Contemporary Curriculum, Phenomenological Methods, Qualitative Research Methods in Education.

[2] Our questionnaire on "teaching qualitative research methods in colleges of education" began in the spring of 1989, when we developed 20 open-ended questions asking respondents about themselves as qualitative researchers and as qualitative research methods teachers, about the history and status of qualitative research and qualitative research methods classes in their college, and about the students they teach and advise. We piloted the questionnaire with seven well-known qualitative researchers who varied in their methodological approaches. The following remark captures their general response, "I enjoyed answering the questions although it took longer than expected—over two hours." Our pilot respondents urged us to continue with the project, but either to make it an interview study or to make the questions closed-ended. We decided to do both. Using our pilot data, we generated a series of "check-the-box" answers for most of the questions, followed by space for comments.

We sent the questionnaire to a sample of professors of education in the United States who were on the *International Journal of Qualitative Studies in Education* subscription list. Seventy-five returned the survey. Unsurprisingly, the most frequent overall comment concerned respondents' resistance to forced-choice items. Nonetheless, few took the time to expand on their checked-off answers. We asked respondents to include copies of course syllabi and other relevant documents; we received 55 course syllabi. Also unsurprisingly, the richest information has come from the interviews. The survey, however, is useful in that it documents patterns in things such as the qualitative education of methods teachers by gender, trends in attitudes of students and other faculty toward qualitative research, and the frustrations and joys (open-ended questions) associated with teaching qualitative research.

[3] Anthropologists might prefer the term "ethnocentrism," but that term is too associated with culture for our purposes.

[4] We use the phrase "social science perspective" throughout this chapter to refer to a kind of inquiry used to understand and interpret meaning in the social world. The term does not refer to methods of empirical explanation used in the natural sciences. We understand that many would insist that a social science perspective must reflect a more positivistic than humanistic stance. They would want to rule out the very elements we want to rule in, such as meaning, mind, and intersubjectivity. We acknowledge the difference in our perspectives but insist that a social science that rules out meaning neglects the most fundamental elements of its subject matter.

[5] For a brief discussion of the use of film in qualitative methods courses, see Eisner (1991).

[6] Bronowski had great respect for inspiration and, for that reason, was interested in romantic poets such as Blake, who claimed that the imagination was the highest expression of the human spirit. Others, of course, were suspicious of imagination and claimed it should have no place in scientific work. For example, Sir Francis Bacon (1605/1975) warned that imagination is a wily guide that would lead unsuspecting researchers almost anywhere except to truth. "The imagination," he wrote, "being not tied to the laws of matter, may at its pleasure join which nature hath severed and sever that which nature hath joined, and so make unlawful matches and divorces of things" (quoted in Hutchinson and Webb, 1990:314). For Bronowski, however, imagination is an implement of science, not a substitute for it.

[7] Self-selection may end, however, with changes in degree programs research requirements. Our survey indicates that some programs require all doctoral students to take at least one qualitative research class.

Acknowledgments

We appreciate the time and effort contributed by colleagues who completed our questionnaire and/or agreed to be interviewed. We are particularly indebted to Robert R. Sherman, Paul Kleine, Nobuo Shimahara, and Anselm Strauss, who read earlier versions of this chapter and made helpful suggestions.

Appendix: List of Texts Used in National Qualitative Research Methods Courses and Reported on the Glesne/ Webb Survey

Agar, M. H. (1980). *The professional stranger: An informal introduction to ethnography.* New York: Academic Press.

Agar, M. H. (1986). *Speaking of ethnography.* Beverly Hills, CA: Sage Publications.

Becker, H. S. (1986). *Writing for social scientists: How to start and finish your thesis, book, or article.* Chicago: University of Chicago Press.

Berger, P. L., and Luckmann, T. (1967). *The social construction of reality: A treatise in the sociology of knowledge.* New York: Doubleday.

Bernard, H. R. (1988). *Research methods in cultural anthropology.* Newbury Park, CA: Sage Publications.

Bogdan, R. C., and Biklen, S. K. (1982). *Qualitative research for education: An introduction to theory and methods.* Boston: Allyn & Bacon.

Burgess, R. G. (Ed.). (1984). *The research process in educational settings: Ten case studies.* New York: Falmer Press.

Carr, W., and Kemmis, S. (1986). *Becoming critical: Education, knowledge, and action research.* Philadelphia: Falmer Press.

Cooper, H. M. (1984). *The integrative research review: A systematic approach.* Beverly Hills, CA: Sage Publications.

Darroch, V., and Silvers, R. J. (Eds.). (1982). *Interpretive human studies: An introduction to phenomenological research.* Washington, DC: University Press of America.

Dobbert, M. L. (1982). *Ethnographic research: Theory and application for modern schools and societies.* New York: Praeger.

Douglas, J. D. (1985). *Creative interviewing.* Beverly Hills, CA: Sage Publications.

Emerson, R. M. (Ed.). (1983). *Contemporary field research: A collection of readings.* Boston: Little, Brown.

Fetterman, D. M. (1989). *Ethnography step by step.* Newbury Park, CA: Sage Publications.

Fetterman, D. M., and Pitman, M. A. (Eds.). (1986). *Educational evaluation: Ethnography in theory, practice, and politics.* Beverly Hills, CA: Sage Publications.

Fitz-Gibbon, C. T., and Morris, L. L. (1987). *How to design a program evaluation.* Newbury Park, CA: Sage Publications.

Glaser, B. G., and Strauss, A. L. (1967). *The discovery of grounded theory; strategies for qualitative research.* Chicago: Aldine.

Goetz, J. P., and LeCompte, M. D. (1984). *Ethnography and qualitative design in educational research.* Orlando, FL: Academic Press.

Guba, E. G., and Lincoln, Y. S. (1981). *Effective evaluation.* San Francisco: Jossey-Bass.

Guba, E. G., and Lincoln, Y. S. (1989). *Fourth generation evaluation.* Newbury Park, CA: Sage Publications.

Hammersley, M., and Atkinson, P. (1983). *Ethnography: Principles in practice.* New York: Tavistock.

Homans, G. C. (1967). *The nature of social science.* New York: Harcourt, Brace and World.

Kuhn, T. S. (1970). *The structure of scientific revolutions* (2nd ed.). Chicago: University of Chicago Press.

Lincoln, Y. S., and Guba, E. G. (1985). *Naturalistic inquiry.* Beverly Hills, CA: Sage Publications.

Lofland, J., and Lofland, L. H. (1984). *Analyzing social settings: A guide to qualitative observation and analysis* (2nd ed.). Belmont, CA: Wadsworth.

Marshall, C., and Rossman, G. B. (1989). *Designing qualitative research.* Newbury Park, CA: Sage Publications.

McCall, G. J., and Simmons, J. L. (1969). *Issues in participant observation: A text and reader.* Reading, MA: Addison-Wesley.

Mehan, H., and Wood, H. (1975). *The reality of ethnomethodology.* New York: Wiley.

Merriam, S. B. (1988). *Case study research in education: A qualitative approach.* San Francisco: Jossey-Bass.

Miles, M. B., and Huberman, A. M. (1984). *Qualitative data analysis: A sourcebook of new methods.* Beverly Hills, CA: Sage Publications.

Patton, M. Q. (1980). *Qualitative evaluation methods.* Beverly Hills, CA: Sage Publications.

Patton, M. Q. (1987). *How to use qualitative methods in evaluation.* Newbury Park, CA: Sage Publications.

Patton, M. Q. (1990). *Qualitative evaluation and research methods* (2nd ed.). Newbury Park, CA: Sage Publications.

Pfaffenberger, B. (1988). *Microcomputer applications in qualitative research.* Newbury Park, CA: Sage Publications.

Phillips, D. C. (1987). *Philosophy, science, and social inquiry: Contemporary methodological controversies in social science and related applied fields of research.* New York: Pergamon.

Powdermaker, H. (1966). *Stranger and friend; the way of an anthropologist.* New York: W. W. Norton.

Punch, M. (1986). *The politics and ethics of fieldwork.* Beverly Hills, CA: Sage Publications.

Schatzman, L., and Strauss, A. L. (1973). *Field research; strategies for a natural sociology.* Englewood Cliffs, NJ: Prentice-Hall.

Schwartz, H., and Jacobs, J. (1979). *Qualitative sociology: A method to the madness.* New York: Free Press.

Sherman, R. R., and Webb, R. B. (1988). *Qualitative research in education: Focus and methods.* New York: Falmer Press.

Spindler, G. (Ed.). (1988). *Doing the ethnography of schooling: Educational anthropology in action.* New York: Holt, Rinehart & Winston.

Spindler, G., and Spindler, L. (Eds.). (1987). *Interpretative ethnography of education: At home and abroad.* Hillsdale, NJ: Lawrence Erlbaum.

Spradley, J. P. (1979). *The ethnographic interview.* New York: Holt, Rinehart & Winston.

Spradley, J. P. (1980). *Participant observation.* New York: Holt, Rinehart & Winston.

Spradley, J. P., and McCurdy, D. W. (1972). *The cultural experience: Ethnography in complex society.* Chicago: Science Research Associates.

Strauss, A. L. (1987). *Qualitative analysis for social scientists.* New York: Cambridge University Press.

Van Maanen, J. (1988). *Tales of the field: On writing ethnography.* Chicago: University of Chicago Press.

Whyte, W. F. (1984). *Learning from the field: A guide from experience.* Beverly Hills, CA: Sage Publications.

Willis, G. (Ed.). (1978). *Qualitative evaluation: Concepts and cases in curriculum criticism.* Berkeley: CA: McCutchan.

Yin, R. K. (1989). *Case study research: Design and methods* (rev. ed.). Newbury Park: Sage Publications.

References

Agar, M. (1986). *Speaking of ethnography.* Beverly Hills, CA: Sage Publications.

Atkinson, P. (1990). *The ethnographic imagination: Textural constructions of reality.* London: Routledge.

Atkinson, P. (1991). Supervising the text. *International Journal of Qualitative Studies in Education, 4*(2).

Bacon, F. (1605/1975). *Advancement of learning.* Atlantic Highlands, NJ: Humanities Press.

Ball, S. (1990). Self-doubt and soft data: Social and technical trajectories in ethnographic fieldwork. *International Journal of Qualitative Studies in Education,* 3(3), 157–171.

Barzun, J. (1959). *The house of intellect.* New York: Harper and Brothers.

Barzun, J. (1983). *A stroll with William James.* Chicago: University of Chicago Press.

Becker, H. S. (1986). *Writing for social scientists: How to start and finish your thesis, book, or article.* Chicago: University of Chicago Press.

Berger, P. L. (1977). *Facing up to modernity: Excursions in society, politics, and religion.* New York: Basic Books.

Berger, P. L., and Berger, B. (1972). *Sociology: A biographical approach.* New York: Basic Books.

Berger, P. L., and Kellner, H. (1981). *Sociology reinterpreted: An essay on method and vocation.* Garden City, NY: Anchor Press: Doubleday.

Berger, P. L., Berger, B., and Kellner, H. (1973). *The homeless mind: Modernization and consciousness.* New York: Vintage Books.

Bernstein, R. J. (1976). *The restructuring of social and political theory.* Philadelphia: University of Pennsylvania Press.

Blumer, H. (1969). *Symbolic interactionism: Perspective and method.* Berkeley: University of California Press.

Brodkey, L. (1987). *Academic writing as social practice.* Philadelphia: Temple University Press.

Bronowski, J. (1956). *Science and human values.* New York: Harper and Row.

Bronowski, J. (1978). *The origins of knowledge and imagination.* New Haven, CT: Yale University Press.

Clifford, J., and Marcus, G. E. (Eds.). (1986). *Writing culture: The poetics and politics of ethnography.* Berkeley: University of California Press.

Dewey, J. (1939). Philosophy and culture. *In* J. Ratner (Ed.), *Intelligence in the modern world* (pp. 245–255). New York: Modern Library.

Eisner, E. W. (1991). *The enlightened eye: Qualitative inquiry and the enhancement of educational practice.* New York: Macmillan.

Eisner, E. W., and Peshkin, A. (Eds.). (1990). *Qualitative inquiry in education: The continuing debate.* New York: Teachers College Press.

Ellul, J. (1964). *The technological society.* New York: Vantage.

Fuller, T. (Ed.). (1989). *The voice of liberal learning: Michael Oakshott on education.* New Haven, CT: Yale University Press.

Garfinkel, H. (1964). Studies of the routine ground of everyday activities. *Social Problems,* 11, 225–250.

Geertz, C. (1973). *The interpretation of cultures.* New York: Basic Books.

Geertz, C. (1983). *Works and lives: The anthropologist as author.* Cambridge: Polity Press.

Gehlen, A. (1980). *Man in an age of technology,* P. Lipscomb (Trans.). New York: Columbia University Press.

Glaser, B. (1978). *Theoretical sensitivity.* Mill Valley, CA: Sociology Press.

Glaser, B., and Strauss, A. (1967). *The discovery of grounded theory.* Chicago: Aldine.

Glesne, C., and Webb, R. B. (in press). Who's teaching qualitative research courses and what's being taught? *The International Journal of Qualitative Studies in Education.*

Goetz, J. P., and LeCompte, M. D. (1984). *Ethnography and qualitative design in educational research.* Orlando, FL: Academic Press.

Goffman, E. (1961). *Asylums: Essays on the social situation of mental patients and other inmates.* Garden City, NY: Anchor.

Goodson, I. (1989). Teachers' lives. *In* B. Allen and J. P. Goetz (Eds.), *Qualitative research in education* (pp. 150–159). Athens: University of Georgia, College of Education.

Greene, M. (1988). Qualitative research and the use of literature. *In* R. R. Sherman and R. B. Webb (Eds.), *Qualitative research in education: Focus and methods* (pp. 175–189). London: Falmer Press.

Guba, E. (1990). *The paradigm dialogue.* Newbury Park, CA: Sage Publications.

Habermas, J. (1971). *Knowledge and human interest.* Boston: Beacon Press.

Habermas, J. (1981). *The theory of communicative action: Vol. 1, Reason and the rationalization of society,* T. McCarthy (Trans.). Boston: Beacon.

Hammersley, A., and Atkinson, P. (1983). *Ethnography: Principles and practices.* London: Tavistock.

Henry, J. (1965). *Culture against man.* New York: Vintage.

Homans, G. C. (1967). *The nature of social science.* New York: Harcourt, Brace and World.

Howell, J. T. (1973). *Hard living on clay street: Portraits of blue collar families.* Garden City, NY: Anchor Books.

Hutchinson, S., and Webb, R. (1990). Teaching qualitative research. *In* J. Morse (Ed.), *Qualitative nursing research: A contemporary dialogue* (pp. 301–321). Newbury Park, CA: Sage.

James, W. (1890/1950). *The principles of psychology* (Vols. I and II). New York: Dover.

Kestenbaum, V. (1977). *The phenomenological sense of John Dewey: Habit and meaning.* Atlantic Highlands, NJ: Humanities Press.

Kuhn, T. (1970). *The structure of scientific revolutions* (2nd ed.). Chicago: University of Chicago Press.

Latour, B., and Woolgar, S. (1988). *Laboratory life: The construction of scientific facts.* Princeton: NJ: Princeton University Press.

LeCompte, M. D., and Goetz, J. P. (1982). Problems of reliability and validity in ethnographic research. *Review of Educational Research, 52*(1), 31–60.

Luckmann, T. (1978). Philosophy, social science and everyday life. *In* T. Luckmann (Ed.), *Phenomenology and sociology* (pp. 217–253). New York: Penguin.

Lynd, R. S., and Lynd, H. M. (1937). *Middletown in transition: A study in cultural conflict.* New York: Harcourt, Brace.

MacLeod, J. (1987). *Ain't no makin' it: Leveled aspirations in a low-income neighborhood.* Boulder, CO: Westview.

Malinowski, B. (1922). *Argonauts of the western Pacific.* London: Routledge & Kegan Paul.

Mannheim, K. (1932). Review of *Methods in social science. American Journal of Sociology, 38*(2), 273–282.

Mannheim, K. (1936). *Ideology and utopia.* London: Routledge & Kegan Paul.

Mannheim, K. (1971). Education, sociology, and the problem of social awareness. *In* K. Wolff (Ed.), *From Karl Mannheim* (pp. 367–384). New York: Oxford University Press.

Mead, G. H. (1934). *Mind, self and society: From the standpoint of a social behaviorist.* Chicago: University of Chicago Press.

Merton, R. (1957). *Social theory and social structure.* New York: Free Press.

Miles, M., and Huberman, M. (1984). *Qualitative data analysis: A sourcebook of new methods.* Beverly Hills, CA: Sage Publications.

Mills, C. W. (1958). On intellectual craftsmanship. *In* L. Gross (Ed.), *Symposium on sociological theory.* Evanston, IL: Row Peterson.

Mills, C. W. (1959). *The sociological imagination.* New York: Oxford University Press.

Mitchell, R. (Ed.). (1979). *Less than words can say*. Boston: Little, Brown.

Mitchell, R. (1981). *The graves of academe*. Boston: Little, Brown and Company.

Natanson, M. (Ed.). (1962). *Literature, philosophy, and the social sciences*. The Hauge: Martinus Nijhoff.

Natanson, M. (1973). *Phenomenology and the social sciences*. Evanston, IL: Northwestern University Press.

O'Leary, J. P. (1986). The place of politics. *In* J. D. Hunter and S. C. Ainlay (Eds.), *Making sense of modern times* (pp. 179–196). London: Routledge & Kegan Paul.

Ostrow, J. M. (1990). Social sensitivity: A study of habit and experience. Albany: State University of New York Press.

Patton, M. Q. (1990). *Qualitative evaluation and research methods*, (2nd ed.). Newbury Park, CA: Sage Publications.

Peshkin, A. (1986). *God's choice*. Chicago: University of Chicago Press.

Phillips, D. C. (1987). *Philosophy, science, and social inquiry: Contemporary methodological controversies in social science and related applied fields of research*. New York: Pergamon Press.

Popper, K. (1972). *The logic of scientific discovery*. London: Hutchinson.

Ricoeur, P. (1976). *Interpretation theory: Discourse and the surplus of meaning*. Fort Worth: Texas Christian University Press.

Ricoeur, P. (1981). *Hermeneutics and the human sciences: Essays on language, action, and interpretation*. New York: Cambridge University Press.

Riseborough, G. F. (1988). The great Heddekashun war. *The International Journal of Qualitative Studies in Education*, 1(3), 197–224.

Rorty, R. (1979). *Philosophy and the mirror of nature*. Princeton, NJ: Princeton University Press.

Rubin, L. B. (1976). *Worlds of pain*. New York: Basic Books.

Schrag, C. O. (1980). *Radical reflection and the origin of the human sciences*. West Lafayette, IN: Purdue University Press.

Schutz, A. (1962a). Common-sense and scientific interpretation of human action. *In* M. Natanson (Ed.), *The collected papers of Alfred Schutz: Vol. 1: The problem of social reality* (pp. 3–47). The Hague: Nijhoff.

Schutz, A. (1962b). Symbol, reality and society. *In* M. Natanson (Ed.), *The collected papers of Alfred Schutz: Vol. 1. The problem of social reality* (pp. 287–356). The Hague: Nijhoff.

Schutz, A. (1964a). The homecomer. *In* A. Brodersen (Ed.), *The collected papers of Alfred Schutz: Vol. II. Studies in social theory*. (pp. 106–119). The Hague: Nijhoff.

Schutz, A. (1964b). The stranger: An essay in social psychology. *In* A. Brodersen (Ed.), *The collected papers of Alfred Schutz: Vol. II. Studies in social theory* (pp. 91–105). The Hague: Nijhoff.

Schutz, A. (1964c). The well-informed citizen. *In* A. Brodersen (Ed.), *The collected papers of Alfred Schutz: Vol. II. Studies in social theory* (pp. 120–134). The Hague: Nijhoff.

Schutz, A. (1967). *The phenomenology of the social world*, G. Walsh and F. Lehnert (Trans.). Evanston, IL: Northwestern University Press.

Schutz, A. (1970). *Reflections on the problem of relevance*, R. Zaner (Trans.). Evanston, IL: Northwestern University Press.

Sherman, R. R., and Webb, R. B. (Eds.). (1988). *Qualitative research in education: Focus and methods*. London: Falmer Press.

Smith, M. L. (1987). Publishing qualitative research. *American Educational Research Journal*, 24(2), 173–183.

Spradley, J. (1980). *Participant observation*. New York: Holt, Rinehart & Winston.

Strauss, A. (1970). Discovering new theory from previous theory. *In* T. Shibutani (Ed.), *Human nature and collective behavior: Essays in honor of Herbert Blumer*. Englewood Cliffs, NJ: Prentice-Hall.

Strauss, A. (1987). *Qualitative analysis for social scientists*. New York: Cambridge University Press.

Strauss, A. (1988). Teaching qualitative research methods courses: A conversation with Anselm Strauss. *The International Journal of Qualitative Studies in Education*, 1(1), 91–99.

Strauss, A., and Corbin, J. (1990). *Basics of qualitative research: Grounded theory procedures and techniques*. Newbury Park, CA: Sage Publications.

Tesch, R. (1990). *Qualitative research: Analysis types and software tools*. London: Falmer Press.

Twitchell, J. B. (1989). *Preposterous violence: Fables of aggression in modern culture*. New York: Oxford University Press.

Van Maanen, J. (1988). *Tales of the field: On writing ethnography*. Chicago: University of Chicago Press.

Webb, R. B. (1976). *The presence of the past: John Dewey and Alfred Schutz on the genesis and organization of experience*. Gainesville: University of Florida Presses.

Weber, M. (1946). *From Max Weber*, H. H. Gerth and C. W. Mills (Trans.). New York: Oxford University Press.

Williams, T. (1989). *The cocaine kids*. Reading, MA: Addison-Wesley.

Willis, P. E. (1981). *Learning to labor: How working class kids get working class jobs*. New York: Teachers College Press.

Winch, P. (1971). *The idea of social science and its relation to philosophy*. New York: Humanities Press.

Wiseman, F. (1968). *High school* [Film]. New York: Zipporah Films.

Wolcott, H. (1990). *Writing up qualitative research*. Newbury Park, CA: Sage Publications.

Wolfe, T. (1987). *Bonfire of the vanities*. New York: Farrar, Straus, Giroux.

Woolgar, S. (Ed.). (1988). *Knowledge and reflexivity: New frontiers in the sociology of knowledge*. Newbury Park, CA: Sage Publications.

CHAPTER 18

❏ Toward an Ethnology of Student Life in Schools and Classrooms: Synthesizing the Qualitative Research Tradition

Margaret D. LeCompte and Judith Preissle

The Handbook of Qualitative Research in Education

815

Introduction

In his 1978 Presidential Address to the Council on Anthropology and Education, Dell Hymes challenged anthropologists and other researchers engaged in ethnographic studies of education to develop an *ethnology of education* (Hymes, 1980). Reviewing the then current state of ethnographic research in education, he found a great array of excellent studies—individual ethnographies that anthropologists use as the building blocks of ethnologies. Anthropologists had, in fact, studied almost every inhabitant and characteristic of schools and schooling but, as yet, had failed to address the question "After all this work, what do we now know?" Educational ethnographers had not been building on each other's work; as a consequence, their studies failed to enhance our understanding of the field because it was not integrated into more comprehensive theories about teaching and learning.

This chapter is an initial response to that challenge. We will examine that part of the ethnographic literature that describes how children experience life in preschool or day care and elementary and secondary schools. First, we will define what an ethnology is, and then, using two different approaches to analysis of this literature, we will examine a set of representative studies to see what they tell us about the overall experience of children in school. One approach simply looks at the content of the studies to see what topics have been addressed. The other examines the theoretical orientations expressed by or embedded in the studies. Both methods will permit us to begin to isolate patterns and themes that tell us something of "what we already have learned" about children's life in school. The former will indicate areas that have not been studied sufficiently or at all, whereas the latter will show how thinking about schooling in general, and the role of children in it in particular, has changed over time, in the process raising new questions and new ways of defining the constructs isolated in previous research. The studies we review include ethnographic and qualitative research from anthropology, sociology, curriculum theory, and other related disciplines.

What Is an Ethnology?

Ethnology is the comparative analysis of ethnographies within and across cultures. An ethnology is a content analysis of existing ethnographies whose purpose is to generate a broader and deeper understanding of some aspect of people's lives. Ethnologies permit anthropologists to generalize from their data to larger populations; an ethnology is simply the result of multiple comparisons of individual case studies— or ethnographies.

An ethnology of education is a crosscultural examination of some aspect of education using ethnographic data. Constructing one requires a preexisting body of ethnographic literature; thus, the phenomenon under consideration must have been identified previously and must have been studied by ethnographers in a variety of settings. An ethnology could address any of the many subjects that interest educational ethnographers, from teacher behavior in classrooms to organizational characteristics to the norms and values attendant to establishment and support of educational institutions. It would do so, however, not by looking at the specific phenomenon in a particular setting but, rather, by combining the insights of many researchers who had examined the same or similar thing in many settings. In this paper, we have chosen to concentrate on research that addresses the experience of children in schools. It should be stressed that our review of the literature is by no means complete; those studies listed are merely representative of the field.

Studies Used for This Analysis

Over the past thirty years, the study of schools as relatively autonomous social units and the analysis of schooling as a distinct cultural process have generated a pool of data, concepts, and hypotheses that explain how and why students behave in particular ways both within formal school environments and as a result of their experiences in such milieus. These usually are presented in ethnographic accounts that describe participants and document the ongoing social life in schools. They explicitly describe the predominant social processes and social structures by which schools are maintained and generate causal hypotheses to explain the existence of the variables and processes identified.

Sources of data on student behavior and perspectives vary from those few efforts whose sole and explicit purpose is an examination of student subculture to a larger number of studies in which information about students is embedded within an examination of a larger community or a school system. Because of the wide range of studies available, we have set certain guidelines for our review, some of which have evolved as material has been examined. Inclusion in this review is contingent upon data dealing directly with student behaviors and perspectives within or concerning settings supported or maintained by schools: classrooms, formal and norformal extracurricular events, campuses, school-affiliated organizations, etc.

Some important studies have been excluded because, while they raise important issues about children, and they certainly address concerns about student behavior, they do not actually document it. For example, Ogbu's (1974) examination of school failure among poor American minorities in an urban ghetto has not been included because its focus is adult ghetto members and school personnel; data from students is minimal and peripheral. Other studies (e.g., Gay and Cole, 1967; Ward, 1971; McDermott, 1987) have been excluded despite their generalizations about student behaviors and perspectives because substantiating empirical data about children are not reported in the published accounts. In some instances, which we cite, data have been collected physically outside the school setting through such techniques as interviews; however, the subjects remain the students and their relationship to school. Finally, literature that reports experimentally induced behaviors and attitudes among students has not been considered because it was not elicited in natural settings and might well reflect researcher manipulations, rather than actual behavior and beliefs of students.

Four areas of concern have been identified among the studies examined: (1) studies of student perceptions of schools, schooling, and school-related activities as actually reported by the students as well as studies of observable patterns of student–student interaction and their participation in schooling and school-related activities (i.e., as observed and conceptualized by an outside, usually adult, observer); (2) student behavior as a function of teacher–student interactions; (3) crosscultural studies, which examine student behavior as a function of congruity with or discontinuity between student cultural background and the organizational and cultural configurations predominant in educational settings; (4) studies that examine student behavior and belief as it is linked to patterns of opportunity and constraint in the larger sociocultural, political, and economic arena of society at large; and (5) studies that describe student behavior and learning as socially constructed in the course of interaction with students, teachers, and others.

While we have sorted studies into these five general areas, some are relevant to more than one identified area; in these cases, we have tried to discuss them in terms of what we feel is their primary focus. We make some reference to places where they overlap. We also apologize for studies that, however excellent and to the point, we may have missed. We make no claim to have done a comprehensive survey of the literature; rather, we wish to spell out some of the parameters of the emerging ethnology toward which we work.

Constructing an Ethnology of Children's Life in School

Ethnology begins with content analysis. First, the content under consideration must be mapped and then categorized before it can be arranged in patterns and enumerated. The first step in creating an ethnology, then, is to examine the collection of studies under consideration to determine the extent to which they share common concepts, approaches, terminology, and research concerns. This is the approach which we have taken in the first part of this chapter. In the second part, we group the studies according to their underlying theoretical premises, because we believe that it is important to begin with an attempt to determine the explicit or implicit theoretical frames that inform each of the studies under consideration. This is because the theories guiding the research often dictate not only the kinds of questions to be asked, but also the methods deemed appropriate and the saliency and legitimacy of concepts, types of data, and units of analysis. Thus, if the theoretical frame can be determined, a more systematic basis for the content analysis can be established, one that clarifies and controls the ideological premises guiding the choice of questions and interpretation of results.

A Content Analytic Approach to Ethnographic Research on Children in School

Assembling the literature on children in school quickly reveals one important theme: Despite the overwhelming volume of research in education, a remarkably small percentage of the studies specifically address what children do, feel, or think about in school. The majority of those that do are experimental or quasi-experimental studies of knowledge and skills acquisition, oriented to evaluation of various forms of curriculum delivery. In the ethnographic literature, studies addressing the behavior of children as mediated or organized by teachers and as influenced by cultural congruency with the school—our categories two and three—are most numerous. They generally have been directed at figuring out how to make children more receptive to the subject matter that schools teach. More recently, phenomenological and interpretive researchers have begun to examine how students themselves view school—our first category—and critical, postmodern, and feminist researchers have begun to examine the links between student behavior and belief and the larger socioeconomic context of schooling—our category four. However, until very recently, few researchers actually talked to children about these matters or described them in terms of the categories children themselves use to describe what they do and how they feel about school experiences. Rather, they tended to use data elicited directly from students to support their own critical interpretations of what went on in school. In the following pages, we discuss a selection of research studies in an attempt to develop an integrated statement of their common themes and interpretations.

Toward an Ethnology: Common Themes and Concepts

Category One: Student Perceptions of Their Participation in Schools and Classrooms

The following studies analyzed student descriptions of their life in schools and classrooms (Burnett, 1969; Coleman, 1961; Cox, 1980; Cusick, 1973; Davis, 1972; Doyle, 1972; Eckerd, 1988; Fine, 1987; Fine and Zane, 1989; Lesko, 1986; McLeod, 1987; McLaren, 1980; Page, 1989; Parrott, 1972; Powell, Farrar, and Cohen, 1985; Woodhouse, 1987). Cusick's (1973) ethnography of a midwestern high school, based on 6 months of participant observation, reported that student attention and loyalty focused on an involvement with the disparate friendship cliques that characterized social organization in the school. The crucial factor in scheduling the day's activities was the company of at least one other clique member.

Cusick (1973) noted that classroom activity was divided into two areas of concern: the productive subsystem consisting of activities designed to further student acquisition of desired knowledge and behaviors and the maintenance subsystem composed of the rules, regulations, and behaviors that facilitate accomplishment of productive goals. The overwhelming majority of student time was taken up with maintenance rather than productive concerns. Cusick observed that interaction among teachers and students was severely restricted and infrequent, that few students were involved in formal school activities, and that students devised means for achievement of official school goals with minimal compliance to the (mostly maintenance) system.

Salient sociocultural features of the school were subject-matter specialty, vertical social organization with students on the bottom, an assumption by adults of adolescent inferiority, downward flow of communication, batch processing of students, routinization of activities, rules and regulations designed to support routines, a future-oriented reward system, and a physical building design that reflected the preceding elements.

Cusick (1973) suggested that the friendship cliques among students function to fill student needs for participation, interaction, and activity—none of which are adequately provided for by the formal organization of the school. The cliques act as a guide to appropriate behavior, social and academic, supply necessary information about the demands of the larger system, protect the system from having to deal with fundamental needs of the students, and protect the students from the alienating effects of formal school organization.

Cusick's findings are corroborated by the work of Coleman (1961), Foley (1990), Powell et al. (1985), McLaren (1980), and others, who also emphasized the importance of peer-group relationships. Studies such as Davis's (1972) analysis of the salient cultural categories of midwestern junior high school girls, Eckerd's (1988) study of "jocks" and "burnouts," and Holland and Eisenhart's (1990) lengthy ethnography of college-aged women all focused on the preoccupation of adolescents in school with personal relationships. Davis's findings, for example, were based on a lengthy series of unstructured tape-recorded interviews with eight informants. She notes that these students conceptualized their world in terms of kinds of teachers, kinds of students, and the nature of conflict between these two groups.

In these studies, students defined teachers as those who made rules, categorizing them on the basis of appearance, personality, and mannerisms and evaluating them by reference to strictness, making sense, and apparent caring about students. Student involvement with subject matter was a function of how they felt about the quality of teacher–student relationships.

Students were defined as those who followed rules. They were labeled preppies, cool kids, trouble-makers, goody-goodies, brains, "earholes," in-betweens, sads, colored kids, deaf kids (perceived as aloof and conceited, not physically handicapped), jocks, burnouts, freaks, vatos, nerds, dweebs, hoods, greasers, lads, loners, and a whole variety of other terms. These distinctions were based on a number of criteria, including who associated with whom, performance in teacher–student interactions, personal appearance—including hair style and dress, how the informant felt about the individual, how much an individual talked, preferred extracurricular activities, committment to academic achievement, and perceived intelligence and coolness. Davis observed that students labeled only those who were not well known to a given informant; close associates were not tagged in this manner.

Students also viewed school events within a framework of perpetual hostility and conflict. Like Waller's (1932) early characterization of students and staff as "fighting groups," students felt that teachers spent their time "picking on" kids to punish them, to make them be good, to embarrass them, or to publicly establish the hierarchy of student intellectual ability. Students concentrated on devising ways of "acting up," especially with teachers who were disliked or dull. This state of hostility was abated only in rare classes viewed as interesting, in classes where students were kept busy, or by the state of truce defined as being teacher's pet, in which a teacher and a student cooperated by tacitly agreeing to leave each other alone. Davis argued that the fixation on conflict filled a void created by the lack of perceived meaningful activity.

The preoccupation of secondary school students with the previously documented relationships contrasts with Doyle's (1972) analysis of the cultural domains of a third-grade child. Basing her conclusions on a series of unstructured taped interviews with a single informant, an 8-year-old female student in a midwestern elementary school, Doyle reported that elementary children assign three principal categories of meaning to school life: activities, identity, and space.

Rather than being predicated on interpersonal relationships, elementary school activities are regulated by the clock. Activities occur in a predictable, regulated sequence and are divided into groups: work, extra activities, games, lavatory breaks, lunch, gym, show-and-tell, choosing new class officers, and reading *Reader's Digest*. Students themselves are labeled in accordance with behavior exhibited during these activities: behavior during lunch (hot-lunchers, bag-lunchers, and home-lunchers) or teacher-delegated classroom tasks (four kinds of class officers and nine kinds of class helpers). Space achieves salience to the extent that it is available for children's play.

Doyle noted that the nature of activities dictates behavior and space: Certain activities require students to assume particular identities and perform in specified places. She suggested that these are rigidly routinized and unaffected by immediate interests of and personal decisions by the children.

Conceptualization based on activity is also found in Parrott's (1972) discussion of a second-grade recess in a midwestern parochial elementary school and LeCompte's (1980) study of kindergarteners.

Both used data collected from participant observation; Parrot used a series of unstructured interviews with six male 7-year-olds, whereas LeCompte conducted structured interviews with 135 4- and 5-year-olds.

Kindergarteners divided the world of school into work and play activities. Work took place inside, under teacher surveillance; play took place outside, where you could do what you please. Second-graders described recess in terms of three kinds of activity: games, tricks, and goofing around. Games shared common features such as rules, specified roles, definite outcomes, physical boundaries, and penalties for breaking rules. Tricks were characterized by unexpectedness, an assumption of opposing sides, physical contact, and deliberate intentions. Goofing around—all activity lacking teams, competition, and goals (including fighting)—apparently allowed for greatest innovation because of its absence of structure.

These studies suggest that children change their focus of attention sequentially and perhaps developmentally as they progress from elementary school through high school. Younger children conceptualize school experience as types of activity and the structures that support them. Older students shift their attention from structures, tasks, and schedules to relationships with people: They initially attend to both teachers and peers and later almost entirely to peers. Having spent the early years of schooling acquiring skill in the management of what Cusick (1973) labels the maintenance subsystem, students turn their attention to interpersonal relationships. These studies suggest that, regardless of their age, students in school are most preoccupied with factors other than those that constitute the formal academic, occupational, and social goals that adults have for them. Furthermore, they indicate that adults in charge of school attribute different meanings to school than those perceived by their student clients.

Category Two: Student Behavior as Structured by Teachers

The studies discussed in this section are concerned primarily or partially with teacher behaviors and attitudes and the way teachers organize and manipulate student behavior. In each case, the researcher is attempting to discover causal relationships between actions of specific teachers and responses of their students. Within the context of teacher-constructed environments, children's behavior is described and explained (Bennett, 1986, 1991; Borman, 1978; Bossert, 1979; Firestone and Rosenblum, 1988; Goetz, 1976; Leacock, 1969;

LeCompte, 1978, 1980; Mehan, 1979; Powell *et al.*, 1985; Rist, 1970; Smith and Geoffrey, 1968).

Smith and Geoffrey's (1968) microethnography of an urban lower-class group of upper-elementary children was an early example of a participant observation study with simultaneous observations collected by an insider (Geoffrey, the teacher and complete participant) and an outsider (Smith, the observer-as-participant). Their express purpose was to reconstruct the classroom experience from the teacher's perspective; however, they also generated some explanations for student behaviors and responses.

They found that student satisfaction with classroom events was positively related to the amount of personal attention each individual student received from the teacher. A strong relationship existed between affective variables and student displays of acceptable classroom behavior; expressed student esteem for the teacher increased as the amount of personalized interaction increased—and student misbehavior decreased. Smith and Geoffrey's findings have been corroborated by Deyhle (1992), McLeod (1987), Powell *et al.* (1985), and others.

Rist's (1970) longitudinal study of a group of lower-class urban black children from kindergarten through second grade also documented the relationship between student behavior and kinds of teacher–student interaction. Rist conducted observations 1.5 hours weekly during the kindergarten and second-grade years, observing the students four times in their first-grade classroom, interviewing all three teachers, and visiting the children's homes to collect additional observations and obtain data from their parents.

He described how the kindergarten teacher separated the students initially into three groups based on their expected achievement—high, middle, and low. These groups were categorized according to the child's ease of interaction with adults, degree of verbalization in standard American English, teacher-perceived ability to become a leader of peers, physical appearance, ability to participate well in peer groups, and extent to which his or her family was an educated, self-supporting, two-parent family. Rist reported that the high group received more time, attention, and rewards from the teacher while both lower groups received more control messages and less attention and support. His contention was that teacher expectations influence student performance in the two subsequent grades, where the teachers maintained the same three groups and displayed similar differential behavior toward the children in them.

Rist also documented student responses to this differential treatment. Children placed in high-achievement groups scored higher on measures of academic tasks, sought closer contact with the teacher, urged others to comply with the teacher's directives, actively ridiculed children in lower groups, and verbalized perceptions of their own superiority to the other youngsters. Students placed in lower groups performed inadequately on measures of academic tasks, exhibited frequent withdrawal behaviors (both physically and psychologically), expressed verbal and physical hostility, but only toward members of their own group, and rarely described what they learned in school in the classroom, although they did so in their home settings. He concluded that initial placement in reading groups more often than not was made on the basis of subjective criteria imposed by the teacher rather than on actual measured ability. Furthermore, placement established persistent and differential patterns of attitude, achievement, and behavior among students in the various groups; it both perpetuated and enhanced initial differences in achievement among children.

Smith and Geoffrey (1968) observed the effect of positive teacher behaviors on children's actions and attitudes. Rist (1970) extended the examination of teacher effects by documenting both negative and positive outcomes. Leacock's (1969) comparative study of second- and fifth-graders in four different schools as well as Bennett's (1986, 1991) and Borko and Eisenhart's (1986) studies of elementary reading groups substantiated Rist's conclusions (see also Page, 1989).

Leacock headed a team of interdisciplinary researchers who identified schools in contrasting urban neighborhoods: middle-class black, middle-class white, lower-class black, and lower-class white. Their findings were based on lengthy interviews with principals, teachers, and students and on semistructured classroom observations conducted over a 4-month period.

Like Rist, Leacock examined the effects of teacher expectations on student achievement. She focused primarily on teacher behaviors and concluded that low achievement in lower-class schools, black and white, was the result of expectations that middle-class teachers hold for what lower-class students should be like. Anticipating that these children will be unruly and apathetic, teachers emphasize learning to be obedient, conscientious, and respectful—to the exclusion of other goals.

Leacock reported that children in the two middle-class schools performed higher on measures of academic tasks, displayed more personal interest in their teachers, more readily volunteered comments about their own life experiences, and took more initiative in classroom events. Interview data collected from the children revealed that all believed that their teachers were concerned with good and bad behavior, but children in the middle-class schools also believed that teachers were concerned about academic performance. Only the students from the middle-class schools described teacher support for and encouragement of good peer-group relations, but all children expected that their education would result in the achievement of desired occupational goals (cf. Grindal, 1974).

In analyzing sociogram data from these students, Leacock offered an observation of student peer-preference patterns congruent with our previous discussion of how student concerns change from structure to relationships. Preference patterns among second-graders were characterized by a few stars toward whom nearly all children gravitated. By the time children had reached fifth grade, these patterns evolved into disparate friendship cliques composed of small numbers of students, surrounded by a few isolates. This phenomenon could be the precursor of increasing concern for relationships, in that the structure found among older elementary school children provides more opportunity for reciprocal interaction among peers.

Goetz's (1976) microethnography of a rural third-grade classroom designated teacher behaviors and values as significant background influences on student behavior; however, it differed from the studies discussed earlier because it attempted to characterize the student subsystem more comprehensively. Goetz used data collected from 5 months of participant observation in the target classroom, from intermittent tape-recorded interviews with the teacher and the students, and from analysis of pertinent classroom documents. She observed that the teacher attempted to implement a mix of apparently contradictory goals: conformity/creativity; cooperation/individual achievement; autonomy/compliance; and present satisfaction/future orientation.

Student behavior was framed by a common set of core values that characterized the classroom: finishing (assignments), giving right answers, achieving mastery, exhibiting responsibility, seeking positive interaction opportunities, engaging in play–work activities, obtaining approval from others, self-expression, conformity, and maximizing novelty and minimizing tedium. Values were realized through a complex set of behavioral strategies, which varied systematically according to activity context, classroom norms, and locus of decision-making. The latter element formed the basis of an explanatory postulate induced from the data: Students generally behaved so as to minimize actions that they regarded as externally controlled and to maximize actions that they perceived as autonomously chosen. Her attempt to locate motivators for student activity that were independent of teacher directives marked Goetz's study as a radical departure from investigations of classroom interaction.

Each of the ethnographic studies in this group seeks to explain student behavior within some parameters set by teacher expectations, actions, and attitudes. They underscore the significance of affective influences in the elicitation of desired student responses. The earlier studies reflect the embryonic state of classroom ethnographic research; they focus on global characteristics of teachers, students, and events and neglect situational variations, idiosyncratic responses, and indirect external influences. As a group, they emphasize ways in which nonacademic behaviors and attitudes impinge on academic pursuits— the manifest cognitive functions of schooling.

Category Three: Student Behavior as a Function of Cultural Congruity

The studies previously discussed focus on student behavior as a function, at least partially, of a variety of teacher actions and expectations, independent of cultural variables. A different perspective is taken by a growing group of reports that can be divided into two groups according to the degree of congruence between the cultural characteristics of the student populations and the culture of the school (Brice-Heath, 1983; Delgado-Gaitan, 1988; Deyhle, 1986a,b, 1992; Bennett, 1986, 1991; Burnett, 1969; Fordham and Ogbu, 1986; Gibson, 1988; Hollingshead, 1947; Lacey, 1966; Lein, 1975; Matute-Bianchi, 1986; Peshkin, 1978, 1986; Schwartz and Merton, 1974; Sindell, 1974; Shimahara, 1983; Spindler, 1974; Tindall, 1975; Warren, 1967; Werner, 1963; Wolcott, 1967; Wylie, 1964).

The first group that we examine, studies of cultures in conflict, addresses responses to schooling by students whose parent cultures or subcultures exhibit features that vary from the Euro-American middle-class cultural orientation of most formal schools. The second group, studies of congruent cultures, analyzes student behavior among children whose backgrounds are relatively congruent with the culture of the school.

Cultures in Conflict

Each of the reports examined in this section views the relationship between student and school as problematic and interprets any difficulties to be rooted in sociocultural disparities between home culture and school culture. Delgado-Gaitan (1988), who studied Hispanic

children, and Brice-Heath (1985), who compared white and black preschool children in the Piedmont area of the Southeast, for example,
discuss the differences between home and school in how children
learn, are talked to, interact with others, are sanctioned, are rewarded,
and engage in work and play activities. Based on additional fieldwork
that the researchers carried out in the schools, they also suggest that
many of these differences have profound impact on the degree to
which children later succeed in school. Delgado-Gaitan's and Brice-
Heath's studies are unusual in that their analyses of home school
differences are based on very lengthy and extensive (in Brice-Heath's
case, 10 years) fieldwork in the children's homes. Most studies of
cultural discontinuity have had more limited access to home life.

Lein's (1975) examination of language usage among black American migrant children was based on several months of participant observation in a migrant camp and its service school and on the analysis of
systematically collected speech samples from 13 migrant students.
Lein established that migrant youngsters spoke less frequently in
school, relative both to other students and to their own nonschool
usage. They used short, simple sentences in school in contrast to the
complex patterns they used elsewhere, and they adhered to sociolinguistic rules that, although learned at home, are regarded as inappropriate in school. Teachers interpreted these in-school behaviors to
mean that the children had limited academic ability.

The study spelled out a set of general differences in expectation
between behavior found in school and that found in the migrant-camp
home environment. In camp, children had considerable control over
their own schedules and activities; in school, schedules and activities
were determined by adults. At home, migrant children interacted constantly with both older and younger children and often had guardian
responsibilities for younger children. As students, they neither interacted with nor had responsibility for cross-age groups. In camp, responsibility for tasks commonly was shared among a number of individuals; at school, children were accountable only to the teacher for
their own tasks. This underscored a contrasting emphasis on cooperation—in camp—and competition—in school.

Conversation among migrants was deliberate and slow and participated in by all present, whereas school speech was fast-paced and
characterized by lengthy monologues, which limited the participation
of others. Most speech among migrants occurred between same-
generation members, but even in cross-age conversations, speakers
participated equally. In school, the teacher (adult) spoke more than
anyone else and dominated interaction with her different-generation

students. Playful verbal fencing between child and adult, common among migrants, was punished when initiated by students at school.

Although ritualistic threats were commonly used by adult migrants toward their children, threats rarely were carried out and physical punishment was unusual. Negative evaluative statements sufficed as signals for children to cease some behavior; their misdeeds were corrected by explicit statements of what the appropriate behavior should be. Children were rarely compared with one another, and tasks undertaken by children were accepted or rejected on their own merits. In contrast, teachers intended for threats to be statements of consequences. Physical punishment was common in school; students' actions were often corrected by drawing comparisons with the actions of their peers, and teachers used negative evaluative statements to tell students that they should improve their behavior. Lein (1975) suggested that migrant children verbally withdraw and apparently have limited language skills in school because of its alien, contrasting expectations. Unable to implement successfully the sociolinguistic rules learned at home, students retreat behind a protective shield of indifference and apathy.

A similar response is found among Ute (Tindall, 1975) and Navajo (Deyhle, 1986a) adolescent males. Tindall (1975) examined differences in behavior between Ute and Anglo-Mormon basketball players in physical education classes in a Utah high school. He engaged in 6 months of participant observation in the high school and community of Roosevelt, Utah, supplemented by analysis of student responses to specially designed projective plates depicting basketball scenes.

Anglo-Mormon students participated regularly in the pickup basketball games informally led by the physical education teachers. Half the Ute students (who formed approximately 20% of each class) never participated; the remainder played irregularly. Teachers claimed that the Ute did not participate because they were not competitively oriented and lacked the skills to play. Tindall observed that, contrary to these beliefs, Ute students played basketball frequently and well in groups within the Ute community.

In comparing games played by Anglo-Mormons and Utes among themselves, Tindall noted striking differences. Anglo-Mormon games were organized so as to maximize group effectiveness. Anyone who possessed the correct social identity—defined by age, sex, social status, and a minimal skill level—had the right to play. Games were structured to reflect the following set of beliefs: Humans can control others for the benefit of all; groups work together to win; a winning team confers status on even the most unskilled member; skill is acquired by entering games and mastering basketball through practice in the course of group play.

By contrast, Ute games were displays of individual performances with no assigned roles. Granting the right to play was the prerogative of current participants, although social status, skill, and proper decorum of request—as well as the need for additional players to even up a side—were considered in allowing entrance. The game structure reflected the Ute belief that humans cannot and should not control each other, in the way each player operated independently of his teammates, in the assignment of status based on skill regardless of team performance, and in the custom of acquiring skill by playing alone before entering game situations.

Deyhle (1986a) spent the first 5 months of a 3-year study of Native American adolescents "going to school" full time in Border Community. There she got to know the "Breakers," a group of Ute and Navajo students who turned to break-dancing as a way to establish their distinctiveness from the culture of the Anglo student Establishment, to build intragroup solidarity, and to achieve success and recognition, however negative, in a school and community that otherwise ignored and disparaged them.

The refusal of the Breakers to participate in the Anglo student subculture is analogous to the nonparticipation by Utes in high school pickup basketball. Both avoided "playing the game" according to Anglo-Mormon rules and values as a means of establishing themselves as a separate cultural group. To play—or not to break dance—was to label oneself as Anglo-Mormon; not to play—and to break dance in public—established oneself as Ute or Navajo. The effect of these activities is to maintain the two distinct cultures—separate also in the general community—by allowing students to actively communicate their identity to both their fellows and to members of the other group.

Lein (1975), Tindall (1975), and Deyhle (1986a) document instances of cultural discontinuity in which a subgroup withdraws from committed interaction within the school setting. In all cases, the minority group is unable to practice its cultural values in Euro-American classrooms and consequently masks its skills behind a screen of nonparticipation. The Ute and Navajo students differ from the black migrant students Lein studied in using their withdrawal as a demonstration of group solidarity.

A somewhat different response was reported by Wolcott (1967) among a Canadian minority group. He characterized the Kwakiutl Indian village that he studied as experiencing cultural disintegration: The native culture was deteriorating but had not yet been replaced by

Euro-American life-styles. Wolcott's conclusions were based on 1 year's participant observation in a small Kwakiutl village; during this time, he was the sole teacher in the multigraded village elementary school, allowing him access to student records and instructional products as well as to other documentary evidence. These data were supplemented with observations collected as a member of an Indian fishing-boat team during two subsequent summers.

Kwakiutl children were socialized by their parents into a subsistence economy based on mutual help and familial welfare. Relationships were informal and egalitarian; Wolcott described the culture as present-oriented. By contrast, the culture represented by the village school was formal, authoritarian, competitive, and future-oriented. Wolcott described Kwakiutl ambivalence toward the school by documenting how parents view education as positive (literacy leads to occupational opportunities) at the same time that they perceived the school to be different, alien, and threatening to their native culture. Children's behavior in the school reflected this ambivalence.

Accustomed to a traditional curriculum emphasizing reading and math, students expected their teachers to have all the answers, to open school on time, to be honest and dependable, to disapprove of their village, and to keep them busy with repetitive tasks. Teachers also were expected to refrain from excessive talk and dictatorial orders, to assign undemanding tasks, to maintain the accustomed routine, and to abstain from interfering in children's peer interactions. Students socialized teachers to behave in this manner through their reluctance to comply with teacher requests and demands and by directing scolding and mocking remarks at teachers.

The children generally were poor achievers for whom the English language was a primary difficulty. Their attendance and punctuality was erratic, and they delayed completing tasks with both physical and verbal foot-dragging. They resisted teacher attempts to encourage competition and rejected differential praise and expressed little interest in grades. Interpersonal tensions in the village were reflected in the pressure exerted on younger students by older ones to torment and bully each other at school. At other times, children cooperated with and assisted one another.

The children came to hold certain expectations for the way in which schools should be run through experience with a series of white Canadian teachers, and they resisted deviations from these expectations. Simultaneously, when their classroom behavior reflected congruence with Kwakiutl cultural norms, it disrupted the Anglo model. The conflict between teacher and student expectations in this setting impeded student achievement of academic and occupational goals.

While Lein (1975), Tindall (1975), and Deyhle (1986a) observed withdrawal to be the primary response by minority-culture students to hostile or alien school environments, the students Wolcott (1967) studied engaged in active manipulation of the school environment. Kwakiutl children attempted both to integrate their own cultural practices and perspectives into classroom life and to demand from their instructors what they interpreted as normal schoollike activities and behaviors. A primary factor explaining these differences in response may be that Wolcott's school was located within a homogenous native Indian environment; the populations described by Lein, Deyhle, and Tindall are minority groups within a setting claimed by the larger and dominant white population.

Sindell's (1974) study of Cree Indian students contrasts with the three previously discussed in emphasizing the ways in which discontinuities of expectations between home and school and contradictory cultural norms and values may be just as disruptive of parent culture as they are of school culture. Sindell based his study on 14 months of participant observation at a Cree Indian post and in the residential school servicing the post's children; interviews with parents, children, teachers, and counselors; and behavior-rating forms and observational protocols used with students across settings.

At home, Cree children were expected to be self-reliant and to take responsibility for filling their own needs and devising their own amusements; dependency was discouraged. At school, students had to conform to established routines and display submissive, nonexploratory behavior patterns; to satisfy needs for sustenance and amusement, students had to demonstrate that they depended on school personnel.

At home, Cree children had close, affectionate ties with numerous kin representing a range of age groups; they displayed minimal needs for social stimulation. At school, students interacted mostly within large, same-age peer groups and possessed close ties with only two or three adults. They displayed a high need for social stimulation.

At home, tasks were performed cooperatively with extensive sharing of benefits and responsibilities. At school, individual children competed both academically and socially for the range of rewards available. Open expression of aggression is discouraged among the Cree, and corporal punishment is rare. In the residential school, children were exposed to multiple models of openly aggressive behavior. They were subjected to verbal and physical abuse directly from the school personnel (verbal and physical) and observed many stances of aggression in the mass media.

Cree children are exposed to native adult role models at an early age, assume responsibility for meaningful tasks, and imitate more mature, complex adult roles in their play. Play was separated from work in the school and consisted of organized Euro-American group games. Few chores were expected of the students, and they had little contact with adult Euro-American work models.

Sindell suggested that the effects of these differences were most obvious when Cree students reach adolescence. After spending infancy and early childhood with their families, students then alternated between residential school (winter) and native home (summer) for approximately 9 years. After leaving school, their parents expected them to return to the hunting–trapping existence of the subsistence economy, but the years of schooling had socialized young Cree to new needs and aspirations impossible to fulfill in the native environment; it also left them lacking the skills to survive there.

A few studies focus not so much on cultural disparities but on ways in which individuals attempt to resolve the discontinuities between home and school life. Werner's (1963) study of a group of rural southern college students was based on 3 months of participant observation and interviews as well as documentary evidence. All of the students were raised in religiously conservative communities that differed from the cosmopolitan, secularized university that they had chosen to attend. The disparity between the belief system of the university and the rural southern home environments resulted in high states of anxiety among the students. Like Holland and Eisenhart's (1988, 1990) study of southern college women, Werner grouped typical student reactions into an acculturative typology: (1) passive withdrawal: the student focuses on peripheral activities and eventually flunks or drops out (cf. Lein, 1975; Tindall, 1975; (2) reactive: the student attempts to translate what is learned on the university campus into terms meaningful in the home culture, ignoring the differences between them and emphasizing traditional/historical elements to the exclusion of present- and future-oriented features; (3) compensatory: the student repudiates the earlier belief system in a near irrational denial of its validity (cf. Sindell, 1974); (4) adaptive: the student accepts university culture as part of training but maintains a division between this belief system and otherwise retained, original life ways (cf. Wolcott, 1967); and (5) cultural revisionist: the student restructures a new world view, incorporating elements from both the new and the old belief systems.

Werner classified most of the students he observed—all of whom had been associated with a university-affiliated religious center—as cultural revisionists, observing that the majority of them went on to graduate training in eastern urban areas. Although Werner ostensibly examined creative solutions to the problem of culture conflict and considered cultural revision to be an example of such a solution, his results underscore the findings of the other studies in this section. Neither home cultures nor the school culture apparently could assist students confronted with major social discontinuity. The sole option students seemed to have involved conformity to one culture accompanied by rejection of the other.

The problem of the conflict between Euro-American schools and the variety of parent cultures and subcultures served is, however, illuminated by a series of ethnographic studies of minority groups that have achieved high literacy rates through formal schooling and specific native minority individuals—who have resolved this disparity more successfully (e.g., Oriental or Eastern European immigrants in the United States. (Delgado-Gaitan, 1988; Gibson, 1988; Matute-Bianchi, 1986; Schneider and Lee, 1990)

The title of Gibson's (1988) study of Punjabi Sikh students in California, *Accommodation without Assimilation*, highlights this approach. Gibson spent 2 years engaged in participant observation of the students in their homes and schools; she interviewed parents, teachers, administrators, and the students themselves and used school records and other documents. Her results indicated that Punjabi Sikh parents heavily emphasize the need for their children to succeed in school to achieve economic mobility. The parents did so despite the fact they, themselves, did not understand the American school system well, did not participate in school activities or visit the school often, and could not help their students with schoolwork. They also required their children to maintain distinctive cultural patterns at home, patterns that caused their children to be ridiculed at school for their language, dress, food, hair style, patterns of modesty and interaction, and even study habits. Punjabi Sikh students, nonetheless, liked school and were able both to be successful in school and to remain integrated with their home community, participating in celebrations, arranged marriages, and maintaining the distinctive visual appearance of the Sikh community. Delgado-Gaitan's (1988) life histories of Hispanic students also emphasizes the importance of family support and encouragement.

In a slightly different kind of study, Matute-Bianchi (1986) compared successful and unsuccessful Japanese-American and Mexican-American students in California. Japanese-American students received the same encouragement from parents and community to excel and accommodate as Gibson's Punjabi students did; they also had the advantage of being a "favored" minority considered by school personnel to be quiet, hard-working, and respectful. Matute-Bianchi could not find an unsuccessful Japanese-American student. She linked the contrast between successful and unsuccessful Mexican-American students to patterns of ethnic identity and solidarity, indicating that students who were recent migrants or who identified with being Mexican, and those who were more "American," identifying as Americans of Mexican descent, were more successful. These students (or their parents) had had to overcome primary cultural differences of language, unfamiliarity with school rules and curricula, and the like. These primary cultural differences did not constitute a threat to ethnic identity. However, disaffected students, the "Cholos" or Chicanos, felt a less secure ethnic identity to begin with and, as a consequence, chose to reject participation in school culture as a means to maintain the integrity of Chicano identity. Like Fordham and Ogbu's (1986) study of high-achieving black students who were criticized for "acting white," they did not feel that it was legitimate or possible both to participate in the culture of the dominant group—the school—and to maintain one's identity as a Chicano. Deyhle (1989) also found that Navajo students who maintained close ties with culturally traditional grandparents were much less likely to drop out of school. What these studies emphasize is the importance not only of peer group pressures, but also of the stability and integrity of ethnic identity as a precursor to academic success.

Congruent Cultures

In contrast to the ethnographies discussed in the preceding section, the studies that follow document student perspectives and behaviors in instances where the culture of the school is congruent with the parent culture. In certain cases, it is just this congruence that researchers seek to establish.

Spindler (1974) reported that both native and migrant children in a German village school shared a common conceptualization of desired evolving life-styles, which integrated traditional rural perspectives with increasing pressures for urbanization and modernization. Although they adhered to an idealized image of nature and rural culture, these students preferred the comfort and security of modern, urban alternatives in areas such as occupational choice and desirable home sites. Where rural customs did not impinge on convenience and other

pragmatic considerations (e.g., church attendance, community celebrations), traditional behaviors were preferred.

Spindler based his conclusions on intermittent participant observation (using tape recorders and cameras) in the village and the school
conducted over a 3-year period, supplemented by document analysis
of curriculum materials and by interviews and the administration of
the Instrumental Activities Inventory (a semistructured measure of
instrumental and end goals), both used with teachers, students, and
parents.

Spindler characterized parents and teachers as more traditionally
oriented than students but nevertheless approving of the children's
evolving belief system. Spindler suggested that the school advocated
rural values while supporting students' variant choices. He presented
this as an instance of how an institution could allow for changes in the
client population and general culture environment. The balance between tradition and change was reflected in classroom interaction.
Spindler observed that teachers established certain parameters for
student behavior within which children were encouraged to make
many individual choices, thus combining both freedom and constraint
in the social system.

Warren's (1967) study of another German village school contrasts
with Spindler's (1974) findings. Warren spent 1 year in the field, using
participant observation to collect data on the community and the
school. He concluded that the school functioned primarily as an agent
of cultural continuity in which social relationships in village society,
especially with respect to authority, were mirrored in the school. Such
pressures for change that existed were mediated through two institutional leaders, the school principal and the village mayor.

Warren's study corroborated Spindler's general conclusions, but
the content of values and behaviors that Warren observed were somewhat different. The curriculum was fragmented and traditional as compared to the integrated approach taken in Spindler's school. Student
learning was rote and regimented. Relationships between students
and teachers were formal and involved a one-way adult–child communication process. Teachers maintained authoritarian control over
classes, relying on physical punishment and teacher-reinforced peer
sanctions to maintain order and conformity. Students sought opportunities for academic display, primarily in the form of individual recita-
tion. Because children were considered too immature to effectively
employ higher-level cognitive behaviors, factual learning was emphasized.

Warren noted that most of these elements—authoritarianism, assumption of child inferiority, use of physical punishment—were present in the village's familial settings. He attributed their acceptance by students to a continual reinforcement throughout the children's experience—in home, school, and community. As in Spindler's ethnography, he assumed that congruence of cultural norms and values between home and school result in a lack of institutional friction and individual trauma.

The impact on children of adult decisions about school, which are implicit in Spindler (1974) and Warren (1967), also was examined by Lacey (1966) and Willis (1977). Both used extensive participant observation in the field, with structured observational protocols with written questionnaires as additional data collection techniques. They concluded that an unintended effect of heterogeneous grouping in British grammar schools is the formation of what Lacey terms an antigroup of students.

In Lacey's study, 11-year-old boys entered grammar school, forming an undifferentiated homogeneous group selected from a range of elementary schools in which they have all enjoyed a best-pupil status. They retained few associations from their former schools. Their classroom behavior was characterized by eagerness, cooperation with the teacher, and a high level of intragroup competition.

At the conclusion of the first year, these students were separated hierarchically on the basis of exam scores and teacher-perceived ability. The bottom group became highly visible by virtue of frequent public evaluative comments by the school's teachers. By the end of the fourth year, the antigroup of students, Willis's "lads," had solidified. They were characterized by poor academic performance, rejection of school values, and open aggression toward their peers. They expected to withdraw before completion of the school's program, regarded themselves as scholastically unsuccessful, and reported spending less time on schoolwork relative to other students. These boys were more likely to come from working-class families than other students, but the relationship between their social class and school success was not uniformly correlated. Lacey suggested that the formation of this antigroup subculture in the school was initially stimulated by institutional divisions, hastened by expressed teacher expectations, but maintained by peer definitions and responses. The antigroup students were subject to ridicule and differential treatment from the rest of the school's students.

Lacey's and Willis's conclusions support the contentions of Leacock (1969) and Rist (1970), which link student behavior and performance with teacher expectations. However, the antigroup students, or lads, were not a specified stigmatized ethnic or social-class minority. Although these students coalesced into a definable group, their difficulties were considered by the school to be individual rather than group phenomena. Finally, Lacey and Willis emphasized the significance of peer, rather than teacher, expectations in effecting responses from the antigroup students. These studies provoke speculation that, even in a school which serves a relatively homogeneous population and maintains cultural congruence with its community environment, certain institutional practices will result in the formation of a disadvantaged, underdog group. Page (1989), for example, describes group formation in a "heavenly" high school in the United States, where the majority of the lower-track students were white, middle-class children who scored in the third, rather than the fourth, quartile on achievement tests. Despite their relative social advantage, these students—and their teachers—still occupied a "strange netherworld in the academic hierarchy" (Page, 1989:202).

Schwartz and Merten's (1974) and Lesko's (1986) examination of ritual behavior among student groups provided evidence for other status differentiations among adolescents. Schwartz and Merten used participant observation to investigate the function of initiation rites of high school sororities. They concluded that these practices legitimize and validate a girl's social identity. They function to support and maintain status categories among student groups, communicating the sorority member's position at the top of the student hierarchy.

Their findings differ from Lacey's (1966) in that no established relationship exists between this kind of social status and academic performance. Furthermore, the rituals reinforce existing social-class divisions in the community at large. Status assignments already had been created outside school; they were not effected by official school practices. Initiation rites merely reaffirmed the status quo.

The organizational functions of public rituals within student peer groups are also examined by Cox (1980) and Burnett (1969). Burnett engaged in 9 months of participant observation, supplemented by structured and unstructured interviews and questionnaires. Burnett concluded that certain extracurricular events in a small midwestern rural high school function as significant rites of passage and intensification for the students as a group. She described a recurrent annual and 4-year cycle of events that marks transitional periods in adolescent experience.

Pep rallies were interpreted as a ritual means of enabling students and adult school personnel to make the shift from formal school-day relations to the casual, nonauthoritarian structure characteristic of audiences at evening athletic events. The senior trip was viewed as a rite of passage, marking the student's movement from pupil status to that of community member and potential tax-paying supporter of local schools.

Cox's (1980) study defined attendance in kindergarten as a "rite of passage" for young children. Rituals of importance included the first time students ate lunch in the regular cafeteria. In both Burnett's and Cox's work, school rituals, including getting grade cards and ceremonies marking the passage from one grade to the next, defined changing student relationships to the school and an increasing involvement with and membership in the general community. For the students Burnett studied, the final ritual, graduation and its concomitant events, may have represented the adolescent's assumption of occupational status in the community, a departure from the area for employment or further schooling.

Lesko (1986) studied the structure of assemblies, extracurricular activities, and religious services in a parochial high school and indicated that these serve to develop and reinforce school-specific cultural norms of "caring," "love," and "fun" and to reduce tensions that competition among students otherwise would engender.

The group of studies reviewed in this section attempt to document student experience within the school culture, especially as that culture is viewed against the larger frame of the external society. Some schools may represent striking contrasts with various cultural or subcultural groups served, but many schools also function to maintain extraschool social traditions or even to support change in such traditions. Some of the researchers represented earlier seek to analyze this latter phenomenon by identifying how school rituals and ceremonies, values, organizational features, and normative practices match counterpart processes, structures, and functions in the general community.

Category Four: Student Behavior as a Function of Links between School and the Larger Society

Some of the studies cited previously make reference to the links between organization of curricula and activities within schools and patterns of economic domination, gender differentiation, and political and cultural asymmetry in the larger society. These concerns are explicit in the studies cited in the following pages (Borman, 1988, 1991; Foley, 1990; Grindal, 1974; Holland and Eisenhart, 1988, 1990;

LeCompte and Ginsburg, 1986; Peshkin, 1972, 1978; Roman, 1989; Stinchcombe, 1964; Weis, 1990; Willis, 1977)

Grindal (1974), who spent 19 months among the Sisala of Northern Ghana, described educational outcomes as perceived by students. His conclusions are based on participant observation in a tribal town and its public schools and on the results of a series of projective autobiographical essays administered to ninth- and tenth-grade students and their teachers.

Grindal's students believed that completion of an academic career, based on the traditional British model, would lead to success in native society. Education would guarantee access to material and status rewards, would enable individuals to acquire dominance over others, and would provide students with the means to act as benefactors to their familial and tribal groups. Failure to achieve such outcomes was attributed to fate rather than to deficiencies in the educative process or individual activity. Grindal noted that these beliefs were held by secondary-level students despite experiential evidence that possession of various levels of education does not always result in such outcomes (see also Foster, 1965; Clignet and Foster, 1966). Sisala students, operating in the contrasting cultures of Western school and African tribal village, reconcile anomalies by adhering to the belief that participation in one will lead to success in the other.

Slightly different is Peshkin's (1972) and Schildkraut's (1984) analysis of the changes that Western education brought to the Kanuri, when school activities provided new economic opportunities to children but prevented them from carrying out some of their traditional responsibilities in informal market schemes. For example, rather than acting as a purely "modernizing" force, the education of young girls actually acted to further isolate adult women, who used their prepubescent daughters to run errands and engage in trading, which they, secluded in purdah, could not do. Willis (1977), Holland and Eisenhart (1990), and Borman (1988) all examined the "cooling out" function (Clark, 1960) in education, by which students come to lower their expectations for the future in the light of traditional economic and cultural pressures. Willis and Borman examined the ways in which students' perception of their future job possibilities affect both the course of studies they chose and their academic diligence; Willis in particular stressed the role of parent, rather than teacher, models as critical. In both cases, the world outside the school was far more important a determinant of school behavior than was anything occurring within. LeCompte and Ginsburg (1986) also found that the impact of teacher role models at the university was far less important in determining the actual teaching behavior and career aspirations of student teachers than was real-life experience on the job and influences of the student's friends and family.

Holland and Eisenhart (1990) examined how previous high school academic experience, experience with college teachers, and traditional gender-role pressures mediated the scholastic roles that women undergraduates defined for themselves. For all but a few, the failure of college to confirm previous—probably unrealistic—expectations for academic success that they developed in high school caused women students to succumb to dating pressures, lower or sidetrack their occupational aspirations, and often to drop out of school. In this behavior, they were conforming to traditional stereotypes of the secondary role women play to males in contemporary society.

These studies confirm that schools do not exist in isolation from external social and economic forces. They also substantiate that students are acutely aware of the relationship between their social and cultural status and their potential for success after leaving school. The impact of school on students and the outcomes expected—especially for academic success or failure—cannot be understood without a careful analysis of the opportunity structure outside schools.

Category Five: Student Behavior and Learning as a Social Construction

This section includes a range of studies that employ an approach to investigation rather new in education. All of them refuse to accept as given standard functional definitions or labels for the social processes and their participants. All of them primarily concern how reality is defined, interpreted, and constructed by actors in various social and educational situations. Some of the early studies of school desegregation, although more or less descriptive and atheoretical, fall into this category (Clement, Eisenhart, and Harding, 1979; Schofield, 1982; Shimahara, 1983). These studies examine the interaction between cultural ideologies of equality and the reality of social, racial, and cultural differences in schools undergoing court-ordered desegregation. We group these studies here because they describe the way *expectations* had shaped and constrained the participants' subsequent actions and beliefs, confirming old patterns of interracial discomfort and avoidance, in newly desegregated schools. For example, they describe how white students interpreted the loud talking, often expansive movements, and language patterns of black students to be threatening and, thus, as contributing to racial and social polarization within schools. These studies were among the first to suggest that many standard institutional practices in schools, including ability grouping or tracking, contributed to the lower achievement of black students by stratifying knowledge and rewards in schools, adding racial segregation to already existing patterns of segmentation by class and achievement. They also called into question assumptions about the ability of legislated social reform to revolutionize long-standing cultural practices.

Other studies in this group, like some of those discussed by Woods (Chapter 8) Grant and Fine (Chapter 9), and Carspecken and Apple (Chapter 11) in this volume, address the construction of school failure and success through student–teacher and student–student interaction. They employ critical, phenomenological, feminist, and symbolic interactionist perspectives. Fine (1987), Fine and Zane (1989), McLeod (1987), McLaren (1980), and Measor and Woods (1984), for example, all are concerned with the way teachers and students interact, often so as to push students into dropping out of school. These studies describe how students react to negative sanctions for minor infractions of school rules by escalating their misbehavior; the escalation is met by teachers with correspondingly more stringent sanctions until student and teacher tacitly agree that the student is a troublemaker on his or her way to suspension. They also document how students interpret various kinds of teacher inattention to be lack of caring and how they respond by ceasing to care about—or accomplish—their schoolwork. The result is the construction of a stigmatized identity, one that is shared by both the students to whom it is attached and the teachers and staff who participated in its creation.

Other studies focus on the construction of identity—especially gender identity—itself. Lesko (1989) and Roman (1989) document the way young women "become feminine," conforming to general or idiosyncratic norms for gender-specific behavior and bodily presentation. Holland and Eisenhart (1990) discuss how the young college women they studied adopt and adapt to cultural norms dictating their relationships with men and their participation in the labor force.

Some studies, such as that of Bennett (1986, 1991), document how teacher beliefs shape achievement. Bennett studied how elementary school children are assigned to and respond in reading groups. The teacher in her study defined a "good reader" to be someone who sat up straight, followed the words being read with their finger or a ruler, and responded to questions with *verbatim* quotations from the text. Students who excelled in these noncognitive prerequisites for the reading act were judged to be better readers and were placed in higher reading groups, regardless of how well they actually comprehended the text or how fluently they read aloud.

Another body of work elaborates on the research just described by microscopically analyzing the patterns of verbal and nonverbal communication, which frame the construction of reality. Many such works, like those discussed by Erickson (Chapter 5) and Gee, Michaels, and O'Connor (Chapter 6) in this volume, are sociolinguistically informed; they include the study of proxemics and kinesics. Much of this work began with studies of the impact of black English on the achievement of black students (see Ward, 1971). Piestrup (1973), for example, detailed how the degree to which teachers forbade the use of black English in their classrooms was positively associated with the frequency with which students used it. Students whose teachers were relaxed about their nonstandard language use in school tended to lessen their use of dialect, whereas students whose teachers made a point of correcting student language tended to heighten their adherence to black English. Rose (1988) documented why her black college students persisted in using black English for specific purposes in tasks of English composition despite the fact that it harmed their grades; they felt that certain aspects of the black experience just "didn't sound right" in standard English. Mehan (1979) discussed how teachers actually "cued" student responses on individually administered tests by nuances of voice and body language.

The newest group of studies in this category has been reviewed in this volume by Jacob (Chapter 7). They concerned how learning is constructed, how learners define what they are doing, and the meaning that students and teachers attach to themselves as learners and the kinds of learning they undertake. These studies differ from psychologically informed studies of learning in that they situate all learning in its social and cultural context and often focus on the mediation of learning by the cultural meaning and salience of the specific task under consideration. Most of these studies focus on teachers; information about what students think and the meanings they attach to learning have been inferred from observations by adults rather than from actual conversations with them. An exception is Millroy (1990), who became a carpenter's apprentice in South Africa in an attempt to document the mathematical ideas embedded in everyday woodworking activities of the carpenters as well as how those mathematical ideas were taught and learned by the workers. Millroy's ethnographic study documented that the carpenters' mathematics had several unique characteristics that distinguished it from textbook mathematics. These characteristics clearly showed how the culture of the workshop indelibly stamped the mathematical ideas developed there. She also noted that, notwithstanding the unstructured and relaxed context of the workshop, the same patterns of stratification of knowledge and access to information by ethnicity prevalent in formal schooling could be observed in the workshop.

What all these studies do is to provide a missing link, or mechanism, by which phenomena that hitherto could only be associated by statistical correlation can be causally linked. For example, it was well known that low-income students tended to do less well in school, but, barring a belief in the inherent inferiority of poor people, no real mechanism existed to explain why bright poor children did not succeed in school. What research on interaction and social construction did was to provide explanations for how phenomena observable at the level of the social group, such as dropping out of school, were enacted by individuals through the construction of identities and realities that correspond to patterns in the dominant culture.

Summary

This analysis of ethnographic studies of student behaviors and perspectives underscores a number of significant variables in the educative process within formal school settings. Viewed in isolation, each study is a valid description of a cultural setting. Each is also a source for empirically generated and grounded concepts and generalizations that can be investigated across settings using alternative methods. Considered as a group, these reports offer convincing evidence for further examination of particular phenomena. What can they tell us at this point, in answer to Hymes's question, "What have we learned?"

First, students' selective perceptions of what is significant in the school environment is likely to differ from what most adults see. Young children appear to conceptualize classroom experience as a series of maintenance tasks: how, where, and when events take place. They are concerned with establishing the content and nature of their own roles as individuals within these scenarios. They also shed light on the relationship between the child's mastery of maintenance tasks and performance of academic assignments as well as the way children integrate conceptions of maintenance concerns with their perceptions of substantive goals. Some of the critical literature also described how the maintenance skills and identities constructed during primary grades solidify into an accustomed student role, difficult to modify or exchange in later years.

With maturity, expertise in maintenance tasks is assumed, and students turn their primary attention to the nature and manipulation of personal relationships, especially among peers. Acquisition of social skills during puberty is a developmental adolescent task across cultures, so its significance to secondary-level students may be obvious. There is some indication, however, that this preoccupation may influence academic performance (i.e., Coleman, 1961; Lacey, 1966; Holland and Eisenhart, 1990). Some of the studies cited here show how student success, real or perceived, in social affairs affects school learning and achievement of academic goals.

Students across age groups appear to be greatly influenced by affective elements in school and classroom environments. The emotional climate seems to affect motivation, performance, and students' perceptions of the significance of educational tasks. Many studies explore how students vary in their responses to differential affective stimuli as well as attempt to identify the source of this variation—social, cultural, or psychological.

The influence of teacher expectations on student academic performance, social behavior, and attitudes toward school generally is well enough accepted among educators to constitute a significant body of research literature. Some of the studies examined earlier (i.e., Lacey, 1966; Rist, 1970) suggest that peer expectations may also have strong repercussions for student behavior. The studies cited here suggest that peer expectations mirror those of teachers and, to some extent, are independent of teacher influence. They also describe the profound effect of peer expectations on student perceptions and behaviors.

The studies indicate that student behavior and teacher goals are likely to be at odds; even elementary school children act to maximize opportunities for autonomy in the service of coherent identity formation. These actions often conflict with teacher demands for conformity to curricular and social goals inherent in the schooling process. The consequence is that student developmental needs and institutional cognitive goals are inherently contradictory. Many of the studies examined earlier explore the degree of cultural fit and nonfit between the school and the students' home environments. Apparently, certain cultural features characteristic of many groups are common among students who have difficulty in schools: early assumption by children of responsibility for necessary group tasks and for individual scheduling and personal amusements; an emphasis on the cooperative sharing of work obligations; an orientation to present satisfaction rather than future rewards; a learning style that emphasizes careful mimicking of expert role models and mitigates against trial-and-error approaches; expectations that "people like us" never achieve success because subordination is expected and customary; and a social organization composed of informal, cross-age relationships. More studies need to explore which of these characteristics in students' home cultures correlate with difficulty in schools, and whether or not there is variability with different types of student background. Currently, it appears that students respond to cultural lack of fit by withdrawing from adequate school performance (Deyhle, 1986a,b; Sindell, 1974; Tindall, 1975), by totally rejecting parent culture in exchange for that represented by the school, by compartmentalization and accommodation (Gibson, 1988; Matute-Bianchi, 1986; Schneider and Lee, 1990); or—when possible—by coopting school practice to render it closer to parent culture (Wolcott, 1967).

An additional proposition is supported by this research: Students who are better integrated into their home culture achieve higher success in school, even if they are members of stigmatized minority groups. Thus, to the extent that schools can reinforce important home cultural values, the integrity of student identity (and associated levels of esteem and achievement) will be enhanced.

Ethnographic and qualitative studies also document that student response to school is context-dependent; it is a function of how strongly students perceive success in school to be articulated with economic opportunity, of cultural isolation, and of the receptivity of dominant culture groups and school personnel to the cultural, ethnic, and class background of the students.

Finally, the emergence of interactionist and interpretivist forms of culturally and cognitively oriented investigation point out the inextricable link among tasks, teaching, learning, meanings, and social identities. No longer can any component of the teaching–learning process be viewed "out of context," investigated without taking into consideration how people execute them, or understood without eliciting the meaning that people assign to them.

Toward an Ethnology: Common Theoretical and Conceptual Frames

A Theory-Informed Approach to Constructing an Ethnology of Schooling: Some Conceptual Prerequisites

Elsewhere, we have encouraged ethnographers to describe their populations and research context clearly and completely, define their terms adequately, describe their methods, and use concepts and terminology that are more or less comparable to those used by other re-

searchers in the discipline. Where this is impossible, we have suggested that researchers explain why they deviated from convention
and make clear the canons that dictated why they chose otherwise
(LeCompte and Goetz, 1982; Goetz and LeCompte, 1984). We did this
to illuminate the pitfalls of inventing terminology or using terms that
are so idiosyncratic that they apply only in the specific and unique
circumstances under which they were generated or first observed.
Hymes's challenge to create ethnology only makes our concern more
vivid; comparative analysis requires that the units being compared
possess some means for establishing likeness and dissimilarity.

An efficient way for potential ethnologists to begin to trace emerging patterns of thought in the research area, to identify possible biases
in interpretation, and to identify common constructs, categories, and
likenesses and dissimilarities is to examine the theoretical frames that
inform and guide the research and interpretation of results.

Sometimes identifying the theoretical frame is difficult, given conventions in much ethnographic writing, which dictates a pretense at
maintaining the "absent presence" of the researcher, value neutrality,
and descriptive atheoreticism. Some ethnography, and much educational ethnography, appears to have no explicit theoretical framework
whatsoever. Sometimes this occurs because researchers wish to avoid
being accused of merely having searched for data to support their
initial hunches. In other cases, the work genuinely is "merely descriptive" of a phenomenon incompletely known. Investigators also avoid
an initial description of theory because they feel compelled to generate theory only from the data collected in the study, and only after it has
been collected, rather than using it to inform the inquiry process
before and during data collection.

We believe, however, that no research is done in a theoretical
vacuum. In most cases, the omission of a theoretical frame is a consequence of carelessness, lack of self-awareness or knowledge, insensitivity to research participants, or deliberate obfuscation on the part of
the researcher. All ethnographers, even those most wedded to neutrality and whether conscious of them or not, approach the most concrete
empirical description with some set of questions that structure and
direct their investigation. These must first be made explicit and their
consequences traced (Goetz and LeCompte, 1984; 41). We believe that
this can be done and that the frames that shape and guide research can
be determined, even if the process of doing so requires that the studies
be examined within an historical and biographical, rather than a conceptual, context (see LeCompte, 1987).

Theoretical Frames Informing Research on Children in School

While all of the theoretical frameworks that inform social science research can be used to study children in schools, those that concern us most are usually associated with those disciplines most inclined to use ethnographic research—anthropology and sociology. These frameworks include functionalism—especially structural functionalism—conflict theory, symbolic interactionism and phenomenology, and critical theory, including feminist and poststructural approaches. They are listed here more or less chronologically according to the order in which they have come to be used by researchers in educations. One other theoretical frame that has been little used in educational research but that could have great explanatory power is social exchange theory; we do not discuss this frame further because of our inability to find studies that illustrate its use in ethnography.

An important point needs to be made: These theoretical frames often are not mutually exclusive. They inform each other and borrow concepts from one another. Ethnographers may use insights from several frames to structure their research and interpret its findings. For example, much of the current critical theoretical research in education draws heavily on insights regarding the social construction of reality delineated in symbolic interactionist research; similarly, research informed by conflict theory, while eschewing its emphasis on stasis and equilibrium, still uses much the same general conceptual and analytic structure as functionalism. We begin this discussion, then, with an examination of the theoretical frameworks which underly ethnographic research on children's experience in schools. We then attempt to re-sort the studies we have discussed previously into theoretically appropriate categories.

Functionalism

Prior to the early 1970s, ethnographic research on children tended to have a decidedly structural–functional flavor. Researchers were interested in identifying, describing, and enumerating the principle components and processes in educational systems and figuring out "how the system worked." For researchers interested in children, this involved more fully exploring what the role of students was, how they participated in school activities, what functions each of the activities in which they participated had in the larger scheme of things, and what the consequences were for children as a result of their participation in various kinds of educational experiences—curricular or extracurricular. These studies did not question either the form and content of schooling or its function in society, which was seen, on the one hand, as appropriately sorting people by ability into occupational niches and, on the other, as reinforcing what was perceived to be an attitudinal consensus on political organization and relations of domination and subordination. Rather than the phenomenological approaches that have become common in later years, these studies elicited the responses of children to instruments or interviews that were informed by researcher constructs and assumptions about how students behaved. Studies such as those by Burnett (1969), Coleman (1961), Cox (1980), Goetz (1976), Goldman and McDermott (1987), Hollingshead (1949, 1975), LeCompte (1978), Lesko (1986), Peshkin (1972, 1978), Schildkrout (1989), Smith and Geoffrey (1968), Spindler (1973, 1974), Schwartz and Merten (1974), Wolcott (1967), and Wylie (1964) are illustrative.

Conflict Theory

Conflict theorists began to question functional approaches, not so much as to the analytic constructs used, but as to whether or not the interpretations rendered were accurate or beneficial. While most of this research was quantitative and theoretical, rather than ethnographic, it did set the stage for questioning whether or not the purported pay-off to schooling—good jobs in exchange for legitimate effort and high achievement—were perceived as such by students. It also formed the basis for later ethnographic work, informed by symbolic interactionist approaches, which focused on both student definitions of the world of schooling, rather than definitions created by adults to which students were asked to respond, and how the reality of life in school was not given but, rather, constructed in the interaction among teachers, students, and staff. The primary contribution of conflict approaches was to introduce the concepts of assymetries of power and access into research in education. They questioned the "naturalness" or legitimacy and inevitability of the patterns of inequality and inequity to which educational activities contributed. Rather than focusing on the role of schools in transmission of cultural patterns, conflict theorists began to look at cultural reproduction; the change in terminology reflected a new questioning of the status quo. Research on children began to describe the lack of fit between schools and students as a problem of schools, not clients, and to seek ways of redressing it which emphasized changing school organizational patterns and social characteristics, rather than student attitudes and behavior. These studies include those by Borman (1988), Delgado-Gaitan (1988), Deyhle (1986a,b, 1992), Foley (1990), Gibson (1988), Leacock (1969), McLeod (1987), Shimahara (1983), Sindell (1974), Varenne (1982), Weis (1990), and Willis (1977).

Phenomenology and Ethnomethodology

Phenomenological and ethnomethodological approaches set the stage for interactionist research, which followed shortly after. Phenomenological studies of schooling elicited the meanings that participants in the educational process assigned to themselves and what they were doing. However, the research more or less remained within a functional frame; participant definitions were considered givens. While participants and researchers might differ in their depiction and interpretation of the system, the two remained separate—the emic and etic representations of reality. This frame assigned responsibility to researchers for understanding and reporting different realities, but absolved them from participating in their construction. Studies such as those by Goetz (1976) and LeCompte (1980) are illustrative; they elicited and inventoried student categorizations for classroom activities but provided no explanation for how students arrived at their definitions. Similarly, Delgado-Gaitan (1988) describes differences in how children experienced home and school, but, in this particular report, while she suggests that these differences must reciprocally affect each other, she does not elaborate on how this takes place.

Symbolic Interactionism

Perhaps the most profound change in research on children in school was generated by the symbolic interactionists, who changed the focus of research from large-scale functional and quantitative studies to studies of small groups, individuals, and dyadic interaction, often informed by categories and definitions generated by the people being studied. Focusing on the way interaction among people is shaped by the meanings and expectations that they bring to settings, they studied patterns of communication, symbols, and signs. This approach viewed reality as a social construction; because it questioned conventional "scientific" notions of the nature of reality, it called into question common assumptions about the validity of schooling outcomes in everything from test scores to the accuracy of teacher categorizations of students to children's attitudes toward school. Much of the early work had a curricular emphasis and was devoted to understanding specific acts of teaching and learning. Erickson, in Chapter 5 of this volume, documents much of this research. Mehan (1976) and Deyhle (1986b), for example, demonstrated that student test results were as much a product of teacher–student interaction as they were an "objective" depiction of what students knew. Bossert (1979) described how teachers and students organized the task structure of classrooms. Bennett (1986, 1991) studied how student grades in reading are a function of student conformity to teacher conceptualizations of the social behavior required to "show" the teacher one is a good reader, not actual student ability.

Studies such as these led to an interest in the impact on student attitudes of nuances of teacher language and behavior, which in turn led researchers to focus on the reciprocal effects of student–teacher interaction. Borko and Eisenhart (1986), for example, studied how students actually affect and manipulate their teachers in reading groups. In another arena, Erickson (quoting from Piestrup, 1973) describes how a teacher's heavy use of pejorative comments about the use of black dialect actually led to increased use of nonstandard English by students, rather than its hoped-for diminution.

Many studies of school success and school failure have been profoundly influenced by symbolic interactionism. Its emphasis on how the expectations embodied in social roles constrain behavior and interaction, as well as how interaction patterns lead actors to confirm or deny their prior expectations for behavior of others, helped to explain why students—and teachers—act in ways that appear to be counterproductive or even harmful to their identities, reputations, and life chances. Its emphasis on the role of the self of the researcher in all investigatory interaction changed the locus of inquiry from a one-sided preoccupation with those who are studied to a multifaceted concern for how the actions and beliefs of all "stakeholders" or participants affect the research process. The British tradition of sociology of education, which initiated this approach, is exemplified in the work of Lacey (1966) and Measor and Woods (1984) and is described in this volume by Woods (Chapter 8), Quantz (Chapter 10), and Carspecken and Apple (Chapter 11).

Critical and Emancipatory Theory

While these studies had an implicitly critical flavor, it remained for researchers whose work was explicitly influenced by neo-Marxist analysis to introduce what has come to be called critical theory in education and its research tool, termed critical ethnography.[1] These are studies whose express purpose is to expose the sources of inequality in society and how they are produced and reinforced within the schools. They use ethnographic or observational techniques and are deeply influenced by both the methods of the symbolic interactionists and the theoretical approaches of conflict theory. Some are informed by the sociology of knowledge and focus on creating a deeper understanding of the links between school and society (Apple, 1979, 1982, 1988; Apple and Weis, 1983; Weis, 1990). Others are oriented to feminist, postmodern, and post-structural approaches (see Roman, Chapter 12 of this volume; Lesko, 1989). Most of these researchers explicitly enter the field with an agenda—to expose inequities of race, class, and gender, to bring them to the consciousness of the oppressed, and to confront the creators of those inequities. They endeavor to make the class, gender, and ethnic biases and agendas of the researcher transparent to participants. They seek empowerment and strenthened voices for research participants and attempt to participate with those studied in the construction and documentation of the (new) reality that investigatory activities create (Roman, Chapter 12 of this volume). Their purpose is to make research and education transformative and democratic, rather than reproductive and oppressive (McLaren, 1989; Aronowitz and Giroux, 1985; Giroux, 1988). While many of these reserachers and writers purport to be phenomenologically oriented, little of their work on student attitudes, beliefs, and behavior is grounded in actual empirical research with young people. Many of their conclusions are based on inferences that use data from adults and other researchers to support their contentions. They and their agenda also have been criticized for apparently imposing categories and constructs on those they study. Nonetheless, their frameworks have been seminal in much analysis of problems and conflict in contemporary schools.

Summary

We are now left again with Hymes's challenge: What does all this tell us? In the first place, it is clear that in the past three or four decades ethnographic and qualitative research in education has undergone the same theoretical and methodological evolution from functionalism to interpretive and from positivistic to more phenomenological and constructed forms of inquiry as has occurred in the natural and social sciences more generally. Conceptually, this has meant a shift in focus from structure to agency. In the early periods of qualitative and ethnographic research, individual behavior and belief was conceived to be determined primarily by system norms and expectations. In this conceptualization, individuals played little role in enacting their own destiny; to understand individuals, one had to understand how the systems in which they participated operated. The focus of research then was descriptive analysis of *system* processes and components as a means to understand the behavior of *individuals* better. While this research considerably enhanced our understanding of the nomothetic, or institutional, aspects of human life and, in fact, still frames many excellent and useful research studies, the functional framework it employed was unsatisfying, especially in a society whose cultural norms support individual agency and cultural change—despite how much they are honored in the breach rather than in practice. It also failed to address sufficiently the obvious social, economic, and political asymmetries that researchers observed and that did not fit with either conventional American cultural ideology or aspirations.

A solution has been to change the theoretical frame. Researchers have sought out conflict theory, critical theory, phenomenology, and symbolic interactionism as counters to the overly deterministic approach of functionalism. This shift has permitted researchers to broaden their perspective on schools and learning and to ask a whole array of new questions.

The first impact was the "contextualizing" of schools and classrooms. Conflict theory situated schools inextricably within the political economy, demonstrating their interdependence with other aspects of a culture. Symbolic interactionism and critical theory accorded new importance to the actual behavior and beliefs of participants, especially children. As we indicated earlier, only recently have the perspectives and thought processes of children themselves been considered a significant arena for investigation in education. Research in which investigators actually talked to children, eliciting from them their own points of view and using those points of view to frame the research, are even more recent. The change in emphasis from structure to agency has, therefore, been associated with a shift in concern from those in authority to less powerful participants. This, in turn, has reconceptualized the roles of teacher and student, viewing them not as mere system definitions to be assumed and passively enacted by their occupants, but also as the dynamic and negotiated consequence of interaction between people, within a contextualized framework of expectations, past experiences, beliefs, and initial presentation.

Reconceptualization of roles also has begun the integration, as particularly described by Jacob (Chapter 7), Woods (Chapter 8), and Roman (Chapter 12) in this volume of the importance of the role of the self—including the self of the investigator—in all social interactions, including the research process. The move to reflexivity and to self-consciousness in execution in the inquiry process has been a catalyst for a preoccupation with how people think in context, not only during the research process, but also while learning cognitive skills. Finally, the emphasis on thought and action has initiated a movement toward collaboration between researchers and educators in the service of educational research and practice. While this generally goes under the rubric of applied or collaborative research, it is heavily influenced by critical, postmodern, and feminist perspectives. We find it hopeful and encouraging that research in all the modes enumerated in this chapter continue to maintain vigorous traditions, despite considerable controversy and internecine warfare among practitioners and the institutions who practice them. We believe that this multiplicity of outlooks enriches the field.

Conclusions

We have undertaken two tasks in this chapter. First, we clarified and categorized the substantive issues raised in a series of ethnographic and qualitative studies of student behaviors and perspectives. Second, we described the theoretical assumptions and frames that typically have informed ethnographic research and tried to sort the studies referenced in the chapter accordingly. In each section, we have attempted to enumerate what our meta-analysis elicited from the categorization of studies. Our analysis has made one thing very clear: Depending on what the initial questions or agenda may be, researchers vary considerably in the theoretical orientations with which they approach similar sets of phenomena. This variability has enhanced our understanding of educational processes because it has resulted not just in looking at the same phenomenon repeatedly or in different settings, as is typical in ethnology, but also in taking a look at the same phenomenon in many different ways or through many different lenses. It substantiates our belief in the multiple forms of causation and explanation needed to fully explain what goes on in schools and reinforces our conviction that inquiry about the field of education and its settings requires the eclecticism and holism of qualitative and ethnographic research.

Oxymoron terms

Note

[1] We consider the term to be erroneous. The terms ethnography, meaning the research design defined and practiced by anthropologists, and critical, characterizing the transformation-oriented practice of neo-Marxists, are oxymoronic. We prefer to call this approach applied, "educative" (Gitlin, 1989), action, or emancipatory research.

References

Apple, M. W. (1979). *Ideology and curriculum*. Boston: Routledge & Kegan Paul.

Apple, M. W. (1982). *Education and power*. Boston: Routledge & Kegan Paul.

Apple, M. W. (1988). *Teachers and texts*. Boston: Routledge & Kegan Paul.

Apple, M., and Weis, L. (Eds.). (1983). *Ideology and practice in schooling*. Philadelphia: Temple University Press.

Aronowitz, S., and Giroux, H. (1985). *Education under siege*. South Hadley, MA: Bergin and Garvey.

Bennett, K. (1986). An ethnographic study of elementary school reading among Appalachian students. Doctoral dissertation, University of Cincinnati, OH, August.

Bennett, K. P. (1991). Doing school in an urban Appalachian first grade. *In* C. Sleeter (Ed.), *Empowerment through multicultural education*. Albany: State University of New York Press.

Borko, H., and Eisenhart, M. A. (1986). Students conceptions of reading and their reading experience in school. *The Elementary School Journal*, 86, 586–612.

Borman, K. M. (1978). Social control and schooling: Power and process in two kindergarten settings. *Anthropology and Education Quarterly*, 9(1), 38–53.

Borman, K. M. (1988). Playing on the job: Adoelescent work settings. *Anthropology and Education Quarterly*, 19(2), June, 163–181.

Borman, K. M. (1991). *The first "real" job: A study of young workers*. Albany, NY: State University of New York Press.

Bossert, S. T. (1979). *Tasks and social relationships in classrooms: A study of instructional organization and its consequences*. Cambridge: Cambridge University Press.

Brice-Heath, S. (1985). *Ways with words: Language, life, and work in communities and classrooms*. Cambridge: Cambridge University Press.

Burnett, J. H. (1969). Ceremony, rites and economy in the student system of an American high school. *Human Organization*, 28, 1–10.

Clark, B. R. (1960). The "cooling out" function in higher education. *The American Journal of Sociology*, 75(May), 569–576.

Clement, D. C., Eisenhart, M. A., and Harding, J. R. (1979). The veneer of harmony: Social–race relations in a southern desegregated school. *In* R. C. Rist (Ed.), *Desegregated schools: Appraisals of an American experiment* (pp. 15–52). New York: Academic Press.

Clignet, R. P., and Foster, P. (1966). *The fortunate few: A study of secondary schools and students in the Ivory Coast*. Evanston, IL: Northwestern University Press.

Coleman, J. S. (1961). *The adolescent society*. Glencoe, IL: The Free Press.

Cox, T. V. (1980). *Kindergarten, a status passage for American children: A microethnography of an urban kindergarten*. Unpublished doctoral dissertation, Department of Anthropology, University of Georgia. Disssertation Abstracts International 41:1668A–1669A. University Microfilms No. 8023196.

Cusick, P. A. (1973). Inside high school: The student's world. New York: Holt, Rinehart & Winston.

Davis, J. (1972). Teachers, kids, and conflict: Ethnography of a junior high school. In J. P. Spradley and D. W. McCurdy (Eds.), The cultural experience: Ethnography in complex society (pp. 103–119). Chicago: Science Research Associates.

Delgado-Gaitan, C. (1988). The value of conformity: Learning to stay in school. Anthropology and Education Quarterly, 19(4), 354–382.

Deyhle, D. (1986a). Break dancing and breaking out: Anglo, Ute and Navajos in a border reservation school. Anthropology and Education Quarterly, 17, 111–127.

Deyhle, D. (1986b). Success and failure: A microethnographic comparison of Navajo and Anglo students' perceptions of testing. Curriculum Inquiry, 16(4), 366–389.

Deyhle, D. (1989). Pushouts and pullouts: Navajo and Ute school leavers. Journal of Navajo Education, 6, 36–51.

Deyhle, D. (1991). Empowerment and cultural conflict: Navajo parents and the schooling of their children. Qualitative Studies in Education (1991).

Doyle, J. (1972). Helpers, officers, and lunchers: Ethnography of a third-grade class. In J. P. Spradley and D. W. McCurdy (Eds.), The cultural experience: Ethnography in complex society (pp. 147–157). Chicago: Science Research Associates.

Eckerd, P. (1988). Jocks and burnouts: Social categories and identity in the high school. New York: Teachers College Press.

Fine, M. (1987). Silencing in public schools. Language Arts, 64(2), 157–174.

Fine, M., and Zane, N. (1989). Bein' wrapped too tight: Why low-income women drop out of high school. In L. Weis, E. Farrar, and H. Petrie (Eds.), Dropouts from school: Issues, dilemmas and solutions (pp. 23–55). Albany: State University of New York Press.

Firestone, W. A., and Rosenblum, S. (1988). Building committment in urban high schools. Educational Evaluation and Policy Analysis, 10(4), 285–299.

Foley, D. (1990). Learning capitalist culture: Deep in the heart of Texas. Philadelphia: University of Philadelphia Press.

Fordham, S., and Ogbu, J. U. (1986). Black students' school success: Coping with the "burden" of "acting white." The Urban Review, 18(3), 176–206.

Foster, P. (1965). Education and social change in Ghana. Chicago: University of Chicago Press.

Gay, J., and Cole, M. (1967). The new mathematics and an old culture: A study of learning among the Kpelle of Liberia. New York: Holt, Rinehart & Winston.

Gibson, M. A. (1988). Accommodation without assimilation: Punjabi Sikh immigrants in an American high school and community. Ithaca, NY: Cornell University Press.

Giroux, H. (1988). Teachers as intellectuals: Toward a critical pedagogy of learning. Hadley, MA: Bergin and Garvey.

Gitlin, A. (1989). The politics of method: From leftist ethnography to educative research. Qualitative Studies in Education, 2(3).

Goetz, J. P. (1976). Behavioral configurations in the classroom: A case study. Journal of Research and Development in Education, 9(4), 36–49.

Goetz, J. P., and LeCompte, M. D. (1984). Ethnography and qualitative design in educational research. New York: Academic Press.

Goldman, S. V., and McDermott, R. (1987). The culture of competition in American schools. In G. Spindler (Ed.), Education and cultural process: Anthropological approaches (2nd ed., pp. 282–298). Prospect Heights, IL: Waveland Press.

Grindal, B. T. (1974). Students' self-perceptions among the Sisala of Northern Ghana: A study of continuity and change. In G. D. Spindler (Ed.), Education and cultural *process: Toward an anthropology of education* (pp. 331–372). New York: Holt, Rinehart & Winston.

Holland, D., and Eisenhart, M. (1990). *Educated in romance: Women, achievement and college culture.* Chicago: University of Chicago Press.

Holland, D. C., and Eisenhart, M. A. (1988). Moments of discontent: University women and the gender status quo. *Anthropology and Education Quarterly,* 19(2), 115–138.

Hollingshead, A. B. (1947). *Elmtown's youth.* New York: John Wiley & Sons.

Hollingshead, A. B. (1975). *Elmtown's youth and Elmtown revisited.* New York: Wiley.

Hymes, D. (1980). Educational ethnology. *Anthropology and Education Quarterly,* 11, 3–8.

Jackson, P. (1968). Life in classrooms. New York: Holt, Rinehart & Winston.

Lacey, C. (1966). Some sociological concomitants of academic streaming in a grammar school. *British Journal of Sociology,* 17, 245–262.

Leacock, E. B. (1969). *Teaching and learning in city schools: A comparative study.* New York: Basic Books.

LeCompte, M. D. (1978). Learning to work: The hidden curriculum of the classroom. *Anthropology and Education Quarterly,* 9(1), 23–37.

LeCompte, M. D. (1980). The civilizing of children: How young children learn to become students. *The Journal of Thought,* 15(3), Fall, 105–128.

LeCompte, M. D. (1987). Bias in the biography: Subjectivity in ethnographic research. *Anthropology and Education Quarterly,* 18(2), 43–52.

LeCompte, M. D., and Goetz, J. P. (1982). Reliability and validity in ethnographic research. *Review of Education Research,* 52:31–60.

LeCompte, M. D., and Ginsburg, M. (1986). How students learn to become teachers. *In* G. Noblit and W. T. Pink (Eds.), *Schooling in social context: Qualitative studies* (pp. 3–22). New York: Ablex Press.

Lein, L. (1975). "You were talkin' though, oh yes, you was:" Black American migrant children: Their speech at home and school. *Anthropology and Education Quarterly,* 6(4), 1–11.

Lesko, N. (1986). The curriculum of the body: Lessons from a Catholic high school. *In* L. G. Roman and L. K. Christian-Smith, with E. Ellsworth (Eds.), *Becoming feminine: The politics of popular culture* (pp. 123–143). Philadelphia: Falmer Press.

Lesko, N. (1989). Individualism and community: Ritual discourse in a parochial high school. *Anthropology and Education Quarterly,* 17(1), 25–40.

Matute-Bianchi, M. E. (1986). Ethnic identities and patterns of school success and failure among Mexican descent and Japanese-American students in a California high school: An ethnographic analysis. *American Journal of Education,* 95(1), 233–256.

McDermott, R. (1987). Achieving school failure: An anthropological approach to illiteracy and social stratification. *In* G. D. Spindler (Ed.), *Education and cultural process: Anthropological approaches* (pp. 173–204). Prospect Heights, IL: Waveland Press.

McLaren, P. (1980). *Cries from the corridor: The new suburban ghettos.* Toronto: Methuen.

McLaren, P. (1989). *Life in schools.* White Plains, NY: Longmans.

McLeod, J. (1987). *Ain't no makin' it: Levelled aspirations in a low-income neighborhood.* Boulder, CO: Westview Press.

Mehan, H. (1976). Assessing children's school performance. *In* M. Hammersley and P. Woods, (Eds.), *The process of schooling: A sociological reader* (pp. 126–132). London: Routledge & Kegan Paul, in association with the Open University Press.

Mehan, H. (1979). *Learning lessons: Social organization in the classroom.* Cambridge, MA: Harvard University Press.

Measor, L., and Woods, P. (1984). Changing schools: Pupil perspectives on transfer to a comprehensive. Milton Keynes, England: Open University Press.

Millroy, W. L. (1990). *An ethnographic study of the mathematical ideas of a group of carpenters.* Unpublished doctoral dissertation, Department of Education, Cornell University, Ithaca, NY.

Ogbu, J. U. (1974). *The next generation: An ethnography of education in an urban neighborhood.* New York: Academic Press.

Page, R. (1989). The lower-track curriculum at a "heavenly" high school: "Cycles of prejudice." *Journal of Curriculum Studies,* 21(3), 197–221.

Parrott, S. (1972). Games children play: Ethnography of a second-grade recess. *In* J. P. Spradley and D. W. McCurdy (Eds.), *The cultural experience: Ethnography in complex society* (pp. 207–219). Chicago: Science Research Associates.

Peshkin, A. (1972). *Kanuri schoolchildren: Education and social mobilization in Nigeria.* New York: Holt, Rinehart & Winston.

Peshkin, A. (1978). *Growing up American: Schooling and the survival of community.* Chicago: University of Chicago Press.

Piestrup, A. (1973). Black dialect interference and accommodation in first grade (Monograph No. 4). Berkeley CA: Language Behavior Research Laboratory.

Powell, A. G., Farrar, E., and Cohen, D. K. (1985). *The shopping mall high school: Winners and losers in the educational marketplace.* Boston: Houghton Mifflin.

Rist, R. C. (1970). Student social class and teacher expectations: The self-fulfilling prophecy in ghetto education. *Harvard Educational Review,* 40, 411–451.

Roman, L. G. (1989). Intimacy, labor and class: Ideologies of feminine sexuality in the punk slam dance. *In* L. G. Roman and L. K. Christian-Smith, with E. Ellsworth (Eds.), *Becoming feminine: The politics of popular culture* (pp. 143–185). Philadelphia: Falmer Press.

Rose, R. C. (1988). "Syntactic styling" as a means of linguistic empowerment: Illusion or reality? Paper presented at the meetings of the American Anthropological Association, Phoenix, AZ.

Schildkrout, E. (1984). Young traders of northern Nigeria. *In* J. P. Spradley and E. W. McCurdy (Eds.), *Conformity and conflict: Readings in cultural anthropology* (pp. 246–253). Boston: Little Brown.

Schneider, B., and Yongsook Lee (1990). A model for academic success: The school and home environment of East Asian students. *Anthropology and Education Quarterly,* 21(4), 358–377.

Schofield, J. (1982). *Black and white in school: Trust, tension or tolerance?* New York: Praeger.

Schwartz, G., and Merten, D. (1974). Social identity and expressive symbols: The meaning of an initiation ritual. *In* G. D. Spindler (Ed.), *Education and cultural process: Toward an anthropology of education* (pp. 154–175). New York: Holt, Rinehart & Winston.

Shimahara, N. (1983). Polarized socialization in an urban high school. *Anthropology and Education Quarterly,* 14(2), 109–131.

Sindell, P. S. (1974). Some discontinuities in the enculturation of Mistassini Cree children. *In* G. D. Spindler (Ed.), *Education and cultural process: Toward an anthropology of education* (pp. 333–341). New York: Holt, Rinehart & Winston.

Smith, L. M., and Geoffrey, W. (1968). *The complexities of an urban classroom: An analysis toward a general theory of teaching.* New York: Holt, Rinehart & Winston.

Spindler, G. D. (1974). *Schooling in Schonhausen: A study of cultural transmission and instrumental adaptation in an urbanizing German village. In* G. D. Spindler (Ed.),

Education and cultural process: Toward an anthropology of education (pp. 230–271). New York: Holt, Rinehart & Winston.

Stinchcombe, A. (1964). *Rebellion in a high school.* Chicago: Quadrangle Press.

Tindall, B. A. (1975). The cultural transmissive function of physical education. *Anthropology and Education Quarterly, 6*(2), 10–12.

Varenne, H. (1982). Jocks and freaks: The symbolic structure of the expression of social interaction among American senior high school students. *In* G. D. Spindler (Ed.), *Doing the ethnography of schooling* (pp. 210–236). New York: Holt, Rinehart & Winston.

Waller, W. (1932). *The sociology of teaching.* New York: John Wiley.

Ward, M. C. (1971). *Them children: A study in language learning.* New York: Holt, Rinehart & Winston.

Warren, R. L. (1967). *Education in Rebhausen: A German village.* New York: Holt, Rinehart & Winston.

Weis, L. (1990). *Working class without work: High school students in an industrializing economy.* Albany: State University of New York Press.

Werner, F. H. (1963). Acculturation and milieu therapy in student transition. *In* G. D. Spindler (Ed.), *Education and culture: Anthropological approaches* (pp. 259–267). New York: Holt, Rinehart & Winston.

Willis, P. (1977). *Learning to labour: How working class kids get working class jobs.* Farnborough, England: Saxon House.

Wolcott, H. F. (1967). *A Kwakiutl village and school.* New York: Holt, Rinehart & Winston.

Woodhouse, L. (1987). *The culture of the four year old in day care: Impacts on social, emotional and physical health.* Unpublished doctoral dissertation, School of Education, University of Cincinnati.

Wylie, L. (1964). *Village in the Vaucluse: An account of life in a French village.* New York: Harper Colophon Books, Harper and Row.

Index

ISBN 0-12-440570-3

90038

9 780124 405707